FINNEY AND MILLER'S

PRINCIPLES OF ACCOUNTING

INTERMEDIATE

BY **GLENN L. JOHNSON,** PH.D.
THE UNIVERSITY OF KANSAS

AND **JAMES A. GENTRY, JR.,** PH.D., CPA
EMORY UNIVERSITY

FINNEY AND MILLER'S

Principles of ACCOUNTING

INTERMEDIATE

SEVENTH EDITION

PRENTICE-HALL, INC.

Englewood Cliffs, New Jersey

Library of Congress Cataloging in Publication Data

Finney, Harry Anson, 1886–
Finney and Miller's Principles of accounting.

Continues the authors' Finney and Miller's Principles of accounting, introductory.
Includes bibliographical references.
CONTENTS: [1] Intermediate.
1. Accounting. 2. Accounting—Problems, exercises, etc. I. Miller, Herbert E., joint author. II. Gentry, James A. III. Johnson, Glenn Laurence, 1934– IV. Title: Principles of accounting.
HF5635.F538 1974 657 73-21623
ISBN 0-13-317586-3

Finney and Miller's
Principles of ACCOUNTING, Intermediate
Seventh Edition
Glenn L. Johnson and James A. Gentry, Jr.

PRINTED IN THE UNITED STATES OF AMERICA

10 9 8 7 6 5 4 3 2

PRENTICE-HALL INTERNATIONAL, INC., *London*
PRENTICE-HALL OF AUSTRALIA, PTY. LTD., *Sydney*
PRENTICE-HALL OF CANADA, LTD., *Toronto*
PRENTICE-HALL OF INDIA PRIVATE LIMITED, *New Delhi*
PRENTICE-HALL OF JAPAN, INC., *Tokyo*

CONTENTS

PREFACE

When we began this revision, two significant problems confronted us. First, changes in financial reporting since 1965 required major revisions for this edition; and it seemed certain (especially with the inception of the Financial Accounting Standards Board in 1973) that change would continue at the same—if not an accelerated—pace. Second, we faced the challenge of maintaining in this fiftieth-anniversary edition, the high standards set by Finney and Miller for this series over the past half-century.

The resolution of the first problem, while not easy, was clear: The many changes in concepts, procedures, and terminology required by the numerous pronouncements of the American Institute of Certified Public Accountants (AICPA), such as the opinions and statements of the Accounting Principles Board (APB), had to be incorporated into this new edition. This task was sizeable and occasionally, frustrating. The number of APB opinions published while this revision was in progress required frequent rewriting of already revised chapters—including some last-minute changes in proof to reflect the latest opinions. Nevertheless, we are certain that all the necessary changes have been made to provide completely up-to-date coverage of financial accounting.

The second problem was solved by several significant structural changes. We felt that the potential for change in accounting practice required a somewhat more conceptual approach to the subject matter: that is, with a strong foundation in the underlying concepts of financial accounting, future changes in accounting practice could be readily integrated into an overall framework. As an additional requirement, to permit wider latitude in sequence and stress, we felt that this edition should allow greater flexibility in coverage than may have been the case with prior editions.

The first two chapters are optional. They are designed to provide a quick review of introductory accounting, strengthening weaknesses and plugging gaps in knowledge. An appendix illustrating the complete accounting cycle follows these chapters as an overall case review.

The primary organizational change in this edition has been to introduce financial accounting theory at the very beginning of the book in chapter 3 and to provide a totally new—and we believe unique—chapter on valuation in chapter 6. Chapter 3 provides a descriptive framework to which the reader can relate the specific accounting procedures discussed in subsequent chapters, and it is written so that it may be covered at the very beginning of the course or deferred until later. Chapter 6 is designed to provide a frame of reference for evaluating and understanding valuation methods used for particular assets and liabilities as they are discussed throughout the book. An appendix to this chapter serves as a review of the important concepts of compounding and present value.

Each of the basic financial statements is dealt with in a separate chapter. The statement of income and retained earnings (chapter 4) and the statement of financial position (or balance sheet, chapter 5) follow the theory chapter. Chapter 25, covering the statement of changes in financial position, has been written so that it may be covered after chapter 5 by those who prefer to treat financial statements as a single unit. Taking chapter 6 as a foundation, chapter 7 (discounted-cash-flow valuation: bonds) and chapter 8 (discounted-cash-flow: leases) provide material that may be covered in sequence or deferred until later.

After chapter 8 the sequence follows the traditional balance sheet approach from cash to stockholders' equity, but with greater flexibility. Chapters 9 through 19 are written so that they may be covered before the material on valuation (chapters 6, 7, and 8). Because some may prefer to cover stockholders' equity earlier than others, we have written those chapters (20 through 23) so that they too may be rearranged.

The chapters beyond 23 (with the exception of chapter 25) cover special topics: income tax allocation (chapter 24), general price-level adjusted financial statements (chapter 26), and correction of errors and statements from incomplete records (chapter 27) may be covered as appropriate.

To increase the understanding of material that normally poses some difficulty, we have utilized a three-pronged approach throughout the book: namely, to describe, illustrate, and, where feasible, put in equation form. Some specific examples are found in chapter 7 (bonds), 8 (leases), 16 (depreciation), 19 (pensions), and 25 (statements of changes in financial position), as well as the appendix to chapter 6 (review of compound interest concepts). In chapter 25 we have used the T-account method, followed by the work sheet technique consistent with the T-account method in order to increase the reader's understanding of the preparation of the statement of changes in financial position.

We are indebted to Professor Joseph A. Greco (Montclair State College), Douglas R. Haines (Rutgers University), Nils H. Hakansson (University of California, Berkeley) Dennis Gordon (The University of Akron), Orville R. Keister (The University of Akron), and Howard W. Wright (University of Maryland) who provided helpful comments and suggestions on the preliminary outline and some early chapters. We would also like to acknowledge the help of our research assistants, John H. Fisher and Wilmer E. Huffman of the University of Kansas, as well as John L. Green, Robert G. Morgan, and Thomas H. Oxner of the University of Georgia.

We would also like to express our appreciation to Garret White, Accounting Editor, and Fred Dahl, Production Editor at Prentice-Hall.

Finally, we would like to acknowledge the permission of the American Institute of Certified Public Accountants to quote from their publications and to adopt problems from their Uniform CPA Examinations.

GLENN L. JOHNSON
JAMES A. GENTRY, JR.

FINNEY AND MILLER'S

PRINCIPLES OF ACCOUNTING

INTERMEDIATE

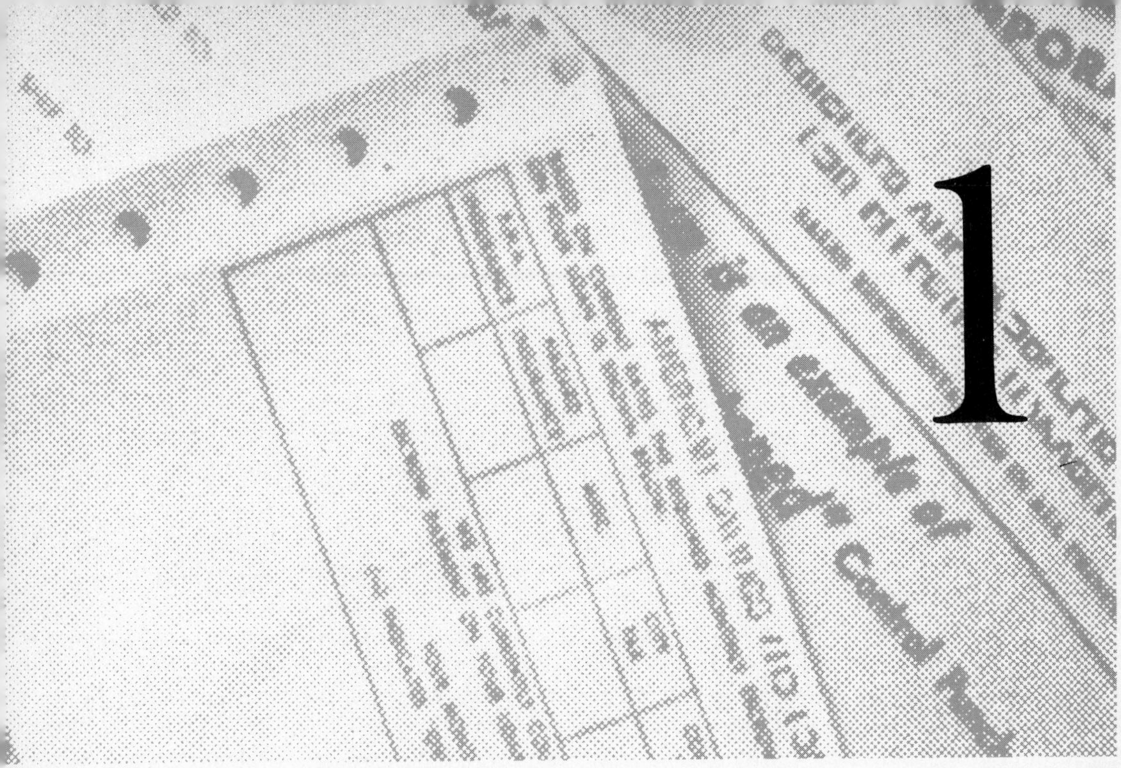

1

Review of Accounting Procedures

The accounting cycle. The principal procedural activities of the accounting process, referred to as the accounting cycle, are as follows:[1]

Journalize—thus providing a chronological record of transactions in books of original entry.

Post—thus classifying and accumulating the results of transactions in the accounts affected.

Prepare a trial balance—thus checking on the equality of the debit and credit balances in the ledger and summarizing the data from the ledger in a convenient form needed for the preparation of the financial statements. If working papers are prepared, the trial balance is entered directly in them.

Record and post the journal entries necessary for adjustments and corrections—thus updating the accounts for such matters as bad debts, depreci-

---

[1] For a basic review of accounting procedures, see Glenn L. Johnson and James A. Gentry, Jr., *Finney and Miller's Principles of Accounting: Introductory*, 7th ed. (Englewood Cliffs, N.J.: Prentice-Hall, Inc., 1970), Chapters 4 and 5.

ation, accruals, and revenue and cost apportionments. If working papers are prepared, the adjusting and correcting entries can be taken directly from them.

Prepare financial statements from the adjusted data—thus reporting on the results of operations for the period (income statement), accounting for the changes in retained earnings during the period and showing the current balance of the account (statement of retained earnings), showing the financial position at the end of the period (balance sheet), and reporting on the sources and uses of a firm's economic resources for the period (statement of changes in financial position). If working papers are prepared, the financial statements can be prepared directly from them.

Record and post the journal entries necessary to close the books—thus updating retained earnings and preparing the revenue, expense, and dividend accounts with zero balances for the start of the next period. If working papers are prepared, the closing entries can be prepared from them.

(Optional) Record and post reversing journal entries—thus facilitating the recording of transactions next period in line with company policy as to recording procedures.

Prepare an after- (post) closing trial balance—thus checking on the equality of debits and credits in the ledger after closing the books.

Since the accounting cycle represents the sequence of accounting procedures during the fiscal period, it is repeated each period. The steps in the accounting cycle will be reviewed in this and the following chapter.

A review of the recording process. The record-keeping function of accounting is based on the fundamental relationship, called the basic accounting equation, expressed as follows:

Assets = Equities

In other words, equities are the source of a firm's funds, and assets are the uses or forms these funds take; hence, sources equal uses and, therefore, assets equal equities.

Assets are defined as future economic benefits, the rights to which are owned or controlled by a firm (or individual). Equities are the sources of and the claims against the firm's assets. Equities are classified into liabilities (creditor claims) and owners' equity (owners' claims or interests). Liabilities are the obligations of a firm (or individual) to render assets or perform services. The excess of the assets over the liabilities of a business is the owners' equity. For a corporation, owners' equity is called stockholders' equity and is classified into paid-in capital and retained earnings.

Paid-in capital is the amount contributed or paid in by the stockholders to the corporation for capital stock. It includes both capital stock (such as preferred stock and common stock), which is reported at par or stated value, and capital in excess of par or stated value.

Retained earnings is that portion of the stockholders' equity attributable to profitable operations. It includes aggregate net income minus any net losses, dividends, and capitalization of retained earnings. It also includes any prior period adjustments made to the retained earnings account.

Thus, for a corporation the basic accounting equation can also be expressed as follows:

$$\textbf{Assets} = \textbf{Liabilities} + \begin{matrix}\textbf{Capital}\\ \textbf{Stock}\end{matrix} + \begin{matrix}\textbf{Capital in Excess of}\\ \textbf{Par or Stated Value}\end{matrix} + \begin{matrix}\textbf{Retained}\\ \textbf{Earnings}\end{matrix}$$

The elements in the basic accounting equation represent broad categories. A business may have anywhere from a few to dozens of different assets, and records must be maintained to show the increases, decreases, and present status of each asset. The same applies to the equities. To record all the increases and decreases in assets, liabilities, capital stock, and retained earnings, accounts are maintained.

Increases in assets and decreases in equities are recorded on the left side of the account, called the debit (*dr.*) side. Increases in equities and decreases in assets are recorded on the right side of the account, called the credit (*cr.*) side. Under the double-entry system of accounting, the recording of each transaction consists of one or more debits and credits, and the totals of the two must be equal in dollar amount. Thus, increases and decreases are recorded in accounts in the manner shown below.

Asset Accounts		=	**Liability Accounts**	
Debits (Increases)	Credits (Decreases)		Debits (Decreases)	Credits (Increases)

+	**Paid-in Capital Accounts**		+	**Retained Earnings Account**	
	Debits (Decreases)	Credits (Increases)		Debits (Decreases)	Credits (Increases)

The difference between the total debits and the total credits in an account is called the balance. Thus, asset accounts normally have debit (left-hand) balances and equity accounts normally have credit (right-hand) balances.

Many business transactions result in revenue or expense. Revenue is an inflow of assets in the form of cash, receivables, or other property from customers or clients, which results from sales of merchandise or the rendering of services, or from investments. Expense is the cost of goods or services used for the purpose of generating revenue. Net income (profit) is the excess of revenues over expenses.

Revenues increase and expenses decrease retained earnings; however, rather than use the retained earnings account directly, it is more convenient to use separate revenue and expense accounts to accumulate the results of revenue and expense transactions. Thus, revenue and expense accounts are in effect "offshoots" or subdivisions of the retained earnings account, and with this relationship in mind, the debit–credit plan for revenue and expense accounts follows logically.

Retained Earnings

Debits (Decreases)	Credits (Increases)
Expenses decrease retained earnings and are recorded as debits	Revenues increase retained earnings and are recorded as credits

Expense Accounts

Debits (Increases)	Credits (Decreases)
Expenses are recorded as debits	

Revenue Accounts

Debits (Decreases)	Credits (Increases)
	Revenues are recorded as credits

In addition to revenues and expenses, dividends also affect retained earnings. Although not an expense, dividends also decrease retained earnings, because they are a return on invested capital to stockholders from profitable operations. Rather than record the dividends directly to retained earnings, a separate dividends account is used to accumulate periodic dividends.

The debit–credit plan can now be summarized using the basic accounting equation as follows:

Assets		=	Liabilities		+	Capital Stock		+	Retained Earnings	
+	−		−	+		−	+		−	+
dr.	cr.		dr.	cr.		dr.	cr.		dr.	cr.

Expenses

+	−
dr.	cr.

Revenues

−	+
dr.	cr.

Dividends

+	−
dr.	cr.

Or, descriptively, the debit–credit plan is as follows:

Debits	Credits
Increases in assets	Decreases in assets
Increases in expenses	Decreases in expenses
Increases in dividends	Increases in liabilities
Decreases in liabilities	Increases in capital stock
Decreases in capital stock	Increases in retained earnings
Decreases in retained earnings	Increases in revenues
Decreases in revenues	

Finally, the debit–credit plan results in the following normal account balances:

Debit Account Balances	Credit Account Balances
Assets	Liabilities
Expenses	Capital Stock
Dividends	Retained Earnings
	Revenues

Accounting records. In general, business records consist of the following:

Documents, or business papers, such as invoices, credit memorandums, bank checks, insurance policies, freight bills, and promissory notes. These furnish detailed information about business transactions, state the terms of contracts, and serve as evidence of the propriety of accounting entries.

Books of original entry, such as the general journal, sales journal, accounts payable journal, and cash receipts and disbursements journals. These books contain chronological records of business transactions and show, among other facts, the accounts to be debited and credited to record the transactions.

Ledgers, both general and subsidiary. These show in detail or in summarized form the debits and credits of each account.

Registers and other supplementary records, such as the notes receivable register, the notes payable register, and the insurance register. These furnish more detailed information than can conveniently be recorded in the accounts. They may also serve as books of original entry, and may take the place of subsidiary ledgers.

Working papers in which information for the periodic statements is assembled.

Periodic statements, which show the results of operations, changes in financial position, and the financial position of the business.

Books of original entry. A book of original entry contains a record of transactions in their chronological order, names the accounts to be debited and credited to record each transaction, and states the debit and credit amounts. The debits and credits shown in the journals are posted periodically to the various accounts.

Ledgers and controlling accounts. A *ledger* is a group of accounts. If a ledger contains accounts (some of which may be controlling accounts rather than detailed accounts) for all the assets, liabilities, and elements of ownership equity of the business, including revenues and expenses, it is called a *general ledger.*

In a large business there are usually several groups of similar accounts. There may be many accounts receivable and accounts payable; if deposits are kept in several banks, an account must be kept for each bank account; it may be desirable to maintain a separate account for each parcel of land, for each building, and for each security investment; there will be numerous selling expense accounts, and numerous general expense accounts; and there may be other groups of kindred accounts.

If all of these accounts are kept in one ledger, the posting work may be too much for one employee. To provide for a division of labor, the following procedure may be applied:

Keep the several accounts of the group in a subsidiary ledger.

Keep a controlling account in the general ledger. It is debited with totals of the charges to the accounts in the subsidiary ledger; it is credited with totals of the credits to the accounts in the subsidiary ledger; and its balance should be equal to the sum of the balances of the accounts in the subsidiary ledger.

The controlling account and subsidiary ledger device also has the advantage of helping to locate errors by isolating them. If the trial balance of the general ledger shows that the general ledger is in balance, but the sum of the balances in a subsidiary ledger does not agree with the balance in its controlling account, it may be presumed (but not definitely known) that the error is in the subsidiary ledger. If the general ledger is not in balance and the subsidiary ledger is in agreement with its control, it may be presumed (but, again, not definitely known) that the error is in the general ledger—someplace other than in the controlling account.

Auxiliary accounts. An auxiliary account is one that is closely related to another (major, or principal) account. Auxiliary accounts are sometimes called *contra,* or *offset,* accounts if the principal account has a debit balance and the auxiliary account has a credit balance, or vice versa. They are sometimes called *adjunct* accounts if the balances of the principal and auxiliary accounts are both debits or both credits.

The sales returns and allowances account is a contra to the sales account. The purchase returns and allowances account is a contra to, and the transportation in account is an adjunct to, the purchases account. The allowance for uncollectibles and accumulated depreciation accounts are contra accounts.

The journal. It is theoretically possible, although not often practicable, to use a two-column journal, often referred to as the general journal, as the only book of original entry. Entries in such a journal are illustrated below.

JOURNAL

19--						
July	1	Cash	10,000	00		
		Capital stock			10,000	00
		Issuance of 100 shares of stock.				
	2	Purchases	2,500	00		
		Cash			2,500	00
		Purchase of merchandise for cash.				

Accountants have given a great deal of thought to the development of books of original entry that effect a division and saving of labor. Two that are used are special journals and special columns. Some illustrations follow.

Special journals. The following sales journal is a special journal that is used as a book of original entry.

SALES JOURNAL

Date		✓	Name	Invoice No.	Debit Accts. Rec. / Credit Sales	
19--						
May	2	✓	R. E. West	1	800	00
	7	✓	G. O. Davis	2	450	00
	12	✓	S. E. Bates	3	600	00
	18	✓	R. E. West	4	850	00
	23	✓	G. O. Davis	5	280	00
	30	✓	R. E. West	6	300	00
					3,280	00
					(10)	(40)

The check marks show that the individual entries have been posted to the customers' accounts in the subsidiary ledger. The number (10) at the foot of the money column shows that the total has been posted to the debit of the accounts receivable controlling account. The number (40) shows that the total has been posted as a credit to the sales account.

Such a journal facilitates a division of labor because one employee can be assigned to recording sales on account. It saves posting work because the column total, instead of the individual entries, is posted to the sales account.

Some of the other special journals that may be kept are:

Sales returns and allowances journal
Purchases journal
Purchase returns and allowances journal
Cash receipts journal
Cash disbursements journal

Special columns. Special columns may be introduced in books of original entry for the following purposes:

For classification of data
To facilitate recording transactions
To save labor in posting

Special columns for these purposes are shown in the cash receipts journal on page 8.

Columns for classification of data are illustrated by the two Sales columns.

The Sales Discounts debit and Interest Revenue credit columns are examples of columns to facilitate recording transactions when the entry includes more than one debit or credit. If no special column is provided, entries may be made in the Sundry sections.

Posting labor is saved when there is more than one entry in a column, because the column total, rather than the individual entries, can be posted to the general

(Left side)

CASH RECEIPTS JOURNAL

Line No.	Date		Explanation	Cash	Sales Discounts	Debits: Sundry Accounts Name	L.F.	Amount
	19—							
1	May	1	Sale	480 00				
2		2	Invoice April 24, less 2%	980 00	20 00			
3		3	Fred White's note	505 00				
4		4	Note discounted at bank	990 00		Interest expense	51	10 00
5								
28		29	Invoice May 21, less 2%	1,470 00	30 00			
29		30	Sales	490 00				
30				29,578 00	298 00			80 00
31				(1)	(47)			

(Right side)

Line No.	Account Credited	Credits: Accounts Receivable ✓	Accounts Receivable Amount	Sales Dept. A	Sales Dept. B	Interest Revenue	Sundry Accounts L.F.	Sundry Accounts Amount
1				280 00	200 00			
2	Frank Brown	✓	1,000 00					
3	Notes receivable					5 00	13	500 00
4	Notes payable						28	1,000 00
5								
28	George White	✓	1,500 00					
29				315 00	175 00			
30			15,875 00	4,860 00	5,645 00	60 00		3,516 00
31			(10)	(45)	(46)	(50)		

ledger. For this reason, a special Accounts Receivable controlling account credit column should usually be provided in the cash receipts journal. Postings of totals of special columns are indicated by writing the account numbers below the totals.

Combined books of original entry and subsidiary records. The voucher register is one of the most frequently used records, combining the features of a book of original entry and the features of a subsidiary record. Many other such dual-purpose books are used in the accounting systems of large enterprises.

When a voucher system is in use, a formal voucher must be prepared and approved before a cash disbursement can be made. As each liability is processed for payment, information is entered on the voucher by various employees. When the voucher form is complete, it describes the transaction that created the liability and shows the work done in verifying the liability and approving it for payment. Each voucher is recorded in the voucher register; the proper asset, expense, or other account is debited, and the vouchers payable account is credited. When the cash disbursement is made (either immediately or at a later date), an entry is made in the cash disbursements journal (sometimes called a check register) debiting Vouchers Payable and crediting Cash, and also crediting Purchase Discounts if a discount is taken.

The form of the voucher register is indicated by the very abridged illustration on page 10.

When a voucher is paid, notations are made in the Date Paid and Check No. columns of the voucher register, in the manner illustrated below.

VOUCHER REGISTER

Voucher No.	Date		Payee	Explanation	Terms	Date Paid		Check No.	Credit Vouchers Payable	
	19—					19—				
7-93	July	6	The Osborne Company	Invoice, July 3	1/10; n/30	July	12	1668	270	00

Entries in the voucher register with no notations in the Date Paid and Check No. columns are "open," or unpaid, items. Their total should agree with the balance in the vouchers payable controlling account in the general ledger. The voucher register thus serves as a subsidiary record that takes the place of the accounts payable subsidiary ledger.

Posting from documents. One illustration should suffice to show how labor can be saved by posting directly from documents. Instead of recording sales in a sales journal and posting therefrom, carbon copies of all sales invoices can be kept in a binder, which thus serves as a sales journal. The amount of each charge sale can be posted directly from the carbon copy of the invoice to the customer's account in the subsidiary accounts receivable ledger, and the total, shown by an adding-machine tape (retained in the binder), can be posted as a debit to the accounts receivable controlling account and as a credit to the sales account.

VOUCHER REGISTER

Voucher No.	Date		Payee	Explanation	Terms	Date Paid	Check No.	Credit Vouchers Payable	Debits				
									Purchases	Transportation In	Sundry Accounts		
											Name of Account	L.F.	Amount
	19—												
7-93	July	6	The Osborne Company.......	Invoice, July 3	1/10; n/30			270 00	270 00				

The entry in the voucher register records a debit to Purchases and a credit to Vouchers Payable, which is another name for Accounts Payable. Voucher registers usually contain many debit columns for accounts that are frequently debited. Only three debit columns are shown in the illustration—one for purchases, one for transportation in, and one for accounts for which no special column is provided.

The cash disbursements entry for the payment of The Osborne Company voucher is shown below.

CHECK REGISTER

Check No.	Date		Payee	Voucher No.	Debit Vouchers Payable	Credits	
						Purchase Discounts	Cash
	19—						
1668	July	12	The Osborne Company..................................	7-93	270 00	2 70	267 30

The procedures reviewed in this chapter to save labor and to permit the division of labor may need further refinement whenever the volume of transactions is large. The recording process may be expedited by the use of accounting machines or electronic devices. Their use does not alter the basic debit–credit process whereby transaction data are recorded, classified, and summarized into meaningful aggregates; they do nothing more than can be achieved through the use of special journals of the type previously illustrated, but they do offer greater speed and economy.

Trial balance and subsidiary ledger schedules. The general ledger trial balance taken periodically serves as a test of the mechanical accuracy of the accounting procedures (to the extent of establishing the equality of debits and credits) and provides a list of account balances to be used in the preparation of statements. If the general ledger is well organized, the account balances will appear in the trial balance in a sequence similar to that in which they will appear in the statements. However, amounts may appear in the statements although they do not appear in the general ledger trial balance—for instance, the sum of the credit balances in accounts in the subsidiary accounts receivable ledger.

The schedules of the subsidiary ledgers are also a test of mechanical accuracy; they establish the agreement of the subsidiary ledgers with their related controlling accounts.

End-of-period cutoff. There must be a correct cutoff at the end of any period for which statements are prepared. That is, the accounts should include entries for all transactions that occurred before the end of the period, and should not include entries for any transactions that occurred after the end of the period. Complete information regarding some transactions may not be available on the last day of the period in which they occurred; for this reason, it is often necessary to wait a few days after the end of the period before completing the recording and posting and taking a trial balance.

Locating errors. An accountant not infrequently discovers that mistakes have been made in the accounts. This becomes apparent if the trial balance does not balance, or if the balance in a controlling account is out of agreement with the sum of the account balances in its subsidiary ledger.

If the general ledger trial balance does not balance, the accountant should perform the following operations, in the order indicated:

(1) Refoot the general ledger trial balance.
(2) Compare the balances shown by the trial balance with those shown by the accounts in the general ledger.
(3) Recompute the balance of the general ledger accounts.
(4) Trace the postings to the general ledger.
(5) Refoot the books of original entry.
(6) See whether the sum of the totals of the debit columns is equal to the sum of the totals of the credit columns of each columnar book of

original entry; if they are not in balance, refoot each column. If this does not disclose the error, see whether the debits and credits in each entry are equal.

When the general ledger is in balance but a subsidiary ledger is out of agreement with its control, the presumption is that the error or errors causing the disagreement are within the subsidiary ledger. In this case the accountant should:

(1) Refoot the schedule of the subsidiary ledger.
(2) See that the balances were carried correctly from the subsidiary ledger to the schedule.
(3) Recompute the balance of each subsidiary ledger account.
(4) Trace the postings to the subsidiary ledger.

ADJUSTING ENTRIES

Cash and accrual bases of accounting. Because statements of operations and financial position are prepared periodically, it is necessary to determine the accounting period to which revenues and expenses are applicable. There are two principal bases for assigning revenues and expenses to accounting periods: the cash basis and the accrual basis.

CASH BASIS: On a pure cash basis, no income is recorded from sales on account until collections are received; purchases are not recorded until payments are made; and no consideration is given to inventories.

Revenue from other sources is regarded as earned in the period in which the cash collection is received. No revenue is regarded as having been earned for services performed unless the cash has been collected. Any cash collections for services to be rendered in the future are regarded as revenue of the period in which the collections are received, even though nothing has been done to earn it.

Expenses are regarded as applicable to the period in which the cash payment is made. No charge for bad debts appears in the operating statement because no revenue is recorded until the receivable is collected. There is no charge for depreciation because the entire cost of a long-lived asset is regarded as an expense of the period in which the purchase disbursement is made.

It is obvious that such an accounting basis is wholly unsatisfactory for a business with material amounts of expenses accrued or prepaid, revenue accrued or collected in advance, long-lived assets, inventories, accounts receivable, or accounts payable.

The so-called cash basis of reporting income for federal income tax purposes, as governed by the law and the regulations, is really a mixed cash-accrual basis. If sales of purchased or manufactured goods are a major source of revenue, recognition must be given to sales on account, purchases on account, and inventories. An expenditure for long-lived assets cannot be taken as a deduction wholly in the period in which the purchase disbursement is made; deductions can be taken only for periodic depreciation and amortization. But consideration need not be given to bad-debt provisions (since the taxpayer may elect the direct write-off method), nor to accrued or deferred revenue or expense.

ACCRUAL BASIS: On the accrual basis of accounting, revenue is regarded as earned in the period in which the sales are made or the services rendered (regardless of when collected), and expenses are regarded as applicable to the period in which they are incurred (regardless of when paid).

The "matching" of revenues and expenses for the purpose of determining net income on an accrual basis often requires the exercise of trained judgment, and not infrequently involves estimates. But it is fundamental that, if the books are to reflect the results of operations and the financial position on an accrual basis, adjusting entries are almost always necessary.

Adjustments and income measurement. The matching process referred to in the previous paragraph is at the heart of the income-measurement function of the accounting process. During the accounting period, transactions are recorded as they take place, based on external evidence (for example, checks, sales slips, invoices, or shipping orders) received or issued. However, to achieve a proper matching of the revenues and expenses for a given period of time, it may be necessary to record certain adjustments to the accounts at the end of the period before preparing the financial statements. In other words, adjusting entries are made to update the accounts to be reported on the financial statements.

Adjustments are made at the end of the accounting period because it is not practical to record deferrals and accruals on a daily or weekly basis, and because such entries are not "triggered" by the receipt or issuance of external business documents, but by an analysis of the accounts.

The adjustment process makes very clear the relationship between the income statement and the balance sheet. It should be emphasized that although the major reason given for end-of-period adjustments is income measurement, the adjustments also affect the balance sheet of the firm. Thus, the failure to record the necessary adjustments will not only misstate the income for the period, but will also result in a misstatement of the end-of-period balance sheet.

The number of adjustments required at the end of the accounting period will vary from firm to firm and from period to period within a firm, but all adjustments may be classified as those required for the following reasons:

(1) Unrecorded revenues that have been earned
(2) Unrecorded expenses that have been incurred
(3) Cost expirations that have previously been recorded as assets or expenses
(4) Earned revenues that have previously been recorded as liabilities or revenues
(5) Provision for losses

It should be noted that certain adjustments require the recording in the accounts of amounts that have not been recorded previously. This is true for items (1) and (2) above. Other adjustments merely require the transfer, or reclassification, of amounts already on the books. This is true for items (3), (4), and (5) above.

Unrecorded revenues. It is quite possible that certain revenues may be earned before they are actually recorded in the accounting records. For example, an interest-bearing obligation such as a note or bond provides for the payment of interest on a specific date or dates. However, the holder of the note or bond is in fact earning interest each day he holds the instrument. There is no reason why he should record the interest earned on a daily basis, and to do so would only involve unnecessary record-keeping expense. It is only at the end of the accounting period, when financial statements are to be prepared, that it becomes necessary to record the interest that has been earned.

Assume that ABC Company holds $50,000 of XYZ Corporation's 7 per cent bonds. The bonds pay interest on April 1 and October 1 of each year, but the accounting period of ABC Company ends on December 31. If the net income of ABC Company is to be properly determined for 19+3, it is necessary that an adjusting entry be made at the end of the year to recognize the interest earned but not previously recorded. Since interest on the bonds was last paid on October 1, 19+3, the amount of the adjusting entry is $875 [($50,000 × .07) × 1/4]. The entry is shown below.

Interest receivable	875	
Interest revenue		875
Accrued interest receivable for three months.		

After this entry is posted to the accounts, they will appear as follows:

		Interest Receivable		Interest Revenue	
19+3					
Dec. 31	Adjusting entry	875			875

It should be noted that failure to record the entry would affect both the income statement (revenues would be understated) and the balance sheet (assets would be understated).

Unrecorded expenses. As a practical matter, not all the expenses of a firm are recorded in the accounting records as they are incurred. For example, a firm incurs wages and salaries expense each day it operates, but the expense is normally recorded only when the total amount owed for a payroll period is paid. It is only when financial statements are to be prepared that it becomes necessary to record any wages and salaries that have been earned by employees but not yet paid to them. Failure to do so would understate both expenses and liabilities.

Assume that ABC Company owes its employees $1,000 at December 31, 19+3, for wages and salaries that have been earned in 19+3, but that will not be paid until the end of the first pay period in 19+4. The following adjusting entry recognizes the expense in 19+3, which is the proper treatment under accrual accounting.

Wages and salaries expense	1,000	
Wages and salaries payable		1,000
Accrued wages and salaries payable at December 31, 19+3.		

After this entry is posted to the accounts, they will appear as shown below.

		Wages and Salaries Expense (Dr.)	Wages and Salaries Expense (Cr.)	Wages and Salaries Payable (Dr.)	Wages and Salaries Payable (Cr.)
19+3					
Various Dates	Expense to date	30,000			
Dec. 31	Adjusting entry	1,000			1,000

Cost expirations. Adjusting entries may be required to apportion a prepayment that will benefit more than one accounting period. The portion of the prepayment that has expired should be reported as an expense of the current period, with the unexpired portion being reported as an asset at the end of the period. The precise form of the adjusting entry required will depend upon the way in which the prepayment was originally recorded.

To illustrate, assume that ABC Company paid $300 at the beginning of 19+3 for a three-year insurance policy. The adjusting entry at the end of the year, to show that the insurance expense for 19+3 amounts to $100, will depend on whether the $300 expenditure was charged to the unexpired (prepaid) insurance account, which is an asset, or to the insurance expense account. The two conditions are illustrated below.

ORIGINAL CHARGE TO AN ASSET ACCOUNT: If the $300 premium payment was debited to the unexpired insurance account, the adjusting entry should transfer the *expired* portion from the asset account to an expense account. The adjusting entry is as follows:

Insurance expense	100	
Unexpired insurance		100
Insurance expired during the year.		

The accounts affected are shown below after the adjusting entry has been posted.

		Unexpired Insurance (Dr.)	Unexpired Insurance (Cr.)	Insurance Expense (Dr.)	Insurance Expense (Cr.)
19+3					
Jan. 2	Original expenditure	300			
Dec. 31	Adjusting entry		100	100	

ORIGINAL CHARGE TO AN EXPENSE ACCOUNT: If the $300 premium payment was originally debited to the insurance expense account, the adjusting entry should transfer the *unexpired* portion from the expense account to an asset account. The adjusting entry is as follows:

Unexpired insurance	200	
Insurance expense		200
Insurance unexpired at the end of the year.		

In this case the accounts appear as shown below after the adjusting entry has been posted.

		Unexpired Insurance		Insurance Expense	
19+3					
Jan. 2	Original expenditure			300	
Dec. 31	Adjusting entry	200			200

In either case, the adjusting entry results in a $200 debit balance in the unexpired insurance account, which would appear as an asset in the balance sheet; and a $100 debit balance in the insurance expense account, which would appear in the income statement.

COST EXPIRATIONS AND CONTRA ACCOUNTS: In the preceding discussion of prepayments recorded as assets, the adjusting entry resulted in a credit to the asset account for the amount of the expiration. Not all cost expirations previously recorded as assets are handled in this manner.

The acquisition of a depreciable asset is recorded by debiting an appropriate asset account, with the cost being transferred to expense over the life of the asset. The adjusting entry for the annual depreciation charge includes a credit to an accumulated depreciation account rather than to the asset account. The accumulated depreciation account is shown on the balance sheet as a deduction from the related asset account balance. The difference between the two accounts is referred to as the "net book value" of the asset.

The adjusting journal entry to record depreciation is shown below, along with the accounts affected by the entry, assuming annual depreciation of $1,500.

Depreciation expense	1,500	
Accumulated depreciation		1,500
To record annual depreciation.		

		Depreciation Expense		Accumulated Depreciation	
19+3					
Jan. 1	Balance from prior periods				6,000
Dec. 31	Adjusting entry..................	1,500			1,500

Earned revenues. The adjusting entry to be made for the apportionment of revenue recorded in advance and to be earned during more than one period depends on the nature of the account that was originally credited.

To illustrate, assume that a magazine publisher made collections of $100,000 during 19+3 for one-, two-, and three-year subscriptions, and that at the end of the year only $40,000 had been earned by the issuance of magazines. The adjusting entry at the end of the year, to show that $40,000 had been earned, will depend on whether the $100,000 was originally credited to Subscriptions Collected in Advance (a liability account) or to Subscriptions Revenue. The two conditions are illustrated below.

ORIGINAL CREDIT TO A LIABILITY ACCOUNT: The adjusting entry should transfer the *earned* portion from the liability account to a revenue account. The entry is illustrated below.

Subscriptions collected in advance....................	40,000	
Subscriptions revenue...........................		40,000
Subscriptions earned during the year.		

The accounts affected by the entry are shown below.

		Subscriptions Collected in Advance (Dr.)	Subscriptions Collected in Advance (Cr.)	Subscriptions Revenue (Dr.)	Subscriptions Revenue (Cr.)
19+3					
Various dates	Advance collections		100,000		
Dec. 31	Adjusting entry	40,000			40,000

ORIGINAL CREDIT TO A REVENUE ACCOUNT: The adjusting entry should transfer the *unearned* portion from the revenue account to a liability account. The entry is illustrated below.

Subscriptions revenue	60,000	
Subscriptions collected in advance		60,000
Subscriptions collected but not earned as of the end of the year.		

After posting the adjusting entry, the accounts affected appear as shown below.

		Subscriptions Collected in Advance (Dr.)	Subscriptions Collected in Advance (Cr.)	Subscriptions Revenue (Dr.)	Subscriptions Revenue (Cr.)
19+3					
Various dates	Advance collections				100,000
Dec. 31	Adjusting entry		60,000	60,000	

In either case, the Subscriptions Revenue balance of $40,000 will be reported in the income statement and the Subscriptions Collected in Advance balance of $60,000 will be reported as a liability in the balance sheet.

Provision for losses. Certain end-of-period adjustments may be required in order to avoid a misstatement of asset amounts. The accounts receivable account balance at any time reports the total amount owed by all customers of the company. However, if any portion of this total is likely to be uncollectible, the accounts should be adjusted to reflect this fact.

Methods of determining the amount of the adjusting entry for uncollectible accounts will be discussed in a later chapter. For the present discussion, we are concerned with the entry to be made once the amount has been estimated. If it is determined that $1,000 is the appropriate amount for the entry, the following adjustment should be recorded.

Bad debts expense	1,000	
Allowance for uncollectibles.....................		1,000
Estimated uncollectible accounts.		

The affected accounts would appear as follows:

		Bad Debts Expense (Dr.)	Bad Debts Expense (Cr.)	Allowance for Uncollectibles (Dr.)	Allowance for Uncollectibles (Cr.)
19+3					
Dec. 31	Adjusting entry	1,000			1,000

The contra account is used to record the reduction in the net realizable value of accounts receivable. This is necessary because a credit to the Accounts Receivable account would require that individual customer accounts in the subsidiary accounts receivable ledger also be credited. However, we do not know which specific customers' accounts will prove to be uncollectible.

The allowance for uncollectibles account would be shown as a deduction from the accounts receivable account in the balance sheet. The bad debts expense account is usually shown as an operating expense in the income statement. An alternative treatment is to show it contra to sales.

Although the adjusting entry for estimated bad debts is necessary in order to avoid overstating the assets, it should be noted that, just as with all other adjusting entries, it also has an income statement effect. Failure to record the adjustment results in an overstatement of net income for the period.

Data for adjustments. A logical question to raise at this point is "Where does the accountant obtain the information required for adjusting entries?" For the experienced accountant this is not as difficult a task as it might appear to be.

We might begin to answer the question in general terms by stating that he wants to be as certain as possible that the income statement reports all revenues earned and expenses incurred and the balance sheet reports all assets and liabilities of the firm. Thus, by scanning the trial balance he may note certain items that are not listed (such as depreciation expense). Certain items found in the trial balance may also indicate the necessity of looking further to see if an adjustment is required. For example, the presence of a notes receivable account would indicate that there might be accrued interest receivable not yet recorded. This would also be true for an investment in bonds account. In addition, a review of the prior year's adjusting entries will often disclose adjustments that are again appropriate.

Ultimately, certain source documents and supporting data must be consulted to determine the *amount* of specific adjustments. Insurance policies may be inspected to determine the amount of premium expirations; depreciable asset records or a depreciation schedule may be used to determine the depreciation charge for the year; and payroll records may be used to determine the amount of accrued wages and salaries payable.

REVERSING ENTRIES

Purpose of reversing entries. It was noted in the list of steps in the accounting cycle at the beginning of this chapter that some of the adjusting entries may be reversed after the books are closed. Reversing entries do not imply that the adjusting entries were incorrect. The purpose of reversing entries, which are made at the beginning of the accounting period with debits and credits exactly opposite from certain adjusting entries made at the end of the previous year, is simply to allow similar transactions to be recorded in the same manner.

For example, it may be company policy for clerical employees to record revenue when the cash is received and to record expenses when the cash is paid during the period, with accruals and other adjusting entries made at the end of the period by an accountant. By the use of reversing entries, the accountant makes it possible for the clerks to follow standard procedures in the recording of large numbers of similar transactions. On the other hand, it should be pointed out that reversing entries are not an absolute necessity and can be avoided if the individuals who record the transactions during the period have some knowledge of accounting.

Illustration. The adjusting entries discussed earlier in this chapter will be used to illustrate the use of reversing entries.

BAD DEBTS AND DEPRECIATION: There is no reason to reverse the entries for bad debts and periodic depreciation. The contra accounts are reported with the related asset accounts to show the net book value of the assets. Failure to reverse the entries will have no effect on the form of subsequent entries for bad debts and depreciation.

UNRECORDED REVENUES: On page 14, an adjusting entry was recorded for interest receivable on bonds. Accrued interest of $875 was receivable at December 31, 19+3, even though it was not actually payable until April 1, 19+4. The interest to be received on April 1 will consist of the following:

For the period October 1, 19+3, to December 31, 19+3	$ 875
For the period January 1, 19+4, to March 31, 19+4	875
Total	$1,750

The portion of the interest applicable to 19+3 has already been recognized as revenue at the time of receipt on April 1, 19+4. Therefore, unless a reversing entry is recorded, it will be necessary to record the receipt as follows:

Cash	1,750	
Interest receivable............		875
Interest revenue		875
To record receipt of interest.		

Normally, the receipt of interest earned would be recorded by a debit to Cash and a credit to Interest Revenue for the entire amount received, a procedure that cannot be followed in this case.

If the December 31, 19+3, adjusting entry is reversed, the receipt on April 1, 19+4, can be recorded just as any other receipt of interest earned is recorded. The appropriate journal entries and the resulting effects on the accounts are shown below.

December 31, 19+3 (adjusting entry):		
Interest receivable	875	
Interest revenue		875
January 1, 19+4 (reversing entry):		
Interest revenue	875	
Interest receivable		875
April 1, 19+4 (receipt of interest):		
Cash	1,750	
Interest revenue		1,750

Date		Interest Receivable (Dr.)	Interest Receivable (Cr.)	Interest Revenue (Dr.)	Interest Revenue (Cr.)
19+3					
Dec. 31	Adjusting entry	875			875
31	Closing entry			875	
19+4					
Jan. 1	Reversing entry		875	875	
Apr. 1	Receipt of interest				1,750

The $875 ($1,750 − $875) credit balance in the interest revenue account reflects the correct amount earned in 19+4. Thus, the effect of the entries is to recognize one half of the interest as revenue in 19+3 and the balance as revenue in 19+4. The fact that the interest revenue account (which normally has a credit balance) has a debit balance of $875 for the first three months of 19+4 is of no significance. The accountant knows that by the end of the accounting period this situation will have changed.

UNRECORDED EXPENSE: An adjusting entry was illustrated earlier (see page 14) recording accrued wages and salaries owed at the end of 19+3 in the amount of $1,000. If we assume that total payroll for the first pay period ending in 19+4 is $2,500, the following entry is required to correctly record the payment unless a reversing entry is recorded.

Wages and salaries payable	1,000	
Wages and salaries expense	1,500	
Cash		2,500
To record payroll.		

However, all other payrolls during the year will be recorded by debiting the expense account and crediting Cash. The use of a reversing entry will allow us to record the first payroll in 19+4 just as we would all others during the year. The entries and accounts are shown below.

December 31, 19+3 (adjusting entry):		
Wages and salaries expense	1,000	
Wages and salaries payable		1,000
January 1, 19+4 (reversing entry):		
Wages and salaries payable	1,000	
Wages and salaries expense		1,000
January 4, 19+4 (payment of payroll):		
Wages and salaries expense	2,500	
Cash		2,500

Date		Wages and Salaries Payable (Dr.)	Wages and Salaries Payable (Cr.)	Wages and Salaries Expense (Dr.)	Wages and Salaries Expense (Cr.)
19+3					
Dec. 31	Adjusting entry		1,000	1,000	
31	Closing entry				1,000
19+4					
Jan. 1	Reversing entry	1,000			1,000
4	Payment of payroll			2,500	

The $1,500 ($2,500 – $1,000) debit balance in the wages and salaries expense account is the correct expense for 19+4, as of January 4. The difference between this amount and the amount paid on January 4 was properly recorded as an expense in 19+3.

COST EXPIRATIONS—PREPAYMENTS: The necessity for reversing adjustments to record the expirations of costs previously recorded will depend upon the way in which the prepayment is recorded. It was assumed in the first adjustment on page 15 that the payment of a $300, three-year insurance premium was originally debited to an asset account, and that one third of the premium had expired at the end of 19+3. After the adjusting entry is recorded, the prepaid portion of the premium is in the asset account. Since it is the policy of the firm to debit premium payments to the asset account, it is desirable to leave the beginning balance for 19+4 in the asset account, and no reversing entry is needed.

If we assume that the $300 was originally debited to the insurance expense account, the purpose of the adjusting entry is to transfer the unexpired portion to the asset account at the end of 19+3 (see entry at the bottom of page 15). A reversing entry is desirable in this case in order to transfer the $200 prepayment at the beginning of 19+4 back into the expense account, so as to prepare it for any additional premium payments that may occur during the year. The effect of the reversing entry on the accounts is illustrated below.

		Unexpired Insurance		Insurance Expense	
19+3					
Jan. 2	Original expenditure			300	
Dec. 31	Adjusting entry	200			200
31	Closing entry				100
19+4					
Jan. 1	Reversing entry		200	200	

The desirability of the reversing entry becomes apparent if we assume that no reversing entry is made, and that an additional premium of $175 is paid in 19+4 and charged (in accordance with the company's previous procedure) to Insurance Expense. An undesirable situation is produced at the end of 19+4 when it is time to record the annual adjusting entry. Part of the apportionable cost is in the unexpired insurance account ($200) and part is in the insurance expense account ($175). This would be a confusing situation, as shown below, which the reversing entry avoids.

		Unexpired Insurance		Insurance Expense	
19+3					
Jan. 2	Original expenditure			300	
Dec. 31	Adjusting entry	200			200
31	Closing entry				100
19+4					
Feb. 1	Additional premium			175	

If an expense prepayment will benefit more than one period, it is advisable to charge the expenditure to an asset account, because a reversal of the adjusting entry will thus be avoided.

EARNED REVENUES: The entries illustrated on pages 16 and 17 show the adjustments required under each alternative for recording revenues received in advance. When the original credit is to an unearned revenue account, the adjusting entry transfers the portion earned to a revenue account. Since the remaining portion is in the liability account and it is the company's policy to credit receipts to this account, there is no reason for a reversing entry.

If the original credit is to a revenue account, the adjusting entry transfers the portion unearned to a liability account. A reversing entry is desirable in this case so that the beginning belance of unearned revenues will be in the account that is normally credited when revenues are received in advance. This is illustrated below.

		Subscriptions Collected in Advance		**Subscriptions Revenue**	
19+3					
Various dates	Advance collections				100,000
Dec. 31	Adjusting entry		60,000	60,000	
31	Closing entry			40,000	
19+4					
Jan. 1	Reversing entry	60,000			60,000

When revenue recorded in advance will be earned during more than one period, it is advisable to credit an unearned revenue account, because a reversing entry will thus be avoided.

2

Review of Working Papers and Closing Procedures

Purpose of working papers. Working papers are a columnar device to facilitate the preparation of financial statements by classifying the account balances according to the statements in which they will appear, and to facilitate the preparation of entries involved in the procedure of adjusting and closing the books. Also, by the recording of adjusting and closing entries from the working papers, errors are minimized in the formal journal and ledger records. Finally, interim period financial statements (such as monthly or quarterly statements) can be prepared from working papers without the necessity of making formal adjusting and closing entries at the end of the interim period.

It should be pointed out that working papers are an informal record and do not replace any formal record or statement. Thus the form in which working papers are prepared depends to some extent on the preference of the accountant. Also, in those cases where there are few ledger accounts and adjusting entries, working papers may not even be prepared.

MERCHANDISING OPERATIONS

Perpetual inventory procedures. The first working papers illustration will be for a merchandising concern using perpetual inventory procedures. The working papers are shown on pages 26 and 27. The steps required to prepare the working papers are listed below.

Step 1. The trial balance was entered in the first pair of columns.

Step 2. The following year-end adjustments were entered in the Adjustments columns.

(a) The allowance for uncollectibles was increased $600.

Bad debts expense	600	
Allowance for uncollectibles		600

(b) Depreciation of delivery equipment was computed at 20 percent of the $4,000 balance in the asset account.

Depreciation—Delivery equipment	800	
Accumulated depreciation—Delivery equipment		800

(c) Insurance premiums were debited to Unexpired Insurance. The expired portion, $440, was transferred to an expense account.

Insurance expense	440	
Unexpired insurance		440

(d) On November 1, the company collected $300 for services to be rendered in making deliveries for another store during November, December, and January. The credit was made to Delivery Fees Collected in Advance. By the end of the year, $200 was earned; it is transferred to a revenue account.

Delivery fees collected in advance	200	
Delivery revenue		200

(e) Accrued salesmen's salaries amount to $500, and accrued office salaries amount to $130.

Salesmen's salaries	500	
Office salaries	130	
Salaries payable		630

(f) Accrued interest on notes receivable is $25.

Interest receivable	25	
Interest revenue		25

Step 3. The Adjustments columns were totaled and the account balances after adjustments were entered in the Adjusted Trial Balance columns. Then these columns were totaled.

Step 4. Each account balance in the Adjusted Trial Balance columns was extended to the appropriate column for the statement in which the balance should appear. Debit balances were extended to debit columns; credit balances were extended to credit columns. (The amount shown as accounts receivable in the Adjusted Trial Balance column is the balance of the controlling account. The subsidiary ledger contains accounts with debit balances totaling $20,000 and accounts with credit balances totaling $500. These amounts were entered in the Balance Sheet columns.)

Step 5. The Income Statement columns were footed; the net income before income tax was entered as a balancing figure and brought down after again footing the columns.

Step 6. The income tax was computed and entered in the Income Statement debit column, and in the Balance Sheet credit column as a liability. If the federal income tax is not recorded until the net income before tax is computed in the working papers, an additional adjusting entry is required and would be recorded as follows:

Federal income tax	3,036	
Income tax payable		3,036

If the income tax was recorded in the accounts before the working papers were prepared, Step 5 would consist merely of footing the Income Statement columns, and Step 6 would be omitted.

Step 7. The net income was entered as a balancing figure in the Income Statement debit column and in the Retained Earnings credit column.

Step 8. The Retained Earnings columns were footed; the amount of the retained earnings at the end of the year was entered as a balancing figure in the Retained Earnings debit column and in the Balance Sheet credit column. The Retained Earnings and Balance Sheet columns were footed.

Some accountants record the adjusting entries in the journal and then apply them to the unadjusted balances in the working papers. Other accountants first enter the adjustments in the working papers and do not record the adjusting entries in the journal until later, when they record the entries to close the books.

If statements are prepared monthly but the books are closed only annually, the monthly adjustments may be applied to the working papers only, without making adjusting entries in the books.

CLOSING ENTRIES. After the annual statements have been prepared, it is cus-

A CORPORATION
Working Papers
For the Year Ended December 31, 19+5

	Trial Balance		Adjustments		Adjusted Trial Balance		Income Statement		Retained Earnings Statement		Balance Sheet	
Cash	9,730				9,730						9,730	
Accounts receivable	19,500				19,500						20,000	500
Allowance for uncollectibles		300		(a) 600		900						900
Notes receivable	5,000				5,000						5,000	
Inventory, December 31, 19+5	30,000				30,000						30,000	
Unexpired insurance	695			(c) 440	255						255	
Delivery equipment	4,000				4,000						4,000	
Accumulated depreciation—delivery equipment		1,600		(b) 800		2,400						2,400
Accounts payable		18,300				18,300						18,300
Delivery fees collected in advance		300	(d) 200			100						100
Capital stock		25,000				25,000						25,000
Retained earnings, December 31, 19+4		9,380				9,380				9,380		
Dividends	2,000				2,000				2,000			
Sales		203,000				203,000		203,000				
Sales returns and allowances	980				980		980					
Sales discounts	1,670				1,670		1,670					
Cost of goods sold	150,000				150,000		150,000					
Salesmen's salaries	12,650		(e) 500		13,150		13,150					
Rent expense	3,000				3,000		3,000					
Advertising	10,200				10,200		10,200					
Delivery expense	3,275				3,275		3,275					
Miscellaneous selling expenses	860				860		860					
Office salaries	3,260		(e) 130		3,390		3,390					
Office expense	930				930		930					
Property taxes	190				190		190					
Interest revenue		60		(f) 25		85		85				
Totals forward	257,940	257,940	830	1,865	258,130	259,165	187,645	203,085	2,000	9,380	68,985	47,200

A CORPORATION
Working Papers (Concluded)
For the Year Ended December 31, 19+5

	Trial Balance		Adjustments		Adjusted Trial Balance		Income Statement		Retained Earnings Statement		Balance Sheet	
Totals brought forward			830	1,865	258,130	259,165	187,645	203,085	2,000	9,380	68,985	47,200
Bad debts expense			(a) 600		600		600					
Depreciation—delivery equipment			(b) 800		800		800					
Insurance expense			(c) 440		440		440					
Delivery revenue				(d) 200		200		200				
Salaries payable				(e) 630		630						630
Interest receivable			(f) 25		25						25	
			2,695	2,695	259,995	259,995	189,485	203,285				
Net income before income tax—down							13,800					
							203,285	203,285				
Net income before income tax—brought down								13,800				
Federal income tax							3,036					3,036
Net income							10,764			10,764		
							13,800	13,800	2,000	20,144		
Retained earnings, December 31, 19+5									18,144			18,144
									20,144	20,144	69,010	69,010

tomary to close the books. This is accomplished by recording and posting closing entries. The purpose of closing entries is to transfer the data contained in the temporary accounts (revenues, expenses, and dividends) to a permanent account (retained earnings). When the closing has been completed, the only accounts showing balances will be the asset, liability, and owners' equity accounts. The revenue, expense, and dividend accounts will be closed; that is, these accounts will have zero balances.

The following illustration of closing entries is based on data in the preceding working papers for A Corporation and uses an income summary account to "summarize" the results of operations in a single account before transferring the income or loss for the period to retained earnings.

Sales	203,000	
Interest revenue	85	
Delivery revenue	200	
Income summary		203,285
To close accounts with credit balances.		
Income summary	192,521	
Sales returns and allowances		980
Sales discounts		1,670
Cost of goods sold		150,000
Salesmen's salaries		13,150
Rent expense		3,000
Advertising		10,200
Delivery expense		3,275
Miscellaneous selling expenses		860
Office salaries		3,390
Office expense		930
Property taxes		190
Bad debts expense		600
Depreciation—Delivery equipment		800
Insurance expense		440
Federal income tax		3,036
To close accounts with debit balances.		
Income summary ($203,285 – $192,521)	10,764	
Retained earnings		10,764
To close the income summary account.		
Retained earnings	2,000	
Dividends		2,000
To close the dividends account.		

The first entry closes all the accounts whose balances were extended to the Income Statement credit column of the working papers.

The second entry closes all the accounts whose balances were extended to the Income Statement debit column of the working papers, and also the income tax expense.

The third entry closes the income summary account.

The last entry closes the dividends account.

An alternative closing procedure will be illustrated later in the chapter.

Periodic inventory procedures. Illustrative working papers for a company that does not maintain a perpetual inventory are shown on page 30. Under such circumstances, the inventory balance shown in the unadjusted trial balance is the beginning inventory. An adjusting entry may be used to determine the cost of goods sold, to remove the beginning inventory from the account balances, and to set up the ending inventory, as shown in the working papers. To simplify the illustration, no other adjusting entries are used. In effect, the adjusting entry shown takes the beginning inventory, adds the net delivered cost of purchases for the period, then deducts the ending inventory to determine the cost of goods sold.

As indicated in the working papers, the cost of goods sold by B Corporation is $32,000. The following schedule confirms this amount.

B CORPORATION
Schedule of Cost of Goods Sold
For the Year Ended December 31, 19+5

Inventory, December 31, 19+4			$ 4,500
Add net cost of purchases:			
Purchases		$30,500	
Add transportation in		1,670	
Total		$32,170	
Deduct:			
Purchase returns and allowances	$770		
Purchase discounts	600	1,370	30,800
Cost of goods available for sale			$35,300
Deduct inventory, December 31, 19+5			3,300
Cost of goods sold			$32,000

There is no liability for income taxes shown on the working papers, because 19+5 was an unprofitable year.

CLOSING ENTRIES: Some accountants do not use an income summary account in the closing process. They credit the net income or debit the net loss directly to Retained Earnings. Such a practice is illustrated in the closing entries for B Corporation below.

Sales	56,000	
Retained earnings	310	
Sales returns and allowances		500
Sales discounts		710
Cost of goods sold		32,000
Transportation out		750
All other expenses		22,350
To close the revenue and expense accounts.		
Retained earnings	2,500	
Dividends		2,500
To close the dividends account.		

B CORPORATION
Working Papers
For the Year Ended December 31, 19+5

	Trial Balance		Adjustments		Adjusted Trial Balance		Income Statement		Retained Earnings Statement		Balance Sheet	
Cash	29,090				29,090						29,090	
Inventory	4,500		(a) 3,300	(a) 4,500	3,300						3,300	
Accounts payable		2,200				2,200						2,200
Capital stock		25,000				25,000						25,000
Retained earnings, December 31, 19+4		8,000				8,000				8,000		
Dividends	2,500				2,500				2,500			
Sales		56,000				56,000		56,000				
Sales returns and allowances	500				500		500					
Sales discounts	710				710		710					
Purchases	30,500			(a) 30,500								
Transportation in	1,670			(a) 1,670								
Purchase returns and allowances		770	(a) 770									
Purchase discounts		600	(a) 600									
Cost of goods sold			(a) 32,000		32,000		32,000					
Transportation out	750				750		750					
All other expenses	22,350				22,350		22,350					
	92,570	92,570	36,670	36,670	91,200	91,200	56,310	56,000				
Net loss								310	310			
							56,310	56,310	2,810	8,000		
Retained earnings, December 31, 19+5									5,190			5,190
									8,000	8,000	32,390	32,390

Proprietorship and partnership working papers. Instead of a pair of columns for the Statement of Retained Earnings, the working papers for a proprietorship have a pair of columns headed, for example, *John Smith, Capital.* The balances of the proprietor's capital and drawing accounts and the net income or net loss for the period are extended to these columns, and the balance of the columns is extended to the Balance Sheet credit column.

Working papers for a partnership contain a pair of similar columns for each partner, showing the balances of the capital and drawing accounts and the division of the net income or net loss.

MANUFACTURING OPERATIONS

The preparation of financial statements for a manufacturing concern differs from that of a merchandising concern in one major respect. The manufacturing firm utilizes production costs in order to manufacture the goods that are ultimately transferred to its finished goods inventory. These costs must be determined before the cost of goods sold can be calculated for the manufacturing firm. This difference will now be illustrated.

The cost of goods sold for a merchandising firm is determined as follows:

$$\begin{pmatrix}\text{Cost of}\\ \text{goods}\\ \text{sold}\end{pmatrix} = \begin{pmatrix}\text{Cost of}\\ \text{beginning}\\ \text{merchandise}\\ \text{inventory}\end{pmatrix} + \begin{pmatrix}\text{Cost of}\\ \text{merchandise}\\ \text{purchased}\end{pmatrix} - \begin{pmatrix}\text{Cost of}\\ \text{ending}\\ \text{merchandise}\\ \text{inventory}\end{pmatrix}$$

For the manufacturing firm, the cost of goods sold is determined as shown below.

$$\begin{pmatrix}\text{Cost of}\\ \text{goods}\\ \text{sold}\end{pmatrix} = \begin{pmatrix}\text{Cost of}\\ \text{beginning}\\ \text{finished goods}\\ \text{inventory}\end{pmatrix} + \begin{pmatrix}\text{Cost of}\\ \text{goods}\\ \text{manufactured}\end{pmatrix} - \begin{pmatrix}\text{Cost of}\\ \text{ending}\\ \text{finished goods}\\ \text{inventory}\end{pmatrix}$$

The cost of goods manufactured during a given period is calculated as follows:

$$\begin{pmatrix}\text{Cost of}\\ \text{goods}\\ \text{manufactured}\end{pmatrix} = \underbrace{\begin{pmatrix}\text{Direct}\\ \text{material}\\ \text{cost}\end{pmatrix} + \begin{pmatrix}\text{Direct}\\ \text{labor}\\ \text{cost}\end{pmatrix} + \begin{pmatrix}\text{Factory}\\ \text{overhead}\\ \text{cost}\end{pmatrix}}_{\substack{\text{Production costs utilized}\\ \text{during the current period}}} + \begin{pmatrix}\text{Cost of}\\ \text{beginning}\\ \text{goods in}\\ \text{process}\end{pmatrix} - \begin{pmatrix}\text{Cost of}\\ \text{ending}\\ \text{goods in}\\ \text{process}\end{pmatrix}$$

The equation above is formalized by a separate financial statement known as the statement of cost of goods manufactured. In order to facilitate the preparation of this statement, the working papers for a manufacturing firm are expanded to allow the classification of the accounts needed to prepare the statement.

The equations above also provide the underlying rationale for the debits and credits recorded in the working papers for cost of goods manufactured and cost of goods sold. For example, the cost of goods manufactured equation above shows ending goods in process as a deduction, which is why ending goods in process is credited in the Cost of Goods Manufactured columns of the working papers shown on page 34. Similarly, the additions to the same equation are shown as debits in the working papers.

There are two ways in which working papers may be prepared for a manufacturing concern. One alternative is to use a single set of working papers to prepare all the financial statements for the firm. This procedure is illustrated below. A second alternative is to prepare separate working papers for each statement.

The adjusting entries for the illustration are presented below. It is assumed that the firm uses a separate asset account (factory supplies) for indirect materials. An acceptable alternative would be to record such supplies in the materials inventory account.

(a) Bad debts expense	300	
Allowance for uncollectibles		300
To add $300 to the allowance account.		
(b) Manufacturing overhead	2,070	
Factory supplies		2,070
Supplies used.		
(c) Manufacturing overhead	910	
Insurance expense	65	
Unexpired insurance		975
Premium expiration for the year. (Manufacturing, $910; General, $65.)		
(d) Manufacturing overhead	2,600	
Accumulated depreciation—Factory buildings		2,600
Depreciation for the year.		
(e) Manufacturing overhead	4,788	
Accumulated depreciation—Machinery and equipment		4,788
Depreciation for the year.		
(f) Depreciation—Office equipment	314	
Accumulated depreciation—Office equipment		314
Depreciation for the year.		
(g) Interest expense—Bonds	250	
Discount on bonds		250
Amortization of discount for the year.		
(h) Rent collected in advance	50	
Rent revenue		50
Earned portion of rent collected in advance.		
(i) Interest receivable	45	
Interest revenue—Notes receivable		45
Interest accrued on notes receivable.		
(j) Interest expense—Notes payable	20	
Interest payable		20
Interest accrued on notes payable.		

The end-of-year inventories were: finished goods, $10,991; goods in process, $13,212; materials, $9,923.

Some expenditures cannot be regarded as entirely manufacturing, selling, or general, but should be apportioned to two or more of these groups on some appropriate basis. In this illustration, property taxes and insurance are apportioned to manufacturing (included in manufacturing overhead) and to general expense (see individual accounts). Stationery and printing expense is apportioned 20 per cent to selling expense and 80 per cent to general expense; the apportionment is indicated by the letters *S* and *G* beside the related amounts in the Income Statement debit column.

Single set of working papers. A single set of working papers for a manufacturing firm is illustrated on pages 34, 35, and 36. As indicated by the illustration, an accountant need not provide for the adjusted trial balance when setting up the column headings in the working papers.

Note the use of the manufacturing overhead control account in the working papers. This assumes that the indirect manufacturing costs utilized during the year, as well as year-end adjustments for indirect manufacturing costs, are recorded in the manufacturing overhead control account. If the control account is not used, it is necessary to use *individual* indirect manufacturing-overhead accounts (for example, Indirect Labor; Heat, Light, and Power—Factory; Repairs to Buildings and Machinery; Property Taxes—Factory; etc.). In the latter case, these individual accounts would be shown in the working papers.

CLOSING THE BOOKS. The closing of the books of a manufacturing firm using the periodic-inventory procedure involves: closing the accounts used in the preparation of the statement of cost of goods manufactured and recording the end-of-period inventories of materials and goods-in-process; closing the accounts used in the preparation of the income statement and recording the end-of-period inventory of finished goods; and closing any other accounts affecting retained earnings. Entries are shown below.

Cost of goods manufactured	150,624	
Purchase returns and allowances	425	
Purchase discounts	675	
Goods in process, ending	13,212	
Materials, ending	9,923	
Goods in process, beginning		8,120
Materials, beginning		6,325
Purchases—Materials		54,630
Transportation in		1,200
Direct labor		65,805
Manufacturing overhead		38,779
To record the cost of goods manufactured and the ending inventory of materials and goods in process.		

INGRAM MANUFACTURING COMPANY
Working Papers
For the Year Ended December 31, 19+5

	Trial Balance		Adjustments		Cost of Goods Manufactured		Income Statement		Statement of Retained Earnings		Balance Sheet	
Cash	27,600										27,600	
Marketable securities	10,000										10,000	
Accounts receivable	35,365										35,365	
Allowance for uncollectibles		650		(a) 300								950
Notes receivable	6,000										6,000	
Inventories:												
Finished goods	12,400						12,400	10,991			10,991	
Goods in process	8,120				8,120	13,212					13,212	
Materials	6,325				6,325	9,923					9,923	
Factory supplies	2,420			(b) 2,070							350	
Unexpired insurance	1,375			(c) 975							400	
Stock of Murdock Sales Company	5,000										5,000	
Land	23,000										23,000	
Factory buildings	65,000										65,000	
Accumulated depreciation— Factory buildings		14,500		(d) 2,600								17,100
Machinery and equipment	53,900										53,900	
Accumulated depreciation— Machinery and equipment		13,600		(e) 4,788								18,388
Office equipment	3,140										3,140	
Accumulated depreciation— Office equipment		750		(f) 314								1,064
Accounts payable		4,000										4,000
Notes payable		5,000										5,000
Rent collected in advance		150	(h) 50									100
Bonds payable		50,000										50,000
Discount on bonds	2,500			(g) 250							2,250	
Capital stock—Preferred		40,000										40,000
Capital stock—Common		75,000										75,000
Capital in excess of par value— Common stock		7,500										7,500
Totals forward	262,145	211,150	50	11,297	14,445	23,135	12,400	10,991			266,131	219,102

INGRAM MANUFACTURING COMPANY
Working Papers (Continued)
For the Year Ended December 31, 19+5

	Trial Balance		Adjustments		Cost of Goods Manufactured		Income Statement		Statement of Retained Earnings		Balance Sheet	
Totals brought forward	262,145	211,150	50	11,297	14,445	23,135	12,400	10,991			266,131	219,102
Retained earnings, December 31, 19+4		18,714								18,714		
Dividends—Common	6,000								6,000			
Dividends—Preferred	2,400								2,400			
Sales		238,625						238,625				
Sales returns and allowances	1,315						1,315					
Sales discounts	1,617						1,617					
Purchases—Materials	54,630				54,630							
Purchase returns and allowances		425				425						
Purchase discounts		675				675						
Transportation in	1,200				1,200							
Direct labor	65,805				65,805							
Manufacturing overhead	28,411		(b) 2,070		38,779							
			(c) 910									
			(d) 2,600									
			(e) 4,788									
Property taxes	64						64					
Advertising	7,320						7,320					
Salesmen's salaries	8,000						8,000					
Salesmen's traveling expenses	4,100						4,100					
Transportation out	850						850					
Miscellaneous selling expenses	875						875					
Officers' salaries	16,500						16,500					
Office salaries	4,200						4,200					
Office supplies expense	312						312					
Stationery and printing expense	415						S- 83 G-332					
Miscellaneous general expenses	561						561					
Interest revenue—Notes receivable		141		(i) 45				186				
Dividends on Murdock stock		400						400				
Interest expense—Bonds	3,000		(g) 250				3,250					
Interest expense—Notes payable	410		(j) 20				430					
Totals forward	470,130	470,130	10,688	11,342	174,859	24,235	62,209	250,202	8,400	18,714	266,131	219,102

INGRAM MANUFACTURING COMPANY
Working Papers (Concluded)
For the Year Ended December 31, 19+5

	Trial Balance		Adjustments		Cost of Goods Manufactured		Income Statement		Statement of Retained Earnings		Balance Sheet	
Totals brought forward			10,688	11,342	174,859	24,235	62,209	250,202	8,400	18,714	266,131	219,102
Bad debts expense			(a) 300				300					
Insurance expense			(c) 65				65					
Depreciation—Office equipment			(f) 314				314					
Rent revenue				(h) 50				50				
Interest receivable			(i) 45								45	
Interest payable				(j) 20								20
			11,412	11,412	174,859	24,235						
Cost of goods manufactured						150,624	150,624					
					174,859	174,859	213,512	250,252				
Net income before income tax—down							36,740					
							250,252	250,252				
Net income before income tax—brought down								36,740				
Federal income tax							11,135					11,135
Net income							25,605			25,605		
							36,740	36,740	8,400	44,319		
Retained earnings, December 31, 19+5									35,919			35,919
									44,319	44,319	266,176	266,176

Cost of goods sold	152,033	
Finished goods, ending	10,991	
Cost of goods manufactured		150,624
Finished goods, beginning		12,400
To record cost of goods sold and ending inventory of finished goods.		
Sales	238,625	
Interest revenue—Notes receivable	186	
Dividends on Murdock stock	400	
Rent revenue	50	
Income summary		239,261
To close revenue accounts to Income Summary.		
Income summary	213,656	
Cost of goods sold		152,033
Sales returns and allowances		1,315
Sales discounts		1,617
Advertising		7,320
Salesmen's salaries		8,000
Salesmen's traveling expenses		4,100
Transportation out		850
Miscellaneous selling expenses		875
Officers' salaries		16,500
Office salaries		4,200
Office supplies expense		312
Stationery and printing expense		415
Bad debts expense		300
Insurance expense		65
Depreciation—Office equipment		314
Property taxes		64
Miscellaneous general expenses		561
Interest expense—Bonds		3,250
Interest expense—Notes payable		430
Federal income tax		11,135
To close expense accounts to Income Summary.		
Income summary	25,605	
Retained earnings		25,605
To transfer net income to Retained Earnings.		
Retained earnings	8,400	
Dividends—Common		6,000
Dividends—Preferred		2,400
To close the dividends accounts.		

Some accountants might not use all the entries just illustrated to close the books of a manufacturing firm. Various alternative closing procedures might combine some of the entries shown.

Financial statements. The financial statements prepared from the working papers of Ingram Manufacturing Company include the statement of cost of goods manufactured, income statement, statement of retained earnings, and balance sheet.

The statement of cost of goods manufactured is different from the other statements, in that it may be viewed as an internal statement that is seldom seen by statement users outside the firm. The other statements are usually included in some form in the firm's annual report to stockholders, which is widely circulated outside the firm.

As indicated earlier in this chapter, the statement of cost of goods manufactured formalizes the calculation of the cost of goods fully completed during the current accounting period. The statement for Ingram Manufacturing Company is illustrated below.

Exhibit D

INGRAM MANUFACTURING COMPANY
Statement of Cost of Goods Manufactured
For the Year Ended December 31, 19+5

Materials:			
Inventory, December 31, 19+4			$ 6,325
Cost of purchases:			
Purchases		$54,630	
Purchase returns and allowances	$425		
Purchase discounts	675	1,100	
Net		$53,530	
Transportation in		1,200	54,730
Total inventory and purchases			$ 61,055
Inventory, December 31, 19+5			9,923
Materials used			$ 51,132
Direct labor			65,805
Manufacturing overhead			38,779
Total manufacturing cost			$155,716
Add goods in process, December 31, 19+4			8,120
Total production cost			$163,836
Deduct goods in process, December 31, 19+5			13,212
Cost of goods manufactured			$150,624

The other financial statements of Ingram Manufacturing Company are presented on pages 39 and 40. The following relationships among the statements should be noted:

(1) The cost of goods manufactured must be determined before the cost of goods sold can be calculated in the income statement.

(2) Net income must be determined in order to calculate the ending retained earnings.

(3) Ending retained earnings must be determined before the balance sheet can be completed.

Exhibit C

INGRAM MANUFACTURING COMPANY
Income Statement
For the Year Ended December 31, 19+5

Gross sales			$238,625
Sales returns and allowances		$ 1,315	
Sales discounts		1,617	2,932
Net sales			$235,693
Cost of goods sold:			
Finished-goods inventory, December 31, 19+4		$ 12,400	
Cost of goods manufactured—Exhibit D		150,624	
Total		$163,024	
Finished goods inventory, December 31, 19+5		10,991	152,033
Gross margin			$ 83,660
Operating expenses:			
Selling expenses:			
Advertising	$ 7,320		
Salesmen's salaries	8,000		
Salesmen's traveling expenses	4,100		
Transportation out	850		
Stationery and printing expense	83		
Miscellaneous selling expenses	875	$ 21,228	
General expenses:			
Officers' salaries	$16,500		
Office salaries	4,200		
Office supplies expense	312		
Stationery and printing expense	332		
Bad debts expense	300		
Insurance expense	65		
Depreciation—Office equipment	314		
Property taxes	64		
Miscellaneous general expenses	561	22,648	43,876
Net operating income			$ 39,784
Nonoperating items:			
Other expenses:			
Interest expense—Bonds	$ 3,250		
Interest expense—Notes payable	430	$ 3,680	
Other revenue:			
Dividends on Murdock stock	$ 400		
Interest revenue—Notes receivable	186		
Rent revenue	50	636	3,044
Income before income tax			$ 36,740
Federal income tax			11,135
Net income			$ 25,605

Exhibit B

INGRAM MANUFACTURING COMPANY
Statement of Retained Earnings
For the Year Ended December 31, 19+5

Retained earnings, December 31, 19+4		$18,714
Add net income for the year—Exhibit C		25,605
Total		$44,319
Deduct dividends:		
Common	$6,000	
Preferred	2,400	8,400
Retained earnings, December 31, 19+5		$35,919

Exhibit A

INGRAM MANUFACTURING COMPANY
Balance Sheet
December 31, 19+5

Assets

Current assets:			
Cash		$ 27,600	
Marketable securities—at the lower of cost or market		10,000	
Accounts receivable	$35,365		
Less allowance for uncollectibles	950	34,415	
Notes receivable		6,000	
Interest receivable		45	
Inventories—at the lower of cost or market:			
Finished goods	$10,991		
Goods-in-process	13,212		
Materials	9,923	34,126	
Factory supplies		350	
Unexpired insurance		400	$112,936
Stock of Murdock Sales Company—at cost			5,000
Property, plant and equipment:			
Land—at cost		$ 23,000	
Factory buildings—at cost	$65,000		
Less accumulated depreciation	17,100	47,900	
Machinery and equipment—at cost	$53,900		
Less accumulated depreciation	18,388	35,512	
Office equipment—at cost	$ 3,140		
Less accumulated depreciation	1,064	2,076	108,488
			$226,424

Equities

Current liabilities:			
Accounts payable		$ 4,000	
Notes payable		5,000	
Federal income tax payable		11,135	
Interest payable		20	
Rent collected in advance		100	$ 20,255
Long-term liabilities:			
Real estate mortgage bonds payable—6%—due December 31, 19+14		$ 50,000	
Less discount on bonds		2,250	47,750
Stockholders' equity:			
Capital stock—$10 par value:			
Preferred—6% cumulative; authorized, 5,000 shares; issued, 4,000 shares	$40,000		
Common—authorized and issued, 7,500 shares	75,000	$115,000	
Capital in excess of par value—Common stock		7,500	
Total		$122,500	
Retained earnings—Exhibit B		35,919	158,419
			$226,424

Note: At the balance sheet date, the company was contingently liable on notes receivable discounted in the amount of $2,000.

Reversing entries. The adjusting entries of Ingram Manufacturing Company were listed on page 32. Reversing entries are recommended for only two of the adjusting entries, as follows:

Entry (i) for interest accrued on notes receivable.

Adjusting entry:

Interest receivable	45	
Interest revenue—Notes receivable		45

Reversing entry:

Interest revenue—Notes receivable	45	
Interest receivable		45

Entry (j) for interest accrued on notes payable:

Adjusting entry:

Interest expense—Notes payable	20	
Interest payable		20

Reversing entry:

Interest payable	20	
Interest expense—Notes payable		20

The reasons why some of the adjusting entries are not reversed are listed below,

Bad debts and depreciation:

Because the allowance for uncollectibles and the accumulated depreciation accounts are contras to the related asset accounts the adjusting entries for bad debts and depreciation are not reversed.

Other cost apportionments—Factory supplies used, expired insurance, and bond discount amortized:

Because the original charges were made to asset or deferred charge accounts, the adjusting entries are not reversed.

Earned revenues—Rent collected in advance:

Because the original credit was made to an unearned revenue account, the adjusting entry is not reversed.

Accrued federal income tax:

Because the liability account is customarily debited when the tax is paid, the adjusting entry is not reversed.

Separate working papers for each statement. If the general ledger trial balance is very long, some accountants prefer to prepare a separate working paper for each of the following statements: statement of cost of goods manufactured, income statement, statement of retained earnings, and balance sheet. This procedure has the advantage of classifying the data so that each statement can be prepared from its own working papers.

APPENDIX THE ACCOUNTING CYCLE ILLUSTRATED

The Graham Corporation was organized on August 1, 19—. On this date the corporation acquired the inventories and long-lived assets of another firm by issuing bonds and capital stock. Transactions for the first month of operations are presented below.

August

1 Acquired the following assets from Patton Company:

Finished goods	$ 75,900
Raw materials	54,700
Land	97,200
Buildings	140,000
Machinery and equipment	155,000
Furniture and fixtures	9,600
	$532,400

1 In exchange for the assets, the corporation issued the following:

5%, First mortgage bonds payable (face value $120,000)	$122,400
41,000 shares of $10 par value common stock	410,000
	$532,400

1 Sold 9,000 shares of $10 par value common stock at par.

2 Advanced T. R. Price, a salesman, $1,000 for traveling expenses.

4 Purchased factory supplies of $3,000 and raw materials of $15,000 from Estee Company on account. Terms are 2/10; n/30, and the corporation records such purchases net of discounts.

4 Received a statement for insurance premiums of $4,920 from Scott Insurance Agency for one year's coverage. Terms are net on receipt of statement.

4 Purchased machinery and equipment for $30,000 from Modern Company, giving a 30-day, 6% note for the entire amount.

5 Paid Scott Insurance Agency the amount owed for premiums.

5 Sale to Arthur King, $16,500. Terms, 2/10; n/30.

9 Sale to Frank Anderson Company, $25,000. Terms, 2/10; n/30.

11 Purchased raw materials on account from Davis and Brown, $22,070. Terms, n/30.

12 Sale to Camp Corporation, $15,950. Terms, 2/10; n/30.

12 Part of the shipment of August 9 was returned by Frank Anderson Company, $1,000.

12 Received payment of $16,170 from Arthur King for sale of August 5.

12 Paid Estee Company in full for the purchase of August 4.

15 Received statement from Supply Company for machine repairs, $117. Terms, n/30.

15 Paid the semimonthly payroll, $13,712:

Gross payroll:			
Direct labor	$9,125		
Indirect labor	3,034		
Sales salaries	2,350		
Officers' salaries	1,200		
Office salaries	750	$16,459	
Less payroll taxes		2,747	$13,712

16 Effective today, part of one of the company's buildings has been rented to Midland Distributors Company for three years, at $400 per month. The first month's rent is collected today.

18 Received a check from Frank Anderson Company for $23,520.

19 Sale to Robertson & Company, $15,300. Terms, 2/10; n/30.

22 A credit memo is issued to Robertson & Company to correct a $500 error in the invoice of August 19.

22 Received the net amount from Camp Corporation for the sale of August 12.

23 Purchased machinery from Franklin Machine Company for $37,800.

Terms: One half in cash before September 1, with a six-month non-interest-bearing note dated August 31 for the balance.

24 Purchased raw materials from Morgan and Walton, $27,700. Terms, 1/10; n/30.

25 Received bill for $400 from Smith Company for installing the machinery purchased from Franklin Machine Company. Terms, E.O.M. (end of month).

29 Paid Smith Company $400.

30 Local Delivery Company bills the company for delivery charges on merchandise sold during August, $169. The charges are payable September 10.

30 Paid $18,900 and gave a six-month non-interest-bearing note for $18,900 to Franklin Machine Company.

31 The August bill from Central Power Company, payable September 10, is analyzed as follows:

Factory light and power	$825
Office light	37
	$862

31 Paid the semimonthly payroll, $13,656:

Gross payroll:			
Direct labor	$9,011		
Indirect labor	2,833		
Sales salaries	2,900		
Officers' salaries	1,200		
Office salaries	750	$16,694	
Less payroll taxes		3,038	$13,656

31 Declared a $1,000 cash dividend, payable September 15, to stockholders of record September 10.

The corporation uses a multicolumn journal, as well as several special journals, to record its transactions. These books of original entry are shown on pages 45–52 as they would appear after the transactions for the month have been recorded and posted. It will be noted that the company uses supplementary records (not shown in this illustration) for detailing manufacturing overhead. The general ledger is shown on pages 53–57.

The books are to be closed at the end of the month and financial statements prepared. After the transactions for the month have been posted, a trial balance is prepared, using the first two columns of the working papers shown on pages 58–60. Data for the month-end adjustments are presented below.

(a) Expired insurance should be charged as follows:

Insurance—Factory	$300	
Insurance—Selling	100	
Insurance—General	10	$410

(b) Salesmen's traveling expenses for the month, $964.
(c) Factory supplies used, $2,710.
(d) Provision for bad debts should be .8% of gross sales.
(e) Accrued interest on notes payable is $135.
(f) Depreciation is computed for a full month on August 1 balances and for a half-month on additions during the month. For the month, the depreciation adjustments are:

Assets	Rate	Amount
Buildings	6%	$ 700
Machinery and equipment	12%	1,892
Furniture and fixtures	12%	96

(g) Accrued property taxes at August 31 are:

Factory	$1,525	
General	140	$1,665

(h) Of the rent collected in advance, $200 has been earned.
(i) Accrued interest on the bonds payable, $500.
(j) Amortization of bond premium, $20.
(k) Ending inventories were as follows:

Raw materials	$66,263
Goods in process	28,302
Finished goods	80,331

(l) The provision for federal income taxes for the month should be $3,244.

The adjustments are entered in the appropriate set of columns in the working papers on pages 58–60. It will also be necessary to record the adjustments in the journal, as shown on pages 50 and 51, although this is normally done after the working papers and statements are completed. The closing entries are recorded in the journal as shown on page 52. Completed financial statements for the company are shown on pages 61 and 62.

SALES JOURNAL
August, 19—

Invoice No.	Date 19—	√	Sold To	Terms	Dr. 1120 Cr. 4001
1	Aug. 5	√	Arthur King	2/10; n/30	16,500
2	9	√	Frank Anderson Company	2/10; n/30	25,000
3	12	√	Camp Corporation	2/10; n/30	15,950
4	19	√	Robertson & Company	2/10; n/30	15,300
					72,750
					√√

CASH RECEIPTS JOURNAL
August, 19—

(Left Side)

Line No.	Date 19—	Explanation	Debits: Cash 1111	Debits: Sales Discounts 4008	Debits: Sundry Accounts: Account No.	Debits: Sundry Accounts: √	Debits: Sundry Accounts: Amount
1	Aug. 1	Issued 9,000 shares of common					
2		stock at par	90,000				
3	12		16,170	330			
4	16	Monthly rental from Midland					
5		Distributors Company	400				
6	18		23,520	480			
7	22		15,631	319			
8			145,721	1,129			
9			√	√			
10							

(Right Side)

Inv. No.	Credits: Accounts Receivable: Name	Credits: Accounts Receivable: √	Credits: Accounts Receivable: Amount 1120	Credits: Interest Revenue 8135	Credits: Sundry Accounts: Account No.	Credits: Sundry Accounts: √	Credits: Sundry Accounts: Amount	Line No.
								1
					3101	√	90,000	2
1	Arthur King	√	16,500					3
								4
					2191	√	400	5
2	Frank Anderson Company	√	24,000					6
3	Camp Corporation	√	15,950					7
			56,450				90,400	8
			√					9
								10

August, 19—

(Left Side)

Line No.	Liability No.	Date 19—	Creditor	Explanation	Terms	Paid Date, 19—	Paid Ck. No.	Credit Accounts Payable 2120	Debit Materials 1171
1	8-1	Aug. 4	Estee Company	Recorded net	2/10; n/30	Aug. 12	6	17,640	14,700
2	8-2	4	Scott Insurance Agency	1-year policies	Cash	5	4	4,920	
3	8-3	11	Davis & Brown		n/30			22,070	22,070
4	8-4	15	Supply Company	For repairs	n/30			117	
5	8-5	23	Franklin Machine Co.	Half cash before 9/1;					
6				half note		30	13	37,800	
7	8-6	24	Morgan and Walton	Recorded net	1/10; n/30			27,423	27,423
8	8-7	25	Smith Company		E.O.M.	29	12	400	
9	8-8	30	Local Delivery Company					169	
10	8-9	31	Central Power Co.		9/10			862	
11								111,401	64,193
12								√	√
13									
14									

(Right Side)

Debit Mf'g. Overhead —Control, 5300 Acc't No.	√	Amount	Debit Selling Expense Acc't No.	√	Amount	Debit General Expense Acc't No.	√	Amount	Sundry Accounts Debit Acc't No.	√	Amount	Sundry Accounts Credit Acc't No.	√	Amount	Remarks	Line No.
									1181	√	2,940				Gross amount: $18,000	1
									1184	√	4,920				Policies dated 8/1	2
																3
5338	√	117														4
																5
									1331	√	37,800					6
																7
									1331	√	400					8
			6051	√	169											9
5315	√	825				7090	√	37								10
		942			169			37			46,060					11
		√														12
																13
																14

CASH DISBURSEMENTS JOURNAL
August, 19—

			Debits					Credits			
					Sundry Accounts			Sundry Accounts			
Check No.	Date 19—	Payee	Liability No.	Accounts Payable 2120	Acc't No.	√	Amount	Acc't No.	√	Amount	Cash 1111
1	Aug. 2	T. R. Price................			1183	√	1,000				1,000
2	5	Scott Insurance Agency...	8-2	4,920							4,920
3	12	Estee Company	8-1	17,640							17,640
4	15	Payroll			5201	√	9,125	2162	√	2,747	13,712
					5300	√	3,034				
					6001	√	2,350				
					7001	√	1,200				
					7002	√	750				
5	29	Smith Company	8-7	400							400
6	30	Franklin Machine Co.	8-5	37,800				2130	√	18,900	18,900
7	31	Payroll			5201	√	9,011	2162	√	3,038	13,656
					5300	√	2,833				
					6001	√	2,900				
					7001	√	1,200				
					7002	√	750				
				60,760			34,153			24,685	70,228
				√							√

JOURNAL
August, 19—

Debits							Credits	
Manufacturing Overhead—Control 5300	Selling Expense	General Expense	Sundry	Date 19—	√		Sundry	Accounts Receivable 1120
			75,900	Aug. 1	√	1151 Finished goods		
			54,700		√	1171 Materials		
			97,200		√	1311 Land		
			140,000		√	1321 Buildings		
			155,000		√	1331 Machinery and equipment		
			9,600		√	1361 Furniture and fixtures		
					√	2501 5% First mortgage bonds	120,000	
					√	2550 Bond premium	2,400	
					√	3101 Common stock	410,000	
						Purchase of assets for bonds and capital stock. Bonds mature in ten years.		
			30,000	4	√	1331 Machinery and equipment		
					√	2130 Notes payable	30,000	
						30-day, 6% note to Modern Company for purchase of machinery.		
			1,000	12	√	4009 Sales returns and allowances		
					√	1120 Frank Anderson Company		1,000
						Return of part of shipment on invoice no. 2.		
			500	22	√	4001 Sales		
					√	1120 Robertson & Company		500
						Correction of error on invoice no. 4.		
			1,000	31	√	3233 Dividends		
					√	2133 Dividends payable	1,000	
						Declaration of 1% dividend payable 9/15 to stockholders of record 9/10.		
			564,900			Totals	563,400	1,500
								√

JOURNAL (CONTINUED)
August, 19—

Debits: Manufacturing Overhead—Control	Debits: Selling Expense	Debits: General Expense	Debits: Sundry	Date 19—		✓	Credits: Sundry	Credits: Accounts Receivable 1120
					Adjusting Entries			
300				Aug. 31	5384 Insurance—Factory	✓		
	100				6084 Insurance—Selling	✓		
		10			7084 Insurance—General	✓		
					1184 Unexpired insurance	✓	410	
					Insurance expired during month.			
	964			31	6083 Salesmen's traveling expenses	✓		
					1183 Salesmen's traveling expense advances	✓	964	
					Expenses for month.			
2,710				31	5381 Factory supplies used	✓		
					1181 Factory supplies	✓	2,710	
					Supplies used.			
		582		31	7029 Bad debts	✓		
					1129 Allowance for uncollectibles	✓	582	
					Provision .8% of gross sales.			
			135	31	8235 Sundry interest expense	✓		
					2135 Interest payable—Notes		135	
					Accrued interest.			
700				31	5329 Depreciation—Buildings	✓		
1,892					5339 Depreciation—Machinery and equipment	✓		
		96			7069 Depreciation—Furniture and fixtures	✓		
					Accumulated depreciation:			
					1329 Buildings	✓	700	
					1339 Machinery and equipment	✓	1,892	
					1369 Furniture and fixtures	✓	96	
					Depreciation for month.			
5,602	1,064	688	135		Totals forward		7,489	

JOURNAL (CONTINUED)
August, 19—

Debits: Manufacturing Overhead—Control 5300	Debits: Selling Expense	Debits: General Expense	Debits: Sundry	Date 19—	√		Credits: Sundry	Credits: Accounts Receivable 1120
5,602	1,064	688	135			Totals brought forward	7,489	
1,525				Aug. 31	√	5380 Taxes—Factory		
		140			√	7080 Taxes—General		
						2180 Property taxes payable	1,665	
						Accrued property taxes.		
			200	31	√	2191 Rent collected in advance		
					√	8191 Rent revenue	200	
						Rent earned.		
			500	31	√	8250 Bond interest expense		
						2150 Bond interest payable	500	
						Interest for the month.		
			20	31	√	2550 Bond Premium		
					√	8250 Bond interest expense	20	
						Amortization of bond premium.		
			3,244	31	√	8251 Provision for federal income taxes		
					√	2181 Estimated federal income taxes payable	3,244	
						Estimated liability.		
7,127	1,064	828	4,099			Totals	13,118	
√								

JOURNAL (CONCLUDED)

August, 19—

Debits: Manufacturing Overhead—Control 5300	Debits: Selling Expense	Debits: General Expense	Debits: Sundry	Date 19—	√		Credits: Sundry	Credits: Accounts Receivable 1120
				Aug. 31		*Closing Entries*		
			80,331		√	1151 Finished goods		
			28,302		√	1161 Goods in process		
			66,263		√	1171 Raw materials		
			72,250		√	4001 Sales		
			200		√	8191 Rent revenue		
					√	1151 Finished goods	75,900	
					√	1171 Raw materials	118,893	
					√	4008 Sales discounts	1,129	
					√	4009 Sales returns and allowances	1,000	
					√	5201 Direct labor	18,136	
					√	5300 Manufacturing overhead—Control	13,936	
					√	6001 Sales salaries	5,250	
					√	6051 Delivery expense	169	
					√	6083 Salesmen's traveling expenses	964	
					√	6084 Insurance—Selling	100	
					√	7001 Officers' salaries	2400	
					√	7002 Office salaries	1500	
					√	7029 Bad debts	582	
					√	7069 Depreciation—F&F	96	
					√	7080 Taxes—General	140	
					√	7084 Insurance—General	10	
					√	7090 Miscellaneous expense	37	
					√	8235 Sundry interest expense	135	
					√	8250 Bond interest expense	480	
					√	8281 Provision for federal income taxes	3,244	
					√	3201 Retained earnings	3,245	
						To record ending inventories and close net income to retained earnings.		
			1,000	31	√	3201 Retained earnings		
					√	3233 Dividends	1,000	
						To close dividends to retained earnings.		

GENERAL LEDGER

Cash **1111**

19—				19—			
Aug. 31		CR	145,721	Aug. 31		CD	70,228

Accounts Receivable **1120**

19—				19—			
Aug. 31		S	72,750	Aug. 31		J	1,500
				31		CR	56,450

Allowance for Uncollectibles **1129**

				19—			
				Aug. 31		J	582

Finished Goods **1151**

19—				19—			
Aug. 1		J	75,900	Aug. 31		J	75,900
31		J	80,331				

Goods in Process **1161**

19—				19—			
Aug. 31		J	28,302				

Raw Materials **1171**

19—				19—			
Aug. 1		J	54,700	Aug. 31		J	118,893
31		AP	64,193				
31		J	66,263				

Factory Supplies **1181**

19—				19—			
Aug. 4		AP	2,940	Aug. 31		J	2,710

Salesmen's Traveling Expense Advances **1183**

19—				19—			
Aug. 2		CD	1,000	Aug. 31		J	964

Unexpired Insurance **1184**

19—				19—			
Aug. 4		AP	4,920	Aug. 31		J	410

Land **1311**

19—							
Aug. 1		J	97,200				

Buildings **1321**

19—							
Aug. 1		J	140,000				

Accumulated Depreciation—Buildings **1329**

				19— Aug. 31		J	700

Machinery and Equipment **1331**

19— Aug. 1		J	155,000				
4		J	30,000				
23		AP	37,800				
25		AP	400				

Accumulated Depreciation—Machinery and Equipment **1339**

				19— Aug. 31		J	1,892

Furniture and Fixtures **1361**

19— Aug. 1		J	9,600				

Accumulated Depreciation—Furniture and Fixtures **1369**

				19— Aug. 31		J	96

Accounts Payable **2120**

19— Aug. 31		CD	60,760	19— Aug. 31		AP	111,401

Notes Payable **2130**

				19— Aug. 4	30-day, 6%	J	30,000
				30	6 mos.; non-interest	CD	18,900

Dividends Payable **2133**

				19— Aug. 31		J	1,000

Interest Payable—Notes **2135**

				19— Aug. 31		J	135

Bond Interest Payable **2150**

				19— Aug. 31		J	500

Payroll Taxes Payable **2162**

				19— Aug. 15		CD	2,747
				31		CD	3,038

Property Taxes Payable **2180**

				19— Aug. 31		J	1,665

Estimated Federal Income Taxes Payable **2181**

				19— Aug. 31		J	3,244

Rent Collected in Advance **2191**

19— Aug. 31		J	200	19— Aug. 16		CR	400

5% First Mortgage Bonds Payable **2501**

				19— Aug. 1		J	120,000

Bond Premium **2550**

19— Aug. 31		J	20	19— Aug. 1		J	2,400

Common Stock
(Authorized issue, 50,000 shares of $10 par value.) **3101**

				19— Aug. 1		J	410,000
				1		CR	90,000

Retained Earnings **3201**

19— Aug. 31		J	1,000	19— Aug. 31		J	3,245

Dividends **3233**

19— Aug. 31		J	1,000	19— Aug. 31		J	1,000

Sales **4001**

19— Aug. 22		J	500	19— Aug. 31		S	72,750
31		J	72,250				
			72,750				72,750

Sales Discounts **4008**

19— Aug. 31		CR	1,129	19— Aug. 31		J	1,129

Sales Returns and Allowances **4009**

19— Aug. 12		J	1,000	19— Aug. 31		J	1,000

Direct Labor **5201**

19—				19—			
Aug. 15		CD	9,125	Aug. 31		J	18,136
31		CD	9,011				
			18,136				18,136

Manufacturing Overhead—Control **5300**

19—				19—			
Aug. 15		CD	3,034	Aug. 31		J	13,936
31		CD	2,833				
31		AP	942				
31		J	7,127				
			13,936				13,936

Sales Salaries **6001**

19—				19—			
Aug. 15		CD	2,350	Aug. 31		J	5,250
31		CD	2,900				
			5,250				5.250

Delivery Expense **6051**

19—				19—			
Aug. 30		AP	169	Aug. 31		J	169

Salesmen's Traveling Expenses **6083**

19—				19—			
Aug. 31		J	964	Aug. 31		J	964

Insurance—Selling **6084**

19—				19—			
Aug. 31		J	100	Aug. 31		J	100

Officers' Salaries **7001**

19—				19—			
Aug. 15		CD	1,200	Aug. 31		J	2,400
31		CD	1,200				
			2,400				2,400

Office Salaries **7002**

19—				19—			
Aug. 15		CD	750	Aug. 31		J	1,500
31		CD	750				
			1,500				1,500

Bad Debts **7029**

19—				19—			
Aug. 31		J	582	Aug. 31		J	582

Depreciation—Furniture and Fixtures **7069**

19—				19—			
Aug. 31		J	96	Aug. 31		J	96

Taxes—General **7080**

19—				19—			
Aug. 31		J	140	Aug. 31		J	140

Insurance—General **7084**

19—				19—			
Aug. 31		J	10	Aug. 31		J	10

Miscellaneous Expense **7090**

19—				19—			
Aug. 31		AP	37	Aug. 31		J	37

Rent Revenue **8191**

19—				19—			
Aug. 31		J	200	Aug. 31		J	200

Sundry Interest Expense **8235**

19—				19—			
Aug. 31		J	135	Aug. 31		J	135

Bond Interest Expense **8250**

19—				19—			
Aug. 31		J	500	Aug. 31		J	20
				31		J	480
			500				500

Provision for Federal Income Taxes **8281**

19—				19—			
Aug. 31		J	3,244	Aug. 31		J	3,244

GRAHAM CORPORATION
Working Papers
For the Month Ended August 31, 19—

	Trial Balance		Adjustments		Cost of Goods Manufactured		Income Statement		Statement of Retained Earnings		Balance Sheet	
1111 Cash	75,493										75,493	
1120 Accounts receivable	14,800										14,800	
1129 Allowance for uncollectibles				(d) 582								582
1151 Finished goods	75,900						75,900	80,331			80,331	
1161 Goods in process						28,302					28,302	
1171 Raw materials	118,893				118,893	66,263					66,263	
1181 Factory supplies	2,940			(c) 2,710							230	
1183 Salesmen's traveling expense advances	1,000			(b) 964							36	
1184 Unexpired insurance	4,920			(a) 410							4,510	
1311 Land	97,200										97,200	
1321 Buildings	140,000										140,000	
1329 Accumulated depreciation—Buildings				(f) 700								700
1331 Machinery and equipment	223,200										223,200	
1339 Accumulated depreciation—Machinery and equipment				(f) 1,892								1,892
1361 Furniture and fixtures	9,600										9,600	
1369 Accumulated depreciation—Furniture and fixtures				(f) 96								96
2120 Accounts payable		50,641										50,641
2130 Notes payable		48,900										48,900
2133 Dividends payable		1,000										1,000
2135 Interest payable—Notes				(e) 135								135
2150 Bond interest payable				(i) 500								500
2162 Payroll taxes payable		5,785										5,785
2180 Property taxes payable				(g) 1,665								1,665
2191 Rent collected in advance		400	(h) 200									200
2501 5% First mortgage bonds payable		120,000										120,000
2550 Bond premium		2,400	(j) 20									2,380
3101 Common stock		500,000										500,000
3201 Retained earnings												
3233 Dividends	1,000								1,000			
4001 Sales		72,250						72,250				
4008 Sales discounts	1,129						1,129					
4009 Sales returns and allowances	1,000						1,000					
5201 Direct labor	18,136				18,136							
5300 Manufacturing overhead—Control	6,809		(f) 700 (f) 1,892 (g) 1,525 (c) 2,710 (a) 300		13,936							
6001 Sales salaries	5,250						5,250					
6051 Delivery expense	169						169					
6083 Salesmen's traveling expenses			(b) 964				964					
6084 Insurance—Selling			(a) 100				100					
7001 Officers' salaries	2,400						2,400					
7002 Office salaries	1,500						1,500					
Totals forward	801,339	801,376	8,411	9,654	150,965	94,565	88,412	152,581	1,000		739,965	734,476

GRAHAM CORPORATION
Working Papers (Concluded)
For the Month Ended August 31, 19—

		Trial Balance		Adjustments		Cost of Goods Manufactured		Income Statement		Statement of Retained Earnings		Balance Sheet	
	Totals brought forward	801,339	801,376	8,411	9,654	150,965	94,565	88,412	152,581	1,000		739,965	734,476
7029	Bad debts			(d) 582				582					
7069	Depreciation—Furniture and fixtures			(f) 96				96					
7080	Taxes—General			(g) 140				140					
7084	Insurance—General			(a) 10				10					
7090	Miscellaneous expense	37						37					
8191	Rent revenue				(h) 200				200				
8235	Sundry interest expense			(e) 135				135					
8250	Bond interest expense			(i) 500	(j) 20			480					
		801,376	801,376	9,874	9,874	150,965	94,565						
	Cost of goods manufactured						56,400	56,400					
						150,965	150,965	146,292	152,781				
	Net income before income tax—down							6,489					
								152,781	152,781				
	Net income before income tax—brought down								6,489				
8281	Provision for federal income taxes							3,244					
2181	Estimated federal income taxes payable												3,244
	Net income							3,245			3,245		
								6,489	6,489	1,000	3,245		
	Retained earnings, August 31, 19—									2,245			2,245
										3,245	3,245	739,965	739,965

Exhibit D

GRAHAM CORPORATION
Statement of Cost of Goods Manufactured
For the Month Ended August 31, 19—

Materials used	$52,630
Direct labor	18,136
Manufacturing overhead	13,936
Total manufacturing cost	$84,702
Deduct goods in process, August 31, 19—	28,302
Cost of goods manufactured	$56,400

Exhibit C

GRAHAM CORPORATION
Income Statement
For the Month Ended August 31, 19—

Sales			$72,250
Deduct:			
Sales discounts		$ 1,129	
Sales returns and allowances		1,000	2,129
Net sales			$70,121
Cost of goods sold:			
Finished goods, August 1, 19—		$ 75,900	
Cost of goods manufactured—Exhibit D		56,400	
Total		$132,300	
Finished goods, August 31, 19—		80,331	51,969
Gross margin			$18,152
Operating expenses:			
Selling expenses:			
Sales salaries	$5,250		
Delivery expense	169		
Salesmen's traveling expenses	964		
Insurance—Selling	100	$ 6,483	
General expenses:			
Officers' salaries	$2,400		
Office salaries	1,500		
Bad debts	582		
Depreciation—Furniture and fixtures	96		
Taxes—General	140		
Insurance—General	10		
Miscellaneous expense	37	4,765	11,248
Net operating income			$ 6,904
Nonoperating items:			
Other expenses:			
Sundry interest expense	$ 135		
Bond interest expense	480	$ 615	
Other revenue:			
Rent revenue		200	415
Net income before income tax			$ 6,489
Federal income tax			3,244
Net income			$ 3,245

Exhibit B

GRAHAM CORPORATION
Statement of Retained Earnings
For the Month Ended August 31, 19—

Net income for the month—Exhibit C	$3,245
Dividends	1,000
Retained earnings, August 31, 19—	$2,245

Exhibit A

GRAHAM CORPORATION
Balance Sheet
August 31, 19—

Assets

Current assets:			
Cash		$ 75,493	
Accounts receivable	$14,800		
Less allowance for uncollectibles	582	14,218	
Inventories:			
Finished goods	$80,331		
Goods in process	28,302		
Raw materials	66,263	174,896	
Factory supplies		230	
Salesmen's traveling expense advances		36	
Unexpired insurance		4,510	$269,383

Property, plant and equipment:

	Cost	Accumulated Depreciation	Net	
Land	$ 97,200		$ 97,200	
Buildings	140,000	$ 700	139,300	
Machinery and equipment	223,200	1,892	221,308	
Furniture and fixtures	9,600	96	9,504	
	$470,000	$2,688		467,312
				$736,695

Equities

Current liabilities:		
Accounts payable	$50,641	
Notes payable	48,900	
Dividends payable	1,000	
Interest payable—Notes	135	
Bond interest payable	500	
Payroll taxes payable	5,785	
Property taxes payable	1,665	
Estimated federal income taxes payable	3,244	
Rent collected in advance	200	$112,070
Long-term liability:		
First mortgage 5% bonds payable	$120,000	
Add bond premium	2,380	122,380
Stockholders' equity:		
Capital stock—$10 par value; 50,000 shares authorized and issued	$500,000	
Retained earnings—Exhibit B	2,245	502,245
		$736,695

Financial Accounting Theory

Introduction. With regard to any field of thought, such as accounting, what is needed is a theoretical structure that unifies the underlying logic or system of reasoning. Such a theoretical structure abstracts from the complexities of the real world in order to achieve a level of simplicity necessary for analysis. Thus theory is useful in explaining, evaluating, and predicting phenomena associated with a given field of thought.

There are two types of theory: normative and descriptive. Normative theory is based on a model (that is, a system or object that is representative of a more complicated system or object) that represents real-world phenomena as they *ought* to exist. Descriptive theory is based on a model that represents real-world phenomena as they exist. Since financial accounting is concerned with the development and communication of financial information to those outside the firm, normative financial accounting theory pertains to what financial information should be developed and communicated and how this should be done. In contrast, descriptive financial accounting theory explains how financial information *is* developed and communicated. For example, descriptive financial accounting theory explains the existing financial accounting models of a firm's financial position (the balance sheet), results of operations (the income statement), and sources and uses of financial resources (the statement of changes in financial position).

This textbook is primarily concerned with descriptive financial accounting theory. Thus a theoretical framework, in the descriptive sense, is needed so as to provide a structure in which accounting practices can be placed and integrated as they are discussed throughout this text. Although descriptive financial theory is provided by *Statement No. 4*[1] and by *Accounting Research Study No. 7*[2], these writings do not provide a manageable and meaningful framework or structure that is conducive to teaching. Moreover, there is no agreement in the accounting profession as to precise terminology with regard to assumptions, postulates, principles, doctrines, procedures, rules, and so on. For these reasons, we present a condensed framework of descriptive financial accounting theory and use terminology that we feel the reader can readily understand. This framework is summarized on page 65 and is discussed below.

Accounting objectives. The accounting profession tends to view the basic objective of accounting as providing useful financial information to aid in making financial decisions. From a financial accounting viewpoint, where the emphasis is on external reporting, this objective is fulfilled by providing financial statements about a business enterprise that can be used by those outside the firm (investors, creditors, and so on) to aid in making financial decisions. From a managerial accounting viewpoint, this objective is also fulfilled by providing financial information to management to aid in their internal financial decision making. Since the subject matter of this textbook is basically financial accounting, we will be primarily concerned with accounting for external reporting purposes.

The accounting objective of providing financial statements to external users has resulted in financial statements that are general-purpose statements. The financial statements are not designed for providing financial information to one specific group of users, but rather to all external users. The primary external users of financial statements are investors and creditors, with others being employers, customers, government, labor unions, and the public in general. Such external users of general-purpose financial statements rely on the financial information provided to aid in making judgments about a business firm's financial position (economic resources, and claims against and interests in those resources), present and future profitability, and general ability to survive and adapt to changing conditions.

A basic problem in an objective of providing useful financial information to those outside the business firm is that different external users have different

---

[1]Accounting Principles Board, "Basic Concepts and Accounting Principles Underlying Financial Statements of Business Enterprises," *Statement No. 4* (New York: AICPA, October 1970).

[2]Paul Grady, "Inventory of Generally Accepted Accounting Principles for Business Enterprises," *Accounting Research Study No. 7* (New York: AICPA, 1965).

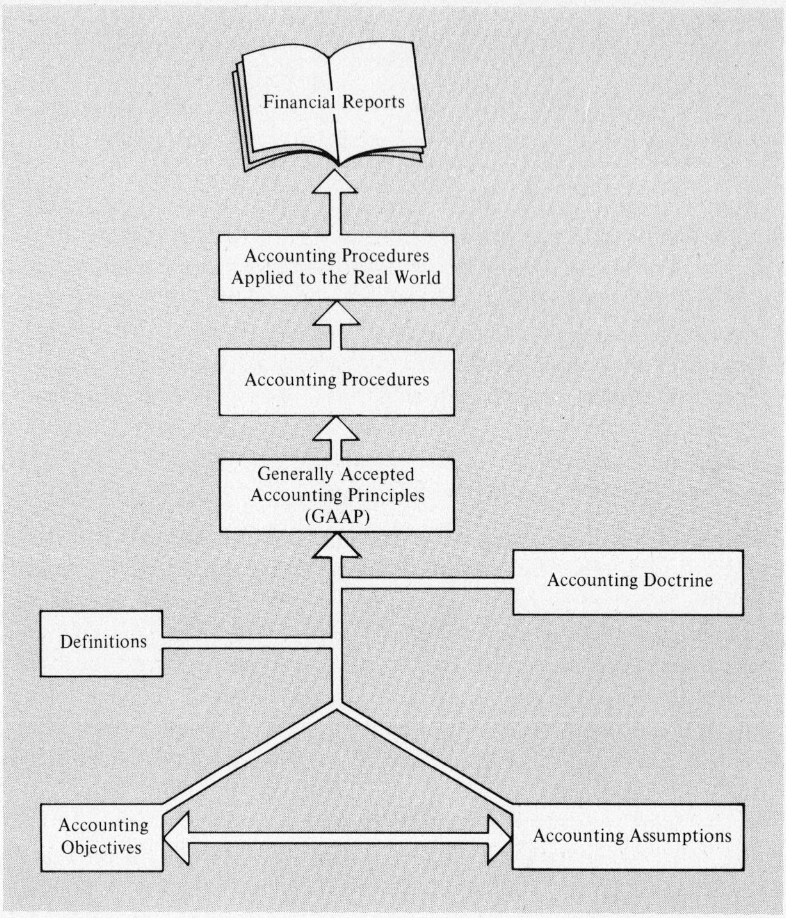

financial objectives. The accountant is faced with providing financial statements to unknown specific users who have multiple objectives. The accountant's approach to this problem is to provide a single set of general-purpose financial statements that contain as much financial information as is practicable within the framework of generally accepted accounting principles (GAAP). The GAAP provide the basis for the final information presented in the financial statements; and the users of the statements, in general, have accepted and used this information so long as it has been in accordance with GAAP. Users of financial statements are assured that the statements have been prepared in accordance with GAAP (as well as fairly presented and consistent applications of such principles) by having certified public accountants (CPAs) in their capacity as independent auditors verify the use of GAAP and so state on the statements in the form of an opinion (audit report) as follows:

To the Board of Directors,
..... Company:

We have examined the balance sheet of ..... Company as of December 31, 19––, and the related statements of income, retained earnings, and changes in financial position for the year then ended. Our examination was made in accordance with generally accepted auditing standards, and accordingly included such tests of the accounting records and such other auditing procedures as we considered necessary in the circumstances.

In our opinion, the accompanying financial statements present fairly the financial position of ..... Company at December 31, 19––, the results of its operations and changes in its financial position for the year then ended, in conformity with generally accepted accounting principles applied on a basis consistent with that of the preceding year.

Finney and Miller
Certified Public Accountants

January 28, 19—

The heavy reliance on GAAP as a foundation for financial-statement preparation and reporting is consistent with the financial accounting viewpoint that funds are entrusted to management by investors and creditors and that accounting serves to report on management's stewardship (responsibility) in the efficient use of the funds. That is, financial accounting is concerned with the fiduciary (trust) relationship between a business enterprise's management and outsiders who represent the general public. Thus, financial statements based on GAAP add credibility to the figures presented in the statements because such principles are independent of management and user's desires as to how the figures should look.

Accounting assumptions. In any field of thought there are certain knowns and unknowns, and the unknowns are filled by assumptions in order to weave together the assumptions and the knowns into a complete theoretical structure.[3] The assumptions are the "givens," that are taken for granted in order that conclusions can be reached despite unavoidable gaps in our knowledge. Thus assumptions are the "building blocks" in the construction of theory.

It should be made clear that there is a strong interrelationship between assumptions and objectives, as is indicated in the diagram on page 64 by the horizontal arrow connecting the two. The point is that the specification of assumptions necessitates some idea of objectives.

---

[3]See William J. Vatter, "Postulates and Principles," *Journal of Accounting Research* (Autumn 1963), pp. 179–97.

The accounting literature generally uses the term *postulates* or *concepts* in place of the term *assumptions,* but defines both terms as basic assumptions. We prefer to use the term *assumptions.* The term *concept* is so general that it is more confusing than helpful. The term *postulates* denotes axioms or hypotheses advanced in a deductive approach; however, descriptive financial accounting theory is based on an inductive approach, not a deductive approach.

Faced with an uncertain world in which there are several alternatives to a given situation, accountants assume that one of these alternatives is the best one, in that it will result in providing useful financial information. For example, accountants assume that money is the best measuring unit of economic activity, not physical attributes nor qualitative attributes that cannot be quantified in terms of money. Such assumptions end up being basically descriptive statements of what accountants do in the environment in which accounting normally operates. From the view of the total environment in which accounting operates, there could be specified a large number of descriptive statements. Many of these statements would be obvious and trivial, and would not *directly* affect the structure of the theory of accounting practice. For this reason, most of the accounting literature limits the specification of assumptions to those directly affecting the theoretical structure of financial accounting; however, this results in incomplete agreement on the specification of assumptions. For example, *Statement No. 4* specifies thirteen assumptions, which are called basic features: accounting entity, going concern, measurement of economic resources and obligations, time periods, measurement in terms of money, accrual, exchange price, approximation, judgment, general-purpose financial information, fundamentally related financial statements, substance over form, and materiality.[4] *Accounting Research Study No. 7* specifies ten assumptions, which are called concepts: a society and government structure honoring private property rights, specific business entities, going concern, monetary expression in accounts, consistency between periods for the same entity, diversity in accounting among independent entities, conservatism, dependability of data through internal control, materiality, and timeliness in financial reporting requires estimates.[5]

Consistent with the theoretical structure proposed on page 64, we specify seven basic accounting assumptions underlying a descriptive theory of financial accounting: specific-separate-entity assumption, going-concern assumption, money-measuring-unit assumption, historical-cost assumption, fiscal-period (periodicity) assumption, revenue-recognition assumption, and the matching assumption. Each assumption is explained below.

SPECIFIC-SEPARATE-ENTITY ASSUMPTION: An entity is a specific unit. An accounting entity is a *specific* unit carrying out economic activity for which an accounting is desired. Thus, an accounting entity can be a specific business firm (a corporation, partnership, or single proprietorship), a specific segment of a business firm (a division, department, sales territory, or the like), a specific consolidated

[4] *Statement No. 4,* pp. 44–53.
[5] Grady, "Inventory of GAAP," pp. 23–44.

group of corporations operating under common control via stock ownership, or a specific nonprofit organization that carries on economic activity. However, in financial accounting, with its emphasis on external reporting, the specific business firm is considered to be the accounting entity. From a managerial accounting viewpoint, the accounting entity is considered to be not only the overall business firm, but also the specific economic subunits within the business firm. Since we are primarily concerned with financial accounting in this textbook, the accounting entity normally discussed will be the business firm.

By assuming that he is accounting for a specific entity, the accountant defines the area of interest. The assumption allows the accountant to narrow his focus of interest. The accountant has to know what he is accounting upon before he can prepare meaningful financial reports. Thus the accountant records, classifies, summarizes, verifies, reports, and interprets the financial data of a specific entity.

Not only does the accountant assume that he is accounting for a specific entity, he also assumes that he is accounting for a specific business firm that is *separate and distinct* from other entities and from the owners, managers, and employees who constitute the firm. In other words, the accountant is accounting for the economic activity of the specific entity, not the personal financial transactions of those who make up the business entity and not the transactions of other entities. Thus the assumption provides the accountant with the basis for distinguishing between specific entity transactions and owners' transactions. This is especially important in single proprietorships and partnerships, where the business entity is *not* considered to be *legally* separate from the owners. Nevertheless, such separateness is assumed in accounting, because the personal transactions of owners should not be allowed to distort the financial statements of the business firm.

This assumption is made not only because it defines the area of interest needed to provide relevant economic information, but also as the result of the difficulty, in some cases, of distinguishing between personal and business transactions. The business activity of a small neighborhood grocery is not easily distinguishable from the personal economic activity of the owner of the store. For example, if the owner lives in the back of his store, how much of the utility bill, property tax, and the like is business expense as opposed to personal expense? The entity assumption means that the accountant assumes he can distinguish between personal and business activity even though in actual practice such a distinction is somewhat arbitrary, as it would be in the grocery store example.

GOING-CONCERN (CONTINUITY) ASSUMPTION: Unless there is specific evidence to the contrary, the accountant assumes, in preparing the financial statements of a particular business firm, that the firm will continue to be in existence in the foreseeable future. This does not imply a permanent continuance of the firm, but rather that the firm will continue in business long enough to complete current plans and fulfill existing commitments.

Since financial statements are prepared periodically for business firms, the accountant can review the situation periodically to determine if the continuity assumption is a reasonable expectation. If a firm is experiencing large and persistent losses, if the future is such that it is unlikely to remain profitable, or if the firm's operations are to be terminated, the accountant abandons the going-concern assumption and does not prepare the normal financial statements. In such situations, the accountant would prepare statements required for receivership and liquidation.

The primary reason for this assumption is that it leads to the presentation of financial information that may aid users of financial statements in making financial decisions with regard to future profitability and financial position of a particular business firm (that is, aid in making financial predictions). In contrast to the going-concern viewpoint, in the normal situation a liquidation viewpoint would not provide useful information for making financial decisions. Thus the going-concern assumption removes a liquidation viewpoint from the preparation of financial statements, so that assets are not reported at forced-liquidation amounts (in which there would be losses) and liabilities are not stated as being immediately payable (where such payments would be in excess of present value).

MONEY-MEASURING-UNIT ASSUMPTION: Accountants assume that money is the best measuring unit of a firm's assets and equities, as well as the changes therein. In other words, in accounting for business transactions, which are changes in a firm's assets and equities, the accountant assumes that money is the best measuring unit of these transactions.

The use of money as the measuring unit in accounting is justified by the functions of money, which are as follows:

A common denominator in that labor hours, pounds, feet, gallons, administrative services, and the like can all be expressed in terms of money.

A medium of exchange that is universally accepted and recognized as the unit of measure for economic activity.

A store of value.

A standard of deferred payment in that loans are expressed in terms of money.

The ultimate expression of the inputs and outputs of a firm, since the inputs and outputs end up eventually being expressed in terms of money.

The assumption results in quantifying in the financial statements only those business activities of a firm that can be measured in terms of money. Those activities that cannot be easily expressed in terms of money are generally thought to be too subjective to measure and report. Thus the financial statements do not provide a complete picture of the business firm, because they do not include such qualitative information as the state of its personnel relations, the firm's position on ecology, the health of its top executives, the quality of its products relative to competing products, the firm's position on racial discrimination, the status of its research and development programs, and the like. Although such qualitative information is not usually expressed in dollars in the body of the financial statements, it is sometimes expressed in footnotes to the figures and by descriptive material that accompanies the financial statements in firms' annual reports. Finally, it can be argued that all measurements involve some compromises, but that the money measuring unit comes closest to meeting overall needs.

It should also be pointed out that the accountant generally limits his money measurements to business transactions, which are loosely defined to include both external and internal transactions as follows: changes in assets and equities arising from external exchange (transfer of assets and equities to or from the firm), internal asset usage and conversion, and internal accounting adjustments (deferrals and accruals). The accountant does not normally view changes in market values and expectations as being business transactions and would not generally record and report them. Some accountants contend that the emphasis on business transactions should be specified as an assumption—the transactions assumption.

By using money as a measuring unit, accountants are assuming either that money is a stable measuring unit, that its instability is immaterial, or that the accountant's function is to account for dollars only and not changes in general purchasing power. In other words, a measuring unit should be a *standard* measuring unit, such as a yardstick, that is stable over time. Unfortunately, because of changes in the general-price level (the proportional change in the price of all goods and services), money is not a stable measuring unit. During periods of inflation (a rise in the general-price level), the general purchasing power (ability to acquire a given quantity of goods and services) of the dollar decreases, and during periods of deflation (a fall in the general-price level) the general purchasing power of the dollar increases. Thus it should be understood that the basic financial statements prepared by accountants are not adjusted for changes in the general purchasing power of the dollar. On the other hand, as we shall discuss in a later chapter, companies may, but are not required to, issue supplementary general-price-level-adjusted financial statements.

HISTORICAL-COST ASSUMPTION: Subject to generally recognized exceptions, and excluding such monetary assets as cash, marketable securities, and receivables, accountants assume that cost is normally the proper money measurement of a firm's assets at acquisition and of asset usage and conversion within the firm. From an accounting-theory viewpoint, cost is an economic sacrifice or foregoing for benefits received or to be received. In actual accounting practice, cost is generally limited to the cash or cash equivalent sacrificed in exchange to obtain assets through purchase (including costs to put in working condition), manufacture, and construction for use. In other words, in accounting practice, cost means acquisition cost, which is the *total* of the exchange prices, or price aggregates, to obtain an asset and render it suitable for its intended use.

Since nonmonetary assets (such as inventory, land, plant and equipment, long-term investments, and deferred charges) are acquired during different time periods, financial records maintained and financial statements prepared subsequent to asset acquisitions reflect past exchange prices, or historical costs. Thus the historical-cost assumption is an assumption that accountants should normally use past-purchase exchange prices (that is, past entry or input exchange prices) in the valuation of a firm's assets.

The historical-cost assumption also normally applies to the valuation of liabilities. In accounting practice, liabilities are generally recorded and reported based on the valuation of the assets received, expenses incurred, or losses incurred (the debit side of the transaction). Since the valuation of the debit side is normally based on the historical-cost assumption, accountants generally record and report liabilities based on historical cost. In other words, a liability is an obligation to convey assets or perform services, and the cash or cash equivalent necessary to discharge the liability is normally used in the valuation of liabilities.

It is also important to emphasize that owners' equity is a residual (assets minus liabilities) and therefore is not independently measured. Thus there is no independent valuation of owners' equity. However, since assets and liabilities are independently measured, based normally on the historical-cost assumption, the assumption also affects the recording and reporting of owners' equity.

Valuation in accounting is the quantification of, and the changes in, assets and liabilities expressed in terms of the money measuring unit. Since business firms operate in a market economy and are not consuming entities, valuation is based on exchange or market prices. However, there are several different types of exchange prices that could be used as the valuation method in accounting. Thus accountants could use past-purchase exchange prices (historical cost), present-purchase exchange prices (replacement cost), present-sale exchange prices (current net realizable prices, present realizable prices in orderly liquidation, or current forced-liquidation prices), or future exchange prices (discounted cash flows). In practice, accountants normally reject all but past-purchase exchange prices because the others are thought to be too subjective; however, note that this is an assumption—the historical-cost assumption.

Accountants justify the historical-cost assumption on the basis of the following arguments:

Cost is objectively determined in the marketplace by rational buyers and sellers acting in arm's-length transactions (no collusion). In other words, cost is not "dreamed up" subjectively by accountants, but is a bargained price objectively determined in the marketplace.

Cost can be verified by other accountants by going into the marketplace (i.e., the test of the marketplace).

Cost approximates value at time of purchase.

From a practical point of view, cost is convenient to obtain, it is conservative, and it is closely related to and consistent with the revenue-recognition (realization) assumption.

Because of these reasons, the subjectivity and impracticality of other valuation methods, and the precedence of acquisition cost in our legal system, historical cost is the normal valuation method used by practicing accountants. On the other hand, there are exceptions to the use of historical cost by accountants, and historical cost is criticized as not providing relevant information for current financial decision-making purposes. Historical cost is further discussed in a later chapter.

FISCAL-PERIOD (PERIODICITY) ASSUMPTION: The economic activity of a business firm is continuous in nature with regard to economic input–output flows through the firm. Given that the primary objective of accounting is to provide economic information useful for financial decision making, the accountant must somehow measure, record, and report on the continuous economic input–output flows of a firm. Obviously, if the accountant could wait until a firm terminated its operations and converted its assets into cash (that is, until the economic input–output flows ceased), net income for the entire life-span of a business would be the excess cash received by the owners over their investment in the business. No estimates or assumptions would be required because there would be no uncertainty.

It should be equally obvious that in most cases accountants do not know when a business will terminate its operations and cannot wait for such termination to prepare internal and external financial reports. Both internal and external financial-decision makers want current financial information to aid them in making financial decisions, and the demand for financial information has forced the accountant to prepare financial reports periodically. In other words, the demand for timely financial information has resulted in the accountant's assuming that he can periodically "stop" the continuous economic activity of a firm in order to prepare an income statement for the current period just ended, a balance sheet (statement of position) as of the end of the period, a statement of changes in financial position (funds statement) for the current period just ended, and the various internal financial reports desired by management for the period. Thus the fiscal-period assumption is an assumption that the life-span of a business firm can be segmented into short-run time periods in order to provide timely financial information to aid in financial decision making.

The accounting period, called the fiscal period, is normally one year, based on either the calendar year or the natural business year (the annual period ends on the lowest point of business activity). In addition, most firms have financial reports prepared monthly for internal purposes and release income data quarterly to the financial press. Note, however, that the use of annual reporting periods by the accountant is part of the fiscal-period assumption, largely based on established business practice, because time periods of other than a year could be just as logically used. Finally, note that the assumption pertains to specifically identifiable time periods and that the time periods are assumed to be of equal length to facilitate comparisons.

There are several implications in periodic reporting via the fiscal-period assumption. First, changes in the assets and equities of a firm during a short-run period, such as a year, do not correspond with changes in cash receipts and disbursements. Thus there are noncash changes in assets and equities during a short-run time period because of credit transactions, the use of long-lived assets, and production. Thus the accountant records changes in assets and equities as they occur during the short-run period, regardless of the cash flows. In other words, the accountant records and reports revenue when earned and expenses when incurred during the period, regardless of cash flows, and then matches the two (expenses are incurred to generate revenue) to derive periodic net income—accrual accounting.

Besides accrual accounting, a second implication of periodic reporting is the use of estimates (approximations) and informed judgment by accountants. Since most firms are engaged in continuous economic activity, the assumption that economic activity can be "stopped" in order to prepare financial statements results in periodic accounting information that should be viewed as short-run approximations of the firm's financial position and progress. Thus the accountant uses such cost allocations as depreciation, amortization, depletion, cost of goods sold, and bad debts to assign costs to present and future periods in order to derive periodic financial reports; however, because of uncertainty, continuity, and jointness of economic activity, there are several logical ways to allocate cost. The selection of a method of cost allocation is by its very nature an approximation, but an approximation that is based on the informed judgment of the accountant.[6]

REVENUE-RECOGNITION (REALIZATION) ASSUMPTION: The continuous nature of the economic activity of a business firm means that the creation of goods and services by a firm is also a continuous-flow process. In other words, the product of a firm (its goods and services) is the *joint* result of the continuous process of planning, investing, producing, storing, providing goods and services to customers, collecting cash, and providing warranty services. The continuous and joint nature of the process of product creation by a firm means that it is impossible to identify a firm's product with any one stage of the product-creation process. And since revenue is the monetary expression of a firm's product (goods and services), it is also impossible to identify revenue generation with any one stage of the product-creation process. Thus given the continuous and joint nature of the revenue-generation process, how does the accountant determine when revenue should be recognized for recording and reporting purposes?

Although there are certain exceptions, the accountant normally assumes that out of the whole revenue-generation process of a firm, he can select one point in time to recognize revenue for recording and reporting purposes, and that such point recognition results in providing useful information for evaluating management's efforts directed toward the generation of revenue. Under normal circumstances, for retail, wholesale, and manufacturing business, the accountant uses the point (date) of sale, when goods are delivered and title passes to the buyer, as the basis for revenue recognition. For service-type businesses, the point of sale is when services are performed. Note, however, that the recognition of revenue at the point of sale is an assumption not only because it is assumed that useful information is provided by recognizing revenue at only one point of the revenue-generation process, but also because there are other points of time when revenue could be recognized. For example, revenue could be recognized when orders are received from customers, during production, when production is completed, or when cash or some other asset is received in payment for the goods sold.

---

[6]It should be pointed out that whereas we have specified accrual accounting, approximation, and judgment as implications of the fiscal-period assumption, they are viewed as basic features of financial accounting in *Statement No. 4* (pp. 46–47). Grady specifies "timeliness in financial reporting requires estimates" as a basic concept (pp. 41–42). Moonitz specifies "Time Period" and "Tentativeness" as basic postulates and relates the two. See Maurice Moonitz, "The Basic Postulates of Accounting," *Accounting Research Study No. 1* (New York: AICPA, 1961), pp. 22, 33–37.

The accountant justifies the use of the point of sale for revenue recognition based on the following arguments:

Generally, by the time the point of sale has been reached, the firm has performed the major economic effort required in the generation of revenue (i.e., by the time of sale economic value has been added by the firm).
At the point of sale, the exchange price provides an objective and verfiable measurement for revenue.
At the point of sale, a conversion takes place—one asset is exchanged for another.
By the time the point of sale has been reached, most of the expenses have been incurred in the generation of revenue, and any remaining expenses are readily determinable.

Although the recognition of revenue is normally based on the point of sale, under certain circumstances accountants recognize revenue during production, when production is completed, and when cash is received. In other words, accountants believe that there are special circumstances in which the recognition of revenues at the point of sale could distort periodic net-income figures, and therefore they allow for exceptions to point-of-sale recognition. Such exceptions are discussed later in the text.

MATCHING ASSUMPTION: Faced with user demand for timely financial information and with the continuous economic input–output flows through a business firm, the accountant assumes a fiscal period over which he can report on the results of operations and at the end of which he can report on the financial position of a firm. Because of the problem of leads and lags in cash flows over a fiscal period, the accountant's primary report on the periodic results of operations is in terms of revenues and expenses—the periodic income statement. Based on the revenue-recognition assumption, revenue is recognized during the period when earned; however, since the generation of revenue is not costless, the accountant also recognizes expenses during the period to derive periodic net income. The recognition of expense during the fiscal period is based on the matching assumption.

The matching assumption is that those goods and services used (expenses) during the fiscal period can be associated with the revenue earned during the same fiscal period and therefore recorded and reported during that fiscal period. Matching is an assumption that expenses can be related to the revenue recognized during the fiscal period. In other words, it is an assumption that expenses can be matched with related revenue during the fiscal period to derive periodic net income or loss. Based on the revenue-recognition assumption, revenue is recognized during the fiscal period, and then, based on the matching assumption, expenses related to that revenue are recognized during the same fiscal period. Based on the historical-cost assumption, goods and services used in the generation of revenue are measured at cost (since expenses are the costs of goods and services used in the generation of revenue over a fiscal period); hence, accountants often refer to the matching of costs (really expenses measured at cost) with revenue.

Matching is an assumption in that accountants assume that there is a cause-and-effect relationship between expense and revenue that allows them to properly determine an association between the two for recording and reporting purposes. In reality, it is impossible to directly associate all expenses with revenue, and because of this impossibility, accountants assume that reasonable matching can be achieved based on the practical and expedient method of distinguishing between direct and indirect costs. Those costs directly associated with a firm's product[7] are expensed during the period when the revenue is earned from the sale of the product, since both the expenses and revenues are associated with the same physical product. For example, in a merchandising firm the cost of the merchandise acquired is treated as a product cost and inventoried as an asset until the product is sold, at which time the product cost is expensed during the same period via cost of goods sold—revenue and expenses are matched during the same time period.

Those costs that cannot be directly associated with the firm's product, such as selling and administrative expenses, are expensed during the time period when the goods and services are used (for instance, when the expenses are incurred). Such expenses are more directly related to the time period than to the product and are therefore called period expenses.[8] Note that this is an indirect matching of expenses with revenue, in that the expenses of the period are matched with revenues of the same period; however, this is period matching rather than matching based on expenses associated with revenues. Such indirect matching is conventionally justified on practical grounds as a reasonable approximation of matching expenses with revenues.

Finally, it should be pointed out that the accrual method of accounting is a natural outgrowth of the fiscal-period, revenue-recognition, and matching assumptions. Because users of financial statements want periodic information on the results of operations, revenue and expenses for the same fiscal period are reported via the income statement. Accrual accounting is the method used to bring about such periodic reporting: Revenue is recognized when earned and expenses are recognized when incurred, regardless of cash flows. Thus, accountants use accrual and deferral accounts and then adjust them at the end of the fiscal period, in order that there be proper matching of revenue and expense to derive periodic net income.

Accounting doctrine. From an accounting-theory viewpoint, accounting principles could be derived logically from given assumptions and objectives. However, in actual accounting practice, accounting principles are modified, but not determined, by accounting doctrine. Accounting doctrines are normative attitudes (ideas) of the

[7]Note that for a manufacturing firm, this would include manufacturing overhead cost utilized, since it is directly related to production in general, even though it is called an indirect manufacturing cost because it is not directly related to any one specific product.

[8]It can be argued that cost of goods sold is also a period expense in that it is an expense of the period; however, it is customary in accounting terminology to refer to period expenses as just including selling and general and administrative expenses.

accounting profession as to what ought to represent good accounting practice.[9] By modifying accounting principles, doctrines provide normative standards by which practicing accountants can apply accounting procedures in a given situation that reflect the collective judgment of the accounting profession.

Accounting doctrines include such normative ideas as materiality, consistency, comparability, objectivity, and conservatism. Because of their normative and ethical flavor, such ideas seem to fit well under the classification of accounting doctrine. However, some accountants would classify such ideas under basic accounting concepts, which incorrectly implies that they are basic assumptions. Other accountants would classify such ideas under accounting principles, but because of their normative and ethical flavor, they differ from the usual accounting meaning of *principle* as a generally accepted guideline. Finally, Hendriksen calls such ideas constraints[10]—which they are in the sense of modifying principles —but constraints do not denote the normative and ethical flavor of such ideas, and it is difficult to stretch the meaning of *constraint* to include such ideas as conservatism.

MATERIALITY: The doctrine of materiality pertains to accountants' not reporting certain economic events in compliance with strict accounting theory when the results are so insignificant that such treatment does not affect the accuracy of the financial statements. In other words, the cost of reporting certain trivial items according to accounting theory outweighs the usefulness of the resulting information. For example, many businesses have a minimum dollar amount below which acquisitions are expensed, even though in theory they should be capitalized as assets. Thus, such office supplies as pencils may be expensed when acquired, even though in theory they should be capitalized and subsequently expensed as they are used.

There are no strict rules for determining when an item is material or immaterial, and there are degrees of materiality depending on the circumstances. Accountants determine whether an item is material or not depending on judgment and common sense. On the other hand, a general guide as to whether an item is material is whether knowledge of it would affect the decisions of informed users of financial statements. Thus, in *Statement No. 4,* materiality is defined as follows: "Financial reporting is only concerned with information that is significant enough to affect evaluations or decisions."[11] Similarly, Grady defines materiality as follows: "A statement, fact, or item is material, if giving full consideration to the surrounding circumstances, as they exist at the time, it is of such a nature that its disclosure, or the method of treating it, would be likely to influence or to 'make a difference' in the judgment and conduct of a reasonable person."[12]

---

[9] See Vatter, "Postulates and Principles," p. 184.

[10] Eldon S. Hendriksen, *Accounting Theory,* 2d ed. (Homewood, Ill.: Richard D. Irwin, Inc., 1970), pp. 106–19.

[11] *Statement No. 4,* p. 48.

[12] Grady, "Inventory of GAAP," p. 40.

CONSISTENCY: The doctrine of consistency is that the same accounting procedures for a given entity should be used from one period to the next. Because there are many areas of accounting in which different procedures are acceptable from the standpoint of approved accounting practice, consistency is desirable in order that comparative analyses of financial statements over time reveal actual changes in underlying economic conditions, instead of changes brought about by the application of different accounting procedures. In other words, consistency is part of accounting doctrine because alternative accounting procedures exist and the application of alternative procedures over time can mislead users of financial statements. For example, if the earnings per share of a company changes from $8 in 19+1 to $9 in 19+2 as the result of switching from expensing to capitalizing advertising expenditures, then such information may be highly misleading to users of financial statements (unless the reason for the change is clearly disclosed).

On the other hand, consistency does not mean that desirable changes in accounting principles or procedures cannot be made. If the accountant believes a change in an accounting procedure will result in more accurate or useful information for decision making, then such a change should be made. However, if such a change is made, then the financial statements should include a footnote describing the change and its dollar effect for the period when the change took place, any material adjustments necessary to reflect the change should be reported as an extraordinary item in the income statement, and net income and earnings per share reflecting the change should be reported.

The importance of consistency in accounting is exemplified by the CPA's opinion that accompanies audited financial statements. An example of such an opinion was presented on page 65, and with regard to consistency, note the last part of the opinion: ". . . in conformity with generally accepted accounting principles applied on a basis consistent with that of the preceding year."

There is some confusion as to the implications of the doctrine of consistency. For example, consistency does *not* require:

The use of consistent accounting procedures by an entity for a given time period. A company can use both straight-line and double-declining depreciation methods and both LIFO and FIFO inventory costing procedures.

The use of consistent accounting procedures by all entities within an industry.

In other words, too much should not be read into the meaning of consistency, since its meaning in accounting is limited to the use of the same accounting procedures through time for a specific entity.

COMPARABILITY (UNIFORMITY): The doctrine of comparability in accounting is that the financial statements of different firms should be based on similar accounting principles and procedures, in order to aid users of financial statements in finding similarities and differences among firms for purposes of financial decision making. For example, if an investor is interested in acquiring common stock in the oil industry, the financial statements of the different oil companies should be based on similar accounting principles and procedures so that they may be used by the investor to aid him in his investment decision. Note, however, that this doctrine does *not* imply strict uniformity, but rather that accounting principles and procedures are similar enough for different companies so that comparisons can be made.

There is controversy in accounting over the doctrine of comparability. For example, Grady includes diversity as a basic concept in *ARS No. 7,* and this seems to be in conflict with the doctrine of comparability. Grady basically argues that given diffusion in decision making in our free society system, numerous alternative accounting procedures, the impossibility of preparing a single manual of instruction to fit the needs of all industry, and the substantial role of judgment and estimation in accounting, diversity is a fact of life in accounting. On the other hand, Grady points out that such diversity in accounting should not stand in the way of attempting to improve the comparability of financial statements.[13]

It is generally agreed by accountants that comparability increases the usefulness of financial information. However, the unresolved question is, How much comparability should accountants strive for and how much diversity should be permitted? On the one hand, some accountants argue that because firms differ with regard to financial conditions, physical conditions, management goals and policies, and economic-flow patterns, comparability is not feasible. On the other hand, other accountants argue that even though diversity exists, comparability does not mean uniformity, so that a reasonable degree of comparability can be achieved, especially with regard to particular industries.

It is important to note that we have discussed comparability in terms of both accounting principles and procedures being similar for different firms. In order to achieve comparability in the financial statements of business firms, it is necessary but not sufficient to have similarity of general guidelines (accounting principles), since much diversity would still exist unless accounting procedures were also similar. The opinions issued by the Accounting Principles Board (APB) are an attempt to increase the uniformity in accounting procedures and thereby increase the comparability of financial statements. The growing number of lawsuits against CPA firms, and the growing critical reactions of users of financial statements with regard to the adverse effect of diverse accounting procedures on financial statements, would seem to indicate that the accounting profession must strive for more uniformity in the preparation and presentation of financial statements or face the possibility of uniformity by government legislation.

OBJECTIVITY: In accounting practice, the doctrine of objectivity is that accounting measurements should be based on evidence that is verifiable by competent persons. The emphasis is on the existence of evidence that verifies the measurement independently of the accountant making the measurement—that is to say, independently of the accountant's subjective valuation and bias. For example, acquisition cost is the objective evidence used by accountants in the valuation of

[13] See Grady, "Inventory of GAAP," pp. 32–35.

long-lived assets, because the purchase price is determined in the marketplace independently of the accountant making the measurement, and because it can be verified in the marketplace by other accountants.

The accounting-practice view of objectivity is accounting doctrine because it has a normative and ethical flavor as to what accountants should do: They should base their measurements on objective evidence. Thus the normative idea of objectivity means that it is not a basic concept, an assumption, nor an accounting principle.

Although the view of objectivity as being verifiable evidence is widely held in accounting practice, another view is that objectivity should be defined as measurement based on a consensus of qualified measurers.[14] This "consensus view" of objectivity attempts to avoid the problem that verifiable evidence can be still subject to personal bias—that you cannot really separate accounting data from the accountant's measurement and processes. On the other hand, the "consensus view" of objectivity does raise some practical problems in its implementation, because there could be a range of values observed by the qualified experts, which provides some measurement problems.

CONSERVATISM: The doctrine of conservatism has traditionally been that where there are reasonable alternatives available, the accountant should select the alternative that is least optimistic with regard to its immediate effect on owners' equity. Thus, if the accountant has a reasonable choice between two asset amounts, he should record the lower of the two (and the reverse for liabilities). Similarly, if there is a reasonable possibility of a loss, then the loss should be recognized in the current period; however, the accountant should not recognize possible gains. In other words, the traditional doctrine of conservatism is that the accountant should recognize all possible losses but anticipate no profit, in order to offset the natural optimism of managers and owners and because it is more dangerous to have optimistic than pessimistic financial statements.

In the past, accountants were primarily concerned with presenting a conservative picture of the financial condition of a business in its balance sheet. They regarded the balance sheet as of primary, and the income statement as of secondary, importance. Moreover, they were inclined to assume that a conservative balance sheet was a good balance sheet for all purposes, and that balance-sheet conservatism automatically resulted in a proper and conservative income statement.

The emphasis upon the balance sheet and upon conservative asset valuations and liability and loss provisions doubtless resulted from the fact that, in the early days of the development of accounting, the services of public accountants were required principally for the preparation of reports for bankers and other grantors of short-term credit, who were primarily concerned with the question of the margin of security. For many years, bankers and other short-term creditors were much more interested in the balance sheet than in the income statement, and they were

---

[14]See Yuji Ijiri and Robert K. Jaedicke, "Reliability and Objectivity of Accounting Measurements," *Accounting Review* (July 1966), pp. 474–83.

naturally disposed to regard balance-sheet conservatism as a safeguard and hence a basic virtue. Accountants were naturally influenced by their attitude.

Although balance-sheet conservatism is still regarded as an accounting virtue, the time-honored emphasis upon the balance sheet and upon conservatism in asset valuations has been subjected to critical reconsideration. One reason for this is the recognition that, with the increase in the number of corporate stockholders who are not active in the management, accounting reports must serve the requirements of investors as well as of short-term creditors. Ultraconservatism may be prejudicial to the interests of stockholders or other security holders who, having been led to believe that the company in which they have made investments is less prosperous than it really is, may sell their securities for less than they are really worth.

Also, with the income statement now receiving the emphasis formerly accorded the balance sheet, accountants have become increasingly aware that adherence to a doctrine of balance-sheet conservatism may result in incorrect, and even unconservative, income statements. If an expenditure or a cost that can be presumed to be essential or beneficial to the operations of more than one period is charged to current income in one period—a procedure that may be conservative from the balance-sheet standpoint—the income statements for all periods are distorted, and the income statements for the periods that are relieved of their just portions of the cost are the opposite of conservative.

The modern view of conservatism is that deliberate understatement is not an accounting virtue, but that when matters of opinion or estimates are involved, the accountant should proceed with caution and not be too optimistic. Or, as Moonitz states, "the proper role of conservatism in accounting is to insure that the uncertainties and risk inherent in any given business situation are given adequate consideration."[15]

On the other hand, the traditional view of conservatism with regard to understatement still permeates accounting practice (as examples, the lower-of-cost-or-market rule, LIFO, expensing items that should be capitalized, recording goodwill only when purchased, and the like) and cannot be dismissed as having disappeared, as Grady attempts to do.[16] In fact, a good case can be presented that conservatism underlies much of existing accounting practice.[17] An informed person should be aware that conservatism exists and plays an important role in existing accounting practice, but that from a normative-theory point of view, deliberate understatement should be eliminated because it is a very crude attempt to offset uncertainty that could be better handled by modern statistical methods; it conflicts with consistency, comparability, and the proper matching of expenses with revenue; and it can result in providing misleading information to users of financial statements.

---

[15]Moonitz, "Basic Postulates," p. 47.

[16]Grady, "Inventory of GAAP," p. 35.

[17]See Robert R. Sterling, "Conservatism: The Fundamental Principle of Valuation in Traditional Accounting," *Abacus* (December 1967), pp. 109–32.

Accounting principles. Accounting principles are general guidelines used in accounting practice that are based on substantial authoritative support. Such support comes from the American Institute of Certified Public Accountants (AICPA), which is the professional organization of the practicing certified public accountant (CPA), government regulatory agencies (such as the Securities and Exchange Commission), and accounting practices that have been accepted and continue to be accepted by the profession. The term *principles* is generally modified by the term *generally accepted* (that is, *generally accepted accounting principles*) in order to convey the substantial support behind them.

It is important to note that in accounting, the term *principle* does *not* mean a fundamental truth or proposition, as it does in the natural sciences, but rather a "general law or rule adopted or professed as a guide to action; a settled ground or basis of conduct or practice."[18] Thus, accounting principles are man-made, in contrast to natural law, and are not rigid. They are constantly evolving, since they are influenced by business practices; the needs of statement users; legislative and government regulation; the opinions and actions of stockholders, creditors, labor unions, and management; and the reasoning and experience of accountants. Such influences affect the assumptions, doctrines, and definitions underlying accounting principles, as well as the resulting accounting procedures. In the final analysis, accounting must serve the needs of society, necessitating continual adaptation to changes in our economic system in order to meet user demand for relevant information for purposes of financial decision making.

Accounting principles have not been deduced from an axiomatic approach, but have evolved. As problems arose in financial reporting, practices were formulated as solutions and either rejected, modified, or accepted by the accounting profession. As such practices became widely used by the accounting profession, they were elevated to the status of GAAP. As time passed, some accounting principles lost the support of the accounting profession and were eliminated from the status of GAAP. This evolutionary process continues today and is going on constantly.

The most authoritative source of GAAP is the Opinions of the Accounting Principles Board (APB) of the AICPA. The APB was formed in 1959 to advance the written expression of what constitutes GAAP in order to narrow the differences between existing accounting practices and in order to settle areas of controversy. From time to time, the board issues an Opinion, consisting of one or several paragraphs describing the principle, accompanied by several pages of explanatory material. In October 1965, the board issued *Opinion No. 6*[19] in which the opinions (51 Accounting Research Bulletins) of its predecessor (the Committee on Accounting Procedure) were adopted, with some revisions, until further notice; however, in recent years the board has issued several Opinions revising the

---

[18]AICPA, *Accounting Research and Terminology Bulletins: Final Edition* (New York: AICPA, 1961), p. 11.

[19]Accounting Principles Board, "Status of Accounting Research Bulletins," *Opinion No. 6* (New York: AICPA, October 1965), pp. 37–51.

original bulletins. In addition, the board has issued several Statements, which are primarily informative in nature, and lack the official pronouncement of Opinions.

GAAP are those principles that have substantial authoritative support, and the Opinions of the APB constitute such authoritative support. The Opinions provide the principal authoritative support for an examining CPA in his capacity as an independent auditor in reporting his opinion as to whether a company's financial statements are consistent with GAAP. If a company's financial statements are found to be consistent with GAAP, the examining CPA can render an unqualified opinion to that effect; otherwise, the report is qualified or an adverse opinion is rendered. If an accounting principle is used that departs from an Opinion of the APB, even though there is other substantial authoritative support for the accounting principle (e.g., the principle is used by other reputable companies or it is a requirement of a regulatory agency, such as the SEC), the auditor's opinions must be qualified for that departure, unless it can be shown that due to unusual circumstances the financial statements would otherwise have been misleading. In such rare situations, the examining CPA's report must describe the departure, the approximate effects of such departure (if practicable), and the reasons why the use of the principle would result in financial statements that are misleading.[20]

Note that when the CPA in his capacity as an independent auditor renders an opinion on a company's financial statements being in conformity with GAAP, he is not only verifying the use of acceptable general accounting guidelines, but also acceptable procedures. The point is that in actual accounting practice, GAAP are viewed as including both acceptable general accounting guidelines and acceptable accounting procedures. On the other hand, most writers in accounting make the distinction between specific accounting procedures and GAAP as general accounting guidelines. For example, an acceptable general accounting principle is that periodic depreciation should be recorded and reported by accountants. The acceptable accounting procedure is the use of either the straight-line method, decreasing-charge method (declining-balance or sum-of-the-year's digits depreciation), increasing-charge method (sinking-fund or annuity depreciation), or production (use) method. In this textbook, GAAP mean acceptable general guidelines and are distinguished from the carrying out of the guidelines via specific accounting procedures.

Two expressions of GAAP are provided by APB *Statement No. 4* and Grady's *Accounting Research Study No. 7*.[21] The former divides GAAP into three levels: pervasive principles (pervasive measurement principles and modifying conventions), broad operating principles (general rules derived from the pervasive principles that govern the application of the detailed principles), and detailed principles (numerous rules and procedures). *ARS No. 7* specifies five objectives of financial accounting and then discusses the GAAP that apply to each of those

---

[20]See Rule 203 in AICPA, *Restatement of the Code of Professional Ethics* (N.Y.: AICPA, 1973), p. 22.

[21]*Statement No. 4*, pp. 1–122; and *ARS No. 7*, pp. 57–67.

objectives. Since both *Statement No. 4* and *ARS No. 7* are quite voluminous, and since such principles are discussed throughout the text, the two works are not further discussed here, but *ARS No. 7* is summarized in an appendix to this chapter.

Recent developments. In May 1972 the council of the AICPA adopted the report of the Study on Establishment of Accounting Principles (also called the Wheat Report). The report recommended the replacement of the Accounting Principles Board (APB) with the Financial Accounting Standards Board (FASB). Whereas the APB consisted of eighteen part-time members, all of whom were CPAs, the FASB consists of seven full-time, well-paid members of which three need not be CPAs. The rationale is to have members on the board who are independent of practicing CPA firms, thereby increasing the board's credibility.

The function of the FASB is to establish *standards* of financial accounting and reporting. Note that the emphasis is on accounting standards; hence, the general guidelines underlying financial accounting probably will become known as "generally accepted accounting standards," instead of principles. Standards are issued by the FASB after an affirmative vote of five of its seven members.

Accounting procedures. Accounting procedures are the specific methods used by accountants in carrying out the general guidelines provided by GAAP. They are the numerous rules specifying how financial data should be recorded, classified, summarized, and reported. In other words, accounting procedures are the detailed methods used by accountants in their daily work.

There is normally more than one acceptable accounting procedure for each generally acceptable accounting principle, as was exemplified above with regard to depreciation. As another example, we can state the generally accepted accounting principle that inventory should be carried on the balance sheet at the lower of cost or market. The acceptable procedure in costing inventory is either FIFO, LIFO, average cost, retail-inventory method, gross-profit method, base-stock method, or some combination of these methods. Accounting procedures are discussed throughout the text.

It should be clear that the diversity in accounting and the problem of comparability in different companies' financial statements are largely the result of the large number of alternative accounting procedures that exist. The issuance of APB Opinions is an attempt to reduce some of the existing alternative accounting procedures.

Finally, the accounting procedures discussed above and throughout the text pertain to financial accounting, with its emphasis on external reporting. For purposes of managerial accounting, it is the accountant's job to provide relevant financial data for the managerial decision at hand, and he is not constrained by the theory of accounting practice: accounting assumptions, objectives, doctrines, principles, and procedures. For example, if a manager is involved with a capital-budgeting problem, the accountant should provide data on future cash flows for the various alternatives and not present financial data based on the theory of financial accounting practice.

Summary. The framework of descriptive financial accounting theory discussed in this chapter is summarized in the illustration below.

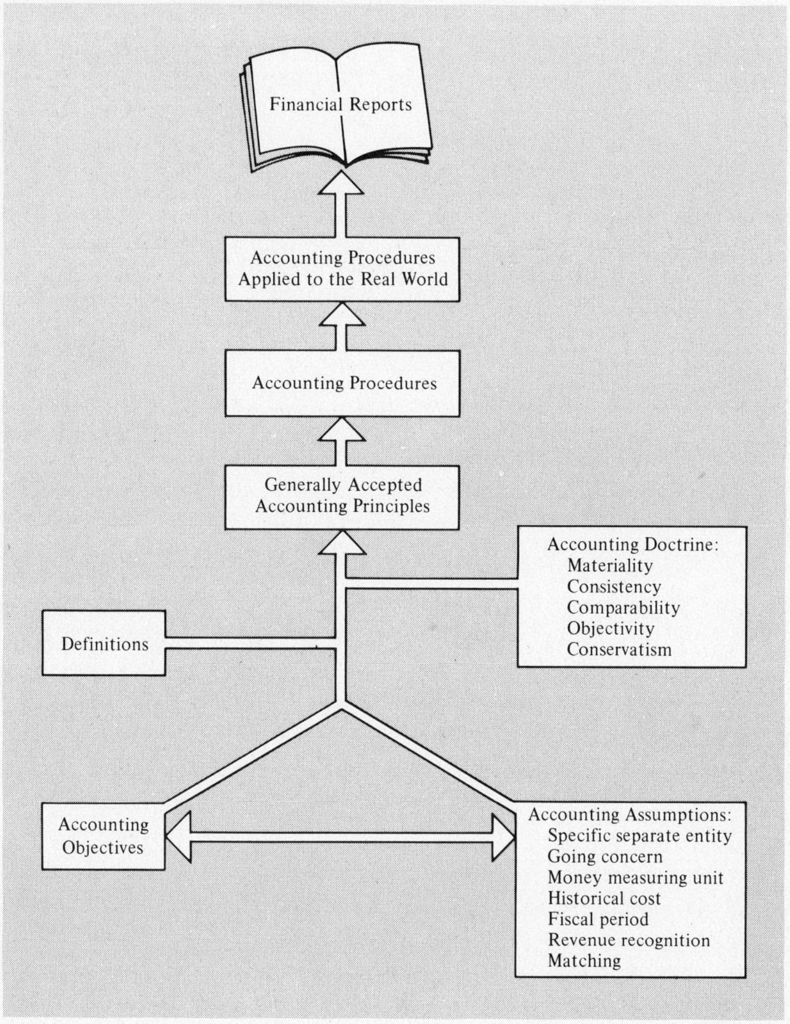

APPENDIX SUMMARY OF GAAP FROM *ARS NO. 7*

Objective A. Account for sales, revenues, income, cost of sales, expenses, gains and losses in such manner as to present fairly the results of operations for the period or periods of time covered.

Principle A-1. Sales, revenues and income should not be anticipated or materially overstated or understated. Accordingly, there must be proper cutoff accounting at the beginning and end of the period or periods.

Principle A-2. Costs of sales and expenses should be appropriately matched against the periodic sales and revenues. It follows that there must be proper cutoff accounting for inventories and liabilities for costs and expenses at the beginning and end of the period or periods.

Principle A-3. Appropriate charges should be made for depreciation and depletion of fixed assets and for amortization of other deferred costs.

Principle A-4. Proper distribution of costs should be made as between fixed assets, inventories, maintenance and expense. Direct costs are usually identifiable and common costs applicable to more than one activity should be distributed on appropriate cost incurrence bases such as time or use factors.

Principle A-5. Contingency provisions and reserves should not be misused as a means of arbitrarily reducing income or shifting income from one period to another.

Principle A-6. Nonrecurring and extraordinary gains and losses should be recognized in the period they occur, but should be shown separately from the ordinary and usual operations.

Principle A-7. There is a strong presumption that all gains and losses will be included in periodic income statements unless they are of such magnitude in relation to revenues and expenses from regular operations as to cause the statements to be misleading.

Principle A-8. Disclose rental charges under material leases and capitalize those which are in effect installment purchases of fixed assets.

Adapted from Paul Grady, "Inventory of Generally Accepted Accounting Principles for Business Enterprises," *Accounting Research Study No. 7* (New York: AICPA, 1965), pp. 57–67.

Principle A-9. If accounting principles in the determination of periodic results have not been consistently maintained, the effect of the change should be stated.

Objective B. Account for the equity capital invested by stockholders through contribution of assets or retained earnings in a meaningful manner on a cumulative basis and as to changes during the period or periods covered. The account structure and presentation in financial statements of a business entity are designed to meet statutory and corporate charter requirements and to portray significant financial relationships.

Principle B-1. In case there are two or more classes of stock, account for the equity capital invested for each and disclose the rights and preferences to dividends and to principal in liquidation.

Principle B-2. From a financial viewpoint the capital invested by stockholders is the corpus of the enterprise and its identity should be fully maintained. Any impairment of invested capital resulting from operating deficits, losses of any nature, dividend distributions in excess of earnings, and treasury stock purchases is accounted for both currently and cumulatively.

Principle B-3. Capital surplus, however created, should not be used to relieve the income account of the current or future years of charges which would otherwise fail to be made thereagainst. There should be no commingling of retained earnings with invested capital in excess of par or stated values.

Principle B-4. Retained earnings should represent the cumulative balance of periodic earnings less dividend distributions in cash, property or stock, plus or minus gains and losses of such magnitude as not to be properly included in periodic earnings. The entire amount may be presumed to be unrestricted as to dividend distributions unless restrictions are indicated in the financial statements.

Principle B-5. Retained earnings may be decreased by transfers to invested capital accounts when formal corporate action has, in fact, changed the composition of the equity capital. Accumulated deficit accounts may be eliminated against invested capital accounts through formal action approved by stockholders, which establishes a new base line of accountability.

Principle B-6. The amount of any revaluation credits should be separately classified in the stockholders' equity section, and it is not available for any type of charge except on reversal of the revaluation.

Principle B-7. Disclose status of stock options to employees or others and changes therein during the period or periods covered.

Objective C. Account for the assets invested in the enterprise by stockholders (through property contributed or retained earnings) and creditors, in a meaningful manner, so that when considered with the liabilities and equity capital of stockholders there will be a fair presentation of the financial position of the enterprise both at the beginning and end of the period. It should be understood that financial position or balance sheet statements do not purport to show either present values of assets to the enterprise or values which might be realized in liquidation.

Principle C-1. Items classified as current assets should be carried at not more than is reasonably expected to be realized within one year or within the normal operating cycle of the particular business. Cash should be segregated between unrestricted and restricted items, and the inclusion of the latter in current assets must be justified by their nature. Receivables should be reduced by allowance accounts to cover expected collection or other losses. Receivables from officers, employees, or affiliated companies should be shown separately. Inventories should be carried at cost or market, whichever the lower. Cost comprises direct costs plus factory overhead costs, and the basis of determination (e.g., LIFO, FIFO, or average) should be stated. Prepaid items should be properly chargeable to future periods.

Principle C-2. Fixed assets should be carried at cost of acquisition or construction in the historical accounts, unless such cost is no longer meaningful. Cost of land should ordinarily be shown separately. Cost of construction includes direct costs and overhead costs incurred, such as engineering, supervision and administration, interest and taxes. Items treated as fixed assets should have at least one year of expected useful life to the enterprise, and normally the life is considerably longer. Practicable yardsticks or criteria should be established in order that consistent distinctions may be made between fixed assets, operating expenses and maintenance. Ordinarily, this should be accomplished by creating a catalogue of property units to current expenses. Items no longer in service should be removed by charge to depreciation reserve or expense in order that fixed assets will represent the cost of properties in service.

Principle C-3. Appropriate provision or allowances should be made in order to charge operations with the investment in depreciable assets over the estimated life thereof. The accumulated allowances, less property retirements, should be shown as a deduction from fixed assets.

Principle C-4. Long-term investments in securities ordinarily should be carried at cost. When market quotations are available, the aggregate quoted amounts should be disclosed. Investments in affiliates should be segregated from other investments.

Principle C-5. The costs of intangible items, such as debt discount and expense, patents, copyrights, research and development (if deferred) and goodwill should be shown separately. Limited-term items should be amortized against earnings over their estimated lives. The policy in regard to amortization of unlimited-term intangibles should be disclosed.

Principle C-6. The nature and extent of hypothecated or pledged assets should be shown.

Objective D. Account for all known liabilities in a meaningful manner in order that their summarization, considered together with the statement of assets and equity invested by stockholders, will fairly present the financial position of the enterprise at the beginning and end of the period.

Principle D-1. All known liabilities should be recorded regardless of whether the definite amount is determinable. If the amounts cannot be reasonably approximated, the nature of the items should be disclosed on the face of the summary of liabilities or by footnote.

Principle D-2. Current liabilities should include items payable within one year or at the end of the operating business cycle used in classification of current assets. Accounts should be shown separately for notes payable to banks, notes payable to others, accounts payable (may include payrolls), Federal income taxes accrued, other accrued taxes, accounts or notes payable to officers, and accounts or notes payable to affiliates.

Principle D-3. Long-term liabilities should be described and due dates and rates of interest shown.

Principle D-4. The nature and extent to which specific liabilities are a preferred lien on assets should be shown.

Principle D-5. Deferred income should be separately classified and described.

Principle D-6. Contingent liabilities of importance should be disclosed.

Objective E. Financial statements should comply with the applicable reporting standards included in generally accepted auditing standards. Reporting to investors should be performed on an entity basis.

Principle E-1. Generally accepted reporting standards applicable to financial statements are set forth in Chapters 7, 8, 9 and 11 of Statements on Auditing Procedure No. 33, which are incorporated in this Inventory.

Principle E-2. Where there is a parent company and one or more subsidiaries, there is a presumption that consolidated statements are more meaningful than separate statements.

Principle E-3. The accounts of consolidated subsidiaries or divisions operating in foreign countries should be translated into dollars at the appropriate rates of exchange.

Principle E-4. Where two or more previously independent entities merge or otherwise combine in such a manner as to constitute a pooling of interests, the new entity inherits the bases of accountability of the constituent entities.

4

Statement of Income and Retained Earnings

Introduction. The fundamental objective of accounting is to provide useful financial information about economic entities to aid in making financial decisions. To those outside the business entity, primarily owners and creditors, such information is provided by general-purpose financial statements.

Financial statements are the end result of the financial accounting process that accumulates, analyzes, records, classifies, summarizes, verifies, reports, and interprets the financial data of the economic activities of a business firm. This financial accounting process is based on generally accepted accounting principles (standards). Over the years, the accounting profession has developed basic patterns of disclosure that, although not completely uniform, aid the statement users in reviewing and analyzing the economic activities of business firms.

Investors, such as stockholders, stockbrokers, investment analysts; creditors, such as banks and other lending institutions; governmental agencies; labor unions; and other interested parties desire information about a business firm's financial position at points in time and about changes in fiancial position during periods of time.

Information about a firm's financial position or status at the end of a fiscal period is reported in the balance sheet (statement of financial position). The results of operations, or operating performance, from a firm's profit-oriented activities during a fiscal period are reported in the income statement. Changes in retained earnings during a fiscal period are reported in the statement of retained earnings, which is often combined with the income statement into a statement of income and retained earnings. The sources and uses of a firm's economic resources during a fiscal period are reported in the statement of changes in financial position (funds statement). Finally, information about a reporting company's accounting policies is provided as an integral part of its financial statements, preferably in a separate summary of significant accounting policies preceding the notes to financial statements.

The aforementioned statements are the *basic* financial statements that companies are required to provide, following generally accepted accounting principles (GAAP). Such financial information includes notes that explain items on the face of the statements, as well as descriptive information that is not quantifiable in terms of money. In addition, varying types of supplemental financial information generally accompany the financial statements, such as pertinent financial ratios and trends, analyses of changes in specific items, financial information adjusted for general-price-level changes, and the like. Most companies widely circulate such financial information as part of their annual reports to stockholders, with the financial statements certified by certified public accountants as being in conformity with GAAP.

Accounting policies. Accounting policies are the *specific* accounting principles and procedures (methods) used by a company to present financial statements in accordance with GAAP. Since the presentation of financial statements is affected by the specific accounting policies used by a reporting company, statement users should be aware of such accounting policies when using financial statements to aid them in their financial decision making. Consequently, Accounting Principles Board (APB) *Opinion No. 22* states that a reporting company's financial statements should include a description of all significant accounting policies as an integral part of the financial statements.[1] Note, however, that such disclosure does not apply to unaudited, interim financial statements where the reporting entity has not changed its accounting policies since the end of its preceding fiscal year.

Per *Opinion No. 22,* disclosure of accounting policies should encompass those accounting principles and procedures that pertain to any of the following:

A selection from existing acceptable alternatives
Principles and methods peculiar to the industry in which the reporting entity operates
Unusual or innovative applications of GAAP

---

[1]Accounting Principles Board, "Disclosure of Accounting Policies," *Opinion No. 22* (New York: AICPA, April 1972), p. 434.

Examples of accounting policies that should be disclosed include those relating to depreciation methods, amortization of intangibles, basis of consolidation, inventory pricing, accounting for research and development costs (including method of amortization), recognition of profit on long-term construction contracts, recognition of revenue from leasing and franchising operations, and translation of foreign currencies.

Although there can be flexibility with regard to format and location of the disclosure of accounting policies, *Opinion No. 22* recommends that they be disclosed in a separate statement of significant accounting policies preceding the notes to financial statements or as the initial note.

Income statement. The income statement, also called the statement of earnings, or profit and loss statement, provides financial information about a firm's profit-directed activities (that is, results of operations) during a fiscal period. It shows the financial changes brought about by profitable (unprofitable) operations during a period of time. Thus the income statement is a model of a firm's operating performance that is used in financial accounting to provide classified summary reports on the results of profit-directed operations for periodic time intervals.

The income-statement model is based on a firm's revenues and expenses during a period, to derive net income (also called profit) or loss. Net income (loss) is the positive (negative) difference between periodic revenues and expenses and is a periodic measure of operating success. If a firm has a profitable year, this means that it was successful in providing goods and services that customers desired, that the goods and services were at prices customers were willing and able to pay, and that the prices were sufficient to provide a margin above operating expenses. By providing classified and summarized information with regard to a firm's periodic revenue, expense, and therefore net income, the income statement presents financial information that is useful in

- Evaluating the operating success of a firm and management's efficiency in conducting operations
- Predicting future net-income flows and future operating success
- Evaluating return on invested capital (net income divided by stockholders' equity)
- Determining whether capital is being maintained in conducting operations

Since revenue and expense are the basic components of the income statement, their meaning should be understood; hence, they are defined as follows:

> *Revenue* is the product (goods and services) created by the firm during a time period. By including conventional accounting timing (i.e., the time of delivery of goods or the time when services are rendered) and considerations of measurement (i.e., the monetary measurement of assets received) into the revenue definition, the usual definition of revenue is

an inflow of assets in the form of cash, receivables, or other property from customers or clients, which results from sales of merchandise or the rendering of services, or from investments (e.g., interest revenue).

Expense is the goods or services used in the generation of revenue during a time period. By including the conventional accounting valuation method of cost in the expense definition, expense is usually defined as *the cost of goods or services used for the purpose of generating revenue during a time period.*

It should be clearly understood that the income statement is a flow statement (that is, revenue and expense flows) over a specific interval of time. In contrast, the balance sheet is a stock (not flow) statement that shows financial position at a given point in time. On the other hand, the income statement is a link between two successive balance sheets via retained earnings, since revenues increase and expenses decrease retained earnings, and therefore, net income (loss) is the net increase (decrease) in retained earnings from profitable (unprofitable) operations for the period. Hence there is a close relationship between net income and changes in retained earnings, even though there are other changes in retained earnings (such as prior-period adjustments and dividend charges) besides that from profitable operations. Because of this close relationship, there has been a growing tendency, at least among the larger companies, to combine the income statement and the statement of retained earnings into one statement: the statement of income and retained earnings. When they are not combined, a separate statement of retained earnings is presented as a basic financial statement that provides financial information about changes in retained earnings during the fiscal period.

AN ILLUSTRATION: An example of a statement of income and retained earnings is presented on the next page for Kansas Company. Obviously, a separate income statement and a separate statement of retained earnings could have been presented just as well.

In the reading of an income statement, such as that for Kansas Company, the accounting assumptions that underlie the preparation of the statement must be kept in mind. For example, the periodic net-income figure ($92,400 for Kansas Company) is an *estimate* of operating performance, because "true" net income cannot be really determined until the business is terminated and liquidated. But accountants have to provide periodic reports on operating performance for investors, creditors, other external readers, and management for purposes of financial decision making. As a result, the accountant assumes that he can segment the operating life of a business firm into periodic time intervals or fiscal periods (January 1 to December 31, 19+5 for Kansas Company) to provide periodic income statements on the results of operations—the fiscal-period assumption. Moreover, because of the difficulties in measuring revenue and expense for a periodic time interval, the accountant uses accrual accounting, estimation, and informed judgment—implications of the fiscal-period assumption.

KANSAS COMPANY
Statement of Income and Retained Earnings
For the Year Ended December 31, 19+5

Net sales			$840,000
Cost of goods sold			520,000
Gross margin			$320,000
Operating expenses:			
Selling expense		$ 80,000	
General and administrative expense (Note A)		85,100	165,100
Net operating income			$154,900
Nonoperating items:			
Add: Interest revenue	$1,600		
Gain on sale of equipment (Note B)	8,000	$ 9,600	
Deduct: Interest expense (Note C)	$6,500		
Loss on sale of bond investment (Note D)	4,000	10,500	900
Income before taxes			$154,000
Federal income taxes			61,600
Net income			$ 92,400
Retained earnings at beginning of year:			
As previously reported		$175,000	
Deduct prior-period adjustment for additional income taxes settled in 19+5 (Note E)		20,000	
As restated			155,000
			$247,400
Deduct: Common stock dividends—cash		$ 30,000	
Common stock dividends—stock		50,000	80,000
Retained earnings at end of year			$167,400
Earnings per common share			$ 6.72

Note A: Includes depreciation expense of $20,000 on building and $35,000 on equipment.

Note B: During 19+5 Kansas Company sold equipment with a net book amount of $30,000 for $38,000, which resulted in an $8,000 gain from sale of equipment.

Note C: Includes $500 bond premium amortization.

Note D: During 19+5 Kansas Company sold some of its bond investments originally costing $15,000 for $11,000, which resulted in a $4,000 loss on sale of investments.

Note E: The balance of retained earnings at December 31, 19+4 has been restated from amounts previously reported to reflect a retroactive charge of $20,000 for additional income taxes settled in 19+5. This amount is the result of expenses deducted for income tax purposes during 19+3 that were not allowed in the tax litigation settled in 19+5. Net income of $70,000 ($7.00 per share) as previously reported for 19+3 should be restated to $50,000 ($5.00 per share).

Since revenue and expense are the main components of the income statement, it must be understood how they are being recognized in the statement. Although there are certain exceptions, revenue ($840,000 sales and $1,600 interest revenue) is normally recognized during the period when sales are made (goods delivered), services rendered, or interest earned—the revenue-recognition assumption. Based on the matching assumption, which is implemented by distinguishing between product cost and period expense, expenses that were incurred to generate that revenue ($520,000 cost of goods sold, $165,100 operating expenses, $10,500 nonoperating expense, and $61,600 income tax expense) during the period are matched with the resulting revenue and gain ($8,000), along with any extraordinary items, to derive periodic net income.

The specific-separate-entity assumption affects the income statement in that the reader immediately knows that the statement is based on the revenue and expense of a specific entity (Kansas Company), independently of the revenue and expense of owners, management, and employees who make up the entity and of other entities. The money-measuring-unit assumption means that only those revenues and expenses that can be quantified in terms of money are on the face of the statement and that they are not adjusted for changes in the general purchasing power of money (inflation and deflation). The historical-cost assumption means that the normal valuation method used in reporting expenses in the income statement is cost incurred and expired in the generation of revenues. The going-concern assumption affects the income statement in that the reporting of expenses that are the result of cost allocations (depreciation expense, expired insurance, etc.) and that are incurred but not paid (liabilities created) is justified because the entity is expected to remain in business at least long enough to use up such assets and pay off such liabilities.

Income-statement format. The two basic formats used in income-statement presentations are the multiple-step and single-step income statements. The multiple-step income statement, as previously illustrated for the Kansas Company, reports various subtotals (for instance, gross margin, net operating income, and income before extraordinary items) in order to show important relationships that exist. For example, gross margin ($320,000 for Kansas Company) indicates the average markup on goods sold (38% = $320,000/$840,000), net operating income ($154,900) shows the income for the normal (regular) and principal activities for which the firm is in business, and net income ($92,400) shows the income from both operating and nonoperating (secondary business) activities. In addition, if any extraordinary items (to be discussed shortly) exist, such items are reported as additions or deductions from income before extraordinary items to derive net income. Income before extraordinary items shows the income from both operating and nonoperating items, but is not distorted by unusual nonrecurring, extraordinary activities. Thus the basic argument for the multiple-step statement is that it provides more useful information in evaluating management efficiency in conducting operations, making income comparisons, and predicting future-income flows, because it provides income information on the normal, recurring operations.

As illustrated on p. 94 (along with a separate statement of retained earnings)

KANSAS COMPANY
Income Statement
For the Year Ended December 31, 19+5

Revenues and gains:		
Net sales		$840,000
Interest revenue		1,600
Gain on sale of equipment (Note A)		8,000
Total revenues and gains		849,600
Expenses and losses:		
Merchandise	$520,000	
Wages, salaries, and employee benefits	110,100	
Depreciation of building and equipment (Note B)	55,000	
Interest (Note C)	6,500	
Loss on sale of bond investment (Note D)	4,000	
Federal income taxes	61,600	
Total expenses and losses		757,200
Net income		$ 92,400
Earnings per common share		$ 6.72

Note A: Same as note B on page 92.
Note B: Same as note A on page 92.
Note C: Same as note C on page 92.
Note D: Same as note D on page 92.

KANSAS COMPANY
Statement of Retained Earnings
For the Year Ended December 31, 19+5

Retained earnings at beginning of year:		
As previously reported	$175,000	
Deduct prior period adjustment for additional income taxes settled in 19+5 (Note E)	20,000	
As restated		$155,000
Net income		92,400
		$247,400
Deduct: Common stock dividends—cash	$ 30,000	
Common stock dividends—stock	50,000	80,000
Retained earnings at end of year		$167,400

Note E: Same as note E on page 92.

for Kansas Company, the single-step income statement groups all revenue at the top of the statement ($849,600), followed by a grouping of all expenses ($757,200). By subtracting total expenses from total revenues (single-step subtraction), net income ($92,400) is shown without any intermediate subtotals. In many cases, the single-step income statement will also show expenses classified by the nature of the expense (as illustrated), instead of by the usual functional classification (such as cost of goods sold, selling expense, and general and administrative expense) employed in multiple-step income statements.

In comparison to the multiple-step statement, the single-step income statement has the practical advantage of being simpler and easier to understand, because it is more compact and relatively uncluttered. It is also contended that the single-step statement has the advantage of treating all revenue and expense alike (that is, does not erroneously imply a priority of expense and revenue as it is contended that the multiple-step statement does), and that it avoids subtotals and titles that do not have universally recognized meaning.

Extraordinary items. *Opinion No. 9* states that all items of profit and loss should be included in the income statement (except for prior-period adjustments), and that extraordinary items should be segregated from the results of ordinary operations. Extraordinary items would be shown separately in the income statement, with disclosure of the nature, tax effects, and amounts thereof.[2] Thus the income statement would disclose the following elements when extraordinary items exist:

Income before extraordinary items
Extraordinary items (less applicable income taxes)
Net income

Opinion No. 9 defined extraordinary items as "events and transactions of material effect which would not be considered as recurring factors in any evaluation of the ordinary operating processes of the business."[3] The Opinion provided examples of extraordinary items (such as, material gains and losses from the sale or abandonment of plant or a significant segment of the business) and examples of gains and losses that would not constitute extraordinary items (such as the write-downs of receivables, inventories, and research and development costs).

The criteria for determining extraordinary items, as well as the intent of the criteria and definitions, per *Opinion No. 9* were found to be difficult to interpret in the actual accounting practice; hence, there were found in practice inconsistent applications of the criteria for the determination of extraordinary items. The result was the reporting of extraordinary items that were definitely prohibited by the Opinion (such as, the write-off of inventories and research and development costs) and that were not intended per the Opinion to be reported as such (for example, the extraordinary reporting of gains and losses on sale of equipment, when

---

[2] Accounting Principles Board, "Reporting the Results of Operations," *Opinion No. 9* (New York: AICPA, December 1966), pp. 112–14.

[3] *Opinion No. 9*, pp. 114–15.

the Opinion referred to gains and losses on sale of plant or a significant segment of the business). Moreover, it was argued that the reporting of extraordinary items was being abused in that companies were letting routine losses pile up and then writing-off inflated losses as extraordinary items to set up profitable operations in the future—the so-called "big-bath" approach to special write-offs.

Because of the difficulty in the interpretation of extraordinary items per *Opinion No. 9,* as well as the abuses in the reporting thereof, current accounting thinking is that extraordinary items are rare. Thus current accounting practice restricts extraordinary items to those material gains or losses (or provisions for losses), in light of the environment in which the entity operates, that are derived from events or transactions distinguished by *both* their unusual nature and by the infrequency of their occurrence:[4]

> Unusual nature. The underlying event or transaction must be clearly unrelated to, or only incidentally related to, the ordinary and typical activities of the entity taking into account the environment in which the entity operates. Such events or transactions possess a high degree of abnormality and are significantly different from the ordinary and typical activities of the entity in light of the entity's environment. The environment is a primary consideration in determining the abnormality and unusual nature of the event or transaction, and includes such factors as the characteristics of the industry, the geographical location, and the nature of governmental regulation in which the entity operates. Because of the different characteristics of the environment, an event or transaction may be unusual for one entity but not for another entity.
>
> Infrequency of occurrence. The underlying event or transaction must be nonrecurring; that is, the event or transaction must be of a type that would not reasonably be expected to recur in the foreseeable future. The primary consideration is the determination of the frequency or probability of occurrence of a particular event or transaction, taking into account the environment in which the entity operates. Consequently, a specific event might meet the infrequency condition for one company, but because of a different probability of occurrence, might not meet the conditions for another company. Also, the reoccurrence of similar events or transactions in a period is evidence of frequency and therefore not an extraordinary item.

Because the effect of the dual criteria for extraordinary items is to eliminate most gains and losses from the extroardinary classification, examples of extraordinary items are few in number. Examples would include material gains or losses (or provisions for losses) resulting from the disposal of a segment of a business

---

[4]Accounting Principles Board, "Reporting the Effects of Extraordinary Events and Transactions," *Exposure Draft: Proposed APB Opinion Ref. No. 1060* (New York: AICPA, November 1972), pp. 5–6.

(such as, a major line of business, geographic location, or class of customer),[5] a major casualty (such as an earthquake), government actions (such as, condemnations or expropriations), and tax-loss carryforwards.[6]

In contrast, because they are usual in nature and may be expected to recur as a consequence of customary and continuing business activities, the following gains and losses, except in rare instances, are *not* extraordinary items:

- Write-down or write-off of receivables, inventories, equipment leased to others, or deferred research and development costs
- Exchange gains or losses from fluctuations of foreign currencies
- Gains or losses on the sale or abandonment of capital assets
- Effects of a strike, including those at competitors and major suppliers
- Adjustment of accruals on long-term contracts
- That portion of the losses on the disposal of a segment of a business, or investment in a subsidiary or joint venture, which should have resulted from a valuation of the assets on a going-concern basis immediately prior to the disposition[7]

ILLUSTRATION: To illustrate the accounting for extraordinary items, assume that a company had uninsured earthquake damage to its plant and equipment of $50,000 during 19+6. Assuming a 40 percent tax rate and that the company had 10,000 shares of common stock outstanding, the loss would be reported as an extraordinary item in the income statement as follows:

Income before extraordinary item	$100,000
Extraordinary item:	
Loss on earthquake damage to plant and equipment, net of applicable taxes of $20,000 (Note C)	30,000
Net income	$ 70,000
Earnings per common share:	
Income before extraordinary item	$ 10.00
Extraordinary item	3.00
Net income	$ 7.00

Note C: During 19+6 Company X incurred earthquake damage to its plant and equipment of $50,000. The damage was uninsured. The resulting book loss of $50,000 was reduced by applicable tax savings of $20,000 to report an extraordinary loss of $30,000.

[5] At the time of this writing there is a controversy as to whether this gain or loss should be reported in a separate classification before the caption "Income before extraordinary items."

[6] Tax-loss carryforwards are treated as extraordinary items per Accounting Principles Board, "Accounting for Income Taxes," *Opinion No. 11* (New York: AICPA, December 1971), p. 173.

[7] *Exposure Draft: Proposed APB Opinion Ref. No. 1060*, p. 6.

Prior-period adjustments. With the exception of prior-period adjustments, APB *Opinion No. 9* states that *all* profit and loss items recognized during the period should be reflected in net income. *Opinion No. 9* states that prior-period adjustments should be reported as adjustments of the beginning retained earnings balance; hence, they would be reported in a separate statement of retained earnings or in the retained earnings section of a statement of income and retained earnings. If comparative financial statements (that is, statements for more than one period) are presented, then prior-period net-income figures, retained earnings balances, and any other affected balances are adjusted to reflect the retroactive application of prior-period adjustments. In addition, disclosure of prior-period adjustments requires the reporting of the associated tax effects, if any, arising from such adjustments.

Prior-period adjustments can be defined as rare, material accounting adjustments arising from prior-period economic events that, because of uncertainty, could not be meaningfully measured at that time, but that are now determinable. *Opinion No. 9* specifies the following four criteria for prior-period adjustments: those material adjustments that

Can be specifically identified with and directly related to the business activities of particular prior periods
Are not attributable to economic events occurring subsequent to the date of the financial statements for the prior period
Depend primarily on determinations by persons other than management
Were not susceptible of reasonable estimation prior to such determinations

Examples of prior-period adjustments would include material, nonrecurring adjustments resulting from the settlement of income taxes, renegotiation proceedings or rate cases, and litigation. Note, however, that prior-period adjustments would *not* include adjustments that are the result of

Using estimates in the normal accounting process (e.g., changes in the estimated remaining useful life of plant and equipment)
Changes in estimations of the realization of assets (e.g., collectibility of accounts receivable or the ultimate recovery of deferred costs), because they are determinable by economic events subsequent to the period when originally recognized
Immaterial changes in provisions for liabilities (e.g., income taxes) made in prior periods, because they are considered part of normal, recurring operations

As a specific example of the reporting of a prior-period adjustment, refer to the statement of income and retained earnings for Kansas Company (see page 92). In this situation, there had been litigation begun in previous years as to the amount of income taxes owed, and it was settled during the current reporting year (19+5). Since it was an unfavorable settlement of $20,000, it is reported as a deduction from beginning retained earnings (as previously reported) to show the adjusted beginning retained earnings balance ($155,000) to which net income for the period ($92,400) can be added to show the ending retained earnings balance ($167,400).

The accounting entry during 19+5 for this prior-period adjustment would be as follows:

Prior-period adjustment—settlement of income taxes (closed to retained earnings)	20,000	
Cash		20,000

Intraperiod income tax allocation. Intraperiod income tax allocation is the assigning (allocating) of the total income tax expense for the period to the items that brought about the tax and the reporting of this association in the financial statements. It is allocation within a period in order to clearly present income before extraordinary items, the extraordinary items, prior-period adjustments to retained earnings, and direct entries to other stockholders' equity accounts, net of applicable income taxes. The total tax expense for the period is allocated to the income statement (to operations and to extraordinary items), statement of retained earnings (prior-period adjustments that have tax effects), and balance sheet (only to the extent that any tax effects exist, a rare occurrence, on direct entries to stockholders' equity accounts other than retained earnings).

The basic argument for intraperiod income tax allocation is that the taxes should follow, on the financial statements, the items that caused the taxes. Following this line of reasoning, if the total tax expense for the period were shown as a deduction to derive income before extraordinary items, this could result in the misstatement of

Income before extraordinary items, because it would be reported net of taxes *not* applicable to current operations

Extraordinary items, because they would be shown gross, instead of net, of applicable taxes

Net income, because it would be reported net of taxes on prior-period adjustments

Adjusted beginning retained earnings, because prior-period adjustments would *not* be net of applicable taxes

Intraperiod income tax allocation is supported by *Opinion No. 11* and *Opinion No. 9*. APB *Opinion No. 11* states that intraperiod income tax allocation should be applied to obtain an appropriate relationship between income tax expense and income before extraordinary items, extraordinary items, prior-period adjustments, and direct entries to other stockholders' equity accounts.[8] *Opinion No. 9* states that extraordinary items disclosed in the income statement should show, on the face of the statement or in notes thereto, the amount of income taxes applicable to the items. In other words, an extraordinary gain results in additional taxes so that the net gain is lower than the book gain by the amount of the taxes. Similarly,

[8] *Opinion No. 11*, p. 175.

an extraordinary loss can be tax deductible; therefore, the book loss is reduced by the tax savings on the loss.

As a specific example of intraperiod income tax allocation, refer to the statement of income and retained earnings for Kansas Company (see page 92). Note the $20,000 additional income taxes treated as a prior-period adjustment to retained earnings of Kansas Company. Thus the total income taxes for Kansas Company are $81,600 ($61,600 + $20,000). Based on intraperiod income tax allocation, the $81,600 total taxes are allocated to operations ($61,600) and to retained earnings ($20,000).

The following entry reflects the income taxes for Kansas Company for 19+5:

Prior-period adjustment—settlement of income taxes (closed to retained earnings)	20,000	
Income taxes	61,600	
Income taxes payable		61,600
Cash		20,000

As a concluding comment on income tax allocation, it should be pointed out that some accountants are opposed to all income tax allocations, because they view income taxes as a distribution of profits (similar to dividends) instead of a business expense. However, they are primarily against interperiod income tax allocation (allocation of taxes between periods), which is the subject matter of a subsequent chapter.

Accounting errors. Material accounting errors are rare for companies that are annually audited by independent certified public accounting firms, since such audits, as well as the company's own internal audits, normally find errors and correct them before the financial statements are issued. Consequently, accounting errors made and discovered during the current accounting period are easily handled by merely reversing the incorrect entries and making the correct entry before the financial statements are issued. On the other hand, there is the problem of how to report during the current period those rare, material accounting errors that were made in previous periods and not discovered until the current period. Obviously, such errors can have a distorting effect on a company's financial statements, especially with regard to trends shown by comparative financial statements.

APB *Opinion No. 20* states that accounting errors made during previous periods and discovered subsequently should be reported as prior-period adjustments.[9] The accounts would be corrected when the error is discovered, the correcting account (such as Correction of prior-period errors) closed to retained earnings, and the correction reported in the retained earnings section of the statement of income and retained earnings (or in the separate statement of retained earnings) as an adjustment to the beginning retained earnings balance. If comparative finan-

---

[9] Accounting Principles Board, "Accounting Changes," *Opinion No. 20* (New York: AICPA, July 1971), pp. 398–99.

cial statements are presented, the statements for each year should be restated (retroactive adjustment) to reflect the correct basis.

An accounting error can be defined as a misapplication of the economic facts existing at the time of recording and reporting an economic event. Examples of accounting errors include:

Use of an *unrealistic* estimate as a result of a misuse of economic information at the time the estimate was made (e.g., the use of an unrealistic estimate of the useful life of plant and equipment in the determination of depreciation)

Mathematical mistakes (e.g., errors in counting or pricing inventory)

Use of an *unacceptable* accounting principle or procedure (e.g., failure to recognize depreciation, accruals, or deferrals)

Classification mistakes (e.g., cost of equipment expensed instead of capitalized)

As an illustration of recording and reporting a material accounting error, assume that a piece of equipment was purchased in 19+5 for $10,000 and was incorrectly expensed at that time. Further assume a ten-year estimated life, no estimated salvage value, straight-line depreciation, and discovery of the error in 19+7. Finally, assume that the income statement for 19+6 had previously reported income before extraordinary items and net income of $60,000 and $40,000, respectively.

Based on the data above, the correcting entry made in 19+7 would be as follows:

Equipment...	10,000	
Depreciation expense (19+7)	1,000	
Accumulated depreciation—equipment (3 years)....		3,000
Correction of prior-period error (to be closed to Retained earnings)		8,000

Prior-period balance sheets reported as comparative statements would be restated to show the asset (Equipment, $10,000) and accumulated depreciation ($2,000 for the 19+6 balance sheet). Comparative income statements would be reported as shown on page 102.

Note that in the presentation shown, previously reported (19+6) income before extraordinary items ($60,000) and net income ($40,000) were adjusted to $59,000 ($60,000 − $1,000) and $39,000 ($40,000 − $1,000), respectively, by correcting for the $1,000 depreciation expense that was not previously reported. Also, note that the prior-period adjustment for 19+6 is $9,000, not the $8,000 used in the 19+7 correcting entry, since beginning (19+6) retained earnings are restated. That is, the beginning retained earnings figure for 19+6 was incorrect because during 19+5, $10,000 was mistakenly expensed and $1,000 depreciation expense was not recorded; hence, net income, and therefore ending retained earnings for 19+5 (beginning retained earnings for 19+6), were understated by $9,000 ($10,000 − $1,000).

PARTIAL COMPARATIVE STATEMENTS OF INCOME AND RETAINED EARNINGS

	19+7	19+6 As Adjusted (Note A)
⋮		
Depreciation expense	$ 1,000	$ 1,000
⋮		
Income before extraordinary items (Note A)	80,000	59,000
⋮		
Net income (Note A)	65,000	39,000
Retained earnings at beginning of year:		
As previously reported	$140,000	$100,000
Add prior-period adjustment for accounting error (Note A)	8,000	9,000
As restated	$148,000	$109,000
Retained earnings at end of year	$213,000	$148,000

Note A: The balance of retained earnings at December 31, 19+6, has been restated from amounts previously reported, to reflect a retroactive credit of $8,000 for a 19+5 accounting error found in 19+7. The error was the result of a $10,000 purchase of equipment during 19+5 that was inadvertently charged to expense instead of being properly capitalized as an asset. As a result of the error, annual depreciation of $1,000 was not recognized during 19+5 and 19+6. The $8,000 prior-period adjustment for 19+7 is the result of beginning retained earnings of 19+6 being understated $9,000 from the carryover from the 19+5 error, and net income for 19+6 being overstated $1,000 by the failure to report depreciation expense, both of which carried over to the 19+7 beginning retained earnings.

Some accountants believe that accounting errors made in previous periods should be reported in the current year's income statement as an extraordinary item, in order that net income reflect all material economic events that occurred or were discovered during the current period. However, such reporting would result in net income being misstated twice because of the error. That is, prior-period's net income would be misstated and current period's net income would be misstated in the opposite direction by the correction.

All-inclusive vs. current-operating concept. Prior to the issuance of *Opinion No. 9* and *Opinion No. 20,* there was a controversy in accounting as to how to report in the financial statements nonrecurring gains and losses, and errors made during prior periods. In other words, what is properly included in the computation of net income for the period? Is the net income for the period affected by unusual, extraneous, and nonrecurring gains and losses, such as an uninsured flood loss? Is the net income for the current period affected by corrections of income-computation errors of prior periods?

For many years accountants adhered to the current-operating concept of net income, believing that corrections of the net income of prior years and unusual, extraneous, and nonrecurring items of income and expense (such as gains and losses resulting from disposals of property, plant, and equipment) should be shown in a separate statement of retained earnings or in the retained earnings section of a statement of income and retained earnings. The procedure of showing all such items as adjustments to retained earnings was considered desirable because the current net income then showed the results of regular operations for the period, unaffected by unusual, extraordinary, or extraneous transactions or by corrections of net income of prior years. Thus the proponents of the current-operating concept of net income supported their position by the following arguments:

In order to measure the efficient utilization of a firm's resources in operating the business to earn a profit, net income should reflect only those transactions that are controllable by management and result from decisions made during the current period. In other words, current operating data provide useful information in the evaluation of management efficiency in operating the business.

Investors and prospective investors are more interested in the net income of a business than in any other one figure shown by the annual statements. And the net income in which they are most interested is that produced by the normal operating activities of the business during the year. Although the net income of one or more years is only one of numerous factors that should be considered in the formation of opinions about prospective earning power, the stated net income should reflect, as nearly as possible, what happened during the year as the result of normal operating transactions. Otherwise, it is difficult to determine the trend of a company's operations and to compare the results of operations of one company with those of other companies.

If the stated net income of one year is affected by a material correction of the net income of a prior year, there is a distortion. The error is compounded, because the current year's net income is overstated or understated to the extent that the net income of the past was understated or overstated. Indicated trends are therefore misleading. When an accountant renders an opinion with respect to the net income for a year, he indulges in an obvious contradiction if the amount of net income he shows in the statement includes a correction of the net income of some other year.

If the stated net income includes extraordinary and extraneous items not likely to recur, the reader of the statement is left to make his own decisions regarding the items that should be excluded to determine the results of normal operations. Although it is often difficult to draw a clear and definite line of demarcation between operating and extraordinary items, management and the trained accountant, familiar with the facts, are in a better position to do so than outsiders can possibly be.

There should be full disclosure of all material extraneous and extraordinary items and corrections of earnings of prior years; such disclosure should be made in a way that will avoid any possible distortion and any confusion in the mind of the reader of the statements regarding the results of the regular operations of the business during the year.

In contrast to the current-operating concept, the proponents of the all-inclusive concept of net income maintained that all items of revenue, expense, gain, or loss are necessary factors in determining net income. They believe that extraordinary and correction items should be included (properly described and segregated) in the determination of net income. They contended that mere size, unusualness, or timing does not convert what would otherwise be an item of revenue, expense, gain, or loss into something else. Thus the proponents of the all-inclusive concept of net income supported their position with the following arguments:

The total of the amounts shown as net income in the statements for a series of years should be the aggregate net income for those years. This will not be the case if corrections of net income of prior years are shown as adjustments to retained earnings rather than as part of the determination of net income. In other words, by providing financial data on the entire historical operations of the business over several years, useful information is provided with regard to determining operating efficiency and predicting future operating performance.

When an accountant charges retained earnings with a loss because he considers it extraordinary or extraneous, he implies that it is nonrecurring. But a study of business history indicates that, over a period of years, such losses do recur, and that the retained earnings charges tend to exceed the retained earnings credits, with the result that the reported net income for a series of years gives an exaggerated impression of a company's earning power.

The line of demarcation between operating items and extraordinary or extraneous items is not clear-cut and is often a matter of opinion. There are many borderline cases. This results in inconsistencies in making interperiod and interfirm comparisons, because the same company can classify an item as nonoperating in one period and as operating in the next period, and because different companies can classify the same item differently. For example, are large inventory losses due to obsolescence part of normal operations or are they unusual, extraordinary losses?

Permitting certain charges and credits to be excluded from the determination of net income creates an opportunity for manipulation or smoothing of annual net-income figures. That is, charges and credits to retained earnings may be made to take the place of income charges and credits properly applicable to the operations of past or future periods.

Many so-called extraordinary or extraneous charges or credits are really closely related to operations over several years. In other words, some so-called extraordinary items are really normal in that they are expected to recur over several years. For example, gains and losses on sale of equipment tend to recur over several years, and they can be viewed as related to operations in that they are corrections of prior years' income charges for depreciation. Similarly, a write-off or write-down of an asset is related to operations in that it relieves future years of amortization charges.

Net-income determination under the all-inclusive concept avoids the problem of subjective judgments by management and accountants concerning what items to include in net income, since all charges and credits are recognized.

By providing information on all the charges and credits to income for the period, the statement user can classify the data to arrive at one income figure suited for his particular needs.

It overcomes the problem of statement users' overlooking important financial data contained in a separate statement of retained earnings under the current-operating concept.

With the issuance of APB *Opinion No. 9* and *Opinion No. 20,* there exists a compromise between the two concepts. With *Opinion No. 9* stating that all profit and loss items, with the exception of prior-period adjustments, should be reflected in net income, the final net-income figure more nearly reflects the all-inclusive concept. The current-operating concept is reflected only to the extent that prior-period adjustments are excluded from the income statement. Similarly, *Opinion No. 20* (to be discussed shortly) is also a compromise between the two concepts, in that on the one hand the accounting treatment of accounting errors (treated as prior-period adjustments), a change in the reporting entity (retroactive adjustment), and certain amortizations (retroactive adjustments) reflect the current-operating concept. On the other hand, the treatment by *Opinion No. 20* of a change in an accounting principle (current-period adjustment shown as an extraordinary item) reflects the all-inclusive concept, while a change in an accounting estimate (prospective adjustment) reflects neither.

Accounting changes. *Opinion No. 20* states that an accounting change is a change in an accounting principle, an accounting estimate, or the reporting entity. An accounting change, as defined by *Opinion No. 20,* does not include a correction of an error in previously issued financial statements.

Prior to *Opinion No. 20,* changes in accounting (as well as accounting errors) were recorded and reported in diverse ways. For example, in order to report accounting changes (and errors) in comparative financial statements, one of three types of adjustments to the financial statements was necessary:

Current adjustment. Report the accounting change as an extraordinary item in the income section (or separate income statement), or as a prior-period adjustment in the retained earnings section (or separate statement of retained earnings), of the current period's statement of income and retained earnings.

Retroactive adjustment. Report the accounting change by restating all prior-period financial statements presented. Any cumulative effect would be reported by restating beginning retained earnings as a prior-period adjustment.

Prospective adjustment. Report the accounting change in the current and future periods' financial statements. There would be no reporting of cumulative effects from prior periods nor restated financial statements from prior periods, since the accounting change is spread over current and future periods.

Moreover, there is a basic conflict in the reporting of accounting changes. On the one hand, it can be contended that accounting principles and procedures should be applied consistently for all periods reported in comparative financial statements; hence, prior-period financial statements should be restated to reflect an accounting change, in order to provide consistent treatment. On the other hand, it can be argued that the restatement of prior-period financial statements for accounting changes results in confusing the statement user and lessening his confidence in the statements.

It should be obvious that the manner in which material accounting changes are recorded and reported affects the presentation of financial statements, especially the trends shown in comparative financial statements. *Opinion No. 20* attempts to provide some consistency in the recording and reporting of accounting changes.

CHANGE IN ACCOUNTING PRINCIPLE: This results from a firm's changing from a previously used generally accepted accounting principle, including procedures (methods) in applying the principle, to a different one for purposes of reporting. Thus there exists a choice between two or more GAAP or procedures. Note, however, that an accounting change does *not* include a change from an unacceptable (that is, unacceptable at the time adopted and therefore an accounting error) to an acceptable accounting principle, the adoption of a principle because of events occurring for the first time or previously immaterial in their effect, and adoption or modification of a principle because of events that are clearly different in substance from those previously occurring.

Concerning the disclosure of a change in an accounting principle, *Opinion No. 20* states that, with certain exceptions, the cumulative effect of the change should be included in the net income of the period by reporting it similarly to an extraordinary item (it is not an actual extraordinary item), between "Extraordinary items" and "Net income" on the income statement. Also, the cumulative effect of the change should be explained and justified by a footnote, reported earnings per share should be adjusted for the change, and income before extraordinary items and net income should be shown on the face of the income statement on a pro forma basis (that is, what the amounts would have been if the new principle or procedure had been used from the very beginning).

As an illustration of a change in an accounting principle, assume that a company has been depreciating equipment ($100,000 cost, 10-year estimated useful life, and no estimated salvage value) on a straight-line basis for two years and changes to double-declining depreciation in the third year (19+8). As shown below, the cumulative effect of the difference between straight-line (10 percent rate) and double-declining (20 percent rate) depreciation for the years 19+6 and 19+7 is $16,000, and would require the following entry in 19+8:

Accounting change—depreciation method........	16,000	
Accumulated depreciation		16,000

	Straight-Line Depreciation	Double-Declining Depreciation	Difference
19+6:			
$100,000 × .10 =	$10,000		
$100,000 × .20 =		$20,000	$10,000
19+7:			
$100,000 × .10 =	10,000		
($100,000 – $20,000) (.20) =		16,000	6,000
Cumulative effect			$16,000
19+8:			
($100,000 – $20,000 – $16,000) (.20) =		12,800	

Ignoring income tax effects (that is, any deferred tax effects), the accounting change in depreciation methods would be reported in the income statements as shown on the next page. The pro forma amounts are determined by adjusting the 19+7 income figures as if the double-declining depreciation method had been in use since 19+6; hence, there is no adjustment needed for 19+8. The pro forma calculations are as follows:

	19+8	19+7
Net income..	$200,000	$150,000
Add straight-line depreciation expenses for 19+7 (i.e., eliminate its effect on 19+7 income)	—	10,000
Deduct double-declining depreciation expense (i.e., include its effect in 19+7 income)	—	(16,000)
Pro forma net income...	$200,000	$144,000

The discussion and illustration of a change in depreciation method is an example of the normal treatment of a change in an accounting principle (that is, current-period adjustment). On the other hand, *Opinion No. 20* specifies certain exceptions to this normal treatment:

> There may be a change in the method of amortization where there is no cumulative effect. For example, a company may adopt a new method of amortization for its new assets, but continue using its old method of amortization for its existing assets. In such a situation, disclosure requires

PARTIAL COMPARATIVE INCOME STATEMENTS

	19+8	19+7
.		
.		
.		
Depreciation expense	$ 12,800	$ 10,000
.		
.		
.		
Income before accounting change	200,000	150,000
Accounting change:		
Cumulative effect on prior years (to December 31, 19+7) of changing from straight-line to double-declining depreciation (Note A)	16,000	—
Net income	$184,000	$150,000
Earnings per common share (100,000 shares outstanding):		
Income before accounting change	$ 2.00	$ 1.50
Accounting change	.16	—
Net income	$ 1.84	$ 1.50
Pro forma amounts assuming accounting change is applied retroactively:		
Net income	$200,000	$144,000
Earnings per common share	$ 2.00	$ 1.44

Note A: Depreciation of equipment has been computed by the double-declining method in 19+8. Depreciation of equipment in prior years, beginning in 19+6, was computed by the straight-line method. The new method of depreciation was adopted to recognize the declining productivity of the equipment in later life as compared to its early life. The effect of the change in 19+8 was to reduce income before accounting change by $2,800 (or three cents per share). The adjustment of $16,000 to apply retroactively the new method is included in income of 19+8. The pro forma amounts shown on the income statement have been adjusted for the effect of retroactive application on depreciation.

a description of the nature of the change, its effect on income before extraordinary items and net income, and its effect on per share amounts.

In rare situations, pro forma amounts are not determinable for individual prior periods. Disclosure requires that the cumulative effect be reported in the income statement of the period of change.

In some cases, the cumulative effect is not determinable. Disclosure will be limited to showing the effect of the change for the current period (including per share data) and an explanation of why the cumulative effect and pro forma data are omitted.

There are special changes where the advantages of retroactive adjustment outweigh the disadvantages. These include a change from LIFO to some other inventory costing method, a change in accounting for long-term construction-type contracts, and a change to or from the "full-cost" method of accounting in extractive industries.

When there is an initial public distribution, and a company wishes to change from one acceptable accounting principle to another in connection with the public offering of shares, disclosure requires retroactive adjustment for all prior-period financial statements. This exemption from the normal treatment of a change in accounting principle is available only once, at the time a company's financial statements are first used for obtaining additional equity capital from investors, effecting a business combination, or registering securities.

One of the main purposes of *Opinion No. 20* is to provide some consistency in the recording and reporting of accounting changes. However, with the large number of exceptions to the specified normal treatment of a change in an accounting principle, with no theoretical basis for such exceptions, the Opinion is weakened considerably.

CHANGE IN AN ACCOUNTING ESTIMATE: This results from a change in an estimate used in recording and reporting financial data, which is the result of subsequent events (therefore distinguishable from an accounting error), such as new or additional information, new developments, or better insight and improved judgment as experience is acquired. Note that a change in accounting principle that is inseparable from the effect of a change in an estimate (for example, a change from capitalizing to expensing research and development costs because of growing uncertainty of future benefits) is treated as a change in an accounting estimate.

Examples of a change in an accounting estimate include a change in estimate for bad debts, useful lives or salvage values of depreciable assets, warranty costs, inventory obsolescence, and deferred costs and revenues.

Because changes in accounting estimates are the result of new information or circumstances, they should be treated as prospective adjustments, a procedure that is in agreement with *Opinion No. 20.* Thus the effect of the change in an estimate is recognized during the period of change and any future periods affected. Note that there is no cumulative adjustment or restatement of prior-period financial statements.

An example of a change in an accounting estimate would be a change in the estimated useful life of a depreciable asset. In such a situation, the remaining book value of the asset (cost minus accumulated depreciation to date) would be depreciated over the new estimated remaining useful life of the asset. Another example would be a change in the estimated rate of bad debts, with the new rate merely used in the current period. Note that these are not examples of accounting errors, since the estimates were reasonable at the time they were made, and are now changed because of new circumstances.

CHANGE IN THE REPORTING ENTITY: Because of a change in what comprises the reporting entity itself, the result is financial statements that are, in effect, those of a different reporting entity. Examples include changing from individual to consolidated or combined financial statements, changes in the subsidiaries that make up the consolidated reporting entity, and changes in the companies included in combined financial statements.[10] Disclosure per *Opinion No. 20* requires retroactive adjustment by restating all prior-period financial statements presented.

Earnings per share. The general meaning of *earnings per share* (EPS) is the amount of net income (earnings) or net loss applicable to each share of common stock. Prior to the issuance of *Opinion No. 9,* EPS data were reported optionally as supplementary information in company's annual reports. *Opinion No. 9* recommended that EPS data be disclosed in the income statement. With the issuance of *Opinion No. 15,* it became mandatory to present earnings-per-share data on the face of the income statement; or more specifically, *Opinion No. 15* states that EPS data should be presented for income before extraordinary items and for net income and recommends presentation for extraordinary items.[11] Thus by virtue of *Opinion No. 15,* EPS data became part of the financial statements for which certified public accounting firms render their opinion as to the financial statements being in conformity with generally accepted accounting principles.

Because the market value of the common stock of a company tends to be influenced by EPS data, investors use EPS data as indicators of the present and future market value of a firm, of present and future company dividends, and of management's effectiveness in conducting operations. For purposes of presenting such EPS data to investors to aid in their investment decisions, accountants traditionally had based such data on historical information. However, this historical emphasis changed with *Opinion No. 15,* since it requires dual presentation (primary EPS and fully diluted EPS), both of which are pro forma in nature (that is, "as if" or "would have been if" . . . had occurred) and imply predictive qualities.

In the case of simple capital structures (just common stock with no dilutive common stock equivalents), EPS data are computed by taking income before extraordinary items (and any changes in accounting principles), extraordinary items and any changes in accounting principles), and net income and dividing each by the weighted average (that is, weighted by the number of months) number of shares of common stock outstanding during the year. To illustrate the computation of weighted average number of shares, assume that Kansas Company had 5,000 common shares outstanding at the beginning of the period, issued 15,000 additional shares on April 1, and issued 5,000 shares on July 1 as the result of a large (25 percent) stock dividend. The weighted average number of shares is equal to 21,250, as shown below:

5,000 shares × 12 months =	60,000	or	5,000 shares × 12/12 of a year = 5,000
15,000 shares × 9 months =	135,000		15,000 shares × 9/12 of a year = 11,250
5,000 shares × 12 months =	60,000		5,000 shares × 12/12 of a year = 5,000
	255,000		
Weighted average shares =	255,000 ÷ 12 months		
=	21,250		21,250

[10]See James A. Gentry, Jr., and Glenn L. Johnson, *Finney and Miller's Principles of Accounting: Advanced,* 6th ed. (Englewood Cliffs, N.J.: Prentice-Hall, Inc., 1971).

[11]Accounting Principles Board, "Earnings per Share," *Opinion No. 15* (New York: AICPA, May 1969), p. 220.

Note that, based on *Opinion No. 9,* an increase in shares as the result of a stock dividend or split should be treated as a change for the *entire* period (retroactive adjustment); hence, the 5,000 shares from the stock dividend are weighted for the full 12 months for Kansas Company.[12] Consequently, the EPS for Kansas Company is computed as follows:

Earnings per common share ($92,400/21,250)	$4.35

Also, EPS data are required on a pro forma basis when there is a change in an accounting principle, per *Opinion No. 20.* For example, refer to the illustration on page 108, where EPS data are presented on the income statement "as if" the accounting change had been applied in the past.

In complex capital structures, dual presentation of EPS data in the form of primary and fully diluted EPS is required per *Opinion No. 15* for both income before extraordinary items and net income. Primary EPS data are the earnings attributable to each share of common stock and dilutive (that is, reduces EPS) common-stock equivalents. Common-stock equivalents are securities that, because of the terms or circumstances under which they were issued, contain provisions that allow their owners to become common stockholders; hence, it is argued that they are equivalent in substance (but not in form) to common stock and should be included in the computation of primary EPS data. Note, however, that common-stock equivalents are included in the computation of primary EPS only if they have a dilutive effect of 3 percent or more.

Examples of common-stock equivalents include all common-stock options and warrants, all common-stock purchase contracts, convertible debt and preferred stock (provided that cash yield at time of issuance is less than two thirds of the bank prime rate at that time), and participating securities.

Fully diluted EPS data are intended to reflect maximum potential dilution by assuming that all contingent issues that would individually reduce EPS had taken place. In comparison to primary EPS, fully diluted EPS show the maximum dilution of earnings that non-common-stock equivalents could create. Note that fully diluted EPS, as well as primary EPS to a lesser extent, are pro forma in nature, since they are on an "as if" basis ("as if" the conversions took place, and "as if" the warrants and options were exercised).

Because the rules for computing primary and fully diluted EPS data are highly technical and complex, and because some of the rules are arbitrary and lack a theoretical basis, it is questionable whether such pro forma EPS data are understandable and therefore more useful to investors and other users of financial statements than are historically based EPS data. On the other hand, such EPS data may make the reader aware of the tentative nature and the importance of estimation in such figures, as well as the difficulty of compressing results of operations into single EPS figures.

---

[12] *Opinion No. 9,* p. 122.

5

Statement of Financial Position (Balance Sheet)

Introduction. The statement of financial position (position statement), traditionally called the balance sheet, provides financial information about a firm's financial position at the end of a fiscal period. It provides information about the accounting entity's financial status or condition at a given date. The balance sheet presents the cumulative financial condition of the business firm, as if a "snapshot" of financial position were taken at a specific date. Thus it is a model of a firm's financial position that is used in financial accounting to provide summary position reports at the end of periodic time intervals.

The accountant's monetary measurement of the financial position of a firm is based on the fundamental accounting equation that assets equal equities (liabilities and owners' equity). At a given point in time, the financial position of a firm can be represented by the firm's total resources (assets) and the claims against or interests in those resources (equities); hence, assets equal equities. Another way to view financial position at a point in time is that funds are provided by creditors (liabilities), owners (preferred and common stock), and profitable operations (retained earnings), and the forms these funds take are represented by assets; hence, sources (equities) equal uses (assets). Thus the balance sheet provides financial information with regard to a firm's economic resources, future commitments, liquidity position, ownership interests, and trends (comparative balance sheets) in financial position.

The basic elements that make up the position statement are defined as follows:

Assets are future economic benefits or service potentials, the rights to which are owned or controlled by an organization (or individual).

Liabilities are future economic obligations of an organization (or individual) to render assets or perform services, where the obligations have resulted from past or current transactions (or events).

Owners' equity is the financial interest of the owners in a firm, and is a residual interest equal to the excess of a firm's assets over its liabilities.

Illustration. An example of the statement of financial position is presented on the next page. Note that comparative balance sheets are shown (for example, December 31, 19+5 and 19+4), a procedure quite common in annual reports in order to provide information on trends in financial position.

Note that the balance sheet is essentially a *historical* report, since it is based on the financial accounting process of recording and reporting past and completed financial transactions of a firm. Thus the balance sheet does *not* show the realizable value of the firm at a specific date. Other than cash, short-term marketable securities, and net accounts receivable (that is, net of allowance for uncollectibles), acquisition cost is the normal valuation method used in reporting assets on the balance sheet—the historical-cost assumption. For example, the balance sheets for Kansas Company show merchandise inventory at FIFO cost, prepayments at unexpired cost, building and equipment at original cost less accumulated depreciation (net book value), land at original cost, and bond investment at cost. Similarly, assets and liabilities are not reported at liquidating values on the balance sheet—the going-concern assumption. For example, Kansas Company reports bonds payable of $107,500, which represents the present value of the future interest and principle payments, not the amount due for current maturity. Thus, because the valuation of assets are not all at actual, or even estimated, realizable values, and because estimates have so much effect on asset and liability accounts, the amount shown in the balance sheets as the owners' equity cannot be regarded as representing "net worth" in the sense of an amount that would be distributable to the owners upon immediate disposal of the assets and payment of the liabilities.

Besides the historical-cost and going-concern assumptions, the effect of the other basic accounting assumptions on the balance sheet should be kept in mind. For example, the position statement is limited to the financial position of a particular economic entity (here, Kansas Company) independent of its owners, managers, and employees and other entities—the specific-separate-entity assumption. Also, the balance sheet represents financial condition at the end of a specific fiscal period and therefore reflects accruals, deferrals, and the tentativeness of estimates—the fiscal-period assumption. Finally, the financial status of a company shown on the face of the balance sheet uses the dollar as the measuring unit, not physical or qualitative data, and the dollar is assumed to be a relatively stable measuring unit with regard to general purchasing power.

KANSAS COMPANY
Comparative Balance Sheets
December 31, 19+5 and 19+4

Assets	19+5		19+4	
Current assets:				
Cash		$ 18,000		$ 20,000
Marketable securities—at cost (market, $1,050)		1,000		—
Accounts receivable	$ 60,000		$ 30,000	
Less allowance for uncollectibles	8,000	52,000	10,000	20,000
Inventory—FIFO cost		110,000		30,000
Prepayments		14,900		19,000
Total current assets		$195,900		$ 89,000
Long-term investments:				
Investment in bonds—at cost		$ 20,000		$ 10,000
Property, plant, and equipment:				
Land		$ 26,000		—
Building	$400,000		$400,000	
Less accumulated depreciation	160,000	240,000	140,000	$260,000
Equipment	$300,000		$350,000	
Less accumulated depreciation	120,000	180,000	105,000	245,000
Total property, plant, and equipment		$446,000		$505,000
Total assets		$661,900		$604,000
Equities				
Current liabilities:				
Accounts payable		$ 35,400		$ 46,000
Notes payable		40,000		25,000
Taxes payable		61,600		50,000
Total current liabilities		$137,000		$121,000
Long-term liabilities:				
Bonds payable—7% interest, due December 31, 19xx	$100,000		$100,000	
Bond premium	7,500		8,000	
Total long-term liabilities		$107,500		$108,000
Stockholders' equity:				
Preferred stock		—		$150,000
Common stock—$10 par value; authorized, 100,000 shares; issued and outstanding, 25,000 shares		$250,000		50,000
Retained earnings		167,400		175,000
Total stockholders' equity		$417,400		$375,000
Total equities		$661,900		$604,000

Balance-sheet format. Balance sheets are generally presented in annual reports in one of two forms: account form or vertical form. The account form lists all the assets on the left-hand side and all the equities on the right-hand side:

Assets		Liabilities	
(details)	$661,900	(details)	$244,500
		Owners' equity	
		(details)	417,400
	$661,900		$661,900

The vertical form lists all the assets first and all equities below, as illustrated for Kansas Company. Another vertical form is a listing of assets followed by a subtraction of a listing of liabilities, followed by the resulting listing of owners' equity. Another variation of the vertical form is a listing of current assets followed by a listing of current liabilities to show net working capital; to this is added a listing of noncurrent assets and the deduction of a listing of noncurrent liabilities to show owners' equity. The latter two variations of the vertical form are illustrated below in condensed form:

Assets	
(details)	$661,900
Less: Liabilities	
(details)	244,500
Total net assets	$417,400
Owners' equity	
(details)	$417,400

Current assets	
(details)	$195,900
Less: Current liabilities	
(details)	137,000
Net working capital	$ 58,900
Noncurrent assets	
(details)	466,000
Net working capital and noncurrent assets	$524,900
Less: Long-term liabilities	107,500
Total net assets	$417,400
Owners' equity	
(details)	$417,400

Balance-sheet classifications. The classifications of assets and equities in the position statement are intended to provide the statement user with relevant summaries of financial data that facilitate the analysis and interpretation necessary for financial decision-making purposes. Although the classifications used in the statement of financial position depend upon the nature of the business and the nature of the items appearing in the position statement, basic patterns of disclosure have developed over the years from accounting practice, and the following classifications are typical.

Assets

CURRENT ASSETS: Cash and other assets that, according to reasonable expectations, will be converted into cash, or will be used, or will expire during the normal operating cycle or one year, whichever is longer. Examples of current assets include cash, short-term marketable securities, receivables from customers, other short-term receivables, inventories, supplies, and short-term prepayments. They are customarily listed on the balance sheet in the foregoing order based on liquidity.

LONG-TERM INVESTMENTS: Investments that do not qualify as a commitment of funds for secondary cash reserves, as do short-term marketable securities, since they are required on a long-term basis to collect funds, to accumulate funds for special purposes, to gain control of another company, to assist in establishing or maintaining good customer or supplier relationships, or for any other purpose that would make their disposal inexpedient. Examples of long-term investments include long-term receivables, bond sinking fund, advances to suppliers, investments in the common stock of another company, investments in bonds, cash surrender value of life insurance, land held for plant expansion, and retired equipment held for sale.

PROPERTY, PLANT, AND EQUIPMENT: Land, depreciable property, and natural resources (wasting assets) of a tangible and relatively long-term nature used in the operations of the business and not intended for sale. Examples are land in use (not for resale), buildings, machinery, equipment, furniture and fixtures, natural resources, and tools. They are customarily listed on the balance sheet with those having the longest use-life being listed first.

INTANGIBLE ASSETS: Long-term assets lacking physical substance that have future economic benefits because of the rights and privileges associated with their possession. Examples are patents, franchises, copyrights, goodwill, leaseholds, leasehold improvements, research and development costs, and organization costs. Leaseholds and leasehold improvements are alternatively classified in practice under property, plant, and equipment.

DEFERRED CHARGES (OTHER ASSETS): Long-term prepayments that represent charges to be included in the determination of net income of subsequent periods covering a time span in excess of one operating cycle or one year, whichever is longer. Examples are prepaid pension costs, deferred income tax charges, machinery rearrangement costs, and bond-issue costs.

Liabilities

CURRENT LIABILITIES: Economic obligations that, according to reasonable expectations, are to be satisfied from current assets or the creation of other current liabilities within the operating-cycle period or one year, whichever is longer. Examples are accounts payable, notes payable, salaries payable, interest payable, income tax payable, advances from customers, rent received in advance, and the current-maturity portion of long-term debt.

LONG-TERM LIABILITIES: Economic obligations the settlement of which extends beyond the normal operating cycle or one year, whichever is longer. Examples are notes payable, bonds payable, mortgages payable, and long-term advances.

DEFERRED CREDITS: Credits to be included in the determination of net income of subsequent periods covering a time span in excess of an operating cycle or one year, whichever is longer. Examples include advance payments from lessees under long-term leases and deferred income tax credits.

Stockholders' Equity

CAPITAL STOCK: Capital contributed (paid-in or invested) by stockholders of the corporation, reported at the par value, or stated value if no par, of the shares outstanding. Examples are preferred stock and common stock.

CAPITAL IN EXCESS OF PAR VALUE (OR STATED VALUE): All capital contributed by stockholders in excess of par value, or stated value if no par, of outstanding shares. Examples are capital in excess of par value—preferred stock; capital in excess of par value—common stock; capital in excess of par value—treasury stock; and capital in excess of par value—donated capital.

RETAINED EARNINGS: That portion of stockholders' equity attributable to profitable operations. It includes aggregate net income minus any net losses, dividends, and capitalization of retained earnings, and plus or minus any prior-period adjustments.

APPROPRIATED RETAINED EARNINGS: The segregation of total retained earnings as a means to disclose that part of retained earnings is restricted and not available for future dividend charges. Note, however, that such appropriations of retained earnings do *not* reduce total retained earnings, but rather segregate retained earnings into two parts: appropriated retained earnings (restricted) and unappropriated retained earnings (unrestricted). Appropriations of retained earnings arise from statutory requirements (such as restrictions equal to the cost of treasury stock), from contractual agreements (restrictions specified by bond indentures), and from formal action of the board of directors in connection with financial planning (appropriations for plant expansion) and/or future contingencies (appropriation for a pending law suit).

UNREALIZED CAPITAL INCREMENT PER APPRAISAL: The increase in capital that results from a write-up of property, plant, and equipment to fair market value. Such an increase is neither contributed capital from stockholders nor retained earnings from profitable operations; therefore, a special capital account (unrealized capital increment per appraisal) is used and reported after retained earnings in the balance sheet. Such upward revaluations are not in accordance with generally accepted accounting principles and therefore occur in only rare circumstances.[1]

Contingencies. A contingency is a possible future economic event. If the possible future event is the result of transactions that have not yet occurred, then accountants do not report the dollar amounts of such events in the balance sheet. If the possible

---

[1] Accounting Principles Board, "Status of Accounting Research Bulletins," *Opinion No. 6* (New York: AICPA, October 1965), p. 42.

future event is the result of some past or current transaction, then contingent assets and liabilities exist, and such contingencies are normally reported in the balance sheet as footnotes, as parenthetical remarks, as contra accounts, or as a special classification between liabilities and stockholders' equity.

A contingent liability is an obligation that, because of some past or current transaction, may arise as the result of some future economic event; hence, the obligation does not actually exist at the balance-sheet date, but may exist in the future. Thus contingent liabilities differ from estimated liabilities (such as product warranties) in that the latter are obligations that exist at the balance-sheet date even though the amount, due date, or both must be estimated. Examples of contingent liabilities include notes receivable discounted, accounts receivable assigned, actual or pending lawsuits against a company, actual or pending additional tax assessments against a company, guarantees of liabilities of other companies, and pending renegotiation of refunds on government contracts.

A contingent asset is a future economic benefit that, because of some past or current transaction, may arise as the result of some future economic event; hence, the right to that future benefit does not exist at the balance-sheet date. Examples of contingent assets include a tax loss carry-forward from previous years, tax refund claims, contingent donations, and lawsuit claims for damages.

The basic problem in the reporting of contingencies is one of uncertainty about whether the future economic event will materialize and whether it will have a material effect on the company. If the contingencies are expected to have a material effect on the company should they materialize, then such contingencies should be included in footnotes to the position statement.

Disclosure after balance-sheet date. Economic events that may have a material effect on the financial statements sometimes occur after the position-statement date but before the statement is issued. Such events should be disclosed in notes to the financial statements. Examples include litigation, mergers, and contracts canceled or negotiated.

Current assets and liabilities. The balance-sheet classification of assets and liabilities into current and noncurrent is based on providing useful financial information with regard to a firm's short-run solvency. Creditors and other statement users are interested in a firm's ability to meet current operating needs, including day-to-day cash needs and payments of obligations as they become due. Cash and near-cash assets (current assets), as well as the financing of current assets via current liabilities, provide some indication of the "circulating capital" used by a firm to maintain day-to-day operations. For example, creditors will often use the balance sheet to calculate the firm's working capital (current assets minus current liabilities) and current ratio (current assets divided by current liabilities) as indicators of liquidity and debt-paying ability. Thus the basis for inclusion in the current-asset and current-liability classifications is important.

The concept of a normal operating cycle is used by accountants to determine the current classifications. The normal operating cycle is the average interval of time it takes to convert cash into product, product into receivables, and receivables back into cash. In other words, business operations consist of a round of conversions: cash to acquire or produce salable inventory, to receivables from sales, and back to cash from collections. For example, if a firm had an inventory turnover (cost of goods sold divided by average inventory) of three (or 12/3 = 4 months), and an accounts receivable turnover (credit sales divided by average receivables) of six (or 12/6 = 2 months), the normal operating cycle would be every six (4 + 2) months.

If the normal operating cycle of a business is less than one year (since there could be several operating cycles within the year), or if the business has no clearly defined operating cycle, then the accounting rule for segregating current assets and current liabilities is one year. If the normal operating cycle is longer than one year (as in tobacco, distillery, and lumber businesses), then the normal operating cycle governs. This is why current assets and current liabilities were previously defined in terms of a normal operating cycle or one year, whichever is longer. Thus short-term marketable securities, accounts receivable, inventory, supplies, and short-term prepayments are classified as current assets, since they will normally be turned over within the normal operating cycle or one year. Similarly, short-term payables, revenue received in advance, and the current maturity of long-term debt are classified as current liabilities, since they will normally be settled from current assets within the normal operating cycle or one year.

There are some theoretical problems in distinguishing current from noncurrent items based on a time interval. For example, should not the current portion of noncurrent assets (for example, next year's depreciation on equipment) be included in the current-asset classification, just as the current portion of long-term debt is included in the current-liability classification? Does not the current portion of equipment enter into current operations in order to generate revenue for the current period? Although the answers to these two questions is yes in theory, the current portion of noncurrent assets does not directly affect cash, near-cash items, or short-term obligations and is therefore excluded from the current-asset classification in current accounting practice. On the other hand, the current portion of long-term debt does not finance short-term operations of the firm, yet it is still included in the current-liability classification in current accounting practice, because it will require cash or cash becoming available for settlement during the operating cycle or one year.

As another example, prepaid insurance is often paid in advance for two to three years. Should the total prepayment be classified as a current asset? In theory, only the current portion (one-half or one-third of cost) should be shown as a current asset, yet in actual accounting practice the total prepayment is generally classified as a current asset and amortized over the two or three years. The point of the foregoing examples is that in distinguishing between current and noncurrent items in actual accounting practice, practical considerations sometimes overrule strict theoretical considerations.

It is also important to note that management's intent plays an important part in distinguishing between current and noncurrent items in current accounting practice, and this is why current assets and liabilities were previously defined to include the words "according to reasonable expectations." For example, if it is the definite intent of management to invest short-term assets in particular long-term uses (for instance, cash and short-term marketable securities to be used subsequently to acquire equipment or pay off long-term debt), then such assets should *not* be classified as current assets; however, there should be a note to the balance sheet explaining why they are classified as noncurrent. Similarly, if it is the definite intent of management that short-term liabilities are to be settled subsequently from particular noncurrent fund accumulations, issuance of common stock, or flotation of long-term debt, then such short-term liabilities should be classified as noncurrent liabilities, with a note to the balance sheet explaining the circumstances.

With regard to management's intent, the point to be made is that current assets are not only liquid assets (in other words, can be converted quickly, easily, and with very little loss into cash), but also free from long-term commitments and thus available for current operations. Because current assets turn over during the operating cycle or one year, management has the opportunity to reinvest them more frequently in current operations than if they were committed for long-term uses. Similarly, current liabilities are the result of short-term financing of current operations and therefore are settled from current assets. Because current liabilities turn over during the operating cycle or one year, management has the opportunity to refinance current operations more frequently than if they were long-term obligations. Although, in total, current assets and liabilities are in a sense long term, because they are continually being turned over, they are short run in the sense that management has the opportunity to recommit them to current operations more frequently than if they were truly long term in nature.

On the other hand, the reliance on management's intent creates certain problems in the current and noncurrent classification scheme. The reason for this is that the accountant's determination of management's intent is somewhat nebulous and can change. For example, short-term marketable securities are classified as current assets if they are highly liquid and if it is management's intent to convert them into cash for use in current operations. However, from a practical point of view, the accountant will often classify short-term marketable securities as current assets even if it is expected that they will not be needed for current operations, provided that they are capable of being converted into cash.

Disclosure of current assets and liabilities. Because there are several generally acceptable valuation methods used in the monetary measurement of current assets, and for purposes of full disclosure, the current-asset classification in the balance sheet should include parenthetical remarks or footnotes indicating the valuation methods used. For example, short-term marketable securities can be reported at cost, at lower of cost or market, or at market. Parenthetical remarks or footnotes should disclose which valuation method is used and preferably indicate the dollar amount of market if cost is used, and vice versa. Similarly, inventories can be reported at different cost bases (FIFO, LIFO, or average cost), at the lower of cost or market, or at estimated cost (such as the retail inventory method), and the balance sheet should disclose which valuation method is employed. An example of such reporting is illustrated below:

Current assets:	
Cash	$10,000
Short-term marketable securities—at cost (market, $15,200)................	15,000
Inventories—at lower of cost or market (FIFO cost, $50,000)...............	45,000

The valuation methods used for the other current assets are assumed to be known (cash and receivables) or not material enough (short-term prepayments) to require disclosure of the valuation method: cash at nominal (face) amount, short-term receivables at net realizable value (amount owed less estimated uncollectibles), and short-term prepayments at unamortized (unexpired) cost.

Balance-sheet disclosure based on GAAP requires the separate reporting of assets and liabilities and does not normally allow the offsetting of assets and liabilities, because it can result in misleading information. Management's intention of using existing cash to pay off a specific note payable does *not* mean that this intention is irrevocable and that the cash should be offset against the note. Such intention may not materialize, and such offsetting overstates the current ratio. For example, if a firm had total current assets of $30,000 and total current liabilities of $10,000, the current ratio would be 3 to 1. However, if cash of $2,000 were reported as a direct deduction of a short-term note payable of $5,000 (that is, the note reported net at $3,000), then this would misleadingly increase the current ratio to 3:5 ($28,000/$8,000). Offsetting is permissible only when there is a legal right of offset (for example, a $1,000 overdraft in one account and a $10,000 cash balance in another account of the *same* bank), or when a company acquires acceptable securities that are, in effect, an advance payment of taxes due in the relatively near future.[2]

Monetary and nonmonetary classification. The basic reason for reporting classified financial information is to provide a grouping of similar items that aids the statement user in understanding and using such information in his financial decision making. With this in mind, it can be argued that the current and noncurrent classification in the balance sheet is too heterogeneous in nature and should be further broken down into monetary and nonmonetary items. For example, the current-asset classification mixes such fixed-dollar claims as cash and accounts receivable with such nonfixed-dollar claims as inventory and short-term prepayments.

Monetary assets are future economic benefits in the form of cash (domestic currency, such as dollars, not foreign currency) and fixed-money claims (number of monetary units in the domestic currency fixed by contract, law, or government) *owned.*[3] Thus, current monetary assets are cash and fixed-money claims owned in which the fixed number of dollars will be available for use during the current operating cycle or one year, whichever is longer. Examples of normal monetary assets include cash, short-term government securities, and accounts receivable. It follows that noncurrent monetary assets include long-term advances of money and long-term investments in bonds.

---

[2]Accounting Principles Board, "Omnibus Opinion—1966," *Opinion No. 10* (New York: AICPA, December 1966), p. 147.

[3]See Glenn L. Johnson, "The Monetary and Nonmonetary Distinction," *Accounting Review* (October 1965), pp. 821–23.

Monetary liabilities are future economic obligations in the form of fixed-money claims *owed.* Thus, current monetary liabilities are fixed-money claims owed that are satisfied by payment within the normal operating cycle or one year, whichever is longer. Examples of current monetary liabilities include the short-term payables (accounts payable, notes payable, salaries payable, and taxes payable) that make up most of the conventional current liability classification. Consequently, noncurrent monetary liabilities include long-term notes payable, bonds payable, and mortgages payable.

Nonmonetary assets are future economic benefits in the form of goods and services to be generated. The future economic benefits of nonmonetary assets result from selling (inventory) or using (plant and equipment) such assets. Thus, current nonmonetary assets are future-service potentials that generate real goods and services only during the current operating cycle or one year, whichever is longer. Examples of current nonmonetary assets include inventory, short-term prepayments, and short-term investments in common stock. Consequently, noncurrent nonmonetary assets include land, buildings, equipment, intangibles, and long-term prepayments.

Nonmonetary liabilities are future economic obligations satisfied by the rendering of real goods and services. Unlike monetary liabilities, nonmonetary liabilities are not satisfied by paying fixed amounts of money by specific due dates. Thus, current nonmonetary liabilities are future economic obligations satisfied by rendering goods and services during the normal operating cycle or one year, whichever is longer. Examples of current nonmonetary liabilities include short-term revenue received in advance and short-term estimated produce warranties. Consequently, noncurrent nonmonetary liabilities include long-term revenue received in advance and long-term estimated product warranties.

Since owners' equity does not represent fixed-money claims owned or owed, the items classified under owners' equity are nonmonetary in nature.

Why make the distinction between monetary and nonmonetary items on the balance sheet? In the first place, monetary items have the common characteristic of being fixed-dollar claims and therefore are reported at their fixed-dollar amounts (short term) or at the discounted present value of their fixed-dollar amounts (long term). In contrast, nonmonetary items, in general, are based on the historical-cost assumption and reported at original cost or unexpired (unamortized) cost. Thus, the reader of the balance sheet should be aware of those assets and equities that are more easily measured in terms of money (monetary items) and those that are affected by the historical-cost assumption. By making the distinction between monetary and nonmonetary items on the balance sheet, it can be argued that the statement user is aided in understanding and therefore analyzing the balance sheet for financial decision-making purposes.

Second, although the current-asset classification provides financial information on the liquidity of a firm, added information on liquidity can be provided by distinguishing between current monetary and nonmonetary assets. Current monetary assets are more liquid than current nonmonetary assets because they consist of cash and near-cash assets that are legal claims to a fixed number of dollars.

Finally, the monetary and nonmonetary classification in the balance sheet aids the statement user in determining the financial effect of future inflation (deflation) on a company. If a company has monetary liabilities that exceed monetary assets, then, other things being equal, the company will benefit financially from inflation. That is, during inflation, a company loses general purchasing power by holding monetary assets (since fixed-dollar amounts acquire fewer future goods and services in general during inflation) and gain general-purchasing power by holding monetary liabilities (since fixed-dollar obligations are paid off in "cheaper" dollars during inflation).[4] Thus, by comparing the monetary assets and liabilities (monetary assets divided by monetary liabilities) presented in the balance sheet, the statement user obtains some indication about how future inflation will affect the company financially.

An example of a balance sheet that includes the monetary and nonmonetary classification is presented on page 125 for Kansas Company. Note that the company improved its liquidity position, as indicated by the increase in the current monetary ratio (current monetary assets divided by current monetary liabilities) from .33 ($40,000/$121,000) in 19+4 to .56 ($76,000/$127,000) in 19+5, as well as by the increase in the current ratio (current assets divided by current liabilities) from .74 ($89,000/$121,000) to 1.43 ($195,900/$137,000). Note also that the company should not, other things being equal, be adversely affected by inflation, since its monetary liabilities exceed its monetary assets; however, as indicated by the monetary ratio (monetary assets divided by monetary liabilities), the proportion of monetary assets to monetary liabilities did increase from .22 ($50,000/$229,000) in 19+4 to .39 ($91,000/$234,500) in 19+5.

Although conventional balance sheets usually do not present monetary and nonmonetary classifications, the distinction between monetary and nonmonetary items is an important concept in accounting that should be understood. Moreover, it can be argued that the balance sheet would provide more useful information if the monetary and nonmonetary classification were included in it. Finally, with APB *Statement No. 3* recommending that supplementary general-price-level financial statements be presented, including the reporting of a general-price-level gain or loss based on monetary items, the monetary and nonmonetary distinction is becoming more important.

Contra and adjunct accounts. Rather than show some items at one amount on the balance sheet, accountants report two amounts in order to provide additional information that is thought to be useful to statement users. For example, accounts receivable are reported on the balance sheet at the gross amount due from customers, the estimated amount of uncollectibles is reported as a separate deduction (contra) from the gross amount, and the difference is reported at the estimated amount to be collected (net realizable value). In this manner, the statement user is provided not only with the expected realizable amount, but also with information regarding

---

[4]See Chapter 26 for a complete discussion of the effect of inflation on the financial statements.

a firm's expected bad-debt experience. Similarly, plant, equipment, and wasting assets (natural resources) are reported on the balance sheet at original cost, estimated accumulated depreciation or depletion is reported as a separate deduction (contra), and the difference is reported at net book value. Thus additional information is provided about original cost, depreciation or depletion policy, and the relative age of the assets. In contrast, only the net book value (cost less accumulated amortization) of intangible assets is normally reported, but where material, the accumulated amortization should be at least reported parenthetically. In fact, there seems to be no objection to also reporting accumulated depreciation and allowance for uncollectibles parenthetically, rather than as separate contra amounts, since the same information is provided.

Since bonds payable are often issued at a discount or premium, the latter should be reported along with the face value of the bonds in the balance sheet, in order to show present value to maturity. Bond discount would be reported as a separate deduction (contra) from, and bond premium would be reported as a separate addition (adjunct) to, the face value of the bonds. It is acceptable to report the bond discount or premium, along with the face value, parenthetically and show the present value of the bonds as a line item on the balance sheet. Bond discount or bond premium should *not* be reported as a deferred charge or a deferred credit, respectively.[5] It is sometimes contended that bond discount is a deferred charge (asset) because it represents prepaid interest; however, it is really unpaid interest, in the sense that the issuing company did not receive that amount (discount), because the nominal rate was lower than the market rate of interest.

Obsolete terminology. In reading position statements, one should be aware of terminology that infrequently appears, but is thought to be obsolete in current accounting usage. For example, the term *reserve* is sometimes used with regard to contra asset accounts (reserve for depreciation or reserve for bad debts) and estimated liabilities (reserve for product guarantees) that appear in balance sheets. However, since the term *reserve* tends to connote "something held for a specific purpose, such as for emergencies," which is not the accounting meaning intended, the term should not be used in that context. On the other hand, the AICPA does recommend the use of the term *reserve* for appropriations of retained earnings (reserve for plant expansion). However, even in this case, the term *reserve* is still misleading and it is preferable not to use it (footnote the appropriation, or use the title "appropriation for plant expansion").

The term *surplus* is sometimes used with regard to retained earnings (earned surplus), contributed capital in excess of par or stated value (paid-in surplus), and unrealized capital increment per appraisal (appraisal surplus). Since the term *surplus* misleadingly connotes an excess, or "that which remains when use or need is satisfied," it should not be used to describe capital accounts in the balance sheet.

Although not considered to be obsolete terminology, the term *fixed assets* is

---

[5] Accounting Principles Board, "Interest on Receivables and Payables," *Opinion No. 21* (New York: AICPA, August 1971), pp. 417–28.

KANSAS COMPANY
Comparative Balance Sheets
December 31, 19+5 and 19+4

	19+5		19+4	
Assets				
Current assets:				
Monetary.				
Cash		$ 18,000		$ 20,000
Marketable securities—at cost (market, $1,050)		1,000		—
Accounts receivable	$ 60,000		$ 30,000	
Less allowance for uncollectibles	8,000	52,000	10,000	20,000
Total current monetary assets		$ 71,000		$ 40,000
Nonmonetary:				
Inventory—FIFO cost		$110,000		$ 30,000
Prepayments		14,900		19,000
Total current nonmonetary assets		$124,900		$ 49,000
Total current assets		$195,900		$ 89,000
Long-term investments:				
Monetary:				
Investment in bonds—at cost		$ 20,000		$ 10,000
Property, plant, and equipment:				
Nonmonetary:				
Land		$ 26,000		—
Buildings	$400,000		$400,000	
Less accumulated depreciation	160,000	240,000	140,000	$260,000
Equipment	$300,000		$350,000	
Less accumulated depreciation	120,000	180,000	105,000	245,000
Total property, plant, and equipment		$446,000		$505,000
Total assets		$661,900		$604,000
Equities				
Current liabilities:				
Monetary:				
Accounts payable		$ 25,400		$ 46,000
Notes payable		40,000		25,000
Taxes payable		61,600		50,000
Total current monetary liabilities		$127,000		$121,000
Nonmonetary:				
Revenue received in advance		$ 10,000		—
Total current liabilities		$137,000		$121,000
Long-term liabilities:				
Monetary:				
Bonds payable—7% interest, due December 31, 19xx	$100,000		$100,000	
Bond premium	7,500		8,000	
Total long-term liabilities		$107,500		$108,000
Stockholders' equity:				
Nonmonetary:				
Preferred stock		—		$150,000
Common stock—$10 par value; authorized, 100,000 shares; issued and outstanding, 25,000 shares		$250,000		50,000
Retained earnings		167,400		175,000
Total stockholders' equity		$417,400		$375,000
Total equities		$661,900		$604,000

often used in balance sheets to convey the asset classification for long-lived assets used in operations and not intended for resale. However, the term is somewhat misleading in that the assets are not really "fixed"; hence, it is probably preferable to use the heading "property, plant, and equipment" or "long-lived assets" in the asset classification in the balance sheet.

Deferred charges. Deferred charges were previously defined as long-term prepayments that represent charges to be included in the determination of net income of subsequent periods covering a time span in excess of the normal operating cycle or one year, whichever is longer. Deferred charges are generally shown in the asset section of the balance sheet as the last asset classification or as part of the other-assets classification.

A basic problem with the deferred-charges classification in the balance sheet is that it is questionable whether such classification provides useful information to statement users. The meaning of deferrals is confusing, and specific deferrals cannot be adequately explained by a line item on the balance sheet. Moreover, the deferred-charges classification contains heterogeneous items, which are not consistently reported in the same way by different companies.

Sometimes such intangible assets as organization costs and research and development costs are included in the deferred-charges classification. Such intangibles should preferably be reported under the intangible-assets classification, rather than under the nebulous deferred-charges classification. Similarly, long-term prepayments that are clearly assets, such as a five-year insurance prepayment, probably would be better disclosed as part of the long-term investments classification, or even as part of an other-assets classification.

In addition to the problem of providing useful information, there is a theoretical problem about how to report those deferred charges that are not really assets. That is, some deferred charges are nothing more than delayed (deferred) debits (charges), arising from the double-entry bookkeeping system, that are unallocated; hence, they are reported as deferred charges and amortized over future periods in order not to affect unduly one period's net income. They are not assets because there is no future-service potential, and in effect, they result in income smoothing. Therefore, they do not logically fit into the basic accounting equation of assets equal equities, nor should they be condoned because of their smoothing effect. Examples include deferred pension costs and deferred income tax charges (that is, arising from interperiod income tax allocation).

Because of the practical problem of providing useful financial information and the theoretical problem that some deferred charges are not really assets, the recording and reporting of deferred charges should be avoided where possible. On the other hand, with the Accounting Principles Board sanctioning the use of deferred pension costs (*Opinion No. 8*) and deferred income tax charges (*Opinion No. 11*), such deferrals will continue to be reported in the balance sheet.

Deferred credits. Deferred credits were previously defined as credits to be included in the determination of net income of subsequent periods covering a time span in excess of an operating cycle or one year, whichever is longer. The disclosure of deferred credits in the balance sheet varies, in that they are reported as a separate classification between liabilities and stockholders' equity, as part of current liabilities, or as part of noncurrent liabilities.

As with the deferred-charges classification, it is questionable whether the deferred-credits classification provides useful information to statement users. The term deferral is confusing and nebulous, specific deferred credits cannot be adequately explained as a line item on the balance sheet, and the reporting of deferred credits varies considerably. Consequently, those so-called deferred credits that can be more meaningfully reported elsewhere should not be reported under the deferred-credits classification. For example, revenue received in advance is a future obligation to provide goods or services; hence, it should be reported as a liability (a current liability if short term, a long-term liability otherwise), not as a deferred credit. Other examples that are reported as deferred credits, but should not be, include bond premium (an addition to the face value of bonds), minority interests arising from consolidated balance sheets (part of stockholders' equity), leasehold advances (liability), refundable deposits (liability), and advances on royalties (liability).

There are also certain deferred credits that are reported on the equity side of the balance sheet, but they are not liabilities (no future obligation) nor stockholders' equities (no owners' claims). They are delayed credits arising from the double-entry bookkeeping system; hence, they are accounted for by deferring them and amortizing them over several periods. However, since such credits do not logically fit into the asset, liability, and owners' equity structure, and since they, in effect, result in income smoothing, the recording and reporting of such deferred credits lacks a theoretical basis. Examples of such deferred credits are deferred income tax credits, deferred investment credits, and pension costs in excess of payments (a liability per *Opinion No. 8,* but there is no legal obligation). On the other hand, since such deferred credits are sanctioned by the Accounting Principles Board, such deferrals will continue to be reported in the balance sheet.

6

Valuation

Introduction. Valuation in accounting is the quantification of, and the changes in, assets and liabilities expressed in terms of the money-measuring unit. Since owners' equity in accounting is the monetary expression of the residual of assets minus liabilities, the valuation of assets and liabilities determines the monetary amounts assigned to owners' equity; hence, there is no independent monetary quantification of owners' equity.

Valuation in accounting should not be confused with *value;* the terms are not synonymous. Whereas valuation is the assigning of dollar amounts to assets and liabilities, value is what those assets and liabilities are worth to a particular person at a particular point in time.[1] Value depends on the personal preferences or sub-

[1]The meaning of *value* in accounting is confusing because of the frequent use of the term *current-value accounting,* to mean the use of current exchange prices as opposed to historical exchange prices. Because there is more than one current exchange price that could be used in accounting, the distinction is made in this chapter between value and valuation to avoid this confusion.

jective utility (that is, a person's utility function) of the person doing the valuing. Since persons control and use resources for their own consumption, what those resources are worth depends on the person's own preferences. In contrast, business firms control and use resources for the purpose of selling goods and providing services, not for their own consumption, and therefore engage in market exchanges to acquire inputs for production and to sell their output. As a result, accountants use exchange prices (the ratio of money to goods exchanged or to be exchanged), not values based on subjective utility, in the valuation process of accounting for business firms.

On the other hand, there is still the question of which exchange price to use in the accountant's valuation process. That is, business firms engage in economic activities in two different markets, a situation that results in two basically different exchange prices. One is exit (output) exchange prices, representing the assets to be received by the firm from the sale of its output (goods and services)—selling prices. The other is entry (input) exchange prices, representing the assets to be sacrificed to obtain other assets (inputs) to be used in operations—purchase prices. Which exchange prices, exit or entry, should be used by accountants in the valuation process?

Not only do exchange prices differ by the market in which they are found, they also differ as to time (the temporal location of prices). Exchange prices can be past, present, or future prices. Consequently, exchange prices can be classified as past, present, or future exit prices and past, present, or future entry prices, as summarized below:

Type of Market	Past Exchange Prices	Present Exchange Prices	Future Exchange Prices
Exit (selling) exchange prices	Historical selling prices	Current selling prices	Future selling prices
Entry (purchase) exchange prices	Historical purchase prices	Current purchase prices	Future purchase prices

Which exchange price (valuation method) is used in the valuation of assets and liabilities will obviously affect balance-sheet presentations. But which valuation method is used also affects the determination of net income. This should be obvious when it is remembered that, ignoring capital changes and dividends, the difference between net assets (assets minus liabilities) at the beginning and the end of the fiscal period equals net income. Asset and liability valuation affects expenses, gains, and losses, and therefore net income. This association between asset and liability valuation and income determination is often referred to in accounting as articulation between the balance sheet and the income statement.

Because differences in asset and liability valuation result in differences in income determination, different valuation methods can be associated with different income figures. Based on the matrix of exchange prices above, we could have six different income figures that result from six different exchange prices. However, this can be reduced to four income figures by combining future selling and purchase prices to derive one income figure based on future exchange prices, and by eliminating historical selling prices, which are not used by accountants in their valuation process and which are irrelevant because they are out of date. Using the income terminology of Edwards and Bell, we can associate four resulting income figures from four valuation methods, as illustrated below:[2]

Type of Market	Valuation Method	Resulting Income Figure
Exit and entry	Future selling and purchase prices	Subjective or economic income
Exit	Current selling prices	Realizable income
Entry	Current purchase prices	Business income
Entry	Historical purchase prices	Realized income

Future exchange prices. Financial-statement preparation based on future exchange prices necessitates predicting a company's future cash receipts (from expected future sales and the rendering of expected future services) and future cash disbursements (expected future acquisitions of factors of production needed to generate cash receipts). Expected future cash receipts and disbursements are based on estimates of future selling prices and acquisition prices, as well as estimates of future quantities.

In order to prepare financial statements based on future cash flows, it is necessary to convert the future cash flows into equivalent dollars today by discounting them to obtain present amount (value). The use of expected cash flows in the valuation process means that there is a time lag (or waiting period) before the actual cash flows occur; hence, future dollars are converted into equivalent present-day dollars by computing the discounted amount (present value) of the future dollars. The concepts of discounting and compounding are reviewed in the appendix to this chapter.

Note, however, that the conventional use of the term *present value* in the context above means "discounted amount" and should not be confused with the term *value.* To avoid this confusion, hereafter in this chapter we will refer to discounted amount, instead of present value, and call such valuation discounted cash-flow valuation, instead of present-value valuation.

Under discounted cash-flow valuation, assets would be reported on the balance sheet at the discounted amount of the expected future cash receipts. Liabilities would be reported at the discounted amount of the expected future cash disbursements. Owners' equity would be reported at the discounted amount of the expected future *net* cash receipts, which is equal to the difference between the discounted amounts of the assets and liabilities.

Net income under discounted cash-flow valuation is equal to the discounted amount of owners' equity at the beginning of the period, multiplied by the interest rate used in discounting the future cash flows, assuming that the predictions of the estimated future cash flows are correct. This is why such income is called subjec-

[2]Edgar O. Edwards and Philip W. Bell, *The Theory and Measurement of Business Income* (Berkeley and Los Angeles: University of California Press, 1961).

tive income, since it is based on the subjective valuation of the firm's net assets at the beginning period, multiplied by the discount rate.[3] It is also called economic income (in the Hicksian sense), because it is the amount that could be paid out to the owners without contracting the business.[4] In other words, by withdrawing cash equal to the net income, the business is as "well off" at the end of the period as it was at the beginning, since the discounted amount of owners' equity remains the same (assuming owners' equity is adjusted for any capital changes).

In order to clarify discounted cash-flow valuation, we turn next to an illustration of such valuation before discussing its advantages and disadvantages.

ILLUSTRATION: Assume that Mr. Staubus wants to start a business that will earn him a 10 percent return on his investment. He finds a business that has assets and liabilities with a five-year life. He estimates the firm's future cash flows to be as follows:

Year	Future Cash Receipts at End of Each Year	−	Future Cash Disbursements at End of Each Year	=	Future Net Cash Inflows at End of Each Year
1	$50,000		$40,000		$10,000
2	50,000		40,000		10,000
3	50,000		40,000		10,000
4	50,000		40,000		10,000
5	50,000		40,000		10,000

By taking the discounted amount of the future receipts, disbursements, and net cash inflows, Mr. Staubus' discounted cash-flow valuation of the assets and liabilities, as well as the resulting owner's equity, is $189,539.35, $151,631.48, and $37,907.87, respectively:[5]

Discounted future cash receipts:

$$\mathbf{\$189{,}539.35 = Rp_{\overline{n}|i} = \$50{,}000\, p_{\overline{5}|.10} = (\$50{,}000)\,(3.790787)}$$

where R = Constant periodic rent (payment or receipt)

$p_{\overline{n}|i}$ = Discounted amount (present value) of an ordinary annuity of $1 for n periods at i rate of interest, obtained from tables

Discounted future cash disbursements:

$$\mathbf{\$151{,}631.48 = \$40{,}000\, p_{\overline{5}|.10} = (\$40{,}000)\,(3.790787)}$$

Discounted future net cash inflows:

$$\mathbf{\$37{,}907.87 = \$10{,}000\, p_{\overline{5}|.10} = (\$10{,}000)\,(3.790787)}$$

In other words, Mr. Staubus pays $37,907.87 for the business in order to earn an expected 10 percent return on his investment, by acquiring assets with a present

[3]Edwards and Bell, *Theory and Measurement,* pp. 38–44.

[4]J. R. Hicks, *Value and Capital* (Oxford: Clarendon Press, 1946), p. 172.

[5]Present-value tables, as well as compound tables, are found in the appendix to this book. Abbreviated tables are also found in the appendix to this chapter.

valuation of \$189,539.35 and assuming liabilities with a present valuation of \$151,631.48. These valuations would be the amounts reported in a balance sheet at the beginning of the period.

If we assume that the business is operating under conditions of certainty (that is, the predicted future cash flows turn out to be exactly correct), during the first year of operations the business would report net income of \$3,790.78. This is equal to a 10 percent return on the discounted amount of owner's equity at the beginning of the period (\$37,907.87 × .10), which reflects the difference between the 10 percent increase in the discounted amount of assets (\$18,953.93 = \$189,539.35 × .10) and liabilities (\$15,163.15 = \$151,631.48 × .10) during the year. Also, note that of the \$10,000 net cash inflow during the year, \$3,790.78 represents net income and \$6,209.22 (\$10,000 − \$3,790.78) represents a recovery of investment.

The balance sheet at the end of the first year would report assets, liabilities, and owner's equity based on the discounted amount, at 10 percent, of the future cash flows for the remaining four years. Specifically, assets, liabilities, and owner's equity would be reported at \$158,493.25, \$126,794.60, and \$31,698.65, respectively, on the balance sheet at the end of the first year:

Discounted future cash receipts:

$$\$158{,}493.25 = \$50{,}000\ p_{\overline{4}|.10} = (\$50{,}000)\,(3.169865)$$

Discounted future cash disbursements:

$$\$126{,}794.60 = \$40{,}000\ p_{\overline{4}|.10} = (\$40{,}000)\,(3.169865)$$

Discounted future net cash inflows:

$$\$31{,}698.65 = \$10{,}000\ p_{\overline{4}|.10} = (\$10{,}000)\,(3.169865)$$

STAUBUS COMPANY
Balance Sheet
December 31, 19+1

Assets (discounted future cash receipts, 10%, 4 years)	\$158,493.25	Liabilities (discounted future cash disbursements, 10%, 4 years)	\$126,794.60
		Staubus, capital	31,698.65
	\$158,493.25		\$158,493.25

STAUBUS COMPANY
Income Statement
For the Year Ended December 31, 19+1

Owner's equity, January 1, 19+1 (discounted future net cash inflows, 10%, 5 years)	\$37,907.87
Rate of return	10%
Net income (10% return on beginning owner's equity)	\$ 3,790.78

In a manner similar to that at the end of the first year, discounted amounts would be calculated at the end of each year until the end of the fifth year, when the discounted amounts would be zero. Financial statements would be prepared from the discounted amounts at the end of each year and the return on beginning owner's equity, which are summarized below for the five years:

Years	Discounted Amount of Assets at Year End	Discounted Amount of Liabilities at Year End	Discounted Amount of Owner's Equity at Year End	10% Return on Beginning Owner's Equity	Capital Recovery
0	$189,539.35	$151,631.48	$37,907.87	$ —	$ —
1	158,493.25	126,794.10	31,698.65	3,790.78	6,209.22
2	124,342.60[a]	99,474.08[b]	24,868.52[c]	3,169.87[d]	6,830.13[e]
3	86,776.85	69,421.48	17,355.37	2,486.85	7,513.15
4	45,454.55	36,363.64	9,090.91	1,735.54	8,264.46
5	0	0	0	909.09	9,090.91

[a]$124,342.60 = $50,000 $p_{\overline{3}|.10}$ = ($50,000)(2.486852)
[b]$ 99,474.08 = $40,000 $p_{\overline{3}|.10}$ = ($40,000)(2.486852)
[c]$ 24,868.52 = $10,000 $p_{\overline{3}|.10}$ = ($10,000)(2.486852) = $31,698.65 − $6,830.13
[d]$ 3,169.87 = $31,698.65 × .10
[e]$ 6,830.13 = $10,000.00 − $3,169.87

The calculation above assumes that the cash balance at the end of the year is paid to the owner, since under conditions of certainty there is no need to keep a cash balance. Note that if the owner withdraws cash at the end of the year equal to the net income for the year, the discounted amount of owner's equity would remain constant at the beginning and end of each year, as illustrated below for year 1:

Beginning discounted owner's equity	$37,907.87
Net income	3,790.78
	$41,698.65
Cash payment to owner equal to net income	3,790.78
Ending discounted owner's equity	$37,907.87

ADVANTAGES: Assets are future economic benefits, and liabilities are future obligations. Companies acquire assets because the discounted amounts of their future economic benefits are expected to be greater than or equal to their current purchase prices. Companies incur liabilities today because it is expected that the resulting assets received will provide future economic benefits that are greater than or equal to the discounted amount of the economic obligations of the liabilities. Since assets are acquired and held and liabilities are incurred because of expectations of future economic benefits, it is conceptually sound that the valuation of such assets and liabilities be based directly on the discounted amount of future economic benefits—discounted cash-flow valuation. In other words, discounted cash-flow valuation is useful as a normative (should-be) model of valuation, since it is based on direct valuation (discounted amount), rather than indirect valuation (discounted amount approximated by using past or current exchange prices), of the expected future economic events.

It can also be demonstrated that current financial decisions cannot be meaningfully made without some expectations of the future. Therefore, to aid investors, creditors, and other statement users in their financial decision making, it can be contended that financial statements should be based on expected future exchange prices—discounted cash-flow valuation.

Discounted cash-flow valuation can be useful to investors in attempting overall firm valuation, to owners in the valuation of single ventures (limited-life businesses formed to accomplish a specific purpose), and to managers for use in their managerial decision models. In addition, discounted cash-flow valuation is of interest to practicing accountants, since it is sanctioned per APB *Opinion No. 21* for monetary assets and liabilities with maturities of more than one year.

DISADVANTAGES: The implementation of discounted cash-flow valuation in the real world is limited to those situations where certainty is approximated. In the real world of uncertainty, how are a firm's estimated cash flows condensed into single dollar amounts and how do they reflect risk? Meaningful estimates of a firm's future cash flows, discount rate, and time horizon for purposes of valuation are highly questionable because of the need to rely on certainty assumptions that are unrealistic (except for certain monetary assets and liabilities).

A major problem with discounted cash-flow valuation is the valuation of individual assets. The valuation of individual assets, except for monetary assets, is practically impossible because of the inseparable and joint contribution of a firm's assets to its net cash inflows. That is to say, how do you identify a firm's future cash flows with particular assets?

Finally, in the real world of uncertainty, where a firm's actual cash flows would be found after the fact to be different from estimated cash flows, it is highly questionable how to report such deviations. But more important, there is the question of whether the reporting of historical deviations between actual and estimated cash flows would provide useful information for financial decision-making purposes. In other words, there would be a mixing of historical deviations and discounted amounts based on future cash flows in the financial statements that would be confusing to statement users.

Current selling prices. Under this approach to asset valuation, as advocated by its leading proponent, Professor Chambers, assets are reported at their present realizable sales prices at the balance-sheet date.[6] Such selling prices are quoted market selling prices of assets of a similar kind under conditions of orderly sale. They are *not* liquidating selling prices under conditions of forced sale. Moreover, the use of selling prices does not assume that assets on hand will necessarily be sold at those

---

[6]Raymond J. Chambers, *Accounting Evaluation and Economic Behavior* (Englewood Cliffs, N. J.: Prentice-Hall, Inc., 1966); and R.J. Chambers, "Second Thoughts on Continuously Contemporary Accounting," *Abacus* (September 1970), pp. 39–55.

prices, but that current quoted market selling prices are used as indicators of present cash equivalents.

As to liability valuation, Professor Chambers argues that liabilities should be reported in the balance sheet at their face amount—the amount owing. In other words, selling-price valuation is used only for asset valuation, whereas liability valuation is based on the amounts owing. The argument is that the debtor company owes the contractual amount regardless of the price at which the debt instruments (such as bonds) are being, or could be, sold in the market. A related argument is that to use the market selling prices of outstanding equities is tantamount to the valuation of the business as a whole, which is not the purpose of the balance sheet.[7] That is, the purpose of the balance sheet is to show current financial position by reporting assets at current selling prices, liabilities at face amount to show the claims against the assets, and stockholders' equity at the residual interest in the assets.

The income statement under selling-price valuation reports the net assets (assets minus liabilities) at the end of the fiscal period, after adjustments for any capital changes and dividends, from which the net assets at the beginning of the period are subtracted to derive net income or loss. Thus, net income is viewed as the result of the valuation of a firm's net assets. The emphasis is on asset valuation, since it is the assets that generate a firm's income, and the change in the valuation of net assets (after adjustments for capital changes) is net income.

ADVANTAGES: The basic argument for selling-price valuation is that rational financial decision making with regard to a business firm necessitates knowledge about the *current* financial condition of the firm, knowledge of which is provided by current balance sheets where assets are stated at current selling prices. As Professor Chambers points out, knowledge about the present financial state of the firm is necessary for informed choice of future economic actions and for informed appraisal of past economic actions.

The present selling prices of a firm's assets provide information with regard to the present financial state of the firm because such prices approximate the cash that could be obtained by the firm—current cash equivalents. Balance sheets based on selling-price valuation of assets provide financial information as to the ability of the firm to expand or contract, the property base for borrowing, the return on current investment, and the financial risk (debt to equity or debt to assets). Or, as Professor Sterling points out, the current selling prices of a firm's assets define the firm's market alternatives, define the investment necessary to maintain the status quo, are a component in indicating financial risk, and are relevant to rational decision models of management, creditors, and investors.[8]

An advantage of using selling-price valuation is that it avoids the arbitrary cost

---

[7]See Kenneth W. MacNeal, *Truth in Accounting* (Philadelphia: University of Pennsylvania Press, 1939), pp. 274–75. Reprinted by Scholars Book Co., Lawrence, Kansas, 1970.

[8]Robert R. Sterling, "Measuring Income and Wealth: An Application of the Relevance Criterion," *Journal of Business Administration* (Spring 1972), pp. 3–23.

allocations necessary under conventional historical cost valuation that reduce the significance of financial information presented in the financial statements. Using quoted market selling prices in the valuation of assets, it is not necessary to use diverse allocation procedures to systematically allocate historical cost to fiscal periods (depreciation, depletion, and amortization), nor is it necessary to allocate the cost of inventory to fiscal periods using diverse inventory-valuation methods (FIFO, LIFO, weighted average, retail-inventory method, lower-of-cost-or-market method, and the like).

Finally, it can be argued that net income cannot be meaningfully measured without proper valuation of a firm's assets. Yet conventional accounting practice emphasizes the matching of revenue and expense to derive net income, which relegates the balance sheet to a meaningless statement of residuals—what is left over. Instead, asset valuation should be based on current selling prices, so that net income is the *result* of the current valuation of the change in net assets (after adjustments for capital changes).

DISADVANTAGES: As to the arguments against current-selling-price valuation, one of the most frequent arguments is that such valuation cannot be applied to all the assets of the firm, since they lack quoted selling prices; therefore, such valuation has meaning only for salable assets. This means that those assets with no quoted selling prices are either reported at a zero amount or not reported at all.

For example, most firms do not have available the selling prices for their plant and equipment, since they are not in the business of selling plant and equipment. Similarly, in many cases there will be no existing selling prices for the goods-in-process inventory of manufacturing firms. Finally, a company may have specialized assets that are useful only to that company, so that there are no existing selling prices for such assets. In fact, specialized assets can be bought and immediately thereafter have a low or zero selling price.

Another argument against current-selling-price valuation is that it results in an income statement that provides little information for financial decision-making purposes, especially with regard to predicting future net income of the firm. In other words, such valuation is essentially a balance-sheet approach, with the income statement relegated to a secondary position of showing only the change in owner's equity (after adjustments for capital changes) from the beginning to the end of the fiscal period. The resulting income statement does not show the revenue inflows and the expense outflows, which are thought to be useful information for financial decision-making purposes. This is not to say that revenue and expense flows could not be shown, but rather that they normally are not shown, under selling-price valuation, in order to avoid the arbitrary allocations that would be necessary to report such flows.

There is also the question of whether current-selling-price valuation results in a balance sheet that really shows the present or current financial status of the firm as claimed. For example, the fact that merchandise inventory has a quoted selling price of $100 a unit, and that there are 1,000 units on hand at the balance-sheet date, does not necessarily mean that the present financial status of the inventory is

$100,000. If all the inventory were sold at the balance-sheet date, the price would be lower because of forced-liquidation prices. If the liquidating price were $50 per unit, would the present financial condition of the inventory be $50,000? Are liquidating prices of assets a better measure of current financial condition than current selling prices under orderly selling conditions, or are liquidating prices unrealistic because most firms will continue in business rather than liquidate?

Another problem with selling-price valuation is whether assets stated at current selling prices can be meaningfully added together on the balance sheet.[9] The presumption under selling-price valuation is that the prices are those under orderly selling conditions in the quantities and combinations normally sold. However, the way the assets are grouped or combined for sale affects the selling price; hence, different combinations or grouping of assets can result in different selling prices. Different selling prices, in turn, result in different asset valuations, raising the question as to whether such valuations can be meaningfully added together on the balance sheet. In other words, selling-price valuation results in aggregation problems, but avoids allocation problems.

Finally, it can be argued that it is inconsistent to report assets at current selling prices and liabilities at face amount. If the objective is to report current financial condition, then liabilities should be reported at their prevailing selling prices.

Current purchase prices. Under current-purchase-price valuation, more commonly called replacement-cost valuation, the market price used in asset valuation is the quoted market exchange price to acquire existing assets held by the firm (replacement in kind). For merchandise inventory, raw materials, and purchased parts, replacement cost is the current quoted purchase price based on normal quantities obtained from normal suppliers at the financial-statement preparation date. For goods-in-process and finished-goods inventories of manufacturing firms, replacement cost is the current cost to manufacture such inventories based on the current purchase prices of raw materials, labor, and factory overhead at the financial-statement preparation date. Where no current purchase prices are available for particular assets held by the firm, then replacement-cost valuation would be approximated by the use of specific price indexes for similar assets or by appraisals.

As to liability valuation under replacement-cost valuation, short-term liabilities would be reported in the balance sheet at face amount (amount owing), because the gains or losses to adjust them to current-purchase-price valuation are usually too small to warrant such adjustments. On the other hand, long-term liabilities would be reported at current purchase prices (current market purchase prices plus commissions), in order to show how much was saved (or additional cost) by borrowing at terms more favorable (or less favorable) than those that currently exist.

With regard to income determination under replacement-cost valuation, net

[9]Kermit Larson and R.W. Schattke, "Current Cash Equivalent, Additivity, and Financial Action," *Accounting Review* (October 1966), pp. 634–41.

income is reported in the income statement so as to show both holding gains and losses (holding assets and liabilities while their purchase prices rise or fall) and operating profit (profit from normal sales of goods and services). As suggested by the leading proponents of replacement-cost valuation, Professors Edwards and Bell, two net-income figures would be reported.[10] One net-income figure, which they called "realized profit," would be based only on realized holding gains and losses (realized by sale or use). The other net-income figure, which they called "business profit," would be based on both current period realized and unrealized (not realized by sale or use) holding gains and losses.

ADVANTAGES: The basic arguments for replacement-cost valuation are that current costs (really current expenses) are matched with current revenue to derive operating income, that holding gains and losses are reported separately in the income statement and not mixed with operating income, and that the assets are reported in the balance sheet at current costs. In other words, the contention is that financial statements based on current costs (replacement-cost valuation) provide more useful information for financial decision-making purposes than do those based on conventional historical-cost valuation. Replacement-cost valuation avoids the problems of historical-cost valuation that result in the mixing of purchase prices of different periods, the mixing of operating and holding gains and losses, and the reporting of out-of-date, and therefore irrelevant, past purchase prices in the balance sheet.

Those accountants favoring replacement-cost valuation contend that the net operating income for the period should be the difference between current revenue and current cost (replacement cost at time of sale) of goods and services utilized (current expense) in the generation of the revenue during the current period. Current expenses should be matched with current revenue because the "true" cost of generating revenue is the cost to acquire goods and services necessary to generate the revenue at the time of sale.

Under replacement-cost valuation, changes in the replacement cost of specific assets are segregated and reported in the financial statements during the period when such price changes occur—holding gains and losses. The argument is that the *timing* of the investment in, the holding of, and the sale or use of assets (as well as liabilities) is part of management's job in operating the business efficiently. Consequently, it is argued that holding gains and losses should be reported in the income statement in order to report on which period's holding activities were successful or unsuccessful.

Under conventional historical-cost valuation, gains and losses for a fiscal period are not generally recognized until the assets are sold or used in production and sold as finished goods. For example, if merchandise inventory that originally cost $10,000 has a replacement cost of $11,000 at year end, there is no recognition of a $1,000 holding gain under conventional historical-cost valuation. If the re-

---

[10] Edgar O. Edwards and Philip W. Bell, *Theory and Measurement.*

placement cost of the inventory is $10,500 when sold in the next period, then under historical-cost valuation there is a $500 holding gain that is not segregated but is mixed with operating income as part of the difference between sales and the historical cost of the inventory. Such valuation results in the failure to report a $1,000 holding gain in the first period and a $500 holding loss in the second period, as well as the mixing of a "net" $500 holding gain ($10,500 – $10,000) with operating income in the second period. In contrast, under replacement-cost valuation, holding gains and losses can be reported for the period when they occur.

By using the conventional revenue-recognition assumption with replacement-cost valuation, only those holding gains and losses that are realized by sale or use are reported in the income statement; hence, net income is the same for both replacement-cost and historical-cost valuation. The only differences between the two valuation methods are that under replacement-cost valuation, realized holding gains and losses are reported separately in the income statement, unrealized holding gains and losses are reported in the stockholders'-equity section of the balance sheet, and nonmonetary assets and long-term liabilities are reported at current replacement cost. Thus, replacement-cost valuation has the practical advantage of being easily adapted to existing accounting practice, since it builds upon conventional historical-cost valuation in both the accounting records and the resulting financial statements, as well as being consistent with generally accepted accounting principles.

On the other hand, some accountants argue that *both* realized and unrealized holding gains and losses should be reported in the income statement. If this were done, then the conventional revenue-recognition assumption would have to be modified by the recognition of holding gains and losses as being earned when the asset is sold or used, or when the end of the accounting period occurs, whichever is first. For example, Edwards and Bell argue that business profit, which includes both realized and unrealized holding gains and losses, should be reported because it results in the reporting of profit not distorted by data from past periods, as well as permitting the determination of which period's holding activities were successful or unsuccessful.

As a final argument for replacement-cost valuation, Professor Bell contends that it is the accountant's function to measure a firm's performance (profits), so that it can be compared with management's plan of operations and thereby provide the means to evaluate the plan.[11] Since current cost (replacement cost) represents the cost of assets management has chosen to use in its plan of operations, then current cost (expense) should be matched with revenue to measure operating success or failure. Once the operating plan has been evaluated, then management can decide whether to attempt to change future performance by selling or holding assets and the like. Consequently, historical-cost valuation is rejected because it does not provide current-cost data to measure performance. Similarly, selling-

[11] Philip W. Bell, "On Current Replacement Costs and Business Income," in *Asset Valuation and Income Determination: A Consideration of the Alternatives,* ed. Robert R. Sterling (Lawrence, Kans.: Scholars Book Co., 1971), pp. 27–30.

price valuation is rejected because it does not measure past economic events that actually occurred, and therefore does not provide the means to evaluate performance in terms of what was expected via management's plan of operations.

DISADVANTAGES: It can be argued that the use of replacement-cost valuation does *not* result in a balance sheet that shows present financial condition necessary for informed financial decision making. Since the firm already holds the assets, asset valuation should not be based on their hypothetical purchase, since such hypothetical purchase prices are not relevant to reporting present financial condition. Purchase prices are not relevant because they do not define the firm's market alternatives, the investment necessary to maintain the status quo, or the ability of the firm to expand or contract.

Another disadvantage of replacement-cost valuation is that it is necessary to make the same type of arbitrary cost allocations that are currently being used in conventional accounting under historical-cost valuation. The only difference is that it is necessary to allocate current, instead of historical, cost to fiscal periods. Thus there remains the question of which depreciation, inventory valuation, and amortization methods are to be used in the preparation of financial statements. In addition, there is allocation associated with the reporting of holding gains and losses, since the reported current-cost depreciation affects the amount of the holding gain or loss reported for the period. The point is that such arbitrary allocations reduce the usefulness of the financial information presented in the financial statements for purposes of financial decision making.

Another problem with replacement-cost valuation is that current purchase prices are not really available for all of a firm's assets. This is especially pertinent with regard to specialized assets and to manufactured inventory. For example, what is the current replacement cost of factory overhead used in the manufacture of goods-in-process?

There is also the question of what exactly replacement cost is. Is it the cost to replace the asset in its present form (replace the exact asset), or the cost of replacing the capacity to produce? This is especially important when there have been technological changes. That is, because of technological changes, a firm's existing equipment may not be able to produce the quality and quantity that new equipment can. In such a situation, what is replacement cost?

Past purchase prices. Under past-purchase-price valuation, more commonly called historical-cost valuation, the market price used in asset valuation is the acquisition cost of an asset at the time of purchase (including costs to put in working condition), manufacture, or construction. It is the *total* of the exchange prices, or price aggregates, to obtain an asset and render it suitable for its intended use. Thus, historical cost is measured by the cash or cash equivalent sacrificed in exchange for obtaining an asset.

Historical-cost valuation of assets is based on past purchase exchange prices (past entry or input exchange prices), where *past* refers to the time of acquisition. Historical-cost valuation is similar to replacement-cost valuation in that both are based on purchase exchange prices, but they differ as to the timing of the purchase and the actual occurrence of the exchange. That is to say, historical-cost valuation is based on *actual past* purchases of assets, while replacement cost is based on *hypothetical* (as if the firm's existing assets were replaced) *current* (at time of financial-statement preparation) purchases of assets. Similarly, historical-cost valuation differs from current-selling-price valuation as to type of market (purchasing market versus selling market), timing (past purchase versus current sale), and actual occurrence of the exchange (actual past purchases versus hypothetical sales of existing assets).

In current accounting practice, historical cost is the normal valuation method used for nonmonetary assets (inventory, property, plant, and equipment), but not for monetary assets (cash, short-term marketable securities, accounts receivable, and bond investment). For example, cash is reported at face amount, short-term marketable securities at the lower of cost or market, accounts receivable at net realizable amount (amounts owing to the firm minus estimated uncollectibles), and bond investment at discounted amount to maturity.

There are also exceptions in current accounting practice to the use of historical-cost valuation for nonmonetary assets. For example, inventory valuation based on the lower-of-cost-or-market procedure uses replacement cost; inventory valuation based on the percentage-of-completion method uses future prices to estimate future costs; inventory valuation of some precious metals and agricultural products is based on net realizable amount (selling price less disposal costs); valuation of common-stock investment is based on the equity method (original cost plus proportional share of investee's net income minus dividends); the valuation of donated assets is based on fair market amount (independent market appraisal); and valuation of land in which valuable mineral or other natural resources are discovered is based on fair market amount.

It should also be understood that when accountants refer to historical-cost valuation of nonmonetary assets in current accounting practice, they do not mean that the original cost is the only amount reported on the balance sheet. Rather, historical cost is the valuation method for nonmonetary assets at time of acquisition and serves as the basis for subsequent cost allocation of such assets to expense or to product. Thus, equipment is reported on the balance sheet at original cost less accumulated depreciation, natural resources at cost less accumulated depletion, and intangibles at an amount net of original cost less amortization to date. Similarly, merchandise inventory is reported on the balance sheet at original cost after adjusting for the costs allocated to merchandise sold (cost of goods sold). Prepayments are reported on the balance sheet at unallocated cost (original cost minus cost allocated to expense).

As to liability valuation, current accounting practice generally records and reports liabilities based on the valuation of the assets received, expenses incurred, or losses incurred (the debit side of the transaction). Since the valuation of the debit side of the transaction is normally based on historical cost, liabilities are generally recorded and reported also at historical cost (the cash or cash equivalent to discharge the liability). Also, long-term liabilities are recorded and reported at the discounted amount of the future interest payments and maturity amount, but since the discount rate used is the effective interest rate at the time of issuance, such valuation is consistent with historical-cost valuation.

With regard to income determination under historical-cost valuation, current accounting practice matches revenue and expenses for the fiscal period to derive net income. Since periodic expenses are measured at cost paid or owed during the fiscal period and at cost allocations of nonmonetary assets, net income reflects a matching of revenue with expenses based on historical-cost valuation. This means that with the emphasis on matching revenue and expense during the fiscal period, the income statement is the primary financial statement in current accounting practice, and the balance sheet ends up being a statement of residuals (unallocated past costs) with regard to the nonmonetary assets.

Also, current accounting practice does not include unrealized gains on the holding of assets and liabilities in the income statement, as well as not segregating realized holding gains on inventory sold. The recognition of unrealized gains would require writing assets up in violation of the historical-cost assumption, as well as of the revenue-recognition assumption. Based on the revenue-recognition and historical-cost assumptions, revenue is normally (there are exceptions) recognized at point of sale, and therefore, gains are normally recognized only when realized by sale or use. On the other hand, based on the doctrine of conservatism, unrealized holding losses on assets for sale are included in the income statement under current accounting practice.

ADVANTAGES: As previously discussed with regard to the historical-cost assumption (Chapter 3), the primary argument for historical-cost valuation is that it is objectively determinable. That is to say, acquisition cost is objectively determined in the marketplace by rational buyers and sellers acting in arm's-length transactions (no collusion). Consequently, acquisition cost is not subjectively determined by accountants, but is a bargained purchase price objectively determined in the marketplace.

Based on the objectivity argument as a foundation, other arguments for historical-cost valuation naturally follow. For example, it is argued that acquisition cost has the advantage of approximating value at time of purchase, since it is a market-determined purchase. It is also argued that historical-cost valuation is verifiable by accountants, because it can be tested in the marketplace. Also, since historical-cost valuation is based on *actual* purchases, it can be argued that such valuation results in financial statements that are less subject to dispute than those using other proposed valuation methods based on hypothetical purchases (replacement cost), hypothetical sales (current selling price), or subjective estimates of future prices (discounted amount).[12]

A frequent argument for historical-cost valuation is that it provides useful financial information for financial decision making, in that knowledge of the past

[12]See Yuji Ijiri, "A Defense for Historical Cost Accounting, " in *Asset Valuation and Income Determination: A Consideration of the Alternatives,* ed. Robert R. Sterling (Lawrence, Kans.: Scholars Book Co., 1971), pp. 1–14.

is necessary to predict the future. Consequently, it is contended that historical-cost data provide useful information for making comparisons for trend analysis, for intracompany analysis (cost comparison among departments), and for inter-company analysis, as well as for comparisons with current-cost data.

Professor Ijiri argues that historical-cost valuation provides an automatic control feature that is missing in other proposed valuation methods.[13] That is to say, historical-cost valuations structured on the double-entry bookkeeping system result in recording changes in the entity's resources by linking together the inputs and outputs so that they can be traced and identified whenever necessary. Thus investors and creditors can rely on the existing accounting system to control the resources of a firm (custodianship function of accounting) in a manner that they can trust to protect their interests.

DISADVANTAGES: Probably the primary criticism of historical-cost valuation is that it results in providing financial information that is irrelevant to making current financial decisions. Historical-cost valuation provides *past* cost data, whereas financial decision making should be based on *current* and *future* financial data. Financial decision-making models used by informed management, creditors, and investors are not based on historical-cost data.

Another criticism of historical-cost valuation is that its primary argument, that acquisition cost is objectively determinable, is true only with regard to a single cash price at acquisition. For example, the total cost of many nonmonetary assets includes costs other than just the exchange price, and these other costs are often difficult to determine objectively (such as the cost of "debugging" a new machine to put it into operating condition). Also, the acquisition cost may include a group of assets, and it is difficult to objectively determine the cost of *each* asset. Moreover, there are difficulties in objectively determining cost when there is no cash consideration sacrificed in exchange and it is necessary to determine the cash equivalent sacrificed (for example, the exchange of land for a machine). Finally, there are assets that are constructed by companies for their own use, and the total cost of such assets, especially the applicable overhead cost, is difficult to determine objectively.

It is also argued that historical-cost valuation results in a balance sheet that does not provide useful financial information about current financial position, since the nonmonetary asset valuations are out of date and merely show remaining unallocated past costs or residuals (book amounts). The balance sheet as a statement of meaningless residuals is the result of the emphasis in current accounting practice to match revenue and expenses (measured at historical cost) to report periodic net income in the income statement. Such matching requires allocation of acquisition costs to periodic expense, and the reporting of unallocated costs on the balance sheet. However, the reporting of such unallocated costs does not show the firm's command over its assets, the assets available to a firm to meet its obligations, nor the nature of a firm's assets that is necessary to evaluate risk—

[13] Ijiri, pp. 4–5, 13.

current financial position. Also, the emphasis on matching and the resulting cost allocations results in reporting deferred charges (and deferred credits) on the balance sheet that are not really assets, because they have no future economic service potential. Similarly, the unamortized cost of intangibles is reported on the balance sheet; this does not indicate future economic potential and raises the question as to whether intangibles should even be reported.[14]

Historical-cost valuation is also criticized because it results in mixing acquisition prices of different time periods on the balance sheet. In other words, nonmonetary assets are acquired during different periods of time, yet the unamortized acquisition costs are added together on the balance sheet as if they were acquired at the same time. Thus it is questionable whether the amounts reported on the balance sheet are very meaningful when summed together.

There is also the question of consistent use of historical-cost valuation in current accounting practice. Since monetary assets are not stated at historical cost, and since there are numerous exceptions to historical-cost valuation of nonmonetary assets, it is contended that financial statements reflect a conglomeration of different valuation methods. Such conglomeration does not result in providing useful financial information for financial decision-making purposes.

Finally, it is argued that the use of historical-cost valuation in conjunction with the revenue-recognition assumption in current accounting practice fails to report holding gains and losses that are useful information for financial decision making. Moreover, by recognizing gains and most losses only when realized by sale or use, realized holding gains and losses are not reported in the proper time period and are not always separately reported (for example, the holding gain on inventory sold).

Illustration. A simplified illustration is presented below, demonstrating the recording and reporting of economic transactions under current-selling-price, replacement-cost, and historical-cost valuation.

Suppose that Sunflower, Inc., was formed with the following assets, stated at acquisition cost, and equities: cash, $10,000; merchandise inventory (4,000 units @$5), $20,000; land, $5,000; building, $65,000; and common stock (1,000 shares at $100 par value), $100,000. At the time of the formation of the business, the replacement cost of the assets approximated original cost, and their selling prices were as follows: merchandise inventory at retail, $40,000; land, $5,100; and building, $66,000.

Assume that during the first year of operations of Sunflower, Inc., the following economic transactions occurred:

(1) There were cash sales of 3,000 units of merchandise inventory at $10 per unit. Replacement cost of the inventory at time of sale was $6 per unit.

---

[14]See Arthur Andersen & Co., *Objectives of Financial Statements for Business Enterprises* (Chicago: Arthur Andersen & Co., 1972), pp. 48–51.

(2) There were 3,500 units of merchandise inventory purchased at \$6 per unit, of which \$9,000 cash was paid and the remainder was on credit. At time of acquisition, the retail selling price of the merchandise inventory was \$10 per unit.

(3) Sunflower, Inc., received cash of \$5,000 by issuing 50 shares of common stock at par value of \$100 a share.

(4) At year end, the replacement cost of inventory was \$7 per unit, of land \$5,500, and of building \$67,000. Also at year end, the selling prices of the assets were as follows: merchandise inventory, \$10.60 per unit; land, \$5,400; and building, \$66,700.

(5) Depreciation on the building was computed by the straight-line method at a rate of 10 percent per year, with no estimated salvage value.

Based upon the data above, general-journal entries are prepared for Sunflower, Inc., for its first year of operation, as illustrated on page 146, under all three valuation methods.

Under current-selling-price valuation, assets are written up or down to reflect current selling prices at the financial-statement preparation date, and merchandise inventory is written up or down at time of sale. For Sunflower, Inc., under current-selling-price valuation, assets were written up to current selling prices at the time the business was started and at the end of the fiscal period. Merchandise inventory was not written up at time of sale, since the inventory was already stated at the current selling price (\$10 per unit).[15] Note that under current-selling-price valuation, there are no individual entries for revenue and expense flows (for example, no depreciation entry), since it is basically a current-balance-sheet approach.

Under replacement-cost valuation, assets and liabilities are written up or down to reflect replacement cost at the financial-statement preparation date, and merchandise inventory is written up or down at time of sale. Such adjustments reflect holding gains and losses on assets and liabilities and are segregated into realized and unrealized holding gains and losses. For Sunflower, Inc., under replacement-cost valuation, assets were not written up or down at the beginning of the business because acquisition cost approximated replacement cost. Inventory was written up at time of sale to reflect the increase in replacement cost, of which \$3,000 was realized by the sale of inventory and \$1,000 was unrealized because of the inventory still on hand. At year end, assets were written up to reflect current replacement cost and were treated as unrealized holding gains. Depreciation on the building was computed on the current replacement cost of \$67,000, not the acquisition cost of \$65,000, which resulted in a \$200 excess of current-cost depre-

---

[15] The use of the current retail inventory price is consistent with Chamber's view that quoted selling prices are indicators of current cash equivalents needed for reporting current financial position. On the other hand, other proponents of current selling-price valuation, such as Sterling, argue that inventory valuation should be based on current selling prices obtainable if all the inventory were sold on the balance sheet date (such prices would in most cases be below retail prices).

	Current-Selling-Price Valuation dr.	Current-Selling-Price Valuation cr.	Replacement-Cost Valuation dr.	Replacement-Cost Valuation cr.	Historical-Cost Valuation dr.	Historical-Cost Valuation cr.
(a) Form business:						
Cash	10,000		10,000		10,000	
Merchandise inventory	20,000		20,000		20,000	
Land	5,000		5,000		5,000	
Building	65,000		65,000		65,000	
Common stock		$100,000		$100,000		$100,000
Inventory	20,000		—		—	
Land	100		—		—	
Building	1,000		—		—	
Exit price valuation		21,100		—		—
(b) Sales:						
Cash (3,000 × $10)	30,000		30,000		30,000	
Sales		—		30,000		30,000
Inventory [($6 – $5) (4,000)]	—		4,000		—	
Realized holding gains [($6 – $5)(3,000)]		—		3,000		—
Unrealized holding gains [($6 – $5) (1,000)]		—		1,000		—
Cost of goods sold (3,000 × $6)	—		18,000		—	
(3,000 × $5)	—		—		15,000	
Inventory		30,000		18,000		15,000
(c) Inventory purchases:						
Inventory (3,500 × $10)	35,000		—		—	
(3,500 × $6)	—		21,000		21,000	
Cash		9,000		9,000		9,000
Accounts payable		12,000		12,000		12,000
Exit price valuation [($10 – $6)(3,500)]		14,000		—		—
(d) Issue common stock:						
Cash	5,000		5,000		5,000	
Common stock (50 × $100)		5,000		5,000		5,000
(e) Asset write up at year end:						
Inventory [($10.60 – $10.00)(4,500)]	2,700		—		—	
[($7 – $6)(4,500)]	—		4,500		—	
Land ($5,400 – $5,100)	300		—		—	
($5,500 – $5,000)	—		500		—	
Building ($66,700 – $66,000)	700		—		—	
($67,000 – $65,000)	—		2,000		—	
Unrealized holding gains		—		7,000		—
Exit price valuation		3,700		—		—
(f) Depreciation:						
Depreciation expense ($67,000 × .10)	—		6,700		—	
($65,000 × .10)	—		—		6,500	
Accumulated depreciation		—		6,700		6,500
Unrealized holding gains ($6,700 – $6,500)	—		200		—	
Realized holding gains		—		200		—
(g) Closing:						
Sales	—		30,000		30,000	
Realized holding gains ($3,000 + $200)	—		3,200		—	
Cost of goods sold		—		18,000		15,000
Depreciation expense		—		6,700		6,500
Retained earnings		—		8,500		8,500

ciation over historic-cost depreciation ($6,700 – $6,500). This $200 was a realized holding gain (or cost saving) because Sunflower, Inc., purchased the building at a price lower than the current replacement cost when the asset services were used. Also, note that there was no write-up or -down of liabilities, since Sunflower, Inc., had no long-term liabilities.

Based on the preceding entries, financial statements are prepared for Sunflower, Inc., under the three valuation methods, as illustrated below and on page 148.

As to the balance sheets, under current-selling-price valuation, assets were written up to current selling prices and the write-ups accumulated in an Exit Price Valuation account, which was reported on the equity side of the balance sheet below common stock. Under replacement-cost valuation, assets were written up to reflect current replacement cost for both realized and unrealized holding gains, with the latter reported below retained earnings on the balance sheet.

With regard to the income statements, note that the income statement under selling-price valuation merely shows the change in net assets (assets minus liabilities) from the beginning to the end of the fiscal period, after adjusting for any capital changes. Thus, the end-of-period net assets ($155,800 – $12,000 = $143,800) are adjusted for the $5,000 increase in common stock, which of course should not be included in net income, and from this is subtracted the net assets at

SUNFLOWER, INC.
Balance Sheet
December 31, 19+1

(Current-Selling-Price Valuation)

Assets			Equities	
Cash		$ 36,000	Accounts payable	$ 12,000
Inventory		47,700	Common stock	105,000
Land		5,400	Exit price valuation	38,800
Building		66,700		
		$155,800		$155,800

(Replacement-Cost Valuation)

Cash		$ 36,000	Accounts payable	$ 12,000
Inventory		31,500	Common stock	105,000
Land		5,500	Retained earnings	8,500
Building	$67,000		Unrealized holding gains	7,800
Less accumulated depreciation	6,700	60,300		
		$133,300		$133,300

(Historical-Cost Valuation)

Cash		$ 36,000	Accounts payable	$ 12,000
Inventory		26,000	Common stock	105,000
Land		5,000	Retained earnings	8,500
Building	$65,000			
Less accumulated depreciation	6,500	58,500		
		$125,500		$125,500

SUNFLOWER, INC.
Income Statement
For the Year Ended December 31, 19+1

	Replacement-Cost Valuation	Historical-Cost Valuation
Sales	$30,000	$30,000
Cost of goods sold	18,000	15,000
Gross margin	$12,000	$15,000
Operating expenses:		
Depreciation	6,700	6,500
Net operating incomes	$ 5,300	$ 8,500
Realized holding gains	3,200	—
Net Income	$ 8,500	$ 8,500

(Current Selling-Price Valuation)

Net assets, December 31, 19+1	$143,800
Less increase in common stock during 19+1	5,000
Net assets adjusted for capital change	$138,800
Less net assets at formation of business	100,000
Net income	$ 38,800

the time the business was formed ($100,000), to derive net income of $38,800. Note how much larger this income figure is than under the other two valuation methods, because of the excess of selling prices over historic and replacement costs, and because no distinction is made between realized and unrealized price gains. Also, it should be observed that no revenue and expense flows are reported, although it is possible to do so, because this would necessitate arbitrary allocations that are to be avoided under current-selling-price valuation.

The income statement for Sunflower, Inc., under replacement-cost valuation reports both revenue and expense flows and holding gains and losses actually realized by sale or use. Reporting only realized holding gains and losses in the income statement is consistent with the revenue-recognition assumption under historical-cost valuation. For example, note that the net income ($8,500) is the same for both replacement-cost and historic-cost valuation, the only difference being that realized holding gains and losses are mixed with net operating income under historic-cost valuation, but segregated under replacement-cost valuation.

On the other hand, it can be argued that both realized and unrealized holding gains and losses should be reported in the income statement under replacement-cost valuation, in order to show them in the proper time period. Thus Edwards and Bell propose the reporting of realized profit, which includes only realized holding gains and losses, and business profit, which includes both realized and unrealized holding gains and losses (called realizable holding gains and losses), as illustrated below:

SUNFLOWER, INC.
Income Statement
For the Year Ended December 31, 19+1

(Current-Replacement-Cost Valuation)

Sales	$30,000
Cost of goods sold	18,000
Gross margin	$12,000
Operating expenses:	
Depreciation	6,700
Current operating profit	$ 5,300

Current operating profit		$5,300
Realized holding gains:		
On inventory	$3,000	
On depreciation	200	3,200
Realized profit		$8,500

Current operating profit		$5,300
Realizable holding gains:		
On inventory	$8,500	
On land	500	
On building	2,000	11,000
Business profit		$16,300

Appendix: Review of Compound Interest Concepts

Purpose of appendix. Among the common long-run financial decisions made by business managers today are those regarding (1) borrowing money today and repaying it over several future time periods, and (2) investing money today to obtain future cash inflows. Accountants, in their capacity as management advisers, must be familiar with compound-interest concepts in order to take into account the time lags between present and future cash flows, and so to properly evaluate borrowing and investment alternatives. Also, the accountant should be cognizant of the effects of compound-interest concepts on the recording and the reporting of depreciation, leases, long-term investments, and long-term debt. Finally, the accountant should understand compound interest, since it plays an important part in many mathematical models that are used to aid managerial decision making.

The understanding of compound interest is so important that its fundamentals are now being taught in introductory accounting courses.[1] Thus, many of the con-

[1] See Glenn L. Johnson and James A. Gentry, Jr., *Finney and Miller's Principles of Accounting: Introductory,* 7th ed. (Englewood Cliffs, N.J.: Prentice-Hall, Inc., 1970), Chap. 27.

cepts discussed in this appendix may be a review for some readers; however, there are some concepts, such as nominal versus effective interest, continuous compounding, and deferred annuities, that may be new to some readers. It is recommended that you read this appendix to review familiar concepts, to learn some new concepts that may have been missed, and to become used to the mathematical notations that are used in the book. The reader who feels that he is up to date on compound interest may want to skip this appendix.

Compound amount. Compound interest is interest earned on any previously earned interest plus the original investment (principal). Periodically as interest becomes due, it is added (compounded or converted) to the original principal plus any previously earned interest, and the larger accumulated amount (called the compound amount, compound sum, or future value) earns interest. For example, if \$1,000 is invested in a savings account at 6 percent interest compounded annually, then the compound amount at the end of year 1 is \$1,060, at the end of year 2 is \$1,123.60, and at the end of year 3 is \$1,191.02, as shown below:

$$\$1{,}000.00 + (\$1{,}000 \times .06 \times 1) = \$1{,}060.00$$
$$\$1{,}060.00 + (\$1{,}060 \times .06 \times 1) = \$1{,}123.60$$
$$\$1{,}123.60 + (\$1{,}123.60 \times .06 \times 1) = \$1{,}191.02$$

The compound-amount calculation can be formalized as follows:

Let i = Rate of interest per period of compounding
n = Number of compound periods
P = Principal single sum invested today
S = Compound amount (sum), or the amount that P accumulates for n compound periods at i interest rate, compounded once per compound period

Then $S = P(1 + i)^n$
$\$1{,}060 = \$1{,}000\,(1.06)^1$

Compound amount of \$1. To avoid the tedious computations of repeated multiplications to derive compound amounts over several time periods, tables of compound amounts of \$1 are available (see Appendix). The tables are really compound amounts of 1, since they can refer to any monetary unit (dollars, pounds, and so on). The tables are constructed by using the compound-amount formula, with \$1 being used for the principal in the formula. To illustrate this, let s be denoted as the compound amount of \$1 that is found in the tables;[2] then,

$$S = P(1 + i)^n$$
$$s = 1(1 + i)^n = (1 + i)^n$$

[2] A common notation for the compound amount of \$1 is a. However, to be consistent mnemonically with the common S symbol for the compound sum, s is used to denote the compound sum (amount) of \$1.

Given any principal amount to be invested today, the pertinent compound amount of $1 can be found in the tables and multiplied by the principal to obtain the compound sum. For example, what is the compound amount of $41,000 invested today for six years at 4 percent interest compounded annually? As shown in the abbreviated table below, the compound amount of $1 for six years at 4 percent interest is 1.265319, and the factor times $41,000 provides a compound amount of $51,878.08.

$$s = (1 + i)^n$$
$$\mathbf{1.265319} = (\mathbf{1.04})^6$$
$$S = P(1 + i)^n = P \cdot s$$
$$\mathbf{\$51{,}878.08} = \mathbf{\$41{,}000}\,(\mathbf{1.04})^6 = \mathbf{\$41{,}000}\,(\mathbf{1.265319})$$

Amount of $1 at Compound Interest

Periods	3%	3½%	4%	4½%	5%	6%
1	1.030000	1.035000	1.040000	1.045000	1.050000	1.060000
2	1.060900	1.071225	1.081600	1.092025	1.102500	1.123600
3	1.092727	1.108718	1.124864	1.141166	1.157625	1.191016
4	1.125509	1.147523	1.169859	1.192519	1.215506	1.262477
5	1.159274	1.187686	1.216653	1.246182	1.276282	1.338226
6	1.194052	1.229255	1.265319	1.302260	1.340096	1.418519
7	1.229874	1.272279	1.315932	1.360862	1.407100	1.503630
8	1.266770	1.316809	1.368569	1.422101	1.477455	1.593848

Compound interest. The compound interest (denoted by I) on an investment is the excess of the compound amount over the principal sum invested, or $I = S - P$. Compound interest can be computed without knowing the compound sum, by multiplying the investment by the factor of the compound amount of $1 minus 1.

$$I = S - P = P(1 + i)^n - P = P[(1 + i)^n - 1] = P(s - 1)$$

For instance, if one wishes to know the compound interest that will be earned on an investment of $100,000 for five periods at 5 percent, the computation below shows it to be $27,628.20.

$$I = P(s - 1)$$
$$\mathbf{\$27{,}628.20} = \mathbf{\$100{,}000}\,(\mathbf{1.276282} - \mathbf{1})$$

or

$$I = S - P$$
$$\mathbf{\$27{,}628.20} = [\mathbf{\$100{,}000}(\mathbf{1.05})^5] - \mathbf{\$100{,}000} = [\mathbf{\$100{,}000}(\mathbf{1.276282})] - \mathbf{\$100{,}000}$$

Frequency of conversion. Since interest is normally stated as an annual rate, money at x percent interest means x percent interest compounded annually, unless otherwise stated. When interest is compounded more than once a year, the more frequent compounding causes the *actual* annual interest rate earned to be greater than the *stated* annual interest rate. In such a case, the stated rate is often referred to as the *nominal annual rate* and the actual rate is called the *effective annual rate.*

To determine the compound sum when interest is compounded more than once a year, the frequency of conversion is used to convert the nominal rate into a rate per compound period, and to convert the number of annual periods into the number of interest or compound periods. The *frequency of conversion* is defined as the number of times interest is compounded or converted into principal during the year. Hence, the frequency of conversion (denoted as m) divided into the nominal rate (r) provides the rate per compound period (i); and the number of years (t) multiplied by the frequency of conversion (m) provides the total number of compound periods (n). Taking into account the frequency of conversion, the compound-amount formula can be restated as follows:

$$S = P(1 + i)^n \quad \text{[annual compounding]}$$

$$= P\left(1 + \frac{r}{m}\right)^{m \cdot t} \quad \text{[}m\text{ compounding per year]}$$

For example, \$1,000 invested for two years at 12 percent interest compounded semiannually, quarterly, or monthly provides a compound sum of \$1,262.48, \$1,266.77, or \$1,269.73, respectively.

$$S = P\left(1 + \frac{r}{m}\right)^{m \cdot t}$$

$$\$1{,}262.48 = \$1{,}000\left(1 + \frac{.12}{2}\right)^{2 \cdot 2} = \$1{,}000(1.06)^4$$

$$= \$1{,}000(1.26248)\text{[semiannual compounding]}$$

$$\$1{,}266.77 = \$1{,}000\left(1 + \frac{.12}{4}\right)^{4 \cdot 2} = \$1{,}000(1.03)^8$$

$$= \$1{,}000(1.26677)\text{[quarterly compounding]}$$

$$\$1{,}269.73 = \$1{,}000\left(1 + \frac{.12}{12}\right)^{12 \cdot 2} = \$1{,}000(1.01)^{24}$$

$$= \$1{,}000(1.26973)\text{[monthly compounding]}$$

Since the nominal annual rate is quite frequently the only rate given, an informed person should be able to calculate the actual annual rate earned (effective annual rate). We know that for every dollar invested, the investor will end up with the original dollar plus the actual interest earned for one year, which is merely the compound sum of \$1 for one year. Therefore, the effective annual rate is equal to the compound sum of \$1 for one year, adjusted for the frequency of conversion, minus 1. Thus, \$1,000 invested for one year at 12 percent interest compounded quarterly provides an effective *annual* rate of 12.5509 percent.

$$\text{Effective annual rate} = \left(1 + \frac{r}{m}\right)^m - 1$$

$$.125509 = \left(1 + \frac{.12}{4}\right)^4 - 1 = (1.03)^4 - 1 = 1.125509 - 1$$

As a final point on the frequency of conversion, it can be argued that interest is really earned every second of the day, so compounding should be done continuously. Consequently, there are some savings and loan companies that pay interest compounded continuously, and there are some financial analysts who use continuous compounding in capital-budgeting problems. However, the familiarity of most businessmen with discrete compounding makes it much more widely used than continuous compounding.

In continuous compounding, the frequency of conversion approaches infinity as a limit. In other words, the frequency of conversion becomes very large and the interest period becomes very short. In such a case, $\left(1 + \frac{r}{m}\right)^{(m/r)}$ approaches the limit e, which is the base of the natural, or Napierian, system of logarithms, as shown below:

$$\begin{aligned} S &= P\left(1 + \frac{r}{m}\right)^{m \cdot t} \\ &= P\left(1 + \frac{r}{m}\right)^{(m/r)(r \cdot t)} \\ &= P \cdot e^{r \cdot t} \end{aligned}$$

where e = natural log = 2.71828

Since there are tables of e^{rt} available, as well as tables of e^x, computations using continuous compounding can easily be made. For instance, in the previous example of \$1,000 invested for two years at 12 percent interest, if interest is assumed to be compounded continuously, the compound sum is equal to \$1,271.20, and the effective annual rate is 12.75 percent.

$$\begin{aligned} S &= Pe^{rt} \\ \$1{,}271.20 &= \$1{,}000(2.71828)^{(.12)(2)} = \$1{,}000(1.2712) \\ \text{Effective rate} &= e^r - 1 \\ .1275 &= (2.71828)^{.12} - 1 = 1.1275 - 1 \end{aligned}$$

Present value. Present value is the opposite of compounding. The compound sum (amount) supplies the answer to the following question: Given the dollar amount of the investment *today,* the interest rate, and the time period, what is the future value (compound sum) of the investment? In contrast, present value supplies the answer to the following question: Given a known *future* amount, the interest rate, and the time period, what is the dollar amount that would have to be invested today to accumulate the future amount?

For example, we know that the compound amount of \$1,000 invested today at 6 percent interest compounded annually for three years is equal to \$1,191.02.

$$S = P(1 + i)^n = \$1{,}000(1.06)^3 = \$1{,}000(1.191016) = 1{,}191.02$$

Thus, the present value of \$1,191.02 three years hence at 6 percent interest compounded annually is equal to \$1,000. Or \$1,191.02 three years from now is *equivalent* to \$1,000 today, since \$1,000 could be invested today to earn 6 percent interest for three years and could accumulate to \$1,191.02. The \$1,000 is also called the *discounted amount* of \$1,191.02.

Since present value is the opposite of compounding, the formula for a compound sum can be used to derive the formula for the present value of a future sum. Hence, it is shown that present value (P) is equal to the known future sum divided by the compound sum of \$1:

$$S = P(1 + i)^n$$

$$P = \frac{S}{(1 + i)^n}$$

$$\$1{,}000 = \frac{\$1{,}191.02}{1.19102}$$

Note that the greater the interest rate (i) or the greater the number of time periods (n), the smaller the present value (P). In other words, a high interest rate and a long time period mean that a small P is needed to accumulate to a known S, in comparison to a small interest rate and a short time period. Obviously, the opposite is true of a compound amount.

Present value of \$1. The present-value formula shows that the present value of a known future sum is equal to the future amount multiplied by 1 over the compound sum of \$1.

$$P = \frac{S}{(1 + i)^n} = S\,\frac{1}{(1 + i)^n}$$

In other words, there is a reciprocal relationship between the compound sum of \$1 (s) and the present value of \$1 (denoted by p).

$$P = S\,\frac{1}{(1 + i)^n} = S\,\frac{1}{s} = S \cdot p$$

where

$$s = (1 + i)^n = \frac{1}{p}$$

$$p = \frac{1}{(1 + i)^n} = \frac{1}{s}$$

For instance, in the previous example of determining the \$1,000 present value of \$1,191.02 three years hence at 6 percent interest, the present value could have been calculated by dividing the compound amount of \$1 into 1 (the reciprocal) and multiplying the quotient (.839619) by \$1,191.02.

$$P = S\,\frac{1}{(1 + i)^n}$$

$$\$1{,}000 = \$1{,}191.02\,\frac{1}{(1.06)^3} = \$1{,}191.02\,\frac{1}{1.191016} = \$1{,}191.02(.839619)$$

Since present-value calculations are so widely used in financial analysis, and to avoid tedious division, tables of present values of \$1 are available (see Appendix) for computational purposes. Given any future amount, the pertinent present-value-of-\$1 factor (obtained from tables), multiplied by the known future amount, equals the present value. For example, what is the present value of \$10,500 five years hence at 5 percent interest? As shown in the abbreviated table below, the present value of \$1 for five years at 5 percent interest is .783526, and this factor multiplied by \$10,500 provides a present value of \$8,227.02.

$$p = \frac{1}{(1 + i)^n} = (1 + i)^{-n}$$

$$.783526 = \frac{1}{(1.05)^5} = (1.05)^{-5}$$

$$P = S \frac{1}{(1 + i)^n} = S(1 + i)^{-n} = S \cdot p$$

$$\$8{,}227.02 = \$10{,}500 \frac{1}{(1.05)^5} = \$10{,}500(1.05)^{-5} = \$10{,}500(.783526)$$

Present Value of \$1

Periods	3%	3½%	4%	4½%	5%	6%
1	.970874	.966184	.961538	.956938	.952381	.943396
2	.942596	.933511	.924556	.915730	.907029	.889996
3	.915142	.901943	.888996	.876297	.863838	.839619
4	.888487	.871442	.854804	.838561	.822702	.792094
5	.862609	.841973	.821927	.802451	.783526	.747258
6	.837484	.813501	.790315	.767896	.746215	.704961
7	.813092	.785991	.759918	.734828	.710681	.665057
8	.789409	.759412	.730690	.703185	.676839	.627412

Compound discount. Similar to compound interest (I), compound discount (denoted by D) is the excess of the compound amount over the present value.

$$D = S - P = I$$

The only difference between compound interest and compound discount is the time perspective; the former is a view of time progressing (P is known) and the latter is a view of time retrogressing (S is known). Compound discount can be calculated by multiplying the known future sum by the factor of 1 minus the present value of \$1.

$$D = S - P = S - S(1 + i)^{-n} = S[1 - (1 + i)^{-n}] = S(1 - p)$$

For instance, what is the compound discount on \$127,628.20 due five years hence at 5 percent interest? The compound discount is \$27,628.20, as shown below, and is the same as the compound interest computed on page 152.

$$D = S[1 - (1 + i)^{-n}] = S(1 - p)$$

$$\$27{,}628.20 = \$127{,}628.20[1 - (1.05)^{-5}] = \$127{,}628.20[1 - .783526]$$

Known amount and present value—compute unknowns. Given the investment today, the future amount, and the rate of interest, the number of required periods can be approximated from the appropriate tables. For example, if a person has \$25,000 to invest today at 5 percent to pay a debt of \$35,177.50, how many years will it take to accumulate enough to pay the loan? As shown below, the compound amount of \$1 (1.4071) is equal to the future amount (\$35,177.50) divided by the present value (\$25,000), and the present value of \$1 (.710681) is equal to the present value (\$25,000) divided by the future amount (\$35,177.50). Once either of these two factors is determined, the approximate amount of either factor can be found in the tables under the given rate column, and by referring to the corresponding periods column, the unknown number of years (7) can be found.

$$S = P(1+i)^n \quad \text{or} \quad P = S(1+i)^{-n}$$

$$(1+i)^n = \frac{S}{P} \qquad (1+i)^{-n} = \frac{P}{S}$$

$$(1.05)^n = \frac{\$35{,}177.50}{\$25{,}000} = 1.4071 \qquad (1.05)^{-n} = \frac{\$25{,}000}{\$35{,}177.50} = .710681$$

Therefore, $n = 7$ **Therefore, $n = 7$**

In a similar manner, given the investment today, the future amount, and the number of periods, the required interest rate can be approximated from the appropriate table. For example, based on the data in the preceding problem, the 1.4071 (or .710681) can be found in the amount-of-\$1 table (or present-value-of-\$1 table) by reading across the 7-periods row, and by referring to the corresponding interest-rate column, the required rate can be found (5 percent).

$$(1+i)^n = \frac{S}{P} \quad \text{or} \quad (1+i)^{-n} = \frac{P}{S}$$

$$(1+i)^7 = \frac{\$35{,}177.50}{\$25{,}000} = 1.4071 \qquad (1+i)^{-7} = \frac{\$25{,}000}{\$35{,}177.50} = .710681$$

Therefore, $i = 5\%$ **Therefore, $i = 5\%$**

The use of tables to find unknowns often does not give exact answers, but the approximate answers are close enough for most decision-making purposes. If more exact answers are needed, interpolation can be used with the tables, or approximate table answers can be avoided by using logarithms.

Series of payments or receipts. The previous discussion has concentrated on single lump-sum cash payments or receipts. We have discussed the compound amount of a known single lump-sum amount (principal) and the present value of a known single lump-sum future amount. However, many investment and borrowing decisions are concerned with a series of cash payments (receipts).

To determine the amount or present value of a series of cash flows, merely sum the compound amount or present value of each individual cash flow. For example, what is the amount at the end of three years of a series of cash deposits of \$900, \$1,500, and \$2,000, made at the end of each year, assuming that the interest rate is 5 percent? The \$4,795.61 solution can be determined by multiplying each cash flow by its pertinent compound amount of \$1 (obtained from tables) and summing them:

Let R **= periodic payment (receipt), usually called rent**

$$\text{Then } S = R_1(1+i)^{n-1} + R_2(1+i)^{n-2} + \cdots + R_{n-1}(1+i)^1 + R_n$$

$$\$4{,}567.25 = \$900(1.05)^2 + \$1{,}500(1.05)^1 + \$2{,}000$$

$$= \$900(1{,}1025) + \$1{,}500(1.05) + \$2{,}000$$

$$= \$992.25 + \$1{,}575 + \$2{,}000$$

Similarly, what amount needs to be invested today to assure a series of cash payments of \$1,100, \$1,500, and \$2,100 at the end of each year for three years, assuming that the interest rate is 6 percent? The \$4,222.22 solution can be determined by multiplying each cash flow by its pertinent present value of \$1 (obtained from tables) and summing:

$$P = R_1 \frac{1}{(1+i)^1} + R_2 \frac{1}{(1+i)^2} + \cdots + R_{n-1} \frac{1}{(1+i)^{n-1}} + R_n \frac{1}{(1+i)^n}$$

$$= R_1(1+i)^{-1} + R_2(1+i)^{-2} + \cdots + R_{n-1}(1+i)^{-(n+1)} + R_n(1+i)^{-n}$$

$$\$4{,}222.22 = \$1{,}100(1.05)^{-1} + \$1{,}500(1.05)^{-2} + \$2{,}100(1.05)^{-3}$$

$$= \$1{,}100(.952381) + \$1{,}500(.907029) + \$2{,}100(.863838)$$

$$= \$1{,}047.62 + \$1{,}360.54 + \$1{,}814.06$$

Annuities. In many instances, the series of cash flows in borrowing and investment situations are constant periodic amounts. In such a situation, we have what is called an *annuity*. An annuity is a series of *equal cash receipts or payments,* called rents, made at *uniform intervals of time,* such as annually, semiannually, or the like, at a *constant interest rate.* For the standard annuity, which is assumed in this book, interest is compounded once each time period, so that the payment (receipt) period is equal to the compound-interest period. Examples of annuities include interest payments on bonds, monthly loan payments, premiums on life insurance, payments to sinking funds, and constant cost savings.

There are several types of annuities, the type being determined by when the periodic payments occur. An *ordinary* annuity exists when the periodic payments (receipts) occur at the *end* of each period. An annuity *due* exists when the periodic payments (receipts) occur at the *beginning* of each period. A *deferred* annuity is one in which the periodic payments (receipts) do not begin until two or more periods have lapsed from the date of the original investment.

Amount of an ordinary annuity. The amount of an annuity is the sum of the compound amount of each rent; that is, the sum of the rents and compound interest thereon. The only difference between the amount of an ordinary annuity and the amount of a series of cash payments (receipts) is that in the former case, each rent is the same amount. Hence, we can use the previously discussed formula for the amount of a series of cash flows and factor out the constant periodic rent (denoted by R) to show that the amount of an ordinary annuity (denoted by S_a) is equal to the constant periodic rent multiplied by the sum of each period's compound amount of \$1, for n total periods.[3]

$$
\begin{aligned}
S_a &= R_1(1+i)^{n-1} + R_2(1+i)^{n-2} \\
&\qquad + \cdots + R_{n-2}(1+i)^2 + R_{n-1}(1+i)^1 + R_n \\
&= R_n + R_{n-1}(1+i)^1 + R_{n-2}(1+i)^2 \\
&\qquad + \cdots + R_2(1+i)^{n-2} + R_1(1+i)^{n-1}
\end{aligned}
$$

Since $R_1 = R_2 = R_3 = \cdots = R_n$

Then $S_a = R[1 + (1+i)^1 + (1+i)^2 + \cdots + (1+i)^{n-2} + (1+i)^{n-1}]$

Note that when rents occur at the end of each period (ordinary annuity), the last rent (R_n) occurs at the end of the last period and no interest is earned on it. This means that the amount of an ordinary annuity has one less interest period than the number of rents.

For example, assume that \$1,000 is to be deposited in a fund on December 31 of each year for four years, and that the interest rate is 3 percent per year, compounded annually. What is the amount of this annuity at the end of four years? Note that this is an ordinary annuity, since payments occur at the end of each year; therefore, the last payment (R_4) will earn no interest, and there will be four rent payments and three interest periods. Using the compound-amount-of-\$1 table, the amount is \$4,183.63, as shown below.

$$
\begin{aligned}
S_a &= R_n + R_{n-1}(1+i)^1 + R_{n-2}(1+i)^2 \\
&\qquad + \cdots + R_2(1+i)^{n-2} + R_1(1+i)^{n-1} \\
&= R_4 + R_3(1+i)^1 + R_2(1+i)^2 + R_1(1+i)^3 \\
\$4{,}183.63 &= \$1{,}000 + \$1{,}000(1.03)^1 + \$1{,}000(1.03)^2 + \$1{,}000(1.03)^3 \\
&= \$1{,}000 + \$1{,}000(1.03) + \$1{,}000(1.0609) + \$1{,}000(1.092727)
\end{aligned}
$$

Or

$$
\begin{aligned}
S_a &= R[1 + (1+i)^1 + (1+i)^2 + \cdots + (1+i)^{n-2} + (1+i)^{n-1}] \\
&= \$1{,}000[1 + (1.03)^1 + (1.03)^2 + (1.03)^3] \\
&= \$1{,}000(1 + 1.03 + 1.0609 + 1.092727) \\
&= \$1{,}000(4.183627) \\
&= \$4{,}183.63
\end{aligned}
$$

Since calculations of the amounts of ordinary annuities are quite common in financial problems, tables are available for the amount of an ordinary annuity of \$1 (see Appendix) to facilitate such calculations. To determine the amount of an ordinary annuity, merely find the pertinent amount of an ordinary annuity of \$1 (denoted by $s_{\overline{n}|i}$) in the table and multiply by the constant periodic rent. For

---

[3] The symbol S is often used to denote both the amount of a single lump sum and of an annuity, with the right-hand side of the equation indicating the former or the latter case. However, to clearly distinguish between the two, the amount of an *annuity* is denoted by S_a in this text.

instance, in the preceding problem of the amount of an ordinary annuity of $1,000 for four years at 3 percent interest, the abbreviated table below shows that the amount of an ordinary annuity of $1 for four years at 3 percent interest is 4.183627, and this factor multiplied by $1,000 equals the amount of $4,183.63. (Note that the 4.183627 factor from the table is the same as that found previously by summing each periodic compound amount of $1).

$$s_{\overline{n}|i} = \text{Amount of an ordinary annuity of \$1 for } n \text{ periods at } i \text{ rate of interest}$$

$$s_{\overline{4}|.03} = 4.183627$$

$$S_a = Rs_{\overline{n}|i}$$

$$\$4{,}183.63 = \$1{,}000 s_{\overline{4}|.03}$$

$$= \$1{,}000(4.183627)$$

Amount of an Ordinary Annuity of $1

Rents	3%	3½%	4%	4½%	5%	6%
1	1.000000	1.000000	1.000000	1.000000	1.000000	1.000000
2	2.030000	2.035000	2.040000	2.045000	2.050000	2.060000
3	3.090900	3.106225	3.121600	3.137025	3.152500	3.183600
4	4.183627	4.214943	4.246464	4.278191	4.310125	4.374600
5	5.309136	5.362466	5.416323	5.470710	5.525631	5.637093
6	6.468410	6.550152	6.632975	6.716892	6.801913	6.975319
7	7.662462	7.779408	7.898294	8.019152	8.142008	8.393838
8	8.892336	9.051687	9.214226	9.380014	9.549109	9.897468

Finally, since the formula for the amount of an ordinary annuity can be written as a constant periodic rent multiplied by the sum of each periodic compound amount of $1, this is equivalent to multiplying a constant by the sum of a geometric progression. Therefore, the formula for the amount of an ordinary annuity can also be written as the constant periodic rent multiplied by the quotient of the compound interest of $1.00 $[(1 + i)^n - 1]$ divided by the interest rate.

$$S_a = R[1 + (1 + i)^1 + (1 + i)^2 + \cdots + (1 + i)^{n-2} + (1 + i)^{n-1}]$$

$$= R\,\frac{(1 + i)^n - 1}{i}$$

$$\$4{,}183.63 = \$1{,}000\,\frac{(1.03)^4 - 1}{.03} = \$1{,}000\,\frac{1.125509 - 1}{.03} = \$1{,}000(4.18363)$$

Amount of an annuity due. Since rents occur at the beginning of each period for an annuity due, the number of interest periods equals the number of rent payments (receipts). This means that for the same number of periods, the only difference between the amount of an ordinary annuity and that of an annuity due is that the latter has *one more interest period.* Assuming a common date today, the first rent under an annuity due begins to earn interest immediately, while the first rent for an ordinary annuity does not begin to earn interest until the end of the first period. Similarly, the last rent payment earns no interest under an ordinary annuity, whereas the last rent for an annuity due earns interest for the last period. In other words, in comparison to the amount of an ordinary annuity, *each rent* of the amount of an annuity due earns interest for one more period. This difference is formalized below.

$$\textbf{Amount of an ordinary annuity} = R_1(1+i)^{n-1} + R_2(1+i)^{n-2} + \cdots + R_{n-1}(1+i)^1 + R_n(1)$$

$$\textbf{Amount of an annuity due} = R_1(1+i)^{n} + R_2(1+i)^{n-1} + \cdots + R_{n-1}(1+i)^2 + R_n(1+i)^1$$

Given this difference of one interest period between the amount of an ordinary annuity and that of an annuity due, the tables for the amount of \$1 for an ordinary annuity, which are readily available, can be used to calculate the amount of an annuity due. To calculate this amount, find the pertinent amount of an ordinary annuity of \$1 for $n + 1$ periods (for the one extra interest period of an annuity due) in the tables and subtract \$1 (for the last noninterest payment of an ordinary annuity of \$1), and the resulting amount of an annuity due of \$1 (denoted by $s_{\overline{n+1}|i} - 1$) is multiplied by the constant periodic rent.

For example, what is the amount of an annuity due of \$1,000 for three years at 5 percent interest? From the table of an amount of an ordinary annuity of \$1, the amount of \$1 for four years ($n + 1$) is 4.310125, and this factor minus 1 equals the amount of an annuity due of \$1 for three years, or 3.310125. The 3.310125 multiplied by \$1,000 equals the amount of \$3,310.13.[4]

$$s_{\overline{n+1}|i} - 1 = s_{\overline{4}|.05} - 1 = 4.310125 - 1 = 3.310125$$
$$S_a = R(s_{\overline{n+1}|i} - 1)$$
$$\$3{,}310.13 = \$1{,}000(3.310125)$$

The difference between the amounts of an ordinary annuity and an annuity due for the same number of periods is that each rent, for the latter, earns interest for one extra period. Hence the amount of an annuity due can also be calculated as follows: Multiply the amount of an ordinary annuity of \$1 by one plus the interest rate for one more period, and the resulting amount of an annuity due of \$1 is then multiplied by the constant periodic rent:

$$S_a = R(s_{\overline{n}|i})(1+i)$$
$$\$3{,}310.13 = \$1{,}000(s_{\overline{3}|.05})(1.05) = \$1{,}000(3.1525)(1.05) = \$1{,}000(3.310125)$$

Known amount—compute the rents. Given the amount of an ordinary annuity or an annuity due, and given tables of the amount of an ordinary annuity of \$1, unknown periodic rents can easily be computed. The formula for the amount of an annuity consists of the future amount, the periodic rent, and the amount of an annuity of \$1 at i rate for n periods; hence, given any two of these three data, the third can be determined. To calculate the unknown periodic rent, divide the known sum of an annuity by the known amount of an annuity of \$1:

[4] To avoid excess symbols, the symbol S_a is used to denote the amount of any type of annuity, with the right-hand side of the equation indicating the particular type of annuity (e.g., ordinary annuity, annuity due, or deferred annuity).

$$S_a = Rs_{\overline{n}|i}$$

$$R = \frac{S_a}{s_{\overline{n}|i}}$$

For example, what contributions must be made at the end of each of eight years to produce a fund of \$25,000 by the end of the eighth year, if the fund earns 5 percent interest, compounded annually? The annual rent has to be \$2,618.05 in order to have \$25,000 at the end of eight years, as shown below:

$$R = \frac{S_a}{s_{\overline{n}|i}}$$

$$\$2{,}618.05 = \frac{\$25{,}000}{s_{\overline{8}|.05}} = \frac{\$25{,}000}{9.549109}$$

As a second example, assume that a man desired to accumulate a fund that will amount to \$100,000 on his sixtieth birthday. He wishes to accumulate this fund by equal deposits on each of his birthdays, from his thirty-fifth through his fifty-ninth, a total of twenty-five deposits. On the assumption that the fund will earn 3 percent interest, compounded annually, what annual deposit should he make? The annual deposit would be \$2,662.90 in order to have \$100,000 on his sixtieth birthday, as shown below. (Note that this is an annuity due and that twenty-six periods require using the table in Appendix.)

$$R = \frac{S_a}{s_{\overline{n+1}|i} - 1}$$

$$\$2{,}662.90 = \frac{\$100{,}000}{s_{\overline{26}|.03} - 1} = \frac{\$100{,}000}{38.553042 - 1} = \frac{\$100{,}000}{37.553042}$$

Present value of an ordinary annuity. The present value of an annuity is a sum that, when invested at compound interest, will provide for the withdrawal of a stated number of rents at equal intervals. The interest earned increases the balance of the investment, and the rent withdrawals reduce it. The withdrawal of the last rent should exhaust the investment.

In an ordinary annuity, each rent is withdrawn at the end of a period, and the present value of the annuity (the sum invested) is computed as of the beginning of the first period (which is one period prior to the date of the first withdrawal). Therefore, unlike the amount of an ordinary annuity, the present value of an ordinary annuity has the same number of interest periods as the number of rents.

It was previously shown that the present value of a series of cash payments (receipts) is equal to the sum of the present value of each cash payment (receipt). By factoring out the constant periodic rent associated with an annuity, the formula for the present value of a series of cash payments (receipts) can be used to show that the present value of an ordinary annuity (denoted by P_a) is equal to the constant periodic rent multiplied by the sum of each period's present value of \$1.[5]

---

[5]Note that to distinguish between the present value of a single lump sum and an annuity, the former is denoted by P and the latter by P_a.

$$P_a = R_1 \frac{1}{(1+i)^1} + R_2 \frac{1}{(1+i)^2} + \cdots + R_{n-1} \frac{1}{(1+i)^{n-1}} + R_n \frac{1}{(1+i)^n}$$
$$= R_1(1+i)^{-1} + R_2(1+i)^{-2} + \cdots + R_{n-1}(1+i)^{-(n+1)} + R_n(1+i)^{-n}$$

Since $R_1 = R_2 = \cdots = R_n$

Then $P_a = R[(1+i)^{-1} + (1+i)^{-2} + \cdots + (1+i)^{-(n+1)} + (1+i)^{-n}]$

Since the sum in the brackets of the foregoing equation is the sum of a geometric progression, the present value of an ordinary annuity can also be written as the constant periodic rent multiplied by the quotient of the compound discount of $1 divided by the interest rate.

$$P_a = R \frac{1-(1+i)^{-n}}{i}$$

For example, how much has to be invested on January 1, 19+6, to provide for the withdrawal of $1,000 on December 31 of each of the years 19+6, 19+7, 19+8, and 19+9, assuming that interest is 3 percent compounded annually? Using the present-value-of-$1 table, the present value is $3,717.10, as shown below:

$$P_a = R[(1+i)^{-1} + (1+i)^{-2} + \cdots + (1+i)^{-(n+1)} + (1+i)^{-n}]$$
$$\$3{,}717.10 = \$1{,}000[(1.03)^{-1} + (1.03)^{-2} + (1.03)^{-3} + (1.03)^{-4}]$$
$$= \$1{,}000[.970874 + .942596 + .915142 + .888487]$$
$$= \$1{,}000(3.717099)$$

Or

$$P_a = R \frac{1-(1+i)^{-n}}{i}$$

$$\$3{,}717.10 = \$1{,}000 \frac{1-(1.03)^{-4}}{.03} = \$1{,}000 \frac{1-.888487}{.03} = \$1{,}000(3.7171)$$

To verify the calculations above, as well as to facilitate understanding of the present value of annuities, the following table of reduction is presented:

19+6:	
January 1—investment	$3,717.10
Add interest—3% of $3,717.10	111.51
Total	$3,828.61
Deduct rent—December 31	1,000.00
Balance, December 31	$2,828.61
19+7:	
Add interest—3% of $2,828.61	84.86
Total	$2,913.47
Deduct rent—December 31	1,000.00
Balance, December 31	$1,913.47
19+8:	
Add interest—3% of $1,913.47	57.40
Total	$1,970.87
Deduct rent—December 31	1,000,00
Balance, December 31	$ 970.87

19+9:

Add interest—3% of $970.87	29.13
Total	$1,000,00
Deduct rent—December 31	1,000.00
Balance, December 31	$ -0-

Since present-value-of-annuity calculations are so commonly used in financial analysis, tables of present value of an ordinary annuity of $1 are available (see Appendix) to facilitate computations. To determine the present value of an ordinary annuity, merely find the pertinent present value of an ordinary annuity of $1 (denoted by $p_{\overline{n}|i}$) in the table and multiply by the constant periodic rent.[6] For instance, in the preceding problem, the abbreviated table below shows that the present value of an ordinary annuity of $1 for four years at 3 percent interest is 3.717098, and this factor multiplied by $1,000 equals the present value of $3,717.10. (Note that the 3.717098 factor from the table is the same, after allowing for rounding, as that found previously by summing each periodic present value of $1.)

$p_{\overline{n}|i}$ = **Present value of an ordinary annuity of $1 for *n* periods at *i* rate of interest**

$$p_{\overline{4}|.03} = 3.717098$$

$$P_a = Rp_{\overline{n}|i}$$

$$\$3{,}717.10 = \$1{,}000(3.717098)$$

Present Value of an Ordinary Annuity of $1

Rents	3%	3½%	4%	4½%	5%	6%
1	.970874	.966184	.961538	.956938	.952381	.943396
2	1.913470	1.899694	1.886095	1.872668	1.859410	1.833393
3	2.828611	2.801637	2.775091	2.748964	2.723248	2.673012
4	3.717098	3.673079	3.629895	3.587526	3.545951	3.465106
5	4.579707	4.515052	4.451822	4.389977	4.329477	4.212364
6	5.417191	5.328553	5.242137	5.157872	5.075692	4.917324
7	6.230283	6.114544	6.002055	5.892701	5.786373	5.582381
8	7.019692	6.873956	6.732745	6.595886	6.463213	6.209794

Present value of an annuity due. Since rents occur at the beginning of each period, the present value of the first rent of an annuity due is not discounted back, because it is already in terms of present value. In contrast, the present value of the first rent of an ordinary annuity is discounted back one period, since the rent occurs at the end of the first period. Thus the number of *discount periods* for the present value of an annuity due is one less than the number of rents, and for the same number of time periods, is one less than the present value of an ordinary annuity. This difference is formalized below.

[6] The symbol $a_{\overline{n}|i}$ is often used to denote the present value of an ordinary annuity of $1. However, to be consistent with the commonly used *P* for present value, the symbol $p_{\overline{n}|i}$ is used in this text to denote the present value of an ordinary annuity of $1.

Present value of an ordinary annuity

$$= R_1 \frac{1}{(1+i)^1} + R_2 \frac{1}{(1+i)^2} + \cdots + R_{n-1} \frac{1}{(1+i)^{n-1}} + R_n \frac{1}{(1+i)^n}$$

$$= R_1(1+i)^{-1} + R_2(1+i)^{-2} + \cdots + R_{n-1}(1+i)^{-(n+1)} + R_n(1+i)^{-n}$$

Present value of an annuity due

$$= R_1(1) + R_2 \frac{1}{(1+i)^1} + \cdots + R_{n-1} \frac{1}{(1+i)^{n-2}} + R_n \frac{1}{(1+i)^{n-1}}$$

$$= R_1(1) + R_2(1+i)^{-1} + \cdots + R_{n-1}(1+i)^{-(n+2)} + R_n(1+i)^{-(n+1)}$$

Given this difference of one discount period between the present value of an ordinary annuity and that of an annuity due, the tables for the present value of \$1 for an ordinary annuity, which are readily available, can be used to calculate the present value of an annuity due. To calculate the present value of an annuity due, find the pertinent present value of an ordinary annuity of \$1 for $n - 1$ periods (for the one less discount period of an annuity due) in the tables and add \$1 (for the first nondiscount payment of an annuity due of \$1), and the resulting present value of an annuity due of \$1 (denoted by $p_{\overline{n-1}|} + 1$) is multiplied by the constant periodic rent.

For example, assume that A, the owner of certain real estate, agrees to lease it to B for five years, beginning January 1, 19+3, at an annual rental of \$1,000, payable January 1 of each year. B accepts the offer and asks A if he is willing to accept (instead of five annual rents) an immediate lump sum equal to the present value of the five rents, discounted at 5 percent. What is the present value of the five rents? From the table of the present value of an annuity of \$1, the present value of \$1 for four years ($n - 1$) is 3.545951, and this factor plus 1 equals the present value of an annuity due of \$1 for five years, or 4.545951. The 4.545951 multiplied by \$1,000 equals the present value of \$4,545.95:

$$p_{\overline{n-1}|i} + 1 = p_{\overline{4}|.05} + 1 = 3.545951 + 1 = 4.545951$$
$$P_a = R(p_{\overline{n-1}|i} + 1)$$
$$\$4{,}545.95 = \$1{,}000(4.545951)$$

Present value of a deferred annuity. A deferred annuity is one that does not begin to produce rents until after the expiration of two or more periods. For instance, "an annuity of five annual rents deferred three years" means that no rents will be paid during the first three years, and that the first of the five rents will be payable at the end of the fourth year.

The amount of a deferred annuity is the same as the amount of an ordinary annuity, since there is no accumulation until the first rent (that is, the deferral period does *not* affect the amount), and therefore will not be discussed further. However, the present value of a deferred annuity is not the same as the present value of an ordinary annuity until the lapse of the deferral period (that is, the deferral period affects present value). In other words, the original investment (or deposit) will earn interest over the deferral period, which is one period less than the number of periods prior to the first payment, assuming payments at the end of each annuity period; therefore, the present-value computation has to account for the interest earned over the deferral period.

To compute the present value of a deferred annuity, multiply the constant periodic rent by the difference that is calculated by taking the present value of an ordinary annuity of \$1 for n (number of rents) plus k (number of deferred periods) periods and subtracting the present value of an ordinary annuity of \$1 for k periods. The latter subtraction eliminates the nonexistent rents during the deferral period, and converts the present value of an ordinary annuity of \$1 for $n + k$ periods to the present value of n rents of \$1, deferred k periods. This can be formalized as follows:

$$\textbf{Present value of a deferred annuity} = R(p_{\overline{n+k}|i} - p_{\overline{k}|i}) = R[(p_{\overline{n}|i})(1+i)^{-k}]$$

For example, on January 1, 19+1, Brown purchases an annuity of five rents of \$1,000 each, the first rent to be payable January 1, 19+5. Although Brown does not receive his first rent until the expiration of four periods, it should be remembered that the first rent of an ordinary annuity is not payable until the expiration of one period; therefore, this annuity is deferred only three periods. What is the present value of the five rents, deferred three periods, with interest computed at the rate of 7 percent per annum? The present value is \$3,346.98, as shown below:

$$P_a = R(p_{\overline{n+k}|i} - p_{\overline{k}|i})$$

$$\$3{,}346.98 = \$1{,}000(p_{\overline{5+3}|.07} - p_{\overline{3}|.07}) = \$1{,}000(5.971299 - 2.624316)$$

$$= \$1{,}000(3.346983)$$

Known present value—compute the rents. The formula for the present value of an annuity consists of the present value, the periodic rent, and the present value of an annuity of \$1 at i rate for n periods; hence, given any two of these three data, the third can be determined. To calculate the unknown periodic rent, divide the known present value of an annuity by the known present value of an annuity of \$1.

$$P_a = Rp_{\overline{n}|i}$$

$$R = \frac{P_a}{p_{\overline{n}|i}}$$

For example, a man owes a debt of \$5,000, bearing 5 percent interest payable annually. He desires to pay the debt and interest in five equal annual installments, beginning one year hence. What equal annual installments will pay the debt and interest? The principal of the debt is the present value of an ordinary annuity; the annual payments are the rents. Therefore, the equal annual installments that will pay the principal and interest are \$1,154.87, computed as below:

$$R = \frac{P_a}{p_{\overline{n}|i}}$$

$$\$1{,}154.87 = \frac{\$5{,}000}{p_{\overline{5}|.05}} = \frac{\$5{,}000}{4.329477}$$

As a second example, assume that on January 1, 19+8, B offers to buy A's summer home for \$5,000, payable in five equal installments, which are to include 5 percent interest on the unpaid balance and a portion of the principal, the first of such payments to be made immediately. How much will each payment be? The \$5,000 principal sum is the present value of an annuity due of five unknown rents. Thus, the equal annual installments are \$1,099.88, as shown below:

$$R = \frac{P_a}{p_{\overline{n-1}|i} + 1}$$

$$\$1{,}099.88 = \frac{\$5{,}000}{p_{\overline{5-1}|.05} + 1} = \frac{\$5{,}000}{3.545951 + 1}$$

As a final example of computing rents, assume that on January 1, 19+4, A invests \$50,000 in an annuity at 4 percent compounded annually. The first rent of the annuity is payable to him January 1, 19+8, or four years after the annuity is purchased. A is buying an annuity of five rents deferred three periods. The present value at 4 percent of an annuity of five rents of \$1 deferred three periods is computed below; it is 3.957654. Thus, the annual rent that A will receive is \$12,633.75:

$$R = \frac{P_a}{p_{\overline{n+k}|i} - p_{\overline{n}|i}}$$

$$\$12{,}633.75 = \frac{\$50{,}000}{p_{\overline{8}|.04} - p_{\overline{3}|.04}} = \frac{\$50{,}000}{6.732745 - 2.775091} = \frac{\$50{,}000}{3.957654}$$

Given present value and rents—compute unknowns. The formula for the present value (or amount) of an annuity can be used to derive the formula for calculating the present value (or amount) of an annuity of \$1. Thus, if the present value (or amount) of an annuity and the constant rent are known, the *unknown present value (or amount) of \$1* can be calculated by dividing the known present value (or amount) by the known rent, as shown below:

$$P_a = Rp_{\overline{n}|i} \quad \text{or} \quad S_a = Rs_{\overline{n}|i}$$

$$p_{\overline{n}|i} = \frac{P_a}{R} \qquad s_{\overline{n}|i} = \frac{S_a}{R}$$

Once the present value (or amount) of an annuity of \$1 is calculated, then, given the interest rate, the number of periods can be determined, or given the number of periods, the interest rate can be determined. For example, if a person wants to invest \$74,932.95 today to insure \$15,000 payments to his mother at the end of each year for the next six years, what is the required interest rate? Dividing the present value (\$74,932.95) by the rent (\$15,000) equals 4.99553, which is the present value of an annuity of \$1 for six periods at *i* rate of interest. Referring to the table for the present value of an annuity of \$1, 4.99553 is found to be between 5.075692 and 4.917324, and referring to the corresponding rate columns, the former is found to be 5 percent and the latter 6 percent. Thus the investor must earn between 5 percent and 6 percent, which by interpolation is found to be $5\frac{1}{2}$ percent.

$$\left.\begin{array}{l} \left.\begin{array}{l} p_{\overline{6}|.05} = 5.075692 \\ p_{\overline{6}|i} = 4.995530 \end{array}\right\} .080162 \text{ difference} \\ p_{\overline{6}|.06} = 4.917324 \end{array}\right\} .158368 \text{ difference}$$

$$i = .05 + \frac{.080162}{.158368}(.06 - .05) = 5\tfrac{1}{2}\%$$

If the periodic rents are not equal, annuity tables cannot be used to find the unknown rate. Also, since the equation for the present value of a series of unequal rents involves i raised to various powers, the solving for i involves a tedious trial-and-error basis.

The rationale used to find the unknown rate is to find that rate that equates the present value of the future rents to the investment today. This is equivalent to finding that rate that makes the present value of all the cash flows (the net present value) equal to zero. That is, find i such that

$$P = R_1(1 + i)^{-1} + R_2(1 + i)^{-2} + \cdots + R_n(1 + i)^{-n}$$

$$= \sum_{t=1}^{n} R_t(1 + i)^{-t}$$

$$0 = -P + \sum_{t=1}^{n} R_t(1 + i)^{-t}$$

For example, in very simple terms, if \$1 is invested today to earn \$1.06 one year hence, then i equals 6 percent, which is the yield or rate of return, since 6 percent equates the future \$1.06 to \$1 today (that is, the net present value is zero).

$$1 = \frac{1.06}{1.06}$$

$$0 = -1 + \frac{1.06}{1.06}$$

Suppose that if \$7,094.41 is invested today, it will bring in future cash flows of \$1,000, \$2,000, \$3,000, and \$2,000 at the end of each year, respectively, for four years. What is the rate of return on this investment? By trial and error, various rates can be used to compute the present value of the cash flows until the rate is found that makes the net present value zero. If 4 percent is tried, the *positive* net present value of \$92.84 (as shown on page 169) indicates that the actual rate must be higher, since the higher the rate, the lower the present value. If 5 percent is tried, the *negative* net present value (shown on page 169) indicates that the actual rate must be lower, since a lower rate would increase the present value. Finally, if 4½ percent is tried, the net present value is *zero,* which indicates that the yield is 4½ percent.

$$0 = -P + \sum_{t=1}^{n} R_t(1 + i)^{-t}$$

At 4%:

$$\$92.84 = -\$7{,}094.41 + \$1{,}000(.961538) + \$2{,}000(.924556) + \$3{,}000(.888996) + \$2{,}000(.854804)$$
$$= -\$7{,}094.41 + \$7{,}187.25$$

At 5%:

$$-\$91.06 = -\$7{,}094.41 + \$7{,}003.35$$

At 4½%:

$$0 = -\$7{,}094.41 + \$7{,}094.41$$

Working with limited tables. AMOUNT OF \$1. If a particular compound amount of \$1 is not in the available tables, it can be computed several ways:

Multiply $1 + i$ successively, or $(1 + i)(1 + i)(1 + i) \cdots$, until n periods is reached. If the total number of periods is large, use the shortcut for computing the power of a number by multiplying together two or more other powers of that number, the sum of whose exponents is equal to the exponent of the power desired. (This shortcut can also be used when particular periods are missing in the tables.)

$$\text{Let } n = m + k$$
$$\text{then } (1 + i)^n = (1 + i)^{m+k} = (1 + i)^m(1 + i)^k$$
$$(1.05)^4 = (1.05)^2(1.05)^2$$

Find the present value of \$1 in the tables for the particular rate and number of periods wanted and divide into 1:

$$\frac{1}{p} = \frac{1}{(1 + i)^{-n}} = (1 + i)^n$$

Find the applicable amount of an annuity of \$1 in the tables ($s_{\overline{n}|i}$) and solve for the unknown $(1 + i)^n$ given n, i, and the formula:

$$s_{\overline{n}|i} = \frac{(1 + i)^n - 1}{i}$$

PRESENT VALUE OF \$1. If a particular present value of \$1 is not in the available tables, it can be computed several ways:

Compute $\frac{1}{1 + i}$ and then successively multiply by $\frac{1}{1 + i}$ until the desired number of periods is reached—i.e., $\left(\frac{1}{1 + i}\right)\left(\frac{1}{1 + i}\right)\left(\frac{1}{1 + i}\right)\cdots$, with the added shortcut that

$$\left(\frac{1}{(1 + i)^1}\right)\left(\frac{1}{(1 + i)^1}\right) = \frac{1}{(1 + i)^2}, \left(\frac{1}{(1 + i)^2}\right)\left(\frac{1}{(1 + i)^2}\right) = \frac{1}{(1 + i)^4}, \ldots$$

Find the compound amount of \$1 in the tables for the particular rate and number of periods wanted and divide into 1:

$$\frac{1}{s} = \frac{1}{(1+i)^n} = (1+i)^{-n}$$

Find the applicable present value of an annuity of \$1 in the tables ($p_{\overline{n}|i}$) and solve for the unknown $(1 + i)^{-n}$ given n, i, and the formula.

$$p_{\overline{n}|i} = \frac{1-(1+i)^{-n}}{i}$$

AMOUNT OF AN ANNUITY OF \$1. If a particular amount of an annuity of \$1 is not in the available tables, it can be computed several ways:

Use the formula $\frac{(1+i)^n - 1}{i}$, where $(1 + i)^n$ can be found in the tables or computed as discussed above.

Given the rate and the number of periods, find the present value of an annuity of \$1 ($p_{\overline{n}|i}$) and the amount of \$1 [$(1 + i)^n$] in the applicable tables and multiply the two together, since $s_{\overline{n}|i} = (1 + i)^n p_{\overline{n}|i}$.

PRESENT VALUE OF AN ANNUITY. If a particular present value of an annunty of \$1 is not in the available tables, it can be computed several ways:

Use the formula $\frac{1-(1+i)^{-n}}{i}$, where $(1 + i)^{-n}$ can be found in the tables or computed as discussed above.

Given the rate and the number of periods, find the amount of an annuity of \$1 ($s_{\overline{n}|i}$) and the present value of \$1 [$(1 + i)^{-n}$] in the applicable tables and multiply the two together, since $p_{\overline{n}|i} = (1 + i)^{-n} s_{\overline{n}|i}$.

Symbols. Many different symbols are used to express amounts and present values. To review the symbols and formulas used in this textbook, and to provide a contrast with some of the symbols used by others, the summary table on page 171 is presented.

The use of any other symbols need not be confusing. For example, if a problem states that

$$v^6 \text{ at } 5\% = .7462$$

it is obvious that the value given is a present value, since it is less than 1; clearly, it is the present value of \$1 at 5 percent, due six periods hence.

Or if the problem states that, at 4 percent, $q^7 = 1.31593178$, it is apparent that the value given is an amount, since it is more than 1; clearly, it cannot be the amount of an annuity of seven rents of \$1, since that amount would exceed 7. It is the amount of \$1 for seven periods.

If a problem states that s_8 at 3 percent is 8.89233605, the value (being in excess of 8) is obviously the amount of an annuity of eight rents of \$1.

Or if the problem states that $a_{\overline{6}|.04 1/2}$ is 5.15787248, the value (being somewhat less than 6) is apparently the present value of an annuity of six rents of \$1.

SYMBOLS AND FORMULAS
Used in this Text

Description	Symbols	Formulas	Symbols Used by Others
Amount of $1	s	$s = (1 + i)^n$	$a, q^n, a_{\overline{n}\rceil i}$
Present value of $1	p	$p = (1 + i)^{-n}$	$v^n, p_{\overline{n}\rceil i}$
Amount of a principal sum	S	$S = P(1 + i)^n$	A, a, S_n
Present value of a future sum	P	$P = S(1 + i)^{-n}$	p
Amount of an ordinary annuity of $1	$s_{\overline{n}\rceil i}$	$s_{\overline{n}\rceil i} = \dfrac{(1 + i)^n - 1}{i}$	$s_{\overline{n}\rceil}$ at i, $s_n, A, A_{\overline{n}\rceil i}$
Present value of an ordinary annuity of $1	$p_{\overline{n}\rceil i}$	$p_{\overline{n}\rceil i} = \dfrac{1 - (1 + i)^{-n}}{i}$	$a_{\overline{n}\rceil i}, a_{\overline{n}\rceil}$ at i, $a_n, P, P_{\overline{n}\rceil i}$
Amount of an ordinary annuity	S_a	$S_a = R \cdot s_{\overline{n}\rceil i} = R\dfrac{(1 + i)^n - 1}{i}$	A, S_n
Present value of an ordinary annuity	P_a	$P_a = R \cdot p_{\overline{n}\rceil i} = R\dfrac{1 - (1 + i)^{-n}}{i}$	A, A_n

Complications in problems. Problems in compound interest and annuities sometimes require careful analysis to determine what tables and procedures to use. Some illustrations of complicating conditions are presented below.

CASE 1: To what amount will an investment of $1,000 accumulate in twenty years if it earns 5 percent, compounded annually, for eight years, 4 percent for the next seven years, and 3 percent for the last five years?

Amount of $1 at 5% for 8 periods	1.47745544
Multiply by amount of $1 at 4% for 7 periods	1.31593178
Amount of $1 at end of 15 periods	1.94423057
Multiply by amount of $1 at 3% for 5 periods	1.15927407
Amount of $1 at end of 20 periods	2.25389609
Amount of $1,000	$2,253.90

CASE 2: Compute the amount of an annuity of fifteen rents of $1 if interest rates are:

Between dates of 1st and 5th rents—5%.
Between dates of 5th and 10th rents—4%.
Between dates of 10th and 15th rents—3%.

Amount of an ordinary annuity of 5 rents of $1 at 5%	5.52563125
Multiply by amount of $1 at 4% for 5 periods	1.21665290
Amount of first 5 rents at end of 10th year	6.72277528
Add amount of an ordinary annuity of 5 rents of $1 at 4%	5.41632256

Amount of first 10 rents at end of 10th year	12.13909784
Multiply by amount of $1 at 3% for 5 periods	1.15927407
Amount of first 10 rents at end of 15th year	14.07254136
Add amount of an ordinary annuity of 5 rents of $1 at 3%	5.30913581
Amount of annuity of $1 at end of 15 years	19.38167717

CASE 3: What is the present value, on January 1, 1979, of an annuity of fifteen rents of $1, payable on December 31 of the years 1979 to 1993, inclusive, if interest rates are as stated below?

1979—1983	5%
1984—1988	4%
1989—1993	3%

Present value, on January 1, 1989, of last 5 rents—present value of ordinary annuity of 5 rents of $1 at 3%	4.57970719
Multiply by present value of $1 at 4% for 5 periods	.82192711
Present value, on January 1, 1984, of last 5 rents	3.76418550
Add present value of ordinary annuity of 5 rents of $1 at 4%	4.45182233
Present value, on January 1, 1984, of last 10 rents	8.21600783
Multiply by present value of $1 at 5% for 5 periods	.78352617
Present value, on January 1, 1979, of last 10 rents	6.43745715
Add present value of ordinary annuity of 5 rents of $1 at 5%	4.32947667
Present value, on January 1, 1979, of the 15 rents	10.76693382

CASE 4: A man makes a series of unequal payments into a fund, which earns interest at increasing rates, compounded annually, all as indicated below:

	Deposits	Interest Rates
December 31, 1979–1983	$1,000	1979–1983 3%
December 31, 1984–1988	1,200	1984–1988 4%
December 31, 1989–1993	1,500	1989–1993 5%

What amount will be in the fund on December 31, 1993?

	First Series	Second Series	Third Series
Years 1979–1983:			
Amount of ordinary annuity of 5 rents of $1 at 3%	5.30913581		
Years 1984–1988:			
Multiply by amount of $1 at 4% for 5 periods	1.21665290		
Amount of ordinary annuity of 5 rents of $1 at 4%		5.41632256	
Amounts, December 31, 1988, per dollar of deposit	6.45937548	5.41632256	
Years 1989–1993:			
Multiply by amount of $1 at 5% for 5 periods	1.27628156	1.27628156	
Amount of ordinary annuity of 5 rents of $1 at 5%			5.52563125

Amounts, December 31, 1993, per dollar of deposit	8.24398181	6.91275261	5.52563125
Deposits	\$1,000.00	\$1,200.00	\$1,500.00
Amounts, December 31, 1993	\$8,243.98	\$8,295.30	\$8,288.45
Summary:			
First series	\$ 8,243.98		
Second series	8,295.30		
Third series	8,288.45		
Total	\$24,827.73		

CASE 5: An individual wants to create a fund, on a 3 percent basis, which will enable him to withdraw \$2,500 per year on June 30, 2000, and each year thereafter to and including June 30, 2020. To provide this fund, he intends to make equal contributions on June 30th of each of the years 1980 to 1999. What contributions must he make?

The amount that will be in the fund on June 30, 1999, is the amount of an ordinary annuity of twenty rents (contributions) at 3 percent. If we knew this amount, we could divide it by the amount of an ordinary annuity of twenty rents of \$1 at 3 percent to determine the contributions. The problem does not state the amount, but we can determine it because we know that it must be the present value of an ordinary annuity of the twenty-one annual rents to be withdrawn, starting June 30, 2000. Therefore, the problem can be solved by the following procedure:

Rents to be withdrawn	\$ 2,500
Multiply by present value of an ordinary annuity of 21 rents of \$1 at 3%	15.41502414
Present value of annuity of 21 rents of \$2,500, or amount to be in the fund on June 30, 1999	\$ 38,537.56
Divide by amount of an ordinary annuity of 20 rents of \$1 at 3%	26.87037449
Annual contributions	\$ 1,434.20

CASE 6: Assume the same facts as before, except that only fifteen contributions are to be made (the last on June 30, 1994); twenty-one withdrawals are to be made, as before, starting on June 30, 2000.

Because of the waiting period, the amount in the fund on June 30, 1994, is the present value of an annuity of twenty-one rents deferred five periods. (Although there are six years between June 30, 1994, and June 30, 2000, there is one period of waiting in an ordinary annuity.) Then the solution proceeds as follows:

Present value of an ordinary annuity of 26 rents of \$1 at 3%	17.87684242
Deduct present value of an ordinary annuity of 5 rents of \$1 at 3%	4.57970719
Present value of an annuity of 21 rents of \$1 deferred 5 periods	13.29713523
Multiply by rent to be withdrawn	\$ 2,500
Amount that should be in the fund on June 30, 1994	\$ 33,242.84
Divide by amount of an ordinary annuity of 15 rents of \$1	18.59891389
Annual contributions	\$ 1,787.35

CASE 7: A bond issue of \$500,000, dated January 1, 1980, is to be paid in five

equal annual installments, beginning December 31, 1991. To provide for these payments, the issuing company will create a fund by making fifteen annual contributions of equal amount on December 31, 1981 to 1995, inclusive. The fund will be on a 4 percent basis. What annual contribution should be made?

To determine the contributions, we must divide some actual, or theoretical, accumulated fund amount by the amount of an annuity of $1 at 4 percent for the number of periods from December 31, 1980, to the date as of which the actual or theoretical fund amount would be accumulated.

The amount that will be in the fund on December 31, 1991, cannot be computed until the unknown contributions are determined; and the amount in the fund on December 31, 1995, will be zero.

However, we do know that if the equal installments of $100,000 to be withdrawn on December 31 of the years 1991 to 1995 were immediately reinvested at 4 percent, they would amount, on December 31, 1995, to $100,000 × 5.41632256 (amount of ordinary annuity of five rents of $1 at 4 percent), or $541,632.26.

Then $541,632.26 is the amount to which the sinking fund would accumulate on December 31, 1995, if no withdrawals were made from it.

And $541,632.26 ÷ 20.02358764 (amount of ordinary annuity of fifteen rents of $1 at 4 percent) = $27,049.71, the annual contribution.

CASE 8: A man invests $1,000 in a fund on December 31 of each of the years 1980 to 1989, inclusive. The fund earns 5 percent per year, compounded semiannually. How much will be in the fund on December 31, 1989?

The effective interest rate per year (the period between deposits) is $(1.025)^2 - 1$, or $1.050625 - 1$, or 5.0625 percent. We have no table at this rate. But we can compute the amount of an annuity of ten rents of $1 at 5.0625 percent by applying the formula $s_{\overline{n}|i} = \dfrac{(1 + i)^n - 1}{i}$.

The amount of $1 for ten periods at 5.0625 percent per period is the same as the amount of $1 for twenty periods at $2\frac{1}{2}$ percent per period. This is shown by the $2\frac{1}{2}$ percent table to be 1.63861644. Then

$$s_{\overline{10}|.050625} = .63861644 \div .050625 = 12.61464572$$

and the accumulated amount in the fund is

$$\$1,000 \times 12.61464572 = \$12,614.65$$

7

Discounted-Cash-Flow Valuation: Bonds

Introduction. As discussed in Chapter 6, conceptually the valuation of assets and liabilities should be based on the discounted amount (present value) of their future cash flows. However, it was also pointed out that the actual implementation of discounted-cash-flow valuation is extremely difficult because of the uncertainty of the future cash flows, discount rate, and time period, as well as the difficulty in isolating future cash flows as being directly attributable to specific, individual assets and liabilities.

On the other hand, because bond contracts specify the time period, interest rate, and amount due at maturity, the future cash outlays associated with the bonds can be objectively estimated. Thus it is possible to use direct valuation of bonds by discounting their future interest payments and maturity amount at the effective rate of interest (yield) when the bonds are issued (debtor) or acquired (investor). Note, however, that by using the effective rate of interest at the time of bond issuance (acquisition), discounted-cash-flow valuation of bonds is consistent with historical-cost valuation. Consequently, it should be understood that this chapter ties in with Chapter 6 on valuation by illustrating the implementation of discounted-cash-flow valuation in the accounting for bonds.

Nature of bonds. A bond is a written contract to pay a fixed future amount (maturity or redemption amount) and fixed future periodic interest. Consequently, companies issue bonds in order to borrow large sums of money for long-term uses, and investors (lenders) acquire bonds in order to earn interest over a long period of time. From the viewpoint of the company issuing bonds, they are a long-term liability, since the obligation to make future payments extends beyond the normal operating cycle or one year, whichever is longer. To the investor acquiring bonds, they are a long-term investment, since the claims to receive future payments extend beyond the normal operating cycle or one year, whichever is longer. Thus the bond issuer and the bond investor represent two sides of the same transaction, a reciprocal relationship, and the accounting for them is conceptually the same; hence, the accounting for both bond investment and bond liability is presented in this chapter.

The terms of the agreement between the borrower (company issuing the bonds) and lenders (investors) are specified in a bond contract, called a bond indenture, which is normally held by a trustee (bank or trust company), who acts as an independent third party to protect the interests of the borrower and lenders involved. The bond indenture normally includes the following:

Amounts authorized to be issued
Maturity amount and date
Interest rate and interest dates
Sinking-fund provisions
Property pledged as security
Trustee's access to issuing company's books and records
Bond certification by trustee
Bond restrictions as to working capital, dividends, and prescribed ratios (such as bonds outstanding to net tangible assets)
Other bond provisions, such as call provisions, conversion privileges, and the like

Because of the large amount of money borrowed, a bond issue is divided into individual bonds with denominations of $100, $1,000, or $10,000 (other denominations can be used), so that more than one lender can participate in the loan. In other words, it is easier to borrow a large sum of money from a number of lenders than it is from a single lender. Thus bonds are sold directly to individual investors, sold to (underwritten by) an investment banker or syndicate who in turn markets the bonds, or sold directly to a financial institution without the aid of an underwriter. In this regard, underwriting consists of one of the following plans: the actual purchase and resale of the bonds by the underwriter, sale of the bonds by the underwriter less a sales commission, or an agreement whereby the underwriter takes over at a certain future time all bonds not sold by the issuing company at that time.

The denomination of a bond, such as $1,000, is called its face or par value, which we will refer to as its *face amount.* The fixed contractual amount of a bond that is payable upon maturity is called the maturity or redemption value, which we will refer to as the *maturity amount.*[1] In the usual situation, where the face amount and maturity amount are the same, the bonds are said to be redeemable at par. In those unusual situations where the maturity amount differs from the face amount, the maturity amount is expressed as a percentage of the face amount with the percentage sign omitted: $100,000 bond, maturity amount 104 (that is, 1.04 × $100,000 = $104,000).

The contractual interest rate of a bond is called its nominal, stated, or coupon rate, and is expressed as an annual rate. Since bond interest is normally paid semiannually, the face amount multiplied by one-half the annual nominal rate is equal to the total interest paid by the issuing company every six months.[2] Consequently, a 6 percent, $100,000 bond pays interest of $3,000 (= $100,000 × .06 × ½ = $100,000 × .03) semiannually.

The actual rate of interest expense incurred by the company issuing the bonds, or the actual rate of interest earned by bondholders, is called the effective or yield rate of interest. It is the prevailing market rate of interest when the bonds are issued or bought; hence, it is the annual interest rate to maturity. The effective rate of interest is the rate that equates the discounted amount of the future interest payments and maturity amount to the price of the bonds. Unlike the nominal interest rate, which is determined by the issuing company and is fixed by contract, the effective interest rate is determined in the money market for bonds of similar risk and maturity.

When bonds are sold (bought) at a price equal to the face amount, the bonds are said to be sold (bought) at par, and the effective interest rate is the same as the nominal interest rate. If bonds are sold (bought) at a price above the face amount, the bonds are said to be sold (bought) at a premium, and the nominal interest rate is greater than the effective interest rate. Conversely, if bonds are sold (bought) at a price below the face amount, the bonds are said to be sold (bought) at a discount, and the nominal interest rate is less than the effective interest rate. In other words, the nominal rate of interest is, in effect, adjusted to the effective interest rate by the market price at which the bonds are sold (bought), since the nominal interest rate and maturity amount are fixed by contract. The prevailing market rate of interest at date of issuance or acquisition determines the bond price.

Types of bonds. Bonds can be classified as to the nature of the business of the debtor (obligor), the nature of the obligation, the evidence of ownership, and the nature of maturity, as illustrated below:

---

[1]Because *value* has several different meanings, it is a highly confusing term that should be avoided where possible; hence, we will use the terms *face amount* and *maturity amount,* instead of *face value* and *maturity value.*

[2]This assumes that one-half the annual nominal rate results in a rate compounded semiannually that is equivalent to the annual rate. Although assumed in actual practice for convenience, in reality this is not true. For example, 3% interest compounded semiannually is equivalent to an annual rate of 6.09% [= $(1.03)^2 - 1$], not 6%.

Bond classification according to the nature of business of obligor:

Governments

Municipals, such as cities and other government subdivisions

Public utilities, such as gas and electric companies, city bus lines, and so forth

Railroads

Industrials, such as manufacturing and trading concerns

Real estate, such as apartments, hotels, office buildings and so forth

Bond classification as to the nature of obligation:

Mortgage bonds. These are bonds secured by a mortgage, whereby the mortgage creates a lien on specified assets as security for the amount borrowed. Mortgages may be used with either notes or bonds. If the borrower is able to find a person who is willing to loan the entire amount desired, the note and mortgage may be used; the note recites the terms of the obligation, and the mortgage serves as the security. Although such obligations secured by mortgages are often called *mortgages payable,* the expression is not strictly correct, and a more precise title would be *long-term mortgage notes.*

If it is necessary to borrow the money from a number of persons, the bond and trust deed are used. The bond issue creates a number of obligations, all of equal rank and all equally secured. However, because there are a number of lenders, because these lenders are not known when the bond issue is being arranged, and because the lenders will change with each transfer of a bond, a mortgage cannot name the lenders personally as the transferees of the pledged property. Therefore, a trust deed, rather than a mortgage deed, is used. Corporations, when borrowing funds on long-term bond issues, generally use the trust deed. By such a deed the corporation conveys the property to a third person, usually a bank or a trust company, as trustee. Upon final payment of the bonds by the corporation, the trustee executes and delivers to the corporation a release deed, whereby the lien on the corporate property created by the trust deed is removed. In the event of a default in payment of the bonds, the trustee may commence foreclosure proceedings for the benefit of the bondholders. It should be understood, therefore, that the issuance of bonds secured by a trust deed is, for all practical purposes, a mortgage transaction and is so considered by law.

Bonds may be secured by first, second, third, and even more mortgages. If the obligations are not met and foreclosure ensues, the proceeds of the property must go first to the satisfaction of the first-mortgage bondholders, any residue to the satisfaction of the second-mortgage bondholders, and so on. Bonds secured by prior liens are called underlying bonds; the others are called junior bonds.

The mere fact that a bond is called a first-mortgage bond does not necessarily mean that it has a lien prior to all others. To illustrate, assume that each of three companies, A, B, and C, has two mortgages on its property. A consolidation is effected by which the three companies are combined, and a new issue of bonds is marketed, secured by a mortgage on all of the property. This issue might be called First Consolidated Bonds, but it is really secured by a third mortgage. On the other hand, assume that first-, second-, and third-mortgage bonds have been issued, and that the first and second have been paid; the third-mortgage bonds really have a first lien on the pledged property.

Collateral trust bonds. Collateral trust bonds are similar to collateral notes in that they are secured by pledged collateral. To illustrate, assume that a corporation holds stocks and bonds of several subsidiaries. The tangible property of the holding company and the subsidiaries may be mortgaged to the point where junior mortgage issues cannot be marketed; therefore, the holding company issues its own bonds and places the stocks and bonds of the subsidiaries in the hands of a trustee as collateral.

Guaranteed bonds. A corporation obligates itself to pay the principal of and interest on its bonds, but it cannot guarantee to do so. If a guarantee is made, it must be made by a third party. Sometimes a holding company will guarantee the principal and interest of the bonds of its subsidiaries, and sometimes a company leasing the property of another company will guarantee the bonds of that company.

Debenture bonds. A debenture bond, or debenture, is merely an unsecured bond. It is similar to an unsecured note, in that it rests on the general credit of the debtor. It may or may not be a safe investment, depending upon the financial condition of the issuing company.

Income bonds. The peculiar feature of an income bond is that the payment of interest is conditional upon the earning of income. If the debtor company's income is not sufficient to pay the interest, there is no obligation to pay interest. The bond may be cumulative or noncumulative. If cumulative, any interest not paid in one year becomes a lien against future earnings; if noncumulative, any interest lost in one year is lost forever. The principal may or may not be secured.

Such bonds are sometimes used in reorganizations, in which a scaling-down of interests results in security holders' taking a less desirable form of security than the one formerly held.

Participating bonds. These are sometimes called *profit-sharing bonds,* because, in addition to assuring the holder a definite rate of return regardless of operating results, they entitle him to participate with the stockholders in the earnings of the company. The participation may be pro rata or limited.

Convertible bonds. A convertible bond gives its holder the right to exchange the bond for some other security, usually common stock, of the issuing company. The bond stipulates the terms on which the transfer can be made—that is, par for par; or par for the bond and book amount (value) for the stock; or par and accrued interest for the bond and par and "accrued" dividends for the stock; or any other arrangement.

Such bonds give the holder a more assured income and secured principal during the development period of the issuing company than he might have as a stockholder, with a right to become a stockholder if the company is successful.

Bond classification as to the evidence of ownership:

Registered bonds:

Registered both as to principal and as to interest. The name of the owner of the bond is registered on the books of the issuing company or its fiscal agent, and interest is paid by check, drawn to the order of the bondholder. This method has the advantage of safeguarding the owner against loss or theft, because the transfer of a stolen bond could be accomplished only by a forgery. On the other hand, a sale and transfer can be made only by assignment and registry, instead of by delivery.

Registered as to principal only. If the bond is registered as to principal only, and coupons for the interest are attached, the owner is safeguarded against loss or theft of principal, and the debtor company is relieved of the burden of issuing interest checks.

No registration—coupon bonds:

Such a bond is transferable by delivery, without endorsement; interest is collected by clipping coupons and presenting them to a bank for deposit or collection.

Bond classification as to the nature of maturity:

Straight or ordinary bonds, which mature all at one time (i.e., a single fixed maturity)

Serial bonds, which provide for the repayment of the maturity amount in periodic installments (i.e., maturity at stated installments)[3]

---

[3]Serial bonds are covered in James A. Gentry, Jr., and Glenn L. Johnson, *Finney and Miller's Principles of Accounting: Advanced,* 6th ed. (Englewood Cliffs, N.J.: Prentice-Hall, Inc., 1971), pp. 343–44.

Callable or redeemable bonds, which provide the issuing company with the option of redeeming (retiring) the bonds at a stated price before the maturity date

Bond valuation. Bond valuation has to do with the accountant's assigning dollar amounts to the bond liability (issuing company's viewpoint) and to the bond investment (investor's viewpoint), as well as to the changes in both, for purposes of recording and reporting. For the company issuing the bonds, valuation is based on the market selling price of the bonds at the time of issuance, and for the bond investor, valuation is based on the market purchase price of the bonds at the time of acquisition.

The market price of a bond depends on the prevailing market rate of interest when the bonds are sold or purchased. This market rate of interest reflects the financial risk (risk of default by the company issuing the bonds) underlying the bonds, and the supply and demand conditions of comparable bonds. The price of bonds adjusts to the prevailing market rate of interest by investors' bid prices, with the prices based on the normal assumption that the terms of the bond contract will be fulfilled in the future. Thus, investors' bid prices for bonds reflect the purchase of the future maturity amount and future periodic interest at the prevailing market rate of interest—the effective or yield rate to maturity. It follows that the price of a bond is equal to the discounted amount (present value) of the future maturity amount and future periodic interest, where the discount rate is the effective interest rate to maturity. It also follows that the effective interest rate is the rate that equates the discounted amount of the future maturity amount and future periodic interest to the price of the bond.

Because the nominal interest rate of a bond is fixed by contract, the nominal rate can differ from the effective interest rate. This is the result of fluctuations in the market rate of interest between the time of getting new bonds ready for issue and the final issuance date, and between the time of original issue and the current dates of buying and selling outstanding bonds. Consequently, the price of a bond will reflect the market rate of interest prevailing when the bonds are issued or acquired, or bought and sold by investors, since this is the yield rate at which investors are willing to acquire the bonds.

If the market rate of interest for comparable securities is above the nominal rate of a bond, then no rational investor will buy the bond at face amount, because he can obtain a higher yield elsewhere. In order for the bond to sell, it has to be sold at enough of a discount off the face amount so that the investor's yield on the bond is equal to the higher market rate of interest for comparable securities. Similarly, if the coupon rate is above the market rate of interest, then the rational bond seller will sell the bond only at enough of a premium above the face amount so that the investor's yield is equal to the lower market rate of interest. Finally, if the coupon rate and market rate are equal, then the bond will sell at face amount (par). In other words, with fixed nominal rates stated on bond certificates, market prices of bonds adjust upward and downward depending on market rates of interest.

The market price of bonds at the date of issuance (or acquisition), which is determined by the yield rate of interest at that time, is used by accountants in the valuation of bonds for reporting purposes. Since the price is equal to the discounted amount (present value) of the future maturity amount and future periodic interest at the effective rate of interest at the date of issuance (acquisition), it is this discounted amount that is reported in the balance sheet. Thus, at the end of a fiscal period, the bonds are reported at their discounted amount over the remaining life of the bonds, with the face amount, nominal interest rate, maturity date, and any discount or premium reported parenthetically. Bonds can also be reported, as is traditionally done, at the face amount plus any premium or less any discount, with the nominal rate and maturity date reported parenthetically.

Note that bond valuation in current accounting practice is based on the effective rate of interest at the time of issuance (acquisition), which means that subsequent changes in the market rate of interest—and therefore changes in the current market price—for similar bonds are ignored in accounting for bonds outstanding or held. This accounting treatment of bonds is consistent with historical-cost valuation, since the bonds are reported at the past exchange price at the time of issuance (acquisition), plus or minus any unamortized bond premium or discount. It is also consistent with the revenue-recognition assumption, since unrealized holding gains or losses on the bonds are not recognized. The underlying rationale of such treatment is that the effective rate at issuance is the committed rate of the issuing company to maturity. Similarly, the effective rate at acquisition is the yield rate of return to maturity on the investor's bond investment.

If bond valuation were based on the current yield rate of comparable bonds at the financial-statement preparation date, then bonds would be reported at current selling price (less selling commissions) or at current replacement cost (including selling commissions). Also, the write-up or write-down of the bonds to current selling price would affect the valuation of net assets (assets minus liabilities) and therefore affect net income (the change in net assets from the beginning to the end of the fiscal period, after adjusting for any capital changes). Under replacement-cost valuation, holding gains and losses on the bonds would be reported to show the additional savings (cost) by borrowing or investing at terms more favorable (less favorable) than those currently existing at the financial-statement preparation date.

ILLUSTRATIONS OF BOND VALUATION: As previously discussed, the price of a bond is equal to the discounted amount of its future periodic interest plus its maturity amount, discounted at the effective rate of interest at the date of issuance or acquisition. It is this price that accountants use in the valuation of bonds for accounting purposes; hence, we now turn to some illustrations of bond valuation.

Assume that a \$100,000 bond issue, consisting of 100 bonds with a face amount of \$1,000 each, bearing 6 percent interest payable semiannually on January 1 and July 1, and due in four years, is sold at par (face amount) on January 1, 19+1. Since the company issuing the bonds receives \$100,000 and the bond investors pay \$100,000 for the bonds, the effective interest rate to be incurred (bond issuer) and earned (bond investors) is 6 percent. Comparable bonds must be yielding 6 percent, or the investors would not be willing to acquire the bonds at par in order to obtain a yield of 6 percent.

Since the bonds have a four-year maturity and pay interest semiannually, the number of interest periods is eight (= 2 × 4 years) and the nominal rate and effective rate are both 6 percent, or 3 percent (= 6%/2) semiannually. Given this information and the fact that the bonds are issued (acquired) at par, the price of the bond issue is equal to the $100,000 face amount, as illustrated below by discounting the future interest payments ($100,000 × .03 = $3,000) and the maturity amount ($100,000) at the 6 percent effective annual rate, or 3 percent semiannually.

Let P = Present amount (value), or discounted amount, of the bonds
F = Face amount of the bonds
r = Nominal (coupon) rate per interest period
i = Effective rate (yield) per interest period
M = Maturity amount
n = Number of interest periods
$p_{\overline{n}|i}$ = Present amount (value), or discounted amount, of an ordinary annuity of $1 for n periods at i rate of interest, obtained from tables (see the appendix at the end of the book)
$(1 + i)^{-n}$ = Present amount (value), or discounted amount, of $1 for n periods at i rate of interest, obtained from tables (see appendix at the end of the book)

$$
\begin{aligned}
\textbf{Then } P &= F \cdot r \cdot p_{\overline{n}|i} + M(1 + i)^{-n} \\
&= (\$100{,}000)(.03)p_{\overline{8}|.03} + (\$100{,}000)(1.03)^{-8} \\
&= (\$3{,}000)(7.019692) + (\$100{,}000)(.789409) \\
&= \$100{,}000
\end{aligned}
$$

As a second illustration, assume that at the time of the issuance of the $100,000 of bonds, the market rate of interest for comparable bonds is 7 percent, instead of 6 percent as in the preceding illustration. Since the nominal rate of interest fixed by the bond contract is only 6 percent, bond investors will not be willing to acquire the bonds at par, because they will demand a rate of return equal to the existing market rate of interest, or 7 percent. To avoid amending the bond contract with its fixed face amount and nominal rate, the bonds will sell at a price below the face amount, whereby the amount of the bond discount (face amount minus price) is such that the bond investors will obtain a yield to maturity on their investment at the 7 percent market rate of interest, or 3½ percent (= .07/2) semiannually. Under such conditions, the bond investors would pay $96,563 for the bonds, instead of the $100,000 face amount, as demonstrated below, because $96,563 is the discounted amount of the future periodic interest ($3,000) and maturity amount ($100,000) at the 7 percent effective annual rate, or 3½ percent semiannually.

$$
\begin{aligned}
P &= F \cdot r \cdot p_{\overline{n}|i} + M(1 + i)^{-n} \\
&= (\$100{,}000)(.03)p_{\overline{8}|.035} + (\$100{,}000)(1.035)^{-8} \\
&= (\$3{,}000)(6.873956) + (\$100{,}000)(.759412) \\
&= \$96{,}563
\end{aligned}
$$

By issuing \$100,000 of bonds for \$96,563, the effective interest expense for the issuing company is at the annual rate of 7 percent, not 6 percent, because the company obtains the use of only \$96,563, but pays interest on the \$100,000 face amount and pays \$100,000 upon maturity. Similarly, if they acquired the \$100,000 bonds at par, the bond investors would earn a yield to maturity of 6 percent; however, since they paid only \$96,563, their yield to maturity is 7 percent, because they recover the \$3,437 (= \$100,000 − \$96,563) bond discount when the bonds mature at \$100,000 and receive periodic interest on the \$100,000 face amount. Thus, when the yield rate exceeds the nominal rate, the bonds sell at a discount, where the amount of the discount is sufficient to make up the difference between the nominal rate specified in the bond contract and the higher market rate of interest that the investors demand. Consequently, the price of the bond issue is also equal to the difference between the nominal and effective interest per semiannual period, discounted at the effective rate of interest per semiannual period, plus the maturity amount, as demonstrated below.

$$
\begin{aligned}
P &= F(r - i)p_{\overline{n}|i} + M \\
&= (\$100{,}000)(.03 - .035)p_{\overline{8}|.035} + \$100{,}000 \\
&= (\$100{,}000)(-.005)(6.873956) + \$100{,}000 \\
&= \$96{,}563
\end{aligned}
$$

As a final illustration, assume that at the time of the issuance of the \$100,000 of bonds, the market rate of interest for comparable bonds is 5 percent. Since the nominal rate of interest fixed by the bond contract (6 percent) is greater than the market rate of interest (5 percent), the rational bond issuer would not be willing to sell the bonds at par. Instead, the bond issue is sold at a premium above the face amount, where the amount of the bond premium (price minus face amount) is such that the bond investors will obtain a yield to maturity on their investment at the 5 percent market rate of interest, or $2\frac{1}{2}$ percent (= .05/2) semiannually. Thus, the bond investors would pay \$103,585, instead of the \$100,000 face amount, as shown below, because \$103,585 is the discounted amount of the future periodic interest (\$3,000) and maturity amount (\$100,000) at the 5 percent effective annual rate, or $2\frac{1}{2}$ percent semiannually.

$$
\begin{aligned}
P &= F \cdot r \cdot p_{\overline{n}|i} + M(1 + i)^{-n} \\
&= (\$100{,}000)(.03)p_{\overline{8}|.025} + (\$100{,}000)(1.025)^{-8} \\
&= (\$3{,}000)(7.170137) + (\$100{,}000)(.820747) \\
&= \$103{,}585
\end{aligned}
$$

By issuing \$100,000 of bonds for \$103,585, the effective interest expense for the issuing company is at the rate of 5 percent, not 6 percent, because the company obtains a \$3,585 (= \$103,585 − \$100,000) premium above the face amount, yet pays interest on the \$100,000 face amount and pays only \$100,000 upon maturity. Similarly, by paying \$103,585 instead of \$100,000 for the bonds, the bond investors' yield to maturity is 5 percent, not 6 percent, because they do not recover the \$3,585 bond premium at maturity (that is, they receive \$100,000, not \$103,585) and receive periodic interest on the \$100,000 face amount. Thus, when the nominal rate exceeds the effective rate, the bonds sell at a premium, where the amount of the premium is sufficient to make up the difference between the nominal rate specified in the bond contract and the lower market rate to which the investors are entitled. Consequently, the price of the bond issue is also equal to the difference between the nominal and effective interest per semiannual period, discounted at the effective rate of interest per semiannual period, plus the maturity amount, as shown below.

$$\begin{aligned}
\mathbf{P} &= F(r - i)p_{\overline{n}|i} + M \\
&= (\$100{,}000)(.03 - .025)p_{\overline{8}|.025} + \$100{,}000 \\
&= (\$100{,}000)(.005)(7.170137) + \$100{,}000 \\
&= \$103{,}585
\end{aligned}$$

It should be pointed out that, to facilitate the computation of bond prices, bond tables can be used. Part of a table for bonds due in four years, bearing different nominal rates (appearing at the top) and different yield rates (shown at the left) is presented below.

FOUR YEARS INTEREST PAYABLE SEMIANNUALLY

Percent Per Annum	3%	3½%	4%	4½%	5%	6%	7%
4.00	96.34	98.17	100.00	101.83	103.66	107.33	110.99
4.10	95.98	97.81	99.63	101.46	103.29	106.94	110.60
4.125	95.89	97.72	99.54	101.37	103.20	106.85	110.50
4.20	95.62	97.45	99.27	101.09	102.92	106.56	110.21
4.25	95.45	97.27	99.09	100.91	102.73	106.38	110.02
4.30	95.27	97.09	98.91	100.73	102.55	106.19	109.83
4.375	95.00	96.82	98.64	100.45	102.27	105.90	109.54
4.40	94.92	96.73	98.55	100.36	102.18	105.81	109.44
4.50	94.56	96.38	98.19	100.00	101.81	105.44	109.06
4.60	94.21	96.02	97.83	99.64	101.45	105.06	108.68
4.625	94.13	95.93	97.74	99.55	101.36	104.97	108.58
4.70	93.87	95.67	97.47	99.28	101.08	104.69	108.30
4.75	93.69	95.49	97.30	99.10	100.90	104.51	108.11
4.80	93.52	95.32	97.12	98.92	100.72	104.32	107.92
4.875	93.26	95.06	96.85	98.65	100.45	104.04	107.64
4.90	93.17	94.97	96.77	98.56	100.36	103.95	107.54
5.00	92.83	94.62	96.41	98.21	100.00	103.59	107.17
5.10	92.49	94.28	96.06	97.85	99.64	103.22	106.80
5.125	92.40	94.19	95.98	97.77	99.55	103.13	106.70
5.20	92.15	93.93	95.72	97.50	99.29	102.86	106.43
5.25	91.98	93.76	95.54	97.33	99.11	102.67	106.24
5.30	91.81	93.59	95.37	97.15	98.93	102.49	106.06
5.375	91.55	93.33	95.11	96.89	98.67	102.22	105.78
5.40	91.47	93.25	95.02	96.80	98.58	102.13	105.69
5.50	91.13	92.91	94.68	96.45	98.23	101.77	105.32
5.625	90.71	92.48	94.25	96.02	97.79	101.33	104.86
5.75	90.30	92.06	93.83	95.59	97.35	100.88	104.41
5.875	89.88	91.64	93.40	95.16	96.92	100.44	103.96
6.00	89.47	91.23	92.98	94.74	96.49	100.00	103.51

Looking down the 6 percent column to the 5 percent line, we will find a figure of 103.59. Multiplying 103.59 by \$100,000 equals \$103,590, which corresponds to the \$103,585 valuation of the \$100,000, 6 percent bond issue sold (bought) to yield 5 percent. The minor difference between the two amounts is due to rounding, and tables are available where there are more decimals.

Accounting for bond issuances and acquisitions. The accounting for a bond issuance is normally handled by debiting cash for the amount received and crediting the bond liability at the face amount, with any difference between the two debited to bond discount or credited to bond premium. The bond liability can also be recorded by debiting cash and crediting the bond liability at the amount received, which is equal to the selling price or discounted amount (present value) of the bond. Except for the setting up of bond premium or discount accounts, the latter method is basically the same as the former method, because the face amount plus bond premium or minus bond discount is equal to the discounted amount of the bond.

The accounting for a bond investment is normally handled at the date of acquisition by debiting bond investment and crediting cash at cost. Since the cost of the investment is the purchase price of the bond, it is also equal to the discounted amount of the bond to maturity. Although it is normally not done, separate bond discount or premium accounts could be set up: Debit bond investment at the face amount, credit cash for the cost, and any difference is debited to bond premium or credited to bond discount.

To illustrate the accounting for a bond issuance and acquisition, we will use the \$100,000, 6 percent, four-year bond issue previously discussed, assuming that the bonds are issued (acquired) on January 1, 19+1, at par, at a discount, and at a premium, and assuming that one investor acquired the whole bond issue, as shown below:

Bond Issuer			Bond Investor		
Issued (acquired) at par:					
Cash	100,000		Bond investment	100,000	
Bonds payable		100,000	Cash		100,000
Issued (acquired) at a discount:					
Cash	96,563		Bond investment	96,563	
Bond discount ..	3,437		Cash		96,563
Bonds payable		100,000			
Issued (acquired) at a premium:					
Cash	103,585		Bond investment	103,585	
Bond premium		3,585	Cash		103,585
Bonds payable		100,000			

Accounting for bond-interest expense and revenue. If bonds are sold (bought) at par, then the interest to be incurred by the bond issuer and to be earned by the bond investor is at the annual nominal interest rate, which is the same as the annual effective interest rate to maturity. In such a case, periodic interest expense (bond issuer) and periodic interest revenue (bond investor) are computed every six months (assuming semiannual interest) by multiplying one-half the nominal interest rate by the face amount.

For example, referring to the $100,000, 6 percent, four-year bonds previously discussed, if the bonds were sold (bought) at par on January 1, 19+1, then the following entries for periodic interest would be made for the first year and each of the subsequent three years, assuming that the fiscal period ends on December 31:

Bond Issuer			Bond Investor		
July 1, 19+1:					
Interest expense........	3,000		Cash	3,000	
Cash ($100,000 × .06 × ½).........		3,000	Interest revenue........		3,000
December 31, 19+1:					
Interest expense	3,000		Interest receivable.........	3,000	
Interest payable....		3,000	Interest revenue........		3,000
January 1, 19+2:					
Interest payable	3,000		Cash	3,000	
Cash................		3,000	Interest receivable		3,000

BOND-DISCOUNT AMORTIZATION. If bonds are purchased (sold) at a discount, this means that the current market rate of interest for comparable bonds is greater than the nominal rate of the bonds. The bond investor is willing to receive future periodic interest at a nominal rate lower than the effective rate at time of purchase, provided that he can purchase the bonds at enough of a discount to make up for the lower future periodic interest receipts. By purchasing the bonds at a discount, the bond investor is lending less money, but will receive the full face amount upon maturity, which increases his yield to maturity and brings it in line with the market rate of interest for comparable bonds at the time of acquisition. Thus, the bond investor's future periodic interest revenue on the bonds will be greater than his future periodic interest receipts, since the former is based on the higher effective rate and the latter is based on the lower nominal rate.

Similarly, by selling the bonds at a discount, the bond issuer has less money available for his use, but will have to pay the full face amount at maturity, which increases the effective rate on the borrowed money. The bond issuer's future periodic interest expense will be greater than his future periodic interest payments, since the former is based on the higher effective rate and the latter is based on the lower nominal rate. In effect, the bond discount represents additional interest that the bond issuer will pay at maturity.

The periodic interest expense for the bond issuer and the periodic interest revenue for the bond investor is equal to the discounted amount (present value) of the bonds at the beginning of the period, multiplied by the effective rate. The difference between the periodic interest expense (revenue) and the periodic interest paid (received) is equal to the periodic amortization of the bond discount. As the bonds approach maturity, this difference increases the discounted amount of the bonds until it is equal to the face amount at maturity.

For example, referring to the $100,000, 6 percent, four-year bonds previously discussed, if the bonds were sold (bought) to yield 7 percent on January 1, 19+1, the interest entries for the first year would be as shown below:

Bond Issuer			Bond Investor		
July 1, 19+1:					
Interest expense ($96,563 × .035)....	3,380		Cash	3,000	
Bond discount ($3,380 − $3,000)		380	Bond investment	380	
Cash ($100,000 × .03)		3,000	Interest revenue........		3,380
December 31, 19+1:					
Interest expense [($96,563 + $380 = $96,943)(.035)]	3,393		Interest receivable.........	3,000	
Bond discount ...		393	Bond investment	393	
Interest payable .		3,000	Interest revenue........		3,393
January 1, 19+2:					
Interest payable........	3,000		Cash	3,000	
Cash		3,000	Interest receivable		3,000

A bond-discount amortization schedule provided below shows periodic interest expense (revenue), periodic bond-discount amortization, and the discounted amount (present value) of the bond issue over its life. Such a schedule not only is useful to illustrate the effect of bond-discount amortization on periodic interest expense (revenue), but also provides data for making periodic interest entries and data on the discounted amount to be reported in the balance sheet.

SCHEDULE OF BOND-DISCOUNT AMORTIZATION UNDER THE EFFECTIVE INTEREST METHOD—$100,000, 6% BONDS SOLD (BOUGHT) TO YIELD 7%

Semiannual Period	Interest Expense (Revenue)	Interest Paid (Received)	Bond-Discount Amortization	Unamortized Bond Discount	Discounted Amount (Present Value) of Bonds
Jan. 1, 19+1				$3,437	$96,563
1	$ 3,380	$ 3,000	$ 380	3,057	96,943
2	3,393	3,000	393	2,664	97,336
3	3,407 [a]	3,000 [b]	407 [c]	2,257 [d]	97,743 [e]
4	3,421	3,000	421	1,836	98,164
5	3,436	3,000	436	1,400	98,600
6	3,451	3,000	451	949	99,051
7	3,467	3,000	467	482	99,518
8	3,482	3,000	482	—	100,000
	$27,437	$24,000	$3,437		

[a] $3,407 = $97,336 × .035
[b] $3,000 = $100,000 × .03
[c] $407 = $3,407 − $3,000
[d] $2,257 = $2,664 − $407
[e] $97,743 = $97,336 + $407
= $100,000 − $2,257

The schedule above shows how the discounted amount (present value) of the bond liability (investment) increases each period until the maturity amount is reached, by the excess of the periodic interest expense (revenue) over the periodic interest paid (received), where the excess is equal to the periodic bond-discount amortization. In other words, the discounted amount of the bond liability (investment) grows each period by the amount of the periodic interest expense (revenue) and declines by the periodic interest paid (received); but since the former is larger than the latter, there is a net increase in the discounted amount of the bond each period. The periodic net increase is the result of the fact that the periodic interest expense (revenue) is based on an effective rate that is greater than the nominal rate used in determining the periodic interest payment (receipt).

In the case of a bond liability, with a separate bond-discount contra account, the periodic bond-discount amortization reduces the bond-discount account each period, and the remaining unamortized bond discount subtracted from the face amount of the bonds is equal to the discounted amount of the bond liability at the end of each period. For the investment, with no separate bond-discount account, the periodic bond-discount amortization is reflected as a direct addition to the discounted amount of the bond investment, so that the bond investment at the end of each period is equal to the discounted amount over the remaining life of the bond.

BOND-PREMIUM AMORTIZATION: If bonds are sold (bought) at a premium, this means that the nominal rate of the bonds is greater than the current market rate of interest for comparable bonds. The bond issuer is willing to pay future periodic interest at a nominal rate higher than the effective rate at time of issuance, provided only that the bond investor pays a premium for the higher future interest payments to be received. By the sale of the bonds at a premium, the future periodic interest expense to be incurred by the bond issuer is lower than the future periodic interest to be paid, because the former is based on the lower effective rate and the latter is based on the higher nominal rate.

Similarly, the bond investor is willing to pay a premium for the bonds in order to receive higher future periodic interest payments than he would receive if the interest payments were based on the lower market rate of interest for comparable bonds. By the payment of a premium for the bonds, the bond investor's future periodic interest revenue is less than his future periodic interest receipts, since the former is based on the lower effective rate and the latter is based on the higher nominal rate.

For example, referring to the $100,000, 6 percent, four-year bonds previously discussed, if the bonds were sold (bought) to yield 5 percent on January 1, 19+1, the interest entries for the first year would be as follows:

Bond Issuer			Bond Investor		
July 1, 19+1:					
Interest expense ($103,585 × .025)	2,590		Cash	3,000	
Bond premium ($3,000 − $2,590)....	410		Bond investment....		410
Cash ($100,000 × .03)		3,000	Interest revenue		2,590

	Bond Issuer		Bond Investor	
December 31, 19+1:				
Interest expense [($103,585 − $410 = $103,175) (.025)]	2,579		Interest receivable ..	3,000	
Bond premium.......	421		Bond investment.		421
Interest payable		3,000	Interest revenue..		2,579
January 1, 19+2:					
Interest payable	3,000		Cash................	3,000	
Cash		3,000	Interest receivable		3,000

A schedule of bond-premium amortization over the life of the bonds is provided below.

In analyzing the schedule, note how the discounted amount (present value) of the bond liability (investment) decreases each period by the excess of the periodic interest paid (received) over the periodic interest expense (revenue), where the excess is equal to the periodic bond-premium amortization, until the maturity amount (face amount) is reached at the maturity date. In other words, the discounted amount of the bond liability (investment) grows each period by the amount of the periodic interest expense (revenue) and declines by the periodic interest paid (received); but since the latter is larger than the former, there is a net decrease in the discounted amount of the bond each period.

In the case of a bond liability, with a separate bond-premium adjunct account,

SCHEDULE OF BOND-PREMIUM AMORTIZATION UNDER THE EFFECTIVE INTEREST METHOD—$100,000, 6% BONDS SOLD (BOUGHT) TO YIELD 5%

Semiannual Period	Interest Paid (Received)	Interest Expense (Revenue)	Bond-Premium Amortization	Unamortized Bond Premium	Discounted Amount (Present Value) of Bonds
Jan. 1, 19+1				$3,585	$103,585
1	$ 3,000	$ 2,590	$ 410	3,175	103,175
2	3,000	2,579	421	2,754	102,754
3	3,000 [a]	2,569 [b]	431 [c]	2,323 [d]	102,323 [e]
4	3,000	2,558	442	1,881	101,881
5	3,000	2,547	453	1,428	101,428
6	3,000	2,536	464	964	100,964
7	3,000	2,524	476	488	100,488
8	3,000	2,512	488	—	100,000
	$24,000	$20,415	$3,585		

[a] $3,000 = $100,000 × .03
[b] $2,569 = $102,754 × .025
[c] $431 = $3,000 − $2,569
[d] $2,323 = $2,754 − $431
[e] $102,323 = $102,754 − $431
= $100,000 + $2,323

the periodic bond-premium amortization reduces the bond-premium account each period, and the remaining unamortized bond premium plus the face amount of the bonds is equal to the discounted amount of the bond liability at the end of each period. For the bond investment, with no separate bond-premium account, the periodic bond-premium amortization is reflected as a direct reduction to the discounted amount of the bond investment, so that the bond investment at the end of each period is equal to the discounted amount over the remaining life of the bonds.

STRAIGHT-LINE AMORTIZATION: Up to this point, the accounting for bond premium or discount amortization has been done by the effective-interest or yield method, which is an acceptable accounting method per APB *Opinion No. 12.*[4] Under this method, periodic interest expense (revenue) is equal to the constant effective rate to maturity multiplied by the discounted amount of the bonds at the beginning of the period, and periodic bond discount or premium amortization is equal to the difference between periodic interest paid (received) and incurred (earned).

On the other hand, the most widely used accounting method for bond premium or discount amortization is the straight-line method. As long as the straight-line method does not cause the results obtained to be materially different from those under the effective-interest method, it is an acceptable method per APB *Opinion No. 21.*[5] Under this method, bond premium or discount is amortized at a constant amount each period, which is equal to the premium or discount divided by the number of future interest periods over the life, or remaining life, of the bonds, and results in a constant periodic interest expense (revenue).

To illustrate straight-line amortization of bond discount, assume again that a $100,000 bond issue, bearing 6 percent interest payable semiannually on January 1 and July 1, and due in four years, is sold (acquired) on January 1, 19+1 to yield 7 percent. The bond-discount amortization schedule and the first-year interest entries under the straight-line method would be as shown on page 192.

Now assume that the same bond issue is sold (acquired) to yield 5 percent. Assuming straight-line amortization, the bond-premium amortization schedule and first-year interest entries would be as shown on page 193.

By a comparison of the bond discount and premium amortization schedules under the straight-line method with those schedules under the effective-interest method (see pages 188 and 190), the periodic difference in reported interest over the life of the bonds under the two methods can be perceived. In the bond-discount case, the straight-line method overstates in the early life of the bond and understates in the later life of the bond the periodic interest expense (revenue). The reverse occurs for the bond-premium case under straight-line amortization.

---

[4]Accounting Principles Board, "Omnibus Opinion—1967," *Opinion No. 12* (New York: AICPA, December 1967), p. 194.

[5]Accounting Principles Board, "Interest on Receivables and Payables," *Opinion No. 21* (New York: AICPA, August 1971), p. 423.

SCHEDULE OF BOND-DISCOUNT AMORTIZATION UNDER THE STRAIGHT-LINE METHOD—$100,000, 6% BONDS SOLD (BOUGHT) TO YIELD 7%

Semiannual Period	Interest Expense (Revenue)	Interest Paid (Received)	Bond-Discount Amortization	Unamortized Bond Discount	Approximate Discounted Amount (Present Value) of Bonds
Jan 1, 19+1				$3,437	$ 96,563
1	$ 3,430	$ 3,000	$ 430	3,007	96,993
2	3,430	3,000	430	2,577	97,423
3	3,430 [a]	3,000 [b]	430 [c]	2,147 [d]	97,853 [e]
4	3,430	3,000	430	1,717	98,283
5	3,430	3,000	430	1,287	98,713
6	3,430	3,000	430	857	99,143
7	3,430	3,000	430	427	99,573
8	3,427	3,000	427 [f]	—	100,000
	$27,437	$24,000	$3,437		

[a] $3,430 = $3,000 + $430
[b] $3,000 = $100,000 × .03
[c] $430 = $3,437 ÷ 8
[d] $2,147 = $2,577 − $430
[e] $97,853 = $97,423 + $430
[f] Rounded down $3

Bond Issuer			Bond Investor		
July 1, 19+1:					
Interest expense ($3,000 + $430)	3,430		Cash	3,000	
			Bond investment	430	
Bond discount ($3,437 ÷ 8)		430	Interest revenue		3,430
Cash ($100,000 × .03)		3,000			
Dec. 31, 19+1:					
Interest expense	3,430		Interest receivable	3,000	
Bond discount		430	Bond investment	430	
Interest payable		3,000	Interest revenue		3,430
Jan. 1, 19+2:					
Interest payable	3,000		Cash	3,000	
Cash		3,000	Interest receivable		3,000

This difference is illustrated at the top of page 194.

What the illustration shows is that the straight-line amortization of bond discount or premium is an averaging process that results in the same interest expense (revenue) each period in spite of changes in the discounted amount of the liability (investment). In contrast, under effective-interest amortization, interest expense (revenue) changes as the discounted amount of the liability (investment) changes over the life of the bonds, since periodic interest is equal to a constant effective rate multiplied by an increasing (bond discount) or decreasing (bond premium) discounted amount. Because bonds are bought and sold based on effective interest rates to maturity, and are not based on straight-line averages, the reporting of bond interest under the effective-interest method is conceptually sound and in line

SCHEDULE OF BOND-PREMIUM AMORTIZATION UNDER THE STRAIGHT-LINE METHOD—$100,000, 6% BONDS SOLD (BOUGHT) TO YIELD 5%

Semiannual Period	Interest Paid (Received)	Interest Expense (Revenue)	Bond-Premium Amortization	Unamortized Bond Premium	Approximate Discounted Amount (Present Value) of Bonds
Jan. 1, 19+1				$3,585	$103,585
1	$ 3,000	$ 2,552	$ 448	3,137	103,137
2	3,000	2,552	448	2,689	102,689
3	3,000[a]	2,552[b]	448[c]	2,241[d]	102,241[e]
4	3,000	2,552	448	1,793	101,793
5	3,000	2,552	448	1,345	101,345
6	3,000	2,552	448	897	100,897
7	3,000	2,552	448	449	100,449
8	3,000	2,551	449[f]	—	100,000
	$24,000	$20,415	$3,585		

[a] $3,000 = $100,000 × .03
[b] $2,552 = $3,000 − $448
[c] $448 = $3,585 ÷ 8
[d] $2,241 = $2,689 − $448
[e] $102,241 = $102,689 − $448
[f] Rounded up $1

Bond Issuer			Bond Investor		
July 1, 19+1:					
Interest expense ($3,000 − $448)..........	2,552		Cash.....................	3,000	
Bond premium ($3,585 ÷ 8)	448		Bond investment		448
Cash ($100,000 × .03)		3,000	Interest revenue		2,552
Dec. 31, 19+1:					
Interest expense	2,552		Interest receivable	3,000	
Bond premium	448		Bond investment		448
Interest payable.......		3,000	Interest revenue		2,552
Jan. 1, 19+2:					
Interest payable	3,000		Cash.....................	3,000	
Cash..................		3,000	Interest receivable ...		3,000

with the reporting of the economic realities of the real world. On the other hand, straight-line amortization has the practical advantages of ease of implementation, ease of understanding, and adequate accuracy.

BONDS ISSUED (BOUGHT) AFTER THE CONTRACT DATE: Up to this point, bond valuation and the accounting for bonds have assumed that the bonds are issued on the date when the bond contract begins. However, bonds are often sold by the issuing company after the legal date of the bond contract, and after the bonds are outstanding they can be bought and sold at any time.

If a company issues bonds after the contract date of the bonds, but on any interest date (such as July 1 or January 1), then the valuation of the bonds (the price) is the discounted amount of the future maturity amount plus the future periodic

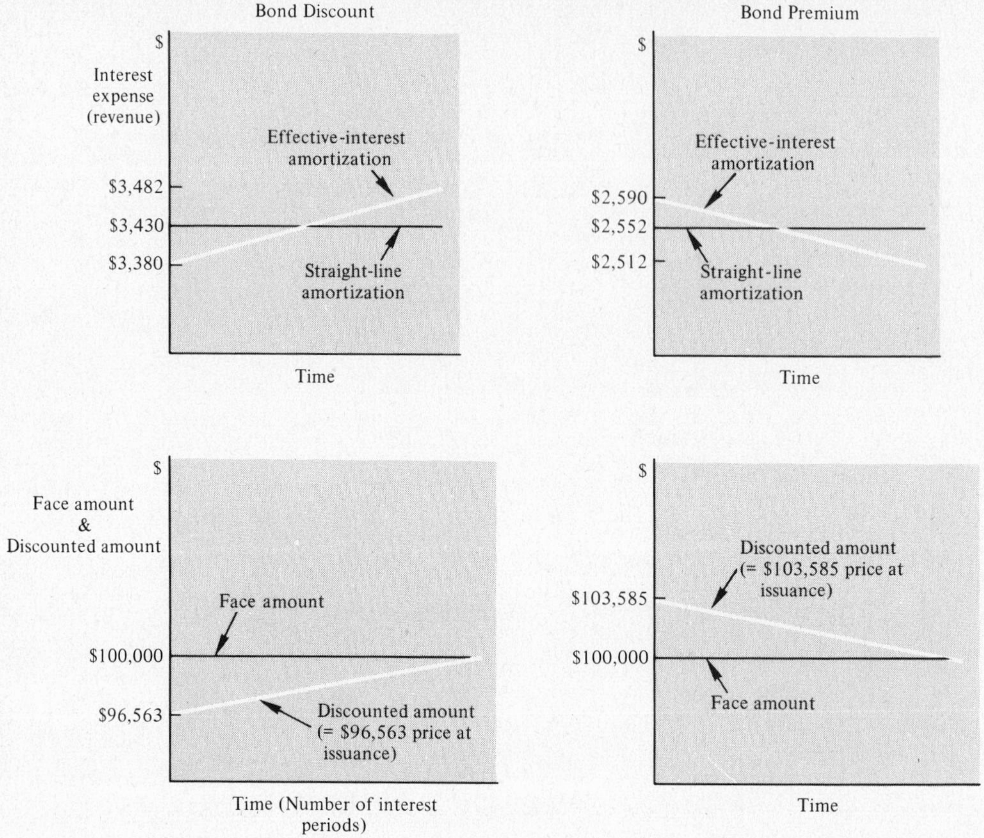

interest over the remaining life of the bonds. For example, if a ten-year bond, paying interest semiannually on January 1 and July 1, is sold on July 1, 19+1 (instead of January 1, 19+1), the price of the bond is equal to the discounted amount over nineteen semiannual interest periods ($9\frac{1}{2} \times 2$). Based on this bond price, the accounting for the bond liability is the same as was previously discussed.

In the case of a bond investor who buys an outstanding bond on an interest date (rather than buying the bond from the issuing company), the price of the bond is equal to the discounted amount of the bond over its remaining life, at the effective interest rate. Based on this bond price, the accounting for the bond investment is the same as was previously discussed.

BOND VALUATION BETWEEN INTEREST DATES: Previous discussion on the determination of the price of a bond assumed that bonds are purchased (sold) on an interest date. However, many bond purchases are made between interest dates. In such instances, the price of a bond is equal to the discounted amount of the bond on the last preceding interest date plus the accrued interest on that discounted amount at the effective rate for the partial period. In other words, the price of a bond between interest dates includes the growth of the discounted amount of the bond over the partial period.

The book amount (value) of the bond between interest dates is not equal to the purchase price of the bond, because the latter includes the interest accrued over the partial period when the buyer did not own the bonds. Thus the book amount of a bond between interest dates is equal to the discounted amount at the date of purchase minus the interest accrued on the face amount at the nominal rate over the partial period. Since the quoted price of a bond is usually the book amount (value) of the bond, the quoted price plus the accrued interest is equal to the purchase (issue) price, often referred to as the flat price.

To illustrate this, assume again a \$100,000 bond issue, bearing 6 percent interest payable semiannually on January 1 and July 1, and due in four years, purchased (sold) on February 1, 19+1 (instead of January 1, 19+1), to yield 5 percent. Thus on February 1, 19+1, the price of the bond issue is \$104,017 and the book amount is \$103,517, as shown below:

Price (discounted amount) at last preceding interest date	\$103,585
Add: Effective interest for one month (\$103,585 × .025 × ⅙)...............	432
Price at February 1, 19+1	\$104,017
Deduct: Nominal interest for one month (\$100,000 × .03 × ⅙).............	500
Book amount (value)	\$103,517

Or the foregoing can be expressed algebraically, as follows:

$$
\begin{aligned}
\textbf{Let } m &= \textbf{Fractional six-month period} \\
\textbf{Then } P &= [F \cdot r \cdot p_{\overline{n}|i} + M(1+i)^{-n}](1 + i \cdot m) \\
&= [(\$100{,}000)(.03)p_{\overline{8}|.025} + \$100{,}000(1.025)^{-8}](1 + .025 \cdot 1/6) \\
&= [(\$3{,}000)(7.170137) + \$100{,}000(.820747)](1.004167) \\
&= (\$103{,}585)(1.004167) \\
&= \$104{,}017 \\
\textbf{Let } B &= \textbf{Book amount of bonds at date of purchase (issue)} \\
\textbf{Then } B &= P - (F \cdot r \cdot m) \\
&= \$104{,}017 - [(\$100{,}000)(.03)(1/6)] \\
&= \$104{,}017 - \$500 \\
&= \$103{,}517
\end{aligned}
$$

Assuming effective-interest amortization, the following journal entries would be made:

Bond Investor			Bond Seller		
February 1, 19+1:					
Bond investment...	103,517		Cash	104,017	
Interest receivable .	500		Interest payable		500
Cash		104,017	Bond premium .		3,517
			Bonds payable..		100,000
July 1, 19+1:					
Cash	3,000		Interest expense....	2,158[b]	
Interest receivable....		500	Interest payable ...	500	
Bond investment		342[a]	Bonds premium....	342[a]	
Interest revenue		2,158[b]	Cash		3,000

[a] \$342 = \$103,517 – [\$103,585 + (\$103,585)(.025) – (\$100,000)(.03)]
[b] \$2,158 = (\$103,585)(.025) – \$432

Balance-sheet presentation. From the viewpoint of a company issuing bonds, the bond liability is reported in the balance sheet under the long-term-liability caption at its discounted amount. The discounted amount is usually reported by showing the face amount of the bonds as a separate-line item, with any unamortized bond discount or premium shown as a separate deduction from or addition to the face amount. The bond liability could also be reported at its discounted amount, with the face amount, any unamortized discount or premium, and the nominal rate reported parenthetically.

From the investor's viewpoint, bonds would be reported in the balance sheet under the long-term-investment caption at their discounted amount. The reported discounted amount would be equal to the original bond cost plus any unamortized bond premium or less any unamortized bond discount to the balance-sheet date. The separate reporting of bond premium or discount is not normally done for bond investments.

To illustrate the balance-sheet presentation of bonds, assume the issuance (acquisition) of $100,000, 6 percent bonds that were sold (bought) two years ago (January 1, 19+1) to yield 5 percent and accounted for under the effective-interest method (see the bond-premium amortization schedule, page 190). The bond investment from the investor's viewpoint and the bond liability from the issuer's viewpoint would be reported on their December 31, 19+2, balance sheets as follows:

Long-term investments:	
Bond investment ($100,000, 6% bond, due Jan. 1, 19+4, unamortized premium $1,881)................	$101,881

Long-term liabilities:		
Bonds payable (6% nominal rate, due Jan. 1, 19+4)........	$100,000	
Unamortized bond premium.....	1,881	$101,881

From the viewpoint of the company issuing bonds, bond premium or bond discount is *not* reported as a deferred credit or a deferred charge, respectively; however, bond-issue costs are reported in the balance sheet as a separate deferred charge.[6] Such bond-issue costs would be amortized in the same manner as the amortization of bond premium or discount.

Also, from the viewpoint of the company issuing bonds, any bonds reacquired but not canceled, called treasury bonds, are reported in the balance sheet as a separate deduction from bonds payable. Treasury bonds are debited at par when reacquired.

Early extinguishment of bond liability. Many bond issuances include a call provision in the bond contract that allows the issuer, at his option, to redeem (pay) the bonds, at a specified price, before the maturity date.[7] Such bonds are referred to as

---

[6] *Opinion No. 21*, p. 423.

[7] The determination of the price of callable bonds from the investor's viewpoint is covered in Gentry and Johnson, *Finney and Miller's Principles of Accounting: Advanced*, 6th ed., pp. 341–43.

callable bonds. Since bonds normally would be called when interest rates have fallen, which is to the disadvantage of the bond investor, who would be faced with reinvesting at lower rates, there is usually a call premium in excess of the maturity amount that must be paid to the investor upon redemption before the maturity date.

The bond issuer can retire bonds by calling them or by purchasing the bonds in the open market. The payment for the retirement of bonds can be obtained from existing liquid assets, from the issuing of common stock, or from issuing new bonds. The replacement of outstanding bonds with new bonds is called *bond refunding*.

In the accounting for the extinguishment of bond liability before the maturity date, it is first necessary to bring the interest and any bond discount or premium amortization up to the date of the redemption. This normally causes no problems, since redemption is usually on an interest date for practical reasons.

Once the interest and amortization are brought up to the redemption date, the accounting for the bond redemption from the issuer's viewpoint is one of removing from the accounts any unamortized bond discount or premium and any unamortized bond-issue costs of the bonds to be redeemed. Any difference between the discounted amount of the bonds carried on the books and the redemption price is recorded as a loss or gain on bond retirement. Similarly, from the bond investor's viewpoint, the discounted amount of the bond investment carried on the books is removed, and any difference between the cash received and the discounted amount of the bond investment is reported as a loss or gain on sale of bonds.

For example, assume that a $10,000 bond with unamortized bond discount of $800 is called on an interest date at 105. Assuming that interest and discount amortization have been brought up to the redemption date and accounted for, the accounting for bond redemption would be as follows:

Bond Issuer			Bond Investor		
Bonds payable	10,000		Cash	10,500	
Loss on bond retirement			Bond investment		9,200
($10,500 − $9,200)...	1,300		Gain on sale of bonds.		1,300
Bond discount		800			
Cash					
($10,000 × 1.05)		10,500			

Note that the loss on bond retirement of $1,300 is the sum of the call premium of $500 (= $10,000 × .05) and the unamortized bond discount of $800. In order to terminate the old bond contract, the issuing company has to pay the $800 additional interest at termination, instead of at maturity, plus a call premium.

The difference between the reacquisition price and the discounted amount of the bonds to be extinguished ($1,300 in the above example) is recognized as a loss or gain in the period of extinguishment per APB *Opinion No. 26*.[8] The Opinion

[8] Accounting Principles Board, "Early Extinguishment of Debt," *Opinion No. 26* (New York: AICPA, October 1972), p. 502.

states that the difference is treated as a loss or gain regardless of whether the proceeds used to achieve the extinguishment were obtained by refunding (retiring outstanding bonds with the proceeds from a new bond issue) or nonrefunding (retiring outstanding bonds with the proceeds obtained from issuing common stock or using existing liquid assets) means. However, prior to this Opinion, accountants recognized the difference as a loss or gain in nonrefunding situations, but for refunding situations they used one of three methods:

Recognize the difference in current income as a loss or gain
Amortize the difference over the remaining original life of the extinguished bond issue
Amortize the difference over the life of the new bond issue

The recognition of the difference as a loss or gain in refunding is based on the argument that canceling of the old bond issue and the issuing of new bonds are separate transactions. The loss or gain emerges from terminating the old bond issue because the old loan cycle has ended; the new bond issue begins a new loan cycle, and therefore only its costs are deferred to future periods.

Another argument for recognizing the difference as a loss or gain in bond refunding is that the cost (call premium plus any unamortized bond discount) of terminating the old bond contract is a loss incurred to terminate an unfavorable bond contract that relates to past transactions; hence, the loss should be recognized when the contract is terminated. Related to this argument is the contention that the market price of the debt has increased as the result of a decline in the market rate of interest, and paying the call price is the most favorable way to extinguish the debt. Since the bond accounts do not reflect current bond prices based on current yield rates, the loss on retirement should be recognized no later than the date of termination. To defer the loss would be to penalize future periods, since the new bonds could be issued at the advantageous rate regardless of the old bond issue.

A problem with recognizing the difference as a loss or gain in bond refunding is that a potential reporting loss may discourage the favorable replacement of high-interest-cost bonds with low-interest-cost bonds. Conversely, the potential for reporting a gain may induce a company to issue high-interest-cost bonds in order to retire outstanding low-interest-cost bonds. Because of this, some accountants argue that the difference should be deferred and amortized over the remaining life of the old bond issue (the cost to terminate was incurred to obtain advantageous low-interest cost over the remaining life of the old bond issue) or over the life of the new bond issue (the new bond issue is merely a continuation of the old bond issue, so costs of both should be prorated over the entire period of indebtedness). But deferring the difference fails to recognize that the future benefits of lower interest cost on the new bond issue in comparison to the old bond issue merely reflect the accounting practice of recording and reporting bonds based on historical interest rates—the effective rate at the time the bonds were issued.

Convertible bonds. These are bonds issued with a convertible feature in the bond contract that permits the bondholder, at his option, to convert the bonds into common stock (or other securities) of the issuing company at a specified conversion price. The ratio of the number of common shares to be received by the bondholder in exchange for each bond is called the conversion ratio, and the conversion ratio divided into the face amount of the bond is equal to the conversion price. The conversion price and ratio are established in the bond contract when the bonds are issued and are usually, but not always, fixed. Convertible bonds generally have the following characteristics:

The contractual interest rate is lower than the market rate of interest for nonconvertible bonds.
The initial conversion price is higher than the market price of the common stock at time of issuance.
The conversion price does not decrease over time (except for stock splits and stock dividends).
The bond issuer retains a call option.

Convertible bonds offer advantages to both the bond issuer and the bond investor. From the bond issuer's viewpoint, financing is obtained at a lower interest rate because of the attractiveness of the convertible feature to the bond investor. If the market price of the convertible stock increases, the bond issuer can force conversion of the bonds by calling the bonds for redemption, and if the market price of the common stock does not increase, the issuer still has the advantage of low-interest-rate financing. From the bond investor's viewpoint, there is the security of holding a debt instrument with its fixed return and maturity amount, coupled with the advantage of being able to convert into common stock should the market price of the stock increase above the conversion price.

From the accounting standpoint, convertible bonds are accounted for at the time of issuance (acquisition), at the time interest on the convertible bonds is incurred (earned), and at the time bonds are converted into common stock.

ISSUANCE (ACQUISITION) OF CONVERTIBLE BONDS: Because convertible bonds are hybrid securities that include both debt and equity characteristics, there is a problem as to how to account for their issuance. At the time of issuance, should convertible bonds be accounted for solely as debt, or should the debt and the conversion option on the bonds be accounted for separately? Per APB *Opinion No. 14,* convertible bonds are accounted for solely as debt, because of the inseparability of the debt and the conversion option.[9] That is, the debt and the conversion option are so interconnected that they should not be accounted for separately. In addition, there is the practical problem of not being able to meaningfully determine (because it is too subjective) what convertible bonds would sell for if the conversion option did not exist.

---

[9] Accounting Principles Board, "Accounting for Convertible Debt and Debt Issued with Stock Purchase Warrants," *Opinion No. 14* (New York: AICPA, March 1969), p. 207.

For example, if 100, 6 percent, four-year $1,000 convertible bonds, paying interest semiannually on January 1 and July 1, were sold to yield 5 percent, the issuance would be accounted for solely as debt, per *Opinion No. 21,* as shown below:

Bond Issuer			Bond Investor		
Cash (see page 184)...	103,585		Bond investment......	103,585	
Bond premium		3,585	Cash		103,585
Bonds payable.....		100,000			

On the other hand, if it could be determined that the bonds could be sold with no convertible feature to yield 7 percent (debit Cash $96,563 and Bond discount $3,437, and credit Bonds payable $100,000), then contrary to *Opinion No. 14,* the separate accounting for debt and the conversion option would be as follows:

Bond Issuer		
Cash	103,585	
Bond discount ($100,000 – $96,563)	3,437	
Bonds payable............		100,000
Additional paid-in capital ($103,585 – $96,563)		7,022

The accounting for periodic interest with regard to convertible bonds is the same as that previously discussed for nonconvertible bonds. Note, however, that periodic interest expense would not be the same if the convertible bonds were accounted for by separating debt and equity, instead of the APB-approved nonseparation. Based on the preceding example, and assuming effective-interest amortization, the difference in periodic interest under nonseparation and separation is illustrated below:

Debt and Equity Not Separated			Debt and Equity Separated		
July 1, 19+1:					
Interest expense ($103,585 × .025)...	2,590		Interest expense ($96,563 × .035)	3,380	
Bond premium ($3,000 – $2,590)...	410		Bond discount ($3,380 – $3,000) ...		380
Cash ($100,000 × .03).		3,000	Cash		3,000

The arguments for separate accounting for the debt and the conversion option are as follows:

The conversion element is a distinct element in the bond contract and has economic worth; hence, to be consistent with the traditional debt and equity classifications, the two should be accounted for separately.

The periodic interest expense should be based only on the debt characteristics of the convertible bonds; hence, debt and equity should be separated.

The separation of debt and equity in accounting for convertible bonds is consistent with the separation of debt and warrants in the accounting for debt with detachable stock purchase warrants per APB *Opinion No. 14,*[10] since they are, in effect, the same.

CONVERSION: In accounting for the conversion of convertible bonds into common stock, it is first necessary to bring any bond premium or discount amortization and accrued interest up to the date of the conversion. This normally causes no problem, since conversion is usually on an interest date for practical reasons.

Once the interest and amortization are brought up to date, the accounting for conversion from the issuer's viewpoint is usually handled by one of two methods. The first method is to reclassify the discounted amount of the bonds (face amount plus unamortized premium or minus unamortized discount) as common stock (at par or stated amount of no par) and additional paid-in capital (for the remainder). Since the book amount of the debt is merely capitalized as stockholders' equity, there is no gain or loss on conversion. The second method is to capitalize stockholders' equity based on the current market price of the bonds or the common stock, with any excess of the current price over the discounted amount of the bonds on the books shown as a loss on conversion.

From the investor's viewpoint, the accounting for conversion is handled by recording the common stock at its current market price. Any difference between the current market valuation and the up-to-date discounted amount of the bond investment given up is reported as a gain or loss on conversion.

To illustrate the conversion of bonds into common stock, assume that 100, 6 percent, four-year $1,000 convertible bonds, paying interest semiannually on January 1 and July 1, were sold to yield 5 percent on January 1, 19+1. The conversion ratio is 20 shares of common stock for each $1,000 bond, which means a conversion price of $50 (= $1,000/20), and the par value of the common stock is $40 a share. If an investor converts 10 bonds into common stock on July 1, 19+3, when the market price of the stock is $60, the following entries would be made, assuming effective-interest amortization (see page 190, period 5):

Bond Issuer			Bond Investor		
Method 1—based on book amount of bonds					
Bonds payable ($1,000 × 10)	10,000		Investment in common stock ($60 × 10 × 20)	12,000	
Bond premium ($14.28 × 10)	143		Investment in bonds ($1,014.28 × 10)		10,143
Common stock ($40 × 10 × 20)		8,000	Gain on bond conversion ($12,000 − $10,143)		1,857
Additional paid-in capital ($10,143 − $8,000)		2,143			
Method 2—based on market price of stock					
Bonds payable	10,000		same as above		
Bond premium	143				
Loss on bond conversion ($12,000 − $10,143)	1,857				
Common stock		8,000			
Additional paid-in capital [($60 − $40)(10 × 20)]		4,000			

The argument for method 1 is that the conversion is merely a transfer from one equity (liability) to another equity (stockholders' equity), which does not change invested capital and should not affect net income. Also, it is argued that

[10]*Opinion No. 14,* p. 209.

when a company issues convertible bonds, it is understood that the proceeds from the bond issue may ultimately represent the consideration for the common stock; hence, upon conversion, merely capitalize bonds into stock. The second method is supported by the argument that the use of current market price provides more relevant information. It is also argued that the conversion ends the cycle for bonds and begins a new cycle for stock, and the new cycle should begin by recording the stock at current market price.

8

Discounted-Cash-Flow Valuation: Leases

Introduction. It was pointed out in the valuation chapter that discounted-cash-flow valuation is conceptually the preferred valuation method, because it takes into account future cash flows. On the other hand, it was also pointed out that discounted-cash-flow valuation is extremely difficult to implement in actual practice unless certainty conditions are approximated. Because such certainty conditions are approximated with regard to long-term, noncancelable financing leases, discounted-cash-flow valuation is employed in actual accounting practice for such leases, but in a manner consistent with the historical-cost assumption.

A lease is a contractual agreement whereby the lessor (owner rentor) grants rights to the lessee (tenant) to use real or personal property for a specified period of time in return for compensation, usually in the form of specified periodic cash payments (rents). Because the lease is a contract between the lessor and lessee, it can vary widely, depending on the lease provisions agreed upon. Typical lease provisions pertain to the following:[1]

Term of lease. The lease may be a short-term lease, extending for a few hours or days (lease of an automobile), or a long-term lease, which ranges from a period of several years to the estimated useful life of the property (buildings, equipment, and the like).

Early termination. The lease may be cancelable or noncancelable. Early termination may require the payment of a specified amount.

Rents. Rental agreements may be at a constant, increasing, or decreasing amount each period. Rents can be at a predetermined amount or vary with some factor (such as sales).

Obligations. The obligations for insurance, taxes, and maintenance of the property may be assumed by either the lessor or the lessee, or divided between them.

Restrictions. As in a bond indenture, there may be restrictions in the lease that limit the lessee's dividend payments, issuance of future debt, incurrence of future leases, and the like.

Lessor's services. The lease contract may state that the lessor shall provide certain services (heat, elevator, and the like) or no services to the lessee.

Default. The lease contract may state that upon default of a lease payment, the lessee is liable for all future payments at once, and, when these are paid, the title of the property transfers to the lessee. Or the lease may state that the lessor is to sell the property and collect from the lessee the difference between the sale price and the lessor's unrecovered cost.

Termination. Alternatives at the end of the lease may vary from none to such alternatives as the right of the lessee to renew, to purchase at fair market value, or to purchase at a specified price.

Lessors engage in lease transactions as an investment (as do financial institutions), to make property operated by the lessor available for profit (as do leasing companies), or to facilitate the sale or use of the lessor's own manufactured product. Lessees engage in leasing activities to acquire property temporarily needed or not otherwise available, to conserve working capital (leasing permits 100 per cent financing), to shift the risks of ownership (such as obsolescence, unprofitable operation, idle capacity, and uncertainty of residual amount), to obtain tax advantages (such as the full deductibility of lease payments, the write-off of the full cost of the property, and the acceleration of deductions), to obtaining buying or servicing advantages, and the like.

In accounting for leases, the problem from the lessor's viewpoint is the allocation of revenue and expense to the accounting periods covered by the lease in order to fairly state the lessor's net income. From the lessee's viewpoint, the ac-

[1] See John H. Myers, "Reporting of Leases in Financial Statements," *Accounting Research Study No. 4* (New York: AICPA, 1964), pp. 10–11.

counting problem is whether the fair presentation of the lessee's financial statements should provide for only the periodic rentals under the terms of the lease, or provide for the asset and liability, as well as the expense of using and financing the property created by the lease. In determining how to account for leases, accountants base the method on the type of the lease—namely, whether it is an operating or a financing lease.

Operating leases. The basic characteristics of an operating lease are as follows:

The lessor retains the usual risks and rewards of ownership of the leased property. Thus the lessor pays for the ownership expenses of the leased property, such as insurance, taxes, and maintenance, and incurs such ownership expense as depreciation.

The lessee has no options at the termination of the lease to acquire the leased property; hence, the lessee has no special purchase rights or lease-purchase options.

The lease is normally cancelable by either party on relatively short notice.

The lease is normally a short-term lease; hence, it does not cover substantially the entire useful life of the leased property.

Because the usual risks and rewards of ownership are *not* passed to the lessee under an operating lease, the lease payments are essentially rentals for services rendered by the lessor on a period-to-period basis. Thus the rents are designed to cover the lessor's ownership expenses plus a normal return for assuming the ownership risks involved. For example, the leasing of computers is normally done under an operating lease, since the lease agreement is usually subject to cancellation on relatively short notice. The lessee is paying rent to use the computer and have it maintained, not to acquire it.

With the operating lease being essentially a rental agreement, the lessor reports the periodic rent receipts as revenue and the lessee reports the periodic rent payments as expense, in their respective income statements. The lessor reports the leased property in the balance sheet under the Property, Plant, and Equipment classification (for example, Leased Asset—Building). Accumulated depreciation on the leased property would be reported in the balance sheet contra to the leased property.[2]

Note that under an operating lease, the lessee does *not* report the leased property as an asset in the balance sheet, since no special property or purchase rights were acquired. Similarly, the lessee does *not* report as a liability the obligation to make future rent payments, since the lease is temporary and cancelable. In other words, the lessee makes rent payments for services rendered each period, and there is no obligation for future unperformed services. On the other hand, information on the details of the operating lease should be disclosed in notes to the financial

---

[2]Accounting Principles Board, "Accounting for Leases in Financial Statements of Lessors," *Opinion No. 7* (New York: AICPA, May 1966), p. 59.

statements, in separate statements or schedules, or parenthetically in the financial statements.

ILLUSTRATIONS: To illustrate the accounting for an operating lease, assume that a building is leased for three years at an annual rental of $10,000 per year, payable at the beginning of each year. The lease agreement is cancelable by either party on three months' notice. The annual depreciation charge on the building is $5,000, and miscellaneous ownership expense is $1,000. Typical lease entries would be as follows:

Lessor			Lessee		
Cash	10,000		Rent expense—leased building	10,000	
Rent revenue—leased building ..		10,000	Cash		10,000
Depreciation expense ..	5,000		—		
Accumulated depreciation—leased building.........		5,000			
Miscellaneous expense (ownership expense)	1,000		—		
Cash		1,000			

Now assume the same type of building lease as above, except that the lessor and lessee agree that the lessee will make an advance payment (down payment) of $10,000 at the inception of the lease, in addition to three annual rental payments of $6,000 at the beginning of each year. The down payment is a liability to the lessor for rent received in advance, and an asset to the lessee for prepaid rent. Thus the advance payment needs to be amortized over the life of the lease in order to reflect periodic rent revenue (lessor) and expense (lessee). Such amortization can be done by either the straight-line method or the effective-interest (present-value) method. The latter is theoretically preferable because it takes into account the time value of money (interest), but the former is more convenient and easier to understand and is used where there is no material difference between the two methods.

Typical lease entries (other than the lessor's entries for depreciation and miscellaneous expenses, previously illustrated) would be as follows:

Lessor			Lessee		
January 1, 19+2:					
Cash................	16,000		Rent expense—leased building	6,000	
Rent received in advance—leased building		10,000	Prepaid rent—leased building	10,000	
			Cash		16,000
Rent revenue—leased building		6,000			
December 31, 19+2: (straight-line amortization)					

Lessor

Rent received in advance—leased building	3,333	
Rent revenue—leased building[a]		3,333

Lessee

Rent expense—leased building[a]	3,333	
Prepaid rent—leased building		3,333

[a]$3,333 = $10,000 ÷ 3

or

(effective-interest amortization, assuming an 8% rate)

Lessor

Interest expense—leased building[b]	512.57	
Rent received in advance—leased building[c]	3,080.33	
Rent revenue—leased building[d]		3,592.90

Lessee

Rent expense—leased building[d]	3,592.90	
Prepaid rent—leased building[c]		3,080.33
Interest revenue[b]		512.57

[b]$512.57 = ($10,000.00 − $3,592.90)(.08)
[c]$3,080.33 = $3,592.90 − $512.57
[d]$3,592.90 = $10,000/$(p_{\overline{n-1}|i} + 1)$ = $10,000/$(p_{\overline{3-1}|.08} + 1)$ = $10,000/(1.783265 + 1)

Note that under effective-interest amortization, the $512.57 interest expense (lessor) represents the interest accrued on the liability (rent received in advance) and the $512.57 interest revenue (lessee) represents the interest accrued on the asset (prepaid rent). The $3,592.90 amortization represents three equal beginning-of-the-year amounts, calculated by dividing the $10,000 advance payment by the present value of an annuity due of $1.00 (see appendix to Chapter 6) at 8 percent for three periods (see Appendix for present-value tables), denoted as $p_{\overline{3-1}|.08} + 1$. Alternatively, the amortization could have been based on an ordinary annuity, or three equal year-end amounts.

As a final illustration of the accounting for an operating lease, assume the same type of building lease as above, except that the lessor makes one lump-sum payment. That is, instead of making three beginning-of-the-year payments of $10,000 each, as in the first illustration, the lessor is willing to make one payment at the inception of the lease. Assuming that the lessor and lessee agree on an interest rate of 8 percent, and since the lump-sum payment is in lieu of three beginning-of-the-year payments, the agreed payment would be equal to $10,000 times the present value of an annuity due of $1 at 8 percent for three periods, or $24,832.65.

Let P_a = Present value (discounted amount) of an annuity
R = Rent payment or receipt at a constant amount per period
$p_{\overline{n-1}|i} + 1$ = Present value of an annuity due of $1 at *i* rate for *n* periods
Then $P_a = R(p_{\overline{n-1}|i} + 1)$
$27,832.65 = ($10,000)($(p_{\overline{3-1}|.08} + 1)$ = ($10,000)(1.783265 + 1)

Typical lease entries (other than the lessor's entries for depreciation and ownership expense, previously illustrated) would be as follows:

Lessor			Lessee		
January 1, 19+2:					
Cash	27,832.65		Prepaid rent—leased building	27,832.65	
Rent received in advance—leased building		27,832.65	Cash		27,832.65
December 31, 19+2:					
(straight-line amortization)					
Rent received in advance—leased building	9,277.55		Rent expense—leased building[a]	9,277.55	
Rent revenue—leased building[a]		9,277.55	Prepaid rent—leased building		9,277.55

[a]$9,277.55 = $27,832.65 ÷ 3

or

Lessor			Lessee		
(effective-interest amortization)					
Rent received in advance—leased building[b]	8,573.39		Rent expense—leased building	10,000.00	
Interest expense—leased building[c]	1,426.61		Prepaid rent—leased building[b]		8,573.39
Rent revenue—leased building		10,000.00	Interest revenue—leased building[c]		1,426.61

[b]$8,573.39 = $10,000.00 − $1,426.61
[c]$1,426.61 = ($27,832.65 − $10,000)(.08)

As previously discussed in the down-payment illustration, effective-interest amortization is theoretically preferable to straight-line amortization, because it takes into account the time value of money (interest). In the example above, the time value of money over the three years is equal to $2,167.35, which is the difference between the discounted amount of $27,832.65 that was paid by the lessor in one lump-sum amount and the $30,000 that would have been paid in three equal installments of $10,000 each.

Financing leases. The basic characteristics of a financing lease are as follows:

The usual risks and rewards of ownership of the leased property are passed to the lessee without a formal transfer of title (the lessor retains formal title to the property). Thus the lessee pays for the ownership expenses of the leased property, such as insurance, taxes, and maintenance, and incurs such ownership expense as amortization of the leased asset. (Unlike the case with an operating lease, these ownership expenses are not covered in the rental payment.)

The lease is noncancelable, or cancelable only upon some remote contingency.

The periodic lease payments over the life of the lease are designed to allow the lessor full recovery of his investment plus a fair return on the investment.

The lease is a long-term lease that normally includes one of the following:

The term of the lease covers essentially the entire useful life of the leased property (salvage is small or nonexistent).

The term of the lease is shorter than the useful life of the leased property, and the lessee has the option to acquire the property at a bargain price or renew the lease at bargain rentals. (This condition is added to be consistent with the accounting for lessees per *Opinion No. 5,* which will be discussed later.)

Under a financing lease, the lessor invests in property and then leases the property to earn a return on that investment. The lessor provides major financing and the lessee obtains a major source of financing. The lessee, in effect, acquires property financed by the lessor, and assumes the risks of ownership without obtaining formal title to the leased property.

For example, such financial institutions as lease-finance companies, banks, and insurance companies provide major financing via financing leases. In addition, as will be discussed in a subsequent section of this chapter, manufacturing companies engage in financing leases to aid in marketing their products.

In accounting for financing leases, at the inception of the lease the lessor transfers the property to a receivable account. Note, however, that the aggregate rentals will exceed the discounted amount of the future rentals, with the excess representing compensation, in the form of interest, to the lessor for investing in the property. Thus the receivable can be set up at the discounted amount of the future rentals (which would equal cost) or at the aggregate future rentals, with the excess over the discounted amount recorded as unearned interest revenue (aggregate rentals minus unearned interest revenue equals the discounted amount). The discounted amount of the future rentals at the beginning of the period, multiplied by the agreed interest rate in the lease contract (assuming a fair rate), would be equal to the periodic interest revenue recognized by the lessor.

In accounting for the lessee under financing leases, the lessee recognizes the leased property as an asset and the obligation to make future periodic payments as a liability, since the lessee, in effect, acquires the property. The asset and liability can be recorded at the discounted amount of the future periodic payments, or the liability can be recorded at the aggregate future periodic payments, offset by a discount on the lease liability (aggregate payments minus the discount on liability equals the discounted amount of the future payments). The lessee recognizes periodic amortization of the leased asset, periodic ownership expenses, periodic interest expense (discounted amount at beginning of the period multiplied by the agreed-on interest rate), and periodic reduction of the liability (periodic payment minus effective interest).

ILLUSTRATION: To illustrate the accounting for a financing lease, assume that a lease-finance company leases equipment costing $44,651.06 for five equal annual receipts of $10,000 each, payable at the beginning of each year. The lease is noncancelable, the lessee assumes the normal ownership expense, and the title to the equipment transfers to the lessee at the end of the term of the lease.

The lessor determined the $10,000 annual receipts based on his earning a 6 percent return on the investment of $44,651.06. Since the payments are made at the beginning of each period, the present value of an annuity due of $1 for five periods at 6 percent interest, divided into the present value of the investment ($44,651.06), is equal to the annual $10,000 receipt.

$$R = P_a/(p_{\overline{n-1}|i} + 1)$$

$$\$10{,}000 = \$44{,}651.06/(p_{\overline{5-1}|.06} + 1) = \$44{,}651.06/(3.465106 + 1)$$

Similarly, the lessee determined the valuation of the leased asset by discounting the future annual payments at the agreed interest rate of 6 percent. That is, since the payments are to be made at the beginning of each period, the $10,000 annual payment, multiplied by the present value of an annuity due of $1 for five periods at 6 percent interest, is equal to the valuation of $44,651.06.

$$P_a = R(p_{\overline{n-1}|i} + 1)$$

$$\$44{,}651.06 = \$10{,}000(p_{\overline{5-1}|.06} + 1) = \$10{,}000(3.465106 + 1)$$

To facilitate the preparation of journal entries, lease-amortization schedules can be prepared by both the lessor and the lessee. In order to illustrate a lease-amortization schedule applicable to both the lessor and the lessee, a schedule with general headings is presented below:

Period	Annual Cash Flow at Beginning of Period	Interest	Amortization	Discounted Amount (Present Value) at End of Period
0				$44,651.06
1	$10,000	$2,079.06[a]	$ 7,920.94[b]	36,730.12[c]
2	10,000	1,603.81	8,396.19	28,333.93
3	10,000	1,100.04	8,899.96	19,433.97
4	10,000	566.03	9,433.97	10,000.00
5	10,000	—	10,000.00	—
	$50,000	$5,348.94	$44,651.06	

[a]$ 2,079.06 = ($44,651.06 − $10,000)(.06)
[b]$ 7,920.94 = $10,000.00 − $2,079.06
[c]$36,730.12 = $44,651.06 − $7,920.94

Note that since annual cash receipts (lessor) and payments (lessee) of $10,000 occur at the beginning of each period, interest accrues each period on the beginning discounted amount minus the $10,000 cash flow; hence, for the last year (period 5), there is no interest. Also, note that interest declines and amortization increases each period, because interest is calculated by multiplying the interest rate by a declining discounted amount.

Assuming that the lessee amortizes the lease rights under the straight-line method ($44,651.06/5 = $8,930.21), that the lessee incurs ownership expenses of $3,000 and $4,000 for years 1 and 2 respectively, and using the amortization schedule above, typical journal entries for the first two years would be as follows:

Lessor			Lessee		
January 1, 19+1:					
Receivables—leased equipment	40,000.00		Lease rights—equipment...........	44,651.06	
Cash.................	10,000.00		Discount on lease obligation	5,348.94	
Equipment....		44,651.06	Lease obligation.		40,000.00
Unearned interest revenue—lease		5,348.94	Cash		10,000.00
			Lease rights—equipment...........	44,651.06	
or					
Receivables—leased equipment	34,651.06		Lease obligation.		34,651.06
Cash.................	10,000.00		Cash		10,000.00
Equipment....		44,651.06			
During 19+1:			Miscellaneous expense (ownership expense)	3,000.00	
—			Cash		3,000.00
December 31, 19+1:			Interest expense—lease................	2,079.06	
Unearned interest revenue—lease ..	2,079.06		Amortization expense—lease	8,930.21	
Interest revenue—lease		2,079.06	Discount on lease obligation		2,079.06
			Lease rights—equipment....		8,930.21
or					
Receivables—leased equipment	2,079.06		Interest expense—lease................	2,079.06	
Interest revenue—lease........		2,079.06	Amortization expense—lease	8,930.21	
			Lease obligation		2,079.06
			Lease rights—equipment....		8,930.21
January 1, 19+2:					
Cash.................	10,000.00		Lease obligation........	10,000.00	
Receivables—leased equipment....		10,000.00	Cash		10,000.00
During 19+2:			Miscellaneous expense	4,000.00	
—			Cash		4,000.00

Lessor			Lessee		
December 31, 19+2:					
Unearned interest revenue—lease	1,603.81		Interest expense—lease	1,603.81	
Interest revenue—lease		1,603.81	Amortization expense—lease	8,930.21	
			Discount on lease obligation		1,603.81
			Lease rights—equipment		8,930.21

or

Lessor			Lessee		
Receivables—leased equipment	1,603.81		Interest expense—lease	1,603.81	
Interest revenue—lease		1,603.81	Amortization expense—lease	8,930.21	
			Lease obligation		1,603.81
			Lease rights—equipment		8,930.21

Note that alternative entries are given above for the lessor. Under the first alternative, as recommended by *Opinion No. 7,* receivables are recorded and reported at the *aggregate* amount to be collected ($40,000 on January 1, 19+1) and are offset by the unearned interest revenue ($5,348.94), which nets to the discounted amount ($34,651.06) of the receivables. Since the receivables are recorded gross, the subsequent accruing of interest revenue is debited to Unearned Interest Revenue instead of to Receivables, and the subsequent cash collections are credited to Receivables. Under the second alternative, the receivables are recorded at their discounted amount ($34,651.06 on January 1, 19+1); hence, the subsequent accruing of interest revenue is debited directly to Receivables for the interest growth on the discounted amount of the asset, and the subsequent cash collections are credited to Receivables.

Similarly, alternative entries are given above for the lessee. Under the first alternative, the lease obligation is recorded at the total amount owing ($40,000 on January 1, 19+1) and is offset by the discount on the lease obligation ($5,348.94), which nets to the discounted amount ($34,651.06) of the lease obligation. Since the lease obligation is recorded gross, the subsequent accruing of interest expense is credited to Discount on Lease Obligation instead of to Lease Obligation, and the subsequent cash payments are debited to Lease Obligation. Under the second alternative, the lease obligation is recorded at its discounted amount ($34,651.06); hence, the subsequent accruing of interest expense is credited directly to Lease Obligation for the interest growth on the discounted amount of the liability, and the subsequent cash payments are debited to Lease Obligation.

From the lessee viewpoint, the accounting for the amortization of the asset, lease rights, is done, as with depreciation, under such conventional methods as straight line and sum-of-the-years' digits. Although not usually done in current accounting practice, the lease rights could be amortized by the effective-interest method, which corresponds to the amortization column shown above in the amortization schedule. Effective-interest amortization of the lease rights would result in reporting the asset at its discounted amount (present value) and reporting periodic amortization expense in line with the discounted amount of the asset, which is consistent with the financing nature of the lease.[3]

Financial-statement disclosure. Under financing leases, the lessor reports the receivables from the lease as an asset, classified into current and noncurrent portions. The current receivable would be next period's cash receipt from the lessee minus the related unearned interest revenue (next period's interest to be earned). The noncurrent receivable, reported under the Investments or the Other Assets classification, would be the remaining cash receipts (cash receipts after next period) minus the remaining unearned interest revenue (interest to be earned after next period).

For example, referring to the amortization schedule on page 210, the lessor would report the lease in the balance sheet at the end of the first year as follows (excluding the explanatory footnotes):

Current assets:		
Receivables—leased equipment	\$10,000.00[a]	
Less unearned interest revenue	1,603.81[b]	8,396.19
Investments (or Other assets):		
Receivables—leased equipment	\$30,000.00[c]	
Less unearned interest revenue	1,666.07[d]	28,333.93

[a]Next period's (period 2) cash receipt from lease of \$10,000.
[b]Next period's (period 2) interest to be earned of \$1,603.81.
[c]Total cash receipts from lease to be collected after next period, or \$10,000 + \$10,000 + \$10,000.
[d]Total interest to be earned after next period, or \$1,100.04 + \$566.03.

Note that the \$8,396.19 current receivable and the \$28,333.93 noncurrent receivable total to \$36,730.12, which is the discounted amount of the receivable at the end of the first year. Thus, if the receivable is recorded and reported at its discounted amount instead of at gross offset by unearned interest revenue, only the \$8,396.19 and the \$28,333.93 would be reported.

As to the balance-sheet reporting of the lessee under a financing lease, the lessee reports the lease rights as an asset under the Intangible Assets classification. As is conventionally done for the reporting of intangible assets, the lease rights would be reported net of accumulated amortization to date, without the latter being reported as a separate-line item. On the other hand, some accountants report lease rights under the Property, Plant, and Equipment classification and report accumulated amortization to date as a separate offset to the lease rights.

The lessee would also report the lease obligation in the balance sheet, classifying the liability into current and noncurrent portions. The current liability of the lease obligation would be next period's cash payment to the lessor minus the related discount on the lease obligation (next period's interest expense). The noncurrent liability, classified under Long-Term Liabilities, would be the remaining

[3]Effective-interest amortization is similar to sinking-fund depreciation. See James A. Gentry, Jr., and Glenn L. Johnson, *Finney and Miller's Principles of Accounting: Advanced* (Englewood Cliffs, N.J.: Prentice-Hall, Inc., 1971), pp. 327–30.

cash payments (cash payments after next period) minus the remaining discount on the lease obligation (interest to be expensed after next period).

For example, referring to the amortization schedule on page 210, and assuming straight-line amortization of the lease rights ($44,651.06/5 = $8,930.21), the lessee would report the lease in the balance sheet at the end of the second year as follows (excluding the explanatory footnotes):

Intangible assets:		Current liabilities:		
Lease rights—equipment........	$26,790.64[a]	Lease obligation—equipment........	$10,000.00[b]	
		Less discount on lease obligation	1,100.04[c]	8,899.96
		Long-term liabilities:		
		Lease obligation—equipment........	$20,000.00[d]	
		Less discount on lease obligation	566.03[e]	19,433.97

[a]$26,790.64 = $44,651.06 − ($8,930.21 + $8,930.21)
[b]Next period's (period 3) cash payment on lease of $10,000.
[c]Next period's (period 3) interest expense of $1,100.04.
[d]Total cash payments to be made on lease after next period, or $10,000 + $10,000.
[e]Total interest expense to be incurred after next period, or $566.03.

Note that the $8,899.96 current liability and the $19,433.97 long-term liability total to $28,333.93, which is the discounted amount of the lease obligation at the end of the second year. Thus, if the liability is recorded and reported at its discounted amount, instead of at gross offset by the discount, only the $8,899.96 and the $19,433.97 would be reported.

With regard to income-statement reporting under a financing lease, the lessor reports periodic interest revenue on the lease and the lessee reports periodic interest expense and amortization expense on the lease. In addition, the lessee reports the periodic ownership expense, such as maintenance, taxes, and insurance, on the leased property.

Balance-sheet reporting under an operating lease has the lessor reporting the lease property as a separate-line item under the Property, Plant, and Equipment classification. Accumulated depreciation on the leased property is reported contra to the leased asset. The lessee, under an operating lease, has no line-item balance-sheet reporting of the lease, since the lessee is merely paying annual rentals and has *not* acquired property or incurred a liability.

Income-statement reporting under an operating lease has the lessor reporting periodic rent revenue and the lessee periodic rent expense. In addition, the lessor reports depreciation expense on the leased property and periodic ownership expense.

In order to disclose sufficient information regarding the present and prospective effect of lease commitments under the operating leases of lessees, details of the lease should be disclosed in notes to the financial statements, in separate statements or schedules, or parenthetically in the financial statements. Such information would disclose the following:[4]

Disclosure of the total rental expense for each period for which an income statement is presented for all leases having initial noncancelable terms of more than one year and for all other leases other than very-short-term leases not expected to be renewed.

Disclosure of the minimum annual rental requirements under lease agreements for each of the five succeeding fiscal years and thereafter by five-year periods for all leases with initial noncancelable terms of more than one year.

The following information should be disclosed as of the close of the latest fiscal year for all leases with initial noncancelable terms of more than one year:

(a) The present values of the net fixed-minimum lease commitments in the aggregate and by major categories of properties
(b) The weighted-average interest rate for the aggregate of all lease commitments included in the amount disclosed under (a) above
(c) The present values of rentals to be received from existing subleases of property included in (a) above

Additional information should be disclosed on the basis for calculating rental payments (if dependent on other than lapse of time), significant renewal or purchase options, guarantees made or obligations assumed, lease restrictions, and any other information necessary to assess the effect of lease commitments upon the financial statements.

Sale and leaseback. A sale-and-leaseback transaction is one by which the owner of property enters into an agreement with another party to sell the property and to simultaneously lease it back. For example, a grocery chain may construct a building according to its specifications, and then sell it to and lease it back from another party without interruption in the use of the building. In exchange for a long-term obligation to make fixed periodic cash payments, the lessee (original owner) frees cash that would otherwise be tied up as an investment in the property, and at the same time receives a full tax deduction on the periodic payments. The lessor (buyer) makes a long-term investment in the property in return for periodic cash receipts sufficient to recover the investment and earn a fair return on it.

The annual lease payments are related to the sale price of the property, because the sale and the leaseback are, in effect, a single economic transaction. Thus *Opinion No. 5* states that the sale and the leaseback usually cannot be accounted for as independent transactions. Any material gains or losses on the property resulting from sale-and-leaseback transactions, together with the related tax effects,

---

[4]Based on Accounting Principles Board, "Disclosure of Lease Commitments by Lessees," *Exposure Draft: Proposed APB Opinion Ref. No. 504* (New York: AICPA, January 1973), pp. 4–5.

should be amortized over the life of the lease as an adjustment of the rental expense (operating lease) or as an adjustment of amortization (financing lease).[5]

ILLUSTRATION: To illustrate the accounting for a sale-and-leaseback transaction, assume that Lessee Company has special equipment constructed for it by another company at a cost of $42,123.64. Upon completion of the equipment on January 1, 19+2, Lessee Company sells the equipment to an investor for $42,123.64 and then immediately leases it back from the investor (lessor). Further assume that the lease is a financing-type lease—that is, it is noncancelable, the lessee assumes the normal ownership expense, and the title to the equipment transfers to the lessee at the end of the term of the lease. It is agreed that the lessor should earn a 6 percent return on his investment; hence, it is agreed that Lessee Company will make annual payments of $10,000 at the end of each year, beginning December 31, 19+2, for five years. The $10,000 annual payment is determined by dividing the present value of the lease ($42,123.64) by the present value of an ordinary annuity of $1.00 for five periods at 6 percent interest ($p_{\overline{5}|.06}$), as shown below:

$$R = P_a / p_{\overline{n}|i}$$
$$\$10{,}000 = \$42{,}123.64 / p_{\overline{5}|.06} = \$42{,}123.64 / 4.212364$$

To facilitate the preparation of journal entries, the lease amortization schedule on page 217 is constructed. (Note that for purposes of comparison, the difference between the schedule shown on page 217 and the schedule on page 210 is that lease payments of the former are at the end of the period, which affects the lease valuation and therefore the interest and the amortization.)

Assuming that Lessee Company amortizes the lease rights under the straight-line method ($42,123.64/5 = $8,424.73), typical journal entries for the first year of the lease would be as follows:

Lessor			Lessee		
January 1, 19+2:					
Receivables—leased equipment	50,000.00		Lease rights—equipment	42,123.64	
Cash		42,123.64	Equipment......		42,123.64
Unearned interest revenue —lease ...		7,876.36	Cash	42,123.64	
			Discount on lease obligation..........	7,876.36	
			Lease obligation		50,000.00
or					
Receivables—leased equipment........	42,123.64		Cash	42,123.64	
Cash		42,123.64	Lease obligation		42,123.64

[5]See Accounting Principles Board, "Reporting of Leases in Financial Statements of Lessee," *Opinion No. 5* (New York: AICPA, September 1964), p. 33.

Period	Discounted Amount (Present Value) at Beginning of Period	Annual Cash Flow at End of Period	Interest	Amortization	Discounted Amount (Present Value) at End of Period
1	$42,123.64	$10,000.00	$2,527.42[a]	$ 7,472.58[b]	$34,651.06[c]
2	34,651.06	10,000.00	2,079.06	7,920.94	26,730.12
3	26,730.12	10,000.00	1,603.81	8,396.19	18,333.93
4	18,333.93	10,000.00	1,100.04	8,899.96	9,433.97
5	9,433.97	10,000.00	566.03[d]	9,433.97	—
		$50,000.00	$7,876.36	$42,123.64	

[a]$2,527.42 = $42,123.64 × .06
[b]$7,472.58 = $10,000.00 − $2,527.42
[c]$34,651.06 = $42,123.64 − $7,472.58
[d]Rounded down 1 cent.

December 31, 19+2:

Lessor			Lessee		
Cash	10,000.00		Lease obligation	10,000.00	
Unearned interest revenue—lease	2,527.42		Interest expense—lease	2,527.42	
Receivables—leased equipment		10,000.00	Amortization expense—lease	8,424.73	
Interest revenue—lease		2,527.42	Cash		10,000.00
			Discount on lease obligation		2,527.42
			Lease rights		8,424.73

or

Lessor			Lessee		
Cash	10,000.00		Lease obligation	7,472.58	
Receivables—leased equipment		7,472.58	Interest expense—lease	2,527.42	
Interest revenue—lease		2,527.42	Amortization expense—lease	8,424.73	
			Cash		10,000.00
			Lease rights—equipment		8,424.73

Opinions No. 5 and No. 7. Up to this point, the discussion on the accounting for leases has been made conceptually consistent between the lessor and the lessee by maintaining the distinction between operating and financing leases. For example, under an operating lease, the lessor accounts for the annual rental revenue and the lessee accounts for the annual rental expense, because the terms of the lease are such that it is *not* in substance a sale-purchase contract. Under a financing lease, the lessor accounts for the lease by setting up a receivable and recognizing revenue, similar to a sale, and the lessee capitalizes the lease rights and the lease obligation, similar to a purchase. Given the same lease contract, the accounting for the lessor and the lessee should be conceptually consistent, which they are if both account for the lease in the same manner (both treat it as a financing lease or both treat it as an operating lease).

The distinction between operating and financing leases is based on APB *Opinion No. 7;* however, the Opinion covers the accounting for lessors, not for lessees. Thus the accounting for lessors so far discussed is consistent with *Opinion No. 7,* and the accounting for lessees has been made consistent with the accounting for lessors (see page 209). That is, the distinction between financing and operating leases per *Opinion No. 7* has been used to account for lessees, even though the opinion does not cover lessees.

The accounting for lessees is covered by APB *Opinion No. 5.* This Opinion does not make the distinction between operating and financing leases, as does *Opinion No. 7.* Instead, *Opinion No. 5* makes the distinction between leases that are in substance installment purchases of property and those that are not. Only if the lease is in effect a purchase can the lessee capitalize the lease rights as an asset and the lease obligation as a liability.

Per *Opinion No. 5,* a lease is in substance a purchase if its terms result in the creation of a material equity in the property for the lessee. Thus a lease is equivalent to a purchase by the lessee if the lease is noncancelable (or cancelable only upon some remote contingency) and either of the two following conditions exist:

The initial term of the lease is materially less than the useful life of the property, and the lessee has the option to renew the lease for the remaining useful life of the property at substantially less than the fair rental amount; or

The lessee has the right, during or at the expiration of the lease, to acquire the property at a price that, at the inception of the lease, appears to be substantially less than the probable fair market value of the property at the time or times of permitted acquisition by the lessee.

Per *Opinion No. 5,* if the lease is noncancelable and if either of the two preceding conditions exist, then the lease is definitely creating material equity for the lessee and is in substance a purchase. In some cases it may be difficult to determine whether material equity is being created by the lease based on the two preceding conditions; hence, *Opinion No. 5* specifies, in addition to the lease being noncancelable, that one or more of the following special circumstances would qualify the lease as in substance a purchase:

The property was acquired by the lessor to meet the special needs of the lessee and will probably be usable only for that purpose and only by the lessee.

The term of the lease corresponds substantially to the estimated useful life of the property, and the lessee is obligated to pay costs, such as taxes, insurance, and maintenance, that are usually considered incidental to ownership.

The lessee has guaranteed the obligations of the lessor with respect to the property leased.

The lessee has treated the lease as a purchase for tax purposes.[6]

Opinion No. 5 is consistent with *Opinion No. 7* with regard to operating leases. Under an operating lease, the lessee is *not* in effect purchasing the property and therefore would not capitalize the lease, which is consistent with the accounting for the lessor as if the lease were *not* in effect a sale. From a very general viewpoint, *Opinion No. 5* is consistent with *Opinion No. 7* with regard to financing leases. In many cases, a financing lease does result in the lessee's in effect purchasing the property and therefore capitalizing the lease, which is consistent with the accounting for the lessor as if the lease *were* in effect a sale.

On the other hand, there is some inconsistency between *Opinion No. 5* and *Opinion No. 7,* which has resulted in a current controversy in accounting practice.

---

[6]*Opinion No. 5,* pp. 30–31.

A lease can qualify as a financing lease per *Opinion No. 7*, and therefore require the lessor to account for the lease as for a sale, and at the same time the terms of the lease can be such that the lessee is not acquiring equity in the property, and therefore is not required to capitalize the lease per *Opinion No. 5*. For example, the lease may be a financing lease, but without options permitting a bargain purchase or the renewal of the lease at bargain rentals by the lessee—thus no equity is created.

Some accountants believe that the requirement of *Opinion No. 5* that equity is created by the lease is inconsistent with *Opinion No. 7*, and instead all financing leases should result in capitalization by the lessee. The same lease should be accounted for in a consistent manner by both the lessor and the lessee. However, given the flexibility of *Opinion No. 5*, lessees are tempted to account for financing leases on an annual rental-expense basis (noncapitalization) in order to avoid showing the lease liability on the balance sheet—a practice called "off-balance-sheet financing." If the lease is noncancelable, covers substantially the full useful life of the property, requires the lessee to assume the costs of ownership, and requires annual payments that cover the lessor's investment in the property plus a fair return, then the lease is a financing lease that should conceptually require the lessee to capitalize it. The lessee is using the lease to finance the acquisition of property rights under his possession and control, which is equivalent to asset acquisition and liability assumption, regardless of bargain-purchase or bargain-rental options that create equity in the property. Moreover, as Leonard Spacek points out in his dissent to *Opinion No. 5*, the creation of equity is equivalent to prepaid rent that should be deferred to applicable periods:

> It is incorrect to assume that only when rental charges are thus determined to be excessive in early periods does a recordable obligation for future payments result, since this leads to the unsupportable conclusion that the payment of prepaid rent creates a liability and the nonexistence of prepaid rent eliminates the liability.[7]

Manufacturer or dealer lessors. Manufacturers and dealers enter into leases with independent lessees to assist in the marketing of their products or services. If the terms of a lease were such as to qualify it as a financing lease, and there were no important uncertainties regarding costs and ownership risk, manufacturers were allowed, per *Opinion No. 7*, to account for it as a financing lease and recognize all revenue and related cost at the time the lease agreement was entered into. Manufacturers naturally prefer accounting for leases as financing-type leases, since revenue is recognized during the period when the lease agreement is made, even though full cash payment has not been received by the lessor and will, in fact, be

---

[7]*Opinion No. 5*, pp. 34–35.

spread out over several years. Note that for the same type of financing lease, the lessor prefers accounting for it as a financing lease to report increased earnings and the lessee prefers accounting for it as an operating lease so as not to have to report the lease obligation as a liability.

Because of questions that arose about the circumstances under which it was appropriate for the manufacturer to account for leases as financing-type leases, the Accounting Principles Board concluded that more specific criteria than that provided by *Opinion No. 7* were needed for determining when a manufacturer or dealer lessor could account for the lease as if it were similar to a sale. Thus the board issued *Opinion No. 27,* which states the following:

> A manufacturer or dealer lessor should account for a lease transaction with an independent lessee as a sale if at the time of entering into the transaction (a) collectibility of the payments required from the lessee is reasonably assured, (b) no important uncertainties, such as those described in paragraph 7 discussed below, surround the amount of costs yet to be incurred under the lease, and (c) any one of the following conditions is present:
>
> (i) The lease transfers title to the property to the lessee by the end of its fixed, noncancelable term; or
>
> (ii) The lease gives the lessee the option to obtain title to the property without cost or at a nominal cost by the end of the fixed, noncancelable term of the lease; or
>
> (iii) The leased property, or like property, is available for sale, and the sum of (1) the present value of the required rental payments by the lessee under the lease during the fixed, noncancelable term of the lease (excluding any renewal or other option) and (2) any related investment tax credit retained by the lessor (if realization of such credit is assured beyond any reasonable doubt) is equal to or greater than the normal selling price or, in the absence thereof, the fair value (either of which may be less than cost) of the leased property or like property; or
>
> (iv) The fixed, noncancelable term of the lease (excluding any renewal option) is substantially equal to the remaining economic life of the property.[8]

Under such leases as described above, per *Opinion No. 27* the lessor recognizes as revenue in the period of sale an amount equal to the discounted amount (present value) of the annual cash receipts to be paid by the lessee during the fixed, noncancelable term (excluding any renewal or other options) of the lease. The cost of the leased property and any estimated related future costs are charged

---

[8]Accounting Principles Board, "Accounting for Lease Transactions by Manufacturer or Dealer Lessors," *Opinion No. 27* (New York: AICPA, November 1972), pp. 509–10.

against revenue during the period of sale, which could result in a loss on the transaction.[9]

A lease may appear to meet the tests of recognition as a sale, but because of the difficulties in evaluating future costs, the risks may be so great that the lease should be accounted for as an operating lease. Examples of such future costs include extensive lessor guarantees on product warranties, guarantees against obsolescence, and the like.

ILLUSTRATION: To illustrate the accounting for a manufacturer lessor, assume that a company manufactures equipment at a cost of $35,095.28. The company sells its equipment for $42,123.64 or leases it to earn 6 percent on the selling price.

Assume that on January 1, 19+2, the company leases a piece of equipment in return for annual year-end payments of $10,000 for five years. The lease is a financing-type lease, in that the lease is noncancelable, the lessee assumes the normal ownership expense, and the title to the equipment transfers to the lessee at the end of the term of the lease. Typical journal entries for the lease on January 1, 19+2, would be as follows. (Note that since the lease data for this illustration are the same as for the sale-and-leaseback illustration on pages 216 and 217, year-end entries, as well as the lease-amortization schedule, would be the same and are therefore not repeated.)

Manufacturer Lessor

Cost of goods sold	35,095.28	
Finished goods ..		35,095.28
Receivables—leased equipment..........	50,000.00	
Lease revenue—equipment....		42,123.64
Unearned interest revenue—lease		7,876.36

Lessee

Lease rights—equipment..........	42,123.64	
Discount on lease obligation	7,876.36	
Lease obligation.		50,000.00

[9] *Opinion No. 27,* pp. 510–11.

Cash and Marketable Securities

CASH

What is cash? In order to be classified as cash, an item must meet the following requirements:

(1) It must be acceptable as a medium of exchange.
(2) It must be available as a source of current funds.

Thus, cash would generally consist of currency and coin, checks, bank drafts, money orders, cashier's checks, and demand deposits in banks.

Certain other items are sometimes incorrectly classified as cash. For example, some concerns make a practice of allowing customers ordering goods by mail to make payment in postage stamps; such remittances should be recorded not as cash, but as postage inventory.

Monies advanced to salesmen or other representatives for traveling and other expense disbursements have ceased to be under the control of management for immediate disbursement for other purposes, and are therefore properly shown in the balance sheet as prepayments or receivables from employees.

The practice of carrying due bills or I.O.U.'s of officers and employees as cash in place of money advanced is improper. They should be shown in the balance sheet as receivables from officers or employees.

Although checks payable to a company are usually included in its cash, there are some exceptions. If a check credited to a customer's account and sent to the bank for deposit is returned by the bank because of insufficient funds, the entry crediting the customer should be reversed. (A reversing entry is not necessary if the check is returned for lack of endorsement.) Postdated checks should not be recorded until the date when they can be deposited. Company officials and others in a position to do so sometimes "pay" the debit balance in their accounts by checks that it is understood will not be deposited. Obviously, if there is any restriction upon the deposit or cashing of a check, the check is not an available source of current funds. Any statement prepared while such a check is held should show the amount thereof as a receivable.

Deposits in savings accounts are usually classified in the balance sheet as cash, notwithstanding the legal right of the bank to demand a certain notice before withdrawal; the classification of such balances as cash appears to be justified, because the bank's right to demand notice is rarely exercised. Demand certificates of deposit may be classified as cash, but time certificates should not be so classified. A portion of the balance on deposit in an ordinary commercial checking account may not be subject to immediate withdrawal because, under the terms of a bank loan, the depositor is obligated to maintain a minimum or compensating balance; notwithstanding such restrictions, it is customary to include the entire bank balance as current cash.

Deposits in closed banks should not be regarded as current cash, nor should balances in foreign banks be so considered if they are subject to any restrictions. If the deposits in foreign banks are available for unrestricted withdrawal, they may be classified as current cash at an amount determined by translation at the current exchange rate.

Cash deposits made in connection with contract or other bids, or deposits made in connection with purchase contracts, should be shown as deposits on contract bids or as advances against purchases, rather than as cash, even though the deposits are returnable in cash under certain circumstances.

A distinction should be made in the balance sheet between cash available for general operating purposes and cash tied up in special-purpose funds. If a fund is to be used for the payment of a current liability, as is the case with money deposited with a trustee for the payment of mortgage interest and taxes on mortgaged property, it should not be merged with the general cash. However, because the debt is a current liability, the special fund can properly be classified under the Current Assets caption, with a statement of the purpose for which it is available. Special funds not available for current purposes, such as a sinking fund for the payment of the principal of a long-term debt, a fund for the retirement of capital stock, or the proceeds of a construction mortgage that are impounded and available for disbursement only for construction work, should not be shown under the Current Assets caption.

Whether notes and acceptances endorsed to a bank should be shown in the balance sheet as cash or as receivables depends on whether the bank took the paper as deposits or merely for collection. Only if the bank credited the depositor's account with the paper may the item properly be included in the cash.

Bank overdrafts. A bank overdraft exists when a depositor issues checks in excess of the amount he has on deposit in his bank account. Under these circumstances, the account is said to be overdrawn. There is some difference of opinion among accountants as to the proper balance-sheet treatment of overdrafts.

If there is only one bank account and this account is overdrawn, the amount of the overdraft must be shown as a liability.

If there are several bank accounts, one or more with overdrafts and one or more with available balances, and if the available balances are in excess of the overdrafts, it has until recently been regarded as permissible to show on the asset side of the balance sheet the excess of the available bank balances over the overdrafts, particularly if it is the company's practice to transfer funds from bank to bank as required. However, this opinion is no longer generally held, and it is now considered better practice to show the bank balances on the asset side and the overdrafts on the liability side. Some accountants still consider it permissible merely to show on the asset side the net available bank funds, provided that reference is made to the overdrafts by the use of some clearly descriptive balance-sheet title, such as "Cash in Banks—Net of Overdrafts."

Some accountants have taken the position that if the company's books show an overdraft, whereas the bank statement shows an available balance (the difference being represented by outstanding checks), such an overdraft may be offset against balances in other banks without disclosure in the balance sheet, disclosure being necessary only if the bank statement shows an overdraft. Such a distinction scarcely seems logical. If the checks are outstanding, the issuing company has no control over them and, so far as available funds are concerned, an overdraft in fact exists. Of course, if the checks have been merely drawn and recorded but have not been issued, and are therefore under the company's control, adjusting entries should be made to restore the amounts thereof to the bank balance and to the accounts payable.

Distorted cash balances. In order to improve the appearance of its balance sheet, a company may resort to the practice of holding its cash book open for a few days after the close of the accounting period and recording as of the last day of the period remittances received after the close of the period. Such a procedure has the effect of overstating the most current asset, cash, by correspondingly understating the less current asset of accounts receivable.

The company may then go one step further by drawing checks after the close of the period for payment of current liabilities, and recording such payments as of the last day of the period.

To illustrate the effect of this practice upon the current position shown by the balance sheet, let us assume that a company holds its cash book open for collections of receivables amounting to $25,000, and for payments totaling $20,000 on current liabilities. The true current position and the distorted position are shown below:

	Correct		Incorrect	
	Amount	Per Cent of Total Current Assets	Amount	Per Cent of Total Current Assets
Current assets:				
Cash	$ 5,000	5.88	$10,000	15.38
Accounts receivable	50,000	58.82	25,000	38.46
Inventories	30,000	35.30	30,000	46.16
Total current assets	$85,000	100.00	$65,000	100.00
Current liabilities:				
Accounts payable	50,000	58.82	30,000	46.16
Net current assets	$35,000	41.18	$35,000	53.84
Dollars of current assets per dollar of current liabilities	$1.70		$2.17	

By this means the company shows a working-capital ratio of 2.17 to 1 instead of 1.70 to 1, and considerably overstates its cash balance and the ratio of cash to total current assets, thus overstating the liquidity of its position.

Cash control procedures. The nature of cash requires that careful control be maintained in order to insure that all cash receipts and disbursements are accounted for. This is accomplished primarily through the operation of an effective system of internal control.

Internal control. A system of internal control consists of a division and integration of procedures to the extent that the activities of various members of an organization are so interrelated that accounting errors and omissions will presumably be detected automatically and the perpetration and concealment of fraud will require collusion.

An adequate system of internal control to safeguard the cash requires a control over both receipts and disbursements. The methods of effecting this control vary greatly; the system described below should be understood to be indicative of the objectives to be attained rather than a procedure to be invariably followed.

The danger of misappropriation of cash is reduced if collusion is made necessary to conceal an abstraction of cash receipts; it is therefore desirable to divide the work of handling cash receipts among several people, whose records must agree. One method of providing such an internal control is indicated below.

(1) All mail receipts and the totals of cash register tapes should be listed and totaled by a trusted employee who is neither the cashier nor a bookkeeper; the letter or other evidence of remittance accompanying each mail receipt should be marked by this employee with the amount of the remittance, initialed by him, and turned over to the accounts receivable bookkeeper, who should also be given duplicates of prenumbered receipts issued to customers for any cash received on account

and rung up on the cash register. The cash should be turned in to the cashier, and a copy of the list mentioned above should be given to the general ledger bookkeeper.

(2) All cash received should be deposited daily. The cashier, after making up the deposit, should submit the deposit slip to the employee mentioned in (1), who should compare the amount of the deposit with the amount of cash received, as shown by his list; if the deposit slip and the list of receipts are in agreement, this employee should initial the deposit slip. When the bank's monthly statement is received, it should be checked by the general-ledger bookkeeper, and the deposits shown by it should be compared by the employee mentioned in (1) with the daily lists prepared by him.

(3) The cashier, the general ledger bookkeeper, and the accounts receivable bookkeeper should be different persons.

(4) An added safeguard may be introduced by having a fifth individual reconcile the bank account.

With such a system of internal control, fraud with respect to collections from debtors cannot be practiced and concealed even for a day without collusion. The first employee has no access to the books and cannot falsify the records to conceal a misappropriation; he cannot expect to withhold funds received from debtors without detection, because the debtors will receive statements or letters from the credit department and will report their remittances. If the cashier withholds any cash, his daily deposit will not agree with the first employee's list or with the general-ledger bookkeeper's cash-receipts record made from the list of receipts. The general-ledger and accounts receivable ledger bookkeepers, having no access to the cash, have no opportunity to misappropriate any of it, and, therefore, have no incentive to falsify their records unless they are parties to collusion.

The bank should be instructed to cash no checks of outsiders payable to the company, but should accept them only for deposit. Checks drawn by the company itself for petty cash or other requirements may be cashed.

Because all receipts are deposited daily in the bank, all disbursements (except from petty cash) must be made by check. Disbursements from petty cash should be approved by someone in authority, and periodic totals thereof should be represented by replenishing checks. The person authorized to sign checks should have no authority to make entries in any of the books; thus a fraudulent disbursement by check could not be concealed without the collusion of two persons. A file of approved invoices, expense bills, and other documents evidencing the propriety of the disbursements should be maintained.

The collusion of a third person in the falsification of disbursements can be made necessary by either of the following methods:

(1) By requiring that all checks shall be signed by one person and countersigned by another.

(2) By allowing checks to be signed by one person, but only upon authorization by another person, evidenced by approved invoices, expense bills,

and so forth. The documents presented to the authorizing person as evidence of the propriety of the disbursement should be initialed or otherwise marked by him to prevent their use a second time.

All checks should be prenumbered. All spoiled, mutilated, or voided checks should be preserved. Some companies even go so far as to require that such checks be recorded in their proper sequence in the cash disbursements record, without entry in the money column but with a notation to the effect that the check is void.

It is advisable to review the system of internal control from time to time to see whether any revisions are desirable as a result of changed operating conditions, and also to determine whether the system of internal control is actually being operated as planned or whether deviations or omissions have been allowed to impair the system.

Cash over and short account. As a part of the system of internal control, frequent and unannounced cash counts should be made by the internal auditing department. Any unlocated differences between the balance per books and the cash on hand and in bank, whether discovered by the accounting staff or by the internal auditing staff, may be set up in a cash over and short account. If all reasonable efforts fail to disclose the cause of the shortage or overage, the account may be closed at the end of the period along with other revenue and expense accounts.

Cash Over and Short should not be charged with an ascertained defalcation; the amount of defalcation should be charged to a special account, which should be written off only in the event to failure to collect from the party responsible therefor or from a bonding company.

Imprest cash systems. In the discussion of internal control, it was stated that all disbursements should be made by check. Petty expenditures not made by checks can nevertheless be represented by checks through the operation of an imprest cash, or petty cash, fund. A check is drawn for an amount that will provide for petty expenditures for a reasonable time, and cashed. The cash is held in the office. The drawing of the check is recorded by a debit to Petty Cash and a credit to the general cash account. As expenditures are made from the petty cash fund, receipts and other memoranda are retained to evidence the nature and propriety of the disbursements. A petty cash book may be kept with a number of columns in which to classify the disbursements, or the classification may be made from the memoranda when the fund is replenished. When the fund is nearly exhausted, another check is cashed for the amount of the expenditures, thus restoring the fund to its original amount; this check is recorded by a credit to the general cash account and debits to various expense or other accounts properly chargeable with the disbursements.

The petty cash fund should be replenished or increased only by check, and never from undeposited cash receipts. The fund should be replenished at the end of each accounting period, even though it is not depleted to the customary replenishing point, so that the disbursements will be recorded in the proper period. If the issuance of a replenishing check is overlooked at the end of the period, an adjusting journal entry may be made, debiting the proper expense or other accounts and crediting Petty Cash; when a replenishing check is issued in a subsequent period, the petty cash account should be debited with the amount with which it was credited in the adjusting entry, and other accounts should be debited with the remainder of the replenishing check. Except for such possible credits and debits, no entries should be made in the petty cash account other than the original debit unless the established amount is increased or decreased.

When the petty cashier requests a replenishing check, he should submit a report of his disbursements, accompanied by receipts or other evidences of the authenticity of the disbursements. This report should be audited, and all the supporting documents should be initialed or otherwise marked by the person who audits the report, so that the petty cashier cannot subsequently use the supporting receipts or other vouchers to obtain a check to which he is not entitled. The internal control over the petty cash fund is also improved by unexpected counts thereof made by the internal auditing staff.

The imprest system can be applied to the control of funds of small or large amounts required at factories, branches, or offices located at a distance from the main office.

ILLUSTRATION: The entries required to account for a petty cash fund are illustrated below.

(1) Establish petty cash fund in the amount of $50.00.

Petty cash	50.00	
Cash		50.00

(2) At the end of the month, cash of $13.85 was on hand. Paid petty cash vouchers totaled $36.00, detailed as follows: postage, $16.17; office supplies, $11.40; freight in, $8.43. The fund is replenished at this time.

Postage expense	16.17	
Office supplies	11.40	
Freight in	8.43	
Cash over and short	.15	
Cash		36.15

(3) It is decided that the fund should be increased to $100.00. A check is drawn for this purpose.

Petty cash	50.00	
Cash		50.00

If for some reason the petty cash fund is not replenished at the end of the accounting period, an adjusting entry should be made in order to record the disbursements made from the fund and to reduce the amount of the asset to be reported on the balance sheet. For example, if entry (2) above is not recorded and it is assumed that the firm's accounting period ends at this time, the following entry is necessary.

Postage expense	16.17	
Office supplies	11.40	
Freight in	8.43	
Cash over and short	.15	
Petty cash		36.15

If it is assumed that the oversight is corrected in the following period and the fund is replenished, the balance in the petty cash account should be increased in order to reflect the original amount of the fund. This is accomplished by the following entry.

Petty cash	36.15	
Cash		36.15

Reconciliation of bank accounts. The balance at the end of the month shown by the bank statement rarely agrees with the balance shown by the depositor's books. The reasons for this are discussed below.

Very frequently, there are items on the depositor's books that do not appear on the bank statement. For instance, there may be outstanding checks (checks written by the depositor that have not yet been presented to the bank for payment), and deposits mailed toward the end of the month may not reach the bank and be recorded on its books until the next month.

Less frequently, there are items on the bank statement that do not appear on the depositor's books. For instance, the bank may have recorded collection or other charges that the depositor may not know about and record until the bank statement is received; or the bank may have credited the depositor with the proceeds of paper left with it for collection, and the notice of collection may not have been received by the depositor before the end of the month.

The purpose of a bank reconciliation is to establish that reconciling items such as those just mentioned are the reason for the difference between the balance per bank statement and the balance per books and, thus, that there is agreement between the bank's records and the depositor's records.

There are two ways in which the bank reconciliation may take place. One is to reconcile both the bank balance and the balance per books to the correct amount. An alternative is to reconcile the bank balance to the balance per books. Both procedures will now be illustrated.

FIRST ILLUSTRATION: In this illustration, the reconciling items are:

A deposit in transit
The outstanding checks
These are items recorded on the books of the depositor but not as yet entered on the bank's records.
The bank charges
The proceeds from a collection made by the bank for the depositor
These are items recorded by the bank but not as yet recorded by the depositor.

If there are items on the books that do not appear on the bank statement and also items on the bank statement that do not appear on the books, it is advisable to reconcile the balance per bank and the balance per books to the correct, or adjusted, balance. Applying this procedure to the information presented in the first illustration, the reconciliation would appear as follows:

ABC CORPORATION
Bank Reconciliation—The City National Bank
December 31, 19+5

Balance per bank statement		$10,361.51
Add:		
Deposit in transit—mailed December 31		9,849.83
Total		$20,211.34
Deduct outstanding checks:		
No. 1264	$1,000.00	
1329	52.80	
1499	84.70	
1510	108.07	
1511	2,500.00	
1512	3,281.70	
1513	3,370.91	
1514	100.80	10,498.98
Correct balance		$ 9,712.36
Balance per books		$ 9,215.33
Add proceeds of draft on J. C. White collected by bank		500.00
Total		$ 9,715.33
Deduct bank charges:		
Telegram	$ 1.80	
Collection charges	1.17	2.97
Correct balance		$ 9,712.36

It should be noted that neither the balance per bank statement nor the balance per books is the correct balance at the end of the month. Therefore, the reconciliation process is not complete until the journal entries necessary to correct the ledger account have been recorded in the journal and posted. The entry required in this case is presented below.

Cash	497.03	
Telephone and telegraph	1.80	
Collection and exchange	1.17	
Accounts receivable (J. C. White)		500.00

SECOND ILLUSTRATION: Using the data from the previous illustration, the bank balance may be reconciled to the balance per books. The bank reconcilation appears below. Since neither the bank balance nor the book balance represents the correct balance, the journal entry shown in the first illustration would also be required in this case.

ABC CORPORATION
Bank Reconciliation—The City National Bank
December 31, 19+5

Balance per bank statement			$10,361.51
Add:			
Deposit in transit—mailed December 31			9,849.83
Bank charges:			
Telegram		$ 1.80	
Collection charges		1.17	2.97
Total			$20,214.31
Deduct outstanding checks:			
No. 1264	$1,000.00		
1329	52.80		
1499	84.70		
1510	108.07		
1511	2,500.00		
1512	3,281.70		
1513	3,370.91		
1514	100.80	$10,498.98	
Add proceeds of draft on J. C. White collected by bank		500.00	10,998.98
Balance per books			$ 9,215.33

THIRD ILLUSTRATION: The following reconciliation of the bank account of Bailey Transformer Company includes several reconciling items not previously mentioned. The books of Bailey Transformer Company showed a balance of $5,900.05 in the First National Bank on September 30, 19+5. There was a deposit of $723.90 in transit. The following checks had not cleared:

No. 2345	$115.21
2347	579.99
2362	300.00

Although check No. 2362 had not cleared, a memo accompanying the bank statement reported that the check had been certified, and consequently charged to the company's account. A check for $350.00 drawn by Bailey Transit Company was improperly charged to Bailey Transformer Company. Check No. 132 for $25.00 was issued in 19+2; it was restored to the bank balance in May, 19+5, as it was believed at that time that, having been outstanding so long, it would not be presented; the entry made in May was a debit to Cash and a credit to Miscellaneous Revenue. This check was paid by the bank in September with the approval of Bailey Transformer Company. Two checks deposited on September 29 were returned: One was a check for $75.50 received from H. E. Gates to apply on account, and returned because there were insufficient funds in the drawer's account to provide for payment of the check; the other was a check for $216.50 received from Henry Bigley, which was returned because it had not been endorsed by Bailey Transformer Company. The latter check was endorsed and redeposited on October 1. Check No. 2357 for $279.20 was improperly recorded as $297.20; the offsetting debit was to Purchases. The bank's service charge for September was $6.75.

The bank reconciliation is shown below.

BAILEY TRANSFORMER COMPANY
Bank Reconciliation—The First National Bank
September 30, 19+5

Balance per bank statement		$5,215.60
Add: Deposit in transit		723.90
Check of Bailey Transit Company charged to our account		350.00
Check of Henry Bigley returned for endorsement		216.50
Total		$6,506.00
Deduct outstanding checks:		
No. 2345	$115.21	
2347	579.99	
2362—certified—$300.00		695.20
Correct balance		$5,810.80
Balance per books		$5,900.05
Add error in recording check No. 2357 as $297.20 instead of as $279.20, the amount for which it was drawn		18.00
Total		$5,918.05
Deduct: N.S.F. check—H. E. Gates	$ 75.50	
Check No. 132 issued in 19+2 restored to cash balance in May, 19+5, but now cleared	25.00	
Monthly service charge	6.75	107.25
Correct balance		$5,810.80

Although check No. 2362 has not cleared the bank, it was certified and charged by the bank to the company's account; therefore, it is not shown as a reconciling item.

The check returned by the bank because of insufficient funds is shown as a deduction from the balance per books, because the check is not good and should be charged back to the maker.

The check returned for endorsement is added to the balance per bank, because the check was immediately endorsed and redeposited.

The following entries should be made.

Cash	18.00	
Purchases		18.00
To correct error in recording Check No. 2357 as $297.20 instead of $279.20.		
Accounts receivable (H. E. Gates)	75.50	
Cash		75.50
To charge Gates with check returned N.S.F.		
Bank service charges	6.75	
Cash		6.75
Charges for September.		
Miscellaneous revenue	25.00	
Cash		25.00
To reverse entry made in May, 19+5, eliminating Check No. 132 from outstanding checks; it has now cleared.		

COMPREHENSIVE RECONCILIATION ILLUSTRATION: This illustration is based on the assumed facts of the first illustration on pages 230 and 231, with the additional information stated below.

Reconciliation—November 30, 19+5:

Balance per bank statement	$11,216.22
Add deposit in transit	7,216.85
Total	$18,433.07
Deduct outstanding checks	6,215.30
Correct balance	$12,217.77
Balance per books	$12,220.92
Deduct bank charges	3.15
Correct balance	$12,217.77

Summary of the depositor's books for December:

Balance in bank, November 30, 19+5	$12,217.77
Add cash receipts—all deposited	47,763.78
Total	$59,981.55
Deduct disbursements—all by check	50,766.22
Balance in bank, December 31, 19+5	$ 9,215.33

Summary of the bank statement for December:

Balance, November 30, 19+5	$11,216.22
Credits for deposits	45,630.80
Total	$56,847.02
Charges for checks, etc.	46,485.51
Balance, December 31, 19+5	$10,361.51

The $45,630.80 total of deposits was determined by running an adding machine tape of the deposits shown on the bank statement.

The $46,485.51 total of checks paid and other charges was determined by running an adding machine tape of them, or by the following computation:

Balance, November 30, 19+5, per bank statement	$11,216.22
Credits for deposits	45,630.80
Total	$56,847.02
Balance, December 31, 19+5, per bank statement	10,361.51
Checks and other charges	$46,485.51

The reconciling items on December 31, 19+5, as in the first illustration, were:

Deposit in transit	$ 9,849.83
Outstanding checks	10,498.98
Bank charges	2.97
Credit for collection made by bank	500.00

The reconciliation procedures described below represent more than a bank reconciliation. There are actually three reconciliations, as follows:

(1) Receipts reported per the bank statement and receipts reported per the books are reconciled to the correct amount.
(2) Disbursements reported per the bank statement and disbursements reported per the books are reconciled to the correct amount.
(3) The cash balance per the bank statement and the balance per the books are reconciled to the correct amount.

The reconciliation statement is shown on page 236. Observe that the first line consists of a summary of the bank statement for December. The first column shows the bank reconciliation at the end of the previous period, after the company recorded the items that were on the bank statement for November but that had not been recorded before the statement was received. The first line in the "per books" section of the reconciliation is a summary of the depositor's cash records for December.

Completion of the reconciliation is as follows:

(1) Receipts
  (a) Per bank. Unrecorded deposits at the end of the *previous* period were recorded by the bank as a receipt in the current period. Therefore, they must be deducted to arrive at the correct amount for receipts of the current period. Unrecorded deposits at the end of the *current* period must be added because they have not yet been recorded as receipts by the bank, although they represent receipts of the current period.
  (b) Per books. The collection of the draft increases receipts of the current period. However, the amount collected has not yet been recorded on the books and must therefore be added.

(2) Disbursements
  (a) Per bank. Checks outstanding at the end of the previous month have been treated as disbursements of the current month by the bank, thus requiring that they be deducted from the disbursements per bank. Outstanding checks for the current month are treated in the opposite manner. Since they have not yet cleared the bank, they must be added to the disbursements per bank in order to determine the correct disbursements total for the month. A check from the previous month that is still outstanding at the end of the current month does not create any particular problem. It will be added as a part of the total checks outstanding at the beginning of the current period and then deducted in the total for the checks outstanding at the end of the period.
  (b) Per books. Bank charges for the current month must be added because they are not included in the disbursements per books.

ABC CORPORATION
Reconciliation of Receipts, Disbursements, and Bank Account
The City National Bank
For the Month of December 31, 19+5

	Balance, November 30, 19+5	Add Receipts	Deduct Disbursements	Balance, December 31, 19+5
Balance per bank	$11,216.22	$45,630.80	$46,485.51	$10,361.51
Unrecorded deposits:				
November 30, 19+5....	7,216.85	7,216.85*		
December 31, 19+5....		9,849.83		9,849.83
Outstanding checks:				
November 30, 19+5....	6,215.30*		6,215.30*	
December 31, 19+5			10,498.98	10,498.98*
Correct balance	$12,217.77	$48,263.78	$50,769.19	$ 9,712.36
Balance per books	$12.217.77	$47,763.78	$50,766.22	$ 9,215.33
December bank charges:				
Telegram			1.80	1.80*
Collection charge			1.17	1.17*
Draft collected by bank....		500.00		500.00
Correct balance	$12,217.77	$48,263.78	$50,769.19	$ 9,712.36

*Deduction.

(3) Bank reconciliation at December 31. The items in the final column of the reconciliation are the same as those illustrated on page 231.

As indicated earlier, an alternative procedure for preparing a bank reconciliation involves reconciling the bank balance to the book balance. This same alternative can also be applied to the comprehensive reconciliation, as illustrated below.

ABC CORPORATION
Reconciliation of Receipts, Disbursements, and Bank Account
The City National Bank
For the Month of December, 19+5

	Balance, November 30, 19+5	Add Receipts	Deduct Disburse-ments	Balance December 31, 19+5
Per bank	$11,216.22	$45,630.80	$46,485.51	$10,361.51
Deposits in transit:				
November 30	7,216.85	7,216.85*		
December 31		9,849.83		9,849.83
Outstanding checks:				
November 30	6,215.30*		6,215.30*	
December 31			10,498.98	10,498.98*
Bank's charges			2.97*	2.97
Proceeds of draft collected by bank..		500.00*		500.00*
Per books	$12,217.77	$47,763.78	$50,766.22	$ 9,215.33

*Deduction.

The three reconciliations are made as follows:

(1) Reconciliation of receipts per bank statement ($45,630.80) with receipts per books ($47,763.78):

The $7,216.85 deposit in transit on November 30 was included in the receipts per books in November; therefore, it is deducted from the receipts per bank for December to reconcile with the receipts per books.

The $9,849.83 deposit in transit on December 31 is added to the receipts per bank to reconcile with the receipts per books.

The $500 collected by the bank for the depositor appeared on the bank statement but was not recorded on the books; therefore, it is deducted from the receipts per bank to reconcile with the receipts per books.

(2) Reconciliation of the disbursements per bank statement ($46,485.51) with the disbursements per books ($50,766.22):

The $6,215.30 of checks outstanding on November 30 were recorded on the books as disbursements prior to December; therefore, they are deducted from the December disbursements per bank to reconcile with the December disbursements per books.

The $10,498.98 of checks outstanding on December 31 are added to the disbursements per bank to reconcile with the disbursements per books.

The $2.97 of bank charges are not included in the disbursements per books; therefore, they are deducted from the disbursements per bank.

(3) The items in the bank reconciliation (last column) are the same as those in the illustration on page 232.

Cash forecasting. The role of cash in maintaining the operations of a firm makes it mandatory that future cash requirements be anticipated. The planning of cash receipts and disbursements makes it possible for a firm to know in advance when it will have cash available in excess of current needs (creating temporary investment possibilities) and when current needs are in excess of available cash (creating the need for borrowing).

One means of forecasting the future cash position of a firm is by analyzing expected future cash receipts and disbursements. This method will now be illustrated.

A company had the following current assets and liabilities on June 30, 19+5:

Cash	$ 3,000
Accounts receivable	8,000
Merchandise	10,000
Accounts payable and accruals	7,000

Some of the merchandise in which the company deals is obtainable only in the summer months, and purchases are therefore high from June to September. The prospective purchases for the next six months are:

July	$10,000
August	9,000
September	8,000
October	6,000
November	5,000
December	4,000

The company wishes to obtain a bank loan, and the bank requests a statement showing the probable date when the loan can be repaid. The company's sales are fairly uniform throughout the year, averaging about $8,000 a month; they are made at an average gross profit of 25 per cent. Expenses paid immediately in cash average about $600 per month. It is assumed that liabilities for purchases and expenses will be paid in the month following that in which they are incurred, and that accounts receivable will be collected in the month following the month of sale.

The company wishes to borrow $5,000 on August 1, and assures the bank that the loan can be repaid at the end of December. The cash forecast upon which this assurance is based is shown on the following page.

MARKETABLE SECURITIES

Types of investments. The rules for the valuation of securities in the accounts and on the balance sheet, and the methods of accounting for investments, depend to some extent on whether the investment is to be held for a short period or for a long period. The following classification reflects this distinction:

(1) Marketable securities (temporary investments):
- (a) Merchandise of a dealer in securities. In this case, the securities represent the stock-in-trade of the dealer and are acquired with the intention of holding them for a relatively short period of time.
- (b) Speculative holdings.
- (c) Investments of surplus funds, forming part of the working capital. Such temporary investments are usually found in industries doing a seasonal business; the excess funds not needed during a slack period are invested temporarily to obtain the income.
- (d) Securities taken on account.

(2) Long-term investments:
- (a) Stock interests in subsidiaries.
- (b) Small holdings maintained for the purpose of establishing business connections.
- (c) Sinking funds and other funds.
- (d) Bonds of outside companies.
- (e) Long-lived assets not used in the operations of the company. An example would be land held for speculation.

Investments may be classified as current assets if they are of a temporary nature, if it is the owner's intention to convert them into cash to meet cash requirements during the operating cycle, and if there is a ready market for them

Forecast of Cash and Current Position
For the Six Months Ending December 31, 19+5

	Cash	Accounts Receivable	Merchandise	Accounts Payable and Accruals	Bank Loan
June 30:					
Balances..........	$ 3,000	$8,000	$10,000	$ 7,000	
July:					
Collections	8,000	8,000*			
Payments.........	7,000*			7,000*	
Sales..............		8,000	6,000*		
Purchases			10,000	10,000	
Expenses				600	
Balances	$ 4,000	$8,000	$14,000	$10,600	
August:					
Bank loan	5,000				$5,000
Collections	8,000	8,000*			
Payments.........	10,600*			10,600*	
Sales..............		8,000	6,000*		
Purchases			9,000	9,000	
Expenses				600	
Balances..........	$ 6,400	$8,000	$17,000	$ 9,600	$5,000
September:					
Collections	8,000	8,000*			
Payments.........	9,600*			9,600*	
Sales..............		8,000	6,000*		
Purchases			8,000	8,000	
Expenses				600	
Balances..........	$ 4,800	$8,000	$19,000	$ 8,600	$5,000
October:					
Collections	8,000	8,000*			
Payments.........	8,600*			8,600*	
Sales..............		8,000	6,000*		
Purchases			6,000	6,000	
Expenses				600	
Balances..........	$ 4,200	$8,000	$19,000	$ 6,600	$5,000
November:					
Collections	8,000	8,000*			
Payments.........	6,600*			6,600*	
Sales..............		8,000	6,000*		
Purchases			5,000	5,000	
Expenses				600	
Balances..........	$ 5,600	$8,000	$18,000	$ 5,600	$5,000
December:					
Collections	8,000	8,000*			
Payments.........	5,600*			5,600*	
Sales..............		8,000	6,000*		
Purchases			4,000	4,000	
Expenses				600	
Bank loan paid....	5,000*				5,000*
Balances..........	$ 3,000	$8,000	$16,000	$ 4,600	$ —

*Deduction.

either on a securities exchange or elsewhere. The mere fact that a security is readily marketable is not sufficient justification for marshalling it among the current assets; the nature of the business of the owning company and the nature and purpose of the investment should be such as to make the current disposal of the security probable. Unless this rule is rigidly adhered to, there is a danger of overstating the working capital by including among current assets securities that, although having a ready market, are really long-term investments. On the other hand, it should be pointed out that the "intention to convert" criterion is often difficult for the accountant to determine in actual practice.

Cost of marketable securities. The cost of any investment includes the purchase price and brokerage, taxes, and other expenditures incident to acquisition. An investment in interest-bearing securities between interest-payment dates will also require that any accrued interest be accounted for. For example, the acquisition of a $1,000 bond at 98, plus other costs of $25 and accrued interest of $10, would be accounted for as follows:

Marketable securities [($1,000 × .98) + $25]	1,005	
Interest receivable	10	
Cash		1,015

Any purchase discount or premium applicable to marketable securities is usually not amortized. This practice is based primarily upon practical considerations. Theoretically, any premium or discount should be amortized, but the failure to do so for marketable securities usually has little effect on income because the securities are held for a short period of time.

Investments in marketable securities may continue to be reported at cost if fluctuations in market prices are relatively minor. Such minor changes in market price can be reported parenthetically in the balance sheet, as shown below.

Current assets:	
Marketable securities—at cost (market value, $51,500)	$51,000

Valuation at the lower of cost or market. Because temporary investments in securities are current assets, it is argued that they should not be shown at amounts above realizable value; hence, their valuation should be at the lower of cost or market for balance sheet purposes when there has been a significant decline in market price. It is not customary to apply the cost-or-market rule to investments by taking the lower value for each item; it is considered sufficient to determine the total valuation of the portfolio at cost and at market and to use the lower of these totals.

Investors cannot take losses from market declines as a tax deduction, but must instead report gains and losses only upon disposal, with the gain or loss being the difference between cost and sales price. Therefore, a record of the cost of the securities should be maintained, and any write-downs to market are preferably made by credit to a contra account rather than to the asset account. The offsetting charge should be made against income.

The reasoning underlying the valuation of marketable securities at the lower of cost or market is that since they are viewed as a reserve source of cash, failure to recognize the decline in market price would have the effect of overstating the cash position of the firm. Also, there is the related point that income should be charged with the decline in value in the period in which the decline takes place, not in the period in which the securities are sold. On the other hand, it should be pointed out that the lower-of-cost-or-market method is logically inconsistent, since it recognizes declines, but not increases, in market price.

Lower-of-cost-or-market valuation procedures are illustrated below.

	Cost	Market
Marketable securities	$86,200	$73,500

The journal entry required to reduce the securities to market in this case would be:

Market loss on securities...........................	12,700	
Allowance for excess of cost of marketable securities over market		12,700

This information could be reported in the balance sheet as follows:

Current assets:	
Marketable securities—at the lower of cost or market (cost, $86,200)..	$73,500

An alternative balance sheet presentation would be:

Current assets:		
Marketable securities:		
Cost......................................	$86,200	
Allowance for excess of cost over market	12,700	
Market		$73,500

The $12,700 loss recorded in the entry above is an unrealized loss and therefore is not deductible for tax purposes. Realization is considered to take place only at the time the securities are actually sold. However, such unrealized losses are reported in the income statement in the period in which they occur. They affect the calculation of net income before charges or credits for extraordinary items.

If the securities acquired at a cost of $86,200 in 19+5 were written down to a market value of $73,500 at December 31, 19+5, and then sold in 19+6 for $72,000, the following entry should be recorded at the time of the sale:

Cash	72,000	
Allowance for excess of cost of marketable securities over market...........................	12,700	
Loss on sale of marketable securities	1,500	
Marketable securities..............................		86,200

In the previous illustration, there was an additional decline in the market price of the securities from the time they were written down to a market valuation of $73,500 until they were sold in the following period. If it is now assumed that the market price increased between the date of the write-down and the date of sale, the entry would reflect a gain on the sale. For example, assuming a sale price of $76,000 for the securities, the following entry would be recorded:

Cash	76,000	
Allowance for excess of cost of marketable securities over market	12,700	
Marketable securities		86,200
Gain on sale of marketable securities		2,500

If securities that are written down to an amount below cost in one period are still on hand at the end of the following accounting period, the appropriate comparison is between the market value at the end of the second period and the amount at which they were carried at the beginning of the period. Normally, additional adjustments would be made only if there had been additional declines in market price.

For example, assume that the marketable securities discussed above were acquired ($86,200 cost) during 19+5 and written down ($73,500 market) at the end of 19+5. Now assume that during 19+6, securities costing $21,550, or one-fourth of the total cost of marketable securities, are sold for $18,000. Following the lower-of-cost-or-market rule, the sale could be recorded as follows:

Cash	18,000	
Allowance for excess of cost of marketable securities over market (¼ × $12,700)	3,175	
Loss on sale of marketable securities	375	
Marketable securities (¼ × $86,200)		21,550

The adjusted basis for lower-of-cost-or-market comparison at the end of 19+6 is now $55,125, as shown below:

Original cost of marketable securities	$86,200	
Less cost of marketable securities sold	21,550	$64,650
Allowance for excess of cost of marketable securities over market	$12,700	
Less adjustment of allowance for marketable securities sold	3,175	9,525
Adjusted basis		$55,125

If the market at the end of 19+6 were $57,000, there would be no increase in the amount at which the securities were reported, since the adjusted basis of $55,125 is lower than the $57,000 market. On the other hand, if the market were $54,000 at the end of 19+6, an additional write-down of $1,125 ($55,125 − $54,000) would be made, since market is below the adjusted basis of $55,125.

The entry at the end of 19+6 would be as follows:

Market loss on securities	1,125	
Allowance for excess of cost of marketable securities over market		1,125

Marketable securities would then be reported on the December 31, 19+6, balance sheet at $54,000, which is the net of the two accounts, as shown on the following page.

	Marketable Securities Account	Allowance Account
Balance, January 1, 19+6	$86,200	$12,700*
Sale of securities during the year	21,550*	3,175
Balance	$64,650	$ 9,525*
Decline recorded at December 31, 19+6		1,125*
Balance, December 31, 19+6	$64,650	$10,650*

*Credit.

One feature of the previous treatment of the sale of marketable securities under the lower-of-cost-or-market method is the mixing of unrealized losses and realized losses. For example, the entry at the bottom of page 241 records a loss of $1,500 on the sale of securities in 19+6. However, this is the difference between the realized loss on the sale of $14,200 (cost of $86,200 less the selling price of $72,000) and the unrealized loss of $12,700 reported in the previous year.

The entry at the top of page 242 reports a gain of $2,500 on the sale. This is the difference between the realized loss of $10,200 (cost of $86,200 less the selling price of $76,000) and the unrealized loss of $12,700 reported in the previous year.

In the example in the middle of page 242, by debiting the allowance account for $3,175 (¼ of $12,700), the conventional treatment shows a $375 loss that results from offsetting the previously recorded, but unrealized, holding loss of $3,175 against a realized loss of $3,550 (¼ of [$86,200 − $72,000]). Although not usually done, this mixing of unrealized and realized losses can be avoided by making no entry to the allowance account upon sale of the marketable securities:

Cash	18,000	
Loss on sale of marketable securities	3,550	
Marketable securities		21,550

If this is done, and it is assumed that the market valuation of the securities remaining on hand at the end of 19+6 is $57,000, then market is above the adjusted basis of $51,950 ($86,200 − $21,550 − $12,700). The following entry is necessary to reflect the facts under the lower-of-cost-or-market rule.

Allowance for excess of cost of marketable securities over market	5,050	
Market gain on marketable securities ($57,000 − $51,950)		5,050

This entry will result in the marketable securities being reported at a net amount of $57,000, which is the difference between the marketable securities account balance of $64,650 ($86,200 − $21,550) and the allowance account balance of $7,650 ($12,700 − $5,050). The market gain account will be closed to Retained Earnings along with other items entering into the determination of net income before extraordinary items.

Valuation at market. Although it is not generally accepted practice to account for marketable securities at an amount in excess of cost, many people argue that it is inconsistent to reduce the carrying amount of the securities to an amount below cost without increasing their carrying amount when market is above cost. Considering the nature of marketable securities as a reserve source of cash, it would appear to the authors that valuation at market is to be preferred. This would certainly enhance the usefulness of a firm's balance sheet as a source of information concerning financial position.

One problem encountered in the use of market valuation for reporting marketable securities is the treatment of any gains recorded at the time the securities are written up to an amount above cost. Such an entry results in a credit to the account Gain in Market Price of Securities. Traditionally, such "unrealiized gains" are not considered appropriate for inclusion in the determination of a firm's periodic income. However, such holding gains could be reported separately from the operating income of the firm.

Determining the cost of securities sold. If several purchases of the same security are made at different prices, a question may arise concerning the gain or loss on the sale of a portion of the holdings. To illustrate, assume that 20 shares of X Company stock were purchased at $100 per share; another 20 shares were subsequently purchased at $125; and 10 shares were later sold at $110. Did the sale produce a gain of $10 per share (the difference between the selling price and the cost of the first shares purchased), or a loss of $15 per share (the difference between the selling price and the cost of the second shares purchased), or a loss of $2.50 per share (the difference between the selling price and the average cost)?

For tax purposes, average costs are not recognized. If the shares sold can be identified as pertaining to the first lot purchased, the transaction can be regarded as producing a gain of $10 per share. If they can be identified as belonging to the second lot purchased, a loss of $15 per share may be reported. If they cannot be identified as pertaining to either lot (which would be the case if the certificates for the two purchases had been converted into a single certificate for all the shares), the shares sold should be regarded as pertaining to the first lot purchased.

This rule, which is obligatory for tax purposes, appears to be reasonable for general accounting purposes. However, average costs are also recognized from the standpoint of general accounting theory.

Offsetting securities against taxes payable. Marketable securities are normally reported as a current asset because of their liquidity. However, the Accounting Principles Board has recognized one instance in which they might be used to offset a liability. This situation exists "when it is clear that a purchase of securities (acceptable for the payment of taxes) is in substance an advance payment of taxes that will be payable in the relatively near future, so that in the special circumstances the purchase is tantamount to the prepayment of taxes."[1]

---

[1]Accounting Principles Board, "Omnibus Opinion—1966" *Opinion No. 10* (New York: AICPA, December 1966), p. 147.

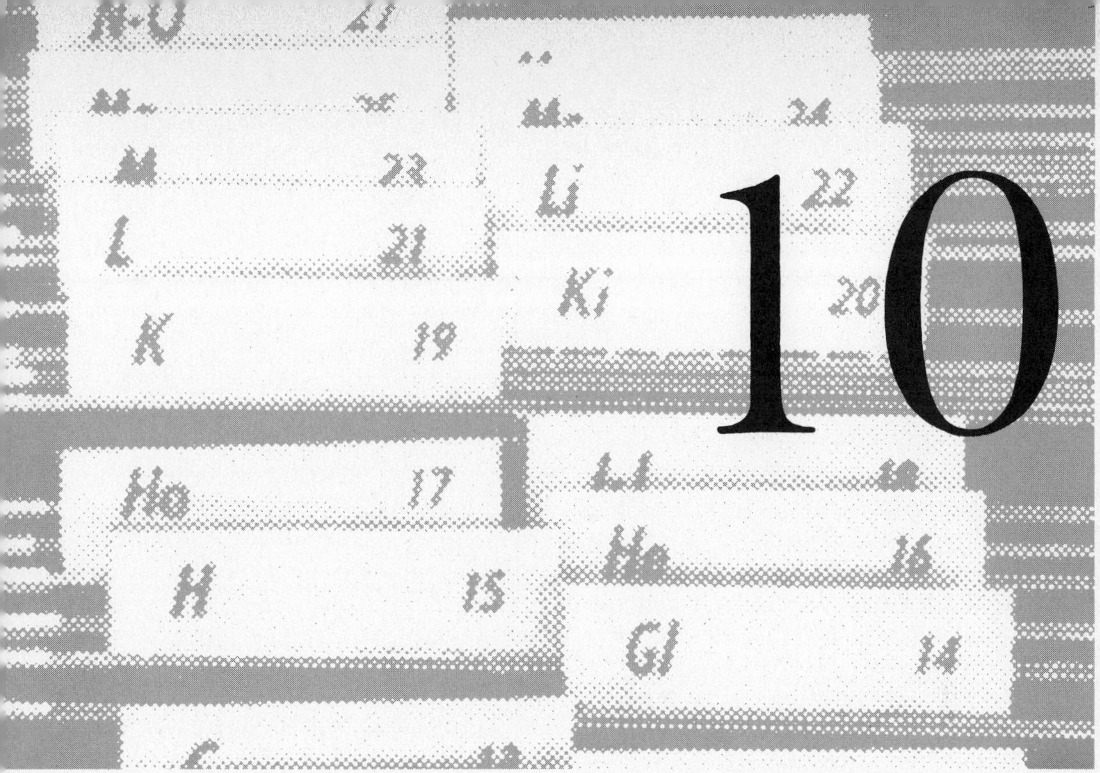

10

Receivables

Introduction. The term *receivables,* in its broadest sense, includes all amounts resulting from transactions that give the firm a claim for future asset inflows, usually in the form of cash. However, due to the variety of transactions that result in receivables, they are normally described more precisely for financial statement purposes. For example, the major source of receivables for most businesses is the sale of goods and services to customers on account. The resulting claim is referred to as a trade receivable and is reported in the balance sheet as an account receivable or note receivable, depending upon the document that serves as evidence of the sale.

There are many other transactions that give rise to receivables but that should not be included as a part of the trade receivables of the firm. Examples of these transactions will be referred to in the following section.

There are basically two problems encountered in the financial statement presentation of receivables: first, the determination of what can properly be included as accounts receivable; and second, the proper designation of receivables as either current or noncurrent.

ACCOUNTS RECEIVABLE

Classification. Because accounts receivable are classified as current assets in the balance sheet, no balances (with a few exceptions mentioned later) should appear as accounts receivable unless they will presumably be converted into cash during the current operating cycle or one year, whichever is longer.

In most businesses, the terms of sale require payment within 30, 60, or 90 days, but in some types of business, the accounts receivable are due in installments over a long period of time. It is considered proper to include in the current assets any "installment or deferred accounts and notes receivable if they conform generally to normal trade practices and terms within the business."[1]

Amounts receivable from officers, directors, and stockholders, except in instances where goods have been sold to them on account for collection in accordance with the regular credit terms, are not likely to be collected with any promptness and should be shown under some noncurrent caption (for example, long-term investments).

Accounts for advances to stockholders, officers, and directors are often found on the books of closely held corporations, particularly if the business was previously conducted as a partnership. The former partners, having become accustomed to taking drawings, continue to do so, not realizing that, whereas partners are allowed to take drawings in any free and easy manner they desire, the profits of a corporation can be legally divided only by the formal declaration of a dividend. Until a dividend is declared, these advances are in the nature of loans, recoverable by creditors in case the corporation is unable to pay its debts.

Advances to subsidiary companies should not be included with customers' accounts in the balance sheet. Advances are usually of a more permanent nature and are not current. To show them in the balance sheet as accounts receivable is likely to be misleading. The casual reader of the balance sheet will probably obtain too favorable an impression of the financial position because of the overstatement of current assets and working capital. On the other hand, a more penetrating reader may compute the ratio of receivables to sales and may gain the unwarranted and unfavorable impression that too great a percentage of the period's sales remains uncollected, and that the receivables are therefore of dubious value.

Receivables resulting from sales to subsidiaries, collectible currently, can be included in accounts receivable under the Current Assets caption.

If special deposits made in connection with contract bids or for other purposes are likely to remain outstanding for considerable periods of time, they should not be classed as current assets.

Some receivables that can properly be classified as current assets should never-

---

[1]Committee on Accounting Procedure, *Accounting Research Bulletin No. 43* (New York: AICPA, 1961), p. 20. See James A. Gentry, Jr., and Glenn L. Johnson, *Finney and Miller's Principles of Accounting: Advanced,* 6th ed. (Englewood Cliffs, N.J.: Prentice-Hall, Inc., 1971), Chapter 14 and Appendix, for discussion of the accounting for installment accounts receivable.

theless be segregated from the receivables from customers. Some of these are debit balances in suppliers' accounts, claims against railroads and other common carriers for damages to goods in transit, uncollected stock subscriptions, currently recoverable deposits made against contract bids, claims for cash refunds, declared dividends receivable on stock investments, insurance claims receivable, and advances on purchases. If the circumstances of a particular case indicate that collection will not be received currently, the item should not be classified under the current caption.

If contingent receivables such as claims under guarantees and amounts thought to be recoverable in litigation are placed on the books as a matter of record, proper consideration should be given to both the question of valuation and the question of classification in the balance sheet. The degree of probability of collection will determine the advisability of establishing an allowance account; the date of probable collection will determine the current or noncurrent classification.

Memorandum charges to consignees for goods shipped on consignment should not be included in accounts receivable, because title to the merchandise has not passed to the consignee and there is no valid claim against him. Receivables from consignees arise only upon the sales of the consigned goods.[2]

It has often been said that the term *accounts receivable* is too inclusive and that it should therefore be abandoned. The term *customers' accounts* has been suggested to take its place. *Trade debtors* has also been suggested as an even better term, because it corresponds with the similar term *trade creditors*.

A distinction should be made between the words *receivable* and *due*. An account receivable is a claim against a debtor. A receivable that is due is a claim that the creditor has a right to collect at the present time. Accounts receivable may be due, or not yet due. Hence, it is undesirable to speak of the total accounts receivable as "receivables due from customers," or by any other expression in which "due" is used improperly.

Valuation of accounts receivable. In the valuation of the total of customers' accounts, consideration should be given to certain possible deductions. These deductions are for:

Uncollectible accounts
Freight
Returns and allowances
Discounts

The deduction for uncollectible accounts is almost invariably applicable; the deductions for freight, returns and allowances, and discounts are applicable only under special circumstances.

Allowance for uncollectibles. The creation of an allowance for uncollectibles account is intended to accomplish two results, namely:

---

[2]See Gentry and Johnson, *ibid.*, Chapter 14, for discussion of the accounting for consignment sales.

To charge the loss by the sale of goods to customers whose accounts prove to be uncollectible against the period that caused the loss
To show the estimated realizable amount of the customers' accounts

It is not always possible, however, to accomplish both these results, as will be shown in the following discussion of methods of estimating the amounts to be credited to the allowance account.

The two customary procedures for computing the periodic credits to the allowance account are indicated below:

(1) Increasing the allowance account by a percentage of the credit sales for the period
(2) Adjusting the allowance account to the amount of loss estimated by aging the accounts receivable and considering supplementary data

Percentage of sales. Credit terms are granted on sales (that is, credit or charge sales) because they result in increased sales volume; however, they also result in some credit sales that prove to be uncollectible—bad debts. Since these bad debts result from sales made during the current period, they should be recognized during the same period in order to obtain a proper matching of revenue and expense. Such matching is attainable under the percentage-of-sales method of estimating bad debts.

Based on past statistics of credit sales, bad debt losses, and bad debt recoveries, as well as an adjustment factor for current business conditions, an estimated percentage relationship between bad debt losses and credit sales can be determined. This percentage estimate of bad debt losses can then be applied at the *end* of the current period to the *actual* credit sales for the current period to derive the estimated dollar amount of bad debts for the period. Based on this estimated bad debts amount, an adjusting entry is made at the end of the period by debiting bad debts and crediting allowance for uncollectibles. Note that the credit to the allowance account results in a current addition to the allowance account over and above what is already in the account based on prior period estimates.

Under the percentage-of-sales method, the estimated bad debts do not represent which particular accounts receivable will prove to be uncollectible. Rather, the estimate is based on the law of large numbers—that, on the average, a certain percentage of actual credit sales will result in bad debts of a certain amount. In other words, the accountant cannot wait to record the bad debts until the specific accounts receivable are found to be uncollectible, because this can occur in subsequent periods and result in improper matching of revenue and expense.

As an example, assume that based on company experience, adjusted for current business conditions, it is estimated that bad debts will be \$6,000, bad debt recoveries \$1,000, and credit sales \$500,000. Thus the estimated percentage relationship of bad debts to credit sales is 1 percent.

$$\textbf{Estimated bad debt percentage} = \frac{\textbf{Estimated bad debts} - \textbf{Estimated bad debt recoveries}}{\textbf{Estimated credit sales}}$$

$$1\% = \frac{\$6{,}000 - \$1{,}000}{\$500{,}000}$$

If actual credit sales during the period were $480,000, the adjusting entry at the end of the period would be as follows:

Bad debts ($480,000 × .01)............................	4,800	
Allowance for uncollectibles		4,800

Further assume that during the subsequent period, $4,000 in accounts receivable prove to be uncollectible. Since the bad debts were properly recognized during the previous period, the actual write-off should not recognize bad debts again. In order to avoid double counting, the write-off is charged against the allowance account, as follows:

Allowance for uncollectibles............................	4,000	
Accounts receivable (Customer's account)...........		4,000

Note that the write-off entry has a zero effect on the financial statements. Obviously, the current period's net income is not affected by the write-off. The balance sheet is not affected, because *both* the allowance for uncollectibles and accounts receivable are reduced by $4,000; hence, the reported net realizable value of the accounts receivable is still the same.

One of the problems in using the percentage-of-sales method is that the estimated percentage of bad debts may become out of date in light of changes in current business conditions. For this reason, when the percentage-of-sales method is used, accounts receivable should be examined (that is, age the accounts receivable) at least once a year to determine whether the amount in the allowance account is adequate. If it is excessive or inadequate, the percentage applied to credit sales should be revised accordingly and used subsequently.

As a final point, some accountants use an estimate of total, rather than credit, sales in deriving the estimated percentage of bad debts. Based on the doctrine of materiality, the difference between a bad debts estimate based on total sales and one based on credit sales may be small, since a lower rate is applied to a higher total actual sales for the period. However, from a theoretical point of view, an estimate of bad debts based on total sales is inappropriate, since cash sales do not generate bad debts. Moreover, a shift in the proportion of cash sales to total sales can distort a bad debts estimate based on total sales.

If statements are prepared monthly, it is important that allowance provisions be made monthly rather than annually; otherwise, the monthly balance sheets may show very inaccurate net valuations of the receivables. Assume that balance sheets are prepared monthly, but no provision for losses on the year's sales is made until the end of the year. Obviously, in all balance sheets prepared before the close of the year, the receivables will be shown without provision for losses on receivables that arose from sales during the year—presumably, the major portion of the receivables. On the other hand, if an adequate allowance account exists throughout the year by reason of provisions in prior years, the year-end provision based on the total sales for the year will produce an excessive allowance account.

Aging accounts receivable. When this method is used, a list of all accounts may be made on working papers, with columns with various headings such as "Not due," "1 to

30 days past due," "31 to 60 days past due," and so forth. All accounts in the subsidiary ledger are then listed, and the component elements of the balances are classified in the proper columns.

A comparative accounts receivable aging schedule, summarizing the data assembled in the working papers, is illustrated below:

Age of Accounts Receivable
December 31, 19+5 and 19+4

	December 31, 19+5		December 31, 19+4	
	Amount	Percent of Total	Amount	Percent of Total
Not due	$15,000	30.93	$20,000	41.67
1 to 30 days past due	12,000	24.74	16,000	33.33
31 to 60 days past due	8,000	16.50	5,000	10.42
61 to 90 days past due	6,000	12.37	4,500	9.38
91 to 120 days past due	4,000	8.25	1,000	2.08
More than 120 days past due	2,000	4.12	1,000	2.08
Bankrupt or with attorneys	1,500	3.09	500	1.04
Total	$48,500	100.00	$48,000	100.00

Using the aging schedule and supplementary information, the balance required in the allowance for uncollectibles account can be determined. Basically, this involves the determination of an estimation of the portion of the accounts in each bracket of the aging schedule likely to become worthless. Experience will usually show that the longer an account is past due, the less the likelihood of collecting the entire amount. However, it may be known that some accounts not yet past due are doubtful, whereas others long past due may be considered collectible.

The estimated balance required in the allowance account at December 31, 19+5, is calculated in the schedule shown below. It is based upon the information in the aging schedule at the top of the page.

Estimated Bad Debt Losses
December 31, 19+5

	Balances	Estimated Loss Percentage	Estimated Loss Amount
Not due	$15,000	1%	$ 150
1 to 30 days past due	12,000	2	240
31 to 60 days past due	8,000	5	400
61 to 90 days past due	6,000	8	480
91 to 120 days past due	4,000	25	1,000
More than 120 days past due	2,000	50	1,000
Bankrupt or with attorneys	1,500	70	1,050
Total	$48,500		$4,320

The information above indicates that the receivables on the books at the end of 19+5 have a net realizable value of $44,180 ($48,500 – $4,320). Since it is assumed that the estimates are based upon the best information available, accounts receivable would be misstated if they were reported at an amount other than $44,180 in the December 31, 19+5 balance sheet.

The adjusting entry required at December 31, 19+5, to record the information above must be for an amount that will result in a credit balance of $4,320 in the allowance for uncollectibles account. Therefore, the amount of the entry will be affected by the balance in the allowance account *prior* to the adjustment. Two possible situations will now be illustrated.

Assume first of all that the allowance account has a *credit* balance of $350 prior to recording the adjusting entry. The amount of the adjustment is $3,970 ($4,320 – $350) and the entry is shown below.

Bad debts	3,970	
Allowance for uncollectibles		3,970

After the entry has been posted, the accounts receivable account and related allowance account will show the following:

Accounts receivable	$48,500	
Less allowance for uncollectibles ($350 + $3,970)	4,320	$44,180

If it is assumed that the allowance account has a $400 *debit* balance prior to recording the adjusting entry, the adjustment must be for $4,720 ($400 + $4,320), or an amount necessary to reflect a credit balance of $4,320 in the allowance account. Although the entry is for a different amount in this case, the accounts will show the following after the entry has been recorded:

Accounts receivable	$48,500	
Less allowance for uncollectibles ($4,720 – $400).	4,320	$44,180

Note that this is the same net amount as shown in the first illustration. This is as it should be, because the balance in the allowance account prior to adjustment does not affect the portion of the accounts receivable estimated to be uncollectible.

This method has the advantage of accomplishing the second of the two objectives stated on page 248, because it results in a fairly accurate valuation of the accounts receivable on the books. Also, the method has the practical advantage of simplicity, and it reflects current business conditions that affect collectibility. However, it may easily result in a failure to distribute losses to the periods during which they were caused. Bad debt losses are caused by making sales to customers who do not pay their accounts. Theoretically, therefore, provision for the loss should be made in the period in which the sales were made. But if the aging method is used, accounts may not appear to be uncollectible until a date subsequent to the period of sale; in that case the loss, or the provision therefor, will not be charged to income until a period subsequent to that of sale. Thus, one period will be credited for the revenue and a later period will be charged for the loss.

Percentage of open accounts. If a company's experience indicates that a certain percentage of the accounts open at any date will ultimately prove uncollectible, the total allowance requirement at any date can be estimated by multiplying the open account balances by the loss experience percentage. The allowance account is then credited with an amount sufficient to increase the existing balance to the estimated required balance. The theory of this method is the same as the theory of the preceding method; the difference lies in the procedure for estimating the total allowance requirement. It is subject to the same theoretical weakness as the aging method, and it is difficult to obtain experience data from which to make a reliable estimate of the percentage to be applied.

Correction of the allowance for uncollectibles account. There may be instances in which it is obvious that the balance in the allowance for uncollectibles account is either greater or smaller than it should be. This situation could arise as a result of the firm's using an inaccurate percentage of credit sales to calculate the amount of the adjusting entry for estimated bad debt losses at the end of the period.

Assume that at the end of the current year, the allowance for uncollectibles account has a debit balance of $2,000 before recording the current year's bad debts expense. This debit balance is the result of using too small a percentage of sales in calculating the bad debts expense in prior years. After giving consideration to the bad debt experience that resulted in the debit balance in the allowance account, assume that the company increases the rate from 2 percent to 3 percent of credit sales.

The Accounting Principles Board has taken the position that a change in an estimate of the type illustrated here should be accounted for "in (a) the period of change if the change affects the period only, or (b) the period of change and future periods if the change affects both."[3] The board goes on to state that amounts pertaining to the estimate reported in prior periods should not be restated.

If the credit sales for the current year amount to $200,000, the required entry, following the treatment recommended by the Board and using the new 3 percent rate, is as follows:

Bad debts (3% of $200,000)	6,000	
Allowance for uncollectibles		6,000

In effect, the errors of prior years are corrected in the current and future years by the use of the new rate. Disclosure of this fact is not required in the income statement for the current year, but is recommended if the effect of the change in the estimate is considered material.

Bad-debt recoveries. If a collection is made on an account once charged off as uncollectible, the customer's account should be recharged with the amount collected, and possibly with the entire amount previously written off if it is now expected that collection will be received in full. The collection should then be credited to the customer's account. These entries are made in the customer's account so that it will show that the debtor has attempted to reestablish his credit by the payment.

---

[3]Accounting Principles Board, "Accounting Changes," *Opinion No. 20* (New York: AICPA, July 1971), p. 397.

What account should be credited when the customer's account is recharged? From the standpoint of theory, the following may be said:

> It is conservative to credit recoveries to the allowance account if the credits to it were determined by multiplying the sales by a percent representing the relation of net bad debt losses (losses less recoveries) to sales. It is not correct if the percent used in computing the provision represents the relation of gross write-offs to sales; in this case, recoveries should be credited to an income account.
>
> If the allowance account was credited by aging the accounts or using a percent representing the relation of losses to account balances, it makes no difference, from a theoretical standpoint, whether recoveries are credited to the allowance account, to the bad debts expense account, or to an income account, as the allowance account balance and likewise the net income will be the same in any case. For, if a recovery is credited to the allowance account, the amount to be charged to expense at the end of the period to raise the allowance account to its required balance will be reduced by the amount of the recovery; if the recovery is credited to the bad debt expense account or to an income account, the charge for the current provision will be correspondingly increased; the net income will be the same by either method.

From a practical standpoint, the choice of methods is usually of no serious consequence, because the allowance balance and the net operating charge for bad debts are usually matters of estimate; the theoretical considerations, therefore, seem to be of no great practical importance unless recoveries are of abnormally large amounts. In fact, recoveries are usually credited to the allowance account.

To illustrate the accounting for recovery of an account previously written off, assume that the $4,000 receivable illustrated in the entry on page 249 is later collected in full. The following entries first reinstate the customer's account and then record the collection.

Accounts receivable (Customer's account)	4,000	
Allowance for uncollectibles		4,000
Cash	4,000	
Accounts receivable (Customer's account)..........		4,000

Freight. Merchants sometimes sell goods f.o.b. destination but ship the goods "freight collect," with an understanding that the purchaser will pay the freight charges to the transportation company and deduct the amount thereof in making his remittance. In such instances, any freight to be deducted in the settlement of accounts that are open at the end of the period should be deducted from the accounts receivable by setting up a contra account with the offsetting debit to the expense account for freight charges.

In this connection, it is worth noting that the customer is entitled to discount on the full amount of the invoice, and not on the amount of the invoice less the freight. If the shipper paid the freight, the invoice would not be subject to a freight deduction, and discount would probably be taken on the whole amount of the invoice. The purchaser should not suffer a loss of discount merely because he pays the freight for the seller.

For example, assume that Company A has a $1,000 receivable at the end of its accounting period on which the customer has paid $25 in freight charges. The freight charges are to be deducted from the amount of the invoice at the time of payment. The following entry by Company A records these facts:

Freight out..	25	
Allowance for freight charges paid by customers		25

The allowance account reflects the fact that the gross amount of the invoice does not represent the amount to be collected and would be shown contra to the accounts receivable account in the balance sheet.

Returns and allowances. Should a contra account be set up to provide for the probable allowances to be credited to customers on accounts open at the end of the period, and for losses represented by the difference between probable credits for returns and the valuation that can properly be placed on the goods returned to inventory? Theoretically, yes, because otherwise the realizable value of the accounts receivable, as well as the net sales, would be overstated. In practice the provision is rarely made.

It is assumed that of the total accounts receivable at the end of the period, goods sold for a price of $2,000 will be returned. The following entry would be recorded to reflect the fact that the gross receivables do not report the amount expected to be collected:

Sales returns and allowances	2,000	
Allowance for sales returns		2,000

Provision for discounts. From a theoretical standpoint, a contra account should be set up for the discounts that will probably be taken on the accounts receivable; otherwise, the net realizable value of the receivables will presumably be overstated. However, the creation of such a contra account is not customary, and the charge to income to set up such an account is not deductible for federal income tax purposes.

For example, if Company A has total accounts receivable of $50,000 at the end of the period, and it is estimated that discounts to be taken on the receivables will amount to $800, the following entry would be recorded:

Sales discounts..	800	
Allowance for sales discounts........................		800

The allowance account would be reported as a deduction from the accounts receivable in the firm's balance sheet.

Discounts on returned sales. Assume that a customer buys goods invoiced at $1,000, subject to a 2 percent discount, and that he pays the invoice within the discount period with a check for $980. Subsequently he returns one-tenth of the goods, which had been billed to him at $100 and which were paid for at the net amount of $98. What credit should he receive? Although this is largely a matter of policy, it would seem that the credit should be $98 if the customer is to be reimbursed in cash, and $100 if the credit is to be traded out. The reason behind this conclusion may be made clearer by assuming that the entire invoice is returned. If a credit of $1,000 were allowed, to be paid in cash, the discount privilege could be abused, for the customer who paid $980 could obtain $1,000 in cash; on the other hand, if a credit of only $980 were allowed, payable in merchandise, the customer would lose the benefit of having paid his bill within the discount period.

The entry to record the return, assuming the customer is to receive a cash refund, is shown below:

Sales returns and allowances	100	
Cash		98
Sales discounts..		2

The credit to Sales Discounts is to remove the discount previously recorded on the portion of the sale that was returned.

Credit balances. If the subsidiary accounts receivable ledger contains accounts with credit balances, the balance of the controlling account will be the difference between the total of the debit balances and the total of the credit balances in the subsidiary ledger. At what figure should the accounts receivable be shown in the balance sheet? The accounts receivable should be shown at the total of the debit balances, and the credit balances should be shown on the liability side of the balance sheet, as a separate item. "Credit Balances of Customers' Accounts" is an appropriate title.

Direct write-off of bad debts. The use of an allowance for uncollectibles account is unique to the allowance method of accounting for bad debt losses. An alternative procedure used by some firms is referred to as the direct-write-off method. The latter method has practical advantages but is theoretically inferior to the method discussed earlier.

The major theoretical deficiency of the direct-write-off method is that it makes no attempt to relate the bad debts expense reported in any period to the credit sales of the period that caused the bad debts. Thus, there is improper matching of revenues and expenses. Also, the direct-write-off method results in an overstatement of the net realizable value of the accounts receivable reported on the balance sheet.

The following entry records the write-off of a $600 bad debt under the direct-write-off method.

Bad debts...	600	
Accounts receivable (Customer's account)		600

If the entire amount is subsequently recovered in the same accounting period, the following entries record the facts:

Accounts receivable (Customer's account)..................	600	
Bad debts		600
Cash	600	
Accounts receivable (Customer's account)		600

The first entry reinstates the account, and the second entry records the receipt from the customer.

If the recovery occurs in a later accounting period, the following entries are necessary:

Accounts receivable (Customer's account)	600	
Bad debt recoveries		600
Cash	600	
Accounts receivable (Customer's account)		600

Bad Debt Recoveries is a revenue item to be reported on the firm's income statement before extraordinary items.

Under the direct-write-off method, no attempt is made at the end of the accounting period to determine what the appropriate charge to income should be for estimated bad debts. Instead, accounts are written off during the period as they are determined to be worthless, by debiting the bad debt expense account and crediting accounts receivable. Thus, a basic characteristic of this method is that the allowance for uncollectibles account is not used at all.

Accounts receivable financing. The accounts receivable of a firm may be used to accelerate the inflow of cash resulting from credit sales. This practice occurs frequently in firms whose growth is hampered by inadequate cash and the inability to obtain additional bank credit. It is also often used by firms in a strong financial condition that are not faced with these problems, as a part of their overall cash management program. There are two widely used procedures by which the accounts receivable may be used to finance current operations to some extent. One method involves the *assignment* of accounts receivable, while the other is referred to as *factoring*.

ASSIGNMENT OF ACCOUNTS RECEIVABLE: Under this procedure, an agreement is made with a finance company to advance funds against accounts receivable for a definite period of time, usually a year, with a provision that the contract can be terminated upon written notice by either the client or the finance company six months prior to the termination date stated in the contract. The contract states the percentage of the accounts that the finance company will advance. The rate ranges from 75 to 95 percent, depending on the quality of the accounts and their average size, as well as the financial status of the client. An 80 percent rate is typical.

In effect, a line of credit is established, and the borrower draws against this as needed. The borrower may be required to sign a note for amounts actually borrowed. The client usually pledges the receivables as collateral to the obligation for the funds advanced, with full recourse to the client if an account is not collected when due.

Such financing is usually done on a nonnotification basis; that is, the client's customer is not informed that his account has been assigned to a finance company. The client makes the collections and agrees to transmit them, in the form in which received, to the finance company, which deposits them. The finance company makes arrangements with its bank to use a code endorsement, so that the checks returned to the customers will bear no evidence that the accounts have been financed.

Because the amount received from the finance company at the time of the financing is less than the amount of the receivables, the client retains an equity in the accounts, which the finance company credits to the client. Any returns, allowances, and discounts reduce the equity. If the equity is exhausted or reduced to an amount that the finance company regards as an inadequate cushion of protection, the client sends the finance company a check in an amount sufficient to create an acceptable equity. When accounts are collected, the related equity may be paid to the client immediately or periodically.

The finance company's charges consist of interest, usually at a daily rate of $\frac{1}{30}$ of 1 percent, applied:

Sometimes to the daily uncollected balances of the accounts; for instance, if the uncollected balances on a certain day totaled \$75,000, the interest charge for the day would be $\frac{1}{30}$ of 1 percent of \$75,000, or \$25.

Sometimes to the cash-advanced element of the daily uncollected balances; for instance, if the amount originally advanced was 80 percent of the accounts, the interest charge for the day would be $\frac{1}{30}$ of 1 percent of (\$75,000 × 80%), or \$20.

Because of the contingent liability that the client assumes in open accounts receivable financing, the transaction is similar in nature to the discounting of notes receivable and may be similarly recorded. To illustrate, assume that \$10,000 of accounts receivable were financed and that \$8,000 in cash was advanced to the client on December 31, 19—. The entry to record the financing would be:

Accounts receivable assigned	10,000	
Accounts receivable		10,000
Cash	8,000	
Payable to finance company		8,000

If a note is actually signed for the amount advanced, the credit in the second entry would be to Notes Payable.

The balance sheet presentation of accounts receivable at this point, assuming that the company has \$20,000 of unassigned accounts, would be:

Current assets:			
Accounts receivable		\$20,000	
Accounts receivable assigned	\$10,000		
Less: Finance company's interest in assigned accounts	8,000	2,000	\$22,000

The subsidiary ledger should indicate the accounts that have been assigned.

The balance sheet should disclose, preferably by a footnote, the contingent liability on the financed accounts. This is always the total of the uncollected balances of the assigned accounts, minus the equity. The footnote might state:

> On December 31, 19—, the company was contingently liable in the amount of \$8,000 on accounts receivable financed.

If it is assumed that collections on the assigned accounts during January were \$2,000 (gross amount) less cash discounts of \$40, and that there were sales returns of $175, the following entry would be required:

Cash	1,960	
Sales discounts	40	
Sales returns and allowances	175	
Accounts receivable assigned		2,175

The company would be required to remit the cash collected to the finance company, along with the finance charge for the month. Assuming the finance charge to be $80 (1 percent of the amount financed for the month), the following entry would record the payment to the finance company:

Financing expense	80	
Payable to finance company	1,960	
Cash		2,040

The contingent liability to be shown in a balance sheet footnote at this point is computed as follows:

Uncollected balances of assigned accounts:			
Original amount		$10,000	
Deduct:			
Collections—including cash discounts.	$2,000		
Returns and allowances	175	2,175	$7,825
Deduct equity in assigned accounts:			
Original amount		$ 2,000	
Deduct:			
Returns and allowances	$ 175		
Cash discounts	40	215	1,785
Contingent liability			$6,040

The discussion above is descriptive of the usual procedures in the assignment of accounts receivable. There are some variations of the procedures among finance companies.

FACTORING: Factoring is the outright purchase of receivables by a factor, which is a financing company in the business of purchasing trade receivables. The purchase is made on a notification basis, and the customer makes his remittances directly to the factor, who assumes the responsibility of keeping the receivable records and collecting delinquent accounts.

Before merchandise is shipped to a customer, the client requests the factor's credit approval. If it is obtained, the account is sold to the factor immediately after shipment of the goods. The factor credits the client's account for the amount of the invoice less the amount of the permitted cash discount, and less the factor's commission and a holdback intended primarily to absorb charges for returns and allowances. The percent of holdback (applied to the face of the account minus cash discount and commission) is a matter of agreement, but is normally about 10 percent. After there is no further prospect of returns and allowances or anything else that reduces the amount of the receivable, any remaining balance in the holdback is returned to the client. The client assumes no responsibility for loss.

The factor's compensation consists of:

Commission, which is a percentage of the net amount of the invoice—the gross amount minus available cash discount. The commission is a charge for the service of passing on credits, assuming all credit risks, and keeping the accounts. It usually varies from 1 percent, or somewhat less, to 2 percent or more, depending upon the amount of work and risk involved. Customary rates are $1\frac{1}{8}$ percent or $1\frac{1}{4}$ percent.

Interest, which is computed—usually at 8 percent per annum or at an equivalent daily rate—on amounts withdrawn by the client before the due date. Withdrawals can be made on the due date, interest free. After the due date, interest accrues to the client on any amounts not withdrawn.

The "due date" of a single invoice is ten days after the date on which the discount period expires. Clients frequently sell several invoices to a factor at the same time. It then becomes necessary to compute the average due date. This is done as follows:

(1) Select an arbitrary "focal date"; the most convenient focal date is the last day of the month preceding the earliest due date of any of the invoices.
(2) Determine, for each invoice, the number of days between the focal date and the date on which the discount period expires.
(3) Multiply the net amount (gross amount minus available discount) of each invoice by the number of days between the focal date and the date when the discount period expires, to determine an amount called *dollar-days*.
(4) Add the net invoice amounts.
(5) Add the dollar-days amounts.
(6) Divide the dollar-days total by the net invoice total. The quotient is the number of days between the focal date and the average discount period expiration date.
(7) Add ten days to this quotient to determine the average "due date."

To illustrate, assume that four invoices, all subject to 2 percent discount if paid within ten days, are sold to a factor on August 28. The computation (using August 31 as the focal date) of the average due date is shown below:

Invoice Date	Latest Discount Date	Invoice Amount Gross	Invoice Amount Net	Days Between Focal Date and Latest Discount Date	Dollar-Days
Aug. 28	Sept. 7	$1,000	$ 980	7	6,860 ($980 × 7)
26	5	1,500	1,470	5	7,350
25	4	2,500	2,450	4	9,800
30	9	3,000	2,940	9	26,460
		$8,000	$7,840		50,470

50,470 ÷ 7,840 = 6.4 (rounded off to 6) Days from focal date to average discount period expiration date.

September 6 + 10 = September 16, the average "due date."

Assuming that the commission rate is $1\frac{1}{4}$ percent and that the holdback rate is 10 percent, the client's entry to record the factoring will be:

Sales discounts (2% of $8,000)	160.00	
Factoring commission ($1\frac{1}{4}$% of $7,840)	98.00	
Factor's holdback [10% of ($8,000–$160–$98)]	774.20	
Receivable from factor	6,967.80	
Accounts receivable		8,000.00

As the borrower draws cash from the factor, he will be charged interest on the amounts drawn. For example, continuing the illustration, it is assumed that $3,000 is drawn and the applicable interest is $5. The following entry would be recorded:

Cash	3,000.00	
Interest expense	5.00	
Receivable from factor		3,005.00

This leaves a balance of $3,962.80 ($6,967.80 – $3,005.00) that the borrower may draw against. In addition to this amount, the factor's holdback, less any charges for any items that reduce the amount of the receivable, will be paid to the borrower soon after the due date. It is assumed in the current illustration that the factor remits the amount of the holdback, less sales returns of $250.00. The following entry records the receipt of the balance:

Cash ($774.20 – $250.00)	524.20	
Sales returns and allowances	250.00	
Factor's holdback		774.20

OTHER MEANS OF ACCOUNTS RECEIVABLE FINANCING: In addition to the procedures described in the preceding paragraphs, there are two other ways in which the accounts receivable of a firm may be used to obtain cash. One of these involves the use of accounts receivable as collateral for loans obtained from lenders. This is referred to as pledging the accounts, and should be disclosed in the balance sheet by either a footnote or parenthetical notation.

Firms in serious financial straits may sometimes resort to the outright sale of their accounts receivable. The cost of this arrangement is quite high, as the selling firm usually receives an amount that is considerably less than the face amount of the accounts sold. Under the usual agreement, the buyer takes the accounts without recourse to the seller.

NOTES AND ACCEPTANCES RECEIVABLE

Definitions. A *note* is defined by the Uniform Negotiable Instruments Law as follows:

> A negotiable promissory note within the meaning of this act is an unconditional promise in writing made by one person to another, signed by the maker, engaging to pay on demand or at a fixed or determinable future time a sum certain in money to order or to bearer.

A *bill of exchange* is defined by the same law as follows:

> A bill of exchange is an unconditional order in writing addressed by one person to another, signed by the person giving it, requiring the person to whom it is addressed to pay on demand or at a fixed or determinable future time a sum certain in money to order or to bearer.

After a bill of exchange has been accepted by the drawee, it becomes an acceptance.

A *trade acceptance,* as defined by the Federal Reserve Board, is a "bill of exchange, drawn by the seller on the purchaser, of goods sold, and accepted by such purchaser."

Terminology. Because bills of exchange, instead of notes, have been commonly used in England, the terms *bills receivable* and *bills payable* found their way into American terminology. However, the terms *notes receivable* and *notes payable* have now come into general use as more exactly indicative of the form of paper most in use here. If the bulk of a company's paper is in the form of notes, there is no serious objection to recording a few acceptances in the note accounts. But if acceptances are frequently used, it may be desirable to distinguish between the two classes of paper in the accounts by the terms *notes receivable* and *acceptances receivable,* and *notes payable* and *acceptances payable.*

Advantages of trade acceptances. Banks usually prefer to discount a customer's trade acceptance receivable rather than to discount his own note payable—for two reasons. First, the acceptance is two-name paper, a primary liability of the acceptor and a secondary liability of the drawer. Second, it is "self-liquidating"; because the acceptance arose out of a purchase of goods, it is assumed that sales will provide the funds with which to pay the paper.

From the standpoint of the selling merchant, the trade acceptance is preferable to the open account because (1) it is a written promise to pay a stated amount at an agreed date; (2) it relieves the seller of the financial burden of tying up a considerable portion of his capital in customers' accounts, because acceptances can be discounted at the bank more readily and more cheaply than accounts receivable can be assigned; and (3) it may reduce losses from bad debts.

Because trade acceptances are assumed to have a better credit standing than notes receivable, since the nature of their origin makes them presumably self-liquidating, it may be advisable to show them as separate items in the balance sheet if they are of any considerable amount.

Dishonored notes. When a note has reached its maturity and been presented to the maker without being collected, it is said to have been *dishonored.* It should then be taken out of the notes receivable account and transferred to the customer's account by the following entry:

Accounts receivable (John Doe)	500	
Notes receivable		500
To charge Doe's dishonored note back to his account. (The purpose of this entry is to show the dishonor of the note in Doe's account for purposes of credit information.)		

If the dishonored note bore interest, the interest revenue account should be credited and the maker of the note should be debited. This should be done in order to maintain a record of the interest earned and the total amount receivable from the debtor. If any protest fees were paid, they should be charged to the maker. Any amount regarded as uncollectible should be written off.

It has been suggested that dishonored notes be passed on to a dishonored notes receivable account, thus:

Dishonored notes receivable	500	
Accounts receivable (John Doe)		500
To transfer the note to a dishonored-notes account.		

This entry takes the item out of the accounts receivable, which are assumed to be current and collectible, and shows its true nature as a past-due note.

Credit limit on notes and accounts. When the credit department fixes a maximum credit limit for a customer, and when customers settle their accounts by notes, it may be desirable to keep the records in such a way as to show the combined liability of each customer on notes and on account. This purpose can be accomplished by providing customers' accounts with two debit and two credit columns, the inner columns to be used as memorandum note columns. When a customer is credited with a note in the outer credit column, he is also charged in the inner, or memorandum, debit column. When he pays the note, Notes Receivable is credited and a memorandum entry is made in the inner credit column of the customer's personal account. Thus, the balance of the outer columns will show the customer's liability on open account, and the balance of the inner columns will show his liability on notes.

Notes receivable valuation. In theory, all notes receivable (and payable) should be reported in the balance sheet at the present value of the future principal (face value) and interest payments of the notes. If a note is interest-bearing and the stated interest rate reflects the prevailing market rate of interest for similar notes (that is, there is no discount or premium), then the present value of the note to maturity is equal to the face value (principal amount specified in the note). In such a case, the face value of the note can be properly reported in the balance sheet, since it reflects present value. For example, assuming that the market interest rate is 7 percent, a one-year 7 percent $1,000 note receivable has a present value to maturity equal to the face value of $1,000, since the present value of the principal ($1,000) plus interest ($70 = $1,000 × .07 × 1) is equal to $1,000 ($1,070/1.07).

In contrast, if a note receivable is non-interest-bearing (no stated interest rate) or has a stated rate that is different from the prevailing market rate appropriate to similar notes, then the face value of the note does not equal the present value of the note to maturity. The difference between the present value to maturity and the face value of the note is a discount or premium; hence, the face value of the note is *not* the proper valuation to be reported in the balance sheet. In such a case, if the note were reported at face value, then the sales price (purchase price) and profit (cost) to the seller (buyer) during the current period, and interest revenue (expense) during subsequent periods, would be misstated. For example, a one-year, non-interest-bearing $1,000 note receivable, in effect, has the interest included in the face of the note. If the market rate for equivalent notes is 7 percent, then this rate can be used to impute the present value to maturity, or $934.58 ($1,000/1.07), and the discount, or $65.42 ($1,000 – $934.58), on the note. In theory, the discount should be amortized over the life of the note and the note reported in the balance sheet at face value minus unamortized discount to approximate present value to maturity.

Assume now that the $1,000, one-year, non-interest-bearing note previously discussed is a trade note receivable dated January 1 and that the fiscal period of the firm holding the note ends June 30.

In theory, the note should be recorded and reported at present value to maturity based on the imputed interest rate of 7 percent. This can be done two ways, by either recording the note directly at present value to maturity, or recording at the face value and setting up a contra notes receivable account for the discount on notes receivable. Both methods will result in reporting the note at present value to maturity on the balance sheet. The discount could be amortized using either a semiannual rate of 3.5 percent (.07/2) or the straight-line method. Assuming the use of a semiannual rate of 3.5 percent, the following entries would be made:

19+1			
Jan. 1	Notes receivable [present value, $1,000 $(1.035)^{-2}$ = $1,000(.93351)]	933.51	
	Sales		933.51
or	Notes receivable (face value)	1,000.00	
	Discount on notes receivable ($1,000 – $933.51)		66.49
	Sales		933.51
June 30	Notes receivable ($933.51 × .035)	32.67	
	Interest revenue		32.67
or	Discount on notes receivable	32.67	
	Interest revenue		32.67
19+2			
Jan. 1	Notes receivable [($933.51 + $32.67)(.035)]	33.82	
	Interest revenue		33.82
	Cash	1,000.00	
	Notes receivable		1,000.00
or	Discount on notes receivable	33.82	
	Interest revenue		33.82
	Cash	1,000.00	
	Notes receivable		1,000.00

At June 30, 19+1, the end of the fiscal year, the note receivable would be reported in the balance sheet directly at present value to maturity ($966.18 = $933.51 + $32.67) or at face value ($1,000) minus the discount ($33.82 = $66.49 – $32.67), to show the $966.18.

In contrast to the treatment just illustrated, APB *Opinion No. 21* states that normal receivables and payables not exceeding approximately one year (short term)—that is, transactions with customers or suppliers in the normal course of business that are due in customary trade terms—are exceptions (there are other exceptions also) to the requirement of the Opinion that receivables and payables should be reported at face value plus premium or minus discount.[4] Hence, normal short-term trade receivables and payables can be recorded and reported at face value. Such accounting treatment is not theoretically correct, but is based on practical considerations. The difference between the present value and face value of normal short-term trade receivables and payables is immaterial (doctrine of materiality), and the difference tends to average out over time as such receivables and payables recur.

This means that the note receivable referred to in the previous illustration would be recorded as follows:

Jan. 1, 19+1	Notes receivable	1,000	
	Sales		1,000
Jan. 1, 19+2	Cash	1,000	
	Notes receivable		1,000

Note that at June 30, 19+1, the end of the fiscal period, the note receivable would be reported in the balance sheet at the $1,000 face value, instead of present value of $966.18 ($933.51 + $32.67) as shown on page 263 and interest earned for six months, imputed at 7 percent ($32.67), is ignored.

In contrast to normal short-term trade receivables and payables, *Opinion No. 21* was issued to set forth the proper accounting for receivables and payables (such as secured and unsecured notes, mortgage notes, debentures, bonds, equipment obligations, and some accounts receivable and payable) whose face value does not reasonably represent the present value of the consideration given or received in exchange. The difference between the face value and present value to maturity of such receivables and payables is either a discount or premium resulting from interest not being stated; an unreasonable stated interest rate; face value that is materially different from the cash sales price of property, goods, or services exchanged; or face value that is materially different from the market value of the receivables or payables. Per *Opinion No. 21*, the proper valuation of such receivables or payables should be the fair value of the property, goods, or services exchanged, or the market value of the receivables or payables, whichever is more clearly determinable. If neither can be clearly determined, then the valuation of the receivables or payables should be based on the present value of the future payments, using an imputed interest rate (a market rate of interest for similar receivables or payables).

As an example, assume that a company sells, for $10,000, land that had a cost of $8,000 and receives a non-interest-bearing note receivable due two years hence.

---

[4]Accounting Principles Board, "Interest on Receivables and Payables," *Opinion No. 21* (New York: AICPA, August 1971), p. 418.

Since the seller is willing to wait two years before receiving the $10,000, clearly the land is not worth $10,000, because of the time value of money; hence, the land and note receivable should not be recorded at the $10,000 face value of the note. If the market rate of interest for similar notes is 7 percent, then the present value of the note can be determined to be $8,734.39.

$$\begin{aligned} P &= Sp_{n(i)} = \$10{,}000p_{2(.07)} = \$10{,}000(.873439) \\ &= \$8{,}734.39 \end{aligned}$$

The note would be recorded at the time of sale as follows:

Notes receivable	8,734.39	
Land		8,000.00
Gain on sale of land		734.39

Or:

Notes receivable	10,000.00	
Discount on notes receivable		1,265.61
Land		8,000.00
Gain on sale of land		734.39

The discount would be amortized over the two-year life of the note.

Bank discount. The bank discount and the proceeds of a note or acceptance discounted at a bank are computed as follows:

Compute the maturity value (M) of the note.

The value of a non-interest-bearing note is its face (F); hence, maturity value equals face value (i.e., $M = F$).

The value of an interest-bearing note is its face (F) plus interest (I), at the rate (r) stated by the note, for the full time (t) of the note, or

$$M = F + I = F + (F \cdot r \cdot t) = F(1 + r \cdot t)$$

Compute the bank discount (D); this is equivalent to interest, on the value at maturity (M) and at the discount rate (d), for the discount period (t), or

$$D = M \cdot d \cdot t$$

Deduct the discount (D) from the value at maturity (M) to derive the proceeds (P) received by discounting the note, or

$$P = M - D = M - (M \cdot d \cdot t) = M(1 - d \cdot t)$$

Three illustrations are given below. In each case the principal of the note is $600, its date is June 15, it is due in 60 days (on August 14), and it is discounted on June 27. The discount period is 48 days, which is equal to the term of the note (60 days) minus the 12 days the note is held before it is discounted. The discount rate is 6 percent. The first column shows the computation if the note does not bear interest; the second column shows the computation if the note bears 4 percent interest; the third column shows the computation if the note bears 7 percent interest.

	No Interest	4% Interest	7% Interest
Value at maturity (M):			
Face of note (F)	$600.00	$600.00	$600.00
Interest (I) on face for term of note ($I = F \cdot r \cdot t$):			
None..............................			
At 4% for 60 days ($600 × .04 × 60/360)..........................		4.00	
At 7% for 60 days ($600 × .07 × 60/360)..........................			7.00
Value at maturity ($M = F + I$)....	$600.00	$604.00	$607.00
Bank discount (D) at 6% for 48 days ($D = M \cdot d \cdot t$):			
On $600 ($600 × .06 × 48/360)	4.80		
On $604 ($604 × .06 × 48/360)		4.83	
On $607 ($607 × .06 × 48/360)			4.86
Proceeds ($M - D$)........................	$595.20	$599.17	$602.14

Note that by calculating the discount on the maturity value, and then deducting the resulting discount from the maturity value, the proceeds for each note are smaller then the present value of the maturity value. This gives the bank a slightly higher effective rate of interest than the stated discount rate. In theory, the proceeds should be equal to the present value of the maturity value—that is, $M/(1 + d \cdot t)$. However, as in the examples above, the difference between the proceeds and the present value of the maturity value is usually immaterial for short-term and relatively small notes.

Notes receivable discounted. When a note or an acceptance receivable is discounted, the credit should be made to Notes Receivable Discounted or Acceptances Receivable Discounted, to show the contingent liability resulting from the endorsement.

The traditional method of recording the discounting of a note or an acceptance receivable involved a debit to Interest Expense or a credit to Interest Revenue for the difference between the *face* of the paper and the proceeds. Entries made in this manner, based on the foregoing illustrations, are shown below:

Cash	595.20	
Interest expense..	4.80	
Notes receivable discounted..........................		600.00
Cash	599.17	
Interest expense	.83	
Notes receivable discounted..........................		600.00
Cash	602.14	
Interest revenue..		2.14
Notes receivable discounted..........................		600.00

Such entries do not appear to give adequate expression to the facts if the paper is interest-bearing. They ignore the interest earned between the date of the note and the date of discounting. They also ignore the fact that we are parting with two assets (the note and the accrued interest) and that there is a loss or gain equal to the difference between the total amount of these assets and the proceeds of the note.

Referring to the 4 percent note, the facts are:

Assets parted with:	
Face of note	$600.00
Accrued interest on $600 for 12 days (June 15 to June 27) at 4%	.80
Total	$600.80
Proceeds	599.17
Loss	$ 1.63

and the following entries would appear desirable:

Interest receivable	.80	
Interest revenue		.80
Cash	599.17	
Loss on discounting notes receivable	1.63	
Interest receivable		.80
Notes receivable discounted		600.00

Note that the $1.63 debit and the $.80 credit net to $.83, which is the debit to interest expense using the conventional entries previously discussed.

Referring to the 7 percent note, the facts are:

Proceeds		$602.14
Assets parted with:		
Face of note	$600.00	
Accrued interest at 7% for 12 days	1.40	
Total		610.40
Gain		$ .74

and the following entries should be made:

Interest receivable	1.40	
Interest revenue		1.40
Cash	602.14	
Interest receivable		1.40
Notes receivable discounted		600.00
Gain on discounting notes receivable		.74

Note that the credits of $1.40 and $.74 total to $2.14, which is the amount credited to interest revenue using the conventional entries previously illustrated.

If an interest receivable account is debited by an adjusting entry at the close of a prior period for an interest accrual applicable to the note being discounted, the amount of the credit to Interest Receivable in the entry to record the discounting should be the sum of the prior accrual and the interest accrued since the date of the adjusting entry.

Contingent liability in the balance sheet. The usual disclosure of the contingent liability on discounted notes is to show on the asset side only the notes receivable on hand, with a footnote indicating the contingent liability, thus:

Current assets:	
Notes receivable (Note B)	$4,000

Note B. The company was contingently liable on December 31, 19+1, in the amount of $1,000 on customers' notes discounted.

Some accountants indicate the contingent liability on discounted paper by a deduction in the balance sheet, thus:

Current assets:		
Notes receivable	$5,000	
Less notes receivable discounted	1,000	
Notes receivable on hand		$4,000

Payment by maker. If a discounted note is paid by the maker, the contingent liability should disappear from the endorser's books. This is accomplished by debiting Notes Receivable Discounted and crediting Notes Receivable.

Because notice of dishonor must be given to the endorser promptly in order to hold him, the endorser may safely assume that a discounted note has been paid at maturity unless he receives notice to the contrary within a few days after the maturity of the paper.

Payment by endorser. Assume that the $600 note bearing 7 percent interest, the proceeds of which were computed on page 266, could not be collected from the maker, and that the bank obtained collection from the endorser. Assume that the total collected included the face, the $7 interest payable on the note, and protest fees of $4.30. The endorser's entries are:

Accounts receivable (maker)	611.30	
Cash ($600.00 + $7.00 + $4.30)		611.30
Payment of note discounted June 27, and interest and protest fees		
Notes receivable discounted	600.00	
Notes receivable		600.00
To eliminate the note and the contingent liability from the accounts		

Endorsement without recourse. According to the Uniform Negotiable Instruments Law:

> Every person negotiating an instrument by delivery or by a qualified endorsement, warrants:
>
> (1) That the instrument is genuine and in all respects what it purports to be;
>
> (2) That he has a good title to it;
>
> (3) That all prior parties had capacity to contract;
>
> (4) That he has no knowledge of any fact which would impair the validity of the instrument or render it valueless.

As compared with the contingent liability arising from an unqualified endorsement, these warranties implied by an endorsement without recourse impose so slight a liability that it is usually ignored, and notes transferred by such endorsements are credited to Notes Receivable instead of to Notes Receivable Discounted.

Inventory: Basic Cost Methods

Introduction. Inventory may be defined as all goods held for sale to customers or held for the manufacture of goods for sale to customers. Accounting for the inventory of a business firm includes the procedures for the valuation of inventory based on cost, departures from cost (other valuation methods), and estimations of inventory. This chapter discusses inventory valuation based on cost. Chapters 12 and 13 cover inventory valuation based on noncost and estimating methods of valuation, respectively.

Inventory and income determination. The inventory amounts reported on a firm's financial statement have a significant impact on both the balance sheet and the income statement. The same amount reported on the balance sheet as the ending inventory is used to calculate the cost of goods sold in the income statement. Thus, any misstatement of inventory amounts will affect the income reported for the period. Such errors, if not corrected, will also affect the income of the following period, because the incorrect amount is used in the determination of cost of sales for the following period.

Classification of inventories. Certain business firms acquire their inventory items from suppliers in condition for resale to customers. Wholesale and retail businesses are examples of such firms, which are usually referred to as *trading* concerns. The term *inventory,* or *merchandise inventory,* is used to designate such goods held by trading concerns.

Manufacturing firms acquire goods in a state that requires additional work be performed before the completed inventory unit is ready for sale to customers. The classification of the inventory of such firms is discussed below.

Finished goods consist of manufactured articles that are completed and ready for sale. The cost of these units includes, in addition to the cost of materials, labor and manufacturing overhead costs utilized to complete them.

Goods in process consist of partially manufactured goods. The cost of such goods includes the materials, labor, and overhead costs utilized to bring them to their present state of completion.

Raw materials consist of items purchased for use in the manufacturing process but on which no work has yet been done by the firm inventorying them. This usually includes only those items that become an integral part of the completed product.

It should be pointed out that the classification of a given item will depend upon the firm in whose inventory it is contained. For example, an automobile manufacturer may have on hand a supply of batteries to be used in each automobile completed. These would properly be reported as a part of the firm's raw materials inventory. However, prior to their sale they would have been reported as finished goods inventory of the company that manufactured them.

If parts are manufactured before they are required, and are held for future use in manufacturing, they may be classed as finished goods, but they are usually included in the materials inventory.

Reference to the balance sheet of a manufacturing company, illustrated on page 40, indicates that, in addition to the three classes of inventory just discussed, there is a separate item, referred to as factory supplies, reported separate from the inventories, but still within the Current Assets section. Factory supplies, sometimes referred to as manufacturing supplies, are distinguished from raw materials as indicated below.

Materials can be directly associated with, and become a part of, the finished product; and they are used in sufficient amounts to make it practicable to allocate their costs to the product.

Some manufacturing supplies, like lubricants, are used indirectly in the process of manufacture and do not become part of the finished product. Some other things classified as manufacturing supplies, like paint and nails, do become part of the finished product, but the amounts involved are so insignificant that it is impracticable to attempt to allocate their costs directly to the product; however, they find their way into the product cost as part of the manufacturing overhead.

Supplies that will be charged to selling and general expense are of a somewhat different nature. Shipping supplies and office supplies are examples. Although these are more appropriately classified as short-term prepayments, they are often shown as supplies under the Current Assets caption.

Some companies classify under the Inventories caption of the balance sheet any advances made to vendors against purchase commitments. This seems to be of doubtful propriety, because the company does not have title to the related merchandise. Such advances should probably appear in the balance sheet after the inventories. Current assets, with the exception of prepayments, are usually marshalled under the current caption in the order of their liquidity—cash, receivables, and inventories. Advances on purchase commitments are less current than goods on hand. Wherever the advances appear, they should be clearly distinguished from debit balances in suppliers' accounts resulting from merchandise returns, overpayments, and other similar causes. Prepayments are shown as the last item under the current caption.

Inventory determination. The amount reported for the inventory of any firm at the end of the accounting period is the result of two different steps, both of which involve unique procedures and related problems. The first step is the determination of quantities on hand. The second step involves the determination of the dollar amount at which the quantities on hand will be reported.

Inventory contents. What should be included in the inventory, and what should be excluded therefrom? The general rule is that the inventory should include all goods to which the company holds title, wherever they may be.

If goods sold under contract or ordered by customers for future delivery are being held in stock, it is important to determine whether title has passed. The mere fact that the goods have been segregated from other merchandise may or may not mean that title has passed to the vendee. If title has passed, the goods should be excluded from the inventory; if title has not passed, they should be included.

On the other hand, goods that have been ordered but not received at the balance sheet date may properly belong in the inventory. If the goods are in transit, the general rule as to passing of title is as follows: If the goods were shipped f.o.b. shipping point, they belong to the purchaser; if they were shipped f.o.b. destination and have not arrived at the destination, they belong to the seller. If merchandise purchases are in transit and title has passed, it is advisable to postpone the completion of the inventory tabulation until the merchandise has been received and checked into stock; this procedure will avoid inventory errors arising from differences between merchandise merely invoiced to the company and merchandise received in good condition. Because the completion of the inventory taking normally requires some time, the checking of the receipt of merchandise in transit will not ordinarily cause any delay.

Inventory errors. Two types of errors may result from failure to include all owned goods in the inventory.

First, the purchase may be correctly recorded, and the goods may be incorrectly omitted from the ending inventory. This omission, of course, results in an understatement of net income and assets (ending inventory) by the same amount.

Second, the purchase may *not* be recorded, and the goods may be incorrectly omitted from ending inventory. This omission does not result in an understatement of net income, because the purchases and the closing inventory are equally understated. The practice is to be condemned, however, because it understates current assets (inventory) and current liabilities (accounts payable) in the balance sheet. Thus, the current financial position appears more favorable than the facts really warrant, partly because the working capital ratio is overstated, and partly because, in many instances, the accounts payable will have to be paid before the merchandise is sold and converted into cash.

There are also two types of errors that may result from the inclusion of items in the inventory that should not be included.

First, a purchase may be recorded that should not have been, with the merchandise incorrectly included in the ending inventory. This has no effect on net income, because the purchases and ending inventory are overstated by the same amount and offset one another in the determination of cost of goods sold. The effect on the balance sheet is that assets (inventory) and liabilities (accounts payable) will be overstated by the same amount.

Second, the purchase may *not* be recorded, with the merchandise being incorrectly included in ending inventory. Since ending inventory is overstated, both net income and assets are overstated by the same amount.

Purchase discounts and cost. From a theoretical standpoint, purchase discounts represent reductions in the cost of merchandise. However, practical considerations often result in some other treatment of the discounts.

NET METHOD: The net method of recording merchandise purchases is based upon the logical argument that the true cost of the merchandise is the net amount to be paid according to the terms of purchase. For example, if goods are purchased at a list or invoice price of $1,000, with terms of 2/10; n/30, the purchaser may acquire the goods at a cost of $980 [$1,000 − ($1,000 × .02)]. If for some reason the purchaser does not pay within the discount period, thus having to pay $1,000 to acquire the goods, the additional $20 represents the cost of an additional 20 days of credit and can be viewed as an expense associated with the way in which merchandise acquisitions are financed. Moreover, the failure to take purchase discounts results in a high annual interest rate, which is 36 percent in the case just illustrated.

$$I = p \cdot r \cdot t$$

$$\$20 = \$1{,}000 \cdot r \cdot 20/360$$

$$r = 36\%$$

If the purchase above is paid for within the discount period, the following entries would be recorded, assuming the use of perpetual inventory procedures:

Inventory	980	
Accounts payable		980
To record purchase net of discount.		
Accounts payable	980	
Cash		980
To record payment within the discount period.		

If the payment is made after the discount period has elapsed, the second entry would record the payment of $1,000 as follows:

Accounts payable	980	
Discounts lost	20	
Cash		1,000

The use of this method will result in the cost of sales and the inventory being reported at the true net cost. The discounts that are not taken will be reported as a separate item and should properly be treated as a financial expense item on the income statement, in the same manner as interest expense.

In order to correctly state the liability associated with merchandise purchases, it may be necessary to record an adjusting entry at the end of the period as a result of lost discounts associated with invoices that have not yet been paid. For example, assume that the $1,000 purchase referred to earlier was made on December 15, and the invoice remains unpaid at December 31. The invoice is not yet past due, but the discount period has passed, and the payment that must be made in the following period is $1,000, not $980. The following entry will record these facts:

Discounts lost	20	
Accounts payable		20

As a practical matter, the entry above is seldom recorded.

GROSS METHOD: Traditionally, merchandise acquisitions were recorded at the total invoice price, with recognition given to the discounts taken. A $1,000 purchase and the related payment within the discount period would be recorded as follows:

Inventory	1,000	
Accounts payable		1,000
To record purchase at invoice amount.		
Accounts payable	1,000	
Purchase discounts		20
Cash		980
To record payment within the discount period.		

At one time, it was widespread practice to treat the discounts taken as an item of revenue, although there is no theoretical justification for this. Revenue results from the sale of goods or services, not from acquisitions. The most widespread treatment of the discounts taken under this method is as a reduction in the cost of goods sold by treating purchase discounts as contra to the purchases account.

Theoretically, the discounts should be allocated between the cost of goods sold and the ending inventory, a refinement that is uncommon in practice.

From a theoretical standpoint, the major argument against the gross method is that it results in an overstatement of the cost of merchandise and the related liability. It also fails to disclose discounts that are not taken, an item of information that may be helpful in appraising how well a firm is managed. For example, the payment of the $1,000 invoice after the discount period had elapsed would be recorded as follows:

Accounts payable....................................	1,000	
Cash		1,000

This weakness is the major reason for the increased use of the net method, which reports separately the discounts not taken. However, because the overstatement under the gross method is usually not significant, and because of the theoretical need under the net method for adjusting entries that are usually not material, the gross method is still widely used in practice.

Incidental costs. Cost includes not only the purchase price but also any additional costs necessary to placing the goods on the shelves. These incidental costs include duties, freight or other transportation costs, storage, insurance while the goods are being transported or stored, and costs incurred during any aging period. The total of these items is clearly an addition to the total purchase price of all goods; it is not a simple matter, however, to apply the incidental costs to individual purchases and to determine what portion of the total incidental costs is applicable to the goods in the inventory. Some incidental costs may be easily applied to the particular goods on which the costs were incurred. Other costs may be prorated on a percentage basis; such a distribution is not likely to be strictly accurate, because the incidental costs are not usually incurred in amounts exactly proportionate to the cost of the merchandise. Greater accuracy may be obtained by an attempt to apply each bill to its corresponding invoice, but this procedure usually involves more labor and cost than are warranted by the slightly greater degree of accuracy.

Theoretically, there is some justification for regarding the cost of operating the purchasing department as part of the cost of the merchandise acquired and including an element of such cost in the inventory valuations. However, such a procedure is not usually regarded as practicable or advisable. In the first place, it involves the allocation of general overhead to the purchasing department and thus raises questions as to an equitable determination of the cost of operating the department. In the second place, such a procedure necessitates the apportioning of the purchasing department cost to the various purchases during the period and to the various classes of goods in the inventory at the end of the period, and questions arise as to an appropriate basis for the apportionment of such costs.

If the incidental costs are immaterial, the accountant will consent to either their inclusion or their exclusion for inventory-pricing purposes, on a consistent basis. This does not mean that all incidental costs must be treated alike; for instance, it is acceptable to include freight and exclude storage costs, or vice versa. And it does not follow that, if freight charges are included in computing one section of the inventory, they must be included in computing the other sections of the inventory; but if freight charges are included in pricing an inventory or any section of an inventory, then that practice should be consistently followed over the years.

Apportioned costs. A special problem arises when a whole, acquired at a lump price, is divided into parts that, because of differences in nature or in quality, are to be sold at different prices. To determine a cost for the parts sold and a cost for the parts remaining in the inventory, it is necessary to make an apportionment of the lump-sum price.

To illustrate, assume that land is purchased, developed, and subdivided into cemetery lots. The total cost, assumed to be $60,000, may be apportioned to individual lots in the ratio of selling price, thus:

Selling Price Per Lot	Number of Lots	Product	Percent of Total	Apportioned Cost Total	Apportioned Cost Per Lot
$200	40	$ 8,000	8	$ 4,800*	$120**
500	60	30,000	30	18,000	300
600	80	48,000	48	28,800	360
700	20	14,000	14	8,400	420
Total		$100,000	100	$60,000	

*8% of $60,000
**$4,800 ÷ 40

Lost costs. Cost for inventory purposes may be less than the total original cost because, under some circumstances, it may be apparent that the costs invested in the inventory may not be fully recoverable. This condition may be the result of style changes, technological improvements, deterioration, spoilage, or damage attributable to storm or fire. Whatever the cause, the implication is the same: All or a portion of a cost outlay for merchandise or goods on hand has been lost.

A strict cost basis would be unrealistic if it required all items in the inventory to be priced at full cost irrespective of their potential realizable value. To avoid stating a current asset at an amount in excess of its realizable value, it is customary, even though the basis is described as a cost basis, to price inventory items below cost whenever it is apparent that the cost outlay cannot be recovered through sale in the ordinary course of business. This subject is discussed in greater detail in the following chapter.

Manufacturing costs. The purchase price of materials and merchandise bought can, of course, be determined from invoices. But the cost of goods in process and the cost of finished goods can be determined only by keeping accurate cost records showing costs of materials, labor, and factory overhead assignable to the product.

Some companies have followed the practice of omitting manufacturing overhead from the inventory valuation, on the theory that this is a conservative procedure. There seems to be no more propriety in omitting the overhead element of manufacturing cost than in omitting the materials or labor cost.

VARIABLE (DIRECT) COSTING: Traditional cost accounting procedures allocate to each unit of manufactured product the three elements of manufacturing costs—materials, labor, and overhead. These procedures are referred to as absorption costing or full costing, because each unit bears or "absorbs" its share of total manufacturing costs. In recent years, an increasing number of manufacturing firms have adopted procedures referred to as *variable or direct costing,* which treat certain manufacturing costs in a different manner from their treatment under absorption costing.

Advocates of variable costing contend that manufacturing costs should be divided into two main categories, variable and fixed, and that no portion of the latter should be assigned to inventories or used in computing the inventory valuation. Following this plan, fixed manufacturing costs (those that do not vary with changes in the volume of output) would be treated as expenses of the period, as selling and administrative expenses are treated; only variable costs would be considered when determining cost for inventory purposes. Those arguing in favor of variable costing point out that the procedure minimizes the problem of overhead application (which, in practice, is often arbitrary and questionable), because fewer costs are subject to allocation. However, the strongest argument is that variable costing lends itself to more meaningful cost analyses. For example, changes in the volume of output usually result in considerable fluctuations in unit costs. This effect is primarily attributable to the impact of fixed costs, which are mostly beyond the control of management, at least in the short run. As a consequence, the usefulness of unit cost data is impaired, because management is not able to determine readily whether a change in unit cost is the result of a change in volume or the result of poor control over those costs that are subject to management's control. On the other hand, variations in unit costs under variable costing would signal cost variations presumably subject to managerial control, because fixed costs would be expensed and not included in unit cost data. But the point remains that under variable costing, a portion of the costs of manufacturing would be ignored for inventory-valuation purposes—which is not a commendable result, considering the effects on financial statements.

The allocation of the total production costs during a period to those goods that have been completed and to those that remain in process is admittedly a difficult problem. Elaborate cost records may be used for this purpose. In the absence of such records, it may be necessary to compute unit costs, for purposes of inventory pricing, from general accounting and production data. If there were goods in process at the beginning and/or the end of the period, and if there was any change in the quantity or stage of completion of the goods in process at the two dates, unit costs of goods completed during the period cannot be computed by dividing the total manufacturing costs for the period by the number of units of product completed during the period. Consideration must be given to the inventories of goods in process at the beginning and end of the period, and to the stages of completion thereof.

STANDARD COSTS: It is not uncommon for manufacturing concerns to price their goods in process and finished goods inventories by using standard costs.

There are several varieties of standard costs; they may be developed by relying on time and motion studies, past costs and manufacturing performances, expected costs and manufacturing performance, theoretical costs, or some combination thereof. They may be described as predetermined costs or estimated costs.

To illustrate, the material requirements for a given product are computed and the quantity required to complete one unit of product is priced, perhaps at current purchase prices or at expected purchase prices. Labor cost per unit of product is similarly developed, perhaps by reference to production studies or past performance. And finally, estimated overhead is allocated on the basis of an expected or average volume of production.

As products are completed, the finished goods are charged to the inventory account on the basis of their standard costs. Actual costs probably will differ from predetermined costs, with the result that cost-variance balances will develop in the accounts. These variances are commonly closed to Cost of Goods Sold. For inventory-pricing purposes, it is desirable to review standard costs periodically to see that they do not deviate significantly from actual costs.

INVENTORY COST SELECTION

Introduction. The total cost of the merchandise on hand during any period is the sum of the cost of the beginning inventory and the cost of the additions to inventory during the period. The basic problem involved in costing the ending inventory is determining a proper cost amount for the items on hand. In other words, the problem involves the allocation of costs between the units still on hand at the end of the period and the units sold during the period.

If all units on hand during the period had the same unit cost, a very unrealistic assumption, then inventory costing would be a very simple process. Once the total number of units on hand was determined, they would be costed at the per-unit amount, which would be the same for the units sold during the period. However, since identical goods may be purchased or produced at different costs, inventory costing is usually a more complex procedure.

The first step in inventory costing is the selection of one of several possible costing methods. Each method is based upon an assumption concerning the order in which inventory costs flow through the accounting records. This cost flow can be quite different from the order in which the goods themselves move through the firm. For example, in many business firms, the physical flow of goods must be first-in, first-out, owing simply to the nature of the product. A food store would be a very good example of such an operation.

There is no requirement that the assumed cost flow reflect the actual flow of units in the firm. The major consideration in the selection of a costing method is how well it reflects periodic income.[1]

---

[1]This is the position of the American Institute of Certified Public Accountants, as stated in paragraph 29 of *Accounting Research Bulletin No. 43*. The American Accounting Association has taken the position that the assumed cost flow should approximate the physical flow of goods.

Several methods of selecting the costs that are to be regarded as applicable to the inventory are discussed in the following sections.

For purposes of illustration, assume that the inventory and purchases data are as shown below:

Beginning inventory:	100 units at $1.00	$100
First purchase:	200 units at 1.10	220
Second purchase:	250 units at 1.20	300
Third purchase:	100 units at 1.25	125
Fourth purchase:	150 units at 1.30	195
Total	800	$940

There are 200 units in the ending inventory.

Specific identification. If the goods on hand can be identified as pertaining to specific purchases or specific production orders, they may be inventoried at the costs shown by the invoices or the cost records. Specific identification requires the keeping of records by which goods can be definitely identified and their costs determined.

Although this method appears to have an excellent logical foundation, it is often impossible or impracticable to apply. It also has the disadvantage of allowing profit manipulation by the arbitrary selection of low or high cost items for ending inventory.

Last invoice price. Under this method, the cost applicable to the last purchase transaction is used to price the entire inventory quantity. In other words, $1.30 would be applied to the 200 units in the inventory. If there is a rapid physical turnover of the inventory in the normal course of the business, and the goods are sold in approximately the same order in which they are acquired, the last invoice price may closely approximate the results produced by the use of the specific-identification method, with much less clerical effort.

Simple-average method. The simple arithmetical average of the unit prices is determined by adding the unit costs of the beginning inventory and all purchases, and dividing by the number of purchases plus one (for the beginning inventory). Using the foregoing data, the simple average unit cost and the inventory valuation are computed as follows:

$$\text{Unit Cost} = \frac{\$1.00 + \$1.10 + \$1.20 + \$1.25 + \$1.30}{5} = \$1.17$$

$$\text{Inventory valuation} = \$1.17 \times 200 = \$234$$

This is a rather illogical method, because the unit prices applicable to large and small purchases are given the same weight in the computation.

Weighted-average method. The cost of the purchases plus the beginning inventory is divided by the total units purchased plus those in the beginning inventory, and a weighted-average unit cost is thus determined. Applied to the foregoing data, this method produces an inventory valuation computed as follows:

Total cost—\$940
Total units—800
Unit cost = \$940 ÷ 800 = \$1.175
Inventory valuation = \$1.175 × 200 = \$235

Because the costs determined by the weighted-average method are affected by purchases early in the period as well as those toward the end of the period, there may be a considerable lag between purchase costs and inventory valuations. Thus, on a rising market, the weighted-average costs will be less than current costs, and on a falling market, the weighted-average costs will be in excess of the current costs.

Moving-average method. This method may be used when perpetual inventories are kept, new unit-average costs being computed after each purchase. Assume that the purchases stated in the preceding illustration and the sales were made in the sequence set forth in the following tabulation, which shows how the moving-average unit costs are computed. Each sale is costed out at the latest computed moving-average cost, and the resulting inventory valuation is on the moving-average unit-cost basis.

	Units	Unit Cost	Amount	Moving-Average Cost
Beginning inventory	100	\$1.00	\$100.00	\$1.00
First purchase	200	1.10	220.00	
Inventory	300		\$320.00	1.0666
First sale	175	1.0666	186.67	
Inventory	125		\$133.33	
Second purchase	250	1.20	300.00	
Inventory	375		\$433.33	1.1555
Second sale	275	1.1555	317.78	
Inventory	100		\$115.55	
Third purchase	100	1.25	125.00	
Inventory	200		\$240.55	1.2028
Third sale	50	1.2028	60.14	
Inventory	150		\$180.41	
Fourth sale	100	1.2028	120.28	
Inventory	50		\$ 60.13	
Fourth purchase	150	1.30	195.00	
Inventory	200		\$255.13	1.27565

Because the cost applied to the inventory is affected to some extent by the cost of all purchases, there is (as in the weighted-average method) a lag between market prices and inventory valuations. However, the lag is less pronounced in the moving-average method than in the weighted-average method.

WIDELY FLUCTUATING COSTS: A modification of the moving-average cost computation is peculiarly suited for the determining of monthly inventory valuations when unit costs vary widely from month to month because of differences in the quantity of production. To illustrate, let us assume that a company manufactures a product that sells heavily in warm months and poorly in cold months, and that its production fluctuates with sales. The following are the quantities and the monthly costs of production during two years:

	19+4			19+5		
	Units Produced	Total Cost	Unit Cost	Units Produced	Total Cost	Unit Cost
January	100	$ 1,660	$16.600	90	$ 1,705	$18.944
February	115	1,738	15.113	75	1,688	22.507
March	220	2,232	10.145	250	2,195	8.780
April	3,200	8,745	2.733	3,720	10,503	2.823
May	4,600	11,935	2.595	4,360	11,700	2.683
June	5,950	13,665	2.297	6,325	15,260	2.413
July	6,300	15,060	2.390	6,720	16,800	2.500
August	6,750	15,855	2.349	7,310	18,215	2.492
September	5,200	13,470	2.590	6,205	16,225	2.615
October	850	4,170	4.906	960	4,515	4.703
November	300	2,475	8.250	412	2,925	7.100
December	140	1,940	13.857	125	2,025	16.200
Totals and averages	33,725	$92,945	2.756	36,552	$103,756	2.839

High unit costs appear in the months of low production because a large fixed overhead is distributed over a small number of units.

The inventories at the close of the year can be valued at the average costs for the year: $2.756 at the end of 19+4, and $2.839 at the close of 19+5. But what basis can be used for the valuation of monthly inventories, if monthly statements are desired? Obviously, the monthly unit costs would not be appropriate, because of their wide fluctuation. Nor would it be entirely correct to use, in the 19+5 monthly statements, the average cost for 19+4 ($2.756), because 19+5 costs appear to be on a higher level, as evidenced by the higher average for the year ($2.839).

A moving-average cost, computed in the manner illustrated below, appears suitable for such a situation.

	Units			Cost			
	This Year (Add)	Last Year (Deduct)	Twelve Months	This Year (Add)	Last Year (Deduct)	Twelve Months	Moving Average
Year 19+4			33,725			$ 92,945	$2.756
Year 19+5:							
January	90	100	33,715	$ 1,705	$ 1,660	92,990	2.758
February	75	115	33,675	1,688	1,738	92,940	2.760
March	250	220	33,705	2,195	2,232	92,903	2.756
April	3,720	3,200	34,225	10,503	8,745	94,661	2.766
May	4,360	4,600	33,985	11,700	11,935	94,426	2.778
June	6,325	5,950	34,360	15,260	13,665	96,021	2.795
July	6,720	6,300	34,780	16,800	15,060	97,761	2.811
August	7,310	6,750	35,340	18,215	15,855	100,121	2.833
September	6,205	5,200	36,345	16,225	13,470	102,876	2.831
October	960	850	36,455	4,515	4,170	103,221	2.831
November	412	300	36,567	2,925	2,475	103,671	2.835
December	125	140	36,552	2,025	1,940	103,756	2.839

The moving-average cost (using January as an example) is computed as follows:

	Units	Cost
Total—Twelve months ended December 31, 19+4...	33,725	$92,945
Add amounts for January, 19+5	90	1,705
Total	33,815	$94,650
Deduct amounts for January, 19+4	100	1,660
Total—Twelve months ended January 31, 19+5	33,715	$92,990

$92,990 ÷ 33,715 = $2.758

The use of such a moving-average cost eliminates the irrational fluctuations in inventory values that would result from pricing the monthly inventories at the widely varying unit costs of production during the busy and slack seasons. The moving-average costs are preferable to the average cost of the preceding year, because the moving averages are affected by the factors that increased the average yearly unit costs from $2.756 in 19+4 to $2.839 in 19+5.

In the application of this moving-average cost theory, the sales each month, as well as the inventory at the end of the month, should be costed on the moving-average basis. This method will result in overabsorptions and underabsorptions of cost in the monthly statements, and will probably require an adjustment at the end of the year for the net overabsorption or underabsorption. For example, the underabsorption for January 19+5 (costing the opening inventory at the $2.756 average for 19+4, and the sales and the January 31 inventory at the January average of $2.758) would be determined as follows:

Inventory, December 31, 19+4	1,200 units at $2.756	$3,307.20
January production	90 units at actual cost	1,705.00
Total	1,290 units	$5,012.20
January sales	120 units at $2.758	$ 330.96
Inventory, January 31, 19+5	1,170 units at $2.758	3,226.86
Total		$3,557.82
Underabsorption of costs		$1,454.38

The cumulative underabsorptions and overabsorptions of cost during the year, computed similarly, are shown below.

End of:	Underabsorption or Overabsorption*
January	$1,454.38
February	2,933.04
March	4,443.56
April	4,651.80
May	4,231.09
June	1,799.21
July	301.50*
August	2,820.76*
September	4,159.78*
October	2,362.54*
November	611.94*
December	1,051.46

The cumulative adjustment for the year, $1,051.46, is only slightly more than 1 percent of the actual costs for the year.

First-in, first-out (FIFO) method. This method is based upon the assumption that inventory costs should be assigned to units sold in the order in which the costs were incurred. Thus, the cost of goods on hand at the end of the period represents the cost of the most recent acquisitions. Using the data on page 279, the cost of the ending inventory is calculated as follows:

From the fourth purchase: 150 units at $1.30	$195.00
From the third purchase: 50 units at $1.25	62.50
Total	$257.50

This method has been considered desirable because it produces an inventory valuation that is in conformity with price trends; because the inventory is priced at the most recent costs, the pricings follow the trend of the market.

A perpetual-inventory record maintained on the first-in, first-out basis appears below:

Perpetual Inventory—First-in, First-out Basis

	Quantity			Cost		
Date	Into Stock	Out of Stock	Balance	Into Stock	Out of Stock	Balance
June 1			100			$100.00
5	200		300	$220.00		320.00
8		175	125		$182.50	137.50
13	250		375	300.00		437.50
18		275	100		317.50	120.00
23	100		200	125.00		245.00
25		50	150		60.00	185.00
26		100	50		122.50	62.50
29	150		200	195.00		257.50

The cost of the first sale consisted of:

100 units at $1.00 each (beginning inventory)	$100.00
75 units at $1.10 each (first purchase)	82.50
Total	$182.50

The inventory after the first sale consisted of 125 units at a cost of $1.10 each. The cost of the second sale consisted of:

125 units at $1.10 each (first purchase)	$137.50
150 units at $1.20 each (second purchase)	180.00
Total	$317.50

The inventory after the second sale consisted of 100 units at a cost of $1.20. The cost of the third sale consisted of:

50 units at $1.20 (second purchase)	$ 60.00

The inventory after the third sale consisted of:

50 units at $1.20 (second purchase)	$ 60.00
100 units at $1.25 (third purchase)	125.00
Total	$185.00

The same computational procedure would be applied to the fourth sale and fourth purchase for the month.

The first-in, first-out method can be applied without great difficulty even though perpetual inventories are not maintained; it is necessary only to determine prices shown by the most recent invoices for quantities sufficient to equal the number of units in the inventory.

Last-in, first-out (LIFO) method. This method assigns the cost of the most recent goods purchased to the units sold. Thus, to cost the ending inventory, the accountant refers to the cost data applicable to the beginning inventory, and uses cost data applicable to purchases of the current year only in case the ending inventory is larger than the beginning inventory.

Consider the following facts:

	Quantity	Cost	Total
Beginning inventory	1,000	$ 8	$8,000
Purchases during the current period:			
First purchase	250	9	2,250
Second purchase	300	10	3,000
Third purchase	100	13	1,300
Fourth purchase	200	14	2,800

The following illustrates the approach used under the last-in, first-out method if the ending inventory consists of 1,300 units.

	Quantity	Cost	Total
Beginning inventory	1,000	$ 8	$ 8,000
First purchase	250	9	2,250
Part of the second purchase	50	10	500
Total			$10,750

Advocates of the method maintain that during periods of changing costs and prices, more meaningful income statements are produced if "current" costs are applied to current sales, thus achieving a better matching of expense and revenue. To illustrate the point by a simple and rather arbitrary example, let us assume that a company sells one unit of a commodity each year. At the beginning of the first year, it bought one unit for $1 and marked it to sell for $1.50, as a gross margin of $.50 was considered necessary to cover expenses and leave the desired profit. Before any sale was made, the company purchased another unit for $1.05, and raised the selling price to $1.55. It then sold one unit for $1.55.

By the FIFO method, the gross margin would be computed thus:

Sale	$1.55
Cost of unit sold	1.00
Gross margin	$ .55

And the inventory would be priced at a cost of $1.05.

By the LIFO method, the gross margin would be computed thus:

Sale	$1.55
Current cost of unit sold	1.05
Gross margin	$ .50

And the inventory would be priced at a cost of $1.00.

The purchase and sale operations for a period of eight years are tabulated below; the period embraces a cycle in which costs went from $1.00 to $1.50 and back to $1. The goods were always sold at a price $.50 above the cost of the most recent purchase. The tabulation also shows the gross margin on the FIFO and LIFO bases. (The costs applied against the sales are indicated by letters in the "Purchases" and "Gross Margin" columns.)

				Gross Margin			
Year	Purchases		Sales	FIFO Basis		LIFO Basis	
1	A	$1.00					
	B	1.05	$1.55	A	$0.55	B	$0.50
2	C	1.15	1.65	B	0.60	C	0.50
3	D	1.30	1.80	C	0.65	D	0.50
4	E	1.50	2.00	D	0.70	E	0.50
5	F	1.30	1.80	E	0.30	F	0.50
6	G	1.15	1.65	F	0.35	G	0.50
7	H	1.05	1.55	G	0.40	H	0.50
8	I	1.00	1.50	H	0.45	I	0.50
					$4.00		$4.00

The aggregate gross margins for the eight years were the same in this instance, because the first and the last purchase costs were the same.

It will be observed that the FIFO method resulted in the showing of widely fluctuating gross margins even though the company continually adjusted its selling prices to keep them closely related to current purchase costs. The advocates of the LIFO method would say that it is unrealistic, when the quantity of yearly sales is uniform and sales prices are adjusted in conformity with cost changes, to show annual gross margins varying as widely as $.70 and $.30. The opponents of the LIFO method would say that it is unrealistic to price a commodity in the inventory, for balance-sheet purposes, at a remote cost not representative of current costs. For instance, at the end of the fourth year in the illustration, the inventory cost under LIFO would be $1.00, whereas under the FIFO method, the same inventory would be shown at a 50 percent higher cost, or $1.50, which would be a more current, meaningful representation of the investment in the inventory.

Another reason advanced in support of the LIFO method is that, on a rising market, a portion of the net income shown under the FIFO method is necessarily plowed back into the inventory, and, although such net income amounts are legally available for dividends, it may be inexpedient, from the working-capital standpoint, to distribute them. The LIFO method tends to keep out of the stated net income any amounts that are not realized in the sense of being represented by a net increase in current assets other than merchandise. To make this point clear, let us refer to the foregoing illustration and assume that the company whose purchases and sales are stated there began its life with the balance sheet shown below.

Cash	$2.00	Capital stock	$2.00

After the first purchase, its balance sheet appears as follows:

Cash	$1.00	Capital stock	$2.00
Inventory	1.00		
	$2.00		$2.00

By the end of the fourth year, the company has made additional purchases totaling $5 and sales totaling $7. Assume, to simplify the case, that it has incurred no expenses and paid no dividends; therefore, its cash has increased $2, and it has a cash balance of $3. Under the FIFO method, its net income for the four years will amount to $2.50, and its balance sheet will be as follows:

Cash	$3.00	Capital stock	$2.00
Inventory	1.50	Retained earnings	2.50
	$4.50		$4.50

If cash in the amount of the entire retained earnings is now distributed as a dividend, the balance sheet will be:

Cash	$ .50	Capital stock	$2.00
Inventory	1.50		
	$2.00		$2.00

After the first purchase, the company had one unit in its inventory and $1 in cash; it now has one unit of inventory and $.50 in cash. It is not inconceivable that the continuance of such a procedure might result in leaving the company with inadequate cash to carry on successful operations. Of course, the company could limit its dividends to $2, but are not the stockholders perhaps justified in feeling that there is something deficient or peculiar in a situation in which reported earnings cannot be distributed without risking the impairment of working funds?

Under the LIFO method, the earnings for the four years are shown at $2, the inventory is valued at $1, and the balance sheet appears as follows:

Cash	$3.00	Capital stock	$2.00
Inventory	1.00	Retained earnings	2.00
	$4.00		$4.00

The company can now pay out its entire stated earnings and be in the same asset position as it was after the first purchase—with one unit of merchandise and $1 in cash.

Income taxes should be included in any consideration of LIFO and FIFO. And an assumption that a period of increasing prices is followed by a period of relative price stability (and not by a period of declining prices, as was assumed in the preceding example) would be more realistic. Under such conditions, the FIFO method will result in the reporting of larger earnings and the payment of more income taxes over the years than if the LIFO method were adopted. These are important considerations for management to weigh, but they should not be the determinants of what constitutes good accounting theory.

Unsettled LIFO problems. The argument between LIFO and FIFO seems to be a question of whether current costs should be regarded as applicable to the inventory to be shown in the balance sheet (FIFO method) or be matched against current revenue in the income statement (LIFO method).

The LIFO method places the emphasis on the income statement, but its effect on the balance sheet, and particularly on the working capital shown therein, should not be overlooked.

If a sustained price rise follows an adoption of the LIFO method, the dollar balance reported for inventories among the current assets will be substantially less than current costs. Although the LIFO advocates contend that achieving a more appropriate matching of expense against revenue is such an important objective that it offsets the "incorrect" balance-sheet results, the fact remains that, conceivably, inventory quantities might eventually be priced at such "old" costs as to produce a misstatement of working-capital position that would be seriously misleading. To some extent, this could be remedied by disclosing current costs for the inventory parenthetically or in a footnote to the balance sheet. This proposal is resisted in some quarters because of the clerical burden it would impose in computing the inventory on two bases. It would be possible to avoid this burden by permitting the use of estimates for purposes of parenthetical disclosure of current costs for the inventory.

In discussions of LIFO, there seems to be a tacit assumption that a company will adopt the LIFO method when prices are relatively low although rising. But suppose a company adopts LIFO when the price level is not at a low point. Under these conditions, it is conceivable that subsequent price declines might bring the replacement costs below the cost level prevailing at the time the company adopted the LIFO method. In this event, should the LIFO costs be used for inventory pricing, or should those costs be reduced to coincide with the newer and lower replacement costs? A strict application of the LIFO method would preclude such a reduction, because the matching of current costs against current revenues would thereby be disturbed. However, there is reason to expect that, as with all so-called cost bases of inventory pricing, accountants would sanction a reduction in LIFO costs when it was apparent that the valuation of a current asset would otherwise be overstated.

A disturbing problem arises whenever a company using the LIFO method fails, for some reason, to maintain its usual inventory position, resulting in a smaller ending inventory than beginning inventory. If the inventory quantity is drawn down after a significant price rise, a strict application of the LIFO method would result in matching some old, low costs against current revenues produced by selling goods at current prices. To illustrate, let us assume the following conditions:

Inventory, January 1—1,000 units priced on the LIFO basis at $100 each.......	$ 100,000
Purchases during the year—10,000 units at an average cost of $150 each.........	1,500,000
Sales during the year—10,300 units at an average selling price of $175 each......	1,802,500
Inventory, December 31—700 units priced on the LIFO basis at $100 each......	70,000

Here we face a situation in which current revenues may be charged with some current costs and with some old costs, as shown below:

Sales—10,300 units.......................................		$1,802,500
Cost of sales:		
10,000 units at current costs—$150 each ..	$1,500,000	
300 units at old costs —$100 each ..	30,000	1,530,000
Gross margin		$ 272,500

This partial matching of old costs against current revenue would cause some distortion in the net income of the period in which the inventory reduction occurred, because current revenue would not be entirely matched with current costs. Moreover, if the inventory reduction was only temporary and the inventory was replenished in the near future at current costs, a comparison of the replenished inventory with the prior inventory might create a misleading impression, for an equal inventory quantity would be set forth in the accounts at a higher dollar figure—15 percent higher in the illustration being developed here. This is demonstrated by the following computation, based on the assumption that the inventory was replenished by the purchase of 300 units at $150 each:

Inventory before temporary reduction:		
1,000 units at $100 each		$100,000
Inventory after replenishment:		
700 units at $100 each	$70,000	
300 units at $150 each	45,000	115,000

In some instances, an inventory reduction, or "liquidation," may be involuntary, resulting from such uncontrollable causes as shortage of supply or delivery delays owing to strikes. In other instances, the quantity reduction may be voluntary, management expecting more favorable purchase prices in the near future. In either case, the inventory quantity impairment could very likely be temporary; and it would seem to be regrettable if income statement and balance sheet distortions were to result from the mere fact that inventory quantities happened to be temporarily low at the end of the accounting period.

Adherents of LIFO accounting, concentrating on the fundamental objective of matching current costs with current revenues, advocate dealing with such a situation by charging Cost of Goods Sold with current costs, even though some of the goods sold were carried in the accounts at old, lower costs. Referring to the preceding illustration, they would record an entry similar to the following:

Cost of sales (10,300 units at $150 each)........	1,545,000	
Inventory (to reduce balance in this account to LIFO cost of 700 units at $100 each)..		30,000
Excess of replacement cost over LIFO cost of basic inventory temporarily liquidated ($50 × 300)		15,000
Purchases		1,500,000

When the inventory was replenished by the purchase of 300 units, at the current price of $150 per unit, the entry would be:

Inventory (300 units at $100—LIFO cost)	30,000	
Excess of replacement cost over LIFO cost of basic inventory temporarily liquidated	15,000	
Cash		45,000

The income statement would then show the following:

Sales—10,300 units..	$1,802,500
Cost of goods sold—10,300 units at current cost of $150 each	1,545,000
Gross margin	$ 257,500

The consequences of making entries of the nature indicated above can be shown by a comparison of the results produced without making the foregoing entries and the results obtained by making the entries:

	Without Suggested Entries	With Suggested Entries
Sales..	$1,802,500	$1,802,500
Cost of goods sold	1,530,000	1,545,000
Gross margin	$ 272,500	$ 257,500
Inventory before replenishment	$ 70,000	$ 70,000
Excess replacement cost reserve		15,000
Inventory after replenishment..................................	115,000	100,000

The account Excess of Replacement Cost Over LIFO Cost of Basic Inventory Temporarily Liquidated would be shown in the balance sheet among the current liabilities.

It should be pointed out that firms often avoid the LIFO problem of ending inventory being smaller than beginning inventory by purchasing inventory near the end of the period in sufficient quantities to insure that the ending inventory is at least equal to the beginning inventory. Thus, it is contended that LIFO results in inventory manipulation by management in order to affect profits.

LIFO layers. The technique of inventory valuation applying the LIFO method can perhaps be best indicated by a graphic presentation of the inventory base and layers at successive dates, as shown on page 290.

We shall assume that the LIFO base inventory consisted of 1,000 units acquired at an average cost of $10 per unit.

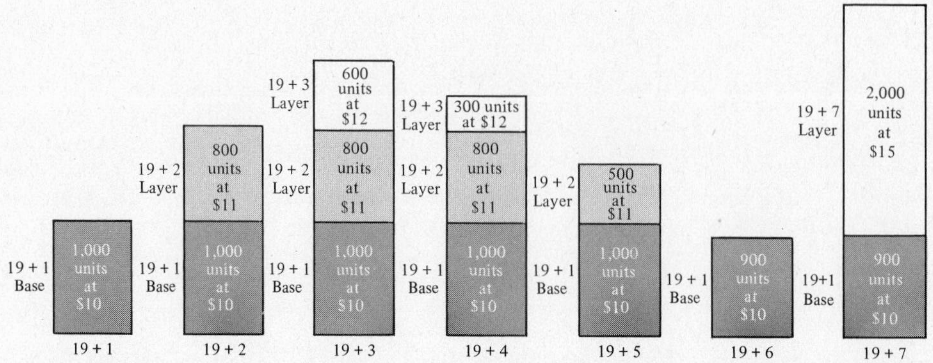

On December 31, 19+2, one year later, the inventory consisted of 1,800 units: the 19+1 base of 1,000 units, and the 19+2 incremental layer of 800 units priced at 19+2 costs.

On December 31, 19+3, there were 2,400 units in the inventory, consisting of the 19+1 base, the 19+2 layer, and a 600-unit layer priced at 19+3 LIFO cost.

On December 31, 19+4, the inventory had decreased. On the last-in, first-out basis, the decrease came out of the 19+3 layer, reducing that layer to 300 units.

On December 31, 19+5, the inventory had further decreased. The 19+3 layer was gone, and only 500 units of the 19+2 layer remained.

On December 31, 19+6, the inventory had again decreased, and consisted only of 900 units of the 19+1 base.

On December 31, 19+7, the inventory had increased 2,000 units. This 2,000-unit increment must be regarded as a new layer, to be priced at 19+7 LIFO cost.

Costing LIFO layers. Three alternatives are acceptable in costing an incremental layer. The following data are used to illustrate the application of the alternatives:

Current year's purchases:

Date	Quantity	Cost	Total
January 10	250	$ 9	$2,250
May 15	300	10	3,000
September 20	100	13	1,300
December 27	200	14	2,800
Total	850		$9,350

Average cost—$9,350 ÷ 850 = $11.

Current year's inventory increase (layer)—300 units.

Alternatives:

(1) The incremental quantity is assumed to relate to the first acquisitions of the current year.

Amount to be used in computing new layer of LIFO inventory:

250 × $ 9 =	$2,250
50 × $10 =	500
LIFO cost	$2,750

(2) Average costs for the current year may be used.

Amount to be used in computing new layer of LIFO inventory:

300 × \$11 = \$3,300

(3) The incremental quantity is assumed to relate to the last acquisitions of the current year.

Amount to be used in computing new layer of LIFO inventory:

200 × \$14 =	\$2,800
100 × \$13 =	1,300
LIFO cost	\$4,100

Alternative (1) seems to be the most logical, because it follows the last-in, first-out assumption. However, all three alternatives are acceptable for federal income tax purposes; as a result, all three methods are used in practice.

Once the aggregate dollar amount for any given layer has been determined, it remains unchanged until all or some portion of the layer is sold or utilized.

Adopting LIFO. If a company changes its inventory costing method, the resulting effect on net income should be computed and disclosed in the financial statements for the year in which the change was made. This requirement makes it necessary to compute the ending inventory by both the old method and the new method. Thus, if a company decides to abandon FIFO and adopt LIFO as of December 31, 19+5, it will be necessary to calculate the December 31, 19+5, inventory by both the FIFO and LIFO methods.

Having made the decision to adopt LIFO as of December 31, 19+5, how are LIFO costs computed? An acceptable method is to refer to the beginning inventory (December 31, 19+4) for this information. The cost figures used there are assumed to be the appropriate costs to apply to the ending inventory quantities not in excess of the December 31, 19+4, inventory quantity. In other words, the beginning inventory of the year in which LIFO is adopted is used as the LIFO base inventory. For reasons of expediency, the beginning (December 31, 19+4) inventory unit costs are averaged in order to arrive at uniform unit-cost data. For example, assume the facts shown below in connection with an abandonment of first-in, first-out and the adoption of the last-in, first-out inventory method for 19+5 and subsequent years.

December 31, 19+4, inventory (FIFO):

Article		Quantity	Unit Costs	Total	Average Unit Costs
A		1,000	\$ 9	\$ 9,000	
		500	10	5,000	
		500	12	6,000	
	Total—A......	2,000		\$20,000	\$10
B		800	24	\$19,200	
		400	27	10,800	
	Total—B......	1,200		\$30,000	25
	Total...........			\$50,000	

19+5 purchases:

	Quantity A	Quantity B	Cost A	Cost B	Total
February 1	1,000		$11		$ 11,000
March 1		600		$28	16,800
June 15	4,000		12		48,000
August 20		1,500		29	43,500
November 25	1,500		13		19,500
December 10		1,200		30	36,000
Total purchases					$174,800

December 31, 19+5, inventory:

Quantity: 2,100 units of A
1,100 units of B

Costing on Last-In, First-Out Basis

Article	Explanation	Quantity	Inventory Price	Total
A	LIFO base quantity at established LIFO cost	2,000	$10	$20,000
	From February 1 purchase	100	11	1,100
	Total—A	2,100		$21,100
B	LIFO base quantity is not exceeded, so entire December 31, 19+5 quantity is priced at established LIFO cost	1,100	25	27,500
	Total			$48,600

Costing on First-In, First-Out Basis

Article	Explanation	Quantity	Inventory Price	Total
A	From November 25 purchase	1,500	$13	$19,500
	From June 15 purchase	600	12	7,200
	Total—A	2,100		$26,700
B	From December 10 purchase	1,100	30	33,000
	Total			$59,700

Computation of effect of change in inventory method on 19+5 net income before income taxes:

Inventory, December 31, 19+5, first-in, first-out	$59,700
Inventory, December 31, 19+5, last-in, first-out	48,600
Net effect—decrease in net income before income taxes	$11,100

The effect on net income (either before or after income taxes) produced by a change in inventory method is generally disclosed by a footnote to the financial statements.

Base-stock method. The base-stock (sometimes called "normal-stock") method is founded on a theory that may be described as follows: If a company considers that its inventory of a certain commodity should never normally fall below 100 units, the

100 units are the base stock, and no increase in the market replacement cost of this base stock should be regarded as realized income because, like fixed assets, the base stock cannot be disposed of if the business is to continue operations. To avoid the taking of any profit on such "unrealized" market increases, the base-stock quantities should be costed for inventory purposes at not more than the lowest cost experienced. It should be noted that the base quantity is the minimum quantity a given business needs to carry on normal operations, not an average inventory quantity.

Units sold or issued for manufacture are costed out at the most recent acquisition cost; in this regard, the base-stock method is similar to the last-in, first-out method, because current costs are matched against current revenues. For this reason, the base-stock method (which was developed before the last-in, first-out method) is sometimes regarded as the precursor of the LIFO method.

The operation of the base-stock method may be illustrated as follows:

	Units	Unit Price	Amount
First purchase (and base-stock quantity).	100	$1.00	$100.00
Second purchase	200	1.10	220.00
Total	300		$320.00
First sale	175	1.10	192.50
Inventory	125		$127.50
Third purchase	250	1.20	300.00
Total	375		$427.50
Second sale	275	1.20	330.00
Inventory	100		$ 97.50
Fourth purchase	100	1.25	125.00
Total	200		$222.50
Third sale	50	1.25	62.50
Inventory	150		$160.00

Observe that, after the second sale, and as a result of costing out 275 units at the most recent unit cost of $1.20, although only 250 units were purchased at so high a cost, the inventory of 100 units—the base quantity—is priced at less than the original base cost of $100.

The results disclosed above are those that would result from a perpetual inventory record. The perpetual inventory record would be adjusted from time to time, at least annually, to conform to the results of a physical inventory, for which the pricing procedure usually adopted is as follows:

If quantities are in excess of base stock:

Base-stock quantities at base price,
Plus excess quantities at current cost.

For instance, if there are 150 units in the inventory, the valuation would be determined as follows:

100 units at $1.00	$100.00
50 units at 1.25	62.50
150	$162.50

If quantities are less than base stock:

> Base-stock quantities at base price,
> Less deficient quantities at current cost.

For instance, if there are 95 units in the inventory, the valuation would be determined as follows:

100 units at $1.00	$100.00
5 units at 1.25	6.25
95	$ 93.75

The computations above disclose the primary contrasting feature of the base-stock method and the LIFO method. Under LIFO procedures, if the ending-inventory quantity is less than the beginning-inventory quantity, the entire quantity is priced by using the LIFO unit costs used in the beginning inventory. No use is made of current costs or costs applicable to recent purchases.

Because the base price should be the lowest cost experienced, a reduction of market costs below the originally adopted base price should result in the adoption of the new and lower cost as the base price.

The base-stock method is not in general use and is not acceptable for income tax purposes.

Under the base-stock method, the costs used are ordinarily lower—often substantially lower—than current market costs. As a consequence, the inventory shown in the balance sheet may be misleading. This is also typical of LIFO. It would seem equally appropriate, as suggested in the case of LIFO, to disclose by footnote the approximate difference between the amount shown and the valuation on a current-cost basis, or by stating parenthetically the inventory on a current-cost basis. Such disclosure is not required by present reporting standards.

"NIFO." NIFO is an abbreviation for "next-in, first-out." Thus far, NIFO has not attained a status of acceptability as an inventory-costing method. As the expression indicates, under this approach cost of sales would be computed by using replacement costs. As a result, income would be measured by matching current revenues and the replacement costs of the goods sold.

The argument for NIFO is founded on reasoning that can be summarized in the following manner. Assume that a merchant has on hand an article that cost $10. Suppose that it is sold for $15. If the merchant is going to continue in business, he must replace the article sold. Assume that the replacement cost is $12. Under these conditions, a proponent of NIFO would argue that conventional accounting misstates gross margin by reporting it as $5 (because $2 of the $5 reported gross margin is needed to maintain the inventory), and that gross margin and net income would be more truthfully reported if the article sold were "costed" at the $12 replacement cost. The $3 gross margin thus reported under the NIFO method would measure the real gain produced by the sale, because of the elimination of the "fictitious" profit element that would have to be used merely to maintain a normal inventory.

12

Inventory: Valuation Methods

Introduction. The preceding chapter discussed the various costing procedures that may be used to calculate the cost of a firm's inventory. This chapter is devoted to coverage of the procedures involved when inventory is to be valued at an amount other than its cost.

Lower of cost or market. Once the cost of a firm's inventory has been determined using an acceptable costing method, it is necessary to determine whether or not cost is an appropriate amount to be used for financial statement purposes. A departure from cost is generally considered acceptable when the current cost of buying or producing the inventory (referred to as *market*) is less than the inventory cost as determined by an appropriate costing method.

Definition of market. Depending upon the circumstances, market value for purposes of inventory valuation may be determined in one of the following ways:

Purchase or replacement basis:

This basis applies to purchased merchandise or materials. It has been defined by the Treasury Department for tax purposes as follows: "Upon ordinary circumstances and for normal goods in an inventory, 'market' means the current bid price prevailing at the date of the inventory for the particular merchandise in the volume in which usually purchased by the taxpayer." The restriction concerning quantity is important; if it were omitted, inapplicable market values might be used.

Replacement is probably a better word than *purchase,* as it is broad enough to include the incidental acquisition costs, such as freight and duties, which are properly included with the purchase price in the inventory computation.

Reproduction basis:

This basis applies to manufactured goods and goods-in-process. It is determined on the basis of market prices for materials, prevailing labor rates, and current overhead.

Realization basis:

For some items in the inventory, such as obsolete or repossessed merchandise, a purchase or reproduction market value may not be determinable, and it may be necessary to accept, as an estimate of market value, the prospective selling price minus all prospective costs to be incurred in conditioning and selling the goods, and minus a reasonable profit.

Limits on market. There are certain limits on the application of market values to inventories. These have been stated by the Committee on Accounting Procedure of the AICPA in *Bulletin No. 43* as follows:

> As used in the phrase *lower of cost or market* the term *market* means current replacement cost (by purchase or by reproduction, as the case may be), except that:
>
> (1) Market should not exceed the net realizable value (i.e., estimated selling price in the ordinary course of business less reasonably predictable costs of completion and disposal); and
> (2) Market should not be less than net realizable value reduced by an allowance for an approximately normal profit margin.[1]

It should be noted that the first exception places an upper limit or ceiling on the market figure to be used, and the second one determines a lower limit or floor for the market figure. The purpose of the latter is to insure that losses are recognized only when they have been sustained.

---

[1]Committee on Accounting Procedure, *Accounting Research Bulletin No. 43* (New York: AICPA, 1961), p. 31.

NORMAL PROFIT: The preceding quotation from *Bulletin No. 43* refers to "an approximately normal profit margin." This expression is used in the statement that, if market is lower than cost, in no event should the figure used for inventory pricing be less than net realizable value (estimated selling price less reasonably predictable costs of completion and disposal) reduced by an allowance for an approximately normal profit margin. For example, this calculation would be made as follows for an item having an estimated selling price of $100 and estimated disposal costs of $30, assuming that a normal profit is 20 percent of selling price.

Estimated selling price	$100
Less estimated disposal costs	30
Net realizable value	$ 70
Less normal profit ($100 × 20%)	20
Net realizable value less normal profit	$ 50

The use of a normal profit concept seems somewhat unfortunate. How is a "normal" profit determined? By whom? What is the normal profit margin for General Motors Corporation? Can an estimate of a normal profit margin be more than a matter of individual opinion?

There is an additional troublesome feature in the use of normal profit. If an inventory is reduced to "net realizable value reduced by an allowance for an approximately normal profit margin," then in the period of sale a normal profit will be reported, if the sales price is correctly forecast. Such results, however, may be somewhat misleading, because they are attributable to a method of inventory costing. It seems logical to price the inventory at less than cost if it is clearly apparent that the investment in inventory cannot be recovered. But why adopt an accounting procedure that reduces an inventory figure to such an extent that a profit will probably be reported in the subsequent period?

If December 31 was the close of the accounting period and the goods in question had been sold on December 29, a loss would have been reported. If the goods are costed in the inventory to permit a normal profit when sold, and they are sold on January 5, a profit is reported. The close of an accounting period and the application of an accounting convention have thus made a loss transaction appear to be profitable. By understating profits or overstating losses in one year, a larger profit can be reported in a subsequent year.

It may be relevant to note that this result would arise only if market were below net realizable value. If market is above net realizable value, then cost is reduced to net realizable value without further reduction to provide for an approximately normal profit. The goods thus reduced would be sold at no loss in the period of sale. Only when market is below net realizable value will the inventory be reduced to produce a subsequent accounting profit.

ILLUSTRATION: The following illustration shows how the limits previously mentioned would be applied to five different inventory items. The underlined amounts are those to be used for inventory valuation purposes.

	Items				
	1	2	3	4	5
(a) Cost	.72	.85	.85	.68	.84
(b) Market–cost to replace at inventory date	.76	.80	.70	.65	.83
(c) Selling price less estimated cost to complete and sell (ceiling)	.82	.82	.82	.82	.82
(d) Selling price less estimated cost to complete and sell and normal profit margin (floor)	.73	.73	.73	.73	.73

Explanation:

Item 1—Cost is used because it is lower than market.
Item 2—Market is used because it is lower than cost, not greater than (c), and not less than (d).
Item 3—Market is less than cost, but it is not used because it is lower than (d). Price (d) is used because it measures the limit of reduction.
Item 4—Market is lower than cost; it is not used because it is less than (d). But, because cost is less than (d), cost is used.
Item 5—Market is lower than cost, but it is higher than (c); therefore, (c) is used.

Discussion of lower of cost or market. The lower-of-cost-or-market method of inventory valuation conforms with an old rule of accounting conservatism often stated as follows: Anticipate no profit and provide for all possible losses. If market purchase prices decline, it is assumed that selling prices will decline with them; reducing the inventory valuation to market purchase price reduces the profit of the period when the cost price decline took place and transfers the goods to the next period at a price that will presumably permit the earning of a normal gross margin on their sale. If the market purchase price increases, the inventory is valued at cost, so that a profit will not be anticipated.

The lower-of-cost-or-market method has been, in the past, one of the most generally accepted applications of conservative accounting principles. It was developed and widely accepted during the long period when bankers and other creditors were primarily concerned with the balance sheet and when relatively little consideration was given to the income statement. With the emphasis thus placed on the balance sheet, the major emphasis was on a conservative valuation of the assets shown therein. The valuation of the inventory at the lower of cost or market is unquestionably conservative from the balance sheet standpoint.

To obtain this balance sheet conservatism, all other considerations were ignored or their importance was minimized. It was recognized that the lower-of-cost-or-market approach was subject to question on the ground of consistency; to absorb against current gross margins an unrealized and even problematical loss on unsold merchandise, while ignoring an unrealized potential increase in gross margin that might result from a rising market, was recognized as inconsistent; but such an inconsistency was regarded as of no concern when questions of conservatism were at issue. It was recognized that, even from the balance sheet standpoint, the method resulted in inconsistencies and in valuations that were not comparable. Different items in an inventory might be priced on different bases—some at cost and some at market; the inventories of the same concern at two dates might be priced on different bases—at cost on a rising market and at market on a falling market—and a comparison of the balance sheet valuations might therefore lead to incorrect interpretations; the inventories of two concerns might be priced on different bases, because they were acquired at different dates, and therefore not be comparable. But all inconsistencies of this nature were considered unimportant in comparison with considerations of conservatism in the valuation of each inventory.

However, income performance has become increasingly recognized as a significant measure of debt-paying ability and investment desirability. As a consequence, bankers, other creditors, business management, and stockholders are becoming increasingly concerned with the income statement—and not only with the income statement for a single period, but with the trend of earnings as shown by a series of income statements. For this reason, the propriety of the lower-of-cost-or-market method is being questioned.

Accountants are now raising the question as to whether, giving consideration to the income statements for a series of periods, the lower-of-cost-or-market method is as conservative as it formerly seemed to be. If, at the close of one period, the market value of the inventory is less than its cost, the reduction of the inventory valuation to market undoubtedly produces a conservative balance sheet valuation and a conservative computation of income in the statements for that period. But what is the effect on the income statement of the subsequent period? The effect may be so great a distortion of stated earnings of successive periods as to render a series of income statements definitely misleading.

To illustrate, assume that, at the beginning of January, merchandise was purchased at a cost of $100,000; that half the goods were sold in January for $75,000: that the remaining half were sold in February for $73,000; and that the inventory at the end of January, which cost $50,000, had a replacement cost of $40,000. The statement at the top of the next page shows:

In the first column, the computation of gross margins for the two months under the lower-of-cost-or-market method.

In the second column, the computation of gross margins for the two months with the inventory stated at cost.

The balance sheet valuation of the inventory at the end of January on the lower-of-cost-or-market basis instead of on the cost basis ($40,000 instead of $50,000), and the resulting statement of gross margin for January ($15,000 instead of $25,000), may be accepted as conservative. But is the February income statement on the lower-of-cost-or-market basis (showing $33,000 of gross margin instead of $23,000) conservative? And would not the statements for the two months on the lower-of-cost-or-market basis give a misleading impression as to the trend of operations to anyone who did not realize that the increase in profit

	With Inventory at Lower of Cost or Market	With Inventory at Cost
January:		
Sales	$75,000	$75,000
Cost of goods sold ($100,000 of purchases, minus the inventory)	60,000	50,000
Gross margin	$15,000	$25,000
February:		
Sales	$73,000	$73,000
Cost of goods sold (consisting of the opening inventory)	40,000	50,000
Gross margin	$33,000	$23,000

shown by the statements was caused by the write-down of the inventory and the consequent transfer of profits from January to February?

The lower-of-cost-or-market inventory valuation method is founded on the assumption that a decrease in market purchase costs will be accompanied by a similar decrease in selling prices before the disposal of the inventory. This was not the case in the foregoing illustration, and in the actual conduct of business affairs it is frequently not the case. Therefore, there is a trend toward the opinion that it is not necessary or desirable to reduce the inventory valuation to market if there is no probability that sales prices will also decrease; there is also some trend of opinion in favor of the idea that reduction to market is unnecessary even though some decline in selling prices has occurred or can be expected, if the inventory can probably be disposed of at a selling price that will include the cost and some profit. And there is even some opinion that reduction to market is unnecessary if the inventory can probably be disposed of without loss.

Some accountants, therefore, believe that, instead of assuming that a decrease in selling prices will promptly follow a decrease in cost, consideration should be given to the trend in selling prices, and that the inventory valuation should not be reduced unless selling prices have decreased at the balance sheet date or unless it is expected that they will decrease sufficiently after that date and before the disposal of the inventory to cause a loss.

If a decrease in the realizable value of the inventory is in prospect, balance sheet conservatism undoubtedly requires a reduction in the inventory valuation; however, bearing in mind the importance of the income statement, there still remains the question as to whether the customary procedure, of reducing the inventory valuation by an accounting method that also reduces the gross margin of the period in which market costs declined, is desirable. The question of distortion of profits between periods still remains. To illustrate, let us return to the foregoing case in which the inventory at the end of January cost $50,000 and had a replacement cost of $40,000. In that illustration, it was assumed that the selling prices in February were depressed only $2,000 in spite of the $10,000 decrease in replacement costs. Let us now assume that the selling prices decreased $10,000—an amount equal to the decrease in inventory valuation. Statements are presented below:

	With Inventory at	
	Lower of Cost or Market	Cost
January:		
Sales	$75,000	$75,000
Cost of goods sold	60,000	50,000
Gross margin	$15,000	$25,000
February:		
Sales	$65,000	$65,000
Cost of goods sold	40,000	50,000
Gross margin	$25,000	$15,000

The figures in the "Cost" column seem to reflect the facts more truly: The company made less profit in February than in January because of the decrease in selling prices. The "Lower of Cost or Market" column tells a very strange story: The company made more profit in February than in January, notwithstanding the decrease in selling prices that occurred in February.

It seems to the authors that accountants might expect that the shift in emphasis from the balance sheet to the income statement would produce a similar shift in emphasis in the accounting approach to inventory valuation. When the emphasis was on reporting financial position, the approach to the inventory problem was one of valuation for purposes of properly reflecting financial position. Under these conditions, cost or market, whichever is lower, seemed well suited. With the emphasis currently on the measurement of net income, the accountant logically gives preeminent consideration to those procedures associated with the assignment or "matching" of costs against related revenues. With the emphasis on a matching of costs and revenues, it would seem that the approach should be shifted to one of determining the portion of the total merchandise cost outlay for a period that should be charged against current revenues and the portion that should be assigned to future periods. The emphasis, thus, would not be one of inventory "valuation," but of cost assignment, the residue being carried forward to apply to future periods.

To some extent, this shift in approach to inventory pricing has occurred. Cost or market, whichever is lower, is receiving less support from accountants and is being refined in a number of ways, all in the direction of not reducing the cost figure unless a loss on the inventory investment is clearly in prospect.

Application of lower of cost or market. There are three ways in which the lower-of-cost-or-market method may be applied to a firm's inventory: (1) application to each item in the inventory, (2) application to each major category in the inventory, and (3) application to the total for the entire inventory. Application to each item in the inventory is the most widely used procedure in practice. Whichever procedure is adopted, it should be used consistently.

Each of the three procedures for applying the method will now be illustrated.

(1) By comparing the cost and market for each item in the inventory, and using the lower figure.

DETERMINATION OF LOWER OF COST OR MARKET—ITEM-BY-ITEM METHOD

		Unit Price		Extended		Lower of Cost
	Quantity	Cost	Market	Cost	Market	or Market
Men's clothing:						
Suits	200	$40	$37			$ 7,400
Coats	100	35	31			3,100
Jackets......	50	15	17			750
Hats	80	5	6			400
Ladies' clothing:						
Dresses	300	10	12			3,000
Suits	100	40	38			3,800
Coats	80	30	32			2,400
Robes.......	60	5	5			300
Inventory at lower of cost or market						$21,150

(2) By comparing the total cost and market for major inventory categories, and using the lower figure.

DETERMINATION OF LOWER OF COST OR MARKET—CATEGORY METHOD

		Unit Price		Extended		Lower of Cost
	Quantity	Cost	Market	Cost	Market	or Market
Men's clothing:						
Suits	200	$40	$37	$ 8,000	$ 7,400	
Coats	100	35	31	3,500	3,100	
Jackets......	50	15	17	750	850	
Hats	80	5	6	400	480	
Total				$12,650	$11,830	$11,830
Ladies' clothing:						
Dresses	300	10	12	$ 3,000	$ 3,600	
Suits	100	40	38	4,000	3,800	
Coats	80	30	32	2,400	2,560	
Robes.......	60	5	5	300	300	
Total				$ 9,700	$10,260	9,700
Inventory at lower of cost or market						$21,530

(3) By comparing the total cost and market for the entire inventory, and using the lower figure.

**DETERMINATION OF LOWER OF COST OR MARKET—
TOTAL INVENTORY METHOD**

		Unit Price		Extended		Lower of Cost
	Quantity	Cost	Market	Cost	Market	or Market
Men's clothing:						
Suits	200	$40	$37	$ 8,000	$ 7,400	
Coats	100	35	31	3,500	3,100	
Jackets......	50	15	17	750	850	
Hats	80	5	6	400	480	
Ladies' clothing:						
Dresses	300	10	12	3,000	3,600	
Suits	100	40	38	4,000	3,800	
Coats	80	30	32	2,400	2,560	
Robes.......	60	5	5	300	300	
Total				$22,350	$22,090	$22,090

Once the valuation of an item for inventory purposes is at an amount below cost, the lower amount becomes a "new" cost for accounting purposes. Such items should not be reinstated to their original cost in a subsequent period.

Accounting for inventory losses. When inventories are stated below cost under the lower-of-cost-or-market method, there are two different inventory items to be accounted for in the firm's income statement. One of these is the *cost* of the inventory sold during the period, and the other is the *loss* resulting from the difference between cost and market of the inventory still on hand.

Preferably, these two items should be accounted for and reported separately on the firm's income statement. In practice, this is not always done. The loss is sometimes included as a part of cost of goods sold, which in effect tends to bury the loss rather than disclose it. The different methods of accounting for the lower-of-cost-or-market method will now be illustrated.

No separation of inventory losses. Assume that a firm using the lower-of-cost-or-market method has suffered a $10,000 loss because of falling market prices. Facts pertaining to this situation are as follows:

Cost of goods available for sale..............	$100,000	
Ending inventory:		
At cost	50,000	} $10,000 loss
At lower of cost or market	40,000	
Sales	80,000	
Operating expenses and income taxes	16,000	

If there is no separate disclosure of the $10,000 loss, it is simply included as a part of the cost of goods sold. Assuming the use of perpetual inventory procedures, this would be accomplished as follows:

Inventory account at cost.......................	$50,000
Inventory at lower of cost or market	40,000
Required reduction in an inventory account...	$10,000

Entry: Cost of goods sold	10,000	
Inventory........................		10,000

It should be noted that the use of perpetual inventory procedures would require the adjustment of unit costs in the subsidiary inventory records to reflect the $10,000 reduction.

The firm's income statement will appear as follows:

Sales	$80,000
Cost of goods sold	60,000
Gross margin	$20,000
Operating expenses and income taxes	16,000
Net income	$ 4,000

The inventory loss of $10,000 is merged with the cost of goods sold. This procedure, although correctly stating the net income, gives a misleading impression of the cost of goods sold and gross margin.

Separation of inventory losses. An alternative to the treatment just illustrated is to record the $10,000 loss in a separate account. The required reduction in the inventory account would be recorded as follows, assuming the use of perpetual inventory procedures:

Loss on reduction of inventory to lower of cost or market	10,000	
Inventory		10,000

With separate disclosure, the income statement will appear as follows:

Sales	$80,000
Cost of goods sold	50,000
Gross margin	$30,000
Loss on reduction of inventory to lower of cost or market	10,000
Gross margin less inventory loss	$20,000
Operating expenses and income taxes	16,000
Net income	$ 4,000

It should be noted that under this treatment there is no separate reporting of the decline in the balance sheet. The ending inventory is reported at the lower-of-cost-or-market amount, which is then carried forward to the following year as the beginning inventory. A refinement of the separate reporting of inventory losses involves the use of a contra-inventory account.

In order to illustrate such a balance sheet account, assume again that a perpetual inventory record was maintained in the case just cited. The relevant accounts, in summary form, would appear as follows at year end.

INVENTORY

Beginning inventory plus purchases (goods available for sale)—debits totaling	100,000	Cost of goods sold—credits totaling	50,000

COST OF GOODS SOLD		
Goods sold—debits totaling	50,000	

When a contra account procedure is used, the inventory account is maintained at cost, and the reduction to market is achieved by crediting a contra account as follows:

Loss on reduction of inventory to lower of cost or market	10,000	
Allowance for reduction of inventory to lower of cost or market		10,000

The income statement would be prepared in the manner illustrated previously, in which the loss is set forth separately. In the balance sheet, the inventory would be shown at cost, and the reduction would be subtracted therefrom, as follows:

Inventory, at cost	$50,000	
Less allowance for reduction of inventory to lower of cost or market	10,000	$40,000

The contra asset account remains open and its balance is carried forward.

In order to carry the illustration forward, assume that the following data relate to the next year:

Beginning inventory—at cost	$ 50,000
Purchases	70,000
Cost of goods available for sale	$120,000
Ending inventory:	
At cost	60,000
At lower of cost or market	52,500
Sales	96,000
Operating expenses and income taxes	28,500

As indicated, the difference at the end of the second year between cost ($60,000) and the lower of cost or market ($52,500) is $7,500. The contra account, however, would continue to show the $10,000 credit balance carried forward from the previous year. Accordingly, the following entry is required to reduce the contra account balance to $7,500.

Allowance for reduction of inventory to lower of cost or market	2,500	
Gain from reduction in inventory allowance		2,500

The income statement for the second year is presented on the next page. As in the income statement for the preceding year, the cost of goods sold is stated at cost, with the effect of the lower-of-cost-or-market inventory valuation method disclosed separately. In this instance, the $2,500 gain from reduction in the inventory allowance account would be added to the gross margin.

Sales	$96,000
Cost of goods sold	60,000
Gross margin	$36,000
Gain from reduction in inventory allowance	2,500
Total	$38,500
Operating expenses and income taxes	28,500
Net income	$10,000

The inventory would be presented in the accompanying balance sheet as follows:

Inventory, at cost	$60,000	
Less allowance for reduction of inventory to lower of cost or market	7,500	$52,500

DISCUSSION OF ALTERNATIVE PROCEDURES: The first observation to be made from the foregoing discussion is that the net income of the firm is not affected by the choice of a method to account for the lower of cost or market. However, the choice does cause differences to appear within the income statement.

Although the first method illustrated has the practical advantage of simplicity, as indicated earlier, it does not distinguish between inventory costs (related to items sold) and the inventory loss (related to items on hand). Thus gross margin is misstated, and this obviously affects gross margin percentage calculations. Also, from a practical point of view, the first method has the disadvantage of necessitating adjustments of the subsidiary perpetual inventory records.

The second method illustrated above (separate reporting of inventory losses without the use of an allowance account) does overcome the major disadvantage of the first method, in that inventory losses are reported separately. However, the method does result in an inconsistent treatment of beginning and ending inventories. To illustrate, assume that the facts given on page 303 pertain to the year 19+2. The result was a $10,000 loss during the year because of falling market prices. In calculating the cost of goods sold for 19+2, the actual cost of the ending inventory ($50,000) was subtracted from the cost of goods available for sale ($100,000), resulting in cost of goods sold of $50,000. Thus, the ending inventory is shown at cost in the calculation, with the $10,000 market loss being reported as a separate item in the income statement. This treatment is illustrated below:

Sales	$80,000
Cost of goods sold ($100,000 – $50,000)	50,000
Gross margin	$30,000
Loss on reduction of inventory to lower of cost or market	10,000
Gross margin less inventory loss	$20,000
Operating expenses and income taxes	16,000
Net income	$ 4,000

In the following year, the beginning inventory will be reported at $40,000 (cost of $50,000 less the market loss of $10,000), or at the lower of cost or market. The ending inventory for the following year will be reported at cost in calculating the cost of goods sold. Thus, the same basis is not used for reporting beginning and ending inventories.

Although the original cost of the inventory on hand is not maintained in the accounts under these methods, it should be shown in some manner in the balance sheet. A parenthetical notation is widely used for this purpose.

The principal advantage of the use of the allowance account to report inventory declines is that it presents complete information concerning such declines in both the income statement and the balance sheet. Actual cost of the inventory is maintained in the accounts, inventory at the beginning and ending of each period is consistently reported at the lower of cost or market, and original gross margin is maintained in the income statement. It is for these reasons that the method is considered to be theoretically superior to other alternatives.

On the other hand, the allowance method has the disadvantage of not reporting the actual gain or loss in the period it occurred. For example, refer to the illustration on page 305 where a gain of $2,500 is reported for the second year, when there was an actual loss of $7,500.

Reserve for future market declines. The inventory market declines discussed thus far in this chapter represent declines that had taken place prior to the balance sheet date. The allowance account illustrated on pages 305 and 306 was established for the purpose of reporting such declines. The word "reserve" is sometimes used to describe the account, but such terminology is incorrect. The allowance account is properly established by a charge to income, so that net income is computed in accordance with the lower-of-cost-or-market basis of inventory valuation.

An account for price declines that have already taken place must be distinguished from an account set up to reflect anticipated, prospective, or possible inventory price declines. Regarding the latter type of account, the Committee on Accounting Procedure has stated:

> It has been argued with respect to inventories that losses which will have to be taken in periods of receding price levels have their origins in periods of rising prices, and that therefore reserves to provide for future price declines should be created in periods of rising prices by charges against the operations of those periods. Reserves of this kind involve assumptions as to what future price levels will be, what inventory quantities will be on hand if and when a major price decline takes place, and finally, whether loss to the business will be measured by the amount of the decline in prices. The bases for such assumptions are so uncertain that any conclusions drawn from them would generally seem to be speculative guesses rather than informed judgments. When estimates of this character are included in current costs, amounts representing conjecture are combined with others representing reasonable approximations.[2]

---

[2]*Accounting Research Bulletin No. 43*, p. 42.

The same statement would be equally true with respect to estimates of possible price declines made during periods of declining prices. Such estimates are necessarily based on assumptions regarding the extent of the decline, its duration, the inventory quantity affected, and the response of selling prices to the decline.

Although the terminology is outdated, some firms do use the term "reserve" in describing accounts that are established in anticipation of possible future losses attributable to inventory declines. Actually, such accounts represent an appropriation of retained earnings and should be described as such. An appropriate account title might be "Retained Earnings Appropriated for Possible Future Inventory Losses." Such an account is established by debiting Retained Earnings and should be shown as a part of the stockholders' equity in the firm's balance sheet.

What disposition should be made of the appropriation account thus created? It should be returned to Retained Earnings whether or not the declines occur. If they do not occur, the appropriation is thus proved to have been unnecessary. But if they do occur, the loss should be charged against the operations of the period during which the market decline took place.

For example, if a firm states its inventory at the lower of cost or market, and if, at the end of 19+5, the cost of the inventory is $50,000 and the replacement cost is $40,000, the books should be closed and the income for 19+5 ascertained on the basis of an inventory valuation of $40,000. If there is a prospect of additional market declines, an appropriation may be set up out of Retained Earnings. Theoretically, the appropriation should be returned to Retained Earnings during or at the end of 19+6, since it pertains to the beginning inventory for the year. As a practical matter. if it is felt that there should also be some appropriation pertaining to inventories on hand at the end of 19+6, the appropriation account may simply be adjusted to the desired balance at the end of the year.

Obsolete and depreciated merchandise. Regardless of the inventory-costing method adopted, merchandise that has become obsolete or has depreciated because of shopwear or damage should be excluded entirely from the inventory if it is unsalable or cannot be utilized in production. If it can be sold at a reduced price, a conservative estimate of realizable value may be assigned to it. The loss on goods that have been damaged or have become obsolete should be taken in the period when the loss developed.

The question of the proper treatment of write-downs for losses on obsolete, shopworn, or otherwise damaged goods requires some consideration. If write-downs are required as a result of shopwear, style changes, or other operating causes, they should be treated as a charge against income. On the income statement, they should be reported either as a reduction of gross margin or as a separate loss item.

Goods repossessed in a worn or damaged condition should be priced for inventory purposes at an amount not in excess of the net realizable value (estimated selling price in the ordinary course of business, less reasonably predictable costs of reconditioning and disposal). It is also acceptable, and logically justifiable, to reduce the net realizable value by an allowance for an approximately normal profit margin. Such a procedure would place the repossessed merchandise on a basis comparable with that of new merchandise.

Scrap. The valuation of scrap material presents some special problems. If the scrap cannot be sold or used, it should, of course, be given no inventory amount. If it can be sold, it can be priced for inventory purposes on a net realization basis.

If the scrap is used in the manufacture of a by-product, the entire original cost of the material may be charged to the main product; in that case, the cost of the by-product will be computed without the inclusion of any charge for scrap material used, and no valuation should be placed on the scrap for inventory purposes. Or the original cost of the material may be charged in part to the main product and in part to the by-product; in that case, the scrap can be given an inventory value. It is important that consistency be maintained, and that the error of charging the main product with the entire cost of the material and also placing a valuation on the scrap in the inventory not be committed. Such a procedure obviously would result in an inflation of asset values and profits to the extent of the valuation placed on the scrap.

Goods in foreign countries. If a company operates a branch or factory in a foreign country, the problems of inventory costing already discussed are applicable, and in addition, the company must meet the problem of translating values stated in a foreign currency to values stated in domestic currency.

In general, it may be said that the translation should be made by applying to the foreign currency valuation the exchange rate current on the balance sheet date. This general rule requires some modification. Some companies keep the accounts of foreign branches in such a manner as to show the dollar cost of the foreign money used for the payment of manufacturing costs.

Inventory valuation based on selling price. In some lines of industry, such as meat packing, in which material costs cannot be specifically allocated to joint products, practical considerations may make it advisable or even necessary to determine the inventory valuation on the basis of the relative selling prices of the various commodities. Although selling prices in such cases serve as a convenient basis for the determination of inventory valuations, conservatism requires at least the deduction of a sufficient allowance for marketing and transportation charges to be incurred; and, to avoid an anticipation of profits, the deductions from selling prices should include a provision for profits.

Valuation of the inventory at selling prices less a provision for disposal costs is often regarded as acceptable practice if production costs are difficult to determine and the product has a ready marketability. This condition is recognized as prevailing in farming. It is therefore considered acceptable practice in the valuation of crops and livestock. Any other procedure might involve practical impossibilities of inventory valuation, and might result in imposing the burden of production on one period while waiting until a succeeding period to record the related income. Valuation at selling prices is also used for precious metals, such as gold and silver, because of their ready marketability.

Unrealized profits in inventories. When the process of manufacturing involves the transfer of work in process from one department to another, the transfer amount is sometimes based on the price at which products at that stage of completion could be obtained from outside suppliers. This amount may be used for the purpose of comparing manufacturing costs with a presumptive acquisition cost to see whether a manufacturing department is an advantageous or "profitable" one to maintain. A system of bonus payments may be in effect, the bonuses being determined by the difference between manufacturing costs and suppliers' prices. Although such a basis for pricing interdepartmental transfers may be desirable for purposes of management, all such unrealized profits should be excluded from the inventory valuation for balance sheet and income statement purposes.

Variations in inventory pricings and the doctrine of consistency. We have seen that there are various acceptable methods of inventory pricing. Inventories may be priced at cost, at the lower of cost or market, at cost or less, or on a basis of selling prices. The cost figures may be affected by such matters as the treatment of freight, purchase discounts, and incidental expenditures, and by the choice of the method to be used in the selection of costs for inventory purposes. The lower of cost or market may be determined on a basis of individual items, inventory categories, or inventory totals.

Although the amount of permissible variation in inventory pricing by different companies is somewhat disturbing, the matter is not as serious as it might seem, because the doctrine of consistency requires that the basis and method of inventory pricing adopted by each company be consistently applied by it over the years, or that the effect of any departure from consistency, if material, be disclosed. The doctrine of consistency thus reduces the troublesome consequences that might otherwise develop from having a variety of acceptable inventory procedures.

Long-term contracts. A special inventory-valuation problem arises for businesses engaged in the construction of bridges, ships, dams, and similar assets that generally require more than one annual accounting period for their completion. There are two generally accepted accounting methods for dealing with such contracts:

The completed-contract method—No income is recorded until the contract is completed; hence, cost is the valuation basis for any work in process.

The percentage-of-completion method—Income is recorded as the work progresses; hence, the asset accounts will include an increment above cost for the amount of income recorded.

COMPLETED-CONTRACT METHOD: Under this method, the balance sheet will show the construction costs incurred to date less progress billings (revenue billed on construction contracts) as a current asset after accounts receivable, but before inventory, and labeled "Cost of uncompleted contracts in excess of related billings." In those cases where progress billings exceed the accumulated contract costs, the excess is shown as a current liability and labeled "Billings on uncompleted contracts in excess of related costs." If there are several contracts, some of which have costs to date that are less than and others greater than progress billings, then *both* a current asset and a current liability should be reported in the balance sheet.

Accounting for long-term contracts under the completed-contract method will now be illustrated. The illustration is based upon the following data:

CONTRACT DATA

Work under the contract was started in year 1 and completed in year 3.

Contract price	$500,000	
Estimated contract costs:		
At start of project	$400,000	
At end of year 1	400,000	
At end of year 2	420,000	
(Notice that the contract cost estimates are subject to change as the work progresses.)		
Actual costs to complete contract:		
Incurred in year 1	$100,000	
Incurred in year 2	194,000	
Incurred in year 3	121,000	$415,000
Progress billings:		
Based on percentage of completion.		
Year 1 (25% completed)	$125,000	
Year 2 (70% completed)	225,000	
Year 3 (100% completed)	150,000	
Collections on progress billings:		
Year 1	112,500	
Year 2	202,500	
Year 3	185,000	

The following accounts may be used in the accounting for the long-term contract:

Account Title	Purpose
Construction in Progress	Debited for costs identified with the performance of the contract
Accounts Receivable from Progress Billings	Debited for progress billings
Progress Billings	Credited for progress billings
Income from Completed Contracts	Credited for income on contracts *completed* during the fiscal period

Journal entries for each of the three years are shown below:

	Year 1		Year 2		Year 3	
(1) To record construction costs associated with the contract:						
Construction in progress	100,000		194,000		121,000	
Cash (or other asset accounts such as Materials and Supplies)		100,000		194,000		121,000

	Year 1		Year 2		Year 3	
(2) To record progress billings for the work performed:						
Accounts receivable from progress billings	125,000		225,000		150,000	
Progress billings		125,000		225,000		150,000
(3) To record the cash collected:						
Cash............................	112,500		202,500		185,000	
Accounts receivable from progress billings...........		112,500		202,500		185,000
(4) To record income in period of completion:						
Progress billings					500,000	
Construction in progress....						415,000
Income from completed contracts						85,000

It was noted in the contract data given on page 311 that the progress billings were based on the percentage of completion. The amount of the entry for the progress billings each year is calculated as follows:

Year 1—25% of $500,000	$125,000
Year 2—(70% − 25%) of $500,000..............................	$225,000
Year 3—(100% − 70%) of $500,000..............................	$150,000

In keeping with the basic rule that no revenue is recognized until the contract is completed, note that no income from the contract is reported in years 1 and 2. Income is not recognized until year 3, when the contract is completed. Thus, at the end of the third year it is necessary to close those accounts related to the contract and recognize the income earned, as shown in entry (4). The amounts shown in entry (4) are calculated as follows:

Progress billings: $125,000 + $225,000 + $150,000 = $500,000
Construction in progress: $100,000 + $194,000 + $121,000 = $415,000
Income from completed contracts: $500,000 − $415,000 = $85,000

The information pertaining to the contract would be reported in the balance sheet at the end of each year as follows:

	Year 1	Year 2	Year 3
Current assets:			
Accounts receivable from progress billings	$12,500	$35,000	—
Current liabilities:			
Billings on uncompleted contracts in excess of related costs..........	$25,000	$56,000	—

The amount reported as accounts receivable from progress billings is the difference between the charges to receivables (based on revenues billed) and the amounts collected, which is calculated for each year as follows:

Year 1: $12,500 = $125,000 – $112,500
Year 2: $35,000 = $12,500 + $225,000 – $202,500
Year 3: 0 = $35,000 + $150,000 – $185,000

The amount reported as billings on uncompleted contracts in excess of related costs is the difference between construction costs incurred and the progress billings (except for the year of completion), which is calculated as follows for years 1 and 2:

Year 1: $25,000 = $100,000 – $125,000
Year 2: $56,000 = $194,000 – ($25,000 + $225,000)

The completed-contract method has the advantage of eliminating the estimates inherent in the percentage-of-completion method. Thus it is consistent with the doctrine of conservatism, in that it avoids profit estimates that may never materialize. Profits are recognized only when the right to full payment is unconditional. The method is also consistent with the revenue-recognition and historical-cost assumptions, because no revenue is recognized prior to the point of sale (completion), and construction costs are reported at historical cost (less related billings) on the balance sheet.

The major disadvantage of the method lies in the fact that, because income is recorded in the year of completion, the amounts reported as net income for several successive years may vary widely even though operations were fairly uniform through the years. Consequently, net income could be low during years of construction (when the largest proportion of work is being done) and high during the year of completion (when a small proportion of the work is done). Also, net income could be negative (net loss) during years when no construction is completed, because of administrative expenses. Although income is not recorded under this method before completion, provision should be made in any period for foreseeable losses.

PERCENTAGE-OF-COMPLETION METHOD: Under this method, income is recorded as work is performed. Long-term contracts generally specify the timing and amounts of bills that may be submitted to the customer as the work progresses. Such progress billings do not, as a rule, provide a reasonable basis on which to record income. The percentage of completion, which is used as the basis for income recognition, is generally determined by one of the following methods:

(1) By a comparison of costs incurred to date with total estimated costs for the entire contract
(2) By a study of engineering data pertinent for a determination of stage of completion for the project

In making a choice between these two methods for determining the percentage of completion, it should be pointed out that method (1) might not be appropriate for certain contracts. This would be true in those instances where a major portion of the cost of materials must be incurred in order to begin construction. Thus, a substantial portion of the costs of the contract might have been incurred, but very little of the work actually done. The Committee on Accounting Procedure of the American Institute of CPAs has stated:

> *Costs* as here used might exclude, especially during the early stages of a contract, all or a portion of the cost of such items as materials and subcontracts if it appears that such an exclusion would result in a more meaningful periodic allocation of income.[3]

The percentage-of-completion method will now be illustrated, using method (1) above for calculating the completion percentage. The illustration is based on the same contract data shown on page 311 and used in the previous illustration.

Information in the illustration indicates that the contract was completed at a total cost of $415,000. Given a contract price of $500,000, the total income to be allocated over the three-year period is $85,000; this is, of course, the same amount recorded in the third year under the completed-contract method. Allocation of the income to the three years is as follows:

INCOME DETERMINATION

	Year					
	1		2		3	
Contract price		$500,000		$500,000		$500,000
Deduct:						
Accumulated contract costs	$100,000		$294,000		$415,000	
Estimated cost to complete contract	300,000	400,000	126,000	420,000	-0-	415,000
Total income from contract (estimated in years 1 and 2)		$100,000		$ 80,000		$ 85,000
Percent complete (Accumulated costs ÷ Total estimated costs):						
Year 1—$100,000 ÷ $400,000		25%				
Year 2—$294,000 ÷ $420,000				70%		
Year 3—Contract complete						100%
Income from contract—earned to date		$ 25,000		$ 56,000		$ 85,000
Income assigned to prior periods				25,000		56,000
Periodic income from contract		$ 25,000		$ 31,000		$ 29,000

[3]Committee on Accounting Procedure, *Accounting Research Bulletin No. 45* (New York: AICPA, 1955), p. 4.

The first three journal entries illustrated on page 311 for each of the three years under the completed-contract method would also be required for the percentage-of-completion method. In addition, it is necessary at the end of each year to recognize a portion of the income from the contract. The income determination schedule above shows the amount of income to be recognized each year. The entries to record the income earned over the three years is shown below:

	Year 1		Year 2		Year 3	
Construction in progress	25,000		31,000			
Income from construction contracts		25,000		31,000		
Progress billings.....					500,000	
Construction in progress						471,000
Income from construction contracts						29,000

The income of $29,000 for year 3 is the difference between the balance in the progress billings account of $500,000 ($125,000 + $225,000 + $150,000) and the balance in the construction in progress account of $471,000, with the latter calculated as follows:

Year 1 contract costs	$100,000
Year 1 income recognized	25,000
Year 2 contract costs	194,000
Year 2 income recognized	31,000
Year 3 contract costs	121,000
Total	$471,000

As for the balance sheet under the percentage-of-completion method, accounts receivable from progress billings are reported in the same manner as under the completed-contract method; hence, the reporting of the receivables illustrated on page 312 also applies to the percentage-of-completion method.

Unlike the completed-contract method, the construction in progress account includes the income recognized each year. Thus, the difference between construction costs incurred and progress billings that is reported as a current asset (Cost of Uncompleted Contracts in Excess of Related Billings) or a current liability (Billings on Uncompleted Contracts in Excess of Related Costs) is affected by the income recognized each period, and is calculated as follows:

Construction in progress less related billings = **Total construction costs incurred** + **Total income earned under percentage-of-completion method** − **Total progress billings**

= **Ending balance in construction in progress account** − **Ending balance in progress billings account**

If total construction costs incurred plus total income earned is greater than total billings, the difference is reported as a current asset; if it is less, the difference is reported as a current liability.

In the illustration, the total amount billed is the same as the balance in the construction in progress account because partial billings are based on percentage of completion. As a result, there is no difference to report as a current asset or liability in the balance sheet, as illustrated below:

Year 1: 0 = \$100,000 + \$25,000 − \$125,000
Year 2: 0 = \$294,000 + \$56,000 − \$350,000
Year 3: 0 = \$415,000 + \$85,000 − \$500,000

If a loss on a contract is in prospect, provision should be made for the total loss, not for portions thereof computed on a percentage-of-completion basis.

Note that the percentage-of-completion method results in an *exception* to the historical-cost and revenue-recognition assumptions that are conventionally used in current accounting practice. That is, by including periodic income earned with the construction costs incurred in the construction in progress account, construction costs less related billings are not reported in the balance sheet at historical cost. Also, by the recognition of periodic income during construction, revenue is recognized prior to the point of sale (completion of contract).

GENERAL MATTERS: It will be noted in the previous illustrations that the amount received in cash each year was less than the amount billed to the customer. In fact, the cash received in each of the three years was 90 percent of the amount billed. This is quite common in the construction of long-term projects and is viewed as a means of protecting the customer by allowing him to retain some percentage of the contract price until the job is completed according to the terms and specifications in the contract.

Some contracts provide for cash advances from the customer before any work is performed under the contract. Such advances should be shown among the liabilities on the contractor's books. Each time a progress billing is made, the advances account would be reduced. Accounts Receivable from Progress Billings would be debited for the difference between the billable revenue and the applicable portion of the advance. Thus, if an advance was received equal to 20 percent of the contract price, the contract advances account would be debited subsequently for 20 percent of each progress billing. For example, assume that a 20 percent advance in the amount of \$5,000 is received. A subsequent progress billing covering \$10,000 of work would be recorded as follows:

Accounts receivable from progress billings	8,000	
Contract advances (20% of \$10,000)	2,000	
Progress billings......................................		10,000

If a contract is on a cost-plus basis, there is no hazard in recording income on an uncompleted contract; but if a contract is on a flat-price basis, there is usually an element of hazard in doing so because of the possibility that unforeseen costs may turn a prospective profit into a smaller profit or into a loss.

The hazards of recording income on uncompleted contracts may, of course, be eliminated or minimized if the work to be done, or the product to be delivered, is divisible into identifiable units to which portions of the total contract price are definitely applicable. In some such cases, completion alone may provide a sufficient basis for income recognition, particularly if acceptance is reasonably assured and delivery is merely a routine operation. If the contract calls for the construction and delivery of a single unit, such as a ship, the contract may call for inspections by the customer as the work progresses, with reports of any exceptions, and may provide for progress payments at certain stated completion stages; in such instances, the hazards of recording income as the work progresses are somewhat minimized.

Although, from the standpoint of a going concern, it is always conservative to defer the taking of any income until the contract is completed, consideration should be given to the fact that such conservatism may work an injustice on partners or stockholders. If a partner is to retire before the completion of a contract and is to sell his interest to the remaining partners, he should, in fairness, receive some benefit for the income to be reasonably regarded as applicable to work done up to the date of his retirement. Because stockholders of a corporation may change before the completion of a long contract, there may also be a responsibility on the part of the corporate management to recognize the question of fairness involved.

Rigid adherence to a policy of recording no income from contracts until they are completed not only may impose unreasonable hardships on partners or stockholders, but may result in the showing of income from period to period quite at variance with the operating facts. For instance, if we assume that a company is engaged throughout one year on a single contract that was uncompleted at the end of the year, the recording of no income at the end of the year would result in showing a loss if administrative overhead expenses were charged off. The income statement of the succeeding period would also show a distorted picture, because it would include income resulting largely from the activities of the prior period. The assumed conditions of this illustration have been made somewhat extreme to emphasize the point. The fact that the distortion may be concealed because other contracts are being carried on concurrently only emphasizes the necessity of recognizing the conditions.

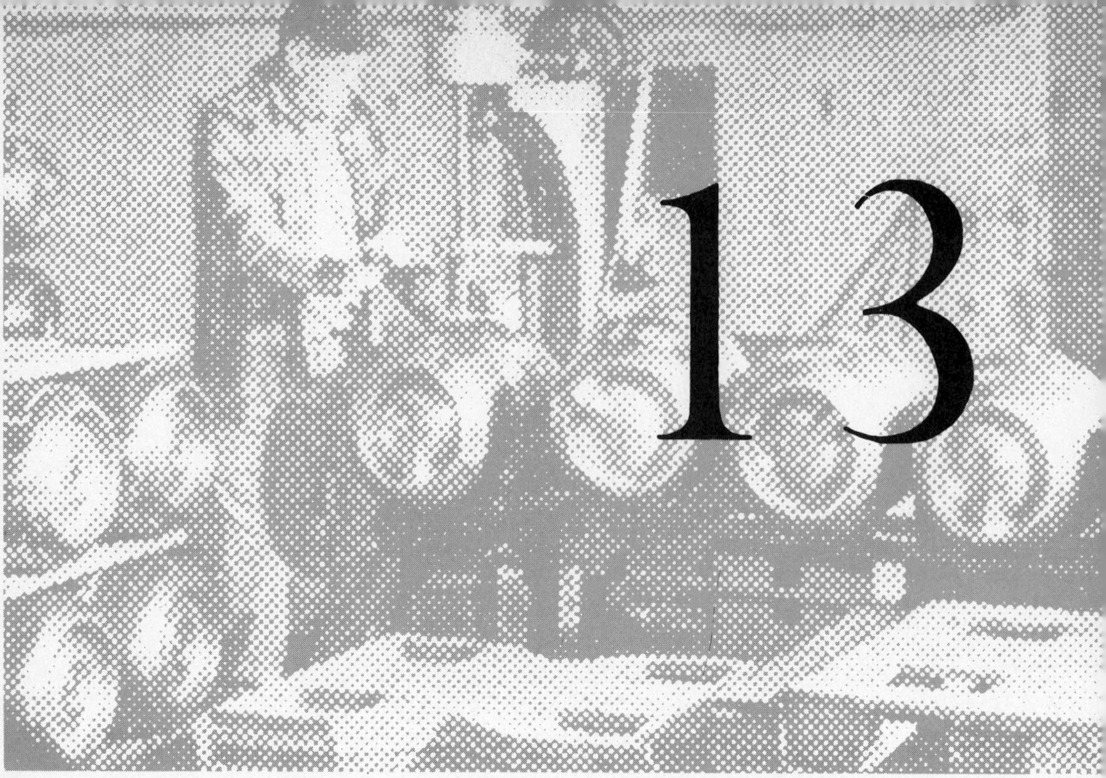

13

Inventory: Estimating Methods

Introduction. Situations frequently arise in which the accountant employs estimating procedures to develop inventory quantities and costs. For example, when inventories are destroyed by fire or other casualty, the gross-margin method can be used to estimate merchandise on hand. Merchandising firms that deal in a large number of different items use the retail-inventory method to estimate merchandise on hand, especially during the fiscal period, in order to avoid the cost and delay of taking a physical inventory that would otherwise be necessary every time the determination of ending inventory (and therefore cost of goods sold) was desired. The principal inventory-estimating methods and the circumstances under which they are used are discussed in the following pages.

Gross-margin method. The gross-margin method of approximating an inventory is based on the assumption that the percentage of gross margin should be approximately the same in successive periods. This does not mean that the gross margin should be exactly the same, because the amount of margin will depend upon the volume of sales; it means only that the rate of gross margin on sales is assumed to be uniform. If, for instance, the rate of gross margin has been uniformly about 25 percent of the sales for a number of past years, it is assumed that the rate was 25 percent during the current period. If this assumption is in reasonable conformity with the facts, then it should be possible to approximate, with a fair degree of accuracy, the inventory at the end of the current period.

To illustrate, assume the following data:

Inventory—January 1	$ 10,000
Purchases for the year	94,000
Net sales for the year	124,000
Average rate of gross margin in recent years, 25% of sales.	

What should be the approximate inventory on December 31?

Inventory—January 1		$ 10,000
Purchases		94,000
Total		$104,000
Deduct approximate cost of goods sold:		
Sales—net	$124,000	
Less estimated gross margin:		
25% of $124,000	31,000	93,000
Approximate inventory—December 31		$ 11,000

If the gross-margin percentage is stated in terms of cost (gross margin divided by cost of goods sold) or markup on cost, instead of in terms of sales as illustrated above, then the markup on sales can be easily determined and applied as shown. Thus, if the markup on cost is estimated to be $33\frac{1}{3}$ percent, then markup on sales (gross margin divided by sales) is 25 percent, computed as follows:[1]

$$\textbf{Markup percentage on sales} = \frac{\textbf{Markup percentage on cost}}{\textbf{1 + markup percentage on cost}}$$

$$25\% = \frac{33\frac{1}{3}\%}{1 + 33\frac{1}{3}\%}$$

Or, since sales must be equal to the sum of cost (100 percent) and gross margin on cost ($33\frac{1}{3}$ percent), then cost of goods sold (100 percent) is approximately equal to sales divided by $1.33\frac{1}{3}$, and ending inventory is approximately equal to cost of goods available for sale minus cost of goods sold:

$$\textbf{Cost of goods sold} = \$124{,}000/1.33\tfrac{1}{3} = \$93{,}000$$

$$\textbf{Ending inventory} = \$104{,}000 - \$93{,}000 = \$11{,}000$$

[1]Similarly, if the percentage markup on sales is known, then the percentage markup on cost can be computed as follows:

$$\textbf{Markup percentage on cost} = \frac{\textbf{Markup percentage on sales}}{\textbf{1 − Markup percentage on sales}}$$

$$33\tfrac{1}{3}\% = \frac{25\%}{1 - 25\%}$$

If the rate of gross margin is a composite produced by selling several types or classes of merchandise at different gross-margin rates, sales and purchases data must be classified by gross-margin classes. The gross-margin method is applied to each inventory class. To illustrate, assume the following:

> Article A is marked to produce a gross margin of 20%.
> Article B is marked to produce a gross margin of 40%.
> Last year's gross margin on all sales was 25%.

Computation of Inventories—Gross-Margin Method
Current Year

	A	B	Total
Inventory—January 1	$15,000	$ 25,000	$ 40,000
Purchases for the year	80,000	120,000	200,000
Total	$95,000	$145,000	$240,000
Deduct approximate cost of goods sold:			
Sales—net	$90,000	$210,000	$300,000
Less estimated gross margin:			
20% of $90,000	18,000		18,000
40% of $210,000		84,000	84,000
Approximate cost of goods sold	$72,000	$126,000	$198,000
Approximate inventory—December 31	$23,000	$ 19,000	$ 42,000

If the data had not been classified by commodity, the combined inventory would have been estimated at $15,000, as illustrated below:

		Combined
Inventory—January 1 ($15,000 plus $25,000)		$ 40,000
Purchases for the year ($80,000 plus $120,000)		200,000
Total		$240,000
Deduct approximate cost of goods sold:		
Sales ($90,000 + $210,000)—net	$300,000	
Less estimated gross margin:		
25% of $300,000	75,000	225,000
Approximate inventory—December 31		$ 15,000

In the illustration above, the average rate of gross margin of the business as a whole for the preceding year was an unreliable measure to apply in approximating inventories for the current year because of the significant change that occurred in the average rate of gross margin. Last year's gross margin on all sales was 25 percent, whereas the gross margin on all sales for the current year is probably in the neighborhood of 34 percent. This is evident from the following computation:

Sales, current year—net	$300,000	100%
Approximate cost of goods sold ($72,000 + $126,000)	198,000	
Approximate gross margin	$102,000	34%

If there are any conditions present in the current year that would result in a change in the rate of gross margin, the gross-margin method, since it is based on prior gross-margin data, will not produce reliable inventory approximations.

USES OF GROSS-MARGIN METHOD: The gross-margin method may be used by an auditor as one of the means of verifying an inventory; for instance, referring to the illustration on page 319, if the December 31 inventory submitted to the auditor was $25,000, whereas the gross-margin method indicated that the inventory should be approximately $11,000, either a satisfactory explanation of the increase in the rate of gross margin would have to be forthcoming, or the auditor would have reason to believe that the inventory was overstated. An ending inventory of $25,000 would imply that the gross margin had increased to 36 percent, in contrast to the 25 percent rate that had prevailed in past periods.

The gross-margin method can also be used to approximate the cost of inventory destroyed by fire or lost through theft. In the case of fire loss, the valuation of inventory is necessary not only to estimate the amount of the loss, but also as the basis for any insurance claim that may exist. For example, assume that Fisher Sales Corporation lost most of its inventory in a fire on December 31, 19+6, before the year-end inventory was taken. The corporation's books disclose the following:

Beginning inventory	$ 51,000
Purchases during the year	173,000
Purchase returns	16,150
Sales	209,000
Sales returns	5,000

The corporation's pricing policy during the year was such that its markup on sales 24 percent. Undamaged merchandise salvaged was marked to sell at $6,000, and damaged merchandise marked to sell at $4,000 had an estimated realizable value of $900. Based on the gross-margin method, the estimated inventory loss was $47,350, computed as follows:

Goods available for sale ($51,000 + $173,000 − $16,150)		$207,850
Deduct approximate cost of goods sold:		
Net sales ($209,000 − $5,000)	$204,000	
Less estimated gross margin ($204,000 × .24)	48,960	155,040
Estimated ending inventory		$ 52,810
Deduct:		
Cost of undamaged merchandise ($6,000 × .76)	$ 4,560	
Realizable value of damaged merchandise	900	5,460
Estimated inventory loss arising from fire		$ 47,350

The gross-margin method is also widely used to estimate ending inventory (and therefore cost of goods sold) for interim financial statements. This is more practical than taking a physical inventory count at the end of each month in order to prepare monthly financial statements, because of the excessive cost of such physical counts.

After the sales budget is developed, a company may use the gross-margin method to derive budget estimates of cost of goods sold, gross margin, and inventory.

Finally, merchandise turnovers based on the average of the inventories at the beginning and end of the year will be inaccurate if the year-end inventories differ materially in amount from those carried during the year. This error will be avoided if the average of monthly inventories is used. If such inventories are not available, they may be estimated by the gross-margin method.

EFFECT OF LIFO ON THE GROSS-MARGIN METHOD: If a company is using the LIFO inventory method, the gross-margin method for approximating an ending inventory in terms of LIFO costs can be used only with extreme caution. This situation is attributable to the fact that, typically, the relation of LIFO inventory costs to selling prices is considerably at variance with the relation of recent purchase prices to selling prices. Suppose that a company establishes a pricing policy of selling, for $10 each, articles that currently cost $6 to acquire at wholesale. If the company has been on a LIFO basis for a considerable period of time, the articles might conceivably be carried in the beginning inventory at $3 each. If it should develop in any given year that more items were sold than were purchased, the resulting net reduction in the inventory would produce a distortion in the actual gross margin, because some of the goods sold would have been assigned to cost of sales at $3 each, thus inflating the gross margin.

For example, assume the following case, in which goods are sold for $10 each and the gross-margin rate for several preceding periods was 40 percent:

Sales, at $10 each, 6,000 units		$60,000
Cost of goods sold:		
Inventory, January 1, 2,000 units at $3 each	$ 6,000	
Purchases for the year at $6 each, 5,000 units	30,000	
Total	$36,000	
Inventory, December 31, 1,000 units at $3 each	3,000	33,000
Gross margin		$27,000

The gross-margin rate indicated by the example above is 45 percent. If this distorted gross-margin percentage were used in the following period to estimate the inventory by the gross-margin method, the results would be unreliable. To illustrate, assume that 5,000 units were sold during the following year, and that sufficient units were purchased to cover the quantity sold. An estimate of the ending inventory by the gross-margin method would indicate an inventory of $5,500, whereas in fact the inventory would be $3,000, an error of 83 ⅓ percent.

Inventory, January 1, 1,000 units at $3 each		$ 3,000
Purchases for the year at $6 each, 5,000 units		30,000
Total		$33,000
Deduct approximate cost of goods sold:		
Sales, at $10 each, 5,000 units	$50,000	
Less estimated gross margin of 45%	22,500	27,500
Approximate inventory, December 31		$ 5,500

Under LIFO procedures, the ending inventory would be priced as follows:

Inventory, December 31, 1,000 units (see computation below) at $3 each...	$3,000

Computation of Inventory Quantity

	Units
Inventory, January 1	1,000
Purchases for the year	5,000
Total	6,000
Sales	5,000
Inventory, December 31	1,000

Incidentally, the accountant should realize that with the LIFO method, management can intentionally distort gross margin and net income by deliberately curtailing purchases and thereby "dipping into" the LIFO base quantity.

Retail-inventory method. The so-called retail method of inventory pricing is frequently used in department and other retail stores; it is suitable for use by wholesalers also. It is not suitable, however, for manufacturing businesses, because the articles purchased are not immediately priced for resale.

With records showing the opening inventory and purchases at both cost and retail, it is possible to determine a ratio of cost to retail, the uses of which are described below:

(1) To estimate the inventory at any time without taking a physical inventory; the procedure is as follows:

	Cost	Retail
Inventory at beginning of period	$ 10,000	$ 15,000
Purchases during the period	110,000	185,000
Totals	$120,000	$200,000
(Ratio of cost to retail—60%)		
Sales		180,000
Estimated inventory at retail		$ 20,000

Inventory computation—60% of $20,000 = $12,000.

The retail method makes it possible to prepare monthly, weekly, or even daily estimates of the inventory. Such estimates may be useful for purposes of inventory control and formulating purchasing policy.

(2) To permit pricing a physical inventory at marked selling prices and reducing the selling-price valuation by applying to it the ratio of cost to retail. Using retail prices eliminates the necessity of marking costs on the merchandise, referring to invoices, and dealing with the problem of identical merchandise acquired at different costs.

Physical inventories, priced by the retail method, should be taken from time to time (at least annually) as a check on the accuracy of the estimated inventories determined by the procedure described under (1) above. If the inventory determined by procedure (2) is less than the amount estimated by procedure (1), the difference may be attributable to "shrinkages" resulting from theft, breakage, or other causes. However, the difference may be attributable in part to errors in the retail-inventory records or in the physical inventory priced at retail.

TERMINOLOGY: The foregoing illustration ignores the problem created whenever changes are made in selling prices after the original selling prices have been placed on the goods. The fact that businessmen do revise or modify prices of goods on hand necessitates an understanding of the following terms:

Original retail is the price at which the goods are first offered for sale.
Markups are additions that raise the selling price above the original retail.
Markdowns are deductions that lower the price below the original retail.
Markup cancellations are deductions that do not decrease the selling price below the original retail.
Markdown cancellations are additions that do not increase the selling price above the original retail.

To illustrate, assume the following:

The goods cost $100.	
The original retail price was	$140
There was a markup of	20
Which advanced the selling price to	$160
There was a markup cancellation of	5
Which reduced the selling price to	$155
The selling price was further reduced $30:	
This included a markup cancellation of	15
Which reduced the selling price to original retail	$140
It also included a markdown of	15
Which reduced the selling price to	$125
There was a markdown cancellation of	5
Which increased the selling price to	$130

Markups minus markup cancellations may be referred to as *net markup;* markdowns minus markdown cancellations may be referred to as *net markdown.*

A clear understanding of markups, markup cancellations, markdowns, and markdown cancellations, and a careful differentiation thereof in the records, is necessary because, in determining the ratio of cost to retail, it is customary to include markups and markup cancellations, but to ignore markdowns and markdown cancellations. To illustrate, assume the following:

	Cost	Retail
Inventory at beginning of period	$20,000	$ 30,000
Purchases	80,000	120,000
Markups		10,000
Markup cancellations		(2,000)
Markdowns		(7,000)
Markdown cancellations		1,000

The percentage to be used in computing the inventory by the retail method (including net markups and excluding net markdowns) is determined as follows:

	Cost	Retail
Inventory at beginning of period	$ 20,000	$ 30,000
Purchases..	80,000	120,000
Markups		10,000
Markup cancellations............................		(2,000)
Totals..	$100,000	$158,000

(Ratio of cost to retail: $100,000/$158,000 = 63.29%)

Markon is the difference between the cost and the original retail plus net markups. In the example above, the markon is $58,000; the percentage of markon is 36.71 ($58,000 ÷ $158,000); and the ratio of cost to retail is the complement of this percentage, or 63.29 percent. This rate is used in the following inventory computation:

	Cost	Retail
Inventory at beginning of period	$ 20,000	$ 30,000
Purchases..	80,000	120,000
Markups		10,000
Markup cancellations............................		(2,000)
Totals (Cost ratio, 63.29%)	$100,000	$158,000
Markdowns		(7,000)
Markdown cancellations.........................		1,000
Remainder		$152,000
Sales		120,000
Estimated inventory at retail.....................		$ 32,000

Inventory computation: 63.29% of $32,000 = $20,253.

WHY MARKDOWNS ARE IGNORED IN THE COMPUTATION OF COST RATIO: The intent of the retail-inventory method, as conventionally applied, is so to compute the inventory that its sale at prevailing prices will yield at least the normal or prevailing rate of gross margin. The dollar amounts thus determined are intended to conform generally to the cost-or-market rule.

Referring to the preceding illustration, let us compute by four different methods the percentages that might be applied to the inventory at selling price, and note which method produces an inventory figure that conforms most nearly to the lower of cost or market. (See the table at the top of the next page.)

It is obvious that the lowest inventory figure is obtained by the second method, in which net markups are used and net markdowns are ignored in the computation of the cost ratio. But is such a procedure merely conservative without being logical? Two illustrations bearing on this question follow.

	Use Markups and Markdowns	Use Markups but Not Markdowns (as above)	Use Markdowns but Not Markups	Use Neither Markups Nor Markdowns
Original retail:				
Inventory	$ 30,000	$ 30,000	$ 30,000	$ 30,000
Purchases	120,000	120,000	120,000	120,000
Markups—net	8,000	8,000		
Markdowns—net	(6,000)		(6,000)	
Totals (*a*)	$152,000	$158,000	$144,000	$150,000
Cost (*b*)	100,000	100,000	100,000	100,000
Cost ratio (*c*) = (*b*) ÷ (*a*)	65.79%	63.29%	69.44%	66.67%
Inventory at retail (*d*)	$ 32,000	$ 32,000	$ 32,000	$ 32,000
Computed inventory (*e*) = (*c*) × (*d*)	21,053	20,253	22,221	21,334

ILLUSTRATION WITH MARKUPS: Markups in retail prices are presumably related to market increases in wholesale prices; the inventory should, therefore, be priced at cost. In the following illustration, it is assumed that half the merchandise was sold:

	Cost	Retail
Opening inventory and purchases	$60,000	$ 90,000
(Cost ratio, ignoring markups = $60,000/$90,000 = 66⅔%)		
Markups—net		10,000
Total		$100,000
(Cost ratio, including markups = $60,000/$100,000 = 60%)		
Sales		50,000
Estimated inventory at retail		$ 50,000

Inventory figure:
At rate ignoring markups: 66⅔% of $50,000 = $33,333.
At rate including markups: 60% of $50,000 = $30,000.

The $33,333 figure is affected by the rise in market prices (denominator is lower, so rate is higher) and is incorrect per the lower-of-cost-or-market rule; the $30,000 figure is on a cost basis, and is correct because cost is lower than market. Therefore markups should be used in the determination of the cost ratio.

ILLUSTRATION WITH MARKDOWNS: Markdowns may be necessitated by market decreases in wholesale prices; if such a situation exists, the inventory (if it is to conform to cost or market, whichever is lower) should be reduced to market:

	Cost	Retail
Opening inventory and purchases	$60,000	$90,000
(Cost ratio, ignoring markdowns = $60,000/$90,000 = 66⅔%)		
Markdowns—net		10,000
Remainder		$80,000
(Cost ratio, including markdowns = $60,000/$80,000 = 75%)		
Sales		40,000
Estimated inventory at retail		$40,000

Inventory figure:
At rate ignoring markdowns: 66⅔% of $40,000 = $26,667.
At rate including markdowns: 75% of $40,000 = $30,000.

The $26,667 figure was affected by the decrease in market price (denominator is higher, so rate is lower), and is appropriate in view of the fact that the traditional objective of the retail method is to approximate the results produced by the lower-of-cost-or-market method. It therefore appears that markdowns should not be used in determining the cost ratio.

Retail method is based on averages. The retail-inventory method is based on the assumption that an average cost ratio can appropriately be applied to the selling price of the inventory. Some factors that might tend to make the assumption unwarranted are discussed in the following paragraphs.

DEPARTMENTAL RATES: The first point to be considered is the possible effect of differences in departmental rates of markon. The retail-inventory method assumes that high-cost-ratio goods and low-cost-ratio goods will be found in the same proportions in the final inventory as in the total of goods offered for sale. But let us assume the following conditions:

	Department A		Department B		Total	
	50%-Cost-Ratio Merchandise		80%-Cost-Ratio Merchandise		72.5% Average Cost Ratio	
	Cost	Retail	Cost	Retail	Cost	Retail
Opening inventory and purchases (or total offered for sale)	$25,000	$50,000	$120,000	$150,000	$145,000	$200,000
Sales		45,000		105,000		150,000
Estimated inventory at retail		$ 5,000		$ 45,000		$ 50,000

It will be noted that the proportions of high-cost-ratio goods and low-cost-ratio goods are not the same in the closing inventory as in the total goods offered for sale. Instead, the proportions are those shown below:

	50% Cost Ratio	80% Cost Ratio
Offered for sale:		
Amounts—at selling price	$50,000	$150,000
Percentages: $50,000/$200,000	25%	
$150,000/$200,000..........		75%
Final inventory:		
Amounts—at selling price	$ 5,000	$ 45,000
Percentages: $5,000/$50,000.............	10%	
$45,000/$50,000		90%

Under such circumstances, it is desirable to keep departmental records, in order that a separate computation can be made for the inventory of each department, thus:

Department A inventory: 50% of $ 5,000 = $ 2,500
Department B inventory: 80% of $45,000 = $36,000

Without the necessary departmental records, the inventory figure would be misstated, thus:

72.5% (average cost ratio) of \$50,000 = \$36,250

SPECIAL-SALE MERCHANDISE: Special sales of merchandise carrying low rates of markon may distort the average. To illustrate, assume the conditions shown below:

	Merchandise At Normal Cost Ratio—50%		Special-Sale Merchandise 90% Cost Ratio		Total (58% Average Cost Ratio)	
	Cost	Retail	Cost	Retail	Cost	Retail
Opening inventory and purchases .	\$40,000	\$80,000	\$18,000	\$20,000	\$58,000	\$100,000
Sales..............		61,000		19,000		80,000
Estimated inventory at retail ...		\$19,000		\$ 1,000		\$ 20,000

Again we find that the proportions of high-cost-ratio and low-cost-ratio merchandise in the inventory and in the total of goods offered for sale are not the same, but are as follows:

	50% Cost Ratio	90% Cost Ratio
Offered for sale:		
Amounts—at selling price	\$80,000	\$20,000
Percentages: \$80,000/\$100,000	80%	
\$20,000/\$100,000		20%
Final inventory:		
Amounts—at selling price	\$19,000	\$ 1,000
Percentages: \$19,000/\$20,000	95%	
\$ 1,000/\$20,000		5%

An attempt to compute the inventory by use of the average cost ratio of 58 percent would produce erroneous results, as shown below:

Using average rate:		
58% of \$20,000		\$11,600
Using separate rates:		
50% of \$19,000	\$9,500	
90% of \$ 1,000	900	
Total..		\$10,400

Under such circumstances, it is usually considered desirable to set up separate records and to make a separate inventory computation for special-sale merchandise, as if such special merchandise constituted a department by itself.

SALES OF MARKED-UP AND MARKED-DOWN GOODS: Let us assume that, after all the merchandise of a department is marked at a uniform original retail, half the merchandise is given an additional markup and the other half is marked down;

let us also assume that 70 percent of the sales are made from marked-down merchandise and only 30 percent from marked-up merchandise. Obviously, under such circumstances, it is fallacious to assume that high-cost-ratio goods and low-cost-ratio goods will be found in the same proportions in the final inventory as in the total of goods offered for sale; and the retail method in such instances would give fallacious results.

PERIOD COVERED BY COMPUTATION: A year is too long a period to embrace in the inventory computation unless approximately the same rate of markon prevails throughout the year. This situation will not exist if, for example, different rates of gross margin are made on spring- and fall-season sales, or if extensive markdowns are made during one period of the year and extensive markups are made during another season.

The illustration below indicates the desirability of making interim inventory computations if the rate of markon is not fairly uniform throughout the year.

If the inventory is computed semiannually:

	Cost	Retail
First six months:		
Opening inventory	$100,000	$150,000
Purchases	300,000	450,000
Totals	$400,000	$600,000
(Cost ratio: $400,000/$600,000 = 66⅔%)		
Markdowns		20,000
Remainder		$580,000
Sales		500,000
Estimated inventory at retail		$ 80,000

Inventory computation, June 30: 66⅔% of $80,000 = $53,333.

	Cost	Retail
Second six months:		
Opening inventory	$ 53,333	$ 80,000
Purchases	400,000	500,000
Markups		25,000
Totals	$453,333	$605,000
(Cost ratio: $453,333/$605,000 = 74.9311%)		
Sales		385,000
Estimated inventory at retail		$220,000

Inventory of computation, December 31:
74.9311% of $220,000 = $164,848.

If the inventory is computed annually:

	Cost	Retail
Opening inventory	$100,000	$ 150,000
Purchases	700,000	950,000
Markups		25,000
Totals	$800,000	$1,125,000
(Cost ratio: $800,000/$1,125,000 = 71.1111%)		

	Cost	Retail
Markdowns		20,000
Remainder		$1,105,000
Sales		885,000
Estimated inventory at retail		$ 220,000

Inventory computation, 71.1111% of $220,000 = $156,444.

The inventory figure of $156,444, obtained by the foregoing computations covering the full year, is erroneous. Although the average cost ratio during the whole year was about 71 percent, the cost ratio for the second half of the year was about 75 percent.

It is apparent that, in this instance, the use of a cost ratio applicable to only the last half of the year will result in the determination of an inventory valuation more nearly approximating the lower of cost or market at the end of the year. By the application of the average cost ratio, 71 percent, the December 31 inventory computation is unjustifiably affected by the low cost ratio of the first half-year.

If the rates of markon vary during the year, it is obvious that monthly, or even more frequent, inventory computations will produce more correct results than can be obtained by annual computations.

EXTENDED ILLUSTRATION: The following statement shows the treatment of various elements in the computation of inventory by the retail method:

		Cost	Retail
Opening inventory		$ 65,000	$100,000
Purchases		350,000	520,000
Returned purchases		(10,000)	(14,800)
Transportation in		2,500	
Markups			12,500
Markup cancellations			(3,000)
Totals		$407,500	$614,700
(Cost ratio: $407,500/$614,700 = 66.2925%)			
Deductions:			
Sales	$511,000		
Less returned sales	7,000		$504,000
Markdowns	$ 5,000		
Less markdown cancellations	1,500		3,500
Total deductions			$507,500
Estimated inventory at retail			$107,200

Inventory computation: 66.2925% of $107,200 = $71,066.

FREIGHT, DISCOUNTS, RETURNS: Transportation and other charges that, in accordance with accounting theory, are proper additions to merchandise costs should be added to purchase costs in the retail records. If cash discounts are regarded as deductions from purchases, the purchases should be shown net in the retail-inventory records. If such discounts are regarded as financial income, they should not be included in the retail-inventory computations.

Purchases should be entered at cost and at retail in the inventory computation;

returned purchases should be similarly shown. Returned sales should be deducted from sales to obtain a net sales figure for use in the computation.

LIFO-retail method. When an accountant applies the LIFO concept to the retail method, he must use procedures that are somewhat different from those used under the conventional-retail method.

First difference:

Include markdowns as well as markups in the determination of the cost ratio.

As previously stated, the conventional-retail method produces an inventory valuation that closely approximates the amount that would be obtained by taking a physical inventory and pricing the goods at the lower of cost or market. LIFO, on the other hand, is a cost method. It is possible to modify the retail method to produce results reasonably conforming to a cost basis by *including markdowns* as well as markups in the determination of the cost ratio.

Second difference:

Ignore the beginning inventory in the determination of the cost ratio.

After the LIFO method has been in use for a period of time, the difference between current costs and the "old" costs that are considered by the LIFO method to be applicable to the inventory becomes quite significant. Since the cost ratio is intended to indicate the current relationship between costs and selling prices, the beginning-inventory data are not used in the computation of the cost ratio because their inclusion could have a distorting effect on the cost ratio.

If a conventional-retail procedure has been in operation and a decision is reached to change to a LIFO-retail procedure, then the beginning inventory of the year in which the change is to be made must be restated on a cost basis by the application of the retail method as modified by the differences explained above. This is illustrated below, where it is assumed that the data pertain to the year prior to the current-year switch from the conventional-retail method to the LIFO-retail method.

	Conventional Retail		LIFO Retail	
	Cost	Retail	Cost	Retail
→ Inventory—beginning of year ..	$ 3,200	$ 5,500	Omitted from cost ratio	
Purchases........................	15,600	24,500	$15,600	$24,500
Transportation in	400		400	
Markups		2,000		2,000
	$19,200	$32,000		$26,500
Conventional cost ratio: $19,200 ÷ $32,000.......	(60%)			
Markdowns		2,500		2,500
Remainder			$16,000	$24,000

	Conventional Retail		LIFO Retail	
	Cost	Retail	Cost	Retail
LIFO cost ratio:				
$16,000 ÷ $24,000			(66⅔%)	
→ Inventory—beginning of year				5,500
Total goods, at retail		$29,500		$29,500
Sales		23,500		23,500
Inventory at retail—end of year		$ 6,000		$ 6,000
Applicable cost ratio		60%		66⅔%
Inventory valuation		$ 3,600		$ 4,000

Since the ending inventory last year (the beginning inventory this year) was $3,600 using the conventional-retail method, it is necessary to make a $400 ($4,000 − $3,600) current-year adjusting entry to convert it to the $4,000 LIFO basis.

It will be noted that the markups and markdowns were applied, in the foregoing computation of the LIFO cost ratio, to the selling price of the goods purchased, although they presumably applied in part to the opening inventory. Obviously, this is not strictly correct; however, the slight theoretical impropriety is usually ignored.

The practice of disregarding the beginning inventory when computing the cost ratio is a feature of the LIFO-retail method and, therefore, is followed in all subsequent years and not confined merely to the computation of the base or beginning LIFO inventory.

SUBSEQUENT INVENTORIES—NO CHANGES IN THE PRICE LEVEL: The basic operational features of LIFO are not affected by the retail-method application. Distinctions must be maintained between the base inventory and any subsequent layers or increments to the inventory. The cost ratio of a particular period is used only to convert the layer of that period to cost. If there is no increase in the inventory in a given year, the cost ratio of that year is not used in converting the inventory from retail to cost.

The schedule on the next page, covering a six-year period after the adoption of LIFO, illustrates the application of LIFO procedures to the retail-inventory method.

Because the inventory at retail is now smaller than when the LIFO method was established, the 66⅔ percent cost ratio prevailing at that time is applicable, and the inventory at the end of the sixth period is stated at a LIFO cost of 66⅔ percent of $4,800, or $3,200.

Year	Cost Ratio For Year	Inventory at Retail	Base-Period Inventory at Retail	Increments at Retail (Reference to Year)	Applicable Cost Ratio	LIFO Cost Layers	LIFO Cost Base	Inventory Total
Base	66⅔%	$ 6,000	$6,000		66⅔%		$4,000	$4,000
1	70	8,000	6,000	$2,000 (1)	70	$1,400	4,000	5,400
2	75	9,000	6,000	2,000 (1)	70	1,400		
				1,000 (2)	75	750	4,000	6,150
3	80	12,000	6,000	2,000 (1)	70	1,400[a]		
				1,000 (2)	75	750[b]		
				3,000 (3)	80	2,400[c]	4,000	8,550[d]
4	78	10,000	6,000	2,000 (1)	70	1,400		
				1,000 (2)	75	750		
				1,000 (3)	80	800	4,000	6,950
5	73	7,000	6,000	1,000 (1)	70	700	4,000	4,700
6	69	4,800	6,000					
			1,200[e]					
			4,800		66⅔		3,200	3,200

[a]$1,400 = $2,000 × .70
[b]$750 = $1,000 × .75
[c]$2,400 = $3,000 × .80
[d]$8,550 = $1,400 + $750 + $2,400 + $4,000
[e]A $1,200 reduction of base, or $6,000 − $4,800.

SUBSEQUENT INVENTORIES—CHANGES IN THE LEVEL OF SELLING PRICES: In the preceding illustration, it was assumed that the level of retail selling prices remained unchanged during the entire period. When retail prices are not stable, it is necessary to make use of retail price indexes to adjust the inventory to a retail valuation that would have been shown by the retail records if there had been no change in selling prices.

To illustrate, assume that the retail records of a store showed the following:

	Cost	Retail	Cost Ratio
Purchases	$21,000	$28,000	75%
Base inventory, December 31, 19+4	4,000	6,000	
Total		$34,000	
Sales		25,200	
Inventory at retail, December 31, 19+5		$ 8,800	

Assume, also, that the retail index applicable to this business was 100 for 19+4 and 110 for 19+5.

We first reduce the December 31, 19+5, inventory at retail to the basis of 19+4 selling prices:	
$8,800 ÷ 1.10	$8,000
And then deduct the December 31, 19+4, inventory at retail	6,000
To determine the inventory increment in terms of 19+4 selling prices	$2,000
The inventory increment in terms of 19+5 selling prices was $2,000 × 1.10 =	$2,200

The December 31, 19+5, inventory priced at $8,800 retail can now be reduced to LIFO cost as follows:

	LIFO Cost	Retail
Segment equal to base inventory:		
On 19+4 price basis		$6,000
Old cost	$4,000	
Price inflation		600

	LIFO Cost	Retail
Incremental segment:		
At retail		2,200
At LIFO cost—determined by applying the cost ratio of the period—75% of $2,200	1,650	
Total	$5,650	$8,800

EXTENDED ILLUSTRATION: The AB Store adopts the retail-inventory method and LIFO in 19+5. Its December 31, 19+4, inventory was $80,000 at cost and $130,000 at retail. Inventory computations at three subsequent dates are shown below. The illustration has been simplified by omitting some of the items usually found with the retail method, such as transportation in and markups and markdowns. Applicable index numbers were as follows:

19+4	100	19+6	110
19+5	104	19+7	105

	Cost	Retail	Cost Ratio
Data for 19+5:			
Purchases	$240,000	$400,000	60%
Inventory—beginning of year (which is the base inventory)	80,000	130,000	
Total		$530,000	
Sales		389,600	
Inventory—end of year		$140,400	
Reduction to LIFO cost:			
19+5 inventory in terms of 19+4 prices—$140,000 ÷ 1.04		$135,000	
19+4 inventory (base)	$ 80,000	130,000	
Increment in inventory:			
In terms of 19+4 prices		$ 5,000	
In terms of 19+5 prices—$5,000 × 1.04		$ 5,200	
At LIFO cost—60% of $5,200	3,120		
19+5 inventory at LIFO cost	$ 83,120		
Data for 19+6:			
Purchases	$260,400	$420,000	62%
Inventory—beginning of year	83,120	140,400	
Total		$560,400	
Sales		408,600	
Inventory—end of year		$151,800	
Reduction to LIFO cost:			
19+6 inventory in terms of 19+4 prices—$151,800 ÷ 1.10		$138,000	
19+4 inventory (base)	$ 80,000	130,000	
Increment over 19+4 inventory		$ 8,000	
Portion of increment arising in 19+5 (see above)	3,120	5,000	

	Cost	Retail	Cost Ratio
Portion of increment arising in 1966:			
In terms of 19+4 prices		$ 3,000	
In terms of 19+6 prices—$3,000 × 1.10		$ 3,300	
At LIFO cost—62% of $3,300	2,046		
19+6 inventory at LIFO cost	$ 85,166		
Data for 19+7:			
Purchases	$292,500	$450,000	65%
Inventory—beginning of year	85,166	151,800	
Total		$601,800	
Sales		463,200	
Inventory—end of year		$138,600	
Reduction to LIFO cost:			
19+7 inventory in terms of 19+4 prices—$138,600 ÷ 1.05		$132,000	
19+4 inventory (base)	$ 80,000	130,000	
Increment over 19+4 inventory—regarded under LIFO theory as acquired in 19+5:			
In terms of 19+4 prices		$ 2,000	
In terms of 19+5 prices—computed by using 19+5 price index—$2,000 × 1.04		$ 2,080	
At LIFO cost—reduced by using 19+5 cost ratio—60% of $2,080	1,248		
19+7 inventory at LIFO cost	$ 81,248		

Dollar-value LIFO. As described in Chapter 11, the LIFO-inventory method is a unit-LIFO method, in that the quantity on hand is the basis used to determine the increments or reductions in the LIFO inventory. This requires considerable clerical detail, because increments and reductions must be determined for each item in the inventory. Thus, if a business stocks 100 different articles, a record of base and layer quantities must be maintained for each article. To avoid this handicap, dollars may be used as a measure of increments or reductions in a LIFO inventory.

For example, assuming no change in the price level during the current year, if last year's inventory was $1,000 (at cost) and this year's was $1,100 (at cost), it can be inferred that the inventory has increased 10 percent. Under LIFO, this would mean that we have an additional layer to deal with. In a sense, this approach views an inventory as a pool or aggregate, in contrast to an item-by-item approach. In practice, the inventory would probably be divided by broad product categories or by departments, with separate LIFO bases and layers for each grouping.

Of course, the price level changes. So before we can compare the dollar amount of a current inventory with the dollar amount of a previous inventory to determine whether there has been an increase or decrease, the two inventories being compared must be stated in dollars "of the same size." This could be done by the use of index numbers that measure the extent of changes in the price level. For instance, if it were known that the prices of goods purchased for resale had increased 10 percent during the current year, an inventory of $11,550, priced by using the current year's costs, could be converted to last year's price level by dividing by 1.10; thus, $11,550 ÷ 1.10 = $10,500.

If last year's inventory amounted to $10,000, the comparison between the $10,500 amount and the $10,000 amount would indicate that the inventory had increased 5 percent, or by $500 in terms of last year's prices. For purposes of determining the LIFO inventory, this layer should be stated in terms of the current year's price level, or $550, which is computed by multiplying $500 by 1.10.

Because price-index numbers are not available for many industries or lines of business, some alternative device must be applied for measuring price change as it affects the inventory of a particular business. The approach used is to compute an inventory first in terms of current costs, and second in terms of the costs prevailing when LIFO was adopted.

For example, if the current inventory amounts to $110,000 at current costs, and to $100,000 in terms of costs prevailing when the LIFO method was adopted (see below), it can be concluded that as far as this company is concerned, prices of inventory items have gone up 10 percent.

Inventory

		Unit Costs		Total	
Description	Current Quantity	Current Period	Prevailing When LIFO Was Adopted	At Current Costs	At Costs Prevailing When LIFO Was Adopted
A	80	$3.00	$2.75	$ 240	$ 220
B	100	2.45	2.25	245	225
C	200	5.50	5.00	1,100	1,000
				$110,000	$100,000

In the previous paragraph it was stated that each inventory is computed twice—once using the current year's costs and again using costs prevailing when the LIFO method was adopted. It should be pointed out that only a representative sample of the inventory need be thus double-priced, because the purpose of the extra computation is to obtain an index or measure of price change. It should also be mentioned that, as a practical matter, some provision must be made for the effects of discontinued and new products in developing a measure of price change.

The basic techniques of dollar-value LIFO are illustrated below. Zero is used to designate the year when LIFO was adopted.

	Inventory of Year			
	0	1	2	3
Priced by using costs of year 0	$10,000			
Priced by using costs of year 1		$10,710		
Priced by using costs of year 2			$11,340	
Priced by using costs of year 3				$11,880

	Inventory of Year			
	0	1	2	3
Priced by using costs of year 0	$10,000	$10,500	$10,800	$10,800
Index of price change since year 0, when LIFO was adopted:				
$10,710 ÷ $10,500		102		
$11,340 ÷ $10,800			105	
$11,880 ÷ $10,800				110

Inventory—LIFO cost:

Year 0	$10,000

Year 1:

By comparing the year 1 inventory with the year 0 inventory, both stated in dollars of the same price level (year 0), it is seen that there has been an increment to the inventory. This layer amounts to $500 ($10,500 − $10,000) in terms of the price level at year 0. But a new layer must be computed in terms of the current price level, or $500 × 1.02.

Year 1 layer	$ 510
Base	10,000
Inventory—LIFO cost	$10,510

Year 2:

By comparing year 2 and year 1 inventories, both stated in dollars of the same price level (year 0), it is seen that there has been a further increment to the LIFO inventory. The year 2 layer amounts to $300 ($10,800 − $10,500) in terms of the price level when LIFO was adopted. To convert to the year 2 price level, the $300 is multiplied by 1.05.

Year 2 layer ($300 × 1.05)	$ 315
Year 1 layer	510
Base	10,000
Inventory—LIFO cost	$10,825

Year 3:

By comparing year 3 and year 2 inventories, both stated in dollars of the same price level (year 0), it is seen that there has been no change in the aggregate inventory ($10,800 − $10,800). Therefore, the LIFO inventory for year 3 is the same as for year 2.

Inventory—LIFO cost	$10,825

INVENTORY REDUCTIONS: Reductions in LIFO inventories are subtracted first from the most recent layer (or layers, depending on the extent of the reduction), and, after all layers have been utilized, then from the base inventory. To show how a reduction is handled under dollar-value LIFO, continue the illustration for an additional year and assume that the inventory for year 4 is as follows:

Priced using costs of year 4	$11,770
Priced using costs of year 0	$10,700

By comparing year 4 and year 3 inventories, both stated in dollars of the same price level (year 0), it is seen that there has been a reduction of $100 ($10,800 −

$10,700). This reduction is taken from the year 2 layer, as follows:

Year 2 layer stated in terms of year 0 prices	$300
Reduction occurring during year 4	100
Remaining layer	$200
Price index for year 2	1.05
Remainder of year 2 layer in terms of LIFO cost	$210

Inventory—LIFO cost:	
Year 4:	
Year 2 layer	$ 210
Year 1 layer	510
Base	10,000
Inventory—LIFO cost	$10,720

Investments—Stocks and Funds

Introduction. Certain matters relative to investments have been discussed in previous chapters. Reference to the classification of investments on page 218 shows that they can be divided into two categories: (1) marketable securities (temporary investments), which were discussed in Chapter 9; and (2) long-term investments. Long-term investments in bonds were discussed in Chapter 7. This chapter deals with the accounting for long-term investments in stocks and funds.

In contrast to marketable securities, which are reported in the balance sheet as current assets, the investments discussed in this chapter are reported under a separate Investments caption. The distinction between the two categories of investments also has other accounting implications, which will be discussed in this chapter.

INVESTMENTS IN STOCKS

Cost. The cost of an investment in stock includes brokerage, taxes, and other expenditures related to acquisition. If securities are purchased through a broker on margin account, the books and the balance sheet should reflect as an asset the full cost of the securities and not merely the margin deposit. The unpaid balance should be shown as a liability. Similarly, if securities are purchased on an installment contract, it is important to record as an asset the full cost of the securities.

If two or more classes of securities are purchased for a single lump-sum payment, market prices may be used for the purpose of apportioning the cost. For example, if 100 shares of common stock and 100 shares of preferred stock of a company are bought at a total price of $22,050 at a time when the preferred stock has a market price of $105 per share and the common stock has a market price of $140 per share, the total purchase cost may be apportioned as follows:

Market price of preferred stock ($105 × 100 shares).........	$10,500
Market price of common stock ($140 × 100 shares).........	14,000
Total	$24,500

105/245 × $22,050 =	$ 9,450	Cost assigned to preferred stock
140/245 × $22,050 =	12,600	Cost assigned to common stock
	$22,050	Total cost

If only one of the classes of securities acquired has an ascertainable market price, the lump price may be apportioned by allocating the known market price to the one class of securities, and the remainder of the price to the securities with no ascertainable market price. If neither of the securities has a known market price, it may be necessary to postpone any apportionment of the purchase price until at least one market price can be established.

ADJUSTMENTS OF COST: After stock investments are made, any subsequent assessments paid or any contributions made for the purpose of eliminating a deficit or for other reasons should be added to the original cost. Any receipts from the issuing corporation representing a return of capital should be deducted from the original cost.

Exchanges. In accordance with the terms of issuance, securities of one class may be convertible at the option of the holder into other securities of the same company. Accountants are in agreement that, if no fair market value at the date of conversion is determinable for either class of securities, the securities received should be recorded at the cost or carrying amount of the securities parted with.

For example, assume that an investment in 100 shares of the convertible preferred stock of X Company had an original cost of, and is being carried on the books at, $100 per share, or a total of $10,000. If the preferred stock is exchanged for 100 shares of common stock of the same company and no market price can be determined for either class of stock, the following entry would be recorded:

Investment in common stock of X Company	10,000	
Investment in preferred stock of X Company...		10,000

The effect of this treatment is to simply transfer the cost of the stock given up to the stock acquired; thus, there is no gain or loss upon conversion.

Where it is possible to obtain market prices, the new securities acquired in an exchange should be recorded at their fair market value (quoted market price times number of shares), or the fair market value of the stock exchanged, using the market price that is more clearly determinable. Using the information in the preceding example, it is now assumed that the common shares acquired have a current price of $125 per share.

The decision to convert probably results in some changes in the rights of the investor. The position of a common stockholder relative to voting, dividends, and such matters is generally different from that of a preferred stockholder. Accordingly, there is some justification for the opinion that a new basis of accountability should be established for the investment at conversion, by recording the common stock at its fair market value of $12,500 ($125 × 100 shares) and recording a gain of $2,500, as illustrated in the following entry:

Investment in common stock of X Company (100 shares × $125 per share)........................	12,500	
Investment in preferred stock of X Company (100 shares × $100 per share)......		10,000
Gain on conversion of X Company stock ...		2,500

Not all accountants agree with this treatment of an exchange of stock. They argue that the asset given up (preferred stock) has been replaced with a similar asset (common stock) and that there is no realization of a gain or loss. Current income tax laws contain provisions such that many gains and losses on the exchange of stock do not have to be reported for tax purposes.

In reorganizations and mergers in which the exchange of securities is not made at the option of the holder as the exercise of a privilege granted under the terms of issuance of the securities held, the entry for the exchange of the securities will depend primarily upon whether the holder remains in essentially the same position with respect to his equities after the exchange as before. If his status remains practically unchanged, the security received can be placed on the books at the cost or carrying amount of the security relinquished, and no gain or loss need be recognized. If, however, the holder's status is materially affected by reason of a change in the number or nature of the securities held before and after the transaction, the newly acquired securities should be recorded at their fair market value, and the difference between the fair market value and the carrying amount of the old securities should be recorded as a gain or loss.

Stock warrants and rights. A legal right to purchase stock at a stated price during a specified period may be granted in the form of a stock purchase warrant or a stock right. Such warrants or rights are issued by corporations, and are generally transferable and thus may be purchased or sold by investors as are shares of stock.

ACCOUNTING FOR STOCK WARRANTS: The words *warrants* and *rights* are often used interchangeably. The term *warrant* is generally used when the privilege of purchasing shares of common stock, at a price that is potentially attractive, is issued with some other form of security, such as a bond or preferred stock. For example, each bond issued by a corporation may have a warrant attached that enables the holder of the warrant to purchase a specified number of shares of the company's common stock at a stated price during a period of time. Initially, the stated purchase price may be above the prevailing market price of the stock, in which case the warrants will probably have no immediate worth. They will become valuable should the market price of the common stock increase and exceed the purchase price stated in the warrants. However, if the warrants have a market price when acquired, the cost of the "investment package" should be allocated between the security acquired (the bond or the preferred stock, as the case may be) and the warrant, by using relative market prices, as previously shown on page 340. When warrants are purchased separately in the securities market, their cost is debited to a suitably described asset account. The asset is accounted for as are other investments. A gain or loss may result from their subsequent sale. The warrants account is credited, as is cash, when the warrants are used to purchase from the corporation the common stock described in the warrants.

The entries below, related to the assumed facts, illustrate the proper accounting for stock warrants purchased in a securities market:

Cost of warrants purchased—$1,000. 200 warrants permitting purchase of 400 shares of common stock for $20 per share.		
Cost of stock warrants	1,000	
Cash		1,000
Sale of 100 warrants—$600.		
Cash	600	
Cost of stock warrants		500
Gain on sale of stock warrants		100
Use of remaining 100 warrants to purchase 200 shares of stock for $4,000.		
Investment in common stock	4,500	
Cost of stock warrants		500
Cash		4,000

ACCOUNTING FOR STOCK RIGHTS: Stock rights are issued to existing stockholders, giving them the privilege of subscribing for additional shares of the same class of stock held. A corporation would not issue stock rights to its shareholders unless it wished to secure additional capital. As noted earlier, rights are generally transferable; thus, a person need not be a stockholder of a corporation to hold or exercise its rights. Stock rights are usually valuable, because the price at which the stock is offered to the rightholders is generally below the price prevailing for such shares in the securities market.

A stockholder receives one right for each share owned; if he owns 50 shares of stock, he will receive 50 rights. The rights will specify the quantity of stock that may be purchased with each right. More than one right may be required to purchase one additional share of stock. For example, five rights may be needed to purchase one share of stock.

The announcement of the granting of the rights states the date when the stock records will be closed to determine the stockholders of record to whom the rights will be issued, and also the later date when subscriptions will be payable. Between the date of the announcement and the date of the issuing of the rights, the stock and the rights are inseparable, and the stock is dealt in "rights-on." After the rights are issued, the stock is dealt in "ex-rights," and the rights are dealt in separately. During the period in which the stock is selling rights-on, no special problems arise, because any transactions involve the stock and the rights as a unit. After the rights are issued and the stock is selling ex-rights, problems arise that require an apportionment of the cost of the originally acquired stock between the stock and the rights. This is done on the basis of the market price of the right and the market price of the share ex-rights at the time of the issuance of the rights. For instance, assume that an investor owns 10 shares of stock for which he paid a total of $1,200.

Cost of share of stock owned	$120
Market prices on date of issuance of rights:	
Right	30
Stock	150
Apportionment of $120 cost:	
Right—$^{30}/_{180}$ of $120	20
Stock—$^{150}/_{180}$ of $120	100
Apportioned cost of 10 rights	200

When the apportioned cost of the rights is ascertained, it is advisable to record an entry setting up a cost of stock rights account, thus:

Cost of stock rights	200	
Investment in stock of X Company		200
Receipt of stock rights.		

The investment in stock of X Company account and the cost of stock rights account will then appear as follows:

Investment in Stock of X Company

Cost of 10 shares	1,200	Apportioned cost of rights	200

Cost of Stock Rights

Apportioned cost of rights	200		

Assume that each right entitled the holder to purchase one share of stock for $120, and that he exercised the rights. The cost of the new shares should be regarded as including the disbursement made to the issuing corporation therefor and the $200 apportioned cost of the rights. The entry for the acquisition of the 10 new shares is:

Investment in stock of X Company	1,400	
Cost of stock rights		200
Cash		1,200
Purchase of stock for cash and rights.		

The first shares of stock acquired are now regarded as having a cost of $100 each, and the new shares acquired are regarded as having a cost of $140 each.

Now assume that instead of using the rights, the holder sold them at their market price of $30 each. The entry would be:

Cash	300	
Cost of stock rights		200
Gain on sale of stock rights		100
Sale of stock rights.		

If the holder of rights is careless enough to neither use them nor sell them but allows them to lapse, the apportioned cost of the rights should be written off as a loss.

As stated above, the right pertaining to each share may entitle the holder to purchase only a fraction of a share; for instance, each right may entitle the holder to purchase one tenth of a share. The holder of four shares would, in such a case, receive rights entitling him to purchase four tenths of one share. The cost to be assigned to each right would be determined in the manner illustrated above. The holder of the rights may:

Buy additional rights to enable him to buy a full share. The cost of the new share will include the apportioned cost of his rights for four tenths of a share, plus the cost of the rights for six tenths of a share, plus the subscription price.

Sell his rights for four tenths of a share, in which case he should compute his gain or loss and record an entry for the sale of the rights in the manner illustrated above.

Dividends on stock investments. Dividends are usually declared on one day, and payable on a subsequent day, to stockholders of record at some intermediate date. At which of these dates should the dividends be recorded as revenue to the stockholder? Revenue should not be recorded until the date of record, because the stock may be sold before that date and the right to receive the dividend be thereby lost. At the date of record, an entry can be made debiting Dividends Receivable and crediting Dividend Revenue.[1] When the dividend is collected, the entry is to debit Cash and credit Dividends Receivable.

Dividends received in property should be recorded at the fair market value (quoted market price of property or similar property, or if not determinable, independent appraisal) of the property received. Dividends received from companies engaged in the exploitation of assets subject to depletion may consist partly of income and partly of a return of capital. The portion representing a liquidating dividend should be so designated by the corporation and should be recorded by the recipient as a reduction of the cost of the stock investment.

Stock received as a dividend. Stockholders may receive additional shares as a result of a stock dividend. As a general rule, stock dividends are not income to the recipients

---

[1]This procedure assumes that the investment is accounted for using the cost method. Another method of accounting for stock investments is discussed later in this chapter.

from either the general accounting or the income tax standpoint. There is no distribution of assets of the corporation, but merely a change in the component elements of the stockholders' equity. Far from being a distribution from retained earnings, a stock dividend constitutes a notice to stockholders that a portion of the retained earnings will not thereafter be available for dividend charges.

If a person owns 100 shares out of a total of 1,000 outstanding shares, and if the corporation issues a 25 percent stock dividend, the stockholder's shares are increased to 125 and the total outstanding shares are increased to 1,250; but as far as the stockholder is concerned, he still has a 10 percent interest in the corporation, and the only effect of the stock dividend is an increase in the number of shares by which his equity is represented. Therefore, the receipt of a stock dividend should not be recorded by any entry increasing the carrying amount of the investment or recognizing revenue. The only necessary record of the dividend received is a notation in the investment account indicating the increase in the number of shares held.

In the case of stock acquired at various times and at different prices, if some of the shares are sold, and the shares sold cannot be identified as pertaining to any particular lot, the cost of the shares sold can be determined, for purposes of computing gain or loss, on the first-in, first-out basis. How should stock received as a dividend be dealt with in applying this method? If 100 shares were purchased in 19+3 at $100 each, another 100 shares were purchased in 19+4 at $125 each, another 100 shares were acquired in 19+5 at a cost of $150 per share, and a 25 percent stock dividend was received in 19+6, the 75 shares received as a dividend should not be regarded as having been acquired in 19+6. They should be associated with the shares on which they were received as a dividend. Thus, the three purchases should now be regarded as follows:

Date	Shares Purchased	Cost	Shares Owned	Adjusted Cost per Share
19+3	100	$10,000	125	$ 80
19+4	100	12,500	125	100
19+5	100	15,000	125	120

If bonds or other similar evidences of indebtedness are received as a dividend, proper accounting and the tax regulations require that they be recorded as assets and revenue at their fair market value.

Dividends payable in stock or in cash at the option of the stockholder, and taken in stock at his option, are regarded as taxable income. Likewise, a stock dividend is taxable to the extent that it is distributed in discharge of preference dividends for the distributing corporation's current or preceding tax year.

Accounting for stock investments subsequent to acquisition. Traditionally, most investments in stocks were accounted for by recording them at cost and carrying them at cost, except in cases where there was evidence of a permanent major decline in their price, a procedure referred to as the cost method. However, in those instances in which the investment represents more than 50 percent of the voting stock of a company, a parent–subsidiary relationship is considered to exist. The company owning the stock (parent) is in a position to control the operations of the company whose stock is held (subsidiary), owing to ownership of more than half the voting stock.

Rather than using the cost method, some parent companies have used the equity method to account for their investments in subsidiaries and their income or loss thereon. Each of these methods will now be discussed.

Cost method. From a legal standpoint, a parent and its subsidiary are separate entities. The net income or loss of the subsidiary is not a part of the net income or loss of the parent; dividends received from the subsidiary are revenue to the parent. If the parent company adopts the cost method of accounting for its investment in the subsidiary and its revenue thereon, it will carry the investment at cost and will record dividends as revenue. To illustrate:

Company P organizes a subsidiary, Company S, and acquires its entire stock issue by an investment of $100,000.

Investment in stock of Company S.............	100,000	
Cash......................................		100,000
Acquisition of stock of subsidiary.		

During the first year of its operation, the subsidiary earns a net income of $30,000 (for which the parent makes no entry) and pays a dividend of $5,000.

Cash	5,000	
Dividend revenue.............................		5,000
Dividend from subsidiary.		

The dividend revenue account is closed to Retained Earnings, as are other revenue accounts.

During the second year, the subsidiary loses $15,000 (the parent records no entry) and pays a dividend of $5,000 based on retained earnings produced by the earnings of the preceding year.

Cash	5,000	
Dividend revenue.............................		5,000
Dividend from subsidiary.		

During the third year, the subsidiary loses $12,000 and pays no dividends. The parent company records no entry.

The foregoing entries under the cost method are summarized below:

	Investment	Cash	Dividend Revenue	Retained Earnings
First year: Investment.....	$100,000	$100,000*		
Subsidiary net income —no entry				
Subsidiary dividend ...		5,000	$5,000*	
Closing entry			5,000	$5,000*

	Investment	Cash	Dividend Revenue	Retained Earnings
Second year: Subsidiary net loss—no entry				
Subsidiary dividend ...	5,000	$5,000*		
Closing entry		5,000	5,000*	
Third year: Subsidiary net loss—no entry				

*Credit.

This accounting procedure conforms strictly to the legal realities of separate corporate entities. However, when this method is used, the balance in the investment account will not reflect the underlying book amount of the subsidiary's net assets. The changing amounts of subsidiary net assets and the unchanging balance of the parent's investment account are compared below:

	Net Assets of Subsidiary	Parent's Investment Account
First year:		
Investment by parent........................	$100,000	$100,000
Increase in subsidiary's net assets resulting from net income	30,000	
Decrease in subsidiary's net assets resulting from payment of dividend..............	5,000*	
Balance at end of year.......................	$125,000	$100,000
Second year:		
Decrease in subsidiary's net assets resulting from loss	15,000*	
Decrease in subsidiary's net assets resulting from payment of dividend.....	5,000*	
Balance at end of year......................	$105,000	$100,000
Third year:		
Decrease in subsidiary's net assets resulting from loss	12,000*	
Balance at end of year.......................	$ 93,000	$100,000

*Deduction.

Of even greater consequence is the fact that the dividends recorded by the parent company as income bear no relation to the results of the subsidiary's operations. The parent company is in a position to dictate the dividend policy of the subsidiary. Therefore, as long as the subsidiary has retained earnings available for dividend charges, the parent, by determining the dividends to be paid to it, can take into revenue any amounts it may desire, instead of recording the net income or loss resulting from the subsidiary's operations.

Assume that a company, instead of organizing a subsidiary, purchases the stock of a company that has been in existence for some time. Assume, also, that the dividends paid by a subsidiary after the acquisition of its stock by the parent company exceed its earnings since that date. How should the parent company record the portion of the dividend that was based on retained earnings accumulated prior to acquisition? Although such a dividend appears to have a legal status of income to the parent company, accountants are in general agreement that such a dividend should not be recorded as revenue, but should be regarded as a partial recovery of cost and should be credited to the investment account.

It should be recognized that a parent company may not own all the outstanding stock of a subsidiary; there may be a minority interest in the subsidiary. Under such circumstances, the parent company will receive only its share of the dividends paid by the subsidiary.

Equity method. The equity method gives recognition to the fact that subsidiary earnings increase the subsidiary net assets that underlie the investment, and that subsidiary losses and dividends decrease these net assets. The parent's entries under this method increase and decrease the balance in the investment account in accordance with increases and decreases in the underlying subsidiary net assets. Also, the amounts shown as income or loss on the investment each year correspond with the amounts shown as income and loss by the subsidiary. To illustrate, assume the same facts as those in the illustration of the cost method. The entries are indicated below:

	Investment	Cash	Subsidiary Income	Retained Earnings
First year:				
Investment..........	$100,000	$100,000*		
Subsidiary net income..........	30,000		$30,000*	
Subsidiary dividend	5,000*	5,000		
Closing entry........			30,000	$30,000*
Balance at end of year..............	$125,000			
Second year:				
Subsidiary net loss..	15,000*		$15,000	
Subsidiary dividend	5,000*	5,000		
Closing entry........			15,000*	15,000
Balance at end of year..............	$105,000			
Third year:				
Subsidiary net loss..	12,000*		$12,000	
Closing entry........			12,000*	12,000
Balance at end of year..............	$ 93,000			

*Credit.

When entries are made by the parent company in this manner, the changes in the balance of the investment account keep pace with the changes in the net assets of the subsidiary, and the amounts recorded by the parent as income or loss on the investment are in accordance with the income or loss of the subsidiary instead of arbitrary amounts transferred from the subsidiary to the parent as dividends. This accounting procedure undoubtedly reflects the economic realities. The only objection to the equity method is that it violates the legal realities, because the parent's retained earnings account is affected by subsidiary earnings and losses although it can legally be affected only by subsidiary dividends.

The Committee on Accounting Procedure of the AICPA took the position in 1959 that the equity method was preferable in accounting for investments in unconsolidated subsidiaries in consolidated statements.[2] However, the committee recognized both methods as being acceptable, and the cost method continued to be widely used. Recent Opinions of the Accounting Principles Board have had the effect of specifying under what conditions each method is acceptable and generally require that the equity method be used by the parent to account for investments in subsidiaries.

> The Board reaffirms the conclusion that investors should account for investments in common stock of unconsolidated domestic subsidiaries by the equity method in consolidated financial statements, and the Board now extends this conclusion to investments in common stock of all unconsolidated subsidiaries (foreign as well as domestic) in consolidated financial statements. . . . The Board also concludes that parent companies should account for investments in the common stock of subsidiaries by the equity method in parent-company financial statements prepared for issuance to stockholders as the financial statements of the primary reporting entity.[3]

At the same time, the board went even further and concluded that the equity method should be used, under certain circumstances, even when stock ownership is less than 50 percent.

> The Board concludes that the equity method of accounting for an investment in common stock should also be followed by an investor whose investment in voting stock gives it the ability to exercise significant influence over operating and financial policies of an investee even though the investor holds 50% or less of the voting stock.[4]

---

[2]Committee on Accounting Procedure, "Consolidated Financial Statements," *Accounting Research Bulletin No. 51* (New York: AICPA, August 1959), pp. 46–47.

[3]Accounting Principles Board, "The Equity Method of Accounting for Investments in Common Stock," *Opinion No. 18* (New York: AICPA, March 1971), pp. 353–54.

[4]*Opinion No. 18*, p. 355.

Evidence of the ability to exercise significant influence would include "representation on the board of directors, participation in policy-making processes, material intercompany transactions, interchange of managerial personnel, or technological dependency."[5] Another consideration mentioned is the investor's extent of ownership in relation to the concentration of other shareholdings.

Obviously, the decision as to whether or not significant influence is present involves subjective judgments. To achieve some degree of uniformity in the application of this extension of the use of the equity method, the board concluded that "an investment (direct or indirect) of 20% or more of the voting stock of an investee should lead to a presumption that in the absence of evidence to the contrary an investor has the ability to exercise significant influence over an investee."[6] For investments of less than 20 percent, it is necessary to show that the ability to exercise significant influence is present. In other words, for stock investments consisting of 20 to 50 percent of the voting stock, the equity method is used; for investments of less than 20 percent, the cost method is used (or possibly the market-value method, explained in a subsequent section); and for investments of more than 50 percent, consolidated statements are prepared and the investment account is eliminated. In determining the voting interest of an investor, only those voting securities presently outstanding should be considered.

Valuation of stock investment. It was noted in Chapter 9 that declines in the market price of temporary investments in stock are normally reflected in the accounts, since the securities are viewed as a reserve source of cash. However, market declines are not as significant in the accounting for long-term stock investments. Declines that are considered minor or temporary need not be reported in the accounts, since the market may recover prior to sale of the stock.

Serious declines in the market prices of long-term stock investments should be reflected in the accounts, particularly in those cases where the recovery of cost is unlikely. This should be done no matter whether the investor uses the cost or the equity method. The credit to record the decrease in valuation should be made to a contra account rather than to the asset account, so as to preserve a record of cost for tax purposes. To illustrate, assume that stock costing $100,000 has declined to a market valuation of $80,000, and it is decided that the decline should be recorded. The following journal entry should be booked:

Market loss on securities.......................	20,000	
Allowance for excess of cost of long-term investments over market		20,000
Provision for decline in market price.		

The investment may be shown on the asset side of the balance sheet, thus:

[5] *Opinion No. 18*, p. 355.
[6] *Opinion No. 18*, p. 355.

Investment in stocks:		
Cost	$100,000	
Less allowance for excess of cost of long-term investments over market	20,000	$80,000

or as follows:

Investment in stocks—at market, cost $100,000	$80,000

Any subsequent adjustments of the contra account because of additional changes in market prices would be handled in the same manner as discussed in Chapter 9 concerning temporary investments.

If, for any reason, declines in the market price of long-term or temporary investments in securities are not recorded in the accounts, and the securities are stated in the balance sheet at a valuation other than market, it is important to state the market valuation parenthetically.

Market-value method. A third method of accounting for investments in stocks, referred to as the market-value method, was also mentioned in *Opinion No. 18.* The method, which is used only in special situations, is summarized below:

(1) Dividends received on the stock investment are treated as revenue by the investor.

(2) Changes in the market price of the stock investment are treated as revenues or losses by the investor.

The Accounting Principles Board concluded that "further study is necessary before the market-value method is extended beyond current practice."[7] Current use of the method is restricted to those situations in which there is less than majority ownership of stock.

Consolidated financial statements. The ownership of a controlling interest in a subsidiary by a parent company means that although there are two separate legal entities, there is a single economic entity, under unified management and control. Under such circumstances, consolidated financial statements are considered preferable to either the separate statements of the parent or the statements of the parent accompanied by separate statements of the subsidiary. "There is a presumption that consolidated statements are more meaningful than separate statements and that they are usually necessary for a fair presentation when one of the companies in the group directly or indirectly has a controlling financial interest in the other companies."[8]

The subject of consolidated statement preparation is covered in detail in the *Advanced* volume of this series.[9] Basically, the procedure involves the elimination

[7] *Opinion No. 18,* p. 352.

[8] *Accounting Research Bulletin No. 51,* p. 41.

[9] James A. Gentry, Jr., and Glenn L. Johnson, *Finney and Miller's Principles of Accounting: Advanced,* 6th ed. (Englewood Cliffs, N.J.: Prentice-Hall, Inc., 1971), Chap. 5–12.

of the parent's investment account against the related equity of the subsidiary, elimination of intercompany transactions, and a combining of the remaining accounts in the separate financial statements of the companies.

It should be noted at this point that the use of the equity method as opposed to the cost method of accounting for a parent's investment in the subsidiary has no effect at all on either the decision to consolidate or the resulting consolidated financial statements. The Accounting Principles Board has stated, "The equity method is not, however, a valid substitute for consolidation and should not be used to justify exclusion of a subsidiary when consolidation is otherwise appropriate."[10]

BUSINESS COMBINATIONS

Conditions during the period following World War II have been conducive to the combining of businesses. The urge to expand, the appeal of diversification, the interest in improving competitive position, the desire to acquire managerial talent, income tax considerations, and the prospect of economies of larger scale operations are some of the incentives leading to the bringing together of two or more businesses. These arrangements have included the formation of new corporations, the exchange of corporate shares, and the merger of several corporations, to mention only a few of the procedures used.

Accountants' services in combinations. When businesses are exploring the desirability of combining, the books of account provide information of importance in the negotiations. The book amounts of assets and the past earnings serve as a logical starting point in forecasting the contributions the several companies will make to the combination.

It is at this point that the services of an accountant are often required, to give assurance that generally accepted accounting principles have been applied and that the data for the several companies are on a reasonably uniform basis. Adjustments of recorded data may be necessary. Errors may have been made. The necessity for some adjustments may arise because of differences in accounting policies. Other adjustments may be needed in order to avoid the possibility of producing misleading impressions by unusual transactions.

For these reasons, certain accounts should be analyzed in considerable detail. For example, the accountant should analyze the depreciation accounts of the several companies to determine whether the depreciation policies are acceptable and comparable. If differences are revealed, the effect of these differences on book values and reported earnings must be computed in order to place the accounting data on a reasonably comparable basis. Similarly, the stockholders' equity accounts should be analyzed for unusual or nonrecurring items and for evidence of any entries reflecting appraisals or write-downs.

The following list suggests some of the areas where differences are most likely

[10] *Opinion No. 18*, p. 354.

to be discovered:

(1) Depreciation and maintenance policies
(2) Provision for uncollectible accounts
(3) Inventory-pricing policy
(4) Accounting for intangibles
(5) Valuation of investments
(6) Provisions for contingencies or losses
(7) Officers' salaries
(8) Differences in accounting policy—such as capitalizing or expensing certain expenditures
(9) Long-lived asset valuations in the accounts—cost or appraisal
(10) Accrual and prepayment policies
(11) Accounting for unusual and nonrecurring items

It should be recognized that differences in the areas above may not be an indication of incorrect or improper accounting. There are many areas where generally accepted accounting principles permit alternative accounting procedures. In other words, books of account may lack comparability because of clerical mistakes, incorrect accounting, or the application of equally acceptable alternatives. In any event, comparability of accounting data is the objective when a combination is being developed.

After reasonable comparability of accounting data has been achieved, as a general rule the interested parties endeavor to use the data relative to assets, liabilities, and earning power in an intelligent fashion in arriving at a program for effecting the combination. Accountants and business management recognize that book amounts, even when determined on a comparable basis, are not the only matters to be given consideration. Technological changes and the decline in purchasing power of money, to mention only two matters, may substantially impair the significance of recorded amounts. The earning power of a business may warrant a total valuation for the business in excess of that shown by the books. The valuation of an individual asset may be estimated by considering such matters as its condition, its remaining use-life, its replacement cost, and its resale price. But considering the business as a whole, an estimate of earning power is particularly relevant in determining valuation, and in most cases, such estimates are feasible.

If the accountant is asked to review estimates of earning power, the following list is illustrative of the possible considerations:

(1) Will any items of expense be higher or lower after the combination is effected?
(2) Will key personnel continue with the new or continuing company?
(3) What is the trend of earnings? of sales? of selling prices? of unit costs?
(4) Will any products or productive capacity be discontinued? If so, what will be the effect on earnings?

Accounting for business combinations. There are two ways in which business combinations may be accounted for, depending upon the circumstances. The two methods are not alternatives for a given combination. Certain combinations must be accounted for as *purchases,* whereas others are accounted for as *poolings of interests.* The Accounting Principles Board has stated:

> The Board concludes that the purchase method and the pooling of interests method are both acceptable in accounting for business combinations, although not as alternatives in accounting for the same business combination. A business combination which meets specified conditions requires accounting by the pooling of interests method. A new basis of accounting is not permitted for a combination that meets the specified conditions, and the assets and liabilities of the combining companies are combined at their recorded amounts. All other business combinations should be accounted for as an acquisition of one or more companies by a corporation. The cost to an acquiring corporation of an entire acquired company should be determined by the principles of accounting for the acquisition of an asset. That cost should then be allocated to the identifiable individual assets acquired and liabilities assumed based on their fair values; the unallocated cost should be recorded as goodwill.[11]

It should be noted that in the prior discussion of parent–subsidiary relationships in this chapter, it was assumed that the acquisition of the subsidiary's stock represented a purchase.

Business combination treated as a purchase. In effect, the Accounting Principles Board has stated that a business combination must be treated as a purchase *unless* the combination meets certain conditions specified by the board. The basic characteristic of the purchase method of accounting for a combination is that one company is considered to have acquired another company. In such a case, the following procedures are used:

> The acquiring corporation records at its cost the acquired assets less liabilities assumed. A difference between the cost of an acquired company and the sum of the fair values of tangible and identifiable intangible assets less liabilities is recorded as goodwill. The reported income of an acquiring corporation includes the operations of the acquired company after acquisition, based on the cost to the acquiring corporation.[12]

There are two very important implications for the financial statements of the combined companies when the acquisition of the subsidiary is treated as a pur-

---

[11] Accounting Principles Board, "Business Combinations," *Opinion No. 16* (New York: AICPA, August 1970), p. 283.

[12] *Opinion No. 16,* p. 284.

chase. First, since the retained earnings of the subsidiary at acquisition are considered to have been purchased, the retained earnings balance at acquisition is eliminated, and no part of it may be carried to the consolidated balance sheet of the combined companies. Second, if goodwill is recorded as a result of the combination, it must be charged off against income in the future. In *Opinion No. 17,* issued at the same time as the Opinion dealing with business combinations, the Accounting Principles Board stated that such goodwill should be charged off systematically to the period benefited, but that the period of amortization should not exceed 40 years.[13]

Several reasons have been advanced in favor of the purchase method. Generally, one of the companies relinquishes control over its assets and operations. If the combination results from a bargained transaction between independent parties, then the bargained cost to the acquiring company would seem to be the significant amount to be recognized. Thus, the amounts at which assets and liabilities are carried by the acquired company are inappropriate for carrying the assets and liabilities forward.

PURCHASE ILLUSTRATION: To illustrate the treatment of a business combination as a purchase, it is assumed that Company S had the following assets and equities at January 1, 19+3:

Assets			Equities	
Cash		$10,000	Accounts payable	$ 5,000
Inventory		15,000	Capital stock	60,000
Plant and equipment:			Retained earnings	20,000
Cost	$80,000			
Less accumulated depreciation	20,000	60,000		
		$85,000		$85,000

On this date, Company P pays $120,000 for all the stock of Company S. At the same time, it is determined that the inventory of Company S has a fair market value of $12,000, and the plant and equipment has a fair market value, net of accumulated depreciation, of $85,000. Thus, Company P paid $18,000 in excess of the fair market value of the net assets acquired, determined as follows:

Fair market value of assets acquired:	
Cash	$ 10,000
Inventory	12,000
Plant and equipment (net)	85,000
Total	$107,000
Less liabilities assumed	5,000
Fair market value of net assets	$102,000
Excess of acquisition price over fair market value of net assets ($120,000 – $102,000)	$ 18,000

[13]Accounting Principles Board, "Intangible Assets," *Opinion No. 17* (New York: AICPA, August 1970), p. 334.

The following entries are required in order to prepare a consolidated balance sheet for the combined companies as of the date of the stock acquisition by Company P. The entries are recorded *only in the consolidated working papers.*

(a) To eliminate the investment account of Company P, the stockholders' equity of Company S, and recognize the amount paid in excess of the book amount of the net assets:

Capital stock (Company S)	60,000	
Retained earnings (Company S)	20,000	
Excess of cost over book value of net assets acquired	40,000	
Investment in Company S		120,000

The $40,000 debit in the entry is simply the difference between the amount paid for all the stock of Company S ($120,000) and the book amount of the net assets acquired ($80,000). It is important to note that Company S still carries the assets and equities on its books at the amounts shown in the condensed balance sheet on page 355. The fair market values referred to on page 355 are to be reflected only in the consolidated balance sheet prepared for the combined companies.

(b) To adjust Company S assets to their fair market value and recognize the balance of the excess paid as goodwill:

Plant and equipment (net)	25,000	
Goodwill	18,000	
Inventory		3,000
Excess of cost over book value of net assets acquired		40,000

The purpose of this entry is to allocate the difference between cost and the book value of the equity acquired to specific items to the extent possible. This could be done for $22,000 (increase in plant and equipment of $25,000 less decrease in inventory of $3,000) of the total difference of $40,000. The portion not allocated to specific items is recorded as goodwill on the consolidated balance sheet.[14] This goodwill must be amortized on future consolidated income statements prepared for the combined companies.

It should be noted that treatment of the acquisition as a purchase has the following implications for the consolidated balance sheet: (1) Assets of the acquired company (Company S) are reported on the consolidated balance sheet at their fair market value at the date of acquisition; and (2) The retained earnings balance of the acquired company at date of acquisition is completely eliminated and no part of the at-acquisition amount appears on the consolidated balance sheet.

A combination may take place by the distribution of assets (primarily cash) by the acquiring company. However, it is also possible that the combination can be

[14]The authors believe it would be more descriptive to label the portion of the excess not allocated to specific items as "Portion of excess of cost of subsidiary stock over book amount thereof at acquisition not assigned to specific subsidiary assets."

effected by the issuance of stock of the acquiring company. Proponents of the purchase treatment argue that, even in this case, the transaction is a purchase in substance and should be accounted for as such. Many accountants are opposed to the use of the purchase method in those instances involving an exchange of stock. The problem of measuring the fair market value of the property acquired or the consideration given in exchange may be very difficult under these circumstances. It then becomes quite difficult to determine the valuation of goodwill and other unidentifiable intangible assets.

Business combination treated as a pooling of interests. The basic characteristic of the pooling-of-interests method of accounting for a business combination is that the ownership interests of two or more companies are considered to have been joined by an exchange of equity securities. The combination is not considered to have resulted in a purchase, since the companies involved did not disburse resources as a part of the transaction. The following procedures are used to record the combination:

> Ownership interests continue and the former bases of accounting are retained. The recorded assets and liabilities of the constituents are carried forward to the combined corporation at their recorded amounts. Income of the combined corporation includes income of the constituents for the entire fiscal period in which the combination occurs. The reported income of the constituents for prior periods is combined and restated as income of the combined corporation.[15]

The pooling treatment causes some important differences in the financial statements of the combined companies when compared with the purchase method. The assets and liabilities are reported at the book amounts at which they were previously carried, after adjustments necessary to apply accounting principles consistently to the assets and liabilities of all companies involved. As a result of this, there will be no goodwill resulting from the combination. Also, the total retained earnings of the combined companies at the date of the combination may be less, but never more, than the sum of the retained earnings of the parent and subsidiary.

The major argument for the pooling concept is that it is an arrangement among different stockholder groups whereby each group that gives up its existing interest receives in exchange an interest in the assets of another of the combined companies. For example, B Company may be combined with A Company, with B Company's stockholders surrendering their stock in exchange for the stock of A Company. Another arrangement might be the formation of C Company to combine the operations of A Company and B Company, with stockholders of the old

---

[15] *Opinion No. 16*, pp. 284–85.

companies receiving C Company stock in exchange for their stock. In effect, their equity interests have been pooled. Proponents of the pooling concept contend that since there is no newly invested capital and the former ownership continues, there is no basis for viewing the transaction as a purchase.

Some accountants oppose the pooling method because they doubt that it is in fact supported by a concept. "In their view it has become essentially a method of accounting for an acquisition of a company without recognizing the current costs of the assets, including goodwill, underlying the transaction."[16] Its greatest flaw has been described as follows:

> The most serious defect attributed to pooling of interests accounting by those who oppose it is that it does not accurately reflect the economic substance of the business combination transaction. They believe that the method ignores the bargaining which results in the combination by accounting only for the amounts previously shown in accounts of the combining companies. The acquiring corporation does not record assets and values which usually influence the final terms of the combination agreement with consequent effects on subsequent balance sheets and income statements.[17]

The specified conditions under which the Accounting Principles Board has stated that the pooling of interests method must be used have been classified by the board into three groups, as follows:

I. Attributes of the combining companies
   A. Each of the combining companies is autonomous and has not been a subsidiary or division of another corporation within two years before the plan of combination is initiated.
   B. Each of the combining companies is independent of the other combining companies.

II. Manner of combining interests
   A. The combination is effected in a single transaction or is completed in accordance with a specified plan within one year after the plan is initiated.
   B. A corporation offers and issues only common stock with rights identical to those of the majority of its outstanding voting common stock in exchange for substantially all of the voting common stock interest of another company at the date the plan of combination is consummated.
   C. None of the combining companies changes the equity interest of the voting common stock in contemplation of effecting the combina-

[16] *Opinion No. 16*, p. 292.
[17] *Opinion No. 16*, p. 293.

tion either within two years before the plan of combination is initiated or between the dates the combination is initiated and consummated; changes in contemplation of effecting the combination may include distributions of stockholders and additional issuances, exchanges, and retirements of securities.

D. Each of the combining companies reacquires shares of voting common stock only for purposes other than business combinations, and no company reacquires more than a normal number of shares between the dates the plan of combination is initiated and consummated.

E. The ratio of the interest of an individual common stockholder to those of other common stockholders in a combining company remains the same as a result of the exchange of stock to effect the combination.

F. The voting rights to which the common stock ownership interests in the resulting combined corporation are entitled are exercisable by the stockholders; the stockholders are neither deprived of nor restricted in exercising those rights for a period.

G. The combination is resolved at the date the plan is consummated and no provisions of the plan relating to the issue of securities or other consideration are pending.

III. Absence of planned transactions

A. The combined corporation does not agree directly or indirectly to retire or reacquire all or part of the common stock issued to effect the combination.

B. The combined corporation does not enter into other financial arrangements for the benefit of the former stockholders of a combining company, such as a guaranty of loans secured by stock issued in the combination, which in effect negates the exchange of equity securities.

C. The combined corporation does not intend or plan to dispose of a significant part of the assets of the combining companies within two years after the combination other than disposals in the ordinary course of business of the formerly separate companies and to eliminate duplicate facilities or excess capacity.[18]

The board noted that all the conditions listed above must be met in order for a combination to be accounted for as a pooling of interests.

POOLING-OF-INTERESTS ILLUSTRATION: In order to illustrate the pooling treatment of a business combination, the same balance sheet information assumed for Company S on page 355 will be used. However, it is now assumed that instead of purchasing the stock of Company S, Company P acquires all the outstanding stock of Company S by issuing 7,000 shares of Company P's $10 par value com-

---

[18] *Opinion No. 16,* pp. 295–304.

mon stock. Assuming that all the conditions listed on pages 358 and 359 are met, the combination must be treated as a pooling of interests.

First, it should be noted that the way Company P records the acquisition of the Company S stock will be different from that in the purchase treatment previously illustrated, as shown below:

Purchase			Pooling		
Investment in Company S stock	120,000		Investment in Company S stock	70,000	
Cash		120,000	Common stock		70,000

The total par value of the additional stock issued becomes the basis for recording the stock acquired. The only entry required in the preparation of a consolidated balance sheet at acquisition is as follows:

Common stock (Company S)	60,000	
Retained earnings (Company S)	10,000	
Investment in Company S stock		70,000

Treatment of the combination as a pooling of interests causes the account balances of the companies to be combined without adjustment, assuming that they are stated in conformity with generally accepted accounting principles. Thus, the assets and liabilities of Company S are carried to the consolidated balance sheet at the same amounts reported on the books of Company S. As a result, the total retained earnings reported on the consolidated balance sheet at acquisition exceed the retained earnings of the parent company alone. Of Company S's retained earnings, $10,000 has in effect been capitalized from a consolidated standpoint, by crediting the capital stock account of the parent for an amount $10,000 greater than the par value of the Company S stock acquired. The remaining $10,000 of Company S's retained earnings will be included in the total retained earnings on the consolidated balance sheet.

Although the preceding illustration deals only with the impact of the purchase and pooling treatments on the balance sheet prepared for the combined companies, the difference in treatment has some important implications for the income statements prepared for the combined companies. It has already been mentioned that any goodwill recorded as a result of the purchase treatment must be amortized in future periods, thus reducing the consolidated income of the companies. Also, under the pooling treatment, income of the combined corporation will include the income of the acquired company for the entire period in which the acquisition takes place; whereas under the purchase treatment, only the parent's share of subsidiary income since acquisition would be included.

INVESTMENTS IN FUNDS

Classes of funds. This section deals with special-purpose funds that are represented by assets (usually cash) set aside for a specific use. These funds always represent assets and should be reported as such on the balance sheet.

Funds may be classified as follows:

(1) As to the use to be made of the assets in the fund:
- (a) Payment of an existing liability
- (b) Payment of a contingent liability
- (c) Payment for an asset or a service
- (d) Retirement of capital stock

(2) As to obligatory or voluntary creation:
- (a) Obligatory—required by contract
- (b) Voluntary—created by action of the management

Funds in the balance sheet. Funds should be classified in the balance sheet as current assets if they are created for the payment of current liabilities or for current expenditures. Thus, periodic deposits for the payment of bond interest or for the payment of taxes on property mortgaged as security for a short-term or a long-term liability should properly be shown as current assets.

Funds for the payment of long-term indebtedness should be shown in the balance sheet as a noncurrent account.

It has been suggested that a fund established for plant expansion should be shown under the Property, Plant, and Equipment caption. This seems unsound, because the fund is not being used as a plant asset, and its inclusion under that caption would distort any ratios involving long-lived assets. Moreover, funds set aside by the management for plant expansion can be diverted by the management to other purposes.

Companies are sometimes required to deposit funds for the payment of current interest on long-term indebtedness and taxes on the mortgaged property, as well as for the repayment of the principal of the indebtedness. In such instances, it seems advisable to divide the fund into two parts for balance sheet presentation, the funds available for current purposes being shown under the Current Assets caption and the remainder being shown under a special noncurrent caption.

Accounting for funds. The accounting entries required in the operation of funds are usually not complicated. Typical fund transactions may include the following:

(1) The transfer of assets to the fund.
(2) The investment of fund cash in fund securities.
(3) The collection of revenue earned by the fund. The entries for this transaction may include the amortization of premium or discount on fund securities.
(4) The payment of expenses incurred in the operation of the fund.
(5) The application of the fund to its intended purpose.

Entries for these transactions are illustrated in the appendix to this chapter.

The discussion in prior chapters with respect to the valuation of stocks and bonds held as investments applies equally to securities held in special funds. If a fund is established for the payment of a current liability or for other current expenditures, the principles governing the valuation of temporary investments apply. If securities in a fund are to be held for a considerable period of time, the principles applicable to long-term investments should govern their valuation in the accounts.

Funds for the payment of existing liabilities. Funds may be created for the payment of current liabilities. For example, such funds may be accumulated to meet bond interest requirements.

Funds for the payment of long-term liabilities are more common. Funds for the retirement of long-term liabilities may be classified as follows:

(1) Sinking funds. A sinking fund, strictly defined, consists of assets set aside, together with the accumulated earnings thereon, for the payment of an existing liability at its maturity.

(2) Redemption funds. A redemption fund consists of assets set aside for the piecemeal retirement of obligations. The resources of the fund may be applied to meet serially maturing obligations or to purchase outstanding obligations of the company.

The distinction between sinking funds and redemption funds is interesting as a matter of precision in terminology. However, usage modifies meanings, and business usage seems to have sanctioned the extension of the term *sinking fund* to include funds used in the periodic retirement of bonds and other obligations, and funds for the retirement of capital stock.

Sinking funds are usually administered by a trustee. Sometimes the company itself retains custody and control of the fund, but this plan is seldom entirely satisfactory to the creditors for whose protection the fund is being accumulated.

Sinking fund contributions. The amount of the periodic contribution to the sinking fund is usually stipulated in the trust indenture. The following requirements are typical:

(1) A certain number of cents per unit of output. This method of computing the periodic contributions is often required by the trust indenture when the bonds are secured by a mortgage on wasting assets such as mines and timberlands; the contributions are based on the number of tons mined or of thousand feet of timber cut. Thus, the sinking fund increases as the physical security backing the mortgage decreases. But because operations may not be carried on with sufficient rapidity to provide an adequate fund at the maturity of the bonds, a minimum annual contribution may be required.

(2) A percentage of the annual earnings. This method is frequently used in connection with so-called sinking funds for the retirement of preferred stock. From the standpoint of bondholders, it is not satisfactory to make the provision for the repayment of the bonds conditional upon the uncertain earnings of the business, although in the long run it might be advisable to allow the debtor corporation to make small contributions in poor years with offsetting large contributions in good years; otherwise, the drain upon the working capital when uniform contributions are required even in poor years may handicap the com-

pany in its operations and make it impossible for the company to meet its future contribution requirements.

(3) An equal annual amount computed by dividing the total required fund by the number of years of the life of the bonds. For instance, if a fund of $20,000 is to be provided in ten years, the annual addition to the fund will be $2,000. The first year, the contribution out of general cash will be $2,000, but the interest earned on the fund will reduce the subsequent contributions from the general cash.

(4) An equal annual contribution computed on an actuarial basis. The method of computing the periodic contributions required to produce a fund of a given amount is explained in the authors' *Principles of Accounting: Advanced,* 6th edition.

Theoretical accumulation. Often a company will prepare a schedule showing a theoretical accumulation of its sinking fund. Such a schedule is presented below for a sinking fund to be created by deposits computed on an actuarial basis and intended to accumulate to $20,000 in a ten-year period. It is assumed that all deposits in the fund can be invested in securities on the dates of the deposits, that 5 percent interest will be earned on all investments from the dates of their acquisition to the date of their disposal at the end of the fund period, and that no gains or losses will be realized when the securities are converted into cash.

Schedule of Accumulation

End of Year	Debit Fund	Credit Cash	Credit Income	Total Fund
1	$ 1,590.09	$ 1,590.09		$ 1,590.09*
2	1,669.59	1,590.09	$ 79.50	3,259.68
3	1,753.07	1,590.09	162.98	5,012.75
4	1,840.73	1,590.09	250.64	6,853.48
5	1,932.76	1,590.09	342.67	8,786.24
6	2,029.40	1,590.09	439.31	10,815.64
7	2,130.87	1,590.09	540.78	12,946.51
8	2,237.42	1,590.09	647.33	15,183.93
9	2,349.29	1,590.09	759.20	17,533.22
10	2,466.75	1,590.09	876.66	19,999.97
	$19,999.97	$15,900.90	$4,099.07	

$$*S = s_{\overline{n}|i} \cdot R$$
$$R = S/s_{\overline{n}|i}$$
$$= \$20,000/s_{\overline{10}|.05} = \$20,000/12.57789$$
$$= \$1,590.09$$

Actual accumulation. Actually, a sinking fund planned as above will not accumulate with any such mathematical exactness. Conditions in the securities markets may delay the prompt investment of sinking fund cash. The fund assets may earn more or less than the expected interest rate. Gains may be realized or losses incurred when the securities in the fund are converted into cash at the end of the fund period. For all these reasons, the actual accumulation of the fund cannot be expected to conform with the theoretical accumulation.

If the sinking fund is required by contract, the contract may call for supplemental contributions whenever the fund is below its scheduled level. If the sinking fund is a voluntary one, the management of the company may make supplemental contributions at its discretion.

Investment in company's own bonds. Investments for the sinking fund may be made in the securities of other companies or in the very bonds the fund is intended to retire. If the sinking fund trustee or manager can obtain the company's own bonds at favorable prices, it is advisable to do so if the company is in a strong financial condition, because the risk associated with an investment in outside securities is thereby eliminated. If the company is not in good financial condition, there is some question regarding the propriety of acquiring the company's own bonds for the fund, because such a transaction may be regarded as giving preference to the bondholders whose bonds are acquired.

The Accounting Principles Board has taken the position that the acquisition of the firm's own bonds by the use of sinking fund assets is an early extinguishment of debt. The difference between the price paid to acquire the bonds and the net amount at which they are carried on the firm's books (face amount plus unamortized premium or minus unamortized discount) is a gain or loss to be recognized in the period in which the bonds are acquired by the sinking fund.[19]

Sinking funds for principal and interest. Companies are sometimes required to place with a sinking fund trustee monthly deposits for the payment of the semiannual interest as well as the principal of the bonds. In such instances, it should be remembered that making a deposit with a trustee does not constitute payment of the interest any more than it constitutes payment of the principal. The total funds on deposit with the trustee should be shown on the asset side of the balance sheet, and the liability for accrued unpaid interest as well as for principal should be shown on the liability side of the balance sheet. The liability for principal and interest cannot be eliminated from the balance sheet until the trustee has applied the funds to the payment of the liability.

Dividend restrictions. Indentures executed in connection with long-term debt obligations frequently place a restriction on the payment of dividends while the obligation is outstanding. At one time, it was common practice for the restriction to take the form of a requirement that the company make periodic transfers from Retained Earnings to a separate account representing an appropriation of retained earnings. A proper title for the appropriation account is Retained Earnings Appropriated for Bond Retirement. Such restrictions are now more commonly

---

[19]Accounting Principles Board, "Early Extinguishment of Debt," *Opinion No. 26* (New York: AICPA, October 1972), p. 502. The board stated in *Opinion No. 26* that the criteria in its *Opinion No. 9,* "Reporting the Results of Operations," should be used to determine whether the loss or gain on early extinguishment of debt should be reported as an extraordinary item. See Chapter 4 for additional discussion of *Opinion No. 9.*

disclosed by parenthetical comments in the balance sheet or by a balance sheet footnote.

Funds for payment of contingent liabilities. Funds for the payment of contingent liabilities are rarely encountered. A deposit by a contractor to guarantee the performance of work in accordance with specifications is an illustration of an obligatory fund for the payment of a contingent liability. A fund for the payment of damages that may result from an adverse decision of a pending patent-infringement suit is an illustration of a voluntary fund created for the payment of a contingent liability.

Funds for payment for an asset or a service. Sometimes the directors of a corporation adopt the policy of establishing a fund for the acquisition of plant assets. A building fund, machinery fund, or similar fund account may then be put on the books.

Funds for the payment of services may be compulsory or voluntary. They are compulsory if the establishment of the fund is based on a contract with outsiders. For example, leases frequently contain clauses requiring the immediate deposit of cash to be applied in payment of rent for subsequent (often the last) years of the lease. Cemeteries frequently sell lots under agreements that a certain portion of the sale price shall be deposited with a trustee as a fund to provide perpetual care.

Funds for future expenditures chargeable to expense accounts may be created voluntarily, by authorization of the management. A fund for research is an example.

It is important that the operation of a fund of the type mentioned here not be confused with the proper measurement of revenue and expense. Assume that a cemetery sells lots under an agreement that $50 shall be set aside from the proceeds of the sale of each lot until a fund of $90,000 is accumulated; and that, when all the lots are sold, the fund shall be turned over to a trustee and the revenue used to provide perpetual care of the cemetery. Assume that the cemetery contains 3,000 lots having a uniform selling price. The fund should be provided from the sale of the first 1,800 lots, because $50 × 1,800 = $90,000. But each of the 3,000 lots should bear its share of the cost of perpetual care; therefore, the charge to expense should be made at the rate of $90,000 ÷ 3,000, or $30 per lot. As each of the first 1,800 lots is sold, entries should be made as follows:

Perpetual care fund	50	
Cash		50
To record the required contribution to the fund.		
Perpetual care expense	30	
Perpetual care liability		30
To charge operations with the pro rata cost of perpetual care of lot sold.		

After 1,800 lots have been sold, the fund should be $90,000 and the liability should be $54,000. No further contributions to the fund need be made, but the $30 expense entry will have to be made when each of the remaining 1,200 lots is sold. When all the lots have been sold, there will be a $90,000 fund and a $90,000 liability; the fund will have been accumulated in accordance with the contract, and the liability will have been credited in accordance with the expense accrual.

Stock-redemption funds. The redemption-fund method has long been used for the retirement of bonds, and is also used for retiring preferred stock. The provisions of the stock issue may require that a definite amount of stock shall be retired annually, but it is doubtful whether this requirement could be enforced against the corporation if earnings were inadequate and creditors' rights were jeopardized. More frequently, the amount of stock to be retired annually is based upon the amount of the net income of the preceding year; it may be a fixed percentage of the net income, or it may be determined by a sliding scale of rates.

Fund arrearages and deposit requirements. If fund deposits required by contract are in arrears, the balance sheet should disclose this fact. It should also disclose the amount, if material, of any deposits required to be made soon after the balance sheet date and therefore constituting a demand upon the current assets. Footnotes are probably the best device for making such disclosures. Such footnotes might be somewhat as follows: "On (the balance sheet date) the company was in arrears as to sinking fund deposits in the amount of $10,000"; or, "The company is obligated to make a deposit of $15,000 on (a date subsequent to the balance sheet date) to a fund for the retirement of its preferred stock."

CASH SURRENDER VALUE OF LIFE INSURANCE

Life insurance as an investment. It has long been recognized that a business firm has several good reasons for insuring the lives of its owners and certain key employees. Some of the more important reasons are listed below.

(1) To provide funds for the purchase of the shares of a deceased stockholder in a close corporation, and thus keep the stock under the control of interested parties.

(2) To provide funds for the payment of the capital interest of a deceased partner, without placing an undue strain on the working capital.

(3) To compensate for the loss which might result from the death of an important member of the organization.

In order for the business to be named as the beneficiary it must have an insurable interest in the life of the person insured. An insurable interest exists if the business has a reasonable ground for expecting some financial benefit or advantage from the continued life of the insured.

There are basically two elements in the type of insurance normally purchased by firms on the lives of employees, commonly referred to as "ordinary" life policies. One of these, obviously, is the insurance protection obtained. The other is a form of investment evidenced by an increasing *cash surrender value* of the policy as it remains in force. The cash surrender value is the amount which the insurance company will pay to the insured upon surrender and cancellation of the policy. Since the insuring company incurs certain costs associated with the writing of a policy, there may be no cash surrender value during the first two or three years the policy is in force.

In addition to the cash surrender value, ordinary life insurance policies also have a *loan value*.

The *loan value* is the amount which the insurance company will loan on a policy maintained in force. The loan value at any date is equal to the cash surrender value at the end of the policy year, minus discount thereon for the period of time from the loan date to the end of the policy year. If a policy has a cash surrender value at the end of the third year, it has a loan value at the beginning of the third year, after the payment of the third year's premium. The following table shows assumed cash surrender values on a $50,000 ordinary life policy. Values are given here for only the earlier years of the policy. The loan values at the beginning of each year were computed by discounting the end-of-year cash value at 6 percent; that is, the cash value which will be available one year after making the premium payment was divided by 1.06 to determine the loan value at the beginning of the policy year.

Year	Cash Surrender Value at End of Year	Loan Value at Beginning of Year
1	—	—
2	—	—
3	$1,590.50	$1,500.47
4	2,151.00	2,029.25
5	2,908.00	2,743.40
6	3,647.00	3,440.57

Accounting for the cash surrender value of life insurance. The accounting relative to the carrying of life insurance policies requires recognition of both the expense and investment elements. The net premium paid to the insurance company less the increase in the cash surrender value during the year is the net insurance expense for the year.

Premiums paid may be charged to Insurance Expense or Unexpired Insurance. If the policy is carried with a mutual insurance company, the gross premium will likely be reduced by a dividend declared by the insuror. Any such dividends should be treated as a reduction in the amount of the premium for the period. In practice, theoretical considerations are often secondary to the practicalities involved in accounting for life insurance premiums.

In order to illustrate the accounting for an ordinary life insurance policy, the amounts presented in the schedule above will be used. It is further assumed that the annual premium of $1,405.50 is due on October 1 and that the firm closes its books annually on September 30.

Although the policy has no cash surrender value until the end of the third year, the premium payments for each of the first three years obviously must be made in order to provide a cash surrender value of $1,590.50 at the end of three years. In the absence of additional information, the total increase in the cash surrender value during the first three years can be allocated equally to each year. As a matter of convenience, this can be done at the beginning of each year at the time the annual premium payment is recorded. Entries for years 1, 2, and 3 would be as shown at the top of the following page.

	Year 1		Year 2		Year 3	
Life insurance expense	875.33		875.33		875.34	
Cash surrender value of life insurance	530.17		530.17		530.16	
Cash		1,405.50		1,405.50		1,405.50

The amount charged to Life Insurance Expense each year is the difference between the premium payment and the portion of the increase in cash surrender value recognized.

For year 4 and each succeeding year, the debit to Cash Surrender Value of Life Insurance can be determined from the schedule appearing on page 367. For year 4, the amount of the increase is \$560.50 (\$2,151.00 – \$1,590.50). This is recorded at the beginning of the year at the time the annual premium is paid. The entry would be as follows:

Life insurance expense	845.00	
Cash surrender value of life insurance	560.50	
Cash		1,405.50

It has been assumed in the preceding discussion that the cash surrender value was recorded at the beginning of the year at the time the premium payments were made. As an alternative, the premium payment could be recorded by debiting the entire amount to the life insurance expense account. An entry could then be recorded at the end of the year to recognize the increase in cash surrender value applicable to each year. If the company followed the alternative of debiting premium payments to the unexpired insurance account, it would be necessary to record an adjusting entry at the end of the accounting period to transfer the premium to the expense account. This procedure may be preferable when the period covered by the premium does not correspond with the firm's accounting period.

Collection of the proceeds of a life insurance policy requires that the cash surrender value be removed from the books. It is also necessary to recognize as a gain the excess of the proceeds received over the cash surrender value. To illustrate, assume that the policy used in the previous illustration becomes payable at the end of the fifth year due to the death of the insured. It is assumed that the increase in the cash surrender value for the fifth year has already been recorded. The following entry records the cancellation of the policy.

Receivable from insurance company (face amount of the policy)	50,000.00	
Cash surrender value of life insurance (amount accumulated per schedule)		2,908.00
Gain on settlement of life insurance policy (\$50,000.00 – \$2,908.00)		47,092.00

The gain would be reported as a separate item on the firm's income statement. If the death of the insured does not coincide with the end of the policy year, the premium paid for the year will normally be pro-rated and the unused portion refunded. This would have the effect of increasing the amount of the receivable in the entry above and would result in a corresponding credit to the account debited for the premium payments.

The cash surrender value of life insurance is normally reported as a part of the investments of a firm. This is in keeping with the nature of the policy, which is purchased with the intention of holding it until the death of the insured, or at least so long as the insured remains with the firm.

Income tax laws do not allow a firm to deduct as an expense those premiums paid for insurance policies on employees when the company is the beneficiary. Should the policy be surrendered prior to the death of the insured, the amount received is taxable only to the extent that it is greater than the premium payments made. The proceeds of a policy paid upon the death of the insured are exempt from income taxes.

APPENDIX
ACCOUNTING FOR SINKING FUNDS

Sinking fund entries. The operations of a sinking fund consist of making contributions to the fund, investing in securities, collecting revenue, paying expenses, disposing of fund securities, and using the cash fund for its intended purpose, such as the retirement of bonded indebtedness. Entries for these transactions, assuming that the fund is being accumulated to pay off bonded indebtedness, are illustrated below:

Contributions of cash:		
Sinking fund cash	xx,xxx.xx	
Cash		xx,xxx.xx
Purchase of securities:		
Sinking fund securities—A B bonds ..	xx,xxx.xx	
Sinking fund cash		xx,xxx.xx
(Entry if securities are purchased at par and without accrued interest. Purchases at a premium or discount and purchases with accrued interest are considered later.)		

Collection of income:		
Sinking fund cash	xxx.xx	
Sinking fund revenue		xxx.xx
(Entry for revenue on securities purchased at par.)		
Payment of expenses:		
Sinking fund expense	xxx.xx	
Sinking fund cash		xxx.xx
(Entry if expenses are paid from fund cash.)		
Sinking fund expense	xxx.xx	
Cash		xxx.xx
(Entry if expenses are paid from general cash.)		
Disposal of sinking fund securities:		
Sinking fund cash	xx,xxx.xx	
Sinking fund securities		xx,xxx.xx
(Entry if securities are sold at carrying value.)		
Sinking fund cash	xx,xxx.xx	
Loss on sinking fund securities.......	xxx.xx	
Sinking fund securities		xx,xxx.xx
(Entry if securities are sold at a loss.)		
Sinking fund cash	xx,xxx.xx	
Gain on sinking fund securities.		xxx.xx
Sinking fund securities		xx,xxx.xx
(Entry if securities are sold at a gain.)		
Cancellation of bonds at maturity:		
Sinking fund cash	x,xxx.xx	
Cash		x,xxx.xx
(Entry if sinking fund cash after disposal of securities is inadequate for retirement of bonds.)		
Bonds payable	xxx,xxx.xx	
Sinking fund cash		xxx,xxx.xx
(Entry for retirement of bonds.)		
Cash	x,xxx.xx	
Sinking fund cash		x,xxx.xx
(Entry if any residue remains in the fund and is returned to general cash.)		

The sinking fund revenue and sinking fund expense accounts should be closed at the end of each period to Retained Earnings.

Purchases between interest dates. If securities are purchased for the sinking fund at par plus accrued interest, the following entry is required:

Sinking fund securities	xx,xxx.xx	
Interest on sinking fund securities	xxx.xx	
Sinking fund cash		xx,xxx.xx
(Entry for purchase of sinking fund securities between interest dates.)		

At the date of the first collection of interest, the following entry is made:

Sinking fund cash	xxx.xx	
Interest on sinking fund securities .		xxx.xx
Sinking fund revenue		xx.xx
(Entry for first interest collection when securities were purchased between interest dates.)		

Amortization of premium or discount. If bonds are purchased for the sinking fund at a premium or a discount, the sinking fund securities account should be charged with their cost. Entries for the collection of interest and amortization of premium or discount will be as follows:

Sinking fund cash	x,xxx.xx	
Sinking fund securities............		xx.xx
Sinking fund revenue		x,xxx.xx
(Entry for semiannual interest collection on sinking fund securities purchased at a premium.)		
Sinking fund cash	x,xxx.xx	
Sinking fund securities..................	xx.xx	
Sinking fund revenue		x,xxx.xx
(Entry for semiannual interest collection on sinking fund securities purchased at a discount.)		

Cash and accrual basis. If the interest dates on securities purchased for the sinking fund do not coincide with the dates of closing the company's books, adjusting entries may be made for accrued interest. For instance, assuming that interest at 5 percent on $150,000 of bonds in the fund is due on October 31 and April 30, and that the books are closed on December 31, entries could be made as illustrated below:

December 31:		
Interest receivable—Sinking fund securities	1,250	
Sinking fund revenue		1,250
(Entry for accrual of interest at closing date.)		
April 30:		
Sinking fund cash	3,750	
Interest receivable—Sinking fund securities................................		1,250
Sinking fund revenue		2,500
(Entry for collection of interest.)		

Fund with trustee. If the sinking fund is placed in the hands of a trustee, the company's records generally will not show the individual transactions relating to the purchase and sale of securities and to the earnings and expenses of the fund. The records will show the deposits made with the trustee and summary entries for the revenues and expenses as reported periodically by the trustee.

15

Long-Lived Assets: Acquisitions and Disposals

Introduction. Such long-lived assets as property, plant, and equipment, often referred to as fixed assets, normally have the following characteristics:

(1) They are relatively permanent in nature.
(2) They are used in the operation of the business.
(3) They are not intended for sale.

A building used as a factory is an example of property, plant, and equipment; it has all three of the characteristics listed above. Land held as a prospective site for a future plant, however, is classified as a long-term investment, not as property, plant, and equipment. Although it is permanent in nature and is not intended for sale, it is not used in the operation of the business. A factory building no longer used in operations is not classified as property, plant, and equipment because it is not used in the operation of the business. Instead, it should be reported on the balance sheet under Other Assets.

Classification of long-lived assets. Long-lived assets may be classified into two major groups, according to the nature of the asset. *Tangible* long-lived assets are those that have bodily substance. *Intangible* long-lived assets are those that have no bodily substance, but have future economic benefits because of the rights they afford the possessor.

Tangible long-lived assets include land, buildings, machinery, tools, patterns, delivery equipment, furniture and fixtures, and other similar property having physical substance. Intangible long-lived assets include goodwill, patents, copyrights, trademarks, franchises, and other similar assets having no bodily substance but having future benefits because of the rights inherent in them.

Long-lived assets may be further classified as follows:

(1) Tangible:
  - (a) Property, plant, and equipment
    - (i) Subject to depreciation
      Examples: Buildings, machinery, tools and equipment, delivery equipment, furniture and fixtures
    - (ii) Not subject to depreciation
      Example: Land
  - (b) Natural resources, subject to depletion
    Examples: Timber tracts, mines, oil wells

(2) Intangible:
  Examples: Patents, copyrights, franchises, leasehold improvements, goodwill, trademarks

This is the first of four chapters dealing with matters related to long-lived assets. In this chapter, we shall be concerned primarily with matters related to the acquisition and disposal of tangible long-lived assets. Chapter 16 discusses the depreciation and depletion of long-lived assets; Chapter 17 covers revaluations of such assets; and Chapter 18 deals with the subject of intangible assets.

Valuation of long-lived assets. Long-lived assets are usually reported in the accounts at one of the following bases of valuation:

(1) Cost
(2) Cost less depreciation, depletion, or amortization

At one time, it was a fairly common practice for companies to write up the amounts at which long-lived assets were reported in such a way as to reflect higher current prices. This was normally done by having the asset appraised and using the appraisal as the basis of the write-up. Such a practice is not considered acceptable accounting at the present time, although some accountants feel that a departure from cost may be necessary for more accurate reflection of current prices of assets in a firm's balance sheet. Departures from the cost basis will be discussed in Chapter 17.

Cost of long-lived assets. It is obvious that the first problem encountered in the accounting for long-lived assets is the determination of cost. Cost is defined as the cash or its equivalent given up to acquire the asset and get it to the place and into the condition for which it was purchased. Thus, the total cost may include several items other than the invoice price of the asset.

Since the cost of an asset is determined normally in a bargained transaction between a buyer and a seller, it is considered to be the best measure of the firm's investment in the future services embodied in the asset.

The initial cost of a long-lived asset is said to be capitalized, or to represent a capital expenditure, since it is charged to the asset account rather than to an expense account in the period of acquisition. Expenditures are capitalized if they benefit one or more future accounting periods; hence, they are incurred to produce income in one or more future periods. On the other hand, expenditures associated with long-lived assets that do not benefit future accounting periods are expensed during the current period (so-called revenue expenditures), because they are incurred to obtain only the current period's income.

The distinction between capitalizing and expensing an outlay is important in the determination of periodic net income, because the former will be charged against income in future periods as a result of periodic depreciation. Thus, the effect of treating the entire cost of a long-lived asset as an expense of the current period would be to understate net income in the period of acquisition, and overstate net income in the future periods benefited by the use of the asset. As a practical matter, many firms distinguish between capital and revenue expenditures by selecting some arbitrary amount as the dividing line between the two types. For example, any expenditure of less than $50 may be charged to expense even though one or more future periods may benefit from it (doctrine of materiality).

Determination of acquisition cost. A definition of cost does not completely answer the question of just what is involved in measuring the cost of a long-lived asset. It was stated in the definition on page 374 that assets may be acquired for cash *or its equivalent*. Thus, in certain instances, it may be necessary to make adjustments to the cash price; or perhaps the transaction does not involve the payment of any cash. Starting with the situation that involves the outright purchase for cash, we will now consider the various means whereby long-lived assets may be acquired.

Acquisition for cash. If long-lived assets are purchased for cash, the problem of determining the cost is relatively simple, because no question arises concerning the valuation of what is parted with in exchange for the asset. Cost includes the purchase price and all incidental payments, such as freight, installation charges, and other items to be discussed in detail in the sections of this chapter devoted to specific assets.

CASH DISCOUNTS: It was noted in the discussion of inventories in Chapter 11 that cash discounts represent reductions in the cost of the inventory, even though they are not always treated as such in practice. Regardless of what treatment is accorded cash discounts on merchandise acquisitions, any cash discount related to the acquisition of a long-lived asset should be recorded as a cost reduction. For example, if an item of equipment is purchased for an invoice price of $10,000, subject to a 2 percent discount for payment within 15 days, it is possible to acquire the asset for a net cost of $9,800 [$10,000 – ($10,000 × .02)]. Should the buyer elect not to pay within the discount period, the additional $200 he pays should not be treated as a part of the cost of the equipment, but should be accounted for as discounts lost, and reported as a separate item of financial expense.

ACQUISITION FOR A LUMP SUM: If several assets are acquired in one purchase at a lump-sum price, it is necessary to apportion the cost to the various assets in order to show costs not subject to depreciation, or subject to depreciation at various rates. The apportionment of cost can be made on the basis of an appraisal by outside appraisers or by company officials. For instance, if land, buildings, and machinery are acquired at a cost of $120,000, and if they are appraised at $15,000, $60,000, and $75,000, respectively, the cost can be apportioned in the ratio of the appraisal of each class of assets to the total appraisal. The computation is shown below:

	Appraisal		Apportioned	
Assets	Amount	Percent	Cost	
Land	$ 15,000	10%	$ 12,000	($120,000 × .10)
Buildings	60,000	40	48,000	
Machinery	75,000	50	60,000	
Total	$150,000	100%	$120,000	

Acquisition on credit terms. Long-lived assets may be acquired under various deferred payment arrangements. If the asset is offered at a cash price and at a higher credit price, and is purchased at the credit price, the cash price should be recorded as the cost of the asset, with the difference being recorded as interest expense. For example, assume that an asset can be purchased for a cash price of $1,000, or by signing a one-year, 6 percent note payable. The acquisition should be recorded as follows:

Equipment	1,000	
Notes payable		1,000

When the note is paid, the additional amount paid ($60) should be charged to interest expense.

An alternative arrangement might be an installment contract requiring the payment of equal installments over a period of time. For example, an item of equipment is purchased under a contract that calls for five annual installments of $1,187 and an annual interest rate of 6 percent. The total amount paid is $5,935 ($1,187 × 5), but a portion of this is obviously the interest paid for deferring payment. The cost of the asset is the present value (discounted amount) of the five payments discounted at a rate of 6 percent. This is calculated as follows:

Present value of an annuity of $1 for five periods at 6 percent =	$4.2123[1]	
Present value of an annuity of $1,187 for five periods at 6 percent =	$5,000	($4.2123 × $1,187)

The following entry would be necessary to record the acquisition of the asset:

[1]See table in Appendix.

Equipment	5,000	
Installment notes payable		5,000

At the end of the first year, the payment of $1,187 would be recorded as follows:

Interest expense ($5,000 × .06)	300	
Installment notes payable	887	
Cash		1,187

The interest element included in the second annual payment is determined by applying the applicable rate (6 percent) to the amount of the liability at the beginning of the year. The entry to record the second payment is shown below:

Interest expense [($5,000 − $887) × .06)]	247	
Installment notes payable	940	
Cash		1,187

The same procedure would be followed for all subsequent payments on the contract.

In some instances, the deferred payment arrangement may not specify the rate of interest to be charged. However, if the total contract price is in excess of the cash price of the asset, the excess represents the charge for deferring payments and should be recorded as interest expense, not as a part of the cost of the asset. This difference can be easily determined if a cash price is quoted. Even when no cash price is quoted, a deferred payment arrangement is normally assumed to include some charge for financing. The Accounting Principles Board has issued an Opinion stating what the accounting treatment should be under these circumstances, as well as those instances in which the terms of the note do not appear to be in line with current economic realities. The board has stated:

> When a note is exchanged for property, goods, or service in a bargained transaction entered into at arm's length, there should be a general presumption that the rate of interest stipulated by the parties to the transaction represents fair and adequate compensation to the supplier for the form of the transaction to prevail over its economic substance and thus would not apply if (1) interest is not stated, or (2) the stated interest rate is unreasonable, or (3) the stated face amount of the note is materially different from the current cash sales price for the same or similar items or from the market value of the note at the date of the transaction. In these circumstances, the note, the sales price, and the cost of the property, goods, or service exchanged for the note should be recorded at the fair value of the property, goods, or service or at an amount that reasonably approximates the market value of the note, whichever is the more clearly determinable. That amount may or may not be the same as its face amount, and any resulting discount or premium should be accounted for as an element of interest over the life of the note.[2]

[2] Accounting Principles Board, "Interest on Receivables and Payables," *Opinion No. 21* (New York: AICPA, August 1971), p. 421.

The board went on to state that the present value of such a note "should be determined by discounting all future payments on the notes using an imputed rate of interest."[3] Since there is no specific interest rate that could applied in all circumstances, the board set forth some general guidelines to be used. These are summarized as follows:

(1) Credit standing of the issuer
(2) Restrictive covenants in the credit instrument
(3) Collateral, payment, and other terms pertaining to the debt
(4) Prevailing rates for similar instruments of issuers with similar credit ratings
(5) The rate at which the debtor can obtain financing of a similar nature from other sources at the date of the transaction
(6) The prevailing market rates for the source of credit that would provide a market for sale or assignment of the note
(7) The prime or higher rate for notes that are discounted with banks, giving due weight to the credit standing of the maker
(8) Published market rates for similar quality instruments (in the case of bonds)
(9) Current rates for instruments with substantially identical terms and risks that are traded in open markets (in the case of bonds)
(10) The current rate charged by investors for first- or second-mortgage loans on similar property.[4]

In amortizing any discount or premium resulting from the procedures used to determine the present value of the debt instruments, the method is the same as that previously illustrated in this chapter. A constant rate should be applied to the amount of the debt outstanding at the beginning of each period.

CONDITIONAL SALES CONTRACTS: A conditional sales contract is an arrangement whereby the seller of property retains legal title until all payments called for under the contract are completed. In the event that the buyer does not make payments as required by the contract, the seller may repossess the property in order to satisfy the unpaid balance on the contract.

In accounting for asset acquisitions under this arrangement, it is normally assumed that the buyer has every intention of paying the contract in full. Therefore, the acquisition is recorded by debiting the asset account for the cost of the asset and recognizing the liability under the contract. This payment arrangement would normally include some charge for financing, whether specifically stated or not, and such charges should be recorded as interest expense, not as a part of the cost of the asset.

LEASE-PURCHASE ARRANGEMENTS: As was noted in Chapter 8, business firms frequently acquire long-lived tangible assets under a lease agreement. It is not

---

[3] *Opinion No. 21*, p. 422.
[4] *Opinion No. 21*, pp. 422–423.

uncommon for the lease agreement to provide that the lessee may acquire title to the asset at the end of the lease, usually by an additional cash payment. This may simply represent a form of deferred payment, requiring that both the asset and the lease obligation be recorded on the books of the lessee.

Acquisition by trade-in. It is a very common practice for business firms to acquire assets by trading old assets as partial payments for the assets acquired. The cost of the new asset in this case is the sum of the following amounts: (1) any cash paid, and (2) the cash price of the old asset given up. This sum represents the cash equivalent of the consideration parted with to acquire the new asset.

Trade-in allowances on old assets sometimes confuse the determination of the cost of the new asset, because such allowances may not measure the cash equivalent of the old asset. They may be intentionally overstated in order to make certain price concessions to the buyer. It is important that the new asset be recorded at the cash equivalent of the consideration given up to acquire it, and not an inflated amount resulting from an artifically high trade-in allowance. Use of the higher trade-in allowance as a part of the cost of the new asset will result in a higher original cost, and therefore higher depreciation charges over the life of the new asset.

To illustrate the proper accounting for the acquisition of a new asset involving the trade-in of an old asset, assume the following facts:

Old asset:	
Cost	$5,000
Accumulated depreciation	3,000
Net book value	2,000
Secondhand market price	1,800
Trade-in allowance	2,300
List price of new asset	6,000
Cash payment	3,700

Using the rule stated previously for determining the cost of the new asset, the following entry would record the trade:

Asset account [new asset ($1,800 + $3,700)]	5,500	
Accumulated depreciation	3,000	
Loss on trade of assets	200	
Asset account (old asset)		5,000
Cash		3,700

Although the new asset acquired had a list price of $6,000, the firm gave up cash or its equivalent of only $5,500 (cash paid plus cash equivalent of the old asset) to acquire it. The loss recognized in the entry is the difference between the amount at which the old asset is reported on the books (cost of $5,000 less accumulated depreciation of $3,000, or $2,000) and the cash equivalent of the old asset at the time it is disposed of ($1,800). The loss would be reported on the firm's income statement.

The cost basis of the new asset in the illustration above will not be the same for federal income tax purposes. The tax method of recording the exchange is discussed in a later section of this chapter.

Acquisition by issuance of securities. When a corporation acquires long-lived assets by issuing its own bonds or stock, there may be some question as to just how the cost of the assets acquired should be determined.

If some of the stock or bonds is sold to third parties for cash at approximately the same time that similar securities are issued for other property, the cash price of the securities is indicative of their worth, and long-lived assets acquired by issuance of securities may be placed on the books at the valuation thus established. This is consistent with the general rule that assets are recorded at the cash or equivalent given up to acquire them.

If there is no way to determine the cash equivalent of the securities given in exchange for the assets, the most objective measure of the cost of the assets would be an independent appraisal of the assets acquired. Thus, cost is measured by the fair market value of the asset acquired, rather than the fair market value of the consideration given up. This obviously represents an estimate of cost, but is considered to be the best possible measure under the circumstances.

Finally, if it is impossible to determine either the valuation of the consideration given up or the valuation of the asset acquired, it will be necessary for the board of directors to establish the cost to be assigned to the asset. Under these circumstances, the directors may decide to use the par or stated value of the securities issued for the assets.

The law allows the directors of a corporation a large measure of discretion in the valuation of property taken in payment for stock. Creditors may, at some later date, attack the valuation in court in an attempt to show that the stock was really issued at a discount, and that the stockholders are liable for the discount. However, this is a contingency that the company's accountant cannot anticipate by insisting upon a valuation less than that approved by the directors and setting up an account with discount on stock.

The public accountant's position is somewhat different. He would probably be considered guilty of misrepresentation if he gave an unqualified opinion regarding financial statements containing gross inflations of asset amounts. He cannot be expected to assume the responsibility of placing an acceptable valuation on the assets, but he can be expected to qualify his report.

A major point to be made from the discussion above is that the par, face, or stated value of securities issued in exchange for assets does not necessarily measure the worth of the assets acquired. There may be a premium or discount on the securities, depending upon their current market prices. Failure to follow the rules previously discussed will result in a misstatement of asset cost, in addition to the misstatement of the bonds or stock.

For example, assume that a corporation issues bonds having a face amount of \$80,000 in exchange for land. If it is determined that the bonds are currently selling at 90, the acquisition should be recorded as follows:

Land (90% of \$80,000)	72,000	
Bond discount	8,000	
Bonds payable		80,000

It was pointed out in the previous chapter that in some instances, the acquisition of assets may result in the assets acquired being recorded at the amount at which they are carried on the books of the previous owner. This occurs in a business combination that is treated as a pooling of interests.

Acquisition by construction. Firms frequently construct assets for their own use. Some of the reasons for this are to use idle plant and personnel, to save a part of the cost that would be incurred if the asset were purchased, and to obtain the asset sooner or of a better quality than if it were purchased. There are several special accounting problems encountered when assets are self-constructed.

OVERHEAD AS AN ELEMENT OF COST: There is no question but that the cost of a self-constructed asset includes the material and labor costs incurred. However, there is some difference of opinion as to the extent to which manufacturing overhead should be included as a part of the cost.

Some accountants argue that long-lived assets should be charged only with the factory overhead specifically incurred in their manufacture. This is sometimes referred to as the incremental-overhead approach. Those who support this approach maintain that the manufacture of plant and equipment cannot be carried on without incurring some overhead costs that would not otherwise be incurred. Although there are many fixed charges that would not be increased, there are variable costs that are more or less proportionate to the utilization of the factory facilities. The cost of power is one illustration. It would be improper to load the cost of finished goods with costs that were not incurred in their manufacture and that would not have been incurred if plant and equipment had not been produced.

To charge long-lived assets with part of the normal factory overhead that would be incurred even if the assets were not constructed would result in a corresponding reduction in the overhead charged to the cost of goods manufactured, and a corresponding increase in the profits on the items sold. Because this additional profit would be the result of a charge to the long-lived assets for the factory overhead capitalized, the company would be increasing its reported profits as a result of the self-construction of long-lived assets.

Some accountants argue that the assets constructed for the firm's own use should be charged with factory overhead on the same basis and at the same rate that is charged to goods manufactured for sale. Thus, no special cost exemptions are granted, and this treatment avoids undercosting the long-lived assets to be used by the firm. This procedure would be followed even when the cost of goods manufactured for sale will be relieved of a portion of the overhead costs that would otherwise be charged.

The degree to which plant capacity is being utilized may determine the ultimate treatment of manufacturing overhead as it is related to self-construction of assets. If the construction utilizes what would otherwise be idle capacity, a very good case can be made for charging the asset with a portion of all overhead costs.

The authors are of the opinion that variable manufacturing overhead should be charged to assets constructed for the firm's own use. However, it is doubtful that this method is the most widely used in practice.

THE CONSTRUCTION-PERIOD CONCEPT: The accounting principle that sanctions the capitalization of all expenditures during the construction period applies particularly to buildings. It was at first regarded as applying to a building constructed before the company commenced operations, and it was defended on two grounds: First, if a company was engaged only in the construction of a plant, all its expenditures (even those that, during operations, would be regarded as administrative expenses) were incurred for the purpose of construction and hence were properly capitalizable; second, a company should not be required to begin operations with a deficit. The concept is now regarded as also applying to plant additions made while operations are in progress; however, it is not intended that this should result in any favoritism to regular operations.

A period sometimes elapses between the completion of a plant and its occupancy or other utilization as an income-producing asset of the business, and management sometimes desires to capitalize expenses during that period. If operations are being conducted elsewhere, there seems little justification for such a capitalization. If operations have not been commenced, the situation may be somewhat different, and it is sometimes regarded as permissible to capitalize, after completion of construction, some expenditures that would normally be charged to income. For instance, if occupancy of a factory building is necessarily postponed for some time after its completion, capitalizing the carrying charges until the date of occupancy may be sanctioned. However, the construction-period concept should not be abused by capitalizing carrying charges over a long interim period. A long waiting period should probably be recognized as an indication that executive planning was poor, that the building has proved to be a losing venture, and that losses should be taken into the accounts. Even if interim-period costs appear to be properly capitalizable, it is probably preferable to record them as deferred charges instead of including them in long-lived asset costs.

Although a building or other long-lived asset may deteriorate to some extent during the construction period, it is customary to ignore such depreciation in the accounts, and to spread the depreciation charges over the period of utilization. There would certainly be no object in making a charge for depreciation during the construction period and recapitalizing such charges by adding them back to the cost of the asset as a construction-period cost.

INTEREST DURING CONSTRUCTION: Utility commissions permit utility companies to charge the long-lived asset accounts with interest costs incurred during the construction period, regardless of whether the construction is done by the company itself or by a contractor. In addition to interest on funds borrowed to finance the new asset, regulatory commissions often approve the capitalization of an interest allowance for the utility's own funds devoted to the construction activity. When permitted, such implicit interest is debited to the asset being constructed, and credited to a special revenue account. Capitalization of interest is permitted because no revenue is earned by the asset during construction to cover the cost of capital. Because the interest cannot be recovered before the asset is put to use, the utility is permitted to recover it by including it in the investment on which it is permitted to take depreciation and on which its allowed earnings are based.

Although no similar reason exists for allowing nonregulated companies to capitalize interest incurred during the construction period, the sanction of utility commissions has been carried over to such companies without a consideration of the difference in conditions. However, there is this difference: Regulated companies have been permitted to capitalize implicit interest (computed on the company's own funds used in construction) as well as interest actually paid; the capitalization of implicit interest by nonregulated companies has not been sanctioned.

Interest paid, by any kind of business, is not a necessary cost of construction. Interest could be avoided by the issuance of additional capital stock. Utilities are permitted to capitalize interest in order that rate-fixing bodies will give it proper consideration in determining future rates and earnings; nonregulated businesses do not need to capitalize interest for any such reason, because they are permitted to earn what they can.

Considering interest on indebtedness, incurred by a nonregulated business to obtain funds for construction, as a part of the cost of tangible assets has little justification in theory. Some attempt has been made to justify it under the concept that all costs during the construction period can be capitalized; but interest is a money cost, not a construction cost, and it can be avoided by an additional investment of equity capital. However, the practice is now so well established that it is rarely challenged.

The issue concerning the propriety of capitalizing interest in the case of nonregulated companies generally arises during the "startup" period, when the new business has construction activity but little, if any, revenue. During such a period, capitalization has some theoretical appeal because it can lead to a better matching of revenue and expense. The authors are of the opinion that if any interest is capitalized, the accountant should capitalize both implicit and explicit interest. However, assuming that justification is found to support the capitalization of interest during an organizational period, it would be better if the amount were charged to an intangible asset rather than to a tangible asset as part of its cost.

LOSS OR GAIN ON CONSTRUCTION: There may be some instances in which the full costs of construction of an asset should not be capitalized. For example, if a firm undertakes the construction of an asset that it could purchase for $50,000, and the total construction costs are in excess of this amount, it is normally the actual cost and not the alternative purchase price that represents the amount to be capitalized. However, if the total construction cost of the asset should turn out to be materially in excess of the cost anticipated, it is proper to charge the excess cost as a loss in the period of construction.

If, on the other hand, the asset that could be purchased for $50,000 is constructed for $45,000, no gain on construction is recognized. Although it is inconsistent with the treatment of a loss, it is argued that the difference of $5,000 is a saving that will be recognized over the life of the asset in lower depreciation charges.

Acquisition by donation and discovery. Corporations sometimes receive gifts of long-lived assets, either from their stockholders or from cities that attract industries by providing them with plants or with sites for plants. It has long been established practice to record such assets at their fair market value, which may have to be determined by an appraisal. It has been argued that such accounting is a departure from the cost basis. However, because the purpose of accounting is to reflect accountability, it would seem proper for management to report some amount for all assets for which it is accountable. The fair market value of property acquired by gift properly measures the accountability for the asset.

Gifts of assets may be unconditional or conditional. If they are unconditional, the recipient obtains immediate title to them, and the gift should be recorded by debiting the asset account for an appropriate amount and crediting an account titled Donated Capital. For example, if land appraised for $35,000 is contributed to a firm, the following entry records the acquisition:

Land	35,000	
Donated capital—Acquisition of land		35,000

Gifts of long-lived assets from a city are frequently subject to some condition, such as continued operations over a stated period of time, or the employment of a certain minimum number of employees for a specified number of years. To illustrate, assume that a business is given factory land and buildings on condition that it employ at least 100 employees each year for five years. Any entries made to record the contingent gift should clearly indicate that title has not been obtained and that no addition to the owners' equity has been assuredly realized. This can be done by the following entry:

Contingent asset—Land	20,000	
Contingent asset—Buildings	80,000	
Contingent donated capital		100,000

If title is obtained at the end of the five-year period, the balances in the contingent asset accounts should be transferred to the land and buildings accounts, and the contingent owners' equity should be transferred to Donated Capital. It would be improper to transfer one fifth of the contingent equity to Donated Capital annually, because the stipulated conditions must be met during each of the five years. Failure to comply with the requirements during any one year will cause a forfeiture.

Long-lived assets acquired by gift should be depreciated on the basis of appraisal valuations recorded in the accounts. But if the gift is conditional, should depreciation be provided on the assets before the date on which title is obtained? It might be contended that such depreciation should be ignored, because production costs should not be charged with depreciation of assets not owned. On the other hand, if no depreciation is provided during this period, high depreciation charges, sufficient to compensate for the lack of such charges during the period before title was acquired, will be necessary during the period of use following the acquisition of title. These high charges will introduce an element of variation in income charges during two periods of similar operating conditions and will load the total depreciation on the period of ownership rather than on the entire period of use. The authors are, therefore, of the opinion that operations during the period prior to the acquisition of title should be charged with depreciation.

The worth of land owned by a company may increase significantly as the result of the discovery of previously unknown natural resources. An example would be the discovery of oil. Under these circumstances, the original cost of the asset might not be proper for reporting assets and determining income. The land should be reappraised and the appraisal increase recorded in the accounts. For example, assume that the discovery of oil reserves results in an increase of $100,000 in the value of the land. The following entry should be recorded:

Land—Appraisal increase (oil reserves)	100,000	
Unrealized capital increment—Appraisal of land		100,000

The subject of asset appraisals is discussed in detail in the following chapter.

ACQUISITION OF SPECIFIC ASSETS

Most of the discussion up to this point has dealt with general principles applicable to the acquisition of long-lived assets. Problems encountered in the acquisition of specific assets will now be discussed.

Real Estate. Rights in real estate may be classified as follows:

(1) Freehold estates:
  (a) Estates in fee simple, or estates of inheritance, which descend to one's heirs
  (b) Estates for life
(2) Estates less than freeholds, otherwise known as *leaseholds.*

Only freeholds can properly and legally be considered real property, to be recorded under the heading of Land. Leaseholds are personal property, and are considered later under the classification of intangible assets. Persons holding leaseholds for long periods of time are likely to consider them as freeholds, but the legal distinction should not be lost sight of in the accounts.

ACCOUNTS: Land and buildings should not be carried in a single account called "Real Estate." Separate accounts should be opened for the land and the buildings, because land does not depreciate and does not have to be insured, whereas buildings do depreciate and should be insured.

Although land valuation does not decrease as a result of use and the passing of years, losses may be incurred as a result of obsolescence or a sort of supersession. Neighborhoods change, and there are consequent declines in income productivity. Although it would probably be improper for a business to make regular provisions for such obsolescence, it might be advisable for management to observe neighborhood changes, give consideration to the possibility that obsolescence is in prospect, and make provisions therefor. Any such occurrence would presumably affect the valuation of the buildings as well as the valuation of the land.

Land. If any land is held for speculative purposes, or with the intention of using it for future plant extensions, such land should be distinguished in the accounts from land in use as a plant site. The distinction can be made by using such account titles as Land, and Land Held for Future Plant Site. Plant-site land should be shown in the balance sheet under the Property, Plant, and Equipment caption; land held for speculation or possible plant expansion should be shown under Long-Term Investments.

Not only should plant-site and speculative land be separated in the accounts, but various premises should be recorded in separate accounts if there are a considerable number of them. Although one general ledger account for plant land and one for nonplant land may be sufficient, subsidiary records of some kind should be kept, particularly if some of the parcels of land are mortgaged and others are not.

If natural resources are acquired and the land will have a residual value after the wasting asset is exhausted, the portion of the cost applicable to the land itself should be set up in a separate account.

Cost is the generally accepted basis of accounting for land. Cost includes the purchase price, broker's commission, fees for examining and recording title, surveying, draining, clearing (less salvage), and landscaping.

Expenditures for land improvements may be charged to the land account if the expenditures result in the addition of costs that are not subject to depreciation. If depreciation must be considered in relation to such expenditures, an account titled Land Improvements should be opened. Such an account would be charged with expenditures for fences, water systems, and sidewalks, and with paving costs.

Assessments for such local benefits as paving and street lighting are often spread so wide geographically that property owners who benefit little, if any, from an improvement are required to contribute to the cost. It would seem that a proper valuation of the land would exclude the cost of such assessments, and that they should be treated as expenses, although for federal income tax purposes special assessments are not recognized as allowable deductions.

Land costs should include any interest, accrued at the date of purchase, on mortgages or other encumbrances on the land, and apportioned to the purchaser.

In the case of land being held for speculation or for future plant-site use, the question arises concerning the treatment of taxes and other carrying charges. It is certainly a conservative procedure to charge off such carrying costs immediately. On the other hand, it may be reasonably contended that, since the purpose of buying such land is either to take advantage of a rising market or to obtain the property when it is available, the carrying charges are proper additions to the cost, particularly because the land produces no income against which the expenses can be charged.

It is often stated that such charges should not be added to the land account unless the market price is increasing sufficiently to cover both the original cost and the subsequent carrying charges. However, if the land is being held for plant purposes, market prices have no bearing on the proper valuation for accounting purposes, because the land may properly be carried at the total of all costs up to the time a plant is constructed on it and occupied. In other words, it is not the liquidating basis of market that governs, but the going-concern basis. If the land is being held for speculation, the eventual gain or loss is the difference between selling price and cost plus carrying charges. If the carrying costs are charged against income from other sources, and if the books show a gain or loss on the sale equal to the difference between purchase and sale prices, both the gain or loss from the speculation and the income from other sources are distorted.

For federal income tax purposes, the taxpayer has the option of capitalizing the carrying charges on vacant land that produces no revenue, or treating them as deductible expenses.

Although the accounts with land should reflect cost, the market price of land held for speculation or plant expansion, if substantially below cost, should be shown parenthetically in the balance sheet or be otherwise disclosed. This need not be done in the case of land on which present facilities are located, because, from the going-concern standpoint, market prices of long-lived assets need not be given recognition.

Buildings. If a building is purchased, cost includes the purchase price plus all repair charges incurred in making good depreciation that occurred before the building was purchased, as well as all costs of alterations and improvements.

If a building is constructed instead of purchased, the cost includes the material, labor and supervision, and other costs, or the contract price, and a great variety of incidentals, some of which are mentioned below:

(1) If land and an old building that is to be razed are purchased at a flat price, the total cost may be charged to the land. The cost of wrecking, minus any proceeds from the sale of salvage, should be charged to the land account. If an old building, formerly occupied by the business, is replaced, the loss on the retirement of the old building should not be capitalized and included in the cost of the new building.

(2) If property is purchased subject to an existing lease, and the building is to be razed to make room for a new structure, any payments made to tenants to induce them to vacate before the expiration of the lease may be included in the cost of the new building.

(3) Costs of excavation should be charged to the building, rather than to the land.

(4) Costs of building permits and licenses may be capitalized.

(5) Costs of temporary buildings used for construction offices or as tool and material sheds may be capitalized, but the cost of temporary buildings used for operations during the construction of the permanent buildings should be absorbed in operations.

(6) Architects' fees and superintendents' salaries are a part of the cost.

(7) The cost of construction of a building can properly include all insurance premiums applicable to the construction period, including premiums

on insurance against claims for damages or accidents. If no insurance is carried, any disbursements made in settlement of such claims can be capitalized unless their amount is so excessive as to inflate grossly the valuation of the building.

(8) As indicated on page 382, certain expenditures that ordinarily would be charged to expense may be capitalized if made during the construction period.

(9) Interest accrued during the construction period on bonds or other obligations assumed or issued to obtain funds for construction purposes may be capitalized; the proportion of bond discount applicable to the construction period may be similarly treated.

Machinery. The cost of machinery includes the purchase price, freight, duty, and installation costs. If machinery has to be operated for a time for the purpose of breaking it in and testing it, the costs of such necessary preliminary operation may be capitalized.

The records for machinery should be kept in considerable detail, to provide information concerning location, price, and condition for insurance purposes, and to supply information concerning life and repairs for depreciation purposes. Depreciation rates are at best only estimates, which should be revised as the history of the business furnishes statistics on which more accurate estimates may be based. Hence, adequate statistical records should be kept. A subsidiary plant ledger should be maintained, with a page or card for each machine. Each unit of equipment should be tagged or otherwise marked with a number that will definitely identify it, and the same identifying code number should appear in the subsidiary ledger. The subsidiary plant ledger should contain the following information, part of which will be posted from books of original entry and part of which will be recorded merely as memoranda:

Name of machine
Number (to identify the machine)
Location
Manufacturer
Manufacturer's guarantee period
From whom purchased
Date of installation
Purchase price
Cost of installation
Other elements of original cost
(The total of these elements in all subsidiary accounts is controlled by the asset accounts in the general ledger.)
Types of machine tools used with the equipment
Service and depreciation data:
  Estimated life
  Actual life
  Estimated salvage
  Actual salvage
Depreciation rate

Periodic depreciation provision, and accumulated amount provided to date (The total in all subsidiary accounts is controlled by accumulated-depreciation accounts in the general ledger.)
Ordinary and extraordinary repairs, with information regarding date, cost, and nature
Information concerning abnormal operating conditions, such as overtime work, affecting depreciation and the operating life of the asset

Such records provide data desirable for insurance purposes and are extremely helpful in proving a claim for loss. The service information is valuable as a guide to future purchases, and the information concerning actual life and actual salvage realized upon the disposal of the asset is helpful in making future estimates of depreciation rates to be applied to similar equipment.

The data concerning total depreciation provided up to any given date are valuable for two reasons:

(1) To avoid overdepreciating any asset. For instance, the general ledger may contain a machinery account with a debit balance of $50,000, and an accumulated depreciation—machinery account with a credit balance of $20,000. On the average, the machinery is 40% depreciated. But this is an average of old and new machinery. Some of the old machinery may have been fully depreciated; for example, one machine costing $1,000 may have been depreciated at 10% per annum for ten years. Reference to the subsidiary record for this machine will disclose this fact, and no further depreciation will be taken on the machine.

(2) To show the depreciated book value of each unit of machinery, in order that the gain or loss on disposals can be accurately determined.

The subsidiary records should, in some cases, be carried to greater detail than for a single unit of equipment. If the unit of equipment consists of various parts subject to different depreciation rates, and if the costs of the various elements can be ascertained, it is advisable to keep the records in such a way as to show the portions of cost subject to the various depreciation rates. A jet liner is a good illustration of a long-lived asset for which subdivided subsidiary records can be kept; the turbines will require replacement before the remainder of the aircraft. Depreciation of long-lived assets is discussed in detail in the following chapter.

If entries are made in the general ledger to give effect to an appraisal, the subsidiary plant ledger should thereafter be kept on both a cost and an appraisal basis. The cost basis should be retained for income tax purposes, and the appraisal-basis data will be required for purposes of maintaining an agreement between the general ledger controlling accounts and the subsidiary records.

Tools. Tools may be divided into two classes: machine tools and hand tools. Machine tools are really a part of the machine and may, therefore, be charged to the machinery account. However, they usually wear out much more rapidly than the machine and are easily lost or stolen, hence they often have to be replaced; and because they are similar to hand tools in these respects, it is usually better to carry both classes of tools in the tools account.

As the element of loss and theft plays a large part in determining the cost of tool replacements, it is usually advisable to abandon the idea of applying a depreciation rate to the tools, and to substitute the physical-inventory method. The tools on hand at the close of the period are listed and valued at cost, with an allowance for wear and tear, and the tools account is written down to the value thus ascertained.

Patterns. Some patterns are used for regular stock work, and thus have a long-term cost that can be charged to the asset account and reduced by depreciation charges. Other patterns are made for special jobs and should be charged to the cost of the jobs and not to the patterns account. Although it may be possible, and even perhaps probable, that orders will be repeated for the special jobs, conservatism results in charging the pattern cost to the first order.

Furniture and fixtures. This account should be charged with the cost of relatively permanent property such as showcases and counters, shelving, display fixtures, safes, and office equipment. It is preferable to have a store fixtures account and an office fixtures account, in order that the depreciation charges may be properly allocated as selling and administrative expenses. Unless carefully watched, these accounts may become inflated with charges for trivial items and with rearrangement and replacement costs that add no value.

Delivery equipment. What was said with regard to subsidiary records for machinery applies equally to records for delivery equipment. Service records are particularly important in furnishing data on which a per-mile depreciation rate may be based. Parts, such as tires, requiring frequent replacement may be charged off as expenses rather than capitalized and subjected to depreciation.

Containers. Concerns that deliver goods in containers, such as milk bottles, vinegar and oil barrels, cement sacks, steel tanks, drums, carboys, and bakers' baskets, face the problem of accounting for such property.

The record of returnable containers in customers' hands may be kept in a purely memorandum manner without making any charges to the customers' accounts. If, as in the retail milk business, there are no billings to customers and there is a high percentage of loss, the containers may be regarded as operating supplies rather than long-lived assets, and the loss thereon should be determined by periodical inventories. If containers not billed to customers are carried in the accounts as long-lived assets, a liberal allowance should be set up for the loss incurred from the customers' failure to make returns.

It is not uncommon to bill customers for containers shipped to them, with the understanding that full credit will be granted upon return of the container. The entries on the following page, for a sale and for a return of containers, illustrate such an arrangement.

Accounts receivable	1,075	
Sales		1,000
Allowance for returnable containers		75
To record a sale.		
Allowance for returnable containers	75	
Accounts receivable		75
To record a return of containers.		

The Allowance for Returnable Containers should be deducted in the balance sheet from the receivables for containers.

Customers sometimes pay for and retain the containers billed to them. The entries for such a collection will depend upon whether the billings were at cost or above cost. Referring to the preceding illustration and assuming that the billing was at cost, the entry for a collection for the containers would be:

Cash	75	
Accounts receivable		75
To record the collection.		
Allowance for returnable containers	75	
Containers		75
To relieve the asset of the cost of containers sold.		

If the billing was above cost (say, $25 above cost), the second entry would be:

Allowance for returnable containers	75	
Containers		50
Revenue from containers sold		25

It will be noted that there are no debits to an accumulated depreciation account in the foregoing entries relieving the asset account for the containers sold. This is so because containers are usually carried in the accounts on an inventory basis; in other words, no accumulated depreciation account is provided, and the asset account is adjusted periodically to a valuation determined by preparing a physical inventory of the containers on hand and those with customers, and making an estimate of their condition.

If customers are billed for the containers, their accounts may be kept in such a manner as to distinguish between balances receivable from customers in cash and balances to be settled by the return of containers. It may be convenient also to provide a separate column in the sales journal for charges to customers for containers.

If cash deposits for returnable containers are collected from customers when sales are made, the amount collected should be credited to a liability account, such as Customers' Container Deposits. When the deposit is refunded upon the return of the containers, the customers' container deposits account is debited and Cash is credited.

It may be the company's experience that some containers are never returned, perhaps because of breakage or disappearance while in the customer's possession. Under such circumstances, periodic adjusting entries are required to reduce the liability account and the containers account. If the required deposit exceeds cost, the difference will be credited to Revenue from Containers Sold in the adjusting entry. To illustrate such an adjusting entry, assume the following facts:

Cost of containers	$10 per unit	
Cash deposit required of customers	$15 per unit	
Estimated number of containers that will not be returned	100	
Customers' container deposits	1,500	
Containers		1,000
Revenue from containers sold		500
Adjusting entry for estimated nonreturns.		

EXPENDITURES DURING ASSET LIFE

After long-lived assets are acquired, expenditures related to their use will have to be made. Some of these expenditures will be normally recurring items, which were probably anticipated at the time the asset was acquired. Others will be of a special or nonrecurring type.

The major accounting problem relating to expenditures during the life of an asset is whether the expenditure should be expensed in the period incurred, or whether it should be capitalized by debiting either the asset or the related accumulated depreciation account. This distinction is important for reasons already discussed on page 375. In many instances, subjective judgments may be necessary in order to make the decision concerning a specific expenditure.

Additions. An addition is something that does not merely replace a thing previously owned. Additions include entirely new units and extensions, expansions, and enlargements of old units. Thus, an entirely new building is an addition; so, also, is an enlargement of an existing building.

An expenditure for an addition consisting of an entirely new unit presents no accounting problems other than those relative to the determination of cost, which have been discussed previously. It is a capital expenditure, and the cost of the addition is chargeable to an asset account.

If an addition is an extension, expansion, or enlargement of an old unit, some special problems may arise; for instance, it may be necessary to tear out walls between the old and new portions of the building, or change roof structures, or increase the capacity of water pipes in the old building in order to provide plumbing facilities in the addition. Should the asset accounts be relieved of any of the old costs? The answer is, generally, no. A negative answer may have some theoretical justification; it may be contended that it is correct to regard all costs, old and new, less salvage from demolished or reconstructed portions of the old structure, as costs of the enlarged building. But it is probable that practical considerations are the usual reason for the negative answer; in most cases, it is not feasible to break down the cost of an entire building to determine the cost applicable to some relatively minor portion of that cost.

Improvements and betterments. The essential difference between an addition and an improvement or a betterment is that in an addition there is an increase in quantity, whereas in an improvement or a betterment there is a substitution with an increase only in quality. The new thing is better than the old one was when it was acquired. There is an improvement or betterment when a tile roof is substituted for wooden shingles, or shatter-proof glass is substituted for ordinary glass, or high-wattage electric light bulbs are substituted for bulbs of low wattage.

The proper accounting treatment of improvements and betterments depends upon whether they are of a major or a minor nature. Major expenditures, such as those for a better roof or better glass, should be capitalized; minor expenditures, such as those for better light bulbs, should be charged to expense.

In the recording of major improvements, the cost of the item replaced should be eliminated from the asset account, and the cost of the new property should be charged to it. If the accumulated depreciation on the replaced asset can be determined, it should be eliminated from the accounts. There should be no duplication of capitalized installation costs.

If plant assets are acquired in a run-down condition and rehabilitation expenditures are made, these expenditures result in improvements and are a proper charge to the asset accounts. Even if the expenditures are made over a considerable period of time, it is still proper to capitalize them as long as they result in an improved condition of the property or improved operating effectiveness as compared with the status at the time of acquisition. However, if the rehabilitation program extends over a long period, it is important to distinguish carefully between true rehabilitation costs and repairs. The charges to the property accounts for rehabilitation expenditures should be net of any amount recovered from salvage.

Replacements. A replacement also involves a substitution; but unlike the case with an improvement or a betterment, the new thing is no better than the old one was when it was acquired. Replacements are of three kinds:

(1) Replacements of whole units.
Amounts related to the old asset are removed from the accounts.
(2) Replacements of parts, which may be regarded as ordinary repairs.
These are discussed in the next section.
(3) Extensive replacements of parts, which constitute extraordinary repairs.
These also are discussed in the next section.

Repairs. Repairs usually involve replacements of parts, but repairs may be made without replacements. Repairs are of two classes: ordinary and extraordinary.

Ordinary repairs are intended maintenance expenditures that are incurred to obtain the benefits (services) expected from the assets when initially acquired. They are frequently encountered and usually involve relatively small sums of money. They require charges to operations. They may be accounted for in either of two ways:

(1) The expenditures may be charged to expense when made.
(2) An allowance procedure may be used.
Because repair costs vary from year to year, normally increasing with the life of the asset, and also vary from month to month (because

repair work may be done during slack operating periods), it may be desirable to equalize the expense over the life of the asset or during a year by the creation of an allowance account. The periodic charge to Operations and credit to the allowance account should be determined by estimating the total of such repair expenditures to be made during the entire life of the asset, or during a year, and apportioning the provisions in equal periodic amounts. Actual expenditures for repairs are recorded by debiting the allowance account. Although such an apportionment procedure may be desirable for the purpose of equalizing the expense, the charges to operations for the creation of the allowance account are not deductible for income tax purposes. The tax deduction must be based on the actual expenditures charged to the allowance account.

The theoretically ideal method of recording extraordinary repairs is to eliminate the cost of the replaced parts from the asset account, relieve the accumulated depreciation account of the depreciation provided thereon, and charge the asset account with the entire cost of the repairs, including the cost of the new parts. This can be done if the subsidiary records provide the necessary information regarding the cost of, and the depreciation provided on, individual parts. In cases in which the necessary information is not available, it has been regarded as acceptable accounting to charge the expenditures to the accumulated depreciation account, based on the concept that the extraordinary repairs extend the life of the asset beyond the originally estimated period; in other words, the extraordinary repairs make good a portion of the depreciation for which provision has been made in the accumulated depreciation account. When this treatment is accorded to extraordinary repairs, it must be recognized that the procedure is a departure from strict theoretical correctness, because it ignores the difference between the cost of the original asset and the cost of the replacement, does not give consideration to the question of the adequacy of the remaining balance in the accumulated depreciation account as a provision for depreciation to date, and does not squarely face the question of the probable length of the period of extended usefulness and the related question of any necessary revision in the depreciation rate.

Repairs and maintenance. A theoretical distinction between repairs and maintenance is sometimes made, maintenance being directed to keeping the assets in good condition and repairs being directed to putting them back into good condition. Maintenance is preventive; repairs are curative. The theoretical distinction is usually difficult to maintain in the accounts.

Reinstallation costs. If machinery is rearranged in the factory for the purpose of improving the "routing" and thus reducing the time and cost of production, a question arises with respect to the proper treatment of the reinstallation expense. Presumably, the cost of one installation will already have been charged to the machinery account. Theoretically, therefore, the cost, or the undepreciated remainder of the cost, of the first installation should be removed from the accounts, and the reinstallation cost should be capitalized by a charge to the machinery account.

DISPOSAL OF LONG-LIVED ASSETS

Determining book amount. Whenever depreciable assets are disposed of, whether by sale, trade, abandonment, sale for scrap, or as the result of a casualty loss, it is first necessary that the book amount (value) of the asset be determined as of the date of disposal. Only if this is done can the gain or loss on disposal be properly determined. Thus, it may be necessary to recognize depreciation for the current accounting period, since depreciation is normally recorded only at the end of the period.

The calculation of depreciation for fractional periods will be discussed in the following chapter. However, for purposes of illustrating the disposal of a depreciable asset, four possible methods of computing depreciation for part of a year will now be illustrated. All four methods assume the use of the straight-line method, and are based on the following facts:

Asset cost	$4,000
Scrap value..	0
Date of acquisition................................	April 1, 19+5
Annual depreciation rate	20%
Date of disposal...................................	November 15, 19+9

(1) Fractional-period depreciation is computed on acquisitions from the date of acquisition to the end of the period. Fractional-period depreciation is computed on disposals from the beginning of the period of disposal to the date of the disposal.

The depreciation charges to December 31, 19+8, would have been:	
19+5—9/12 of 20% of $4,000	$ 600
19+6	800
19+7	800
19+8	800
The depreciation to be recorded at the date of disposal would be:	
19+9—10½/12 of 20% of $4,000	700
And the amount to be charged to the accumulated depreciation account in the entry for the disposal would be	$3,700

(2) Depreciation is computed at the annual rate on the opening balance in the asset account, plus or minus depreciation at one-half the annual rate on the net additions or deductions during the year. *This is equivalent to computing depreciation on acquisitions and disposals for a half year, regardless of the date of the acquisition or the disposal.*

The depreciation charges to December 31, 19+8, would have been:	
19+5—½ of 20% of $4,000	$ 400
19+6	800
19+7	800
19+8	800
The depreciation to be recorded at the date of disposal would be:	
19+9—½ of 20% of $4,000	400
And the amount to be charged to the accumulated depreciation account in the entry for the disposal would be	$3,200

(3) Depreciation is computed at the annual rate on the opening balance in the asset account. *Thus, no depreciation is taken on acquisitions in the year of acquisition, and a full year's depreciation is taken on disposals.*

The depreciation charges to December 31, 19+8, would have been:	
19+5	$ 0
19+6—20% of $4,000	800
19+7	800
19+8	800
The depreciation to be recorded at the date of disposal would be:	
19+9	800
And the amount to be charged to the accumulated depreciation account in the entry for the disposal would be	$3,200

(4) Depreciation is computed at the annual rate on the closing balance in the asset account. *This is equivalent to computing depreciation for a full year on acquisitions, regardless of the date of acquisition, and taking no depreciation on disposals in the year of disposal.*

The depreciation charges to December 31, 19+8, would have been:	
19+5—20% of $4,000	$ 800
19+6	800
19+7	800
19+8	800
The depreciation to be recorded at the date of disposal would be:	
19+9	0
And the amount to be charged to the accumulated depreciation account in the entry for the disposal would be	$3,200

Whichever method is adopted by a firm, it must be followed consistently.

In addition to determining the book amount of the asset as of the date of disposal, it is also necessary to remove both the accumulated depreciation and the cost of the asset from the records. Any gain or loss on the disposal will be recognized as a part of the entry to relieve the accounts of these amounts.

Sale of an asset. To illustrate the sale of a long-lived asset, the facts used in the preceding section will be assumed. It will be further assumed that the firm uses method (1), shown on page 395, to compute fractional-period depreciation, and that the asset was sold for $500 on November 15, 19+9. The following entries record the depreciation for the period and the sale:

Depreciation expense	700	
Accumulated depreciation		700
Cash	500	
Accumulated depreciation	3,700	
Asset		4,000
Gain on disposal of assets		200

The amount of the gain recorded in the entry above is the difference between the amount received ($500) and the book amount of the asset as of the date of disposal ($4,000 – $3,700 = $300). Gains and losses resulting from the disposal of assets should be reported in the firm's income statement as separate items.

Trade of an asset. The trade of assets for similar assets was discussed earlier in this chapter. It was noted at that time that a gain or loss may result from the trade. The transaction recorded in the entry on page 379 resulted in a $200 loss on the trade, and the new asset had a basis of $5,500, which was the sum of the cash value of the old asset ($1,800) and the cash paid ($3,700).

For income tax purposes, no gain or loss is recognized when an asset is traded for a similar asset. The cost of the new asset for tax purposes is the sum of the book amount of the old asset and the cash expenditure made in the transaction. The facts presented on page 379 show the net book amount of the old asset to be $2,000 at the time of trade, and an additional cash payment of $3,700. The entries under both methods of recording the trade are illustrated below:

	Recognition of Gain or Loss		No Recognition of Gain or Loss	
Asset (new asset)	5,500		5,700	
Accumulated depreciation	3,000		3,000	
Loss on trade of assets	200			
Asset (old asset)		5,000		5,000
Cash		3,700		3,700

The effect of the income tax treatment is to spread any gain or loss on the trade over the life of the new asset by adjusting the cost basis of the new asset. This will result in a different annual depreciation charge than if the gain or loss were recognized.

Casualty losses and insurance. Long-lived depreciable assets are sometimes lost owing to catastrophic events such as fires and floods. Such losses are referred to as involuntary conversions of assets.

If such a loss is uninsured, the only entry required in the accounting records is to relieve the accounts of the cost and accumulated depreciation and recognize the loss, after first recording any depreciation for the present period. In this case, the amount of the loss is the book amount of the asset at the date of the loss.

To illustrate the accounting procedure applicable to insured losses, assume the following facts related to a building that was destroyed by fire:

Cost	$100,000
Accumulated depreciation	30,000
Net book amount	70,000
Amount of insurance	75,000
Valuation for insurance-settlement purposes	77,000
Settlement received	75,000

The following facts should be noted concerning the amounts above: First, the building apparently has a fair market value ($77,000) in excess of its book amount ($70,000), which would frequently be the case. Second, no matter what the current value of the building is, the maximum recovery will be limited to the amount of the coverage ($75,000).

At the time of the loss, the following entry should be recorded:

Fire loss	70,000	
Accumulated depreciation—Building	30,000	
Building		100,000

This entry relieves the accounts of the amounts pertaining to the asset destroyed and establishes the fire loss account.

Care must be taken in recording the insurance proceeds. Although the proceeds received from the insurance company ($75,000) are in excess of the book amount of the asset destroyed ($70,000), the $5,000 can hardly be viewed as a gain. Instead, it should be credited to an account titled Excess of Insurance Proceeds over Book Amount of Assets Destroyed. This account should be reported as a separate item on the firm's income statement. The following entry records the receipt of $75,000 from the insurance company:

Cash	75,000	
Fire loss		70,000
Excess of insurance proceeds over book amount of assets destroyed		5,000

COINSURANCE: In the preceding illustration, it was assumed that the asset was completely destroyed by fire. However, because losses are usually only partial, there is a tendency to insure for only a portion of the value of the property. To combat this tendency, insurance companies have developed coinsurance clauses providing that, if the insured does not carry an amount of insurance equal to a specified percentage (for instance, 80 percent) of the insurable value of the property, the insurance company will be obligated to reimburse the insured for only a fraction of any loss suffered. In other words, if the insured does not carry insurance in an amount equal to the coinsurance requirement, he is regarded as being himself a coinsurer with the insurance company, carrying a portion of the risk. For example, if, under an 80 percent coinsurance policy, the insured carries insurance equal to only 70 percent of the insurable value of the property at the date of the loss, he is a coinsurer. Of any loss, seven eighths will be borne by the company and one eighth by the insured; however, the company will not be liable for more than the face of the policy. If the amount of insurance carried is 80 percent of the insurable value of the property, the company will be liable for all losses up to the face of the policy.

The operation of an 80 percent coinsurance clause is illustrated below:

First illustration:

Insurable value of property at date of loss	\$10,000
Policy	8,000

Since the amount of insurance carried satisfies the coinsurance clause, the insurance company is liable for all losses up to \$8,000.

Second illustration:

Insurable value of property at date of loss	\$10,000
Policy	8,500

In this illustration, the insurance carried exceeds the coinsurance clause requirement. Hence, the insurance company is liable for all losses up to \$8,500.

Third illustration:

Insurable value of property at date of loss	\$10,000
Policy	7,000
Loss	4,000

Here the insurance carried is less than the coinsurance clause percentage, being equal to only 70 percent of the insurable value of the property. Therefore, the insured is a coinsurer for $^1/_8$ of any loss up to \$8,000. Hence, the insurance company's liability is $^7/_8$ of \$4,000, or \$3,500.

Fourth illustration:

Insurable value of property at date of loss	\$10,000
Policy	6,500
Loss	4,000

As in the preceding illustration, the insurance carried is less than the coinsurance clause percentage, in this case being equal to 65 percent of the insurable value of the property. Accordingly, the insured is a coinsurer for $^{15}/_{80}$ of any loss up to \$8,000. Hence, the insurance company's liability is $^{65}/_{80}$ of \$4,000, or \$3,250.

Fifth illustration:

Insurable value of property at date of loss	\$10,000
Policy (same as above)	6,500
Loss	Total

$^{65}/_{80}$ of \$10,000 is \$8,125, but the policy is for only \$6,500; hence, the insurance company's liability is \$6,500.

From these illustrations, the following general rule may be derived. The insurance company's liability under a policy with an 80 percent coinsurance clause can be determined as follows: When the policy is less than 80 percent of the insurable value of the property, multiply the loss by a fraction the numerator of which is the face of the policy and the denominator of which is 80 percent of the insurable value of the property. The product is the liability of the company, except that the liability cannot be more than the face of the policy. If the insured amount is 80 percent or more of the insurable value of the property, the coinsurance clause does not affect the settlement.

When the policy contains a coinsurance clause, it is important to watch for changing values of the insured property, caused either by additional purchases or by increases in replacement costs. To illustrate, assume that property was purchased at a cost of $5,000 and insured for $4,000 under a policy containing an 80 percent coinsurance clause. Later, when the property had an insurable value of $8,000, it was partially destroyed, with a loss of $4,000. Settlement would be made as follows:

Insurable value	$8,000
80% thereof..	6,400

Company's liability: $^{40}/_{64}$ of $4,000, or $2,500.

Although of particular importance in fire insurance, coinsurance clauses may be included in policies for other types of insurance. An 80 percent coinsurance rate was used in the preceding illustrations because it is the usual rate in fire insurance policies; other coinsurance rates are also used—for example, 70 percent and 90 percent.

Abandonment of assets. Long-lived assets are sometimes retired from service without being sold or even removed from the locations where they were formerly used. If they are retained as standby units, the cost and depreciation provisions applicable to them may be retained in the accounts. If, however, their usefulness as operating assets is at an end, their salvage or recovery value should be estimated and set up in an abandoned property account, with appropriate entries to relieve the asset and accumulated depreciation accounts of the cost and recorded depreciation and to record the estimated loss or gain.

16

Long-Lived Assets: Depreciation and Depletion

DEPRECIATION

Introduction. Tangible long-lived assets, such as plant and equipment, are assets used in the operations of the business over several years. Such assets are acquired to be used in operations, rather than to be sold, because of their future service potential to aid in generating revenue. However, the future service potential of such assets is limited by their finite lives. Thus, the acquisition of such assets by a firm represents the acquisition of a store of economic-service potentials in which the services are used over the life of the assets.

As plant and equipment are used over their useful lives, there is a decline in the service potential of the assets. In other words, the future service potential of such assets declines or expires as the assets are used in operations to generate revenue. Based on the historical-cost, fiscal-period, and matching assumptions, the cost of the expired service potential of such assets is periodically matched with revenue for purposes of income determination. That portion of the total cost of plant and equipment that is systematically assigned to expense or inventory each period is called *depreciation*. Thus, depreciation represents the decline in service potential of tangible long-lived assets during the fiscal period, and the periodic decline is recognized via systematic cost allocation.

The decline in the service potential of tangible long-lived assets (other than land) is the result of physical deterioration and obsolescence, which limit their useful lives as tangible long-lived assets and cause depreciation. The physical deterioration of an asset is caused by wear and tear from operation, decay from the passage of time, and damage or destruction from accidents; hence, the result is a decline in the quantity or quality, or an increase in the unit cost, of the asset's output. Obsolescence pertains to events external to the asset itself that limit its continued use, even though it is still physically capable of use. Causes of obsolescence are changes in technology (the asset is superseded by a more efficient asset), changes in consumer tastes (the asset's product is superseded by other products), expansion in operations (the asset is inadequate), and any other event or condition that renders the continued use of a physically capable asset uneconomical or impracticable. Since both physical deterioration and obsolescence limit the useful lives of tangible long-lived assets, both should be recognized in the accounting for depreciation.

The problem in accounting for depreciation arises because assets are acquired as lump-sum bundles of future services, but the services are used up slowly over the life of the assets. Periodic income would be distorted if the assets were fully written off to expense during the period of acquisition or during the period of retirement. Consequently, the accountant assigns the cost of tangible long-lived assets to annual periods that benefit from the utilization of the assets in generating revenue over their useful lives. Note, however, that this is cost allocation, not asset valuation. It is cost allocation in that the total cost of an asset, such as equipment, is divided into parts and each part is assigned to expense or inventory in order to match expense with revenue. Since there are an infinite number of ways to divide up cost, the accounting profession limits the number of cost-allocation methods that are acceptable in the determination of periodic depreciation. Acceptable depreciation methods are discussed later in this chapter.

From a theoretical viewpoint, depreciation is *arbitrary* cost allocation. If it were possible to determine the net revenue contribution of each tangible long-lived asset for each period of its life, there would be a rational basis for allocating the cost of each asset. However, because all the assets contribute jointly to overall revenue generation, and because of the uncertainty of each asset's future periodic revenues, operating costs, maintenance and repair costs, and their interactions, it is impossible to come up with the *one* rational basis for cost allocation. On the other hand, as discussed in Chapter 6, arbitrary cost allocations, such as depreciation, could be avoided if accountants used selling-price valuation, instead of historical-cost valuation. Note, however, that the cost-allocation problem would not be avoided by using replacement-cost valuation.

Factors of depreciation. Because of the impossibility of estimating an asset's future net revenue contribution, the accountant abstracts from this difficulty by basing the annual depreciation charge on three factors: the depreciation base, the estimated salvage, and the estimated life of the asset. For purposes of computation, depreciation is viewed as a function of these three factors, which determine the total depreciation to be provided and the period over which the total depreciation is to be spread. The amount charged to each period depends upon the apportionment method adopted; hence, the apportionment method is the specified functional relationship between these three factors.

THE DEPRECIATION BASE: The base generally used for the computation of depreciation is cost, which includes installation and other capitalized incidental expenditures. The base may also include an allowance for removal costs at the expiration of the life of the asset, although it is more customary to apply such costs as a reduction of the realization from salvage.

Replacement or appraisal valuations are sometimes used as the depreciation base. The propriety of the use of such bases is discussed in the next chapter.

In the interest of a more exact computation of depreciation provisions, the plant records may be subdivided so that they show, not merely the total cost or other depreciation base of all tangible long-lived assets of a certain class, but also the cost or other base of various units having different expected service lives. With such information, various rates can be applied to depreciate different structural elements or subtotals of cost.

SALVAGE: The salvage (also called residual or scrap value) of an asset is the amount that can be recovered by its disposal when it is taken out of service. The estimated salvage to be used in the computation of depreciation should be net after estimated costs of dismantling and removal are deducted.

Although salvage should theoretically be taken into consideration in determining the total amount of cost expiration to be charged to operations during the life of an asset, it is frequently ignored. This may be justified if the salvage is small or not subject to reliable estimate, or if the dismantling and removal costs cannot be accurately estimated.

ESTIMATED LIFE: The life of a tangible long-lived asset will be affected by repairs, and the repair policy should be taken into consideration when the life is being estimated. Estimated life may be stated in any one of the following ways:

(1) Time periods, as years or months
(2) Operating periods, or working hours
(3) Units of output

Estimating the life of a tangible long-lived asset requires consideration of both physical deterioration and obsolescence. In essence, it is the period of expected economic usefulness that governs. Plates used in the printing of a book may be in usable condition long after the sale of the book has ceased, but their cost should be charged to operations during the period when sales are made. Patterns and molds, although physically usable for years, may have a life for production purposes only during the manufacture of one annual model.

Depreciation methods. The following methods of apportioning depreciation by periods are the ones we shall discuss:

Straight-line	Reducing-charge (accelerated depreciation)
Working-hours	Inventory
Production	Retirement basis

The annuity and sinking-fund methods will not be discussed here, because of their infrequent use in actual accounting practice. They are described in *Principles of Accounting: Advanced.*

The following symbols are used in the formulas discussed in this chapter:

C = Cost
S = Salvage
n = Estimated life (periods, working hours, or units of product)
r = Rate of depreciation (per period, per working hour, or per unit of product)
D = Depreciation per period

For purposes of illustration, it will be assumed that:

The cost of an asset is \$6,000;
The estimated salvage is \$400; and
The estimated life is eight years (except in two illustrations in which the life is stated in terms of working hours and units of product).

In the illustrations of methods in which the life is expressed in operating hours or units of product, the necessary additional information is furnished.

Straight-line method. This is the simplest and most commonly used method. It results in spreading the total depreciation equally over all periods of life, unless the periodic charge is adjusted because of abnormal operating activities. The formula for computing the periodic depreciation charge is:

$$D = (C - S)/n = (\$6{,}000 - \$400)/8 = \$700$$

or

$$D = \frac{1}{n}(C - S) = r(C - S)$$

$$= \tfrac{1}{8}(\$6{,}000 - \$400) = (.12\tfrac{1}{2})(\$6{,}000 - \$400) = \$700$$

The table at the top of page 405 shows the accumulation of depreciation.

In practical applications of the straight-line method, the salvage is sometimes ignored, and a rate determined from the estimated life of the asset is applied to cost. Thus, in the foregoing illustration, the rate would be $12\frac{1}{2}$ percent, and the annual depreciation would be $12\frac{1}{2}$ percent of \$6,000, or \$750.

The straight-line method has the advantage of simplicity. Moreover, because it has been widely used, a considerable body of experience data is available for the determination of straight-line depreciation rates applicable to various classes of tangible long-lived assets. It is also argued that because the straight-line method

Table of Depreciation—Straight-Line Method

End of Year	Debit Depreciation Expense	Credit Accumulated Depreciation	Total Accumulated Depreciation	Carrying Amount
				$6,000
1	$ 700	$ 700	$ 700	5,300
2	700	700	1,400	4,600
3	700	700	2,100	3,900
4	700	700	2,800	3,200
5	700	700	3,500	2,500
6	700	700	4,200	1,800
7	700	700	4,900	1,100
8	700	700	5,600	400
	$5,600	$5,600		

is time-oriented, it is better suited to take into account the growing importance of obsolescence.

On the other hand, the straight-line method does have disadvantages: It does not take into account asset usage, and it results in the misleading appearance of an increasing rate of return on total invested capital.

Working-hours method. This method recognizes the fact that property, particularly machinery, depreciates more rapidly if it is used full-time or overtime than if it is used part-time. Not only is the wear and tear greater, but there is less opportunity for making repairs. Moreover, the full-time and overtime years get more benefit from the asset than do the part-time years. In the application of this method, the total number of working hours of which the machine is capable of operating is estimated, and a charge per hour is determined by the following formula:

$$r = \frac{C - S}{n}$$

For example, if it is assumed that the asset used for illustrative purposes is expected to have an operating life of 22,400 working hours, the depreciation rate per hour of use is computed in this manner:

$$r = \frac{\$6{,}000 - \$400}{22{,}400}$$
$$= \$.25$$

The table on the following page shows the number of hours the asset was used during each of eight years, and the depreciation provided on the basis of working hours.

Production method. This method is similar to the working-hours method in that it distributes the depreciation among the periods in proportion to the use made of the asset during each period. The estimated life is stated

Table of Depreciation—Working-Hours Method

Year	Hours Worked	Debit Depreciation Expense	Credit Accumulated Depreciation	Total Accumulated Depreciation	Carrying Amount
					$6,000
1	2,600	$ 650	$ 650	$ 650	5,350
2	2,900	725	725	1,375	4,625
3	3,400	850	850	2,225	3,775
4	2,400	600	600	2,825	3,175
5	1,800	450	450	3,275	2,725
6	2,700	675	675	3,950	2,050
7	3,000	750	750	4,700	1,300
8	3,600	900	900	5,600	400
	22,400	$5,600	$5,600		

in units of product or service, and the rate of depreciation is a rate per unit. The figures of the illustration of the working-hours method can serve as an illustration of this method also, if we assume that the estimated life is stated as 22,400 units of product (instead of working hours), and that the figures in the "Hours Worked" column represent units of finished goods produced. The depreciation rate is then $.25 per unit, and the depreciation each year is computed by multiplying the number of units produced by the rate per unit.

The production method is peculiarly suitable to the depreciation of assets for which the total service units can be rather definitely estimated and when the service is not uniform by periods. The method might, for instance, be appropriately applied in depreciating automobile tires on a mileage basis.

If a tangible long-lived asset is subject to obsolescence, the production method appears to be an illogical procedure if intended to account for both physical deterioration and obsolescence, because obsolescence presumably develops on a time basis rather than on the basis of units of output. During a period of small production, the depreciation charges might be less than the amount that should be provided for obsolescence on the basis of the lapse of time, and this inadequacy might not be compensated for in periods of larger production.

Reducing-charge methods (accelerated depreciation). A depreciation procedure by which larger charges are made during the early years of the life of a tangible long-lived asset than during the later years of its life was originally supported by the following reasoning: The cost of the use of a tangible long-lived asset includes depreciation and repairs; the sum of these charges should be a fairly uniform amount year by year; because repairs tend to increase with the age of the asset, the depreciation charge should decrease, so that the increasing repair charges and the depreciation charges will tend to equalize each other and produce a uniform total charge. This may be sound conceptually, but it assumes that repairs will increase in the same amount that the depreciation charges decrease; perhaps they will, but it is likely to be a matter of luck. If it is desirable to equalize the total repair and depreciation charges, it would seem better to create two allowances: one for depreciation (accumulated depreciation) and another for repairs (allowance for repairs). Such a plan is subject to the objection that it may be difficult to estimate accurately the total future repair cost; but with statistics showing past experience, it should be no more difficult to do this than to estimate depreciation. Such a repair allowance would not be deductible for federal income tax purposes.

Diminishing-charge methods were sometimes advocated also on the ground that the large charge in the early part of an asset's life was desirable to correspond with the large initial reduction in valuation from a cost basis to a second-hand market basis. This argument seems to be in conflict with the general accounting principle that current market valuation need not be given consideration in the accounting for tangible long-lived assets.

A new concept in support of diminishing-charge procedures developed after World War II. It may have had its origin in the fact that some companies made large expenditures for tangible long-lived assets at postwar prices that were relatively high, with the hope of making large immediate profits by supplying goods to meet the accumulated postwar demand. It was contended that such expenditures would not have been made except for the prospect of such quick profits, and that a proper matching of revenue and costs required making relatively large depreciation charges during this profitable postwar period.

This concept was then expanded until the argument was stated somewhat as follows: Because management cannot foresee the conditions that will exist during the entire physical life of a tangible long-lived asset, its decisions regarding the advisability of making large capital expenditures are often determined by the prospects of economic usefulness during a much shorter period; immediate prospects of profits may warrant taking a chance with respect to later periods; larger depreciation charges should be made in the earlier periods than in the later ones, because the expenditures were made with these early periods primarily in mind.

In depreciation discussions there is increasing emphasis on the concept that, because new assets are generally capable of producing more revenue than old assets are, a better matching of revenue and expense is achieved by larger depreciation charges in the early periods when assets have their greatest economic usefulness. Such a depreciation procedure is often referred to as accelerated depreciation, meaning essentially that depreciation charges follow a pattern that is constantly decreasing, although initially greater than those under the straight-line method.

Although it can be conceptually argued that accelerated depreciation should be used because tangible long-lived assets are normally characterized by declining revenue contribution and operating efficiency and increasing repair and maintenance costs, it is still arbitrary cost allocation in the sense that there are an infinite number of ways to calculate a declining depreciation charge. Moreover, it is not the conceptual arguments, but the income tax regulations, that have had the greatest influence on the use of accelerated depreciation. That is, accelerated depreciation results in greater annual depreciation charges in the early life of a tangible long-lived asset, and since such charges are tax-deductible, money is saved that would otherwise be used to pay taxes. Of course, over the whole life of an asset, the total depreciation and therefore the total tax savings would be the same; however, because of the time value of money (the interest effect), the tax savings in the early life of an asset are, in effect, an interest-free loan over the period the taxes are postponed. On the other hand, it can be correctly argued that income tax laws should not govern accounting depreciation methods; but since depreciation is cost allocation with no real theoretical basis for choosing one depreciation method over another, depreciation methods influenced by practical tax considerations are just as acceptable as any other systematic cost-allocation method.

Four methods of providing a diminishing depreciation charge are illustrated in the following sections. These methods are:

(1) Declining-balance
(2) Double-declining-balance
(3) Sum-of-the-years'-digits
(4) Diminishing-rates-on-cost

DECLINING-BALANCE METHOD: Under this method, a fixed or uniform rate is applied to the carrying amount of the asset. The depreciation rate to be used in this method is computed by the following formula:

$$\begin{aligned} r &= 1 - \sqrt[n]{S \div C} \\ &= 1 - \sqrt[8]{\$400 \div \$6{,}000} \\ &= 1 - \sqrt[8]{.0666\tfrac{2}{3}} \end{aligned}$$

A table of logarithms must be used to extract the eighth root of $.0666\frac{2}{3}$:

Log $.0666\frac{2}{3}$	8.8239088	− 10
Add	70	− 70
Divide by 8:	8)78.8239088	− 80
	9.8529886	− 10, which is log .712834

Then $r = 1 - .712834$
$= .287166$
$= 28.7166\%$

This rate is applied at the end of the first period to cost, and thereafter to the carrying amount at the beginning of each successive period, as shown by the table at the top of page 409. Thus, the depreciation charge the first year is $28.71\frac{2}{3}$ percent of \$6,000; the second year, it is $28.71\frac{2}{3}$ percent of \$4,277.

The formula requires the use of estimated salvage. If an asset is assumed to have no salvage, a nominal salvage of \$1 can be used.

DOUBLE-DECLINING-BALANCE METHOD: As a practical matter, the depreciation rate used under the declining-balance method is not likely to be used when a higher rate is permissible for income tax purposes. Federal income tax regulations allow for certain assets the use of a depreciation rate not exceeding *twice* that acceptable as a straight-line rate, provided that the asset is not depreciated below

Depreciation Table—Uniform Rate on Diminishing Amount

Rate: $28.71\frac{2}{3}\%$

Year	Debit Depreciation Expense	Credit Accumulated Depreciation	Total Accumulated Depreciation	Carrying Amount
				$6,000.00
1	$1,723.00	$1,723.00	$1,723.00	4,277.00
2	1,228.21	1,228.21	2,951.21	3,048.79
3	875.51	875.51	3,826.72	2,173.28
4	624.09	624.09	4,450.81	1,549.19
5	444.87	444.87	4,895.68	1,104.32
6	317.12	317.12	5,212.80	787.20
7	226.06	226.06	5,438.86	561.14
8	161.14	161.14	5,600.00	400.00
	$5,600.00	$5,600.00		

its estimated salvage.[1] Thus, twice the straight-line rate is applied annually to the carrying amount of the asset (cost minus accumulated depreciation) at the beginning of the period; hence, with a constant doubled rate applied to a declining book balance, the depreciation method is called the double-declining-balance method.

To illustrate the double-declining-balance method using the data previously given (asset cost of $6,000, and an eight-year estimated useful life), the double-declining rate would be 25 percent ($2 \times .12\frac{1}{2}$) and depreciation would be

$1,500.00 for the first year ($6,000 × .25);
$1,125.00 for the second year [($6,000 − $1,500) (.25)];
$843.75 for the third year [($6,000 − $1,500 − $1,125) (.25)];

and so on, as shown in the table below:

Depreciation Table—Double-Declining Balance

Year	Debit Depreciation Expense	Credit Accumulated Depreciation	Total Accumulated Depreciation	Carrying Amount
				$6,000.00
1	$1,500.00	$1,500.00	$1,500.00	4,500.00
2	1,125.00	1,125.00	2,625.00	3,375.00
3	843.75	843.75	3,468.75	2,531.25
4	632.81	632.81	4,101.56	1,898.44
5	474.61	474.61	4,576.17	1,423.83
6	355.96	355.96	4,932.13	1,067.87
7	266.97	266.97	5,199.10	800.90
8	200.23	200.23	5,399.33	600.67
	$5,399.33	$5,399.33		

[1] At the time of this writing, the tax regulations allow the use of the double-declining-balance method for depreciable property other than new realty (buildings) acquired after July 24, 1969, that have an estimated useful life of three years or more. For new realty, the declining-balance rate is limited to $1\frac{1}{2}$ times the rate applicable to the straight-line rate unadjusted for salvage.

The double-declining-balance method can be expressed by formula as follows:

Let B = **Book or carrying amount of asset**

t = **1, 2, . . . , n annual time periods**

Then $D_t = (B_{t-1})(2)(1/n) = (B_{t-1})(2/n) = (B_{t-1})(r)$

$D_3 = (B_{3-1})(2)(1/8) = (B_2)(2/8) = (\$3{,}375)(.25) = \$843.75$

Or $D_t = (D_{t-1})(1 - 2/n) = (D_{t-1})(1 - r)$

$D_3 = (D_{3-1})(1 - 2/8) = (\$1{,}125)(1 - .25) = \$843.75$

Note that in the illustration above, the carrying amount of the asset is \$600.67 after eight years. If the salvage at the end of eight years were \$400, there would be an excess of carrying amount over salvage of \$200.67 (\$600.67 – \$400.00). If the salvage were a large amount, such as \$700, then under the double-declining-balance method, the eighth-year depreciation charge would not be \$200.23. Such a charge would reduce the carrying amount to \$600.67, which would be below the \$700 salvage and would not be allowable for income tax purposes. Instead, the eighth-year depreciation charge would be \$100.90 (\$800.90 – \$700.00), which would reduce the carrying amount to the \$700 salvage.

The carrying amount of the asset can be made to equal the salvage amount by switching from the double-declining-balance method to the straight-line method before the end of the asset's estimated useful life. Such switching is allowable for income tax purposes. On the other hand, such switching would result in an early tax savings only if the annual straight-line depreciation charges were greater than the double-declining depreciation charges during the asset's later life.[2] In the illustration above, the switch could be made in the seventh year, because the annual straight-line depreciation charge would be \$333.94, which is greater than the \$266.67 double-declining depreciation charge. In other words, the switch from the double-declining-balance method to the straight-line method should be made during the year when

$$\frac{\textbf{Carrying (book) amount} - \textbf{Estimated salvage}}{\textbf{Remaining useful life}} \geq \textbf{Double-declining depreciation for that year}$$

$$(\$1{,}067.87 - \$400.00)/2 \geq \$266.97$$

$$\$333.94 \geq \$266.97$$

---

[2]It can be demonstrated mathematically that a switch is not recommended when the salvage at the end of the useful life of the asset exceeds the carrying amount of the asset under the double-declining-balance method. Furthermore, if the salvage is zero, it can be demonstrated that the year to switch is equal to the midpoint of the useful life plus one, or $n/2 + 1$. For assets with an estimated salvage that does not exceed the terminal carrying amount under the double-declining-balance method, the year to switch is determined by comparing the annual depreciation under both the double-declining-balance and the straight-line methods until the latter exceeds the former; however, this will occur somewhere between the halfway point of the useful life plus one and the end of the useful life of the asset. See George A. Taylor, *Managerial and Engineering Economy* (Princeton, N.J.: D. Van Nostrand Company, Inc., 1964), pp. 306–10.

The table below summarizes the depreciation for years 7 and 8 after the switch to the straight-line method:

Year	Debit Depreciation Expense	Credit Accumulated Depreciation	Total Accumulated Depreciation	Carrying Amount
⋮	⋮	⋮	⋮	⋮
6	$ 355.96	$ 355.96	$4,932.13	$1,067.87
7	333.94	333.94	5,266.07	733.93
8	333.93*	333.93*	5,600.00	400.00
	$5,600.00	$5,600.00		

*Rounded down one cent.

SUM-OF-THE-YEARS'-DIGITS METHOD: This method is more readily understood if it is first illustrated. Based on the data previously given,

Add the numbers representing the periods of life:
Thus, $1 + 2 + 3 + 4 + 5 + 6 + 7 + 8 = 36$
Use the sum thus obtained as a denominator.
Use as numerators the same numbers taken in inverse order:
Thus, $^{8}/_{36}$, $^{7}/_{36}$, etc.
Multiply the total depreciation ($C - S$) by the fractions thus produced.

Depreciation Table—Sum-of-the-Years' Digits

Year	Fraction of $5,600.00	Debit Depreciation Expense	Credit Accumulated Depreciation	Total Accumulated Depreciation	Carrying Amount
					$6,000.00
1	$^{8}/_{36}$	$1,244.45	$1,244.45	$1,244.45	4,755.55
2	$^{7}/_{36}$	1,088.89	1,088.89	2,333.34	3,666.66
3	$^{6}/_{36}$	933.33	933.33	3,266.67	2,733.33
4	$^{5}/_{36}$	777.78	777.78	4,044.45	1,955.55
5	$^{4}/_{36}$	622.22	622.22	4,666.67	1,333.33
6	$^{3}/_{36}$	466.67	466.67	5,133.34	866.66
7	$^{2}/_{36}$	311.11	311.11	5,444.45	555.55
8	$^{1}/_{36}$	155.55	155.55	5,600.00	400.00
	$^{36}/_{36}$	$5,600.00	$5,600.00		

The sum-of-the-years'-digits method results in a declining periodic depreciation charge because a declining fraction (a declining depreciation rate) is applied to cost minus salvage (a constant depreciation base) each period. The declining fraction is the result of a declining numerator, consisting of the remaining years of useful life from the beginning of the year, and a constant denominator, consisting of the sum of the series of years making up the useful life of the asset (an arithmetic progression). Thus, the method results in cost minus salvage declining by a constant percentage and the periodic depreciation charge declining by a constant amount each period. For example, in the illustration above, cost minus salvage of

$5,600 declines by a constant 1/36 (27.78 percent) each period, which reduces the periodic depreciation expense by a constant amount of $155.56 (1/36 of $5,600).

The sum-of-the-years'-digits method can be expressed by formula as follows:

$$D_t = \frac{(n - t) + 1}{n(n + 1)/2}(C - S)$$

$$D_4 = \frac{(8 - 4) + 1}{8(8 + 1)/2}(\$6{,}000 - \$400) = (5/36)(\$5{,}600) = \$777.78$$

As a final point, in comparison to the double-declining-balance method, the annual depreciation charge under the sum-of-the-years'-digits method is not as large during the early life of an asset; however, if the asset has a long life, eventually the annual depreciation charge can become larger under the sum-of-the-years'-digits method.

DIMINISHING-RATES-ON-COST METHOD: No formula can be given for determining the rates, as they are chosen arbitrarily when the depreciation program is set up. The following table shows how the method operates, the rate arbitrarily chosen for each year being shown in the table.

Depreciation Table—Diminishing Rates on Cost

Year	Rates	Debit Depreciation Expense	Credit Accumulated Depreciation	Total Accumulated Depreciation	Carrying Amount
					$6,000
1	$15\frac{2}{3}$%	$ 940	$ 940	$ 940	5,060
2	$14\frac{2}{3}$	880	880	1,820	4,180
3	13	780	780	2,600	3,400
4	12	720	720	3,320	2,680
5	11	660	660	3,980	2,020
6	10	600	600	4,580	1,420
7	9	540	540	5,120	880
8	8	480	480	5,600	400
	$93\frac{1}{3}$%	$5,600	$5,600		

Note that under this method, the salvage is expressed as a percentage of cost ($6\frac{2}{3}$ percent); hence, the total of the periodic rates ($93\frac{1}{3}$ percent) and the salvage percentage must be 100 percent.

The method is used where the decline in the service potential of the asset can be reasonably estimated to determine the periodic rates. The method is not widely used because of the difficulty in estimating rates that correspond with the decline in service potential.

Fractional-period depreciation under accelerated methods. If an asset to be depreciated by the sum-of-the-years'-digits method is acquired during the year, it is customary to compute the depreciation applicable to the partial period as follows:

(1) Compute the depreciation for a full year.

(2) Take a fraction thereof, the fraction being representative of the partial year since acquisition.

To illustrate the application of this procedure, assume that the following data relate to a company whose accounting year is the calendar year.

Asset cost	$3,000
Date of acquisition	April 1, 19+5
Sum of years' digits (1 + 2 + 3 + 4 + 5)	15
The salvage is immaterial	-0-

Depreciation for 19+5—$750.

Depreciation for first full year:

$^5/_{15}$ of $3,000 = $1,000

Portion applicable to 9 months starting April 1, 19+5:

$^9/_{12}$ of $1,000 = $750

Such fractional-period computations are needed in subsequent years, as is illustrated by computing the depreciation for 19+6, the first full calendar year after acquisition.

Depreciation for 19+6—$850.

Depreciation for 3 months ending March 31, 19+6:		
Depreciation for first full year	$1,000	
Applicable to 19+5—above	750	
Applicable to 19+6	$ 250	$250
Depreciation for second full year:		
$^4/_{15}$ of $3,000 = $800		
Portion applicable to 9 months starting April 1, 19+6:		
$^9/_{12}$ of $800 =		600
Total		$850

Fractional-period depreciation presents no problem under the declining-balance method. Assume that the applicable rate for the asset above is 20 percent. The depreciation for the 9 months starting April 1, 19+5 is $^9/_{12}$ of the amount for the first full year, or $450 [($^9/_{12}$)(.20)($3,000)]. For subsequent calendar years, depreciation is computed by applying the rate to the carrying amount at the beginning of the calendar year. The following partial table based on the assumed data is illustrative:

Period	Depreciation Expense	Accumulated Depreciation	Carrying Amount	Rate = 20%
			$3,000	
April 1–December 31, 19+5	$450	$ 450	2,550	
19+6	510	960	2,040	
19+7	408	1,368	1,632	

Inventory method. When a business owns numerous, relatively inexpensive tangible long-lived assets of a given class, such as small tools, a physical-inventory approach to depreciation can be justified on practical grounds. The large number of assets in use, the typical frequent reductions due to breakage and disappearance, and the resulting volume of replacements during each year make it both difficult and expensive to attempt to maintain records of individual units of such property showing accumulated depreciation thereon. As an alternative, periodic inventories are taken to determine the number of usable assets on hand. Next, a valuation formula, devised by the company's accountants and based somewhat on past experience, is applied. The objective of the valuation formula is to produce realistic depreciation charges and carrying amounts. The valuation of assets at a specific percentage of cost is an example. Or a more sophisticated plan, based on age groupings with varying percentages, may be applied. As a general rule, depreciation is recorded by writing down the asset account to its depreciated amount. Thus, no use is made of a contra account for accumulated depreciation.

The valuation formula should not give undue weight to physical deterioration. Likewise, care should be taken to avoid the use of market prices, second-hand prices, or replacement costs. The objective is to assign cost, on a reasonable basis, to the periods benefited. Showing appraisal or realizable amounts in the accounts is not the objective of a depreciation method.

This method of computing depreciation is sometimes referred to as the *appraisal* method. This is an unfortunate label, because it implies that depreciation charges are related in some way to what assets are worth. If depreciable assets were stated on the basis of their worth, the method could result in a depreciation charge that was a composite of cost exhaustion and market-price fluctuations. Giving effect, in the computation of income, to unrealized appreciation resulting from market increases is not to be condoned merely because the appreciation is buried in the depreciation provision; the fact that the market fluctuation is netted in the depreciation and the effect thereby obscured makes the practice even more subject to censure.

Because the inventory method does not result in a systematic allocation of cost, it is not a recommended method. Its only use in practice is limited to asset accounts representing numerous small-unit cost items.

Retirement and replacement systems. The retirement and replacement systems of dealing with depreciation have numerous advocates in the public utility field. In effect, these procedures give no recognition to depreciation until the end of the life of the asset. They are akin to providing no allowance for uncollectibles and charging ascertained losses to operations.

Under the retirement system, operations are charged with the cost, less salvage, of plant units retired during the period, and new assets acquired are charged to the property accounts at cost. Under the replacement system, operations are charged with the cost of the new assets acquired as replacements, less the salvage recovery on the old assets. Of the two methods, the retirement system is preferable, because it produces property account balances that reflect the cost of assets in use rather than the cost of assets replaced.

Retirement or replacement systems are perhaps peculiarly suited to the public utility field, because the tangible long-lived assets of utilities include large numbers of units of relatively small valuation in any location (poles, conduits, and so forth), and the distinction between maintenance and replacements is often confused by borderline cases. Such systems may also be advocated by utilities because property valuations have a direct bearing upon the rates sanctioned by controlling commissions, and utility companies are indisposed to admit that accumulated depreciation, which may reflect a percentage of depreciation acceptable for general accounting purposes but in excess of the percentage of accrued physical deterioration, is a justifiable deduction from investment for purposes of rate making.

The two principal objections to these procedures are these: First, operations are relieved of any charge for the expiration of asset costs until the period of retirement; as a consequence, the operating results of the early periods are relieved of normal charges, and the asset valuations are stated in the balance sheet without any recognition of accrued depreciation. Second, instead of operations being charged by periods with a uniform cost for the services of the tangible long-lived asset, operations become charged with variable amounts determined by the necessity for, or the policy with respect to, replacements.

Lapsing schedules. An often-used device for determining the annual amounts of depreciation and keeping track of the accumulated depreciation is known as a *lapsing schedule.* A common form of lapsing schedule is illustrated on page 416.

The operation of a lapsing schedule is probably self-evident. When an asset is acquired, pertinent facts relating to it are entered in the schedule, and the depreciation charges for the entire use-life period are extended across the schedule by years. Annual depreciation charges are determined each year by adding the current year's column. If an asset is retired before it has been fully depreciated, the depreciation charges applicable to the remaining estimated useful life are subtracted in the "Annual Depreciation" columns. This is demonstrated in the illustrative schedule where the Ford truck was traded in on January 3, 1976.

Composite or group depreciation. Instead of computing depreciation for each separate asset (referred to as *unit depreciation*), companies with a large number of tangible long-lived assets frequently find it clerically convenient to apply a single, average depreciation rate to the collective cost of a group of assets. In such cases, an average rate is applied to a number of similar or dissimilar assets (that is, having similar or dissimilar characteristics and service lives). If the assets are similar, this is called *group depreciation;* if they are dissimilar, *composite depreciation.*

Under group or composite depreciation, a single asset account and a single accumulated depreciation account are established for the collective assets. Thus the book amount (value) pertains to the collective assets, not individual assets, and accumulated depreciation applies to the entire asset class, not to any specific asset. Subsequent asset acquisitions are charged to the single asset account at cost. Subsequent asset retirements are credited to the single asset account at cost, with offsetting debits to Accumulated Depreciation at cost less any salvage realized and to Cash for the salvage recovered. Unlike the case with unit depreciation, no gain or loss is recognized upon asset retirement.

Depreciation is computed by multiplying the average rate by the balance in the single asset account at the beginning of the period, regardless of the age of the individual assets that make up the group. The depreciation rate is based on the average life of the collective assets.

Delivery Equipment
Lapsing Schedule

Date	Description	Use Life	Depreciable Cost	Annual Depreciation 1973	1974	1975	1976	1977	1978	1984	1985
7/1/73	Ford truck	4 years	2,800	350	700	700	700	350			
1/3/74	Dodge wagon	4 years	3,200		800	800	800	800			
7/2/74	Chevrolet truck	4 years	2,600		325	650	650	650	325		
4/1/75	Plymouth wagon	4 years	2,880			540	720	720	720		
1/3/76	Ford truck traded in—below						700*	350*			
1/3/76	Ford truck	4 years	3,000				750	750	750		
	Total depreciation			350	1,825	2,690	2,920	2,920	1,795		

Since the accounting procedures for determining the periodic depreciation expense are essentially the same for both group and composite depreciation, an example of composite depreciation is shown below to illustrate both methods.

Asset	Cost	Salvage	Total Depreciation	Estimated Life	Annual Depreciation (Straight-Line)
A	$20,000	$5,000	$15,000	20 years	$ 750
B	12,000	2,000	10,000	10 years	1,000
C	8,000	2,000	6,000	8 years	750
D	2,100	100	2,000	4 years	500
	$42,100	$9,100	$33,000		$3,000

$3,000 ÷ $42,100 = .07125, the composite, or average, depreciation rate.
$33,000 ÷ $3,000 = 11, the composite, or average, life.

The annual depreciation for the first year would be $3,000, which is equal to cost times the composite rate, or $42,100 × 7.125 percent. Note that if there were no changes in the asset account, annual depreciation of $3,000 would accumulate to $33,000 over the average life of eleven years, and the assets would be depreciated to the total estimated salvage, or $9,100. On the other hand, with normal retirements and replacements of assets, the actual average service life of the assets would be influenced by company policy with regard to repairs and replacements.

To illustrate the computation of annual depreciation when there are retirements and replacements, assume that asset D in the illustration above is retired with salvage recovery of $100 and is replaced by an asset costing $2,500, which is reflected by the following entries:

Cash	100.00	
Accumulated depreciation ($2,100 – $100)	2,000.00	
Asset account		2,100.00
Asset account	2,500.00	
Cash		2,500.00

Since depreciation is computed on the balance in the asset account at the beginning of the period, the depreciation for the following year would be $3,028.13, and the following entry would be made for that year:

Depreciation expense [($42,100 – $2,100 + $2,500)(.07125)]	3,028.13	
Accumulated depreciation		3,028.13

In addition to assuming replacement with similar assets, a basic assumption underlying group or composite depreciation, which should be supported by past experience, is that any underdepreciation of assets retired early will be offset by overdepreciation on assets that prove to have a longer life than was estimated. Based on this assumption, it is argued that operating results are more meaningfully presented by this method, because, unlike unit depreciation, it does not recognize gains and losses that result from normal variations in asset lives.

On the other hand, one of the primary disadvantages of group and composite depreciation is that the averaging process can result in significant cumulative errors from average that may go undetected. This is especially true of composite depreciation, where the operating lives of the assets can have a fairly wide range. Consequently, firms using group or composite depreciation have to revise their depreciation rate from time to time in order to bring the balance in the asset account in line with the accumulated depreciation account.

Finally, it should be pointed out that the primary argument for group or composite depreciation in terms of clerical convenience has been weakened by the advent of the computer. Even for a company with a large number of tangible long-lived assets, unit-depreciation property records are feasible via the use of company computers. However, this does not deny the fact that accounting depreciation is cost allocation, and group or composite methods do result in systematic cost allocation.

DEPLETION

Introduction. Natural resources, such as those from mines, timber tracts, or oil wells, are wasting assets in the sense that they are moving toward exhaustion as they are being physically removed from the property and becoming the product to be sold. Since natural resources are normally acquired by a lump-sum payment, but are normally extracted over several years, the accounting problem, similar to depreciation, is one of cost allocation. It is a problem of allocating the cost of the exhaustion of natural resources to fiscal periods.

Based on the historical-cost, fiscal-period, matching, and revenue-recognition assumptions, the accountant assigns the cost of the natural resources to inventory and recognizes the cost of the natural-resource inventory sold during the fiscal period (similar to cost of goods sold) and the cost of the natural-resource inventory still on hand at the end of the fiscal period. The systematic allocation of the cost of a wasting asset to expense and to inventory is called *depletion.* Depletion represents the exhaustion of the cost of a wasting asset resulting from the conversion of the natural resource into inventory. Thus, depletion is similar to depreciation in that both represent cost allocations for purposes of income determination.

The depletion base. The depletion base is the total cost (or in some cases, the appraised amount) of the wasting asset minus the estimated salvage of the land after the natural resources have been removed. Development costs, such as those incurred in the removal of surface earth for strip-mining operations, the sinking of shafts, drilling of wells, and timbering of mines, should be set up in the accounts separately from the original cost of the wasting asset. They should be written off in amounts proportionate to the write-offs of the original cost of the wasting asset if the developments will render service throughout the entire life of the wasting asset. They should be written off over a shorter period if their usefulness will expire before the wasting asset is completely depleted.

If development expenditures prove fruitless, as in the case of the drilling of a dry well, they should be written off. It is not acceptable to carry forward any lost costs. However, if a company is engaged more or less continuously in developmental work of the type in which only a fraction of the projects can be expected to be successful, it can be argued that the cost of the unsuccessful projects is a necessary cost to secure the successful projects. Therefore, the cost of fruitless efforts need not be written off immediately but can be assigned to the successful developments, provided that a record exists showing a reasonable number of successes.

If the cutting of a tract of timberland is deferred to obtain the benefit of growth, it is permissible to capitalize the costs of protection, insurance, and administrative expenses incurred in connection with the tract.

Development costs may be incurred after operations begin. Three procedures are used in dealing with such costs. A deferral may be set up for the estimated aggregate development costs to be incurred during the life of the property, so that this aggregate cost will be spread ratably over each unit of product. Or development costs incurred after operations begin can be capitalized when the expenditures are made, and the depletion charge may be adjusted. Or they may be charged to current income.

After operations begin, a careful distinction must be made between operating expenses and expenditures that may be regarded as development costs to be capitalized.

Depletion methods. Depletion is usually computed by dividing the cost or appraised amount of the wasting asset, minus estimated salvage of the land, by the estimated number of tons, barrels, thousand feet, or other units in the asset, thus determining a unit depletion charge. The total depletion charge for each period is then computed by multiplying the unit charge by the number of units converted during the period into inventory.

To illustrate, assume that $95,000 is paid for a mine that is estimated to contain 300,000 tons of available deposit and have an estimated salvage of $5,000. The unit depletion charge is:

$$(\$95{,}000 - \$5{,}000) \div 300{,}000 = \$.30$$

If 20,000 tons are mined in a given year, the depletion for that year would be $.30 × 20,000, or $6,000, and the following entry would be made:

Depletion cost	6,000	
Accumulated depletion		6,000

For purposes of correct income determination, the depletion deduction must be based on the number of units sold. Depletion applicable to the units not sold is included in the cost of the inventory. Amortization of drilling and development costs, as well as the costs associated with the removal of the resource from its natural location to the company's inventory, are also part of inventory cost.

For example, if 15,000 tons are sold from the 20,000 tons mined in the illustration above, and if there are other production costs of $8,000, then the cost of the natural resource sold and the cost of the ending natural-resource inventory would be as follows:

	Total Cost	Cost Per Unit
Cost of goods sold:		
Depletion (20,000 × \$.30)	\$ 6,000	\$.30
Material, labor, and overhead costs.	8,000	.40
Total production cost...............	\$14,000	\$.70
Ending inventory (5,000 × \$.70) ...	3,500	
Cost of goods sold (15,000 × \$.70) .	\$10,500	

This would be reflected by the following entry:

Cost of goods sold.......................	10,500	
Inventory in process.....................	3,500	
Depletion cost		6,000
Material, labor, and overhead costs.		8,000

Depreciation of plant. Depreciation must, of course, be provided on buildings and machinery located on a wasting asset. If the life of the wasting asset is estimated to be less than the life of the plant, it is customary to accept the life of the wasting asset as the life of the plant for depreciation purposes. This is based on the concept that the plant will have only a salvage amount when it is no longer needed for operations in its present location. As the life of the wasting asset is contingent upon the amount of annual operations, the depreciation of the plant may be computed on the same basis that is used for depletion; that is:

$$\textbf{Annual depreciation} = (\textbf{Cost} - \textbf{Salvage}) \times \frac{\textbf{Units extracted during year}}{\textbf{Total estimated units}}$$

Wasting-asset write-ups. Writing up wasting assets because of increases in market valuation is subject to the same objections that apply to writing up other long-lived assets for the same reason. However, write-ups to reflect discovery value and accretion are generally regarded as permissible.

Discovery value is a term applicable in situations where property that was acquired at a mere land cost is found to contain deposits of natural resources, or when deposits are found to be more extensive than they were believed to be when purchased.

Accretion is a term particularly applicable to timber tracts. For many years, timber tracts were generally regarded as wasting assets, because it was the custom to cut tracts without reforestation, and the recording of accretion was not considered to be in accordance with good accounting. Now that many companies that are dependent on a constant supply of forest products have adopted a policy of maintaining timber tracts from which successive crops are harvested on a partial and selective basis, timber tracts are no longer always wasting assets. When timber tracts are operated on a crop basis, accountants consider it acceptable accounting to charge the asset account with amounts representing growth accretion.

If wasting assets are written up to reflect discovery value or accretion, the asset write-up should be offset by a credit to an unrealized increment account. Depletion will thereafter be based on the appraised amount. There is some opinion to the effect that the credit for the unrealized increment should be considered as part of the permanent capital of the enterprise. Traditional conservative accounting requires that no portion of this credit balance find its way to Retained Earnings until the depletion charges have accumulated to an amount equal to the cost of the asset; thereafter, transfers may be made from Unrealized Increment to Income or Retained Earnings in amounts equal to the periodic depletion. It is less conservative, although usually regarded as permissible, after charging Operations with depletion on the appraised amount, to transfer immediately from the unrealized increment account to Income or Retained Earnings the portion of the periodic depletion charge representing so-called "realized appreciation." Realized appreciation is determined by applying the following formula:

Depletion rate based on appraisal minus depletion rate based on cost, times number of units sold

If the depletion charge based on appraised amount is $.08 per unit of ore, and the depletion charge based on cost is $.05 per unit, and 100,000 units are mined, $8,000 of depletion would be charged. If the 100,000 units are sold, a transfer of $3,000 would be made from Unrealized Increment to Income or Retained Earnings.

In making the entry for realized appreciation, the accountant should give recognition to inventories. For instance, assume that the data above apply to the first year of a company's operations, and that 10,000 units remain in the inventory; the transfer entry would be:

Unrealized appreciation of ore in mine (100,000 × $.03)	3,000	
Allowance for unrealized appreciation in inventory (10,000 × $.03)		300
Realized appreciation or Retained earnings (90,000 × $.03)		2,700

If, during the second year of operations, the same quantity is mined but the inventory is reduced to 5,000 units, the transfer entry would be:

Unrealized appreciation of ore in mine (100,000 × $.03)	3,000	
Allowance for unrealized appreciation in inventory (5,000 × $.03)	150	
Realized appreciation or Retained earnings [(10,000 + 100,000 − 5,000) ($.03)]..........		3,150

Depletion and dividends. Companies operating wasting assets are permitted to pay dividends in amounts equal to accumulated net income plus accumulated depletion charges. Corporations paying such dividends should inform their stockholders that the dividends represent a partial return of capital. If such piecemeal capital payback could not legally be made to the stockholders during the exploitation of the natural resource, the corporation would be obliged to hold the funds until the exhaustion of the property. This might be advisable if the corporation expected to acquire and operate another similar piece of property, but not otherwise. The law, therefore, allows the corporation to follow the financial policy best suited to its plans, basing this permission on the assumption that the creditors, knowing the nature of the business, are in a position to protect their interests.

Depletion must, of course, be provided as an expense before net income can be known. The fact that dividends can be paid in an amount equal to cumulative net income and depletion has given rise to the too-prevalent belief that depletion need not be recognized as an expense for accounting purposes. When it is remembered that the cost of a wasting asset is, in effect, the cost of a long-time supply of raw material, it becomes apparent that the omission of a depletion charge is equivalent to the omission, by a manufacturing company, of a charge for the cost of the materials used.

The fact that companies operating wasting assets can legally pay dividends to the extent of cumulative net income and depletion has given rise to the expression, "dividends paid out of depletion reserves." Such dividends are in no sense paid out of the accumulated depletion account. They may be equal to the depletion charges, but when it is recognized that the accumulated depletion account is a contra account reflecting a decrease in an asset resulting from operations, it becomes obvious that dividends cannot be paid out of, or charged to, the accumulated depletion account. They should be charged to a special account that will clearly indicate that they represent a distribution of the invested capital.

For example, assume the following summarized data:

Assets	$500,000
Accumulated depletion	50,000
	$450,000
Liabilities	$110,000
Capital stock	300,000
Retained earnings	40,000
	$450,000

Dividends of $90,000 ($50,000 + $40,000) could be declared, and would be recorded as follows:

Retained earnings	40,000	
Return of capital to stockholders—Dividends	50,000	
Dividends payable		90,000

The return of capital of $50,000 would be reported in the balance sheet as a deduction from capital stock.

Percentage depletion. The federal income tax regulations with respect to depletion are too extensive and complex to be discussed here, other than to mention the existence of percentage or statutory depletion. Percentage depletion is the annual tax-deductible depletion charge that is computed by multiplying a fixed percentage by gross margin. Under current tax regulations at the time of this writing, the fixed percentages are specified (such as 22 percent of gross margin for oil and gas wells), but the depletion cannot exceed 50 percent of the taxable income from the property, excluding depletion. Note that as long as the property is generating income, percentage depletion is allowable for tax purposes, and the cumulative deductions can greatly exceed the property cost; hence, percentage depletion is not acceptable for accounting purposes.

17

Long-Lived Assets: Revaluations

Revision of depreciation rates. The discussion of depreciation charges in the preceding chapter shows that calculation of the annual depreciation on any asset involves the use of estimates concerning the useful life of the asset and its salvage amount, if any. The accuracy of these estimates will obviously not be known until the asset is retired from service.

However, during the life of the asset, it may become evident that changes should be made in the original estimates of useful life and/or salvage amount, resulting in annual depreciation charges different from those previously recorded. Such situations have been dealt with by the Accounting Principles Board in its *Opinion No. 20.* The board has stated that changes in accounting estimates such as service lives and salvage amounts of depreciable assets "should be accounted for in (a) the period of change if the change affects that period only, or (b) the period of change and future periods if the change affects both. A change in an estimate should not be accounted for by restating amounts reported in financial statements of prior periods or by reporting pro forma amounts for prior periods."[1]

---

[1]Accounting Principles Board, "Accounting Changes," *Opinion No. 20* (New York: AICPA, July 1971), p. 397.

Under this procedure, no changes will be made in the depreciation charges recorded in prior years. Several possible situations involving changes in the service life of a depreciable asset will now be discussed.

RETIREMENT OF ASSET PRIOR TO END OF ESTIMATED SERVICE LIFE: If a depreciable asset is retired from use prior to the end of its estimated useful life, any excess or deficiency in the depreciation of prior years will be known at that time. For example, an asset costing \$10,000, with an estimated useful life of ten years and zero salvage, is depreciated at the rate of \$1,000 per year under the straight-line method. Assume that at the end of eight years, the asset is of no further use and is disposed of without any proceeds being received. The book amount of the asset at the end of the eight years would be \$2,000 (\$10,000 − \$8,000). Had an eight-year life been used to compute the annual depreciation charge, the annual depreciation would have been \$1,250 (\$10,000 ÷ 8 years) and there would have been no gain or loss on the disposal, as the book amount would have been zero at the end of eight years. In fact, a loss of \$2,000 will be recognized on the disposal, calculated as the difference between the book amount of the asset (\$2,000) and the proceeds received (zero).

USE OF ASSET BEYOND ESTIMATED SERVICE LIFE: Just the opposite of the preceding illustration would be the case in which an asset that has been fully depreciated is used beyond the original estimated useful life. Assume that the asset referred to in the example above is used for two additional years, making its total service life 12 years rather than ten. This would indicate that the annual depreciation for the first ten years the asset was used should have been \$833.33 (\$10,000 ÷ 12 years), rather than \$1,000. However, no adjustment is made in the depreciation recorded in the first ten years, and no additional depreciation is recorded in years 11 and 12.

REVISION OF ESTIMATED SERVICE LIFE: Assume now that the asset previously referred to has been in use for five years, at which time it is decided that the asset can be used for a total of 12 years, or an additional seven years from this date. The undepreciated portion of the cost of the asset is \$5,000, determined as follows:

Cost	\$10,000
Accumulated depreciation (\$1,000 × 5)	5,000
Book amount	\$ 5,000

Under the treatment required by the Accounting Principles Board, future depreciation charges are determined by taking the undepreciated portion of the cost and depreciating it over the years remaining in the estimated useful life. Thus, the annual depreciation for years 6 through 12 would be \$714.29 (\$5,000 ÷ 7 years).

The position taken by the Accounting Principles Board in *Opinion No. 20* reaffirmed the Board's position in *Opinion No. 9* when it stated that "changes in the estimated remaining lives of fixed assets affect the computed amounts of depreciation, but these changes should be considered prospective in nature and not prior-period adjustments."[2]

The basic argument underlying the treatment recommended by the board is that estimates are required in various areas of accounting in order to determine periodic net income. The effect of future events cannot be known, so judgment is exercised to make estimates when necessary. The depreciation charges of prior years were based upon the best information available at the time. It may be necessary that estimates be changed when additional experience and information are available.

Not all accountants agree that the method just discussed is the proper way to account for revisions of estimated useful life. They argue that the method compensates for misstatements of depreciation in prior periods by misstating future charges in the opposite direction. In order to avoid this, an alternative procedure is advocated. It involves the following steps: (1) correction of the depreciation charges of prior years, and (2) reporting the depreciation charge for current and future periods as it would have been if the revised estimate of useful life had been used from the beginning.

To illustrate this alternative, the previous facts are repeated:

Asset cost	$10,000
Original estimate of service life	10 years
Original estimate of salvage	zero
Depreciation method	straight-line

Early in the sixth year, it is estimated that the total life of the asset will be 12 years. The following entry is recorded to correct the depreciation charges of prior years:

Accumulated depreciation	833.35	
Correction of prior years' earnings		833.35

The amount of the correction is calculated as follows:

Actual depreciation taken, using a 10-year life [($10,000 ÷ 10) × 5]	$5,000.00
Depreciation that would have been recorded using a 12-year life [($10,000 ÷ 12) × 5]	4,166.65
Excess depreciation recorded in years 1–5	$ 833.35

The annual depreciation recorded for years 6 through 12 is determined as follows:

Adjusted book amount after correction of prior years' depreciation:	
Cost	$10,000.00
Less accumulated depreciation	4,166.65
Undepreciated portion of cost	$ 5,833.35
Annual depreciation charge ($5,833.35 ÷ 7)	$ 833.33

[2]Accounting Principles Board, "Reporting the Results of Operations," *Opinion No. 9* (New York: AICPA, December 1966), p. 116.

DEPARTURES FROM HISTORICAL COST

Valuation methods. The subject of valuation was discussed at length in Chapter 6. The distinction made at that time between valuation and value should be repeated. Valuation involves the process of assigning dollar amounts to assets and liabilities, whereas value is what those assets and liabilities are worth to a particular individual at a specific point in time.

The advantages and disadvantages of various valuation methods, including historical-cost valuation, were discussed in Chapter 6. Under the historical-cost method, cost is measured by the cash or cash equivalent sacrificed in exchange to obtain an asset. In current accounting practice, historical cost is the valuation method used for property, plant, and equipment items. This normally involves the systematic allocation of the historical cost of depreciable assets over their estimated service lives. The reader is referred to pages 142–143 for discussion of the specific advantages and disadvantages of the method.

Departures from historical-cost valuation. It should be obvious from previous chapters that historical-cost valuation is not always used for all assets. Departures are very widespread in accounting for monetary assets. For example, cash is reported at face amount, short-term marketable securities at the lower of cost or market, accounts receivable at net realizable value, and bond investment at discounted amounts to maturity.

Many people, both accountants and nonaccountants, feel that there are situations in which departures from historical-cost valuation would result in more meaningful amounts for long-lived assets in the financial statements.

Before proceeding, it will be helpful to clarify the meaning of certain terms that frequently enter the discussion of possible departures from the historical-cost valuation of assets. First of all, asset amounts may be adjusted because of *general-price-level changes*. However, this represents, not a departure from historical-cost figures, but instead, an attempt to adjust historical-cost amounts so as to report assets at amounts measured in dollars of the same "size."[3] Such adjustments should not be viewed as an approach to reporting assets at *current market prices,* which are measured by current selling or buying prices under orderly selling or buying conditions.

The term *current value* is widely used in the literature dealing with possible alternatives to historical-cost amounts. It is intended to refer to the use of current exchange prices as opposed to historical exchange prices. However, the term actually has no precise meaning, because there are different current exchange prices that could be used.

The concept of *fair value* frequently enters into discussion of procedures to be used to report property, plant, and equipment items at an amount other than historical cost. Fair value can be defined as the exchange price that a well-informed buyer and seller would agree upon, and is not necessarily the same as the

---

[3]The subject of accounting for general-price-level changes is discussed in Chapter 26.

price at which an asset is currently selling. Appraisal amounts represent a means of approximating the fair value of an asset. Appraisal procedures can also be viewed as a current-market valuation method for assigning dollar amounts to assets. Many people advocate the use of appraisal figures for reporting certain assets in financial statements.

Asset appraisals. The use of appraisal amounts in financial statements has been advocated for many years. In fact, beginning during World War I and continuing until the late 1920's, the practice of reporting assets at appraised amounts was quite common. Many accountants felt that appraisals could be recorded in the accounts and reported in the balance sheet if the increase in asset amounts resulting from the appraisals was not credited to retained earnings. However, many such appraisals were followed by write-downs during the depression of the 1930's. Since that time, accountants as a group have been very reluctant to advocate the use of appraisal amounts in financial statements.

Although the authors of *Accounting Research Study No. 3,*[4] published in 1962, offered some theoretical support in favor of the restatement of long-lived assets in terms of current replacement costs, the prevailing attitude of most accountants reflects agreement with the position expressed by the AICPA as long ago as 1940. This position was reaffirmed by the Accounting Principles Board in 1965, when it stated, "The Board is of the opinion that property, plant, and equipment should not be written up by an entity to reflect appraisal, market or current values which are above cost to the entity."[5] Still, there are instances in which firms have used appraisal amounts for reporting certain assets, thus warranting discussion of the procedures involved.

Appraisals are usually made for the purpose of determining *reproduction cost new* and *sound value.* Reproduction cost new is the computed cost of replacing the asset in its present location at current production costs. Sound value is reproduction cost new less the depreciation to date on such amount, using the estimated useful life and salvage resulting from the appraisal. *Condition percent* is the present percentage of sound value to reproduction cost. The determination of reproduction cost new and sound value may be desired for tax, insurance, sale, consolidation, credit, or other purposes, in addition to the unusual case in which the appraisal amount is to be recorded in the accounts.

In order to illustrate the calculation of the amounts referred to in the preceding paragraph, assume that an asset originally acquired for $40,000 is being depreciated over a ten-year life, using the straight-line method and zero salvage. At the end of five years, the asset has a net book amount of $20,000. If at this date the asset is appraised at a reproduction cost of $45,000 and a total useful life of 15 years, the following can be determined:

---

[4]Robert T. Sprouse and Maurice Moonitz, "A Tentative Set of Broad Accounting Principles for Business Enterprises," *Accounting Research Study No. 3* (New York: AICPA, 1962), pp. 32–34.

[5]Accounting Principles Board, "Status of Accounting Research Bulletins," *Opinion No. 6* (New York: AICPA, October 1965), p. 42.

Reproduction cost new (per appraisal)	\$45,000
Sound value [\$45,000 − ($^5/_{15}$ × \$45,000)]	30,000
Condition percent (\$30,000 ÷ \$45,000)	67%

The amount of appreciation to be recorded in the accounts is the amount by which the sound value exceeds the revised book amount of the asset after giving effect to the new information concerning useful life. This is calculated as follows:

Sound value	\$30,000
Less revised book value: [\$40,000 − ($^5/_{15}$ × \$40,000)]	26,667
Appreciation	\$ 3,333

Recording appreciation in the accounts. As noted earlier, current accounting practice does not sanction the writing up of asset amounts to reflect appraisal increases. However, appraisals may reveal information concerning estimated useful lives of long-lived assets that will be used as a basis for revising future depreciation computed on cost, leaving original cost undisturbed. To illustrate, assume the following facts pertaining to an asset:

Original cost (being depreciated over an 8-year life using the straight-line method)	\$10,000
Accumulated depreciation at end of 5 years (\$10,000 × $^5/_8$)	6,250
Reproduction cost new (determined at end of 5 years after acquisition)	15,000
Estimated total useful life (determined at end of 5 years after acquisition)	15 years

This information may be used to calculate future depreciation charges as follows:

Original cost	\$10,000
Accumulated depreciation	6,250
Undepreciated cost	\$ 3,750
Annual depreciation charge for years 6–15. (\$3,750 ÷ 10)	\$ 375

The proper accounting treatment in this situation was discussed earlier in this chapter, under the heading of "Revision of estimated service life." The same procedures could be used to give effect to changes in the estimated salvage amount revealed by an appraisal.

Before we discuss the procedures used to record appraisal increases in the accounts, some consideration should be given to the relation between the recording of such increases and the determination of periodic net income. The offsetting credit for an increase in an asset amount resulting from an appraisal is to an equity account titled Appraisal Capital or Unrealized Capital Increment. In determining income in future periods, it is necessary to consider the increased asset amount in calculating annual depreciation. The Accounting Principles Board has stated that "whenever appreciation has been recorded on the books, income should be charged with depreciation computed on the written-up amounts."[6] Thus, the an-

[6] *Opinion No. 6*, p. 42.

nual depreciation charge will now include depreciation on the original cost as well as on the appraisal increase. The usual procedure is to segregate the appraisal increase from the original cost, so as not to lose sight of the latter. A separate accumulated depreciation account is used to record the depreciation on the appraisal increase recorded on the books. For tax purposes, the depreciable base will still be original cost, and any gain or loss on disposal will be determined by the book amount based upon depreciated original cost.

To illustrate the recording of appraisal increases, assume the following information pertaining to a building:

Original cost (being depreciated over a 20-year life using the straight-line method)	\$50,000
Accumulated depreciation at end of 8 years (\$50,000 × $^8/_{20}$)	20,000
Undepreciated cost	\$30,000
Reproduction cost new (determined at end of 8 years after acquisition)	\$60,000

It is also assumed that the appraisal did not result in any change in the estimated total useful life. Therefore, the sound value of the asset at this time is \$60,000 minus \$24,000 (\$60,000 × $^8/_{20}$), or \$36,000. The entry to record the information on the books is presented below:

Building—Appraisal increase (\$60,000 − \$50,000)	10,000	
Accumulated depreciation—Building—Appraisal increase (\$24,000 − \$20,000)		4,000
Unrealized capital increment—Appraisal of building (\$10,000 − \$4,000)		6,000

The credit of \$4,000 to the accumulated depreciation account in the entry above represents the depreciation on the appraisal increment for the eight years the asset has been in use, or \$10,000 × $^8/_{20}$. The credit to the unrealized capital increment account represents the increase in equity resulting from the increase in the net amount at which the building is reported on the books. It should be noted that the capital increment is different from the two major sources of owners' equity—paid-in capital and retained earnings—in that it did not result from an inflow of assets to the firm. This is the reason it is designated as unrealized capital.

The entry to record annual depreciation after the appraisal is shown below:

Depreciation expense—Building (\$60,000 ÷ 20)	3,000	
Accumulated depreciation—Building—Cost (\$50,000 ÷ 20)		2,500
Accumulated depreciation—Building—Appraisal increase (\$10,000 ÷ 20)		500

Another accounting question raised by the recording of appraisal increments on the books concerns the disposition of the unrealized capital increment. If the entry illustrated above is the only entry recorded each year, the effect of recording the appraisal increase will be to reduce the reported income by \$500 annually. At the end of the estimated life of 20 years (12 years after the appraisal), both the original cost of \$50,000 and the appraisal increment of \$10,000 will have been fully depreciated, and the unrealized capital increment of \$6,000 will still be on the books. When the asset is retired, it would seem necessary to dispose of the capital increment in some manner.

The basic question here is whether or not the appraisal increment should be reported as a part of the realized income of the firm. Some accountants argue that the increment should not be reported on the firm's income statement. They advocate that the increment be transferred to retained earnings over the remaining life of the asset. This would be accomplished by the following entry, recorded each year for years 9 through 20.

Unrealized capital increment—Appraisal of building........	500	
Retained earnings..		500

The amount of this entry is the same as the portion of the increment being charged to depreciation expense each year. The effect of this procedure is to transfer the entire increment of $6,000 to retained earnings over the 12-year period the asset was in use after the appraisal. There is an inconsistency inherent in this method, in that depreciation expense on the income statement is based upon the higher appraisal amount, but the retained earnings balance at the end of each year will be the same as if no increment had been recorded.

An alternative treatment of the appraisal increment is to report the amount of the increment realized through depreciation charges each year on the firm's income statement by use of a special revenue account. Under this procedure, it is possible to report the results of operations based on original-cost depreciation. This approach might be viewed as first reporting the higher depreciation on appraisal amounts and then adjusting the net income upward (by use of the special revenue account) to reflect the lower original-cost depreciation. The ultimate effect, of course, is the same as for the first procedure discussed—an increase in retained earnings by the amount of the depreciation taken on the appraisal increment.

Appraisal increments viewed as permanent changes. Not all accountants feel that the two alternatives just discussed represent the proper treatment of appraisal increments. There are those who argue that such increments should be viewed as permanent capital and should not be transferred, either directly or indirectly, to retained earnings.[7] The recording of the higher appraisal amounts is viewed as establishing a new accounting basis for the assets. The increment is not considered an unrealized amount, but rather permanent capital that should not be affected by the use or sale of the asset. The credit to record the increment in this case would be to a capital adjustment account.

Pros and cons of revaluation. The major argument for the use of appraisal amounts in the accounts is directly related to the annual depreciation charge and the maintaining of a given level of productive capacity. Although depreciation accounting does not represent a provision for the replacement of assets, it is certainly true that

[7] A minority of the Committee on Accounting Procedure of the AICPA took this position in *Accounting Research Bulletin No. 43* (New York: AICPA, 1953).

assets must be replaced as they are retired, and such replacement must take place at the then-current price. Failure to charge operations for amounts sufficient to replace the assets used to produce income has the effect of impairing the real capital of the firm.

It is also argued that failure to include current market valuations in the financial statements impairs the comparability of financial data among firms. Owing to the fact that different companies have assets acquired at different times, intercompany comparisons may be misleading. For example, one firm may appear to be better managed simply because its assets on the average were acquired at a lower cost than were those of a competitor.

Some people believe that without information concerning current market valuations, business management may not be able to make certain decisions in the best interest of the firm. For example, the difference between depreciation charges on historical cost and the depreciation on current market valuations may be significant in certain management decisions.

Many accountants are opposed to the introduction of current market valuations in the accounts primarily because of their subjectivity. They view historical cost as an objective amount that is relatively easy to measure. Thus far, there has been considerable difference of opinion as to just what measure of current market valuation would be the appropriate one to use. Appraisal amounts, which have been discussed in this chapter, represent one possible measure.

Those opposed to current market valuation feel that comparability of financial data among firms might be more difficult if such valuation is allowed. Some firms might choose to incorporate the amounts into their records, while others may decide to retain historical cost. This problem was noted by the Committee on Accounting Procedure of the AICPA in considering the question of appraisal amounts and related depreciation.

It can also be argued that the recording of annual depreciation amounts and the replacement of assets are two different matters. Obviously, management can and does use current-value information in making operating decisions. In many managerial decisions, the depreciation charge on historical cost is irrelevant.

A concluding note should be made at this point. The foregoing discussion has been concerned primarily with the use of amounts other than historical costs for reporting long-lived assets in the financial statements. It should be remembered that there is also the important question facing accountants today of whether financial statements should be adjusted for general-price-level changes. The subject of adjustments for general-price-level changes has been referred to previously and is discussed in detail in Chapter 26.

Asset write-downs. It is possible that the current market valuation of certain long-lived assets may be significantly below the amounts at which they are carried in the accounting records. This situation may require that the asset amounts be restated in order to produce more meaningful accounting data in the future. This can be accomplished in the same manner as that previously illustrated for upward revaluations. For depreciable assets, both the asset account and the related accumulated depreciation account are usually affected, and stockholders' equity would be reduced as a result of the revaluation.

Notwithstanding the theoretical treatment mentioned in the preceding paragraph, accounting practice, based on the doctrine of conservatism, appears to sanction reporting the unrealized loss resulting from downward revaluations as charges against income in the period in which the revaluation takes place. The loss would be reported in the firm's income statement, and full disclosure of the attendant circumstances should be made. Note, however, that the recognition of such unrealized losses in current accounting practice is generally with regard to assets that are to be sold (such as inventory), rather than long-lived assets.

QUASI REORGANIZATIONS

Purpose of quasi reorganizations. A quasi reorganization takes place as a means of establishing a new basis of accountability for assets, so as to give the corporation a fresh start. Usually, the firm is in financial difficulty—perhaps as the result of depressed business conditions generally, or perhaps as the result of losses that have created such a large deficit that the firm has little chance of being able to accumulate earnings for dividend charges within the foreseeable future.

For example, during a time of business depression, a firm might have been operating unprofitably, and it may currently be unable to utilize its productive facilities to operate at a profit, given the historical-cost amounts now recorded on the books. A number of the assets of an unprofitable business, acquired during more prosperous times, may be carried on the books at amounts considerably higher than their future service potential. Under such circumstances, the board of directors might order a number of significant changes, possibly including the removal or reassignment of managerial personnel, the abandonment of certain facilities, and the adjustment of the company's capital structure in an attempt to regain business health. A new basis of accountability for assets is normally a part of this fresh start toward profitable operations.

Under such conditions, the question arises as to whether financial statements prepared in accordance with generally accepted principles of accounting will always result in meaningful reports. What is the merit of continuing to charge depreciation or amortization on cost if it is likely that a share of such cost outlays has in fact become a "lost" cost? If this is the case, should not the loss be taken now, instead of being taken gradually by continuing the depreciation or amortization charges on the basis of the old costs? Will not future operating results be misstated by a failure to give recognition now to any lost costs? Also, if a corporation has a sizable deficit (debit balance in the retained earnings account), is there any merit in a requirement that such deficit be carried forward under all circumstances? Instead of carrying forward in the accounts the handicaps associated with the past, why not, in conjunction with a plan of action to alter the business to conform with its new environment, permit a fresh start in the accounts? If a business is in fact making a fresh start in its operating affairs, it seems desirable that the basis of accountability for its assets and stockholders' equity be similarly adjusted to coincide with the new conditions.

To bring some of the questions above into sharper focus, assume that a corporation's books show the condition summarized below:

Long-lived assets, after deducting depreciation and amortization	$2,000,000
Other assets	700,000
Less liabilities	1,000,000*
Net assets	$1,700,000
Capital stock	$1,500,000
Capital in excess of par (or stated) value	500,000
Less debit balance in retained earnings account	300,000*
Stockholders' equity	$1,700,000

*Deduction.

It is also assumed that the investment in long-lived assets (the $2,000,000 carrying amount above) probably cannot be recovered from future operations. In short, the present management would not invest $2,000,000 to acquire the existing long-lived assets because it is unlikely that such an outlay would be recovered from the use of those facilities.

Consider first the matter of the deficit. To eliminate the deficit, the company *could* transfer its net assets to a newly organized corporation in exchange for the capital stock of the new company, which might begin its corporate existence with the following account balances:

Long-lived assets	$2,000,000
Other assets	700,000
Less liabilities	1,000,000*
Net assets	$1,700,000
Capital stock	$1,500,000
Capital in excess of par (or stated) value	200,000
Stockholders' equity	$1,700,000

*Deduction.

One thing would be accomplished: The deficit would be eliminated. But what about the reduction of the carrying amount of the long-lived assets to more realistic amounts? The transfer of assets to a new corporate entity obviously sanctions a change in asset valuations; but should accounting rules insist upon the creation of a new corporate entity before the historical continuity of any of the account balances can be interrupted?

Quasi reorganization procedures. In general, the answer to the question above is no. Within the framework of generally accepted accounting, a quasi reorganization allows a fresh start in an accounting sense, without the expenses and other disadvantages incident to the creation of a new corporate entity. It has the following characteristics:

(1) The existing corporate entity is not disturbed.
(2) Recorded asset amounts may be readjusted (downward) to conform to present conditions.
(3) Typically, a deficit is eliminated.
(4) A quasi reorganization requires complete disclosure of the effects it has had on the accounts.

As the characteristics above imply, a quasi reorganization is something less formal than a legal reorganization. The accounting result of a quasi reorganization is in substance the same *as if* a legal reorganization *had* occurred.

What formalities, if any, are required to effect a quasi reorganization? *Accounting Series Release No. 25* of the Securities and Exchange Commission states that "it has been the Commission's view for some time that a quasi reorganization may not be considered to have been effected unless ... the entire procedure is made known to all persons entitled to vote on matters of general corporate policy and the appropriate consents to the particular transactions are obtained in advance in accordance with the applicable law and charter provisions."

A quasi reorganization is often brought about without legal formalities of any kind. If the company has capital in excess of par (or stated) value that is legally available for dividends, the offsetting of the operating deficit against such "excess" does not affect the net amount legally available for dividends. On the other hand, the change in the capital structure may be such as to necessitate obtaining an amendment of the corporate charter.

As indicated above, a quasi reorganization enables a company to eliminate a deficit. The deficit may be attributable to operating losses or to the recognition of other losses. A deficit need not exist in the accounts before a quasi reorganization is effected; the deficit may develop as a result of asset write-downs recorded as part of the quasi-reorganization entries. In other words, if assets are overvalued in the accounts, a write-down of such assets to current market valuation should be a part of the quasi reorganization. It is a part of the fresh start. The write-down establishes a new and current measure of management's accountability; it gives recognition to a loss that occurred prior to the quasi reorganization; it enables the company to compute its operating charges for depreciation and amortization on the basis of values as of the date of the fresh start; and such a write-down may produce a debit balance in the retained earnings account.

To illustrate asset write-downs in connection with a quasi reorganization, let us return to the preceding illustration and assume that the long-lived assets carried at \$2,000,000 would be more properly reported at \$1,600,000, considering the new conditions. Assume that, in order to create an amount of capital in excess of par (or stated) value sufficient to provide for writing down the long-lived assets to current market valuation and for eliminating the operating deficit, the capital stock is reduced from \$1,500,000 to \$1,000,000. If the stock has a par value, the reduction can be accomplished by reducing the number or the par value of the shares outstanding, or by changing from a par to a no-par basis and assigning to the no-par shares an aggregate stated value less than the aggregate par value of the shares formerly outstanding. If the stock is without par value, the number of outstanding shares or the stated value per share may be reduced.

Entries to record the quasi reorganization are shown below:

Capital stock	500,000	
Capital in excess of par (or stated) value........		500,000
To record the capital stock reduction from $1,500,000 to $1,000,000.		
Retained earnings	400,000	
Long-lived assets		400,000
To record the reduction in the book amount of the long-lived assets from $2,000,000 to $1,600,000.		
Capital in excess of par (or stated) value...............	700,000	
Retained earnings		700,000
To write off the debit balance in Retained Earnings against the capital-in-excess account.		

These entries produce the following account balances:

Long-lived assets	$1,600,000
Other assets..	700,000
Less liabilities...	1,000,000*
Net assets	$1,300,000
Capital stock	$1,000,000
Capital in excess of par (or stated) value.....................	300,000
Stockholders' equity	$1,300,000

*Deduction.

Any reduction in the book valuation of long-lived or other assets that is made in connection with a quasi reorganization should represent a real loss incurred prior thereto; any write-down in excess of such an incurred loss would have the unjustifiable result of relieving subsequent operations of proper charges for depreciation, amortization, or other costs and thus would result in an overstatement of earnings subsequent to the reorganization. In other words, an unjustifiable debit to Capital in Excess of Par (or Stated) Value at the time of the quasi reorganization would ultimately result in an unjustifiable addition to Retained Earnings. However, it is considered proper to provide for losses and expenses that can reasonably be assumed to have been incurred in the past, although the amounts thereof may not be definitely determinable at the date of the quasi reorganization. Unrequired balances in such accounts should ultimately be transferred to a capital-in-excess account.

If, subsequent to a quasi reorganization, it is desired to make additional write-downs in the valuation of assets owned at the time of the reorganization, is it permissible to make such write-downs against the Capital in Excess? The general opinion seems to be that the results of operations may be misstated unless caution is exercised, and that such subsequent write-downs should be charged to a capital-in-excess account only in case they can be definitely established as representing decreases in value that occurred prior to the quasi reorganization but were not recognized or measurable at that time.

On the other hand, suppose that an asset, written down to its estimated realizable value as a part of a quasi reorganization, is subsequently sold for more than its new carrying amount. Is such excess of sales proceeds over the new carrying amount a gain, or does it represent a correction of the quasi reorganization write-down? If the sale occurs soon after the quasi, the selling price may be a better indication of asset valuation at the time of the quasi than the estimate used, in which case the sale should be viewed as providing a basis for a correction of the quasi entries. If the accountant had known the future sale price at the time of the quasi, he probably would have used that amount for the write-down. Then there would have been no "gain" when the asset was sold. In those cases in which a deficit was eliminated by the quasi reorganization, it would be logical to carry the net credit from the sale to a capital-in-excess account. Of course, if it can be established that the asset increased in price since the quasi reorganization, then the excess should be accounted for as a gain.

In the statements rendered at the close of the period in which a quasi reorganization was effected, there should be disclosure of all facts relative to the quasi—particularly the amount of the operating deficit eliminated. In the statements for that period and subsequent periods, the retained earnings should be "dated": The statements should show that the retained earnings have been accumulated since the date as of which a quasi reorganization took place, with a deficit eliminated from the accounts. The disclosure may be made as follows:

Retained earnings—Accumulated since December 31, 19+1, the date of a quasi reorganization	$xxxx

How long such dating should be continued has not been determined, but a maximum period of ten years has been mentioned.[8] It has also been suggested that the dating should be continued until the company has established a new earnings record.

As noted earlier, a quasi reorganization is comparable to a new start. If a deficit in the retained earnings account is eliminated at that time, the historical distinction maintained in the accounts between paid-in capital and stockholders' equity resulting from earnings is disrupted. The date of the quasi reorganization is the starting point for a new record of retained earnings. Should it also be the date of a fresh start in the capital in excess of par (or stated) value accounts? Prior to a quasi reorganization, there might have been several capital-in-excess accounts that classified the paid-in elements of the stockholders' equity according to source; it appears to be acceptable to show any capital in excess remaining after the quasi reorganization in a single account, indicating in the title of this account that its balance is the aggregate capital in excess of par (or stated) value remaining at the date of the fresh start. Any capital in excess arising after the quasi reorganization should be classified by source in new accounts.

---

[8]Committee on Accounting Procedure, "Discontinuance of Dating Earned Surplus," *Accounting Research Bulletin No. 46* (New York: AICPA, February 1956), p. 11.

What about charges to any capital in excess carried forward after a quasi reorganization? As a general rule, the source of capital-in-excess accounts is an important criterion in establishing the kinds of charges that can be made to such accounts. For example, prior to a quasi reorganization, a premium paid on the retirement of preferred stock could be charged against any capital in excess traceable to preferred stockholders, under the concept that it would be equitable to consider the retirement premium as a return of capital originally invested by the preferred stockholders. But in the opinion of the authors, if charges have been made to capital-in-excess accounts during a quasi, that destroys the classification according to source, and no attempt should subsequently be made to identify any capital-in-excess residue according to source.

The question is sometimes raised of whether or not assets may be written up in connection with a quasi reorganization. Accounting sanction of quasi reorganizations has been based on a recognition of the desirability of allowing corporations to make a fresh start if they have incurred substantial losses or if their assets are materially overstated. Although firms occasionally write up some assets as long as the adjustments as a whole result in a net write-down, the procedure is generally discouraged. No approval has been given to a net write-up.

Assets whose amounts are changed as a part of a quasi reorganization retain their historical-cost basis for tax purposes. Thus, depreciation for tax purposes would remain the same.

18

Intangibles

Nature of intangible assets. Intangible assets are those assets that do not have physical substance. They are of benefit to a firm because of the special rights they afford the owner and the resulting contribution they make to the income of the firm. Examples of intangible assets are patents, copyrights, leaseholds, trademarks, and goodwill. Although such assets do not have physical substance, they may have considerable worth.

Traditionally, intangible assets were classified into two groups: those having a limited term of existence and those having an unlimited term of existence. However, the Accounting Principles Board has now dropped this distinction.

> The Board believes that the value of intangible assets at any one date eventually disappears and that the recorded costs of intangible assets should be amortized by systematic charges to income over the periods estimated to be benefited.... The period of amortization should not, however, exceed forty years.[1]

[1] Accounting Principles Board, "Intangible Assets," *Opinion No. 17* (New York: AICPA, August 1970), pp. 339–40.

Thus, not only did the board decide that all intangible assets have a finite life, but that 40 years is the maximum life for accounting purposes. At the same time, the board recognized that it may not be possible to determine at acquisition just what the maximum life of some intangible assets would be. For example, certain intangibles have definite legal lives that can be used as a basis for determining the period of time over which they will be amortized. Even though the useful life may be considerably shorter than the legal life, it is usually possible to state the estimated useful life in years. Such assets are considered to have determinate life.

However, for some assets, such as goodwill, the life is neither infinite nor specifically limited. Such assets are considered to be of indeterminate life. Even if circumstances indicate that the life of such assets is likely to be in excess of 40 years, the board stated that the cost of these assets "should be amortized over the maximum period of forty years, not an arbitrary shorter period."[2]

Identifiable and unidentifiable intangibles. In *Opinion No. 17,* the board also noted that certain intangible assets may be identified and given descriptive names. Examples cited were patents, franchises, and trademarks. Such assets may be acquired individually, or as part of a group of assets, or as part of an entire firm. Various *identifiable* intangible assets will be discussed later in this chapter.

The board also noted that certain types of intangible assets are *unidentifiable,* in that they lack specific identifiability, and that such assets could not be acquired individually. The best example of this type of asset is commonly referred to as goodwill and represents the excess of cost of an acquired company over the total of the identifiable net assets. This intangible asset will be discussed in greater detail in a later section of this chapter.

Accounting for intangible assets. As already indicated, a firm may acquire intangible assets by purchasing them. It is also possible that a firm may develop such assets itself. No matter whether the intangible is purchased or developed, there are basically three accounting problems associated with intangible assets. These are (1) determination of initial cost, (2) accounting for the cost under normal business conditions, and (3) accounting for the cost in those circumstances where there are significant and permanent declines in future service potential.

Acquisition cost. In keeping with principles discussed in previous chapters concerning the acquisition of assets, intangible assets acquired from others should be recorded at cost. For transactions involving cash, the cost of an intangible asset is measured by the cash paid. When payment includes assets other than cash, including stock issuances, the general rule is that cost is the fair market value of the consideration given up or the fair market value of the property acquired, whichever can be more clearly determined. If several intangibles are acquired in a lump-sum purchase, or if intangibles are acquired with other assets, a separate cost should be established for each intangible acquired.

The accounting for those intangible assets developed within the firm depends

---

[2] *Opinion No. 17,* p. 340.

upon whether or not they are identifiable. The Accounting Principles Board has stated:

> The Board concludes that a company should record as assets the costs of intangible assets acquired from other enterprises or individuals. Costs of developing, maintaining, or restoring intangible assets which are not specifically identifiable, have indeterminate lives, or are inherent in a continuing business and related to an enterprise as a whole—such as goodwill—should be deducted from income when incurred.[3]

Amortization. The major problem in the amortization of intangible assets is the determination of useful life. Many factors affect the periods to be benefited by such assets. Some of the factors that should be considered are listed below:

(1) Legal, regulatory, or contractual provisions may limit the maximum useful life.
(2) Provisions for renewal or extension may alter a specified limit on useful life.
(3) Effects of obsolescence, demand, competition, and other economic factors may reduce a useful life.
(4) A useful life may parallel the service life expectancies of individuals or groups of employees.
(5) Expected actions of competitors and others may restrict present competitive advantages.
(6) An apparently unlimited useful life may in fact be indefinite and benefits cannot be reasonably projected.
(7) An intangible asset may be a composite of many individual factors with varying effective lives.[4]

The Accounting Principles Board has stated that straight-line amortization should be used unless some other method is shown to be more appropriate. Both the amortization method and the useful life should be disclosed in the financial statements.

Significant decline in valuation. The estimated useful lives of intangible assets should be evaluated periodically to ensure that they are realistic. When circumstances indicate that a change in the estimate is warranted, the change should be accounted for in the same manner as changes in the useful life of tangible assets. These procedures were discussed in Chapter 17. However, even when estimates are changed, the total useful life for accounting purposes may not exceed 40 years after acquisition.

---

[3] *Opinion No. 17*, p. 340.
[4] *Opinion No. 17*, p. 340.

There have been instances in which, in the name of conservatism, very large write-downs of intangible assets took place soon after their acquisition. This was done either by a lump-sum write-down, or by amortization over an arbitrarily short period. However, present practice does not sanction this treatment, primarily because of the income distortion that can result.

If circumstances indicate that a significant and permanent decline has taken place in the valuation of the intangible asset, then a charge can be made against the income of the firm. However, the Accounting Principles Board has stated that "a single loss year or even a few loss years together do not necessarily justify an extraordinary charge to income for all or a large part of the unamortized cost of intangible assets."[5]

The foregoing discussion has dealt with matters of a general nature concerning intangible assets. The accounting for specific intangibles will now be discussed.

Patents. Patents may be productive of earnings through the reduction of manufacturing costs or by the creation of a monopolistic condition that permits the charging of prices favorable to the patent owner. Income may be earned directly from patents through royalties collected under license agreements.

If a patent is acquired by purchase, its cost is the purchase price. If it is obtained by the inventor, its cost is the total of experimental costs, costs of working models, and costs of obtaining the patent, including drawings, attorneys' fees, and filing fees.

A patent has no proven future economic benefits until it has stood the test of an infringement suit. The cost of a successful suit may be charged to the patents account as representing an additional cost of establishing the patent. If litigation costs incurred or other expenditures made in protecting a patent are charged to the patents account as additions to the cost, the amortization procedure should be such as to ensure writing off these additional costs at the expiration of the life of the patent. Although the cost of litigation in successfully defending a patent case seems logically to be a proper addition to the cost of the patent to be set up and amortized over the patent's remaining life, decisions in income tax cases do not so recognize it, but require that it be expensed in the tax year in which it is incurred.

If the suit is unsuccessful and the patent is thereby proved to be worthless, both the cost of the suit and the unamortized cost of the patent should be written off.

Patents are issued for a period of 17 years, and this is thus the maximum legal life. If a patent is purchased some time after it is granted, the purchaser will use the remaining life as the maximum legal life. Practical considerations may dictate that the cost be amortized over a shorter period of time than its legal life. Such would be the case when the patent pertains to a product that will be marketable only during a current fad.

If the article patented is subject to the danger of being superseded by some other invention, the element of supersession should be taken into consideration

---

[5] *Opinion No. 17,* p. 341.

as a probable factor in making the effective life of the patent shorter than its legal life.

If the owner of a patent finds that the product manufactured under it is not in demand and cannot be profitably marketed, the patent has no future economic benefits even though its legal life has not expired; in such a case it should be written off.

A patent is sometimes purchased for the purpose of controlling the patent and thus preventing the manufacture of a competing article. Such a patent should be written off over its life unless the sole purpose of its purchase was to provide additional protection during the remaining life of a patent already owned; in that case, the cost of the new patent should be written off over the remaining life of the old patent.

If an additional patent is obtained that is so closely related to a former patent that it in effect extends the life of the basic patent, any unamortized balance of the cost of the old patent remaining in the account at the date of obtaining the new one may be carried forward and written off over the life of the new one. This procedure can properly be adopted only in case there is a reasonable certainty that the productivity of the original patent will continue through the life of the new patent. In the absence of such certainty, the old patent should be amortized over the remainder of its own life.

The entry to record the amortization of patents is a debit to Patents Expense and a credit to the asset account. The credit could be to a contra account, such as Accumulated Patent Amortization, but this is not usually done in practice.

Copyrights. A copyright gives its owner the exclusive right to produce and sell reading matter and works of art. The fee for obtaining a copyright is only a nominal amount, insufficient to justify an accounting procedure of capitalization and amortization. Costs sufficient in amount to justify such a procedure do arise, however, when copyrights are purchased.

Copyrights are issued for 28 years and can be renewed for an additional 28 years. However, publications rarely have an active market for a period as long as 28 years, and it is usually regarded as advisable to write off the copyright cost against the income from the first printing. The nature of certain publications may justify a less conservative procedure.

Trademarks. Trademarks may be registered, but they are valid under the common law without registry if the claimant is able to prove his prior use of the mark. Continuous use gives the user the right to the trademark. Trade names, labels, and brand names are similar intangibles.

When such an asset is developed within the firm, its cost includes all developmental costs, as well as any cost incurred in defending the user's right to the asset. If the asset is purchased, it is recorded at the amount paid. Although trademarks do not have a definite life, it is common practice to amortize their cost over a relatively short period of time.

Organization costs. There are certain expenditures associated with the organization of a corporation. These include attorneys' fees, payments to the state, and the costs of printing and promoting the sale of stock. Traditionally, such costs were viewed as a sheer loss, to be written off as soon as possible. This normally resulted in the amortization of organization costs within a relatively short time period after organization, a treatment that can be theoretically justified only on the assumption that the early years are the only ones benefited by the expenditures.

Presumably, the benefits will continue for the entire life of the firm. This would allow amortization over the maximum period of 40 years specified by the Accounting Principles Board.

Research and development costs. Many businesses maintain research departments and make significant expenditures for basic and applied research and for the development of new or improved products or manufacturing processes. Future periods often benefit from such outlays, and, if a proper matching of revenue and expense is to be achieved, capitalization and subsequent amortization may be necessary. On the other hand, the accountant must exercise caution and not carry an amount forward as an asset unless there is a reasonable expectation that it will be recoverable from future operations.

The difficulty of accounting for research and development costs is probably apparent. It is an area in which there is no deficiency of accounting principles; it is the inherent uncertainties and complexities that make it difficult to justify a specific dollar-and-cents answer in most actual cases. Often the problem is centered on the matter of identifying the costs associated with a particular project or a particular achievement. But even when cost identification is possible, uncertainty about the magnitude of the future benefits and the length of time over which such benefits may be expected to be realized lends appeal to the conservative solution of expensing such costs as incurred, rather than capitalizing any portion of them.

Most companies follow this procedure, with the probable result that the assets of some firms are understated, in that certain costs that will contribute to future revenues are not reported as assets. The income statement of the firm is also affected, since there is no attempt to charge the expenditures against the income of the periods benefited. Since research and development costs are discretionary in nature, the practice of charging them against revenues as incurred could also lead to income manipulation. Income could be directly affected in any period by the decision to reduce such expenditures temporarily.

Some firms operate research departments for the purpose of developing patentable devices. There are three approaches that may be used in accounting for the costs associated with these departments:

(1) Assign the entire cost of the department to the patents obtained, based on the concept that since all the research activity was directed to achieving successes, the costs of the research are properly assignable to the successes.

(2) Maintain records so that costs applicable to work that results successfully in a patent can be capitalized and the remaining costs can be charged to expense. (If this method is used, expenditures can be charged initially to an account with a title such as Unallocated Re-

search Costs, from which transfers can be made to the patents account or to an expense account when the proper allocation of the costs is ultimately determined.)

(3) Charge all the research costs to expense as they are incurred, either based on the concept that competing concerns presumably are conducting similar research and that such outlays are necessary to keep abreast of the industry, or in recognition of the impracticability of attempting to make cost determinations for specific patents.

The strongest theoretical argument can be made for the second approach. However, practical considerations have resulted in the third approach being the most widely used. Present income tax laws allow the taxpayer either to deduct research and development costs in the period incurred or to capitalize them. If the latter procedure is followed, the costs may be amortized over a minimum of five years.

Leaseholds. A lease is a contract that grants the lessee the right to possession and use of the leased property for a specified period. This right is a personal-property right, referred to as a leasehold. The accounting for long-term leases has been discussed in detail in Chapter 8.

Leasehold improvements. Leases frequently provide that the lessee shall pay the costs of any alterations or improvements of the leased real estate, such as new fronts, partitions, and built-in shelving. Such alterations and improvements become a part of the real estate and revert to its owner at the expiration of the lease. The lessee obtains only the intangible right to benefit by the improvements during the life of the lease. The lessee should therefore charge such expenditures to a leasehold improvements account, which should be amortized over the life of the lease or the useful life of the improvements, whichever is shorter.

Buildings constructed by a lessee on leased land revert to the owner of the land at the expiration of the lease. The lessee should spread their cost, by proportionate charges, over the life of the lease, unless it is expected that the buildings will become useless before the lease has expired, in which case the cost should be systematically written off during the estimated life of the buildings.

Although leasehold improvements increase the future service potential of the property of the lessor, it seems advisable for the lessor to postpone making any entries therefor in his accounts until the expiration of the lease. The owner obtains no benefit from the improvements until the expiration of the lease, and may receive no benefit even then because of depreciation, obsolescence, or lack of increase in rent or rentability.

Goodwill. The intangible asset goodwill is considered to exist when a firm is able to earn a rate of return on its investment that is in excess of the normal rate of return for other firms in the industry.

The list of sources or causes of goodwill includes everything that could contribute to an attractive earnings result. Some of these sources are satisfactory customer relations, location, manufacturing efficiency, good employee relations, marketing or production "know-how," and weak or ineffective competition.

Goodwill may be developed internally by a firm, or it may be purchased. However, only in the latter case may goodwill be recorded in the accounts. It is sometimes contended that when a concern conducts an extensive advertising campaign for the purpose of developing business, and spends a sum greatly in excess of a normal advertising expenditure, the purpose is to create goodwill, and the amount by which the cost of the campaign exceeds a normal advertising expenditure can be capitalized as goodwill. Even if such a procedure were theoretically acceptable, the practical difficulties involved in its application are so great as to make it a dangerous one. What will be the normal advertising expenditure necessary to retain the business after the conclusion of the campaign? It is easy to be optimistic about this matter, but there is always a danger that future advertising costs may be much greater than expected. The portion of the expenditure capitalized as goodwill will then be found to be excessive, and the net income of the past will have been overstated. Perhaps the most reasonable compromise is to set up a portion of the campaign cost as a deferred charge, to be written off over the periods that the advertising may reasonably be expected to benefit.

Although businesses customarily spend considerable sums for the purpose of creating goodwill, or at least in the hopes that such expenditures will ultimately result in an advantage to them over their competition, it is generally impossible to establish any direct relationship between the expenditures and the creation of goodwill. Therefore, disbursements made in an attempt to create goodwill are expensed.

> The Board concludes that a company should record as assets the costs of intangible assets acquired from others, including goodwill acquired in a business combination. A company should record as expenses the costs to develop intangible assets which are not specifically identifiable.[6]

It was noted earlier in this chapter that goodwill is the most common example of an unidentifiable intangible asset, and that such assets may not be acquired singly. Thus, the only goodwill given recognition in the accounts is that specifically paid for in connection with the purchase of a business, a product line, or some group of assets. Or it may be described as the excess of the cost of an acquired company over the sum of the identifiable net assets acquired.

> The cost of unidentifiable intangible assets is measured by the difference between the cost of the group of assets or enterprise acquired and the sum of the assigned costs of individual tangible and identifiable intangible assets acquired less liabilities assumed. Cost should be assigned to all specifically identifiable intangible assets; cost of identifiable assets should not be included in goodwill.[7]

---

[6] *Opinion No. 17*, p. 334. Some firms recognize internally developed goodwill by recording it in the accounts at the nominal amount of one dollar.

[7] *Opinion No. 17*, p. 339.

In the final analysis, the price agreed upon between the buyer and the seller of a business firm or a group of assets is a matter of bargaining between the two parties. However, if this price includes an amount that cannot be assigned using the procedures mentioned in the preceding section, they must have come to some agreement as to how this excess, commonly referred to as goodwill, was determined. Of course, the amount paid for goodwill could be arbitrarily agreed upon without formal computation; but the chances are that it is the result of carefully prepared computations. The concept of probable future earnings is important in such computations.

Probable future earnings. When the purchaser of a business pays a price for goodwill, he is not paying for the excess earnings of the past, but for the probable excess earnings of the future. The accomplishments of the past, however, may furnish the best available evidence of the probable accomplishments in the future, and hence it is customary to estimate the future earnings on the basis of past net-income data. In making a statement of past earnings that is to be used as the basis for computing the goodwill, the following points should be considered:

First: The results of operations for one preceding year are not a sufficient basis for estimating future results of operations, because a statement for one year would not disclose fluctuations in earnings. On the other hand, not too many past years should be included in the base if the earnings of the more remote years were affected by conditions at variance with present conditions or trends.

Second: All extraordinary and nonoperating gains and losses should be excluded. If income is earned on investments, such as securities or real estate, the fair market value of the assets should govern their sale price, and the income received from them should be excluded from the net income used in computing the goodwill.

Third: If any known facts point to a possible difference between past and future income results, these facts should be considered.

Have the earnings been derived from sales of articles protected by patents, copyrights, licenses, or royalty agreements? If so, how long will such protection continue in the future? To what extent does the success of the business depend upon its present location, and what tenure of the premises is assured either by ownership or by lease? What is the trend of competition in the field? Are there any prospects of changes in labor conditions?

If management salaries have not been deducted by the seller, or if the salaries have been merely nominal, deductions should be made for the management salaries to be paid by the purchaser, provided that these salaries are reasonable.

If the success of the business in the past has been due largely to the personality or business ability of the old management, and if those who are responsible for this success are not to go with the business to the new owners, this fact should be considered in estimating future earnings.

If the long-lived assets of the business are to be transferred to the purchaser at a higher price than that at which they have been carried on the seller's books, recognition should be given to the fact that higher depreciation charges will be required in the future, and that future net income will be diminished as a consequence.

The effects that the matters above will have on future income taxes should also receive consideration.

Fourth: Consideration should be given to the trend of earnings, and perhaps to the trend of some of the important items of revenue and expense. It is unwise to accept the average net income of a number of past years as the basis of a goodwill computation without giving consideration to variations and the trend of earnings. This fact may be shown by the following illustration:

Schedule of Net Income Amounts

	Co. A	Co. B	Co. C	Co. D
19+1	$ 25,000	$ 19,100	$ 30,000	$ 10,000
19+2	40,000	19,800	25,000	15,000
19+3	19,000	20,400	20,000	20,000
19+4	2,000*	20,200	15,000	25,000
19+5	18,000	20,500	10,000	30,000
Total	$100,000	$100,000	$100,000	$100,000
Average	$ 20,000	$ 20,000	$ 20,000	$ 20,000

*Loss.

Although each of these concerns has made an average net income of $20,000 per year, it is evident that it would be unwise to pay the same amount for the goodwill of each business. Company A's earnings show a wide range of fluctuation, from $40,000 net income in 19+2 to a loss of $2,000 in 19+4. Such a history furnishes very poor evidence of stable earnings in the future.

Company B's earnings, on the other hand, are very uniform year by year and show a slight tendency to increase. Assuming that a net income of $20,000 represents more than a normal return on the assets, it would be reasonable and safe to make a payment for B's goodwill based on an average net income of $20,000.

Company C probably has no goodwill, because its earnings are steadily declining, and if the decline continues in the same fashion for two more years, there will be no net income whatever.

Company D, on the other hand, probably has the most goodwill of all (assuming equal assets), because its earnings are steadily increasing. In fact, just as it would be unwise for a purchaser to pay for goodwill based on the average of the earnings of Company C, which are on the decline, so also would it probably be unfair to the seller to base the goodwill of Company D on the average earnings, because the earnings are steadily increasing. The indication is that future earnings will be considerably more than the average.

If an accountant is called upon to prepare a statement of the average net income of a business for purposes of computing goodwill, he should, as a general rule, submit a statement showing the net income of each year as well as the average net income. A statement of only the average is likely to be misleading, because it fails to furnish information concerning the variation and trend of the earnings.

Methods of computation. The methods of computation illustrated below indicate factors and procedures that may be considered by the purchaser and seller during the negotiations. The illustrations are based on the following assumed facts: The purchaser and the seller of a business have agreed that the valuation of the assets, other than goodwill, shall be \$100,000; the net income figures for the five years next preceding the date of sale were \$19,000, \$19,500, \$19,000, \$21,500, and \$21,000, or an annual average of \$20,000.

(1) *Years' purchase of excess earnings.* Assume that the valuation of the goodwill is to be based on three years' purchase of the past earnings in excess of 12½ percent of the assets other than goodwill. This may mean net income in excess of 12½ percent of the assets actually held during each of the three years, or net income in excess of 12½ percent of the \$100,000 price determined as the valuation of the assets other than goodwill; the latter is the more logical basis. Assuming that the latter basis is agreed upon, the amount to be paid for the goodwill will be computed as follows:

Year Preceding Sale	Net Income	12½% of Assets	Excess
Third	\$19,000	\$12,500	\$ 6,500
Second	21,500	12,500	9,000
First	21,000	12,500	8,500
Total payment for goodwill			\$24,000

(2) *Years' purchase of average excess earnings.* Assume that the valuation of the goodwill is to be based on three years' purchase of the average earnings of the past five years in excess of 12½ percent of the \$100,000 agreed valuation of the assets other than goodwill. This method is similar to the preceding one except that averages are used. The goodwill computation is as follows:

Average earnings of past 5 years	\$20,000
Deduct 12½% of \$100,000	12,500
Excess	\$ 7,500
Multiply by number of years of purchase	3
Goodwill	\$22,500

(3) *Capitalized earnings, minus assets.* Assume that the purchaser and the seller agree upon 12½ percent as a normal or basic rate, and that they decide to base the valuation of the business upon a capitalization, at that rate, of the average income for the past five years.

The goodwill will be computed as follows:

Capitalization of average income, or total valuation of business: \$20,000 ÷ $12\frac{1}{2}\%$	\$160,000
Deduct agreed valuation of net assets other than goodwill	100,000
Goodwill	\$ 60,000

(4) *Excess earnings capitalized.* A serious theoretical objection can be raised to the preceding method. This objection may be made apparent by dividing the total purchase price into two parts and noting what the purchaser of the business obtains in return for his payment.

	Net Assets	Earnings
For the first \$100,000 of the purchase price, the purchaser receives:		
Assets other than goodwill	\$100,000	
Prospective income of $12\frac{1}{2}\%$ thereof		\$12,500
For the remaining \$60,000 of the purchase price, the purchaser receives:		
An intangible asset of goodwill	60,000	
Prospective income of $12\frac{1}{2}\%$ thereof		7,500

For the first \$100,000, the purchaser acquires assets that presumably will have some realizable amount even if the prospective earnings fail to materialize; for the \$60,000, the purchaser acquires an asset that presumably will have no future economic benefit if the prospective earnings fail to materialize. It therefore appears that if $12\frac{1}{2}$ percent is a fair rate for the capitalization of the first \$12,500 of income, a higher rate should be used for the capitalization of the remaining \$7,500. The use of two rates is illustrated by the following computation of goodwill; it is assumed that the purchaser and the seller have agreed that $12\frac{1}{2}$ percent is a fair rate for the capitalization of earnings accompanied by assets other than goodwill, and that the remaining earnings should be capitalized at 25 percent.

Average earnings of past 5 years	\$20,000
Deduct earnings regarded as applicable to assets other than goodwill—$12\frac{1}{2}\%$ of \$100,000	12,500
Remaining earnings, regarded as indicative of goodwill	\$ 7,500
Goodwill = \$7,500 ÷ 25%	\$30,000

Excess earnings may be divided into brackets, and graduated rates may be used in capitalizing them: Earnings at the higher levels are capitalized at a higher rate (and thus given a lower capitalized value) than earnings at lower levels because of the greater danger that they will not continue. This procedure is illustrated below:

Excess earnings regarded as indicative of goodwill (as above)	\$ 7,500
Goodwill:	
Capitalization of first \$5,000 at 25%	\$20,000
Capitalization of remaining \$2,500 at 50%	5,000
Total goodwill	\$25,000

There are certain observations that should be made concerning the foregoing methods. First of all, methods (3) and (4) suffer from the implicit assumption that the excess earnings will continue indefinitely. This is most probably unrealistic. Even when the firm is able to sustain operations at such a level over a long period of time, it is unlikely that the excess earnings of later years could be attributed to factors existing at the time the present transaction took place. Thus, the normal expectation is that the goodwill acquired will disappear over a period of time. The methods may be refined, as was done in method (4), to give consideration to this fact by using a higher capitalization rate than normal. The use of the higher rate will produce a lower capitalized amount.

Methods (1) and (2) have inherent in them the idea that excess earnings are likely to be realized from the present transaction for only a limited number of years. The goodwill is considered to represent a stream of future amounts to be received over a certain number of time periods. However, no attempt is made to measure the present value of the amounts to be received.

(5) *Discounted amount.* The soundest theoretical method for measuring goodwill is to determine the discounted amount (present value) of the excess earnings expected to be realized in the future. This involves a determination of the amount of excess earnings, the time period over which they will be realized, and the choice of an appropriate discount rate.

Using the previous illustration, it is now assumed that excess earnings of $7,500 per year will be realized for the next five years. A return of 12½ percent is considered necessary to attract investment capital into the industry. Goodwill should then be valued as follows:

Excess earnings per year	$7,500
Present value of $1 per year for 5 years at 12½%	3.561
Present value of future excess earnings ($7,500 × 3.561)	$26,707.50

Valuation of other assets. If goodwill is to be computed based on the capitalization of earnings in excess of a normal return on the assets other than goodwill, consideration must be given to the valuation of the other assets, and a decision must be reached as to what is a normal income rate.

For general accounting purposes, cost (less depreciation, amortization, and so forth) is, in most instances, regarded as the proper basis for the valuation of assets, but this may not be the proper basis when asset valuations are being determined for purposes of goodwill computation.[8] For that purpose, current appraisal amounts are more appropriate. If they are not used, the difference between the fair present value of the assets and their book amount will find its way into the valuation of the goodwill. This can be a matter of considerable importance to the purchaser, because the amortization of goodwill is not deductible for income tax purposes.

---

[8]The Accounting Principles Board, in "Business Combinations," *Opinion No. 16* (August 1970), dealt with the problems associated with recording assets acquired in business combinations. See Chapter 14.

Normal rate of return. What is the normal or basic rate of return to be earned before a business can be regarded as having goodwill? This is purely a matter of opinion. The basic or normal income is, fundamentally, the amount that would attract proprietorship capital equal to the agreed valuation of the assets other than goodwill. It varies with different businesses because of variations in hazards and other conditions peculiar to industries. Moreover, no two investors might hold the same opinion as to the normal rate of income applicable to any one business. The determination of the basic rate applicable to assets other than goodwill, and of the rate to be used in the capitalization of excess earnings, is, therefore, a matter of bargaining between the purchaser and seller.

It should be noted that if the purchaser is to assume any of the liabilities of the business selling the assets, a deduction therefor is made to arrive at the net payment for the assets.

Amortization of goodwill. The Accounting Principles Board has taken the position that all intangible assets should be amortized over a period not exceeding 40 years. The reasoning in the case of goodwill is that the excess earnings representing the goodwill purchased will not last indefinitely; and the goodwill should be amortized over the period in which the purchased excess earnings will be realized.

Straight-line amortization is normally used. However, the proper accounting for goodwill and its amortization, under the present-value method illustrated previously, will result in an increasing amortization charge each year. To illustrate, assume that the amount paid for goodwill was $26,707.50, the amount calculated on page 450. Amortization for the first year would be calculated as follows:

Excess earnings	$7,500.00
Less return on carrying amount of goodwill ($26,707.50 × .125)	3,338.44
Amortization of goodwill	$4,161.56

The following entry would be recorded:

Amortization of goodwill	4,161.56	
Goodwill		4,161.56

Amortization for the second year would be calculated as follows:

Excess earnings	$7,500.00
Less return on carrying amount of goodwill [($26,707.50 − $4,161.56) × .125]	2,818.24
Amortization of goodwill	$4,681.76

Not all accountants agree that goodwill should be amortized. Some would argue that purchased goodwill should remain on the books as long as the excess earnings continue. It would be written off only when there was positive evidence that it no longer existed. At the other extreme is the position that owing to the very subjective nature of goodwill, it should be written off immediately at the date of acquisition, a treatment that results in the distortion of earnings during the years the excess earnings are realized. Present practice does sanction the write-off of goodwill because of unusual events during a reporting period.

Disposal of goodwill. It is unlikely that goodwill can be disposed of separately from the firm as a whole. This is due to its nature as an unidentifiable asset.

> However, a large segment or separable group of assets of an acquired company or the entire acquired company may be sold or otherwise liquidated, and all or a portion of the unamortized cost of the goodwill recognized in the acquisition should be included in the cost of the assets sold.[9]

Franchises. Under a franchise arrangement, one party (the franchisor) grants certain rights to a second party (the franchisee). A recent industry accounting guide published by the AICPA stated that the franchise agreement "gives the franchisee the right to use the trademark, trade name, patents, processes, know-how, etc., of the franchisor for a specified period of time or perpetually."[10] Such agreements are tailored to fit specific situations, and some are quite complex.

Some of the more common items found in franchise agreements are listed below:

(1) Rights transferred by the franchisor
(2) The amount and terms of payment of initial franchise fees
(3) Amount or rate and terms of payment of continuing franchise fee or royalty
(4) Services to be rendered by the franchisor initially and on a continuing basis
  (a) Assistance in the selection of a site
  (b) Assistance in obtaining facilities, including related financing
  (c) Assistance in advertising
  (d) Training of the franchisee's personnel
  (e) Preparation of information concerning operations, administration, and record keeping
  (f) Bookkeeping and advisory services
  (g) Various quality-control programs
(5) Acquisition of inventory, supplies or equipment, and terms of payment

---

[9] *Opinion No. 17*, p. 341.

[10] Committee on Franchise Accounting and Auditing, "Accounting for Franchise Fee Revenue," (New York: AICPA, 1973), p. 3. Industry accounting guides are published for the guidance of AICPA members in examining and reporting on financial statements within a given industry. Although the industry guides do not have the same status as Accounting Principles Board Opinions, institute members are put on notice that they may be called upon to justify departures from the recommendations contained in the guides.

(6) Cancellation of franchise, reacquisition of franchise, or acquisition of franchisee[11]

The significant increase in franchising operations in recent years has resulted in the need for additional work in developing appropriate accounting procedures. The major problem area has been the accounting for revenue received from the sale of franchises by the franchisor, and this is the specific point to which the industry accounting guide was directed.

Accounting for franchises by the franchisee. Franchises should not appear on the books of the franchisee unless a payment, either direct or indirect, was made in obtaining them. The total cost of a franchise includes legal fees and other costs incidental to its acquisition.

A franchise may be perpetual or it may be granted for a definite time period. In the former case, the period of amortization would be the 40-year maximum specified by the Accounting Principles Board. If a definite time period is specified, this should govern the period of amortization. When the grantor of the franchise retains the right to terminate the franchise at any time, amortization should take place over a relatively short period of time.

In addition to the original cost, franchise agreements may require that periodic payments be made to the franchisor. Such payments represent expenses to be charged against income as they are incurred. Any property improvements required of the franchisee should be capitalized and then written off over the life of the franchise.

Accounting for franchises by the franchisor. The major problems encountered in the accounting for franchises are associated with the franchisor. The following discussion of these problems is based upon the AICPA industry accounting guide previously referred to.

REVENUE FROM INITIAL FRANCHISE FEES: It is a very common arrangement for the franchisee to pay an initial fee to the franchisor at the time the franchise is granted. In some cases, only a portion of the fee is paid in cash, with the balance being represented by some form of receivable. This creates the following accounting problems:

(1) The time at which the fee is properly regarded as earned
(2) The assurance of collectibility of the receivable arising from any unpaid portion of the fee[12]

At one time, it was a very common practice to recognize as revenue the entire amount of the initial fee when the franchise was sold. However, this treatment could, and often did, lead to serious problems for franchisors in those cases where the fee was never paid in full. There were even instances in which the franchisee never began operations at all. Prior to publication of the industry accounting

[11] "Accounting for Franchise Fee Revenue," pp. 3–4.
[12] "Accounting for Franchise Fee Revenue," p. 5.

guide, an increasing number of accountants supported the practice of deferring recognition of the initial fee as revenue until the franchisee actually began operations.[13]

The institute's Committee on Franchise Accounting and Auditing discusses several different proposals that have been advanced concerning the timing of the recognition of the initial fee as revenue. It notes that the sale of a franchise is different from other sales transactions only in that it becomes very difficult to determine just when the transaction has been completed:

> The usual sale of a franchise is linked to certain conditions, such as the performance of certain services, which affect the consummation of the transaction in much the same way as delivery, installation, or meeting certain qualitative specifications affect the consummation of a conventional sale of equipment. Perhaps the most difficult aspect of accounting for the sale of a franchise is determining when these conditions have been sufficiently met so that the franchise sales agreement may be regarded as consummated and the fee regarded as irrevocably earned.[14]

The committee went on to recommend that the franchisor recognize revenue from the sale of a franchise when he has substantially performed any material conditions required of him by the contract. For the franchisor, substantial performance means that all the following facts are true:

(1) He has no remaining obligation or intent—by agreement, trade practice, or operation of law—to refund any cash already received or to excuse nonpayment of any unpaid notes.
(2) Substantially all the initial services of the franchisor required by the contract have been performed.
(3) Any other conditions that affect consummation of the sale have been met.[15]

Substantial performance will obviously occur at different times for different franchisors. However, the committee felt that conservatism justifies the presumption that substantial performance by the franchisor would normally not take place prior to the time the franchisee actually begins operations.

In dealing with the likelihood of collection of any unpaid portion of the initial

---

[13]The basis for this treatment was an article written by Archibald E. MacKay and published in the January 1970 issue of the *Journal of Accountancy*. The author of the article also served as chairman of the institute's Committee on Franchise Accounting and Auditing, which produced the industry accounting guide.

[14]"Accounting for Franchise Fee Revenue," p. 7.

[15]"Accounting for Franchise Fee Revenue," p. 8.

franchise fee, the committee noted that this was a matter of judgment based upon the facts in each case. Whenever possible, the sale of a franchise under a deferred-payment arrangement should be accounted for in the same manner as any other sale of this type. This requires that the revenue be reported when the sale has been consummated and that appropriate provision be made for estimated losses. This is consistent with the position of the Accounting Principles Board concerning the installment method of accounting, as stated in its *Opinion No. 10.*[16] It is possible, of course, that in exceptional cases there will be no reasonable basis for estimating the degree of collectibility of the deferred portion of the franchise sales price. Under these circumstances, one of the alternative methods referred to by the board in *Opinion No. 10* would be appropriate.[17]

COSTS RELATED TO FRANCHISE SALES: The objective in accounting for franchise sales is basically the same as that in accounting for any sale—reporting revenues and related costs in the same accounting period. However, costs associated with the sale of franchises may present an accounting problem, owing to the timing of their incurrence. The procedures previously discussed call for the recognition of franchise-fee revenue when substantial performance on the part of the franchisor has taken place, but many of the costs associated with the franchise sale may be incurred prior to this time.

The procedures to be followed in accounting for costs associated with franchise sales are summarized below:

(1) Direct costs relating to specific franchise sales for which revenue has not yet been recognized should be deferred.

(2) Indirect costs of a regular and recurring nature that are incurred irrespective of the level of sales, such as general selling expenses and administrative expenses, should be expensed as incurred.

(3) Costs should not be deferred without reference to anticipated revenue and its realizability. The amount of deferred costs should not be permitted to exceed anticipated revenues less estimated additional costs related thereto.

(4) Costs associated with franchise sales, but not to be incurred until after the period in which substantial performance by the franchisor takes place, should be accrued and charged against income no later than the period in which the related revenues are recognized.[18]

DISCLOSURE MATTERS: Franchisors are subject to the usual disclosure practices

---

[16] Accounting Principles Board, "Omnibus Opinion—1966," *Opinion No. 10* (New York: AICPA, December 1966). The board reaffirmed the position contained in Chapter 1A of *Accounting Research Bulletin No. 43* that the installment method of accounting for sales is acceptable only in exceptional cases.

[17] The board specifically mentioned the installment method and the cost-recovery method. Under the latter method, no profit is recognized from the sale until costs have been recovered.

[18] "Accounting for Franchise Fee Revenue," p. 17.

applicable to other firms. There are also additional disclosure requirements related to the unique nature of franchise operations.

> Disclosure should be made of the basis of accounting for all important aspects of transactions with franchisees, such as recognition of initial franchise fees, deferred costs, continuing fees or royalties, etc. In addition, a general disclosure should be made of the nature of all significant commitments and obligations arising from franchise agreements, including a reference to services which the franchisor has agreed to provide relative to agreements which have not yet been substantially performed.[19]

Because of the different nature of initial franchise fees and continuing royalties from the franchisee or product sales to the franchisee, initial franchise fee revenues should be segregated from other franchising revenues. Also, if any portion of the unpaid balance of initial franchise fees is being accounted for under the installment method or the cost-recovery method, this should be disclosed. Other disclosures relate to the activities of franchisors who not only sell franchises but also operate certain outlets of their own.

Prepayments and deferred charges. In discussing the classification of assets within a firm's balance sheet in Chapter 3, it was noted that short-term prepayments were listed as current assets. Examples of short-term prepayments are insurance premiums and rent that are paid in advance. They are normally recurring expenditures that will be charged to expense over a relatively short period of time.

Long-term prepayments are normally reported under a completely separate caption on the balance sheet—frequently Deferred Charges or Other Assets. Prepayments of this type usually occur less frequently than the short-term prepayments and are normally written off over a longer period of time. Examples of long-term prepayments are prepaid pension costs, deferred income tax expense, bond-issue costs, and machinery-rearrangement costs.

---

[19] "Accounting for Franchise Fee Revenue," p. 19.

19

Liabilities and Pensions

LIABILITIES

Introduction. Liabilities are future economic obligations of a business firm (or individual) to render assets or perform services. The basic essentials in accounting for liabilities are the inclusion of all liabilities in the balance sheet and the proper valuation of the reported liabilities. The exclusion of liabilities from the balance sheet is a problem accountants have tried carefully to avoid, because it makes the balance sheet appear more favorable than it is in reality, and this is misleading to financial-statement users. The problem of liability valuation has been somewhat neglected in actual accounting practice, because of the emphasis on income determination. That is, too often the primary concern has been with the debit side of transactions (the charge to expense or assets), and the offsetting credit to a liability has been merely determined by the debit, as a sort of afterthought.[1] For example, certain

[1]See Maurice Moonitz, "The Changing Concept of Liabilities," *Journal of Accountancy* (May 1960), p. 41.

deferred credits are reported as if they were liabilities, but in reality they are merely credits offsetting the debits needed for expense allocation—a form of income smoothing. On the other hand, as evidenced by APB *Opinion No. 21,* current accounting practice is becoming more concerned about the proper valuation of liabilities.

Conceptually, the valuation of liabilities should be at the discounted amount (present value) of the future cash payments or equivalents. In terms of providing useful information for decision-making purposes, a strong conceptual case can be made for reporting liabilities at current market prices, by using the interest rate prevailing for similar liabilities at the balance-sheet date to discount the future cash flows. However, because of the uncertainty of future interest rates and the effect on reported income of fluctuating gains and losses on the holding of liabilities, actual accounting practice does not report liabilities based on current exchange prices.

Per *Opinion No. 21,* accountants report long-term monetary liabilities (such as long-term notes payable, bonds payable, and mortgage notes payable) at their discounted amount. Although such valuation is discounted-cash-flow valuation, it is not *current* discounted-cash-flow valuation (except at the date the liability is incurred), since the discount rate used to report the liability over its term is the interest rate prevailing at the time the liability is incurred (for example, the yield rate at the time bonds are issued). Thus it is discounted-cash-flow valuation that is consistent with historical-cost valuation, since a historical interest rate is used as the discount rate for valuation purposes.

In contrast to that of long-term monetary liabilities, *Opinion No. 21* does not require the valuation of normal trade payables (due in approximately one year or less) at their discounted amount. Thus the valuation of short-term liabilities in actual accounting practice is usually at their face amount (maturity amount or amount payable in the future), which is consistent with historical-cost valuation. Although conceptually the valuation of current liabilities should be at their discounted amount, it is argued that since current liabilities are normally payable within a short period of time, the difference between their discounted amount and face amount is usually immaterial.

In addition, *Opinion No. 21* does not require discounted-cash-flow valuation of deposits or progress payments on construction contracts, security deposits, liabilities between parent and subsidiary companies, product warranties, deferred income tax credits, and liabilities in which interest rates are affected by the tax attributes or legal restrictions prescribed by a government agency (such as tax-exempt obligations).[2] Such liabilities are normally reported at their face amount.

Basic characteristics of liabilities. Although conceptually liabilities are future economic obligations to render assets or perform services, current accounting practice recognizes as liabilities only those obligations that are capable of objective mone-

[2]Accounting Principles Board, "Interest on Receivables and Payables," *Opinion No. 21* (New York: AICPA, August 1971), p. 418.

tary measurement—the doctrine of objectivity. To provide objectivity in the recording and reporting of liabilities, current accounting practice relies on the completed transaction; therefore it recognizes as liabilities only those with future obligations resulting from past or current transactions (completed transactions). Thus, *liabilities* in current accounting practice can be defined as future economic obligations of an organization (or individual) to render assets or perform services, where the obligations have resulted from past or current transactions (or events). More specifically, liabilities in current accounting practice have the following characteristics:

An obligation exists at the present time as the result of some past transaction. Thus an obligation that may arise from some future transaction or event is not a liability in accounting. An obligation contingent upon some future event may never materialize and therefore lacks the objectivity of a completed transaction.

There exists a future obligation to render assets acceptable to the payee. The discharge of the future obligation can take the form of a future cash payment, a future performance of services, a future delivery of noncash assets, a future offset of the obligation by an amount owing to the company by the creditor, a future forgiveness (very rare), or a future substitution of one obligation for another.

The liability is capable of measurement in terms of money at a definite amount or at a reasonably estimated amount. Thus, legal debt has a definite maturity amount, and estimated liabilities are subject to close approximation even though the exact amount is not known.

The unconditional right of offset does *not* exist. Accountants do not recognize as liabilities executory contracts in which the lack of performance by one party relieves the other party of performance. For example, operating leases are cancelable upon short notice by either the lessor or the lessee; hence, if the lessor withdraws his property, the lessee has no future obligation to continue the rent payments. Similarly, current contracts to acquire future long-lived assets are not future obligations, since neither party has performed.

The creditor(s) and due date(s) are either known or are capable of reasonable estimation. For example, as to debt, the creditor and due date are specifically known; as to estimated liabilities, the group (such as the customer group for product warranties) and the time period (such as the warranty period) can be reasonably estimated.

It is important to note that the accounting viewpoint of liabilities, as described above, is broader than the legal concept of a liability. The law defines a liability as a debt: an obligation to pay a fixed sum of money on a definite determinable date, plus interest; one's legal obligation to pay another. With the exception of legal liabilities with an unconditional right of offset, all legal liabilities (debts) are accounting liabilities, but not all accounting liabilities are legal liabilities. For example, liabilities from the accounting viewpoint include estimated liabilities (such as under product warranties) and equitable obligations (such as refunds on damaged or returned goods made to maintain customer goodwill), even though no legal obligation may exist.

It is also important to keep in mind the accounting distinction between equities, owners' equity, and liabilities. The source of a firm's assets is its equities, and the equity source is represented by equity holders' interests in or claims against the firm. Equities include both liabilities (specific or creditor equity) and owners' equity (residual equity), with the former representing the financing of assets by creditors and the latter the financing of assets, including profitable operations, by owners' investments. Whereas liabilities must be paid (or the firm can be thrown into bankruptcy) and are recurring (they are continually being incurred and repaid), there is no legal obligation to repay the investments of the owners unless the firm is liquidated. If the firm is liquidated, creditors' claims are satisfied first and owners are legally entitled to any remaining assets. Thus owners' equity is a residual interest in or a residual claim against the firm, whereas liabilities are specific interests in or specific claims against the firm. Also, whereas the firm is legally responsible to pay any interest specified by creditor agreements, owners (such as stockholders) are entitled to a return on their investment (such as dividends) at the discretion of the company (the board of directors of a corporation); hence, there is no legal obligation to pay dividends (unless declared) as there is for interest on liabilities.

Because liabilities ultimately require payment in one form or another, the date of payment provides a means of classifying them into current, long-term, and contingent liabilities. We now turn to a discussion of these liability classifications.

Current liabilities. As previously defined and discussed in Chapter 5, current liabilities are economic obligations that, according to reasonable expectations, are to be satisfied from current assets or the creation of other current liabilities within the operating-cycle period or one year, whichever is longer. For purposes of discussing the accounting for current liabilities, it is useful to classify them by their principal types, as follows:

Known current liabilities with definite amounts. Because of the existence of written or implied contracts or legal statutes, the amount of such liabilities and the due dates are reasonably certain. With the amount of cash needed to discharge the liability known (except for deferred revenue), the accounting problem with regard to such liabilities is one of making sure they are not omitted from the balance sheet. Examples of such current liabilities are as follows:

- Accounts payable
- Short-term notes payable
- Current maturities of long-term liabilities
- Cash dividends payable
- Returnable deposits
- Accrued liabilities

Payroll taxes and income taxes withheld
Property taxes payable
Deferred revenue (revenue received in advance)

Known current liabilities with amounts dependent on operations. Because the amount of certain liabilities is dependent upon annual income, the liabilities cannot be measured in dollar terms until the end of the fiscal period. Thus the amounts of such liabilities can be reasonably determined at the end of the fiscal period, but require estimation for interim-period financial statements. Examples of such current liabilities are as follows:

Income taxes payable
Sales taxes payable
Employee bonuses payable

Known current liabilities with amounts estimated (estimated liabilities). These are liabilities that definitely exist, because they have arisen from a past transaction and have a future obligation, but their *exact* amounts, and in some cases the exact due dates and payees, are not determinable. The fact that the amount is not exactly determinable does *not* justify ignoring the liability or reporting it merely as a footnote. Thus the accounting problem is one of obtaining the most objective evidence necessary for estimating the amount of the liability. Such evidence consists of the company's past experience, the experience of similar companies, or special research studies. Examples of such current liabilities are as follows:

Estimated liability under product warranties
Estimated liability for premium claims outstanding

ACCOUNTS PAYABLE: These are the amounts owing from the purchase of goods, supplies, and services in the normal course of business. They are liabilities that result from the normal trade obligations of the firm and that are on a recurring basis; hence, they are referred to as "open" payables, in that a formal debt instrument (such as a note) is not required every time goods are purchased on credit. Accounts payable arise because of the time lag between the receipt of the purchased goods and the payment. Since the time lag is generally 30 to 60 days, accounts payable are normally recorded and reported at their face amount, rather than at the conceptually preferred discounted amount.

The recording of accounts payable resulting from the purchase of goods should be made when title to the goods passes; however, for practical purposes, the recording of purchases and the accounts payable is usually made when the goods are received. Consequently, the accountant must make sure that purchases at the end of the fiscal period are properly recorded so that liabilities, as well as inventory, will not be understated.

Since the reporting of liabilities on the balance sheet is based on showing the *source* of financing, accounts payable should be reported separately from other payables. For example, bank loans and loans from officers, stockholders, or employees should be reported separately from the accounts payable. In this way, the extent of the financing from each source is presented in the balance sheet.

SHORT-TERM NOTES PAYABLE: Promissory notes are obligations that are formalized by a written promise to pay a certain sum of money, usually with interest, by a certain date. Notes that are payable within the current operating cycle or one year, whichever is longer, are classified as current liabilities—short-term notes payable.

In order to show short-term notes payable on the balance sheet by source, notes should be segregated as to whether they are trade notes payable (notes to trade creditors for the purchase of goods and services) or other notes payable. The latter include notes issued to banks for loans; notes issued to officers, stockholders, and employees; or notes issued for special purposes, such as for the purchase of equipment.

Short-term notes payable that are interest-bearing are reported in the balance sheet at their face amount, with any accrued interest on such notes reported as interest payable (an accrued liability). The face amount of interest-bearing notes is equal to the discounted amount (present value) of the notes, since the face amount plus interest discounted at the specified interest rate (assuming a fair rate) is equal to its present value.

If the face amount of a note does not represent the discounted amount of the consideration received in exchange, the note should be reported at its discounted amount, not at its face amount. An exception to this is trade notes payable, which, per *Opinion No. 21,* are reported at their face amount because of their short-term duration. The circumstances under which the face amount differs from the discounted amount of a note are those in which the note is non-interest-bearing or the stated interest rate for the note is not the appropriate interest rate to reflect the transaction.

For example, assume that a company acquires equipment on credit by issuing a $20,000 non-interest-bearing, one-year note. Because the $20,000 face amount of the note includes both the purchase price and the interest for the deferring of the payment for one year, the equipment and the note would both be overstated by the amount of the implicit interest if they were recorded and reported at $20,000. Assuming that an 8 percent rate is applicable for such transactions (an imputed rate per *Opinion No. 21*), the transaction should be recorded and reported as follows:

Date of acquisition of equipment:		
Equipment ($20,000/1.08)	18,518.52	
Discount on notes payable ($20,000.00 − $18,518.52)	1,481.48	
Notes payable (face amount)		20,000.00
End of first month:		
Interest expense ($18,518.52 × .08 × $^1/_{12}$)	123.46	
Discount on notes payable		123.46
Balance sheet reporting at the end of one month:		
Current liabilities:		
Other notes payable—for equipment	$20,000.00	
Less discount on notes payable ($1,481.48 − $123.46)	1,358.02	$18,641.98

As a final point, notes payable may be secured by assets pledged as collateral. Such pledged assets are limited in their use and sale until the note is discharged, and in the event of bankruptcy, the cash realized by the pledged assets would be first applied to the related note payable. The reporting of the secured note payable can be made by footnoting the pledged asset (including information on the related note) or, preferably, by parenthetical remarks for both the pledged asset and the note, such as the following:

Investments:		Current liabilities:	
Land held for resale (pledged for $2,000 note payable)	6,000	Notes payable—For equipment (secured by land)	2,000

CURRENT MATURITIES OF LONG-TERM LIABILITIES: Long-term debt that matures within the next fiscal year should be reported as a current liability. When only a part of the long-term debt matures within the next twelve months, such as for serial bonds, the amount to be paid next year is reported as a current liability, and the remaining balance is reported as a long-term liability. On the other hand, current maturity would not be reported as a current liability if it is to be payable out of a noncurrent retirement fund, retired from the proceeds of a new bond issue (refunding), or converted into capital stock. In such situations, there would be no use of current assets for the current maturity; hence, it would continue to be reported as a long-term liability.

CASH DIVIDENDS PAYABLE: At the date of declaration of a cash dividend by the board of directors of a corporation, a legal liability is assumed by the corporation to pay the dividend, and the stockholders are, in effect, creditors with regard to the amount of the declared dividends. Since cash dividends declared are normally paid within the next fiscal period, they are reported in the balance sheet as current liabilities.

Dividends in arrears on cumulative preferred stock are not a liability of a corporation, because they have not been formally declared by the board of directors. Such arrearages are normally reported by a footnote to the cumulative preferred stock in the balance sheet, since they usually have to be paid before any cash dividends on common stock can be paid.

Stock (not cash) dividends declared are not reported as a liability in the balance sheet. Stock dividends are not a liability because there is no future obligation of the corporation to distribute assets and because they are revocable by the board of directors any time prior to issuance. Stock dividends declared, but not issued, are reported in the balance sheet as part of stockholders' equity, by footnote, or by a parenthetical remark.

RETURNABLE DEPOSITS: Because the current assets of a company may include returnable deposits from customers and employees, a current liability (or long-term liability, depending on the time element) should be recognized until the deposits are returned. Deposits may be received from customers as guarantees for possible damage to property left with them, to cover payment of unpaid future obligations, or for performance of a contract or service. Deposits may be received from employees for the return of company property (such as keys), for club memberships, or for locker privileges.

ACCRUED LIABILITIES: These are expenses incurred, but not paid, during the fiscal period, which came into existence as a result of past contractual agreements, past services received, or tax laws. For example, interest on a loan accrues during the fiscal period and is an expense of the period and a liability (interest payable) at the end of the fiscal period if it is not payable until a subsequent fiscal period. Similarly, salaries are usually paid after the services have been performed; hence, at the end of the fiscal period, there are usually accrued salaries payable for the salary expense incurred but not paid until the next fiscal period.

In recording accrued liabilities, separate accounts are used, such as Interest Payable, Salaries Payable, Property Taxes Payable, Payroll Taxes Payable, Income Taxes Withheld, Income Taxes Payable, Sales Taxes Payable, and Employee Bonuses Payable. On the other hand, with the exception of accrued taxes, accruals are generally reported under one combined heading (Accrued Liabilities) in the Current Liabilities section of the balance sheet.

Because of special problems in the accounting for such accruals as payroll taxes, income taxes withheld, and property taxes, they are discussed below. Accruals in which the amount is dependent on operations (such as income taxes payable, sales taxes payable, and employee bonuses payable) are discussed subsequently.

PAYROLL TAXES AND INCOME TAXES WITHHELD: The Federal Insurance Contributions Act (FICA) requires employers to deduct a tax from the pay of each employee, to match the employee contribution, and to remit both to the government. This Social Security tax provides retirement pay and survivor benefits to contributors. In addition, employers must pay a tax under the Federal Unemployment Tax Act (FUTA) to provide unemployment insurance. Also, employers must pay taxes to provide state unemployment insurance. Finally, employers are required under federal and state income tax laws to withhold income taxes from the pay of each employee.

To illustrate the accounting for payroll taxes and income taxes withheld, assume that a company has a March taxable payroll of \$10,000, the FICA rate is 5.85 percent, the FUTA rate is .58 percent, the state unemployment rate is 2.7 percent, and the income tax withholdings are \$1,100. The following entries exemplify the recording of the accrued liabilities resulting from payroll taxes and income tax withholdings:

Salary expense	10,000	
Employee income taxes payable		1,100
FICA taxes payable (\$10,000 × 5.85%)		585
Cash		8,315
Payroll taxes expense	913	
FICA taxes payable (\$10,000 × 5.85%)		585
State unemployment taxes payable (\$10,000 × 2.7%)		270
FUTA taxes payable (\$10,000 × .58%)		58

When the taxes are remitted, cash is credited and the payables are debited. Any unremitted taxes result in reporting the payables on the balance sheet under the Current Liabilities classification.

PROPERTY TAXES PAYABLE: Local government units (such as city and county) tax real and personal property, based on assessed value, as their primary source of revenue. Such property taxes become a legal liability of the property owner as of a given date, referred to as the lien date, which is established by law as the date on which the taxes become a lien against the property.

In accounting for property taxes, the two main problems are when the liability should be recorded and to which period the tax expense should be charged. Since the legal liability of the property taxes arises at the lien date, the liability should be recognized then; however, some accountants argue that the liability accrues throughout the tax year. The tax expense should be charged to the fiscal period of the taxing authority, because such expenses are associated with the right to use property during that period.

In some cases, property taxes may have to be estimated. For example, the government unit may not send out its tax bills until several months after the beginning of its fiscal period, or it may be in the process of revising tax rates. In such situations, property taxes are often estimated based on the existing rates and then adjusted later.

To illustrate the accounting for property taxes, assume that a company is subject to property taxes by the city and county governments. The fiscal year of the government units is from July 1 to June 30. Property taxes of $48,000 are assessed against the company's property on January 1, 19+4, become a lien on July 1, 19+4, and are payable in two equal installments on October 1 and December 1, 19+4. Depending on whether the company recognizes the property-tax liability on the lien date or accrues it monthly, and recognizing the property-tax expense over the fiscal period of the taxing authority, the company would make the following entries:

Tax Liability Recognized at Lien Date			Tax Liability Accrued Monthly		
Entry for July 1, 19+4:					
Deferred property taxes	48,000				
Property taxes payable		48,000			
Entry for the end of July, August, and September 19+4:					
Property tax expense ($48,000/12)..........	4,000		Property tax expense	4,000	
			Property taxes payable............		4,000
Deferred property taxes		4,000			
Entry for October 1, 19+4:					
Property taxes payable ..	24,000		Property taxes payable...	12,000	
Cash ($48,000 × ½).		24,000	Deferred property taxes .	12,000	
			Cash		24,000
Entry for the end of October and November 19+4:					
Property tax expense	4,000		Property tax expense.....	4,000	
Deferred property taxes		4,000	Deferred property taxes...............		4,000

	Tax Liability Recognized at Lien Date			Tax Liability Accrued Monthly		
Entry for December 1, 19+4:						
	Property taxes payable ..	24,000		Deferred property taxes .	24,000	
	Cash		24,000	Cash		24,000
Entry for the end of December 19+4 and for the end of January, February, March, April, May, and June 19+5:						
	Property tax expense	4,000		Property tax expense.....	4,000	
	Deferred property taxes		4,000	Deferred property taxes..............		4,000

DEFERRED REVENUE (REVENUE RECEIVED IN ADVANCE): Revenue collected in advance of the sale of goods or the performing of services is a liability. Such deferred revenue is a future obligation to render assets or perform services before revenue becomes earned—unearned revenue. If the future obligation is not met, a liability exists to refund the advance payments. Examples of deferred revenue include payments received in advance for interest, rent, magazine subscriptions, and tickets. Since such deferred revenue normally becomes earned within the current operating cycle or one year, whichever is longer, it is classified as a current liability in the balance sheet. Note, however, that the terms *deferred revenue, revenue collected in advance,* and *unearned revenue,* as used by accountants and businessmen, are somewhat misleading, because it is assets, not revenue, that are really received in advance.

As was pointed out in the balance-sheet chapter, there is a Deferred Credits classification that is sometimes presented in the balance sheet between Liabilities and Stockholders' Equity. Among other things, such a classification can include deferred revenue; however, this is not recommended, since short-term deferred revenue should be reported as part of current liabilities. Deferred revenue is a liability, not a deferred credit.

INCOME TAXES PAYABLE: Federal and state income taxes for corporations are conditional on annual income; hence, the amount of income taxes owed to the government is not known until the end of the fiscal period. Thus it is necessary at the end of the period to make an adjusting entry debiting Income Tax Expense and crediting Income Taxes Payable, which is a current liability reported in the balance sheet. The amount of the income taxes payable is computed per the tax return, which may not be the same as the income tax expense, depending on whether there is any interperiod income tax allocation (discussed in Chapter 24). Also, there are no income taxes payable reported for a single proprietorship or a partnership, since the proprietor or partners are taxed on their personal income, including their share of the profits of their business.

Although the income tax owed is determinable at the end of the fiscal period based on annual income, it is an estimate in the sense that the tax is subject to the review and approval of the government taxing agency. Thus normal, recurring differences between estimated and owed income taxes can be accounted for during the period in which the differences are determined. However, if there are material, nonrecurring adjustments or settlements of income taxes, per *Opinion No. 9* they should be treated as prior-period adjustments and taken to Retained Earnings.

SALES TAXES PAYABLE: With the existence of sales taxes imposed by state and local governments, businesses act as agents for the government authorities in the collection of sales taxes on the transfers of tangible personal property and on certain services. Thus businesses have a liability for the sales taxes collected from customers that are to be remitted to the government.

In accounting for sales taxes, the business may set up a sales taxes payable account to accumulate the sales-tax collections at the time sales are made. Such an account would reflect the liability for sales taxes owed to the government. For example, if the sales-tax rate were 3 percent, then sales of $10,000 would be recorded as follows:

Cash (or accounts receivable)	10,300	
Sales		10,000
Sales taxes payable ($10,000 × .03)		300

If the sales taxes payable as recorded differ from the sales taxes as computed by the government unit, then the liability account is adjusted by recognizing a gain or loss on sales-tax collections.

Many companies, in accounting for sales taxes, do not segregate the sales taxes payable at the time sales are made. An adjusting entry is made at the end of the period, segregating the sales taxes from the sales and setting up the liability. For example, if a company had sales of $300,000 during the fiscal period, and if the sales-tax rate is 3 percent, then the $300,000 includes $8,738 [$300,000 − ($300,000/1.03)] in sales taxes and would be segregated as follows:

Sales	8,738	
Sales taxes payable		8,738

In addition to sales taxes, the state or local government may require a company to remit a use tax on goods that it acquires for its own use from sellers outside the authority of the taxing unit (that is, outside the local sales-tax law). For example, assume that a company acquires equipment for $5,000 from a seller outside the state, and that there exists a 3 percent state use tax. The following entry reflects the setting up of the use-tax liability:

Equipment	150	
Use taxes payable		150

EMPLOYEE BONUSES PAYABLE: In addition to regular salaries and wages, some companies pay bonuses to officers, managers, or employees. Such bonuses accrue to the employees at the end of the fiscal period and therefore should be recorded by charging an operating expense (such as Employee Bonuses Expense) and crediting a current liability (such as Employee Bonuses Payable), pending payment at the beginning of the next fiscal period.

Although bonuses are an operating expense as well as a tax-deductible expense, they are generally calculated on the basis of the net income (or revenue) for the period and are therefore a form of profit sharing. Since the bonuses are based on net income, the accountant should make sure that the bonus agreements with the employees specifically state how income is to be calculated in determining the bonuses. In other words, is the net income for bonus purposes determined before or after taxes, and before or after the bonuses themselves?

For example, assume that a company has net income for the year of \$200,000 before bonuses and income taxes. Further assume that the company has a bonus agreement with its employees to pay 10 percent of net income after bonuses and income taxes, and that the company's tax rate is 40 percent. The bonuses would be \$11,320.75, calculated and recorded as follows:

$$\begin{aligned}
\textbf{Let } B &= \textbf{Bonus} \\
T &= \textbf{Taxes (income)} \\
\textbf{Then } B &= (.10)[\$200{,}000 - B - ((.40)(\$200{,}000 - B))] \\
&= (.10)[\$200{,}000 - B - (\$80{,}000 - .40B)] \\
&= \$20{,}000 - .10B - \$8{,}000 + .04B \\
1.06B &= \$12{,}000 \\
B &= \underline{\underline{\$11{,}320.75}} \\
\textbf{and } T &= (.40)(\$200{,}000.00 - \$11{,}320.75) \\
&= \underline{\underline{\$75{,}471.70}}
\end{aligned}$$

Employee bonuses expense	11,320.75	
Employee bonuses payable		11,320.75
Income taxes expense	75,471.70	
Income taxes payable		75,471.70

ESTIMATED LIABILITY UNDER PRODUCT WARRANTIES: Products are often sold under a guarantee or warranty to provide free repair service or replacement during a specified period if the products are defective. At the point of sale, a company has incurred a liability arising from the promise to make good the product sold.

Although warranties represent future costs (after-sale costs) the amount of which is not definitely known, they are the result of past transactions (the sales) and normally can be reasonably estimated as to amount, time period (because of the warranty period), and payee (the customer group). Consequently, to avoid understating liabilities and overstating periodic income, warranty costs should be accounted for during the period of sale by debiting Product Warranty Expense, which matches expense with revenue, and crediting Estimated Liability Under Product Warranties at the estimated amount. As the actual warranty costs are subsequently incurred, they are charged against the estimated liability account. Any differences between the actual and estimated amounts are changes in accounting estimates and are treated as prospective adjustments, per *Opinion No. 20.*

If warranty costs are relatively immaterial and the warranty period is relatively short, many companies charge warranty costs to expense as they are actually incurred. This modified cash-basis method of accounting for warranty costs is conceptually incorrect, because no liability is recognized and the warranty expense is not necessarily matched during the period with the sales revenue that resulted in the warranties. The popularity of the modified cash-basis method is based on expediency and the fact that it is the only method recognized for income tax purposes.

ESTIMATED LIABILITY FOR PREMIUM CLAIMS OUTSTANDING: In order to stimulate the sale of their products, some companies offer premiums to their customers in return for product labels, boxtops, wrappers, coupons, or certificates. The premiums may consist of dishes, silverware, toys, or other goods, and in some cases, cash payments.

In accounting for premiums, a company has an inventory of premiums (such as Premiums—Silverware) carried at cost, and when the premiums are redeemed, Premium Expense (a selling expense) is charged and Inventory credited at cost. If the premiums expire during the accounting period, no accounting adjustments are needed; however, if premiums are still outstanding at the end of the fiscal period and they are material in amount, an estimate should be made to recognize the liability and to match expense with revenue. In such a situation, at the end of the fiscal period, Premium Expense is debited and Estimated Liability for Premium Claims Outstanding is credited at the estimated cost.

Long-term liabilities. These are obligations extending beyond the current operating cycle or one year, whichever is longer; hence, unlike current liabilities, they will not be currently discharged from current assets. Examples of long-term liabilities include bonds payable, mortgage notes payable, and long-term notes payable, as well as any existing long-term deferred revenue or product warranties.

Since the accounting for bonds payable is quite similar to the accounting for mortgage notes payable and long-term notes payable, and since the accounting for bonds was thoroughly discussed in Chapter 7, no further discussion on these liabilities is presented. However, unlike the case with bonds payable, it should be pointed out that in current accounting practice, long-term deferred revenue and product warranties are not recorded and reported at their discounted amount (present value).

Contingent liabilities. When conditions are such that a possible liability may arise, depending upon some future events or circumstances (such as a pending lawsuit), the potential liability or possible future obligation is called a contingent liability. In such situations, there have been no past transactions that have resulted in the current existence of a liability, and at the balance-sheet date there is no legal liability; hence, from the accounting viewpoint, contingent liabilities are not really liabilities and should not be reported as such in the balance sheet. Instead, such potential claims are reported in the balance sheet as footnotes, parenthetical remarks, as contra accounts, or as a special classification (Contingent Liabilities) between Liabilities and Stockholders' Equity, with any estimated amounts not included in the balance sheet totals (that is, reported "short").

Although a legal liability for contingent liabilities does not exist at the balance-sheet date, accounting liabilities include more than just legal debt; they also include estimated liabilities. Therefore, the question arises as to the difference between estimated and contingent liabilities, since the former are recognized as liabilities in accounting, and the latter are not. The accounting distinction between an estimated and a contingent liability is one of whether a liability currently exists (estimated liability), or may exist in the future, contingent upon some future event (contingent liability). The distinction is *not* one of whether the amount is definite or indefinite, since a potential liability with a known amount is still a contingent liability if there is no obligation currently existing.

On the other hand, from a conceptual viewpoint the distinction as to whether a liability currently exists or is dependent on future events is not clear-cut. Estimated liabilities are dependent on future events (for example, future costs under product warranties are dependent on the future event of the product's being defective), yet accountants recognize them as liabilities. However, accountants do not recognize estimated liabilities if the future claim is highly unlikely. Consequently, the conceptual difference between an estimated and a contingent liability is that with the former there is a high probability and with the latter there is a low probability that a future claim will materialize.

Some of the more common contingent liabilities, or sources thereof, are mentioned below:

Notes receivable discounted. The proper procedure for recording the discounting of notes receivable was discussed in Chapter 10.

Accounts receivable assigned. The proper procedures for recording the assignment of accounts receivable was also discussed in Chapter 10.

Accommodation endorsements. If a person or representative of a firm cosigns a note, then default by the original maker of the note obligates the cosigner to make payment. Such endorsements can be recognized per the usual treatment for contingent liabilities. However, some accountants prefer to formally recognize such a contingency by debiting a receivable from the party accommodated and crediting a contingent liability, such as Liability Under Endorsements. Such offsetting accounts can be reported "short," so that their amounts are not included in the balance-sheet totals, or ignored in the balance sheet (except by footnote or parenthetically) as merely memorandum accounts.

Pending lawsuits.

Additional taxes.

Purchase commitments. A contingent liability for the full purchase price exists when a firm orders goods for future delivery. Such a contingency can be recognized similarly to other contingent liabilities; however, since a contingent asset also exists, the contingent liability is usually ignored. On the other hand, if a loss is clearly in prospect from the purchase commitment because of declining prices, current accounting practice recognizes the loss (the excess of the commitment price over the market price at the date of delivery) with an offsetting credit to a liability, such as Provision for Losses on Purchase Commitments. Note that the latter is set up as a liability, not a contingent liability, since the loss has actually developed and can be measured.

Contracts for long-lived-asset acquisitions. If, at the balance-sheet date, a company is committed in a material amount on contracts for plant construction or for other long-lived-asset acquisitions, disclosure should be made in a balance-sheet footnote. Although such commitments do not involve prospective losses for which a provision is required, disclosure is important because the use of funds for additions to long-lived assets may significantly affect the working capital.

PENSIONS

Introduction. A pension plan is an arrangement by which a company provides benefits to its retired employees, whereby the retirement benefits can be estimated in advance based on the provisions of company pension documents or company pension practices. Although most pension plans are written plans, a pension plan would exist if it were based on well-defined, although perhaps unwritten, company policy. Note, however, that a pension plan does not include a company's practice of paying retirement benefits to selected employees in amounts determined on an employee-by-employee basis at or after retirement.[3]

A pension plan normally contains a provision that when the employee reaches a specified age, he can retire and receive a determinable amount, usually in the form of monthly payments, during his retirement years. In addition, many pension plans include death and disability benefits.

Pension plans can be funded or unfunded, with the former being the usual case. Under an unfunded plan, the company makes payments directly to its retired employees as they become due. If the employer company establishes its own pension trust fund for the payment of pension benefits, it is still an unfunded plan, because it is under the control of the company rather than of an independent third party.

Under a funded plan, the company makes payments to a funding agency—such as a specific corporate trustee, individual trustee, or an insurance company, which provides the facilities for the accumulation of assets, including the income earned by the fund (called *interest*). Or the funding agency, such as a specific life insurance company, provides the facilities for the purchase of pension benefits and thereby assumes the obligation for payments of the benefits as they become due. The latter situation is referred to as an insured plan, since the employer company purchases a pension system from an insurance company, which contracts to meet and guarantee a specified level of pension benefits.

---

[3]Accounting Principles Board, "Accounting for the Cost of Pension Plans," *Opinion No. 8* (New York: AICPA, November 1966), p. 68.

The employee's cost under a pension plan depends on whether the plan is contributory or noncontributory; the employee bears part of the cost of the former, and the employer bears all the cost of the latter. Since most pension plans are established so as to qualify under the Internal Revenue Code, employees' pension benefits are not subject to income tax, and the employer's contributions are tax-deductible. Also, an employee's benefits are said to be vested when the benefits are no longer contingent upon his continued employment by the company. Depending on the pension plan, vested benefits can occur when the employee retires, has worked a specified number of years, or has reached a certain age.

With this background in mind, we now turn to the basic problems in the accounting for pensions: the reporting of the economic effects of the pension plan in the financial statements, and the timing problem of the allocation of the employer's pension cost to periodic expense.

Valuation of pensions. In theory, a pension plan results in future benefits to a company in the form of reduced employee turnover and absenteeism, and improved employee work because of increased loyalty and goodwill to the company; hence, the discounted amount of such future benefits should be conceptually capitalized as an asset. Similarly, in theory, the discounted amount of the expected future payments to be made to employees during their retirement years is a liability of the firm.

Because of the uncertainty of the future benefits to be derived from a pension, and therefore the extreme difficulty in measuring such future benefits, accountants are not willing to capitalize future pension benefits as an asset on the balance sheet. Similarly, because of the uncertainty and the conditional nature of future retirement payments to employees, accountants are not willing to report the discounted amount of the future payments as a liability on the balance sheet. Just as future wage and salary payments to employees are conditional upon continued employment by the firm, future pension payments are conditional upon continued employment until pension benefits are vested.

It should also be pointed out that a company's liability for pension obligations varies from company to company. Those companies that assume the direct responsibility of payments of the benefits specified in the pension plan are liable for paying the specified retirement benefits regardless of the amounts funded. On the other hand, most pension plans limit the company's legal obligation to the payment of benefits equal to the assets in the pension fund; hence, if the pension fund is inadequate to meet the benefits stated in the pension plan, benefits are reduced as specified in the plan and the company has no further legal obligation. In spite of this, experience shows that if a company continues in business, the pension benefits are not usually reduced to conform to the legal liability.

Because of the practical problems in measuring future retirement payments, accountants report pensions based on funding (financing) methods. The financing methods used in reporting pensions are those consistent with accrual accounting.

Accrual basis. Prior to 1965, the accounting for pension cost was in general on a discretionary cash basis, whereby the periodic pension expense was equal to the cash paid for pension benefits during each fiscal period. Since the cash paid during the fiscal period was influenced by the earnings for the period and the availability of cash, the periodic expense could fluctuate from period to period at the discretion of management's financing of the pension benefits. Because such fluctuations in periodic pension expense can result in distorting the periodic net income reported, the financing of pension benefits should not be the determinant of the annual pension expense.

Accountants are now generally agreed that the discretionary cash basis of accounting for pension cost should not be used, and instead pension cost should be accounted for on the accrual basis. That is, the charging of annual pension cost to expense (often referred to as the provision for pension cost) is similar to the allocation of other costs to expense, and requires accounting judgment and estimation in line with basic accounting assumptions (fiscal-period, matching, cost, and going-concern assumptions).

Conceptually, a company's total pension cost is equal to the discounted amount of the future retirement payments that are to be made to eligible employees per the agreed pension plan during their retirement years. This total pension cost, of course, is uncertain because of unknown future events, such as the length of life of retired employees, employees leaving or dying before retirement, the addition of new employees, and changes in the pension plan itself. However, by the use of actuarial methods, total pension cost can be estimated by determining the amount that must be put into a fund, including the earnings on the fund, sufficient to pay the agreed retirement benefits as they become due.

Assuming that total pension cost can be reasonably estimated by actuarial methods, there still remains the accounting problem of assigning the total pension cost to periodic expense. In other words, accountants view pension cost as an expense of conducting business operations, and therefore such cost should be charged to expense each fiscal period on an accrual basis in order to match revenue and expense. However, since it is impossible under current accounting practice to match perfectly pension expense with revenue, accountants *allocate* pension cost to periodic expense. Thus the allocation of pension cost to expense is similar to other allocations made in accounting, such as depreciation, depletion, amortization, and cost of goods sold, the only difference being that pension cost is based on future cash flows.

It should be pointed out that the allocation of pension cost to periodic expense, like other cost allocations, is arbitrary. Because there are an infinite number of allocation methods possible, there is no real theoretical basis supporting one allocation method over another. Hence, the argument for the allocation of pension cost in current accounting practice reduces to the contention that it should be based on a systematic allocation method to avoid the income distortion that would result from pension charges based on management discretion. Note, however, that systematic cost allocation is a form of income smoothing.

With regard to the allocation of pension cost, accountants make the distinction between normal, past-service, and prior-service costs. We now turn to a discussion of these costs.

Normal and past-service cost. Normal cost is the annual pension cost assigned, under the actuarial cost method in use, to years subsequent to the date of the adoption or amendment of a pension plan. Normal cost is a current-service cost, since it is based on the benefits to employees arising from services currently performed. Thus, normal cost is the pension cost assigned to the current period for services performed by the employees during that year.

In contrast to normal cost, past-service cost is the pension cost assigned, under the actuarial cost method in use, to years prior to the inception of the pension plan. Past-service cost arises when a company, after being in business several years, adopts a pension plan that gives credit to employees for their prior years of service. Thus, past-service cost is similar to a "catch-up" cost determined at one point in time (the date of the inception of the pension plan) and therefore may involve significant amounts.

Similar to past-service cost is prior-service cost. Prior-service cost is the pension cost assigned, under the actuarial cost method in use, to years prior to the date of a particular actuarial valuation. When a pension plan is amended to take into account changes in retirement benefits, such amendment requires an actuarial valuation of the plan.[4] The pension cost assigned to periods prior to the date of the actuarial valuation (amendment date), including any remaining past-service cost, is prior-service cost. Because the two types of cost are similar, the accounting for prior-service cost is similar to the accounting for past-service cost.

The relationship between past-service, prior-service, and normal pension costs is illustrated below:

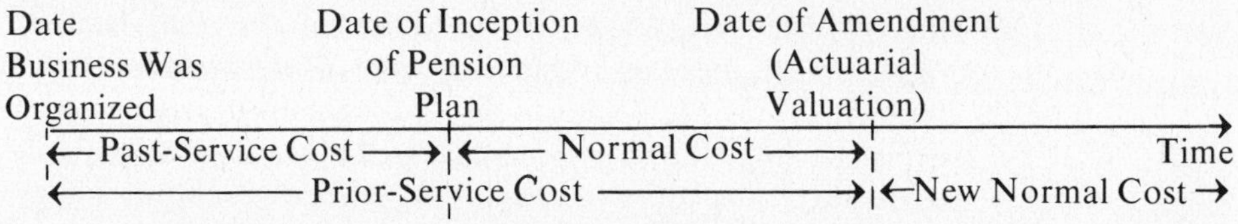

Accounting for pension cost. With regard to normal cost, there is general agreement among accountants that the periodic pension expense, based on accrual accounting, should reflect the cost of future retirement benefits arising from employees' services after the inception of a pension plan. Thus the normal pension cost is accrued annually, with the cost determined by an actuarial cost method consistent with accrual accounting.

In contrast, the question of how to account for past-service cost has caused some controversy, with two opposing points of view as to the nature of pension cost.[5] One point of view is that pensions are a form of supplemental compensa-

---

[4]Per *Opinion No. 8,* p. 99, actuarial valuation is the process by which an actuary estimates the present value of benefits to be paid under a pension plan and calculates the amounts of employer contributions or accounting charges for pension cost.

[5]See *Opinion No. 8,* pp. 69–72; and Ernest L. Hicks, "Accounting for the Cost of Pension Plans," *Accounting Research Study No. 8* (New York: AICPA, 1965), pp. 31–55.

tion to existing employees; hence, the annual pension expense should be based on the estimated future benefit payments to be made to the existing employees at the time of the pension plan's adoption or amendment. In other words, the annual provision for pension cost would be on a full accrual basis, since there would be recognition of expected future payments for employee services rendered before (past- or prior-service cost) and after (normal cost) the adoption (or amendment) of the plan. Past- (prior-) service cost would be accounted for over the remaining service lives of those employees working for the firm at the time of the adoption (or amendment) of the plan. Thus the contention is that past- (prior-) service cost is part of the cost of providing pensions for the employees initially covered, and that the future periods benefited by the past- (prior-) service element is related, in large part, to the periods in which the employees will complete their employment.

The other point of view is that pensions are a means of promoting efficiency by providing retirement benefits, or are the fulfillment of a social obligation by business firms. Thus pension costs are associated with the pension plan itself (rather than with specific employees) and therefore with the continuing employee group as a whole. The contention is that there is no need to make provisions for past-service cost, since the provision for pension cost based on normal cost plus interest on any unfunded prior-service cost is sufficient to meet, on a continuing basis, all benefit payments under the plan. The reason for this is that the actuarial determination of future benefit payments is based on the mass of employees moving through the plan over the years, not on specific employees. Moreover, it is also contended that the future periods benefited by granting past-service credit are indefinite in length; hence, past-service cost is analogous to an intangible asset that need not be amortized.

In analyzing past-service cost, two points should be made. First, the term *past-service cost* is misleading, because such cost is not a cost of past periods. The firm did not benefit during the periods prior to the inception of the plan, because the employees were not working under a pension plan at that time. Hence, past-service cost should *not* be treated as a prior-period adjustment where such cost would be charged against retained earnings. Second, the contention that the provision for past-service cost should be based on the amount necessary to keep the plan continuing is not theoretically sound, because it confuses the provision for pension cost with the method of financing the pension plan. If past-service benefits are granted to employees, then a cost exists and should be accrued, even though full funding may not be necessary. Consistent with accrual accounting, the cost of past-service benefits granted to employees should be systematically allocated over the remaining service lives of the employees who will receive pensions based in part on past service.

Minimum and maximum provisions. In an apparent compromise between the two opposing viewpoints discussed above as to the nature of pension cost, *Opinion No. 8* states that the annual provision for pension cost (periodic pension expense) should be based on an accounting method that uses an acceptable actuarial cost method that results in a provision between specified methods for calculating minimum and maximum charges. The minimum and maximum provisions are as follows:[6]

Minimum. The annual provision for pension cost should not be less than the total of:

(1) Normal cost
(2) An amount equivalent to interest on any unfunded prior-service cost
(3) If indicated, a provision for vested benefits

Maximum. The annual provision for pension cost should not be greater than the total of:

(1) Normal cost
(2) Ten percent of past-service cost, until fully amortized
(3) Ten percent of the amounts of any increases or decreases in prior-service cost arising on amendment of the pension plan, until fully amortized
(4) Interest equivalents on the difference between provisions (pension expense) and amounts funded

The minimum provision per *Opinion No. 8* is in line with the point of view that pension expense should be at an annual amount that will keep the pension plan on a continuing basis. Also, note that the interest on the unfunded past-service cost in the minimum provision keeps the unfunded past-service cost from growing, since it maintains the original present value of such cost relative to the future benefits applicable to the past periods. Finally, it is interesting to note that the practical effect of existing tax requirements is that on a cumulative basis, normal cost plus interest on any unfunded prior-service cost must be funded, which is equivalent to the minimum provision.

The maximum provision per *Opinion No. 8* is in line with the point of view that pension expense should be on a full accrual basis and therefore take into account both prior-period cost and normal cost. Although income tax laws should not determine accounting practice, it is interesting to note that the ten-year minimum period (10 percent amortization) for amortizing past-service cost per the maximum provision is consistent with the Internal Revenue Code section that allows a maximum annual tax deduction of 10 percent of past-service cost for qualified pension plans. Finally, the interest equivalents in the maximum provision pertain to the increase (the interest that would have been earned on the fund if the amount funded had not been less than the pension expense) or the decrease (the excess interest earned on the pension fund because the amount paid to the fund exceeded the pension expense) in pension expense. The excess of the pension expense over the amount funded is reported as an accrued pension liability, and the reverse situation is reported as a prepaid pension cost.

As a final comment on the minimum and maximum provisions, it should be obvious that with annual pension expense being reported by companies at either of two extremes or somewhere in between, diversity rather than comparability in reporting is the end result.

---

[6] *Opinion No. 8*, pp. 73–74.

ILLUSTRATION: To illustrate the minimum and maximum provisions, assume that a company adopts a pension plan on January 1, 19+5. Based on actuarial computations, the annual normal pension cost is $40,000, and the present value of past-service cost is $500,000 on January 1, 19+5. Further assume that the company agrees to pay a designated trustee at the end of each year an amount equal to the normal cost plus interest on any unfunded past-service cost. The fund is expected to earn 5 percent on its investments. Depending on whether management decides to fund past-service cost, and assuming that management decides to use either the minimum or maximum provision for annual pension expense, the following journal entries would be made for the first two years of operation under the pension plan:

Minimum provision, past-service cost unfunded:			
19+5:	Pension expense [$40,000 + ($500,000 × .05)]	65,000	
	Cash		65,000
19+6:	Same entry as above		
Minimum provision, past-service cost to be funded:			
19+5:	Pension expense (normal cost)	40,000	
	Deferred pension cost—Payments in excess of pension expense ($540,000–$40,000)	500,000	
	Cash		540,000
19+6:	Pension expense (normal cost)	40,000	
	Cash (normal cost + zero interest)		40,000
Maximum provision, past-service cost unfunded:			
19+5:	Pension expense [$40,000 + ($500,000 × .10)]	90,000	
	Accrued pension cost—Pension expense in excess of payments ($90,000 – $65,000)		25,000
	Cash [$40,000 + ($500,000 × .05)]		65,000
19+6:	Pension expense [$40,000 + ($500,000 × .10) + ($25,000 × .05)]	91,250	
	Accrued pension cost—Pension expense in excess of payments ($25,000 × 1.05)		26,250
	Cash		65,000
Maximum provision, past-service cost to be funded:			
19+5:	Pension expense [$40,000 + ($500,000 × .10)]	90,000	
	Deferred pension cost—Payments in excess of pension expense ($500,000 × .90)	450,000	
	Cash ($500,000 + $40,000)		540,000
19+6:	Pension expense [$90,000 – ($450,000 × .05)]	67,500	
	Deferred pension cost—Payments in excess of pension expense ($67,500 – $40,000)		27,500
	Cash (normal cost + zero interest)		40,000

In analyzing the entries above, note that for the minimum provision, if past-service cost is funded, then the pension expense does not include any interest on unfunded past-service cost. Under the maximum provision, note the effect of interest equivalents on the annual pension expense subsequent to the first year (19+6). Under the maximum provision with the past-service cost unfunded, the pension expense for 19+6 is increased by the interest that would have been earned on the pension fund if $25,000 had been funded in 19+5; hence, the interest equivalent for 19+6 is $1,250 ($25,000 × .05). Similarly, under the maximum provision with the past-service cost funded in 19+5, the pension expense for 19+6 is decreased by the interest earned on the pension fund for the excess payment of $450,000; hence, the interest equivalent for 19+6 is $22,500 ($450,000 × .05).

Although the illustration above assumes that the amount funded each year is equal to normal cost plus interest on any unfunded past-service cost, this does not have to be the case. Management may decide to fund more or less than this. For example, assume the same data as above except that the annual payment is $40,000. Under the minimum provision and past-service cost unfunded, the following entries would be made:

19+5: Pension expense [$40,000 + ($500,000 × .05)]	65,000	
Accrued pension cost—Pension expense in excess of payments ($65,000 − $40,000).............................		25,000
Cash (agreed payment)...		40,000
19+6: Pension expense [$40,000 + (($500,000 + $25,000) (.05))].......	66,250	
Accrued pension cost—Pension expense in excess of payments [($500,000 + $25,000) (.05)]		26,250
Cash (agreed payment)...		40,000

Since the cash payment in 19+5 was $25,000 less than the pension expense, the interest on unfunded past-service cost for 19+6 is equal to the 5 percent rate multiplied by the total of the past-service cost ($500,000) and the accrued pension cost ($25,000) that were unfunded during 19+6, or $26,250.

It should be remembered that the illustrative entries above, other than the last example, pertain only to a company that elected to recognize the annual pension expense at either the minimum or maximum amount per *Opinion No. 8*. Since the annual pension expense can be in between the minimum and maximum provisions, it is the company's accountants that must make sure that the actuarially determined annual pension expense is within the limits. If it is not within the limits, the closest limit would probably be used.

Financial-statement presentation of pensions. *Opinion No. 8* states emphatically that the annual pension expense should be based on an acceptable actuarial cost method, which is essentially a method of funding the pension plan. Similarly, per *Opinion No. 8,* the difference between the amount charged against income (pension expense) and the amount paid (funded) is reported in the balance sheet as Accrued (pension expense exceeds payment) or Prepaid (payment exceeds pension expense) Pension Cost, as previously illustrated. Any prepaid pension cost would be reported in the balance sheet under the Other Assets or Deferred Charges classification. Any accrued pension cost would be reported in the balance sheet under the Long-Term Liabilities classification. Consequently, it should be obvious that the reporting of pensions in the income statement (Pension Expense) and the balance sheet (Prepaid or Accrued Pension Cost) is primarily influenced by the funding of the pension plan.

Opinion No. 8 states that, in addition to reporting any accrued pension cost as a liability, if the vested-benefit obligation exceeds the amounts funded or accrued, the excess should be reported in the balance sheet as *both* a long-term liability (such as Vested Pension Benefits Payable) and as an asset (such as Deferred Vested Pension Cost) under the Other Assets or Deferred Charges classification. Except for this situation of reporting the legal obligation of vested benefits, per *Opinion No. 8* unfunded prior-service cost is not a liability reported in the balance sheet. Also, it should be pointed out that the vested-pension liability would usually arise only in the early years of a pension plan, where there is significant unfunded past-service cost.

Opinion No. 8 also states that because pension plans are important in understanding the financial statements of a company, the following disclosures should be made in the financial statements or the footnotes thereto:

A statement that such a plan exists, identifying or describing the employee groups covered

A statement of the company's accounting and funding policies

The provision for pension cost for the period

The excess, if any, of the actuarially computed value of vested benefits over the total of the pension fund and any balance-sheet pension accruals, less any pension prepayments or deferred charges

Nature and effect of significant matters affecting comparability for all periods presented, such as changes in accounting methods (actuarial cost method, amortization of past- and prior-service cost, treatment of actuarial gains and losses, etc.), changes in circumstances (actuarial assumptions, etc.), or adoption or amendment of a plan[7]

Actuarial gains and losses. Because pension costs are based on actuarial assumptions that reflect expectations of future events, there can be deviations between planned and actual pension costs, as well as changes in underlying assumptions with regard to the future as conditions change. Thus, adjustments may be needed annually to reflect actual experience, and may be needed from time to time to revise actuarial assumptions applicable to the future. Such adjustments are referred to as actuarial gains and losses. Examples that would give rise to actuarial gains and losses include substantial investment gains or losses, changes in interest rates, plant closings, and changes in actuarial assumptions with regard to employee turnover, mortality, and the like.

The accounting for actuarial gains and losses concerns the timing of their recognition with regard to pension cost. Such actuarial gains and losses could be recognized by adjusting current-period pension cost (immediate-recognition method), by spreading them at the net amount over current and future periods via normal or prior-service cost (spreading method), or by averaging them at a net amount to normal cost (averaging method).

---

[7]*Opinion No. 8,* p. 84.

Opinion No. 8 states that actuarial gains and losses should be reflected in the provision for pension cost in a consistent manner that reflects the long-range nature of pension cost. Thus, *Opinion No. 8* states that actuarial gains and losses should be spread over the current year and future years (recommending ten to twenty years) or averaged. Under the average method, an average of annual net gains and losses, based on past experience and future expectation, is applied to the normal cost. Note that such treatment of actuarial gains and losses is a form of income smoothing.

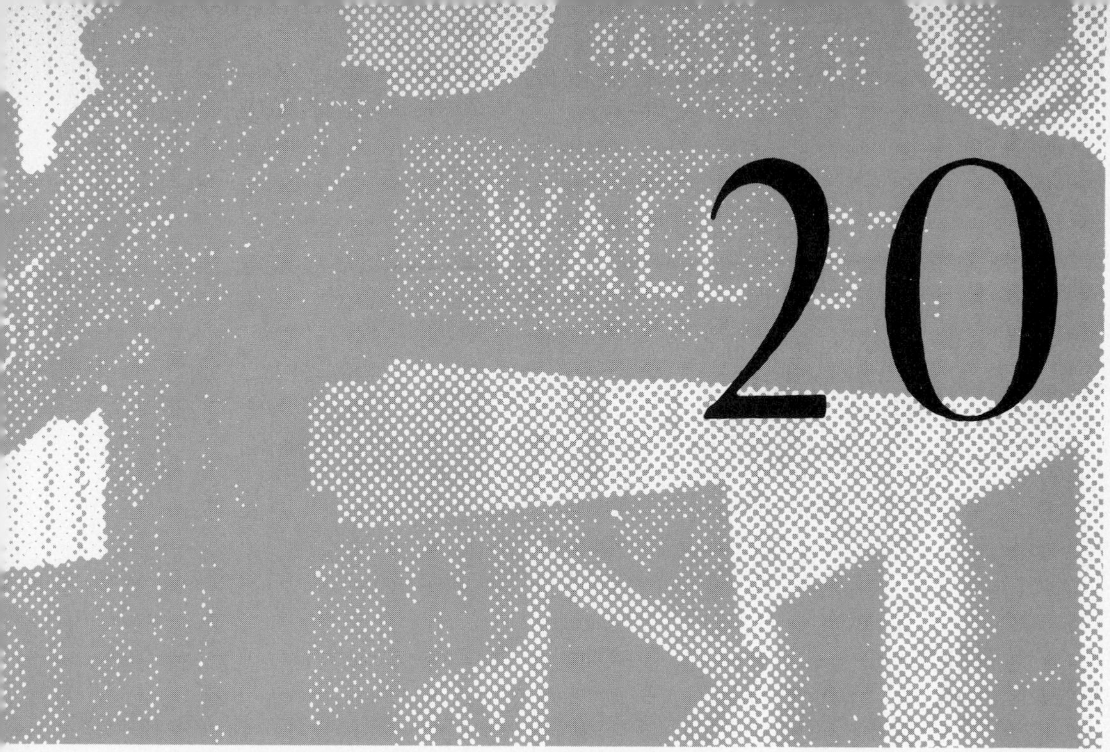

20

Stockholders' Equity: Capital Stock

Introduction. There are three forms of business organization widely used in this country—sole proprietorship, partnership, and corporation—with the last being by far the most prevalent among large companies. The major reasons for the popularity of the corporate form are the limited liability of stockholders (generally, personal assets of the stockholder are not available to satisfy corporate creditors) and the ease with which large sums of capital can be put together to finance large-scale business operations. The corporate form of organization has long been unique in that it is recognized as a distinct entity in the eyes of the law. As a result of this recognition, the corporation continues to exist even though the ownership of stock may change.

Still, most business transactions are recorded in the same manner for any business firm with respect to the effect of the transaction on assets and liabilities. It is in the area of owners' (stockholders') equity that the greatest difference is found between the accounting for the corporate form of organization and that for other forms. This is the first of four chapters that will discuss the accounting for stockholders' equity in detail.

Organization of a corporation. The organization of a corporation is governed by the laws of the respective states. The procedure differs in the various states, and normally the services of an attorney should be used to be certain that the applicable laws are complied with.

In general, the following steps are involved:

(1) An application, signed by a required number of incorporators, is filed with a designated state officer. The application states, among other things:
   (a) The name of the corporation
   (b) The nature of the business it is desired to conduct
   (c) The amount of the authorized capital stock, and the number of shares into which it is to be divided
   (d) The names and addresses of the original subscribers to the stock
   (e) The assets paid into the corporation by those original subscribers

(2) If the application is approved, a charter (which is often the approved application itself) is received from the state officer with whom the application was originally filed. This charter evidences the fact that the corporation has been organized and is authorized to conduct business.

(3) A meeting of the incorporators (or stockholders) is held for the purpose (among other things) of electing directors.

(4) A meeting of the directors is held, and officers are elected.

(5) Capital stock certificates are issued.

Sources of stockholders' equity. In the final analysis, there are basically two sources of stockholders' equity: (1) amounts paid into the corporation by stockholders (referred to as contributed capital), and (2) retained earnings resulting from profitable operations.[1] It is possible in rare circumstances that unrealized capital increments may result from asset appraisals, as was discussed in Chapter 17. However, such revaluations are not in accordance with generally accepted accounting principles at the present time.

Traditionally, a major consideration in the accounting for corporate equity is the idea of showing as clearly as possible the source of the equity. Both the selection of account titles and the balance sheet presentation of stockholders' equity are influenced by this objective. For some firms, only a few accounts may be needed to account for the equity, whereas some corporations may require quite a large number of accounts. This will ultimately be determined by the nature of the stock transactions affecting the firm.

Rights of stockholders. Stockholder investments in a corporation are represented by shares of capital stock that entitle their holders to some or all of certain basic rights. The most important stockholder rights are these:

---

[1]The term *earned surplus* is sometimes used by corporations to designate retained earnings. However, the AICPA has specifically recommended that the term not be used.

(1) The right to vote at stockholders' meetings, and thus to participate in the management.
(2) The right to share in the earnings; that is, to receive dividends when they are declared by the directors.
(3) The right to participate in any additional issues of stock of the class owned, proportionately to one's holdings at the date of the additional issue (known as the "preemptive right"). This right is often abridged or withheld.
(4) The right to share in the distribution of the assets of the corporation upon dissolution.

If there is only one class of stock, these rights are enjoyed proportionately, share and share alike, by all stockholders. If there are two or more classes of stock, one class may enjoy more or less than its proportionate share of certain rights.

Par value stock. When the corporate form of business organization came into widespread use in the latter part of the nineteenth century, laws required that shares of stock be given a par value. This is a purely arbitrary amount, selected by the organizers of the firm, that determines the number of shares into which a total capital amount will be divided. For example, if the charter authorizes a total capital of $100,000, and the organizers want this amount to be represented by 100,000 shares, the par value per share will be set at $1. A par value of $5 per share will result in 20,000 shares ($100,000 ÷ $5). When par value stock is to be sold, both the charter and the stock certificates must specify the par value per share.

Inherent in these early laws was the idea that because of the limited liability of the owners, the creditors of a corporation should have some amount (legal or stated capital) to which they could look as the minimum amount of capital to be maintained in the firm. This concept is discussed later in this chapter. Some states even held that if par value stock was sold for an amount below par value, creditors could require stockholders to pay the additional amount if the firm could not pay the creditors' claims.

No-par value stock. In 1912, New York became the first state to enact legislation allowing the sale of stock without a par value. This resulted from the abuse of par value stock by unscrupulous promoters. Although there is no necessary relation between the par value of a share of stock and the "worth" of the stock, many people simply could not resist the appeal of what they saw as a bargain in being able to purchase par value stock at an amount below par.

The rationale underlying the laws allowing the sale of no-par stock was that the investor would be forced to examine new stock issues to determine the worth of the stock, in order to decide what he would pay for it. The confusion between par value and the worth of the stock would thus be eliminated. Most states now allow the sale of no-par stock, but the laws of the various states are not uniform.

No-par value stock with a stated value. Some states allow the sale of no-par value stock but require that the stock be given a stated value per share. Generally, the board of directors has the right to designate a stated value. In some states, the amount the directors elect to establish as stated value per share cannot be less than a minimum set forth in the law—for example, $5 per share. As will be seen later, the accounting for such stock is basically the same as accounting for par value stock.

Terminology. Before proceeding, we shall use the following illustration to clarify the use of several terms used in reference to stockholders' equity. Assume that the charter of a corporation authorizes the firm to issue 100,000 shares of stock, 70,000 of which have been issued to stockholders. Of the shares issued, 2,000 have been reacquired by the corporation from the shareholders and are held by the firm. This information is summarized below:

Authorized shares total 100,000. This is the maximum number that may be issued without amending the firm's charter.

Issued shares total 70,000. These shares have been issued to stockholders sometime in the past.

Unissued shares total 30,000. These shares have never been issued, but may be issued any time in the future that the corporation wishes.

Treasury shares total 2,000. These shares have been issued by the corporation, have been reacquired by the firm from stockholders, and are presently held by the corporation. Accounting for treasury stock is discussed in Chapter 23.

Outstanding shares total 68,000. These shares are currently held by stockholders. The amount represents the total number of shares that have been issued (70,000), less the shares that have been reacquired and are held by the firm (2,000).

Legal or stated capital. In addition to the emphasis on source, which, as noted earlier, is a primary consideration in the accounting for stockholders' equity, the concept of legal or stated capital is important.

Among the advantages of the corporate form of business organization is that of limited liability, which means that the stockholders normally cannot be held personally liable for the debts of the corporation. Because the law gives stockholders this immunity, it is only fair that creditors should be given some assurance that the corporation will not be permitted to make payments or distributions to its stockholders that will reduce the stockholders' equity below a stipulated amount known as *legal* or *stated capital.* In the absence of any restriction on the amount of assets that can be returned to shareholders, the directors of a corporation in financial difficulty could strip the corporation of most of its assets by declaring dividends or by using company funds to purchase or retire the corporation's capital stock, to the benefit of shareholders and the detriment of creditors. In general, there is less risk associated with a creditor's claim if there is a prescribed amount of stockholders' equity that cannot be reduced by payments or distributions to the shareholders.

The amount of the stated capital is determined by the law of the state in which the corporation is organized. Because there is considerable variation in the state laws on this matter, only the more common definitions are mentioned here.

In the case of par value shares, stated capital is usually defined as *an amount equal to the aggregate par value of the shares issued.*

In the case of no-par shares, stated capital is *the aggregate credited to the capital stock accounts.* The amounts thus credited may equal

(1) the total received for the shares issued, or

(2) an amount based on a stated value per share.

Stated capital can be reduced (provided that the action complies with the provisions of the state corporation act) by a reduction in the number of issued shares or in their par or stated value; by changing par value shares to no-par shares with a lower stated value than the former par; or by changing no-par shares to par shares with a par less than the former stated value.

It should be noted that the existence of legal provisions regarding stated capital reduces, but does not eliminate, the risk of loss by creditors. Stated capital can be impaired by unprofitable operations. Also, some of the assets may not be available to satisfy the claims of general creditors, because the directors of the corporation may have mortgaged or otherwise pledged them as security for specific obligations.

Because stated capital is a legal concept, and because there is considerable variation in the state laws, it is impracticable to deal exhaustively with the subject in an accounting text; it must suffice to call attention to the fact that the treatment of matters related to stated capital is governed by the law of the state in which the company is incorporated.

Classes of stock. The two principal classes of stock are common and preferred. The term *common stock* is applicable to corporate shares that have no preferences. If all the stock is of one class, there are obviously no preferences, and all the shares are common.

Preferred shares have one or more preferences over the common shares. Thus, preferred stockholders may enjoy certain preferential rights in the sharing of earnings (dividends) or in the distribution of assets in liquidation. On the other hand, preferred stockholders may have no rights, or only limited rights, to vote.

The fact that preferred stock is usually nonvoting is one reason for its wide use by corporations to obtain additional capital investments. The common stockholders can thus avoid dilution of their voting interests. Another reason is the opportunity for financial leverage often afforded by preferred stock.

Preferred stock and dividend payments. Stock that is preferred as to dividends entitles its holders to a dividend at a specified rate on the par value, or of a specified amount per share if it is a no-par value stock, before dividends are paid on the common stock. For example, a 6 percent, $100 par value preferred stock entitles the holder to a $6 per share dividend ($100 × .06) before common dividends are paid. If the stock were no-par, it would stipulate that the dividend was $6 per share.

A preference as to dividends is not an assurance that dividends will be declared and paid. No stockholder, whether holding preferred or common shares, has an unconditional right to receive a dividend, for two reasons. First, the payment of dividends on stock of any class depends upon whether the corporation has a legal right to pay a dividend. Second, even though the corporation has a legal right to pay a dividend, the directors, after giving due consideration to matters of corporate policy and cash requirements, may decide that it would be inexpedient to distribute funds to the stockholders. In general, the stockholders' only remedy is to bring an action in a court of equity, and undertake to present evidence to prove that dividends have been unjustifiably withheld. This has not proved to be much of a remedy, because courts have shown a reluctance to order dividend payments. For this reason, dividends should not be regarded as accruing prior to their declaration.

A company cannot guarantee the payment of dividends on its preferred stock. However, dividends on the stocks of one company are sometimes guaranteed by another company; for instance, Company A, in connection with a lease of facilities of Company B, may guarantee the payment of dividends on Company B's stock.

CUMULATIVE AND NONCUMULATIVE STOCK: If preferred stock is cumulative, any preferred dividends not paid in any given year must be paid in the future before any dividends can be paid on the common stock. If a partial dividend is paid, the unpaid portion accumulates. If preferred stock is noncumulative, a dividend lost in one year is lost forever.

For example, assume that a corporation has the following stock outstanding:

Preferred—1,000 shares, \$100 par value, 6% dividend rate
Common—5,000 shares, \$25 par value

Under these conditions, dividends of \$6,000 each year (1,000 shares × \$6) are required to pay the preferred stockholders. If the corporation declares dividends of \$4,000, \$8,000, and \$11,000, respectively, for three consecutive years, the dividends will be allocated as follows:

	Cumulative Preferred Stock	Noncumulative Preferred Stock
Year 1:		
Preferred stock	\$4,000	\$4,000
Common stock	0	0
Year 2:		
Preferred stock	\$8,000	\$6,000
Common stock	0	2,000
Year 3:		
Preferred stock	\$6,000	\$6,000
Common stock	5,000	5,000

The cumulative feature of the preferred stock is important in year 2 because it requires that the preferred stockholders be paid a total of \$8,000 (\$2,000 not paid in year 1, plus \$6,000 for year 2) before the common stockholders receive any dividends. The \$2,000 not paid in year 1 is referred to as "dividends in arrears." Methods of disclosing preferred dividends in arrears will be discussed in the next chapter. As shown in year 3 in the illustration, the cumulative feature is meaningless in any year in which there are no dividends in arrears and the current year's dividend is sufficient to pay the full dividend on the preferred stock.

PARTICIPATING AND NONPARTICIPATING STOCK: Preferred stock may be participating or nonparticipating. Participating preferred stock will share with the common stock in any dividends paid after the common has received a dividend at the preference rate. That is, if the preferred is entitled to dividends of 6 percent on par, and if both preferred and common have received 6 percent dividends, an additional payment on the common stock would require an additional payment on the preferred stock. Preferred stock may be fully participating (that is, entitled to dividends at a rate on par value, or in an amount per share on no-par stock, equal to that paid on the common stock); it may be partially participating (that is, a maximum may be placed on the total dividends that may be paid annually on the preferred stock); or it may be nonparticipating. If preferred stock is nonparticipating, its holders are entitled to dividends at the preference rate (par value stock) or amount (no-par stock) and no more, regardless of the rate at which dividends are paid on the common stock.

To illustrate, it will be assumed that a corporation has the same stock outstanding as shown in the illustration on page 486; that is, outstanding preferred stock with a total par value of $100,000 (1,000 shares × $100) and common stock with a total par value of $125,000 (5,000 shares × $25). If all dividends have been paid on the preferred stock in prior years, and the firm declares a total dividend of $20,000 for the current year, the allocation between preferred and common stock would be as follows:

	Preferred Dividends	Common Dividends
(A) Preferred stock, nonparticipating:		
First $6,000 ($100,000 × 6%)	$6,000	
Balance ($20,000 − $6,000)		$14,000
Totals	$6,000	$14,000

Under these circumstances, the preferred stockholders receive the stipulated dividend of 6 percent on the total par value of the stock. Any dividends in excess of this amount will be paid to the common stockholders.

	Preferred Dividends	Common Dividends
(B) Preferred stock, participating up to a maximum of 8%:		
First $6,000 ($100,000 × 6%)	$6,000	
Next $7,500 ($125,000 × 6%)		$ 7,500
Next $4,500 [($100,000 + $125,000) × 2%]	2,000*	2,500*
Balance of $2,000 [$20,000 − ($6,000 + $7,500 + $4,500)]		2,000
Totals	$8,000	$12,000

*Any dividends in excess of $13,500 are allocated 100/225 to preferred stock and 125/225 to common stock, up to the point at which the preferred stock has received an 8 percent dividend.

In this case, the maximum dividend the preferred stock can receive is $8,000 ($100,000 × 8 percent). However, it shares in the additional 2 percent dividend only after the common stockholders have been paid a rate, calculated on par value, that is equal to the preference rate paid to the preferred stock.

	Preferred Dividends	Common Dividends
(C) Preferred stock, fully participating:		
First $13,500 [($100,000 + $125,000) × 6%]......	$6,000	$ 7,500
Balance of $6,500 ($20,000 − $13,500):		
100/225 × $6,500..............................	2,889*	
125/225 × $6,500..............................		3,611*
Totals...	$8,889	$11,111

*Rounded.

The preferred dividend is higher in this case than in the two previous illustrations, because there is no limitation on the rate that can be paid to the preferred stockholders. The only requirement is that the common stock be paid the preference rate of 6 percent before the preferred can participate.

Preferred stock and liquidation. Stock that is preferred as to assets entitles its holders to payment in liquidation before any payments are made to the common stockholders. The fact that stock is preferred as to dividends does not make it also preferred as to assets; this preference must be specifically stated.

Some stock that is preferred as to assets in liquidation is preferred not only to the extent of par, or a stated liquidation value in the case of no-par stock, but also with respect to cumulative dividends in arrears. Therefore, in the event of liquidation, the holders of such preferred stock are entitled to a distribution equal to such dividends even though the company has no retained earnings.

To illustrate this feature of preferred stock, assume that Poor Corporation has the following condensed balance sheet just prior to liquidation:

Assets	$100,000	Liabilities	$ 30,000
		Preferred stock (6%, $50 par value)	25,000
		Common stock ($10 par value)..........	50,000
		Deficit.................	5,000*
	$100,000		$100,000

*Deduction.

Assuming that the preferred stock is cumulative and that dividends have not been paid for one year prior to liquidation, the preferred stockholders are entitled to $28 per share (par value of $25, plus the dividends of $3) in liquidation. Of course, they would be paid only after the creditor claims had been satisfied, but before the common stockholders receive any payment. If the firm is able to convert its assets to cash equal to their book amount, the final distribution of the assets in liquidation would be as follows:

Creditors		$ 30,000
Preferred stock:		
Par value	$25,000	
Dividend (500 shares × $3)	1,500	26,500
Common stock [$100,000 − ($30,000 + $26,500)]		43,500
Total		$100,000

Not only do the common stockholders have to absorb the deficit of $5,000, but they must also absorb the additional dividend paid to the preferred stockholders.

Special features of preferred stock. Various classes of preferred stock may be issued. If there are first and second preferred stocks, the rights of the second preferred are subject to the rights of the first preferred, although the rights of all preferred stockholders are superior, in certain particulars, to the rights of common stockholders.

Corporations sometimes obtain an authorization of a certain number of shares of preferred stock with the right to issue portions thereof from time to time with different features—for instance, with different dividend rates. Thus, a company may obtain an authorization for the issuance of 10,000 shares of $100 par value preferred stock; it may immediately issue 4,000 shares designated as 5 percent series; later it may issue 4,000 shares designated as 6 percent series; and still later it may issue the remaining 2,000 shares designated as $5\frac{1}{2}$ percent series.

As the right to vote is one of the basic rights of stockholders, preferred stock carries this right unless it is specifically withheld. Corporations organized in certain states cannot withhold the right to vote.

Preferred stock sometimes carries the right of conversion into bonds or common stock. This right is intended to make the investment an attractive one. For instance, if the stock is cumulative and participating, the holder has the chance of sharing in the earnings of a successful business, but his dividend revenue is dependent upon earnings, and he has no security for his principal; if earnings prove to be small, the privilege of conversion into bonds allows him to obtain a security that makes his revenue independent of earnings and affords greater safety as to the principal. Or, if the preferred stock is nonparticipating, and earnings prove to be good, the right to convert into common stock allows the holder to switch to a type of investment having full participation in the larger earnings. Accounting for convertible stock is discussed in the next chapter.

Preferred stock may be subject to gradual retirement, through the operation of a redemption fund (frequently called a *sinking fund*), or otherwise. Or it may be redeemable at the option of the corporation; in other words, the stock may be made callable after a certain date and at a stipulated or determinable price. If the issue is called, all dividends in arrears must usually be paid if the stock is cumulative, and the right to redeem cannot be exercised if creditors' rights would thereby be jeopardized. Charter clauses that provide for redemption of stock should be made permissive and not obligatory, because a corporation cannot enter into an unconditional contract to pay off its stockholders.

The terms of issuance of preferred stocks frequently contain provisions intended to safeguard the interests of the preferred stockholders. For instance, the consent of the preferred stockholders may be required before the management can participate in a merger or change the nature of the company's operations. The most customary restrictive provisions have to do with the payment of cash dividends on common stock or the retirement of common shares or their acquisition as treasury stock. The restrictions take various forms. For instance, the payment of common dividends or reductions of outstanding common shares may not be permissible if contributions to preferred stock retirement funds are in arrears; or if the working capital is less than a stated amount or less than a certain multiple of the preferred dividend requirements; or if the net tangible assets are less than a certain multiple of the liquidating value of the preferred stock; or if the equity available for dividends is less than a stipulated amount.[2] This last restriction often takes the form of "freezing" the equity available for dividends at the date of issuance of the preferred stock, by providing that dividend payments on and retirements of common shares, or their acquisition as treasury stock, can be made only to the extent of the increase in retained earnings since that date.

Recording stockholder investments. The following types of accounts are used in connection with investments by stockholders.

CAPITAL STOCK ACCOUNTS: A separate account is set up in the ledger for each class of stock authorized. The account title should be broadly descriptive of the stock. The number of shares authorized and pertinent details regarding the stock are indicated by a memorandum notation in the account. Thus, if a corporation is authorized to issue 10,000 shares of $25 par value, 5 percent cumulative preferred stock and 50,000 shares of no-par common stock with a stated value of $10 per share, the ledger accounts would be set up as shown below:

Preferred Stock

(Authorized issue, 10,000 shares,	$25 par, 5% cumulative)

Common Stock

(Authorized issue, 50,000 no-	par shares, $10 stated value)

Capital stock accounts are credited when the stock certificates are issued to the stockholders; the accounts are credited with the par or stated value of the shares issued or, in the case of no-par stock without stated value, the aggregate price paid for the shares issued.

PAID-IN CAPITAL ACCOUNTS: Amounts received in excess of the par or stated value of shares are credited to paid-in capital accounts, the titles of such accounts indicating the source of the credits. Thus, if par value preferred shares are issued for an amount in excess of par, Capital in Excess of Par Value—From Preferred Stock Issuances would be a suitable account title. The excess is frequently referred

[2] In most instances, this equity would represent retained earnings only. However, in some states it might also include certain paid-in capital amounts.

to as a premium on the sale of the stock. If no-par common shares are issued at a price in excess of their stated value, the account credited for the excess could be described as Capital in Excess of Stated Value—From Common Stock Issuances.

In order to illustrate the entry required to record the sale of stock, let us assume that a corporation sells 1,000 shares of common stock at a price of $14 per share. Depending upon the nature of the stock, the sale would be recorded as follows:

	$10 Par Value		No-par Value		No-par Value with a $5 Stated Value	
Cash	14,000					
Common stock (1,000 × $10)		10,000				
Capital in excess of par value—From common stock issuances		4,000				
Cash			14,000			
Common stock			14,000			
Cash					14,000	
Common stock (1,000 × $5)						5,000
Capital in excess of stated value—From common stock issuances						9,000

Stock may sometimes be issued for less than its par value. However, this is very rare, for the following reasons:

(1) In many states such issuance is illegal.

(2) In states where it is legal, stockholders to whom the stock was issued at a discount generally face a contingent liability. Should the corporation become insolvent, they may be held personally liable to the corporation's creditors for amounts equal to such deficiency. As a general rule, the contingent liability does not pass to a subsequent holder unless he had notice of the discount or should have known about it.

If capital stock is issued for less than par value, the discount should be debited to a separate account (the word "discount" and the class of stock involved should appear in the account title) and shown as a deduction in the Stockholders' Equity section of the balance sheet. The sale of 5,000 shares of $10 par value common stock for $9 per share would be recorded as follows:

Cash	45,000	
Discount on common stock	5,000	
Common stock (5,000 × $10)		50,000

Balance sheet presentation of stock accounts. The balance sheet should show the following information for each class of stock:

(1) The par value, if any, or the fact that the stock is without par value, in which case the stated value, if any, should be shown.

(2) The special rights appertaining to any class of stock.

(3) The number of shares authorized; the number issued and outstanding (which will differ from the number issued if there is any treasury stock); and the number, if any, subscribed for but not issued.

(4) The capital in excess of par or stated value, if any, applicable to each class of stock.

(5) The balances of any subscriptions receivable.

Stock subscriptions. Time may elapse between the date when subscriptions for stock are received and the date when they are collected and the stock is issued. Under such circumstances, there is a need for accounts to show the amount receivable from the subscribers and the shares that have been subscribed for but as yet are unissued. The accounts to be used under such circumstances are described below:

Subscriptions Receivable:

When subscriptions are received, this account is debited with the aggregate price of shares subscribed.

As collections are received from subscribers, the account is credited.

Common (or Preferred) Stock Subscribed:

When subscriptions are received, this account is credited with the par or stated value or, in the case of no-par stock without stated value, the subscription price of the shares subscribed.

When stock certificates are issued, this account is debited and Common (or Preferred) Stock is credited.

The credit balance in this account shows the par or stated value or subscription price, as the case may be, of the shares subscribed for but not issued.

The account is shown in the Stockholders' Equity section below the presentation for the stock issued.

Common (or Preferred) Stock:

When certificates are issued, this account is credited with the par or stated value or aggregate subscription price of the shares represented by the certificates. In other words, whatever amount was credited to the stock subscribed account when the shares were subscribed for is credited to the Common (or Preferred) Stock account when the shares are issued.

ILLUSTRATION: Subscriptions are received for 200 shares of no-par common stock with a stated value of $10 per share. The subscription price is $12 per share.

Subscriptions receivable	2,400	
Common stock subscribed		2,000
Capital in excess of stated value—From common stock issuances		400
Subscriptions for 200 shares at $12 per share.		

Each subscriber pays one third of the subscription price.

Cash	800	
Subscriptions receivable		800
Partial collection of subscriptions receivable.		

Each subscriber pays the balance of the subscription price.

Cash	1,600	
Subscriptions receivable		1,600
Collection of balance of subscriptions receivable.		
Common stock subscribed	2,000	
Common stock		2,000
Issuance of 200 shares after collection of subscriptions in full.		

A corporation may issue stock before the subscriber has paid in full for the subscribed shares. A variety of terms or conditions may be set forth in subscription agreements concerning the requirements that must be satisfied before the shares are issued. Whatever the conditions, when they are satisfied and the shares are issued, the stock subscribed account is debited and the capital stock account is credited.

BALANCE SHEET PRESENTATION: Where should uncollected subscriptions receivable be shown in the balance sheet? If it is expected that the subscriptions will be collected, they can be shown on the asset side. If collection is expected in the relatively near future, it is customary to show the subscriptions receivable as a current asset, but they should be clearly shown as subscriptions to capital stock, and not as ordinary accounts receivable. If there is no immediate intention to call upon the subscriber for the uncollected balances of their subscriptions, the subscriptions may still be shown on the asset side of the balance sheet, but not as a current asset.

However, if there is some question of whether the uncollected balances will ever be called, or whether they are collectible, it is preferable to exclude them from the assets and show them as a deduction in the Stockholders' Equity section, in some manner similar to the following:

Stockholders' equity:		
Capital stock:		
Preferred—6% cumulative, participating; par value, \$100; authorized, 1,000 shares; issued and outstanding, 750 shares	\$75,000	
Less uncollected subscriptions	15,000	\$ 60,000
Common—No-par value; authorized, 5,000 shares; issued and outstanding, 3,100 shares, at stated value of \$50		155,000
Total		\$215,000
Capital in excess of stated value—From common stock issuances		31,000
Total		\$246,000

Forfeited subscriptions. A subscriber may fail to pay his subscription in full. The accounting procedure depends upon the law of the state of incorporation. To illustrate, assume that the following transactions occur:

A. B. Jones subscribes at par for five common shares with an aggregate par value of \$500.
He pays \$200 and defaults.
The shares are issued to another for \$480.
The expenses incurred as a result of the default are \$30.

In some states, the subscriber is allowed a specific time to complete his payments; if he remains delinquent at the close of that period, he is entitled to no refund, whether or not the shares are issued to another. The entries would be:

Subscriptions receivable	500	
Common stock subscribed		500
Subscription of A. B. Jones.		
Cash	200	
Subscriptions receivable		200
Collection from Jones.		
Common stock subscribed	500	
Subscriptions receivable		300
Capital in excess of par value—Forfeited subscriptions to common stock		200
Forfeiture of subscription.		
Cash	480	
Capital in excess of par value—Forfeited subscriptions to common stock	20	
Common stock		500
Issuance of stock to another.		
Capital in excess of par value—Forfeited subscriptions to common stock	30	
Cash		30
Expense incurred as a result of default by subscriber.		

In other states, an effort must be made to find another subscriber for the forfeited shares. If the corporation is successful, the amount received from the original subscriber, minus any discount and expense incurred as a result of the default, must be refunded to him. The entries required under these conditions would be:

Subscriptions receivable	500	
Common stock subscribed		500
Subscription from A. B. Jones.		
Cash	200	
Subscriptions receivable		200
Collection from Jones.		
Common stock subscribed	500	
Subscriptions receivable		300
Liability to defaulted subscriber		200
Default by stock subscriber.		
Cash	480	
Liability to defaulted subscriber	20	
Common stock		500
Stock issued to another.		
Liability to defaulted subscriber	30	
Cash		30
Expense incurred as a result of default by subscriber.		
Liability to defaulted subscriber	150	
Cash		150
Refund to Jones.		

There is also the possibility that the defaulting subscriber may be entitled to receive the number of shares that his partial payments will pay for in full. Referring to the preceding illustration, the subscriber would receive shares with a par value of $200, and the following entry would be made:

Common stock subscribed	500	
Subscriptions receivable		300
Common stock		200
Issuance of shares and cancellation of balance of defaulted subscription.		

But assume that Jones had paid $230 on his subscription. The immediately preceding entry would become:

Common stock subscribed	500	
Subscriptions receivable		270
Common stock		200
?		30

If the law required that Jones be reimbursed for the $30, a liability account (or Cash) would be credited with the $30. If the $30 was forfeited by Jones, a capital-in-excess account would be credited.

Sale of different stocks as a unit. Corporations sometimes sell different types of securities as a "package" for a single price. Examples would be common stock and preferred stock sold as a unit, or bonds and stock sold as a unit. Under these circumstances, it is necessary that the total amount received be allocated to the different securities in some logical manner.

If the fair market value of each security can be determined, the total amount received should be allocated to the securities by using the relative market prices. Under this method, the sale of 1,000 shares of $100 par value common stock, currently selling for $110 per share, and 100 shares of $50 par value preferred stock, currently selling for $53 per share, would be allocated as shown below. It is assumed that the total amount received for the stock was $110,000.

Market price of common stock (1,000 × $110)	$110,000
Market price of preferred stock (100 × $53)	5,300
Total	$115,300
Sale price allocated to common stock ($110,000/$115,300 × $110,000)	$104,940
Sale price allocated to preferred stock ($5,300/$115,300 × $110,000)	5,060
Total	$110,000

The sale of the stock would be recorded as follows:

Cash	110,000	
Preferred stock (100 × $50)		5,000
Common stock (1,000 × $100)		100,000
Capital in excess of par value—From preferred stock issuances		60
Capital in excess of par value—From common stock issuances		4,940

There may be instances in which the market prices of both securities cannot be determined. For example, if only the market price of the common stock in the previous example could be determined, this would be used as the basis for allocating a portion of the total amount received to the common stock. The remainder of the sale price would then be allocated to the preferred stock. But if a market price cannot be determined for either class of stock in the transaction, then allocation must be made on some arbitrary basis. The relative par values of the total number of shares issued may be the only basis available in this case.

The same procedures just discussed apply to transactions in which stock and bonds are sold as a unit. It is possible, of course, that the application of the procedures might result in the recording of a discount on one or both of the securities. However, if the corporation is organized in a state where stock discount is illegal, the records would probably indicate that the stock was issued at par and that the bonds were issued at a discount. As a practical matter, the transactions are usually managed in some manner that avoids any debit to a discount account.

Stock issued for property. When stock is issued for noncash assets, a valuation problem may arise. If a valuation is placed on the property in an arm's-length transaction, and if related facts do not make the valuation questionable, it may be accepted for purposes of determining the entry to be made to record the transaction. In other cases, the valuation may be based on the fair market value of the property or the fair market value of the stock, whichever is more readily determinable. The price at which other shares of the same class were issued for cash (or were the subject of a stock exchange transaction) at about the time when stock was issued for property may be a good evidence of fair market value. Such evidence is not conclusive, however; instances have been known in which a few shares have been issued for cash at a price in excess of fair market value, in a transaction not at arm's length, for the very purpose of attempting to establish an inflated stock valuation to support an inflated asset valuation.

The existence of a par value for stock and the accounting necessity for balancing the books have been responsible for much inflation in the recorded valuations of assets acquired by issuance of stock. If the property acquired is not worth the par of the stock, a discount-on-stock account should appear on the books; such an account is not likely to appear, however, because directors are disposed toward the valuation of property at the par of the stock. The law allows directors great latitude in exercising their discretion as to the value of property taken for stock. The general rule of law has been that courts will not overrule the directors' valuation even when creditors are trying to prove that par value stock was in reality issued at a discount, unless valuations have been grossly excessive and unless fraud is apparent. There is, however, a growing tendency for courts to scrutinize the valuations of assets taken for stock when creditors are attempting to prove that stock was issued for property at a discount.

The Securities and Exchange Commission has taken a more positive attitude and has frequently found that statements were misleading when property taken for stock was set up at arbitrary and inflated values. This attitude has strengthened the position of the accountant, even in cases outside the jurisdiction of the commission. Although it may still be impossible for an accountant to insist on the recording of noncash assets at a fair cash value lower than the directors' valuation thereof, an independent public accountant should give serious consideration to the advisability of mentioning the facts in his report, particularly in view of the increasing degree of responsibility that government agencies and the public are expecting him to assume.

Stock issued for services. What should be the basis of valuation for stock given to an employee for services? Should it be the par or stated value, the market price, the book amount, the cost to the company (if treasury stock is used), or the fair market value of the services?

The fair market value of the services is the most logical basis, but the market price of the stock is presumptive evidence of the worth of the services, because the corporation foregoes the opportunity to sell the stock at the market price. In other words, the issuance of stock to the employee seems tantamount to issuing the stock for cash and giving the cash to the employee.

For income tax purposes, the fair market value of the stock at the date of receipt is revenue to the recipient. Consistency would presumably require that this be recognized by the corporation as the cost of the services. However, the market price at the date when the contract was made is a more logical basis; cost to a subscriber paying in installments of cash would be the cost at the date of the subscription, and there seems to be no difference between a cost payable in installments of cash and a cost payable in installments of services.

Revenue should be charged with the determined valuation of the services or stock; a capital stock account should be credited with the par or stated value of the stock; and a paid-in capital ("excess") account should be credited with any excess of the total charge for the services over the amount credited to capital stock. A paid-in capital account should be credited just as it would be with any excess of cash received for stock over its par or stated value.

The cost of treasury stock given for services is not a proper basis for a charge to revenue unless this cost happens to represent the fair market value of the services.

Assessments on stockholders. Under certain circumstances, a corporation may make an assessment against its stockholders. The method of recording the collection of assessments paid by stockholders depends upon whether the stock was originally issued at a discount. If it was not issued at a discount, the amount received should be credited to a paid-in capital account with some such title as Donated Capital—Stockholders' Assessments. If the stock was originally issued at a discount, a portion of the assessment equal to the discount should be credited to the discount account, and only the remainder, if any, should be credited to donated capital.

Change from par to no-par. Most state laws permit corporations with par value stock outstanding to change to a no-par basis, or vice versa.

If a change from a par to a no-par basis consists merely of calling in shares that had been issued at par and issuing an equal number of no-par shares with a stated value equal to the par value of the old shares, the only entry required is one closing out the par value stock account and opening a new account with the same balance. For instance, assume that a company's authorized issue consists of 1,000 shares of common stock of $100 par value, and that 600 shares were issued at par and are outstanding; assume also that the charter is amended to cancel the old par value shares and authorize the issuance of 1,000 shares of no-par value; assume further that the directors assign a stated value of $100 per share to the no-par stock. The only entry required is:

Common stock	60,000	
Common stock		60,000

The old and new common stock accounts appear as follows:

Common Stock

(Authorized issue, 1,000 shares, $100 par value)

Date	600 shares converted to shares of no-par value	60,000	Date	600 shares issued	60,000

Common Stock

(Authorized issue, 1,000 no-par shares, $100 stated value)

			Date	600 shares issued	60,000

Assume that 2,000 no-par shares were authorized and that they were given a stated value of $50 per share. The journal entry to record the conversion would be the same as that shown above. The 2,000 shares of no-par stock authorized and the 1,200 shares issued would be shown in the new common stock account.

If a company changing from a par to a no-par basis has any stockholders' equity accounts resulting either from operations or from transactions in the stock that is being converted to a no-par basis, the balances of these accounts should not be transferred, in whole or in part, to capital stock unless the directors authorize such a transfer entry or take some formal action that is equivalent to authorizing such an entry. Any such transfers usually would be made first from any capital-in-excess or other paid-in capital accounts resulting from transactions in the par value shares that are being converted to a no-par basis; the remainder should be transferred from Retained Earnings. To illustrate, assume that a company has the following accounts:

Common stock (1,000 shares of $100 par value)	100,000
Capital in excess of par value—From common stock issuances	25,000
Retained earnings	40,000

Assume also that the par value shares are called in and that 3,000 shares of no-par common stock are issued with a stated value, established by resolution of the directors, of $50 per share. This would mean a declaration of $150,000 as stated capital. The entry for the conversion would be:

Common stock	100,000	
Capital in excess of par value—From common stock issuances	25,000	
Retained earnings	25,000	
Common stock		150,000

After a change from a par basis to a no-par basis has been recorded, any balance remaining in a capital-in-excess account or any other paid-in capital account related to the par value shares converted should be transferred to new accounts, because the reference in the old account titles to a kind of stock no longer outstanding would be confusing.

If a company with par value stock and an accumulated deficit from operations changes its capital structure to no-par stock with a stated value less than the par value of the stock previously outstanding, thus creating a paid-in capital, the law may permit the elimination of the deficit by charge to such paid-in capital. If the par value stock was issued at a discount, the permission to change to a no-par basis might carry an implied permission to eliminate the discount account; this is a matter of law.

Incorporation of a going concern. For various reasons, the owners of a going concern may decide to incorporate the business. When this is done, the books of the old firm may be retained by the corporation, or the owners may decide that the old books will be closed out and new records opened for the corporation.

As a preliminary step, it is usually necessary to adjust some of the accounts of the old firm in order to bring them into conformity with the valuations agreed upon for the purpose of transfer to the corporation. Such adjustments should be carried to the capital account(s) of the previous owner (sole proprietorship) or owners (partnership).

To illustrate, assume that A and B, who have been operating a partnership for some time, decide to expand the business by incorporating and selling stock to outsiders. The partners share profits and losses equally. Just prior to incorporation, the books are closed and the following after-closing trial balance is prepared:

A AND B
After-Closing Trial Balance
December 31, 19+5

Cash	2,000	
Accounts receivable	21,000	
Allowance for uncollectibles		2,000
Merchandise inventory	59,000	
Land	20,000	
Building	75,000	
Accumulated depreciation		15,000
Accounts payable		10,000
Notes payable		6,000
A, capital		60,000
B, capital		84,000
	177,000	177,000

The corporation's charter authorizes 5,000 shares of $100 par value common stock. All the partnership's assets and liabilities are to be transferred to the corporation in exchange for 1,600 shares of stock. It is agreed that in order to reflect fair market values, the following adjustments should be made in the asset amounts prior to transferring them to the corporation: Net accounts receivable should be decreased by $1,000, which will be accomplished by increasing the balance in the allowance for uncollectibles account; Land should be increased by $4,000; and the amount at which the building is reported should be increased by $5,000, which will be done by decreasing the balance in the accumulated depreciation account. In addition to the stock issued to the partners, the corporation sold 1,000 shares to the public at $110 per share.

Before we proceed, it should be pointed out that the basis for the adjustment of the amounts at which assets are reported on the partnership books, and subsequently transferred to the corporation, is the fact that the partnership is in effect selling its assets to the new firm, or corporation. Although it has been assumed that stock is sold to the public at the time of incorporation, one should not get the idea that a corporation can arbitrarily adjust asset amounts each time it issues additional stock.

Assuming that the partnership books are to be retained by the corporation, the following entries are required to record the incorporation:

(a) To adjust partnership accounts prior to incorporation:

Land	4,000	
Accumulated depreciation	5,000	
Allowance for uncollectibles		1,000
Capital adjustment account		8,000

(b) To allocate the net result of asset adjustments to the partners in the profit–loss ratio:

Capital adjustment account	8,000	
A, capital		4,000
B, capital		4,000

(c) To record the goodwill, indicated by the difference between the current price of the stock issued to the partners and the net assets transferred to the corporation:

Goodwill	24,000*	
A, capital		12,000
B, capital		12,000

*Valuation of stock issued to partners (1,600 shares × $110 current price)		$176,000
Less valuation of net assets transferred:		
Assets:		
Cash	$ 2,000	
Accounts receivable ($21,000 − $3,000)	18,000	
Merchandise inventory	59,000	
Land ($20,000 + $4,000)	24,000	
Building ($75,000 − $10,000)	65,000	
Total	$168,000	
Less liabilities ($10,000 + $6,000)	16,000	152,000
Excess		$ 24,000

The goodwill is credited to the partners' capital accounts in the profit–loss ratio used by the partnership. At this point, the partners' capital accounts appear as follows:

	A, Capital	B, Capital
Balance per partnership trial balance	$60,000	$ 84,000
Add: Increase resulting from asset adjustments	4,000	4,000
Increase resulting from recording goodwill	12,000	12,000
Balance	$76,000	$100,000

(d) To record issuance of stock to partners:		
A, capital	76,000	
B, capital	100,000	
Common stock (1,600 × $100)		160,000
Capital in excess of par value—From common stock issuances		16,000
(e) To record sale of 1,000 shares of stock at $110:		
Cash	110,000	
Common stock (1,000 × $100)		100,000
Capital in excess of par value—From common stock issuances		10,000

If new books are to be opened for the corporation, entries (a), (b), and (c) illustrated above will be the same. However, it will then be necessary to close all accounts for the partnership and establish a receivable for the stock to be received from the corporation. The receipt of the stock and its distribution to the partners will then be recorded. At the same time, the new books for the corporation will record the assets received and liabilities assumed and show a payable to the partnership for the stock to be issued. Finally, the issuance of the stock to the partnership and to outsiders will be recorded. This procedure is illustrated on the following page beginning with entry (d).

Old Partnership Books			New Corporation Books		
(d) To record adjusted amounts transferred:					
Allowance for uncollectibles	3,000		Cash	2,000	
Accumulated depreciation	10,000		Accounts receivable	21,000	
Accounts payable	10,000		Merchandise inventory	59,000	
Notes payable	6,000		Land	24,000	
Receivable from AB Corporation	176,000		Building	75,000	
Cash		2,000	Goodwill	24,000	
Accounts receivable		21,000	Allowance for uncollectibles		3,000
Merchandise inventory		59,000	Accumulated depreciation		10,000
Land		24,000	Accounts payable		10,000
Building		75,000	Notes payable		6,000
Goodwill		24,000	Payable to AB Partnership		176,000
(e) To record issuance of stock to partnership:					
Stock of AB Corporation	176,000		Payable to AB Partnership	176,000	
Receivable from AB Corporation		176,000	Common stock		160,000
			Capital in excess of par value—From common stock issuances		16,000
(f) To record distribution of stock to partners:					
A, capital	76,000				
B, capital	100,000				
Stock of AB Corporation		176,000			
(g) To record sale of 1,000 shares at $110 per share:					
			Cash	110,000	
			Common stock		100,000
			Capital in excess of par value—From common stock issuances		10,000

21

Stockholders' Equity: Rights, Warrants, Options, and Convertibles

Nature of stock rights and warrants. The accounting treatment of stock rights and stock warrants from the point of view of the investor was discussed in Chapter 14. *Stock rights* result from the preemptive right of stockholders to protect their proportionate ownership interest. They are issued to existing shareholders and convey the privilege of subscribing for additional shares of the same class of stock currently held. One right is issued for each share of stock, so that the owner of 100 shares of common stock would receive 100 rights. The corporation has the power to prescribe how many rights will be required to purchase one additional share. Thus, if ten rights are required to purchase each share, the owner of the 100 shares previously referred to would be able to purchase only ten additional shares of stock.

A *stock warrant* is a security giving the holder the right to purchase shares of stock of the corporation at a specified price. Warrants are most frequently used when the privilege of purchasing common stock is issued with some other form of security, such as a bond or preferred stock.

Reasons for issuing rights and warrants. Rights and warrants are issued by corporations under the following circumstances:

(1) After a decision to issue additional shares. This is related to the preemptive right discussed earlier. In some states, the corporation's charter may restrict the preemptive right.

(2) Concurrently with the issuance of securities of a class other than those obtainable by exercise of the warrant.

(3) To personnel in connection with employment contracts. These are commonly referred to as *stock options*.

If a corporation has outstanding stock rights or warrants that have not been exercised, its balance sheet should indicate the number of shares of stock reserved to meet the issuance requirements to which it is committed by the rights or warrants.

Let us examine some of the accounting problems related to the issuance and redemption of stock rights and warrants.

Preemptive stock rights. No entry need be made upon the issuance of rights evidencing the preemptive right of stockholders to acquire additional shares of the same class held by them. Entries required upon the issuance of the shares when the rights are exercised are the same as those to record the initial sale of stock if par value shares are paid for by the stockholders at par or more, or if no-par shares are paid for at an amount at least equal to the stated value. But assume that the rights entitle the stockholders to acquire, at $25 per share, no-par stock to be recorded at a stated value of $30; upon issuance of the shares, a transfer from retained earnings to capital stock of $5 per share would be required, regardless of the market price of the stock at the time of issuance.

It is common practice to offer the stock at a price below the present market price, thus insuring that most, if not all, of the stock will be sold to existing stockholders. Stock rights have an expiration date and are worthless if not exercised by that date.

Since stockholders are not required to exercise their preemptive right, it is possible that not all stock to be sold by use of the rights will be purchased by existing stockholders. In order to insure that the entire issue is sold, the corporation may enter into an agreement with a party referred to as an underwriter, who agrees to purchase stock not sold to existing stockholders.

Stock warrants issued with other securities. When stock warrants are issued in connection with the sale of preferred stock or bonds, it may be necessary to assign to the warrants a portion of the amount received from the sale of the securities. The treatment accorded the warrants will depend upon whether or not a valuation can be determined for them.

It has previously been noted that a stock warrant entitles the holder to purchase stock of the corporation at a specified price. Thus, the worth of a warrant to the holder depends upon whether or not it enables the buyer to acquire stock at a price below the price at which it is sold in the market. In some instances, the warrant may have potential worth, depending upon the future market price of the stock that can be purchased. In other cases, the warrant's benefit to the holder may be immediate, because of the present relationship between the market price of the stock and the price at which it can be purchased by use of the warrant.

Preferred stock and stock warrants. Assume that a corporation issues 1,000 shares of preferred stock at $105 per share, with warrants entitling the holders to acquire 1,000 shares of no-par value common stock at $25 per share. It is further assumed that the common stock is currently selling at $24 per share. Depending upon the expiration date of the warrants, they may be highly speculative in nature and have an immediate cash market. However, the market price of the warrants cannot be objectively determined at this time. In this case, the sale of the preferred stock would be accounted for in the same manner as the sale of stock without the warrants. The entry is shown below:

Cash (1,000 × $105)	105,000	
Preferred stock (1,000 × $100)		100,000
Capital in excess of par value—From preferred stock issuances		5,000

The entire sale price of the preferred stock is assigned to the stock, rather than allocated between the stock and the warrants. If the warrants have an expiration date and are not exercised by that date, no entry is required for the expiration, since they had not been recorded in the accounts.

Using the preceding illustration, assume now that the common stock was selling at $27 per share at the time the preferred stock was issued. In this case, a valuation of $2 each can be assigned to the warrants, since they allow the holder to purchase for $25 per share common stock that is selling at $27. The buyer of the preferred stock is assumed to be paying $105 for a "package" that includes a warrant worth $2 and a share of preferred stock worth $103. This serves as a basis for the following entry to record the sale of the preferred stock:

Cash (1,000 × $105)	105,000	
Preferred stock (1,000 × $100)		100,000
Capital in excess of par value—From preferred stock issuances (1,000 × $3)		3,000
Common stock warrants outstanding (1,000 × $2)		2,000

If all the outstanding warrants are subsequently exercised, resulting in the sale of 1,000 shares of no-par value common stock at $25 per share, the following entry would be recorded:

Cash	25,000	
Common stock warrants outstanding	2,000	
Common stock		27,000

The common stock warrants outstanding account is a part of the stockholders' equity of the corporation. It would be reported as an element of paid-in capital in the firm's balance sheet.

Should the market price of the common stock, which was assumed to be $27 per share at the time the preferred stock was sold, fall below $25 per share before the warrants are exercised, there would be no reason for the holders to exercise them. The following entry would be required upon the expiration of the warrants:

Common stock warrants outstanding	2,000	
Paid-in capital from expired stock warrants		2,000

Note that thus far the discussion has dealt with the issuance of an equity security (preferred stock) that carried with it the privilege of purchasing another equity security (common stock). The procedures discussed are deficient in that they ignore the effect the speculative nature of the warrants may have on their price. It is quite possible that the warrants will have a price different from (normally greater than) the amount assigned to them under the procedures previously discussed. To the extent that this is the case, the valuation assigned to the preferred stock is higher than it should be. Where there is an active market for the warrants at the time they are issued, an argument can be made for using the price thus established as a basis for allocating a portion of the sale price of the preferred stock to the warrants.

Bonds and detachable stock warrants. An increasing number of corporate bond issues contain features conveying special privileges to the bondholders. One of these is the conversion feature, allowing conversion of the debt security into an equity security. This was discussed in Chapter 7. Another feature is the issuance of bonds that have stock purchase warrants.

When stock warrants are issued with bonds of the corporation, the buyer acquires a debt security that carries with it the privilege of purchasing an equity security. The warrants will usually result in a lower cash interest cost for the debt than would be the case without the warrants. In its discussion of these bond features, the Accounting Principles Board stated:

> Unlike convertible debt, debt with detachable warrants to purchase stock is usually issued with the expectation that the debt will be repaid when it matures. The provisions of the debt agreement are usually more restrictive on the issuer and more protective of the investor than those for convertible debt. The terms of the warrants are influenced by the desire for a successful debt financing. Detachable warrants often trade separately from the debt instrument. Thus, the two elements of the security exist independently and may be treated as separate securities.[1]

The viewpoint of the board was as follows:

---

[1] Accounting Principles Board, "Accounting for Convertible Debt and Debt Issued with Stock Purchase Warrants," *Opinion No. 14* (New York: AICPA, March 1969), p. 208.

> The Board is of the opinion that the portion of the proceeds of debt securities issued with detachable stock purchase warrants which is allocable to the warrants should be accounted for as paid-in capital. The allocation should be based on the relative fair values of the two securities at time of issuance. Any resulting discount or premium on the debt securities should be accounted for as such.[2]

The decision of the board is based upon the separate nature of the debt security and the warrants. They are traded separately in the market. Also, the normal expectation is that the debt will remain outstanding until maturity, at which time it will be repaid whether the warrants are exercised or not. The usual arrangement is such that the future market price of the stock to be purchased with the warrants will determine whether or not they are ultimately exercised.

To illustrate the method recommended by the Accounting Principles Board, assume that a corporation sells a \$100,000, ten-year, 6 percent bond issue at 102. Each \$1,000 bond has a warrant that allows the purchase of one share of the firm's common stock for \$32. The common stock has a par value of \$25 and is now selling for \$27 per share. Immediately after the sale of the bonds, each bond has a market price of \$1,015 without the warrant, and the warrants have a market price of \$5 each. In this case, the allocation of the proceeds would be as follows:

Bonds (100 × \$1,015)	\$101,500
Warrants (100 × \$5)	500
Total	\$102,000

The following entry records the sale of the bonds:

Cash (\$100,000 × 1.02)	102,000	
Bonds payable		100,000
Premium on bonds payable (100 × \$15)		1,500
Common stock warrants outstanding (100 × \$5)		500

The premium on the bonds would be amortized over the life of the bonds, as discussed in Chapter 7. Assuming that all the warrants are ultimately exercised, the following entry records the issuance of the common stock:

Cash (100 × \$32)	3,200	
Common stock warrants outstanding	500	
Common stock (100 × \$25)		2,500
Capital in excess of par value—From common stock issuances		1,200

Should any of the warrants not be exercised prior to the expiration date, any

[2] *Opinion No. 14*, p. 209.

balance in the warrants outstanding account applicable to such warrants would be transferred to a paid-in capital account, as illustrated on page 506.

It should be noted in the illustration that the measure of fair value used was the market price of the bonds and the warrants at the time they were issued. Also, note that the sum of the market values of the two securities was exactly equal to the total proceeds from the sale of the bonds. Only by coincidence would this be true in practice.

Using the same illustration, it is now assumed that immediately after the bonds are sold, they have a market price of $1,010 each without the warrants, which have a market price of $15 each. Allocation of the total sale price is as follows:

Market price of bonds (100 × $1,010)	$101,000
Market price of warrants (100 × $15)	1,500
Total	$102,500
Allocation of proceeds:	
Bonds ($102,000 × 101,000/102,500)	$100,507*
Warrants ($102,000 × 1,500/102,500)	1,493*
Total	$102,000

*Rounded.

The sale of the bonds is recorded as follows:

Cash	102,000	
Bonds payable		100,000
Premium on bonds payable ($100,507 − $100,000)		507
Common stock warrants outstanding		1,493

The following entry records the exercise of all the stock warrants:

Cash (100 × $32)	3,200	
Common stock warrants outstanding	507	
Common stock (100 × $25)		2,500
Capital in excess of par value—From common stock issuances		1,207

Bonds and nondetachable stock warrants. The foregoing discussion of stock warrants issued with bonds assumed that there was a separate market for the warrants. However, if the warrants are not detachable from the debt security and the latter must be surrendered in order to exercise the warrant, the Accounting Principles Board has stated that the two securities taken together are substantially equivalent to convertible debt and should be accounted for as such. But the board went on to state that "when convertible debt is issued at a substantial premium, there is a presumption that such premium represents paid-in capital."[3]

Employee stock option plans. Corporations may adopt stock option plans whereby employees meeting the stated requirements are granted options to purchase a given

[3] *Opinion No. 14,* p. 209.

number of shares of the company's capital stock during some specified time period at stated prices. Sometimes such a plan is used as a means of raising additional capital, but it is used more often as an incentive or as a device to obtain a more widespread ownership of the corporation's stock by its employees, with a consequent increased employee interest in the corporation's activities. If the market value of the corporation's stock should increase above the purchase price set forth in the option, those holding options would be in the attractive position of being able to invest in the corporation's stock at less than the then currently prevailing market price.

For many years now, the federal income tax laws have included provisions relating to employee stock option plans. Such provisions are necessary in order to set forth the tax consequences that follow from the sale of shares of stock that the seller acquired through a stock option plan. The tax consequences depend on how the gain or loss is figured and whether all or some portion thereof is a capital gain or loss.

In order to avoid income tax consequences unfavorable to employees, the stock option plans are usually designed to comply with the income tax provisions. Under present tax laws, three types of employee stock options qualify for special income tax treatment. These are:

(1) Qualified stock options. These plans are designed to enable executive employees to obtain an interest in the corporation.
(2) Employees stock-purchase plans. These plans are designed primarily to enable employees to acquire stock of the employer corporation at a price below the prevailing market price.
(3) Restricted stock options. These are similar to employee stock purchase plans, but generally had to be granted prior to January 1, 1964. They have a maximum limitation on the exercise period that is longer than those of stock purchase plans.

If the option qualifies for special tax treatment, the employee is taxed only when the stock thus acquired is finally disposed of; and even then, the income reported may be taxed at a special rate under the capital gains provisions of the tax laws.

AICPA and stock option plans. The Committee on Accounting Procedure of the AICPA first issued a pronouncement related to stock option plans in November 1948.[4] Because of a 1950 tax change related to certain types of options and stock purchase plans, there was a significant increase in the number of such plans. This resulted in a revised bulletin by the committee in 1953, which became Chapter 13B of *Accounting Research Bulletin No. 43.*[5] This revised bulletin dealt primarily with what have come to be called traditional stock option plans, in which

---

[4]Committee on Accounting Procedure, "Accounting for Compensation in the Form of Stock Options," *Accounting Research Bulletin No. 37* (New York: AICPA, November 1948).

[5]Committee on Accounting Procedure, "Accounting Research and Terminology Bulletins," final ed., *Accounting Research Bulletin No. 43,* (New York: AICPA, 1961).

both the number of shares covered by the option and the purchase price of the shares are known at the date the option is granted, and there is a specified period during which the option must be exercised. Such options are usually considered to be granted for future services of the employees receiving them.

The period since the issuance of the revised bulletin has been characterized by stock option plans of increasing complexity. Many of these plans have provisions incorporating variable factors that can be determined only by future events. Examples are plans in which the number of shares covered by the plan varies with future events, and plans in which the option price is variable. These developments led to a recent Opinion by the Accounting Principles Board dealing with the subject of stock issuances to employees.[6] The board's Opinion might be considered an extension of the earlier pronouncement dealing with this subject, since the Opinion specifically stated that the 1953 bulletin remains in effect for traditional stock option and stock purchase plans. The board did redefine the measure of compensation involved in option plans as stated in the earlier bulletin.

The major purpose of the Opinion was to deal with practices that have evolved since the prior pronouncement.

> This Opinion recognizes certain practices that evolved after Chapter 13B of ARB No. 43 was adopted and applies the principles of that chapter to other plans in which the number of shares of stock that may be acquired by or awarded to an employee and the option or purchase price, if any, are known or determinable at the date of grant or award. It also specifies the accounting for (a) plans in which either the number of shares of stock or the option or purchase price depends on future events, and (b) income tax benefits related to stock issued to employees through stock option, purchase, and award plans.[7]

The Opinion is applicable to plans that are referred to by the terms *stock option, stock purchase, stock bonus,* or *stock award* plans. However, the treatment is basically the same for all of these; and the authors will use the term *stock options* in the additional discussion of the subject.

Stock options as a form of compensation. Traditionally, there was a tendency to view stock options as a form of additional compensation for officers and other employees. Although the 1953 bulletin of the Committee on Accounting Procedure recognized that not all option plans were intended primarily as a form of compensation, the plans that did represent compensation were the major problem addressed. The title of the bulletin was "Compensation Involved in Stock Option and Stock Purchase Plans."

---

[6] Accounting Principles Board, "Accounting for Stock Issued to Employees," *Opinion No. 25* (New York: AICPA, October 1972).

[7] *Opinion No. 25,* p. 469.

The Accounting Principles Board's Opinion introduced the terms *compensatory,* used to refer to plans whose primary purpose is to compensate employees; and *noncompensatory,* used in reference to plans that are not intended primarily as compensation.

Noncompensatory plans. The board made a distinction between noncompensatory plans and compensatory plans by listing four characteristics that are essential in a noncompensatory plan. Any plan that does not possess each of the characteristics is classified as compensatory. These characteristics are:

(1) Substantially full-time employees meeting limited employment qualifications may participate (executives, and employees owning a specified percent of the outstanding stock, may be excluded).
(2) Stock is offered to eligible employees equally or based on a uniform percentage of salary or wages (the plan may limit the number of shares of stock that an employee may purchase through the plan).
(3) The time permitted for exercise of an option or purchase right is limited to a reasonable period.
(4) The discount from the market price of the stock is no greater than would be reasonable in an offer of stock to stockholders or others.[8]

A plan having these characteristics can be viewed as having as its primary purpose either to raise additional capital or to obtain a greater ownership of the firm's stock among its officers and other employees. The board concluded that there is no compensation for services to be recognized by the corporation in recording the issuance of stock under such a plan, the same conclusion that had been reached in the 1953 bulletin. This appears reasonable, since the employee purchasing the stock has to pay the same price as anyone else to whom it might be made available at this time. The sale of stock under a noncompensatory plan would be recorded in the same manner as the sale of stock to anyone else.

Compensatory plans. The tendency to view stock options as a form of additional compensation for officers and other employees raises an important theoretical consideration. The Committee on Accounting Procedure stated:

> To the extent that such options and rights involve a measurable amount of compensation, this cost of services received should be accounted for as such. The amount of compensation involved may be substantial and omission of such costs from the corporation's accounting may result in overstatement of net income to a significant degree.[9]

This results in two accounting problems associated with stock options: first,

---

[8] *Opinion No. 25,* p. 470.
[9] *Accounting Research Bulletin No. 43,* p. 119.

the question of when the options should be recorded in the accounts; and second, the determination of the amount at which they should be recorded.

Appropriate date for recording stock options. The selection of a date for recording the options is important because the option period may be several years in length; and the valuation selected at one point during the period might be quite different from that selected at another point. In considering this question, the Committee on Accounting Procedure noted six different dates that might be considered:

(1) The date of the adoption of an option plan
(2) The date on which an option is granted to a specific individual
(3) The date on which the grantee has performed any conditions precedent to exercise of the option
(4) The date on which the grantee may first exercise the option
(5) The date on which the option is exercised by the grantee
(6) The date on which the grantee disposes of the stock acquired.[10]

The committee concluded that the date of the grant is the appropriate time for determining the compensation represented by the stock option. There are two arguments in favor of this date. First, when the stock option is part of an employment agreement, it is assumed that the parties to the agreement had in mind a valuation of the option on the date of the contract. Second, the corporation has had the alternative of selling the stock that must be used to satisfy the option; however, as of the date of the grant, the firm gives up this principal alternative use of the shares.[11]

The Accounting Principles Board extended the discussion of the appropriate date so as to include plans that might have these variable factors, stating:

> The measurement date for determining compensation cost in stock option, purchase, and award plans is the first date on which are known both (1) the number of shares that an individual employee is entitled to receive, and (2) the option or purchase price, if any. That date for many or most plans is the date an option or purchase right is granted or stock is awarded to an individual employee and is therefore unchanged from Chapter 13B of ARB No. 43. However, the measurement date may be later than the date of grant or award in plans with variable terms that depend on events after date of grant or award.[12]

In an appendix to the Opinion, the board emphasized that it felt the most important distinction made in the Opinion to have been the dividing of com-

[10]*Accounting Research Bulletin No. 43*, p. 121.
[11]*Accounting Research Bulletin No. 43*, p. 122.
[12]*Opinion No. 25*, p. 472.

pensatory plans into those in which the amount of compensation is measured at the date of the grant and those in which the amount depends upon subsequent events.

Several special situations were discussed by the board. One such case involves the use of the end of the fiscal period as the effective date of the award, rather than the date of the grant. This can be done if the following conditions are met:

(1) The award is provided for by the terms of an established formal plan.
(2) The plan designates the factors that determine the total dollar amount of awards to employees for the period (for example, a percent of income), although the total amount or the individual awards may not be known until the end of the period.
(3) The award pertains to current service of the employee for the period.[13]

Under these circumstances, the year-end date becomes the date on which the compensation represented by the options should be measured.

Measuring compensation represented by stock options. If stock options are considered to represent a form of additional compensation to the recipient, then it is necessary that the compensation, which represents an additional item of expense to the issuing corporation, be measured. It was the opinion of the Committee on Accounting Procedure that "the value to the grantee and the related cost to the corporation of a restricted right to purchase shares at a price *below* the fair value of the shares at the grant date may for the purposes here under discussion be taken as the excess of the then fair value of the shares over the option price."[14]

The committee felt that quoted market prices of stock were usually the major consideration in determining the fair value of shares, but recognized that in some instances it would not be possible to obtain meaningful market prices. In such cases, the committee stated, other valuation methods should be used.

The Accounting Principles Board reaffirmed the basic position of the Committee on Accounting Procedure concerning the way compensation involved in stock options should be measured, but narrowed the meaning of the term "fair value."

> Compensation for services rendered that a corporation receives as consideration for stock issued through employee stock option, purchase, and award plans should be measured by the quoted market price of the stock at the measurement date less the amount, if any, that the employee is required to pay.... If a quoted market price is unavailable, the best estimate of the market value of the stock should be used to measure compensation.[15]

[13] *Opinion No. 25*, p. 473.
[14] *Accounting Research Bulletin No. 43*, p. 123.
[15] *Opinion No. 25*, pp. 471–72.

In practice, many firms that issue stock options do not recognize any compensation. One reason for this is that present tax laws are such that for many plans, maximum tax benefits result only if the option price is set at 100 percent of the market price of the stock at the time the option is granted. Thus, the procedures previously discussed will result in no excess of the quoted market price over the amount that the employee is required to pay. In many cases, it is argued that the amount to be recorded as compensation is not material.

Recording compensation represented by stock options. The foregoing discussion has differentiated between stock option plans under which the amount of the compensation is measured at the date of the grant and those under which the amount will depend upon events after the date of the grant. However, once the amount of the compensation is determined, there is still the problem of when it should be charged against income. Both types of plans normally presume that the employee will perform current or future services, and the compensation represented by the plan should be reported as an expense over the period the employee performs the related services. The total consideration received for stock issued under such plans is the sum of (1) the compensation recognized, and (2) any cash paid by the employee.

Compensation measured at date of grant. It is assumed that a corporation grants options for 5,000 shares of its $10 par value common stock to certain executives on January 1, 19+1, when the stock is selling for $26 per share. The options stipulate a price of $30 per share for the stock and must be exercised between January 1, 19+3, and December 31, 19+5, at which time they expire. Those receiving the options must be employed by the corporation at the time the options are exercised.

The amount of compensation to be recognized under the plan is zero, because there is no excess of the quoted market price over the amount that the employee must pay to acquire the stock. As indicated earlier, this is usually true for stock options, because of present income tax laws.

Changing the illustration above, assume now that the option price is set at $22 per share. The amount of compensation to be recognized is $20,000, calculated as follows:

Market price of stock at date of option (5,000 × $26)	$130,000
Option price of stock (5,000 × $22)	110,000
Compensation to be recognized	$ 20,000

It is possible, of course, that employees participating in such a plan are being compensated for services rendered in the past, as well as current and future services. As a practical matter, it is probably impossible to measure accurately the portion of the compensation applicable to past periods. Unless the plan specifies the period for which payment is being made, the compensation should be allocated as can best be determined from the existing circumstances.

The facts in the illustration above would seem to indicate that the recipients of the options are being compensated for services to be rendered during the period from January 1, 19+1 to December 31, 19+5. Obviously, the employees must remain employed until January 1, 19+3, the beginning of the exercise period. It is possible, of course, that once the exercise period begins, employees may exercise the options and then leave the firm, but the likelihood of this occurrence cannot be known with any degree of certainty at the date of the grant.

The only entry required on the date the options are granted is a memorandum entry recording the terms of the grant. The $20,000 compensation represented by the options is to be recorded over a five-year period. The following entry is required in each of the five years, to allocate the total compensation represented by the plan:

Salaries expense ($20,000 ÷ 5)	4,000	
Unexercised stock options		4,000

It is assumed that all the options are exercised near the end of the option period. The entry to record issuance of the stock is shown below:

Cash (5,000 × $22)	110,000	
Unexercised stock options	20,000	
Common stock (5,000 × $10)		50,000
Capital in excess of par value—From common stock issuances		80,000

It should be noted that the total amount recorded as consideration for the stock issued is the sum of the cash paid by the employees, plus the compensation recognized over the five years.

It is possible that the options might not be exercised, as would be the case if the price of the stock fell below $22 prior to January 1, 19+3, the beginning of the exercise period, and remained below that level for the balance of the option period. Under these circumstances, the following entry would be required at the end of 19+5:

Unexercised stock options	20,000	
Paid-in capital from unexercised stock options		20,000

The amount recorded in this entry is "paid-in" because the employees contributed services to the firm in exchange for the right to purchase shares of stock at a specified price. Their failure to exercise the options owing to a price decline that took place after the option plan was agreed upon does not alter the fact that the options were considered to be an element of compensation. In practice, firms may make new options available at a lower price when there is a significant decline in the market price of the stock.

Since it was assumed in the preceding illustration that all the options could be exercised anytime after January 1, 19+3, it is possible that the employees will exercise them very early in the exercise period. If all the options are exercised on the earliest possible date, the entry at the top of the following page would record the issuance of the stock on January 1, 19+3:

Cash (5,000 × $22)	110,000	
Unexercised stock options ($4,000 × 2)	8,000	
Unearned compensation from exercised stock options	12,000	
Common stock (5,000 × $10)		50,000
Capital in excess of par value—From common stock issuances		80,000

The debit of $12,000 to the unearned compensation account in the entry above is the portion of the compensation represented by the options that will be earned by the employees during the three-year period beginning January 1, 19+3, and should be reported as a separate reduction of stockholders' equity.[16] The stock has been issued to the employees prior to the end of the five-year period over which the compensation is to be allocated. The unearned compensation is charged to expense over the balance of the five-year period, assuming that the employees remain with the firm, by the following entry, recorded at the end of 19+3, 19+4, and 19+5:

Salaries expense	4,000	
Unearned compensation from exercised stock options		4,000

Should the employees who received the options not remain with the firm for the balance of the exercise period, the question arises as to the proper disposition of the unearned compensation account. The Accounting Principles Board's Opinion states that any adjustments required for earlier estimates of the annual compensation represented by the options must be made to the firm's compensation expense in the current period.[17]

Assuming that the employees who exercised the options leave the firm at the end of 19+4, the procedure called for by the board would be applied as follows:

Total compensation represented by the options	$20,000
Less compensation reported in years 19+1, 19+2, 19+3 ($4,000 × 3)	12,000
Balance to be reported as compensation in the current year	$ 8,000

Although it was presumed initially that the element of compensation represented by the options was applicable to a five-year period, it now develops that the employees worked only four years; and the $20,000 compensation is considered to be applicable to this four-year period. The following entry would be recorded by the firm at the end of 19+4:

Salaries expense	8,000	
Unearned compensation from exercised stock options ($20,000 − $12,000)		8,000

[16] *Opinion No. 25*, p. 475.

[17] *Opinion No. 25,* p. 475. The basis of the board's statement is its "Accounting Changes," *Opinion No. 20* (New York: AICPA, July 1971), pp. 397–98.

Compensation measured at date other than date of grant. It has been noted previously that for some stock option plans, the number of shares covered by the grant and/or the option price might not be known at the date of the grant. Under these circumstances, the amount of compensation is measured on the date that both the number of shares and price per share become known. The amount of the compensation is determined by the difference between the quoted market price of the stock on this date and the price to be paid by the recipient of the option. The compensation should be charged to expense "over the period the employee performs related services."[18]

This treatment creates the problem of having to recognize a portion of the compensation as expense before the total amount of the compensation is known. The board has stipulated that the following procedures should be used in this case:

> Estimates of compensation cost are recorded before the measurement date based on the quoted market price of the stock at intervening dates. Recorded compensation expense between the date of grant or award and the measurement date may either increase or decrease because changes in quoted market price of the stock require recomputations of the estimated compensation cost.[19]

Thus, just as in the previous illustration, compensation expense recorded in one period may have to be adjusted in accordance with information that becomes known at a later date. Any such adjustments are made by adjusting the compensation expense reported for the current period.

Stock options and treasury stock. The pronouncement of the Committee on Accounting Procedure stated that the measurement of compensation involved in stock option plans was the same whether treasury stock or unissued shares were used to satisfy the option holders. The Accounting Principles Board reaffirmed this basic position, stating that the cost of treasury stock distributed under an option plan could not be used to measure the amount of compensation represented by the option.

One exception to this rule is the situation characterized by the three conditions listed on page 511. Under these circumstances, the amount of compensation "may be measured by the cost of stock that the corporation (1) reacquires during the fiscal period for which the stock is to be awarded, and (2) awards shortly thereafter to employees for services during that period."[20]

Stock options and income taxes. Current tax laws concerning the deductibility of compensation related to stock option plans can be summarized as follows:

(1) The corporation can deduct as compensation expense only the amount reported by the employee as ordinary income.

---

[18] *Opinion No. 25*, p. 485. [19] *Opinion No. 25*, p. 485. [20] *Opinion No. 25*, pp. 472–73.

(2) The deduction is allowed only in the year in which the employee reports the income.

This creates two problems for financial statement purposes: First, if the amount of the compensation represented by the options on the books of the corporation is exactly equal to the amount of income reported by the employee, the result is a difference in the timing of deductions for tax purposes and reporting purposes. This requires income tax allocation, a subject discussed in detail in Chapter 24.

The second and more difficult problem is the situation in which the amount ultimately reported by the employee as ordinary income, and thus deductible by the corporation for tax purposes, is different from the compensation expense deducted on the firm's books. This is likely to be the case in most instances, because the rules for determining the taxable income from stock options are completely different from the procedures discussed in this chapter for calculating the compensation to be deducted by the corporation. The treatment of differences of this type is summarized below:

(1) If a tax reduction is related to an amount that is deductible for tax purposes but not deductible in reporting net income, the reduction should be added to a capital-in-excess of par or stated value account.
(2) If the tax reduction is less than it would be if the amount of compensation reported on the books were deductible for tax purposes, the difference should be deducted from a capital-in-excess account to the extent that the account has previously been credited for reductions referred to in (1) above.[21]

Disclosure of stock options. Financial statements should disclose the pertinent facts pertaining to stock option plans. These include the number of shares covered by options outstanding, the number of shares related to options that are exercisable, and the option price per share. Information should also be presented concerning any options that were exercised during the period. The means of disclosure varies in practice from brief footnotes to very detailed explanations.

The preceding discussion of stock options has introduced two accounts that are unique to accounting for option plans. One of these is the "unexercised stock options" account. This should be reported on the balance sheet as a part of the firm's stockholders' equity. The account will ultimately be removed from the records, either by the issuance of stock or by transferring any portion applicable to expired options to some other equity account. It was noted on page 516 that the account "unearned compensation from exercised stock options" is reported as a separate deduction from stockholders' equity.

Concluding note. Some basic questions can be raised concerning the present state of accounting for stock option plans. Earlier discussion in this chapter stated that in many instances, the firm granting the options actually records no compen-

---

[21] *Opinion No. 25*, p. 476.

sation, because of the impact the tax laws have on the determination of the option price. Even when there is a difference between the market price of the stock and the option price, it is very doubtful that this is a good measure of the compensation element represented by the option. It is unlikely that the employee would part with the option, even if he had the right to do so, for this difference.

Also, there is the question of how to account for stockholder transactions with third parties that result in some benefit to the corporation. For example, stock might be issued to an officer of the firm to induce him to do something for the benefit of the firm, but the source of the stock is not the corporation. It may come from the chairman of the board or a member of a family that has a large stock holding in the firm. The Accounting Principles Board has not issued an opinion dealing with this situation, but the AICPA apparently plans to issue an accounting interpretation in this area.[22] In general, the interpretation will call for the treatment of such transactions as contributions to capital. The offsetting debit would be accounted for in the same manner as compensatory stock plans. The compensation cost associated with such unrestricted stock would be amortized over the anticipated period the employee would render services, but not more than five years.[23]

Convertible securities. Some bonds and stocks are convertible into other securities of the issuing corporation at the option of the holder. The conversion of bonds into stock of the corporation was discussed in Chapter 7. The present discussion will deal with preferred stock that is convertible into common stock.

The entries required to record conversion of preferred stock into common stock will depend upon the specified conversion ratio. The following general rules are applicable to the accounting for such conversions:

(1) Conversions should not result in an increase in retained earnings. Retained earnings may be decreased by the conversion.
(2) All amounts related to the stock being converted are transferred to accounts associated with the new securities being issued.

To illustrate the conversion of preferred stock, assume that a corporation has the following stockholders' equity:

Preferred stock, $50 par value, 4,000 shares	$200,000
Capital in excess of par value—From preferred stock issuances	10,000
Common stock, $10 par value, 50,000 shares	500,000
Capital in excess of par value—From common stock issuances	100,000
Retained earnings	800,000

[22]Accounting interpretations are issued in answer to accounting questions of general interest to accountants. They do not require the formal procedures of an Accounting Principles Board Opinion and can thus be issued on a more timely basis. Although they are not pronouncements of the Accounting Principles Board, AICPA members may be called upon to justify departures from the interpretations.

[23]AICPA, *Accounting Research Association Newsletter,* March 14, 1973.

This information indicates that the preferred stock originally sold for $52.50 per share [($200,000 + $10,000) ÷ 4,000]. It will first be assumed that one share of the preferred can be converted into five shares of common stock. If half the preferred shares are converted, the following entry would be recorded:

Preferred stock ($200,000 ÷ 2)	100,000	
Capital in excess of par value—From preferred stock issuances ($10,000 ÷ 2)	5,000	
Common stock ($10 × 10,000)		100,000
Capital in excess of par value—From common stock issuances		5,000

In this case, it is necessary to remove one-half the balances from the equity accounts applicable to the preferred stock. This amounts to $105,000, which is now considered to represent the consideration received by the firm for the additional 10,000 shares of common stock issued.

The illustration will be changed slightly by assuming that the conversion ratio is four shares of common stock for each share of preferred stock. If one-half the preferred stock is converted, the entry is as shown below:

Preferred stock ($200,000 ÷ 2)	100,000	
Capital in excess of par value—From preferred stock issuances ($10,000 ÷ 2)	5,000	
Common stock ($10 × 8,000)		80,000
Capital in excess of par value—From common stock issuances		25,000

As the result of a four-for-one conversion ratio, only 8,000 additional shares of common stock were issued. However, the total amount recognized as consideration for the common stock is still $105,000, or the amount applicable to the preferred shares converted.

Finally, let us assume that the conversion ratio is six shares of common stock for each share of preferred, and that one-half the preferred stock is converted. This is recorded by the following entry:

Preferred stock ($200,000 ÷ 2)	100,000	
Capital in excess of par value—From preferred stock issuances ($10,000 ÷ 2)	5,000	
Retained earnings	15,000	
Common stock ($10 × 12,000)		120,000

The conversion ratio requires that 12,000 additional shares of common stock be issued, resulting in a credit of $120,000 to the common-stock account. Since the equity applicable to the preferred stock converted is only $105,000, it is necessary that $15,000 ($120,000 − $105,000) be transferred from the retained earnings account in order to maintain the legal capital of the firm.

When a corporation has convertible securities outstanding, it is necessary that shares be available to meet the conversion requirements. Full disclosure should be made of the conversion requirements and the way in which they will be met.

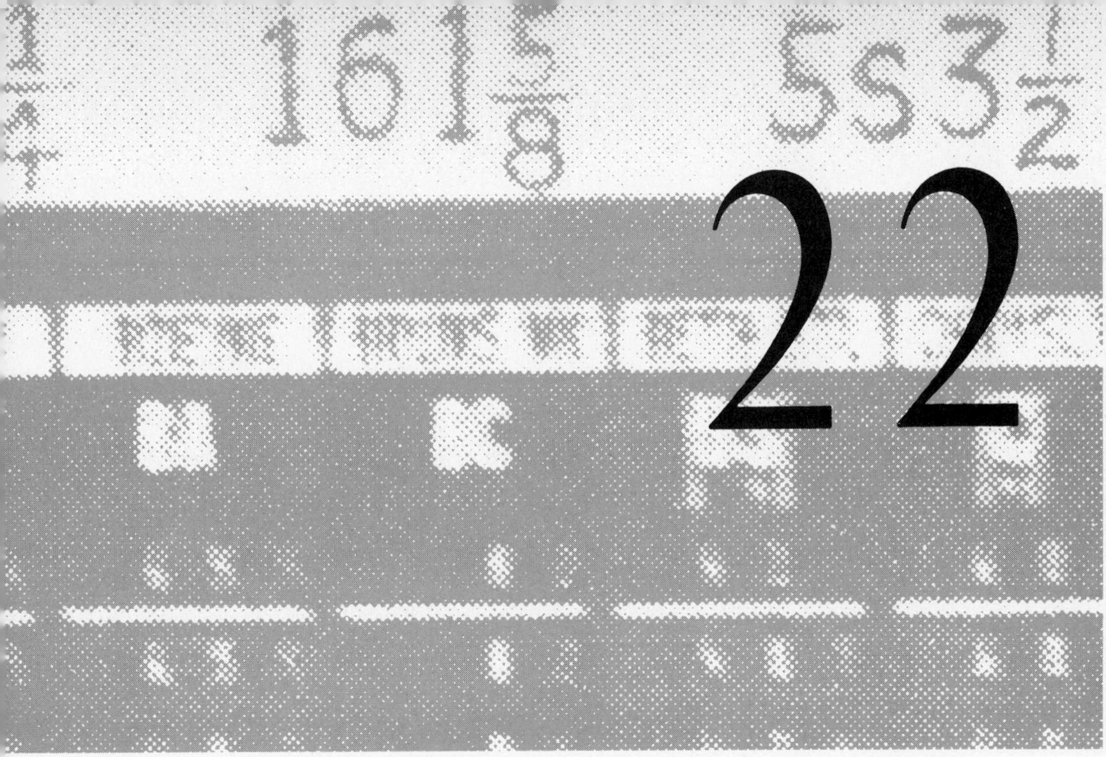

22

Stockholders' Equity: Retained Earnings and Dividends

Nature of retained earnings. Retained earnings represent the retained portion of the corporation's current and prior years' net income, plus or minus the cumulative effect of charges and credits assigned to retained earnings. Owing to the cumulative nature of retained earnings, it is possible that at any point in time it can be a negative amount even though the firm has experienced periods in which operations were quite profitable. Such a negative amount is commonly referred to as a *deficit*.

Next to the periodic transfer of net income or net loss to the retained earnings account, the most frequently recurring entry is a charge for dividends. There are certain instances in which adjustments related to prior periods may be directly charged or credited to Retained Earnings.

Some transactions involving the corporation's own stock result in a reduction in retained earnings. One example of this, involving conversion of preferred stock, was illustrated in the preceding chapter. As another example, suppose that a corporation's capital stock consists of $10 par value stock, which was issued some time ago at par, and that the firm has no additional paid-in capital. The board of directors could, after complying with the applicable legal provisions, change the par value stock to no-par stock with a stated value of $15 per share. Thus, for each share of stock outstanding, $5 of retained earnings is capitalized, or transferred to some other stockholders' equity account.

Terminology. It was noted in Chapter 20 that the term *earned surplus* is sometimes used by corporations to designate retained earnings, even though the AICPA has specifically recommended that the term no longer be used. The major disadvantage of using the word *surplus* in reference to the earnings of a firm is the connotation it conveys as representing an "excess" amount.

A point that was made previously but is important enough to repeat here is the emphasis on sources in accounting for stockholders' equity. Previous chapters introduced several different stockholders' equity accounts that are used to carry out this objective. Examples were paid-in capital accounts resulting from the sale of stock for an amount in excess of par or stated value, forfeiture of payments on stock subscriptions, assessments on stockholders, and expiration of stock options. Additional accounts will be introduced in the next chapter. These accounts are used to clearly identify the source of the equity resulting from various transactions. It should also be emphasized that none of these items represents a source of retained earnings.

Dividends. Dividends represent some form of distribution to the stockholders of a corporation, resulting in a charge against some equity account. They generally involve the outflow of assets, usually cash, but this is not always the case. Because dividends can take different forms, it is important that precise terminology be used when referring to them. Several different types of dividends will be discussed in the following pages.

Legal rather than accounting considerations determine the maximum amount of the equity available for dividend charges at any given time. However, the classification of stockholders' equity by source, previously referred to, provides information that may be absolutely essential to this determination. For example, in most states, dividends must be charged against the retained earnings of the firm; but some states allow certain paid-in capital amounts to be used for this purpose. Stockholders should have the right to assume that retained earnings are being used as the basis of dividends unless they are informed to the contrary.

When the term *dividend* is used alone, it normally refers to a dividend paid in the form of cash. However, dividends may take the form of noncash assets; liabilities of the corporation, such as notes; or shares of stock of the firm. A special form of dividend, referred to as a *liquidating dividend,* actually returns a portion of the stockholders' equity other than retained earnings to them. If any source of equity other than retained earnings is being used as the basis for the dividend, it should be specifically identified.

Dividend policy. The board of directors of a corporation controls the firm's dividend policy, determining the timing, amount, and type of dividend distributions. The directors must obviously operate within the applicable legal provisions, but the courts have generally given them considerable freedom to determine just when it is appropriate to declare a dividend. Stockholder suits attempting to force the payment of larger dividends have met with little success. Legal precedent seems to have established that the financial considerations involved in the payment of a dividend are something that can best be evaluated by the board.

Declared dividends a liability. The notice of the declaration of a dividend should state the date of the declaration, the date on which the stock records will be closed to determine the stockholders of record, and the date on which the dividend will be paid.

After a cash dividend has been legally declared and notice of the declaration has been given to the stockholders, the unpaid dividend ranks as a liability and should be shown as such in the balance sheet. A declared but unpaid dividend is a current liability if it is payable in cash, in short-term scrip or notes, or in property classified as a current asset.

The declaration of a dividend can be rescinded by the directors if no one but the directors has knowledge of the declaration. It can be rescinded by the stockholders at any time before the date of payment.

The fact that cash has been deposited with a trustee or fiscal agent for the payment of a dividend does not justify the omission of the liability from the balance sheet. The depositary is the agent of the company, not of the stockholders; a deposit with the company's agent does not constitute payment to the stockholders. This rule applies to the total dividend prior to the payment date, and any unpaid dividends thereafter.

If a corporation becomes insolvent before the payment of a legally declared dividend of which the stockholders had notice, the stockholders will be entitled to share pro rata with unsecured creditors in the payment of declared dividends and debts. For instance, if there are unpaid dividends of $5,000, other liabilities of $45,000, and assets of $40,000, distribution should be made as follows:

To stockholders:	$^4/_5$ of \$ 5,000, or \$ 4,000
To creditors:	$^4/_5$ of \$45,000, or \$36,000

But this rule will not hold if the corporation was insolvent when the dividend was declared, or if the dividend was illegal, or if notice of the declaration was not given to the stockholders until after the company became insolvent.

If, when the corporation is solvent, a fund is set aside for the payment of a declared dividend, and if the company becomes insolvent before the fund is used for the designated purpose, the fund will be considered a trust fund for the stockholders, and will not be available for payments to general creditors.

Legality of dividends. In general, the laws seek to prohibit the impairment of stated capital by the payment of dividends. The legality of a dividend declaration may depend upon current earnings, retained earnings, or the satisfaction of certain conditions relating to aggregate stockholders' equity, or it may be determined by other statutory provisions, such as that the fair market value of the assets must exceed the liabilities of the corporation. The legality of a cash dividend is not dependent upon the amount of the corporation's cash. The adequacy of the cash balance has a bearing on the financial expediency of paying a dividend, but not on the legal right to declare one.

As discussed in Chapter 4, certain types of transactions give rise to gains that are classified as extraordinary. Generally, these are included with earnings from regular operations for purposes of determining the availability of earnings as a source of dividend charges.

Current net income is the normal source of dividend charges. However, dividends can ordinarily be declared based upon earnings in prior periods, even though there is a net loss for the current period. Some states allow the payment of dividends equal to the current year's net income, even though the firm has an accumulated deficit from prior years.

If losses have impaired the legal or stated capital of the firm, most states prohibit the payment of dividends. The impairment may be remedied by profitable operations and abstaining from the payment of dividends, or by taking the proper legal action to reduce the stated capital.

Retained earnings that normally would be available for dividend charges may become temporarily or permanently not so available. Such restrictions may be imposed by law or may result from contracts. A legal restriction results in many states from the acquisition of treasury stock, a matter that will be discussed in the following chapter. The board of directors may take action that will make earnings temporarily not available for dividend charges. This is discussed later in this chapter.

The various types of dividend distributions that a corporation may make to its shareholders will now be discussed.

Cash dividends. Most dividends are in the form of a cash payment to the shareholders. The effect of the dividend is to decrease the cash balance of the firm and to reduce the stockholders' equity as the result of a charge to Retained Earnings in most cases.

To illustrate the accounting for a cash dividend, assume that a corporation has 1,000 shares of 6 percent, $50 par value preferred stock and 10,000 shares of no-par value common stock outstanding. On November 15, 19+2, the board of directors declares dividends of $3 per share on the preferred stock and $5 per share on the common stock. The date of record is December 20, 19+2, and the date of payment is January 15, 19+3.

The date of declaration establishes the liability of the firm for the dividends, which would be recorded as follows:

Preferred stock dividends	3,000	
Common stock dividends	50,000	
Dividends payable—Preferred		3,000
Dividends payable—Common		50,000

Both the preferred and the common dividends could be recorded in a single dividends account and dividends payable account. At the end of the accounting period, it is necessary that the dividends accounts be closed to Retained Earnings. As a result, many firms record the declaration of a dividend by debiting the retained earnings account at the declaration date. This will be done in subsequent illustrations in this chapter.

No entry is required by the firm on the date of record. This is simply the date that establishes to whom the dividend checks will be mailed, information that is taken from the corporation's stock records.

The dividend liability that was recorded on the declaration date is satisfied on the date of payment. The following entry is recorded at that time, assuming that two different liability accounts were established for the dividends:

Dividends payable—Preferred	3,000	
Dividends payable—Common	50,000	
Cash		53,000

Dividends paid in noncash assets. Dividends that result in the distribution of assets other than cash are commonly referred to as *property dividends.* They have the same effect on the firm's assets and retained earnings as do cash dividends.

Property dividends may take the form of any asset the directors designate, but they are most frequently paid in the form of securities of other firms. Dividends received in property other than cash are generally taxable to the recipients at the fair market value of the property. However, there is some question as to whether the corporation paying the dividend should record the dividend at the book amount of the property or at its fair market value.

The prevailing practice in the past has been to record the dividend at the book amount of the property, based upon the argument that no arm's-length transaction has taken place. However, some accountants are inclined to the view that the property should be adjusted to its fair market value on the books of the corporation before the payment of the dividend is recorded. This has the same effect on the firm's books as if the property had been sold and the cash used to pay dividends.

A peculiar problem may arise if a company has outstanding participating preferred stock and common stock, and pays a property dividend on one class of shares and a cash dividend on the other. For instance, assume that a company has outstanding $100,000 par value of common stock and participating preferred stock of an equal par value; that it distributes as a dividend to the common stockholders certain investment securities carried at $6,000 but having a fair market value of $10,000; and that a matching cash dividend is to be paid to the preferred stockholders. Because equity would require that the preferred stockholders receive a cash dividend of $10,000, and because the accounts should show that the two classes of stock participated equally in the dividends, it would probably be desirable to write up the securities to their market value before distributing them as a dividend to the common stockholders.

If the securities are to be adjusted to their fair market value, the following entries would be recorded:

Investments	4,000	
Gain on disposal of investments		4,000
Retained earnings	20,000	
Dividends payable—Preferred		10,000
Dividends payable—Common		10,000
Dividends payable—Preferred	10,000	
Dividends payable—Common	10,000	
Cash		10,000
Investments		10,000

Liability dividends. Dividends may be distributed in the form of bonds, notes, or scrip. Bonds or notes so issued usually have a definite maturity and bear interest; scrip dividends may or may not have a definite maturity, and may or may not bear interest. When scrip or some other evidence of short-term indebtedness is issued as a dividend, it is usually done for the purpose of maintaining the appearance of a regular dividend when cash is temporarily not available for payment. The issuance of long-term securities as a dividend is not common; such securities are occasionally issued to convert retained earnings available for dividends into funded debt. The issuance of evidences of indebtedness as a dividend may require the authorization of the stockholders.

Liquidating dividends. Dividends that represent a return to the stockholders of a portion or all of the capital they have invested in the firm (as opposed to a dividend that represents a distribution of the earnings of the firm) are referred to as *liquidating dividends*. Intentional liquidating dividends are intended to return all the capital to the stockholders because the company is discontinuing operations, or to return a portion thereof to the stockholders because the scope of the business is being reduced and the total capital is no longer required. If a liquidating dividend is paid, stockholders should be informed of its nature. It is desirable to set up a special account to show the amount of capital returned by liquidating dividends. In the balance sheet, it can be shown in the Stockholders' Equity section contra to the accounts credited with the capital invested by the stockholders.

Liquidating dividends may be unintentional, as in the case in which, although intended to be dividends based upon retained earnings, they are in reality a distribution of a portion of the capital invested by stockholders. The payment of such dividends may result from accounting errors that have overstated earnings.

Stock dividends. A stock dividend represents the distribution of additional shares of stock to current stockholders. The stockholders do not pay any additional amount to the firm for the stock, and assets and liabilities are not affected by the declaration of stock dividends. Total stockholders' equity of the firm is also unaffected, although there will be a transfer of certain amounts within the stockholders' equity accounts.

If all a corporation's stock is of one class, a stock dividend does not change the individual stockholder's interest in the stockholders' equity. It merely increases the number of shares by which his interest is represented. If a company has more than one class of stock, the issuance of a stock dividend to shareholders of one class may alter the stockholders' interests, particularly if the dividend is paid in shares of another class.

Stock dividends are stated as a percentage of the number of shares outstanding and are issued to existing stockholders in proportion to their stock holdings. For example, if a firm with 100,000 shares of common stock outstanding declares a 10 percent stock dividend, it will issue 10,000 additional shares of the common (10 percent of 100,000). A stockholder who currently owns 2,500 shares of the firm's stock will receive an additional 250 shares (10 percent of 2,500).

Reasons for stock dividends. The primary reason for stock dividends is the desire on the part of the management to issue to the stockholder some evidence of an increase in stockholders' equity without paying a cash dividend. There may be very valid reasons why management wishes to use cash for purposes other than a dividend payment. This is especially true for so-called growth companies. It may also be true for an established company that has regularly paid cash dividends in the past but for some reason does not wish to, or perhaps cannot, pay cash dividends in the current period.

The effect of a stock dividend is to permanently capitalize a portion of the firm's retained earnings; and management may use a stock dividend to achieve this result when it is deemed desirable to do so. It is also possible that management may use the stock dividend to achieve a reduction in the market price per share by increasing the number of shares outstanding. This might result when the stock dividend is relatively large. However, the desired reduction in market price is usually achieved by a stock split, which is discussed later in this chapter.

Accounting for stock dividends. The principal question accountants face in accounting for stock dividends is the determination of the amount or amounts that should be transferred from certain stockholders' equity accounts to other stockholders' equity accounts. The laws differ in their requirements. In some cases, stock dividends are intended merely to convert paid-in capital into capital stock; such dividends have no effect on retained earnings, and no accounting problems arise in recording them.

We are here concerned with the important problems that arise in connection with the issuance of stock dividends that are presumed to constitute a capitalization of retained earnings. In such cases, the laws usually specify a minimum amount that must be transferred from retained earnings to legal or stated capital. With respect to par value stock, the legal minimum is usually par. With respect to no-par value stock, the legal minimum may be the minimum amount at which the stock could be issued, or the stated value per share of the stock of the same class previously outstanding. In the case of preferred stock, it is often the liquidating price.

But the minimum transfers required by law are not always regarded by accountants as sufficient to meet the requirements of proper accounting. In its treatment of this matter, the Committee on Accounting Procedure concerned itself only with the most frequently encountered type of stock dividend, namely, common shares issued as a dividend to common shareholders. The committee placed considerable weight on a belief that "many recipients of stock dividends look upon them as distributions of corporate earnings and usually in an amount equivalent to the fair value of the additional shares received. Furthermore, it is to be presumed that such views of recipients are materially strengthened in those instances, which are by far the most numerous, where the issuances are so small in comparison with the shares previously outstanding that they do not have any apparent effect upon the share market price and, consequently, the market value of the shares previously held remains substantially unchanged."[1] In other words, the recipients do not view stock dividends as mere capitalizations of retained earnings, but consider them as a distribution of earnings much like ordinary dividends except that shares of stock are received in place of cash.

The committee therefore recommended that "where these circumstances exist, the corporation should in the public interest account for the transaction by transferring from earned surplus [retained earnings] to the category of permanent capitalization (represented by the capital stock and capital surplus [other paid-in capital] accounts) an amount equal to the fair value of the additional shares issued."[2]

The committee made no reference to the date, period of time, or sources of information that should be used in determining the fair value per share. Presumably, this is a matter requiring the exercise of professional judgment. Certainly, recent market prices and trends would be important factors to consider. However, it would seem desirable to eliminate the influence of temporary conditions that may have distorted the current values of corporate shares. In practice, the current market price of the stock is generally used.

It should be noted that the position stated above was based on the expectation that the additional shares issued as a stock dividend have no influence on the market price of the stock. This raises the question of just when the dividend does have some influence on the market price. Obviously this point is very difficult, perhaps impossible, to determine. In fact, the committee distinguished those stock dividends that are likely to have no influence on the market price of the stock from those that are likely to influence the price, by selecting a range rather than a specific point. The committee concluded that it could be assumed in most cases that stock dividends of less than 20 or 25 percent of the number of shares previously outstanding would not affect the market price per share.

The position of the committee concerning larger stock dividends was that "where the number of additional shares issued as a stock dividend is so great that it has, or may reasonably be expected to have, the effect of materially reducing the share market value, ... The transaction clearly partakes of the nature of a stock split-up [and] under such circumstances there is no need to capitalize earned surplus [retained earnings] other than to the extent occasioned by legal requirements."[3]

To illustrate the accounting entries under these recommendations, assume that a company has 10,000 authorized shares of common stock of $10 par value, of which 6,000 shares are outstanding; also assume that a 10 percent stock dividend (600 shares) is declared and immediately issued. Assuming that the shares issued in this illustration have a market price of $12 each, the entry to record the distribution of the stock dividend is:

---

[1]Committee on Accounting Procedure, "Accounting Research and Terminology Bulletins," final edition, *Accounting Research Bulletin No. 43* (New York: AICPA, 1961), p. 51.

[2]*Accounting Research Bulletin No. 43*, p. 51.

[3]*Accounting Research Bulletin No. 43*, p. 52.

Stock dividends (to be closed to Retained Earnings)	7,200	
Common stock		6,000
Capital in excess of par value—From stock dividends		1,200
Issuance of a 10% dividend: 600 shares of $10 par value stock having a market price of $12 each.		

If time intervenes between the declaration and issuance of the stock dividend, the entries should be:

At date of declaration:

Stock dividends	7,200	
Stock dividend payable		6,000
Capital in excess of par value—From stock dividends		1,200
Declaration of 10% stock dividend to stockholders of record on December 31, 19+4; shares to be issued February 1, 19+5.		

At date of issuance:

Stock dividend payable	6,000	
Common stock		6,000
Issuance of 600 shares as a stock dividend.		

Assume that the stock was without par value and that it had been given a stated value of $7.50 per share; the entry to record the dividend would be:

Stock dividends	7,200	
Common stock		4,500
Capital in excess of par value—From stock dividends		2,700
Issuance of a 10% dividend; 600 shares of no-par value stock (stated value, $7.50 per share) having a market price of $12 each.		

Assume now that the firm, with common stock having a stated value of $7.50 per share, declares a 50 percent stock dividend. Although the market price of the stock is $12 per share prior to the stock dividend, it is likely that the dividend will have the effect of reducing the market price per share. The entry to record the dividend would be:

Stock dividends (3,000 × $7.50)	22,500	
Common stock		22,500
Issuance of a 50% dividend; 3,000 shares of no-par value stock (stated value, $7.50 per share).		

This is in keeping with the treatment discussed earlier. However, some firms go beyond the minimum legal requirements in this situation and capitalize retained earnings equal to the average paid-in capital per share for the shares outstanding prior to the dividend.

Stock dividends that have been declared but not yet issued should be reported as a part of the stockholders' equity of the firm if a balance sheet is prepared between the date of declaration and the date of distribution. Using the illustration above involving a 10 percent dividend and a $10 par value stock, the Stockholders' Equity section of the balance sheet would appear as follows:

Stockholders' equity:			
Common stock—$10 par value; authorized, 10,000 shares.			
Issued, 6,000 shares	$60,000		
To be issued February 1, 19+5, as a stock dividend—600 shares	6,000	$66,000	
Capital in excess of par value—From stock dividends		1,200	
Retained earnings		11,000	$78,200

The treatment of the stock dividend illustrated above is obviously different from that of a cash dividend, which is reported as a liability of the corporation. The major reason for this is that the declaration of the stock dividend does not result in a claim against the assets of the firm.

Fractional shares. When stock dividends are issued, it is usually impossible to issue full shares to all the stockholders. For instance, if a stock dividend of one share for each ten shares outstanding is to be issued, the holder of three shares could not receive a full share, and the holder of 25 shares would be entitled to receive two full shares and a fractional ($^1/_2$) share. Sometimes corporations will pay cash to the stockholders in lieu of fractional shares. Or they may issue special certificates for the fractional shares. Such special certificates customarily provide that no voting or dividend rights attach to the fractional shares. Often corporations sponsor an arrangement enabling the recipients of fractional shares to sell them, or to buy the needed additional fractional interest to obtain full shares.

Assume in the illustration at the top of page 529 that, although the dividend declaration contemplated the issuance of 600 dividend shares, it was necessary to issue special fractional share certificates equivalent to 60 shares. The entry for the distribution of the full shares and the special certificates for fractional shares should be:

Stock dividend payable	6,000	
Common stock		5,400
Fractional share certificates—Common		600
Issuance, as a stock dividend, of 540 full shares and special certificates for fractional shares equivalent to 60 shares.		

When any of the stockholders have acquired special certificates aggregating full shares, these can be presented to the corporation in exchange for regular stock certificates. Entries similar to the following should be made for such exchanges.

Fractional share certificates—Common	100	
Common stock		100
Issuance of 10 shares in exchange for special certificates covering that number of full shares.		

The right to exchange the special certificates for full shares may expire at a specified date. Returning to the foregoing illustration, assume that special certificates amounting to five shares, issued with the dividend shares, expire. A $50 balance remains in the fractional share certificates—common account. What disposition should be made of it? The declaration of a stock dividend capitalizes a portion of the retained earnings. If, under the law of the state of incorporation, the declaration of the dividend cannot be in part rescinded, the aggregate amount of retained earnings to be capitalized (in part by credit to Common Stock and in part by credit to Capital in Excess of Par Value—From Stock Dividends) is irrevocably determined. If the amount credited to Common Stock is reduced because of the expiration of fractional share certificates, the amount credited to paid-in capital should be correspondingly increased. The entry to clear the fractional share certificates—common account would then be:

Fractional share certificates—Common	50	
Capital in excess of par value—From stock dividends		50
Lapse of fractional share certificates covering 5 full shares of common stock.		

If it is legally possible for the directors to rescind the dividend to the extent of the full shares not issued, and this is done, the following entry would be in order:

Fractional share certificates—Common	50	
Capital in excess of par value—From stock dividends	10	
Retained earnings		60
Return to Retained Earnings of amount of stock dividend related to lapsed fractional share certificates.		

Stock splits. A stock split is distinguished from a stock dividend in that the former usually involves replacing all currently outstanding shares of a given class of stock with a larger number of shares, the larger number being a multiple of the number of shares previously outstanding. At the same time, there is a corresponding reduction in the par or stated value of the shares, so that the *total* par or stated value of all shares outstanding does not change. Whereas a stock dividend involves the transfer of a portion of the stockholders' equity from Retained Earnings to other equity accounts, a stock split does not change the balance in any stockholders' equity accounts:

Common stock; 10,000 shares, $10 par value	$100,000
Capital in excess of par value—From common stock issuances	40,000
Retained earnings	125,000

After a two-for-one stock split, the equity accounts would appear as follows:

Common stock; 20,000 shares, $5 par value	$100,000
Capital in excess of par value—From common stock issuances	40,000
Retained earnings	125,000

No formal journal entry is required to record a stock split. A memorandum entry in the capital stock account is sufficient to note the larger number of shares now outstanding and the corresponding reduction in the par value per share.

Stock splits frequently occur when a corporation's stock has so high a market price as to interfere with trading. If, for example, a corporation's stock has a market price of $500 per share, the market at such a price may be limited. To increase the market, the corporation may call in its outstanding shares and issue new shares at the rate of five for one. As a consequence, the market price will probably be reduced to approximately $100 per share, and public trading may be facilitated.

It is possible that a corporation might use the term "stock dividend" to describe a distribution of stock so large that it has the same effect on the market price as would a stock split. For example, a 100 percent stock dividend would double the number of shares outstanding, as would a two-for-one stock split. The Committee on Accounting Procedure recommended "that in such instances every effort be made to avoid the use of the word dividend in related corporate resolutions, notices, and announcements and that, in those cases where because of legal requirements this cannot be done, the transaction be described, for example, as a split-up effected in the form of a dividend.[4]

Dividend restrictions. It was noted earlier in this chapter that there are various reasons why a corporation may find itself restricted as to the amount of cash dividends it can pay. These are summarized below:

(1) Contracts:
 (a) With creditors. For instance, bond indentures, in addition to requiring the establishment of a sinking fund for the payment of the bonds, may place a limitation on the amount of dividends that may be paid; the purpose is to prevent the impairment of working capital that might result from cash deposits in the sinking fund and cash disbursements for dividends.
 (b) With preferred stockholders. Retirable preferred stock is sometimes issued; a restriction on dividend payments to common stockholders may be imposed to preserve funds to meet the stock-retirement commitment with the preferred stockholders.

(2) Law. The statutes of many states prescribe that dividend payments and disbursements for the acquisition of treasury shares must not impair the stated capital.

(3) Voluntary action of the directors:
 (a) To indicate that dividends will be limited in order to accumulate funds for plant expansion or other purposes.
 (b) To indicate the existence of a contingency that may result in a loss, but a contingency so problematical that a charge to current revenue would not be justified.

At one time it was common practice to recognize restrictions on dividend payments by the transfer of a portion of retained earnings to separate accounts. This is referred to as the *appropriation of retained earnings* and is discussed in the next

---

[4] *Accounting Research Bulletin No. 43*, p. 52.

section of this chapter. Currently prevailing practice is to disclose any dividend restrictions by means of footnotes to the financial statements.

Appropriations of retained earnings. In the absence of any restrictions, the balance in a firm's retained earnings account represents the maximum amount of dividends that can be paid. Although some states allow certain paid-in capital accounts to be used as a basis for so-called dividends, this is not a dividend in the strict sense.

No matter what the balance in the retained earnings account, a firm must have sufficient cash available for the payment of dividends. Thus, a firm with a very large retained earnings balance may not be able or may not wish to pay cash dividends.

One way in which corporate management can convey to financial statement users the fact that not all retained earnings should be viewed as a basis for dividends is to transfer a portion of the balance to other retained earnings accounts. Examples of such appropriation accounts are Retained Earnings Appropriated for Retirement of Preferred Stock, Retained Earnings Appropriated for Plant Expansion, and Retained Earnings Appropriated for Contingencies. Transfers to such accounts are recorded as follows:

Retained earnings	100,000	
Retained earnings appropriated for retirement of preferred stock		100,000

It should be emphasized that the entry above has no effect on either the total retained earnings or the total stockholders' equity of the firm. Any appropriation account balance is still a part of the retained earnings of the firm. It should also be pointed out that the entry does not establish a cash fund to be used to retire the preferred stock. It simply indicates that a portion of the retained earnings is no longer available to be used as a basis for dividend payments.

When the conditions that prompted the appropriation of retained earnings no longer exist, the amount appropriated should be transferred back to the retained earnings account. Using the previous illustration, the following entry should be recorded after the preferred stock is retired:

Retained earnings appropriated for retirement of preferred stock	100,000	
Retained earnings		100,000

It is important that retained earnings appropriation accounts not be debited for amounts that should be charged against income and reported on the firm's income statement. For example, the board of directors of a corporation may take action to establish an appropriation for contingencies due to an unsettled lawsuit in which the firm is the defendant. Should the case be decided against the firm, the settlement should be charged to the proper loss account and reported on the firm's income statement. At the same time, the balance in the appropriation account should be transferred back to Retained Earnings.

RESERVES: The term *reserve* has in the past been used in many different ways in accounting terminology. Examples of such usage are listed below:

Reserve for depreciation (Accumulated depreciation)
Reserve for doubtful accounts (Allowance for uncollectibles)
Reserve for income taxes (Estimated income taxes payable)
Reserve for retirement of preferred stock (Retained earnings appropriated for retirement of preferred stock)

The first three examples listed are no longer considered proper uses of the term *reserve*. The fourth example, which actually represents an appropriation of retained earnings, is still considered acceptable and is frequently found in published financial statements. The authors are of the opinion that the term *reserve* should not be used in the stockholders' equity section of the balance sheet.

Retained earnings appropriations and future losses. The use of the account Retained Earnings Appropriated for Contingencies was illustrated earlier in connection with a situation that may result in a future loss, depending upon the outcome of a pending lawsuit. Another situation that involves the appropriation of retained earnings and possible future losses is found when a company that has tangible assets distributed in a large number of locations decides upon a policy of self-insurance. Although the firm must bear all losses incurred, the decision is a sound one in those instances where the actual losses over a period of time are less than the premiums that would have to be paid if insurance coverage was purchased. An example of a company that might decide upon such a policy would be a chain of retail stores with many different locations.

Once management has made the decision to self-insure, it may also decide to appropriate retained earnings in the amount of the maximum expected loss to be incurred at any one time. For example, if this amount was estimated to be $50,000, the following entry would be recorded:

Retained earnings	50,000	
Retained earnings appropriated for self-insurance		50,000

Actual losses incurred as a result of a self-insurance program should be charged to a loss account and reported on the firm's income statement in the period the loss occurred. The appropriation account established in the entry above should not be used to absorb amounts that should be charged against income. If an asset costing $30,000 and one-third depreciated is completely destroyed by fire, the following entry is recorded:

Fire loss	20,000	
Accumulated depreciation	10,000	
Asset		30,000

Some accountants argue that a firm following a policy of self-insurance should record an entry each period charging Insurance Expense for the amount that would have to be paid if the firm purchased insurance coverage. The credit would be to a liability account that might be titled Estimated Claims from Self-Insurance. When losses are actually incurred, they are debited to the liability account.

This procedure appears to have little theoretical support. A company that does not purchase insurance coverage does not incur a premium expense, and no loss is incurred unless a fire or accident occurs.

Appropriated retained earnings in the balance sheet. It has already been noted that the appropriation of retained earnings does not change either the total retained earnings or the total stockholders' equity of a firm. Such restrictions of retained earnings are reported in the balance sheet as shown below:

Retained earnings:	
Appropriated for:	
Retirement of preferred stock	$ 50,000
Plant expansion	100,000
Self-insurance	50,000
Total	$200,000
Unappropriated	500,000
Total retained earnings	$700,000

Footnote disclosure of dividend restrictions. The primary use of the various retained earnings appropriation accounts is to convey to the users of a firm's financial statements information concerning the possible uses of retained earnings. This indicates that management does not view the entire retained earnings balance as a basis for dividend payments. The same information can be conveyed in the form of footnotes to the financial statements, and many people argue that this is preferable to the creation of a large number of additional retained earnings accounts. An example follows:

Retained earnings (See Note A) $700,000

Note A:

In view of the extensive addition to the company's manufacturing facilities now being planned, the directors have earmarked $300,000 of the retained earnings as not available for dividend purposes.

Preferred dividends in arrears. If dividends on cumulative preferred stock are in arrears, the balance sheet should disclose the fact, because common stockholders are entitled to know the prior claims of preferred stockholders against the retained earnings. Disclosure is usually made by a footnote, with some wording similar to the following: "On (the balance sheet date) dividends on the preferred stock were in arrears since (date)"; or, "No dividends have been paid on the preferred stock since (date)"; or, "On (the balance sheet date) dividends on the preferred stock were in arrears in the amount of $ ____________." If the company has retained earnings that exceed the preferred dividend arrearage, disclosure may be made as follows:

Retained earnings:		
Equal to dividends in arrears on preferred stock	$12,000	
Remainder	35,000	$47,000

In this connection it may be noted that partial dividends may be paid on preferred stock, as was illustrated in Chapter 20.

Liquidating price of stock. In the event of liquidation, the preferred stockholders may be entitled to receive, in addition to cumulative dividends in arrears, an amount in excess of the valuation at which the stock is shown in the balance sheet. For instance, the stock may have a par value of $100 per share, but carry a preference right to $110 per share in liquidation; or no-par stock carried in the balance sheet at $50 per share may have a liquidating price of $60 per share.

When preferred stock has a liquidating price greater than the amount at which it is shown in the balance sheet, a clear disclosure of that fact should be made in the balance sheet, or in a footnote appended thereto. Disclosure (parenthetically in the balance sheet or by footnote) may be made by stating the total dollar amount of the liquidating price; or by stating the excess of the total liquidating price over the total par or other amount at which the stock is shown in the balance sheet; or by stating the number of shares outstanding and the liquidating price per share.

If the aggregate liquidating price of the preferred stock, plus any preferred dividends in arrears, exceeds the par or stated value of the junior stocks and the total retained earnings (so that the holders of such junior stocks have no liquidating equity in the company), this fact should be clearly disclosed.

There may be a dividend restriction on retained earnings in an amount equal to the excess of the liquidating price of the preferred stock over its par or stated value. For instance, assume that the outstanding preferred stock has a par value of $100,000 and a liquidating price of $110,000, and that the company has retained earnings of $25,000. There may be a $10,000 restriction on the retained earnings, so that dividends of only $15,000 can be paid. The balance sheet or an appended footnote should so state if such a restriction exists. If the company has paid-in capital that was created by transactions in the preferred stock, such paid-in capital may reduce the restriction on retained earnings.

If there are more than two classes of stock, two of the classes may have liquidating prices in excess of the amounts at which they are shown in the balance sheet. Disclosures such as those mentioned above should then be made with respect to both such classes of stock.

Stockholders' Equity: Miscellaneous Topics

Treasury stock. Treasury stock is a corporation's own stock, once issued and later reacquired but not cancelled. Technically, it is still classed as issued stock, although no longer outstanding. It will be noted that there are three important elements in this definition:

(1) Treasury stock must be the company's own stock; holdings of stock of other companies should not be called "treasury stock."

(2) The stock must have been issued; unissued stock should not be called "treasury stock." There are several reasons why a distinction should be maintained between unissued stock and treasury stock: Stockholders' preemptive rights do not apply to treasury stock; treasury shares may be returned to an outstanding status without stockholders' authorization; treasury stock and unissued stock have wholly different relations to legal or stated capital (as discussed hereafter); and if treasury stock was fully paid when originally issued, it can be reissued at a discount without imposing any discount liability on the new owner.

(3) The stock must not have been cancelled. Cancellation is effected by procedures specified by the law. In some cases, cancellation may result in reducing the authorized issue of stock; in other cases, the shares remain authorized, the only reduction being in the issued shares, which constitute the legal or stated capital of the corporation.

Treasury stock may be acquired by donation, by purchase, or in settlement of a debt. Stockholders may donate to the corporation stock that it may sell to obtain working capital, or they may donate stock to be given as a bonus to the purchasers of other securities, or for other reasons. It may be purchased to buy out a stockholder, to reduce the total capital, or to acquire shares needed for profit-sharing or employee-pension programs.

Treasury stock is not an asset. Although treasury stock is occasionally shown in balance sheets as an asset, it is generally recognized that the purchase of treasury stock does not result in the acquisition of an asset, but causes a reduction in the stockholders' equity. Treasury shares may have a ready marketability and may be reissued, just as unissued shares may be issued; and it seems obvious that treasury stock, like unissued stock, is not an asset but merely a possible source of additional funds. A corporation that acquires its own stock obviously cannot acquire the basic rights inherent in stock ownership: the right to vote, the right to participate in dividend distributions, the preemptive right, and the right to receive a proportionate share of the corporation's assets in the event of liquidation.

The general rule that treasury stock is not an asset may not appear to be so obvious in certain cases. For example, companies may acquire treasury shares for the purpose of reissuing them to employees. This is done to encourage employee interest and support in the affairs of the company; the price of the shares to the employees may be slightly below current market price, and the company may help the employees by using some sort of installment plan to spread the payment for the shares over a period of time. The accounts of the company may show a long history with such a plan and a steady turnover of the treasury shares. Although some firms report such holdings of treasury stock as an asset, the authors are of the opinion that such treatment is improper.

There may be rare instances in which the general rule stated above does not apply. This possibility was recognized by the Committee on Accounting Procedure, whose position was reaffirmed by the Accounting Principles Board.[1] For example, assume that a corporation has a bonus agreement with its officers and employees providing that the bonus liability, after being determined, must be satisfied by distributing shares of the company's stock to those who have earned a bonus. Under these circumstances, assuming that the corporation had no unissued shares or that it preferred not to increase the number of shares outstanding, the

---

[1]See Committee on Accounting Procedure, "Accounting and Research and Terminology Bulletins," final edition, *Accounting Research Bulletin No. 43* (New York: AICPA, 1961), p. 12; and Accounting Principles Board, "Status of Accounting Research Bulletins," *Opinion No. 6* (New York: AICPA, October 1965), p. 40.

bonus liability would be satisfied in two steps: Cash would be used to acquire treasury shares; then treasury shares would be transferred to those entitled to a bonus, thus satisfying the liability. As a practical matter, there would probably be a time interval between the acquisition and the disposition of the treasury shares. Under the circumstances described above, the treasury shares have the capacity to directly satisfy or remove a liability, which is a characteristic associated with certain kinds of assets—for instance, cash. Perhaps it would be reasonable to permit a company to show as an asset treasury shares (at cost) equal to the amount of liability that will be settled in the near future by transfer of treasury shares to officers and employees. However, the Committee on Accounting Procedure stated that any dividends on stock reported in this manner "should not be treated as a credit to the income account of the company."[2]

Treasury stock terminology. It has long been customary to speak of *purchases* and *sales* of treasury stock. However, because treasury stock is not an asset, there is a certain inappropriateness in the use of these words in connection with treasury stock. Some effort has been made to substitute other terminology, such as *contraction of capital* for *purchase,* and *reissue* for *sale.* If a disposal of treasury stock is called a reissue instead of a sale, the words *gain* and *loss* seem equally inappropriate as labels for the difference between the cost and the selling price of treasury shares. However, official pronouncements of the AICPA still refer to "gains" and "losses" on treasury stock.

Accounting for treasury stock transactions. There are two acceptable methods of accounting for treasury stock: (1) the par value method and (2) the cost method. No matter which method is used, the basic theoretical consideration is that treasury stock transactions "relate to the capital of the corporation and do not give rise to corporate profits and losses."[3] Thus, under no circumstances should transactions involving treasury stock result in an increase in the retained earnings of the firm. As will be seen from the following discussion, it is possible that treasury stock transactions may decrease Retained Earnings.

The Accounting Principles Board set forth in its *Opinion No. 6* the practices it considered appropriate in keeping with current developments in accounting for treasury stock.[4] The Opinion did not supersede, but merely expanded, the prior AICPA pronouncement.

The board recognized two ways in which the acquisition of treasury stock might be viewed. First is the situation in which the stock is acquired for either formal or constructive retirement. Under constructive retirement, there may be no intention to formally retire the stock in accordance with applicable laws. The Opinion considered two different situations that might arise in such acquisitions, depending upon the relationship between the purchase price and the par or stated value of the stock.

---

[2] *Accounting Research Bulletin No. 43,* p. 12.
[3] *Accounting Research Bulletin No. 43,* p. 14.
[4] *Opinion No. 6,* pp. 40–41.

EXCESS OF PURCHASE PRICE OVER PAR OR STATED VALUE: When the amount paid for the treasury shares is in excess of their par or stated value, the firm has the following alternatives:[5]

(1) Allocate the excess between paid-in capital and retained earnings. The amount allocated to paid-in capital should not be more than the sum of (a) all paid-in capital arising from previous retirements and net "gains" on sales of treasury stock of the same issue; and (b) the pro rata portion of paid-in capital, capitalization of stock dividends, etc., on the same issue.
(2) Charge the entire amount of the excess to Retained Earnings in recognition of the fact that a corporation can always capitalize or allocate retained earnings for such purposes.

EXCESS OF PAR OR STATED VALUE OVER PURCHASE PRICE: If the amount paid for the stock is less than the par or stated value, the difference should be credited to an appropriate paid-in capital account.

The procedures outlined above normally result in a debit to the treasury stock account for the par or stated value of the shares acquired. As a result, they represent what is commonly referred to as the par value method of accounting for treasury stock. Illustrative entries for this method will be presented in the next section of this chapter.

A second way of viewing treasury stock acquisitions exists when the purpose is other than formal or constructive retirement, or when the final disposition is yet to be decided. Under such circumstances, the acquisition may be accorded the same treatment as that appropriate for retired stock, or the cost of the stock may be shown separately as a deduction from total stockholders' equity.[6] The latter treatment is known as the cost method and will be illustrated later in this chapter.

Par value method. The basic argument for the par value method of accounting for treasury stock is that the acquisition results in a reduction in the capital of the corporation. Just as the capital was increased by the original sale of the stock, the acquisition by the firm of its own stock in effect reverses the prior sale, and the decrease should be recorded. Although the treasury shares may later be reissued, that represents a completely separate transaction from the acquisition.

The American Accounting Association took the following position in favor of the par value method:

> The acquisition of its own shares by a corporation represents a contraction of its capital structure. However, statutory requirements are particularly restrictive in this area of corporate activity and, to an important degree, are controlling in the reporting of such transactions. Preferably, the outlay by a corporation for its own shares is reflected as

[5] *Opinion No. 6*, p. 40.
[6] *Opinion No. 6*, p. 40.

a reduction of the aggregate of contributed capital, and any excess of outlay over the pro rata portion of contributed capital as a distribution of retained earnings. The issuance of reacquired shares should be accounted for in the same way as the issuance of previously unissued shares; that is, the entire proceeds should be credited to contributed capital.[7]

ACQUISITION OF STOCK: To illustrate the par value method, assume that a company's stock was originally issued at $80 per share, of which $75, the par value per share, was credited to Common Stock, and $5 per share was credited to Capital in Excess of Par Value—From Common Stock Issuances. If 100 shares were acquired at $85 per share, the entry would be:

Treasury stock	7,500	
Capital in excess of par value—From common stock issuances ($5 × 100)	500	
Retained earnings	500	
Cash		8,500
Acquisition of 100 treasury shares.		

The debit to the treasury stock account represents the par value of the shares acquired. The capital in excess account is debited for the amount credited to the account at the time the 100 shares were originally sold. Any amount paid in excess of the amount for which the stock originally sold, in this case $5 per share, is debited to Retained Earnings. The treasury stock account title should indicate the class of stock if more than one class has been issued.

REISSUANCE AT PAR VALUE: When treasury stock is accounted for using the par value method, it is necessary that the treasury stock account be credited for par value when the stock is reissued. If all the 100 shares were reissued at a price of $75 per share, the following entry would be recorded:

Cash	7,500	
Treasury stock		7,500

REISSUANCE AT A PRICE IN EXCESS OF PAR VALUE: Reissuance of the treasury shares at a price of $90 per share would be recorded as follows:

Cash	9,000	
Treasury stock		7,500
Capital in excess of par value—From treasury stock transactions		1,500

Note the similarity of this entry to the entry to record the original sale of stock. The capital in excess account used in the entry is labeled so as to clearly indicate the source of the $1,500 paid in excess of the par value of the stock.

[7]"Accounting and Reporting Standards for Corporate Financial Statements and Preceding Statements and Supplements" (Columbus, O.: American Accounting Association, 1957), p. 7.

REISSUANCE AT A PRICE BELOW PAR VALUE: If it is assumed that the shares are reissued at a price of $70 per share, which is less than the par value, we face a problem that does not arise in connection with an original issue. In the latter case, a discount on common stock account would be debited for the difference of $5 per share, as was illustrated in Chapter 20. It was also noted earlier that stockholders to whom stock is sold at a discount generally face a contingent liability for the amount of the discount.

However, in the case of the reissuance of treasury stock at an amount below par value, no such contingent liability exists. Proper treatment of the difference between the reissue price and the par value would be to debit Capital in Excess of Par Value to the extent that it is sufficient to absorb the difference. Any amount not charged to the capital in excess account should be debited to Retained Earnings.

To illustrate this treatment, assume that the firm used in the preceding illustration had originally sold 5,000 shares of common stock at $80 per share, resulting in a credit of $25,000 (5,000 × $5) to Capital in Excess of Par Value—From Common Stock Issuances. After recording of the acquisition of the 100 treasury shares at $85 per share, the capital in excess account has a credit balance of $24,500. If the treasury stock is reissued at $70 per share, the following entry is recorded:

Cash	7,000	
Capital in excess of par value—From common stock issuances	500	
Treasury stock		7,500

Cost method. Under the cost method of accounting for treasury stock, acquisition of the stock is viewed as the first of two transactions. The general expectation is that the shares will later be reissued. In the meantime, the cost of the shares will be recorded in the treasury stock account and will remain there until the shares are disposed of in some manner.

ACQUISITION OF STOCK: The accounting for treasury stock acquisitions under the cost method is, of course, very simple. Assume that 100 shares of treasury stock of $100 par value were acquired at $85 per share. Regardless of whether the stock has or has not a par value, and regardless of the amount received for the stock when it was issued and the amount credited to the capital stock account at that time, the entry for the purchase is merely:

Treasury stock	8,500	
Cash		8,500
Acquisition of 100 treasury shares.		

REISSUANCE AT COST: The reissuance of treasury stock accounted for under the cost method requires that the cost of the stock be removed from the treasury stock account. Assuming that the shares mentioned above are reissued at a price of $85 per share, the entry is:

Cash	8,500	
Treasury stock		8,500

REISSUANCE AT A PRICE IN EXCESS OF COST: If the shares are reissued at a price of $90 per share, the entry is:

Cash	9,000	
Treasury stock		8,500
Capital in excess of par value—From treasury stock transactions		500

Note again that the capital in excess account is clearly described as to source.

REISSUANCE AT A PRICE BELOW COST: The Accounting Principles Board has stated that when the cost method is used and the stock is reissued at a price below cost, "'losses' may be charged to capital surplus (additional paid-in capital) to the extent that previous net 'gains' from sales or retirements of the same class of stock are included therein, otherwise to retained earnings."[8]

In practice, the accounts debited for the difference depend on the laws of the state of incorporation, in addition to the paid-in capital accounts on the firm's books. Although a logical case can be made for charging the difference first to any additional paid-in capital resulting from previous treasury stock transactions and next to retained earnings, it is well established that such differences may be charged to any other additional paid-in capital account related to the same class of stock as the treasury shares, provided that such capital is available for dividends and therefore is not a part of legal capital. The latter condition is pertinent because the amount of legal capital is governed by statute and not necessarily by the results of treasury stock transactions.

If additional paid-in capital is not a part of legal capital under the laws of the state of incorporation, and if a company has additional paid-in capital resulting from the issuance of shares of the same class or resulting from other transactions in shares of that class, the difference between cost and the reissuance price can be assigned in the following sequence:

First, to any additional paid-in capital resulting from previous treasury stock transactions in the same class of shares

Next, to any other additional paid-in capital accounts applicable to the same class of shares, but not a part of legal capital

Finally, to Retained Earnings

Three different cases are presented on page 544 to illustrate the accounting for the reissuance of treasury stock at a price below its cost.

	Case		
	1	2	3
Stockholder's equity accounts:			
Common stock, 10,000 shares issued, $10 stated value	$100,000	$100,000	$100,000
Capital in excess of stated value—From common stock issuances	10,000	60,000	1,000

[8] *Opinion No. 6*, p. 41.

	Case 1	Case 2	Case 3
Capital in excess of stated value—From treasury stock transactions	2,000	None	None
Retained earnings	38,000	10,000	49,000
Treasury stock, 100 shares, at cost	2,500	1,500	2,400

Case 1: Treasury shares are reissued at $23 per share.

Cash	2,300	
Capital in excess of stated value—From treasury stock transactions	200	
Treasury stock		2,500
Reissuance of 100 shares of treasury stock at $23 per share.		

Case 2: Treasury shares are reissued at $12 per share.

Cash	1,200	
Capital in excess of stated value—From common stock issuances	300	
Treasury stock		1,500
Reissuance of 100 shares of treasury stock at $12 per share.		

Case 3: Treasury shares are reissued at $10 per share.

Cash	1,000	
Capital in excess of stated value—From common stock issuances	1,000	
Retained earnings	400	
Treasury stock		2,400
Reissuance of 100 shares of treasury stock at $10 per share.		

Treasury stock with no par or stated value. If a corporation has outstanding no-par stock without a stated value, accounting for treasury stock transactions is identical to the procedures followed under the cost method for stock with a par or stated value. The treasury stock account is debited for cost when the stock is acquired and credited for cost when the stock is reissued. If reissuance is at a price in excess of cost, the difference is credited to Paid-in Capital—From Treasury Stock Transactions. Should the stock be reissued at a price below cost, the difference is assigned using the same rules shown on page 543 for stock with a par or stated value.

Since the par value method presupposes a par or stated value for the stock, it cannot be applied to the situation in which the firm has no-par stock without a stated value. Thus, the cost method is normally used. Some companies follow the procedure in this case of debiting the treasury stock account at the time of purchase for the original sales price of the stock, a procedure that might be viewed as an adaptation of the par value method. However, this creates a unique situation if the stock is reissued at a price in excess of cost. The difference should be credited to the capital stock account, based upon the reasoning that the reissuance should be viewed in the same manner as the original sale of stock.

Treasury stock and legal or stated capital. The concept of legal or stated capital was discussed in Chapter 20. It is a measure of creditor protection, intended to give the creditors assurance that a minimum capital will be maintained as a safeguard for the payment of liabilities—subject, of course, to the risk that unprofitable operations could impair the minimum capital as well as cause a weakening of financial position that could make it difficult for the company to meet its obligations. If the intended protection for creditors is to be effective, it is necessary to limit the amount that can be paid out to stockholders. Therefore, the laws that establish and define stated capital have usually placed a limitation on the combined disbursements for dividends and acquisitions of treasury shares. In a large majority of the states, the limitation is related to retained earnings. In some states, acquisitions of treasury stock can be made only to the extent of the retained earnings; in other states, they can be made to the extent of all classes of capital available for dividends.

The differing effects of a dividend and a treasury stock acquisition on the retained earnings of a corporation should be noted. Assume that a company has retained earnings of $25,000 and pays a $12,000 dividend; the retained earnings are reduced to $13,000. If, on the other hand, it pays $12,000 for treasury stock, the retained earnings are still $25,000, but $12,000 thereof is restricted and cannot be used for dividends or additional treasury-stock acquisitions. It is possible to remove the restriction by either disposing of the treasury shares or cancelling them (restoring them to the status of unissued shares) and thereby reducing the stated capital; a corporation may effect a reduction of stated capital by filing with the proper state authorities a certificate of reduction or otherwise complying with the statutory requirements.

The restriction of retained earnings available as a basis for dividend payments owing to the acquisition of treasury stock may be disclosed parenthetically, by the appropriation of retained earnings, or by a footnote. As noted in the preceding chapter, use of the appropriation procedure requires that the amount of the appropriation be transferred back to Retained Earnings as the treasury stock is reissued. For example, if a company acquired 500 shares of treasury stock at a cost of $33 per share, the following entry would be recorded:

Retained earnings (500 × $33)	16,500	
Retained earnings appropriated for cost of treasury stock		16,500

If 200 shares of the stock are reissued, the following entry should be recorded:

Retained earnings appropriated for cost of treasury stock (200 × $33)	6,600	
Retained earnings		6,600

The various alternatives for reporting the retained earnings restriction will be illustrated in the following section.

Balance sheet presentation of treasury stock. The balance sheet presentation of treasury stock involves not only the reporting of the treasury stock account, which has a debit balance, but also the disclosure of any dividends restriction that might result from state laws. Various alternatives for reporting the latter were mentioned in the preceding section. Presentation of the treasury stock account, which should be reported within the stockholders' equity section, depends upon whether the par value method or the cost method is being used.

To illustrate the alternatives, assume that a company's accounts contain the following balances:

Common stock—$100 par value; 1,000 shares authorized and issued	$100,000
Capital in excess of par value—From common stock issuances	15,000
Retained earnings	25,000

and that the company purchases 100 treasury shares for $12,000.

Under the par value method, acquisition of the stock results in a debit of $2,000 ($12,000 cost, less $10,000 par value) to the capital in excess account. The balance in the treasury stock account, which represents the par value of the shares held, is reported as a deduction from the capital stock account, as shown below:

Stockholders' equity:		
Common stock—$100 par value; 1,000 shares authorized and issued	$100,000	
Less treasury stock, 100 shares at par value	10,000	$ 90,000
Capital in excess of par value—From common stock issuances		13,000
Retained earnings (of which $12,000, the cost of treasury stock, is restricted)		25,000
Total stockholders' equity		$128,000

In this case, the retained earnings restriction resulting from treasury stock acquisitions is reported parenthetically.

Using the information in the preceding illustration, assume now that the firm uses the cost method. The entire cost of the treasury shares is debited to the treasury stock account, which is reported as a deduction from total paid-in capital and retained earnings. This treatment is illustrated below, along with the use of an appropriation of retained earnings to disclose the restriction on dividends:

Stockholders' equity:		
Common stock—$100 par value; 1,000 shares authorized and issued		$100,000
Capital in excess of par value—From common stock issuances		15,000
Retained earnings:		
Appropriated for cost of treasury stock	$12,000	
Unappropriated	13,000	25,000
Total		$140,000
Less treasury stock, at cost		12,000
Total stockholders' equity		$128,000

Disclosure of the restriction on dividends by use of a footnote would result in the following balance sheet presentation, in which it is still assumed that the cost method is used to account for the treasury stock:

Stockholders' equity:	
Common stock—$100 par value; 1,000 shares authorized and issued	$100,000
Capital in excess of par value—From common stock issuances	15,000
Retained earnings (see Note)	25,000
Total	$140,000
Less treasury stock, at cost	12,000
Total stockholders' equity	$128,000

Note: Dividends are restricted to the amount of the retained earnings less the cost of treasury stock held.

It should be noted that the total stockholders' equity is the same no matter which method is used to account for the treasury stock or which procedure is used to disclose the dividends restriction.

Cancellation of treasury stock. If a corporation complies with the required legal formalities and cancels any reacquired shares, the capital stock account should be debited for the amount credited thereto when such shares were issued, except that, in the case of no-par stock without a stated value, an average issuance price is acceptable unless the shares being cancelled can be traced to a specific issuance, in which case the issuance price should be used to record the cancellation.

It is also necessary to debit any related paid-in capital accounts for any amount specifically traceable to the shares being cancelled; or, in those cases in which it is impossible or impracticable to make such an identification, it is acceptable to debit the related paid-in capital accounts for the pro rata portions thereof applicable to the shares being cancelled. To balance the entry, the retained earnings account is charged, or, if a credit is needed to balance the entry, a special paid-in capital account is used. In any event, it is unacceptable to handle the cancellation of shares in a fashion that would increase retained earnings.

The cancellation of treasury shares will be illustrated using the facts in the preceding section, in which it was assumed that 100 shares having a par value of $100 each were acquired at a price of $120 per share. Under the par value method, the balance in the treasury stock account prior to cancellation of the stock would be $10,000. Cancellation of the shares is recorded by the following entry:

Capital stock (100 × $100)	10,000	
Treasury stock		10,000

If the treasury stock had been recorded at cost, the cancellation is recorded as follows:

Common stock (100 × $100)	10,000	
Capital in excess of par value—From common stock issuances (100 × $15)	1,500	
Retained earnings	500	
Treasury stock		12,000

It is assumed in the entry above that the 1,000 shares issued had been sold at $115 each. If this were not known, one-tenth of the balance in the capital in excess account, which is applicable to the shares being retired, should be removed.

Cancellation of treasury shares purchased for an amount less than their par or stated value and accounted for using the par value method would be recorded in the same manner as illustrated previously, when it was assumed the price paid was in excess of par. For example, it is now assumed that the 100 shares were purchased at a price of $90 per share. The balance in the treasury stock account just prior to cancellation is still $10,000, and the cancellation is recorded by the following entry:

Common stock (100 × $100)	10,000	
Treasury stock		10,000

However, if the stock is accounted for using the cost method, the entry to record cancellation of the shares results in debits to paid-in capital accounts ($10,000 + $1,500) in excess of the balance in the treasury stock account ($9,000). A special paid-in capital account is used to balance the entry, as shown below:

Common stock (100 × $100)	10,000	
Capital in excess of par value—From common stock issuances (100 × $15)	1,500	
Treasury stock		9,000
Capital in excess of par value—From cancellation of common stock.		2,500

Any appropriation of retained earnings owing to the acquisition of treasury stock should be reversed upon cancellation of the shares.

Donated treasury stock. If treasury stock is recorded at cost, it is obvious that no debit to a treasury stock account can be made for donated stock. However, a memorandum notation of the number of shares acquired should be made in that account.

The *usual* methods of recording reissuances are stated below:

If the treasury shares consist wholly of donated stock, the entire proceeds of reissue are credited to a paid-in capital account.

If purchased and donated shares are held and the shares reissued are specifically identified as donated shares, the entire proceeds are credited to Paid-in Capital. If the shares reissued are not specifically identified as donated shares, Paid-in Capital can be credited with the excess of the reissuance price over a cost computed on the first-in, first-out basis or on an average basis.

The word *usual* was included in the sentence above to provide for a possible exception. Stock is sometimes issued to the organizers of a corporation for non-cash assets, and a portion of the stock is then donated to the company to be reissued to provide working capital. This procedure was often used by mining and other speculative companies before the introduction of no-par stock made the expedient unnecessary. If such a company undertook to issue par value stock to the public, the stock usually had to be offered at a discount to make it attractive. But if unissued stock were issued at a discount, the purchasers might be liable for the discount, and this contingency might detract from the marketability of the stock. Such companies therefore resorted to the "treasury stock subterfuge." By issuing all the stock for the mine or other property and reacquiring part of it as treasury stock, the reacquired stock became, theoretically at least, fully paid treasury stock that could be reissued at a discount. To credit paid-in capital with the proceeds of the reissuance of such donated stock is of doubtful propriety. The financial position of the business would doubtless be more truly reflected if the proceeds of the reissuance were credited to the account with the property that was received when the stock was originally issued, because the property was obviously overvalued.

Under the par value method, donated treasury stock is recorded following the same procedures used for purchased treasury stock, except that the credit is to Donated Capital. Reissuance of the stock at a price other than the par or stated value is recorded by either debiting or crediting the difference to the donated capital account.

Cancellation of outstanding stock. By taking the appropriate legal action, a corporation may purchase and cancel stock that is held by stockholders. Such action occurs infrequently for common stock, but the cancellation of preferred stock is rather common.

Many preferred stock issues contain a feature that makes the stock callable at the option of the corporation. Normally, the call feature can be exercised only after a certain date has passed, and at a call price that is stipulated or can be determined. It was noted in Chapter 20 that if the stock is cumulative, any dividends in arrears must usually be paid at the time the stock is called. The procedures to record the cancellation of preferred stock when the firm exercises its call option can be summarized as follows: Remove all paid-in capital amounts applicable to the called stock from the accounts. If the total of these amounts is less than the amount paid to call the stock, the difference is debited to Retained Earnings. If the total is in excess of the amount paid, a special paid-in capital account is credited for the difference. An appropriate title for such an account would be Paid-in Capital from Cancellation of Preferred Stock.

Book amount (value) per share of stock. The following describes the approach ordinarily used by accountants in computing book amount per share: What would the stockholders receive on a per-share basis if the company were liquidated without gains, losses, or expenses—in other words, if the cash available for distribution, after the payment of all liabilities, were exactly equal to the stockholders' equity shown by the balance sheet?

Computations of book amount per share must give consideration to the rights of various classes of stockholders. It is impracticable to give more than a few typical illustrations—enough to indicate the nature of the problems involved.

If there is only one class of stock, the book amount per share is computed by dividing the total stockholders' equity (or book amount of all of the stock) by the number of shares outstanding. The total book amount of all the shares should include any appropriations of retained earnings.

Assume that the stockholders' equity of a corporation is composed of the following:

Common stock—2,000 shares outstanding		$200,000
Capital in excess of par value—From common-stock issuances		50,000
Retained earnings:		
Appropriated for bond retirement	$60,000	
Appropriated for contingencies	25,000	
Unappropriated	65,000	150,000
Total stockholders' equity		$400,000

The book amount per share is $400,000 ÷ 2,000, or $200.

The computation is not so simple if there are common and preferred shares outstanding. It is then necessary to determine the portion of the stockholders' equity, or aggregate book amount, applicable to the preferred stock, divide this amount by the number of shares of preferred stock outstanding to determine the book amount per share of the preferred, and divide the remainder of the stockholders' equity by the number of common shares outstanding to determine the book amount per share of the common.

The determination of the portion of stockholders' equity applicable to the preferred stock consists of a computation of the amount the preferred stockholders would be entitled to receive if the company were liquidated without gain or loss. This involves consideration of the following questions:

What preference rights do the preferred stockholders have with respect to dividends? Is the preferred stock cumulative or noncumulative? If it is cumulative, are there any dividends in arrears? If there are dividends in arrears, are there retained earnings from which they can be paid? Is the preferred stock participating or nonparticipating?

What preference rights do the preferred stockholders have with respect to assets in liquidation?

There are so many combinations of conditions, and consequently so many answers to these questions, that it is impracticable to illustrate them all. A few illustrations are shown below.

FIRST ILLUSTRATION: The stockholders' equity of a company on June 30, 19+5, consisted of the following:

Preferred stock—6% cumulative, nonparticipating; $100 par value; 1,000 shares outstanding	$100,000
Common stock—$100 par value; 1,000 shares outstanding	100,000
Retained earnings	50,000
Total	$250,000

Preferred dividends have been paid to December 31, 19+4.

Under the terms of issuance of the preferred stock, it can be called at 105; but in the event of liquidation, it is entitled only to par and unpaid cumulative dividends. Some accountants believe that the book amount per share of preferred should be based on the call price plus the unpaid dividends. If this procedure is adopted, the book amounts per share will be computed as follows:

Total stockholders' equity		$250,000
Portion applicable to preferred stock:		
Call price	$105,000	
Unpaid dividends for six months	3,000	
Total		108,000
(Book amount per share = $108,000 ÷ 1,000 = $108)		
Remainder applicable to common stock		$142,000
(Book amount per share = $142,000 ÷ 1,000 = $142)		

But a call price does not seem appropriate. A call price for preferred stock is applicable when the preferred stock is to be retired but the common stock is to remain outstanding. Therefore, it seems preferable to ignore call prices and make the computations as follows:

Total stockholders' equity		$250,000
Portion applicable to preferred stock:		
Par value	$100,000	
Unpaid dividends for six months	3,000	
Total		103,000
(Book amount per share = $103,000 ÷ 1,000 = $103)		
Remainder applicable to common stock		$147,000
(Book amount per share = $147,000 ÷ 1,000 = $147)		

A call price should be distinguished from a liquidating amount. If the preferred stockholders in the foregoing illustration were entitled to receive $105 per share in the event of liquidation, this amount should be used in the computation.

SECOND ILLUSTRATION: The stockholders' equity of a company on December 31, 19+5, consisted of the items listed below:

Preferred stock—6% cumulative, participating; $100 par value; 1,000 shares outstanding	$100,000
Common stock—No par value; stated value, $50 per share; 3,000 shares outstanding	150,000
Retained earnings	50,000
Total	$300,000

After 6 percent dividends are paid on the preferred stock, the common stockholders are entitled to receive $3 per share; thereafter, the two classes of stock are entitled to participate in dividends in the ratio of $2 per preferred share to $1 per common share; because there are 1,000 shares of preferred and 3,000 shares of common outstanding, the participation ratio is $2,000 to $3,000, or $^2/_5$ to the preferred and $^3/_5$ to the common. Dividends for the first six months of 19+5 have been paid on the preferred stock; no dividends have been paid for 19+5 on the common stock. The computations are made as follows:

		Preferred	Common
Par or stated value		$100,000	$150,000
Retained earnings:			
Total	$50,000		
Amount required for preferred dividend for second six months of 19+5	3,000*	3,000	
Portion required for dividends on common stock for year	9,000*		9,000
Remainder—divisible ²⁄₅ and ³⁄₅	$38,000	15,200	22,800
Total		$118,200	$181,800
Shares outstanding		1,000	3,000
Book amount per share		$ 118.20	$ 60.60

*Deduction.

THIRD ILLUSTRATION: Assume the same facts as in the second illustration, except that the retained earnings are only $7,000. The computations would then be made as follows:

		Preferred	Common
Par or stated value		$100,000	$150,000
Retained earnings:			
Total	$7,000		
Deduct amount required for preferred dividend for second six months of 19+5	3,000	3,000	
Remainder	$4,000		
Because the common stockholders are entitled to receive dividends of $3 per share before any participating dividends are paid on the preferred stock, and because the remaining $4,000 of retained earnings is not sufficient to pay such a dividend on the common stock, the entire remaining $4,000 is applicable to the common stock			4,000
Total		$103,000	$154,000
Shares outstanding		1,000	3,000
Book amount per share		$ 103.00	$ 51.33

FOURTH ILLUSTRATION: The stockholders' equity of a company on December 31, 19+5, consisted of the following:

Preferred stock—6% cumulative, nonparticipating; no par value; stated value, $50 per share; 1,000 shares outstanding	$ 50,000
Common stock—No par value; stated value, $10 per share; 10,000 shares outstanding	100,000
Deficit	20,000*
Total	$130,000

*Deduction.

Dividends of $25,000 are in arrears on the preferred stock.

Before book amounts per share can be computed, it is necessary to know whether the preferred stockholders are entitled, in the event of liquidation, to the dividends in arrears notwithstanding the existence of the deficit. If they are entitled to the dividends in arrears, the book amounts should be computed as follows:

Total stockholders' equity		$130,000
Portion applicable to preferred stock:		
$50 × 1,000	$50,000	
Dividends in arrears	25,000	
Total		75,000
(Book amount per share = $75,000 ÷ 1,000 = $75)		
Remainder applicable to common stock		$ 55,000
(Book amount per share = $55,000 ÷ 10,000 = $5.50)		

If the preferred stockholders are not entitled to the dividends in arrears, the book amounts should be computed as follows:

Total stockholders' equity	$130,000
Portion applicable to the preferred stock: $50 × 1,000	50,000
(Book amount per share = $50,000 ÷ 1,000 = $50)	
Remainder applicable to common stock	$ 80,000
(Book amount per share = $80,000 ÷ 10,000 = $8)	

It is obvious that accounting errors or improprieties will affect the book amount per share. The AICPA has stated:

> *Book value* (amount) is the amount shown on accounting records or related financial statements at or as of the date when the determination is made, after adjustments necessary to reflect (1) corrections of errors, and (2) the application of accounting practices which have been consistently followed.[9]

Appraisal increments. The procedures used in recording appraisal amounts in the accounting records were discussed in Chapter 17. It was noted at that time that some accountants advocate crediting the increment to an unrealized capital increment account and transferring the amount to Retained Earnings over the remaining life of the asset. Other accountants advocate recording the increment as a credit to a capital adjustment account. No matter which alternative is followed, any balance in the unrealized capital increment account or the capital adjustment account should be reported as a part of the stockholders' equity of the firm.

Comprehensive illustration of stockholders' equity. The following illustration shows the balance sheet treatment of various matters affecting the stockholders' equity.

---

[9]Committee on Terminology, "Book Value," *Accounting Terminology Bulletin No. 3* (New York: AICPA, August 1956), p. 39.

Stockholders' equity:		
Capital stock:		
Preferred stock—6% participating, cumulative; par value, $100; authorized and issued, 1,000 shares	$100,000	
Common stock—No par value; stated value, $10; authorized and issued, 10,000 shares, of which 500 shares are in the treasury	100,000	$200,000
Capital in excess of par or stated value:		
From preferred stock issuances	$ 5,000	
From common stock issuances	27,000	
From treasury stock transactions—Common	2,000	
From stock dividends	4,000	38,000
Retained earnings:		
Appropriated:		
For contingencies	$ 25,000	
For plant extensions	15,000	
Not available for dividends—Equal to cost of treasury stock	7,500	
Total	$ 47,500	
Unappropriated	132,000	179,500
Total		$417,500
Deduct cost of treasury stock—Common		7,500
Stockholders' equity		$410,000

In published financial statements, it is often necessary to combine or group some of the related stockholders' equity accounts. This is acceptable provided that the subtotals for paid-in capital and retained earnings are clearly set forth and that any restrictions or appropriations of retained earnings are disclosed. If there are any accounts showing unrealized increments in asset amounts, they should be clearly labeled and presented below the subtotal for retained earnings and above any treasury shares. Such accounts are rarely found, because it is considered unacceptable to write up assets to reflect appraisal amounts.

24

Income Tax Allocation

Introduction. This chapter is not concerned with the preparation of income tax returns or with the computation of the amount to be shown in the balance sheet as the liability for taxes currently payable under federal and state income tax laws. Rather, it considers the question of the amount to be shown in the income statement as income tax expense.

The accounting problem in the reporting of income tax expense is that a corporation's net income before taxes as it is reported in its income statement (pretax accounting income) can be materially different from its taxable net income reported in its income tax return. If there is a material difference, then the reporting in the income statement of the *same* income tax expense as that owed to the government (debit Income Tax Expense and credit Income Taxes Payable) results in a reported income tax expense that bears no normal relationship to the reported net income before taxes. The accounting profession views such disclosure as misleading to income-statement users and therefore applies income tax allocation procedures to bring the reported income tax expense in line with the net income before taxes reported in the income statement.

In light of the different objectives between government in its taxing capacity and accounting in its financial reporting capacity, it is not surprising that taxable income and pretax accounting income differ. Taxable income is determined by law and is a legal concept based on government objectives with regard to revenue needs and public policies. Pretax accounting net income is based on GAAP in order to provide useful financial information on the results of operations of a business firm. Because of these different objectives, different methods and procedures have developed for the determination of pretax accounting income and taxable income.

The differences between pretax accounting income and taxable income can be classified into four categories:

There are differences that arise from certain items that are included in taxable income for the period, but receive special treatment for financial reporting (accounting) purposes. For example, accountants directly associate their related tax effects when reporting the following items: income before extraordinary items and extraordinary items (income statement), prior-period adjustments (statement of retained earnings), and direct entries to other stockholders' equity accounts (balance sheet). This allocation of the total income tax expense for the period between financial statements is called *intraperiod income tax allocation.*

There are differences that arise from the *timing* of charges and credits to income. For example, certain transactions affect pretax accounting net income in one reporting period, but affect taxable net income in a different reporting period. These timing differences are accounted for by interperiod income tax allocation.

There are *permanent* differences that arise because certain items are included in pretax accounting income (or taxable income), but are never included in taxable income (or pretax accounting income). These permanent differences are *not* accounted for by interperiod income tax allocation.

There are differences that arise from loss recognition for income tax purposes. Income tax rules provide that a net operating loss of one period may be deducted in determining the taxable income of other periods.

Intraperiod income tax allocation. Per APB *Opinion No. 11,* the total income tax expense for a fiscal period should be allocated to income before extraordinary items, extraordinary items, prior-period adjustments, and certain direct entries to other stockholders' equity accounts.[1] Note that this intraperiod income tax allocation is allocation within a fiscal period, not between fiscal periods. Such allocation results from the *separate* reporting of these items, because it is argued that more useful information is provided if the tax follows the items causing the tax. In other words, the objective of income tax allocation within a period is to obtain an ap-

---

[1] Accounting Principles Board, "Accounting for Income Taxes," *Opinion No. 11* (New York: AICPA, December 1967), p. 175.

propriate relationship between income tax expense and income before extraordinary items, extraordinary items, prior-period adjustments, and other direct entries to stockholders' equity accounts.

For example, assume that Kaw Corporation has income tax expense of $75,100 for the current year, based on corporate income tax rates of 22 percent on the first $25,000 of taxable income and 48 percent on amounts above $25,000 of taxable income (the rates in existence at the time of this writing), as shown below:

Income tax on net operating income:		
22% of $25,000 =	$ 5,500	
48% of ($110,000 − $25,000) =	40,800	$46,300
Income tax savings on deductible extraordinary loss:		
48% of $40,000 =		(19,200)
Income tax on taxable gain from prior-period adjustment:		
48% of $100,000 =		48,000
Total income tax expense and payable		$75,100

The statement of income and retained earnings for Kaw Corporation without and with intraperiod income tax allocation would be as follows:

KAW CORPORATION
Statement of Income and Retained Earnings
For the Year Ended December 31, 19xx

	Without Intraperiod Allocation		With Intraperiod Allocation	
Sales		$600,000		$600,000
Cost of goods sold		360,000		360,000
Gross margin		$240,000		$240,000
Operating expenses		130,000		130,000
Net operating income before taxes and extraordinary item		$110,000		$110,000
Income taxes		75,100		46,300
Income before extraordinary item		$ 34,900		$ 63,700
Extraordinary item:				
Loss on tornado damage (net of applicable taxes of $19,200*)		40,000		20,800
Net income (loss)		$ (5,100)		$ 42,900
Beginning retained earnings as previously stated	$300,000		$300,000	
Prior-period adjustment:				
Gain on settlement of legal suit (net of applicable taxes of $48,000*)	100,000		52,000	
Beginning retained earnings as restated		400,000		352,000
Ending retained earnings		$394,900		$394,900

*Parenthetical remark would be shown with intraperiod allocation.

In analyzing this statement without intraperiod income tax allocation, several questions on tax effects would immediately come to mind. For example, since the corporate tax rate is approximately 50 percent, why are income taxes reported at $75,100 on only $110,000 net operating income before taxes and extraordinary item? Does this mean that income before extraordinary item of $34,900 is understated because income taxes are overstated? Is the extraordinary loss before or after taxes? Is the prior-period gain before taxes so that the tax effect is included in net income and results in its misrepresentation?

In contrast, in analyzing the statement with intraperiod income tax allocation, it can be readily perceived that income taxes of $46,300 relate to the $110,000 net operating income before taxes and extraordinary item, at the approximate corporate rate of 50 percent; hence, income before extraordinary item of $63,700 seems to reasonably follow. Similarly, it is readily seen that the extraordinary loss of $20,800 is net of taxes of $19,200, or a total tax-deductible loss of $40,000. Also, the prior-period gain of $52,000 is easily seen to be net of taxes of $48,000, or a total taxable gain of $100,000; hence, net income of $42,900 has not been distorted by the tax effect of this prior-period gain. Consequently, failure to allocate the total income tax expense would result in the misrepresentation of income before extraordinary item, extraordinary item, and retained earnings.

The primary argument for intraperiod income tax allocation is that it results in the presentation of more useful information in the financial statements. This argument pertains especially to the reporting of income before extraordinary items, because this income figure should be free from the distortion of unusual and nonrecurring gains and losses and their related tax effects in order that it can be used by investors and others in predicting future income flows. In addition, it is argued that if taxes were not allocated within the period, financial-statement users would be misled as to the net effect on the firm of extraordinary gains and losses and prior-period adjustments.

Three final points on intraperiod income tax allocation can be made. First, it should be pointed out that intraperiod allocation is universally accepted by the accounting profession and is not a controversial issue. Second, it is interesting to note that if a complete, all-inclusive concept of income were used by the accounting profession, there would be no need for intraperiod allocation between the income statement and retained earnings. Finally, it could be argued that the consistent application of intraperiod allocation would require allocation between net operating income (for purposes of better prediction) and nonoperating items (net of tax reporting) in multistep income statements. However, this is not done in practice.

Interperiod income tax allocation. Interperiod tax allocation is based on the same concept as intraperiod tax allocation: Taxes should follow the income that caused the taxes. Whereas allocation within the fiscal period (intraperiod allocation) is a straightforward problem that reduces to one of statement location, interperiod tax allocation is a more difficult problem that arises when the year for tax recognition differs from the year of accounting recognition.

When there are certain revenues and expenses that are recognized in one period following GAAP and in different periods following income tax rules, the taxes payable for the fiscal period do not represent the income tax expense that should be reported for financial-statement purposes. Thus, interperiod income tax allocation is necessary to allocate income taxes between current and future periods in order that, for financial-statement purposes, the reported taxes follow the reported income on which they are based. This process of apportioning income taxes among periods is called *interperiod income tax allocation.*

Differences occur in the timing of the recognition of certain revenues and expenses for accounting purposes versus tax purposes because accounting principles with regard to revenues and expenses do not agree in all instances with income tax rules, and because a corporation may adopt one accounting method for income tax purposes and another method in its books and financial statements. The latter cause is quite prevalent, since corporations will normally elect to avoid paying taxes early by selecting those methods for tax purposes that delay recognition of revenue or accelerate recognition of expense, even though they use other methods for purposes of financial-statement reporting.

Interperiod income tax allocation is specified per APB *Opinion No. 11* when there are timing differences that cause pretax accounting net income to differ from taxable net income, and therefore accounting income tax expense to differ from taxes payable.[2] For financial-statement purposes, the tax expense for the period should include the tax effects of transactions that are included in the determination of current-period pretax net income; thus, the tax effects of some of these transactions are recognized for accounting purposes in periods before or after they are recognized for income tax purposes. In such cases, the differences between pretax accounting net income and taxable net income should be recognized in the periods in which the differences *arise* and in the periods in which the differences *reverse.* In other words, these differences are timing differences in that they originate in one period and reverse or turn around in one or more subsequent periods.

In order to account for these timing differences via interperiod income tax allocation, accountants establish deferred charge or credit accounts for the difference between the income tax expense following GAAP and income taxes payable following income tax rules for the current period in which the differences originate. The deferred charge or credit accounts reflect the tax differences that are carried forward on the balance sheet until they are reversed in future periods.

As a simplified illustration to introduce the accounting for interperiod income tax allocation, assume that a corporation has pretax accounting net income of $80,000 for years 19+5 and 19+6 and a corporate income tax rate of 50 percent, and that a $10,000 expense item was deductible for income tax purposes in 19+5, but was recognized as an expense for accounting purposes in 19+6. Partial income statements reflecting the $10,000 timing difference with and without interperiod income tax allocation would be as follows:

---

[2]*Opinion No. 11*, p. 169.

	19+5		19+6	
	Interperiod Tax Allocation	Without Tax Allocation	Interperiod Tax Allocation	Without Tax Allocation
Net income before taxes	$80,000	$80,000	$80,000	$80,000
Income taxes:				
50% of $80,000 =	40,000			
50% of ($80,000 – $10,000) =		35,000*		
50% of $80,000 =			40,000	
50% of ($80,000 + $10,000) =				45,000*
Net income	$40,000	$45,000	$40,000	$35,000

*Income tax expense and payable per tax return.

Year-end entries to reflect the interperiod income tax allocation above would be as follows:

19+5 entry:

Income tax expense	40,000	
Deferred income tax credit		5,000
Income taxes payable		35,000

19+6 entry:

Income tax expense	40,000	
Deferred income tax credit	5,000	
Income taxes payable		45,000

Note that with interperiod allocation, the income tax expense for financial reporting purposes ($40,000) is in line with the pretax accounting net income ($80,000). Without interperiod tax allocation, the income tax expense (19+5, $35,000; and 19+6, $45,000) does not follow the pretax accounting net income, but instead, reflects the amount payable to the government. Thus, interperiod tax allocation results in the matching of the income tax expense with the revenue for the appropriate period and is therefore consistent with the accounting recognition of other expenses on an accrual basis. In addition, note that the $5,000 tax difference, as reflected by the deferred income tax credit, reverses itself in 19+6, which is consistent with the going-concern and fiscal-period assumptions.

To illustrate the reverse situation of a deferred income tax charge, assume the same data as above except that the $10,000 expense is recognized in 19+5 for accounting purposes (therefore, the 19+5 pretax income of $80,000 is after the $10,000 expense item), but it is not deductible for tax purposes until 19+6. Partial income statements reflecting the $10,000 timing difference with and without interperiod tax allocation and the year-end tax-allocation entries would be as shown on the next page.

Examples of timing differences. Timing differences result from either accounting pretax net income exceeding taxable net income or taxable net income exceeding accounting pretax net income. The former (latter) is caused by revenues or gains that are

	19+5 Interperiod Tax Allocation	19+5 Without Tax Allocation	19+6 Interperiod Tax Allocation	19+6 Without Tax Allocation
Net income before taxes	$80,000	$80,000	$80,000	$80,000
Income taxes:				
50% of $80,000 =	40,000			
50% of ($80,000 + $10,000) =		45,000*		
50% of $80,000 =			40,000	
50% of ($80,000 − $10,000) =				35,000*
Net income	$40,000	$35,000	$40,000	$45,000

*Income tax expense and payable per tax return.

19+5 entry:

Income tax expense	40,000	
Deferred income tax charge	5,000	
Income taxes payable		45,000

19+6 entry:

Income tax expense	40,000	
Deferred income tax charge		5,000
Income taxes payable		35,000

included in taxable income later (earlier) than they are included in pretax accounting income, or by expenses or losses that are deducted in determining taxable income earlier (later) than they are deducted in determining pretax accounting income.

Specific examples of timing differences, classified as to their tax effect, are summarized below:

(1) Pretax accounting income exceeds taxable income for the fiscal period; therefore, accounting tax expense exceeds taxes payable and results in a deferred income tax credit.

(a) Revenues or gains are recognized during the current period for financial reporting (accounting) purposes, but are deferred to later periods for tax purposes.

(i) Revenues on long-term contracts are recognized for accounting purposes based on the percentage-of-completion method, but are deferred for tax purposes based on the completed-contract method.

(ii) Gross margins on installment sales are recognized for accounting purposes at the time of sale, but are deferred for tax purposes to the periods when collected.

(iii) Income of foreign subsidiaries is recognized for accounting purposes during the current period when earned, but is deferred for income tax purposes until the period remitted.

(b) Expenses or losses are deducted for tax purposes in the current period, but are not recognized for financial reporting (accounting) purposes until later periods.

(i) Accelerated-depreciation methods are used for tax purposes, but straight-line depreciation is used for accounting purposes.

(ii) Research and development costs are deducted for tax purposes when incurred, but are deferred (capitalized) and amortized for accounting purposes.

(iii) Interest and taxes during construction are deducted for tax purposes when incurred, but are included in the cost of assets for accounting purposes.

(2) Taxable income exceeds pretax accounting income for the fiscal period; therefore, taxes payable exceed accounting tax expense and result in a deferred income tax charge.

(a) Revenues or gains are included in taxable income during the current period, but are deferred to later periods for financial reporting (accounting) purposes.

(i) Revenue received in advance (unearned or deferred revenue), such as rents, royalties, fees, dues, and service contracts, are taxed during the period when collected, but are deferred for accounting purposes to later periods, when earned.

(ii) Profits on intercompany transactions are taxed when reported in separate returns, but are eliminated for accounting purposes (consolidated statements) for those assets remaining within the group.

(b) Expenses or losses are recognized during the current period for financial reporting (accounting) purposes, but are deductible for tax purposes in later periods.

(i) Estimated warranty costs are expensed for accounting purposes during the current period of sale, but are deductible for tax purposes during later periods when actually paid.

(ii) Pension expense is accrued for accounting purposes during the current period, but is deductible for tax purposes when later contributed to the pension fund.

(iii) Expenses for deferred compensation, profit sharing, bonuses, and vacation and severance pay are recognized for accounting purposes when accrued, but are deductible for tax purposes during later periods when actually paid.

ILLUSTRATION: Assume that H.E. Miller Company, engaged in the construction business, uses the percentage-of-completion method in its financial statements and the completed-contract method for its income tax return. Assume also the facts presented below:

H.E. MILLER COMPANY

	Contract	Year Started	Year Completed	Estimated (and Actual) Total Profit
Construction contracts:				
	I	19+5	19+6	$ 80,000
	II	19+6	19+8	200,000
	III	19+7	19+8	120,000

	19+5	19+6	19+7	19+8
Percentage of completion during year:				
I	50%	50%		
II		30	40%	30%
III			75	25
Net income before income tax, reported in the financial statements (total estimated profit multiplied by percentage of completion during year):				
I	$40,000	$ 40,000		
II		60,000	$ 80,000	$ 60,000
III			90,000	30,000
	$40,000	$100,000	$170,000	$ 90,000
Income reported in income tax returns (total profit on contracts completed during the year):				
I		$ 80,000		
II				$200,000
III				120,000
	—	$ 80,000	—	$320,000
Income tax actually payable—50% rate	—	$ 40,000	—	$160,000

A review of the data will reveal the potential distortion of some of the amounts shown in the financial statements if H. E. Miller Company were to report as tax expense only the tax actually payable currently. For example, no income tax expense or liability would be shown in the 19+5 financial statements. By the end of 19+7, the company would have reported accumulated earnings before income taxes of $310,000 ($40,000 + $100,000 + $170,000) on the three contracts, but only $40,000 of income tax thereon would have been charged. Furthermore, the 19+7 balance sheet would show no income tax liability, although the company is subject to future tax on $230,000 of income already reported in its income statements. The $230,000 amount is the difference between the aggregate net income before income taxes for the years 19+5, 19+6, and 19+7 ($310,000) and the income reported in the 19+6 income tax return ($80,000).

Based on accrual accounting, a proper matching of revenue and expense requires that the income tax expense follow the income. Income that will ultimately be taxable should not be reported in the financial statements as though it were tax-free. Thus, income taxes should be allocated on an accrual basis as follows:

	19+5	19+6	19+7	19+8
Income statement:				
Net income before income tax	$40,000	$100,000	$170,000	$ 90,000
Income tax expense	20,000	50,000	85,000	45,000
Net income	$20,000	$ 50,000	$ 85,000	$ 45,000
Balance sheet:				
Income tax payable		$ 40,000		$160,000
Deferred income tax credit	$20,000	30,000	$115,000	
	$20,000	$ 70,000	$115,000	$160,000

To acquire an impression of the potential distortion involved in this matter, compare the net income figures above with the amounts that would be reported without the application of income tax allocation procedures.

	19+5	19+6	19+7	19+8
Income statement:				
Net income before income tax	$40,000	$100,000	$170,000	$ 90,000
Income tax actually payable	-0-	40,000	-0-	160,000
Net income (loss)	$40,000	$ 60,000	$170,000	$(70,000)
Balance sheet:				
Income taxes payable	-0-	$ 40,000	-0-	$160,000

If H. E. Miller Company uses income tax allocation procedures, the journal entries for the income tax charges and payments would appear as shown below:

19+5 tax expense:		
Income tax expense	20,000	
Deferred income tax credit		20,000
19+6 tax expense:		
Income tax expense	50,000	
Income taxes payable		40,000
Deferred income tax credit		10,000
Income tax for 19+6 paid:		
Income taxes payable	40,000	
Cash		40,000
19+7 tax expense:		
Income tax expense	85,000	
Deferred income tax credit		85,000
19+8 tax expense:		
Income tax expense	45,000	
Deferred income tax credit	115,000	
Income taxes payable		160,000
Income tax for 19+8 paid:		
Income taxes payable	160,000	
Cash		160,000

Observe the following with respect to the income tax allocation procedures just described:

In each year, the tax expense to be shown in the income statement is the amount that would be payable if the accounting procedures used in the books were also applied in the tax return.

In each year in which the tax expense shown in the income statement exceeds the tax liability for the year, the excess is credited to a deferred income tax credit account.

In each year in which the tax liability exceeds the tax expense shown in the income statement, the excess is debited to the deferred income tax credit account.

Methods of applying interperiod tax allocation. The preceding discussion and illustration of interperiod income tax allocation is based on the *deferred method,* which is the specified method per APB *Opinion No. 11.* Under the deferred method, the tax effects of current timing differences are recognized in the period and at the tax rates in effect when the timing differences originate; hence, these tax effects are deferred during the period when they originate and are allocated to future periods when the timing differences reverse.

Another method of interperiod income tax allocation is the *liability method.* Under this method, the tax effects of timing differences are based on the tax rates expected to be in effect during the periods when the timing differences reverse. The initial computations of the tax effects of timing differences during the period of origination are considered to be tentative and subject to future adjustment if tax rates change or new taxes are imposed. The tax effects of timing differences are viewed as either liabilities for taxes payable in the future or assets for prepaid taxes. Although the method has some conceptual merit in terms of taking into account future tax rates, it is a questionable method, because the tax effects of timing differences are not really assets or liabilities. The method is not recommended per *Opinion No. 11.*

The *net-of-tax method* is another method of interperiod income tax allocation. Under this method, the tax effects of timing differences are viewed as reductions of the related assets or liabilities that gave rise to them. In other words, the tax effects of timing differences are viewed as factors in the valuation of specific assets or liabilities. Although the method probably has at least as much conceptual merit as the deferred method, there is the conceptual problem that tax effects are only one of many factors that affect the valuation of assets and liabilities. The method is not recommended per *Opinion No. 11.*

Comprehensive and partial interperiod tax allocation. Comprehensive interperiod income tax allocation is specified per *Opinion No. 11.* Under comprehensive allocation, the tax effects of *all* timing differences are recognized in order to have a consistent and timely matching of expense with revenue for purposes of income determination.

In contrast, partial interperiod income tax allocation is based on the assumption that income tax expense for the period should be the same as the income taxes payable for the period. The only exceptions would be specific nonrecurring differences between taxable income and pretax accounting income that would cause a material misstatement of income tax expense and net income, and then only if such differences are reasonably expected to be paid as income taxes (or recovered as a reduction of income taxes) within a short period of time (around five years). Partial allocation is rejected in practice because of its emphasis on cash outlays rather than accrual accounting.

Permanent differences between taxable and accounting income. Income tax regulations exempt certain accounting revenues from taxation (nontaxable revenues), disallow certain accounting expenses as tax deductions (nondeductible expenses), and allow certain deductions that are not accounting expenses (nonexpense deductions). These differences are either included in the tax return but never in the income statement, or included in the income statement but never in the tax return. Since these differences are not timing differences, they do not reverse in future periods; hence, they are permanent differences that do not affect future periods and do not require interperiod tax allocation. Examples of permanent differences are the following:

Nontaxable revenue, such as interest earned on state or municipal bonds
Nondeductible expenses, such as the amortized portion of premiums paid on officers' life insurance, or a corporation's lobbying expenses
Nonexpense deductions, such as the excess of statutory depletion over cost depletion

Operating losses and tax allocation. Federal income tax regulations provide that operating losses (subject to various adjustments) can be carried back against the income of previous years (three years at the time of this writing) and carried forward against the income of years following the loss (five years at the time of this writing). An operating-loss carryback can result in a corporation's receiving a refund of taxes paid in previous years. If the loss exceeds the income of previous years to which it is carried back, then it can be carried forward to future profitable periods and reduce the taxes that would otherwise be payable for those years. Consequently, when such operating losses are carried back or forward, an income tax allocation problem arises because pretax accounting income and taxable income (after deducting the operating loss carryback or carryforward) will differ for the period to which the loss is applied.

In the case of an operating-loss carryback, the refund (or claim to a refund) of past taxes paid is the result of the operating loss for the current period; hence, the amount of the refund should be reported in the financial statements for the current loss period. Because the refund is virtually certain (it is both measurable and currently realizable), *Opinion No. 11* states that the loss should be recognized in the determination of net income (loss) for the loss period.[3]

To illustrate the operating-loss carryback, assume that a company has a net operating loss of $30,000 for the current year, and that after tax adjustments, it is

[3] *Opinion No. 11*, p. 122.

able to carry back $20,000 of the loss against taxable income of a prior year. Assuming a 50 percent tax rate, the tax refund would be $10,000 and would be recorded and reported as follows:

Entry:

Receivable for refund of income taxes	10,000	
Refund of income taxes due to loss carryback ..		10,000

Income-statement reporting:

⋮	⋮
Net loss before income tax effect	$(30,000)
Less estimated refund of prior year's income taxes due to loss carryback	10,000
Net loss	$(20,000)

In the case of an operating-loss carryforward, the carryforward is the result of the operating loss of the current period; hence, the potential tax saving is the result of the current period's loss and should be recognized during the loss period. This could be done by recognizing the potential tax benefit as a receivable (debit Receivable for Tax Refund on Carryforward) and as a reduction of the operating loss (credit Tax Carryforward) during the current period when the loss occurred. The tax carryforward account would be closed to Income Summary and reported in the income statement as a line item after Net Loss Before Income Tax Effect.

This treatment of operating-loss carryforwards is recommended per *Opinion No. 11* only in unusual circumstances, when realization is assured beyond any reasonable doubt at the time the loss carryforwards arise.[4] Because the tax benefit of carryforwards will be realized only if there are future profitable years to which the carryforwards can be applied, *Opinion No. 11* states that in usual circumstances, the tax benefits should not be recognized until the periods when they are actually realized, and then they should be reported as extraordinary items in the income statement of the carryforward periods. Consequently, the recommended treatment of carryforwards in usual circumstances is based on the doctrine of conservatism, because of the uncertainty of the future realization of the tax benefits. On the other hand, such treatment is probably too conservative (the usual circumstances could be recognition of the carryforward in the loss period, and the unusual circumstances could be recognition in the carryforward periods), is inconsistent with the treatment of carrybacks, and implies a correction of prior periods' losses, yet the carryforwards are not reported as prior-period adjustments, but as extraordinary items.

To illustrate the specified treatment of carryforwards per *Opinion No. 11*, assume that a corporation has a $20,000 loss carryforward from last year, a tax rate of 50 percent, and net income before taxes of $60,000 during the current year. The

[4] *Opinion No. 11*, p. 173.

recording and reporting of the $10,000 (50 percent of $20,000) tax carryforward would be as follows:

Entry:

Income tax expense	30,000	
Tax carryforward (extraordinary item)		10,000
Income taxes payable		20,000

Income-statement reporting:

⋮	⋮
Net operating income before taxes and extraordinary item	$60,000
Income taxes	30,000
Net income before extraordinary item	$30,000
Extraordinary item:	
Tax carryforward	10,000
Net income	$40,000

Disclosure of tax allocation. Balance-sheet disclosure of tax-allocation procedures relates primarily to the reporting of the deferred charges or credits arising from timing differences, and the reporting of refunds of past taxes or offsets to future taxes arising from carrybacks or carryforwards. Per *Opinion No. 11,* the reporting of deferred income tax charges or credits requires classification into net current and net noncurrent amounts, based on whether the related assets or liabilities are current or noncurrent. For example, if estimated warranty cost is classified as a current liability, then the related deferred income tax charge should be reported as a current item. With regard to reporting refunds of past taxes or offsets to future taxes, they should be classified as current or noncurrent, based on when realization is expected to occur during the normal operating cycle or one year, whichever is longer.

Per *Opinion No. 11,* income-statement disclosure of tax-allocation procedures should show the income tax expense for the period, consisting of taxes estimated to be payable, tax effects of timing differences, and tax effects of operating losses. These components of income tax expense should be allocated to Income Before Extraordinary Items and to Extraordinary Items and presented as either separate-line items in the income statement, or as combined amounts with disclosure of the components by parenthetical remarks or footnotes to the financial statements.

Evaluation of tax allocation. Intraperiod income tax allocation is widely accepted by practicing accountants and accounting theorists and is not a controversial issue. There is general agreement by the accounting profession that the tax benefits of operating losses should be recognized during the loss period when realization is virtually certain; however, as previously explained, there is some controversy among accounting theorists as to the recognition of the tax benefits of loss carryforwards to the period when actually realized. Interperiod income tax allocation is widely accepted by the accounting profession, especially in light of *Opinion No. 11;* however, it is a controversial issue among accounting theorists and deserves further discussion.

PRINCIPAL ARGUMENTS IN FAVOR OF INTERPERIOD INCOME TAX ALLOCATION: The basic argument for interperiod income tax allocation is that income taxes are an expense of a firm earning income subject to taxes; therefore, income taxes should be accounted for in the same manner as are other expenses. Consistent with the fiscal-period assumption, income tax expense should be recognized during the period when the income is earned that gave rise to the taxes, which implies the use of accruals, deferrals, and estimates necessary to identify the expense with the proper time period. Similarly, consistent with the matching assumption, expenses such as income taxes, which cannot be directly identified with revenue, are recognized as period expenses and matched indirectly with the revenue for the period. Finally, consistent with the going-concern assumption, the firm is expected to continue profitable operations subject to taxes, pay these taxes, and continue to be taxed in the future; hence, timing differences will probably be offset in the future.

A second argument for interperiod income tax allocation is the accountant's concern with net-income distortion. The accountant does not like to see net income made different by a procedure adopted only for tax purposes. This fairly common case arises when a company makes a substantial investment in new equipment and depreciates it using an accelerated method for tax purposes only. This reduces significantly the current income tax payments. If the tax expense is reported for accounting purposes without tax allocation, the stated net income has been made higher merely by the adoption of a procedure for tax purposes. Such distorted net-income figures would be widely publicized, generally in the form of earnings per share or rate of return on investment, without the disclosure that the apparently favorable showing is really the result of a tax device.

A final argument for interperiod tax allocation is that the tax effects of timing differences are temporary, and such temporary differences should not be allowed to distort reported net income. For example, in the case of a company using double-declining depreciation for tax purposes and straight-line depreciation for accounting purposes, income that will ultimately be taxable (as the periodic difference cancels out in time) should not be reported in the financial statements as though it were tax-free. In other words, because there is only a temporary postponement of taxes, not a permanent tax reduction, the income statement should show tax expense at the amount normally paid on pretax accounting income.

PRINCIPAL ARGUMENTS AGAINST INTERPERIOD INCOME TAX ALLOCATION: A prime argument against interperiod tax allocation is that it results in the reporting of undefined deferred charges and credits in the balance sheet in order to smooth or normalize reported net income by shifting tax effects from one period to the next. Income determination and valuation are not separable, yet the accounting profession's undue emphasis on the income statement has resulted in the use of allocation methods (such as interperiod tax allocation) that leave the balance sheet a meaningless statement of residuals. Deferred income tax charges are not assets, since the government does not recognize such charges as tax prepayments, and deferred income tax credits are not liabilities, since the credits do not represent obligations to the government.

Another argument against interperiod tax allocation is that income taxes are not an expense of doing business, but a distribution of profits similar to dividends. Since such taxes arise only if income is earned, they are not a voluntary and controlled expense, but an involuntary distribution of income. Furthermore, unlike normal expenses, taxes do not generate revenue; however, it can be argued that taxes represent payment for government services (that is, the government provides a favorable economic climate to conduct profitable operations), but this can be rebutted by the fact that firms receive these services regardless of the amount of their taxes. Thus, if income taxes are not an expense, then interperiod tax allocation is not necessary and income taxes should be based on the legal concept of taxable income, not accounting income.

A final argument against interperiod tax allocation is that the tax effect of timing differences do not always reverse or balance out as assumed by the deferred method; therefore, there are timing differences that are really permanent rather than temporary. For example, if a firm uses straight-line depreciation for reporting purposes and accelerated depreciation for tax purposes, and if the firm consistently replaces assets as they are fully depreciated (a stable firm), then the deferred income tax credit will build up rapidly and then level off and result in a permanent tax savings. Furthermore, if the firm expands and increases its investment in depreciable assets, then the deferred income tax credit will grow and not level off, and a permanent tax savings is even more probable.

Because it is unlikely that amounts treated as tax deferments will be precisely balanced off by opposite differences in the future between the books and the tax return, there is a strong possibility that the balance sheet will include, more or less permanently, residuals from the effects of tax-allocation procedures. In time, such deferred amounts would tend to become meaningless, unless some type of adjustment of the amounts is made.

To illustrate the argument above, assume that a corporation replaces one fully depreciated asset on the first of each year and as a result always has five assets in use. The assets cost $150,000 each; a five-year estimated life is assumed. Also, the sum-of-the-years'-digits method of depreciation is adopted for tax purposes in 1975; the straight-line method is continued in the books. The tax policy thus applies to all assets acquired after December 31, 1974. The effect of this regular replacement of assets on deferred taxes is shown below, followed by a partial lapsing schedule showing the details of the tax-return depreciation for the years 1975–1979.

Table of Depreciation and Deferred Tax—A Group of Assets

Year	Number of Assets Owned	Aggregate Cost of Assets in Use	Depreciation per Tax Return	Depreciation per Books	Difference	Tax Effect—50% Rate	Cumulative Tax Saving
1973	5	$750,000	$150,000	$150,000	$ -0-	$ -0-	$ -0-
1974	5	750,000	150,000	150,000	-0-	-0-	-0-
1975*	5	750,000	170,000*	150,000*	$20,000	10,000	10,000
1976	5	750,000	180,000	150,000	30,000	15,000	25,000
1977	5	750,000	180,000	150,000	30,000	15,000	40,000
1978	5	750,000	170,000	150,000	20,000	10,000	50,000
1979	5	750,000	150,000	150,000	-0-	-0-	50,000
1980	5	750,000	150,000	150,000	-0-	-0-	50,000
1981	5	750,000	150,000	150,000	-0-	-0-	50,000
							etc.

*Sum-of-years'-digits method adopted for tax purposes in 1975.

Partial Lapsing Schedule
Tax-Return Depreciation—Sum-of-Years'-Digits Method Starting in 1975

Year Asset Acquired	Cost	Depreciation 1975	1976	1977	1978	1979
1971	$150,000	$ 30,000				
1972	150,000	30,000	$ 30,000			
1973	150,000	30,000	30,000	$ 30,000		
1974	150,000	30,000	30,000	30,000	$ 30,000	
1975	150,000	50,000	40,000	30,000	20,000	$ 10,000
1976	150,000		50,000	40,000	30,000	20,000
1977	150,000			50,000	40,000	30,000
1978	150,000				50,000	40,000
1979	150,000					50,000
		$170,000	$180,000	$180,000	$170,000	$150,000

Note the "Cumulative Tax Saving" column in the table, which shows that for a group of assets, a postponed tax is in fact a tax savings from the point of view of a going concern. Thus, a gradual turnover occurs among the assets, and the cumulative tax saving does not show any tendency to return to zero.

In contrast to the "Cumulative Tax Saving" column, note that the "Difference" column in the table shows that tax and accounting differences tend to cancel out for *individual* assets. This is the basis for the argument by the supporters of interperiod tax allocation that the makeup of the deferred tax amounts revolves, or turns over. Although the differences reverse and are replaced by similar differences, the initial differences do reverse and can be identified and recognized as timing differences. A basic problem with this counterargument is that it assumes that the deferred income tax credit turns over like accounts payable, but that, unlike accounts payable, the deferred credit is not a liability.

25

Statement of Changes in Financial Position

Introduction. The statement of changes in financial position, traditionally called the *funds statement,* provides financial information about the sources and uses of a firm's financial resources (changes in assets and equities) during a fiscal period. Such a statement presents all the significant changes in a firm's financial position during a time period that result from financing and investing activities, including internal financing provided by operations. Thus, the statement is a model of a firm's significant changes in financial position that is used in financial accounting to provide summary input–output financial-resource-flow reports for periodic time intervals.

Per APB *Opinion No. 19,* the statement of changes in financial position is a basic financial statement that should be presented for all profit-oriented businesses for each period in which an income statement is presented.[1] The statement should be presented because the financial information on the financing and investing

---

[1]Accounting Principles Board, "Reporting Changes in Financial Position," *Opinion No. 19* (New York: AICPA, March 1971), pp. 373–74.

activities of a business firm that it provides is essential in aiding financial-statement users in making economic decisions concerning the firm.

By reporting on the individual sources and uses of a firm's financial resources, the statement of changes in financial position provides useful information to investors, creditors, and other external statement users (as well as to management) with regard to investing and financing practices, financial risk, and future financial-resource flows. The statement, especially a comparative statement, provides information about management's policies as to types of financial resources acquired, how they were employed in the business, and how they were financed; hence, the statement is useful in evaluating management's success in investing in and financing operations.

More specifically, the statement aids financial-statement users in its answers to financial questions about the firm that they need in order to make rational financial decisions, such as the following: Has management been modernizing its plant and equipment, and if so, how has such modernization been financed? Does management tend to finance new assets primarily from internal operations, from debt, or from common-stock issues? Is the firm's financial-resource inflow from operations so small in comparison to financial-resource inflow from debt financing that the firm's financial risk is too high? Has the firm been relying too heavily on common-stock issues to finance expansion, and not taking advantage of leverage via low-cost debt financing? Has there been a shift in methods of financing? Why is the working-capital position so low in light of the firm's profitable operations? Why is the firm paying such large dividends, acquiring its own stock, or retiring debt early in spite of low internal financing from operations? Why has such a large proportion of the firm's financial resources been used to acquire land? Does the decreasing trend in internal financing from operations indicate serious financial problems in the future? Do the unusual increases in such working-capital items as receivables and inventories indicate potential liquidity problems?

Although the statement of changes in financial position provides useful information for financial decision-making purposes, so do the other basic financial statements; hence, it supplements, but does not supplant, the statement of income and retained earnings and the balance sheet. That is, the statement of changes in financial position provides financial information that is either not available or only indirectly available in piecemeal form from the other financial statements.

For example, the income statement reports on the results of operations for the period, which are affected by allocations resulting from accruals and deferrals to match revenue and expense to report net income, but it does not report on internal financing via cash or working capital generated from operations. Also, the income statement reports gains and losses on sales of investments, equipment, and the retirement of long-term debt, but it does not report the proceeds received from such sales or the amount paid to retire debt. In addition, there are significant changes in financial resources that are not reported in the income statement because they lack a gain-or-loss element, such as acquisition of equipment, issuance of stock, and the like. In contrast, such significant investing and financing activities are reported in the statement of changes in financial position.

Similarly, the balance sheet reports on financial condition as of a given date, but it does not report the financial changes in assets and equities, and it does not show the investing and financing activities that caused such changes. Comparative balance sheets show net changes in particular assets and equities, but do not show directly their individual increases and decreases. For example, if equipment were reported in last year's balance sheet at $200,000 and this year's balance sheet at $250,000, it is readily perceived that there has been an increase of $50,000. However, the comparative balance sheets would not show that the $50,000 net change was the result of a new-equipment addition costing $75,000 and the sale of $25,000 in old equipment for $30,000. In contrast, individual increases and decreases in assets and equities are included in the statement of changes in financial position.

Thus, the statement of changes in financial position provides a systematic presentation in narrative form of all the firm's significant operating, financing, and investing transactions that changed its financial position during the period. It provides a link between the income statement and the balance sheet by tying together net income, gains, and losses with changes in assets and equities. The statement also provides a link between successive balance sheets, by reporting on all significant changes in financial position between two balance-sheet dates.

Financial-resource-flow concepts. In order to prepare a statement that reports on the individual sources and uses of a firm's financial resources, the accountant needs a financial-resource-flow concept that defines what is meant by changes in financial resources. By defining the concept of financial resources, the accountant can then use the concept in determining the kinds of changes in financial resources that should be included in the statement of changes in financial position.

Traditionally, the financial-resource-flow concept, referred to as *funds flow,* was normally defined in terms of working capital (current assets minus current liabilities), in some cases in terms of cash, and in fewer cases in terms of current monetary assets (cash plus short-term marketable securities plus accounts receivable) or net current monetary assets (current monetary assets minus current monetary liabilities). For example, if financial resources were defined in terms of working capital, individual changes in net current resources during the fiscal period would be reported in the statement of changes in financial position, traditionally referred to as the *funds statement.* Increases in working capital would be reported as sources of working capital, and decreases in working capital would be reported as uses of working capital during the period, and the difference between the total sources and the total uses would be reported as the increase or decrease in working capital for the period. The so-called funds statement would be based on the funds-flow concept of working capital. In a similar manner, if funds flow were defined in terms of cash or current monetary assets, the definition would be used to determine the individual sources and uses of funds and report them, along with the reconciled difference, in the funds statement.

On the other hand, the traditional concept of funds flow, defined in terms of changes in working capital or cash, is too narrow a concept of financial-resource flow. That is, there are significant changes in financial resources that can occur during a fiscal period that affect neither working capital nor cash, and therefore would be omitted from the statement of changes in financial position. For example, equipment acquired in exchange for debt or common stock, debt retired in exchange for common stock, and the like are significant changes in financial resources that do not affect working capital or cash.

Another problem with a narrow concept of funds flow in terms of working capital is that individual changes *within* working capital are not disclosed in the funds statement. By defining funds flow as working capital, the funds statement reports on the changes in amount of working capital, but not the changes within working capital. In other words, working capital is similar to a pool of liquid financial resources (net current assets), and it is the changes in the size of this "pool," not within the "pool," that are reported in the funds statement. Thus, such a funds statement does not provide useful information on unusual changes in individual working-capital items, such as large increases in receivables, inventories, accounts payable, and the like, which can be useful indicators of potential trouble in working-capital management.

APB *Opinion No. 19* was issued to overcome these problems associated with a narrow concept of financial-resource flows. The opinion states that the statement of changes in financial position should be based on a broad concept embracing all changes in financial position. Thus, the statement should disclose all the important financing and investing activities of an entity during the fiscal period, regardless of whether working capital or cash is directly affected. The statement should report as separate-line items the financing and investing aspects of all significant transactions that affect financial position during the period. Moreover, to convey this broad concept of financial-resource flows, the opinion recommends that the title of the statement should be "Statement of Changes in Financial Position," not "Funds Statement" or "Statement of Sources and Uses of Funds."

The financial-resource-flow concept (funds-flow concept) defined per *Opinion No. 19* is all changes in financial position. However, what is really meant is a funds-flow concept defined as all *significant* changes in financial position arising from *external* transactions. The "significant changes" in the definition is necessary because not all changes are included in the statement. For example, stock dividends literally change stockholders' equity (retained earnings decreased and common stock increased), but they are not considered to be a significant change included in the statement. "Changes ... arising from external transactions" is necessary in the definition because changes in assets and equities arising from internal accounting entries are not included in the statement. Such internal accounting transactions include depreciation, amortization of intangibles, bond discount or premium amortization, and increases or decreases in deferrals. Although these internal accounting adjustments change assets and equities, they are not the result of a current-period external transaction that affects cash or working capital. They are similar to intrafirm transactions.

Working capital or cash from operations. *Business operations* refers to a firm's normal business transactions to generate revenue and to incur expenses necessary for revenue generation in order to derive profits. Business operations can generate internal financing for a firm, since operations are an important source of new liquid assets (liquid resources). In other words, a firm's profitable business operations can generate cash and working-capital inflows that can be used in the operations of the business. To the extent that sales generating cash or working capital exceed expenses requiring an outlay of cash or working capital during the fiscal period, there is a net increase in cash or working capital provided from operations for the period. This net increase in cash or working capital for the period has traditionally been referred to as *funds provided from operations.*

On the other hand, unprofitable operations can reduce cash or working capital. To the extent that sales generating cash or working capital are less than expenses requiring an outlay of cash or working capital during the fiscal period, the net decrease represents *funds used in operations.*

Funds provided from (used in) operations show how profitable (unprofitable) operations have been reflected in changes in cash or working capital, and therefore changes in financial position. Hence, funds provided from (used in) operations are a link between the income statement and the balance sheet by showing changes in financial position resulting from operations during the fiscal period. Since funds provided from (used in) operations reflect changes in financial position, they are consistent with the broad concept of financial-resource flows in terms of significant changes in financial position per *Opinion No. 19.* Thus, *Opinion No. 19* states that the statement of changes in financial position should prominently disclose cash or working capital provided from (used in) operations for the period, exclusive of extraordinary items.[2]

It should be understood that neither net income nor income before extraordinary items is synonymous with cash or working capital provided from (used in) operations. Net income includes both ordinary items (normal, recurring revenues and expenses) and extraordinary items (unusual, nonrecurring gains and losses), whereas funds provided from (used in) operations include only ordinary items. Also, most extraordinary items included in net income do not affect cash or working capital and therefore would not be included in funds provided from (used in) operations.

On the other hand, income before extraordinary items is similar to cash or working capital provided from (used in) operations in that it does not include extraordinary items, but differs in that it includes such expenses as depreciation, amortization of intangibles, and bond-discount amortization, which do not affect cash or working capital (so-called nonfund expenses). Based on accrual accounting, such nonfund expenses are legitimately reported in the income statement, but because they do not use or provide cash or working capital during the period, they are excluded from cash or working capital provided from (used in) operations. In other words, such nonfund expenses arise from internal accounting adjustments, whereas cash or working capital provided from (used in) operations arises from revenue and expenses from external transactions that normally affect working capital.

It should also be understood that funds provided from (used in) operations

---

[2] *Opinion No. 19,* p. 374.

defined in terms of working capital are not the same as those defined in terms of cash. Working capital provided from (used in) operations reports on the excess (deficiency) of revenues providing working capital minus expenses using working capital during the fiscal period, exclusive of extraordinary items. Thus, it is the net change in the working-capital pool as a result of operations that is reported in working capital provided from (used in) operations; hence, changes within working-capital items (individual changes in current assets and current liabilities) are not shown. To overcome this problem, *Opinion No. 19* states that when the statement of changes in financial position shows working capital provided from (used in) operations, a separate schedule of individual changes in current assets and current liabilities should be provided.[3]

In contrast to working capital provided from (used in) operations, cash provided from (used in) operations reports on the excess (deficiency) of revenue providing cash minus costs and expenses using cash during the fiscal period, exclusive of extraordinary items. Because net changes in the elements of working capital that are related to operations, other than cash (such as receivables, inventories, and payables), are noncash adjustments (to be subsequently explained), *Opinion No. 19* states that such changes should be disclosed in appropriate detail in the body of the statement of changes in financial position.[4] Thus, cash provided from (used in) operations would be reported in the statement in such a manner that the individual net changes in current assets (other than cash) and current liabilities that are related to operations would be shown. Note, however, that such reporting results in excluding individual changes in working-capital elements from cash provided from (used in) operations; hence, cash and working capital provided from (used in) operations are not the same. Funds provided from (used in) operations reported in the statement of changes in financial position will differ depending on whether a working-capital or cash format is used.

ILLUSTRATION OF WORKING CAPITAL FROM OPERATIONS: In order to illustrate the differences between working capital provided from (used in) operations, income before extraordinary items, and net income, assume the following data:

Sales (collections from customers, $230,000)		$250,000
Cost of goods sold (payments for inventory purchased, $125,000)		140,000
Gross margin		$110,000
Operating expenses:		
Expenses paid in cash	$15,000	
Accrued expenses (accrued expenses paid, $26,000)	20,000	
Depreciation	10,000	
Amortization of goodwill	1,000	46,000
Net operating income		$ 64,000

[3] *Opinion No. 19,* p. 376.
[4] *Opinion No. 19,* p. 376.

Nonoperating items:		
Loss on sale of equipment	$ 600	
Loss on bond redemption	1,000	
Interest on bonds (bond premium amortization, $100)	400	2,000
Income before extraordinary item		$ 62,000
Extraordinary item:		
Loss on flood damage (net of applicable taxes of $1,200)		1,800
Net income		$ 60,200

Additional data:
- Increase in accounts receivable of $20,000
- Decrease in inventory of $10,000
- Increase in accounts payable of $5,000
- Decrease in accrued liabilities of $6,000

In determining working capital provided from (used in) operations, the source of working-capital inflow is revenue, because both cash sales and sales on account (increase in accounts receivable) increase working capital. Uses of working capital are expenses that reduce working capital, which include expenses that are paid in cash, reduce noncash current assets (cost of goods sold reduces inventory), and increase current liabilities (accrued expenses). Thus, working capital provided from (used in) operations can be determined by starting with revenue and subtracting expenses requiring working capital, which, based on the data above, is $74,500, shown as follows:[5]

Working capital provided from operations	=	**Revenue generating working capital**	–	**Expenses requiring an outlay of working capital**
$74,500	=	**$250,000**	–	**[$140,000 + $15,000 + $20,000 + ($100 + $400)]**

Alternatively, working capital provided from (used in) operations can be determined by starting with income before extraordinary items and adding charges not requiring an outlay of working capital and subtracting credits not generating working capital. Income before extraordinary items is based on accrual accounting and therefore does not represent working capital provided from (used in) operations; hence, it is adjusted for non-working-capital items to reflect working capital provided from (used in) operations. That is, income before extraordinary items is reduced by certain charges that do not decrease working capital (depreciation, amortization of intangibles, bond-discount amortization, loss on sale of long-lived assets, decreases in deferred charges, and increases in deferred credits), and increased by certain credits that do not increase working capital (bond-premium amortization, gain on sale of long-lived assets, increases in deferred charges, and decreases in deferred credits). Consequently, working capital provided from operations, based on the data above, can also be determined as follows:

[5]See Glenn L. Johnson, "Funds-Flow Equation," *The Accounting Review* (July 1966), pp. 510–17.

$$\begin{array}{lclclcl} \textbf{Working capital provided from operations} & = & \textbf{Income before extraordinary items} & + & \textbf{Charges not requiring an outlay of working capital} & - & \textbf{Credits not generating working capital} \\ \$74{,}500 & = & \$62{,}000 & + & \left(\begin{array}{c}\$10{,}000 + \$1{,}000 \\ + \$600 + \$1{,}000\end{array}\right) & - & \$100 \end{array}$$

Consistent with *Opinion No. 19,* working capital provided from (used in) operations would be reported in the statement of changes in financial position as follows:

Working capital provided from operations:		
Income before extraordinary items		$62,000
Add charges not requiring an outlay of working capital:		
Depreciation	$10,000	
Amortization of goodwill	1,000	
Loss on sale of equipment	600	
Loss on bond redemption	1,000	
	$12,600	
Deduct credits not generating working capital:		
Amortization of bond premium	100	12,500
Working capital provided from operations for period, exclusive of extraordinary items		$74,500

Note that the $100 bond-premium amortization is subtracted from income before extraordinary items. The reason for this is that the actual bond interest paid is $500, which is a reduction of working capital, but the bond-interest expense is only $400 because of the bond-premium amortization. Hence, in terms of working capital, income before extraordinary items is too high by $100 and must be reduced.

Working capital provided from (used in) operations can also be determined by starting with net income and adjusting for non-working-capital items. The basic difference between starting with net income instead of income before extraordinary items is that the former includes non-working-capital gains and losses from extraordinary items that must be eliminated. This is demonstrated as follows:

$$\begin{array}{lclclcl} \textbf{Working capital provided from operations} & = & \textbf{Net income} & + & \textbf{Losses on extraordinary items not requiring an outlay of working capital} & - & \textbf{Gains on extraordinary items not generating working capital} \\ & & & + & \textbf{Charges not requiring an outlay of working capital} & - & \textbf{Credits not generating working capital} \\ \$74{,}500 & = & \$60{,}200 + \$1{,}800 - 0 & & & & \\ & & + (\$10{,}000 + \$1{,}000 + \$600 + \$1{,}000) - \$100 & & & & \end{array}$$

ILLUSTRATION OF CASH FROM OPERATIONS: In determining cash provided from (used in) operations, the sources of cash inflow are cash sales and collections on accounts receivable arising from sales on account. Uses of cash flow are cash paid for inventory and cash paid for expenses. Consequently, cash provided from (used in) operations can be determined by starting with cash collections from customers (including cash sales) and subtracting cash expenses. Using the data on pages 577 and 578, cash provided from operations is $63,500, shown as follows:

Cash provided from operations	=	**Collections from customers**	–	**Cash paid for inventory purchases**	–	**Expenses paid for in cash**
$63,500	=	**$230,000**	–	**$125,000**	–	**[$15,000 + $26,000 + ($100 + $400)]**

where:

Collections from customers	=	**Net sales**	±	**Add decrease or subtract increase in accounts receivable**
$230,000	=	**$250,000**	–	**$20,000**
Purchases	=	**Cost of goods sold**	±	**Add increase or subtract decrease in inventory**
$130,000	=	**$140,000**	–	**$10,000**
Cash paid for inventory purchases	=	**Purchases**	±	**Add decrease or subtract increase in accounts payable**
$125,000	=	**$130,000**	–	**$5,000**
Cash paid for accrued expenses	=	**Accrued expense**	±	**Add decrease or subtract increase in related accrued liability**
$26,000	=	**$20,000**	+	**$6,000**
Cash paid for prepayments	=	**Operating expense**	±	**Add increase or subtract decrease in related short-term prepayment**
0	=	**0**	±	**0**

Alternatively, cash provided from (used in) operations can be determined by starting with income before extraordinary items and adding (subtracting) items not requiring (generating) cash. Included in the latter are non-working-capital, and therefore noncash, expenses (depreciation, bond-discount amortization, and the like) previously discussed and, in addition, net changes in individual current assets and current liabilities related to operations. These net changes, along with noncash expenses, are added to and subtracted from income before extraordinary items, to convert it from an accrual basis to a cash basis.

The net changes in working-capital elements that are *added* to income before extraordinary items (or net income, if there are no extraordinary items) are given below, along with explanations for the underlying rationale for so doing:

Increase in accounts payable. The cash paid for inventory during the period was less than the cost of goods sold charged against revenue in determining income for the period by the amount of the net increase in accounts payable. Consequently, the net increase is added to income to adjust it to reflect cash paid during the period for inventory purchased.

Increase in accrued expenses. The cash paid for the expenses (such as wages paid) during the period was less than the expenses (such as wage expense) charged against revenue in determining income for the period by the amount of the net increase in the related current payables (such as wages payable). Hence, the net increase is added to income to adjust it to reflect the cash paid during the period for the expense.

Decrease in current prepayments. The cash paid for the prepayments (such as prepaid insurance) during the period was less than the expenses (such as expired insurance) charged against revenue in determining income for the period by the amount of the net decrease in prepayments. Thus, the net decrease is added to income to adjust it to reflect the cash paid during the period for the prepayments.

Decrease in accounts receivable. The cash received during the period for goods and services sold was greater than the revenue recognized in determining income for the period by the amount of the net decrease in accounts receivable. Consequently, the net decrease is added to income to adjust it to reflect cash collected from customers during the period.

Decrease in inventory. Inventory purchases during the period were less than the cost of goods sold charged against revenue in determining income for the period by the amount of the net decrease in inventory. Hence, the net decrease is added to income to adjust it to reflect inventory purchases during the period. Note that the net change in inventory and the net change in accounts payable are, in effect, combination adjustments, since the former adjusts income to reflect inventory purchases and the latter adjusts the purchases reflected in income to cash paid during the period for inventory purchases.

The net changes in working-capital elements that are *subtracted* from income before extraordinary items (or net income when there are no extraordinary items) are the opposite of those given above for additions to income, with the same type, but opposite, rationale. The net changes during the period that are subtracted include a decrease in accounts payable, a decrease in accrued expenses, an increase in current prepayments, and an increase in inventory.

Assuming the data on pages 577 and 578, cash provided from operations would again be $63,500 (as previously shown on page 580), calculated as follows:

Cash provided from operations	=	**Income before extraordinary items**	+	**Charges not requiring an outlay of cash**	−	**Credits not generating cash**
	±	**Add net increase or subtract net decrease in accounts payable**	±	**Add net increase or subtract net decrease in accrued expenses**		
	±	**Add net decrease or subtract net increase in current prepayments**	±	**Add net decrease or subtract net increase in accounts receivable**		

Add net decrease or
± subtract net increase
in inventory

$63,500 = $62,000 + ($10,000 + $1,000 + $600 + $1,000)
− $100 + $5,000 − $6,000 + 0 − $20,000 + $10,000

Consistent with *Opinion No. 19,* cash provided from (used in) operations would be reported as the first item in the statement of changes in financial position, as follows:

Cash provided from operations:		
Income before extraordinary items		$62,000
Add charges not requiring an outlay of cash:		
Depreciation	$10,000	
Amortization of goodwill	1,000	
Loss on sale of equipment	600	
Loss on bond redemption	1,000	
Increase in accounts payable	5,000	
Decrease in inventory	10,000	27,600
		$89,600
Deduct credits not generating cash:		
Amortization of bond premium	$ 100	
Increase in accounts receivable	20,000	
Decrease in accrued liabilities	6,000	26,100
Cash provided from operations for period, exclusive of extraordinary items		$63,500

Extraordinary items. As discussed in Chapter 4, current accounting thinking is that extraordinary items are rare and are generally limited to acts of God: losses from tornadoes, hurricanes, floods, and the like. Because such losses do not affect cash or working capital, they do not need to be reported in the statement of changes in financial position. Also, because the statement of changes in financial position begins with income before extraordinary items, which is before such losses, there is no adjustment to income before extraordinary items for such losses to derive cash or working capital provided from operations (they do not have to be added back).

For example, the income statement data on page 578 show an extraordinary loss on flood damage of $1,800. This $1,800 loss has no effect on cash or working capital and should *not* be reported as a use of cash or working capital. Also, since the statement of changes in financial position would usually begin with the income before extraordinary item of $62,000, which is before the $1,800 extraordinary loss, there is *no* adding back of the $1,800 to the $62,000 to derive cash or working capital from operations.

On the other hand, per *Opinion No. 11,* tax carry-forwards on prior years' operating losses are reported as extraordinary items (see Chapter 24). In terms of cash or working capital, this means that income tax expense, based on accrual accounting, is too high and income before extraordinary items is too low by the amount of the tax carry-forward. Thus, the tax carry-forward could be treated as an adjustment to income before extraordinary items by adding it back to derive cash (also the net change in taxes payable would be an adjustment of income before extraordinary items) or working capital provided from operations.

Other sources of cash or working capital. In addition to cash or working capital provided from operations, other sources of cash or working capital would be individually reported in the statement of changes in financial position. Examples of such sources would be proceeds (cash or working capital) received during the current period from the sale of investments, sale of plant and equipment, issuances of long-term notes payable, issuance of bonds payable, issuance of preferred stock, and issuance of common stock. In other words, sources of cash or working capital are provided by decreases in noncash or noncurrent assets, increases in liabilities or noncurrent liabilities, and increases in owners' equity; however, not all such decreases or increases affect cash or working capital. On the other hand, decreases in current assets (such as inventory) or increases in current liabilities (such as accounts payable) would not be included, because they would be shown in the cash provided from (used in) operations or in the separate schedule of changes in working-capital elements when working capital provided from (used in) operations is reported.

Sales of long-lived assets are *not* considered, in current accounting thinking, to be extraordinary; hence, any resulting gains or losses are included in the income statement before income before extraordinary items (or net income if there are no extraordinary items). Consequently, as previously explained and illustrated, such gains or losses are reported in the statement of changes in financial position as adjustments of income before extraordinary items in order to derive cash or working capital provided from (used in) operations. Thus, it is the proceeds received from the sale, not the gains or losses, that are reported in the statement of changes in financial position as a source of cash or working capital.

For example, assume that equipment with an original cost of $10,000 and accumulated depreciation to date of $7,000 was sold for $2,400 during the current period, which would result in a book loss of $600 [$2,400 – ($10,000 – $7,000)], as illustrated in the entry below:

Cash	2,400	
Loss on sale of equipment	600	
Accumulated depreciation—Equipment	7,000	
Equipment		10,000

The $2,400 would be reported as a source of cash or working capital, not the $600, and the $600 would be reported as an adjustment to income before extraordinary items in deriving cash or working capital provided from (used in) operations.

If bonds are issued at a premium or a discount during the current period, the proceeds received are, respectively, greater or less than the change in bonds payable, assuming separate bond premium or discount accounts. For example, if a $10,000 bond was issued at 98, the cash received would be $9,800, as summarized in the entry at the top of page 584, and this is the amount reported in the statement of changes in financial position, not the $10,000.

Cash	9,800	
Bond discount	200	
Bonds payable		10,000

Similarly, if common stock (or preferred stock) is issued at a price above par (or stated value of no-par stock), it is the amount received, not the change in common stock at par, that is reported in the statement of changes in financial position. For example, if a $100,000 par value common-stock issue was sold for $105,000, as summarized in the entry below, the $105,000, not the $100,000, would be reported in the statement of changes in financial position.

Cash	105,000	
Common stock		100,000
Capital in excess of par value		5,000

Similar to the issue of capital stock at a price above par is the resale of treasury stock at a price above cost. For example, if treasury stock was acquired at a cost of $10,000 and then sold during the current period for $12,000, as summarized in the entry below, it is the $12,000, not the $10,000 change in treasury stock, that would be reported in the statement of changes in financial position.

Cash	12,000	
Treasury stock		10,000
Capital in excess of par value		2,000

Although infrequent and not always affecting cash or working capital, prior-period adjustments can be a source of cash or working capital. For example, if a legal suit initiated several years ago is settled favorably during the current period for $30,000, as summarized by the entry below, the $30,000 is a source of cash or working capital.

Cash	30,000	
Retained earnings (prior-period adjustment)		30,000

Such sources as those given above can be reported in the statement of changes in financial position as follows:

Sources of financial resources:		
Cash (or working capital) provided from operations [Details as previously illustrated]		$ 63,500
Cash (or working capital) provided from other sources:		
Sale of equipment	$ 2,400	
Issuance of bonds	9,800	
Issuance of common stock	105,000	
Sale of treasury stock	12,000	
Favorable settlement of prior-period lawsuit (net of applicable taxes of $12,000)	18,000	$147,200

Other uses of cash or working capital. In addition to cash or working capital used in operations, other uses of cash or working capital are individually reported in the statement of changes in financial position. Examples of such uses would be outlays (cash or working capital) during the current period to make investments, purchase plant and equipment, retire long-term debt, retire common stock, retire preferred stock, repurchase common stock (treasury stock), and to pay or declare cash dividends. In other words, uses of cash or working capital are the result of increases in noncash or noncurrent assets, decreases in liabilities or noncurrent liabilities, and decreases in owners' equity; however, not all such increases or decreases affect cash or working capital. On the other hand, purchases of current assets (such as temporary investments, inventory, and prepayments) and payments of current liabilities (such as accounts payable and accrued liabilities) would not be included, because they would be shown in the cash provided from (used in) operations or in the separate schedule of changes in working capital elements when working capital provided from (used in) operations is reported.

If bonds payable are retired during the current period by paying a call premium, the actual outlay would be greater than the decrease in bonds payable. For example, if $10,000 of bonds payable were retired by paying a $1,000 call premium, the $11,000 outlay, as summarized in the entry below, would be reported in the statement of changes in financial position, not the $10,000 decline in bonds. Note that the $1,000 loss on bond redemption does not affect cash or working capital, but as previously illustrated, is an adjustment of income to derive cash or working capital provided from (used in) operations.

Bonds payable..	10,000	
Loss on bond redemption..............................	1,000	
Cash		11,000

Similarly, if common stock is retired by paying an amount in excess of par value (or stated value of no-par stock), the outlay would be greater than the decline in common stock. For example, if $20,000 par value common stock were retired by paying $25,000 cash, the $25,000 outlay, as summarized in the entry below, would be reported in the statement of changes in financial position, not the $20,000 decline in common stock.

Common stock..	20,000	
Additional paid-in capital	5,000	
Cash		25,000

The reporting of cash dividends in the statement of changes in financial position depends on whether a cash or working-capital format is used. If a cash format is used, then only dividends paid during the current period would be reported as a use of cash in the statement. If a working-capital format is used, then only dividends declared during the current period would be reported as a use of working capital in the statement. That is, dividends declared increase the current-liability dividends payable, which is a reduction of working capital, and is therefore a use of working capital. However, the actual payment of the dividend does not affect the working-capital pool (unless both declared and paid in the current period), since both the current-asset cash and the current-liability dividends payable are reduced.

For example, assume that cash dividends of $15,000 are declared and $10,000 dividends paid during the current period. With a working-capital format, $15,000 would be reported in the statement of changes in financial position as a use of working capital. With a cash format, $10,000 would be reported in the statement as a use of cash. The effect of cash dividends is summarized as follows:

				Use of Cash	Use of Working Capital
Declaration:	Retained earnings	15,000			
	Dividends payable...........		15,000		$15,000
Payment:	Dividends payable	10,000			
	Cash...........................		10,000	$10,000	

Although infrequent and not always affecting cash or working capital, prior-period adjustments can be a use of cash or working capital. For example, if a legal suit initiated several years ago is settled unfavorably during the current period for $40,000, as summarized by the entry below, the $40,000 is a use of cash or working capital.

Retained earnings (prior-period adjustment)	40,000	
Cash		40,000

Such uses as those given above can be reported in the statement of changes in financial position as follows:

Cash (or working capital) applied:		
Retirement of bonds payable....................	$11,000	
Retirement of common stock....................	25,000	
Dividends on common stock	10,000	
Unfavorable legal settlement of prior-period lawsuit (net of applicable taxes of $16,000)...	24,000	$70,000

Noncash investing and financing transactions. Up to this point, the sources and uses of financial resources (changes in assets and equities) have been expressed in terms of changes in cash or working capital, and can be summarized as follows:

Sources of cash or working capital:
- Provided from operations
- Provided from sale of long-lived assets (investments, plant, and equipment)
- Provided from issuing long-term debt
- Provided from issuing capital stock (common or preferred)
- Provided from sale of treasury stock

Uses of cash or working capital:
- Used in operations
- Used to acquire long-lived assets
- Used to retire long-term debt
- Used to retire capital stock
- Used to reacquire capital stock (treasury stock)
- Used to pay or declare cash dividends on capital stock

It is important to note that most external investing and financing transactions affect working capital. For example, external operating transactions during the current period give rise to revenue and expenses that affect working capital and ultimately cash. Nonoperating, external financing and investing transactions during the current period normally affect cash and therefore working capital. Because most external financing and investing transactions increase or decrease working capital or cash, most changes in assets and equities can be expressed in terms of working capital or cash and therefore make up most of the sources and uses of financial resources presented in the statement of changes in financial position.

On the other hand, it is one thing to express *most* significant changes in financial position in terms of working capital or cash, and it is another thing to express *all* significant changes in financial position in terms of working capital or cash. If the statement of changes in financial position were based on a narrow concept of working capital or cash, only the sources and uses of working capital or cash summarized above would be presented. However, as previously discussed, *Opinion No. 19* states that the statement should be based on a broad concept, embracing all significant changes in assets and equities, regardless of whether cash or working capital is affected. That is, significant, external noncash or non-working-capital changes in assets and equities should also be presented in the statement in order to provide a complete picture of changes in financial position between balance-sheet dates.

What are significant, external noncash or non-working-capital changes in assets and equities? Examples would include long-lived assets acquired in exchange for debt or capital stock, bonds or preferred stock converted into common stock, long-lived assets (such as investments) exchanged for other long-lived assets (such as land), debt retired in exchange for capital stock, or assets received as gifts.

As a specific example, assume that a company acquires land with a fair market value of $40,000 by issuing $40,000 no-par common stock in exchange for the land. As shown by the entry below, there is no $40,000 decrease in cash (or working capital) to acquire the land, and there is no $40,000 increase in cash (or working capital) by issuing common stock. There is a zero effect on cash, yet this is a significant external investing (land acquired) and financing (common stock issued) transaction.

Land	40,000	
Common stock		40,000

In order to report such significant, external noncash (non-working-capital) transactions in the statement of changes in financial position per *Opinion No. 19,* such transactions can be viewed hypothetically as consisting of two parts: one part the use and the other part the source of financial resources. Thus, the example of land acquired by issuing common stock could be viewed as shown below:

Cash	40,000	
Common stock		40,000
Land	40,000	
Cash		40,000

Note that sources equal uses, so that the entries are "in and out," because both the financing and investing parts of the transaction are reported.

Assuming a cash format, the significant, external noncash transaction can be reported in the statement of changes in financial position as follows:

VATTER COMPANY
Statement of Changes in Financial Position
For the Year Ended December 31, 19XX

Sources of financial resources:		
Cash provided from operations:		
[Details as previously illustrated]	$ 63,500	
Cash provided from other sources:		
[Details as previously illustrated]	147,200	
Financial resources provided, not affecting cash:		
Common stock issued to acquire land	40,000	
Total financial resources provided for period		$250,700
Uses of financial resources:		
Cash applied:		
[Details as previously illustrated]	$ 70,000	
Financial resources applied, not affecting cash:		
Land acquired by issuing common stock	40,000	
Total financial resources applied for period		110,000
Increase in financial resources (cash) for period		$140,700

Assuming a working-capital format, the exchange of common stock for land would be reported in a complete statement of changes in financial position as follows:

VATTER COMPANY
Statement of Changes in Financial Position
For the Year Ended December 31, 19XX

Sources of financial resources:			
Working capital provided from operations:			
Income before extraordinary items		$ 62,000	
Add charges not requiring an outlay of working capital:			
Depreciation	$ 10,000		
Amortization of goodwill	1,000		
Loss on sale of equipment	600		
Loss on bond redemption	1,000	12,600	
		$ 74,600	
Deduct credit not generating working capital:			
Bond premium amortization		100	
Working capital provided from operations for period, exclusive of extraordinary item		$ 74,500	
Other sources of working capital:			
Sale of equipment	$ 2,400		
Issuance of bonds	9,800		
Issuance of common stock	105,000		
Sale of treasury stock	12,000		
Favorable legal settlement of prior-period lawsuit (net of applicable taxes of $12,000)	18,000	147,200	
Financial resources provided, not affecting working capital:			
Common stock issued to acquire land		40,000	
Total financial resources provided for period			$261,700

Uses of financial resources:			
Working capital applied:			
Retirement of bonds payable	$ 11,000		
Retirement of common stock	25,000		
Dividends declared on common stock	15,000		
Unfavorable legal settlement of prior-period lawsuit (net of applicable taxes of $16,000)	24,000	$ 75,000	
Financial resources applied, not affecting working capital:			
Land acquired by issuing common stock		40,000	
Total financial resources applied			115,000
Increase in financial resources (working capital) for period			$146,700

Preparation of the statement. There are two basic methods in the preparation of the statement of changes in financial position: the T-account method and the work-sheet method. The T-account method, developed by Professor William J. Vatter, has the advantage of being clear and easy to understand, because it is a logical method that builds upon reconstructing and summarizing the transactions made during the period that affected financial resources. The work-sheet method is the traditional method and has the advantage of preserving working papers in a form that most accountants are familiar with in using for future reference, such as in an audit. Also, some accountants prefer to use the work-sheet method when there are numerous adjustments and complications, although it can be argued that the T-account method can handle them just as well.

It should be pointed out that the T-account method and the work-sheet method are merely *aids* in the preparation of the statement of changes in financial position. They are not required and they are not part of the formal journals and ledgers of a company. Thus, instead of using either method, an accountant may prepare the statement of changes in financial position by merely making supplementary computations, by using equations, and the like.

We now turn to a discussion and illustration of a modified version of Vatter's T-account method, which will then be followed by a presentation of a work-sheet method that is consistent with the T-account method.

T-account method. The statement of changes in financial position shows the changes in assets and equities between two balance-sheet dates; hence, comparative balance sheets show the beginning balance, ending balance, and net change in each asset and equity. However, the net change shown in comparative balance sheets does not show the individual increases and decreases in assets and equities, which are reported in the statement of changes in financial position.

Each asset and equity account reported in comparative balance sheets can be viewed as having a beginning balance (from last year's balance sheet) and an ending balance (from current year's balance sheet). If the increase (or decrease) in the asset or equity is known, then given the beginning and ending balances, the decrease (or increase) can be determined, because of the following relationship of each balance-sheet account:

Beginning balance of account + **Increase in account** − **Decrease in account** = **Ending balance of account**

Beginning balance of account + **Increase in account** = **Ending balance in account** + **Decrease in account**

For example, if land had a beginning balance of $10,000 and an ending balance of $15,000, and it was known that land costing $3,000 was sold, it is easily deduced that land must have been acquired for $8,000, as shown below:

$10,000 + Increase = $15,000 + $3,000

Increase = $8,000

Similarly, if bonds payable had a beginning balance of $50,000 and an ending balance of $20,000, and it was known that bonds issued at par during the period amounted to $10,000, it is easily seen that $40,000 in bonds were retired:

$50,000 + $10,000 = $20,000 + Decrease

Decrease = $40,000

The relationship that beginning balance plus increases equals ending balance plus decreases can also be viewed in terms of T-accounts. For asset accounts, the beginning balance (B) and increases would be debits, and the ending balance (E) and decreases would be credits, and would be just the opposite for equity accounts. The T-accounts for the two examples above would be as follows:

Land

B	10,000	E	15,000
	?		3,000
			18,000

Bonds Payable

E	20,000	B	50,000
	?		10,000
			60,000

Land

B	10,000	E	15,000
	8,000		3,000
	18,000		18,000

Bonds Payable

E	20,000	B	50,000
	40,000		10,000
	60,000		60,000

The T-account method is based on the idea that cash (working capital) is changed only if a noncash (noncurrent) account changes. By analyzing the changes in the noncash (noncurrent) accounts, the changes in cash (working capital) can be determined. Therefore, by setting up T-accounts for the noncash (noncurrent) asset and equity accounts, the changes in these accounts can be analyzed to determine whether there has been a change in cash (working capital), and if so, what the causes are of the change in cash (working capital). These causes of changes in cash (working capital) that are traced from the changes in the noncash (non-current) T-accounts are the basis for preparing the formal statement of changes in financial position under the T-account method.

The steps in the T-account method can be summarized as follows:

(1) Decide whether a cash or working-capital format is to be used.

T-account, which puts the latter in balance. This ending balance is the cash (working capital) provided from or used in operations.

(2) If a working-capital format is to be used, prepare a schedule of changes in working-capital elements, which should be formally reported per *Opinion No. 19,* that indicates the net increase or decrease in working capital for the period that is reconciled in the statement of changes in financial position. If a cash format is used, no separate schedule of working-capital elements is needed.

(3) Set up a large T-account for cash (or working capital) and post beginning and ending balances. The beginning and ending balances can be obtained from the cash account in the ledger or from comparative balance sheets. Beginning and ending working-capital balances are obtained from the schedule of working-capital changes constructed in (2).

(4) Set up a large T-account for cash (or working capital) from operations. This is the only T-account that does not have any beginning or ending balances posted to it, since it includes only income adjustments.

(5) Set up T-accounts for all noncash (non-working-capital) assets and equities, and post beginning and ending balances from comparative balance sheets or from the ledger.

(6) Reconstruct summary entries of the transactions that were made during the current period and post to the T-accounts. Number the entries for ease in locating errors.

(a) Make the first entry in the T-accounts by debiting the cash (or working capital) from operations T-account and crediting the retained earnings T-account for net income (or income before extraordinary items, if extraordinary items exist). The opposite would be done for a net loss.

(b) Make entries to the cash (or working capital) from operations T-account for the noncash (non-working-capital) items that are needed to adjust net income (or income before extraordinary items) to cash (working capital) provided from or used in operations. The data needed for these entries are obtained from the accounting records.

(c) The other summary entries are reconstructed from the accounting records and posted to the T-accounts. All entries that affect cash (or working capital) are posted to the cash (working-capital) T-account. Entries that have no effect on cash (or working capital), other than those mentioned in (d) below, are posted to the T-accounts for completeness, since this serves as a check in balancing all the T-accounts.

(d) All significant, external noncash (non-working-capital) transactions are reconstructed and posted on an "in and out" basis to the cash (working capital) T-account.

(e) When all the T-accounts, other than Cash (or Working Capital) and Cash (or Working Capital) from Operations, are in balance, the ending balance in the cash (working capital) from operations T-account is closed to the cash (working-capital)

(7) All entries that are made to the cash (working capital) from operations T-account are labeled as to their cause. Debits to the account include net income (or income before extraordinary items, if extraordinary items exist) and net-income adjustments for such noncash (non-working-capital) charges as depreciation, bond-discount amortization, amortization of intangibles, loss on sale of long-lived assets, loss on bond retirement, and the like. Credits to the account are net-income adjustments for such noncash (non-working-capital) credits as bond-premium amortization, gain on sale of long-lived assets, gain on bond retirement, and the like. If there is a net loss (or loss before extraordinary items) instead of net income, this would be credited to the account and the subsequent debits and credits would be for noncash (non-working-capital) adjustments to the net loss to convert it to cash (working capital) provided or used in operations. An ending debit balance in the cash (working capital) from operations T-account represents cash (working capital) provided from operations, and is closed by debiting the cash (working-capital) T-account and crediting the cash (working capital) from operations T-account. The opposite would be done for an ending credit balance, which represents cash (working capital) used in operations.

(8) All entries that are made to the cash (working-capital) T-account are labeled as to their cause. Debits to the account represent sources of cash (or working capital) and include cash (working capital) provided from operations; proceeds from incurring long-term liabilities, issuing common stock, selling treasury stock, selling long-lived assets and the like; and significant, external noncash (non-working-capital) transactions such as common stock issued for land, land exchanged for equipment, common stock issued to retire preferred stock, and the like. Credits to the account represent uses of cash (or working capital) and include cash (working capital) used in operations; outlays to acquire long-lived assets, retire long-term liabilities, retire common stock, acquire treasury stock, and the like; and significant, external noncash (non-working-capital) transactions such as land acquired by issuing common stock, equipment acquired in exchange for land, preferred stock retired by issuing common stock, and the like.

(9) When all the T-accounts are in balance, the statement of changes in financial position can be prepared directly from the labeled entries in the cash (working-capital) T-account, making sure it is in good form. The details for reporting cash (working capital) provided from operations are obtained from the labeled entries in the cash (working capital) from operations T-account.

ILLUSTRATION: In Chapter 4, an illustrative statement of income and retained earnings, and in Chapter 5, illustrative comparative balance sheets for Kansas Company, were presented. These statements, as reproduced on pages 593 and 594, and additional data (assumed to be obtained from the accounting records of

KANSAS COMPANY
Comparative Balance Sheets
December 31, 19+5 and 19+4

Assets		19+5		19+4
Current assets:				
Cash		$ 18,000		$ 20,000
Marketable securities—at cost (market, $1,050)		1,000		—
Accounts receivable	$ 60,000		$ 30,000	
Less allowance for uncollectibles	8,000	52,000	10,000	20,000
Inventory—FIFO cost		110,000		30,000
Prepayments		14,900		19,000
Total current assets		$195,900		$ 89,000
Long-term investments:				
Investment in bonds—at cost		$ 20,000		$ 10,000
Property, plant, and equipment:				
Land		$ 26,000		—
Building	$400,000		$400,000	
Less accumulated depreciation	160,000	240,000	140,000	$260,000
Equipment	$300,000		$350,000	
Less accumulated depreciation	120,000	180,000	105,000	245,000
Total property, plant, and equipment		$446,000		$505,000
Total assets		$661,900		$604,000

Equities		19+5		19+4
Current liabilities:				
Accounts payable		$ 35,400		$ 46,000
Notes payable		40,000		25,000
Taxes payable		61,600		50,000
Total current liabilities		$137,000		$121,000
Long-term liabilities:				
Bonds payable—7% interest, due December 31, 19xx	$100,000		$100,000	
Bond premium	7,500		8,000	
Total long-term liabilities		$107,500		$108,000
Stockholders' equity:				
Preferred stock		—		$150,000
Common stock—$10 par value; authorized, 100,000 shares; issued and outstanding, 25,000 shares		$250,000		50,000
Retained earnings		167,400		175,000
Total stockholders' equity		$417,400		$375,000
Total equities		$661,900		$604,000

KANSAS COMPANY
Statement of Income and Retained Earnings
For the Year Ended December 31, 19+5

Net sales			$840,000
Cost of goods sold			520,000
Gross margin			$320,000
Operating expenses:			
Selling expense		$ 80,000	
General and administrative expense (Note A)		85,100	165,100
Net operating income			$154,900
Nonoperating items:			
Add: Interest revenue	$1,600		
Gain on sale of equipment (Note B)	8,000	$ 9,600	
Deduct: Interest expense (Note C)	$6,500		
Loss on sale of bond investment (Note D)	4,000	10,500	900
Income before taxes			$154,000
Federal income taxes			61,600
Net income			$ 92,400
Retained earnings at beginning of year:			
As previously reported		$175,000	
Deduct prior-period adjustment for additional income taxes settled in 19+5 (Note E)		20,000	
As restated			155,000
			$247,400
Deduct: Common stock dividends—cash		$ 30,000	
Common stock dividends—stock		50,000	80,000
Retained earnings at end of year			$167,400
Earnings per common share			$ 6.72

Note A: Includes depreciation expense of $20,000 on building and $35,000 on equipment.

Note B: During 19+5 Kansas Company sold equipment with a net book amount of $30,000 for $38,000, which resulted in an $8,000 gain from sale of equipment.

Note C: Includes $500 bond premium amortization.

Note D: During 19+5 Kansas Company sold some of its bond investments originally costing $15,000 for $11,000, which resulted in a $4,000 loss on sale of investments.

Note E: The balance of retained earnings at December 31, 19+4 has been restated from amounts previously reported to reflect a retroactive charge of $20,000 for additional income taxes settled in 19+5. This amount is the result of expenses deducted for income tax purposes during 19+3 that were not allowed in the tax litigation settled in 19+5. Net income of $70,000 ($7.00 per share) as previously reported for 19+3 should be restated to $50,000 ($5.00 per share).

Kansas Company) presented below serve as the data base needed to prepare the statement of changes in financial position. Note, however, that the additional data could have been deduced from the T-accounts, given the comparative balance sheets, the statement of income and retained earnings, and the notes thereto.

Additional data:

Bond-premium amortization was $500.
Equipment originally costing $50,000 with accumulated depreciation of $20,000 was sold for $38,000.
Bond investment originally costing $15,000 was sold for $11,000.
There was a prior-period adjustment that resulted from the unfavorable settlement during 19+5 of an income tax suit initiated in 19+3.
Dividends declared and paid on common stock during 19+5 were $30,000.
Bonds were acquired as a long-term investment at a cost of $25,000.
Land was acquired for $26,000.
Preferred stock of $150,000 was retired by issuing common stock of $150,000.
There was a common-stock (not cash) dividend of $50,000.

CASH FORMAT: Assuming that a cash format is to be used, a large T-account for cash is set up, and the beginning balance of $20,000 (see the 19+4 balance sheet) and the ending balance of $18,000 (see the 19+5 balance sheet) are posted to the cash T-account, as shown on page 596. (Note that this $2,000 decline in cash during 19+5 will be explained by the statement of changes of financial position.) T-accounts are set up for each noncash asset and equity account, and beginning and ending balances (see the comparative balance sheets) are posted to the T-accounts. Summary entries for the year are reconstructed and posted to the T-accounts until they are in balance. The entries are numbered, and every time an entry affects cash, the debit or credit to cash is labeled as to the cause.

In order to explain the numbered entries to the T-accounts shown on pages 596 and 597, the entries are given below in general journal form and then explained:

(1) Entry:

Cash from operations (Net income)	92,400	
Retained earnings		92,400

Analysis: To avoid the detail of cash revenues and expenses, accountants employ a shortcut by starting with the net income (or income before extraordinary items, if extraordinary items exist) reported in the income statement and then in subsequent entries adjust it to reflect cash provided from (used in) operations. Retained Earnings is obviously credited, since, as a summary entry, it reflects the closing process whereby income increases retained earnings.

(2) Entry:

Cash from operations (depreciation)	55,000	
Accumulated depreciation—Building		20,000
Accumulated depreciation—Equipment		35,000

Cash

(Sources)		(Uses)	
Beginning balance	20,000	Ending balance	18,000
(11) Proceeds from sale of equipment	38,000	(13) Outlay for additional income taxes settled in 19+5—prior-period adjustment	20,000
(12) Proceeds from sale of bond investment	11,000	(14) Outlay for dividends on common stock	30,000
(17) Common stock issued to retire preferred stock	150,000	(15) Outlay for bond investment	25,000
(a) Cash provided from operations	50,000	(16) Outlay to purchase land	26,000
		(17) Preferred stock retired by issuing common stock	150,000
	269,000		269,000

Cash From Operations

(Net income and net income adjustments for noncash charges)		(Net income adjustments for noncash credits)	
(1) Net income	92,400	(3) Bond-premium amortization	500
(2) Depreciation	55,000	(4) Increase in marketable securities	1,000
(7) Decrease in prepayments	4,100	(5) Increase in accounts receivable	32,000
(9) Increase in notes payable	15,000	(6) Increase in inventory	80,000
(10) Increase in taxes payable	11,600	(8) Decrease in accounts payable	10,600
(12) Loss on sale of bond investment	4,000	(11) Gain on sale of equipment	8,000
		(a) Balance	50,000
	182,100		182,100

Marketable Securities

B	—	E	1,000
(4)	1,000		
	1,000		1,000

Net Accounts Receivable

B	20,000	E	52,000
(5)	32,000		
	52,000		52,000

Inventory

B	30,000	E	110,000
(6)	80,000		
	110,000		110,000

Prepayments

B	19,000	E	14,900
		(7)	4,100
	19,000		19,000

Bond Investment

B	10,000	E	20,000
(15)	25,000	(12)	15,000
	35,000		35,000

Land

B	—	E	26,000
(16)	26,000		
	26,000		26,000

Building

B	400,000	E	400,000

Acc. Depr.—Bldg.

E	160,000	B	140,000
		(2)	20,000
	160,000		160,000

Equipment

B	350,000	E	300,000
		(11)	50,000
	350,000		350,000

Acc. Depr.—Equip.

E	120,000	B	105,000
(11)	20,000	(2)	35,000
	140,000		140,000

Accounts Payable

E	35,400	B	46,000
(8)	10,600		
	46,000		46,000

Notes Payable

E	40,000	B	25,000
		(9)	15,000
	40,000		40,000

Taxes Payable

E	61,600	B	50,000
		(10)	11,600
	61,600		61,600

Bonds Payable

E	100,000	B	100,000

Bond Premium

E	7,500	B	8,000
(3)	500		
	8,000		8,000

Preferred Stock

E	—	B	150,000
(17)	150,000		
	150,000		150,000

Common Stock

E	250,000	B	50,000
		(17)	150,000
		(18)	50,000
	250,000		250,000

Retained Earnings

E	167,400	B	175,000
(13)	20,000	(1)	92,400
(14)	30,000		
(18)	50,000		
	267,400		267,400

Analysis: Depreciation expense, which should be reported in the income statement (see Note A to the income statement), is debited to Cash from Operations not as a source of cash, but as an adjustment to net income that was previously debited to Cash from Operations. In terms of cash flow, net income is too low by $55,000 and is, in effect, corrected by debiting (adding to net income) Cash from Operations. Although depreciation is a legitimate expense for the income statement, as a cost allocation it does not require an outlay of cash. The cash outlay occurred when the building and equipment were originally acquired, not when they were depreciated. The credits to Accumulated Depreciation are merely reconstructing the original credits that were made to increase Accumulated Depreciation by the amount of periodic depreciation. Note that the $20,000 credit could have been deduced, since it balances the accumulated depreciation—building T-account.

(3) Entry:

Bond premium	500	
Cash from operations (bond-premium amortization)		500

Analysis: Bond-premium amortization is credited to Cash from Operations not as a use of cash, but as an adjustment to net income that was previously debited to Cash from Operations. In terms of cash flow, net income is too high by $500 and is, in effect, corrected by crediting (subtracting from net income) Cash from Operations. Bond-premium amortization correctly reduces periodic interest expense to be reported in the income statement; however, in terms of interest paid, the bond-interest expense is too low and net income is therefore too high by the amount of the amortization. The debit to Bond Premium merely reconstructs the original debit made to reduce Bond Premium by the amount of the amortization. Note that the $500 debit could have been deduced, since it balances the bond-premium T-account.

(4)–(10) Entries:

(4)	Marketable securities	1,000	
	Cash from operations (increase in marketable securities)		1,000
(5)	Accounts receivable	32,000	
	Cash from operations (increase in accounts receivable)		32,000
(6)	Inventory	80,000	
	Cash from operations (increase in inventory)		80,000
(7)	Cash from operations (decrease in prepayments)	4,100	
	Prepayments		4,100
(8)	Accounts payable	10,600	
	Cash from operations (decrease in accounts payable)		10,600

(9)	Cash from operations (increase in notes payable)	15,000	
	Notes payable		15,000
(10)	Cash from operations (increase in taxes payable)	11,600	
	Taxes payable		11,600

Analysis: The net increases and decreases in working-capital elements (as determined by the difference between beginning and ending balances in the T-accounts) are debited and credited to Cash from Operations in order to adjust net income to Cash from Operations. As previously illustrated and explained on pages 579–582, changes in current assets and current liabilities related to operations are reflected in the income statement via revenues and expenses. In order to convert revenues to cash collected from customers and expenses to cash paid for expenses, as reflected by cash provided from operations, the net changes in the working-capital elements are debited and credited to Cash from Operations. The offsetting debits and credits to Cash from Operations merely reconstruct the summary increases and decreases in the working-capital elements for the year. Note that these offsetting debits and credits are obtained directly from the current-asset (other than cash) and current-liability T-accounts and balance the accounts.

(11) Entry:

Cash (proceeds from sale of equipment)................	38,000	
Accumulated depreciation—Equipment	20,000	
Equipment		50,000
Cash from operations (gain on sale of equipment)...		8,000

Analysis: The entry is reconstructed as originally made except that Cash from Operations is credited for the gain on sale of equipment. In terms of cash flow, net income is too high by $8,000 and is, in effect, corrected by crediting (subtracting from net income) Cash from Operations. Thus, the $38,000 will be reported as a source of cash, but the $8,000 is an adjustment of net income, not a cash source. Also, note that the $20,000 debit can be deduced by analyzing the accumulated-depreciation T-account, since it takes a $20,000 debit to balance the account to $140,000. Similarly, the $50,000 credit can be deduced, since it is needed to balance the equipment T-account.

(12) Entry:

Cash (proceeds from sale of bond investment).......	11,000	
Cash from operations (loss on sale of bond investment).......................................	4,000	
Bond investment		15,000

Analysis: The $11,000 is a source of cash. The $4,000 loss, as reported in the income statement, reduces net income, but does not affect cash. In terms of cash flow, net income is too low by the amount of the $4,000 loss; hence, net income that was originally debited to Cash

From Operations is, in effect, corrected by debiting (adding to net income) Cash from Operations. The $15,000 credit merely reconstructs the original credit to reduce the asset.

(13) Entry:

Retained earnings (prior-period adjustment)	20,000	
Cash (settlement of income tax suit)		20,000

Analysis: The $20,000 is a use of cash during the current period to pay the settlement of an income tax suit arising from a prior period. The debit to Retained Earnings reflects the prior-period adjustment, as reported in the statement of income and retained earnings. The entry is reconstructed as made during the period.

(14) Entry:

Retained earnings	30,000	
Cash (dividends paid on common stock)		30,000

Analysis: The $30,000 dividends paid on common stock is a use of cash. The debit to Retained Earnings reflects the declaration of the dividends, and the credit to Cash reflects the payment of the dividends, since the dividends were both declared and paid during the current period. The entry reconstructs the end result of the original entry or entries, although other accounts (such as Dividends and Dividends Payable) may have been used during the year.

(15) Entry:

Bond investment	25,000	
Cash (investment in bonds)		25,000

Analysis: The $25,000 paid to acquire bonds for investment purposes is a use of cash. The entry reconstructs the original entry made. Note that the $25,000 debit could have been deduced, because it takes $25,000 to balance the debits to $35,000 in the bond-investment T-account.

(16) Entry:

Land	26,000	
Cash (purchase of land)		26,000

Analysis: The $26,000 paid to acquire land is a use of cash. The entry reconstructs the original entry made. Note that the $26,000 debit, as the balancing item, could have been deduced from the land T-account.

(17) Entry:

Preferred stock	150,000	
Cash (issue common stock to retire preferred stock)	150,000	
Common stock		150,000
Cash (retire preferred stock by issuing common stock)		150,000

Analysis: The original entry made during the year was a debit to Preferred Stock and a credit to Common Stock for $150,000; hence, there was no effect on Cash. However, because this was a significant change in equities that should be reported, the entry above is made "in and out" (Cash is both debited and credited for $150,000) in order that it will be included in the cash T-account and therefore included in the statement of changes in financial position as a source and use of financial resources. It is a significant, external noncash transaction.

(18) Entry:

Retained earnings (stock dividend)	50,000	
Common stock		50,000

Analysis: The entry reconstructs the original stock-dividend entry. The entry is not really needed because it does not affect cash and it is not considered significant enough to be included in the statement of changes in financial position; hence, it is *not* entered "in and out" similar to entry (17). The entry is made for completeness in order that all the T-accounts balance as an indicator that no entries were omitted.

(a) Entry:

Cash	50,000	
Cash from operations		50,000

Analysis: Up to this point, all the T-accounts, except for Cash and Cash from Operations, are in balance. This entry closes out the cash from operations T-account to the cash T-account, and puts the latter in balance. Since the $50,000 is the ending *debit* balance in the cash from operations T-account, it represents the cash provided from operations for the period. Since cash provided from operations is a source of cash, it is debited to the cash T-account. Note that the $50,000 is the result of starting with net income and then adjusting net income for noncash charges and credits to convert it to cash provided from operations, as shown in the cash from operations T-account and as summarized by the $50,000 debit to the cash T-account.

The formal statement of changes in financial position, using a cash format, can now be formally prepared by reading the labeled entries from the cash T-account. Debits to the cash T-account are sources, and credits are uses, of cash.

Since the formal statement normally begins with cash provided from operations, this is the first item that is obtained from the cash T-account, although it is in summarized form. Thus, if the details of the cash provided from operations are to be reported (for example, to tie it in with the net income reported in the income statement), then the details are obtained by reading the labeled entries from the cash from operations T-account. Some accountants contend that it is better to report the cash provided from operations as a single-line item without the details, because the latter are more confusing than helpful to the readers of the statement. For example, the reporting of depreciation as a noncash item is often misinterpreted to mean that it is a source of cash, when it is not; it is an adjustment to net income to convert it to cash provided from operations. Other than cash provided from operations, all other sources and uses are obtained from the cash T-account.

The formal statement of changes in financial position, using a cash format, for Kansas Company is presented below and on the top of page 603. Although subheadings are used to make the statement clearer, many companies merely list the sources and uses without any subheadings. Also, it should be pointed out that although the basic form of the statement is the same for all companies, the detailed presentations of the statement vary from company to company, depending upon their particular circumstances.

WORKING-CAPITAL FORMAT: A basic difference between a working-capital format and a cash format is the financial resources provided from (used in) operations. Sales on account, cost of goods sold, accrued expenses, and the expired portion (expense) of short-term prepayments are all included in working capital provided from (used in) operations (they affect working capital), but are not in-included in cash provided from (used in) operations (they do not affect cash). On the other hand, the net changes in working-capital items are adjustments to net income to derive cash provided from (used in) operations, but they do not affect the working-capital pool. For example, the payment of accounts payable, the purchase of inventory on account (accounts payable) or by cash, bad-debt write-offs, bad-debt estimates, and dividends paid on dividends declared in the previous period all have a zero net effect on the working-capital pool; hence, in a working-capital format, they are not reported in the statement of financial position. Instead, such changes within the working-capital pool are reported in a separate schedule of working-capital changes, which shows the individual changes in working-capital items that are not shown in the statement of changes in financial position. This separate schedule also shows the overall change in the working-capital pool for the period, but the individual causes of the overall change in the working-capital pool are explained in the statement of changes in financial position (assuming a working-capital format).

KANSAS COMPANY
Statement of Changes in Financial Position
For the Year Ended December 31, 19+5
[Cash Format]

Sources of financial resources:		
Cash provided from operations:		
Net income		$ 92,400
Add charges not requiring an outlay of cash:		
Depreciation	$55,000	
Loss on sale of bond investment	4,000	
Decrease in prepayments	4,100	
Increase in notes payable	15,000	
Increase in taxes payable	11,600	89,700
		$182,100

Deduct credits not generating cash:			
Bond-premium amortization	$ 500		
Gain on sale of equipment	8,000		
Increase in marketable securities	1,000		
Increase in accounts receivable	32,000		
Increase in inventory	80,000		
Decrease in accounts payable	10,600	132,100	
Cash provided from operations for period		$50,000	
Cash provided from other sources:			
Sale of equipment	$38,000		
Sale of bond investment	11,000	49,000	
Financial resources provided, not affecting cash:			
Common stock issued to retire preferred stock		150,000	
Total financial resources provided for period			$249,000
Uses of financial resources:			
Cash applied:			
Income tax settlement	$20,000		
Dividends on common stock	30,000		
Investment in bonds	25,000		
Purchase of land	26,000	$101,000	
Financial resources applied, not affecting cash:			
Preferred stock retired by issuing common stock		150,000	
Total financial resources used for period			251,000
Decrease in financial resources (cash) for period			$ (2,000)

Referring to the Kansas Company's comparative balance sheets, a separate schedule of working-capital changes can be prepared, as shown below, and reported, as shown on page 608.

	December 31 Balances		Changes in Working Capital	
	19+5	19+4	Increase	Decrease
Current assets:				
Cash	$ 18,000	$ 20,000		$ 2,000
Marketable securities	1,000	—	$ 1,000	
Accounts receivable	60,000	30,000	30,000	
Allowance for uncollectibles	(8,000)	(10,000)	2,000	
Inventory	110,000	30,000	80,000	
Prepayments	14,900	19,000		4,100
Total current assets	$195,900	$ 89,000		
Current liabilities:				
Accounts payable	$ 35,400	$ 46,000	10,600	
Notes payable	40,000	25,000		15,000
Taxes payable	61,600	50,000		11,600
Total current liabilities	$137,000	$121,000		
Working capital	$ 58,900	$ (32,000)		
Increase in working capital				90,900
			$123,600	$123,600

WORKING CAPITAL

(Sources)		(Uses)	
Beginning balance	(32,000)	Ending balance	58,900
(4) Proceeds from sale of equipment	38,000	(6) Outlay for additional income taxes settled in 19+5—prior-period adjustment	20,000
(5) Proceeds from sale of bond investment	11,000	(7) Outlay for dividends on common stock	30,000
(10) Common stock issued to retire preferred stock	150,000	(8) Outlay for bond investment	25,000
(a) Working capital provided from operations	142,900	(9) Outlay to purchase land	26,000
		(10) Preferred stock retired by issuing common stock	150,000
	309,900		309,900

Working Capital from Operations

(Net income and net income adjustments for non-working-capital charges)		(Net income adjustments for non-working-capital credits)	
(1) Net income	92,400	(3) Bond-premium amortization	500
(2) Depreciation	55,000	(4) Gain from sale of equipment	8,000
(5) Loss on sale of bond investment	4,000	(a) Balance	142,900
	151,400		151,400

Bond Investment

B	10,000	E	20,000
(8)	25,000	(5)	15,000
	35,000		35,000

Land

B	—	E	26,000
(9)	26,000		
	26,000		26,000

Building

B	400,000	E	400,000

Acc. Depr.—Bldg.

E	160,000	B	140,000
		(2)	20,000
	160,000		160,000

Equipment

B	350,000	E	300,000
		(4)	50,000
	350,000		350,000

Acc. Depr.—Equip.

E	120,000	B	105,000
(4)	20,000	(2)	35,000
	140,000		140,000

Bonds Payable

E	100,000	B	100,000

Bond Premium

E	7,500	B	8,000
(3)	500		
	8,000		8,000

Preferred Stock

E	—	B	150,000
(10)	150,000		
	150,000		150,000

Common Stock

E	250,000	B	50,000
		(10)	150,000
		(11)	50,000
	250,000		250,000

Retained Earnings

E	167,400	B	175,000
(6)	20,000	(1)	92,400
(7)	30,000		
(11)	50,000		
	267,400		267,400

Note that there was a negative working-capital balance for 19+4 of $32,000 and a positive working-capital balance of $58,900 for 19+5; hence, the change in working capital from the end of 19+4 to the end of 19+5 was $90,900 ($32,000 + $58,900). The $90,900 increase in the working-capital pool will be explained by the statement of changes in financial position (using a working-capital format), whereas the schedule of working-capital changes shows the individual changes within the working-capital pool.

Using the T-account method, a large T-account is set up for working capital, as shown on page 604, and the beginning negative balance of $(32,000) is debited and the ending balance of $58,900, which are obtained from the schedule of working-capital changes, is credited to the working-capital T-account. A large T-account is set up for working capital from operations. Individual T-accounts are set up for all the noncurrent assets and noncurrent equities (non-working-capital items), and beginning and ending balances (see the comparative balance sheets) are posted to the noncurrent T-accounts. Summary entries reconstructing the transactions for the year are posted to the T-accounts until they are in balance, with all entries made to the working-capital and working capital from operations T-accounts labeled. The statement of changes in financial position is then formally prepared from the working-capital T-account, with the details of the working capital provided from operations obtained from the working capital from operations T-account.

Since most purchases (sales) of long-lived assets, issuances (retirements) of long-term debt, issuances (retirements) of capital stock, and sales (acquisitions) of treasury stock affect cash, which is part of the working-capital pool, they also affect working capital. Thus, other than operations, the sources and uses of financial resources for Kansas Company are the same under the working-capital format as under the cash format, as shown on the formal statement on page 607.

Although it is true for Kansas Company, this does not mean that, other than operations, sources and uses of cash and working capital are always the same. For example, a piece of equipment may be sold on account (short-term note receivable), which is a working-capital source, but not a cash source. Also, land may be purchased by paying $5,000 and issuing a short-term note payable of $4,000, which is a $9,000 use of working capital, but only a $5,000 use of cash.

The difference between cash and working capital provided from (used in) operations is that the former includes individual net changes in the working-capital elements in order to convert net income to cash provided from (used in) operations. This difference can be demonstrated by reconciling cash and working capital provided from operations for Kansas Company, as shown below:

Cash provided from operations (see page 603)		$50,000
Add working-capital deductions:		
Increase in marketable securities	$ 1,000	
Increase in accounts receivable	32,000	
Increase in inventory	80,000	
Decrease in accounts payable	10,600	123,600
		$173,600

Deduct working-capital additions:		
Increase in notes payable	$15,000	
Increase in taxes payable	11,600	
Decrease in prepayments	4,100	30,700
Working capital provided from operations (see below)		$142,900

KANSAS COMPANY
Statement of Changes in Financial Position
For the Year Ended December 31, 19+5
[Working-Capital Format]

Sources of financial resources:			
Working capital provided from operations:			
Net income		$ 92,400	
Add charges not requiring an outlay of working capital:			
Depreciation	$55,000		
Loss on sale of bond investment	4,000	59,000	
		$151,400	
Deduct credits not generating working capital:			
Bond-premium amortization	$ 500		
Gain on sale of equipment	8,000	8,500	
Working capital provided from operations for period		$142,900	
Working capital provided from other sources:			
Sale of equipment	38,000		
Sale of bond investment	11,000	49,000	
Financial resources provided, not affecting working capital:			
Common stock issued to retire preferred stock		150,000	
Total financial resources provided for period			$341,900
Uses of financial resources:			
Working capital applied:			
Income tax settlement	$20,000		
Dividends on common stock	30,000		
Investment in bonds	25,000		
Purchase of land	26,000	$101,000	
Financial resources applied, not affecting working capital:			
Preferred stock retired by issuing common stock		150,000	
Total financial resources used for period			251,000
Increase in financial resources (working capital) for period			$ 90,900

(See the top of page 608 for the accompanying formal statement of the schedule of working-capital changes.)

Work-sheet method. As was previously discussed, the work-sheet method is the traditional method used in the preparation of the statement of changes in financial position. It has the advantage of presenting working papers that leave a trail for future reference (such as in an audit) that most accountants are familiar with. On the other hand, there are two problems: First, there are several versions of the work-sheet

KANSAS COMPANY
Schedule of Working-Capital Changes
December 31, 19+5 and 19+4

	December 31 Balances		Changes in Working Capital	
	19+5	19+4	Increase	Decrease
Current assets:				
Cash	$ 18,000	$ 20,000		$ 2,000
Marketable securities	1,000	—	$ 1,000	
Accounts receivable	60,000	30,000	30,000	
Allowance for uncollectibles	(8,000)	(10,000)	2,000	
Inventory	110,000	30,000	80,000	
Prepayments	14,900	19,000		4,100
Total current assets	$195,900	$ 89,000		
Current liabilities:				
Accounts payable	$ 35,400	$ 46,000	10,600	
Notes payable	40,000	25,000		15,000
Taxes payable	61,600	50,000		11,600
Total current liabilities	$137,000	$121,000		
Working capital	$ 58,900	$(32,000)		
Increase in working capital				90,900
			$123,600	$123,600

method; and second, the traditional work-sheet methods require complex reversing and reclassifying entries that are not as clear and understandable as the T-account method, which requires merely reconstructing the normal transactions during the year via normal summary entries.

In order to take advantage of the logic underlying the T-account method, the work-sheet method presented here makes use of the same techniques as the T-account method. The work sheets for Kansas Company are presented on pages 610–611 (cash format) and 612–613 (working-capital format), and the resulting statements of changes in financial position would be the same as previously illustrated.

The first two columns in the work sheets contain the comparative balance-sheet data, and the second two contain the net changes in the balance-sheet items from the beginning to the end of the year. Note that the net changes are listed in a manner consistent with the beginning and ending balances posted to the T-accounts under the T-account method. That is, under the T-account method, a net increase (decrease) in an asset (equity) results in an ending (beginning) credit balance in the T-account that is larger than the beginning (ending) debit balance; hence, the net increases in assets and the net decreases in equities are treated as credits in the net-change columns of the work sheets. Similarly, decreases in assets and increases in equities are shown as debit net changes in the work sheets. By listing the net changes in this manner, it is possible to avoid the reversing and reclassifying entries necessary under traditional work-sheet methods.

The third pair of columns in the work sheets is for the transactions reconstructed and summarized for the period, and contains the same entries that are made to the T-accounts under the T-account method. The information needed to explain these entries is written below the listing of the comparative balance-sheet items and is classified as indicated. The dollar amounts pertaining to this information are carried horizontally to the fourth pair of columns, which shows the sources and uses of cash or working capital. If a working-capital format is used, then there is a fifth pair of columns to which the individual working-capital elements are horizontally carried, which serves as the basis for preparing the separate schedule of working-capital changes. All remaining debits and credits under the transactions columns are cancelled by the debit and credit net changes under the net-change columns, because when the two are added together horizontally, they sum to zero.

Debit Balances	December 31 Balances 19+5	19+4	Net Changes Debit(a)	Credit(b)	Transactions Debit	Credit	Financial Resources Source	Use
Cash	18,000	20,000	2,000				2,000	
Marketable securities	1,000	—		1,000	(4) 1,000			
Accounts receivable (net)	52,000	20,000		32,000	(5) 32,000			
Inventory	110,000	30,000		80,000	(6) 80,000			
Prepayments	14,900	19,000	4,100			(7) 4,100		
Bond investment	20,000	10,000		10,000	(15) 25,000	(12) 15,000		
Land	26,000	—		26,000	(16) 26,000			
Building	400,000	400,000	—	—				
Equipment	300,000	350,000	50,000			(11) 50,000		
	941,900	849,000						
Credit Balances								
Accumulated depreciation—Building	160,000	140,000	20,000			(2) 20,000		
Accumulated depreciation—Equipment	120,000	105,000	15,000		(11) 20,000	(2) 35,000		
Accounts payable	35,400	46,000		10,600	(8) 10,600			
Notes payable	40,000	25,000	15,000			(9) 15,000		
Taxes payable	61,600	50,000	11,600			(10) 11,600		
Bonds payable	100,000	100,000	—	—				
Bond premium	7,500	8,000		500	(3) 500			
Preferred stock	—	150,000		150,000	(17) 150,000			
Common stock	250,000	50,000	200,000			(17) 150,000 (18) 50,000		
Retained earnings	167,400	175,000		7,600	(13) 20,000 (14) 30,000 (18) 50,000	(1) 92,400		
	941,900	849,000	317,700	317,700				

Cash provided from operations:				
Net income	(1) 92,400			
Add (deduct) noncash adjustments to net income:				
Depreciation	(2) 55,000			
Bond-premium amortization		(3) 500		
Gain from sale of equipment		(11) 8,000		
Loss on sale of bond investment	(12) 4,000		50,000	
Increase in marketable securities		(4) 1,000		
Increase in accounts receivable		(5) 32,000		
Increase in inventory		(6) 80,000		
Decrease in prepayments	(7) 4,100			
Decrease in accounts payable		(8) 10,600		
Increase in notes payable	(9) 15,000			
Increase in taxes payable	(10) 11,600			
Other sources and uses of cash:				
Proceeds from sale of equipment	(11) 38,000		38,000	
Proceeds from sale of bond investment	(12) 11,000		11,000	
Outlay for income tax settlement		(13) 20,000		20,000
Outlay for dividends on common stock		(14) 30,000		30,000
Outlay for bond investment		(15) 25,000		25,000
Outlay to purchase land		(16) 26,000		26,000
Sources and uses of financial resources, not affecting cash:				
Common stock issued to retire preferred stock	(17) 150,000		150,000	
Preferred stock retired by issuing common stock		(17) 150,000		150,000
	826,200	826,200	251,000	251,000

Note: the amounts of the items from Net income through Increase in taxes payable are bracketed to the single total 50,000.

[a] Decreases in assets and increases in equities are shown as debit net changes.
[b] Increases in assets and decreases in equities are shown as credit net changes.

Debit Balances	December 31 Balances 19+5	19+4	Net Change Debit[a]	Credit[b]	Transactions Debit	Credit	Financial Resources Source	Use	Working-capital Changes Decrease	Increase
Cash	18,000	20,000	2,000						2,000	
Marketable securities	1,000	—		1,000						1,000
Accounts receivable (net)	52,000	20,000		32,000						32,000
Inventory	110,000	30,000		80,000						80,000
Prepayments	14,900	19,000	4,100						4,100	
Bond investment	20,000	10,000		10,000	(8) 25,000	(5) 15,000				
Land	26,000	—		26,000	(9) 26,000					
Building	400,000	400,000	—	—						
Equipment	300,000	350,000	50,000			(4) 50,000				
	941,900	849,000								
Credit Balances										
Accumulated depreciation—Building	160,000	140,000	20,000			(2) 20,000				
Accumulated depreciation—Equipment	120,000	105,000	15,000		(4) 20,000	(2) 35,000				
Accounts payable	35,400	46,000		10,600						10,600
Notes payable	40,000	25,000	15,000						15,000	
Taxes payable	61,600	50,000	11,600						11,600	
Bonds payable	100,000	100,000	—	—						
Bond premium	7,500	8,000		500	(3) 500					
Preferred stock	—	150,000		150,000	(10) 150,000					
Common stock	250,000	50,000	200,000			(10) 150,000 (11) 50,000				
Retained earnings	167,400	175,000		7,600	(6) 20,000 (7) 30,000 (11) 50,000	(1) 92,400				
	941,900	849,000	317,700	317,700						

Working capital provided from operations:						
Net income	(1) 92,400					
Add (deduct) non-working-capital adjustments to net income:						
Depreciation	(2) 55,000		142,900			
Bond-premium amortization		(3) 500				
Gain from sale of equipment		(4) 8,000				
Loss on sale of bond investment	(5) 4,000					
Other sources and uses of working capital:						
Proceeds from sale of equipment	(4) 38,000		38,000			
Proceeds from sale of bond investment	(5) 11,000		11,000			
Outlay for income tax settlement		(6) 20,000		20,000		
Outlay for dividends on common stock		(7) 30,000		30,000		
Outlay for bond investment		(8) 25,000		25,000		
Outlay to purchase bond		(9) 26,000		26,000		
Sources and uses of financial resources, not affecting working capital:						
Common stock issued to retire preferred stock	(10)150,000		150,000			
Preferred stock retired by issuing common stock		(10)150,000		150,000		
	671,900	671,900				
Increase in working capital				90,900	90,900	
			341,900	341,900	123,600	123,600

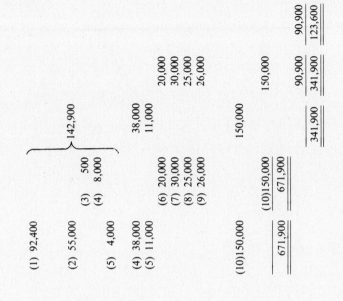

ⓐDecreases in assets and increases in equities are shown as debit net changes.
ⓑIncreases in assets and decreases in equities are shown as credit net changes.

26

General Price-Level Adjusted Financial Statements

Introduction. As we pointed out in Chapter 3 in the discussion of the money-measuring-unit assumption, the functions of money justify its use as a measuring unit in accounting. However, it was also pointed out that a measuring unit should be stable over time and that money is not a stable measuring unit. By using money as a measuring unit, accountants are assuming either that money is a stable measuring unit, that its instability is immaterial, or that the accountant's function is to account for dollars only and not changes in purchasing power.

In a simple barter economy, the exchange of commodities would be expressed in terms of awkward ratios of exchange. For example, so many loaves of bread would be equal to so many pounds of meat, so many pounds of meat equal to a pair of shoes, and so forth. Thus in a barter economy, ratios of exchange would function as values in exchange. In contrast to a barter economy, in a modern economy money is used as one of the commodities, and all other commodities are expressed in terms of money as the common denominator. The result is ratios of exchange in the form of prices, where prices are nothing more than values in exchange expressed in terms of money.[1] For example, if a good is priced at $50, an exchange of $50 will command the good. The power of money to command goods and services is the exchange value of money. Money is an exchange value.

Money (for example, the dollar in the United States) is the measuring unit of the ability to command goods and services in the marketplace at a point in time. The dollar is a measuring unit of economic "size" or economic "length," where "size" and "length" refer to the real goods and services that the dollar can command. However, the dollar as the measuring unit of economic "size" or "length" is not stable as is, for example, the yardstick of physical size, since the dollar has no prescribed economic "size" or "length." This is because its ability to command goods and services can change over time. The ability of the dollar to command commodities changes over time as the result of the fact that the dollar itself is a commodity; hence, its exchange value changes, as do all commodities, with changes in supply and demand. In addition, the exchange value of the dollar changes as the result of government influence over the supply of money via the Federal Reserve System and the Treasury Department.

The general purchasing power of the dollar refers to the ability of the dollar to command goods and services in general. Because the number of dollars needed to acquire goods and services in general changes over time, the general purchasing power of the dollar changes from day to day, month to month, quarter to quarter, and year to year. When the prices of all goods and services (the general-price level) rise on the average (inflation), the purchasing power of the dollar falls, in that it takes more dollars to acquire on the average the same goods and services in general. Similarly, when the general-price level falls (deflation), the exchange value of the dollar rises (an increase in general purchasing power), because it takes fewer dollars on the average to acquire the same goods and services in general. Thus the dollar is an unstable measuring unit, in that it can represent different amounts of general purchasing power at different points in time. In other words, because of inflation and deflation, the purchasing power of the dollar today differs from the purchasing power of the dollar, say, ten years ago, nine years ago, eight years ago, and so on. The purchasing power of 1970 dollars is not the same as the purchasing power of 1960. 1950, 1940, or 1930 dollars.

Based on the money-measuring-unit assumption, accountants use the dollar as the unit of measurement and generally assume that fluctuations in the dollar's purchasing power will be so insignificant as not to undermine its usefulness as a unit of measurement. Thus the accounting process adds, subtracts, and compares account balances without making any allowance for the instability of the dollar. The result is financial statements expressed in terms of diverse amounts of general purchasing power. Although financial statements show dollars of "mixed and varying dimensions," it is doubtful whether statement users make any allowances for this fact (the so-called "money illusion"). There is, therefore, a potentially

[1] See AICPA, "Reporting the Financial Effects of Price-Level Change," *Accounting Research Study No. 6* (New York: AICPA, 1963), pp. 18–19.

dangerous situation that financial statements could be misleading because of the instability of the money measuring unit, especially during periods of significant inflation and deflation.

Price indexes. Because of the instability of the dollar, what is needed is a method for measuring the changes in the purchasing power of the dollar over time. In order to measure *directly* changes in the exchange value of the dollar over time, it would be necessary that a marketplace exist where dollars of different years could be bought and sold; a marketplace where, say, one 19+2 dollar could be exchanged for two 19+9 dollars.[2] Since there is no marketplace to provide direct exchange rates for dollars of different years, we *indirectly* measure changes in the purchasing power of the dollar over time via the use of index numbers. In other words, the use of money as a commodity to facilitate calculation and exchange creates the problem that there is no direct measure of the exchange value of money over time, and we are forced to use the indirect measure of general-price-level indexes.

A general-price-level index is an index that measures the exchange ratio between money (that is, the domestic currency, which is the dollar in the United States) and all the goods and services it can acquire at specific points in time. Because general-price-level indexes reflect changes in the prices of all goods and services at different points in time, such indexes provide an indirect measure of the changes in the purchasing power of money. For example, if the general-price-level index changes from 100 (really 100%) at the end of 19+1 to 150 at the end of 19+7, the 50 percent increase in the general-price level indicates that the purchasing power of the dollar in 19+7 is two-thirds (the reciprocal of the index, 1/1.50, or 100/150) what it was in 19+1—a one-third decline in the purchasing power of the dollar to approximately 67 cents. Similarly, if the general-price level changes from 100 to 200, the doubling of general prices reflects a decline in the purchasing power of the dollar of one half (1 − 1/2.00) over the time period.

Note that in order to measure an increase or decrease in the general-price level, it is necessary to compare the prices of all goods and services as of a specific date to the prices of all goods and services as of an established base period. In other words, general-price-level indexes for current periods are expressed as percentages of the general-price level at a given base period. The base-period index is usually assigned an index number of 100 (100%), and the indexes of subsequent periods are expressed as percentages of the base-period index, as was illustrated in the two examples in the preceding paragraph. Since a current general-price-level index is expressed as a percentage, its reciprocal (one over the current index) represents purchasing power, as was also illustrated above.

It should now be obvious that the dollar is a commodity whose purchasing power varies inversely with the level of general prices (as measured by general-price-level indexes) of the commodities for which it can be exchanged. Thus general-price-level indexes provide a measure of the degree of inflation (a rise in the general-price level) and deflation (a fall in the general-price level) and, there-

---

[2] *ARS No. 6*, p. 9.

fore, a measure of the inverse relationship of the purchasing power of the dollar. During periods of inflation, the general-price level increases, and it takes more dollars to acquire the same goods and services (a decrease in purchasing power); while during deflation, it takes fewer dollars to acquire the same commodities (an increase in purchasing power).

Although there are several price indexes available (for example, Gross National Product Implicit Price Deflator, Consumer Price Index, Wholesale Price Index, and Composite Construction Index), the GNP (gross national product) Implicit Price Deflator is the most "general" price index available. It is the only index that represents a weighted average of *all* the goods and services exchanged in *all* segments of the U.S. economy; therefore, it is the most comprehensive index currently compiled of the general-price level in the United States.

The GNP Deflator measures the relationship between the total value of all goods and services produced in a given year, expressed in current-purchasing-power dollars (current-period prices), and the total value of the same goods and services expressed in base-year-purchasing-power dollars (base-period prices). Since prices have to be averaged to derive index numbers, such as the GNP Deflator, the prices are weighted by the related quantities exchanged at these prices based on formulas. For the GNP Deflator, a Paasche-type formula is used; hence, besides being comprehensive, it has the further advantage of being based on current weights that change every year.[3]

The GNP Deflators are available on a quarterly and yearly basis in the *Survey of Current Business,* and are prepared by the U.S. Department of Commerce, Office of Business Economics. Although GNP Deflators are not available monthly, they can be approximated monthly by using the Consumer Price Index (CPI). The CPI is based on a sample that measures the average change in the retail prices of a "market basket" of approximately 300 goods and services purchased by city wage-earner and clerical-worker families in 46 cities in the United States. The CPI is prepared monthly by the Bureau of Labor Statistics of the U.S. Department of Labor, and it is available in the *Monthly Labor Review,* as well as the *Survey of Current Business.* Because of its "market basket" approach and its use of a fixed-weight formula, the CPI as a general-price-level index is not as satisfactory as is the GNP Deflator. However, over the long run the two indexes tend to approximate each other, even though they may change at different rates in the short run.

An illustration. To aid in understanding general-price-level indexes, a highly simplified price index is constructed on the next page. It is assumed in the illustration that the given goods and services are all the goods and services of a particular economy or a representative sample, so that we can refer to the resulting index as a general-price-level index.

Note that the 108 general-price-level index derived is a weighted-average relation between money and all goods and services (or a representative sample); therefore, it reflects a weighted-average change in the prices of all goods and ser-

[3] *ARS No. 6,* pp. 70–115.

Goods and Services	Current-Year Price (a)	Base-Year Price (b)	Relative Weights (c)	Current-Year Amount (a × c)	Base-Year Amount (b × c)
#1	$20	$18	50	$1,000	$ 900
#2	5	6	30	150	180
#3	10	10	10	100	100
#4	8	6	20	160	120
#5	15	14	40	600	560
				$2,010	$1,860

Base-year price index: 100% = 1.00 = 100
Current-year general-price index: $2,010/$1,860 = 1.08 = 108% = 108
Increase in general-price level: 108 − 100 = 1.08 − 1.00 = .08 = 8%
Purchasing power of the dollar: 100/108 = 1/1.08 = .93 = 93 cents
Decline in general purchasing power: 100 − 93 = 1.00 − .93 = .07 = 7%

vices during the time interval. Since a general-price index is a weighted average of the prices of all goods and services, a change in the index (for instance, from 100 to 108) reflects a proportional change in the prices of all goods and services—a change in the general-price level. Similarly, because the exchange value of money (the purchasing power or price of money) has to be expressed by all the goods and services for which it can be exchanged, the price of money (for example, 93 cents) is reflected by a weighted average of the prices of all goods and services in the ratio in which they affect the general-price level; hence, there is a reciprocal relationship between the price of money and the general-price-level index (1/1.08).

The illustration above clearly points out that changes in the individual prices of commodities do not have to move in the same direction nor by the same percentage of change as the change in the general-price level. For example, note that for commodity #2 there was a decline in price and for commodity #3 no change in price, yet the general-price level increased on the average by 8 percent. Changes in the individual prices of commodities reflect changes in the value of those commodities, but such changes should not be confused with changes in the general-price level. A change in the general-price level is a proportional change in the prices of all goods and services, not a change in the value of a specific good or service.[4]

The failure to recognize the distinction between general and specific price-

[4]Part of the confusion between a general and a specific price change is due to the latter's being the result of the *combined* effect of a relative price change (a change in the price of a commodity relative to all other commodities) and a change in the general-price level, and it is difficult in the real world (as opposed to normative theory) to separate these two effects on specific prices. For example, if the specific price of a commodity increased 10 percent during a time period when general prices increased 4 percent, then the "real" increase in value was only 6 percent. The 10 percent dollar increase in value was the result of the combined effect of a 6 percent relative price increase (110/104 − 1) and a 4 percent decline in the purchasing power of the dollar (1 − 1/1.04). See Edgar O. Edwards and Philip W. Bell, *The Theory and Management of Business Income* (Berkeley, Calif.: University of California Press, 1961).

level changes has led to the contention that financial statements should not be adjusted for general-price-level changes because such statements reflect current values that are highly subjective. But such a contention is incorrect, for general-price-level adjustments are merely costs measured in terms of dollars of general purchasing power at time of acquisition, restated into equivalent dollars of current general purchasing power. The historical-cost assumption is not violated, since the restatement of costs into dollars of current purchasing power does not represent current values.

For example, if land was acquired for $40,000 in 19+1 when the general price level was 100, and if the general-price level is currently 108 for 19+4, then the general-price-level-adjusted balance for land would be $43,200 ($40,000 × 1.08). Because of the 8 percent inflation with its 7 percent decline in the purchasing power of the dollar, land that cost $40,000 in 19+1 is equivalent to a cost today of $43,200. The $43,200 does not represent the value of the land, since the cost of the land is merely restated in terms of the 19+4 general purchasing power of the dollar. Similarly, the $3,200 difference does not represent a gain and it has no significance per se; it is equivalent to the nonsense statement that the difference between 1 yard and 4 feet is 3. General-price-level adjustments are pure scale adjustments, transformations, and restatements of financial data from one unit of measurement (such as 19+1 dollars) to another (such as 19+4 dollars).[5]

Some history. It is frequently contended that changes in the general-price level have not been significant enough to undermine the stable-dollar assumption made by accountants. However, by analyzing changes in the general-price level, as shown by the GNP Deflator below, it is highly questionable whether changes in the general-price level have been insignificant.

Year	Deflator	Year	Deflator	Year	Deflator	Year	Deflator
1929	50.6	1940	43.9	1951	85.6	1962	105.7
1930	49.3	1941	47.2	1952	87.5	1963	107.1
1931	44.8	1942	53.0	1953	88.3	1964	108.9
1932	40.3	1943	56.8	1954	89.6	1965	110.9
1933	39.3	1944	58.2	1955	90.9	1966	113.9
1934	42.2	1945	59.7	1956	94.0	1967	117.6
1935	42.6	1946	66.7	1957	97.5	1968	122.3
1936	42.7	1947	74.6	1958	100.0	1969	128.2
1937	44.5	1948	79.6	1959	101.6	1970	135.3
1938	43.9	1949	79.1	1960	103.3	1971	141.6
1939	43.2	1950	80.2	1961	104.6	1972	145.9

Source: U.S. Department of Commerce, *Survey of Current Business,* issued monthly. Data above are annual averages; however, quarterly averages are also available since 1947.

As illustrated above during the 1958–1972 period, the general level of prices increased approximately 46 percent, signifying approximately a 31 percent decline in the purchasing power of the dollar, and an annual compound rate of increase

[5]See Maurice Moonitz, "Price-Level Accounting and Scales of Measurement," *Accounting Review* (July 1970), pp. 465–75.

of approximately 2½ percent. Because of the discoveries and innovations that grew out of World War II and postwar developments, comparisons of GNP Deflators before 1945 are probably not too reliable.[6] Hence, if we compare the change in the general-price level during the 1945–1972 period, the general level of prices increased approximately 144 percent—approximately a 59 percent decline in the purchasing power of the dollar and an annual compound rate of increase of approximately 3¼ percent.

It should be apparent that the United States has experienced inflation in recent years. As of 1972, not since 1949 has there been a decline in the general-price level as measured by the annual GNP Deflator. It is frequently argued that with the Full Employment Act of 1946 and the setting up of the Council of Economic Advisors, the U.S. government has a built-in bias toward inflation. That is, the economic policy of the government is primarily concerned with attempting to keep unemployment at a low level, even if this means the existence of some inflation.

On the other hand, it is also contended that even though the United States has experienced inflation in recent years, the inflation has tended to be relatively moderate. For example, the annual compound rate of increase in general prices during the 1958–1972 period has been only approximately 2½ percent. However, this overlooks the fact that even moderate annual changes in the level of general prices have a cumulative effect on financial statements. In other words, companies hold assets over several years, and the cumulative effect of moderate annual changes in general prices can have a material effect on the reporting of such assets on the balance sheet and the matching of such "old" dollar expenses with revenue on the income statement.[7]

Implications of the instability of the dollar. Before proceeding further with a reexamination of the assumption regarding the stability of the unit of measurement used in accounting, it seems fundamental to inquire about some of the implications arising from the known fact that the purchasing power of the dollar varies. For instance, we know that the dimensions of the unit of measurement vary through time, but what effect, if any, does this have on the data shown in the financial statements? As a means of clarifying this point, consider the following situations.

SITUATION A: Suppose that the following situation occurred:

In 19+1, X purchased some land for $10,000.
In 19+9, X sold the land for $20,000.

First, assume that the general purchasing power of the dollar did not change during the period of time that the land was owned by X. Did X make a gain? The answer, clearly, is yes. Because the dollars spent and those received had the same purchasing power, X now has twice as much purchasing power.

Second, analyze the transaction assuming that the general purchasing power

[6] See Accounting Principles Board, "Financial Statements Restated for General Price-Level Changes," *Statement No. 3* (New York: AICPA, 1969), p. 33.
[7] *Statement No. 3*, pp. 6–7.

of the dollar declined 50 percent between 19+1 and 19+9. Did X make a gain? Under such circumstances, it is apparent that X has not increased his purchasing power. But it is a fact that X has 10,000 more dollars after the sale of the land than he invested in the land in 19+1. In a "nominal" sense, there has been a gain of $10,000; in a "real" sense, there has been no gain. (Of course, with a stable price level, nominal and real results would coincide.)

Under prevailing accounting practices, a gain of $10,000 would be reported as a result of the purchase and sale of the land; no consideration would be given to the change in the dimensions of the unit of measurement. The following question seems to be pertinent: Which definition of "gain" should be used in accounting?

SITUATION B: Assume that a service business is organized to operate on a "cash basis"; that is, no credit is extended to customers, and the business needs only one long-lived asset in its business operations. The long-lived asset is purchased for $16,000 and is depreciated over its eight-year useful life. Condensed income statements and dividends data covering the eight-year period since organization are presented below. For convenience, the results of each year are identical.

	Year			Aggregate for
	1	2 3 4 5 6 7	8	8-Year Period
Revenue from services	$42,000		$42,000	$336,000
Salaries and wages	$30,000		$30,000	$240,000
Depreciation	2,000	Each year is	2,000	16,000
All other expenses	8,000	identical.	8,000	64,000
Net operating income	$ 2,000		$ 2,000	$ 16,000
Income tax	600		600	4,800
Net income	$ 1,400		$ 1,400	$ 11,200
Dividends	$ 1,400		$ 1,400	$ 11,200

A condensed statement of sources and uses of working capital for the company for the eight-year period would appear as follows:

Working-capital sources:	
Net income before extraordinary items	$11,200
Add—Expenses not requiring an outlay of working capital in the current period:	
Depreciation charges	16,000
Working capital provided from operations for the period, exclusive of extraordinary items	$27,200
Working-capital uses:	
Dividends	11,200
Increase in working capital (in this case, cash)	$16,000

The income statements report that the company earned $11,200 in the eight-year period. An identical amount was distributed to the owners as dividends. But suppose that during the eight-year period the general-price level increased 70 percent, and that the company found that $27,200 was needed to replace the fully depreciated and worn-out long-lived asset. This price represents a 70 percent increase in the number of dollars needed to replace the long-lived asset. Thus, in order to replace the fully depreciated asset, the company would have to borrow \$11,200 (\$27,200 – \$16,000), or raise additional capital from stockholders in that amount. Management and stockholders might justifiably inquire whether the eight-year period had, in reality, been profitable. Was the aggregate net income \$11,200, or \$0? (Could it be rightfully contended that the "income" tax was in reality a tax on capital?)[8]

The illustration above raises questions with regard to the matching assumption. Is it proper to match annual depreciation expense stated in terms of "old" general-purchasing-power dollars (19+1 dollars in the illustration) with periodic revenue stated in terms of more current general-purchasing-power dollars? Does logic not require that expense matched against revenue be stated in dollars of current general purchasing power? In other words, under conventional accounting procedures, some expenses, like wages and rent, are stated in relatively current general-purchasing-power dollars, whereas other expenses, like depreciation and, to a lesser extent, cost of goods sold, are stated in terms of "old" general-purchasing-power dollars.

The illustration also points out the problem of comparative financial statements. Many of the dollar amounts shown in comparative statements are "old" dollars. Thus, comparative statements provide an example of accounting data that are relatively more susceptible to misunderstanding as a consequence of variations in the dollar's general purchasing power.

An increasing number of businesses regularly present partial or complete comparative financial statements covering a considerable number of years. Comparative financial statements for a ten-year period are fairly common. Some companies regularly report selected accounting data for a period exceeding thirty years. There are instances where selected yearly data, such as sales, are shown in each annual report for the entire life of the corporation.

When there have been significant movements in the general-price level, it is obvious that annual data covering several years lose much of their comparability. For example, in the illustration above, revenue is reported at \$42,000 each year for eight years. But has revenue really remained steady, given the fact that the general-price level increased 70 percent over the eight-year period? By adjusting the 19+1 revenue in terms of 19+8 purchasing power (\$42,000 × 1.70), it becomes obvious, as shown at the top of the next page, that revenue has not been maintained over the eight-year period.

Finally, the illustration raises the question as to the reporting of long-lived assets in the balance sheet. Should the long-lived asset's net book value (cost

[8]It should be pointed out that, although the \$27,200 replacement cost is used to illustrate the problem of financial reporting during periods of inflation, the dollar amount of replacement cost or selling price is not relevant to the question of whether general-price-level adjustments should or should not be made. This point will become more clear as the reader progresses through the chapter.

Unadjusted Data	19+8 Current Year	19+1 (Seven Years Ago)
Revenue	$42,000	$42,000
Adjusted Data		
Revenue	$42,000	$71,400

minus accumulated depreciation) be reported in the balance sheet based on "old" dollars (that is, the $16,000 acquisition cost)? In other words, each year the net book value of the long-lived asset ($14,000, $12,000, $10,000, and so on) is reported in the balance sheet in terms of "older" dollars (19+1 dollars) and added together with other assets that represent different purchasing-power dollars. It is obvious that it would be improper to add dollars and francs, yards and meters, or 2,000-pound tons (short tons) and 2,240-pound tons (long tons); however, this is what is done in accounting when dollars of differing dimensions are added and subtracted without regard to the instability of the dollar.

SITUATION C: The point of mixing dollars of various dimensions on the balance sheet can be further emphasized by the reporting treatment of similar assets acquired at different dates. Such assets are added together and reported on the balance sheet as if they were acquired when the general purchasing power of the dollar was the same. For example, the land account, shown below, would be reported on the current balance sheet at $500,000. But did management invest the same amount of general purchasing power in each parcel of land?

Land

19+1	100,000	
19+2	100,000	
19+3	100,000	
19+4	100,000	
19+5	100,000	
	500,000	

If the general-price level increased 40 percent from 19+1 to 19+5, at an approximate annual rate of 10 percent per year, then it should be clear, as shown below, that management did not invest the same amount of general purchasing power in each parcel of land. However, most users of financial statements would probably interpret the $500,000 in land reported on the balance sheet as representing dollars of current general purchasing power.

Land (Adjusted for General-Price-level Changes)

19+1	(100,000 × 140/100)	140,000	
19+2	(100,000 × 140/110)	127,000	
19+3	(100,000 × 140/120)	117,000	
19+4	(100,000 × 140/130)	108,000	
19+5	(100,000 × 140/140)	100,000	
		592,000	

SITUATION D: Suppose that Company Y had cash of $20,000 at the beginning of the current year and that during the year there were cash receipts of $15,000 and cash disbursements of $10,000. Further suppose that the general-price-level index was 110 at the beginning of the year and 120 at the end of the year. As shown in conventional balance sheets, cash would be reported at $20,000 as of the end of the prior year and at $25,000 as of the end of the current year. Given that inflation of 9 percent (10/110) occurred during the current year, does the $25,000 reported cash clearly show the cash position of the company?

The answer is yes, to the extent that the dollar is legal tender by law, and the reporting of the $25,000 at face value shows the cash position in terms of current general purchasing power as of the current balance-sheet date. However, what is not shown in conventional financial statements is that the holding of cash during periods of inflation results in a general-purchasing-power loss. During periods of inflation it takes more dollars to acquire the same goods and services in general than it did before the inflation occurred; hence, dollars held during inflation lose general purchasing power and result in a general-price-level loss. Thus Company Y, as shown below, suffered a general-purchasing-power loss of $2,000 by holding cash during the year when inflation occurred. That is, by restating the beginning balance and changes in cash into the general purchasing power of the dollar at the end of the year, the difference between the restated and actual (the actual is automatically in terms of current general purchasing power) ending cash balance is the general-price-level gain or loss.

	Unadjusted Dollars		Adjustment		Amounts Adjusted for General-Price-Level Changes
Beginning cash balance	$20,000	×	120/110	=	$21,800
Cash receipts*	15,000	×	120/115	=	15,600
Subtotal	$35,000				$37,400
Cash disbursements*	(10,000)	×	120/115	=	(10,400)
Ending cash balance	$25,000				$27,000
Cash balance adjusted for general-price-level changes					$27,000
Actual cash balance					25,000
General-price-level loss on holding cash					$ 2,000

*Cash receipts and disbursements occurred evenly throughout the year, so that the average index (115) could be used in the adjustments.

Now assume that in addition to the cash transactions discussed above, Company Y also had transactions in accounts payable during the current year. Specifically, assume that Company Y had accounts payable of $10,000 at the beginning of the year and increases and decreases in accounts payable during the year of $8,000 and $6,000, respectively. Given that inflation of 10 percent occurred during the current year, does the $12,000 accounts payable reported in the conventional balance sheet at the end of the year clearly show the liability?

The answer is yes, to the extent that accounts payable represent fixed claims in terms of legal tender by law (the dollar), and the $12,000 shows the monetary amount owing. However, what is not shown in conventional statements is that the holding of accounts payable during periods of inflation results in a general-purchasing-power gain. During periods of inflation, dollars with less purchasing power ("cheaper" dollars) are used to pay off liabilities. In other words, the company, in effect, has the use of "borrowed" dollars with greater purchasing power than the dollars subsequently used to extinguish the debt; hence, there is a general-price-level gain. Thus Company Y, as shown below, benefited by a general-purchasing-power gain of $980 by holding accounts payable during the year when inflation occurred.

	Unadjusted Dollars		Adjustment		Amounts Adjusted for General-Price-Level Changes
Beginning accounts payable balance...	$10,000	×	120/110	=	$10,900
Increases*	8,000	×	120/115	=	8,320
Subtotal	$18,000				$19,220
Decreases*	6,000	×	120/115	=	6,240
Ending accounts payable balance......	$12,000				$12,980
Accounts payable balance adjusted for general-price-level changes					$12,980
Actual accounts payable balance					12,000
General-price-level gain on accounts payable					$ 980

*Increases and decreases in accounts payable occurred evenly throughout the year, so that the average index (115) could be used in the adjustments.

By combining the purchasing-power loss on the holding of cash and the purchasing-power gain on the accounts payable, we can determine the net general-price-level gain or loss for Company Y. Thus Company Y suffered a net general-purchasing-power loss of $1,020 ($2,000 − $980). As will be discussed subsequently, such a net general-price-level gain or loss is not reported in the basic financial statements, but is reported in supplementary general-price-level income statements.

Monetary assets and liabilities. Although the preceding example (Situation D) illustrates the concept of a general-price-level gain or loss, it is unrealistic in that there are more items than just cash or accounts payable that determine the net general-purchasing-power gain or loss. The determination of the net general-price-level gain or loss is based on distinguishing between monetary and nonmonetary assets and liabilities.[9]

Monetary assets are cash and fixed-money claims owned; hence, they are claims to a fixed number of dollars that represent general purchasing power. Similarly, monetary liabilities are fixed-money claims owed; therefore, they are obligations to pay a fixed number of dollars in the future. Because monetary assets and liabilities are fixed-money claims, the dollar amounts of such claims do not change during periods of inflation and deflation; however, the ability to convert such

[9]Refer to Chapter 5, pages 121–123, for a discussion of monetary items.

claims into goods and services (that is, their purchasing power) is affected by changes in the general price level. Monetary assets include cash, short-term government bonds, accounts receivable, and long-term investments that pay fixed interest (bonds) or dividends (preferred stock). Monetary liabilities include the usual payables classified as current liabilities (such as accounts, notes, salaries, interest, and taxes payable) and long-term debt, such as bonds and mortgages payable.

During a period of inflation (or deflation), a firm that has monetary assets that exceed monetary liabilities experiences a net general-price-level loss (or gain). The firm loses more general purchasing power on the holding of monetary assets than the general purchasing power it gains from its monetary liabilities. Similarly, if monetary liabilities exceed monetary assets during a period of inflation, the company gains more on the purchasing-power decline of its monetary liabilities than it loses on the purchasing-power loss of its monetary assets. Thus the net general-price-level gain or loss provides an indication of how well the management of a company is reacting to the financial effects of inflation or deflation. In other words, during inflation, management should attempt to maintain monetary liabilities in excess of monetary assets, other things being equal, and show a net general-price-level gain.

The actual calculation of the net general-price-level gain or loss can be made in the same manner as was done for cash and accounts payable in Situation D above, except that it is done for all monetary assets and liabilities. (This will be illustrated later in the chapter.) In other words, the beginning balance of each monetary item, as well as its increases and decreases, are restated into end-of-period purchasing-power dollars, and the difference between the restated and the actual ending balance is the general-price-level gain or loss on that monetary item. The algebraic sum of all the individual gains and losses is the net general-price-level gain or loss. As will be illustrated later, a shortcut method in calculating the net general-price-level gain or loss is the preparation of a source and application of net monetary items.

Comments supporting conventional accounting. Since the dollar is an unstable measuring unit, why don't accountants prepare and present as the basic financial statements those statements that are adjusted for changes in the general price level? To answer this question, we need to examine some of the arguments used by accountants to support the conventional accounting practice of not adjusting the basic financial statements for general-price-level changes.

The point is made that prevailing accounting practices have worked well over the years, and as a consequence, conventional financial statements are widely used and respected. It is argued that the reason for this is that during most periods, the change in the general purchasing power of the dollar has been so gradual as to have had no discernible effect on financial statements.

It is also noted that many legal rules and agreements have been established within the framework of generally accepted accounting. There is some question of whether significant revisions could be made in the way the dollar is used in accounting without the revision of numerous statistics and a multitude of contracts, primarily because the level of earnings would be affected by the change. Income bonds, which provide for the payment of interest only if earned, and profit-sharing agreements are illustrative of contractual arrangements that would need reconsideration.

Some accountants make a point of the fact that, relatively speaking, there are not many "old" dollars in the account balances shown in a current year's financial statements. Therefore, the fact that the dimensions of the dollar have changed does not necessarily lead to a conclusion that financial statements are significantly affected. Old dollars are most likely to be found in the account balances related to plant and equipment. But even in this group, the tendency of business management to adopt conservative estimates of useful life removes a considerable portion of the outlays from account balances within ten years. Amounts invested in long-lived assets not subject to depreciation or amortization are of slight concern in this matter because they do not enter into the determination of periodic net income.

The point is made by some accountants that general-price-level changes make it necessary to interpret the results of operations and financial position with greater discrimination, but that users of accounting reports must assume the responsibility for interpreting accounting data. They believe it is the function of accounting to record expenditures and their assignment to expense in cost dollars, which amounts can be adjusted and modified by statement users if desired to serve their objectives and needs. In other words, accounting accounts for dollars, not the general purchasing power of the dollar.

It is the contention of some accountants that the effect on financial statements of the decline in the purchasing power of the dollar in recent years has been offset by the use of such conservative accounting procedures as accelerated depreciation methods, underestimates of useful life of depreciable and amortizable assets, LIFO inventory costing, and the expensing of outlays that could be capitalized (research and development, advertising, and the like). That is, during periods of inflation, net income can be overstated by the matching of "old" dollar expenses with relatively current revenue dollars, but this overstatement is offset by conservative accounting procedures. Thus the contention is that to adjust financial statements for changes in general purchasing power, in addition to the use of conservative accounting procedures, would be an overreaction to the effects of inflation and could result in reducing reported profits below acceptable levels.[10]

Some of the arguments against general-price-level adjustments have confused such adjustments with methods of current valuation. That is, some accountants contend that general-price-level adjustments are not acceptable because they result in values that are highly subjective; however, this is incorrect, since such adjustments do not result in current values, but in costs restated to reflect current general purchasing power. On the other hand, there are some accountants who con-

---

[10]See Moonitz, "Price-Level Accounting," p. 471.

tend that general-price-level adjustments should not be allowed until current valuation methods are also allowed, since it is argued that both are needed.

Another argument used against general-price-level adjustments is that there are no suitable tools available to make such adjustments; hence, if such adjustments are made, they will be more confusing than helpful to financial-statement users. That is, it is contended that there are no suitable general-price-level indexes available to make such adjustments, and that the use of available index numbers in making general-price-level adjustments would confuse statement users.

It is true that there are no perfect general-price-level indexes available. For example, general-price-level indexes do not generally account for changes in the quality of goods and the appearance of superior goods over time; there is the problem of weighting the goods and services to derive index numbers; and there is the problem of whether a general-purchasing-power concept is applicable to firms, since the management of firms really do not have the choice to invest and reinvest capital for all types of goods and services. On the other hand, it is one thing to say that there are no perfect general-price-level indexes available, while it is another thing to say that there are indexes available that are reliable enough for accounting purposes. Both *ARS No. 6* and *Statement No. 3* state that the GNP Deflator is a general-price-level index to use in the preparation of supplementary general-price-level financial statements.[11]

Related to the argument of confusing statement users is the contention that periodic revisions of account balances for general-price-level changes would cause the results of management's decisions and general-price-level fluctuations to become so commingled in the resulting financial statements that the consequences of management's decisions would not be discernible in the financial statements. In other words, financial statements adjusted for general-price-level changes might result in statement users' inability to determine clearly whether management was effective or ineffective.

Finally, it can be argued that businessmen generally do not favor financial statements adjusted for general-price-level changes because they think in terms of dollars and are held accountable for their success and failure in terms of dollars. Thus, since businessmen prefer "dollar accounting" rather than "general-purchasing-power accounting," accountants should not present financial statements adjusted for general-price-level changes as the basic financial statements.

General-price-level financial statements. Conventional financial statements are generally historical-dollar financial statements, in that the individual items reported in the statements are stated in terms of dollars of the period in which these items originated. Based on the money-measuring-unit assumption, dollars are used as the measuring unit in conventional financial statements even though such dollars represent diverse amounts of general purchasing power. Thus, changes in the general purchasing power of the dollar are ignored in conventional financial statements.

---

[11] *ARS No. 6,* p. 112; and *Statement No. 3,* p. 14.

In contrast to conventional financial statements, general-price-level financial statements are adjusted for changes in the general purchasing power of the dollar. The individual items in such statements are stated in terms of the general purchasing power of the dollar as of the current year-end reporting date (the latest balance-sheet date). Thus, general-price-level financial statements are stated in terms of dollars representing the *same* amount of general purchasing power (so-called common-dollar or uniform-dollar accounting). On the other hand, it should be stressed again that adjustments for changes in the general purchasing power of the dollar do *not* result in general-price-level financial statements that report current values.

Current thinking in accounting with regard to general-price-level adjustments is reflected by Accounting Principles Board (APB) *Statement No. 3*. In this Statement, the board states that general-price-level financial statements, or pertinent information from such statements, present useful information not found in the traditional financial statements. The board recommends that general-price-level information be presented *in addition to* the basic historical-dollar financial statements. Note that this is a recommendation, not a requirement, for the presentation of supplementary general-price-level information, and that the presentation of such information is not at present required to be in conformity with generally accepted accounting principles.[12]

In the preparation of supplementary general-price-level financial statements, *Statement No. 3* recommends the GNP Deflator as the general-price-level index to be used in adjusting for changes in the general purchasing power of the dollar. The deflator for the last quarter of the current year can be used as the index to approximate the current general purchasing power of the dollar as of the latest balance-sheet date. Thus, nonmonetary items in the balance-sheet and income-statement items, expressed in terms of historical dollars, can be adjusted for changes in the general purchasing power of the dollar by the following multiplication:

$$\textbf{Item to be adjusted} \times \frac{\textbf{Current year-end deflator (i.e., 4th quarter deflator of current year)}}{\textbf{Deflator at date of originating transaction (i.e., deflator for the quarter when transaction occurred)}}$$

Based on the doctrine of materiality, for those acquisitions (such as inventory purchases), revenues, and expenses that are acquired, earned, or incurred fairly evenly throughout the current year, the general-price-level adjustment can be based on the *average* deflator for the current year (the transactions, in effect, occur at the average general-price level for the year) as follows:

[12] An exception is where inflation or deflation has been so great in some countries that general-price-level financial statements should be presented, in conformity with GAAP, as the basic foreign-currency financial statements of companies operating in those countries, when the statements are intended for statement users in the United States. *Statement No. 3*, pp. 12–13.

$$\textbf{Item to be adjusted} \times \frac{\textbf{Current year-end deflator (i.e., 4th quarter deflator of current year)}}{\textbf{Average deflator for current year}}$$

In addition, annual average indexes can be used in place of quarterly indexes where the results would not be materially different.

Since current year-end monetary items are automatically stated in terms of current general purchasing power, no general-price-level adjustments are necessary for them. That is, current year-end monetary items are reported in the general-price-level balance sheet at the same amounts in which they are reported in the historical-dollar balance sheet. On the other hand, monetary items, as well as nonmonetary items and income statement items, that appear in prior periods' general-price-level financial statements have to be updated to reflect current general purchasing power, for purposes of presenting comparative general-price-level financial statement. Such updating is done by the "roll-forward" procedure of multiplying each prior-period item as follows:

$$\textbf{Prior-period item to be adjusted} \times \frac{\textbf{Current year-end deflator (i.e., 4th quarter deflator of current year)}}{\textbf{Prior year-end deflator (i.e., 4th quarter deflator of prior year)}}$$

The fact that current year-end monetary items do not have to be adjusted for changes in the general-price-level does *not* mean that there is no general-price-level gain or loss. As previously explained, the holding of monetary items by a company during a period in which the general-price level changes results in a net general-price-level gain or loss. *Statement No. 3* recommends that the net general-price-level gain or loss be included in current net income and reported as a separate item in the general-price-level income statement.

With regard to the presentation of general-price-level information, *Statement No. 3* recommends that it should be presented in a manner that will facilitate the comparison of general-price-level information with other general-price-level information. Since historical-dollar and price-level information are based on two different money measuring units, the former diverse and the latter uniform dollars, it is confusing to compare the two directly. Thus *Statement No. 3* recommends that general-price-level financial statements be presented in separate schedules and not in columns parallel to historical-dollar statements.

Two final points with regard to general-price-level financial statements should be made. First, it should be noted that general-price-level information is presented in terms of dollars of *current* general purchasing power (that is, prior years' and current year's financial data are presented in terms of current year-end general purchasing power) and not in terms of dollars of the same general purchasing power at some other date. It is argued that current general-purchasing-power dollars are more relevant and more easily understood by statement users. Second, general-price-level financial statements are based on *complete* general-price-level adjustments, not "piecemeal" adjustments. In other words, it would be misleading to present general-price-level information based on partial adjustments in which some items (such as depreciation) are adjusted and others are not.

AN ILLUSTRATION: Suppose that we wish to adjust the historical-dollar financial statements of Jayhawk, Inc., for the years 19+7 and 19+8 in order to provide supplementary general-price-level financial statements. We are given the historical-dollar financial statements of Jawhawk, Inc. (see below and the top of page 632), and assume that we compile the following necessary additional information:

Equipment of $210,000 was acquired in 19+4 when the general-price-level index (i.e., the GNP Deflator) was 105. Additional equipment of $30,000 was acquired at the beginning of 19+7 when the index was 110. Depreciation of equipment is computed at 10 percent of cost, with no expected salvage value.

Inventory is costed on the FIFO basis. Purchases of inventory during a year are made fairly evenly throughout the year, so that the average annual general-price-level index can be used.

All revenues and expenses (except depreciation and cost of goods sold) are earned or incurred fairly evenly throughout a year, so that the average annual general-price-level index can be used.

The business was begun in 19+3 when the general-price-level index was 100.

JAYHAWK, INC.
Comparative Balance Sheets
December 31, 19+6–19+8

Assets	19+8		19+7		19+6	
Current assets:						
Cash	$ 40,000		$ 50,000		$ 40,000	
Accounts receivable	150,000		126,000		100,000	
Inventory	80,000	$270,000	60,000	$236,000	55,000	$195,000
Plant & equipment:						
Equipment	$240,000		$240,000		$210,000	
Less accumulated depreciation	111,000	129,000	87,000	153,000	63,000	147,000
		$399,000		$389,000		$342,000
Equities						
Current liabilities:						
Current payables		$ 50,000		$ 40,000		$ 29,000
Long-term liabilities:						
Bank loan		40,000		60,000		60,000
Stockholders' equity:						
Common stock	$200,000		$200,000		$200,000	
Retained earnings	109,000	309,000	89,000	289,000	53,000	253,000
		$399,000		$389,000		$342,000

JAYHAWK, INC.
Comparative Statements of Income and Retained Earnings
For the Years Ended December 31, 19+8 and 19+7

	19+8		19+7	
Sales		$500,000		$480,000
Cost of goods sold	$320,000		$300,000	
Depreciation	24,000		24,000	
Other expenses (including interest and taxes)	126,000	470,000	120,000	444,000
Net income		$ 30,000		$ 36,000
Beginning retained earnings		89,000		53,000
Subtotal		$119,000		$ 89,000
Deduct dividends		10,000		—
Ending retained earnings		$109,000		$ 89,000

The general-price-level index data are as follows:

Year	GNP Deflator Annual Average	GNP Deflator 4th Quarter Average
19+3	100	
19+4	105	
19+5	108	
19+6	109	110
19+7	114	120
19+8	124	126

What we would want to do is adjust the historical-dollar financial statements of Jayhawk, Inc., into dollars of general purchasing power as of the end of 19+8. However, in order to demonstrate the "roll-forward" procedure, assume that we first want to present the 19+7 general-price-level financial statements (dollars of general purchasing power as of the end of 19+7), even though this is an additional step. In other words, most companies presenting comparative general-price-level financial statements would adjust the current-year historical-dollar financial statements into "current dollars" and update prior years' general-price-level financial statements in order to present comparative statements.

19+7 statements. Since we want to present general-price-level financial statements for the year 19+7, it is necessary to adjust the historical-dollar financial data by multiplying each item by the ratio of the current year-end index (and for 19+7 it is 120) to the pertinent index when the transaction originated. To avoid calculating this ratio every time we need to make an adjustment, we can calculate conversion factors and use them in making the necessary adjustments. As shown on page 633, conversion factors are merely the current year-end index divided by the other index numbers.

		GNP Deflator		
Year	Quarter	Annual Average	4th Quarter Average	Conversion Factors
19+3		100		120/100 = 1.20000
19+4		105		120/105 = 1.14286
19+5		108		120/108 = 1.11111
19+6		109		120/109 = 1.10092
19+7		114		120/114 = 1.05263
19+6	4th		110	120/110 = 1.09091
19+7	4th		120	120/120 = 1.00000

We are immediately faced with a problem—the need to determine the beginning retained earnings balance for 19+7, adjusted for general-price-level changes. In order to avoid the impractical alternative of restating all prior years' financial statements since the company was begun, we can compute the beginning retained earnings for the first year in which general-price-level statements are prepared as a balancing amount.[13] Thus, as shown at the top of page 634, the historical-dollar balance sheet for 19+6 is restated into 19+7 dollars by adjusting all items except retained earnings and determining retained earnings as the balancing amount of $44,188.

Having calculated the beginning retained earnings adjusted for general-price-level changes, we need to calculate the general-price-level gain or loss in order to prepare a general-price-level statement of income and retained earnings for 19+7. As was previously explained, the difference between the current year-end monetary items unadjusted and the monetary items held during the year adjusted for general-price-level changes is the general-purchasing-power gain or loss. In order to facilitate the computation of the general-price-level gain or loss, *Statement No. 3* recommends the use of a format consisting of a statement of sources and applications of net monetary items.[14] Such a format is illustrated at the bottom of page 634, and shows that there was a general-price-level loss on the holding of net monetary assets during 19+7 of $4,803.

In calculating the general-price-level loss, note that the monetary items for the year-end 19+6 are merely restated into 19+7 year-end dollars, and that the increases (sales) and decreases (purchases, other expenses, and equipment acquired) in monetary items during 19+7 are adjusted for changes in the general-price level by the use of the appropriate index numbers. The difference between the restated net monetary items ($80,803) and the actual net monetary items ($76,000), which are automatically in terms of current purchasing-power dollars, is the general-price-level loss ($4,803). Also note that merchandise purchases of $305,000 were determined by the use of the cost-of-goods-sold formula in which beginning inventory plus purchases minus ending inventory equals cost of goods sold:

$$\begin{aligned} \$55{,}000 + P - \$60{,}000 &= \$300{,}000 \\ P &= \$305{,}000 \end{aligned}$$

[13] *Statement No. 3,* p. 36.
[14] *Statement No. 3,* p. 40.

JAYHAWK, INC.
General-Price-Level Restatement—19+7
Working Balance Sheet—19+6

	Historical		Conversion Factor[a]		Restated to 12/31/+7 Dollars
Assets					
Cash	$ 40,000	×	1.09091	=	$ 43,636
Accounts receivable	100,000	×	1.09091	=	109,091
Inventory	55,000	×	1.10092	=	60,551
Equipment	210,000	×	1.14286	=	240,001
Less accumulated depreciation	(63,000)	×	1.14286	=	(72,000)
	$342,000				$381,279
Equities					
Current payables	$ 29,000	×	1.09091	=	$ 31,636
Bank loan	60,000	×	1.09091	=	65,455
Common stock	200,000	×	1.20000	=	240,000
Retained earnings	53,000				44,188
	$342,000				$381,279

JAYHAWK, INC.
General-Price-Level Restatement—19+7
General-Price-Level Gain or Loss

	12/31/+6 Historical		12/31/+6 Conversion Factor[a]		12/31/+6 Restated to 12/31/+7 Dollars	Historical 12/31/+7
Net monetary items:						
Cash	$ 40,000	×	1.09091	=	$ 43,636	$ 50,000
Accounts receivable	100,000	×	1.09091	=	109,091	126,000
Current payables	(29,000)	×	1.09091	=	(31,636)	(40,000)
Bank loan	(60,000)	×	1.09091	=	(65,455)	(60,000)
	$ 51,000				$ 55,636	$ 76,000
General-price-level gain or loss:						
Net monetary items—12/31/+6	$ 51,000	×	1.09091	=	$ 55,636	
Add sales	480,000	×	1.05263	=	505,262	
	$531,000				$560,898	
Deduct:						
Purchases of merchandise	$305,000	×	1.05263	=	$321,052	
Other expenses	120,000	×	1.05263	=	126,316	
Equipment acquired	30,000	×	1.09091	=	32,727	
	$455,000				$480,095	
Net monetary items—restated—12/31/+7					$ 80,803	
Net monetary items—historical—12/31/+7	$ 76,000				76,000	
General-price-level loss					$ 4,803	

[a] 1.09091 = 120/110 = 4th quarter 19+7 index/4th quarter 19+6 index
1.10092 = 120/109 = 4th quarter 19+7 index/19+6 average index
1.14286 = 120/105 = 4th quarter 19+7 index/19+4 average index
1.20000 = 120/100 = 4th quarter 19+7 index/19+3 average index
1.05263 = 120/114 = 4th quarter 19+7 index/19+7 average index

JAYHAWK, INC.
General-Price-Level Restatement—19+7
Working Statement of Income and Retained Earnings

	Historical		Adjustment[b]		Restated to 12/31/+7 Dollars
Sales	$480,000	×	1.05263	=	$505,262
Operating expenses:					
Cost of goods sold	$300,000		{$55,000 × 1.10092 + $245,000 × 1.05263}		$318,445
Depreciation	24,000		{$21,000 × 1.14286 + $3,000 × 1.09091}		27,273
Other expenses	120,000	×	1.05263	=	126,316
	$444,000				$472,034
Net operating income	$ 36,000				$ 33,228
General-price-level loss	—				4,803
Net income	$ 36,000				$ 28,425
Retained earnings—12/31/+6	53,000				44,188
Retained earnings—12/31/+7	$ 89,000				$ 72,613

JAYHAWK, INC.
General-Price-Level Restatement—19+7
Working Balance Sheet—19+7

Assets	Historical		Adjustment[b]		Restated to 12/31/+7 Dollars
Cash	$ 50,000	×	1.00000	=	$ 50,000
Accounts receivable	126,000	×	1.00000	=	126,000
Inventory	60,000	×	1.05263	=	63,158
Equipment	240,000		{$210,000 × 1.14286 + $30,000 × 1.09091}		272,728
Less accumulated depreciation	(87,000)		{$84,000 × 1.14286 + $3,000 × 1.09091}		(99,273)
	$389,000				$412,613
Equities					
Current payables	$ 40,000	×	1.00000	=	$ 40,000
Bank loan	60,000	×	1.00000	=	60,000
Common stock	200,000	×	1.20000	=	240,000
Retained earnings	89,000				72,613
	$389,000				$412,613

[b] 1.05263 = 120/114 = 4th quarter 19+7 index/19+7 average index
1.10092 = 120/109 = 4th quarter 19+7 index/19+6 average index
1.14286 = 120/105 = 4th quarter 19+7 index/19+4 average index
1.09091 = 120/110 = 4th quarter 19+7 index/4th quarter 19+6 index
1.20000 = 120/100 = 4th quarter 19+7 index/19+3 average index

Given the beginning retained earnings adjusted for general-price-level changes and the general-price-level loss, we can prepare the general-price-level statement of income and retained earnings. The working statement is shown at the top of page 635. Note that the restated cost of goods sold of $318,445 is calculated by separating the beginning inventory sold ($55,000) and the inventory sold from current purchases ($245,000) and multiplying by the appropriate indexes.[15] Similarly, the restated depreciation expense of $27,273 is calculated by separating the depreciation on the original equipment acquired ($21,000) and the depreciation on the recent equipment acquisition ($3,000) and multiplying by the appropriate indexes. Also note that the working statement provides us with the ending retained earnings balance ($72,613) needed for the preparation of the general-price-level balance sheet.

The preparation of the general-price-level balance sheet is shown at the bottom of page 635. Note that the arrows in the working papers indicate how the restated figures tie together, as well as indicating the steps in the preparation of general-price-level financial statements.

JAYHAWK, INC.
General-Price-Level Statement
of Income and Retained Earnings
For Year Ended December 31, 19+7

	General-Price-Level Basis (Restated to 12/31/+7)
Sales	$(+7) 505,262
Operating expenses:	
Cost of goods sold	$ 318,445
Depreciation	27,273
Other expenses	126,316
	$ 472,034
Net operating profit	$ 33,228
General-price-level loss	4,803
Net income	$ 28,425
Retained earnings—19+6	44,188
Retained earnings—19+7	$ (+7) 72,613

[15]The calculation of the restated cost of goods sold can be verified as follows:

	Historical		Conversion Factor*		Restated to 12/31/+7 Dollars
Beginning inventory	$ 55,000	×	1.10092	=	$ 60,551
Purchases	305,000	×	1.05263	=	321,052
Goods available	$360,000				$381,603
Ending inventory	60,000	×	1.05263	=	63,158
Cost of goods sold	$300,000				$318,445

*1.10092 = 120/109 = 4th quarter 19+7 index/19+6 average index
1.05263 = 120/114 = 4th quarter 19+7 index/19+7 average index

JAYHAWK, INC.
General-Price-Level Balance Sheet
December 31, 19+7

	General-Price-Level Basis (Restated to 12/31/+7)
Assets	
Current assets:	
Cash	$(+7) 50,000
Accounts receivable	126,000
Inventory	63,158
Total current assets	$ 239,158
Long-lived assets:	
Equipment	$ 272,728
Less accumulated depreciation	99,273
Net	$ 173,455
Total assets	$(+7) 412,613
Equities	
Current liabilities:	
Current payables	$(+7) 40,000
Long-term liabilities:	
Bank loan	$ 60,000
Stockholders' equity:	
Common stock	$ 240,000
Retained earnings	72,613
Total stockholders' equity	$ 312,613
Total equities	$(+7) 412,613

The formal general-price-level financial statements for 19+7 are presented on page 636 and above. Note the use of (+7) to indicate that the statements are in terms of 19+7 dollars.

19+8 STATEMENTS: Assume that the 19+8 fiscal period has just ended and that we are ready to prepare comparative general-price-level financial statements for the years 19+7 and 19+8 in terms of the general purchasing power of the dollar as of December 31, 19+8. Since the restated 19+7 financial statements are in terms of dollars of general purchasing power as of December 31, 19+7, we can begin by restating the 19+7 statements into 19+8 dollars. This is shown on page 638. Note that the restatement is done by the "roll-forward" procedure, in which each restated (19+7) item is multiplied by the ratio of the current year-end index (126) to the prior year-end index (120), which is a conversion factor of 1.05. The result is that the 19+7 financial statements are restated to dollars of general purchasing power as of December 31, 19+8. Also note that this "rolling forward" of 19+7 financial data provides the restated beginning retained earnings figure ($76,244) needed for the 19+8 general-price-level financial statements.

We are now ready to prepare the general-price-level financial statements for 19+8. The conversion factors needed for the 19+8 restatement are as follows:

Year	Quarter	GNP Deflator Annual Average	GNP Deflator 4th Quarter Average	Conversion Factors
19+3		100		126/100 = 1.26000
19+4		105		126/105 = 1.20000
19+5		108		126/108 = 1.16667
19+6		109		126/109 = 1.15596
19+7		114		126/114 = 1.10526
19+8		124		126/124 = 1.01613
19+6	4th		110	126/110 = 1.14545
19+7	4th		120	126/120 = 1.05000
19+8	4th		126	126/126 = 1.00000

JAYHAWK, INC.
General-Price-Level Restatement—19+8
Working Statement of Income and Retained Earnings—19+7

	Restated to 12/31/+7 Dollars		Conversion Factor*		Restated to 12/31/+8 Dollars
Sales	$505,262	×	1.05	=	$530,525
Operating expenses:					
Cost of goods sold	$318,445	×	1.05	=	$334,367
Depreciation	27,273	×	1.05	=	28,636
Other expenses	126,315	×	1.05	=	132,632
	$472,033				$495,635
Net operating income	$ 33,229				$ 34,890
General-price-level loss	4,803	×	1.05	=	5,043
Net income	$ 28,426				$ 29,847
Retained earnings—12/31/+6	44,187	×	1.05	=	46,397
Retained earnings—12/31/+7	$ 72,613				$ 76,244

JAYHAWK, INC.
General-Price-Level Restatement—19+8
Working Balance Sheet—19+7

Assets	Restated to 12/31/+7 Dollars		Conversion Factor*		Restated to 12/31/+8 Dollars
Cash	$ 50,000	×	1.05	=	$ 52,500
Accounts receivable	126,000	×	1.05	=	132,300
Inventory	63,158	×	1.05	=	66,316
Equipment	272,728	×	1.05	=	286,364
Less accumulated depreciation	(99,273)	×	1.05	=	(104,236)
	$412,613				$433,244
Equities					
Current payables	$ 40,000	×	1.05	=	$ 42,000
Bank loan	60,000	×	1.05	=	63,000
Common stock	240,000	×	1.05	=	252,000
Retained earnings	72,613	×	1.05	=	76,244
	$412,613				$433,244

*1.05 = 126/120 = 4th quarter 19+8 index/4th quarter 19+7 index.

The conversion factors at the top of page 638 are applied in the same manner that was used in restating the 19+7 statements.

The working papers for the 19+8 restatement are presented on pages 640 and 641. As shown at the top of page 640, we begin by determining the general-price-level loss of $4,350. The source and application of net monetary items format used in determining the general-price-level loss is identical to the 19+7 format, and the same items are used with the exception of the $10,000 dividends for 19+8. It is assumed that the dividends were declared and paid at the end of 19+8, so that they are already stated in "current dollars."

The general-price-level loss of $4,350 and the "rolled-forward" beginning retained earnings, previously determined, of $76,244 are used in preparing the statement of income and retained earnings, as shown at the bottom of page 640 and the top of page 641. Note that the restated cost of goods sold of $330,509 is calculated by separating the beginning inventory sold ($60,000) and the inventory sold from current purchases ($260,000) and multiplying by the appropriate indexes.[16] Similarly, the restated depreciation expense of $28,032 is calculated by separating the depreciation on the original equipment acquisition ($21,000) and the depreciation on the 19+7 acquisition ($3,000) and multiplying by the appropriate indexes. Also note that the restated ending retained earnings balance of $82,782 is determined; this is needed for the general-price-level balance sheet.

The working statement for the general-price-level balance sheet for 19+8 is shown on page 641. The restated equipment cost of $286,634 is calculated by separating the cost of the original equipment ($210,000) and the 19+7 acquisition ($30,000) and multiplying by the appropriate index numbers. Similarly, the restated accumulated depreciation of $132,872 is calculated by separating the depreciation on the original equipment acquired ($105,000) and the depreciation on the 19+7 acquisition ($6,000) and multiplying by the appropriate index numbers.

The formal comparative general-price-level financial statements for 19+8 and 19+7 are presented on page 642. In contrast to the comparative historical-dollar income statements for these two years (see page 632), the comparative general-price-level income statements show that sales, cost of goods sold, and other expenses declined, instead of increasing, from 19+7. Similarly, net income for 19+8 in the adjusted income statement ($16,538) is considerably lower than the 19+8 net income shown in the historical-dollar income statement ($30,000).

---

[16]The restated cost-of-goods-sold figure of $330,509 can be verified as follows:

	Historical		Conversion Factor		Restated to 12/31/+8 Dollars
Beginning inventory	$ 60,000	×	1.10526	=	$ 66,316
Purchases	340,000	×	1.01613	=	345,483
Goods available	$400,000				$411,799
Ending inventory	80,000	×	1.01613	=	81,290
Cost of goods sold	$320,000				$330,509

JAYHAWK, INC.
General-Price-Level Restatement—19+8
General-Price-Level Gain or loss

	12/31/+7 Historical		Conversion Factor[a]		Restated to 12/31/+8 Dollars	Historical 12/31/+8
Net monetary items:						
Cash	$ 50,000	×	1.05000	=	$ 52,500	$ 40,000
Accounts receivable	126,000	×	1.05000	=	132,300	150,000
Current payables	(40,000)	×	1.05000	=	(42,000)	(50,000)
Bank loan	(60,000)	×	1.05000	=	(63,000)	(40,000)
	$ 76,000				$ 79,800	$100,000
General-price-level gain or loss:						
Net monetary items—12/31/+7	$ 76,000	×	1.05000	=	$ 79,800	
Add sales	500,000	×	1.01613	=	508,065	
	$576,000				$587,865	
Deduct:						
Purchases of merchandise	$340,000	×	1.01613	=	$345,483	
Other expenses	126,000	×	1.01613	=	128,032	
Dividends	10,000	×	1.00000	=	10,000	
	$476,000				$483,515	
Net monetary items—restated—12/31/+8					$104,350	
Net monetary items—historical—12/31/+8	$100,000				100,000	
General-price-level loss					$ 4,350 →	

JAYHAWK, INC.
General-Price-Level Restatement—19+8
Working Statement of Income and Retained Earnings

	Historical		Adjustment[a]		Restated to 12/31/+8 Dollars
Sales	$500,000	×	1.01613	=	$508,065
Operating expenses:					
Cost of goods sold	$320,000		{$60,000 × 1.10526 + $260,000 × 1.01613}		$330,509
Depreciation	24,000		{$21,000 × 1.20 + $3,000 × 1.14545}		28,636
Other expenses	126,000	×	1.01613	=	128,032
	$470,000				$487,177
Net operating income	$ 30,000				$ 20,888
General-price-level loss	—				4,350 ←

	Historical		Adjustment[a]		Restated to 12/31/+8 Dollars
Net income	$ 30,000				$ 16,538
Retained earnings—12/31/+7	89,000				76,244
	$119,000				$ 92,782
Dividends	10,000	×	1.00000	=	10,000
Retained earnings—12/31/+8	$109,000				$ 82,782 →

[a]1.05000 = 126/120 = 4th quarter 19+8 index/4th quarter 19+7 index
1.01613 = 126/124 = 4th quarter 19+8 index/19+8 average index
1.10526 = 126/114 = 4th quarter 19+8 index/19+7 average index
1.14545 = 126/110 = 4th quarter 19+8 index/4th quarter 19+6 index

JAYHAWK, INC.
General-Price-Level Restatement—19+8
Working Balance Sheet—19+8

Assets	Historical		Adjustment[b]		Restated to 12/31/+8 Dollars
Current assets:					
Cash	$ 40,000	×	1.00000	=	$ 40,000
Accounts receivable	150,000	×	1.00000	=	150,000
Inventory	80,000	×	1.01613	=	81,290
Total current assets	$270,000				$271,290
Long-lived assets:					
Equipment	$240,000		{$210,000 × 1.20 + $30,000 × 1.14545}		$286,364
Less accumulated depreciation	(111,000)		{$105,000 × 1.20 + $6,000 × 1.14545}		(132,872)
Net	$129,000				$153,492
Total assets	$399,000				$424,782
Equities					
Current liabilities:					
Current payables	$ 50,000	×	1.00000	=	$ 50,000
Long-term liabilities:					
Bank loan	$ 40,000	×	1.00000	=	$ 40,000
Stockholders' equity:					
Common stock	$200,000	×	1.26000	=	$252,000
Retained earnings	109,000				82,782 ←
Total stockholders' equity	$309,000				$334,782
Total equities	$399,000				$424,782

[b]1.01613 = 126/124 = 4th quarter 19+8 index/19+8 average index
1.20000 = 126/105 = 4th quarter 19+8 index/19+4 average index
1.14545 = 126/110 = 4th quarter 19+8 index/4th quarter 19+6 index
1.26000 = 126/100 = 4th quarter 19+8 index/19+3 average index
1.10526 = 126/114 = 4th quarter 19+8 index/19+7 average index

JAYHAWK, INC.
Comparative General-Price-Level Statements of Income and Retained Earnings
For the Years Ended December 31, 19+7—19+8

	General-Price-Level Basis (Restated to 12/31/+8)	
	19+8	19+7
Sales	$(+8)508,065	$(+8)530,525
Operating expenses:		
Cost of goods sold	$ 330,509	$ 334,367
Depreciation	28,636	28,636
Other expenses	128,032	132,632
	$ 487,177	$ 495,635
Net operating income	$ 20,888	$ 34,890
General-price-level loss	4,350	5,043
Net income	$ 16,538	$ 29,847
Retained earnings, beginning of year	76,244	46,397
	$ 92,782	$ 76,244
Less dividends	10,000	—
Retained earnings, end of year	$(+8) 82,782	$(+8) 76,244

JAYHAWK, INC.
Comparative General-Price-Level Balance Sheets
December 31, 19+7—19+8

	General-Price-Level Basis (Restated to 12/31/+8)	
Assets	Dec. 31, 19+8	Dec. 31, 19+7
Current assets:		
Cash	$(+8) 40,000	$(+8) 52,500
Accounts receivable	150,000	132,300
Inventory	81,290	66,316
Total current assets	$ 271,290	$ 251,116
Long-lived assets:		
Equipment	$ 286,364	$ 286,364
Less accumulated depreciation	132,872	104,236
Net	$ 153,492	$ 182,128
Total assets	$(+8)424,782	$(+8)433,244
Equities		
Current liabilities:		
Current payables	$(+8) 50,000	$(+8) 42,000
Long-term liabilities:		
Bank loan	$ 40,000	$ 63,000
Stockholders' equity:		
Common stock	$ 252,000	$ 252,000
Retained earnings	82,782	76,244
Total stockholders' equity	$ 334,782	$ 328,244
Total equities	$(+8)424,782	$(+8)433,244

This is explained by the rising general-price level (inflation), so that the adjusted income statement includes expenses that are restated upward to a greater extent (that is, equipment and beginning inventory were acquired when the general-price-level was lower) than the relatively current dollar revenues, as well as the fact that the general-price-level loss is not reported in the historical-dollar income statement. The point is that the analysis of general-price-level financial statements can lead to different conclusions from the one derived from analyzing diverse-dollar conventional financial statements.

Correction of Errors: Statements From Incomplete Data

CORRECTION OF ERRORS

Accounting errors. It is inevitable that errors will be made in the accounting records of a business firm. However, internal audit procedures and the annual examination of financial statements by independent auditors normally find and correct the errors prior to the issuance of financial statements. The correction of errors under these circumstances is normally a simple process and the errors have no effect on the financial statement amounts.

Still, there are instances in which material errors are not discovered in the period in which they occurred, raising the question of how they should be corrected when discovered and how the effect of the correction should be reported in the financial statements. This is important because of the distorting effect the errors can have on financial statements, especially when comparative statements are presented.

Description of errors. The accounting problems created by the necessary correction of errors that affected prior financial statements are not limited to matters of statement location and disclosure; the accounting techniques involved warrant explanation and illustration.

Many mistakes affecting financial statements are merely classification errors: Examples are loans to officers recorded or classified as trade accounts receivable, or salesmen's salaries charged to Office Salaries. Even though undetected, errors of this type have no effect on the net income of the period in which the error is made. Mistakes of a more significant nature result in incorrect net income amounts. Of course, such mistakes also affect the balance sheet. If the net income is overstated as a result of accounting errors, the retained earnings are overstated on the companion balance sheet. If retained earnings are overstated, the net assets are overstated—by overstatement of assets, understatement of liabilities, or a combination thereof. An understatement of net income and retained earnings is accompanied by a balance sheet understatement of net assets.

The subject of accounting errors was discussed briefly in Chapter 4, at which time an accounting error was defined as a misapplication of the economic facts existing at the time of recording and reporting an economic event. The examples of accounting errors listed at that time will be repeated here:

(1) Use of an *unrealistic* estimate as a result of a misuse of economic information at the time the estimate was made (e.g., the use of an unrealistic estimate of the useful life of plant and equipment in the determination of depreciation)
(2) Mathematical mistakes (e.g., errors in counting or pricing inventory)
(3) Use of an *unacceptable* accounting principle or procedure (e.g., failure to recognize depreciation, accruals, or deferrals)
(4) Classification mistakes (e.g., cost of equipment expensed instead of capitalized)

It should be noted that each type of error listed above not only misstates net income for the period in which the error is made but also misstates some balance sheet amount at the end of the period.

Errors affecting net income. Errors that affect the income statement for a period and the balance sheet at the end of the period are of two kinds:

(1) Errors that overstate (or understate) the net income of one period and correspondingly understate (or overstate) the net income of the following period. These are *counterbalancing* errors; although the net income for each period and the balance sheet at the end of the first period are incorrect, the net income for the two periods combined is correct, and the balance sheet at the end of the second period is correct. This assumes that the same income tax rates will prevail in both periods.

For an example of a counterbalancing error, assume that an accountant overlooks the accrual of $1,000 of interest expense as of December 31, 19+4. In 19+5, the interest applicable to 19+4 is paid and charged to Interest Expense. The net income before income tax for 19+4 is overstated $1,000 and the net income before income tax for 19+5 is understated $1,000. By the end of 19+5 the error has been counterbalanced; the total net income for the two years is unaffected (unless different income tax rates are applicable), and the balance sheet at the end of 19+5 is correct. The following income statement data illustrate the counterbalancing produced by the oversight above:

	With Counterbalancing Errors ($1,000 of 19+4 Interest Expense Recorded in 19+5)			Without Errors		
	19+4	19+5	Total	19+4	19+5	Total
Net income before interest and income tax	$8,000	$8,000		$8,000	$8,000	
Interest expense	2,000	4,000		3,000	3,000	
Net income before income tax	$6,000	$4,000		$5,000	$5,000	
Income tax—25% assumed for both years	1,500	1,000		1,250	1,250	
Net income	$4,500 +	$3,000 =	$7,500	$3,750 +	$3,750 =	$7,500

(2) Errors that overstate or understate the net income of one period and are not counterbalanced by a corresponding understatement or overstatement of the net income of the succeeding period. Such errors leave the retained earnings and one or more asset or liability accounts inaccurate until an entry is made to correct the errors, or, in the case of long-lived assets, until they are disposed of or become fully depreciated —either of which removes the effects of the error from the account balances.

For example, assume that the depreciation charged to operations and credited to an accumulated depreciation account in 19+4 was too small. As a result, the net income for 19+4 was overstated; this error will not be automatically counterbalanced by any corresponding understatement of net income in 19+5. Therefore, retained earnings will remain overstated and the accumulated depreciation will remain understated until a correcting entry is made or until the asset involved is disposed of or becomes fully depreciated.

Prior period adjustments. In reporting errors that have caused misstatements of the net income of prior periods, the accountant first considers the materiality of the amounts involved. If the errors are not material in amount, they may be absorbed in the income statement of the year of discovery without disclosure. This procedure is permissible if the current income statement will not thereby be appreciably distorted. However, it should be noted that several immaterial errors may have a cumulative effect that is material.

The procedures to be followed in reporting material errors were specified by the Accounting Principles Board in *Opinion No. 20:*

> The Board concludes that correction of an error in the financial statements of a prior period discovered subsequent to their issuance should be reported as a prior period adjustment.[1]

Under this procedure, the effect of the error on the net income of a prior period would be debited or credited to the account Correction of Prior Period Errors. This account is then closed to the retained earnings account and reported as an adjustment to the beginning retained earnings balance of the current period. If comparative financial statements are being presented, the statements for each year should be restated to reflect the corrected amounts, a procedure referred to as retroactive application of the prior period adjustment.

In order to illustrate the recording and reporting of a material accounting error, the illustration presented in Chapter 4 will be used. Assume that an item of equipment having a ten year estimated life and zero estimated salvage value, and to be depreciated using the straight-line method, was purchased on January 1, 19+5, for $10,000. Rather than being debited to the asset account, the cost was erroneously expensed. The firm's income statement for 19+6 previously reported income of $60,000 before extraordinary items and net income of $40,000.

The correcting entry to be recorded in 19+7 would be as follows:

Equipment	10,000	
Depreciation expense (19+7)	1,000	
Accumulated depreciation—Equipment (3 years × $1,000)		3,000
Correction of prior period error (to be closed to Retained Earnings)		8,000

Should a December 31, 19+6, balance sheet be presented along with the financial statements for 19+7, it would be restated to show the asset Equipment at $10,000 and Accumulated Depreciation—Equipment of $2,000 (depreciation for 19+5 and 19+6). Comparative income statements would appear as shown at the top of the next page.

The following comments are pertinent to the presentation above. The previously reported 19+6 net income before extraordinary items ($60,000) and net income ($40,000) were adjusted downward to $59,000 and $39,000, respectively. This is because $1,000 depreciation expense applicable to 19+6 was not previously reported. Also, the adjustment to the previously reported beginning retained earnings for 19+6 is $9,000, not the $8,000 shown in the correcting entry. This is the amount by which the error affected ending retaining earnings for 19+5, or the cost of the asset erroneously expensed ($10,000), less the depreciation expense not recorded ($1,000).

---

[1]Accounting Principles Board, "Accounting Changes," *Opinion No. 20* (New York: AICPA, July 1971), pp. 398–99.

Partial Comparative Statements of Income and Retained Earnings

	19+7	19+6 As Adjusted (Note A)
⋮		
Depreciation expense	$ 1,000	$ 1,000
⋮		
Income before extraordinary items (Note A)	80,000	59,000
⋮		
Net income (Note A)	65,000	39,000
Retained earnings at beginning of year:		
As previously reported	$140,000	$100,000
Add: Prior period adjustment for accounting error (Note A)	8,000	9,000
As restated	$148,000	$109,000
Retained earnings at end of year	$213,000	$148,000

Note A: The balance of retained earnings at December 31, 19+6, has been restated from amounts previously reported to reflect a retroactive credit of $8,000 for a 19+5 accounting error found in 19+7. The error was the result of a $10,000 purchase of equipment during 19+5 that was inadvertently charged to expense instead of being properly capitalized as an asset. As a result of the error, annual depreciation of $1,000 was not recognized during 19+5 and 19+6. The $8,000 prior-period adjustment for 19+7 is the result of beginning retained earnings of 19+6 being understated $9,000 from the carryover from the 19+5 error and net income for 19+6 being overstated $1,000 by the failure to report depreciation expense, both of which carried over to the 19+7 beginning retained earnings.

Not all accountants agree with the preceding treatment of accounting errors made in prior periods. They advocate reporting the correction in the current year's income statement, so that net income reflects all material economic events that occurred or were discovered during the current period. The reader is referred to the discussion in Chapter 4 of the all-inclusive versus current-operating concepts of the income statement.

Illustration of correction of errors of prior periods. Assume that the A. B. Company found it necessary to replace its accountant at the end of 19+6, before the financial statements had been prepared. The new accountant was informed that the company follows the accrual basis of accounting, and he determined that adjusting entries were required to give recognition to depreciation ($2,200), accrued wages ($250), and office supplies on hand ($400). After recording these adjustments, the new accountant prepared the adjusted trial balance below.

THE A. B. COMPANY
Adjusted Trial Balance
December 31, 19+6

Cash	17,615	
Inventory, end of year	16,200	
Office supplies on hand	400	
Furniture and fixtures	28,300	
Accumulated depreciation		12,305
Accounts payable		11,390
Accrued wages payable		250
Capital stock		30,000
Retained earnings		6,650
Dividends	6,000	
Sales		124,000
Cost of goods sold	90,550	
Wages	15,280	
Office-supplies expense	1,375	
Depreciation	2,200	
Other expense	6,675	
	184,595	184,595

At this point, the accountant discovered that his predecessor had committed several errors in the preparation of financial statements for previous years. He had (1) failed to make adjusting entries for accrued wages and office supplies on hand; (2) miscalculated depreciation for 19+3 and 19+4; and (3) made clerical errors in computing the inventories as of December 31, 19+4 and 19+5.

In order to determine the effects of these mistakes, the accountant develops the following information:

Accrued wages of prior periods:

No entries for accrued wages were made at the end of 19+3, 19+4, or 19+5; such wages were charged to the wages expense account in the following year, when they were paid. The overlooked accruals amounted to:

December 31:	
19+3	$175
19+4	215
19+5	230

The counterbalancing effects on net income as a result of failing to adjust for accrued wages are shown in the schedule at the top of the following page.

The schedule reveals that, as a result of the failure to make adjusting entries for accrued wages, the December 31, 19+3 retained earnings were overstated $175, the 19+4 reported net income was overstated $40, the 19+5 reported net income was overstated $15, and (unless a correction is made) the current year's net income will be understated $230 as a result of the accrued wages as of December 31, 19+5, being charged to the 19+6 wages expense account.

	December 31, 19+3, Retained Earnings Were Overstated	Net Income Was Overstated–Understated* 19+4	19+5	19+6 Net Income Will Be Understated*
Failure to adjust for accrued wages:				
December 31, 19+3	175	175*		
December 31, 19+4		215	215*	
December 31, 19+5			230	230*
Net overstatement		40	15	

Office supplies on hand:

No recognition was given to the amount of office supplies on hand at the end of 19+3, 19+4, or 19+5. As a result, all purchases of office supplies were treated as an expense in the year of purchase, whether or not they were used in that period. The overlooked amounts on hand were:

December 31:	
19+3	$365
19+4	415
19+5	505

The counterbalancing effects are shown below:

	December 31, 19+3, Retained Earnings Were Understated*	Net Income Was Overstated–Understated* 19+4	19+5	19+6 Net Income Will Be Overstated
Failure to inventory office supplies:				
December 31, 19+3	365*	365		
December 31, 19+4		415*	415	
December 31, 19+5			505*	505
Net understatement*...		50*	90*	

Merchandise inventories:

Year-end inventories were understated and overstated as follows:

December 31:	
19+4—understated....................	$1,390
19+5—overstated	615

The counterbalancing effects are shown at the top of the following page.

	Cost of Goods Sold Was Overstated–Understated* 19+4	19+5	Net Income Was Overstated–Understated* 19+4	19+5	19+6 Net Income Will Be Understated*
Error in computing merchandise inventory:					
December 31, 19+4—understated	1,390	1,390*	1,390*	1,390	
December 31, 19+5—overstated..............		615*		615	615*
Net overstatement–understatement*	1,390	2,005*	1,390*	2,005	

As the schedule above reveals, an understated ending inventory will understate earnings for the current period and overstate earnings for the following period, and vice versa.

Depreciation:

Depreciation for 19+3 was overstated $160.
Depreciation for 19+4 was understated $200.
Depreciation for 19+5 was correct.

The effects of depreciation errors on net income work themselves out only when the depreciating asset is disposed of or becomes fully depreciated. In the case of the A. B. Company, no assets subject to depreciation have been disposed of or become fully depreciated during the 19+3–19+6 period. As a result, the depreciation errors have had the following effects:

	December 31, 19+3, Retained Earnings Were Understated*	Net Income Was Overstated–Understated* 19+4	19+5	December 31, 19+6, Accumulated Depreciation Will Be Understated*
Error in computing depreciation:				
19+3—depreciation overstated	160*			40* (both errors combined)
19+4—depreciation understated.......		200		

In order to determine the net effect of all the errors on the financial statements, a work sheet similar to the example on page 652 may be prepared.

Such a work sheet is useful for two purposes: It shows whether the net effect of the errors is sufficiently material to require disclosure; and it assembles the information required for statement-correction purposes. In this instance, the work sheet shows that:

(1) By the end of 19+5, all errors except the following were counterbalanced:
December 31, 19+5 wage accrual ignored—$230
December 31, 19+5 office supplies on hand omitted—$505

THE A. B. COMPANY
Work Sheet to Determine Effect of Errors
on Prior and Current Years' Financial Statements
Overstatement–Understatement*

	References	Prior Years' Financial Statements			19+6 Financial Statements If No Corrections Are Made		
			Net Income		Income Statement	Balance Sheet	
		Retained Earnings December 31, 19+3	19+4	19+5	Net Income	Accumulated Depreciation	Retained Earnings
Failure to adjust for accrued wages:							
December 31, 19+3	a	175	175*				
December 31, 19+4	b		215	215*			
December 31, 19+5	c			230	230*		
Failure to inventory office supplies:							
December 31, 19+3	d	365*	365				
December 31, 19+4	e		415*	415			
December 31, 19+5	f			505*	505		
Errors in computing merchandise inventory:							
December 31, 19+4—understated	g		1,390*	1,390			
December 31, 19+5—overstated	h			615	615*		
Errors in computing depreciation:							
19+3—depreciation overstated	i	160*				} 40*	40
19+4—depreciation understated	j		200				
Net overstatement–understatement*		350*	1,200*	1,930	340*	40*	40

Note: The small letters appearing in the work sheet are key references used later in the chapter in illustrative working papers.

December 31, 19+5 inventory overstated—$615
19+3 depreciation overstated—$160
19+4 depreciation understated—$200

(2) By the end of 19+6, all errors except the depreciation misstatements will have been counterbalanced. However, the net income for 19+6 will be understated by $340 as a result of the 19+5 errors relating to wages, office supplies, and the merchandise inventory.

Procedure If Corrections Are to Be Absorbed in the Current Year's Income Statement Without Disclosure

Assume that the errors of prior years are not considered sufficiently material to require disclosure, and that those not already counterbalanced will be allowed to affect the 19+6 income statement, without listing or otherwise disclosing them. Therefore, only the depreciation errors will need correcting; the other errors have been counterbalanced or will be counterbalanced in 19+6 by the operation of normal accounting procedures.

The following correcting entry will be required:

Depreciation expense		40	
Accumulated depreciation			40
To correct for:			
Underdepreciation in 19+4	$200		
Overdepreciation in 19+3	160		
Net	$ 40		

The income statement and statement of retained earnings for 19+6 shown below are based on the adjusted trial balance shown on page 649, as modified by the depreciation correction. Balance sheets are not presented in the examples in this chapter because there are no special features to illustrate.

THE A. B. COMPANY
Income Statement
For the Year Ended December 31, 19+6

Sales		$124,000
Cost of goods sold		90,550
Gross margin		$ 33,450
Expenses:		
Wages	$15,280	
Office supplies expense	1,375	
Depreciation	2,240	
Other expense	6,675	25,570
Net income		$ 7,880

THE A. B. COMPANY
Statement of Retained Earnings
For the Year Ended December 31, 19+6

Retained earnings, December 31, 19+5	$ 6,650
Net income—per income statement	7,880
Total	$ 14,530
Dividends	6,000
Retained earnings, December 31, 19+6	$ 8,530

Procedure If Errors Are Disclosed as Prior Period Adjustments

If the errors are considered material enough to be reported as prior period adjustments, then correcting entries will be recorded in the current period for all the errors not counterbalanced as of the *beginning* of the current period. It is assumed in this case that a separate entry is to be recorded from each correction. An alternative would be to record a single entry showing the net effect of all errors on the beginning balance in the retained earnings account.

The following entries would be recorded as of the end of 19+6:

Correction of prior period error—19+5 wage accrual	230	
Wages		230
To remove wages applicable to 19+5.		
Office-supplies expense	505	
Correction of prior period error—Office supplies improperly expensed in 19+5		505
Supplies on hand at beginning of year.		
Correction of prior period error—Inventory overstatement—December 31, 19+5	615	
Cost of goods sold		615
To correct the cost of goods sold because of the error in the beginning inventory.		
Correction of prior period error—Depreciation errors	40	
Accumulated depreciation		40
To correct accumulated depreciation account for errors made in computing depreciation for 19+3 and 19+4.		

Depending upon the number of corrections required, working papers may be used to facilitate the preparation of financial statements for the current year. These are presented on the following page. The statement of retained earnings prepared from the working papers is presented on page 656. The balance sheet and income statement are not shown because there would be nothing unusual in either their form or their content.

Closing entries. When the correction items are shown as prior period adjustments, the revenue and expense accounts and the income summary account will be closed in the usual manner. The correction accounts will be closed to Retained Earnings, as follows:

Retained earnings	380	
Correction of prior period error—Office supplies improperly expensed	505	
Correction of prior period error—19+5 wage accrual		230
Correction of prior period error—Inventory overstatement, December 31, 19+5		615
Correction of prior period error—Depreciation errors		40
To close correction-of-prior-period-errors accounts.		

THE A. B. COMPANY
Working Papers
For the Year Ended December 31, 19+6

	Adjusted Trial Balance		Corrections*		Income Statement		Statement of Retained Earnings		Balance Sheet	
Cash	17,615								17,615	
Inventory, end of year	16,200								16,200	
Office supplies on hand	400								400	
Furniture and fixtures	28,300								28,300	
Accumulated depreciation		12,305		(i–j) 40						12,345
Accounts payable		11,390								11,390
Accrued wages payable		250								250
Capital stock		30,000								30,000
Retained earnings		6,650						6,650		
Dividends	6,000						6,000			
Sales		124,000				124,000				
Cost of goods sold	90,550			(h) 615	89,935					
Wages	15,280			(c) 230	15,050					
Office supplies expense	1,375		(f) 505		1,880					
Depreciation	2,200				2,200					
Other expense	6,675				6,675					
	184,595	184,595								
Correction of prior period errors:										
19+5 wage accrual			(c) 230				230			
Office supplies improperly expensed in 19+5				(f) 505				505		
Inventory overstatement, December 31, 19+5			(h) 615				615			
Depreciation errors			(i–j) 40				40			
			1,390	1,390	115,740	124,000	6,885	7,155		
Net income					8,260			8,260		
					124,000	124,000	6,885	15,415		
Retained earnings, December 31, 19+6							8,530			8,530
							15,415	15,415	62,515	62,515

*The small letter references are to individual items in the work sheet on page 652.

THE A. B. COMPANY
Statement of Retained Earnings
For the Year Ended December 31, 19+6

Retained earnings, December 31, 19+5:			
Per books			$ 6,650
Corrections of prior-period errors:			
Add:			
Office supplies improperly expensed in 19+5			505
Total			$ 7,155
Deduct:			
19+5 wage accrual		$230	
Inventory overstatement, December 31, 19+5		615	
Depreciation:			
Insufficient provision in 19+4	$200		
Excess provision in 19+3	160	40	885
As adjusted			$ 6,270
Net income—per income statement			8,260
Total			$14,530
Dividends			6,000
Retained earnings, December 31, 19+6			$ 8,530

For 19+6, the retained earnings account would show the following amounts:

Retained Earnings

19+6			19+6		
12/31	Correction accounts	380	1/ 2	Balance	6,650
12/31	Dividends	6,000	12/31	From Income Summary	8,260

The year-end account balance is $8,530, which agrees with the statement of retained earnings.

Procedure If Statements for Prior Years Are to Be Revised

It was noted earlier in this chapter that when material errors have been made in prior periods and comparative financial statements are to be presented, the statements for each year affected by the errors should be restated to reflect the corrected amounts. Waiving the question of whether the errors illustrated are significant, the A. B. Company case will be used to show how revised statements may be prepared. Although some of the errors affected the 19+3 statements, we shall assume (in order to shorten the illustration somewhat) that 19+4 is the first year for which revised statements are to be presented. The working papers used in the preparation of revised statements for 19+4 are presented on the following page.

Note the following about the working papers:

(1) The amounts shown in the first two money columns were copied from the financial statements prepared before the discovery of the errors in the statements of prior years.

THE A. B. COMPANY
Working Papers to Revise Financial Statements
For the Year Ended December 31, 19+4

	Per Statements		Corrections*		Revised Statements	
Income Statement						
Sales		114,500				114,500
Cost of goods sold	84,100			(g) 1,390	82,710	
Expenses:						
Wages	13,200		(b) 215	(a) 175	13,240	
Office supplies expense	1,620		(d) 365	(e) 415	1,570	
Depreciation	1,745		(j) 200		1,945	
Other expense	7,035				7,035	
	107,700	114,500			106,500	114,500
Net income—down	6,800				8,000	
	114,500	114,500			114,500	114,500
Statement of Retained Earnings						
Retained earnings, beginning of year		5,000				5,000
Correction of prior period errors			(a) 175	(d) 365 (i) 160		350
Net income—brought down		6,800				8,000
Dividends	6,000				6,000	
	6,000	11,800			6,000	13,350
Retained earnings, end of year—down	5,800				7,350	
	11,800	11,800			13,350	13,350
Balance Sheet						
Cash	12,545				12,545	
Inventory, end of year	15,700		(g) 1,390		17,090	
Office supplies on hand			(e) 415		415	
Furniture and fixtures	27,000				27,000	
Accumulated depreciation		7,945	(i) 160	(j) 200		7,985
Accounts payable		11,500				11,500
Accrued wages payable				(b) 215		215
Capital stock		30,000				30,000
Retained earnings—brought down		5,800				7,350
	55,245	55,245	2,920	2,920	57,050	57,050

*The small letter references are to individual items in the work sheet on page 652.

(2) The corrections were taken from the work sheet prepared by the new accountant to determine the effects of the errors he discovered. (See page 652.) The key references refer to that work sheet. The necessary corrections are repeated here to make it easier to follow the working papers.

(a)} Corrections required because of failure to adjust for accrued
(b)} wages

(d)} Corrections required because of failure to give recognition to
(e)} office supplies on hand

(g) Correction required because of clerical error in computing merchandise inventory

(i)} Correction required because of errors in computing depreciation
(j)} provisions

(3) The three errors affecting the December 31, 19+3 retained earnings are applied to the December 31, 19+3 retained earnings figure of $5,000 (corrections a, d, and i). All other errors affect 19+4 income statement or balance sheet accounts.

Working papers to revise the 19+5 financial statements are presented on page 659. In connection with these working papers, note that when the beginning-of-year retained earnings has been properly corrected, the revised amount, $7,350 ($5,800 + $1,550), agrees with the end-of-year revised retained earnings figure shown in the working papers to revise the financial statements for the year ended December 31, 19+4 (page 657).

The final step in the presentation of comparative statements for 19+4, 19+5, and 19+6 is to prepare the statements for 19+6. Working papers for 19+6 were presented earlier, on page 655. However, it was assumed at that time that all corrections were to be reported in 19+6 financial statements, rather than preparing corrected statements for prior years. When revised statements are prepared for earlier years, the only requirement for the current year is that the amounts reported reflect the retroactive application of the prior period corrections. This would be done for the current year by reporting the effect of the retroactive adjustment on the beginning retained earnings balance, a procedure previously illustrated on page 648.

Income taxes and correction of prior period errors. In order to facilitate concentration on the correction problem, income taxes have been ignored in the foregoing discussion. However, it should be recognized that the discovery of certain errors may result in a change in the income tax liability for one or more prior periods. The disclosure of prior period adjustments requires that the associated tax effects be reported. This was discussed in Chapter 4.

THE A. B. COMPANY
Working Papers to Revise Financial Statements
For the Year Ended December 31, 19+5

	Per Statements		Corrections*		Revised Statements	
Income Statement						
Sales		116,000				116,000
Cost of goods sold	85,050		(g) 1,390		87,055	
			(h) 615			
Expenses:						
Wages	14,100		(c) 230	(b) 215	14,115	
Office supplies expense	1,715		(e) 415	(f) 505	1,625	
Depreciation	2,160				2,160	
Other expense	6,125				6,125	
	109,150	116,000			111,080	116,000
Net income—down	6,850				4,920	
	116,000	116,000			116,000	116,000
Statement of Retained Earnings						
Retained earnings, beginning of year		5,800				5,800
Correction of prior period errors			{(i–j) 40	(e) 415}		1,550
			{(b) 215	(g) 1,390}		
Net income—brought down		6,850				4,920
Dividends	6,000				6,000	
	6,000	12,650			6,000	12,270
Retained earnings, end of year—down	6,650				6,270	
	12,650	12,650			12,270	12,270
Balance Sheet						
Cash	15,455				15,455	
Inventory, end of year	16,100			(h) 615	15,485	
Office supplies on hand			(f) 505		505	
Furniture and fixtures	28,000				28,000	
Accumulated depreciation		10,105		(i–j) 40		10,145
Accounts payable		12,800				12,800
Accrued wages payable				(c) 230		230
Capital stock		30,000				30,000
Retained earnings—brought down		6,650				6,270
	59,555	59,555	3,410	3,410	59,445	59,445

*The small letter references are to individual items in the work sheet on page 652.

STATEMENTS FROM INCOMPLETE RECORDS

Single-entry records. Not all business firms keep their accounting records using a complete double-entry system of accounts. Under the so-called single-entry record keeping system, the minimum essentials consist of accounts with debtors and creditors and a record of cash receipts and disbursements. Other accounts, records, and memoranda may be maintained, but a bookkeeping system short of a complete set of double-entry accounts is still regarded as a single-entry system.

Single-entry income statement. The single-entry method of determining the net income for a period is as follows:

(1) Prepare a statement of assets and liabilities as of the beginning of the period, and a similar statement as of the end of the period. From these statements, the owner's equity at the beginning and end of the period can be determined. Information regarding accounts receivable, accounts payable, and cash, required for these statements, can be obtained from the ledger and cash records. Information concerning other assets and liabilities must be obtained from any available information.

(2) Add the owner's equity at the beginning of the period and the additional investments during the period; the total represents the proprietor's gross contribution to the business for the period.

(3) Add the owner's equity at the end of the period and the owner's withdrawals during the period; the total represents the amount made available to the owner as the result of contributions and business operations.

(4) Compute the difference between the totals determined in (2) and (3); this difference is accepted as the net income or loss for the period.

First illustration:

Owner's equity, end of period		$12,000
Add drawings		1,000
Total		$13,000
Deduct:		
Owner's equity, beginning of period	$10,000	
Additional investments	500	10,500
Net income		$ 2,500

Second illustration:

Owner's equity, beginning of period		$10,000
Additional investments		1,800
Total		$11,800
Deduct:		
Owner's equity, end of period	$11,000	
Drawings	300	11,300
Net loss		$ 500

Statements in double-entry form. If certain information is available, it is possible to prepare an income statement as if double-entry records had been maintained. A record of cash receipts and disbursements can be used to obtain the following data:

An analysis of the cash receipts will show:
- Cash sales
- Collections from customers
- Receipts from other sources

An analysis of the cash disbursements will show:
- Cash purchases
- Payments to creditors
- Payments for expenses
- Other disbursements

This information, plus data concerning accounts receivable, accounts payable, inventories, and such other matters as accrued and deferred items at the beginning and end of the period, can be used to prepare the income statement.

Computation of sales. Several illustrations will now be presented showing the computation of sales by the use of data shown by the cash and receivable records.

BASIC ILLUSTRATION. This first illustration shows the basic procedure.

Cash sales		$ 75,000
Sales on account:		
Collections from customers	$80,000	
Less accounts receivable, beginning of period	8,100	
Collections from sales for the period	$71,900	
Add accounts receivable, end of period	8,000	79,900
Total sales		$154,900

The computation can be somewhat simplified, as follows:

Cash sales	$ 75,000
Add collections from customers	80,000
Total	$155,000
Less decrease in accounts receivable	100
Sales	$154,900

This chapter will show how a systematic set of working papers can be prepared to assemble all the data required for an income statement in double-entry form. Such working papers consist of three sections:

- Comparative balance-sheet data
- Cash receipts and disbursements data
- Income-statement data

The balance-sheet and cash data are first entered in the working papers in the manner shown on the following page.

Income Statement Working Papers
For the Year Ended December 31, 19+5

	Comparative Balance Sheet			
	December 31,		Year's Changes—Net	
	19+5	19+4	Debit	Credit
Balance sheets:				
Assets:				
Accounts receivable ...	8,000	8,100		100
			Cash	
			Debit	Credit
Cash:				
Cash sales			75,000	
Collections on accounts receivable			80,000	
			Income Statement	
			Debit	Credit
Income statement:				

The $154,900 credit offsetting the amounts shown in the last two columns of the working papers above is then entered in the Income Statement section of the papers, in the manner shown below. Observe that the amounts are given a cross-reference letter (A) so that the items entering into the computation of the $154,900 can be traced.

Income Statement Working Papers
For the Year Ended December 31, 19+5

	Comparative Balance Sheet			
	December 31,		Year's Changes—Net	
	19+5	19+4	Debit	Credit
Balance sheets:				
Assets:				
Accounts receivable	8,000	8,100		100 A
			Cash	
			Debit	Credit
Cash:				
Cash sales			75,000 A	
Collections on accounts receivable			80,000 A	
			Income Statement	
			Debit	Credit
Income statement:				
Sales				154,900 A

NOTES RECEIVED FROM CUSTOMERS. If notes are taken from customers, the difference between the notes receivable at the beginning and the end of the period, as well as the change in the accounts receivable, must be taken into the computation of sales.

Income Statement Working Papers
For the Year Ended December 31, 19+5

	Comparative Balance Sheet			
	December 31,		Year's Changes—Net	
	19+5	19+4	Debit	Credit
Balance sheets:				
Assets:				
Accounts receivable	5,000	5,600		600 A
Notes receivable	3,000	2,500	500 A	
			Cash	
			Debit	Credit
Cash:				
Cash sales			75,000 A	
Collections on accounts receivable			60,000 A	
Collections on notes receivable			20,000 A	
			Income Statement	
			Debit	Credit
Income statement:				
Sales				154,900 A

RETURNS AND ALLOWANCES. Assume the same facts as in the preceding illustration, except that an analysis of the accounts receivable showed credits of $350 for returns and allowances.

Income Statement Working Papers
For the Year Ended December 31, 19+5

	Comparative Balance Sheet			
	December 31,		Year's Changes—Net	
	19+5	19+4	Debit	Credit
Balance sheets:				
Assets:				
Accounts receivable	5,000	5,600		600 A
Notes receivable	3,000	2,500	500 A	
			Cash	
			Debit	Credit
Cash:				
Cash sales			75,000 A	
Collections on accounts receivable			60,000 A	
Collections on notes receivable			20,000 A	

	Income Statement	
	Debit	Credit
Income statement:		
Sales returns and allowances................	350 A	
Sales		155,250 A

The $350 debit was entered in the Income Statement debit column, and the $155,250 entered in the credit column was the amount necessary to balance the debits and credits.

CASH DISCOUNTS ON SALES. Assume the same facts as in the immediately preceding illustration; in addition, there were cash discounts on sales amounting to $450.

Income Statement Working Papers
For the Year Ended December 31, 19+5

	Comparative Balance Sheet			
	December 31,		Year's Changes—Net	
	19+5	19+4	Debit	Credit
Balance sheets:				
Assets:				
Accounts receivable	5,000	5,600		600 A
Notes receivable	3,000	2,500	500 A	

	Cash	
	Debit	Credit
Cash:		
Cash sales	75,000 A	
Collections on accounts receivable	60,000 A	
Collections on notes receivable	20,000 A	

	Income Statement	
	Debit	Credit
Income statement:		
Sales returns and allowances................	350 A	
Sales discounts	450 A	
Sales		155,700 A

BAD DEBTS. Assume the same facts as in the preceding illustration; also assume that $1,200 of accounts had been removed from the ledger as uncollectible. This removal, of course, affected the change in the accounts receivable during the year. If no consideration is given to this matter, the sales will be understated and the loss from bad debts will be ignored.

Income Statement Working Papers
For the Year Ended December 31, 19+5

	Comparative Balance Sheet			
	December 31,		Year's Changes—Net	
	19+5	19+4	Debit	Credit
Balance sheets:				
Assets:				
Accounts receivable	5,000	5,600		600 A
Notes receivable	3,000	2,500	500 A	
			Cash	
			Debit	Credit
Cash:				
Cash sales			75,000 A	
Collections on accounts receivable			60,000 A	
Collections on notes receivable			20,000 A	
			Income Statement	
			Debit	Credit
Income statement:				
Sales returns and allowances			350 A	
Sales discounts			450 A	
Bad debts			1,200 A	
Sales				156,900 A

Computation of purchases. Two illustrations are presented below showing the computation of purchases.

BASIC ILLUSTRATION. The first illustration shows the basic procedure.

Cash purchases		$ 3,600
Purchases on account:		
Payments to trade creditors	$92,700	
Less accounts payable, beginning of period	5,900	
Payments for purchases during the period	$86,800	
Add accounts payable, end of period	5,500	92,300
Total purchases		$95,900

The computation can, of course, be simplified by merely deducting the decrease in accounts payable during the year, thus:

Cash purchases	$ 3,600
Add payments to trade creditors	92,700
Total	$96,300
Less decrease in accounts payable	400
Purchases	$95,900

The working-paper treatment is shown on the following page.

Income Statement Working Papers
For the Year Ended December 31, 19+5

	Comparative Balance Sheet			
	December 31,		Year's Changes—Net	
	19+5	19+4	Debit	Credit
Balance sheets:				
Liabilities:				
Accounts payable—Trade	5,500	5,900	400 B	

	Cash	
	Debit	Credit
Cash:		
Cash purchases		3,600 B
Payments to trade creditors		92,700 B

	Income Statement	
	Debit	Credit
Income statement:		
Purchases	95,900 B	

NOTES, RETURNS AND ALLOWANCES, AND CASH DISCOUNTS. This illustration is based on the same facts as the preceding one, with the following additions:

Notes were given to trade creditors.
Purchase returns and allowances amounted to $1,400.
Purchase discounts amounted to $1,675.

Income Statement Working Papers
For the Year Ended December 31, 19+5

	Comparative Balance Sheet			
	December 31,		Year's Changes—Net	
	19+5	19+4	Debit	Credit
Balance sheets:				
Liabilities:				
Accounts payable—Trade	3,000	3,900	900 B	
Notes payable—Trade	2,500	2,000		500 B

	Cash	
	Debit	Credit
Cash:		
Cash purchases		3,600 B
Payments on accounts payable—Trade		79,800 B
Payments on notes payable—Trade		12,900 B

	Income Statement	
	Debit	Credit
Income statement:		
Purchase returns and allowances		1,400 B
Purchase discounts		1,675 B
Purchases	98,975 B	

Inventories. The working-paper treatment of the inventories at the beginning and end of the period is illustrated below:

Income Statement Working Papers
For the Year Ended December 31, 19+5

	Comparative Balance Sheet			
	December 31,		Year's Changes—Net	
	19+5	19+4	Debit	Credit
Balance sheets:				
Assets:				
Merchandise inventory	16,000	15,460	540 C	
			Cash	
			Debit	Credit
Cash:				
			Income Statement	
			Debit	Credit
Income statement:				
Inventory, December 31, 19+4			15,460 C	
Inventory, December 31, 19+5				16,000 C

Completed illustration. The working papers on this and the next page combine those in the last illustrations of the computation of sales and purchases and the illustration of the treatment of inventories. It is now also assumed that the expenses for the year were $50,000—all paid in cash.

H. W. BROWN
Income Statement Working Papers
For the Year Ended December 31, 19+5

	Comparative Balance Sheet			
	December 31,		Year's Changes—Net	
	19+5	19+4	Debit	Credit
Balance sheets:				
Assets:				
Cash	12,740	4,040	8,700	
Accounts receivable	5,000	5,600		600 A
Notes receivable—Trade	3,000	2,500	500 A	
Inventory	16,000	15,460	540 C	
	36,740	27,600		
Equities:				
Accounts payable	3,000	3,900	900 B	
Notes payable—Trade	2,500	2,000		500 B
Owner's equity	31,240	21,700		9,540
	36,740	27,600	10,640	10,640

	Cash Debit	Cash Credit
Cash:		
Cash sales	75,000 A	
Collections on accounts receivable	60,000 A	
Collections on notes receivable—Trade	20,000 A	
Cash purchases		3,600 B
Payments on accounts payable		79,800 B
Payments on notes payable—Trade		12,900 B
Expenses		50,000 D
Increase in cash		8,700
	155,000	155,000

	Income Statement Debit	Income Statement Credit
Income statement:		
Sales returns and allowances	350 A	
Sales discounts	450 A	
Bad debts	1,200 A	
Sales		156,900 A
Purchase returns and allowances		1,400 B
Purchase discounts		1,675 B
Purchases	98,975 B	
Inventory, December 31, 19+4	15,460 C	
Inventory, December 31, 19+5		16,000 C
Expenses	50,000 D	
Net income	9,540	
	175,975	175,975

Accrued revenue and expense. The illustration below shows the working-paper treatment of accruals:

Income Statement Working Papers
For the Year Ended December 31, 19+5

	Comparative Balance Sheet			
	December 31,		Year's Changes—Net	
	19+5	19+4	Debit	Credit
Balance sheets:				
Assets:				
Accrued interest receivable	85	60	25 E	
Liabilities:				
Accrued wages payable	700	625		75 F
Accrued interest payable	45	58	13 G	

	Cash Debit	Cash Credit
Cash:		
Interest on notes receivable	330 E	
Wages		9,500 F
Interest on notes payable		625 G

	Income Statement	
	Debit	Credit
Income statement:		
Interest revenue		355 E
Wages	9,575 F	
Interest on notes payable	612 G	

Revenue and cost apportionments. The following illustration shows the treatment of revenues collected in advance and expenses paid in advance:

Income Statement Working Papers
For the Year Ended December 31, 19+5

	Comparative Balance Sheet			
	December 31,		Year's Changes—Net	
	19+5	19+4	Debit	Credit
Balance sheets:				
Assets:				
Unexpired insurance	650	435	215 H	
Liabilities:				
Rent collected in advance	300	400	100 I	

	Cash	
	Debit	Credit
Cash:		
Insurance policy purchased..................		400 H

	Income Statement	
	Debit	Credit
Income statement:		
Insurance expense............................	185 H	
Rent revenue		100 I

Depreciation. The best procedure for dealing with depreciation expense is to include in the Comparative Balance Sheet columns the accumulated depreciation at the beginning and end of the year.

Income Statement Working Papers
For the Year Ended December 31, 19+5

	Comparative Balance Sheet			
	December 31,		Year's Changes—Net	
	19+5	19+4	Debit	Credit
Balance sheets:				
Assets:				
Store equipment......................	35,000	30,000	5,000	
Accumulated depreciation—Store equipment.......................	6,300*	4,800*		1,500 J

*Deduction.

	Cash	
	Debit	Credit
Cash:		

	Income Statement	
	Debit	Credit
Income statement:		
Depreciation—Store equipment........	1,500 J	

Allowance for uncollectibles. A preceding illustration (page 664) showed the treatment of bad debts when no Allowance for Uncollectibles was included in the Comparative Balance Sheet columns, and accounts determined to be uncollectible were simply removed from the ledger. The following illustration shows the procedure if the Comparative Balance Sheet columns contain an allowance account. The illustration assumes that:

Accounts receivable in the amount of $1,000 were removed from the ledger as uncollectible.

It was believed that the allowance required for the remaining accounts should be $1,500. This is $300 more than was believed necessary a year ago.

The $1,000 must be included in the computation of the sales, as explained on page 664. The bad-debts expense is the sum of the $1,000 of accounts found to be worthless and the $300 increase in the allowance account.

Income Statement Working Papers
For the Year Ended December 31, 19+5

	Comparative Balance Sheet			
	December 31,		Year's Changes—Net	
	19+5	19+4	Debit	Credit
Balance sheets:				
Assets:				
Accounts receivable	30,000	25,000	5,000 K	
Allowance for uncollectibles	1,500*	1,200*		300 L

*Deduction.

	Cash	
	Debit	Credit
Cash:		
Collections on accounts receivable	95,000 K	

	Income Statement	
	Debit	Credit
Income statement:		
Bad debts	{ 300 L 1,000 K	
Sales..................................		101,000 K

Statement of proprietor's capital or retained earnings. If it is desired to prepare a statement of the proprietor's capital, the working papers may be expanded in the manner illustrated below:

HENRY BARTON
Income and Proprietor's Capital Statements Working Papers
For the Year Ended December 31, 19+5

	Comparative Balance Sheet			
	December 31,		Year's Changes—Net	
	19+5	19+4	Debit	Credit
Balance sheets:				
Assets:				
Cash	7,600	3,600	4,000	
Accounts receivable	25,000	21,000	4,000 A	
Inventory	40,000	38,000	2,000 C	
	72,600	62,600		
Equities:				
Accounts payable	15,000	20,000	5,000 B	
Henry Barton, capital	57,600	42,600		15,000
	72,600	62,600	15,000	15,000

	Cash	
	Debit	Credit
Cash:		
Collections on accounts receivable	125,000 A	
Payments on accounts payable		70,000 B
Expenses		45,000 D
Drawings		6,000 E
Increase in cash		4,000
	125,000	125,000

	Income Statement	
	Debit	Credit
Income statement:		
Sales		129,000 A
Purchases	65,000 B	
Inventory, December 31, 19+4	38,000 C	
Inventory, December 31, 19+5		40,000 C
Expenses	45,000 D	
Net income—down	21,000	
	169,000	169,000

	Statement of Proprietor's Capital	
	Debit	Credit
Statement of proprietor's capital:		
Balance, December 31, 19+4—per balance sheet		42,600
Net income		21,000
Drawings	6,000 E	
Balance, December 31, 19+5	57,600	
	63,600	63,600

If the business is a corporation and it is desired to prepare a statement of retained earnings, the working papers may be prepared in the manner shown below:

THE BARTON COMPANY
Income and Retained Earnings Statements Working Papers
For the Year Ended December 31, 19+5

	Comparative Balance Sheet			
	December 31,		Year's Changes—Net	
	19+5	19+4	Debit	Credit
Balance sheets:				
Assets:				
Cash	7,600	3,600	4,000	
Accounts receivable	25,000	21,000	4,000 A	
Inventory	40,000	38,000	2,000 C	
	72,600	62,600		
Equities:				
Accounts payable	15,000	20,000	5,000 B	
Capital stock	30,000	30,000		
Retained earnings	27,600	12,600		15,000
	72,600	62,600	15,000	15,000

	Cash	
	Debit	Credit
Cash:		
Collections on accounts receivable	125,000 A	
Payments on accounts payable		70,000 B
Expenses		45,000 D
Dividends		6,000 E
Increase in cash		4,000
	125,000	125,000

	Income Statement Debit	Income Statement Credit
Income statement:		
Sales		129,000 A
Purchases	65,000 B	
Inventory, December 31, 19+4	38,000 C	
Inventory, December 31, 19+5		40,000 C
Expenses	45,000 D	
Net income—down	21,000	
	169,000	169,000

	Retained Earnings Debit	Retained Earnings Credit
Retained earnings statement:		
Balance, December 31, 19+4—per balance sheet		12,600
Net income		21,000
Dividends	6,000 E	
Balance, December 31, 19+5	27,600	
	33,600	33,600

ASSIGNMENT MATERIAL

CHAPTER 1

QUESTIONS

1. Briefly describe the accounting cycle.
2. What are the rules for recording increases and decreases in the following accounts: assets, liabilities, paid-in capital, expenses, and revenues.
3. Would the normal balance be found on the debit or credit side of the following accounts: assets, liabilities, capital stock, retained earnings, dividends, revenues, and expenses.
4. Describe the relationship between a controlling account and a subsidiary ledger.
5. What are the advantages of using special journals or books of original entry?
6. Describe the way in which a voucher system operates.
7. What is the difference between the cash basis and accrual basis of accounting?
8. What is the relationship between end-of-period adjustments and income measurement?
9. List five types of adjusting entries.
10. Give an example of the following types of adjustments: (a) Unrecorded revenues, (b) Unrecorded expenses.
11. Assume the payment of $1200 for a three-year insurance premium. What is the purpose of the adjusting entry at the end of the first year in each of the following cases: (a) The $1200 was originally debited to an asset account (b) The $1200 was originally debited to an expense account.
12. Give examples of two ways in which an adjusting entry for earned revenues might be recorded and state under what circumstances each would be appropriate.
13. Describe why reversing entries are frequently used as a part of the accounting cycle.
14. What is the purpose of a trial balance?
15. Describe the use of a contra account. Give an example of a contra account.

PROBLEMS

Problem 1-1. The following selected accounts were taken from the ledger of Crowder Company.

(1) Cash
(2) Accounts receivable
(3) Allowance for uncollectibles

(4) Notes receivable
(5) Merchandise inventory
(6) Equipment
(7) Accumulated depreciation—Equipment
(8) Accounts payable
(9) Interest payable
(10) Capital stock
(11) Capital in excess of par value
(12) Retained earnings
(13) Sales
(14) Sales returns and allowances
(15) Purchases
(16) Depreciation expense
(17) Office salaries

Required:

Indicate whether the accounts normally have debit or credit balances.

Problem 1-2. Selected accounts from the ledger of Brooks Company are presented below:

(1) Cash
(2) Petty cash
(3) United States Government bonds
(4) Accounts receivable
(5) Allowance for uncollectibles
(6) Merchandise inventory
(7) Unexpired insurance
(8) Delivery equipment
(9) Accumulated depreciation—Delivery equipment
(10) Notes payable
(11) Accounts payable
(12) Capital stock
(13) Retained earnings
(14) Sales
(15) Sales returns and allowances
(16) Advertising expense
(17) Delivery expense
(18) Office supplies expense
(19) Office salaries
(20) Interest revenue

Required:

Indicate for each of the accounts whether increases are recorded as debits or credits.

Problem 1-3. Holden Company uses a two-column journal and the following special journals:

Sales journal
Purchases journal
Cash receipts journal
Cash disbursements journal.

The following transactions took place during May 19+4.

(1) Sold merchandise on account.
(2) Paid one year's rent in advance.
(3) Paid salaries for the month.
(4) Purchased merchandise on account.
(5) Received rent from the occupants of office space rented by the firm.
(6) Purchased merchandise for cash.
(7) Paid supplier for merchandise previously purchased on account.
(8) Received payment for merchandise previously sold on account.
(9) Issued capital stock for cash.
(10) Sold merchandise for cash.
(11) Purchased a delivery truck for cash.
(12) Gave a supplier a note payable for the balance owed from a prior month.

Required:

Indicate the journal in which each of the transactions should be recorded.

Problem 1-4. Selected transactions of Maxton Company for the month of June 19+1 are presented below.

19+1
June 1—5,000 additional shares of common stock, with a par value of $100 per share, were issued for $505,000 cash.
3—Delivery equipment costing $2,500 was purchased from Milton Truck Company for cash.
4—Merchandise was purchased from Elton Supply Company for $815. A check was issued at this time for $500. The unpaid amount was recorded as a liability.
7—Merchandise was sold on account to Expansive Corporation for $600.
9—A 30-day, non-interest-bearing note for $600 was received from Expansive Corporation (see June 7 transaction).
15—Merchandise was sold on account to Forbes Manufacturing Company for $925.
17—A $300 premium was paid to Surety Insurance Company for a two-year policy on the office equipment.
21—$100 was collected from Forbes Manufacturing Company to apply on account. Because of the bankruptcy of this customer, the balance of its account was determined to be uncollectible (see June 15 transaction).
23—A dividend of $1.50 per share was declared, payable July 31 to shareholders of record July 15, on the 9,500 shares of common stock outstanding.
30—Depreciation on the delivery equipment for the month was $30.
30—The interest accrued on notes receivable for the month was $10.

Required:

Record the transactions in two-column journal form.

Problem 1-5. Burns Company, which closes its books on December 31, had the following selected transactions take place during 19+1.

January 1—Paid $1,620 for a three-year insurance policy. Payment was debited to the insurance expense account.
April 1—Received a $3,000 advance from a customer. The receipt was credited to the sales account. One-half of the advance had been earned at December 31, 19+1.

June 1—	Received $3,600 rent for the period June 1, 19+1 to May 31, 19+2 from the occupant of a building owned by the company. The receipt was credited to the rent revenue account.
December 31—	Recorded $400 accrued interest receivable on bonds of the Cook Company. Interest of $600 will be received on the next interest payment date, March 1, 19+2.
December 31—	Recorded $1,015 in accrued salaries for the last two days of 19+1. The next payroll will be paid on January 3, 19+2.

Required:

Prepare the January 1, 19+2 reversing entries resulting from the transactions.

Problem 1-6. On pages 678 and 679 are the voucher register, check register, and journal of Baxter Company for the month of November, 19+3.

Required:

(a) Post from these records to the general ledger.
(b) Prepare the November 30, 19+3 trial balance.

Problem 1-7. The following trial balance was taken from the accounts of Fast and Slow Company as of June 30, 19+5, the end of the firm's annual accounting period.

FAST AND SLOW COMPANY
Trial Balance
June 30, 19+5

Cash	18,684	
Marketable securities	30,000	
Accounts receivable	8,300	
Allowance for uncollectibles		330
Notes receivable	1,700	
Inventory—June 30, 19+4	7,150	
Prepaid rent	1,000	
Land	5,000	
Buildings	40,000	
Accumulated depreciation—Buildings		20,000
Machinery	75,000	
Accumulated depreciation—Machinery		15,000
Vouchers payable		19,600
Long-term notes payable		4,500
Bonds payable		50,000
Capital stock		100,000
Retained earnings		12,725
Sales		89,070
Purchases	86,624	
Purchase returns and allowances		1,618
Transportation in	480	
Sales salaries	19,909	
Advertising expense	6,500	
Office salaries	11,988	
Insurance expense	580	
Interest expense	120	
Interest revenue		192
	313,036	313,036

(continued on page 680)

VOUCHER REGISTER

Voucher No.	Date	Payee	Explanation	Terms	Date Paid	Check No.	Credit Vouchers Payable	Debits: Purchases	Debits: Transportation In	Sundry Accounts: Account	Sundry Accounts: L.F.	Sundry Accounts: Amount
					19+3							
11-1	Nov. 2	Emory & Company . .	Invoice 312	2/10; n/30	Nov. 9	3	1,400.00	1,400.00				
11-2	3	R. & P. Railroad		Cash	3	1	38.00		38.00			
11-3	6	Hoot Advertising. . . .		Cash	6	2	350.00			Advertising		350.00
11-4	10	Esther Equipment Co.	Invoice Nov. 10	n/30			680.00	680.00				
11-5	12	Edson Electric Co. . . .		Cash	12	4	35.00			Electricity		35.00
11-6	16	Arbor Sales.	Invoice 491	2/10; n/30	25	7	1,060.00	1,060.00				
11-7	20	H. E. Lanson	Rent for Nov.	Cash	20	5	150.00			Rent		150.00
11-8	23	J. B. Benson	Note dated Aug. 15		23	6	1,200.00			Notes payable		1,200.00
11-9	27	Decker & Decker. . . .	Invoice 184	n/30			970.00	970.00				
11-10	30	Payroll	For month		30	8	800.00			Wages payable		800.00
							6,683.00	4,110.00	38.00			2,535.00

CHECK REGISTER

Check No.	Date	Payee	Voucher No.	Debit Vouchers Payable	Credits: Purchase Discounts	Credits: Cash
	19+3					
1	Nov. 3	R. & P. Railroad	11-2	38.00		38.00
2	6	Hoot Advertising	11-3	350.00		350.00
3	9	Emory & Company	11-1	1,400.00	28.00	1,372.00
4	12	Edson Electric Co.	11-5	35.00		35.00
5	20	H. E. Lanson	11-7	150.00		150.00
6	23	J. B. Benson	11-8	1,200.00		1,200.00
7	25	Arbor Sales.	11-6	1,060.00	21.20	1,038.80
8	30	Payroll.	11-10	800.00		800.00
				5,033.00	49.20	4,983.80

JOURNAL

Debits: Accounts Receivable	Debits: Vouchers Payable	Debits: General Ledger	Date	L.F.		Credits: General Ledger	Credits: Vouchers Payable	Credits: Accounts Receivable
		5,000.00	19+3 Nov. 6		Cash			
					Capital stock	5,000.00		
					Sale of stock.			
1,940.00			10		Morrison Works Company			
					Sales	1,940.00		
					Sale of merchandise.			
	100.00		13		Esther Equipment Co.			
					Purchase returns and allowances...............	100.00		
					Merchandise returned today.			
	1,200.00		14		Vouchers payable			
					Notes payable	1,200.00		
					10-day, non-interest-bearing note given to J. B. Benson			
		940.00	19		Notes receivable			
					Morrison Works Company .			940.00
					30-day, 7% note received.			
		800.00	30		Wages expense			
					Wages payable..............	800.00		
					To record wages expense for month.			
1,940.00	1,300.00	6,740.00				9,040.00		940.00

Problem 1-7 (continued):

Additional information:

(1) It is estimated that 6 percent of the outstanding accounts receivable will be uncollectible.

(2) Buildings and machinery are to be depreciated at annual rates of 5 percent and 10 percent, respectively.

(3) The rent is paid on January 1 each year for one year in advance.

(4) The securities held pay interest at an annual rate of 6 percent on March 1 and September 1.

(5) Of the balance in the insurance expense account, $408 is the amount of the premium for a two-year policy purchased on April 1, 19+5.

(6) Salaries accrued on June 30, 19+5, are as follows:

Sales salaries	$925.
Office salaries	$480.

(7) The accrued interest on notes receivable amounts to $40.

(8) The balance in the advertising expense account represents the cost of advertisements which will appear in the October, November, and December issues of a monthly magazine during 19+5.

(9) The interest on the notes payable, amounting to $240 per year, is payable July 1 and January 1.

(10) The bonds payable were issued on May 1, 19+5, and bear interest at an annual rate of 7 percent, payable May 1 and November 1.

Required:

Prepare the June 30, 19+5 adjusting journal entries.

Problem 1-8. The following data were taken from the records of Mayfield Company for the year ended June 30, 19+5.

Sales on account	$18,000
Notes received to settle accounts	2,000
Purchases on account	19,900
Accounts receivable determined to be worthless	1,200
Payments to creditors	16,500
Discounts allowed by creditors	1,300
Merchandise returned by customers	810
Collections received to settle accounts	12,300
Notes given to creditors in settlement of accounts	1,100
Provision for uncollectible accounts	900
Interest paid on notes payable	130
Merchandise returned to suppliers	350
Payments made on notes payable	400
Discounts permitted to be taken by customers	240
Collections received in settlement of notes	1,800

Required:

Using the information above, set up controlling accounts for accounts receivable and accounts payable and record the amounts to be shown in the controlling accounts for the year.

Problem 1-9. The monthly column totals of the special journals and the complete journal of Ames Company for the month of August are given on page 681.

JOURNAL

Accounts Payable	General Ledger	Date	L.F.		General Ledger	Accounts Receivable
		19+5				
	12,400 7,600	Aug. 1		Purchases Store fixtures Capital stock ..... Payment with merchandise and store fixtures.	20,000	
198		8		Carter & Co. Purchase returns and allowances ... Merchandise returned	198	
	100	16		Sales returns and allowances Paschal Brothers.. Allowance on damaged merchandise. Credit memo No. 1		100
	1,500	20		Notes receivable Paschal Brothers.. 5%, 60-day note in payment of account ..		1,500
	50	27		Sales returns and allowances Sims, Inc. .... Credit memo No. 2		50

Sales Journal:
- Column total .... $ 5,900

Accounts Payable Journal:
- Column totals:
  - Accounts Payable $10,450
  - Purchases 10,100
  - Sundry:
    - Store fixtures 350

Cash Disbursements Journal:
- Column totals:
  - Cash $10,278
  - Purchase Discounts 74
  - Accounts Payable 8,752
  - Purchases 300
  - Sundry:
    - Store rent 400
    - Salaries 900

Cash Receipts Journal:
- Column totals:
  - Cash $24,202
  - Sales Discounts 58
  - Accounts Receivable 2,900
  - Sales 1,360
  - Sundry:
    - Capital stock 20,000

Required:

Present T-accounts as they would appear in the general ledger after the monthly postings had been completed.

Problem 1-10. Fox Corporation has authorized common stock of 40,000 shares with a par value of $50. On June 15, 19+1, 8,000 of these shares are outstanding. The chart of accounts used by the corporation is presented below.

Cash	Capital Stock
Petty Cash	Capital in excess of par value
Accounts Receivable	Retained Earnings
Allowance for Uncollectibles	Sales
Notes Receivable	Sales Returns and Allowances
Merchandise Inventory	Sales Discounts
Bond Sinking Fund	Purchases
Land	Transportation In
Buildings	Purchase Returns and Allowances
Accumulated Depreciation—Buildings	Purchase Discounts
Furniture	Depreciation Expense—Buildings
Accumulated Depreciation—Furniture	Depreciation Expense—Furniture
Vouchers Payable	Selling Expense
Notes Payable	Office Expense
Interest Payable	Miscellaneous General Expense
Mortgage Payable	Interest Revenue
Bonds Payable	Bond Interest Expense

Selected transactions for the months of June and July are presented below:

19+1

June 16—Merchandise was sold on account to M. M. White for $380.

17—A petty cash fund of $100 was set up by drawing a check for this amount.

18—Merchandise was purchased from Stoney Corporation for $800; terms, 2/10; n/30.

19—A check for $10,000 was issued to the sinking fund trustee to set up a sinking fund for the retirement of the 20-year, 7 percent bonds, issued one year ago for $200,000.

20—A 60-day, 6 percent note was received from M. M. White in settlement of his account.

22—Merchandise was sold to Rapid Grow Company for $730; terms, 2/10; n/30.

23—The corporation issued 1,200 additional shares of capital stock for $62,000 cash.

25—Rapid Grow Company returned merchandise with an invoice amount of $200.

26—Furniture was purchased on account for $5,500.

27—Furniture purchased on June 26, with an invoice price of $1,200, was returned to the seller.

30—1,500 shares of capital stock were issued for the following assets and liabilities of a going business:

Merchandise inventory	$35,400
Land	11,600
Buildings	50,000
Mortgage payable	22,000

July 1—Rapid Grow Company settled its account in full.

9—The following expenses were paid: repairs, $123; advertising, $160; bond interest expense, $10,000.

14—The petty cash fund was reimbursed after payment of the following expenses:

Office expense	$35
Transportation in	48

16—The account with Stoney Corporation was settled in full.

Required:

For each of the transactions, state:

(a) The book of original entry in which the transaction would be recorded if the following journals were used:

Sales	Voucher register
Sales returns and allowances	Check register
Cash receipts	Journal

(b) The general ledger accounts which would be debited and credited.

Problem 1-11. The trial balance and adjusted trial balance of Hicks Company on December 31, 19+4, are presented below.

	Trial Balance December 31, 19+4		Adjusted Trial Balance December 31, 19+4	
Cash	142,285		142,285	
Accounts receivable	19,900		19,900	
Allowance for uncollectibles		1,230		1,400
Unexpired insurance	500		375	
Interest receivable			25	
Truck rental paid in advance			155	
Tools	1,150		890	
Land	5,000		5,000	
Buildings	129,000		129,000	
Accumulated depreciation—Buildings		32,200		34,700
Accounts payable		15,400		15,400
Salaries and wages payable				800
Interest payable				20
Dividends payable				6,000
Office space rental collected in advance				2,000
Purchases	132,225		132,225	
Purchase returns and allowances		880		880
Truck rental	900		745	
Salaries and wages	82,000		82,800	
Interest expense	110		130	
Bad debts			170	
Depreciation—Buildings			2,500	
Insurance			125	
Tools expense			260	
Dividends			6,000	
Capital stock		200,000		200,000
Retained earnings		95,000		95,000
Sales		158,000		158,000
Office space rental revenue		10,000		8,000
Interest revenue		360		385
	513,070	513,070	522,585	522,585

Required:

Present the December 31, 19+4 adjusting entries in journal form.

Problem 1-12. Below is information from the accounts of Eastern Company as of December 31, 19+2, the close of its accounting period.

(1) The machinery account has a balance of $75,000. Part of this amount consists of machinery acquired on October 1, 19+2, at a cost of $26,000. Machinery has been depreciated at a rate of 8 percent per year, and the new machinery is to be depreciated at one-fourth the annual rate.
(2) Rent of $6,600 for one year in advance was paid on October 31, 19+2, the debit at that time being made to the expense account.
(3) The balance in the supplies account on December 31, 19+1, after adjustment, was $7,200. Additional supplies costing $3,500 were purchased during 19+2 and charged to Supplies Expense. An inventory of supplies, taken on December 31, 19+2, showed the amount on hand to be $4,500.
(4) The allowance for uncollectibles account has a credit balance of $300. It is estimated that 3 percent of the $19,700 of accounts receivable outstanding on December 31, 19+2, will be uncollectible.
(5) A twenty-year 6 percent bond issue in the amount of $200,000 was sold at face value on August 1, 19+2, with interest payable on February 1 and August 1.
(6) A five-year insurance premium of $1,000 was paid on May 31, 19+1 for coverage effective on that date. The entire amount was debited to the unexpired insurance account.

Required:

Prepare the December 31, 19+2 adjusting entries.

Problem 1-13. Roswell Company closes its books semiannually on June 30 and December 31. On April 1, 19+2, the company borrowed $10,000 at the bank, giving a one-year 6 percent note. The note was paid at maturity and the interest payment thereon was charged to Interest Expense. The company had no other interest-bearing indebtedness during 19+2. On June 1, 19+2, the company rented out some storage space, receiving the $1,800 annual rental in advance. The company's accountant credited the receipt to Rent Revenue. On October 1, 19+2, a premium of $576 was paid for a three-year fire insurance policy effective that date. This was a renewal of an identical policy and is the only insurance carried. A debit of $576 was made to Insurance Expense, which was consistent with the entry made three years earlier for the insurance premium.

Required:

Prepare adjusting entries and the related reversing entries based on the data above for the accounting periods ended June 30, 19+2, and December 31, 19+2.

Problem 1-14. The June 30, 19+8 unadjusted trial balance of Cook Company is presented below.

COOK COMPANY
Unadjusted Trial Balance
June 30, 19+8

Cash	1,600
Merchandise inventory	4,800
Office supplies inventory	250
Unexpired insurance	270
Land	7,500

Store fixtures	3,000	
Accumulated depreciation—Store fixtures		1,200
Accounts payable		7,170
Interest payable		40
Salaries payable		800
Rent received in advance		2,400
Long-term bank loan—6%		6,000
Common stock		6,000
Retained earnings	3,035	
Sales		40,000
Cost of goods sold	27,000	
Store rent expense	1,400	
Salaries expense	12,000	
Advertising expense	140	
Insurance expense	45	
Office supplies expense	220	
Interest expense	350	
Land rent revenue	1,000	
	63,610	63,610

The company pays salaries of $1,000 per month.

On September 1, 19+6, the company signed a six-year lease agreement relating to a portion of the land owned by the company. The $1,200 yearly rental is payable in advance and the $1,200 amounts received on September 1, 19+6 and 19+7 were credited to Rent Received in Advance.

The company carries only one insurance policy. The $270 premium for the three-year renewal policy dated January 1, 19+8, was charged to Unexpired Insurance.

The company spent $220 on office supplies during the year ended June 30, 19+8.

On July 1, 19+7, two adjusting entries dated June 30, 19+7 were reversed.

Required:

After analyzing the unadjusted trial balance, prepare the reversing entries that could have been made as of July 1, 19+7, and also show the reversing entries that were made.

CHAPTER 2

QUESTIONS

1. Describe two different procedures that may be used to close a firm's books.
2. How will the working papers prepared for a firm using perpetual inventory procedures differ from those prepared for a firm using periodic inventory procedures?
3. What is the purpose of accounting working papers?
4. What is the major difference between working papers prepared for a manufacturing concern and those prepared for a merchandising firm?
5. How is the cost of goods manufactured during a given period calculated for a manufacturing firm?
6. Briefly describe the financial statements prepared for a manufacturing concern.

7. What elements make up the difference between the cost of goods manufactured and the cost of goods sold in the case of a manufacturing business?

8. Describe two different procedures that might be used to present a firm's income tax expense in the working papers.

9. How do the closing entries of a manufacturing firm differ from those of a merchandising concern?

10. In what ways are the working papers for a proprietorship different from those for a corporation?

11. How is the goods-in-process inventory of a manufacturing firm reported in its financial statements?

12. Describe the procedures followed in balancing the Income Statement columns, Statement of Retained Earnings columns, and the Balance Sheet columns in the working papers of a company having net income for the period.

PROBLEMS

Problem 2-1. The trial balance of a proprietorship is presented below.

J. L. MURRAY
Trial Balance
December 31, 19+1

Cash	27,744	
Accounts receivable	11,300	
Allowance for uncollectibles		604
Inventory, December 31, 19+1	14,150	
Long-term investments	37,500	
Land	2,500	
Buildings	14,000	
Accumulated depreciation—Buildings		6,300
Accounts payable		7,150
Mortgage payable		2,500
J. L. Murray, capital		88,400
Drawings	3,000	
Sales		48,055
Sales returns and allowances	990	
Cost of goods sold	24,735	
Salaries and wages	9,950	
Advertising	1,250	
Transportation out	2,260	
Office expense	1,600	
Supplies expense	2,000	
Interest revenue		155
Interest expense	185	
	153,164	153,164

Additional information:

(1) It is estimated that 8 percent of the outstanding accounts receivable will be uncollectible.

(2) When the buildings were purchased nine years ago, it was estimated that they would have a life of 20 years.

(3) $175 of salaries and wages have accrued on December 31, 19+1.
(4) Interest accrued on the long-term investments is $250.

Required:

(a) Working papers.
(b) Closing entries, using the income summary account.

Problem 2-2. The following list of account balances and supplementary data are taken from the records of The Boston Company as of June 30, 19+9.

Accounts receivable	$ 2,905
Accumulated depreciation—Equipment	1,960
Allowance for uncollectibles	230
Bond interest expense	500
Bonds payable	10,000
Cash	5,498
Common stock	17,000
Dividends	500
Equipment	19,600
Interest revenue	40
Inventory—June 30, 19+8	1,640
Notes receivable	1,460
Property taxes expense	200
Purchases	7,950
Purchase returns and allowances	280
Rent expense	1,200
Repairs expense	330
Retained earnings—June 30, 19+8	1,908
Salaries expense	4,200
Sales	14,760
Sales discounts	172
Sales returns and allowances	134
Shipping supplies	1,183
Transportation in	106
Vouchers payable	1,400

Supplementary data:

(1) The bonds payable were issued on May 1, 19+7, and mature ten years from that date. They bear interest at 6 percent, payable May 1 and November 1.
(2) The allowance for uncollectibles is to be increased to $400.
(3) The equipment is being depreciated at the rate of 5 percent per year.
(4) On June 30, 19+9, the shipping supplies inventory is determined to be $950.
(5) The inventory on June 30, 19+9, is $1,810.

Required:

Prepare working papers for the year ended June 30, 19+9. Ignore federal income taxes.

Problem 2-3. Presented below is a summary of the account balances of O'Malley Supply Company on December 31, 19+9.

Accounts payable	$ 19,900
Accounts receivable	22,600
Accumulated depreciation—Buildings	7,000

Advertising expense	2,500
Allowance for uncollectibles	1,208
Buildings	28,000
Capital stock	150,000
Cash	55,488
Dividends	6,000
Freight out	4,520
Interest revenue	310
Interest expense	370
Inventory—December 31, 19+9	28,300
Land	5,000
Long-term investments	75,000
Mortgage payable	5,000
Office expense	3,200
Cost of goods sold	49,470
Retained earnings—December 31, 19+8	26,800
Salaries and wages expense	19,900
Sales	96,110
Sales returns and allowances	1,980
Supplies expense	4,000

Additional information:

(1) It is estimated that 8 percent of the outstanding accounts receivable will be uncollectible.

(2) When the buildings were purchased five years ago, it was estimated that they would have a life of twenty years.

(3) $350 of salaries and wages have accrued on December 31, 19+9.

(4) Interest accrued on the long-term investments is $500.

(5) The company is obligated to pay a federal income tax amounting to 50 percent of its net income before the income tax.

Required:

(a) Working papers for the year ended December 31, 19+9.

(b) Closing entries assuming the firm does not use an income summary account.

Problem 2-4. Using the trial balance and supplementary data below, prepare working papers for the year ended June 30, 19+8. All of the accounts required are included in the trial balance.

REGAL SALES COMPANY
Trial Balance
June 30, 19+8

Cash	37,370	
Marketable securities	60,000	
Accounts receivable	16,600	
Allowance for uncollectibles		660
Interest receivable		
Inventory	34,300	
Prepaid rent	4,000	
Unexpired insurance		
Land	10,000	
Buildings	80,000	

Accumulated depreciation—Buildings		40,000
Equipment	150,000	
Accumulated depreciation—Equipment		30,000
Accounts payable		43,174
Salaries payable		
Bond interest payable		
Income tax payable		
Bonds payable		100,000
Capital stock		100,000
Capital in excess of stated value		10,000
Retained earnings, June 30, 19+7		33,450
Dividends	3,000	
Sales		198,140
Cost of goods sold	82,200	
Sales salaries	39,818	
Advertising expense	13,000	
Office salaries	23,976	
Insurance expense	1,160	
Depreciation—Buildings		
Depreciation—Equipment		
Bad debts expense		
Rent expense		
Interest revenue		
Interest expense		
Federal income tax		
	555,424	555,424

Additional information:

(1) Buildings and equipment are to be depreciated at 8 percent and 10 percent per annum, respectively.

(2) The rent is paid on January 1 each year for one year in advance.

(3) The securities held pay interest at 8 percent per annum on March 1 and September 1. They were acquired on their issuance date, which was March 1, 19+8.

(4) Of the balance in the insurance account, $840 is the amount of the premium for a two-year policy purchased on March 1, 19+8.

(5) Salaries accrued on June 30, 19+8 are as follows: Sales salaries, $650; Office salaries, $960.

(6) The company's bank reconciliation prepared on June 30, 19+8, is presented below:

Balance per books		$37,370
Deduct:		
N.S.F. check of customer	$1,000	
Deposit not recorded by bank	750	1,750
Balance per bank statement		$35,620

(7) The bonds payable were issued on May 1, 19+8, and bear interest at 6 percent per annum, payable May 1 and November 1.

(8) It is estimated that 6 percent of the outstanding accounts receivable will be uncollectible.

(9) The applicable income tax rate is 20 percent.

Problem 2-5. The following account balances were selected from the unadjusted December 31, 19+3 trial balance of Ames Manufacturing Company:

Inventories—December 31, 19+2:	
Finished goods	$18,910
Goods in process	12,356
Materials	8,612
Purchases—Materials	62,850
Purchase returns and allowances	918
Purchase discounts	614
Freight in	5,420
Direct labor	82,309
Manufacturing overhead	41,626
Heat, light, and power	980
Property taxes	450
Freight out	4,012
Bad debts	1,080
Insurance expense	140

Adjustments are to be made as follows:

Accrued wages:	
Direct labor	$ 2,100
Indirect labor	640
Depreciation:	
Buildings	$ 4,200
Machinery	9,650
Tools	1,800

Expense allocations are to be made as follows:

	Manufacturing	Selling	Administration
Depreciation—Buildings	80	10	10

Inventories on December 31, 19+3:

Finished goods	$25,610
Goods in process	8,400
Materials	10,250

Required:

(a) Partial working papers for the year ended December 31, 19+3 showing the Cost of Goods Manufactured columns.

(b) All journal entries to close the accounts associated with the manufacturing operations of the firm.

Problem 2-6. The adjusted and unadjusted trial balances of Ely Supply Company on March 31, 19+4 follow. The inventory on this date was $48,650.15.

ELY SUPPLY COMPANY

	March 31, 19+4			
	Adjusted Trial Balance		Unadjusted Trial Balance	
Cash	92,189.15		92,189.15	
Accounts receivable	61,480.00		61,480.00	
Allowance for uncollectibles		5,891.10		3,303.40
Notes receivable	8,700.00		8,700.00	
Interest receivable	200.00			
Inventory—March 31, 19+3	44,400.25		44,400.25	
Unexpired insurance	600.00		900.00	
Land	9,200.00		9,200.00	
Buildings	100,000.00		100,000.00	
Accumulated depreciation—Buildings		10,000.00		7,500.00
Accounts payable		39,605.35		39,605.35
Salaries and wages payable		1,200.00		
Rentals collected in advance		425.00		
Capital stock		200,000.00		200,000.00
Retained earnings		53,566.45		53,566.45
Dividends	10,000.00		10,000.00	
Sales		180,142.75		180,142.75
Sales returns and allowances	2,450.60		2,450.60	
Sales discounts	3,770.45		3,770.45	
Purchases	129,310.05		129,310.05	
Purchase discounts		2,140.00		2,140.00
Transportation in	3,605.20		3,605.20	
Insurance	300.00			
Salaries and wages	19,800.00		18,600.00	
Depreciation—Buildings	2,500.00			
Office expenses	4,900.80		4,900.80	
Repairs	1,745.50		1,745.50	
Postage	960.95		960.95	
Freight out	1,455.00		1,455.00	
Bad debts	2,587.70			
Rental revenue		6,375.00		6,800.00
Interest revenue		810.00		610.00
	500,155.65	500,155.65	493,667.95	493,667.95

Required:

(a) Closing entries required as of March 31, 19+4, the end of the firm's accounting period. The firm does not use an income summary account.

(b) Reversing entries as of April 1, 19+4.

Problem 2-7. The following trial balance was taken from the ledger of The Uptown Manufacturing Corporation on December 31, 19+2, before adjusting entries were posted.

THE UPTOWN MANUFACTURING CORPORATION

Trial Balance
December 31, 19+2

Cash	57,744	
Accounts receivable	19,110	
Allowance for uncollectibles		816
Inventories—December 31, 19+1:		
Finished goods	2,090	
Goods in process	12,663	
Materials	18,901	
Unexpired insurance	420	
Land	20,000	
Buildings	94,600	
Accumulated depreciation—Buildings		12,510
Machinery and equipment	106,640	
Accumulated depreciation—Machinery and equipment		29,810
Office equipment	4,600	
Accumulated depreciation—Office equipment		1,030
Accounts payable		9,610
Bonds payable		50,000
Capital stock		200,000
Retained earnings		25,824
Dividends	5,000	
Sales		407,371
Purchases—Materials	128,126	
Purchase discounts		2,410
Transportation in	4,090	
Direct labor	183,200	
Manufacturing overhead	42,732	
Heat, light, and power	3,380	
Taxes—Property	728	
Sales salaries and expense	14,641	
Advertising	3,938	
Miscellaneous selling expense	1,014	
Office salaries	9,525	
Office supplies	1,816	
Bank charges	75	
Telephone and telegraph	948	
Postage	400	
Interest expense	3,000	
	739,381	739,381

Additional information:

(1) Inventories on December 31, 19+2:

Finished goods	$ 3,115
Goods in process	11,981
Materials	19,110

(2) Data for adjusting entries:

(a) It was estimated that \$1,956 of the accounts receivable outstanding on December 31, 19+2, would be uncollectible.

(b) Depreciation for 19+2:

Buildings	\$ 2,400
Machinery and equipment	4,600
Office equipment	850

(c) Insurance premiums expired during the year amounted to \$200.

(d) Office salaries of \$650 were accrued on December 31, 19+2.

(e) The corporation was liable for \$200 of interest expense on December 31, 19+2.

(3) The following expenses are to be allocated as indicated:

	Manufacturing	Selling and	General
Insurance	75	10	15
Depreciation—Buildings	80	5	15

(4) The corporation was liable for federal income tax in the amount of 20 percent of its net income before income tax.

Required:

(a) Working papers for the year ended December 31, 19+2.

(b) Closing entries using an income summary account.

Problem 2-8. The following trial balance was taken from the books of Denby and Carter on December 31, 19+7:

DENBY AND CARTER
Trial Balance
December 31, 19+7

Cash	13,290	
Petty cash	200	
Accounts receivable	35,350	
Allowance for uncollectibles		800
Notes receivable	6,000	
Inventory (December 31, 19+6)	51,000	
Advertising supplies	2,400	
Furniture and fixtures	17,000	
Accumulated depreciation—Furniture and fixtures		4,300
Delivery equipment	16,400	
Accumulated depreciation—Delivery equipment		7,000
Accounts payable		15,710
Bank loans		20,000
Delivery income collected in advance		440
D. H. Denby, capital		25,500

D. H. Denby, drawings	8,400	
K. B. Carter, capital		18,400
K. B. Carter, drawings	6,000	
Sales		302,630
Sales returns and allowances	1,470	
Sales discounts	2,580	
Purchases	190,600	
Purchase returns and allowances		1,990
Purchase discounts		1,430
Cost of goods sold		
Advertising	21,400	
Delivery expense	6,250	
Miscellaneous selling expense	1,920	
Rent expense	9,600	
Taxes	420	
Office salaries	6,300	
Office expense	1,320	
Interest revenue		600
Interest expense	900	
	398,800	398,800

Supplementary data:

(1) $240 of delivery income collected in advance applies to 19+8.
(2) Depreciation to be provided for 19+7:
 10 percent of furniture and fixtures
 20 percent of delivery equipment
(3) It is estimated that $1550 of the accounts receivable will probably prove uncollectible.
(4) Advertising supplies of $1600 remain unused.
(5) Office expense includes $240 for a two-year insurance policy to May 1, 19+9.
(6) All interest for 19+7 has been paid.
(7) Inventory, December 31, 19+7, $50,400.
(8) The partnership agreement provides for the division of earnings in the ratio of two-thirds to Denby and one-third to Carter.

Prepare working papers for the year, omitting the use of Adjusted Trial Balance columns.

Problem 2-9. The trial balance and necessary facts for the adjustments on December 31, 19+9 of The Empire Manufacturing Corporation appear below.

THE EMPIRE MANUFACTURING CORPORATION
Trial Balance
December 31, 19+9

Cash	36,180	
Accounts receivable	35,840	
Allowance for uncollectibles		2,900
Inventories—December 31, 19+8:		
Finished goods	10,400	
Good in process	7,310	
Materials	5,220	
Machinery and equipment	70,000	

Accumulated depreciation—Machinery and equipment		12,500
Office fixtures	4,400	
Accumulated depreciation—Office fixtures		1,360
Accounts payable		24,470
Capital stock		100,000
Retained earnings		14,880
Dividends	2,000	
Sales		192,200
Purchases—Materials	83,410	
Direct labor	51,600	
Rent	800	
Manufacturing overhead	27,380	
Selling expenses	9,500	
General expenses	4,270	
	348,310	348,310

Inventories—December 31, 19+9:

Finished goods	$12,300
Goods in process	8,110
Materials	7,700

20 percent of the corporation's net income before income tax must be paid as federal income tax.

Facts for adjustments:

(1) $400 is to be added to the allowance for doubtful accounts.
(2) Depreciation on the machinery and equipment for 19+9 is $5,000.
(3) Depreciation on the office fixtures for 19+9 is $510.

Required:

(a) Working papers on December 31, 19+9.
(b) Closing entries on December 31, 19+9, using an income summary account.

Problem 2-10. The following trial balance was taken from the books of Smith-Perry Company on December 31, 19+8:

SMITH-PERRY COMPANY
Trial Balance
December 31, 19+8

Cash	11,460	
Accounts receivable	13,755	
Allowance for uncollectibles		1,140
Notes receivable	11,000	
Interest receivable	165	
Inventory—December 31, 19+7	41,650	
Store fixtures	40,750	
Accumulated depreciation—Store fixtures		8,150
Accounts payable		16,120
Bank loans		5,000

D. H. Smith, capital		44,180
D. H. Smith, drawings	3,000	
K. B. Perry, capital		40,100
K. B. Perry, drawings	2,400	
Sales		196,550
Sales returns and allowances	1,940	
Sales discounts	585	
Purchases	145,830	
Purchase returns and allowances		2,020
Cost of goods sold		
Advertising	6,500	
Salesmen's salaries	22,800	
Miscellaneous selling expenses	1,315	
Rent expense	6,000	
Taxes	360	
Office salaries	3,000	
Office expense	890	
Interest expense	210	
Interest revenue		350
	313,610	313,610

Supplementary data:

Accrued interest on the bank loans is $25.

Office expense includes $150 for a one-year insurance policy purchased November 1, 19+8.

Of the accounts receivable, $100 should be written off and the balance should have a $1,400 allowance for bad debts.

Depreciation is computed at 10 percent.

There are 3,000 advertising brochures on hand that relate to 19+9-model products that will be handled by Smith-Perry Company. The cost of the brochures, $800, was charged to Advertising.

The interest receivable shown in the trial balance is the amount for December 31, 19+7. The amount accrued as of December 31, 19+8, is $150.

The December 31, 19+8 inventory is $46,110.

The partners share profits and losses equally.

Required:

(a) Working papers for the year ended December 31, 19+8.
(b) Closing entries using an income summary account.
(c) Reversing entries.

Problem 2-11. From the following trial balance, taken from the books of Metalfab Company as of June 30, 19+5, prepare working papers.

METALFAB COMPANY
Trial Balance—June 30, 19+5

Cash in bank	19,505	
Petty cash	250	
Accounts receivable	115,656	
Allowance for uncollectibles		5,400
Notes receivable	1,500	

Inventories, July 1, 19+4:		
Finished goods	13,800	
Goods in process	18,000	
Materials	9,250	
Land	13,050	
Buildings	30,000	
Accumulated depreciation—Buildings		4,740
Machinery	20,255	
Accumulated depreciation—Machinery		4,950
Office furniture	3,075	
Accumulated depreciation—Office furniture		1,525
Tools	5,250	
Dies and jigs	1,500	
Patents	17,000	
Accumulated amortization—Patents		3,500
Accounts payable		20,050
Notes payable		41,200
Bonds payable		50,000
Capital stock		75,000
Retained earnings		26,969
Sales		637,512
Sales returns and allowances	20,130	
Sales discounts	5,450	
Materials purchased	256,300	
Purchase discounts		4,080
Transportation on materials	10,100	
Direct labor	204,080	
Indirect labor	23,800	
Repairs—Machinery	1,080	
Insurance—Buildings	250	
Factory expense	1,955	
Insurance—Machinery	460	
Power, heat, and light	13,050	
Taxes—Land and buildings	2,400	
Repairs—Buildings	350	
Salesmen's salaries	22,050	
Travel—Salesmen	8,450	
Transportation out	2,550	
Insurance—Merchandise	600	
Payroll—Office	10,600	
Officers' salaries	11,500	
Telephone and telegraph	925	
Bank charges	455	
Office employees' surety bonds	160	
Postage expense	1,900	
Stationery and printing	1,245	
Interest expense	7,200	
Interest revenue		205
	875,131	875,131

Additional information:

(1) Inventories on June 20, 19+5, were:

Tools	$ 4,000
Dies and jigs	1,300
Finished goods	12,950
Goods in process	11,600
Materials	14,050
Postage	325

(2) Accounts receivable aggregating $2,031 were determined to be uncollectible. It was estimated that 8 percent of the remaining outstanding accounts would become uncollectible.

(3) Accrued property taxes on June 30, 19+5 were as follows:

Land and buildings	$600
Machinery	400
Office furniture	50

(4) Wages had been earned, but not paid on June 30, 19+5, in the following amounts:

Salesmen	$1,050
Officers	1,000
Office	630
Factory:	
Direct labor	4,450
Indirect labor	560

(5) The bonds payable bear interest at 8 percent, payable April 1 and October 1. Interest had been paid to June 30, 19+5, on all notes payable with the exception of one 5 percent note for $4,000, which was issued on April 1, 19+5.

(6) Unexpired insurance premiums on June 30, 19+5, were as follows:

Buildings	$150
Merchandise	380
Office employees' surety bonds	90
Machinery	320

Allocate the merchandise insurance as follows: 70 percent to manufacturing and 30 percent to selling.

(7) Depreciation is provided at the following rates (applied to ending asset account balances):

Buildings	3%
Machinery	10%
Office furniture	12%

(8) Patents are amortized over the legal life of 17 years.

(9) Interest accrued on notes receivable amounted to $30 on June 30, 19+5.

(10) All costs associated with the ownership and use of the land and buildings (including power, heat, and light) are allocated as follows:

Manufacturing	80%
Selling	6%
General	14%

(11) The declaration of a 6 percent cash dividend on June 28, 19+5, payable on July 15, 19+5, was not recorded.

(12) The federal income tax for the fiscal year ended June 30, 19+5, was estimated to be $3,600.

Problem 2-12. From the following adjusted trial balance and list of reversing entries:

(a) Prepare working papers, starting with the unadjusted trial balance, without using adjusted trial balance columns.

(b) Prepare closing entries without using an income summary account.

S. E. COOK AND COMPANY
Adjusted Trial Balance
December 31, 19+7

Cash	27,700	
Accounts receivable	42,260	
Allowance for uncollectibles		2,200
Interest receivable	110	
Inventory—December 31, 19+6	21,600	
Unexpired insurance	400	
Long-term investments	5,000	
Delivery equipment	25,000	
Accumulated depreciation—Delivery equipment		10,000
Accounts payable		18,390
Notes payable		4,500
Commissions collected in advance		1,400
Rent payable		800
Capital stock		75,000
Retained earnings		7,860
Dividends	3,000	
Sales		111,700
Sales returns and allowances	4,810	
Sales discounts	5,600	
Purchases	78,000	
Purchase returns and allowances		2,800
Purchase discounts		4,050
Transportation in	1,400	
Salesmen's salaries	19,370	
Depreciation—Delivery equipment	2,500	
Insurance	200	
Rent	3,200	
Office supplies expense	2,940	
Bad debts expense	1,200	
Interest revenue		450
Commissions revenue		5,400
Interest expense	260	
	244,550	244,550

The inventory on December 31, 19+7, was $23,460.
The company's liability for federal income tax for 19+7 was $2,500.
Reversing entries as of January 1, 19+8:

(1) Interest revenue	110	
Interest receivable		110

(2) Commissions collected in advance	1,400	
Commissions revenue		1,400
(3) Rent payable	800	
Rent		800

Problem 2-13. The trial balance on the following pages is that of Riffon Corporation taken from its accounting records as of December 31, 19+2.

RIFFON CORPORATION
Trial Balance
December 31, 19+2

Cash	17,700	
Accounts receivable	82,260	
Allowance for uncollectibles		3,003
Notes receivable	17,000	
Inventories—December 31, 19+1:		
Finished goods	31,218	
Goods in process	23,314	
Materials	14,602	
Investments	20,808	
Land	23,000	
Factory buildings	54,000	
Accumulated depreciation—Factory buildings		13,000
Machinery	32,600	
Accumulated depreciation—Machinery		12,010
Factory tools	4,215	
Salesroom equipment	8,240	
Accumulated depreciation—Salesroom equipment		710
Office furniture	11,300	
Accumulated depreciation—Office furniture		2,700
Patents	10,200	
Goodwill	10,000	
Bond discount	13,500	
Accounts payable		18,306
Notes payable		15,000
First mortgage bonds		75,000
Capital stock—Preferred ($100,000 authorized)		75,000
Capital stock—Common ($200,000 authorized)		100,000
Retained earnings		13,615
Dividends—Preferred	3,000	
Dividends—Common	5,000	
Sales		465,184
Sales returns and allowances	30,310	
Sales discounts	13,821	
Purchases—Materials	270,810	
Purchase returns and allowances		28,400
Purchase discounts		5,020
Transportation in	4,200	
Direct labor	14,209	
Indirect labor	6,370	
Superintendence	6,000	
Heat, light, and power	2,400	
Factory supplies expense	3,703	

Repairs	1,410	
Taxes	500	
Insurance	2,000	
Advertising	16,000	
Salesmen's traveling expense	1,500	
Salesmen's salaries	18,000	
Commissions—Salesmen	7,240	
Freight out	10,210	
Delivery expense	5,800	
Miscellaneous selling expenses	2,301	
Office salaries	4,217	
Officers' salaries	21,000	
Telephone and telegraph	1,830	
Office supplies expense	1,500	
Contributions	200	
Miscellaneous general expenses	810	
Rent revenue		5,600
Interest expense	4,250	
	832,548	832,548

Additional information:

(1) Inventories—December 31, 19+2:

Finished goods	$ 900
Goods in process	31,214
Materials	11,200
Tools	2,700

(2) Depreciation for 19+2:

Factory buildings	$ 1,620
Office furniture	1,130
Salesroom equipment	660
Machinery	3,912

(3) An allowance for doubtful accounts equal to 5 percent of the accounts receivable is considered adequate.

(4) Apportionments:

	Manufacturing	Selling	General
Repairs	70%	20%	10%
Taxes	20	75	5
Insurance	60	30	10

(5) Assume that the federal income tax rate for 19+2 is 50 percent.

Required:

(a) Working papers for the year ended December 31, 19+2.

(b) Adjusting journal entries as of December 31, 19+2.

(c) Closing entries as of December 31, 19+2. The firm uses an income summary account.

(d) Reversing entries as of January 1, 19+3.

CHAPTER 3

QUESTIONS

1. What is theory and of what use is it?
2. What is the distinction between normative and descriptive theory? How does this distinction apply to accounting?
3. Accounting is so practically oriented that there is no need for normative theory. Descriptive theory is sufficient in accounting. Do you agree with these statements?
4. What are the basic differences between accounting objectives, assumptions, doctrines, principles, and procedures? Briefly compare and contrast.
5. What are assumptions and what role do they play in theory? What are accounting assumptions and what role do they play in the theory of accounting practice?
6. What is accounting doctrine and what role does it play in the theory of accounting practice?
7. What do accountants mean by generally accepted accounting principles (GAAP)?
8. With regard to GAAP and substantial authoritative support, answer the following questions.
   (a) What do accountants mean by substantial authoritative support?
   (b) Can substantial authoritative support exist for accounting principles that differ from APB Opinions?
9. Why is money not a stable measuring unit? How do accountants justify their use of an unstable money measuring unit?
10. With regard to.the revenue-recognition assumption, answer the following questions.
    (a) What is the point of sale?
    (b) Do accountants always recognize revenue at the point of sale?
    (c) What are the arguments for recognizing revenue at the point of sale?
    (d) From a strict theoretical point of view, when is revenue earned by the firm?
11. Answer the following questions with regard to the doctrine of consistency.
    (a) Does consistency mean that changes in accounting procedures cannot be made?
    (b) Does consistency mean the use of consistent procedures in a given time period?
12. How are departures from APB Opinions disclosed in the financial statements?
13. With regard to the going-concern assumption, answer the following questions.
    (a) What are the arguments for the "going concern" as a basic accounting assumption?
    (b) Does the going-concern assumption imply the use of historical cost?
14. What is meant by the statement that the fiscal-period assumption implies the use of estimates and informed judgments by accountants?
15. Answer the following questions with regard to the doctrine of comparability.
    (a) Does comparability mean uniformity in accounting principles and procedures for different firms?
    (b) What is the controversy in accounting over the doctrine of comparability?
    (c) Does comparability mean the use of similar accounting principles and procedures by different firms?

16. By using money as the measuring unit, the financial statements prepared by accountants do not give a complete picture of the firm. What does this statement mean?

17. With regard to the doctrine of objectivity, answer the following questions.

(**a**) What is the difference between the traditional accounting view of objectivity as verifiable evidence and the consensus view of objectivity? Compare and contrast the two.

(**b**) Are the verifiable evidence and consensus views of objectivity compatible?

18. The specific-separate-entity assumption is so obvious that it need not be specified as a basic accounting assumption. Do you agree with this statement?

19. Answer the following questions with regard to the historical-cost assumption.

(**a**) What is cost?

(**b**) Is cost objectively determinable and verifiable?

(**c**) Is cost always used by accountants in the valuation of assets and liabilities?

20. What is meant by the statement that accounting principles are not derived by deductive logic, but are evolved?

21. With regard to conservatism, answer the following questions.

(**a**) What is the difference between the traditional and modern views of the doctrine of conservatism?

(**b**) Is conservatism a basic virtue of accounting?

22. Since it is impossible to directly associate all expenses with revenue, how do accountants match expenses with revenue in actual practice?

23. There is no need for a descriptive theory of accounting because it merely rationalizes existing accounting practice. Do you agree with this statement?

24. Is historical cost conservative?

25. What is the difference between matching and accrual accounting?

26. How can conservatism be used as an argument against the doctrine of conservatism?

27. There is no need for the accounting doctrine of materiality, since it amounts to stating the obvious: anything that is not material is immaterial. Do you agreee with this statement?

28. The accounting treatment of period expenses is an approximation, based on practical considerations, of associating expenses with revenue. What are some of these practical considerations that are used to justify such indirect matching?

29. What is the independent valuation method used by accountants for owners' equity?

30. Professor Sterling argues that the "going concern" is a prediction, not an assumption. What must he be arguing?

31. Is the distinction between deductive and inductive models synonymous with the distinction between normative and descriptive theory?

32. With regard to models, answer the following questions.

(**a**) What is a model?

(**b**) How does a model relate to theory?

(**c**) What are two approaches to model analysis?

(**d**) Are financial statements models?

PROBLEMS

Problem 3-1. You are given below eight multiple choice statements. Select the correct answer to complete each statement and indicate the corresponding letter on a separate sheet of paper (e.g., 1-a, 2-a, etc.).

(1) Opinions of the Accounting Principles Board (APB) apply only to items that are (a) immaterial, (b) in excess of ten percent of net income, (c) material and significant, (d) in excess of twenty percent of net income, (e) none of the above.

(2) The matching assumption is best illustrated by (a) not recognizing any expense unless some revenue is realized, (b) associating effort (cost) with accomplishment (revenue), (c) recognizing prepaid rent received as revenue, (d) establishing an allowance for future market decline, (e) none of the above.

(3) The APB (Accounting Principles Board) has been functioning for more than a decade. The best statement as to its current position with respect to generally accepted accounting principles is that (a) Accounting Research Bulletins (issued by its predecessor) remain in effect if not specifically modified or rescinded, (b) Accounting Research Bulletins are no longer in effect, (c) compliance with its pronouncements has become mandatory, (d) it has rendered opinions covering all of the generally accepted accounting principles, (e) none of the above.

(4) The concept of matching means (a) that all expense should be allocated to accounting periods on the basis of the effect on net income, (b) that costs should be carried forward to future accounting periods if they have not resulted in revenue during the current accounting period, (c) that if costs are charged off as expenses in the accounting period when they are actually incurred, they will be matched properly with the revenues actually earned during that accounting period, (d) that costs which can be associated directly with specific revenue should be carried forward in the balance sheet until the associated revenue is recognized, (e) none of the above.

(5) Footnotes to financial statements should *not* be used to (a) describe the nature and effect of a change in accounting principles, (b) identify substantial differences between book and tax income, (c) correct an improper financial statement presentation, (d) indicate basis for asset valuation, (e) none of the above.

(6) Accounting assumptions are (a) "givens" that are taken for granted in order that conclusions can be reached despite unavoidable gaps in our knowledge, (b) facts, (c) generally accepted doctrines, (d) deductive ideas of the accounting profession as to what ought to represent good accounting practice, (e) none of the above.

(7) The doctrine of consistency requires (a) use of consistent accounting procedures by an entity for a given time period, (b) use of consistent accounting procedures by all entities within an industry, (c) use of the same accounting procedure for a given entity from one period to the next, (d) all of the above, (e) none of the above.

(8) In forming his opinion on the financial statements of Kille Corporation, a CPA must decide whether an accounting treatment proposed by Kille has substantial authoritative support. The CPA is most likely to accept a source as constituting substantial authoritative support if it is (a) a pronouncement by an industry regulatory authority, (b) an accounting research study published by the AICPA, (c) a speech or article by the managing partner of a national CPA firm, (d) an Accounting Principles Board Opinion, (e) none of the above.

Problem 3-2. You are given below seven multiple choice statements. Select the correct answer to complete each statement and indicate the corresponding letter on a separate sheet of paper (e.g., 1-a, 2-a, etc.).

(1) A client has proposed an accounting treatment. The situation is not reviewed in the usual primary sources of substantial authoritative support. In this case the the most authoritative support available is (a) research studies of authoritative professional societies, (b) accounting textbooks and reference books, (c) predominant practice within the industry or business in general, (d) the company's treatment of similar transactions in prior years, (e) none of the above.

(2) Charging off a wastebasket with an estimated useful life of 20 years as an expense of the period when purchased is an example of the application of the (a) consistency doctrine, (b) matching assumption, (c) materiality doctrine, (d) historical-cost assumption, (e) none of the above.

(3) The allowance for cash discounts, which would appear as a deduction from accounts receivable on a balance sheet and would be based on an estimate of cash discounts to be taken on accounts receivable, is an example of the application of the (a) consistency doctrine, (b) matching assumption, (c) materiality doctrine, (d) revenue-recognition assumption, (e) none of the above.

(4) Expensing a tank of gas is a use of the (a) conservatism doctrine, (b) materiality doctrine, (c) consistency doctrine, (d) revenue-recognition assumption, (e) none of the above.

(5) In his auditor's report the CPA states that he has examined the (a) books and other records of the client, (b) financial statements of the client, (c) financial condition and operating results of the client, (d) clients' transactions, adjustments, and summaries thereof for the audit period, (e) none of the above.

(6) The assigning of the cost of natural-resources to inventory is based on the (a) matching assumption, (b) fiscal-period assumption, (c) revenue-recognition assumption, (d) historical-cost assumption, (e) all of the above, (f) none of the above.

(7) Accounting doctrines are (a) inductive ideas of the accounting profession as to what ought to represent good accounting practice, (b) pronouncements by the Financial Accounting Standards Board, (c) "givens" that are taken for granted in order that conclusions can be reached despite unavoidable gaps in our knowledge, (d) deductive attitudes of the accounting profession as to what ought to represent good accounting practice, (e) none of the above.

Problem 3-3. You are given below seven multiple choice questions. Select the correct answer to each question and indicate the corresponding letter on a separate sheet of paper (e.g., 1-a, 2-a, etc.).

(1) In the transactions approach to income determination, income is measured by subtracting the expenses resulting from specific transactions during the period from revenues of the period also resulting from transactions. Under a strict transactions approach to income measurement, which of the following would not be considered a transaction? (a) sale of goods on account at 20 percent markup, (b) exchange of inventory at a regular selling price for equipment, (c) adjustment of inventory in lower-of-cost-or-market-inventory valuations when the market is below cost, (d) payment of salaries, (e) none of the above.

(2) Which one of the following has the most relevance in deciding how indirect costs

should be assigned to a product? (a) avoidability, (b) causality, (c) controllability, (d) linearity, (e) none of the above.

(3) Which of the following is *not* an accounting assumption? (a) conservatism, (b) going concern, (c) matching, (d) historical-cost, (e) none of the above.

(4) An item is material if it is (a) in excess of ten percent of net income, (b) significant enough to affect evaluations or decisions, (c) in excess of twenty percent of net income, (d) unlikely to influence the judgment of a reasonable person, (e) none of the above.

(5) The systematic allocation of the cost of tangible long-lived assets over the life of the assets is *not* based on the (a) historical-cost assumption, (b) fiscal-period assumption, (c) revenue-recognition assumption, (d) matching assumption, (e) none of the above.

(6) An exception in the auditor's report because of the lack of consistent application of generally accepted accounting principles most likely would be required in the event of (a) a change in the rate of provision for uncollectible accounts based upon collection experience, (b) the original adoption of a pension plan for employees, (c) inclusion of a previously unconsolidated subsidiary in consolidated financial statements, (d) the revision of pension plan actuarial assumptions based upon experience, (e) none of the above.

(7) Present accounting theory is (a) normative, (b) nonexistent, (c) descriptive, (d) lacking a theoretical framework, (e) none of the above.

Problem 3-4. You are given below seven multiple choice questions. Select the correct answer to each question and indicate the corresponding letter on a separate sheet of paper (e.g., 1-a, 2-a, etc.).

(1) What is the principal disadvantage of using the percentage-of-completion method of recognizing revenue from long-term contracts? It (a) is unacceptable for income tax purposes, (b) violates the revenue-recognition assumption, (c) gives results based upon estimates that may be subject to considerable uncertainty, (d) is likely to assign a small amount of revenue to a period during which much revenue was actually earned, (e) none of the above.

(2) An unqualified standard short-form report by a CPA normally does not explicitly state (a) the CPA's opinion that the financial statements comply with generally accepted accounting principles, (b) that generally accepted auditing standards were followed in the conduct of the audit, (c) that the internal control system of the client was found to be satisfactory, (d) the subjects of the audit examination, (e) none of the above.

(3) The primary responsibility for the adequacy of disclosure in the financial statements and footnotes rests with the (a) partner assigned to the engagement, (b) auditor in charge of field work, (c) staffman who drafts the statements and footnotes, (d) client, (e) none of the above.

(4) Conventionally accountants measure income (a) by applying a value-added concept, (b) by using a transactions approach, (c) as a change in the value of owners' equity, (d) as a change in the purchasing power of owners' equity, (e) none of the above.

(5) The term "revenue recognition" conventionally refers to (a) the process of identifying transactions to be recorded as revenue in an accounting period, (b) the process of measuring and relating revenue and expenses of an enterprise for an accounting period, (c) the earning process which gives rise to revenue

realization, (d) the process of identifying those transactions that result in an inflow of assets from customers, (e) none of the above.

(6) The valuation basis used in conventional financial statements is (a) market value, (b) original cost, (c) replacement cost, (d) a mixture of cost and other valuation methods, (e) none of the above.

(7) Expensing of insurance premiums paid for insurance protection over the next year is a violation of the (a) conservatism doctrine, (b) historical-cost assumption, (c) revenue-recognition assumption, (d) matching assumption, (e) fiscal period assumption, (f) none of the above.

Problem 3-5. You are given below seven multiple choice questions. Select the correct answer to each question and indicate the corresponding letter on a separate sheet of paper (e.g., 1-a, 2-a, etc.).

(1) When work to be done and costs to be incurred on a long-term contract can be estimated dependably, which of the following methods of revenue recognition is preferable? (a) sales method, (b) installment method, (c) percentage of completion method, (d) completed contract method, (e) none of the above.

(2) Which one of the following methods of determining bad debts expense does not match expense and revenue? (a) charging bad debts with a percentage of sales under the allowance method, (b) charging bad debts with a percentage of accounts receivable under the allowance method, (c) charging bad debts with an amount derived from aging the accounts receivable under the allowance method, (d) charging bad debts as accounts are written off as uncollectible, (e) none of the above.

(3) Which of the following should be recognized as an accountable event in financial statements according to generally accepted accounting principles (assume all amounts are material)? (a) receipt of a stock dividend, (b) decline in market valuation of investments held, (c) increase in market valuation of investments held, (d) decrease in selling price of finished goods inventory and a normal profit is expected on the new price, (e) none of the above.

(4) The entity assumption is applicable (a) only to the legal aspects of business organizations, (b) only to the economic aspects of business organizations, (c) only to business organizations, (d) wherever accounting is involved, (e) none of the above.

(5) The consistency doctrine requires that (a) expenses be reported as charges against the period in which they are incurred, (b) the effect of changes in accounting upon income be properly disclosed, (c) extraordinary gains and losses should not appear on the income statement, (d) accounting procedures be adopted which give a consistent rate of return, (e) none of the above.

(6) The going-concern assumption is the basis for the rule that (a) treasury stock should not be recorded in the balance sheet as an asset; (b) net income should include all gains and losses during a year; (c) the cost of insurance on a machine in transit should be capitalized as part of the cost of the machine in the accounts; (d) goodwill should be amortized over a period of years; (e) none of the above.

(7) The specific-separate-entity assumption is the basis for the rule that (a) personal transactions of owners, managers, and employees are separate and distinct from the firm's transactions; (b) revenue is recognized at time of sale; (c) inventories are recorded at lower of cost or market; (d) patents should be amortized over a period of years; (e) none of the above.

Problem 3-6. You are given below some accounting doctrines. Select the doctrine(s) that justifies the following accounting procedures and indicate the corresponding letter(s) on a separate sheet of paper.

(a) Materiality
(b) Consistency
(c) Comparability
(d) Objectivity
(e) Conservatism

(1) Lower of cost or market
(2) Expensing of repair tools when acquired
(3) Prohibition against switching from LIFO to FIFO to LIFO
(4) Recording of expected losses but not profits
(5) Reporting of those items which are significant enough to affect decisions
(6) Providing of summary of accounting principles and procedures with financial statements
(7) Use of past acquisition prices
(8) Use of similar accounting procedures by different firms for the same situation
(9) Recording goodwill only when purchased
(10) Use of point-of-sale for revenue recognition
(11) Use of estimating procedures for valuation of inventory

Problem 3-7. You are given below seven accounting assumptions. Select the assumption(s) that justifies the following accounting procedures and indicate the corresponding letter(s) on a separate sheet of paper.

(a) Specific-separate-entity assumption
(b) Going-concern assumption
(c) Money-measuring-unit assumption
(d) Historical-cost assumption
(e) Fiscal-period (periodicity) assumption
(f) Revenue-recognition assumption
(g) Matching assumption

(1) Amortization of intangibles
(2) Point-of-sale used as point at which receivables are recorded
(3) Consolidated statements
(4) Reporting of liabilities at their discounted amount
(5) Use of past acquisition prices
(6) Accrual accounting
(7) Quantifying only those business activities that can be measured in terms of money
(8) Use of inventory accounts
(9) Transactions approach
(10) Cost centers
(11) Periodic reporting
(12) General-price-level changes
(13) Not reporting assets at liquidating prices
(14) Valuation
(15) Establishment of allowance for uncollectibles
(16) Recording of deferred income taxes
(17) Capitalization of research and development

Problem 3-8. The following two statements have been taken directly or with some modification from the accounting literature. All of them either are taken out of context, involve circular reasoning and/or contain one or more fallacies, half-truths, erroneous comments, conclusions or inconsistencies (internally or with generally accepted principles or practices).

Statement 1

Accounting is a service activity. Its function is to provide quantitative financial information which is intended to be useful in making economic decisions about and for economic entities. Thus the accounting function might be viewed primarily as being a tool or device for providing quantitative financial information to management to facilitate decision making.

Statement 2

Financial statements that were developed in accordance with generally accepted accounting principles, which apply the doctrine of conservatism, can be free from bias (or give a presentation that is fair with respect to continuing and prospective stockholders as well as to retaining stockholders).

Required:

Evaluate each of the above numbered statements as follows:

(a) List the fallacies, half-truths, circular reasoning, erroneous comments or conclusions and/or inconsistencies; and

(b) Explain by what authority and/or what basis each item listed in part (a) above can be considered to be fallacious, circular, inconsistent, a half-truth or an erroneous comment or conclusion. If the statement or a portion of it is merely out of context, indicate the context(s) in which the statement would be correct.

Problem 3-9. *Opinion No. 11* issued by the Accounting Principles Board states that except in unusual circumstances no recognition should be given to the tax benefit of a loss carryforward (may reduce income tax expense in the future that would otherwise be owed on income of those years) until this tax benefit is actually realized.

Recognition of the benefit would create an asset.

Required:

(a) Explain the meaning of asset as the term is used within generally accepted accounting principles.

(b) Whether or not a tax loss carryforward should be a determinant of net loss of the loss period must be decided by weighing the doctrine of conservatism and the going-concern assumption.

(1) Under what conditions should conservatism prevail? Discuss.

(2) Under what conditions should the going concern prevail? Discuss.

Problem 3-10. The Aim Corporation, a farm corporation, produced the following in its first year of operations:

	Selling Price Per Bushel
9,000 bushels of wheat............................	$2.40
6,000 bushels of oats..............................	1.40

During the year it sold two-thirds of the grain produced and collected three-fourths of the selling price on the grain sold; the balance is to be collected in equal amounts during each of the two following years.

Additional data for the first year:

Wealth at beginning of year 1	$100,000
Wealth at end of year 1	115,000
Depreciation on productive plant and equipment	3,000
Other production costs (cash)	4,500
Miscellaneous administrative costs (cash)	3,600
Grain storage costs	—
Selling and delivery costs (incurred and paid at time of sale) per bushel	.10
Additional stockholder investments during year 1	—
Dividends paid to stockholders during year 1	10,000
Income taxes	—

The Aim Company is enthusiastic about the accountant's concept of matching costs and revenues; it wishes to carry the idea to the extreme and to match with revenues not only all direct costs but also all indirect costs such as those for administration.

(1) If revenues were recognized when production is complete (i.e., inventory is carried at net selling price), income computed in accordance with the chosen matching objective for the first year would be (a) $21,600, (b) $17,900, (c) $17,400, (d) $7,400, (e) none of the above.

(2) If revenue were recognized on the sales basis, income computed in accordance with the chosen matching objective for the first year would be (a) $10,400, (b) $9,900, (c) $9,400, (d) $7,400, (e) none of the above.

(3) If revenue were recognized on the cash-collection basis, income computed in accordance with the chosen matching objective for the first year would be (a) $10,700, (b) $6,900, (c) $8,700, (d) $12,900, (e) none of the above.

(4) If revenue were recognized when production is complete, income computed in accordance with the conventional matching assumption for the first year would be (a) $21,600, (b) $18,400, (c) $17,900, (d) $7,400, (e) none of the above.

(5) If revenue were recognized on the sales basis, income computed in accordance with the conventional matching assumption for the first year would be (a) $10,400, (b) $6,300, (c) $8,700, (d) $12,900, (e) none of the above.

(6) If revenue were recognized on the cash-collection basis, income computed in accordance with the conventional matching assumption for the first year would be (a) $8,700, (b) $6,300, (c) $4,400, (d) $6,900, (e) none of the above.

(7) Recently the company's president was introduced to a noted British economist who convinced him that the accountant's accrual approach to measuring income in fact was merely a partial accrual and that full accrual would require consideration of changes in "wealth," which was defined as "the present value of expected net future receipts." Following this it was suggested that a full accrual income for a period would be determined to be the amount that could be spent during a period while leaving wealth unchanged. Income measured in this way for the first year would be (a) $30,000, (b) $25,000, (c) $20,000, (d) $15,000, (e) none of the above.

Problem 3-11. Kwik-Bild Corporation sells and erects shell houses. These are frame structures that are completely finished on the outside but are unfinished on the inside except for flooring, partition studding and ceiling joists. Shell houses are sold chiefly to customers who are handy with tools and who have time to do the interior wiring, plumbing, wall completion and finishing and other work necessary to make the shell houses livable dwellings.

Kwik-Bild buys shell houses from a manufacturer in unassembled packages consisting of all lumber, roofing, doors, windows and similar materials necessary to complete a shell house. Upon commencing operations in a new area, Kwik-Bild buys or leases land as a site for its local warehouse, field office and display houses. Sample display houses are erected at a total cost of from $3,000 to $7,000 including the cost of the unassembled packages. The chief element of cost of the display houses is the unassembled packages, since erection is a short low-cost operation. Old sample models are torn down or altered into new models every three to seven years. Sample display houses have little salvage value because dismantling and moving costs amount to nearly as much as the cost of an unassembled package.

Required:

(a) A choice must be made between (1) expensing the costs of sample display houses in the period in which the expenditure is made and (2) spreading the costs over more than one period. Discuss the advantages of each method.

(b) Would it be preferable to amortize the cost of display houses on the basis of (1) the passage of time or (2) the number of shell houses sold? Explain.

Problem 3-12. The general ledger of Enter-tane, Inc. a corporation engaged in the development and production of television programs for commercial sponsorship, contains the following accounts before amortization at the end of the current year:

Account	Balance (Debit)
Sealing Wax & Kings	$51,000
The Messenger	36,000
The Desperado	17,500
Shin Bone	8,000
Studio Rearrangement	5,000

An examination of contracts and records revealed the following information:

(1) The first two accounts listed above represent the total cost of completed programs that were televised during the accounting period just ended. Under the terms of an existing contract Sealing Wax and Kings will be re-run during the next accounting period, at a fee equal to 50 percent of the fee for the first televising of the program. The contract for the first run produced $300,000 of revenue. The contract with the sponsor of The Messenger provides that he may, at his option, re-run the program during the next season at a fee of 75 percent of the fee on the first televising of the program.

(2) The balance in The Desperado account is the cost of a new program that has just been completed and is being considered by several companies for commercial sponsorship.

(3) The balance in the Shin Bone account represents the cost of a partially completed program for a projected series that has been abandoned.

(4) The balance of the Studio Rearrangement account consists of payments made to a firm of engineers which prepared a report relative to the more efficient utilization of existing studio space and equipment.

Required:

(a) State the underlying accounting assumption that is applicable to the first *four* accounts.
(b) What accounting doctrine is applicable to the recording and reporting of The Messenger? Explain.
(c) How would you report each of the first *four* accounts in the financial statements of Enter-tane, Inc.? Explain.
(d) In what way, if at all, does the Studio Rearrangement account differ from the first four? Explain.

Problem 3-13. Mr. Erik, owner of Erik's Retail Hardware, states that he computes income on a cash basis. At the end of each year he takes a physical inventory and computes the cost of all merchandise on hand. To this he adds the ending balance of accounts receivable because he considers this to be a part of inventory on the cash basis. Using this logic he deducts from this total the ending balance of accounts payable for merchandise to arrive at what he calls inventory (net).

The following information has been taken from his cash-basis income statements for the years indicated:

	19+4	19+3	19+2
Cash received	$173,000	$164,000	$150,000
Cost of goods sold:			
Inventory (net), Jan. 1	$ 8,000	$ 11,000	$ 3,000
Total purchases	109,000	102,000	95,000
Goods available for sale	$117,000	$113,000	$ 98,000
Inventory (net), Dec. 31	1,000	8,000	11,000
Cost of goods sold	$116,000	$105,000	$109,000
Gross margin	$ 57,000	$ 59,000	$ 63,000

Additional information is as follows for the years indicated:

	19+4	19+3	19+2	19+1
Accounts receivable, Dec. 31	$ 8,000	$ 6,000	$ 5,000	0
Accounts payable for merchandise, Dec. 31	33,000	20,000	13,000	0

Calculate the gross margin for the years 19+4, 19+3, and 19+2 under accrual accounting.

Problem 3-14. The following income statement was prepared from the check records of J. G. Hampton at the end of his first year of operations.

HAMPTON AND COMPANY
Income Statement
Year Ended December 31, 19+1

Sales	$85,000
Cost of goods sold	68,000
Gross margin	$17,000

Expenses:		
Equipment	$10,000	
Salaries and wages	17,500	
Utilities	6,500	
Supplies	2,500	36,500
Net loss		($19,500)

Mr. Hampton is perplexed by the large apparent loss. He finds the results of operations as presented to be inconsistent with the net income he has obtained in managing a similar business for others during the past ten years. Your investigation reveals the statement was prepared on a cash basis:

(1) Sales represent only cash collected from customers; in addition to these collections, $8,600 of uncollected receivables were outstanding on December 31, 19+1.
(2) Cost of goods sold represents the total merchandise purchased in 19+1, of which $7,500 was on hand at December 31, 19+1.
(3) The equipment was purchased on January 1 and is expected to have a life of ten years.
(4) The salaries and wages for December of $1,575 have not been paid.
(5) The utilities for December of $525 have not been paid.
(6) Of the total supplies purchased, $1,500 are still on hand.

Required:

Prepare a revised income statement on the accrual basis.

Problem 3-15. Accounting records are kept and financial statements prepared based upon GAAP. Following is the balance sheet for Wild Bill's, Inc. as of December 31, 19+3. The statement was prepared by the bookkeeper who was taking a correspondence course in accounting and reading current magazines about what information is desired by the various users of financial statements. In trying to furnish relevant information to all the various users of financial statements, the bookkeeper may have departed from GAAP.

WILD BILL'S, INC.
Balance Sheet
For the Year Ended December 31, 19+3
Assets

Current assets:			
Cash on hand and in bank		$ 29,275	
Cash value of life insurance		560	
Accounts receivable	$ 88,500		
Less: allowance for uncollectibles	3,540	84,960	
Inventories:			
Iron Ore (LIFO)	$ 68,500		
Chemicals (FIFO)	32,775		
Other materials (cost or market whichever is lower)	50,000		
Finished goods (net realizable value)	90,225	241,500	$ 356,295
Long-term investments:			
Marketable securities—temporary (market value)		$ 75,000	
Land-held for future use (cost)		25,000	100,000

Property, plant and equipment:			
Land (resale value)		$125,000	
Buildings (adjusted for general price-level changes)		400,000	
Equipment, group I (replacement cost)	$ 90,000		
Equipment, group II (adjusted for general price-level changes)	125,000	215,000	740,000
Deferred charges:			
Supplies on hand*		$ 500	
Prepaid insurance (liquidation value)		3,204	
Goodwill		1	3,705
Total assets			$1,200,000

Equities

Current liabilities:			
Accounts payable (net of discount)		$ 98,000	
Warranties payable (estimated cost)		12,000	
Dividend payable		12,500	
6% Mortgage-payment due 12 months (plus interest)		11,660	$ 134,160
Long-term liabilities:			
Bonds payable, 6%, 10 years (present value)		$ 88,000	
Bonds payable, 7%, 20 years (face value)	$250,000		
Less bond discount	3,750	246,250	334,250
Deferred credits:			
Accumulated depreciation—building		$ 30,000	
Accumulated depreciation—equipment, group I		54,000	
Accumulated depreciation—equipment, group II		25,000	109,000
Stockholders' equity:			
Capital stock, $100 stated value, 5,000 shares		$500,000	
Capital in excess of stated value		95,000	
To balance		27,590	622,590
Total equities			$1,200,000

*All over $10 cost per classification.

Wild Bill's, Inc. was formed January 1, 19+1 and immediately purchased an operating business. Included in the purchase price was $100,000 for the land used in the business, the building, group I equipment, certain inventories, and goodwill amounting to $25,000.

Required:

(a) Which items are listed incorrectly? For those listed under the wrong classification discuss how they should have been listed.

(b) List the accounts which are given that deviate from the historical-cost assumption, and then state which of these deviations are acceptable methods of presentation under GAAP.

(c) Explain the figure "To balance."

(d) Evaluate the adjustments for general price-level changes.
(e) Evaluate the presentation of bonds payable.
(f) What accounting doctrine was used in reporting the supplies on hand?
(g) What accounting doctrine applies to the method used to report other materials?

Problem 3-16. Following is the income statement for the year 19+3 for Wild Bill's, Inc. whose balance sheet was given in the preceding problem.

WILD BILL'S, INC.
Income Statement
December 31, 19+3

Revenue:		
Cash received on account	$737,250	
Dividends from investment in stock	750	$738,000
Less: Cost of goods sold:		
Beginning inventory	$228,000	
Purchases	351,500	
Merchandise available for sale	$579,500	
Less: Ending inventory	241,500	338,000
Gross margin		$400,000
Expenses:		
Research and development cost	$ 4,000	
Salaries and wages	200,000	
Interest	23,440	
Utilities	45,260	
Organizational costs	1,500	
Bond discount	2,500	
Advertising	10,000	
Freight in	4,500	
Settlement of prior years' income taxes	6,300	
Dividends	12,500	
Property taxes	4,250	
Freight out	1,400	
Equipment purchased	1,500	
Settlement of prior periods' legal claims	5,000	
Depreciation	40,500	
Goodwill	24,999	387,649
Net income		$ 12,351

Required:

(a) Are the amounts shown for revenue correct? Discuss what you consider should appear as revenue.
(b) Which items are not classified properly? Discuss.
(c) Are there any expenses which are not proper for this period? Discuss.
(d) Are there any items listed which should be separated as extraordinary items? Discuss.
(e) Are there any items listed which should not be included in the income statement? Discuss.

CHAPTER 4

QUESTIONS

1. How does the income statement differ from the balance sheet, statement of retained earnings, and the statement of changes in financial position?
2. What are revenue, expense, and net income?
3. Why is it important for financial statement users to be aware of accounting policies?
4. What is the difference between an income statement and a statement of income and retained earnings?
5. What is the difference between a single-step and a multiple-step income statement?
6. What is the distinction between the following?
   (a) Revenue and expense
   (b) Cost, expense, and loss
   (c) Product cost and period expense
7. What are the objectives of income reporting?
8. How do accounting assumptions underlie the preparation of the income statement?
9. What is the distinction between an extraordinary item, a prior-period adjustment, and an accounting error, and how do they differ as to their accounting treatment?
10. What is the distinction between a change in an accounting principle, estimate, or entity, and how do they differ as to their accounting treatment?
11. What are the arguments against the current-operating and the all-inclusive concepts of income?
12. What is income tax allocation?
13. Per *Opinion No. 15* earnings-per-share data are no longer primarily based upon historical information. What does this statement mean?
14. How does the income statement of a manufacturing firm differ from that of a merchandising firm?
15. The income statement is a flow model, while the balance sheet is a stock model. What does this statement mean?
16. A firm has been depreciating an asset under the straight-line method for four years, based on an estimated useful life of ten years. It is now determined that the estimated useful life should have been fifteen years; hence, it is proposed that prior years' depreciation be corrected and current and subsequent years' depreciation be the correct depreciation based on a fifteen year useful life. Is this treatment in line with GAAP?
17. Where would the following be reported in the income statement?
   (a) Loss on sale of equipment
   (b) Gain on bond retirement
   (c) Gain on sale of a major division of a company
   (d) Loss on uninsured hurricane damage
   (e) Tax effect on (d) above
   (f) Loss on annual uninsured flood damage
   (g) Charge for depreciation omitted for prior years
   (h) Purchase discounts
   (i) Deferred revenue

(j) Unfavorable settlement of prior years' income taxes
(k) Payments for organizing company
(l) Vacation pay
(m) Collection of life insurance policy upon death of a company officer
(n) Tax loss carryforward
(o) Loss on purchase commitment—contract to buy goods for future delivery and price has declined

18. What do the following statements mean?

(a) Revenue is not really earned at the point of sale.
(b) Expenses cannot really be directly matched with revenue.
(c) Net income cannot really be determined until the firm ceases operation.

19. Net income in the income statement represents income to whom?

20. Income determination and valuation cannot really be separated. What does this statement mean?

PROBLEMS

Problem 4-1. Based on the seven multiple choice statements given below, select the answer that you think will best complete each statement and indicate the corresponding letter on a separate sheet of paper (e.g., 1-b, 2-a, etc.).

(1) Which of the following is characteristic of a change in an accounting estimate? (a) It usually need not be disclosed, (b) It does not affect the financial statements of prior periods, (c) It should be reported through the restatement of the financial statements, (d) It makes necessary the reporting of pro forma amounts for prior periods, (e) none of the above.

(2) During the current year a court decided that employers at the Hart Company's plant, which closed down two years ago, were entitled either to severance pay or to added pension benefits if transferred to other Company operations. The amounts involved are material and afford an example for the current year of (a) a prior-period adjustment of retained earnings, (b) an extraordinary item on the income statement, (c) a contingent liability, (d) a casualty loss on the income statement, (e) none of the above.

(3) Classification as an extraordinary item on the income statement would be most appropriate for the (a) unused portion of a capital loss to be carried forward, (b) substantial write-off of obsolete inventories, (c) sale of investments not acquired for resale, (d) amortization of past service costs of a pension plan, (e) none of the above.

(4) Which one of the following types of losses is excluded from the determination of current period net income? Material losses resulting from (a) transactions in the company's own bonds payable, (b) unusual sales of assets not acquired for resale, (c) the write-off of intangibles, (d) adjustments specifically related to operations of prior years, (e) none of the above.

(5) The bookkeeper of Latsch Company, which has an accounting year ending December 31, made the following errors:

(a) A $1,000 collection from a customer was received on December 29, 19+3, but not recorded until the date of its deposit in the bank, January 4, 19+4.
(b) A supplier's $1,600 invoice for inventory items received in December 19+3 was

not recorded until January 19+4. (Inventories at December 31, 19+3 and 19+4 were stated correctly, based on physical count.)

(c) Depreciation for 19+3 was understated by $900.

(d) In September 19+3 a $200 invoice for office supplies was charged to the Utilities Expense account. Office supplies are expensed as purchased.

(e) December 31, 19+3 sales on account of $3,000 were recorded in January 19+4.

Assume that no other errors have occurred and that no correcting entries have been made. Ignore income taxes. Net income for 19+3 was (a) understated by $500, (b) understated by $2,100, (c) overstated by $2,500, (d) neither understated nor overstated, (e) none of the above.

(6) Selling and general expenses appear on (a) the statement of cost of goods manufactured in the manufacturing overhead section, (b) the income statement in the gross margin section, (c) the income statement as extraordinary items, (d) the statement of retained earnings, (e) none of the above.

(7) An example of the correction of an error in previously issued financial statements is a change (a) from the completed-contract to the percentage-of-completion method of accounting for long-term construction-type contracts, (b) in the depletion rate, based on new engineering studies of recoverable mineral resources, (c) from the sum-of-the-years'-digits to the straight-line method of depreciation for all plant assets, (d) from the installment basis of recording sales to the accrual basis, when collection of the sales price has been and continues to be reasonably assured, (e) none of the above.

Problem 4-2. Based on the seven multiple choice statements given below, select the answer that you think will best complete each statement and indicate the corresponding letter on a separate sheet of paper (e.g., 1-b, 2-a, etc.).

(1) Where financial statements for a single year are being presented (without comparative statements), a prior-period adjustment recognized in the current year ordinarily would (a) be shown as an adjustment of the balance of retained earnings at the start of the current year, (b) affect net income before extraordinary items of the current year, (c) be shown as an extraordinary item on the current year's income statement, (d) be included in an all-inclusive income statement, (e) none of the above.

(2) The occurrence which most likely would have no effect on 19+8 net income (assuming that all involved are material) is the (a) sale in 19+8 of an office building contributed by a stockholder in 19+2, (b) collection in 19+8 of a receivable from a customer whose amount was written off in 19+4, (c) settlement based on litigation in 19+8 of previously unrecognized damages from a serious accident that occurred in 19+6, (d) worthlessness determined in 19+8 of stock purchased on a speculative basis in 19+2, (e) none of the above.

(3) If a company classifies its expenses as cost of goods sold, employee salaries and benefits, depreciation, taxes, purchased services, and other expenses, the classification basis used is by (a) area of responsibility, (b) object of expenditure, (c) services received, (d) function performed, (e) none of the above.

(4) Conventionally, accountants measure income (a) by applying a value-added concept, (b) by using a transactions approach, (c) as a change in the value of owners' equity, (d) as a change in the purchasing power of owners' equity, (e) none of the above.

(5) A general description of the depreciation methods applicable to major classes of depreciable assets (a) is not a current practice in financial reporting, (b) is not

essential to a fair presentation of financial position, (c) is needed in financial reporting when company policy differs from income tax policy, (d) should be included in corporate financial statements or notes thereto, (e) none of the above.

(6) Selling and general administration expenses appear (a) on the income statement in the gross margin section, (b) on the income statement as extraordinary items, (c) in the cost of goods sold section of the income statement, (d) on the income statement before the net operating income line, (e) none of the above.

(7) If long-term investments of a manufacturing company are sold at a gain of $80,000 and this transaction increased income taxes by $20,000, the multiple-step income statement for the period would disclose these effects as (a) nonoperating gain of $80,000 and an increase in income tax expense of $20,000, (b) operating income net of applicable taxes, $60,000, (c) a prior-period adjustment net of applicable taxes, $60,000, (d) an extraordinary item net of applicable taxes, $60,000, (e) none of the above.

Problem 4-3. Indicate whether each item below is (a) an extraordinary item, (b) a prior-period adjustment, or (c) an ordinary income item.

(1) Writeoff of research and development costs from prior years.
(2) Settlement of litigation concerning a sale two years ago.
(3) Gain from a fluctuation in foreign currency.
(4) Loss on the condemnation of property.
(5) Refund from a past year of previously recorded revenue as part of the settlement of a rate case.
(6) Writeoff of goodwill.
(7) Write down of inventory.
(8) Major devaluation of a foreign currency.
(9) Writeoff of a five year old receivable.
(10) Sale of an investment not acquired for resale.
(11) Change in the estimated life of plant equipment.

Problem 4-4. Presented below are the three types of accounting changes plus accounting errors as discussed in *Opinion No. 20.*

(a) Change in accounting estimate
(b) Change in accounting principle
(c) Change in reporting entity
(d) Error correction

Using the appropriate letter above, indicate which category each of the following represents:

(1) Mathematical mistake in computing depreciation.
(2) Change from the use of an unacceptable to the use of an acceptable accounting principle.
(3) Change in acceptable depreciation method.
(4) Change from individual to consolidated financial statements.
(5) Change due to the use of an unrealistic estimate of the life of a cement plant.
(6) Change in the percentage of receivables that will be collectible.
(7) Change from a FIFO to a LIFO inventory costing method.

(8) Change by an oil company to the "full costing" method.
(9) Change due to the failure to record a sale in a prior year.
(10) Change from capitalizing to expensing research and development costs because of growing uncertainty of future benefits.
(11) A change in both a realistic accounting estimate and an acceptable accounting principle.
(12) Change caused by the sale of a major subsidiary company.

Problem 4-5. You have been called in to audit the books of Sandy Company. You discover that no depreciation was taken on a cement kiln that was bought three years ago for $100,000 and was estimated to have no salvage and a ten year life. Sandy Company uses straight-line depreciation. The income figures for the past three years before adjustment for this error are presented below.

	19+6	19+5	19+4
Income before extraordinary items ...	$89,600	$79,200	$111,000
Extraordinary items	8,000	1,800	-0-
Net income	81,600	77,400	111,000
Earnings per share.....................	10.20	8.60	11.10

Required:

(a) Prepare the income and earnings per share part of the 19+6 income statement after correcting the 19+6 income figure.
(b) Prepare the pro forma amounts that would be shown for the previous years income when using comparative income statements.

Problem 4-6. Prepare a combined multiple-step income and retained earnings statement for York Company from the data given below.

YORK COMPANY
Adjusted Trial Balance
December 31, 19+5

Allowance for uncollectibles	950
Accrued interest on notes receivable	45
Accumulated depreciation—factory buildings	17,100
Selling expenses..	21,228
Real estate mortgage bonds—6%, due Dec. 31, 19+10	50,000
Cash..	27,600
Accounts payable...	4,000
Discount on bonds	2,250
Net sales	225,693
Capital in excess of par-common stock	7,500
Dividends received on Stokes stock investment...............	400
Accounts receivable	35,365
Federal income tax payable	13,600
General and administrative expense	12,648
Factory buildings..	65,000
Retained earnings	18,714
Notes payable..	5,000
Land	23,000
Inventories—finished goods	10,991
Office equipment..	3,140
Common stock—$100 par	75,000

Cost of goods sold	152,033
Inventories—goods in process	13,212
Rent collected in advance	100
Accumulated depreciation—office equipment	1,064
Rent revenue	50
Factory supplies	350
Machinery and equipment	53,900
Interest revenue	186
Gain on sale of land	2,000
Interest expense—bonds	3,680
Inventories—materials	9,923
Loss on settlement of income tax liability from 19+2	2,542
Investment in Stoker Company	5,000
Federal income tax	14,600
Prepaid insurance	400
Preferred stock—6% cumulative, $100 par	40,000
Accumulated depreciation—machinery and equip.	18,388
Dividends on common stock	6,000
Mathematical error made in 19+4 that increased cost of goods sold	1,542
Dividends on preferred stock	2,400
Marketable securities—market $11,000	10,000
Notes receivable	6,000
Interest payable	20

Problem 4-7. You are given the following data on Billy Bam Enterprises for the year ended December 31, 19+8.

Common shares outstanding at beginning of year	1,000,000
Nonconvertible preferred stock dividends	$ 20,000
Prime bank rate	8%
Convertible bonds outstanding, 8% issued at face	$7,500,000
Conversion ratio—60 shares of common per each $1,000 bond	
Income before extraordinary items	$4,245,055
Sold common stock: July 1	650,000
December 1	300,000
Gain on insurance recovery due to tornado damage, net of taxes of $4,500	$ 13,000
Prior-period adjustment from unfavorable rate case	$ 100,000

Required:

The earnings per share figures for Billy Bam Enterprises presented as they would be in the firm's income statement.

Problem 4-8. Based on the financial data given below, prepare an income statement for Picitti, Inc. for the year ended December 31, 19+9. The statement is to be in multiple-step form. There are 100,000 common shares outstanding.

Deferred revenue	$ 13,000
Beginning merchandise inventory	14,000
Income taxes—40%	?
Sales tax	11,000
Freight in	1,000
Dividends	22,000
Selling expense	49,000
Sales, including sales tax	403,500

Allowance for uncollectibles	24,000
Change in estimated useful life of selling equipment, additional depreciation charge to be recorded	2,000
Purchases	250,000
Unfavorable legal settlement, previously pending	30,000
General and administration expenses	59,000
Gain on sale of equipment, 25% tax rate applicable	5,000
Ending merchandise inventory	25,000
Change from expensing to capitalizing research and development, amount to be capitalized net of taxes of $2,000	15,000

Problem 4-9. The following information was taken from the books of Kathleen Company. It relates to the year ended December 31, 19+8. All items are net of any income tax effect.

Retained earnings—December 31, 19+7	$281,705
Net loss for the year before items listed below	45,678
Gain on sale of land on July 15, 19+8	28,500
Correction of a mathematical error made in calculating 19+2 interest expense, charged to Retained Earnings and credited to Interest Expense as of June 30, 19+8	15,000
Payment on January 15, 19+8, of dividends declared on December 15, 19+7	18,000
Refund of one-half of deposit with State Highway Commission, the balance being forfeited for defective work on a contract completed in 19+5	12,500
Cumulative change in depreciation from double-declining to to straight-line depreciation for the years 19+5 through 19+8 of $8,000 (of which $1,000 pertains to 19+8)	5,000
Correction of December 31, 19+4 inventory, charged to Retained Earnings and credited to Purchases as of June 30, 19+8	10,000

The board of directors met on December 15, 19+8 and declared a regular dividend of $20,000, payable on January 15, 19+9.

Show how the statement of retained earnings for 19+8 would appear.

Problem 4-10. The following income statement has been prepared by Rio Grande Company as a part of an application for a bank loan.

RIO GRANDE COMPANY
Income Statement
For the Year Ended October 31, 19+5

Revenue		
Net sales		$81,315
Other		9,848
		$91,163
Expenses		
Merchandise	$60,924	
Wages, salaries and employee benefits	8,840	
Depreciation	2,030	
Interest	2,218	
Federal income taxes	7,580	81,592
Net Income		$ 9,571
Earnings per common share		$ 9.57

As the auditor for Rio Grande you find that the other revenue account is composed of a $13,000 gain on the sale of equipment, dividend revenue of $1,555, interest revenue of $343, and a loss on the settlement of an income tax claim from 19+2 of $5,050. Rio Grande estimates that 40 percent of all depreciation and wages, salaries, and employee benefit expense are directly related to the company's sales effort. Assume that the income tax rate is 30 percent on the gain from the sale of equipment and 40 percent on all other items.

Required:

Prepare an income statement in multiple-step form.

Problem 4-11. A newly hired, inexperienced bookkeeper prepared the following income statement for Victory Corporation for the year ended December 31, 19+5.

VICTORY CORPORATION
Income Statement
December 31, 19+5

Sales	$285,822	
Purchase returns and allowances	460	
Purchase discounts	998	
Royalties from patents	3,600	
Interest earned	200	
Increase in inventories of finished goods, materials, and factory supplies	1,234	$292,314
Sundry manufacturing costs	$209,720	
Depreciation—Factory	6,900	
Freight in	1,415	
Sales returns	2,112	
Sales discounts	3,113	
Selling expenses	19,876	
Administrative expenses	14,364	257,500
Net income before income tax		$ 34,814
Income tax		11,500
Net income		$ 23,314
Earnings per share		$ 2.33

The management of the corporation gives you the following additional information and requests that you prepare an income statement in good form.

Inventories—December 31, 19+5	
Finished goods	$ 9,788
Materials	8,440
Factory supplies	2,170
Materials used during 19+5, including freight but after deducting purchase discounts and returns and allowances	73,580
Factory supplies used during 19+5	1,205
Direct labor	57,675
Indirect labor	9,135
Other manufacturing overhead not specifically set forth above	69,845
Purchases during 19+5	
Materials	71,140
Factory supplies	1,925

There was no work in process either at the beginning or at the end of 19+5.

Problem 4-12. Cimmerian Company has decided to change from the FIFO to LIFO inventory costing method for the current year. The net income for the current year (19+4) before extraordinary items and accounting changes is $80,000 using the LIFO method. Below are the net income and inventory figures for the life of the firm.

	19+3	19+2	19+1
Net income reported using FIFO...	$ 30,000	$ 60,000	$ 90,000
Year end inventories on a FIFO basis..............................	130,000	200,000	170,000
Year end inventories on a LIFO basis..............................	110,000	130,000	135,000
Common shares outstanding	10,000	10,000	10,000

Required:

(a) Calculate the net income for the year 19+4.

(b) Prepare comparative net income and earnings per share figures on a pro-forma basis for the firm's last four years.

Problem 4-13. The trial balance given below was taken from the ledger of Scythian and Sarmatian Corporation before adjusting entries were posted at the end of operations for 19+8.

SCYTHIAN AND SARMATIAN CORPORATION
Unadjusted Trial Balance
December 31, 19+8

Cash..	$ 9,730
Accounts Receivable	19,500
Allowance for uncollectibles	700
Notes receivable	5,000
Inventory—December 31, 19+7	30,000
Prepaid insurance..	375
Prepaid interest	120
Delivery equipment...	4,000
Accumulated depreciation—Delivery equipment................	1,600
Bank loans	8,000
Accounts payable...	10,300
Delivery fees received in advance	300
Loss on hurricane damage (net of tax of $667)...................	1,000
Common stock ($10 par)	25,000
Retained earnings—December 31, 19+7	6,470
Dividends	5,000
Sales..	207,000
Sales returns and allowances	980
Sales discounts..	1,670
Purchases	150,000
Purchase returns and allowances....................................	1,300
Purchase discounts	1,210
Salesmen's salary expense	12,650
Warehouse rent expense...	3,000
Advertising expense	10,200
Delivery salary expense..	3,275
Miscellaneous salary expenses	860
Office salary expense..	3,260
Office rent expense..	930

Miscellaneous advertising expense	190
Interest revenue	60
Interest expense	200

The following after-closing trial balance was taken from the same ledger after adjusting and closing entries had been posted.

Cash	$ 9,730
Accounts receivable	19,500
Allowance for uncollectibles	1,300
Notes receivable	5,000
Prepaid insurance	215
Prepaid interest	40
Delivery equipment	4,000
Accumulated depreciation—Delivery equipment	2,400
Bank loans	8,000
Accounts payable	10,300
Delivery fees received in advance	100
Common stock	25,000
Retained earnings	14,042
Inventory	28,650
Salaries payable	630
Interest receivable	25
Federal income tax payable	5,388

Required:

Prepare an income statement for Scythian and Sarmatian Corporation in good single-step form.

Problem 4-14. Khazar Furs net income for the past three years are presented below.

	19+4	19+3	19+2
Net income	$36,790	$41,240	$26,465

The amounts above are before the following error corrections, adjustments, and changes are implemented. Khazar has been assured by the Internal Revenue that the following will have no income tax effect.

(1) Khazar bought a truck January 1, 19+1 for $4,000 with no estimated salvage value and a four year life. The truck was expensed in 19+1. The truck is expected to be scrapped next year.

(2) Khazar lost a court case in 19+4 resulting from the sale of its mink farm in 19+1. Because of this suit, Khazar will have to pay $6,000 by July 30, 19+5.

(3) Khazar has decided to change from the straight-line method of depreciating its cement plant to the double-declining method. This is done for better comparability with other firms in the industry. The following information is taken from Khazar's books.

	19+4	19+3	19+2
Cement plant book value	$98,940	$104,730	$110,520
Salvage	510	510	510
Accumulated depreciation	17,370	11,580	5,790

Original estimate of the life of the plant was 20 years.
Depreciation expense is included in cost of goods sold. There are no inventories.

(4) Khazar, in reviewing its provision for uncollectibles, has decided that changing circumstances require a doubling of its percentage used in calculating bad debts expense for the current and succeeding years. The following information has been taken from the books of Khazar.

	19+4	19+3	19+2
Bad debts expense (before adjustment)	$8,625	$8,295	$13,650

Bad debts expense is included in general and administration expense.

Required:

Prepare the entries required to record each item above.

Problem 4-15. You are given below the income statements for Khazar Furs. Refer to Problem 4-14 and prepare pro forma comparative income statements incorporating the information given in the problem. Khazar has 10,000 common shares outstanding for all three years.

KHAZAR FURS COMPANY
Income Statement
For the Years Ended December 31, 19+4, 19+3, and 19+2

	19+4	19+3	19+2
Net sales	$969,065	$834,880	$911,005
Cost of goods sold	667,940	553,845	612,455
Gross margin	$301,125	$281,035	$298,550
Operating expenses:			
Selling expense	$160,825	$143,060	$179,765
General and administration expense	70,710	53,215	65,680
Total operating expenses	$231,535	$196,275	$245,445
Net operating income	$ 69,590	$ 84,760	$ 53,105
Nonoperating items:			
Deduct: Interest expense	4,400	10,320	9,440
Income before taxes	$ 65,190	$ 74,440	$ 43,665
Federal income taxes	28,400	33,200	17,200
Net income	$ 36,790	$ 41,240	$ 26,465

CHAPTER 5

QUESTIONS

1. Assets are future service potentials. What is meant by future service potential?
2. What are assets, equities, liabilities, and owners' equity?
3. What is the distinction between liabilities and owners' equity?
4. Are assets reported in the balance sheet at original cost?
5. How do accounting assumptions underlie the preparation of the balance sheet?
6. Answer the following questions with regard to the normal operating cycle.

(**a**) What is the normal operating cycle?
(**b**) How is the concept of a normal operating cycle used to differentiate between current and noncurrent items?
(**c**) If a firm had a normal accounts receivable turnover of four and a normal inventory turnover of six, approximately how many months would the normal operating cycle be?

7. Answer the following questions with regard to contingencies.
(**a**) What is a contingent asset?
(**b**) What is a contingent liability?
(**c**) How are contingent assets and liabilities reported in the balance sheet?

8. What are some theoretical problems in distinguishing between current and noncurrent items?

9. Answer the following questions with regard to monetary and nonmonetary items.
(**a**) What are monetary assets and monetary liabilities?
(**b**) During periods of deflation, other things being equal, what is the financial effect of a firm holding monetary assets and monetary liabilities?
(**c**) Are the cash surrender value of life insurance, prepaid insurance, and estimated liability for product warranties monetary items?

10. Why do accountants use contra and adjunct accounts in balance sheet reporting?

11. What is wrong with using the following terms in the balance sheet, and what terms would you recommend be used in their place?
(**a**) Reserve
(**b**) Surplus
(**c**) Net worth

12. What are deferred charges and deferred credits in current accounting practice? Is a deferred charge and a deferred credit literally an asset and a liability, respectively?

13. When would the circumstances be such that the following items would *not* be classified as current assets?
(**a**) Cash
(**b**) Receivables
(**c**) Investments in marketable securities
(**d**) Inventory

14. Other than liabilities that extend beyond one year or the normal operating cycle, whichever is longer, what are some examples of liabilities that should *not* be classified as current liabilities?

15. Consider the following definition: Current assets consist of cash and other assets that presumably can be converted into cash within one year without interference with the regular operations. Is this an acceptable definition?

16. The price received for a business entity usually differs from the amount shown on the records for the owners' equity. Why does the sale price of a going concern normally differ from the book amount (value) even where GAAP have been followed in keeping the business records?

17. In the preparation of a balance sheet of a dealer in office furniture, to be used for credit purposes, you ascertain that for the past twenty years his stock in trade has had an average turnover of once every three years. Would you include the said stock in trade among the current assets? Would it make any difference in your method of handling the inventory if you were told that the balance sheet was not to be used for credit purposes?

18. Although the balance sheet presents primarily historical information, what are some examples of items reported in the balance sheet that are not strictly historical in nature?

19. Where would the following be reported in the balance sheet?

(**a**) Bonds issued with restrictive covenants after the formal balance sheet date, but before the balance sheet is issued
(**b**) Merchandise held on consignment
(**c**) A donated truck
(**d**) Pension fund on deposit with a trustee
(**e**) Subscriptions receivable that are unlikely to be collectible
(**f**) Contract for plant construction
(**g**) Equipment retired from use and held for sale
(**h**) Bank overdraft
(**i**) Contract for goods ordered for future delivery

20. With the current emphasis in accounting on the income statement, the balance sheet has become a residual statement that is nothing more than a step between two income statements. With regard to this statement, answer the following questions.

(**a**) Why has the income statement grown in importance and the balance sheet declined in importance in current accounting practice?
(**b**) What is meant by the statement that the balance sheet has become relegated to a statement of residuals?
(**c**) How can it be argued that if exit-price valuation were used the balance sheet would be restored to prominence?

PROBLEMS

Problem 5-1. You are given below eight multiple choice questions. Select the correct answer to each question and indicate the corresponding letter on a separate sheet of paper (e.g., 1-a, 2-c, etc.).

(1) Which of the following is not a current asset? (a) inventory, (b) unexpired insurance, (c) interest receivable, (d) cash surrender value of life insurance, (e) none of the above.

(2) A restriction of retained earnings is most likely to be required by the (a) exhaustion of potential benefits of the investment credit, (b) purchase of treasury stock, (c) payment of last maturing series of a serial bond issue, (d) amortization of past service costs related to a pension plan, (e) none of the above.

(3) An item which is not a contingent liability is (a) notes receivable discounted, (b) accommodation endorsements on customer notes, (c) additional compensation that may be payable on a dispute now being arbitrated, (d) estimated claims under a service warranty on new products sold, (e) none of the above.

(4) Companies that carry no insurance against insurable casualty losses sometimes use an amount called "reserve for self-insurance." In preparing a balance sheet this amount preferably would appear as a (a) liability, (b) part of retained earnings, (c) deduction from the cash surrender value of insurance account, (d) deferred credit, (e) none of the above.

(5) Of the following items, the one which should be classified as a current asset is (a) trade installment receivables normally collectible in 18 months, (b) cash designated for the redemption of callable preferred stock, (c) cash surrender value of a life insurance policy of which the company is beneficiary, (d) a deposit on machinery ordered, delivery of which will be made within six months, (e) none of the above.

(6) Stock warrants outstanding should be classified as (a) liabilities, (b) reductions of capital contributed in excess of par value, (c) capital stock, (d) additions to contributed capital, assuming that the value of the warrants can be properly allocated, (e) none of the above.

(7) If a company converted a short-term note payable into a long-term note payable, this transaction would (a) decrease only working capital, (b) decrease only working capital and the current ratio, (c) increase only working capital, (d) increase both working capital and the current ratio, (e) none of the above.

(8) Of the following items, the one which should be classified as a current liability is (a) an accommodation endorsement on a demand note issued by an affiliated company, (b) a cash dividend declared before the balance-sheet date when the date of record is subsequent to the balance-sheet date, (c) unfunded past service costs of a pension plan to the extent that benefits have not vested and the costs have not been charged to operations, (d) dividends in arrears on cumulative preferred stock, (e) none of the above.

Problem 5-2. You are given below multiple choice questions. Select the correct answer to each question and indicate the corresponding letter on a separate sheet of paper (1-e, 2-a, etc.).

(1) The basis for classifying assets as current or noncurrent is the period of time normally elapsed from the time the accounting entity expends cash to the time it converts (a) inventory back into cash, or 12 months, whichever is shorter; (b) receivables back into cash, or 12 months, whichever is longer; (c) tangible fixed assets back into cash, or 12 months, whichever is longer; (d) inventory back into cash, or 12 months, whichever is longer; (e) none of the above.

(2) When a portion of inventories has been pledged as security on a loan (a) the value of the portion pledged should be subtracted from the debt, (b) an equal amount of retained earnings should be appropriated, (c) the fact should be disclosed but the amount of current assets should not be affected, (d) the cost of the pledged inventories should be transferred from current assets to noncurrent assets, (e) none of the above.

(3) The test of marketability must be met before securities owned can be properly classified as (a) debentures, (b) treasury stock, (c) long-term investments, (d) current assets, (e) none of the above.

(4) An example of an item which is not a liability is (a) dividends payable, (b) advances from customers on contracts, (c) accrued estimated warranty costs, (d) the portion of long-term debt due within one year, (e) none of the above.

(5) Which of the following items is a current liability? (a) bonds (for which there is an adequate sinking fund classified as a long-term investment) due in three months, (b) bonds due in three years, (c) bonds (for which there is an adequate equity reserve) due in eleven months, (d) bonds to be refunded when due in eight months, there being no doubt about the marketability of the refunding issue, (e) none of the above.

(6) The receipt of "revenue in advance" creates (a) a deferred credit, (b) an increase in retained earnings, (c) an asset, (d) a liability, (e) none of the above.

(7) A contingent liability is normally shown as (a) a deferred charge, (b) a current liability, (c) a long-term liability, (d) a footnote on the balance sheet, (e) none of the above.

Problem 5-3. You are given below multiple choice questions. Select the correct answer to each question and indicate the corresponding letter on a separate sheet of paper (1-d, 2-e, etc.).

(1) Marketable securities held to finance future construction of additional plants should be classified on a balance sheet as (a) current assets, (b) property, plant, and equipment, (c) intangible assets, (d) investments and funds, (e) none of the above.

(2) A contingent liability (a) has a most probable value of zero but may require a payment if a given future event occurs, (b) definitely exists as a liability but its amount and/or due date is indeterminate, (c) is commonly associated with operating loss carry-forwards, (d) is not disclosed in the financial statements, (e) none of the above.

(3) Which of the following is an example of a deferred credit? (a) bond discount, (b) minority interest, (c) deferred investment credits, (d) revenue received in advance, (e) none of the above.

(4) On April 15, 19+4 the Rest-More Corporation accepted delivery of merchandise which it purchased on account. As of April 30 the Corporation had not recorded the transaction or included the merchandise in its inventory. The effect of this on its balance sheet for April 30, 19+4 would be (a) assets and owners' equity were overstated but liabilities were not affected, (b) owners' equity was the only item affected by the omission, (c) assets and liabilities were understated but owners' equity was not affected, (d) assets and owners' equity were understated but liabilities were not affected, (e) none of the above.

(5) An example of an item which is not an element of working capital is (a) accrued interest on notes receivable, (b) treasury stock, (c) goods in process, (d) temporary investments, (e) none of the above.

(6) Plant assets may properly include (a) deposits on machinery not yet received, (b) idle equipment awaiting sale, (c) property held for investment purposes, (d) land held for possible use as a future plant site, (e) none of the above.

Problem 5-4. The owner of Verdugo Centers, Inc. has compiled the following comparative data.

	December 31	
Assets	19+9	19+8
Cash in bank	$ 4,000	$ 6,000
Accounts receivable	30,000	20,000
Allowance for uncollectibles	(1,500)	(1,000)
Inventory—FIFO	60,000	45,000
Investment securities	10,000	4,000
Delivery equipment	25,000	20,000
Accumulated depreciation	(6,000)	(5,000)
Liabilities		
Accounts payable	$32,500	$15,000
Mortgage payable		10,000

Upon inquiry you learn the following:

(1) The mortgage is on the owner's residence. It was paid by a check drawn on the store's account for \$10,100, which included the interest due for 19+9. Interest expense for 19+8 was \$400.

(2) The investment securities were paid for by the owner's wife with her personal funds.

(3) The capital stock account for 19+8 and 19+9 had a balance of \$30,000, and the retained earnings balance at the end of 19+8 was \$34,000.

(4) The increase in delivery equipment was accounted for by the acquisition on December 31, 19+9 of an additional delivery truck costing \$5,000. Only \$3,000 of the store's funds were spent for this purpose, since a \$2,000 trade-in allowance was granted on a convertible previously used by the owner's son while in college. The car had a fair market value of \$1,500, which was paid to the son from the firm's bank account.

Required:

Prepare comparative balance sheets in good form for the years 19+9 and 19+8.

Problem 5-5. The balance sheet below has been incorrectly prepared. Prepare a balance sheet in good form for the Bearded One Company.

BEARDED ONE COMPANY
Balance Sheet
February 29, 19+5

Cash	\$ 62,212.31
Petty Cash	2,000.00
Accounts receivable	169,213.00
Inventories—at lower of cost or market	313,955.30
Current installment of bonds payable	10,000.00
Fixed assets:	
Land at cost	69,998.63
Factory building	155,666.15
Less reserve for depreciation	(59,865.90)
Machinery	490,900.00
Less reserve for depreciation	(113,215.13)
Total assets	\$1,100,864.36
Accounts payable	45,003.41
Notes payable	150,000.00
Federal income tax payable	56,859.35
Bonds payable	140,000.00
Capital stock	500,000.00
Reserve for doubtful accounts	17,422.17
Earned surplus	191,579.43
Total liabilities	\$1,100,864.36

Problem 5-6. The trial balance below was taken from the books of Hittite Company after adjusting and closing entries had been posted.

Trial Balance
December 31, 19+5

Cash	9,730
Accounts receivable	13,525
Allowance for uncollectible accounts	1,300

Notes receivable	4,000
Prepaid insurance	255
Marketable securities—at cost (market $18,000)	3,000
Truck	4,000
Accumulated depreciation—truck	2,400
Patents	4,000
Accounts payable	7,300
Revenue received in advance	600
Common stock (no-par, authorized, issued, and outstanding 500 shares)	25,000
Retained earnings	16,042
Inventory	28,650
Salaries payable	630
Bonds payable (11% bonds, due December 31, 19+9)	8,000
Bond premium	500
Deferred federal income tax credit	5,388

Required:

Prepare a balance sheet in good form, including monetary and nonmonetary classifications.

Problem 5-7. As of December 15, 19+6, the stockholders of Goth Company approved an agreement with Vandal, Incorporated, for the purchase of a patent. The purchase price was $500,000. The payment consists of 3,000 shares of authorized, but unissued, common stock of the company and $200,000 in cash, which the company expects to obtain from a seven-year loan from an insurance company. The settlement date is January 15, 19+7. Either company may withdraw from the agreement before that date.

On January 15, 19+7 before the auditors had completed the audit of Goth's books, a $30,000,000, 6 percent bond issue due in twenty years was sold to yield 6 percent.

There is a pending court case that Goth is a defendant in involving the disposal of a subsidiary of Goth in 19+2. Goth's potential liability is $1,000,000. The lawyers retained by Goth to defend this case believe Goth has adequate defenses.

Required:

Prepare the disclosures you believe would be needed in connection with Goth's 19+6 financial statements.

Problem 5-8. Prepare a balance sheet in good form from the trial balance of York Company given in Problem 4-6.

Problem 5-9. The following are the statements of Blue Velvet Company.

BLUE VELVET COMPANY
Balance Sheet
January 1, 19+8

Assets

Current assets	$ 35,000
Buildings and equipment	48,000
Accumulated depreciation—buildings and equipment	(15,000)
Patents	5,000
	$ 73,000

Equities

Current liabilities	$ 9,000
Capital stock	27,000
Retained earnings	37,000
	$ 73,000

BLUE VELVET COMPANY
Statement of Changes in Financial Position
For the year ended December 31, 19+8

Sources of financial resources:			
Working Capital provided from operations:			
Income before extraordinary items		$20,000	
Add (deduct) items not requiring (generating) an outlay of working capital:			
Depreciation expense	$10,000		
Amortization of patents	1,000	11,000	
Working capital provided from operations for period, exclusive of extraordinary items		31,000	
Working capital provided from other sources:			
Proceeds from issue of first mortgage bonds	$ 5,000		
Proceeds from issue of capital stock	5,000		
Proceeds from sale of plant	7,000		
Total working capital provided from other sources for period		17,000	
Financial resources provided, not affecting working capital:			
Common stock issued to acquire land		3,000	
Total financial resources provided for period			$51,000
Uses of financial resources:			
Working capital applied:			
Outlay for dividends on capital stock	$12,000		
Outlay to acquire land	11,000		
Outlay to acquire buildings & equipment	30,000		
Total working capital applied for period		$53,000	
Financial resources applied, not affecting working capital:			
Land acquired by issuing common stock		3,000	
Total financial resources used for period			$56,000
Decrease in working capital for period			($ 5,000)

Accumulated depreciation on the plant sold was $6,000. The gain on the sale of plant was $4,000. Current liabilities on December 31, 19+8 were $9,000.

Required:

Prepare the balance sheet for Blue Velvet Company as of December 31, 19+8.

Problem 5-10. Ball Bearing Company has borrowed $30,000,000 from the Draft Insurance Company. The agreement with the insurance company includes the stipulation that Ball Bearing maintain a current ratio of 3 to 1 at the end of each fiscal period or the loan will become immediately due. The company's CPA firm of Cain, Paul, and Able, has furnished the audited statement for the past fiscal year. Ball Bearing Company has questioned the statement as it shows a current ratio less than 3 to 1.

Ball Bearing Company has asked you to explain why the following were not included in current assets or were included in current liabilities. Give your reasons for agreeing or disagreeing with Ball Bearing.

(1) A prepayment of $1,000 of an insurance contract that covers the next two years was excluded.

(2) Cain, Paul, and Able excluded $10,000 of receivables and $20,000 of inventory as they would have been turned over within a year, but after the current operating cycle.

(3) A $100,000 loan was included in current liabilities. Ball Bearing has a commitment from a bank to refinance this loan for an additional three years.

(4) Since the current portion of long-term debt is a current liability, the current portion of plant (i.e., next year's depreciation of $10,000,000) should be shown as a current asset. This was done.

(5) Short-term marketable securities of $1,000,000 were excluded and management does not believe they will be needed for current operations. They are available for conversion into cash.

Problem 5-11. The following unadjusted trial balance was taken from the books of Harry the Hun Company on December 31, 19+7.

HARRY THE HUN COMPANY
Unadjusted Trial Balance
December 31, 19+7

	Debits	Credits
Cash	11,460	
Accounts receivable	13,755	
Allowance for uncollectibles		1,140
Notes receivable	11,000	
Interest receivable	165	
Inventory—December 31, 19+6	41,650	
Store fixtures	40,750	
Accumulated depreciation—store fixtures		8,150
Accounts payable		16,120
Bank loans		5,000
Capital stock (no-par, 100,000 shares, issued, authorized, and outstanding)		44,180
Retained earnings		40,100
Dividends	5,400	
Sales		196,550

	Debits	Credits
Sales returns & allowances	1,940	
Sales discounts	585	
Purchases	145,830	
Purchase returns & allowances		2,020
Advertising	6,500	
Salesmen's salaries	22,800	
Miscellaneous selling expenses	1,315	
Rent expense	6,000	
Taxes	360	
Office salaries	3,000	
Office expense	890	
Interest expense	210	
Interest revenue		350
	313,610	313,610

After adjusting entries were made, the following entries were made to close the books.

	Debits	Credits
Sales	196,550	
Purchase returns and allowances	2,020	
Interest revenue	335	
Inventory, December 31, 19+7	46,110	
Sales returns and allowances		1,940
Sales discounts		585
Inventory, December 31, 19+6		41,650
Purchases		145,830
Advertising		5,700
Salesmen's salaries		22,800
Miscellaneous selling expenses		1,315
Rent expense		6,000
Taxes		360
Office salaries		3,000
Office expense		765
Interest expense		185
Bad debts		360
Depreciation		4,075
Retained earnings		10,450
Retained earnings	5,400	
Dividends		5,400

Required:

Prepare in good form the balance sheet of Harry the Hun Company as of December 31, 19+7.

Problem 5-12. The trial balance presented below was taken from the books as of December 31, 19+5, after the recording of adjusting and closing entries.

SCHLIEMAN CORPORATION
Trial Balance (After Closing)
December 31, 19+5

Cash in bank	21,316
Office cash funds	1,000
Marketable securities	21,000

	Debits	Credits
Advances and deposits	16,000	
Trade accounts receivable	133,400	
Allowance for uncollectibles		14,500
Notes receivable	15,000	
Interest receivable	240	
Receivable from officers and employees	4,189	
Inventories:		
Finished product	96,210	
Product in process	48,012	
Materials	68,311	
Manufacturing supplies	14,016	
Office supplies	4,220	
Sinking fund for bond retirements	25,000	
Land	20,000	
Building	121,900	
Accumulated depreciation—Building		28,320
Machinery	211,418	
Accumulated depreciation—Machinery		129,040
Office furniture and fixtures	41,315	
Accumulated depreciation—Office furniture and fixtures		18,490
Patents	43,015	
Prepayments and deferrals	26,248	
Accounts payable		39,316
Notes payable		40,000
Interest payable		2,860
Withholding and F.I.C.A. taxes payable		2,115
Income tax payable		38,400
Advances from customers		6,000
4% bonds payable		100,000
Capital stock		300,000
Retained earnings		162,769
Appropriations for plant expansion		50,000
	931,810	931,810

The average period of time elapsing from the purchase of raw materials until the accounts arising from the sale of product manufactured from such materials are collected is approximately eight months.

The corporation owns the following marketable securities on December 31, 19+5:

United States Treasury Notes acquired for investment of seasonally idle cash	$ 8,000
Capital stock of Sales Company, owned as a participant in a co-operative marketing program	13,000

The corporation has advanced $15,000 to A-Z Machine Company to cover the cost of design drawings on machinery for a new product.

The corporation has a $1,000 deposit with the state Workman's Compensation Fund. (This deposit must be maintained as long as the corporation remains in business.)

Of the notes receivable, $6,000 represents three notes of equal face value arising from the sale of excess production equipment. These notes mature on June 30th of each of the succeeding three years.

The amount shown as being receivable from officers and employees includes \$2,189 receivable from employees for merchandise sold on regular credit terms. The balance represents an advance (without interest) to the president, without definite maturity. You are informed that no expectation of current collection exists.

The corporation's inventory of finished product includes \$5,000 representing the undepreciated cost of manufacturing machinery no longer needed by the company and being offered for sale.

The corporation has received a cash offer of \$15,000 for one of its patents with a book value of \$9,000. The management has indicated it will probably accept the offer.

The prepayments and deferrals account includes:

Cash surrender value of life insurance	\$12,018
Unexpired insurance premiums	12,040
Unamortized bond discount	2,190
	\$26,248

Included in the Notes Payable account are:

Bank loan—due June 30, 19+6	\$30,000
Loan from the insurance company with which insurance on the lives of corporation executives is carried	10,000
(There is no intention to repay this loan in the near future)	

The amount received from a customer for product to be delivered in April, 19+6, is shown in the Advances from Customers account.

The bond issue will be retired from sinking fund assets in ten annual installments beginning September 1, 19+6.

Required:

Prepare a balance sheet for Schlieman Corporation from the above data.

Problem 5-13.

EVANS COMPANY
Balance Sheet
December 31, 19+7

Assets

Current assets:		
Cash	\$ 49,400	
Accounts receivable	120,300	
Inventories	218,600	\$388,300
Property, plant, and equipment		491,100
Deferred charges		42,500
		\$921,900

Liabilities and Stockholders' Equity

Current liabilities:		
Accounts payable	\$ 78,800	
Note and interest payable thereon	50,500	
Income taxes payable	35,000	\$164,300
Reserves		196,200
Stockholders' equity:		
Capital stock	\$500,000	
Retained earnings	61,400	561,400
		\$921,900

Recast the balance sheet, using a form that shows the monetary and nonmonetary distinction in light of the information presented below:

(1) Accounts receivable include $50,000 advanced to Automation Corporation on a contract with that company to construct special manufacturing equipment for Evans Company.

(2) The details of the items included in inventories are as follows (stated at cost):

Finished goods	$ 74,800
Goods in process	21,200
Materials	96,200
Machinery under construction by company for its use	26,400
	$218,600

Finished goods costing $50,000 are held in a bonded warehouse as security for the note payable to the bank.

(3) Included in property, plant, and equipment are the following:

Land	$ 50,000
Building	110,200
Machinery	290,400
Office fixtures	40,500
	$491,100

(4) Deferred charges include:

Cash surrender value of life insurance	$ 18,000
Unamortized cost of patents	20,000
Prepaid insurance	2,200
Other current expense prepayments	2,300
	$ 42,500

(5) Accounts payable include advances by customers on unfilled current orders in the amount of $12,400.

(6) The note payable is a six-month note payable to Third National Bank and is due on March 1, 19+8 in the amount of $50,000; interest thereon is payable at maturity at 6%.

(7) Included in reserves are:

Accumulated depreciation:		
Building	$ 51,700	
Machinery	108,300	
Office fixtures	31,200	$191,200
Allowance for uncollectibles		5,000
		$196,200

(8) The company has 75,000 shares of authorized common stock with a par value of $10, of which 50,000 shares were issued at par.

Problem 5-14. The December 31, 19+5 adjusted trial balance of Static Company is presented below.

STATIC COMPANY
Adjusted Trial Balance
December 31, 19+5

Cash	83,100	
Accounts receivable	36,400	
Allowance for uncollectibles		1,945
Inventory—December 31, 19+4	19,800	
Prepaid rent	400	
Long-term investments	52,000	
Delivery equipment (at cost)	20,000	
Accumulated depreciation—Delivery equipment		8,000
Accounts payable		14,620
Notes payable		4,050
Salaries payable		1,000
Withholding and F.I.C.A. tax liabilities		5,687
Federal unemployment tax liability		38
State unemployment tax liability		85
Capital stock—Common		150,000
Retained earnings		16,630
Dividends	11,000	
Sales		119,140
Sales returns and allowances	965	
Bad debts	675	
Freight out	1,330	
Purchases	68,980	
Purchase returns and allowances		660
Advertising	1,400	
Salesmen's salaries	12,935	
Depreciation—Delivery equipment	4,000	
Miscellaneous selling expense	800	
Office salaries	5,750	
Payroll taxes expense—General	175	
Office expense	610	
Rent	1,000	
Miscellaneous general expense	340	
Interest revenue		290
Purchase discounts		770
Interest expense	110	
Sales discounts	1,145	
	322,915	322,915

Supplementary data:

(1) Since the company's organization, the inventories have consistently been valued at cost. In January, 19+5, it was decided to convert the inventory valuations to a basis of cost or current market, whichever is lower. In the past years the current price of the inventories was greater than cost. The first inventory to be valued in this manner was the one taken on December 31, 19+5, which amounted to $25,700. If this inventory had been valued at cost, it would have amounted to $28,350.

(2) Cash in the amount of $5,000 has been placed in escrow as a guaranty on a contract. The contract will be completed in 19+8.

(3) The outstanding accounts receivable include $4,000 from directors.
(4) The company is presently involved in litigation arising from a negligence claim of $10,000 for injuries which a customer received from use of an article sold by the Static Company.
(5) The stock is common and has a par value of $200; 750 of the 1,000 shares authorized are outstanding.
(6) On December 31, 19+5, the company had purchase commitments outstanding in the amount of $14,000.
(7) On the balance sheet date, the market value of the long-term investments was $48,000.
(8) Federal income tax for 19+5 is estimated at $10,000.

Required:

(a) Prepare an income statement for the year ended December 31, 19+5.
(b) Prepare a balance sheet as of December 31, 19+5.

Problem 5-15. Argo Sales Corporation has in recent prior years maintained the following relationships among the data on its financial statements:

(1) Gross margin rate on net sales	40%
(2) Net income rate on net sales	10%
(3) Rate of selling expenses to net sales	20%
(4) Accounts receivable turnover (sales ÷ ending accounts receivable)	8 per year
(5) Inventory turnover (cost of goods sold ÷ ending inventory)	6 per year
(6) Acid-test ratio	2 to 1
(7) Current ratio	3 to 1
(8) Quick-asset composition: 8% cash, 32% marketable securities, 60% accounts receivable	
(9) Asset turnover (sales ÷ year end total assets)	2 per year
(10) Ratio of total assets to intangible assets	20 to 1
(11) Ratio of accumulated depreciation to cost of fixed assets	1 to 3
(12) Ratio of accounts receivable to accounts payable	1.5 to 1
(13) Ratio of working capital to stockholders' equity	1 to 1.6
(14) Ratio of total debt to stockholders' equity	1 to 2

The Corporation had a net income of $120,000 for 19+8 which resulted in earnings of $5.20 per share of common stock. Additional information includes the following:

(1) Capital stock authorized, issued (all in 19+2), and outstanding: Common, $10 per share par value, issued at 10% premium; Preferred, 6% nonparticipating, $100 per share par value, issued at a 10% premium
(2) Market value per share of common at December 31, 19+8: $78
(3) Preferred dividends paid in 19+8: $3,000
(4) Times interest earned in 19+8: 33
(5) The amounts of the following were the same at December 31, 19+8 as at January 1, 19+8: inventory, accounts receivable, 5% bonds payable—due 19+10 and total stockholders' equity
(6) All purchases and sales were "on account."

Required:

a. Prepare in good form the condensed balance sheet for December 31, 19+8 presenting the amounts you would expect to appear on Argo's financial statements (ignoring income taxes). Major captions appearing on Argo's balance sheet are: Current Assets; Property, Plant, and Equipment; Intangible Assets; Current Liabilities; Long-term Liabilities; and Stockholders' Equity. In addition to the accounts divulged in the problem, you should include accounts for Prepayments, Accrued Expenses, and Administrative Expenses.

CHAPTER 6

QUESTIONS

1. Is value synonymous with valuation?

2. Answer the following questions with regard to exchange prices.

(**a**) Why do accountants use exchange prices in the valuation process?
(**b**) What is meant by the statement that exchange prices differ by the market in which they are found and by temporal location?

3. What is the meaning of each of the following types of income?

(**a**) Subjective or economic income
(**b**) Realizable income
(**c**) Business income
(**d**) Realized income

4. With regard to discounted cash-flow valuation, answer the following questions.

(**a**) What is discounted cash-flow valuation?
(**b**) What are the advantages of discounted cash-flow valuation?
(**c**) What are the disadvantages of discounted cash-flow valuation?
(**d**) Is discounted cash-flow valuation used in current accounting practice?

5. With regard to selling-price valuation, answer the following questions.

(**a**) What is selling-price valuation?
(**b**) What are the advantages of selling-price valuation?
(**c**) What are the disadvantages of selling-price valuation?
(**d**) Is selling-price valuation used in current accounting practice?

6. With regard to replacement-cost valuation, answer the following questions.

(**a**) What is replacement-cost valuation?
(**b**) What are the advantages of replacement-cost valuation?
(**c**) What are the disadvantages of replacement-cost valuation?
(**d**) Is replacement-cost valuation used in current accounting practice?

7. With regard to historical-cost valuation, answer the following questions.

(**a**) Does historical-cost valuation mean recording and reporting assets at original cost only? If not, what does it mean?
(**b**) What are the advantages of historical-cost valuation?
(**c**) What are the disadvantages of historical-cost valuation?
(**d**) Is the valuation of monetary assets and liabilities in current accounting practice consistent with historical-cost valuation?

(e) What are some exceptions to historical-cost valuation in current accounting practice?

8. If replacement-cost valuation were used in accounting, then this would necessitate modifying the revenue-recognition assumption. What does this statement mean?
9. Under historical-cost valuation, what is meant by the statement that by recognizing gains and most losses only when realized by sale or use, realized holding gains and losses are not reported in the proper time period and are not always separated?
10. Although selling-price valuation avoids allocation problems, there are aggregation problems. What does this statement mean?
11. Is replacement cost the cost to replace the asset in its present form, or the cost of replacing the capacity to produce?
12. The recording and reporting of short-term marketable securities would seem to be a prime example for the use of selling-price valuation; however, the accounting profession continues to reject such valuation for short-term marketable securities. Why do short-term marketable securities appear to be suitable for selling-price valuation? Why do you think the accounting profession rejects selling-price valuation for short-term marketable securities?
13. Although it is sometimes argued that current accounting practice fails to recognize unrealized holding gains and losses, in fact unrealized holding losses are recognized in current accounting practice. Do you agree with this statement?
14. Under replacement-cost valuation, what is meant by the statement that holding gains and losses on depreciable assets are affected by the depreciation method used?
15. Although selling-price valuation avoids allocation problems in general, if a traditional type income statement is to be presented, then there are allocation problems even under selling-price valuation. What does this statement mean?
16. Under replacement-cost valuation, holding gains and losses could be recognized in the income statement in such a manner that the resulting net income would be the same as that under historical-cost valuation. Do you agree with this statement?
17. Why not base the valuation of a firm's assets and liabilities on the firm's utility function?
18. Answer the following questions with regard to replacement-cost valuation of inventory.
    (a) Replacement-cost valuation would result in eliminating the differences that currently exist between FIFO and LIFO inventory valuation methods. Do you agree with this statement?
    (b) Replacement-cost valuation of inventory meets the objectives of *both* FIFO and LIFO inventory valuation. What does this statement mean?
19. Although periodic net income could differ depending on which valuation method was used, the total income of the firm in the long run would be the same under historical-cost, replacement-cost, and selling-price valuation. Do you agree with this statement?
20. One of the problems in selling-price valuation is which current selling price should be used. Professor Chambers argues for quoted market selling prices of assets of a similar kind under conditions of orderly sale at the balance sheet date. Professor Sterling argues for current selling prices that would be actually obtainable if all the assets were sold at the balance sheet date under orderly conditions. What is the basic difference between these two approaches to selling-price valuation? Evaluate.

PROBLEMS

Problem 6-1. You are given below seven multiple choice questions. Select the correct answer to each question and indicate the corresponding letter on a separate sheet of paper (e.g., 1-a, 2-c, etc.).

(1) Proponents of historical costs maintain that in comparison with all other valuation alternatives for general purpose financial reporting, statements prepared using historical costs are more (a) objective, (b) relevant, (c) indicative of the entity's purchasing power, (d) conservative, (e) none of the above.

(2) One concept of income measurement suggests that income be measured by determining the net change over time in the present discounted value of net cash flow expected to be received by the firm. Under this concept of income, which of the following, ignoring income taxes, would not affect the amount of income for a particular period? (a) providing services to outsiders and investment of the funds received, (b) production of goods or services not yet sold or delivered to customers or clients, (c) windfall gains and losses due to external causes, (d) the method used to depreciate property, plant, and equipment, (e) none of the above.

(3) Assuming that the ideal measure of short-term receivables in the balance sheet is the discounted amount of the cash to be received in the future, failure to follow this practice usually does not make the balance sheet misleading because (a) most short-term receivables are not interest-bearing, (b) the allowance for uncollectible accounts includes a discount element, (c) the amount of the discount is not material, (d) most receivables can be sold to a bank or factor, (e) none of the above.

(4) Proponents of current selling prices maintain that in comparison with all other valuation alternatives for general purpose financial reporting, statements prepared using exit prices (a) are more objective, (b) better match current costs with current revenue, (c) better provide knowledge about the current financial condition of the firm, (d) are verifiable, (e) none of the above.

(5) Which of the following is advocated as an advantage of replacement-cost valuation: (a) defines the market alternatives available to the firm, (b) holding gains and losses are reported separately, (c) verifiable by accountants, (d) based on future cash flows, (e) none of the above.

(6) Which one of the following valuation methods is never used in current accounting practice: (a) current selling prices, (b) discounted cash flows, (c) replacement costs, (d) all of the above, (e) none of the above.

(7) Selling-price valuation results in an income statement that (a) is based on the matching assumption, (b) is the result of the valuation of a firm's net assets at two points in time, (c) normally excludes holding gains or losses to avoid allocation problems, (d) is equal to the discounted amount of owners' equity multiplied by the interest rate, (e) none of the above.

Problem 6-2. You are given below seven multiple choice questions. Select the correct answer to each question and indicate the corresponding letter on a separate sheet of paper (e.g., 1-a, 2-c, etc.).

(1) As discussed in the chapter, valuation in accounting is (a) synonymous with value, (b) the quantification of, and the changes in assets, liabilities, and owners equity, (c) the use of earnings power, (d) based on subjective utility, (e) none of the above.

(2) Current-value accounting (a) refers to the use of exit prices, (b) refers to general-price-level adjusted financial statements, (c) is ambiguous, (d) is synonymous with historical-cost valuation, (e) none of the above.

(3) The valuation method used in accounting affects income determination. Historical-cost valuation results in a net income figure that can be described as (a) realized income, (b) economic income, (c) realizable income, (d) business income, (e) none of the above.

(4) In current accounting practice, the valuation method used for bonds payable is (a) historical cost, (b) current market price to acquire, (c) discounted cash-flow valuation at current yield rates, (d) maturity amount, (e) discounted cash-flow valuation at yield rates at issuance, (f) none of the above.

(5) One of the following is *not* an advantage of replacement cost valuation: (a) holding gains and losses are reported, (b) allocations are not necessary, (c) nonmonetary assets are reported at current entry prices, (d) current costs (expenses) are matched with current revenue in the income statement, (e) none of the above.

(6) One of the following valuation methods uses only future exit prices: (a) discounted cash flow, (b) current selling price, (c) current replacement price, (d) historical cost, (e) none of the above.

(7) Which one of the following is *not* an advantage of the use of discounted cash-flow valuation: (a) based on direct valuation, (b) sanctioned for long-term monetary assets and liabilities per APB *Opinion No. 21,* (c) based on expectations of the future, (d) requires certainty of future cash flows, (e) none of the above.

Problem 6-3. You are given the following alternative valuation methods: (a) discounted cash-flow valuation based on yield to maturity, (b) lower-of-cost-or-market method, (c) net realizable value (estimated selling prices minus costs of disposal), (d) historical cost, (e) future selling prices, (f) future purchase prices (costs), (g) current selling prices, (h) none of the above. Match the letter(s) of the valuation method(s) used in actual accounting practice to the following.

(1) Accounts payable
(2) Short-term marketable securities
(3) Long-term construction contracts accounted for under the percentage-of-completion method
(4) Goodwill
(5) Inventory of gold
(6) Discovery value of oil found on land owned
(7) Merchandise inventory
(8) Donated asset
(9) Accounts receivable
(10) Long-term bonds payable
(11) Land
(12) Cash
(13) Liability for product warranties
(14) Obsolete machinery held for resale
(15) Financing-type lease for lessee

Problem 6-4. Presented below are comparative income statements for Eden Company using historical-cost valuation.

EDEN COMPANY
Comparative Income Statements
For the Year Ended December 31, 19+5 and 19+4
(Historical-Cost Valuation)

	19+5		19+4	
Revenue		$70,000		$50,000
Cost of goods sold	$20,000		$15,000	
Depreciation, machinery	10,000		10,000	
Depreciation, building	5,000	35,000	5,000	30,000
		$35,000		$20,000

The replacement cost of the goods sold during 19+4 and 19+5 was $18,000 and $22,000, respectively. At year end 19+4 and 19+5 the realizable holding gains on the inventory were $20,000 and $25,000, respectively. The depreciation under replacement-cost valuation on the machinery was $15,000 in 19+5 and $14,000 in 19+4. In 19+4, and 19+5 the realizable holding gains on the machinery were $40,000 and $50,000 at year end. The depreciation under replacement-cost valuation on the building was $6,000 in 19+5 and $5,000 in 19+4. At year end 19+4 and 19+5 the realizable holding gains on the building were zero and $10,000.

Required:

Complete the income statement presented below by filling in the required amounts.

EDEN COMPANY
Comparative Income Statement
For the Year Ended December 31, 19+5 and 19+4
(Replacement-Cost Valuation)

		19+5		19+4
Sales				
Cost of goods sold				
Gross margin				
Operating expenses				
Depreciation, machinery				
Depreciation, building				
Current operating profit				
		19+5		19+4
Current operating profit				
Realized holding gains				
On merchandise inventory				
On depreciation, machinery				
On depreciation, building				
Realized profit				

		19+5		19+4
Current operating profit		____		____
Realizable holding gains		____		____
On inventory	____		____	
On machinery	____		____	
On building	____	____	____	____
Business profit		____		____

Problem 6-5. The owner of Verma Enterprises wants you to prepare a discounted cash-flow balance sheet for her firm.

VERMA ENTERPRISES
Balance Sheet
December 31, 19+5
(Historical-Cost Valuation)

Current assets:		Current liabilities:	
Cash	$16,000	Accounts payable	$20,000
Accounts receivable	10,000	Salaries payable	16,000
Merchandise inventory, at cost	11,000	Stockholders' equity:	
Prepaid insurance	1,000	Capital stock, 2,500 shares issued and outstanding	10,000
Property, plant, and equipment	10,000	Retained earnings	2,000
	$48,000		$48,000

Verma wants an 8 percent rate of return on her investment. The amount receivable will be paid July 1, 19+6. Verma estimates that the inventory will be sold at $20,000 and all the receivables from sales will be collected on December 31, 19+6. There is no cash inflow associated with the prepaid insurance amount. Accounts payable of $10,000 will be paid on July 1, 19+6 and $10,000 on December 31, 19+6. The firm pays the previous month's salary on the first of the month. Verma has leased the property, plant, and equipment for its remaining life. The cash flows are estimated to be as follows:

Year	Inflow	Outflow
1	$20,000	$5,000
2	20,000	5,000
3	20,000	5,000
4	20,000	5,000
5	20,000	5,000
6	20,000	5,000

All cash flows occur at the end of the year.

Required:

(a) Prepare a balance sheet for Verma Enterprises as of December 31, 19+5 based on discounted cash-flow valuation.

(b) What would the net income for Verma be in the year 19+6?

Problem 6-6. Loral Company's major stockholder has become interested in the financial position of her firm. After reading an accounting textbook she has decided that a balance sheet and income statement based on current selling-price valuation would provide more useful financial information. She has asked you to prepare these statements from the following information:

LORAL COMPANY
Balance Sheet
December 31, 19+6 and 19+5
(Historical-Cost Valuation)

	19+6	19+5		19+6	19+5
Cash	$ 500	$ 1,000	Accounts payable.	$ 1,000	$ 1,000
Accounts receivable ...	10,000	7,000	Bank loans payable	11,500	11,500
Inventory (100 units) ..	5,000	4,000	Bonds payable	10,000	10,000
Prepaid insurance	100	150	Capital stock	10,000	10,000
Land	10,000	10,000	Retained earnings	11,100	8,650
Building and equipment	20,000	20,000			
Less accumulated depreciation	(2,000)	(1,000)			
	$43,600	$41,150		$43,600	$41,150

Assume that selling-price valuation is the same as historical-cost valuation for the cash, accounts payable, accounts receivable, and bank loans payable. The market price of the capital stock is $25,000 and $20,000 for 19+6 and 19+5, respectively. The firm's selling price for its inventory as of December 31, 19+6 and 19+5 is $60 and $50 per unit, respectively. The firm has calculated that it could sell its remaining assets or satisfy the remaining liabilities for the remaining amounts.

	19+6	19+5
Prepaid insurance	$ -0-	$ -0-
Land	11,000	9,000
Buildings and equipment	33,000	35,000
Bonds payable	9,000	10,000

Required:

Prepare a balance sheet for 19+6 and the income statement for the year ended December 31, 19+6 using current selling-price valuation. Use current selling prices for both assets and long-term liabilities.

Problem 6-7. Sommer Company made the following purchases during 19+3.

Date	Number of Units	Cost per Unit
January 1	1000	$1.00
February 29	520	1.10
April 26	630	1.20
September 8	720	1.25
December 23	100	1.25

Sommer Company sales were:

Date	Number of Units	Sales Cost
January 3	800	$2.00
September 9	1170	2.20
December 25	300	2.30

The following valuations have been made on a per unit basis as of December 31, 19+3.

	Valuation per Unit
Replacement cost	$1.30
Orderly sale in the normal course of business	2.50
Forced sale	1.80
Immediate liquidation	1.25

Sommer uses the LIFO periodic valuation method.

Required:

(a) What would the cost of goods sold figure and ending inventory amount be under replacement-cost valuation?

(b) What would the cost of goods sold figure and ending inventory amount be under current selling-price valuation?

(c) Justify the amounts you obtained in Part (b).

(d) Is the replacement-cost valuation in Part (a) affected by the use of the FIFO, instead of LIFO, inventory method?

Problem 6-8. Miller Trunk Company owns a patent for a coin counting machine. The patent has a remaining life of four years. Mr. Miller estimates the future cash flows from the patent to be as follows:

Year	Cash Receipts Received at the End of Each Year	Cash Disbursements Made at the End of Each Year	Net Cash Inflows at the End of Each Year
1	$60,000	$40,000	$20,000
2	50,000	40,000	10,000
3	50,000	35,000	15,000
4	40,000	30,000	10,000

Required:

Prepare a table with columns listing the assets, liabilities, owner's equity, and net income for Miller Trunk Company for each of the remaining four years of its life, assuming a 6 percent discount factor. Any excess cash is withdrawn at the end of each period.

Problem 6-9. Marcia Brown Corporation specializes in making high risk loans. Marcia Brown has obtained some of its capital by issuing, at a discount, noninterest-bearing notes. Marcia Brown then loans these funds to firms in return for noninterest-bearing notes, which Brown then discounts.

The stockholders have decided to liquidate the company. To obtain favorable tax treatment the liquidation must take place within a year. As of January 1, 19+3 there are still some assets that will not be liquidated within the one-year period allowed. Smith has offered to buy the remaining assets of the company. The company's stockholders have agreed to this proposal with the stipulation that Smith must also assume the remaining liabilities of the company. Thus it is agreed that Smith will purchase the assets and assume the liabilities of Marcia Brown Corporation on January 1, 19+3, and he will pay a price that will earn him a 6 percent return on his investment.

As of January 1, 19+3 the firm's assets consist of five noninterest-bearing notes with maturity amounts as follows: $10,000, $30,000, $25,000, $15,000, and $55,000. These notes, respectively, become due December 31 of each of the following years: 19+3, 19+4, 19+5, 19+6, and 19+7.

The liabilities that exist as of January 1, 19+3 consist of four noninterest-notes with the following maturity amounts: $5,000, $25,000, $10,000, and $5,000. The maturity amounts, respectively, become due December 31 of each of the following years: 19+3, 19+4, 19+5, and 19+6.

Required:

(a) Prepare any entries that would be needed to record Smith's purchase of the assets and liabilities of Marcia Brown Company on January 1, 19+3.

(b) Prepare any journal entries needed to record Smith's transactions from January 1, 19+3 to December 31, 19+7, assuming that all notes are paid in full and that all cash is withdrawn at the end of each year. Further assume that the year-end closing is December 31 of each year.

Problem 6-10. Lynn Corporation has asked you to prepare income statements using replacement-cost valuation. You are given the following income statement data for the years ended December 31.

LYNN CORPORATION
Comparative Income Statements
For the Years Ended December 31, 19+3, 19+2, and 19+1
(Historical-Cost Valuation)

	19+3		19+2		19+1	
Revenue		$110,000		$80,000		$70,000
Expenses:						
Wages and salaries	$35,000		$32,000		$25,000	
Cost of goods sold	18,000		15,000		8,000	
Depreciation-machinery	10,000		10,000		10,000	
Depreciation-building	8,000		8,000		8,000	
Materials	2,000	73,000	2,000	67,000	1,000	52,000
Net Income		$37,000		$13,000		$18,000

The machinery was bought at the beginning of 19+1 for $150,000 and is depreciated on a straight-line basis over a fifteen year period at $10,000 a year. The building was acquired in 19+1 for $88,000 and is depreciated on a straight-line basis over an eleven year period, at $8,000 a year. The replacement cost of the machinery if bought in 19+2 would have been $180,000 and if bought in 19+3 it would have been $225,000. The replacement cost of the building in 19+2 and 19+3 would have been $121,000 and $143,000. You may assume that revenue, wages and salaries, and materials are already based on the current prices of the years in question. The historical cost net income figures above include $3,000, $2,000, and $1,000 of realized inventory holding gains for 19+3, 19+2, and 19+1, respectively. At the end of 19+3 the excess of replacement cost over historical-cost valuation of the inventory was $2,000. The realizable holding gains on inventory of $1,000 at the end of 19+2 and 19+1 are included in the realized holding gains for 19+3 and 19+2, respectively.

Required:

Prepare comparative income statements for the years 19+1, 19+2, and 19+3 using replacement-cost valuation.

Problem 6-11. The B & Q Company was organized on July 1, 19+2. Under the partnership agreement $900,000 was provided by Beke and $600,000 by Quinn as initial capital; income and losses were to be shared in the same ratio as the initial capital contributions. No additional capital contributions have been made.

The June 30, 19+8 balance sheet follows:

Assets

Cash	$ 500,500
Accounts receivable, net	950,000
Inventory (LIFO basis)	1,500,000
Prepaid insurance	18,000
Land	58,000
Machinery and equipment, net	1,473,500
	$4,500,000

Equities

Current liabilities	$1,475,000
Beke, capital	1,815,000
Quinn, capital	1,210,000
	$4,500,000

Beke and Quinn are considering selling their business but are concerned that the financial statements do not reveal its current worth. You have been requested to assist in determining the current value of the assets. You compile the following information in addition to the asset section of the balance sheet:

(1) An aging of accounts receivable disclosed the following:

Fiscal Year	Amount	Allowance for Doubtful Accounts
19+5	$ 40,000	$ 35,000
19+6	125,000	105,000
19+7	160,000	67,500
19+8	925,000	92,500
	$1,250,000	$300,000

A review of past experience shows that all receivables over two years old have been uncollectible, those over one year old have been 50 percent collectible, and those less than one year old have been 90 percent collectible. The receivables may be sold at 90 percent of the collectible amount.

(2) The inventory level has been increasing and its cost has been determined using the LIFO flow assumption. The cost of the LIFO layers at the average price for the indicated year of acquisition and the inventory price increases have been as follows:

LIFO Layers		Price Increases	
Fiscal Year Acquired	Cost	Period	Increase
19+4	$ 60,000	19+4–19+8	20%
19+5	150,000	19+5–19+8	18
19+6	240,000	19+6–19+8	15
19+7	350,000	19+7–19+8	11
19+8	700,000	19+8	5
	$1,500,000		

Inventory can be sold at 120 percent of current average cost.

(3) Machinery was purchased in fiscal years 19+4, 19+6, and 19+7 for $500,000, $850,000, and $660,000, respectively. The straight-line depreciation method and a ten-year estimated life have been used for all machinery with a half year of depreciation taken in the year of acquisition. The experience of other companies over the last several years indicates that the machinery can be sold at 125 percent of its book value.

(4) An independent appraisal made in June 19+8 valued land at $70,000.

(5) The unexpired portion of the company's insurance may be canceled and the premiums refunded.

Required:

Prepare a comparative statement of assets showing historical costs and current values at June 30, 19+8.

Problem 6-12. Thorne Transit, Inc. has decided to inaugurate express bus service between its headquarters city and a nearby suburb (one-way fare $.50) and is considering the purchase of either 32- or 52-passenger buses, on which pertinent estimates are as follows:

	32-Passenger Bus	52-Passenger Bus
Number of each to be purchased.......	6	4
Useful life..............................	8 years	8 years
Purchase price of each bus (paid on delivery).........................	$80,000	$110,000
Mileage per gallon.....................	10	7½
Estimated salvage per bus.............	$ 6,000	$ 7,000
Drivers' hourly wage..................	$ 3.50	$ 4.20
Price per gallon of gasoline............	$ .30	$ .30
Other annual cash expenses	$ 4,000	$ 3,000

During the four daily rush hours all buses would be in service and are expected to operate at full capacity (state law prohibits standees) in both directions of the route, each bus covering the route 12 times (6 round trips) during that period. During the remainder of the 16-hour day, 500 passengers would be carried and Thorne would operate only 4 buses on the route. Part-time drivers would be employed to drive the extra hours during the rush hours. A bus traveling the route all day would go 480 miles and one traveling only during rush hours would go 120 miles a day during the 260-day year.

Required:

(a) Prepare a schedule showing the computation of estimated annual revenue of the new route for both alternatives.

(b) Prepare a schedule showing the computation of estimated annual drivers' wages for both alternatives.

(c) Prepare a schedule showing the computation of estimated annual cost of gasoline for both alternatives.

(d) Assume that your computations in parts (a), (b), and (c) above are as follows:

	32-Passenger Bus	52-Passenger Bus
Estimated revenues.....................	$365,000	$390,000
Estimated drivers' wages...............	67,000	68,000
Estimated cost of gasoline	16,000	18,000

Assuming that a minimum rate of return of 12 percent before income taxes is desired and that all annual cash flows occur at the end of the year, prepare a schedule showing the computation of the present values of net cash flows for the eight-year period; include the cost of buses and the proceeds from their disposition under both alternatives, but disregard the effect of income taxes.

Problem 6-13. Buchholz Inc. was formed with the following assets and equities based on historical cost: Cash $10,000, merchandise inventory (5,000 units @ $4) $20,000, land $15,000, building $73,000, and common stock (1,180 shares at $100 par value) $118,000. The selling prices of the assets at the time of formation were as follows: Merchandise inventory, $40,000; land $15,000; and building $69,000. Acquisition cost approximated the replacement cost of the assets.

During its first year of operations, Buchholz had the following transactions take place:

(1) There were cash sales of 4,000 units of merchandise inventory at $10 per unit. At the time of the sale the firm could have replaced the inventory at a cost of $5 a unit.
(2) A two-year insurance policy was purchased on December 31, 19+1 at a cost of $300. The firm's year end is December 31. The policy can not be resold or terminated for a refund.
(3) A cash dividend of $3,000 was declared and paid.
(4) There were 5,000 units of merchandise inventory purchased at $6 per unit of which $22,000 was on credit and the remainder was cash. At the time of acquisition the selling price of the merchandise inventory was $10 per unit.
(5) Depreciation on the building was taken over an estimated ten year life using the straight-line method. Estimated salvage is zero.
(6) At year end, market prices were as follows:

	Selling Price	Replacement Cost
Inventory (per unit)	$ 12	$ 8
Land	20,000	21,000
Building	72,000	75,000

Required:

(a) Prepare journal entries, as illustrated in the chapter, under the historical-cost, replacement-cost, and current selling-price valuation methods.
(b) Prepare balance sheets and income statements for Buchholz Inc. under all three valuation methods.

Problem 6-14. As the owner of Fisher Corporation you are interested in the effect that the use of replacement-cost valuation would have on your firm's reported results for the years 19+4, 19+3, and 19+2.

Fisher reported the following for 19+4, 19+3, and 19+2:

FISHER CORPORATION
Comparative Income Statements
For the Years Ended December 31, 19+4, 19+3, and 19+2
(Historical-Cost Valuation)

	19+4	19+3	19+2
Sales			
19+4 (15,000 × $110)	$1,650,000		
19+3 (14,000 × $90)		$1,260,000	
19+2 (11,000 × $70)			$770,000
Cost of goods sold			
19+4 (13,000 × $65 + 2,000 × $40)	925,000		
19+3 (13,000 × $50 + 1,000 × $70)		720,000	
19+2 (11,000 × $30)			330,000
Gross margin	$ 725,000	$ 540,000	$440,000
Operating expenses			
Miscellaneous expenses	$ 155,000	$ 120,000	$100,000
Depreciation—building	30,000	30,000	30,000
Depreciation—equipment	10,000	10,000	10,000
Total operating expenses	$ 195,000	$ 160,000	$140,000
Net income before taxes	$ 530,000	$ 380,000	$300,000
Income taxes	265,000	190,000	150,000
Net income	$ 265,000	$ 190,000	$150,000

FISHER CORPORATION
Balance Sheet
December 31, 19+1

Assets

Cash		$ 70,000
Accounts receivable (net)		105,000
Inventory (3000 units @ $25)		75,000
Land		100,000
Building	$900,000	
Less accumulated depreciation	90,000	810,000
Equipment	$250,000	
Less accumulated depreciation	50,000	200,000
Total Assets		$1,360,000

Equities

Accounts payable	$ 100,000
Income taxes payable	65,000
Capital stock	1,000,000
Retained earnings	195,000
Total equities	$1,360,000

(1) Inventory is costed using the LIFO method. Assume that the cost of replacing inventory remained constant during each year. Inventory at the end of each year consisted of:

	Quantity	Historical	Replacement
19+1	3000	$25	$25
19+2	4000	25	40
19+3	4000	25	65
	2000	40	
19+4	4000	25	80
	4000	65	

(2) Miscellaneous expenses remain the same under replacement-cost valuation.

(3) At the time of purchase the life of the building was estimated to be thirty years. It was assumed that there would be no salvage. The straight-line method of depreciation was used.

(4) Depreciation on the equipment was based on a twenty-five year life, assuming no salvage. Straight-line depreciation was used.

(5) The following costs of replacement were determined by reference to the yearly appraisal performed in accordance with Fisher's insurance policy.

	Building	Equipment	Land
19+1	$ 900,000	$250,000	$100,000
19+2	990,000	325,000	110,000
19+3	1,050,000	350,000	121,000
19+4	1,170,000	400,000	138,000

(6) The following year-end balances were taken from the books of Fisher.

	Accounts Receivable	Accounts Payable
19+2	$115,000	$120,000
19+3	205,000	132,000
19+4	265,000	168,000

Income taxes payable at year end were 50 percent of reported net income.

(7) Only realized holding gains and losses are reported in the income statement.

Required:

Using the replacement-cost valuation method:

(a) Prepare the summary entries needed for 19+2, 19+3, and 19+4.

(b) Prepare a balance sheet and income statement for 19+2, 19+3, and 19+4, respectively.

Problem 6-15. The owner of Quick Queen from Quincy, Inc., Ms. Perkins, is interested in the effect of current selling-price valuation on the financial statements for the years 19+4, 19+3, and 19+2.

QUICK QUEEN FROM QUINCY CORPORATION
Comparative Income Statements
For the Years Ended December 31, 19+4, 19+3, and 19+2
(Historical-Cost Valuation)

	19+4	19+3	19+2
Sales			
19+4 (12,400 × $110)	$1,364,000		
19+3 (10,000 × $100)		$1,000,000	
19+2 (8,250 × $90)			$742,500
Cost of goods sold:			
19+4 (10,000 × $65 + 2,400 × $50)	770,000		
19+3 (6,500 × $65 + 3,500 × $35)		545,000	
19+2 (6,000 × $35 + 2,250 × $40)			300,000
Gross margin	$ 594,000	$ 455,000	$442,500
Operating expenses	110,000	120,000	80,000
Miscellaneous expenses	12,000	12,000	12,000
Depreciation—equipment	34,000	34,000	34,000
Total operating expenses	$ 156,000	$ 166,000	$126,000
Net income before taxes	$ 438,000	$ 289,000	$316,500
Income taxes	219,000	144,500	158,250
Net income	$ 219,000	$ 144,500	$158,250

QUICK QUEEN FROM QUINCY CORPORATION
Balance Sheet
December 31, 19+1

Assets

Cash		$ 61,000
Accounts receivable		138,000
Inventory (2125 @ $40)		85,000
Prepayment		6,000
Land		110,000
Buildings	$680,000	
Less accumulated depreciation	34,000	
		646,000
Equipment	$ 90,000	
Less accumulated depreciation	12,000	
		78,000
Total assets		$1,124,000

Equities

Accounts payable	$ 33,000
Income taxes payable	57,000
Bonds payable (due July 1, 19+9)	200,000
Capital stock	400,000
Retained earnings	434,000
Total equities	$1,124,000

(1) Accounts payable and income taxes payable are stated at the amount needed to settle these liabilities. Accounts receivable may be sold at 90 percent of face.

(2) The Quick Queen uses a perpetual FIFO inventory costing method. Inventory at the end of each year was:

		Price per Unit		
	Quality	Historical	Replacement	Sales
19+1	2125	$40	$40	$ 80
19+2	2500	35	50	95
19+3	1500	45	55	110
	2000	50		
19+4	1500	45	65	105
	1000	60		

(3) The prepayment consists of a noncancelable three-year insurance policy that cannot be resold. The amortization of this policy is included in miscellaneous expenses. Miscellaneous expenses in all other cases were cash expenses.

(4) The following current-selling price valuations were determined for the assets that were on the books as of December 31, 19+1:

	Building	Equipment	Land
19+1	$720,000	$120,000	$110,000
19+2	800,000	110,000	130,000
19+3	830,000	145,000	150,000
19+4	800,000	170,000	180,000

(5) Depreciation on the equipment is based on a seven and a half year life. Depreciation on the building is based on a twenty-year life.

(6) The following year end balances were taken from the books:

	Accounts Receivable	Accounts Payable
19+2	$125,000	$100,000
19+3	210,000	95,000
19+4	205,000	140,000

(7) The Quick Queen from Quincy management has estimated that the market price of the bonds payable was 105 percent of face in 19+2, 80 percent of face in 19+3, and 75 percent of face in 19+3. The bonds were sold December 31, 19+1.

(8) On December 31, 19+4 the company purchased specialized machinery to increase its production of Qwaking Qwakeroo dolls. The purchase price of this equipment was $280,000 in notes with a market value of $260,000. Resale value of this equipment was only $40,000 because of its extremely specialized nature. It could only be used to make Qwaking Qwakeroo dolls.

(9) The president of Quick Queen, Ms. Smith, has decided that the valuation of all assets and liabilities should be at current selling prices. For liabilities current selling prices would be the amount needed to settle the liabilities.

Required:

(a) Prepare the summary entries needed for the years 19+2, 19+3, 19+4.

(b) Prepare a balance sheet and income statement for 19+2, 19+3, and 19+4, respectively.

CHAPTER 6 APPENDIX

QUESTIONS

1. Interest provides us with the means to state present-day and future dollars in equivalent terms. What does this statement mean?
2. Is the time value of money normally taken into account in short-run financial decision making?
3. What is meant by the statement that present value is merely the opposite of compounding and vice versa?
4. What is the frequency of conversion and what is its importance?
5. Suppose that you are analyzing an investment that is expected to generate R *unequal,* end-of-year rents for n years at i rate of interest. How would you calculate the compound amount of this series of cash flows? The present value? How would your two answers change if R were *equal,* end-of-year rents?
6. What is continuous compounding? How does it differ from daily compounding?
7. What is the difference between compound interest and compound discount?
8. What are the differences between an ordinary annuity, an annuity due, and a deferred annuity?
9. What is the difference between a nominal annual interest rate and an effective annual interest rate?
10. What does the formula $R\,(p_{\overline{n+k}|i} - p_{\overline{k}|i})$ mean?
11. Can you algebraically prove the equality of the formulas given below?
    (a) $s_{\overline{n}|i} = (1 + i)^n p_{\overline{n}|i}$
    (b) $p_{\overline{n}|i} = (1 + i)^{-n} s_{\overline{n}|i}$

PROBLEMS

Problem 6A-1. To provide a review of compounding, work the following short problems and show all of your computations.

(1) State the rate per interest period and the number of interest periods in each of the following:
   (a) 7 percent per annum compounded annually for 4 years.
   (b) 10 percent per annum compounded semiannually for 5 years.
   (c) 10 percent per annum compounded quarterly for 3 years.
   (d) 15 percent per annum compounded monthly for 2 years.

(2) Refer to the appropriate table and compute the amount to which $1,500 will accumulate for each of the four cases above in part (1).

(3) Compute the effective annual interest rate for each of the four cases above in part (1).

(4) Compute the compound interest for each of the four cases above in part (2).

Problem 6A-2. Suppose that Mr. Jones can invest $1,000 today at 6 percent per year compounded semiannually for two years.

(a) What is the amount to which the $1,000 will accumulate?

(b) Verify the amount calculated in part (a) by presenting a schedule that shows the accumulation period by period. The schedule can be set up using the following format:

Investment	$XXXX
Interest-first period	X
Amount at end of first period	$XXXX
Interest-second period	X
	$XXXX
.	.
.	.
.	.

(c) What would be Mr. Jones's compound interest?

Problem 6A-3. To provide a review of present value, work the following short problems and show all of your computations.

(1) Refer to the appropriate table and compute the present value for each of the four cases below:
   (a) $10,000 due in 18 years at 4 percent compounded annually.
   (b) $1,000 due in 4 years at 6 percent compounded semiannually.
   (c) $2,500 due in 8 years at 4 percent compounded quarterly.
   (d) $1,000 due in 2 years at 6 percent compounded monthly.

(2) What is the compound discount in each of the four cases in part (1)?

(3) Prepare a present-value schedule period by period to verify your computation in part (1)(b) above. The schedule can be set up using the following format:

Investment (present value)	$XXXX
Interest-first period	X
Total at end of first period	$XXXX
Interest-second period	X
	$XXXX
.	.
.	.
.	

Problem 6A-4. Mr. Gentry is the proud father of a new son today. He wants to invest an amount today that will provide his son, on his nineteenth birthday, with $25,000 for his college education.

Required:

(a) If Mr. Gentry can earn 6 percent interest compounded semiannually on his money, how much must he invest today to provide for his son's future college education? Show all computations.

(b) If Mr. Gentry can earn 6 percent interest compounded semiannually on his money until his son reaches his fifth birthday, and then earn 8 percent interest compounded semiannually thereafter, how much must he invest today? Show all computations.

Problem 6A-5. Mr. Winn owes $10,000 at 7 percent interest that is due in 9 years. If the current interest rate is 6 percent compounded quarterly, how much should the creditor receive (i.e., the proceeds) if he decides to sell the note (i.e., discount it)? Show all computations.

Problem 6A-6. To provide a review of the amount of an annuity, work the following short problems and show all of your computations.

(1) Refer to the appropriate table and compute the amount of an *ordinary* annuity for each of the four cases below:
   (a) 13 rents of $1,000 at 7 percent.
   (b) 8 rents of $8,500 at 6 percent.
   (c) 27 rents of $3,750 at 4 percent.
   (d) 4 rents of $400 at $3\frac{1}{2}$ percent.

(2) Verify your computation in part (1)(d) above by preparing an annuity accumulation schedule. The schedule can be set up using the following format:

First period—Deposit	$XXX
Second period—Interest	X
—Deposit	XXX
Subtotal	$XXX
.	.
.	.
.	.

(3) Refer to the appropriate table and compute the amount of an annuity *due* for each of the four cases in part (1) above.

Problem 6A-7. Mr. Hall deposited $100 semiannually in a savings account that paid interest of 6 percent compounded semiannually. The first payment began when his son was six months old and the last payment was made when his son reached his nineteenth birthday. At that time, the accumulated amount was left on deposit to earn interest until his son reached his twenty-first birthday, when the son withdrew the full amount. How much did the son withdraw on his twenty-first birthday? Show all of your computations.

Problem 6A-8. To provide a review on the present value of an annuity, work the following short problems and show all computations.

(1) Refer to the appropriate table and compute the present value of an *ordinary* annuity for each of the four cases below:
   (a) 16 rents of $10,000 at 5 percent.
   (b) 9 rents of $15,000 at 3 percent.
   (c) 41 rents of $7,500 at $2\frac{1}{2}$ percent.
   (d) 3 rents of $9,000 at 7 percent.

(2) Verify your computation in part (1)(d) above by presenting an annuity reduction table (see the format on page 163).

(3) Refer to the appropriate table and compute the present value of an annuity *due* for each of the four cases in part (1).

Problem 6A-9. To review the computation of annual payments of an annuity, work the following short problems and show all computations.

(a) Suppose that an individual wants to have \$150,000 on his 65th birthday. He asks you to tell him how much he must deposit on each birthday from his 58th to 65th, inclusive, in order to receive this amount. Assume an interest rate of $2\frac{1}{2}$ percent.

(b) Suppose that an individual bought a car for \$4,000, agreeing to pay for it in twelve equal monthly installments with interest at 6 percent per year, the first payment to be made immediately. What was the monthly payment?

(c) Suppose that an individual borrowed \$8,000 from a friend, which he agreed to repay on March 1, 19+2. On that date he was unable to pay his friend, so he made the following arrangement with a loan company: The Ever-Ready Loan Company paid the friend the \$8,000 on March 1, 19+2, and the individual agreed to repay the loan in a series of five equal annual payments, such payments being in part interest on the unpaid principal, and in part a payment on the principal. If the interest rate is 4 percent, how much must he pay each year to the loan company if he makes the first payment on March 1, 19+2?

Problem 6A-10. Suppose that there are no tables of amounts and present values at $4\frac{1}{2}$ percent interest available to you, and that you decide to construct your own tables.

Required (show your computations):

(a) Construct a table of amounts of \$1 at $4\frac{1}{2}$ percent for three periods. Carry the figure to six decimal places and show your computations.

(b) Construct a table of present values of \$1 at $4\frac{1}{2}$ percent for three periods. Carry the figures to six decimal places and show your computations.

(c) Using the table in your solution to part (a) above, construct a table of amounts of an ordinary annuity of \$1 at $4\frac{1}{2}$ percent for three periods.

(d) Using the table in your solution to part (b) above, construct a table of present values of an ordinary annuity of \$1 at $4\frac{1}{2}$ percent for three periods.

Problem 6A-11. You are given below two problems on solving for unknowns, assuming that the given compound interest data are the only data available to you. Show all of your computations.

(1) Given that the amount of \$1.00 at $4\frac{1}{2}$ percent for 9 periods is 1.4861, compute the following:
(a) The present value of \$1.00 at $4\frac{1}{2}$ percent for 9 periods.
(b) The amount of an ordinary annuity of \$1.00 at $4\frac{1}{2}$ percent for 9 periods.
(c) The present value of an ordinary annuity of \$1.00 at $4\frac{1}{2}$ percent for 9 periods.

(2) Given that the amount of an ordinary annuity of \$1.00 at $4\frac{1}{2}$ percent for 8 periods is 9.3800, compute the following:
(a) The amount of \$1.00 at $4\frac{1}{2}$ percent for 8 periods.
(b) The present value of \$1.00 at $4\frac{1}{2}$ percent for 8 periods.
(c) The present value of an ordinary annuity of \$1.00 at $4\frac{1}{2}$ percent for 8 periods.

Problem 6A-12. You are given below two problems on solving for unknowns, assuming that the given present value data are the only data available to you. Show all of your computations.

(1) Given that the present value of \$1.00 at $4\frac{1}{2}$ percent for 13 periods is .5643, compute the following:
(a) The amount of \$1.00 at $4\frac{1}{2}$ percent for 13 periods.

(b) The present value of an ordinary annuity of \$1.00 at $4\frac{1}{2}$ percent for 13 periods.
(c) The amount of an ordinary annuity of \$1.00 at $4\frac{1}{2}$ percent for 13 periods.

(2) Given that the present value of an ordinary annuity of \$1.00 at $4\frac{1}{2}$ percent for 6 periods is 5.1579, compute the following:
(a) The present value of \$1.00 at $4\frac{1}{2}$ percent for 6 periods.
(b) The amount of \$1.00 at $4\frac{1}{2}$ percent for 6 periods.
(c) The amount of an ordinary annuity of \$1.00 at $4\frac{1}{2}$ percent for 6 periods.

Problem 6A-13. Mr. Joy plans to deposit \$5,000 in a fund on December 31 of the years 1980 to 1995, inclusive. Determine how much he will have in the fund on December 31, 1995, if interest rates are as follows:

1980–1984, inclusive—5%
1985–1988, inclusive—6%
1989–1995, inclusive—7%

Problem 6A-14. Mr. Moonitz wishes to receive \$6,000 on December 31 of the years 1981 to 1993, inclusive. Determine how much he must invest on January 1, 1981, to assure these annual receipts if the investment earns interest as follows:

1981–1986, inclusive—5%
1987–1990, inclusive—6%
1991–1993, inclusive—7%

Problem 6A-15. Mr. Confused knows how to use compound and present value of annuity tables when the compound period and the payment (receipt) period are the same. He asks you to help him answer the following two questions where the compound period and the payment period differ. Show all of your computations.

(a) What is the amount of an ordinary annuity of 10 annual rents of \$500, with interest at 5 percent compounded semiannually?
(b) What is the present value of an ordinary annuity of 20 annual rents of \$150, with interest at 5 percent compounded semiannually?

CHAPTER 7

QUESTIONS

1. What is the valuation method used in current accounting practice for long-term bonds payable?
2. In the accounting for long-term bond investments, is historical-cost valuation used?
3. What is the valuation method used in current accounting practice for short-term marketable securities, and why does the valuation method differ from that for long-term investments in bonds?
4. With regard to bonds, what do the following terms mean?
   (a) Indenture
   (b) Face amount (value)
   (c) Denomination
   (d) Par amount (value)

(e) Flat price
(f) Call premium

5. With regard to bond interest rates, what is the difference between the current-market rate, the nominal rate, and the effective-interest rate? In your answer, make reference to which, if any, of these rates are constant over the life of the bonds.
6. What is the difference between the following terms?
   (a) Guaranteed bonds and collateral trust bonds
   (b) Registered bonds and nonregistered bonds
   (c) Convertible bonds and callable bonds
   (d) Debenture bonds and guaranteed bonds
   (e) Participating bonds and income bonds
7. Why do bonds sell either at par, a premium, or a discount?
8. Under conventional accounting, the reporting of bond discount or premium differs for bond investments as opposed to bonds payable. What does this statement mean? Could they be reported the same way?
9. With regard to bonds payable, answer the following questions on bond discount.
   (a) How does the amortization of bond discount affect periodic interest expense in relation to periodic interest paid?
   (b) What is the basic objection to the write-off of bond discount by charging retained earnings at the date of issuance, or shortly thereafter?
   (c) If bond discount is amortized using the effective-interest method, will periodic interest expense increase or decrease over the life of the bonds?
   (d) What would be the proper treatment of unamortized bond discount from time to time as holders of convertible bonds exercised their rights to convert them into capital stock?
10. How does the amortization of bond premium on bonds payable and bond investment affect interest expense and interest revenue, respectively?
11. With regard to bond discount and premium amortization under the effective-interest and straight-line methods, answer the following questions.
   (a) What is effective-interest amortization?
   (b) What is straight-line amortization?
   (c) Under either method, what is the period of time over which the amortization is based on?
   (d) In accordance with GAAP, which method is acceptable?
   (e) In general, what is the effect on interest expense and revenue of using effective-interest versus straight-line amortization?
12. With regard to the early retirement of bonds payable, answer the following questions.
   (a) Why would a company want to retire bonds before maturity?
   (b) If bonds are called, why do companies normally have to pay a call premium?
   (c) Is the loss or gain on early retirement reported in the income statement as an extraordinary item?
   (d) If bonds with unamortized bond discount are retired early by paying a call premium, what is the loss on bond retirement equal to?
13. With regard to bond refunding, answer the following questions.
   (a) What is bond refunding?
   (b) In accordance with GAAP, how should the difference between the reacquisition price and the discounted amount of the bonds be accounted for?

(c) What are the arguments for and against deferring the difference between the re-acquisition price and the discounted amount?

14. With regard to convertible bonds, answer the following questions.

(a) Why do companies issue convertible bonds and why are investors willing to buy them?

(b) In accordance with GAAP, how should the issuance of convertible bonds be accounted for?

(c) What are the two methods of accounting for bond conversions and what are the arguments for and against their use?

15. A company issuing bonds establishes the maturity amount (value) and the interest rate. Do you agree with this statement?

16. When bonds are issued at par, the face amount (value) of the bonds is equal to the maturity amount (value) of the bonds. Do you agree with this statement?

17. Since bonds payable and bond investment are reported in the balance sheet at their discounted amount (present value), they therefore reflect current market prices. Do you agree with this statement?

18. The discounted amount (present value) of bonds is equal to the face amount (value) of the bonds. Do you agree with this statement?

19. With regard to bonds issued at a discount, the bond discount represents prepaid interest and therefore should be recorded and reported as a deferred charge and amortized over the life of the bonds. In addition, by separating the bond discount from the bonds payable, the latter will not be reported misleadingly at less than the maturity amount (value). What do you think of these statements?

20. Two companies issue twenty-year, $1,000,000 bonds at par. The nominal and effective interest rates were 4 percent for one company and 8 percent for the other company. Following GAAP, the bonds are reported in the balance sheets of both companies at $1,000,000. In general, what are some theoretical problems in the way accountants report bonds payable in the balance sheet that are implied by this simple example?

PROBLEMS

Problem 7-1. Minoan Company issues $100,000 in bonds on January 1, 19+1 that have a 7 percent coupon rate, pay interest annually on January 1, are due in three years, and are issued to yield 8 percent to maturity. You are given the following present-value data.

Years	Present Value of $1 at 8%	Present Value of An Annuity of $1.00 at 8%
1	.9259	.9259
2	.8573	1.7833
3	.7938	2.5771

Assuming the fiscal period ends December 31, prepare all journal entries needed on the books of Minoan Company for the life of the bonds using the effective-interest method.

Problem 7-2. You are given below seven multiple choice questions. Select the correct answer to each question and indicate the corresponding letter on a separate sheet of paper (e.g., 1-a, 2-a, etc.).

(1) On July 1, 19+2, N Company purchased as an investment two, 6-percent \$1,000 bonds of Y Company. The bonds were dated April 1, 19+2 and are two-year bonds with interest paid each September 30 and March 31. Which of the entries below reflect the purchase of the bonds on July 1, 19+2 at 103½?

(a) Interest receivable	15	
Bond investment	1,035	
Cash		1,050
(b) Bond investment	2,070	
Interest receivable	30	
Cash		2,100
(c) Bond investment	1,095	
Cash		1,035
Accrued interest		60
(d) Bond investment	2,070	
Interest receivable	60	
Cash		2,130
(e) None of the above		

(2) If a bond is purchased at a discount, how does the effective interest rate compare with the nominal rate? (a) higher than, (b) lower than, (c) the same as, (d) none of these.

(3) Which one of the statements below applies to the effective-interest method of amortizing the premium or discount on bonds issued? (a) it provides for a uniform rate of interest expense based upon the beginning debt balance; (b) it is an application of the straight-line method; (c) it is desirable when interest payment dates do not coincide with accounting period dates; (d) it is necessary when there is a partial redemption of the bonds before maturity; (e) none of the above.

(4) If a company issues bonds at a premium, how is the interest expense affected? (a) increased, (b) reduced, (c) unaffected, (d) none of these.

(5) Company H issued \$100,000, 8 percent first-mortgage real estate bonds, payable on March 1, 19+2 at 102½ plus accrued interest. The bonds were dated January 1, 19+2, and are ten year bonds with interest payable each June 30 and December 31. What would be the proper journal entry to record the sale of the bonds on March 1, 19+2?

(a) Cash	102,500	
Bond premium		2,500
Bonds payable		100,000
(b) Cash	97,500	
Bond premium	2,500	
Bonds payable		100,000
(c) Cash	103,833.33	
Bond interest payable		1,333.33
Bond premium		2,500.00
Bonds payable		100,000.00
(d) Cash	104,500	
Bond interest payable		2,000
Bond premium		2,500
Bonds payable		100,000
(e) None of these		

(6) If bonds are initially sold at a discount and the straight-line method of amortiza-

tion is used, what is the effect on interest expense in the earlier years? (a) It will exceed what it would have been had the effective-interest method of amortization been used; (b) it will be less than what it would have been had the effective-interest method of amortization been used; (c) it will be the same as what it would have been had the effective-interest method of amortization been used; (d) it will be less than the nominal rate of interest, (e) none of the above.

(7) On July 1, 19+4, an interest payment date, $10,000 of Cap Company bonds were converted into 200 shares of Cap Company common stock each having a par value of $40 and a market value of $55. There is $400 unamortized discount on the bonds. Under the method using the book amount (value) of the bonds, Cap would record: (a) $1,400 gain, (b) $1,000 gain, (c) no gain or loss, (d) a $1,600 loss, (e) none of the above.

Problem 7-3. On July 1, 19+5 Jones Corporation issued $50,000 of 6 percent bonds. The interest is to be paid semiannually on January 1 and July 1 with maturity of bonds to be 20 years.

Required:

(a) Using the straight-line method of amortization, prepare the entries for Jones Corporation to record the issuance of the bonds under the following conditions:
- (1) Bonds sold at face amount (value)
- (2) Bonds sold at 102.
- (3) Bonds sold at 98.

(b) Referring to the information given in (a) above, prepare the entries in (1), (2), and (3) for the buyer of the bonds.

Problem 7-4. Assuming that Jones Corporation (see problem 7-3) has a fiscal year ending on December 31, you are to prepare the following journal entries for both (a) the seller and (b) the buyer. Prepare all journal entries (except closing) pertaining to the interest payments or accruals of Jones Corporation under the three sales conditions mentioned in problem 7-3 for the first 12 months after issuance.

Problem 7-5. On April 1, 19+3 Smith Corporation issued $75,000 of 20 year, 6 percent bonds. The interest is to be paid semiannually on October 1 and April 1 each year.

Required:

(a) Using the effective-interest method of amortization, prepare the entries for Smith Corporation to record the issuance of the bonds under the following conditions:
- (1) Bonds sold at face amount (value)
- (2) Bonds sold to yield 4 percent
- (3) Bonds sold to yield 8 percent

(b) Referring to the information given in (a) above, prepare the entries in (1), (2), and (3) for the buyer of the bonds.

Problem 7-6. Assuming that Smith Corporation (see problem 7-5) has a fiscal year ending on December 31, you are to prepare the following journal entries for both (a) the seller and (b) the buyer. Prepare all journal entries (except closing) pertaining to the interest payments or accruals of Smith Corporation under the three sales conditions mentioned in problem 7-5 for the first 12 months after issuance.

Problem 7-7. Cuniform and Papyrus Company on January 1, 19+1 issued 20-year, 7 percent convertible bonds, face amount $1,000,000 and issued to yield 8 percent. Interest is payable on January 1 and July 1. The corporation closes its books on December 31. Each $1,000 bond is convertible into 20 shares of Cuniform and Papyrus Company no-par common stock. On July 1, 19+3, $300,000 (face amount) of the bonds are converted and on December 31, 19+3, $700,000 (face amount) of the bonds are converted. A bond amortization table is presented below.

Semiannual Period	Interest Expense (Revenue)	Bond Discount Amortization	Discounted Amount
January 1, 19+1	$ —	$ —	$901,048
July 1	36,042	1,042	902,090
January 1, 19+2	36,084	1,084	903,174
July 1	36,127	1,127	904,301
January 1, 19+3	36,172	1,172	905,473
July 1	36,219	1,219	906,692
January 1, 19+4	36,268	1,268	907,960

Required:

(a) Prepare the entries for the conversions on July 1, 19+3 and December 31, 19+3.

(b) Assume that the market price of Cuniform and Papyrus stock was $50 and $60 on July 1 and December 31, respectively, and prepare the required entries using the market price of the stock.

Problem 7-8. In the course of your examination for 19+9 you find that Tarrant Company retired its outstanding bonds at 102 on July 1. These 4 percent bonds had a face amount of $70,000 and had been issued to yield 6 percent. Interest was to be paid January 1 and July 1. You find the following amount balance on the December 31, 19+8 balance sheet.

Bonds payable.. 56,280.56

What is the entry that Tarrant Company should have made on July 1 to record the retirement of its bonded debt?

Problem 7-9. Alvin Corporation issues $100,000 of 5 percent bonds on January 1, 19+1, due on January 1, 19+6. The interest is to be paid twice a year on July 1 and January 1. The bonds were sold to earn the buyer a yield of 6 percent to maturity.

Required:

(a) Compute the amount of cash received January 1, 19+1 for the bonds and prepare the necessary journal entry for the issuance.

(b) Prepare a table of bond discount amortization using the effective-interest method for the first 3 years (round all figures to the nearest whole dollar).

(c) Prepare all journal entries pertaining to the bonds for the fiscal year ending December 31, 19+3.

Problem 7-10. Refer back to the preceding problem and assume that you are the purchaser of the Alvin Corporation bonds.

Required:

(a) Prepare a table of bond discount amortization for the first three years using the straight-line method.

(b) Prepare all journal entries pertaining to bonds for the first year of purchase.

(c) Prepare all journal entries pertaining to the bonds for the fiscal year ending December 31, 19+3.

Problem 7-11. Thomas Corporation issues $100,000 of 5 percent bonds on January 1, 19+1, due on January 1, 19+6. The interest is to be paid twice a year on July 1 and January 1. The bonds were sold to yield 4 percent. Thomas Corporation closes its books annually on December 31.

Required:

(a) Compute the amount of cash received on January 1, 19+1 and prepare the recording journal entry.
(b) Prepare a table of bond premium amortization for the first three years using the straight-line method.
(c) Prepare all journal entries pertaining to the bonds for the year ending December 31, 19+3.

Problem 7-12. Refer back to the preceding problem and assume you are the purchaser of the bonds sold by Thomas Corporation on January 1, 19+1.

Required:

(a) Prepare a table of bond premium amortization for the first three years using the effective-interest method.
(b) Prepare all journal entries pertaining to the bonds for the first year of purchase.
(c) Prepare all journal entries pertaining to the bonds for the year ending December 31, 19+3.

Problem 7-13. The following entry appeared in the books of Rax Corporation under the date of December 31, 19XX, when exactly one-half of the total life of the bond issue had expired:

Interest expense	2,702.30	
Premium on bonds payable	297.70	
Cash		3,000.00
Semiannual interest on 6% bonds		

In the December 31, 19XX balance sheet the bond premium amount was $7,794.60. The company uses the effective-interest method.

Determine the entry made at the time of the issuance of the bonds for cash.

Problem 7-14. Kansas Corporation is authorized to issue $750,000 of 15 year, 6 percent bonds dated March 1, 19+5. Interest is payable on March 1 and September 1. The entire issue is sold on July 1, 19+5 at 96 plus accrued interest. The fiscal year ends December 31.

Required:

(a) Prepare entries for the seller of the bonds, assuming the straight-line method of amortization.
    (1) Prepare all entries pertaining to the bond issue through December 31, 19+5, the close of the company's accounting period.
    (2) Prepare all entries pertaining to the bond issue during the year ending December 31, 19+6.
(b) Prepare entries for the buyer of the bonds assuming the effective-interest method of amortization.
    (1) Assuming the bonds were sold to yield 5 percent, prepare all entries pertaining to the bond issue through December 31, 19+5.
    (2) Assuming the bonds were sold to yield 5 percent, prepare all entries pertaining to the bond issue during the year ending December 31, 19+6.

Problem 7-15. The president of Mindell Corporation has hired you to calculate some comparative figures on bond investments. For parts (a) and (b) below, determine the price of the bond using two different present-value computations, and use the effective-interest method to prepare the amortization tables.

Required:

(a) Determine the price of a five-year, $10,000 5 percent bond, with semiannual coupons, bought to yield 6 percent. Prepare a table of amortization.

(b) What will be the price of the above bond if it is bought to yield 4 percent? Set up a table of amortization for the life of the bond.

(c) Compute the price, on a 4 percent basis, of a $10,000 5 percent bond, due in 20 years, with interest payable annually. The bond will be redeemed at the end of 20 years at 102.

CHAPTER 8

QUESTIONS

1. With regard to leases, answer the following questions.
   (**a**) What is a lease?
   (**b**) What are the advantages of leasing over buying an asset?
   (**c**) What are the disadvantages of leasing an asset instead of purchasing it?
2. What is the difference between the following lease provisions?
   (**a**) Cancelable lease and noncancelable lease
   (**b**) Lessor assumes obligations and lessee assumes obligations
   (**c**) Short-term lease and long-term lease
   (**d**) Title to leased property remains with lessor and title to leased property transfers to lessee
   (**e**) Lease restrictions and no lease restrictions
3. What are the basic problems in accounting for leases?
4. With regard to operating leases, answer the following questions.
   (**a**) What is an operating lease?
   (**b**) How are operating leases accounted for?
   (**c**) How are operating leases disclosed in the financial statements?
5. With regard to accounting for operating leases, what difference does it make if only annual rental payments are to be made, if a down payment and annual rental payments are to be made, or if the annual rentals are all paid in advance?
6. With regard to financing leases, answer the following questions.
   (**a**) What is a financing lease?
   (**b**) How are financing leases accounted for?
   (**c**) How are financing leases disclosed in the financial statements?
7. Under a financing lease, what difference does it make if the annual receipts (payments) are to be made at the end, instead of the beginning, of each year?
8. With regard to sale and leaseback, answer the following questions.
   (**a**) What is a sale-and-leaseback transaction?

(**b**) What are the advantages of sale and leaseback to the lessee (original owner)?

(**c**) How are material gains and losses accounted for under a sale-and-leaseback transaction?

9. In accordance with GAAP, when should leases be capitalized by the lessee?

10. What are the inconsistencies between *Opinion No. 5* and *Opinion No. 7?*

11. With regard to manufacturer or dealer lessors, answer the following questions.

(**a**) Why do manufacturers and dealers enter into leases with independent lessees?

(**b**) When can a manufacturer or dealer lessor account for a lease as if it were similar to a sale (i.e., a financing lease)?

(**c**) Why do manufacturer or dealer lessors prefer to account for a lease as a financing lease rather than an operating lease?

12. If under an operating lease there is a down payment or rentals are all paid in advance, then effective-interest amortization is theoretically preferable to straight-line amortization. What does this statement mean?

13. In accounting for a lessee under a capitalized lease, the annual interest expense is equal to the difference between the total payments and the discounted amount (present value) of the total payments divided by the life of the lease (i.e., straight-line amortization). Do you agree with this statement?

14. What is meant by off-balance-sheet financing and why does it seem to be compatible with *Opinion No. 5?*

15. In accounting for a lessee under a capitalized lease, should the lease rights be amortized under the straight-line method or the effective-interest method?

16. The amortization of gains or losses over the life of the lease on sale-and-leaseback transactions per *Opinion No. 5* is a form of income smoothing. What does this statement mean?

17. With regard to accounting for the lessee, what is the difference of the effect on periodic income if the lease is an operating lease, the lease rights are capitalized and amortized by the straight-line method, or the lease rights are capitalized and amortized by the effective-interest method?

18. *Opinion No. 5,* in effect, states that "true" leases should not be capitalized because they are executory contracts. What does this statement mean?

19. Contrary to *Opinion No. 5,* it can be argued that the property rights of all noncancelable, long-term leases should be capitalized. What are the arguments for and against such a position?

20. In his dissent to *Opinion No. 5,* what is meant by Leonard Spacek's statement that the creation of equity is equivalent to prepaid rent that should be deferred to applicable periods?

PROBLEMS

Problem 8-1. You are given eight multiple choice questions. Select the correct answer to each question and indicate the corresponding letter on a separate sheet of paper (e.g., 1-a, 2-b, etc.)

(1) Property under construction to be sold and leased back for operating use under a leasing arrangement, which in substance is a purchase, should be reported on a

classified balance sheet under the caption (a) long-term investments, (b) deferred charges, (c) property, plant, and equipment, (d) short-term investments, (e) none of the above.

(2) Under the financing method of accounting for leases, the excess of aggregate rentals over the cost of leased property should be recognized as revenue of the lessor (a) in increasing amounts during the term of the lease, (b) in constant amounts during the term of the lease, (c) in decreasing amounts during the term of the lease, (d) after the cost of leased property has been fully recovered through rentals, (e) none of the above.

(3) When measuring the discounted amount (present value) of future rentals to be capitalized as part of the purchase price in a lease, which is to be accounted for as a purchase, identifiable payments to cover taxes, insurance, and maintenance should be (a) included with future rentals to be capitalized, (b) excluded from future rentals to be capitalized, (c) capitalized but at a different discount rate and recorded in a different account than future rental payments, (d) capitalized but at a different discount rate and for a relevant period that tends to be different than for the future rental payments, (e) none of the above.

(4) In accounting for a lease the account(s) that should appear on the balance sheet of a lessor if he used the financing method, but not if he used the operating method, would be the (a) Investment in leased property account, (b) Investment in leased property and Estimated residual value accounts, (c) Receivables-leased equipment and Investment in leased property, (d) Receivables-leased equipment, (e) none of the above.

(5) Material gains resulting from sale-and-leaseback transactions usually should be accounted for (a) as an ordinary gain of the period of the transaction, (b) as an extraordinary gain of the period of the transaction, (c) by amortizing the gain over the life of the lease, (d) by crediting the gain to the cost of the related property, (e) none of the above.

(6) Which one of the following is *not* a basic characteristic of an operating lease: (a) lessor retains the usual risks and rewards of ownership, (b) lessee has no special purchase rights or lease-purchase options, (c) lessee is acquiring equity in the property, (d) lease is for a short-term, (e) none of the above.

(7) Manufacturers prefer accounting for leases as financing-type leases because (a) the difference between the full cash payments and the cost of the leased property is recognized during the period the lease agreement is made, (b) the gross margin on the leased property is spread over the lease term, (c) the leased property does not appear on the lessor's balance sheet, (d) none of the above.

(8) A company sold property at a price that exceeded book amount (value) and then leased back the property for ten years. The gain resulting from the sale should be recognized (a) in the year of sale, (b) at the end of the ten-year period or termination of the lease, whichever is earlier, (c) over the term of the lease, (d) as a prior-period adjustment, (e) none of the above.

Problem 8-2. Smiley Wiley Company leased a rock crusher on January 1, 19+2 to Van Company. The lease was for a nine-year period, which approximated the useful life of the machine. Smiley Wiley bought the rock crusher for $60,000 and desires a nine percent return. The annual year-end rental was derived as follows:

$$\text{Annual rental} = \$60{,}000/p_{\overline{9}|\,.09} = \$60{,}000/5.995247 = \$10{,}000 \text{ (rounded)}$$

Based on the above data, select the answer that you think will best complete each of the following statements and write the corresponding letter on a separate sheet.

(1) Assuming an operating lease, the January 1, 19+2 entry on the lessor's books would be (a) debit cash and credit interest revenue, $60,000; (b) debit rent expense and credit cash, $60,000; (c) debit lease rights—equipment, $60,000 and discount on lease obligation, $30,000 and credit lease obligation, $90,000; (d) no entry; (e) none of the above.

(2) Assuming a financing lease, the January 1, 19+2 entry on the lessor's books would be (a) debit receivables—lease equipment, $90,000 and credit equipment, $60,000 and unearned interest revenue—lease, $30,000; (b) debit rent expense and credit cash, $10,000; (c) debit cash and credit revenue, $10,000; (d) no entry; (e) none of the above.

(3) Assuming a financing lease, the interest entry on the lessor's books on December 31, 19+2 would be (a) debit cash and credit interest revenue—lease, $10,000; (b) debit interest expense and credit cash, $10,000; (c) debit unearned interest revenue—lease and credit interest revenue—lease, $5,316; (d) debit cash and credit interest revenue—lease, $5,400; (e) none of the above.

(4) Assuming a financing lease and that the lessee uses straight-line amortization (no estimated salvage), the December 31, 19+1 amortization entry on the lessee's books would be (a) no entry; (b) debit lease obligation and credit lease rights—equipment, $10,000; (c) debit amortization expense—lease and credit lease rights, $4,600; (d) debit amortization expense and credit lease rights, $4,684; (e) none of the above.

(5) Assuming a financing lease, the interest entry on the lessee's books on December 31, 19+1 would be (a) debit interest expense—lease and credit discount on lease obligation, $5,400; (b) debit interest expense and credit cash, $10,000; (c) debit unearned interest revenue—lease and credit interest revenue—lease, $5,400; (d) debit unearned interest revenue—lease and credit interest revenue—lease, $10,000; (e) none of the above.

Problem 8-3. The Kaw Valley Mall Company owns and operates a shopping center which cost $2,430,000. It is estimated that the shopping center will have a fifty-year depreciable life. All leases are for a five-year term. The following information pertains to the first year of operation:

Gross rentals	$375,000
Interest on borrowed money	100,000
Maintenance expense	28,000
Insurance expense	12,000
Real estate taxes	83,500

Required:

(a) Are these leases operating or financing leases? Explain.

(b) Prepare the entries that Kaw Valley Mall Company would need to record its operations for the first year.

Problem 8-4. Bovee Builders has entered into a three-year lease for an earthmover. The lease is cancelable by either party upon sixty days' notice. An $11,000 advance payment will be made on January 1, 19+1, and no other payments will be made by Bovee to the lessor of the equipment, Miller Mallets. Miller will earn a 9 percent return.

Required:

Prepare the lease entries over the life of the lease that would be required on the books of the (a) lessor and (b) lessee.

Problem 8-5. Given below is a lease-amortization table.

Period	Annual Cash Flow at Beginning of Period	Interest	Amortization	Discounted Amount (Present Value) at End of Period
0				
1	$ 10,000	$ 5,759.02	$ 4,240.98	$67,590.24
2	10,000	5,334.93	4,665.07	63,349.26
3	10,000	4,868.42	5,131.58	58,684.19
4	10,000	4,355.26	5,644.74	53,552.61
5	10,000	3,790.79	6,209.21	47,907.87
6	10,000	3,169.87	6,830.13	41,698.66
7	10,000	2,486.85	7,513.15	34,868.53
8	10,000	1,735.54	8,264.46	27,355.38
9	10,000	909.08	9,090.92	19,090.92
10	10,000	—	10,000.00	10,000.00
	$100,000	$32,409.76	$67,590.24	—

Required:

(a) Prepare the entry needed to record this lease at the beginning of period one for (1) the lessee, (2) the lessor.

(b) Prepare the entry needed at the end of period two by (1) the lessee, (2) the lessor.

(c) Show how the amortization was calculated in period five.

(d) Prepare the entry needed at the beginning of period seven by (1) the lessee, (2) the lessor.

(e) Show how the interest was calculated in period three.

(f) Show how the discounted amount of the lease payments was calculated in period four.

(g) Prepare the entry needed to record the lease rights amortization in period eight using straight-line amortization.

(h) Prepare the end of period interest entries for (1) the lessee, (2) the lessor in period nine.

(i) Prepare the entry needed to record the lease rights amortization in period five using effective-interest amortization.

Problem 8-6. The Happy Howard Used Car Lot has entered into a three-year lease of a used Edsel with Panton Planatronics. The lease provides for all servicing to be done by Happy Howard. Either party may cancel the lease upon thirty days notice. Panton agreed to pay $1,000 at the inception of the lease in addition to three annual rental payments of $1,000 at the beginning of each year. The Edsel cost $3,000 and will be depreciated by Happy Howard over the term of the lease using the straight-line method, assuming no salvage. The inception of the lease was January 1, 19+1. Happy Howard estimates that the servicing costs will be $250 a year.

Required:

(a) Using effective-interest amortization and assuming an 8 percent rate, prepare the entries for the lessor needed to account for this lease during its three-year term.
(b) Prepare the entries for the lessor needed to account for this lease during its three-year term.

Problem 8-7. Qwaking Qwakeroo Corporation manufactures heavy duty equipment used in construction work. Marsha Company would like to buy a dragline from Qwaking Qwakeroo but is unable to obtain needed financing. The management of Qwaking Qwakeroo has decided to lease a dragline to Marsha for an eleven-year period, which is the useful life of the dragline. The lease agreement calls for a $30,000 payment to be made at the beginning of each year. The lease is noncancelable.

The sales price of the dragline is $192,787.29. Qwaking Qwakeroo manufactured the dragline at a cost of $113,596.32. On January 1, 19+8, the dragline is leased. Marsha will amortize the lease rights using the straight-line method.

Required:

(a) Prepare the entries needed to record the lease on the books of Marsha Company for 19+8.
(b) Prepare the entries needed to record the lease on the books of the Qwaking Qwakeroo Corporation for 19+8.

Problem 8-8. On January 1, 19+5, Paul Pallets signed a seven-year lease agreement for the use of some production equipment. The lessor is to receive a 10 percent return on his investment of $53,552.61. Annual payments are to be made at the beginning of each year. The contract is noncancelable and provides that the lessee is responsible for all maintenance, insurance, and taxes during the term of the lease. The lease term covers the productive life of the equipment. Paul Pallets will amortize the lease rights using the effective-interest method.

Required:

(a) What are the annual payments called for in the contract?
(b) Prepare the journal entries that should be recorded by Paul Pallets on the following dates:
  (1) January 1, 19+5
  (2) December 31, 19+5
  (3) January 1, 19+6

Problem 8-9. On January 1, 19+4, Anita Leasing Company signed a five-year lease agreement for the leasing of some production equipment. The annual payments in the amount of $30,000 are to be made at the end of the year with Anita Leasing earning a 6 percent return on its investment. The lessee is responsible for all maintenance, insurance, and taxes on the equipment. The lease agreement provides that the lessee may acquire the equipment at the end of the lease term for a nominal payment.

Required:

(a) Prepare the journal entry or entries that should be recorded by Anita Leasing Company on the following dates:
  (1) January 1, 19+4

(2) December 31, 19+4
(3) December 31, 19+5

(b) List the accounts and balances relative to the lease agreement as they would appear on the December 31, 19+6 balance sheet of Anita Leasing Company after the December 31, 19+6 payment has been received.

Problem 8-10. On January 1, 19+4, Mills Manufacturing Company signed a five-year lease agreement for the use of some production equipment. The annual payments in the amount of $30,000 are to be made at the end of each year with the lessor to make a 6 percent return on his investment. The Mills Manufacturing Company is to be responsible for all maintenance, insurance, and taxes on the equipment. The asset is to be amortized on a straight-line basis.

Required:

(a) Prepare the journal entry or entries that should be recorded by Mills Manufacturing Company on the following dates:
(1) January 1, 19+4
(2) December 31, 19+4
(3) December 31, 19+5
(4) December 31, 19+7

(b) List the accounts and balances relative to the lease agreement as they would appear on the December 31, 19+7 balance sheet of the lessee after the December 31, 19+7 lease payment has been made.

Problem 8-11. On January 1, 19+2 Sunset Corporation signed a five-year lease agreement for the use of some plant equipment that cost $205,010. The contract calls for payments at the end of each year of $50,000. The lessor is to earn a 7 percent return on his investment and the lessee is responsible for maintenance, insurance, and taxes on the equipment. The company is using the noncancelable lease arrangement as a method of financing the acquisition of the equipment. Sunset uses the effective-interest method to amortize its lease rights.

Required:

(a) Prepare the journal entry or entries that should be made by the Sunset Corporation on the following dates:
(1) January 1, 19+2
(2) December 31, 19+2
(3) December 31, 19+5

(b) List the accounts and balances relative to the lease agreement as they would appear on the December 31, 19+4 balance sheet of the lessee.

(c) List the accounts and balances relative to the lease agreement as they would appear on the December 31, 19+4 balance sheet of the lessor.

Problem 8-12. Steep Park Development Company has entered into an agreement with Trussell Manufacturing Company to build ski lift equipment for its five ski slopes. Because Steep Park Development Company is just getting started and is low on capital funds, Trussell Manufacturing Company has agreed to build and install the ski lifts and related equipment and then lease the total package for a period of ten years. The lease is noncancelable and includes an option to purchase the equipment at the end of the ten-year term for a nominal amount. Payments will be made at the end of each year. The lessee is to assume responsibility for all maintenance, insurance, and taxes related to the ski lifts. The lessor is to earn a 7 percent return on his investment. Steep Park uses straight-line amortization for its lease rights and its fiscal year ends December 31.

The equipment is leased on October 1, 19+1. Total cost of the ski lift equipment was $1,404,716.

Required:

(a) What is the annual payment required?
(b) Prepare the journal entries to record the lease on October 1, 19+1 on the books of Steep Park Development Company.
(c) Prepare the year-end entries needed on December 31, 19+1.
(d) Prepare the journal entries needed on October 1, 19+2.

Problem 8-13. In 19+5 Archibald Freight Company negotiated and closed a long-term base contract for newly constructed truck terminals and freight storage facilities. The buildings were erected to the Company's specifications on land owned by the Company. On January 1, 19+6, Archibald Freight Company took possession of the leased properties.

Although the terminals have a composite useful life of 40 years, the noncancelable lease runs for 20 years from January 1, 19+6 with a favorable purchase option available upon expiration of the lease.

The lease is effective for a 20-year period beginning January 1, 19+6. Advance rental payments of $1,000,000 are payable to the lessor on January 1 of each of the first 10 years of the lease term. Advance rental payments of $300,000 are due on January 1 for each of the last 10 years of the lease. The company has an option to purchase all of these leased facilities for $1 at the completion of the lease. It also must make annual payments to the lessor of $75,000 for property taxes and $125,000 for insurance. The lease was negotiated to assure the lessor a 6 percent rate of return.

Required:

(a) Compute the discounted present amount of the terminal facilities and related obligation as of January 1, 19+6.
(b) Assuming that the discounted amount of terminal facilities and related obligation at January 1, 19+6 was $10,000,000, prepare journal entries for Archibald Freight Company for the year 19+8. Archibald Freight Company closes its books on December 31.

Problem 8-14. Blue Jay Airlines leased five airplanes to be used in their feeder routes on January 1, 19+6. The lease is to run for 10 years with payments of $250,000 to be made at the end of each year and includes an option to purchase the planes at the end of the lease. The Blue Jay Airlines is to be responsible for all maintenance, insurance, and taxes on the planes. The lessor is to earn a 6 percent return on his investment.

Required:

(a) What is the original cost (present value of payments) of the planes?
(b) What accounting method should be used by the lessor to allocate the rental revenues and expenses over the lease periods and why?
(c) Prepare the journal entries that would be recorded on the books of the lessor on the following dates:
   (1) December 31, 19+5

(2) January 1, 19+6
(3) December 31, 19+6

(d) Prepare the journal entries that would be recorded on the books of Blue Jay Airlines on the following dates. Assume straight-line asset amortization and the effective-interest method of reducing the lease obligation.
(1) January 1, 19+6
(2) December 31, 19+6
(3) December 31, 19+7

(e) List the accounts and balances relative to the lease agreement as they would appear on the December 31, 19+9 balance sheet of the lessor.

(f) List the accounts and balances relative to the lease agreement as they would appear on the December 31, 19+9 balance sheet of Blue Jay Airlines.

Problem 8-15. Friedman, Inc. had equipment constructed to its specifications by another company at a cost of $41,001.97. On January 1, 19+4, the date that the equipment was ready for use, Friedman, Inc. sold the equipment to Walters, Inc. and immediately leased it back. The equipment was sold for $41,001.97. Both the lessor and lessee will record the lease using the aggregate amount of the lease payments. The lease contains the following provisions:

(1) Noncancelable
(2) Five year term
(3) Annual year-end payments of $10,000
(4) Title reverts to the lessee at the end of the term of the lease
(5) Lessee is responsible for all maintenance, insurance, and taxes on the equipment
(6) Lease is based on a 7 percent return to the lessor

In addition, Friedman, Inc. amortizes its long lived assets on a straight-line basis.

Required:

(a) In general journal form, prepare entries for both the lessor and the lessee on January 1, 19+4.

(b) In general journal form, prepare the entries for both the lessor and the lessee on December 31, 19+4, which is the end of the fiscal period.

(c) What would have been the cost of the equipment applicable to the lease if the $10,000 annual payments were made at the beginning, instead of at the end, of each year? Do not use the present-value tables.

(d) Based upon the lease valuation in part (c), in general journal form, prepare the entries for both the lessor and the lessee on January 1, 19+1, assuming beginning of the year lease payments of $10,000. Assume that the equipment had cost the same as the lease valuation in part (c).

Problem 8-16. Connable Company owns a piece of land in a fast developing area of town that originally cost them $75,000. They want to build a neighborhood shopping center on the land but do not want to have their cash investment tied up over the forty-year life of the proposed building. Therefore, they manage to work out a sale and leaseback arrangement with the Easy Street Finance Company to cover the entire cost of the shopping center development with a seven percent return on the investment. Connable Company will be responsible for all maintenance, insurance, and taxes during the forty-year lease period and will receive back the title to the property at that time. The building was completed on December 31, 19+1 at a cost of $458,268. On January 1, 19+2, Easy Street Finance

Company paid $533,268 for the shopping center and the lease was signed. Connable Company will amortize the building on a straight-line basis. Terms of the lease provide that it is noncancelable.

Required:

(a) What are Connable Company's annual year-end payments?
(b) Prepare the journal entries needed to record the lease obligation on January 1, 19+2.
(c) Prepare the journal entries that will be needed on December 31, 19+2.
(d) Prepare the journal entries that will be needed on December 31, 19+6.
(e) List the accounts and amounts relative to the leased property as they would appear in the December 31, 19+9 balance sheet after the December 31, 19+9 payment.

CHAPTER 9

QUESTIONS

1. What requirements must an item meet in order to be classified as cash?
2. Explain why it is improper to debit the petty cash account each time the petty cash fund is replenished.
3. What amounts may properly be included as a part of the cost of marketable securities?
4. Assuming that a security is written down to an amount below cost and is still on hand at the end of the following accounting period, what adjustment should be made in the carrying amount at which it is reported in the accounts: (a) If there has been an additional decline in the market price? (b) If the market price has now risen to an amount in excess of the original cost of the security?
5. A company which maintains three different bank accounts has overdrawn one of the accounts at the end of the accounting period. How should the firm's bank balances be reported on the end-of-period balance sheet?
6. What are the basic features of a system of internal control? Describe a method of providing internal control over cash.
7. What are the advantages of using a petty cash fund?
8. What circumstances might cause the amount shown in a firm's cash account to differ from the bank balance as of the same date?
9. Why is a bank reconciliation necessary? Describe two different ways in which a bank reconciliation may be prepared.
10. Investments are classified as marketable securities (temporary investments) and long-term. What are the characteristics of marketable securities?
11. Describe the lower of cost or market method of valuation for marketable securities.
12. What is the purpose of the account Allowance for Excess of Cost of Marketable Securities over Market? Under what circumstances would the account be debited? Under what circumstances would it be credited?

PROBLEMS

Problem 9-1. Oxner Company established a petty cash fund in the amount of $200.00 on June 1, 19+4. An examination of the fund on June 30, 19+4 revealed the following:

Currency and coin		$ 43.57
Paid vouchers:		
Postage	$28.76	
Transportation in	47.34	
Telephone	15.75	
Office supplies	39.89	
Store supplies	19.30	151.04

A check was drawn on this date to replenish the fund and increase it to $250.00. Examination of the fund on July 31, 19+4 revealed the following contents:

Currency and coin		$ 73.80
Paid vouchers:		
Postage	$31.43	
Telephone	17.38	
Office supplies	46.50	
Store supplies	28.99	124.30
Other items:		
Employee's check dated August 10, 19+4	$25.00	
Employees' IOU's	30.00	55.00

A check is drawn to replenish the fund on this date.

Prepare all journal entries required to account for the petty cash fund for the period June 1–July 31, 19+4.

Problem 9-2. The bank account of Howington Company shows a balance of $3,500 on April 30, 19+3. Outstanding checks on this date totaled $2,100. During the month of May the bank reports deposits to the account of $17,000 and charges of $16,500. Included in the charges are a charge of $10 for collections and a charge of $500 representing the repayment of a note due to the bank. Neither of these charges has been recorded by the company. The company has undeposited cash of $1,500 on hand on May 31 and its check book shows disbursements of $17,500 during May.

Required:

(a) Computation of the cash on hand and cash in bank to be reported on the company's May 31, 19+3 balance sheet.

(b) Any necessary journal entries as of May 31, 19+3.

Problem 9-3. Journalize the following transactions and make any necessary adjusting entries in the books of Elton & Veamer, which closes its books annually on March 31.

An imprest petty cash fund was established at $120 on February 8, 19+1.

The composition of the fund on February 28 was as follows:

Currency and coin	$38.30
Vouchers showing expenditures for:	
Postage	24.60
Repairs	35.20
Office supplies	13.50
Sundry office expense	7.40

On this date a check was issued to replenish the fund and to increase its amount to $180.

An examination on March 31 disclosed the following composition of the fund:

Currency and coin	$27.90
Check of company treasurer, dated April 4, 19+1	20.00
Vouchers showing expenditures for:	
Telephone and telegraph	27.30
Office supplies	15.20
Accounts payable	48.00
Postage	31.50
Sundry office expense	12.10

The fund was not replenished on this date.

On April 4, 19+1, the treasurer's check was cashed and the proceeds were added to the petty cash fund. The composition of the fund on April 30 was as follows:

Postage stamps	$ 2.50
Vouchers showing expenditures for:	
Postage	39.10
Telephone and telegraph	35.50
Office supplies	21.40
Accounts payable	48.00
Traveling expense	9.60
Entertainment expense	11.90
Sundry office expense	16.50

A check was drawn to replenish the fund on this date.

Problem 9-4. The following transactions pertain to the marketable securities of Park Company for the year ended December 31, 19+2.

January 14—Purchased 500 shares of A Company common stock a $54 per share, plus costs of $250.

29—Purchased 100 shares of B Company common stock at $32 per share, plus costs of $100.

March 1—Received a cash dividend of $1 per share on the A Company stock.

May 31—Purchased X Corporation bonds at face value of $50,000. The bonds pay interest at an annual rate of 6 percent and mature on October 1, 19+2. Interest was last paid on April 1, 19+2.

July 24—Purchased an additional 300 shares of B Company common stock at $38 per share, plus costs of $300.

October 1—Received the principal and interest payment due on the X Corporation bonds.

November 7—Sold 400 shares of the A Company common stock at $50 per share.

November 9—Received a cash dividend of $2 per share on the B Company stock.

December 3—Sold 250 of the shares of B Company stock acquired on July 24 at a price of $41 per share.

Required:

(a) Journal entries to record the transactions for the year.

(b) The entry required at the end of the year assuming the securities are to be reported at the lower of cost or market. Market prices at December 31 were $57 per share for the A Company stock and $35 per share for the B Company stock.

Problem 9-5. The following information pertains to Goss Company.

	19+9	
	August	September
Bank statement balance—at month end	$ 4,000	$ 4,860
Cash account balance—at month end		3,833
N.S.F. checks returned—at month end	80	160
Outstanding checks—at month end	1,200	1,930
Deposits in transit—at month end	500	850
Bank service charges	8	11
Check #411 was erroneously recorded in the company checkbook and journal as $286; the correct amount is (This check was not outstanding on September 30)		268
Drafts collected by bank (nor recorded by the company until the month following collection)	400	300
Total credits to Cash account	29,705	34,605
Total deposits on bank statement		35,000

Of the outstanding checks on September 30, one check for $200 was certified on September 18.

All disbursements were made by check.

Prepare a reconciliation of receipts, disbursements, and bank account for the month of September, reconciling the balance per bank to the balance per books.

Problem 9-6. The president of Lawton Construction Company has asked you to determine whether there is a shortage of cash on January 31, 19+2. Facts relevant to your investigation are as follows:

The January bank statement shows a final balance of $6,700. A balance of $9,000 appears in the company's Cash account, which includes cash on hand and in bank. A miscellaneous credit of $80 in the bank statement has not been entered in the company books. Deposits amounting to $25,000 were made during January. The bank statement shows deposits of $24,500 received during January. Deposits of $1,000 were in transit on December 31, 19+1.

The following checks, issued during January, are not included among the cancelled checks returned with the January bank statement: #712, $140; #717, $295; #719, $175; #720, $110; #721, $80. Check #604, written for $60 in November and the only outstanding check on December 31, 19+1 was returned as one of the January cancelled checks.

Before leaving for a two-week vacation, the cashier removed all of the cash on hand in excess of $1,325 and prepared the following reconciliation:

Balance per books, January 31, 19+2		$9,000
Add outstanding checks:		
#712	$140	
#717	295	
#720	110	
#721	80	525
		$9,525
Deduct deposits in transit		1,500
		$8,025
Deduct cash on hand		1,325
Balance per bank, January 31, 19+2		$6,700
Deduct unrecorded credit		80
True cash, January 31, 19+2		$6,620

(1) How much did the cashier remove, and how did he attempt to conceal his theft?
(2) Using only the information given, name a specific feature of internal control which apparently was missing.

Problem 9-7. The bookkeeper-cashier of Marcus Distributors absconded on the evening of April 16, 19+5, apparently with a large portion of the company's cash, and has taken with him certain accounting records, including the cash journals and the general ledger. You are called upon to ascertain, if possible, the shortage with which the missing employee may be charged.

From available subsidiary journals and ledgers and other data you obtain the following information:

Balances at close of business, April 16, 19+5:	
Accounts receivable	$ 88,511.00
Accounts payable—Merchandise	41,460.54
Other debtors or creditors	None
Cash in bank, less checks outstanding	19,766.86
Transactions January 1–April 16, 19+5:	
Sales, per receivables clerk	1,175,234.96
Cash sales	None made
Sales allowances in customers' accounts	3,667.26
Cash purchase of furniture, per invoice	600.00
Depreciation provision—3½ months	760.30
Merchandise purchase record total	723,052.84
Expenses paid, supported by paid invoices and payrolls	373,167.36
Cash dividend declared, $10,000, of which $2,000 remains unpaid	8,000.00
Changes in capital stock	None

Cash credits posted to customers' accounts, less deposits reported on statements from the bank during January, February, March, and April (through the sixteenth), amounted to $8,766.84.

A check for $20,000 had been cashed by the bookkeeper shortly before his departure. Although the signatures on the check had been obviously forged, it was paid by the bank and returned with other canceled checks.

In addition to obtaining the amount of the possible shortage, you are asked to prepare a balance sheet as of April 16, 19+5 and income statement for the period January 1, 19+5 through April 16, 19+5. The merchandise inventory at that date has been estimated as having a cost of $82,422.30, which is less than market. Use 50 percent to make provision for income taxes. A balance sheet prepared from the books as of December 31, 19+4, and discovered in the files follows:

MARCUS DISTRIBUTORS
Balance Sheet
December 31, 19+4

Assets

Cash		$ 6,534.98
Accounts receivable		45,246.90
Inventory (cost)		88,071.56
Fixtures	$14,912.52	
Less accumulated depreciation	6,360.84	8,551.68
		$148,405.12

Equities

Accounts payable	$ 22,945.22
Capital stock	100,000.00
Retained earnings	25,459.90
	$148,405.12

Problem 9-8. The following information pertains to the marketable securities of Goldbert Corporation. The company prepares quarterly financial statements and uses the lower-of-cost-or-market method for the valuation of marketable securities.

Date	Cost	Market
January 1, 19+3	$87,000	$87,000
March 31, 19+3	87,000	89,700
June 30, 19+3	87,000	85,600
September 30, 19+3	87,000	86,100
December 31, 19+3	87,000	84,800

Required:

(a) All entries during the year in order to report the securities at the lower of cost or market on the quarterly financial statements.

(b) Presentation of the securities on the balance sheet at the end of each quarter, assuming that any related accounts are to be shown separately in the balance sheet.

(c) Journal entries to record the sale of all the securities under each of the following assumptions:

(1) The securities were sold on August 15, 19+3 for $88,000.

(2) The securities were sold on November 30, 19+3 for $85,000.

Problem 9-9. On November 30, 19+5, the bookkeeper for Barker Company prepared the following statement.

BARKER COMPANY
Bank Reconciliation
November 30, 19+5

Balance per ledger—November 30	$35,862.79
Add:	
Collections received on the last day of November and debited to Cash in Bank on books but not deposited	4,859.83
Debit memo for customer's check returned unpaid (check is on hand but no entry has been made in the books)	200.00
Debit memo for bank service charge for November	11.26
	$41,033.88

Deduct:		
Checks drawn but not paid by bank (see detailed list below)	$4,471.09	
Credit memo for proceeds of a note receivable which had been left at the bank for collection but which has not been recorded as collected	400.00	
Check for an account payable entered on the books as $468.13 but drawn and paid by bank as $706.11	237.98	5,209.07
		$35,824.81
Unlocated difference		200.00
Balance per bank statement—November 30		$35,624.81

Checks Drawn But Not Paid by Bank

No.	Amount	No.	Amount
8210	$638.17	8513	$ 757.98
8407	392.06	8514	316.79
8480	475.00	8515	423.23
8493	107.16	8516	542.55
8511	600.28	8517	417.87
			$4,471.09

Required:

(a) A corrected bank reconciliation.

(b) Journal entries for items which should be adjusted prior to closing the books on November 30.

Problem 9-10. J. R. Allen is contemplating going into business on January 1, 19+3. He plans to sell product X on the installment plan. He will carry no inventory and will pay for the units of X and all associated expenses at the time of sale. Collections will be made in ten equal monthly installments, the first being made on the date of sale.

Mr. Allen prepared the following estimate of sales volume, which is not expected to vary from year to year.

Month	Units	Month	Units
January	40	July	350
February	80	August	300
March	110	September	310
April	175	October	240
May	270	November	190
June	390	December	120

You are given the following additional information:

Selling price of X	$150
Cost of X	100
Selling expense per unit	30
Net profit per unit	20

An important consideration is the amount of cash which Mr. Allen must invest in the proposed business. During 19+3, he intends to invest in a number of ventures. Therefore, it is necessary that Mr. Allen be informed of the extent to which his resources will be needed in this new business.

Assuming that the foregoing figures for sales volume are reliable, compute the minimum cash balance necessary to sustain operations for the first year.

Problem 9-11. An examination of the cash journals, Cash account, cancelled checks, and the February, 19+1 bank statement for Bock Sporting Goods Company produced the following data:

(1) Balance per Cash account, February 29, 19+1, $100 (credit).
(2) Balance per bank statement, February 29, 19+1, $1,866.
(3) Outstanding checks, February 29, 19+1, $3,927.
(4) February service charge, $4.
(5) An N.S.F. check returned by the bank on February 9, was redeposited by mail on February 29 after the maker had assured Bock Sporting Goods Company that the check would be honored. No entries were made on the books. Amount of the check was $638.
(6) Error in the cash journal when deposit of February 7, 19+1 was entered:

Entered as	$4,554
Correct amount	5,455

(7) During February, the bank certified a company check for $293. This check is included among the oustanding checks, above, as it was not among the cancelled checks.
(8) Cash sales proceeds of February 29 were mailed to the bank on that day, $1,817.
(9) On February 17, the bank charged the company's account for a $630 loan made to the company on December 19. Interest, at 6 percent, was deducted in advance, and charged to Interest Expense.
(10) A deposit of Bock Feed Company, $131, was credited by the bank in error to the company's account.
(11) The company has neglected to record two reconciling items which appeared on the January bank statement:
   (a) Collection by bank of a 6 percent, 30-day note and interest, less $1.00 collection fee. Date of note was December 7. Face of note was $400.
   (b) January service charge, $3.
(12) Check #2017, for $386, made payable to a supplier, was reported as lost. The company thereupon ordered the bank to stop payment, and a new check was issued. Subsequently the old check was found and "voided." Accounts Payable was debited when the new check was journalized. Both checks are included among the outstanding checks above.
(13) The bank charged the company $2 as its "stop-payment" fee.
(14) Included among the cancelled checks was a $7 debit memo applicable to Berryland Plumbing Co. for checks printed. The bank, upon being notified of this error and the one described as (10), above, agreed to correct its records.

The books are closed annually on December 31, and proper adjusting entries made. Assume that reversing entries are not made.

No cash was kept on hand.

Required:

(a) Reconciliation of Bock Sporting Goods Company's bank account as of February 29, 19+1.

(b) Journal entries necessary to adjust the company's books to show the correct bank balance as of February 29, 19+1.

Problem 9-12. From the following information, construct a monthly cash budget for Jankowski Stores, Inc., for the three months ended September 30, 19+9.

Jankowski Stores, Inc., purchases merchandise on terms of 1/10; n/60, and regularly takes discounts on the tenth day after the invoice date. For any month's purchases, assume that the tenth day after the invoice date on three-fourths of the purchases falls in the month of purchase, while the discount periods for the remaining purchases overlap into the next month.

The company's sales terms are 2/10; n/30, with the discount period beginning at the end of the month of sale. It has been the company's experience that discounts on 80 percent of billings have been allowed, and that, of the remainder, one-half have been collected during the month following sale and the balance during the second following month. Assume that no collections are made during a month on sales made in the same month.

The average rate of gross margin, based on sales price, is 30 percent. Total sales for the company's fiscal year ended December 31, 19+9, have been estimated at 60,000 units, distributed monthly as follows:

January......	7%	April.........	9%	July..........	5%	October	8%
February	6	May	10	August	8	November...	11
March	7	June	12	September...	9	December ...	8

To insure prompt delivery of merchandise, inventories are maintained during July and August at 5 percent of the estimated annual unit sales, while during the rest of the year they are maintained at 10 percent of the estimated annual unit sales. Thus, the 5 percent level begins with the June 30 inventory, and is increased to 10 percent by the close of August.

Total budgeted selling, administrative, and general expenses for the fiscal year ended December 31, 19+9, are $270,000, of which $60,000 are fixed expenses (inclusive of $12,000 annual depreciation). These fixed expenses are incurred uniformly throughout the year. The other selling, administrative, and general expenses vary with sales. Expenses are paid as incurred, without discounts.

It is assumed that on June 30, 19+9, merchandise inventory, at the 5 percent level, will consist of 3,000 units, to cost $42,000, before discount, and the cash balance will be $105,000.

Problem 9-13. The following information concerning the cash accounts of Kerby Company is available.

1. Balance per bank:

November 30, 19+5	$ 9,285
December 31, 19+5...	9,681

2. Balance per books:

November 30, 19+5	$ 6,184
December 31, 19+5...	9,404

3. Outstanding checks:

November 30, 19+5	$ 3,176
December 31, 19+5	3,752

4. December deposits, per bank statement $67,520
5. December cash receipts, per cash receipts journal $85,255

N.S.F. checks returned by the bank are recorded as a reduction in the cash receipts journal. Those redeposited are recorded as regular cash receipts. Data regarding N.S.F. checks:

Returned by bank in November and recorded by company as a reduction in cash receipts in December, $75.

Returned by bank in December and recorded by company as a reduction in cash receipts in December, $675.

Returned by the bank in December and recorded by company as a reduction in cash receipts in January, $115.

Redeposited by company during December, $400.

6. According to the repayment terms of a large loan with the bank, the bank credits the company's checking account with 80 percent of amount presented for deposit. The remaining 20 percent is applied to reduce the unpaid balance of the loan. The following summary entries for December indicate the company's treatment of the deposits and resulting loan reductions:

Cash in bank	86,005	
Cash on hand		86,005
Recorded in cash receipts journal.		
Bank loan	17,201	
Cash in bank		17,201
Recorded in cash disbursements journal.		

The above summary entries include one deposit in transit on December 31, in the amount of $1,605.

There were no deposits in transit on November 30, 19+5.

There was no undeposited cash on hand on December 31, 19+5.

7. Interest on the bank loan for the month of December charged by bank against the checking account, $914.50.
8. On December 31, 19+5, a $1,161.50 check of Kirbo Company was charged to the company's account in error.

Required:

(a) A reconciliation of receipts, disbursements, and bank account for December 31, 19+5.

(b) December 31, 19+5 adjusting entries relating to the cash accounts of Kerby Company.

CHAPTER 10

QUESTIONS

1. What is the purpose of the allowance for uncollectibles account?
2. You find the following items included among the accounts comprising the accounts receivable control account balance. State how each one should be reported on the firm's balance sheet: Accounts receivable—Employees; Interest receivable—Notes; Rebates received on returned merchandise purchased; Advances to salesmen; Federal tax refund receivable.
3. Should a contra account be established to provide for allowances likely to be credited to customers whose accounts are open at the end of the accounting period? Is this often done and why?
4. Why would a seller prefer a trade acceptance rather than an open account as evidence of a sale?
5. What is the major disadvantage of the direct write-off method of accounting for bad debts?
6. Describe the procedures for calculating the bank discount and the proceeds of a discounted note.
7. Compare the percentage of sales method of estimating bad debt losses with the aging of accounts receivable.
8. Assuming the use of the percentage of sales method, explain the effect a change in the percentage rate used to compute bad debt losses has on the financial statements of the firm.
9. What is meant by the factoring of accounts receivable? How are factored accounts receivable accounted for?
10. What is the justification for recording a non-interest bearing note on the balance sheet at an amount other than the face amount?
11. Assume Beta Corporation obtains cash by the assignment of accounts receivable. Using figures of your own, compute the amount of the resulting contingent liability to be shown by Beta Corporation as a balance sheet footnote.
12. Describe the procedures used to account for a dishonored note receivable.

PROBLEMS

Problem 10-1. The following transactions (in summary) affecting the accounts receivable of Liske Corporation occurred during the year ended January 31, 19+7:

Sales (cash and credit)	$243,610.24
Cash received from credit customers (Customers who paid $120,551.08 took advantage of the discount feature of the corporation's credit terms, 2/10; n/30.)	225,609.87
Cash received from cash customers	86,116.79
Accounts receivable written off as worthless	2,001.14
Credit memoranda issued to credit customers for sales returns and allowances	23,402.69

Cash refunds given to cash customers for sales returns and allowances	6,879.79
Recoveries on accounts receivable written off as uncollectible in prior periods (cash not included in amount stated above)	4,182.45

The following two balances were taken from the January 31, 19+6 balance sheet:

Accounts receivable	$139,227.71
Allowance for uncollectibles	3,986.47

Required:

(a) Journal entries to record the transactions summarized for the year ended January 31, 19+7.

(b) Adjusting journal entry for estimated bad debts on January 31, 19+7. The corporation provides for its net bad debt losses by crediting Allowance for Uncollectibles for 1½ percent of net credit sales for the fiscal period.

Problem 10-2. (a) Prepare a schedule as of October 31, 19+3, for Matthews Sales Company aging the following accounts. Terms in all cases are thirty days.

Aaron

Debits:		
5- 7	a	217.60
7-30	b	124.41
10-10	c	191.20
Credits:		
8- 2	a	217.60
10-16	b	124.41

Beeson

Debits:		
8- 2	a	89.93
8-17	b	110.00

Carlos

Debits:		
9-3	a	716.01
10-7	b	334.52
Credit:		
10-6	a	716.01

Deming

Debits:		
6- 1	a	101.11
6-29	b	27.82
7-20	c	81.76
Credit:		
10- 2	b	27.82

Ealy

Debits:		
4-20	a	100.00
9-16	b	227.65
9-30	c	76.08
Credits:		
7- 3	a	55.00
7-23	a	45.00
10-14	b	200.00

French

Debits:		
7-10	a	97.90
9-15	b	17.44
10-11	c	38.64
Credit:		
9- 2	a	97.90

(b) Matthews Sales Company provides an allowance for doubtful accounts equal to 10 percent of all balances which are 31 to 60 days past due, plus 20 percent of all balances which are more than 60 days past due. An account is regarded as due on the thirtieth day after the invoice date (debits to the above accounts were recorded on the invoice dates). There is a debit balance of $20 in the allowance account on October 31, 19+3. Prepare a journal entry to record bad debts expense for the three months ended October 31, 19+3.

Problem 10-3. The balance sheet of Collins Corporation revealed the following information at the end of 19+3:

Accounts Receivable		$34,950
Less allowance for uncollectibles	$1,460	
Allowance for sales discounts	625	2,085
		$32,865

The company sells on terms of 2/10, n/30. The following percentages along with an aging schedule of accounts receivable are used in estimating the charge to doubtful accounts:

Age of Account	Estimated Loss
Not more than two months overdue	3%
More than two months but less than six months overdue	20
Six months to one year overdue	50
More than one year overdue	90

At the end of the year the company also anticipates sales discounts on all receivables not yet due for payment. In 19+4 the following transactions took place:

Sales on account	$309,305
Cash collected on account	296,715
Cash discounts allowed	4,155
Sales returns and allowances	1,740
Bad debts written off	960
Recovery of bad debts previously written off	170

At the end of the year overdue accounts are as follows:

Not more than two months overdue	$3,900
More than two months but less than six months overdue	935
Six months to one year overdue	790
More than one year overdue	1,100

Required:

(a) The entries required to record the transactions listed above and to adjust the accounts.

(b) The December 31, 19+4 presentation of accounts receivable on the Balance Sheet.

Problem 10-4. The following information is taken from the records of Caribou Company for the year 19+6.

Accounts Receivable (Control)

1/1 Balance after deducting credit balances of $1540	$ 38,360	Collections from customers, including overpayments of $980	435,750
Bad debts recovered	308	Write-offs	780
Cash disbursed for recoverable contract bids	12,600	Collections on carrier claims	938
Goods shipped to customers with 1/1 credit balances	280	Memo entry for consignment sales	2,898
Memo entry for goods shipped on consignment	6,006	Merchandise returns	3,094
Charge sales	444,374	Allowances to customers for shipping damages	1,134
Claims against carriers for shipping damages	1,134		

Allowance for Uncollectibles

Write-offs	780	1/1 Balance	1,078
		Recoveries	308
		Provision	860

Notes Receivable

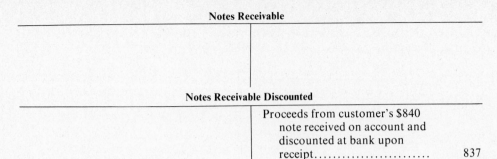

Notes Receivable Discounted

	Proceeds from customer's $840 note received on account and discounted at bank upon receipt........................	837

Compute the amount at which the accounts receivable should be shown on the balance sheet as of December 31, 19+6.

Problem 10-5. The November 30, 19+2 balance sheet of Wesley Corporation appeared as follows:

WESLEY CORPORATION
Balance Sheet
November 30, 19+2

Assets

Cash..		$ 63,049
Receivables		47,860
Inventories..		93,475
Investments, at cost...................................		21,108
Equipment..	$78,100	
Less accumulated depreciation	8,000	70,100
		$295,592

Equities

Accounts payable....................................	$ 40,918
Bonds payable—due June 1, 19+9..................	110,000
Capital stock, par $20	80,000
Capital stock subscribed	20,000
Retained earnings	44,674
	$295,592

An examination of the receivables account revealed that it was composed of items shown below.

Customers' accounts—debit balances	$21,018
Employees' accounts—current.......................	1,600
Advance to officer—noncurrent	850
Selling price of merchandise sent on consignment and not sold by consignees—at 120% of cost.....	6,480
Stockholders' subscriptions—considered collectible within nine months..............................	15,875
Equity in $8,500 of uncollected accounts receivable assigned under guarantee	2,100
Notes receivable:	
On hand—not due	3,564
On hand—past due	1,000

Discounted:		
Indorsed in blank	$ 900	
Indorsed without recourse	916	
Total		$52,487
Deduct:		
Customers' credit balances	$2,721	
Allowance for uncollectibles	1,906	4,627
		$47,860

Prepare a revised balance sheet as of November 30, 19+2.

Problem 10-6. Give necessary journal entries on the books of Max Company for the following:

19+9

February 14—Max Company sold merchandise to Jackson Corporation for $16,800, f.o.b. destination point; terms, 2/10; n/30.

22—Received a check and note from Jackson Corporation. The note, for 90 days at 8 percent, was written for $10,000. Its date was February 21. The remainder of the account was satisfied by the check. Jackson Corporation paid freight of $80, and the cash discount was allowed except for the portion of the account settled by the note.

March 5—Max Company discounted the above note at Third National Bank. Discount rate was 6 percent.

April 11—Max Company discounted its own $4,000 note at Third National Bank. The note was dated April 11, and was for 45 days. Proceeds of $3,975 were received on this date.

30—Max Company closed its books.

May 22—The note from Jackson Corporation was not honored. Upon proper notification from the bank, Max Company paid the note plus a $3 protest fee.

26—Max Company paid its note to the bank.

July 21—Received a check from Jackson Corporation for its full obligation, including interest at 8 percent on the amount owed to Max Company since May 22.

Problem 10-7. Hampton Company was organized in 19+1. All of its sales are on an installment-plan basis which calls for 24 monthly installments.

The company has not made any provision for uncollectible accounts, but has a policy of writing off at year end those accounts on which no collections had been received for two months. The company's sales and bad debt record are shown below:

Year	Installment Sales	Accounts Written Off (Year of Sale)			Recoveries (Year of Sale)
19+1	$ 350,000	$1,925(19+1)			
19+2	875,000	5,250(19+1)	$ 3,500(19+2)		$ 350(19+1)
19+3	1,050,000	1,750(19+1)	14,000(19+2)	4,550(19+3)	1,400(19+2)
19+4	1,137,500	4,200(19+2)	15,750(19+3)	5,250(19+4)	1,750(19+3)
19+5	962,500	9,450(19+3)	17,500(19+4)	4,900(19+5)	2,100(19+4)

Accounts Receivable as of December 31, 19+5;

19+4 Sales	$210,000
19+5 Sales	584,500
	$794,500

The company wishes to change its accounting for uncollectible accounts to an allowance basis and to have the change made effective for its 19+5 financial statements.

Prepare the necessary entry (or entries) as of December 31, 19+5, to effect the change. Ignore income tax considerations.

Problem 10-8. The following information pertains to notes receivable of Village Company for 19+4.

(1) Received a $6,000, 60-day, 8 percent note from Brooks Company. The note is dated October 26.

(2) Received a $1,000, 90-day, 6 percent note from S. S. Smith, a customer. The note is dated October 11 and the maker is Pelter Company. Village Company received the note on November 5, discounting it at a rate of 8 percent.

(3) Received a $8,000, 60-day, non-interest bearing note from Zebra Company. The note is dated November 16.

(4) Received a $1,500, 120-day, 8 percent note dated November 14 from B. Baker, a customer.

Required:

(a) Calculation of the interest revenue earned on the notes as of December 31, 19+4.

(b) The adjusting journal entry required to record accrued interest receivable at December 31, 19+4, the end of the firm's accounting period.

Problem 10-9. The Cambridge Corporation, on June 1, 19+3, assigned the following trade accounts receivable to Flat Fee Finance Company: Alpha, $3,500; Beta, $5,000; Gamma, $6,500; Delta, $4,000; Epsilon, $1,000. After deducting $300 to apply against the payment of finance charges, the finance company remitted $14,700. The agreement with the finance company called for interest of $\frac{1}{30}$ of 1 percent per day on the uncollected balance of each assigned account for the period during which it was assigned and uncollected (including the day on which collection was received). The agreement also provided that The Cambridge Corporation was to pay all accounts which the finance company did not collect within 20 days of the due date. Sales terms of The Cambridge Corporation were 2/15; n/30. Payments received on the assigned accounts by Cambridge Corporation are to be forwarded directly to the finance company without recording them as cash receipts.

On June 6, Beta's account was collected in full, less discount. The collection was transmitted to the finance company. The finance company acknowledged receipt of Beta's collection on June 7, and remitted 20 percent ($1,000) on this account.

On June 9, The Cambridge Corporation notified the finance company that Gamma had been permitted a $300 allowance for damaged merchandise.

On June 12, Gamma paid its account, less discount. The finance company acknowledged receipt of this collection on June 13. Enclosed with the notice, the finance company remitted $1,200 to The Cambridge Corporation.

A check for $900 was received from Zeta on June 16 by The Cambridge Corporation. During 19+2, the Zeta account had been written off against the allowance account, which was maintained by yearly adjustments in anticipation of net bad debt losses.

Alpha paid its account on June 20, without discount. According to a report from the finance company, it received the collection on June 21. A check for $875 was enclosed by the finance company.

On June 26, the finance company reported that the Epsilon account was 20 days overdue. Accordingly, The Cambridge Corporation mailed a check for $750 to the finance company. The check was received on the same day by the finance company.

The Cambridge Corporation closes its books annually on June 30.

Prepare necessary entries for the foregoing transactions on the books of The Cambridge Corporation.

Problem 10-10. On May 31, 19+6, the notes receivable account of Marrett Corporation has a balance of $31,960. Analysis of the account disclosed that $84,500 of notes were received from customers during the fiscal year ended May 31, 19+6, and that $41,600 of these notes were collected from the makers at maturity and $22,100 of the notes were discounted at the bank. Of the notes discounted, $10,400 have been paid by the makers and one note for $3,120, given by Williams Company, was not paid when due. As endorser, the company paid $3,160 to the bank. A three-month 6 percent note for $8,000 was received from an officer of the company. The note was dated December 1, 19+5 and no interest had been recorded.

Partial payments in the amount of $3,300 have been received on notes not yet due, and these collections have been credited to Partial Collections on Notes Receivable, which is shown as a liability on the balance sheet. Such partial collections included $64 of interest.

A customer's note for $5,000 was pledged as collateral for the payment of a bank loan.

Required:

(a) Journal entries necessary to correct the accounts of Marrett Corporation.

(b) Show how the facts regarding all notes discussed above should be disclosed on the firm's May 31, 19+6 balance sheet.

Problem 10-11. Lumpkin Company has hired a new bookkeeper-cashier during the current year. Consequently, when the independent auditor noticed an increase in uncollectible accounts and returns and allowances during the latter part of the year, a further investigation was deemed to be warranted. The following information was obtained from the company's records since the new bookkeeper-cashier was employed.

(1) Accounts receivable beginning balances: X, $348; Y, $222; Z, $174; V, $360; W, $384.

(2) Summary of journal entries per books, with supporting detail:

Cash on hand	12,900	
Sales		12,900
Cash sales; no checks are accepted.		
Accounts receivable	2,328	
Sales		2,328
Sales on account: X, $216; Y, $108 and $144; Z, $90 and $66; W, $252 and $354; N, $210 and $288; and M, $78, $240, and $282.		
Cash on Hand	1,548	
Accounts Receivable		1,548
Collections on Account: X, $348; Y, $222; Z, $156; W, $384 and $228; and N, $210.		

Sales Returns and allowances	228	
Accounts receivable		228
Returns: Y, \$108; Z, \$18; W, \$24; M, \$78.		
Allowance for uncollectibles	378	
Accounts receivable		378
Z, \$90; N, \$288.		
Notes receivable	360	
Accounts receivable		360
60 day, 6 percent note from V.		
Cash in bank	15,228	
Cash on Hand		15,228
Currency: \$12,513. Checks: X, \$348; Y, \$222 and \$108; Z, \$156 and \$90; V, \$364; W, \$384 and \$228; N, \$210 and \$288; M, \$78 and \$240.		
Accounts receivable	360	
Notes receivable		360
V Dishonored note.		

(3) Weekly cash register readings per informal record maintained by sales manager.

\$1,320	\$1,092
1,176	1,500
1,332	1,224
1,596	1,356
1,284	1,260

Prepare any correcting entries necessary.

Problem 10-12. Reaven Industries, Inc., entered into an agreement with Associated Credit Bureaus, Inc., whereby the latter was to purchase trade receivables from the former. The agreed commission was $1\frac{1}{8}$ percent, and interest on advances (measured by the number of days through the date of settlement) was set at 6 percent per year. The holdback was established at 18 percent.

The agreement further provided that the commission, once computed on the "net," could not be raised or lowered due to (1) merchandise returns amounting to less than thirty percent of the invoice, and (2) sales discounts not taken.

Provide all necessary journal entries on the books of Reaven Industries, Inc., for the following unrelated transactions between the two companies.

(1) On January 26, 19+7, five accounts were sold to Associated Credit Bureaus, Inc. Debtors' names and the gross amounts owed were: Abercrombie, \$2,600; Buller, \$4,110; Carr, \$1,950; Dooley, \$2,290; and Easter, \$3,070. Terms of all Reaven Industries, Inc., sales were 1/10; n/30. The invoice dates applicable to the receivables were as follows: Abercrombie, January 25; Buller, January 26; Carr, January 23 (\$820) and January 21 (\$1,130); Dooley, January 19; and Easter, January 26.

In addition to the instructions above, compute the average "due date," using January 28 as the focal date.

(2) On April 23, 19+7, an account receivable from Freeman, \$880, was sold to the factoring company subject to the terms stated above. Invoice date was April 22, 19+7, and terms of all sales of merchandise were 1/10; n/30. Reaven Industries, Inc., requested and received an advance of \$600 from the factoring company on

April 25. On April 28, Reaven Industries, Inc., notified the factoring company that Freeman had been allowed a credit of $30 for returned merchandise. Freeman paid the account directly to the factoring company on May 5, and the factoring company settled its affairs with Reaven Industries, Inc., on the due date.

Problem 10-13. You have just been hired by Morris Company to be its chief accountant. The company is three years old and has never been audited. All transactions for 19+6 have been recorded, but closing entries have not been prepared.

In your preliminary review of the company's accounting system you note the following:

1. A relatively small number of machines has been shipped on consignment. These transactions have been recorded as ordinary sales and billed as such. On December 31 of each year, machines billed and in the hands of consignees amounted to:

19+4	$12,220
19+5	None
19+6	10,686

Sales price was determined by adding 30 percent to cost.

2. Advances to suppliers have been charged to Accounts Receivable. On December 31 of each year, such advances amounted to:

19+4	$4,000
19+5	3,000
19+6	7,600

3. Uncollectible accounts have been recorded on a direct write-off basis. Experience of similar businesses indicates that losses will approximate ¼ of one percent of sales. Accounts written off were:

	Year of Sales		
	19+4	19+5	19+6
19+4	$1,340		
19+5	1,440	$ 960	
19+6	400	3,400	$3,000

During 19+6, Miscellaneous Income was credited $350 for the recovery of an account previously written off. The customer had refused to pay for the February 5, 19+6 sale, alleging that the item ordered had not been delivered. Later the customer discovered that his accountant had made an error, and he mailed a check for $350.

You have decided to adopt the allowance method for uncollectible accounts for all receivables originating subsequent to December 31, 19+5. Thus, uncollectible accounts traceable to 19+4 and 19+5 sales will not be charged to the allowance account.

4. It has been the practice of the company to sell some of its prime accounts receivable to Finance Factors, Inc. The difference between the amount received and the face amount of the receivables sold has been charged to Financial Expense. Financial Expense has been credited whenever "holdback" amounts were subsequently released by Finance Factors, Inc. All withheld amounts are expected to be recovered.

A review of the factoring transactions indicates the following:

Holdback on accounts sold in:

19+4	$ 7,600
19+5	8,900
19+6	10,200

Holdback released by Finance Factors, Inc.:

19+4	$ 4,200
19+5	7,700
19+6	9,400

5. Sales, as shown in the accounts, were as follows:

19+4	$1,689,420
19+5	1,810,064
19+6	3,218,686

Required:

The journal entries suggested by the above data.

Problem 10-14. Journalize the following transactions on the books of Appleby Company. Debit Freight Charges for freight obligations of the seller which are paid by the buyers.

August 19—Sold merchandise to Danforth Sales Company on terms of 2/10; n/30, f.o.b. shipping point. Invoice price was $3,300, and invoice date was August 19.

24—Sold merchandise to Axiom Corp. for $2,180, f.o.b. shipping point. Invoice date was August 24 and terms were 2/10; n/30. This account was immediately assigned, in return for a 75 percent advance, to Old Main Finance Company. Interest was set at $\frac{1}{30}$ of 1 percent per day of the cash advanced.

26—The company authorized credits for sales returns of $110 to Danforth Sales Company and of $230 to Axiom Corp.

27—Sold merchandise to Aspen & Co. for $1,610, f.o.b. shipping point. Invoice date was August 27, and terms were 2/10; n/30. Freight charges of $110 were paid by the buyer.

28—Received a check from Danforth Sales Company in satisfaction of the sale of August 19. It was learned that freight charges, which were paid by Danforth Sales Company, amounted to $60.

30—Sold merchandise to Foothills, Inc., at terms of 2/10; n/30, f.o.b. destination. Invoice price was $2,710, and the invoice date was August 29. Foothills, Inc., paid freight of $75.

31—Adjustments include recognition of expected net bad debt losses, 1 percent of net charge sales. Data available:

Net sales	$300,000
Sales discounts on charge sales	4,000
Sales returns on cash sales	7,000
Sales returns on charge sales	11,000
Net cash sales	60,000

September 1—Sold merchandise to Derby Stores, Inc., for $6,550. Invoice date was September 1; terms were net 30, f.o.b. shipping point. Freight charges of $40 were paid by the buyer.

1—Received 30-day, 6 percent note from Derby Stores, Inc., for $6,550. Date of the note was September 1.

2—Received a check from Axiom Corp. in satisfaction of sale of August 24. It was learned that Axiom Corp. had paid freight charges of $38. The check was immediately forwarded to Old Main Finance Company, which received it on the same day. Therefore, the daily interest charge terminated on September 2.

4—Received a check from Old Main Finance Company in final settlement of the financing arrangement.

5—Sold merchandise to York Retailers, Inc., for $4,000; terms were 2/10; n/30, f.o.b. destination. Invoice date was September 5, and freight charges of $69 were paid by the buyer. The account was immediately sold, without guarantee, to Thompson Factoring Company. The agreed commission was $1\frac{1}{8}$ percent of "net" after all deductions by the buyer, and the holdback was established at 20 percent. Interest of 6 percent per annum was agreed upon for advances. An advance of $2,000 was requested and received from the balance of $3,046.14 against which such advances could be drawn.

8—Received a $2,000 note from Foothills, Inc., and a check in satisfaction of the remainder of the sale of August 29. The note was dated September 7 and carried interest at 5 percent. Its life was 60 days. The cash discount was allowed on that part of the sales price which was paid by check.

11—Learned that Aspen & Co. had suffered several financial setbacks; hence wrote off its account.

12—Discounted the Derby Stores, Inc., note at The Last State Bank. Discount rate was 5 percent.

14—Learned that York Retailers, Inc., had paid its account in full to Thompson Factoring Company.

23—Received from Aspen & Co. a 90-day, 8 percent note for $1,200 and the balance of the account in cash.

25—Received a check from Thompson Factoring Company in settlement of the factoring arrangement.

October 1—Issued our check to The Last State Bank upon learning that the Derby Stores, Inc., note had been dishonored. A $4 protest fee was included in the check.

16—Received from Derby Stores, Inc., payment of the charge of October 1 plus interest thereon from that date at 7 percent.

CHAPTER 11

QUESTIONS

1. In what way is the inventory amount reported on a firm's balance sheet related to the determination of income for the period?
2. List and describe three different types of inventories that would appear on the balance sheet of a manufacturing firm.
3. What are the steps involved in the determination of the inventory of a business firm?
4. Describe two different methods of accounting for purchase discounts.
5. Define the following terms: (1) Incidental costs; (2) Lost costs.
6. Under what conditions might the specific identification method of costing inventory be used?

7. What are the implications of the last-in, first-out inventory costing method for a firm's balance sheet in a period of rising prices?
8. What is the basic theoretical argument in favor of the last-in, first-out method of costing inventory?
9. Describe three alternatives for costing *lifo* inventory layers.
10. What is the basic assumption underlying the first-in, first-out inventory costing method?
11. Distinguish between the simple average, weighted average, and moving average methods of inventory costing.
12. Describe two types of errors caused by failure to include all goods owned in the inventory of a firm.

PROBLEMS

Problem 11-1. The following information pertains to Product Z for the year ended December 31, 19+6.

Inventories:

	Quantity	Amount
December 31, 19+5	9,000	$4,320
December 31, 19+6	13,500	

Purchases during 19+6:

	Quantity	Cost
February 7	6,000	$3,360
April 23	7,500	3,600
July 30	11,250	4,500
September 6	4,500	2,700
December 17	9,000	4,860

Required:

The December 31, 19+6 inventory calculated using each of the following methods:

(a) Simple average
(b) Last invoice price
(c) Specific identification
(d) Weighted average
(e) First-in, first-out
(f) Last-in, first-out

Problem 11-2. Alma Construction Company purchased an undeveloped tract of land on February 12, 19+5 for $1,850,000. Development costs of $2,000,000 were incurred for landscaping, installation of curbs and sidewalks, and other items.

The lots were divided into the following classes: 400 lots to sell for $4,000 each, 700 lots to sell for $3,000 each, 500 lots to sell for $2,000 each.

On December 31, 19+5 the unsold lots consisted of 200 of the $4,000 lots, 100 of the $3,000 lots and 30 of the $2,000 lots.

Prepare a schedule showing the cost of the lots sold and the cost assigned to the unsold lots as of December 31, 19+5. Round all amounts to the nearest dollar.

Problem 11-3. A partial perpetual inventory record of Gunther Company for the month of April, 19+9, is presented below.

	Quantity			Cost		
Date	Into Stock	Out of Stock	Balance	Into Stock	Out of Stock	Balance
April 2....	400		400	$480.00		$480.00
6....	200		600	250.00		
8....		100	500			
11....	300		800	345.00		
15....		200	600			
17....		250	350			
21....	500		850	600.00		
25....		400	450			
28....	300		750	390.00		
30....		175	575			

Required:

Computation of the moving-average unit costs during the month.

Problem 11-4. Crusader Company decided to adopt the last-in, first-out inventory method as of December 31, 19+9. The company also decided that in the application of the *lifo* method it would assume that incremental quantities related to the most recent acquisitions.

Using the following data, compute the December 31, 19+9 inventory, following the *lifo* method. Also determine the effect of the change in inventory method on the 19+9 net income before income taxes.

December 31, 19+8 inventory (*fifo*):

Item	Quantity	Unit Cost	Total
X	300	$5.00	$1,500.00
	200	5.09	1,018.00
	100	5.06	506.00
Total..........................			$3,024.00

19+9 purchases of X:

Date	Quantity	Unit Cost	Total
January 20	400	$5.08	$2,032.00
April 1	420	5.09	2,137.80
June 5	450	5.07	2,281.50
August 25	310	5.08	1,574.80
October 10	300	5.10	1,530.00
December 22	100	5.12	512.00

December 31, 19+9 inventory: 800 units of X

Problem 11-5. Carol Corporation has experienced fluctuating profits in the last two years while using the first-in, first-out inventory costing method. The gross margin for 19+4 was $125,000, but only $40,300 in 19+5. The following comparative data are available.

Inventory:

Date	FIFO	LIFO
December 31, 19+3	$115,000	$115,000
December 31, 19+4	200,000	100,000
December 31, 19+5	171,000	118,000

Management has asked if the last-in, first-out method of inventory costing might stabilize profits.

Compute the gross margin for 19+4 and 19+5 assuming the company had used the last-in, first-out costing method.

Problem 11-6. Medicore Corporation sells only one product. The following amounts were received and sold during 19+9.

	Purchases		
Period	Units	Unit Price	Units Sold
1st Quarter	21,200	$2.10	
2nd Quarter	34,000	2.20	
3rd Quarter	26,800	2.30	
4th Quarter	6,000	2.40	
Total sales for year			80,000

The company expects to pay $2.50 per unit for purchases in the next year.

All purchases were made on the first day of the quarter; the inventory on January 1, 19+9 consisted of 12,000 units priced at a cost of $2.00 each.

The company is contemplating changing its inventory method and has requested its accountant to prepare a statement showing the results of several inventory methods on the income statement for 19+9. The directors inform the accountant that an inventory of 8,000 units would be the minimum the company should have. The sales price of each unit is $3.50.

Prepare a schedule showing the gross margin for 19+9 under each of the following methods:

(a) First-in, first-out
(b) Last-in, first-out
(c) Last invoice price
(d) Weighted average

Problem 11-7. Koko Corporation produces a single product which is very seasonal in its sales pattern. The following information is available concerning production and sales for 19+2 and 19+3. The sales price is $25 per unit.

	19+2				19+3			
	Sales (Units)	Units Produced	Total Cost	Unit Cost	Sales (Units)	Units Produced	Total Cost	Unit Cost
Jan.	250	300	$6500	$21.67	325	375	$6875	$18.33
Feb.	200	200	6000	30.00	250	250	6250	25.00
March	175	200	6000	30.00	200	250	6250	25.00
April	175	150	5750	38.33	200	200	6000	30.00

	19+2				19+3			
	Sales (Units)	Units Produced	Total Cost	Unit Cost	Sales (Units)	Units Produced	Total Cost	Unit Cost
May	200	250	$6250	$25.00	300	325	$6625	$20.39
June	300	350	6750	19.29	400	450	7250	16.11
July......	550	500	7500	15.00	700	650	8250	12.69
Aug.	650	600	8000	13.33	800	750	8750	11.67
Sept.	400	400	7000	17.50	500	500	7500	15.00
Oct.	325	300	6500	21.67	300	375	6875	18.33
Nov.	325	350	6750	19.29	400	450	7250	16.11
Dec.	200	250	6250	25.00	225	300	6500	21.67

Calculate monthly gross margin amounts for 19+3 using a 12-months moving average.

Problem 11-8. A portion of the income statement of Watson Company is presented below. It reveals a much improved gross margin rate compared to that earned by the company in recent years. You are asked to determine the most likely cause of this improvement and to compute the extent of its effect.

WATSON COMPANY
Partial Income Statement
For the Year Ended June 30, 19+9

Sales		$811,350
Cost of goods sold:		
Inventory—June 30, 19+8	$220,740	
Purchases (at an average cost of $22 per unit)...	462,660	
Total	$683,400	
Inventory—June 30, 19+9	142,500	540,900
Gross margin		$270,450

Additional data:

Inventory method—Last-in, first-out with perpetual inventory records.

Inventory—June 30, 19+8:		
Lifo base (19+1)...........	10,000 units at $15.00..........	$150,000
19+4 layer.................	3,000 units at $16.70..........	50,100
19+7 layer.................	1,200 units at $17.20..........	20,640
Total		$220,740
Inventory—June 30, 19+9:		
Lifo base.................	9,500 units at $15.00..........	$142,500

Problem 11-9. September 30, 19+8 marked the end of Beagle Supply Company's accounting year. On this date the company was concluding arbitration proceedings with its employees to settle a strike which had begun one week before. As a consequence of the strike, the errors stated below were made in the computation of the ending inventory. The company does not use a perpetual inventory system.

(1) Merchandise costing $4,200 was received on September 30, 19+8, and was included in the inventory, although the invoice was not recorded until October 5, 19+8.

(2) Included in the inventory was merchandise with a cost of $280 which had been sold on September 25, 19+8, for $340, the title passing to the purchaser at that time. However, the sale was not recorded until October 6, 19+8, when the shipment was made.

(3) Merchandise shipped to customers on September 30, 19+8, f.o.b. destination, was not included in the inventory. This merchandise cost $96 and the sales were recorded at $1,240 on October 3, 19+8.

(4) One lot of merchandise, shipped to the company f.o.b. shipping point, was in transit on September 30, 19+8. This merchandise was recorded at its purchase price of $1,630 on September 30 but was not included in the inventory.

(5) Merchandise costing $415 was inadvertently overlooked when the inventory tabulation was made.

Required:

(a) On the assumption that the company's books were closed September 30, 19+8, without discovery of these errors, a computation of the amount of overstatement or understatement of cost of goods sold which would appear in the income statements for the years ended September 30, 19+8 and 19+9.

(b) On the same assumption as in (a), a computation of the overstatement or understatement of retained earnings on September 30, 19+8 and 19+9.

(c) On the assumption that the errors were discovered before the books were closed on September 30, 19+9, the journal entry necessary to correct the books at that time.

Problem 11-10. The accounting year of Cobb Corporation ended on June 30, 19+9. On this date, all revenue and expense accounts were closed to the income summary account, but the closing of the latter account was delayed until the records could be examined and their accuracy determined.

An examination of the corporation's records for this year led to the discovery of the following facts:

(1) Merchandise costing $840 was excluded from the June 30, 19+9 inventory because the goods had been transferred to the shipping department for crating on June 29, to fill an order which provided that the goods be shipped on July 2, 19+9. The goods will be shipped f.o.b. shipping point.

(2) Merchandise costing $330 was ordered on June 28, 19+9, and included in the June 30, 19+9 inventory, although not received until July 3, 19+9, and not recorded in the corporation's records until then. This merchandise was shipped by the seller on June 29, 19+9, f.o.b. destination.

(3) Merchandise with an invoice price of $1,100 was received on June 26, 19+9, and this amount was included in the June 30, 19+9 inventory. As of July 2, 19+9, $1,100 was credited to Purchase Returns and Allowances, and the merchandise was returned to the seller on this date.

(4) On June 29, 19+9, merchandise costing $860 was shipped by the seller, f.o.b. destination, and was received by Cobb Corporation on June 30. This merchandise was not included in the June 30, 19+9 inventory because no invoice had been received from the seller.

(5) Merchandise with an invoice price of $400 was received on June 30, 19+9, with no entries being made until the condition of the merchandise could be determined, although these goods were included in the June 30, 19+9 inventory. During the course of the examination, these goods were found to be undamaged and in accord with Cobb Corporation's order.

Prepare the journal entries that should be made as of June 30, 19+9, in connection with the above transactions.

Problem 11-11. The Northland Corporation has been using the first-in, first-out method of inventory valuation, but in 19+9 the company decides to price its year-end inventories on the last-in, first-out basis. It plans to price any layers by reference to the first acquisitions of the current year.

The corporation gives you the following pertinent information and requests that you compute the cost of the December 31, 19+9 inventory and also prepare an appropriate footnote, covering the above change, to accompany the financial statements in the corporation's published annual report for the year 19+9.

	Quantity			Unit Purchase Price		
19+8 purchases:	A	B	C	A	B	C
February 20	2,000	4,000		$6.20	$8.50	
April 29		9,000	1,000		8.50	$11.50
June 14	7,000		3,000	6.30		11.50
September 4		13,000	5,000		8.80	12.00
October 19	15,000	4,000	2,000	6.40	8.90	13.00
November 23	3,000			6.50		
December 15	2,000	3,000	1,000	6.60	9.00	13.40
19+9 purchases:						
January 25			500			13.50
March 10	1,000	2,500	1,000	6.70	9.10	13.55
May 16	3,000	4,000		6.75	9.20	
August 8		8,000	2,000		9.25	13.60
October 21	8,000	10,000	6,000	6.76	9.27	13.64
December 12		3,000			9.30	
Inventory quantities:						
December 31:						
19+8	2,500	2,500	2,000			
19+9	3,700	2,400	2,200			

Problem 11-12. Madison Manufacturing Company has been experiencing fluctuating profits due to differences between the volume of sales and the volume of production within a period. Management tends to think of profits as being directly related to sales and finds it difficult to understand when profits are lower during a period of increasing sales due to under-absorbed fixed overhead. To aid in explaining this to management the controller gathered the following data applicable to the years 19+3, 19+4, and 19+5:

Standard production volume	62,500 units
Selling price	$ 2.50 per unit
Standard variable costs at standard volume	$62,500
Standard fixed overhead	$31,250

Operating results:

	19+3	19+4	19+5
Actual sales	50,000 units	62,500 units	75,000 units
Actual production	75,000 units	50,000 units	62,500 units

Prepare partial income statements for each of the three years using both direct costing and absorption costing, assuming actual costs were equal to standard costs. The firm uses the first-in, first-out method for calculating cost of goods sold.

Problem 11-13. The information below was taken from the records of Luttrell Company at December 31, 19+6.

Goods in process, at cost of materials and direct labor	$18,000
Materials in transit (shipped f.o.b. destination)	1,750
Advances to suppliers for purchase commitments	800
Shipping supplies	230
Finished goods in storeroom, at cost, which includes $10,485 of overhead	52,425
Finished goods in transit (shipped out f.o.b. destination, to be billed in 19+9), including $280 freight charge	2,120
Finished goods in hands of consignees (at 140% of cost)	8,400
Finished goods held by salesmen, at selling price (cost, $2,520)	3,200
Unsalable finished goods, at cost	4,910
Materials	26,305
Defective materials returned to suppliers for replacement	8,192
Gasoline and oil for testing finished goods	180
Prepaid machinery rentals	600
Machine lubricants	460

Prepare a partial balance sheet on December 31, 19+6, giving proper disclosure of the above items.

CHAPTER 12

QUESTIONS

1. Under what conditions is a departure from cost considered appropriate for the valuation of inventories?
2. Describe the limits set on market as stated by the Committee on Accounting Procedure of the AICPA.
3. Mention two conditions under which it might be proper to value inventories on the basis of selling prices.
4. Give a brief description of the two generally accepted methods of accounting for long-term contracts.

5. What are the three different ways in which the lower-of-cost-or-market method may be applied to a firm's inventory?
6. What is the major disadvantage of the failure to report inventory market losses separately on a firm's income statement?
7. Give an evaluation of the lower-of-cost-or-market method of inventory valuation.
8. What are the advantages of the use of inventory loss and inventory contra accounts in conjunction with the lower-of-cost-or-market method of inventory valuation?
9. Distinguish between the accounting for inventory price declines which have already taken place at the balance sheet date and possible future market declines.
10. What are two ways of determining the percentage of completion in accounting for long-term contracts?
11. What is the major disadvantage of the completed-contract method of accounting for long-term contracts?
12. How should scrap material be accounted for?

PROBLEMS

Problem 12-1. State, for each of the items listed below, the unit value which would be employed for inventory-pricing purposes, using the lower of cost or market as defined by the Committee on Accounting Procedure of the AICPA.

Item	Original Cost	Replacement Cost	Selling Price	Estimated Cost to Complete and Sell	Normal Profit Margin
a.	$ .67	$ .62	$ .72	$.04	$.03
b.	2.20	2.12	2.22	.12	.08
c.	1.48	1.52	1.72	.12	.06
d.	.22	.20	.24	.03	.01
e.	.93	.87	.97	.05	.04
f.	4.08	4.02	4.52	.33	.18
g.	3.18	3.24	3.52	.18	.06
h.	.44	.42	.46	.05	.02

Problem 12-2. The data presented below were taken from the June 30, 19+9 inventory records of American Code Company.

Category	Merchandise Code Identification	Quantity	Unit Price Cost	Unit Price Market
A	X.	29	$ 16.50	$ 16.00
	Y.	78	4.10	4.30
	Z.	105	2.90	2.80
B	XX.	24	162.10	157.00
	YY.	18	203.00	209.00
	ZZ	12	146.00	143.00
C	I.	294	1.18	1.16
	II.	197	1.37	1.40
	III.	130	1.68	1.70

Price the inventory, using the lower-of-cost-or-market method, applied: (1) Item by item; (2) to categories of inventory; (3) to total inventory.

Problem 12-3. The inventory of Home Furnishing Company on December 31, 19+9, was prepared as shown below:

	Classification	Count	Unit Cost	Unit market to replace on December 31, 19+9	Unit sale price less costs of disposal	Unit sale price less costs of disposal and normal profit margin
Living room suites:	A-1.....	5	$80	$85	$130	$82
	A-2.....	2	70	68	115	69
	A-3.....	4	50	46	72	50
Bedroom suites:	B-1.....	6	60	58	84	61
	B-2.....	1	55	56	82	56
	B-3.....	3	30	35	50	32
	B-4.....	2	35	33	57	34
Dining room suites:	C-1.....	4	85	82	81	78
	C-2.....	2	90	93	104	92
Dinette sets:	C-11 ...	6	40	37	64	42
	C-12 ...	7	30	26	25	22
Tables:	D-1	11	30	35	48	34
	D-2	14	22	24	24	21
	D-3	6	10	9	13	8
	D-4	5	14	15	20	16
Chairs:	E-1.....	22	45	42	63	44
	E-2.....	12	50	35	49	37
Lamps:	F-1.....	17	9	11	14	10
	F-2.....	6	10	9	15	11
	F-3.....	14	7	8	10	8

Compute the December 31, 19+9 inventory, using the lower-of-cost-or-market (by category) method as defined by the Committee on Accounting Procedure of the AICPA.

Problem 12-4. Panama Company uses perpetual inventory procedures to account for its inventory. At the end of 19+7 the firm's inventory had a cost of $88,000. Application of the lower-of-cost-or-market method to the inventory resulted in an inventory amount of $84,300. For the year the firm had goods available for sale of $175,000 and sales of $150,000. Prepare any necessary journal entries and a partial income statement for the year under each of the following assumptions:

(1) There is to be no separation of inventory losses.
(2) Inventory losses are to be reported separately with the inventory account being reduced.
(3) Inventory losses are to be reported separately, but the inventory account is to be maintained at cost.

Problem 12-5. The following information is taken from the records of Vaughn Corporation.

Date	Inventory at Cost	Inventory at Cost or Market
1- 1.............	$24,000	$23,000
1-31.............	26,000	25,000
2-28.............	27,000	24,500
3-31.............	26,500	26,300

The company reports inventory losses separately, but maintains the inventory account at cost. Assuming that the firm prepares monthly income statements, present all journal entries needed to account for the market fluctuations during the three-month period.

Problem 12-6. Ox Company is in the construction business. A long-term contract was entered into in 19+6. The contract price was $700,000 and the company expected to earn $80,000 before taxes. The following data is available:

Year Ended December 31	Cumulative Costs Incurred	Estimated Cost to Complete Contract
19+6	$ 49,600	$570,400
19+7	172,800	467,200
19+8	378,000	252,000

Prepare a schedule computing the income earned in 19+6, 19+7, and 19+8 by Ox Company under the percentage-of-completion method based on costs incurred.

Problem 12-7. The Newport Company manufactures and sells four products. A normal profit margin of 30 percent is usually maintained on each of the four products. Inventories of each are priced at cost or market, whichever is lower.

The following information was compiled as of December 31, 19+1:

Product	Original Cost	Cost to Replace	Estimated Disposal Cost	"Normal" Selling Price*	Expected Selling Price
A	$35.00	$42.00	$15.00	$70.00	$ 80.00
B.............................	47.50	45.00	20.50	95.00	95.00
C.............................	17.50	15.00	5.00	35.00	30.00
D	45.00	46.00	26.00	90.00	100.00

*"Normal" selling price = original cost ÷ (100% − the normal 50% gross margin rate)

Required:

(a) Why are expected selling prices important in the application of the lower-of-cost-or-market rule?

(b) Prepare a schedule containing unit amounts (including "floor" and "ceiling") for determining the lower of cost or market on an individual product basis. The last column of the schedule should contain for each product the unit amount for the purpose of inventory valuation resulting from the application of the lower-of-cost-or-market rule.

Problem 12-8. As of December 31, 19+1 Mercantile Manufacturing had a merchandise inventory of $90,000 at cost and $84,375 based on the lower of cost or market. It was projected that a further decline of $9,375 would take place before the merchandise could be sold. The company made two journal entries to disclose the above situation.

Required:

(a) Give the two journal entries.
(b) What entries should be made if the expected decline in market value occurs in 19+2?
(c) State how both balance sheet accounts created in (a) should have appeared in the December 31, 19+1 balance sheet.
(d) How should the inventory have appeared in the income statement for 19+1?
(e) Give the entries that would be made on December 31, 19+2, if cost and lower of cost or market of the inventory on that date were equal and no future price declines were expected.

Problem 12-9. Creek Construction Company began operations on January 1, 19+5 and took part in the following cash transactions in 19+5.

Cash receipts:	
Proceeds from issuance of capital stock	$ 37,500
Received on contracts	352,500
Cash disbursements:	
Contract costs	$315,450
Construction equipment	33,750
Administrative expenses	16,800

During 19+5, six contracts were signed. The following data pertains to these contracts:

Contract No.	Contract Price	Estimated Cost	Cash Costs to Date	Unpaid Bills 12/31/+5	19+5 Billings	19+5 Collections
1	$ 75,000	$ 63,750	$64,125		$75,000	$75,000
2	105,000	90,000	61,500	$6,000	78,750	73,125
3	95,625	82,315	81,000		95,625	93,750
4	187,500	168,750	75,000	9,375	82,500	67,500
5	33,750	26,250	21,750	1,875	30,375	28,125
6	127,500	112,500	12,075	4,800	18,750	15,000

Other data available:

(1) Billings are made on a percentage-of-completion basis.
(2) A suitable depreciation rate for the construction equipment is 25 percent. The use made of the construction equipment is in proportion to the other construction costs.
(3) Contracts 1 and 3 were completed during 19+5.
(4) Administrative expenses are considered as period costs.

Prepare a balance sheet as of December 31, 19+5 and an income statement for 19+5 based on the completed-contract method. If a provision for income taxes is required, use a rate of 50 percent.

Problem 12-10. Woods Company was organized on January 2, 19+5. The lower-of-cost-or-market inventory method was adopted and was to be applied by comparing the total cost and market for the entire inventory. A contra account was to be used to disclose market losses, the following entry was made as of December 31, 19+5:

Loss on reduction of inventory to lower of cost or market ..	1275	
Allowance for reduction of inventory to lower of cost or market		1275

During 19+6, the following procedures were applied to the Inventory account:

(1) Purchases were charged to the inventory account at cost.
(2) The inventory account was reduced for goods sold by the use of the unit costs applicable to the December 31, 19+5 inventory.

During 19+6, the prices of all categories of goods purchased for resale gradually and steadily increased. Nevertheless, December 31, 19+5 unit cost data were used throughout the year in making the daily computation for the cost of goods sold entry.

By the end of 19+6, costs had increased to such an extent that the accountant for Woods Company became concerned about the prospect of inventory price declines in the near future. He could not believe that the market prices prevailing at year end, the highest for many years, would continue for long. Accordingly, he used the same unit cost data used in pricing the December 31, 19+5 inventory to price the December 31, 19+6 inventory. The inventory dollar amount was thus more conservative and less vulnerable to losses from future price declines.

The December 31, 19+6 inventory priced at December 31, 19+5 costs amounted to $15,000. Because this was lower than the balance in the inventory account at year end, he increased the contra account, set up last year to disclose market losses, by the following journal entry dated December 31, 19+6:

Cost of goods sold	10,425	
Allowance for reduction of inventory to lower of cost or market		10,425

The following T-accounts show, in summary form in some instances, the entries made in compliance with the policies and decisions mentioned above.

Inventory

12/31/+5	Inventory, at cost	14,550	19+6	Cost of goods sold, priced at 12/31/+5 unit costs	179,550
19+6	Purchases, at cost	191,700			

Allowance for Reduction of Inventory to Lower of Cost or Market

			12/31/+5	Disclosure of market losses..............	1,275
			12/31/+6	Special adjustment...	10,425

Cost of Goods Sold

19+6	Cost of goods sold ...	179,550			
12/31/+6	Special adjustment...	10,425			

Prepare a more acceptable estimate of the December 31, 19+6 inventory for use in the 19+6 financial statements. Also adjust the cost of goods sold to conform to your estimate of the December 31, 19+6 inventory. You may assume that the merchandise flow follows a first-in, first-out sequence and that the business is not subject to seasonal volume changes.

Problem 12-11. Western Contractors, Inc. undertakes long-term, large-scale construction projects and began operations on October 15, 19+8 with contract No. 1 its only job during 19+8. A trial balance of the Company's general ledger at December 31, 19+9 is supplied:

WESTERN CONTRACTORS, INC.
Trial Balance
December 31, 19+9

Cash	$ 68,090	
Accounts receivable	136,480	
Cost of contracts in progress	421,320	
Plant and equipment	35,500	
Accumulated depreciation		$ 8,000
Accounts payable		72,728
Billings on contracts in progress		459,400
Capital stock		139,000
Retained earnings		2,862
Selling and administrative expenses	20,600	
	$681,990	$681,990

The following information is available:

(1) The company determines revenue from contracts using the percentage-of-completion method.

(2) At December 31, 19+9 there were three jobs in progress, the contract prices of which had been computed as follows:

	Contract 1	Contract 2	Contract 3
Labor and material costs	$169,000	$34,500	$265,700
Indirect costs	30,000	5,500	48,000
Total costs	199,000	40,000	313,700
Add: Profit in contract	40,000	3,000	30,300
Total Contract price	$239,000	$43,000	$344,000

During the year, billings are credited to Billings on Contracts in Progress. At year end this account is charged for the amount of revenue to be recognized.

(3) All job costs are charged to Costs of Contracts in Progress. Cost estimates are carefully derived by engineers and architects and are considered reliable. Data on costs to December 31, 19+9 are below:

		Incurred to Date		
Contract	Original Estimate	Total	Labor & Materials	Indirect
1	$199,000	$115,420	$ 92,620	$22,800
2	40,000	32,000	26,950	5,050
3	313,700	313,700	265,700	48,000
Totals	$552,700	$461,120	$385,270	$75,850

(4) At December 31, 19+8 accumulated costs on contract 1 were $39,800; no costs had accumulated on contracts 2 and 3.

Required:

(a) A schedule computing the percentage of completion of contracts in progress at December 31, 19+9.
(b) A schedule computing the amounts of revenue, related costs, and net income to be recognized in 19+9 from contracts in progress at December 31, 19+9.
(c) The adjusting journal entries required at December 31, 19+9.

Problem 12-12. Witt Corporation uses the lower-of-cost-or-market inventory method applied by comparing the total cost and market for the entire inventory and using the lower figure. It has been the company's experience that when changes in market occur, such changes are likely to affect all categories of goods carried in stock. In other words, if the price of one type of merchandise declines, similar declines will occur in the prices of the other types of merchandise carried in stock.

Starting in 19+9, the corporation adopted a modified perpetual inventory system, which was to operate as follows:

(1) Purchases to be charged to the inventory account at cost.
(2) Cost of sales to be computed daily and credited to the inventory account. The amount is based on the prices used in the beginning inventory; that is, the prices will be either exclusively cost or exclusively market, depending upon which were used in determining the preceding inventory.
(3) A physical inventory to be taken semiannually and priced at the lower of cost or market, as described in the opening sentence.
(4) The periodical inventory, as computed, to be entered in the accounts by adjusting the inventory account to a balance equal to the ending inventory, with the cost of sales account debited or credited to balance the entry.

The following T-accounts show, in summary form in some instances, the entries made for the six months ended June 30, 19+9, presumably in compliance with the above plan.

Inventory

12/31/+8	Inventory, at market, which is below cost ..	11,500	1/1/ to 6/30/+9	Cost of goods sold, priced at 12/31/+8 market prices	82,850
1/1 to 6/30/+9	Purchases, at cost	89,100	6/30/+9	Adjustment of account balance to equal 6/30/+9 physical inventory, priced at 12/31/+8 market prices, which are below 19+9 costs	6,600

Cost of Sales

1/1 to 6/30/+9	Cost of goods sold.......	82,850			
6/30/+9	Inventory adjustment ...	6,600			

A portion of the June 30, 19+9 physical inventory summary is reproduced below:

		Unit Price		Extended		
Item	Quantity	19+9 Cost	12/31/+8 Market	19+9 Cost	12/31/+8 Market	Lower of Cost or Market
A	20	$ 8	$7	$160	$ 140	
B	30	6	5	180	150	
C	10	10	9	100	90	
...						
Total............				$?	$11,150	$11,150

When quizzed, the bookkeeper said his reason for using December 31, 19+8 market prices in computing the June 30, 19+9 inventory was that the June 30, 19+9 market values were uniformly above cost, while the December 31, 19+8 market prices were uniformly below cost and thus more conservative.

Prepare a more acceptable estimate of the June 30, 19+9 inventory. You may assume that the June 30, 19+9 inventory was representative of the purchases made during the past six months (for instance, if January purchases were 10 percent of the goods purchased in the six months ended June 30, 19+9, you may assume that 10 percent of the goods in the inventory were from January purchases); you may also assume that all of the items in the December 31, 19+8 inventory have been disposed of by June 30, 19+9.

CHAPTER 13

QUESTIONS

1. Under what circumstances are inventory-estimating procedures used and what estimating procedures would be used in such circumstances?
2. With regard to the gross-margin method, answer the following questions.
   (a) What is the gross-margin method?
   (b) What are the assumptions underlying the use of the gross-margin method?
   (c) If the percentage markup on sales is 20 percent, what is the percentage markup on cost?
3. What are some problems in using the gross-margin method when LIFO has been in use?
4. With regard to the conventional retail-inventory method, answer the following questions.
   (a) What is the retail-inventory method?
   (b) What are the assumptions underlying the use of the retail-inventory method?
   (c) What is the cost ratio?
5. What is the distinction between the following?
   (a) Markups and markdowns
   (b) Markup cancellations and markdown cancellations
   (c) Net markup and net markdown

6. Under the conventional retail-inventory method, why are markdowns ignored?
7. What is the distinction between the following?
   (a) Markup cancellations and markdowns
   (b) Percentage markup on sales and percentage markup on cost
   (c) Conventional-retail method and LIFO-retail method
8. With regard to the LIFO-retail method, answer the following questions.
   (a) If a merchandising firm has been using the conventional retail-inventory method and wants to switch to the LIFO-retail method, what are the modifications to the conventional retail-inventory method necessary to accomplish the switch?
   (b) Once a merchandising firm has switched from the conventional retail-inventory method to the LIFO-retail method, how is the latter method applied assuming no material changes in the price level?
9. A company uses the LIFO-retail method. In recent years, selling prices have increased considerably from year to year for the same inventory items. If these changes in selling price are ignored in the inventory computations, what will be the effect on the inventory figure? How would you correct for the above situation in the computation of the inventory under the LIFO-retail method?
10. How would the following be accounted for under the retail-inventory method?
    (a) Sales discounts
    (b) Purchase returns and allowances
    (c) Sales returns and allowances
11. There are two main computations in which the gross-margin method differs from the conventional retail-inventory method. What are these two computations?
12. Is the conventional retail-inventory method a perpetual inventory procedure? Is the gross-margin method a perpetual inventory procedure?
13. The gross-margin method would not generally be considered to be an acceptable inventory valuation method for purposes of financial statement reporting. Why?
14. Is the objective of the conventional retail-inventory method the valuation of inventory at cost?
15. It is argued that the conventional retail-inventory method is subject to the same objections as those made against the lower-of-cost-or market method. What does this statement mean?

PROBLEMS

Problem 13-1. You are given below seven multiple choice statements. Select the correct answer to complete each statement and indicate the corresponding letter on a separate sheet of paper (e.g., 1-a, 2-a, etc.).

(1) To produce an inventory valuation that approximates the lower of cost or market using the conventional retail inventory method, the computation of the ratio of cost to retail should (a) include markups but not markdowns, (b) include markups and markdowns, (c) ignore both markups and markdowns, (d) include markdowns but not markups, (e) none of the above.

(2) The gross-margin method of inventory valuation is invalid when (a) a portion of the inventory is destroyed, (b) there is a substantial increase in inventory during

the year, (c) there is a general price decline during the year, (d) there is no beginning inventory because it is the first year of operations, (e) none of the above.

(3) On April 15, 19+2, a fire destroyed the entire merchandise inventory of John Anderson's retail store. The following data are available:

Sales, January 1 through April 15	$72,000
Inventory, January 1	10,000
Purchases, January 1 through April 15	70,000
Markup on cost	20%

The amount of the loss is estimated to be (a) $24,000, (b) $20,000, (c) $22,000, (d) $8,000, (e) none of the above.

(4) Price index numbers generally are used in connection with the (a) LIFO-retail-inventory method, (b) annuity method of calculating depreciation, (c) amortization of premium or discount of serial bond issues, (d) calculation of past-service costs of pension plans, (e) none of the above.

(5) The retail-inventory method is based on the assumption that the (a) final inventory and the total of goods available for sale contain the same proportion of high-cost- and low-cost-ratio goods, (b) ratio of gross margin to sales is approximately the same each period, (c) ratio of cost to retail changes at a constant rate, (d) proportions of markups and markdowns to selling price are the same, (e) none of the above.

(6) A major advantage of the retail-inventory method is that it (a) permits companies that use it to avoid taking an annual physical inventory, (b) gives a more accurate statement of inventory costs than other methods, (c) hides costs from customers and employees, (d) provides a method for inventory control and facilitates determination of the periodic inventory for certain types of companies, (e) none of the above.

(7) When the conventional retail-inventory method is used, markdowns are commonly ignored in the computation of the cost to retail ratio because (a) there may be no markdowns in a given year, (b) this tends to give a better approximation of the lower of cost or market, (c) markups are also ignored, (d) this tends to result in the showing of a normal profit margin in a period when no markdown goods have been sold, (e) none of the above.

Problem 13-2. You are given below six multiple choice statements which pertain to the following data concerning the retail-inventory method that were taken from the financial records of the Bandit Company.

	Cost	Retail
Beginning inventory	$18,600	$ 30,000
Purchases	91,000	154,000
Freight in	1,400	—
Net markups	—	1,000
Net markdowns	—	1,740
Sales	—	156,760

Select the correct answer to complete each statement and indicate the corresponding letter on a separate sheet of paper (e.g., 1-a, 2-a, etc.).

(1) The ending inventory at retail should be (a) $28,240, (b) $27,980, (c) $27,240, (d) $26,500, (e) none of the above.

(2) If the ending inventory is to be valued at approximately the lower of cost or market, the calculation of the cost to retail ratio should be based on goods available for sale at (1) cost and (2) retail respectively of (a) $111,000 and $186,740, (b) $111,000 and $185,000, (c) $111,000 and $182,260, (d) $109,600 and $184,000, (e) none of the above.

(3) If the ending inventory for the current period at cost amounts to $15,900, it appears that the rate of markon for the current period as compared to that for the preceding period was (a) the same, (b) higher than before, (c) lower than before, (d) indeterminate, (e) none of the above.

(4) If the foregoing figures are verified and a count of the ending inventory reveals that merchandise actually on hand amounts to $25,000 at retail, ignoring tax consequences the business has (a) realized a windfall gain of approximately $1,500, (b) sustained a loss in terms of cost of approximately $900, (c) sustained a loss in terms of cost of approximately $1,500, (d) no gain or loss as there is close coincidence of the inventories, (e) none of the above.

(5) If the LIFO-inventory method were used in conjunction with the data, the ending inventory at cost would be (a) $16,430, (b) $16,060, (c) $15,980, (d) $15,900, (e) none of the above.

(6) Assuming that the LIFO-inventory method were used in conjunction with the data and that the inventory at retail had increased during the period, then the computation of retail in the cost to retail ratio would (a) exclude both markups and markdowns and include beginning inventory, (b) include markups and exclude both markdowns and beginning inventory, (c) include both markups and markdowns and exclude beginning inventory, (d) exclude markups and include both markdowns and beginning inventory, (e) none of the above.

Problem 13-3. You have been engaged to audit the records of Gardner's Department store. The physical inventory was taken under your observation, however, the extension and computation of figures have not been completed to determine the ending inventory valuation. You need to know approximately what the figure will be before these computations will be ready. The store has averaged a 33⅓ percent gross margin over the past five years. The records available show the following data:

Sales	$953,725
Purchases	618,340
Beginning inventory	87,740
Sales returns and allowances	23,050
Freight in	12,250
Purchase discounts	8,360
Purchase returns and allowances	7,520

Required:

Determine the valuation of the ending inventory using the gross-margin method.

Problem 13-4. Accounting data relating to the operations of the shoe department of Campus Corner are presented below. Compute the ending inventory by the retail-inventory method.

Beginning inventory—cost	$12,920
Beginning inventory—sales price	19,105

Purchases—cost	33,771
Purchases—sales price	46,312
Purchase returns and allowances	1,093
Freight in	845
Departmental transfers in—cost	100
Departmental transfers in—sales price	140
Markups	1,207
Markup cancellations	274
Inventory shortage—sales price	704
Sales (including sales of $4,460 of items which were marked down from $5,920)	37,246

Problem 13-5. From the data presented below, for the sports department of Northern Department Store, compute the January 31, 19+5 inventory, using the retail inventory method. Carry percentages to two decimal places.

Inventory—January 31, 19+4:	
Cost	$ 26,250.00
Selling price	43,510.00
Purchases:	
Cost	130,560.00
Selling price	218,440.00
Freight in	3,830.00
Returns:	
Purchases:	
Cost	1,310.00
Selling price	2,460.00
Sales	4,140.00
Cash discounts:	
Purchases	2,410.00
Sales	3,860.00
Markups	5,310.00
Markdowns	8,120.00
Cancellations of:	
Markups	1,860.00
Markdowns	1,290.00
Sales	221,210.00

Problem 13-6. A fire destroyed the entire inventory of Used Furniture Mart during the night of September 10, 19+7. Although most of the accounting records were destroyed, sufficient information was recovered to compute the following balances:

As of June 30, 19+7, the end of the company's accounting period, the inventory valuation was $37,800.

As of September 10, 19+7:

Purchases	$23,180
Sales discounts	120
Freight in	384
Purchase returns and allowances	350
Sales returns and allowances	220
Purchase discounts	140
Sales	55,640

One of the items recovered from the fire was a copy of a condensed income statement for the preceding year.

USED FURNITURE MART
Condensed Income Statement
For the Year Ended June 30, 19+7

Sales		$282,000
Cost of goods sold		163,560
Gross margin		118,440
Deduct:		
Selling expenses	$57,600	
Administrative expenses	27,630	85,230
Net income before income taxes		$ 33,210
Income taxes		8,710
Net income		$ 24,500

Required:

Compute the cost of the inventory destroyed by the fire. Round amounts to nearest dollar.

Problem 13-7. The dollar-value LIFO method of inventory valuation was adopted by the Glenn Company on January 1, 19+3. Its inventory on that date was $75,000. The inventory at December 31, 19+3 was $71,500 based on prices existing on that date. Using the price level at January 1, 19+3 as 100, the price level at December 31, 19+3 was 110.

Required:

(a) Using the dollar-value LIFO method, calculate the amount of inventory at December 31, 19+3.

(b) The inventory prices existing on December 31, 19+4 was $90,000 and the price level was 125. Using the dollar-value LIFO method, calculate the inventory on December 31, 19+4.

Problem 13-8. City Company lost its entire inventory of merchandise by fire early in January, 19+9, before completing the physical inventory that was being taken as of December 31, 19+8. The following information was taken from the books of the company as of December 31, 19+7 and 19+8.

	December 31, 19+7	December 31, 19+8
Inventory—January 1	$ 42,380	$ 45,755
Purchases	159,045	174,433
Purchase returns and allowances	8,021	10,015
Sales	196,677	203,317
Sales returns and allowances	2,402	2,167
Wages	17,743	18,356
Salaries	8,000	9,000
Taxes other than income	3,732	3,648
Rent	5,400	5,400
Insurance	967	982
Light, heat, and water	1,134	1,271
Advertising	4,250	2,680
Interest expense	2,755	3,020
Depreciation expense	1,255	1,280
Furniture and fixtures, net of depreciation	10,065	10,570
Miscellaneous expenses	6,634	6,897

Required:

From the above information, you are to estimate the book amount of the inventory destroyed by the fire, assuming that there were no transactions after December 31, 19+8.

Problem 13-9. Given the following data, compute the inventory for December 31, 19+4, 19+5, 19+6, and 19+7 using the dollar-value LIFO inventory method. The company adopted dollar-value LIFO as of January 1, 19+1. The inventory shown in the December 31, 19+3 balance sheet amounted to $6,000, which was less than the inventory when dollar-value LIFO was adopted.

Inventory Data

	Inventory Computed by Using Average Costs of	
	Current Year	Base Year
December 31, 19+4	$6,804	$6,480
December 31, 19+5	7,128	6,480
December 31, 19+6	7,392	6,600
December 31, 19+7	7,475	6,500

Problem 13-10. Ready Manufacturing Corporation has followed the practice of inventorying its finished goods at selling prices and has applied the same percentage of markup to its goods in process; the company has prepared the following statement on this basis.

READY MANUFACTURING CORPORATION
Income Statement
For the Year Ended December 31, 19+9

Sales			$956,300
Cost of goods sold:			
Raw materials used (at cost)		$221,362	
Direct labor		304,162	
Manufacturing overhead		103,912	
Total manufacturing costs		$629,436	
Work in process (on selling price basis):			
December 31, 19+8	$627,040		
December 31, 19+9	427,350	199,690	
Goods manufactured		$829,126	
Finished goods (at selling prices):			
December 31, 19+8	$165,760		
December 31, 19+9	458,210	292,450	536,676
Gross margin			$419,624
Selling and administrative expenses			367,766
Net income			$ 51,858

Required:

Prepare a corrected statement, assuming that the percentage of markup for the current year is normal. Show supporting computations.

Problem 3-11. Quality Stores Corporation has employed the retail-inventory method in the computation of merchandise inventory for two years. The method was properly initiated by a certified public accountant. The corporation's procedures in applying the retail-inventory method are shown by the summary below covering the two-year period ending January 31, 19+2.

	Data for the Year Ended January 31,			
	19+1		19+2	
	Cost	Retail	Cost	Retail
Beginning inventory	$ 52,100	$ 75,700	$ 58,212	$ 80,850
Purchases—net	274,610	382,800	334,167	439,150
Freight in	3,410		2,801	
Totals.................	$330,120	$458,500	$395,180	$520,000
Cost ratio:				
19+1...........	72%			
19+2...........	76%			
Add net price changes on marked merchandise (Note)		6,550		9,545
Totals.................		$465,050		$529,545
Sales......................		384,200		415,845
Inventory at retail		$ 80,850		$113,700
Inventory computations:				
72% of $80,850 or $58,212				
76% of $113,700, or $86,412				

Note. The records show that net markups exceed net markdowns by 100 percent.

During the month of December, 19+1, the corporation made a purchase of special sale merchandise for $79,200, f.o.b. destination. The special sale merchandise was marked to sell for $90,000, and no changes have been made in such selling prices. As of January 31, 19+2, two-thirds of this special-purchase merchandise has been sold.

The corporation did not take a physical inventory as of January 31, 19+1. A physical inventory was taken as of January 31, 19+2, at retail, but the corporation's accountant made no use of the information. The January 31, 19+2 inventory sheets show the following totals:

Special sale merchandise	$ 30,000
Regular merchandise	81,700
Total inventory, at retail	$111,700

Required:

Compute the January 31, 19+2 merchandise inventory as you would if you were the corporation's auditor. Show computations and carry percentages to two decimal places, for example, 45.85 percent.

Problem 13-12. The Calvert Department Store uses the retail-inventory method. All of the inventory records are kept on a selling-price basis with each department using its own gross-margin code marked on the merchandise. Then at the end of each year a physical inventory is taken by departments and a reconciliation made. The following information is available from the accounting department records:

	Department		
	Bargain Basement	Ladies' Wear	Men's Wear
Beginning inventory at cost ...	$ 75,000	$ 90,000	$ 52,500
Beginning inventory at retail ..	100,000	135,000	75,000
Sales ...	650,000	1,000,500	510,000
Markups ...	60,000	48,500	27,250
Markup cancellations ...	15,000	7,170	12,385
Purchases at cost ...	630,000	984,600	497,385
Markdowns ...	75,000	30,000	25,000
Markdown cancellations ...	20,000	5,270	12,585
Physical inventory at retail ...	278,000	625,000	275,000
Regular rate of gross margin ..	25%	33⅓%	30%

Required:

(a) Determine the ending inventory for each department.

(b) Prepare a reconciliation of book inventory with physical inventory to determine amount of merchandise not accounted for by departments.

Problem 13-13. Duke Corporation adopted the dollar-value LIFO method one year ago. Compute, to two decimal places, the inventories for years 19+2, 19+3, and 19+4. Last year's (19+1) inventory (base) was $17,000.

Inventory Quantities

	Year		
Description	19+2	19+3	19+4
X ...	1,000	1,100	1,100
Y ...	1,200	1,250	1,300
Z ...	1,610	1,700	1,800

Inventory Prices

	Year			
Description	19+1	19+2	19+3	19+4
X ...	$4.00	$4.04	$4.25	$4.40
Y ...	4.60	4.65	4.85	5.05
Z ...	5.00	5.16	5.30	5.49

Problem 13-14. Compute the inventories for Phoenix Company for the dates listed below:

December 31, 19+2, 19+3, and 19+4.

You may assume that the company adopted the LIFO retail-inventory method in 19+2.

Year Ended December 31,	Cost	Retail
19+1:		
Beginning inventory ...	$ 23,920	$ 46,000
Purchases ...	108,000	185,000
Freight in ...	6,080	

Year Ended December 31,	Cost	Retail
Markups—net		2,000
Markdowns—net		3,000
Sales		184,000
19+2:		
Purchases	124,000	230,000
Freight in	9,110	
Markups—net		3,600
Markdowns—net		4,100
Sales		224,500
19+3:		
Purchases	134,800	259,800
Freight in	10,800	
Markups—net		4,100
Markdowns—net		3,900
Sales		247,400
19+4:		
Purchases	148,200	270,400
Freight in	11,100	
Markups—net		4,200
Markdowns—net		4,600
Sales		270,900

Indexes of selling prices on December 31 were:

19+1	100
19+2	102
19+3	106
19+4	110

Problem 13-15. On April 15, 19+6, fire damaged the office and warehouse of King Wholesale Corporation. The only accounting record saved was the general ledger from which the following trial balance was prepared:

KING WHOLESALE CORPORATION
Trial Balance
March 31, 19+6

Cash	7,000	
Accounts receivable	27,000	
Inventory, December 31, 19+5	50,000	
Land	24,000	
Building and equipment	120,000	
Accumulated depreciation		27,200
Other assets	3,600	
Accounts payable		23,700
Other expense accruals		7,200
Capital stock		100,000
Retained earnings		47,700
Sales		90,400
Purchases	42,000	
Other expenses	22,600	
Totals	296,200	296,200

The following data and information have been gathered:

(1) The fiscal year of the Corporation ends on December 31.

(2) An examination of the April bank statement and cancelled checks revealed that checks written during the period April 1–15 totalled $11,600: $5,700 paid to accounts payable as of March 31, $2,000 for April merchandise shipments, and $3,900 paid for other expenses. Deposits during the same period amounted to $10,650, which consisted of receipts on account from customers with the exception of a $450 refund from a vendor for merchandise returned in April.

(3) Correspondence with suppliers revealed unrecorded obligations at April 15 of $8,500 for April merchandise shipments, including $1,300 for shipments in transit on that date.

(4) Customers acknowledged indebtedness of $26,400 at April 15, 19+6. It was also estimated that customers owed another $5,000 that will never be acknowledged or recovered. Of the acknowledged indebtedness, $600 will probably be uncollectible.

(5) The companies insuring the inventory agreed that the Corporation's fire loss claim should be based on the assumption that the overall gross margin ratio for the past two years was in effect during the current year. The Corporation's audited financial statements disclosed the following:

	Year Ended December 31,	
	19+5	19+4
Net sales	$400,000	$300,000
Net purchases	226,000	174,000
Beginning inventory	45,000	35,000
Ending inventory	50,000	45,000

(6) Inventory with a cost of $6,500 was salvaged and sold for $3,000. The balance of the inventory was a total loss.

Required:

Prepare a schedule computing the amount of the inventory fire loss. The supporting schedule of the computation of the gross margin should be in good form.

Problem 13-16. Under your guidance as of January 1, 19+5, Little Corner Sporting Goods Store installed the retail-inventory method of accounting for its merchandise.

When you undertook the preparation of the store's financial statements at June 30, 19+5, the following data were available:

	Cost	Selling Price
Inventory, January 1	$26,900	$ 40,000
Markdowns		10,500
Markups		19,500
Markdown cancellations		6,500
Markup cancellations		4,500
Purchases	86,200	111,800
Sales		122,000
Purchase returns and allowances	1,500	1,800
Sales returns and allowances		6,000

Required:

(a) Prepare a schedule to compute Little Corner Sporting Goods Store's June 30, 19+5 inventory under the LIFO-retail method of accounting for inventories. Note that the beginning inventory is already at cost.

(b) Without prejudice to your solution to part (a), assume that you computed the June 30, 19+5 inventory to be $44,100 at retail and the ratio of cost to retail to be 80 percent. The general price level has increased from 100 at January 1, 19+5 to 105 at June 30, 19+5. Prepare a schedule to compute the June 30, 19+5 inventory at the June 30 price level under the dollar-value LIFO method.

Problem 13-17. Lopez Department Store converted from the conventional retail method to the LIFO-retail-inventory method on January 1, 19+6 and is now considering converting to the dollar-value LIFO inventory method. Management requested during your examination of the financial statements for the year ended December 31, 19+7 that you furnish a summary showing certain computations of inventory costs for the past three years.

Available information follows:

(1) The inventory at January 1, 19+5 had a retail value of $45,000 and a cost of $27,500 based on the conventional retail method.

(2) Transactions during 19+5 were as follows:

	Cost	Retail
Gross purchases	$282,000	$490,000
Purchase returns	6,500	10,000
Purchase discounts	5,000	
Gross sales		492,000
Sales returns		5,000
Employee discounts		3,000
Freight in	26,500	
Net markups		25,000
Net markdowns		10,000

(3) The retail value of the December 31, 19+6 inventory was $56,100, the cost ratio for 19+6 under the LIFO-retail method was 62 percent and the regional price index was 102 percent of the January 1, 19+6 price level.

(4) The retail value of the December 31, 19+7 inventory was $48,300, the cost ratio for 19+7 under the LIFO retail method was 61 percent and the regional price index was 105 percent of the January 1, 19+6 price level.

Required:

(a) Prepare a schedule showing the computation of the cost of inventory on hand at December 31, 19+5 based on the conventional retail method.

(b) Prepare a schedule showing the computation of the cost of inventory on hand at the store on December 31, 19+5 based on the LIFO-retail method. Lopez Department Store does not consider beginning inventories in computing its LIFO retail cost ratio. Assume that the retail value of the December 31, 19+5 inventory was $50,000.

(c) Without prejudice to your solution to part (b), assume that you computed the December 31, 19+5 inventory (retail value $50,000) under the LIFO-retail method at a cost of $28,000. Prepare a schedule showing the computations of the cost of the store's 19+6 and 19+7 year-end inventories under the dollar-value LIFO method.

CHAPTER 14

QUESTIONS

1. When two or more classes of securities are purchased for a single price, how is the cost of each class of security determined?
2. Describe two different methods of accounting for stock investments.
3. Under what circumstances might market declines pertaining to long-term stock investments be recorded on the books of the investor? What procedure is followed to record the decline?
4. What is the proper classification of the account Cost of Stock Warrants? What typical events cause the account to be credited?
5. When some of the company's own bonds have been acquired by a sinking fund established to retire the bonds, how should such bonds be accounted for?
6. Describe two ways in which business combinations may be accounted for. May either alternative be used for any given business combination?
7. If the acquisition of a firm is treated as a purchase, what are the implications for the consolidated balance sheet?
8. To what extent is the use of the equity method to account for stock investments presently recommended?
9. What is the major argument in favor of the pooling of interests treatment of a business combination?
10. In what way does the increase in the cash surrender value of a life insurance policy carried by a firm affect the firm's financial statements?
11. How may dividend restrictions required by bond indentures be disclosed in the financial statements?
12. Without using amounts, present entries required to account for the following sinking funds transactions: (a) contribution of cash to the fund; (b) collection of income of the fund; (c) payment of expenses by the fund; (d) purchase of securities.

PROBLEMS

Problem 14-1. Nederland Corporation acquired common stock of Madison Broadcasting Network as follows:

Date	Shares	Total Cost
November 9, 19+1	150	$4,585.35
June 17, 19+2	80	2,538.80
September 28, 19+3	160	4,057.60

On July 20, 19+3, Madison Broadcasting Network issued a 10 percent stock dividend. On October 2, 19+3, Nederland Corporation sold 210 shares of the stock at $27.75 per share.

The following cash dividends were declared during 19+3:

April 1—40 cents per share to holders of record on April 15, payable on May 4.

September 15—50 cents per share to holders of record on September 30, payable on October 12.
December 2—70 cents per share to holders of record on December 23, payable on January 3, 1961.

No cash dividends were declared during 19+2.

Required:

(a) Determine the gain or loss on the sale, computing the cost of shares sold on the basis of: (a) First-in, first-out; (b) average cost.
(b) Compute the amount of cash received during 19+3 from dividends.
(c) Compute the amount of dividend revenue for 19+3.

Problem 14-2. During 19+4, Pine Point Corporation purchased common stock of Cleaver Corporation as follows:

January 23	250 shares at $48 per share
April 4	200 shares at $50 per share

Cleaver Corporation issued a 20 percent stock dividend on February 28, 19+4.

Common stock rights were issued on September 18, 19+4, entitling holders to purchase one new common share at $39 for each ten shares held. On September 18, 19+4, the rights were being traded at $1 each, and the stock ex-rights was being traded at $49 per share.

On October 2, 19+4, Pine Point Corporation sold 100 rights which pertained to the stock purchase of January 23, 19+4. Sales price was $.90 per right. The corporation paid a brokerage fee of $5 on the sale of the rights. The remaining rights were exercised on October 5, 19+4.

Required:

(a) Computation of gain or loss on the sale of the rights.
(b) Computation of the number of shares in each lot, and the cost basis of each lot as of January 1, 19+5.

Problem 14-3. Tanner Corporation purchased 5,000 shares of Cobble Company's 6 percent cumulative preferred stock with a par value of $150. In order to make the stock more attractive as an investment, Cobble Company gives 1 share of common stock, par value $30, as a bonus for each 2 shares of preferred stock purchased. The total purchase price of the stock was $800,000. At the time of the sale the market price of the common stock was $35 per share. Two months later Tanner Corp. sold 200 of the preferred shares for $148 per share.

Present journal entries to record the information above on the books of Tanner Corporation.

Problem 14-4. Present journal entries to record the selected transactions described below, relating to the sinking fund of Lakeview Apartments, Incorporated.

(1) The payment of $10,000 cash to the sinking fund.
(2) The purchase of securities for the sinking fund for $8,200, including $150 accrued interest.
(3) The payment of $75 from the sinking fund for sinking fund expenses.
(4) The sale for $28,000, including accrued interest of $60, of sinking fund securities having a book amount of $26,400.
(5) The retirement, at par, of $30,000 par value of bonds payable before maturity.

The bonds thus retired were issued at 103. Their carrying value at retirement was 101.

(6) The return to general cash of $920 remaining in the fund after the retirement of the bond issue.

Problem 14-5. Central Corporation organized The Center Sales Company on May 1, 19+6, for the purpose of marketing the products of Central Corporation. The corporation paid $200,000 in cash to the company in exchange for the company's entire issue of authorized capital stock, consisting of 50,000 no-par shares.

The record of net income earned and dividends paid by The Center Sales Company during 19+6, 19+7, 19+8, and 19+9 appeared as follows:

Year Ended December 31,	Net Income	Cash Dividends Paid
19+6	$14,000	$ —
19+7	30,000	10,000
19+8	36,000	24,000
19+9	5,000*	10,000

*Loss.

Prepare a schedule showing the effect of the net income and dividends of The Center Sales Company on the accounts of Central Corporation, assuming that the corporation employs each of the following methods of accounting for its investment in the subsidiary: (1) Cost method; (2) Equity method.

Problem 14-6. "Investment in Capitol Corporation" appeared as follows on the books of Arcade Corporation at the end of 19+8:

Investment in Capitol Corporation

19+8			19+8		
Jan. 2	300 shares	48,060	Mar. 24	1,250 shares at $36	45,000
Mar. 13	1,200 shares	42,600	Apr. 1	400 shares at $36	14,400
Sept. 10		2,560			

Additional information:

(1) On January 26, 19+8, 4 new shares were received in exchange for each old share.

(2) On March 22, 19+8, a 10 percent stock dividend was issued to holders of record on March 5, 19+8.

(3) On August 29, 19+8, rights were issued entitling stockholders to subscribe to one share at $32 for each five shares held. On this date, rights were selling for $.75, and the stock ex-rights was selling for $35.25. During September, Arcade Corporation sold some of the rights at $1.00, crediting Retained Earnings for the proceeds, and exercised the remainder.

(4) On October 26, 19+8, an additional paid-in capital account was created on the books of Capitol Corporation by a reduction of par value of the stock, and a cash dividend of $3 per share was paid on November 18, 19+8, to holders of record on November 1, 19+8, and charged to the newly created additional paid-in capital account.

Prepare all necessary adjusting entries as of December 31, 19+8; assume that *fifo* procedures are applicable when securities are sold.

Problem 14-7. The condensed balance sheet of Wise Company at July 31, 19+8 is presented below.

WISE COMPANY
Balance Sheet
July 31, 19+8

Assets		**Equities**	
Current assets	$110,000	Current liabilities ...	$100,000
Long-lived assets (net)...	86,000	Capital stock	100,000
Investments.............	10,000	Retained earnings...	22,000
Other assets.............	16,000		
	$222,000		$222,000

On this date Owl Company acquired all the stock of Wise Company for a cash payment of $136,000. It was agreed that the assets of Wise Company had fair market values on this date as follows: current assets, $105,000; long-lived assets (net), $96,000; investments, $13,000; and other assets, $15,000.

Required:

(a) The entry on the books of Owl Company to record the acquisition of the Wise Company stock, which represents a purchase.

(b) The entries required on the consolidated working papers to prepare a consolidated balance sheet for the two companies at July 31.

Problem 14-8. On December 31, 19+3, Astro Company purchased all of the capital stock of Rocket Company, consisting of 4,000 shares with a par value of $100 each, for $300,000. The balance sheets of the two companies just after the acquisition appeared as follows:

Assets	Astro Company	Rocket Company
Cash..	$ 50,000	$ 40,000
Accounts receivable	160,000	70,000
Inventories..	152,000	120,000
Investment in Rocket Company....................	300,000	
Land	120,000	60,000
Buildings..	202,000	30,000
	$984,000	$320,000
Equities		
Notes payable......................................	$ 50,000	$ -0-
Accounts payable...................................	104,000	20,000
Capital stock......................................	500,000	400,000
Capital in excess of par value......................	100,000	
Retained earnings (Deficit).........................	230,000	(100,000)
	$984,000	$320,000

The accounts receivable of Rocket Company include $40,000 receivable from Astro Company.

Prepare a consolidated balance sheet for the two companies at December 31, 19+3.

Problem 14-9. On April 1, 19+8, Morse Manufacturing Company acquired 17,000 of the 20,000 oustanding shares of stock of Cody Supply Corporation for $10 per share. On this date the stockholders' equity of Cody Supply Corporation included common stock of $100,000 and retained earnings of $64,500.

On April 25, 19+8, Morse Manufacturing Company received a cash dividend of 50 cents per share which had been declared by Cody Supply Corporation on March 15, 19+8, payable to stockholders of record on April 10, 19+8.

Cody Supply Corporation reported net income of $36,000 for the year ended December 31, 19+8, earned evenly during the year. No additional dividends were declared during the year 19+8.

During 19+9, net income of Cody Supply Corporation amounted to $34,000, and dividends declared were as follows:

April 30—5 percent stock dividend.
October 15—Cash dividend of 80 cents per share.

Required:

(a) All journal entries required on the books of Morse Manufacturing Company during 19+8 and 19+9 to account for the investment using the equity method.
(b) The amount at which the investment would be reported on the balance sheets of Morse Manufacturing Company at December 31, 19+8 and December 31, 19+9.

Problem 14-10. Toot Company purchased 8,000 of the 10,000 outstanding shares of $10 par value capital stock of Midwest Industries on July 1, 19+6, for $11 per share. On January 2, 19+8, Toot Company purchased an additional 1,000 shares for $12 per share. On January 2, 19+9 Toot Company sold 500 shares from its last acquisition for $14 per share.

The earnings and dividend record of Midwest Industries subsequent to July 1, 19+6, was as follows:

	Net Income* (Loss)	Cash Dividends	
		Date Paid	Amount Per Share
Year ended December 31:			
19+6	$ 6,000	December 10	$ .50
19+7	12,800	July 1	1.00
19+8	26,400	September 10	1.20
19+9	(1,000)	September 10	.50

*Assume that net income and loss accrue evenly throughout the year.

Give the journal entries on the books of Toot Company to record the data presented, except closing entries, using the equity method of accounting for the investment in Midwest Industries.

Problem 14-11. The October 1, 19+4 stockholders' equity accounts of Company A and Company B are presented below.

	Company A	Company B
Common stock	$100,000	$200,000
Retained earnings	40,000	60,000
	$140,000	$260,000

On this date Company B acquired all of the stock of Company A by issuing to Company A shareholders 15,000 shares of Company B's $10 par value common stock.

Assuming that the acquisition must be treated as a pooling of interests, prepare the following:

(a) The entry on the books of Company B to record acquisition of the Company A stock.
(b) The entry required for the stockholders' equity accounts on the working papers for a consolidated balance sheet as of October 1, 19+4.
(c) The stockholders' equity section of the consolidated balance sheet prepared at October 1, 19+4.

Problem 14-12. Harold Company purchased a $100,000 life insurance policy on the life of its president on July 1, 19+3, the beginning of its accounting period. Information concerning the policy during the first five years is presented below.

Year	Premium	Dividends	Cash Surrender Value at End of Year
1	$3,000	—	—
2	3,000	—	$1,300
3	3,000	$350	2,900
4	3,000	380	4,400
5	3,000	410	8,000

Premiums are payable annually in advance on July 1. Dividends shown above are deductible in determining the premium to be paid for that year. The president of the company died on January 2, 19+7, at which time a claim was filed with the insurance company. The policy provides that unexpired premiums will be refunded. Full settlement was received from the insurance company on January 20, 19+7.

Prepare all journal entries required to account for the insurance policy on the books of Harold Company for the period July 1, 19+3 to January 20, 19+7.

Problem 14-13. The Rawhide Mining Company was required to create a sinking fund by the deposit of 20 cents for each ton mined; but it was also provided that the fund, at the end of any year, must be $10,000 times the number of years which have elapsed or the accumulated amounts of contributions on a tonnage basis, whichever is larger. Earnings of the fund were not to be considered in measuring this minimum. The fund earned 6 percent a year.

The following record of tons mined was presented:

1st year	35,640 tons
2nd year	44,720 tons
3rd year	56,820 tons
4th year	68,310 tons
5th year	42,380 tons

Required:

(a) A table showing:
  (1) The annual contributions to the fund.
  (2) The annual amounts earned by the fund.
  (3) The balance in the fund at the close of each year.
(b) The journal entry to record the changes in the fund during the third year.

Problem 14-14. After extended negotiations Bock Corporation bought from Carlton Company most of the latter's assets on June 30, 19+1. At the time of the sale Carlton's accounts (adjusted to June 30, 19+1) reflected the following descriptions and amounts for the assets transferred:

	Cost	Contra (Valuation) Account	Book Amount
Receivables......	$ 83,600	$ 3,000	$ 80,600
Inventory........	107,000	5,200	101,800
Land.............	20,000	—	20,000
Buildings	207,500	73,000	134,500
Fixtures and equipment....	205,000	41,700	163,300
Goodwill	50,000	—	50,000
	$673,100	$122,900	$550,200

You ascertain that the contra (valuation) accounts were allowance for uncollectibles, allowance to reduce inventory to market and accumulated depreciation.

During the extended negotiations Carlton held out for a consideration of approximately $600,000 (depending upon the level of the receivables and inventory). However, as of June 30, 19+1 Carlton agreed to accept Bock's offer of $450,000 cash plus 1 percent of the net sales (as defined in the contract) of the next five years with payments at the end of each year. Carlton expects that Bock's total net sales during this period will exceed $15,000,000.

Present journal entries to record the purchase and the first two years payments assuming sales are $3,000,000 both years.

Problem 14-15. Balance sheets of two companies which are negotiating an acquisition are presented below.

Balance Sheets
December 31, 19+3

Assets	Hall Company	Hill Company
Cash	$118,700	$124,800
Accounts receivable	131,800	137,900
Inventories	98,700	164,700
Long-lived assets	294,000	83,000
	$643,200	$130,400
Equities		
Accounts payable	$ 31,500	$ 16,500
Accrued expenses	26,700	28,900
Notes payable	90,000	
Capital stock—$50 par value	300,000	50,000
Paid-in capital in excess of par		10,000
Retained earnings	195,000	25,000
	$643,200	$130,400

As of January 1, 19+4, Hall Company acquired all the stock of Hill Company in exchange for 1,500 shares of Hall Company stock.

Required:

(a) The consolidated balance sheet as of January 1, 19+4, assuming the acquisition is treated as a pooling of interests.

(b) Assuming that Hall Company made the acquisition by paying $85,000 cash for all the stock of Hill Company, prepare the consolidated balance sheet as of January 1, 19+4.

CHAPTER 15

QUESTIONS

1. What are the basic characteristics of long-lived assets?
2. When a long-lived asset is purchased on the installment arrangement, but no interest is specified in the contract, does this mean that the total amount paid under the contract is the total cost of the asset?
3. How is the cost of a new asset determined when it is acquired in a transaction involving the trade-in of an old asset?
4. Describe two different methods of accounting for the acquisition of an asset when a trade-in is involved.
5. How is the cost of an asset determined when it is acquired by the issuance of securities?
6. To what extent should overhead be included as an element in the cost of a long-lived asset constructed by a firm for its own use?
7. Under what circumstances might it be proper to recognize a loss on the construction of an asset? Is it ever proper to recognize a gain on the construction of an asset?
8. Distinguish between an addition to an asset and an improvement in an asset.
9. If an asset is insured under a policy with an 80 percent coinsurance clause and the firm carries insurance equal to at least 80 percent of the insurable value of the property, does this mean that the insurance company will pay 100 percent of all losses incurred?
10. What distinction, if any, should be made in the books and in the balance sheet between land held for speculation and land used as a factory site?
11. What is a conditional sales contract? How should assets acquired under this arrangement be accounted for?
12. What items may properly be included as a part of the cost of the following long-lived assets: (a) buildings; (b) machinery?

PROBLEMS

Problem 15-1. Snopes Company made the following individual purchases:

From *XY* Realty Company:	
Land and buildings	$90,000
From Acme Supply:	
Machinery and office equipment	36,000
From Central Auto Agency:	
Delivery equipment	9,000

The question of apportioning the cost of the purchases among the assets arose, so an appraisal was made, shortly after the assets were purchased, which disclosed the following amounts:

Land	$ 22,500
Buildings	90,000
Machinery	22,500
Office equipment	15,000
Delivery equipment	7,800
Total	$157,800

State the costs properly assignable to each asset and your reasons therefor.

Problem 15-2. Finnesse Company purchased some new machinery. From the following data prepare a schedule showing the proper amount to be capitalized as the cost of the new machinery.

List price of machinery	$12,000
Cash discount available but not taken on purchase	240
Freight on new machinery	125
Cost of removing old machinery	235
Installation costs of new machinery	305
Testing costs before machinery was put into regular operation, including $80 wages of regular machine operator	165
Loss on premature retirement of old machinery	175
Estimated cost of manufacturing similar machinery in company's own plant, excluding overhead	7,500
Estimated cost of manufacturing similar machinery in company's own plant, including overhead	11,800

Problem 15-3. Mixon Corporation acquired a new machine by trading in an old machine and paying $24,000 in cash. The old machine originally cost $40,000 and had accumulated depreciation at the date of exchange of $30,000. The new machine could have been purchased outright for $50,000 cash.

Required:

(a) Journal entries to record the trade-in using (1) the accounting method, and (2) the income-tax method.

(b) Using the accounting method give the journal entry to record the above transaction if the new machine had a list price of $52,000, was commonly selling for $50,000 cash, and Mixon Corporation were allowed $28,000 for its old machine.

Problem 15-4. The delivery trucks account in the ledger of Grand Corporation for the year 19+8 contains the following entries:

Debits

January 1	Trucks 1, 2, 3, 4 at $3,000	12,000
May 1	Truck 5	4,000
September 1	Truck 6	5,000

Credits

September 1	Truck 2	1,800
October 1	Truck 4	1,600

The accumulated depreciation—delivery trucks account had a balance of $5,600 on January 1, 19+8.

Upon analyzing the entries in the account, you find the following facts:

(1) Truck 5 replaced Truck 1, which was junked. Depreciation accrued on January 1 for Truck 1 amounted to $1,400. Truck 5 was purchased for cash.

(2) Truck 2 was traded in for $1,800 on the purchase of Truck 6, costing $5,000; the difference was paid in cash. Depreciation accrued on Truck 2 on January 1 amounted to $600.

(3) Truck 4 was totally destroyed in an accident on October 1. Accumulated depreciation on this truck amounted to $1,000 on January 1; $1,600 was recovered from the insurance company.

The rate of depreciation is 25 percent per year. The company follows the practice of computing depreciation for fractional periods to the nearest full month.

Give journal entries to adjust the accounts in accordance with the above facts, and show balances of the asset and accumulated depreciation accounts as of December 31, 19+8.

Problem 15-5. Prepare journal entries to record the following transactions involving the acquisition of long-lived assets by Niles Company.

(1) Land and buildings were acquired on June 1, 19+9, by the issuance of 5,200 shares of the corporation's $10 par value common stock. The seller had placed a value of $60,000 on the property, one-fourth of which was applicable to the land. The corporation's common stock was quoted at $11 on the stock exchange on June 1, 19+9.

(2) On June 16, 19+9, a tract of land, adjacent to the new plant, was acquired in exchange for an issue of 7 percent debenture bonds, dated June 1, 19+9, with a face value of $60,000. An independent appraisal showed the value of the land to be $58,000.

(3) On July 1, 19+9, an abandoned building was removed from the tract of land acquired in (2). The cost of removal, which was paid in cash, was $3,200, and $1,800 was received from the sale of salvaged materials.

(4) On July 22, 19+9, a machine was purchased for cash. The invoice price thereof was $12,400 and a 2 percent discount was allowed for cash payment. Power and wages applicable to the breaking-in period and the testing period were estimated to be $10 and $90, respectively.

(5) On August 15, 19+9, the company requested an allowance from the Machinery Manufacturing Company because the machine proved lacking in certain performance capabilities. The manufacturer granted a cash allowance of $1,000, which was received on August 31, 19+9.

Problem 15-6. Hooper Corporation purchased a new wrecker to use in providing towing services to industrial vehicles. The following data relating to this wrecker was obtained from the journal of the company.

19+3				
July	1	Machinery	27,000.00	
		Accounts payable		27,000.00
		Purchase of wrecker truck. Terms: 2/30; n/90.		

Date	Account	Debit	Credit
19+3			
5	Transportation	150.00	
	Cash		150.00
	Transportation cost of the wrecker truck		
30	Accounts payable	27,000.00	
	Notes payable		22,500.00
	Cash		4,410.00
	Purchase discounts		90.00
	Renegotiated terms: one-year, 8% note; balance in cash, less discount		
Dec. 31	Depreciation expense—Machinery	1,350.00	
	Accumulated depreciation—Machinery		1,350.00
	Depreciation for six months. Useful life, 10 years.		
19+4			
Jan. 2	Miscellaneous expense	300.00	
	Cash		300.00
	Installation of two-way radio on wrecker truck.		
July 1	Maintenance expense	90.00	
	Cash		90.00
	Installation of rotating warning light on wrecker		
30	truck	22,500.00	
	Notes payable	1,800.00	
	Machinery		24,300.00
	Cash		
Dec. 31	Paid 8% note at maturity	1,485.00	
	Depreciation expense—Machinery		1,485.00
	Accumulated depreciation—Machinery		
	Annual depreciation		
19+5			
Sept. 1	Machinery	675.00	
	Cash		675.00
	Replaced winch motor with a more powerful one to increase the efficiency of wrecker truck. New motor, which cost about 50% more than the smaller, discarded motor, will not extend useful life of the wrecker truck.		
Dec. 31	Depreciation expense—Machinery	1,537.50	
	Accumulated depreciation—Machinery		1,537.50
	Annual depreciation		

Prepare a schedule showing the debits and credits that should appear in the machinery account and the related accumulated depreciation—machinery account as a result of the above transactions. For purposes of depreciation computations, consider any changes in the asset as occurring on the first of the nearest month, and compute depreciation for fractional periods by months.

Problem 15-7. Midwest Flying Service expanded and improved its main hangar during 19+9. The following information, related to this program, is given to you.

(1) On November 15, 19+9, a 60-foot extension to the hangar was completed at a contract cost of $67,000.

(2) During construction, the following costs were incurred for the removal of the old hangar door and the installation of the new one:

(a) Payroll costs arising from use of employees on this project, $1,243.
(b) Payments to a salvage company for removing debris, $330.

(3) The old flooring was resurfaced with a new-type, long-lasting covering at a cost of $4,320.

(4) $1,576 was received from the construction company for assorted materials salvaged from those parts of the hangar that were torn down or remodeled during the construction of the extension.

(5) $140 of payroll costs were incurred in moving the inventory of repair parts to the new storage location in the hangar.

(6) Old heating pipes were replaced at a cost of $3,678, and new blowers were installed for $2,380.

Cost of the old heating pipes removed was determined to be $2,800 with depreciation recorded to date of $1,830. The old blowers, which cost $1,200 and were 60 percent depreciated, can be sold for $200.

(7) $310 was spent on refreshments to celebrate the completion of the expansion program.

Prepare entries in general journal form to record the above facts.

Problem 15-8. Precision Company owns three machines. The cost and accumulated depreciation data relating to the machines are shown below.

Machinery

19+5			
Jan. 2	Machine A	3,000.00	
19+6			
Aug. 1	Machine B	4,000.00	
19+7			
April 1	Machine C	5,000.00	

Accumulated Depreciation—Machinery

	19+5	
	Dec. 31	600.00
	19+6	
	Dec. 31	880.00
	19+7	
	Dec. 31	1,604.00
	19+8	
	Dec. 31	1,783.20

On different dates during 19+9, the machines are traded in on new machines. The company pays cash, less the trade-in allowance, for each new machine. Data on the trade-ins are presented below.

Machine Traded In	Date of Trade-In	List Price of New Machine	Allowance on Old Machine	Cash Price of Old Machine	Accounting Method to Be Followed
A	Feb. 22, 19+9	$3,200	$1,400	$1,200	Income tax rule
B	May 1, 19+9	4,300	1,825	1,700	Recognize cash value of old asset
C	Oct. 10, 19+9	5,500	2,850	2,400	Recognize cash value of old asset

Give the entries required at the time of each trade-in.

Problem 15-9. The partial results of the construction of long-lived assets in Carson Company's plant during 19+6 are shown below.

	Total	Finished Goods	Long-lived Assets
Direct labor	$144,000	$108,000	$36,000
Materials	120,000	72,000	48,000
Overhead	96,000	?	?
Total	$360,000	?	?

Compute the total cost of both finished goods and long-lived assets manufactured by each of the following methods:

(1) No overhead is to be assigned to the long-lived assets.
(2) Normal production of finished goods amounts to 30,000 units. Because of the construction of long-lived assets, finished goods production totaled only 21,000 units in 19+6. The assets are to be charged with the overhead which would have been charged to the 9,000 units which were not produced.
(3) Overhead is to be apportioned in the ratio of direct labor.

Problem 15-10. From the following information prepare a schedule showing, for *each* of the cases given:

(1) Amount paid by insurance company, 80 percent co-insurance in force.
(2) Loss suffered by owner.

Case	Insurable Value of Property	Insurance Coverage	Loss by Fire
A—1	$100,000	$100,000	$100,000
2			80,000
3			40,000
B—1	$100,000	$ 80,000	$100,000
2			80,000
3			40,000
C—1	$100,000	$ 50,000	$100,000
2			80,000
3			40,000

Problem 15-11. Arizona Chemical Company purchases containers at $11 each. These are billed to customers at $15, but the customers are allowed to return them for credit. Customers who pay for the containers are allowed to keep them. The containers must be constantly repaired.

Give the journal entries for the following:

(1) 22,000 containers were purchased and paid for.
(2) $14,000 was spent reconditioning containers.
(3) During the year, billings of $6,420,000 were made, which included $147,000 of charges for containers.
(4) Credits were issued for 8,700 containers returned.
(5) 120 containers were scrapped as beyond repair, and salvage of $120 was obtained from them.
(6) 420 containers were paid for by customers.
(7) A physical inventory of the containers on hand and those with customers showed

the following:

Quantity: 21,000
Depreciated value: 80 percent of cost

Problem 15-12. Spring Water Company delivers its product in large glass containers which are returnable. The containers cost $1.10 each, but are charged to customers at $1.50 each when delivered. A portion of the company's business is on a cash-and-carry basis. Cash customers are required to make a cash deposit of $1.50 for each container. It is the company's experience that cash customers return only 80 percent of their containers.

Data for the two years ended December 31, 19+9, are as follows:

	Year Ended	
	December 31, 19+8	December 31, 19+9
Containers:		
Purchased	3,200	3,500
Delivered with charge sales	30,000	29,400
Used with cash sales	500	550
Returned by charge customers	26,000	26,200
Returned by cash customers	300	310
Destroyed during year by employees	120	110
Collections from charge customers for unreturned containers	$3,600	$3,750
Charges for containers written off as uncollectible		$ 30

Prepare journal entries summarizing all transactions related to containers in the two-year period, including adjusting entries and closing entries.

Problem 15-13. Royal Theater Company purchased some projection equipment on the installment basis. The contract price was $23,610, consisting of a $5,610 down payment and four annual payments of $4,500, beginning one year after the date of purchase. An annual rate of 8 percent is appropriate for calculating the interest element in the contract.

Required:

(a) Assuming the purchase took place on January 1, 19+3, present the entries necessary to record the information above on the books of Royal Theater Company for the period January 1, 19+3 to January 1, 19+7. The Company closes its books annually on December 31. Note: Present value of an annuity of $1 for four years at 8 percent, 3.3121.
(b) The total amount debited to the asset account as the cost of the asset.
(c) The total interest expense applicable to the contract.

Problem 15-14. The manager of the McMain Company has taken out several insurance policies containing an 80 percent co-insurance clause. He desires that you compute for him the amount of insurance which he can collect in each of the following cases:

Assets Insured	Insurable Amount	Agreed Loss Suffered	Insurance Carried
Buildings	$40,000	$24,000	$38,000
Furniture	9,600	7,840	7,200
Machinery	24,000	9,600	16,000
Merchandise	Unknown	Total	12,000

To find the value of the merchandise destroyed, the following additional information is given: Opening inventory, $21,000; purchases for the period, $30,000; sales for the period, $50,000. The agreed gross margin averages 30 percent of sales.

Problem 15-15. Washington Manufacturing Company started in business as of January 1, 19+4, by acquiring three machines having a cost of $5,240, $4,000, and $4,400, respectively. Since that date the company has computed depreciation at 20 percent on the balance of the asset account at the end of each year, which amount has been credited directly to the asset account. All purchases since January 1, 19+4, have been debited to the machinery account and the cash received from sales has been credited to the account.

The following transactions took place.

(1) On September 30, 19+4, a machine was purchased on an installment basis. The cash price was $6,800, but 12 monthly payments of $600 each were made by the company. The difference is considered to represent reasonable interest charges. Only the monthly payments were recorded in the Machinery account starting with September 30, 19+4. Freight and installation charges of $200 were paid and entered in the Machinery account on October 10, 19+4.

(2) On June 30, 19+5, a machine was purchased for $8,000, 2/10; n/30, and recorded at $8,000 when paid for on July 7, 19+5.

(3) On June 30, 19+6, the machine acquired for $5,240 was traded for a larger one having a cost of $9,300. An allowance of $4,300 was received on the old machine, the balance being paid in cash and charged to the machinery account.

(4) On January 2, 19+7, the machine which cost $4,400 was sold for $2,500, but, because the cost of removal and crating was $125, the Machinery account was credited with only $2,375.

(5) On October 1, 19+8, the machine purchased for $4,000 was sold for cash and the cash received was credited to the account.

(6) The balance of the account on January 1, 19+8, was $14,505.50, and on December 31, 19+8, after adjustment for depreciation, it was $10,644.40.

The company has decided that its method of handling its machinery account has not been satisfactory. Accordingly, after the books were closed in 19+8, the management decided to correct the account as of December 31, 19+8, in accordance with usual accounting practices, and to provide depreciation on a straight-line basis with a separate accumulated depreciation account. Straight-line depreciation is estimated to be at the rate of 10 percent per annum computed on a monthly basis, over one-half of a month being considered a full month.

Required:

(a) A schedule showing the balance of the machinery account and of the accumulated depreciation—machinery account as of December 31, 19+8, on the revised basis.

(b) A schedule showing the correct gain or loss on disposals of assets during the five-year period.

(c) A computation of the corrected depreciation expense for the year 19+8 on the new basis.

You are not to consider income tax procedures in your solution.

Problem 15-16. You are engaged in the examination of the financial statements of Rocky Company for the year ended December 31, 19+5. The following schedules for the property, plant and equipment and related accumulated depreciation accounts have been prepared by the client. You have checked the opening balances to your prior year's audit workpapers.

ROCKY COMPANY
Analysis of Property, Plant and Equipment and Related Accumulated Depreciation Accounts
Year Ended December 31, 19+5

Assets

Description	Final 12/31/+4	Additions	Retirements	Per Books 12/31/+5
Land	$ 22,500	$ 5,000		$ 27,500
Buildings	120,000	17,500		137,500
Machinery and Equipment	385,000	40,400	$26,000	399,400
	$527,500	$62,900	$26,000	$564,400

Accumulated Depreciation

Descriptions	Final 12/31/+4	Additions*	Retirements	Per Books 12/31/+5
Buildings	$ 60,000	$ 5,150		$ 65,150
Machinery and Equipment	173,250	39,220		212,470
	$223,250	$44,370		$277,620

*Depreciation expense for the year.

Your examination reveals the following information:

(1) All equipment is depreciated on the straight-line basis (no salvage value taken into consideration) based on the following estimated lives: buildings, 25 years; all other items, 10 years. The company's policy is to take one-half year's depreciation on all asset acquisitions and disposals during the year.

(2) On April 1 the company entered into a ten-year lease contract for a die casting machine with annual rentals of $5,000 payable in advance every April 1. The lease is cancelable by either party (sixty days written notice is required) and there is no option to renew the lease or buy the equipment at the end of the lease. The estimated useful life of the machine is ten years with no salvage value. The company recorded the die casting machinery in the machinery and equipment account at $40,400, the present discounted value at the date of the lease, and $2,020, applicable to the machine, has been included in depreciation expense for the year.

(3) The company completed the construction of a wing on the plant building on June 30. The useful life of the building was not extended by this addition. The lowest construction bid received was $17,500, the amount recorded in the buildings account. Company personnel were used to construct the addition at a cost of $16,000 (materials, $7,500; labor, $5,500; and overhead, $3,000).

(4) On August 18, $5,000 was paid for paving and fencing a portion of land owned by the company and used as a parking lot for employees. The expenditure was charged to the land account.

(5) The amount shown in the machinery and equipment asset retirement column represents cash received on September 5 upon disposal of a machine purchased in July 19+1 for $48,000. The bookkeeper recorded depreciation expense of $3,500 on this machine in 19+5.

(6) Dodge City donated land and building appraised at $10,000 and $40,000 respectively to Rocky Company for a plant. On September 1, the company began operating the plant. Since no costs were involved, the bookkeeper made no entry for the above transaction.

Prepare a schedule to show the correct balances in the asset and accumulated depreciation accounts as of December 31, 19+5.

CHAPTER 16

QUESTIONS

1. With regard to depreciation, answer the following questions.
   (**a**) What is depreciation?
   (**b**) What are the primary factors that cause depreciation?

2. What is the general distinction between depreciation, depletion, and amortization?

3. With regard to wasting assets, answer the following questions.
   (**a**) What are wasting assets?
   (**b**) What are some examples of wasting assets?
   (**c**) When buildings and machinery are used in connection with the operation of a wasting asset, should the depreciation be based on the life of the building and machinery or on the life of the wasting asset?

4. How does depreciation affect the following financial statements?
   (**a**) Income statement
   (**b**) Balance sheet
   (**c**) Statement of changes in financial position

5. Depreciation is the physical deterioration of a tangible, long-lived asset caused by wear and tear and the action of elements. Do you agree with this definition of depreciation?

6. When a company's stock in trade is its wasting assets, why is it considered to be acceptable to determine the amount available for dividends as equal to the sum of accumulated net income and accumulated depletion charges?

7. In determining the results of the operations of a company that requires the use of a large number of perishable tools, how would you proceed in making the assignment of the cost of such equipment to the periods benefited?

8. What is the retirement system of depreciation, particularly as applied by public utilities, and do you approve of such a system?

9. Depletion is accounted for similar to raw materials purchases. What does this statement mean?

10. Depending on the depreciation method used, depreciation may be a variable or fixed cost. What does this statement mean?

11. An electric lamp manufacturing company has charged to cost of manufacturing lamps, as "depreciation," one-fourth of the cost of the filament-filtering machinery acquired a little more than one year ago. The life of the machinery is estimated to be ten years; but, owing to discovery by a competitor of a new process of metal pulling which, although still imperfect, promises to revolutionize the lamp industry, the machinery in question will probably become obsolete within a period of three years. What do you think about the propriety of making such a charge to cost of manufacturing?

12. The chief engineer of a manufacturing firm suggested in a conference of the company's executives that the accountants should speed up depreciation on the machinery in Department 3 because improvements are making those machines become obsolete very rapidly, and it is desirable to have a depreciation fund large enough to cover their replacement. What do you think of the issues raised by the chief engineer?

13. The management of a corporation suggests the reduction or elimination of depreciation charges on plant and machinery on these grounds:

(**a**) Nothing need be written off, because the plant is actually more valuable than it was when acquired, owing to a rise in the cost of similar machinery.

(**b**) Repairs have been fully maintained, and the plant is as good as ever.

(**c**) To charge depreciation to the same extent in a poor year as in a good year will prevent a dividend in the poor year, with a consequent objection from stockholders and a fall in the price of shares.

What do you think of these arguments?

14. A small manufacturing company owned in 19+2 one factory building with a net depreciated cost of $90,000. Equipment was carried at $120,000. Because of expanding business in 19+3, a new building was constructed at a cost of $150,000 and $210,000 of equipment was installed in it. In the period from 19+3 to the end of 19+6, some new equipment was put into the old building and the company continued to operate both plants. Depreciation has been computed on a straight-line basis.

In 19+7 the directors of the company order the old plant shut down because of lack of orders. They propose that they should quit taking depreciation on the old building and equipment. They suggest that, although the old plant is useful, it is not in use and is not wearing out. They also suggest that to take depreciation on it increases their cost, overvalues inventory, and places them in a poor competitive position to bid for business because their costs are high.

What do you think of their proposal and of their arguments?

15. What is the position taken by accountants with regard to the writing up of wasting assets?

16. Since depreciation is a book charge that does not require an outlay of funds, yet it is a charge against revenue, it, in effect, is a source of funds, as shown in the statement of changes in financial position. Do you agree with this statement?

17. Since the *total* depreciation of a tangible, long-lived asset is approximately the same no matter which depreciation method is used, there are no tax advantages to using one depreciation method over another. Do you agree with this statement? Why is the *total* depreciation the same for all depreciation methods?

18. Arguments for and against straight-line depreciation can be based on the fact that many assets have a declining productivity with the passage of time. What does this statement mean?

19. To argue that one depreciation method is superior to another is fruitless, because there are numerous rational methods for the systematic allocation of cost; hence, the accounting profession would be better off to require companies to use only *one* depreciation method. Do you agree with this statement?

20. One of the arguments against the depreciation methods used in current accounting practice is that they fail to take into account the time value of money (i.e., the interest factor). What is this argument? How can the time value of money be accounted for in depreciation accounting? From a normative theory viewpoint, would a depreciation method that takes into account the time value of money be the one best depreciation method?

PROBLEMS

Problem 16-1. You are given below seven multiple choice statements. Select the correct answer to complete each statement and indicate the corresponding letter on a separate sheet of paper (e.g., 1-a, 2-a, etc.).

(1) The straight-line method of depreciation is not appropriate for (a) a company that is neither expanding or contracting its investment in equipment because it is replacing equipment as the equipment depreciates, (b) equipment on which maintenance and repairs increase substantially with age, (c) equipment with useful lives that are not affected by the amount of use, (d) equipment used consistently every period, (e) none of the above.

(2) A principal objection to the straight-line method of depreciation is that it (a) provides for the declining productivity of an aging asset, (b) ignores variations in the rate of asset use, (c) tends to result in a constant rate of return on a diminishing investment base, (d) results in smaller periodic charges to expense than decreasing-charge methods, (e) none of the above.

(3) For income statement purposes depreciation is a variable expense if the depreciation method used for book purposes is (a) units-of-production, (b) straight-line, (c) sum-of-the-year's digits, (d) declining-balance, (e) none of the above.

(4) Each year a company has been investing an increasingly greater amount in machinery. Since there are a large number of small items with relatively similar useful lives, the company has been applying the straight-line depreciation method at a uniform rate to the machinery as a group. The ratio of this group's total accumulated depreciation to the total cost of the machinery has been steadily increasing and now stands at .75 to 1. The most likely explanation of this increasing ratio is that the (a) estimated average life of the machinery is greater than the actual average useful life, (b) estimated average life of the machinery is equal to the actual average useful life, (c) estimated average life of the machinery is less than the actual average useful life, (d) company has been retiring fully depreciated machinery that should have remained in service, (e) none of the above.

(5) On July 10, 19+5 XB Corporation purchased factory equipment installed for $14,600. Salvage was estimated to be $1,000. The equipment will be depreciated over eight years using the double-declining-balance method. Counting the year of acquisition as one-half year, XB would deduct 19+6 depreciation on this equipment of (a) $3,650.00, (b) $3,193.75, (c) $2,975.00, (d) $1,825.00, (e) none of the above.

(6) In those rare instances where appraisal increments in the valuation of plant and equipment have been recorded, depreciation on the appraisal increments should be (a) ignored because the increments have not been paid for and should not be matched with revenue, (b) charged to retained earnings, (c) charged to expense, (d) charged to an appropriation of retained earnings, (e) none of the above.

(7) Chain Hotel Corporation recently purchased Elgin Hotel and the land on which it is located with the plan to tear down the Elgin Hotel and build a new luxury hotel on the site. The cost of the Elgin Hotel should be (a) depreciated over the period from acquisition to the date the Hotel is scheduled to be torn down, (b) written off as an extraordinary loss in the year the Hotel is torn down, (c) capitalized as part of the cost of the land, (d) capitalized as part of the cost of the new Hotel, (e) none of the above.

Problem 16-2. ABC Company acquired a tangible long-lived asset for $120,000. The asset is expected to have a useful life of 10 years with salvage of $10,000. The company is considering whether to use the straight-line, sum-of-the-years'-digits or double-declining method to allocate the cost of the asset over its useful life.

Required:

(a) Compute the depreciation to be used under each of the three methods listed above for the years 19+5 and 19+6 assuming that the asset was purchased on January 1, 19+5.

(b) Compute the depreciation to be used under each of the three methods listed above for the years 19+5 and 19+6 assuming that the asset was purchased on April 1, 19+5.

Problem 16-3. Surface Mining Company purchased a tract of land containing coal veins for $363,000. The tract is estimated to contain 990,000 tons of coal; it is expected that the quantity mined the first year of operations will be one-half of that mined in each succeeding year.

Installations are set up at an additional cost of $77,000. The above transactions took place during the latter part of 19+1. Equipment was purchased early in January 19+2 for $176,000, and operations were started as soon as employees were hired and trained.

It is estimated that the installations could be used for 20 years. However, they will, of necessity, be abandoned when the coal deposits are exhausted. The equipment is estimated to have a useful life of 8 years and can be transferred conveniently to another location.

By the end of 19+2, 90,000 tons had been mined and sold. The company has adopted the production method of depreciation.

Required:

Give the adjusting entries for depletion and depreciation as of December 31, 19+2.

Problem 16-4. A schedule of property, plant, and equipment assets owned by Stewart Manufacturing Corporation is presented below:

	Factory Building	Plant Equipment	Small Tools	Patterns
Total cost	$260,000	$240,000	$78,000	$48,000
Estimated salvage....	$ 20,000	$ 16,000	$ 6,000	$ —
Estimated life in years	40	20	8	4

Required:

(a) Determine the composite life of the assets listed above.

(b) Prepare journal entries for the depreciation of each class of asset for the third year of service life, using the following methods:

Factory building—Straight-line.
Plant equipment—Constant rate of 10 percent on declining balance.
Small Tools—Sum-of-the years'-digits.
Patterns—Diminishing rates on cost: 40-30-20-10 percent.

Support the journal entries with appropriate computations.

Problem 16-5. The following table gives the necessary information to calculate the annual depreciation expense for equipment owned by Flint Hills Manufacturing Company, Inc.

Asset	Cost	Salvage	Estimated Life
A	$ 5,000	$ 600	10 years
B	7,500	300	8 years
C	10,000	900	5 years
D	12,500	914	4 years
E	15,000	1,340	10 years
F	17,500	2,274	15 years

Required:

(a) Compute the composite life and composite depreciation rate for the group of assets listed above.

(b) Prepare the journal entry to record the annual depreciation at the end of the first year.

(c) Assuming the depreciation has been entered using the composite method, prepare the journal entry to record the sale of asset D for cash of $2,500 at the end of the third year.

(d) Assuming the sale of asset D in (c) prepare the journal entry to record the annual depreciation at the end of year three if asset G costing $25,000 with an estimated 6 year life and $2,000 salvage was acquired at midyear.

(e) Assuming the sale of asset D and acquisition of asset G, prepare the journal entry to record the annual depreciation at the end of year four.

Problem 16-6. Pounce Company acquired a machine at the beginning of the year at a cost of $9,960. It was estimated that salvage would be $300. Prepare depreciation tables for 6 years and submit journal entries to record depreciation for the third year under each of the following methods:

(1) Sum-of-the-years' digits; estimated life—6 years.
(2) Working hours; estimated life in working hours—19,320 hours.
(3) Production; estimated life in units of product—77,280 units.

Additional data is given below:

Year	Working Hours	Units of Product
1	2,900	11,600
2	3,250	13,000
3	3,100	12,400
4	3,000	12,000
5	3,410	13,640
6	3,660	14,640

Problem 16-7. The following table gives information concerning the property, plant, and equipment acquisitions and disposals for Georgia Corporation during its first 6 years of business. The company was organized January 1, 19+1.

PROPERTY, PLANT, AND EQUIPMENT

	Acquisitions				Disposals	
Date	Description	Useful Life	Cost	Salvage	Description	Date
1/1/+1	A	4 years	$3,600	$ —	A	12/31/+4
7/1/+1	B	5 years	4,000	—	B	12/31/+5
4/1/+2	C	6 years	5,000	200	C	7/1/+6
7/1/+3	D	10 years	8,000	500		
1/1/+5	E	4 years	4,200	—		
10/1/+6	F	5 years	6,000	500		

Required:

Prepare a lapsing schedule to show the annual depreciation for the first 8 years of the business life of Georgia Corporation using the straight-line method.

Problem 16-8. Bishop Tungsten Company bought a mine estimated to have deposits totaling 3,500,000 tons for $315,000. The company spent $52,500 on developments and improvements at the mine. Of these, two-thirds were estimated to last until the mine was exhausted and the rest were estimated to last five years. During the first year of operations, costs, aside from depreciation and depletion, were $540,000. Of these costs, $80,000 were for general and selling expense. The company mined 125,000 tons, of which it sold 115,000 tons for $620,000.

They ask you to determine:

(a) The net income for the year.
(b) The amount legally available for dividends assuming that the 10,000 tons in inventory were sold at cost.
(c) The amount legally available for dividends if the 10,000 tons in inventory were not sold.

Problem 16-9. General Insurance Agency maintains a separate account in its ledger for typewriters. New typewriters cost $200. As a general rule, the agency uses typewriters for four years and each year sells a number of its oldest typewriters when new ones are being purchased. It has been the agency's experience to realize about $44 from the sale of each such old machine.

Purchases and sales of typewriters for a five-year period are summarized below.

Year	Purchases of New Typewriters	Sale of Old Typewriters	Proceeds from Old Typewriters
19+5	24	14	$560
19+6	18	18	738
19+7	20	20	880
19+8	25	22	990
19+9	22	24	960

You may assume that all purchases and sales of typewriters occur early in January. Under the replacement method the cost of retirements in excess of replacements is added to the cost of replacements before salvage is deducted.

As of December 31, 19+4, the agency owned 80 typewriters; 15 were four years old, 18 were three years old, 22 were two years old, and 25 were one year old.

Prepare a schedule of the annual depreciation charges for the years 19+5 through 19+9, under the following depreciation plans:

(a) Straight-line method. (Ignore pre-19+5 purchases.)
(b) Retirement method.
(c) Replacement method.

Problem 16-10. As an independent public accountant, you have been engaged to prepare certain information relating to the comparison of the following three methods of computing depreciation: (1) Straight-line, (2) Sum-of-the-years'-digits, (3) Double-declining balance.

Required:

(a) Explain these three methods.
(b) Assuming the following information, prepare a summary of the property and accumulated depreciation accounts showing beginning balances, additions and retirements, and ending balances for the years 19+5 and 19+6, based on the three above methods. For the purpose of recording depreciation, take one-half year in the year of acquisition and a full year in year of retirement. Disregard any salvage for depreciation purposes.

			Sales or Retirements	
Year	Property Acquired	Estimated Useful Life	Year of Acquisition	Amount
19+5.........	$50,000	10 years		
19+6.........	20,000	10 years	19+5	$7,000

Problem 16-11. Tom Company purchased a machine with an estimated service life of 10 years for $15,000 and has decided to use double-declining depreciation. The president of the company has heard that in some cases it might be beneficial to switch back to straight-line depreciation at some future date.

Required:

For each of the following situations, determine if a switch to straight-line depreciation is advisable or not, in what year the switch should be made, and the amount of depreciation to be taken in each remaining year after the switch.

(a) The salvage is zero.
(b) The salvage is $2,000.
(c) The salvage is $1,500.
(d) The salvage is $1,000.

Problem 16-12. Presto Diaper Service began operations January 1, 19+1 and immediately purchased 5 especially designed trucks and other equipment. The accountant has decided to simplify his work and will use the group system of recording and computing depreciation on all assets owned by the company. The delivery trucks are expected to have a 5-year life and salvage at the end of five years of $500 each.

The transactions affecting the delivery truck group of assets for the first three years of operation are given below:

(1) January 1, 19+1, purchased 5 trucks at $4,500 each.
(2) December 31, 19+1, recorded annual depreciation.
(3) October 1, 19+2, purchased 2 additional trucks at $5,000 each, with salvage estimated at $750 each.
(4) December 31, 19+2, recorded annual depreciation.
(5) July 1, 19+3, one truck (first purchase) was wrecked and released to the insurance company in return for check for $2,000.
(6) December 31, 19+3, recorded annual depreciation.
(7) December 31, 19+4, recorded annual depreciation.

Required:

(a) Prepare the journal entries for each of the transactions listed above.
(b) Prepare a "T" account for the delivery truck group of assets and one for the corresponding accumulated depreciation, showing the transactions above.

Problem 16-13. Minnesota Corporation began business with the following property, plant, and equipment:

Asset	Cost	Salvage	Estimated Life in Years
Land	$25,000		
Building	70,000	$1,000	25
Machinery	41,930	2,000	10

The company has been in operation 5 years. Instead of recording depreciation on individual assets on the straight-line basis, it adopted a policy of relating depreciation charges to net income by charging as depreciation each year an amount equal to 10 percent of that year's net income before depreciation. This was recorded by a debit to Depreciation and a credit to Accumulated Depreciation.

The net income before depreciation for each of the 5 years was as follows:

Year	Net Income Before Depreciation
1	$20,000
2	37,500
3	52,000
4	73,000
5	68,000

You are to submit the journal entry to correct the books after the close of the fifth year, establishing a separate accumulated depreciation account for each asset, using the straight-line method for the building and the sum-of-the-years'-digits method for the machinery.

Problem 16-14. Milwaukee Tile Company bought a machine for $16,350. The freight-in was $530 and the installation cost was $1,420. The estimated salvage was $300 and the estimated life was 15 years. At the end of the second year, accessories costing $780 were added to the machine in order to reduce operating cost per unit. They neither prolonged its life nor did they have any additional salvage. State what the depreciation will be for the third year under each of the following methods of computing depreciation.

(a) Straight-line method.
(b) Working hours method. Total estimated hours, 36,000. Used the first year, 2,500; the second year, 2,200; the third year, 2,750.
(c) Production method. Total estimated units of production, 67,500, produced the first year, 4,700; the second year, 4,400; the third year, 5,100.
(d) Constant rate on a diminishing-balance method.

$$r = 1 - \sqrt[15]{300 \div 18{,}300} = .2397$$

$$r = 1 - \sqrt[15]{300 \div 16{,}350} = .1657$$

$$r = 1 - \sqrt[13]{300 \div 11{,}358.43} = .2439$$

$$r = 1 - \sqrt[13]{1{,}080 \div 16{,}350} = .2648$$

(e) The sum-of-the-years'-digits method.

Problem 16-15. Canada Oil Corporation purchased a lease on potential oil property for $160,000, and spent $144,000 drilling producing wells on the property. It was estimated that the oil potential of the property was 1,800,000 barrels with a discovery value of $560,000 excluding the costs of property and drilling.

During 19+1, the first year of operations, 90,000 barrels of oil were produced, of which 81,000 were sold. Cash operating costs for the year associated with the removal of oil from its underground location to the company's storage facilities were $40,000, and a net income of $30,000 was earned. In the computation of net income, depletion was based on the discovery value.

Required:

(a) Set up the discovery value of the oil property and determine the cost of oil produced on this basis.
(b) Journal entries to record and amortize all costs and to adjust unrealized appreciation.

Problem 16-16. In 1977 True-Form Plastics Corporation erected a new plant and installed all new equipment prior to beginning operations in January 1978. Among the assets purchased was a special hydraulic press for use in making their plastic products. This press was bought for $22,500 and is expected to have a useful life of twenty years. In December 1981, $2,800 was spent on the press for certain updating improvements, which made the press's current resale price $27,500. Then in December 1993, twelve years later, the press was completely overhauled and rebuilt. As a result of the work done the useful life was estimated to have been extended by five years or until the end of 2002. The cost of the overhaul was $5,375. In January 1999 a fire completely destroyed the plant and equipment. From the insurance proceeds received by the company, $4,500 was for the loss of the hydraulic press. All depreciation was computed on the straight-line basis.

Required:

(a) Prepare the journal entries to record:
    (1) The depreciation on the press for 1978.
    (2) The updating of the improvements added in December 1981.

(3) The annual depreciation for 1982.
(4) The rebuilding of press in December 1993.
(5) The annual depreciation for 1994.
(6) The receipt of the insurance payment for fire loss in 1999.

(b) Show the balances as they would appear on December 31, 1997 for the hydraulic press asset account and the corresponding accumulated depreciation account.

Problem 16-17. Royal Company purchased a lumber tract in April of 19+1 for $5,440,000. A cruise had shown that it held 1,460,000 M feet of lumber. It was estimated that the land, without trees, was worth $60,000. No lumbering operations were conducted on this property until 19+3. During the intervening period, the company spent $73,100 protecting the property.

In January of 19+3, another cruise was made which showed that the available timber had increased by 182,500 M feet. In recognition of this new information, the company added $722,700 to the carrying amount of the tract.

Early in 19+3, the company spent $98,550 on a railroad expected to last, with ordinary maintenance, until the tract was logged. The company took out 150,000 M feet during the year 19+3, of which all but 7,500 M feet were sold at a price of $13 per M feet. The operating costs, exclusive of depletion and depreciation, were $937,000; selling and general expenses were $186,000.

Required:

(a) Prepare the income statement for 19+3.
(b) Prepare the journal entry to record realized appreciation for 19+3.
(c) Prepare the journal entry to record a dividend declaration of $400,000 as of December 31, 19+3. Assume that the company had no retained earnings as of December 31, 19+2.

Problem 16-18. Since its organization, January 1, 19+1, Dodge Corporation purchased nine special-order delivery trucks. The following summary shows the facts relating to the acquisitions and disposals of the delivery trucks.

Number	Date Acquired	Cost	Date Sold	Proceeds
1	January 2, 19+1	$5,000	January 4, 19+5	$510
2	January 2, 19+2	5,000	January 10, 19+6	505
3	January 2, 19+3	5,000		
4	January 2, 19+3	5,500	January 3, 19+7	540
5	January 2, 19+4	6,000	October 2, 19+7	700
6	January 2, 19+5	6,000		
7	July 1, 19+6	6,400		
8	January 2, 19+7	6,500		
9	October 1, 19+7	6,800		

The management of the corporation has been operating with the expectation that the trucks could be sold at the end of four years, which is considered to be the average useful life of the trucks, for 10 percent of cost.

Compute the depreciation expense for 19+7 under the following methods:

(a) Straight-line.
(b) Declining balance, using a 40 percent rate.
(c) Retirement.
(d) Replacement.

CHAPTER 17

QUESTIONS

1. When, during the life of a depreciable asset, it becomes evident that the estimate of useful life originally used is no longer valid, how should the change be accounted for?
2. Distinguish between the terms valuation and value.
3. Under present accounting practice, a change in the estimated useful life of a depreciable asset does not result in an adjustment of prior period income. What is the argument supporting this practice?
4. Define the following terms: (a) reproduction cost new; (b) sound value.
5. Is historical-cost valuation always used in reporting assets in the financial statements of a firm?
6. Without using amounts, present the journal entry required to record an appraisal increase related to an asset used by a firm.
7. Discuss the alternative treatments of the appraisal increment recorded as a credit when appraisal amounts are entered in the accounting records.
8. What are the major arguments for and against the use of appraisal amounts in the accounting records?
9. What is the purpose of a quasi-reorganization?
10. List the characteristics of a quasi-reorganization.
11. Are asset amounts ever written up as the result of a quasi-reorganization?

PROBLEMS

Problem 17-1. Snow Corporation purchased a machine on July 1, 19+1, for $51,000. It was estimated to have a life of 12 years with a $3,000 trade-in value. During 19+4, it became apparent that this machine would be useless after December 31, 19+9, and that it would have no trade-in or salvage value. The chief accountant was instructed to make the necessary corrections when making the annual adjustments for 19+4. The corporation closed its books on December 31 of each year.

Required:

(a) Journal entry for 19+4 depreciation expense, applying Accounting Principles Board Opinion No. 20.

(b) Journal entries for 19+4 to correct prior year's depreciation and record depreciation expense for 19+4.

Problem 17-2. On January 2, 19+1, Ripple Company purchased a machine for $17,550. It was estimated that this asset would have a scrap value of $500 after a service life of 10 years. The company closes its books on a calendar-year basis and records depreciation on its assets by the sum of years' digits method.

Early in 19+5, it became apparent that the original use-life and scrap-value estimates were excessive. On the basis of the information available in 19+5, it was evident that the original estimates should have been for an 8-year service life and a $90 scrap value.

The controller of the company has instructed the chief accountant to make any required corrections or revisions when preparing adjusting entries for 19+5.

Required:

(a) Journal entry for 19+5 depreciation expense applying Opinion No. 20.
(b) Journal entries for 19+5 to correct prior year's depreciation and record depreciation expense for 19+5.

Problem 17-3. Sideways Company purchased a machine on July 1, 19+1, for $52,000. It was estimated to have a life of 10 years with a salvage value of $1,000. During 19+5, it became apparent that this machine would become uneconomical after December 31, 19+9, and that $500 would be a more realistic scrap value. The chief accountant was directed to make allowance for this new determination when making the annual adjustments for 19+5. The company closes its books on December 31.

Required:

(a) Prepare a schedule showing the depreciation charge for the years 19+1, 19+2, 19+5, and 19+6, assuming the following:
(1) Past depreciation is to be corrected in 19+5.
(2) Past depreciation is not to be corrected in 19+5.
(b) Prepare all journal entries for 19+5 for (a) 1 and (a) 2.

Problem 17-4. On January 1, 19+1, Layden Company purchased factory property for $110,000, of which $10,000 was assigned to the Land account. Straight-line depreciation was provided on the basis of an estimated life of 20 years with no scrap value.

On June 30, 19+5, an independent appraisal indicated a replacement value new of $120,000 for the building and a remaining useful life of 20½ years.

Give the entries that should have been made as of June 30, 19+5, assuming that the directors of the company ordered that the appraisal be given recognition in the accounts. Also give the December 31, 19+5 and 19+6 entries for depreciation and the piecemeal transfer of the appraisal increment to Retained earnings.

Problem 17-5. Overseas Corporation acquired a warehouse on January 2, 1975, at a cost of $95,000, of which $10,000 was assigned to land. It was estimated that the scrap value of this structure would be $6,000 at the end of a 25-year life. The company closes its books on a calendar-year basis and records depreciation on its assets by the straight-line method.

Late in 1985, an appraisal of the company's property revealed the replacement cost, new, of this warehouse to be $127,500. The appraisers indicated that such a building should have a scrap value of $3,000 and a total estimated life of 30 years.

The directors of the company request that you prepare entries to record the appraisal as of January 1, 1986, using separate appraisal accounts, the depreciation expense for 1986, and the piecemeal realization appraisal increment on December 31, 1986.

Problem 17-6. Lester Corporation purchased certain real estate on January 1, 19+1, for cash as follows:

Building	$40,000
Land	10,000
Total	$50,000

An appraisal of the property on the basis of the replacement cost, new, was made late in 19+7, and the results of the appraisal were recorded on December 31, 19+7, before the books were closed. The appraisal was as follows:

Building	$ 80,000
Land	22,000
Total	$102,000

Depreciation had been recorded in 19+1 and through 19+6 at 2 percent of cost annually, but the appraisal stated that the rate should have been 3 percent annually.

This real estate was sold by the corporation on June 30, 19+8 for cash. The price agreed on is indicated below:

Building	$ 94,000
Land	16,000
Total	$110,000

Required:

(a) Journal entry to record depreciation on the above property for the year 19+6.

(b) Journal entry to record the 19+7 appraisal, maintaining separate accounts for the appraisal increments.

(c) Journal entries to record depreciation on the basis of replacement cost for the year 19+7, including amortization of the appraisal increment.

(d) Journal entries to be made on June 30, 19+8, at the time of the sale of this property.

Problem 17-7. Simons Corporation, a family-owned corporation, purchased a building on July 1, 1965, for $180,000, of which $24,000 was assigned to the land account. The board of directors adopted a policy of straight-line depreciation for the building.

Early in 1975, the board of directors received an appraisal report which showed that the replacement cost, new, of the building would be $243,000 as of January 1, 1975. The report also stated that the building would have a useful life of 20 years from that date. The board of directors ordered that the appraisal be recorded in the accounts as of January 1, 1975. On the recommendation of the chief accountant, the board also voted that past depreciation was not to be corrected.

The December 31, 1974 balance sheet showed that $78,000 of depreciation had been accumulated on the building.

The property was sold on January 2, 1977, for $145,000.

Required:

(a) Journal entries for the following:
   (1) Depreciation on the building for 1974.
   (2) Depreciation on the building for 1975.
   (3) Amortization of appraisal increment as of December 31, 1975.
   (4) Those arising from the sale of the property.

(b) A partial balance sheet, as of December 31, 1975, showing the location and balances of all accounts relating to the property.

Problem 17-8. Tinker Corporation was organized on July 1, 19+1. 150,000 shares of $10 par value stock were authorized and 100,000 shares were sold at $13 per share on July 1, 19+1.

The June 30, 19+6 balance sheet follows:

Assets

Cash	$ 500,500
Accounts receivable, net	950,000
Inventory (LIFO basis)	1,500,000
Unexpired insurance	18,000
Land	58,000
Machinery, net	1,473,500
	$4,500,000

Equities

Current liabilities	$1,475,000
Capital stock	1,000,000
Capital in excess of par value—from common stock issuances	300,000
Retained earnings	1,725,000
	$4,500,000

During 19+6 the board of directors decided to write up the long-lived assets to reflect their current value. The following information is available:

(1) Machinery was purchased in fiscal years 19+2, 19+4 and 19+5 for $500,000, $850,000 and $660,000, respectively. The straight-line depreciation method and a ten-year estimated life have been used for all machinery with a half year of depreciation taken in the year of acquisition. The experience of other companies over the last several years indicates that the reproduction cost, new, of the machinery is 125 percent of its book value.
(2) An independent appraisal made in June 19+6 valued land at $70,000.

Required:

(a) For each machinery purchase determine:
 (1) Reproduction cost new.
 (2) Sound value.
 (3) Condition per cent.
 (4) Appreciation.
(b) Journal entries for June 30, 19+6 to record the current values of the long-lived assets.
(c) A balance sheet as of June 30, 19+6 reflecting the asset write ups. Do not net accumulated depreciation against the machinery account.

Problem 17-9. South Belt Company had authorized and outstanding 40,000 shares of $25 par value common stock which had been issued at par. On December 31, 19+1, the corporation had an operating deficit of $260,000.

The corporation was in need of additional cash, but the directors felt that borrowing or issuing additional stock was impractical because of the appearance of the balance sheet. For this reason, appropriate procedures were followed during January, 19+2, to obtain authorization of the quasi-reorganization outlined below:

(1) Change the capitalization to 60,000 shares of no par value with a stated value of $15 per share.
(2) Exchange shares on a one-for-one basis.

(3) Write down the long-term investments by $25,000.
(4) Remove the deficit by a transfer from a capital in excess account.

The quasi-reorganization was completed and recorded in the corporation's accounts as of January 2, 19+2.

On February 15, 19+2, the company was able to issue 10,000 shares of stock for $17 per share.

Required:

(a) Journal entries to effect the quasi-reorganization as of January 2, 19+2, and to record the issuance of the shares on February 15, 19+2.
(b) The Stockholders' Equity section of the company's balance sheet as of December 31, 19+2, assuming that the net income for 19+2 was $35,000, and that no dividends were declared during the year.

Problem 17-10. The condensed balance sheet of McCain Company, prior to giving effect to a quasi-reorganization as of September 30, 19+1, is presented below.

McCAIN COMPANY
Balance Sheet
September 30, 19+1

Assets		Equities		
Current assets	$162,200	Current liabilities		$ 90,000
Long-lived assets (net)	263,800	Capital stock	$400,000	
		Retained earnings—deficit	64,000	336,000
	$426,000			$426,000

The quasi-reorganization which was approved included the following actions:

(1) The reduction of the par value of the company's stock from $25 to $15 per share. The new stock was exchanged for the old stock on a one-for-one basis.
(2) The provision of additional depreciation of $20,000.
(3) The recognition of a $9,000 loss on obsolete inventory.
(4) The elimination of the deficit.

During the three months ended December 31, 19+1, the company earned $11,000 which included a $2,000 gain on the scale of the obsolete inventory on October 16, 19+1. Depreciation expense for the three-month period was $6,000.

During the three months, no dividends were declared; no additions to or disposals of the long-lived assets were made; no financing was undertaken. As of December 31, 19+1, the current liabilities amounted to $77,500.

Prepare the December 31, 19+1 balance sheet of McCain Company.

Problem 17-11. Round Company had an authorized issue of 10,000 shares of $50 par value stock, all of which was outstanding. Its condensed balance sheet on August 31, 19+1 was as follows:

ROUND COMPANY
Balance Sheet
August 31, 19+1

Assets		Equities		
Current assets	$142,800	Current liabilities		$126,400
Long-lived assets (net)	523,600	5% bonds payable		200,000
		Capital stock	$500,000	
		Retained earnings—deficit	160,000	340,000
	$666,400			$666,400

In order to eliminate the deficit, the company obtained, during July and August, all the necessary authorizations to change its par value shares to a stated value of $10 and to increase the authorized number of shares to 50,000. Three shares of new stock are to be exchanged for each share of $50 par value stock.

Additional depreciation of $30,000 is to be recorded to bring the carrying amount of the fixed assets into line with present replacement values.

Interest has not been paid on the bonds for two years preceding the balance sheet date, and the bondholders have agreed to accept 2,400 of the new shares of stock in payment of the accrued interest.

The deficit is to be eliminated.

Required:

(a) Journal entries, assuming that all of the matters were effected as of September 1, 19+1.

(b) A balance sheet after recording the journal entries.

Problem 17-12. The June 30, 19+1 condensed balance sheet of Bomar Company is presented below.

BOMAR COMPANY
Balance Sheet
June 30, 19+1

Assets		
Current assets		$ 440,000
Long-term investments—at cost		60,000
Property, plant, and equipment	$1,680,000	
Less accumulated depreciation	640,000	1,040,000
Patent—at cost less amortization		320,000
		1,860,000

Equities	
Bond interest payable	$ 108,000
Other current liabilities	240,000
Bonds payable—19+8	600,000
Common stock—$5 stated value	800,000
Capital in excess of stated value—from common stock issuances	72,000
Retained earnings	40,000
	$1,860,000

One of the products manufactured and sold by the company—the one covered by the patent—was not well received in the market. This caused the company to be unprofitable in recent years, which in turn caused the company to postpone the payment of bond interest for the last three years.

Management decided to discontinue the product, to scrap the related manufacturing facilities, and to write off the patent as worthless. Cost and market studies prepared by management indicated that the company would regain a profitable status if it concentrated on its other products, which were well received by the company's customers.

Management obtained the necessary approvals for the following plan, which was made effective as of July 1, 19+1:

(1) Common stock was assigned a stated value of $2 per share.
(2) The bond interest liability was settled by the issuance of 18,000 shares of the company's common stock (which had a current market price of $6 per share).
(3) The patent was written off.
(4) An appropriation of retained earnings for losses from the disposal of manufacturing facilities and unsold inventory was established in the amount of $200,000.
(5) The deficit was eliminated.

During the year ended June 30, 19+2, the company disposed of all of its manufacturing facilities and inventory related to the discarded product at a loss of $170,000. Its net income from operations for the fiscal year ended June 30, 19+2, was $64,000. No dividends were declared.

Required:

(a) The journal entries recorded as of July 1, 19+1, for the quasi-reorganization.
(b) The Stockholders' Equity section of the June 30, 19+2 balance sheet, including any pertinent disclosures.

CHAPTER 18

QUESTIONS

1. What are intangible assets? Give some examples.
2. Define the term "indeterminate life" as it relates to intangible assets.
3. Distinguish between identifiable and unidentifiable intangible assets.
4. What are some of the factors that should be considered in the determination of useful life of intangible assets?
5. How do the legal life and economic life of an intangible asset affect the accounting for the asset?
6. What costs might properly be considered organization costs for a firm? Describe the accounting treatment of organization costs.
7. Describe three alternatives for accounting for the costs of a research department involved in the development of patentable devices.
8. Define goodwill. List two ways in which goodwill may be acquired by a firm.

9. How is the cost of unidentifiable intangible assets measured?
10. List five different methods for computing goodwill.
11. How is the normal rate of return determined for a firm?
12. Describe two methods of amortizing goodwill.
13. What are the accounting problems associated with the accounting for initial franchise fees?
14. What conditions must exist for a franchisor to have substantially performed his requirements under a franchise contract?

PROBLEMS

Problem 18-1. The research staff of Spooner Manufacturing Company launched an intensive investigation early in 19+1 in order to find a less costly process of manufacturing transistor radios. Research costs amounting to $82,600 were incurred in that year and $189,100 of research costs were incurred during 19+2, until, in October, 19+2, a successful process was developed. A patent was secured on January 3, 19+3. Application fees amounted to $20. On that date, the board of directors decided to amortize the cost of the patent over ten years.

On August 8, 19+3, Spooner Manufacturing Company named its chief competitor as defendant in a patent infringement suit. Legal fees amounting to $8,300 were incurred during 19+3, and $2,600 of legal fees were incurred between January 1, 19+4 and March 10, 19+4, when arguments by opposing lawyers ended. The verdict, announced on June 1, 19+4, was in favor of the plaintiff. The decision was appealed and legal costs of $2,300 were incurred during the last four months of 19+4. The case was adjudicated on October 31, 19+5, when the U.S. Supreme Court ruled against Spooner Manufacturing Company. A rehearing was denied.

Spooner Manufacturing Company closes its books annually on June 30.

Compute the amounts which should be charged to Amortization of Patents for the fiscal years ending June 30, 19+3, 19+4, and 19+5. What journal entries, if any, should have been prepared when the case was finally decided?

Problem 18-2. Prepare a schedule showing the cost, amortization, and net balance of the patents of Stone Company for the period January 1, 19+2 to December 31, 19+7.

The company spent a total of $29,000 developing a basic patent which was applied for on March 1, 19+1.

Additional legal costs incurred in expediting the issue of the patent amounted to $750 by December 31, 19+1.

The patent was issued on January 2, 19+2, and manufacture began on that date.

On April 30, 19+3, the corporation paid $12,750 to attorneys for services in connection with an attempted infringement of this patent.

On July 1, 19+4, the corporation purchased a patent on a closely related improvement of the original patent for $30,000. The patent purchased had 15 years to run from July 1, 19+4. An opinion was given to the firm by competent counsel that this patent will extend the life of the old patent.

To protect its patent position, the company purchased a competing patent on October 1, 19+5. This patent cost the company $64,000 and had 16 years to run from the date of acquisition.

During 19+7, the corporation paid a total of $25,500 to perfect and apply for a modification of the company's original patent. The patent on the modification was issued on January 2, 19+8. It was understood that this patent would extend the period of protected production of the earlier patents over the life of the new patent.

Problem 18-3. Unamortized Organization Costs appears on the books of Norton, Incorporated, on December 31, 19+4, before closing, at $162,000. Debits to the account, all recorded in 19+1, were as follows:

Discount on issuance of common stock	$ 49,000
Attorney's fees for services in connection with organization of the corporation	6,000
Advertising costs	132,000
Charter fee paid to Secretary of State	1,000
Net loss for 19+1	28,000

Two credits, equal in amount, appear in the account and represent amortization adjustments for 19+2 and 19+3 at a percent of the total debits which was specified by the board of directors on December 31, 19+2.

The advertising costs resulted from an intensive "consumer education" campaign conducted early in 19+1. The sales promotion director estimates that the campaign will benefit the five-year period ending December 31, 19+5.

Prepare the necessary entries as of December 31, 19+4, to correct the balance of the above account. The yearly rate of amortization which was established by the board of directors need not be changed.

Problem 18-4. Fabulous Creations, Incorporated had the following debit items in its patents account on January 1, 1977. All of the patents were developed by the corporation.

(1) Cost of developing a patent expiring December 31, 1986	$38,600
(2) Cost of developing a patent expiring June 30, 1989	25,900
(3) Development costs of a patent granted to the corporation on April 1, 1975	19,200
(4) Costs incurred in patent developments prior to 1976, with no resulting patents as of January 1, 1977	22,000
(5) Cost incurred in patent development during 1976 with no resulting patents as of January 1, 1977	8,600

On May 1, 1977, a patent is received on a process which, in effect, will prolong the life of the patent mentioned in (2) above, over the legal life of the new patent. The total cost assignable to this patent includes $13,100 of the costs incurred prior to 1976, $2,600 of the costs incurred during 1976, and $7,600 of the costs incurred in 1977.

During 1977, total patent development costs amounted to $20,800. One project was abandoned in 1977, and it was decided to write off past development costs amounting to $3,900. No entry has been made to give effect to this decision. The corporation does not charge development costs to expense when incurred; it charges these costs to the patents account. Patent amortization has never been recorded.

Required:

(a) Computation of the correct balance in the patents account on December 31, 1977.
(b) Journal entries to correct the patents account on December 31, 1977, and to

establish an account entitled Unallocated Research Costs for any cost not allocated to specific patents. Assume that the books have not been closed.

Problem 18-5. On January 1, 1975, Sheridan Roads Corporation, as lessee, leased real estate, including a building which had been completed in December, 1930, with an expected useful life of 50 years. Under the terms of the lease agreement, the lessee was to make annual rental payments of $12,000. The lease was to run for 25 years without renewal option. The agreement also specified that property taxes, insurance, maintenance and repairs, costs of remodeling, and new construction were to be borne by the lessee. Remodeling costs incurred before occupancy were $34,000.

At the end of the seventh year in the life of the lease, the building was torn down and a new one was erected at a cost of $346,000, including taxes and insurance during the period of construction. The new structure had an estimated life of 30 years, with no scrap value. Two years were required to remove the old and construct the new building.

Sheridan Roads Corporation subleased the buildings during the entire period, except during the construction period; rental income from the old building was $32,000, and from the new building $50,000, per annum. Taxes, insurance, and repairs aggregated $6,000 a year for the old and $9,100 a year for the new building.

Required:

(a) Calculation of the total aggregate net income before income taxes earned by Sheridan Roads Corporation during the life of the lease.

(b) Income statements of Sheridan Roads Corporation for the first and last years of the lease.

Problem 18-6. The management of Edison Company has been negotiating with a prospective purchaser of the company and agreement has been reached on the following items, which deal with the company's earnings performance for five years and also give consideration to expected increases in sales and expenses.

Stockholders' equity, December 31, 19+7	$370,000
Recorded goodwill on company's books was paid for	25,000
Average earnings for the past five years	56,000
Expected increase in yearly sales attributable to recently completed addition to the company's facilities	70,000
Expected increase in annual expenses from the operation of the new facilities, including income taxes	55,000
Normal rate of earnings for the industry	10%
Net tangible assets	335,000

The following formulas are being considered for calculation of the amount of the firm's goodwill.

(1) Purchase of average excess earnings for five years.

(2) Average excess earnings capitalized at the normal profit rate.

(3) Average excess earnings up to $10,000 capitalized at the normal rate, and those above $10,000 capitalized at 20 percent.

(4) Discounted average excess earnings for five years using 10 percent as the discount rate.

Compute the goodwill under each of the four alternatives.

Problem 18-7. The following information pertains to Claghorn, Martin, and Prince Companies at December 31, 19+4.

	Claghorn Company	Martin Company	Prince Company
8% bonds payable (long-term) ..	$112,500	$100,000	—
Capital stock	112,500	90,000	$150,000
Retained earnings (deficit)	45,000	30,000	(30,000)
Total assets	300,000	225,000	150,000
Expected net income after taxes at 50%:			
19+5	36,000	18,750	15,000
19+6	37,500	20,250	16,200
19+7	37,875	21,000	17,496
Anticipated dividend policy for the years 19+5, 19+6, and 19+7 (as a percent of earnings)	60%	40%	none
Normal rate of return on assets .	12%	10%	8%

Prepare calculations to show the following:

(a) Which companies have goodwill?
(b) Which company has the most goodwill?

Problem 18-8. On the basis of the following information, prepare a schedule as of December 31, 1980, showing the estimated future annual net income which Alco Corporation may expect if it acquires the assets of Bark, Incorporated. The estimated future annual net income will be used as a base from which goodwill is to be computed.

Average annual net income for the years 1975–1980, inclusive .	$65,800
Excess of agreed price for building acquired on January 1, 1959, over its book amount (Bark, Incorporated, has been using a depreciation rate of 2½% of cost)	26,100
Expected annual increase in executive salaries to take place upon change of ownership	23,000

On the first business day of 1979, Bark, Incorporated, replaced several of its old machines. The loss of $6,000 resulting from the disposal of the old machines was reported in the 1979 income statement. The loss was attributable to inadequate depreciation taken on the old machines during the eight years they were in use.

Certain patents are to be retained by Bark, Incorporated. However, as a part of the agreement, full rights to these patents will be granted to Alco Corporation under a licensing arrangement, at an estimated annual royalty of $11,000. The company received annual royalties of $8,100 during 1977, 1978, 1979, and 1980. Half of these royalties were received from companies other than Alco Corporation, and the licensee of these patents may expect to continue to collect them.

Problem 18-9. On June 30, 19+1, Holland, Inc., purchased 100 percent of the oustanding common stock of Erickson Corporation for $3,605,000 cash and Holland's common stock having a market value of $4,100,000. At the date of purchase the book amount and fair values of Erickson's assets and liabilities were as follows:

	Book Amount	Fair Value
Cash	$ 160,000	$ 160,000
Accounts receivable, net	910,000	910,000
Inventory	860,000	1,025,186
Furniture, fixtures and machinery	3,000,000	2,550,000
Building	9,000,000	7,250,000
Accumulated depreciation	(5,450,000)	—
Intangible assets, net	150,000	220,000
	$8,630,000	
Accounts payable	$ 580,000	580,000
Note payable	500,000	500,000
5% mortgage note payable	4,000,000	3,710,186
Common stock	2,900,000	—
Retained earnings	650,000	—
	$8,630,000	

By the year end, December 31, 19+1, the net balance of Erickson's accounts receivable at June 30, 19+1, had been collected; the inventory on hand at June 30, 19+1, had been charged to cost of goods sold; the accounts payable at June 30, 19+1, had been paid; and the $500,000 note had been paid.

As of June 30, 19+1, Erickson's furniture, fixtures, and machinery and building had an estimated remaining life of eight and ten years, respectively. All intangible assets had an estimated remaining life of twenty years. All depreciation and amortization is to be computed using the straight-line method.

As of June 30, 19+1, the 5 percent mortgage note payable had eight equal annual payments remaining with the next payment due June 30, 19+2. The fair value of the note was based on a 7 percent rate.

The after-closing trial balances of the two corporations as of December 31, 19+1 are as follows:

	Holland Inc.	Erickson Corporation
Cash	$ 507,000	$ 200,750
Accounts receivable, net	1,890,000	817,125
Interest receivable	—	22,500
Inventory	2,031,000	1,009,500
Investment in Holland 6% bonds payable, net	—	290,000
Investment in subsidiary	7,705,000	—
Furniture, fixtures, and machinery	4,200,000	3,000,000
Buildings	17,000,000	9,000,000
Accumulated depreciation	(8,000,000)	(6,050,000)
Intangible assets, net	—	146,250
Totals	$25,333,000	$8,436,125

Accounts payable	1,843,000	575,875
Interest payable	200,500	100,000
Mortgage notes payable	6,786,500	4,000,000
7½% bonds payable	1,000,000	—
Discount on 7½% bonds payable	(24,000)	—
8¼% bonds payable	3,900,000	—
Common stock	8,772,500	2,900,000
Retained earnings	2,854,500	860,250
Totals	$25,333,000	$8,436,125

Depreciation and amortization expenses for Erickson Corporation from July 1, 19+1 to December 31, 19+1, were $600,000 and $3,730, respectively.

Required:

(a) Computations to determine the amount of goodwill purchased by Holland, Inc., after allocating the purchase price to specific asset(s) of Erickson to the extent possible.

(b) Calculation of the amount at which intangible assets would be reported on a consolidated balance sheet prepared for the companies at December 31, 19+1.

Problem 18-10. Davis Company is negotiating to purchase all of the assets except cash of Brown Company. No great difficulty is anticipated in negotiating prices for specific assets. However, there is some concern on the part of the representatives of Davis Company about the evaluation of Brown Company's earnings as to whether superior earning power from the assets is indicated, because Brown Company has followed different accounting policies from those of Davis Company in several instances.

The representatives of Davis Company believe that the best way to evaluate the earnings potential is to analyze the earnings of the three preceding years and to recompute them following the accounting policies of Davis Company. In addition to the adjustments attributable to the differences in accounting policies, adjustments should be made to remove any distortion introduced into the earnings record by unusual or nonrecurring items, and consideration should be given to any known factors which will affect future earnings.

You are asked to make a determination of the average earnings of Brown Company, based on the earnings for the years 19+6, 19+7, and 19+8, assuming that the policies of Davis Company had been in force and making whatever other revisions seem relevant. It is assumed that the charge for income taxes should be recomputed using the rate applicable to the earnings for 19+8. Also show what the carrying values of the assets, except cash, would have been as of December 31, 19+8.

Relevant financial information and policy differences are set forth below.

BROWN COMPANY
Balance Sheet
December 31, 19+8
Assets

Cash	$ 15,350
Receivables	90,200
Inventory	136,500
Lease of mineral rights	75,000
Long-lived assets	128,150
Accumulated depreciation (deduct*)	62,700*
	$382,500

Equities

Accounts payable	$ 31,150
Liability for 19+8 income taxes	12,000
Bonds payable—5% (issued 7/1/+2)	60,000
Common stock	200,000
Retained earnings	79,350
	$382,500

Net Income After Taxes

19+6	$24,500
19+7	26,250
19+8	28,000

Davis Company has used the last-in, first-out cost as a basis for pricing its inventory. Brown Company has used first-in, first-out. Inventory data for Brown Company under both methods follow.

	Fifo	Lifo
December 31, 19+5	$115,000	$105,000
December 31, 19+6	123,000	109,000
December 31, 19+7	129,000	112,000
December 31, 19+8	136,500	114,500

Brown Company discontinued a small segment of its business at the end of 19+5. It is estimated that 19+6 expenses included $4,000 of charges relating to the discontinuance.

Davis Company has followed a policy of writing off as current expenses all minor equipment items costing less than $300. This was the practice of Brown Company prior to 19+6. In 19+6, Brown changed its policy and expensed only items costing less than $100. Both companies have charged a full year's depreciation in the year of acquisition, regardless of the purchase date, and have used a 10 percent depreciation rate. Items costing between $100 and $300, by year of purchase by Brown Company, were:

19+6	$1,500
19+7	1,000
19+8	2,500

No utilization has as yet been made of the mineral rights held under lease. Development costs incurred in the past two years and charged to expense were: 19+7, $5,000; 19+8, $7,000. Data thus gathered indicate that the leasehold will, without further cost, generate royalty revenue of $12,500 per year for the next ten years.

Problem 18-11. The board of directors of Elkton, Incorporated, has entered into a contract with Prosper Company calling for the sale of the net assets (exclusive of cash) of the company, the consideration therefore to be computed as follows:

Net assets, less cash—at book amounts as adjusted by agreement of the parties.

Goodwill—at an amount computed by capitalizing estimated future excess annual earnings at a rate of 10 percent. Excess annual earnings are defined as the excess of the estimated future net income over an amount equal to 10 percent of the book amount, as adjusted for purposes of the sale, of net assets, including the cash.

You have been retained by the directors to compute the consideration to be received for the total net noncash assets of the company. The information presented below is made available to you for this purpose.

(1) The condensed balance sheet on December 31, 19+8, the effective date of the sale, is as follows:

ELKTON, INCORPORATED
Balance Sheet
December 31, 19+8

Assets		Equities	
Cash	$ 66,000	Accounts payable	$103,500
Accounts receivable—net of allowance of $3,000	47,700	Capital stock	290,000
Inventory	113,000	Retained earnings	64,000
Long-lived assets—net	230,800		
	$457,500		$457,500

(2) Included in administrative expenses for the year 19+7 were nonrecurring legal expenses of $9,000.

(3) It is anticipated that salesmen's salaries will increase in the amount of $13,000 per year.

(4) The average annual net income for the calendar years 19+4–19+8, inclusive, was $52,400.

(5) Through a clerical error, the December 31, 19+8 inventory is understated. The correct valuation is $118,300.

(6) The long-lived assets account comprises land, building, equipment, and showroom facilities. The land is carried at cost, $40,000. The building and equipment, purchased for $268,000 on January 1, 19+1, are to be valued at $198,000, which is replacement cost less depreciation.

(7) The showroom facilities were completed during December, 19+8, at a cost of $30,000. It is expected that the utilization of the additional space will begin early in January, 19+9, with a probable additional annual sales volume resulting therefrom of $16,000, on which a 25 percent gross margin is expected. The only additional expense arising from the use of these facilities will be depreciation on the facilities at the annual rate which the company has been using on the building and equipment.

(8) None of the depreciable long-lived assets is expected to have salvage value.

(9) A 19+5 expenditure of $36,000 for display advertising in trade publications was charged to that year's operations. It is estimated that this expenditure, which will continue to be made each fifth year, was of equal benefit to the operations of each year from 19+5 to 19+9, inclusive. There were no such advertising expenditures made prior to 19+5.

Required:

(a) An estimate of the future annual net income which Prosper Company may expect if it acquires the net noncash assets of Elkton, Incorporated.

(b) A determination of the total consideration to be paid for the net noncash assets of Elkton, Incorporated, in accordance with the terms presented above.

Problem 18-12. Super Burger, Inc., was established in early January, 19+1 for the purpose of franchising a number of short-order food outlets. Franchises of the company are sold under the following arrangements:

(1) The franchisee pays an initial fee of $25,000, of which $5,000 is payable at the date the franchise is sold. The balance is payable in two equal amounts, due six months and twelve months, respectively, after the franchise is sold. Interest is charged on the portion of the fee deferred at an annual rate of 4 percent on the balance outstanding.

(2) The initial franchise fee covers the following services rendered by the franchisor: Site selection, obtaining facilities and financing, training of franchisee's personnel, and the installation of quality control and record keeping systems. In addition, the franchisor reimburses the franchisee for one-half the cost of an initial advertising program, or $3,000, whichever is less.

(3) Franchisees are required to submit a monthly report of sales to the franchisor. An amount equal to one percent of the gross sales for the preceding calendar year or portion thereof must be paid to the franchisor by January 31 of each year.

(4) The franchisee may cancel the agreement any time within one year after the franchise is sold. In this case he will receive a refund of 50 percent of the initial franchise fee, less any direct costs associated with the franchise and incurred by the franchisor.

During the first year of operations, five franchises were sold. Information pertaining to each of these is presented below:

Franchise Number	Date Sold	Date Began Operations	Total Cost of Initial Advertising	Direct Costs Incurred by Franchisor to December 31	Sales to December 31
1	Jan. 15	Sept. 1	$ 8,000	$15,000	$65,000
2	March 20	July 15	5,000	18,000	75,000
3	June 6	—	1,000	8,000	—
4	Sept. 30	Dec. 15	7,000	12,500	10,300
5	Nov. 1	—	10,000	14,300	—

The purchaser of franchise number three cancelled the agreement on August 1. All amounts due the franchisee were refunded to him.

Required:

(a) A schedule showing for each franchise the total revenues and expenses to be reported by Super Burger, Inc., in 19+1. It may be assumed that the franchisor reports revenues from initial franchise fees as follows: (1) one-half on the date when the franchise is sold; (2) the remaining one-half as of the date the franchise begins operations or one year after the franchise is sold, whichever occurs later.

(b) Calculation of net income or loss for the year, assuming general expenses as follows: selling, $30,000; administrative, $40,000.

CHAPTER 19

QUESTIONS

1. With regard to liabilities, answer the following questions.
(**a**) What is a liability?
(**b**) What are the characteristics of liabilities?

2. With regard to pensions, what are the following distinctions?
(**a**) Pension plan and no pension plan
(**b**) Contributory and noncontributory plan
(**c**) Insured and noninsured plan
(**d**) Funded and nonfunded plan

3. With regard to liabilities, what are the following distinctions?
(**a**) Current and long-term liabilities
(**b**) Debt and liabilities
(**c**) Equities and liabilities
(**d**) Estimated and contingent liabilities

4. What is the difference between the accrual basis and the discretionary-cash basis of accounting for pension cost?

5. Are short-term notes payable reported in the balance sheet at their face amount or discounted amount?

6. What is the distinction between normal, past-service, and prior-service cost?

7. When should the current maturity of long-term debt *not* be reported as a current liability?

8. What is the controversy as to how to account for past-service cost?

9. What are accrued liabilities and how do they differ from accrued expenses?

10. With regard to the minimum and maximum provisions per APB *Opinion No. 8*, answer the following questions.
(**a**) What are the minimum and maximum provisions?
(**b**) What is meant by the statement that the minimum and maximum provisions are a compromise between two opposing viewpoints?
(**c**) What are interest equivalents?

11. What are the effects on the financial statements of a failure to show the liability for goods in transit shipped f.o.b. shipping point if the goods are not included in the inventory?

12. With regard to pensions, what are the following?
(**a**) Interest
(**b**) Actuarial gains and losses
(**c**) The period over which past-service costs are normally amortized.

13. If deferred revenue is revenue, then how can it be a liability?

14. Accountants determine pension costs based on funding (financing) methods and then allocate such costs to periodic expense. What does this statement mean?

15. Warranty costs should be charged to expense as they are actually incurred. Do you agree with this statement?

16. A manufacturer of ice cream purchased, on the deferred-payment plan, refrigerator units at a cost of $15,000. All these units were resold to customers at cost. Collections from the customers in payment of the units had been $3,126.18, whereas payments by the manufacturer to the distributor of the units totaled $6,180.31.

You are auditing the books of the manufacturer, who contends that he has no liability to the distributor because he purchased the refrigerator units for his customers and that an asset should appear on his balance sheet as follows:

Advances to customers:	
Payment made for customers' account	$6,180.31
Less cash received from customers	3,126.18
Balance	$3,054.13

Do you believe that your client is correct in his contentions?

17. During the course of an audit as of December 31, 19+7, you find that your client in 19+1 purchased two acres of land adjacent to its present plant for future expansion, subject to a first mortgage, the maturity of which was May 10, 19+5. The mortgage has not been refinanced but has been extended for one year at each May 10th since 19+5, the date of the annual 5 percent interest payment. The bank which owns the mortgage informs you that, subject to the usual interest payment at May 10, 19+8, it will grant the customary one-year extension of the mortgage to May 10, 19+9. Your client is in a good financial position. How will you show the mortgage liability on the balance sheet?

18. From a normative theory viewpoint, what is the proper valuation of pensions? Why is this not done in actual accounting practice?

19. The allocation of pension cost to periodic expense is similar to the depreciation of tangible, long-lived assets and has the same theoretical problems. What does this statement mean?

20. Since accountants are not willing to capitalize future wage commitments, it should be obvious they would not be willing to capitalize future pension benefits and obligations. What does this statement mean?

PROBLEMS

Problem 19-1. You are given below seven multiple choice questions. Select the correct answer to each question and indicate the corresponding letter on a separate sheet of paper (e.g., 1-a, 2-c, etc.).

(1) The Vandiver Corporation provides an incentive compensation plan under which its president receives a bonus equal to 10 percent of the Corporation's income in excess of $100,000 before income tax but after the bonus. If income before income tax and bonus is $320,000 and the effective tax rate is 40 percent, the amount of the bonus would be (a) $32,000, (b) $30,000, (c) $22,000, (d) $20,000, (e) none of the above.

(2) When the fiscal year of the taxpayer is different from that of the taxing authority, the amount of the taxpayer's monthly accrual of property taxes should be based upon (a) the taxpayer's fiscal year, (b) the taxing authority's fiscal year, (c) a 12-month period beginning with the assessment date, (d) a 12-month period beginning with the lien date, (e) none of the above.

(3) Which of the following contingencies need *not* be disclosed in the financial statements or the notes thereto: (a) pending litigation, (b) possibility of a strike, (c) possible assessments of additional taxes, (d) notes receivable discounted, (e) none of the above.

(4) When the following periods are different, the preferable treatment of real and personal property taxes is monthly accrual over the (a) fiscal period of the taxpayer, (b) fiscal period of the taxing authority, (c) year beginning on the assessment date, (d) year ending with the assessment date, (e) none of the above.

(5) A company in accounting properly for pension cost (a) allocates total pension costs systematically and rationally, (b) records fluctuating gains and losses on pension fund investments as they occur, (c) gives recognition to all pension costs for which legal liability exists, (d) establishes a positive relationship between contributions to the fund and the recorded provision, (e) none of the above.

(6) The prior-service cost of a pension plan should be (a) charged to retained earnings as a cost related to the past, (b) amortized over a specified period of years, (c) disregarded except that interest thereon is to be provided currently along with the normal cost, unless all benefit payments can not be met on a continuing basis by such annual provisions, (d) consistently provided within a defined minimum-maximum range in a manner most realistic in the circumstances, (e) none of the above.

(7) In accounting for individual deferred compensation contracts on the accrual basis, cumulative charges to expense during the period of active employment should approximate (a) the present value of future services to be performed, (b) the estimated present value of future payments, (c) the total amount of payments reasonably estimated to be made, (d) an estimated percentage of the employee's cumulative earnings, (e) none of the above.

Problem 19-2. You are given below seven multiple choice questions. Select the correct answer to each question and indicate the corresponding letter on a separate sheet of paper (e.g., 1-a, 2-b, etc.).

(1) When presenting pension plan costs on an income statement, past and present service costs (a) must be shown separately in computing operating income, (b) may be either combined or shown separately, (c) must be separated so that past service costs can be treated as a prior-period adjustment, (d) both should not be included on the income statement for a single year, (e) none of the above.

(2) Immediate recognition, spreading, and averaging are three techniques which affect the annual pension cost provision through the (a) recognition of actuarial gains and losses, (b) determination of the normal cost, (c) amortization of past-service cost, (d) funding of the plan, (e) none of the above.

(3) In accounting for a pension plan any difference between the pension cost charged to expense and the payments into the fund should be reported as (a) an offset to the liability for past-service cost, (b) accrued or prepaid pension cost, (c) an operating expense in this period, (d) an accrued actuarial liability, (e) none of the above.

(4) Past-service benefit costs incurred upon the adoption of a pension plan should be charged to (a) the current period, (b) retained earnings, (c) current and future periods benefited, (d) future periods benefited, (e) none of the above.

(5) With certain of its products, Hite Foods, Inc., includes coupons having no expiration date which was redeemable in merchandise. In the Company's experience, 40 percent of such coupons are redeemed. The liability for unredeemed coupons at December 31, 19+6, was $9,000. During 19+7, coupons worth $18,000 were

issued and merchandise worth $8,000 was distributed in exchange for coupons redeemed. The December 31, 19+7 balance sheet should include a liability of (a) $9,800, (b) $13,000, (c) $8,200, (d) $7,600, (e) none of the above.

(6) Cash dividends are usually declared on one date and payable on a subsequent date to stockholders of record on some intermediate date. At which of the following dates has the corporation incurred a liability: (a) the date the dividend is declared, (b) the date of record, (c) the date the dividend check is mailed by the corporation, (d) the date the dividend check is received by the stockholder, (e) none of the above.

(7) An example of an item which is not a liability is (a) dividends payable in stock, (b) advances from customers on contracts, (c) accrued estimated warranty costs, (d) the portion of long-term debt due within one year, (e) none of the above.

Problem 19-3. You have been engaged to audit the books of Sterling's Sterling Silver Company. During the course of your audit you discover that Sterling has failed to make a provision for payroll expense. You have assembled the following information for the year:

		Income Tax Withholding	
Name	Earnings	State	Federal
M. Perkins	$ 8,500	$200	$600
L. Smith	11,000	300	400
B. Buchholz	5,700	50	100
G. Braun	9,300	75	125
B. Bam	10,000	220	380

The FICA rate is 5.65 percent, the FUTA rate is .4 percent, and the state unemployment rate is 2.7 percent. The books have not been closed for the year under audit. Ignore individual income limits.

Required:

Prepare the entries needed to record the payment of the salaries, the payroll tax expense, and employer withholdings.

Problem 19-4. Grinning Glen Used Car Lot has a policy of paying bonuses to its sales manager and three salesmen. The car lot had net income for the year of $850,000 before bonuses and income taxes. Assume that the income tax rate is 40 percent.

Required:

Compute the bonuses under the following conditions and prepare the entries needed:

(a) Each bonus is 5 percent of income before income taxes and bonuses.
(b) Each bonus is 10 percent of income after income taxes but before bonuses.
(c) Each bonus is 15 percent of income after income taxes and bonuses.
(d) Each bonus is 20 percent of income after bonuses but before income taxes.

Problem 19-5. The following are transactions of Koch Company for the year 19+6:

(1) Koch Company had total sales during the year of $1,915,000. Sales taxes are 3 percent.

(2) The total payroll of Koch for the year was $850,000. (See Problem 19-3 for the applicable rates.)

(3) A movable crane was purchased out of state. Koch must pay a 3 percent use tax on the purchase of this crane. The crane purchase was financed by the issuance of a six-month note for $100,000 that was discounted at 8 percent.

(4) Koch estimates that its federal income tax will be $150,000 of which it has already made four quarterly payments of $30,000 each.

(5) An advance payment of $30,000 was received for merchandise to be delivered the next year.

Required:

Prepare the entries needed to record the above transactions.

Problem 19-6. Pichler Food-A-Rama offers to give its customers a place setting of dinnerware for every hundred dollars of sales (before sales tax) as verified by sales receipts. The cost of each place setting is one dollar and Pichler believes that only 30 percent of the sales receipts will be turned in for dinnerware. This promotion has been in effect for the entire year. Total sales (including a 3 percent sales tax) were $10,984,950. Pichler bought 20,000 dinnerware sets and issued 10,000 of these sets during the year in return for sales receipts.

Required:

(a) Prepare the entries needed to record the sales and sales tax for the year.

(b) Prepare the entries needed to record the transactions affecting Pichler's promotion program.

Problem 19-7. Summerfield Gourmet Shoppe sells vending machines for the industrial market with a five-year warranty covering the replacement of defective parts. Each machine is sold for $1,000 and the experience of the Shoppe has been that .4 percent need parts replaced in the first year, .4 percent in the second year, .1 percent in the third year, .7 percent in the fourth year, and .8 percent in the fifth year at an average cost of $10.

Operations were as follows:

Year	Sales	Warranty Payments
19+1	$1,000,000	$ 4,000
19+2	1,100,000	8,300
19+3	1,150,000	9,800
19+4	1,500,000	19,900

Required:

Prepare the entries that would have been made for each year to record the sales estimated liability under product warranties, and warranty payments.

Problem 19-8. The following are transactions of Liekteig Company for the year 19+8.

(1) On January 23, Liekteig purchased merchandise costing $39,000 from Kathy, Inc. The terms of the purchase were 2/10 E.O.M. Liekteig records its purchases at the net amount.

(2) On February 9, Liekteig acquired equipment in return for a $30,000 note with 12 percent interest deducted in advance (i.e., discounted) and a ninety day maturity.

(3) On March 1, the Board of Directors declared a $75,000 cash dividend, which was payable on April 10 to stockholders of record on March 20.

(4) Sales during the current year were $11,050,000. The state sales tax is 3 percent and the city sales tax is levied at a rate of 5 percent.

(5) Property taxes become a lien on the company's property on July 1. Property taxes of $15,000 become payable in equal installments on August 1 and November 1. Property tax liability is recorded at the lien date.

Required:

Prepare the entries needed to record the above transactions.

Problem 19-9. Bearded One Company had taxable income of $500,000. State income taxes are levied at a rate of 20 percent and Federal income taxes at a rate of 48 percent on income above $25,000 and 22 percent on all other income. State taxes are deductible in computing taxable income for Federal income taxes and Federal income tax is deductible in computing taxable income for the state. Assume the $500,000 is before any deduction for income taxes.

Required:

Prepare the entries needed to record the state and Federal income tax.

Problem 19-10. Oak Street Company is subject to property taxes by the county and city governmental units. Property taxes of $72,000 are assessed against the company's property on January 1, 19+4 and become a lien on May 1, 19+4. Taxes are payable in two equal installments on June 1 and December 31, 19+4. Oak Street Company closes its books on December 31. The fiscal year of the taxing authority is May 1 to April 30.

Required:

(a) Prepare the entries required to record the property tax liability if the liability is recorded at the lien date for Oak Street Company during the year 19+4.

(b) Prepare the entries required for the year 19+4 if Oak Street accrues the property tax expense monthly.

Problem 19-11. Dyer Corporation, a client with a fiscal year ending on June 30, requests that you compute the appropriate balance for its estimated liability under product warranties of June 30, 19+5.

Dyer Corporation manufactures television tubes and sells them with a six-month guarantee under which defective tubes will be replaced without charge. Expenses and losses resulting from the return of tubes sold in the preceding fiscal year are charged to the estimated liability under product warranties while such charges incurred for tubes sold in the current year are debited to the warranty expense account. On June 30, 19+4, the estimated liability under product warranties had a balance of $51,000. By June 30, 19+5, it had been reduced to $1,250.

The company started the current fiscal year expecting 8 percent of the dollar volume of sales to be returned. However, owing to the introduction of new models during the year, this estimated percentage of returns was increased to 10 percent on May 1. It is assumed that no tubes sold during a given month are returned in that month. Each tube is stamped with a date at time of sale so that the warranty may be properly administered. The following table of percentages indicates the likely pattern of sales returns during the six-month period of the warranty, starting with the month following the sale of tubes.

Month following sale	Percentage of Total Returns Expected
First	20
Second	30
Third	20
Fourth through sixth—10% each month	30
Total	100

Gross sales of tubes were as follows for the first six months of 19+5:

Month	Amount
January	$360,000
February	330,000
March	410,000
April	285,000
May	200,000
June	180,000

The company's warranty also covers the payment of freight cost on defective tubes returned and on new tubes sent out as replacements. This two-way freight cost runs approximately 10 percent of the sales price of the tubes returned. The manufacturing cost of the tubes is roughly 80 percent of the sales price, and the estimated salvage of returned tubes averages 15 percent of their sales price.

Problem 19-12. In January, 19+3 you were examining the financial statements of Lang Manufacturing Company for the year ended December 31, 19+2. Lang filed the necessary payroll tax returns for the first three quarters of 19+2 and had prepared drafts of the returns scheduled to be filled by January 31, 19+3.

The following information was available from the general ledger, copies and drafts of payroll tax returns and other sources:

General Ledger:

Account	Balance December 31, 19+2	Composition of Balance
Wages	$121,800	12 monthly entries from payroll summaries
Payroll Taxes Expense	8,382	F.I.C.A. (5.65 percent of $102,500), $5,791.25; state unemployment tax (2.7 percent of $59,000), $1,593; federal unemployment tax (.4 percent of $102,500), $410; amounts withheld from employee by F.I.C.A. tax in October and November and paid to depositary, $578.
Employee's Payroll Taxes Withheld	2,320	December income tax, $1,530; October through December F.I.C.A., $790
Employer's Payroll Taxes Payable	821	December F.I.C.A., $212; October through December state unemployment tax, $199; 19+2 federal unemployment tax, $410

Copies of 19+2 Tax Returns:

	Totals for Year	First Three Quarters (Duplicate Copies of Returns)	Last Quarter (Pencil Draft)
Gross wages	$121,800	$95,870	$25,930
Wages taxable for F.I.C.A.	102,500	88,520	13,980
F.I.C.A. tax	11,583	10,003	1,580
Income tax withheld	15,740	11,490	4,250
Wages taxable for state unemployment tax	59,000	51,640	7,360
Total state unemployment tax (employer only)	1,593	1,394	199
Total federal unemployment tax (employer only)	410		

Information from other sources:

(1) In August 19+2 six laborers were hired to tear down an old warehouse building located on the site where a new warehouse would soon be constructed. The laborers 19+2 wages, totaling $1,000, were charged to the property, plant, and equipment account. Payroll taxes were not withheld.

(2) Included in a 19+2 wages expense account is one month's salary of $1,400 paid to the president on December 30, 19+2 for his 19+1 vacation allowance.

(3) A gross factory payroll of $1,200 through December 31, 19+2 and the related F.I.C.A. taxes (employer and employee) were accrued on the general ledger at the year end for a portion of the week ending January 4, 19+3. Each of the employees included in this payroll earned between $4,000 and $6,000 as a Lang employee in 19+2. The state maximum taxable wage base is $3,900.

(4) In December 19+2 a contractor was paid $2,300 for making repairs to machinery usually made by Company employees and the amount was charged to wages expense. No payroll taxes were withheld.

Required:

(a) Prepare a schedule presenting the computation of total taxable wages to be reported on the 19+2 payroll tax returns for F.I.C.A. and for state unemployment taxes.

(b) Prepare a schedule presenting the computation of the amounts (to the nearest dollar) which should be paid with each of the year-end payroll tax returns to be filed in January 19+3 for (1) F.I.C.A. taxes and income tax withheld, (2) state unemployment tax and (3) federal unemployment tax.

(c) Prepare a schedule to reconcile the differences between the amounts which should be paid with payroll tax returns to be filed in January 19+3 (as computed for "b") and the balances shown at December 31, 19+2 in the related general ledger liability accounts.

Problem 19-13. You are given below a pension past service cost amortization table, assuming a 4 percent rate.

Year	Fourteen-Year Accrual	Reduction for Interest	Past-Pension Expense	Ten-Year Funding	Deferred Charge End of Year Balance Sheet
1	$9,466.92	-0-	$9,466.92	$12,329.09	$ 2,862.17
2	9,466.92	$114.49	9,352.43	12,329.09	5,838.83
3	9,466.92	233.55	9,233.37	12,329.09	8,934.55

Year	Fourteen-Year Accrual	Reduction for Interest	Past-Pension Expense	Ten-Year Funding	Deferred Charge End of Year Balance Sheet
4	$9,466.92	$ 357.38	$9,109.54	$12,329.09	$12,154.10
5	9,466.92	486.16	8,980.76	12,329.09	15,502.43
6	9,466.92	620.10	8,846.82	12,329.09	18,984.70
7	9,466.92	759.39	8,707.53	12,329.09	22,606.26
8	9,466.92	904.25	8,562.67	12,329.09	26,372.68
9	9,466.92	1,054.91	8,412.01	12,329.09	30,289.76
10	9,466.92	1,211.59	8,255.33	12,329.09	34,363.52
11	9,466.92	1,374.54	8,092.38	—	26,271.14
12	9,466.92	1,050.85	8,416.07	—	17,855.07
13	9,466.92	714.20	8,752.22	—	9,102.35
14	9,466.92	364.09	9,102.35	—	-0-

Required:

(a) Show how the fourteen-year accrual of past-service cost was determined if the past service cost was $100,000.

(b) Show how the funding accrual was determined.

(c) Show how the reduction for interest factor was determined in year 2.

(d) Show how the past-pension expense was determined in year 2.

(e) What is the maximum provision for past-pension expense in year 1 given the above information?

(f) What is the minimum provision for past-pension expense in year 1 given the above information?

(g) Assuming that the normal cost was $10,000, what would the entry for pension expense be in year 5?

(h) Show how the deferred charge on the balance sheet would be calculated at the end of year 2.

(i) Show how the deferred charge on the balance sheet would be calculated at the end of year 11.

Problem 19-14. The Channing Sales Corporation adopts an employee pension plan on January 1, 19+5. The data pertaining to the plan are listed below:

(1) The normal pension cost is $100,000 per year.

(2) The discounted amount (present value) of the past-service cost is $308,869 on January 1, 19+5.

(3) The amount paid to the pension trust at the end of each year is equal to the normal pension cost.

(4) The pension fund is expected to earn a 5 percent return.

Required:

(a) Assume that the past-service cost was unfunded on the date of adopting the pension plan. Further assume that the maximum provision per *Opinion No. 8* is used in determining the annual pension cost to be charged to expense. Based on these assumptions and the information given above, prepare in general journal form the entry to record the payment to the pension trust and the provision for pension cost for 19+5.

(b) The same requirement as in (a) above, except that the minimum provision per *Opinion No. 8* is used in determining the annual provision for pension cost.

(c) Under the assumptions in part (a) above, prepare the journal entry to record the annual payment to the pension trust and the provision for pension cost for 19+6.

(d) Under the assumptions in part (b) above, prepare the journal entry to record the annual payment to the pension trust and the provision for pension cost for 19+6.

Problem 19-15. Shattuck Manufacturing Company adopted an employee pension plan on January 1, 19+5. The data pertaining to the plan are listed below:

(1) The annual normal cost is estimated to be $75,000.

(2) The total actuarially determined past-service cost is estimated to be $800,000. The past-service cost will be amortized over 30 years.

(3) The rate of interest on the pension fund is estimated to be 5 percent.

(4) The company will fund the past-service cost over a forty year period.

Required: (Round to nearest dollar.)

(a) Prepare a table giving all needed information for the first five years.

(b) Using the information in the table prepared for (a), prepare the journal entries to record the amount funded in the first and the fifth years and the provision for pension expense.

Problem 19-16. As a result of labor negotiations Tongier Corporation adopts an employee pension plan. The company's actuary has estimated that the past service cost as of January 1, 19+2 is $300,000. The company on January 1, 19+4 amends the plan thereby incurring prior-service costs of $100,000. Normal cost of the plan is $30,000 before amendment and $35,000 after amendment. Interest will be earned at 6 percent.

Required: (Round to the nearest dollar.)

(a) Prepare the entries to record the pension expense under the minimum provision if the plan is (1) funded, (2) unfunded, for the years 19+2, 19+3, and 19+4.

(b) Prepare the entries to record the pension expense under the maximum provision if the plan is (1) funded, (2) unfunded, for the years 19+2, 19+3, and 19+4.

(c) Prepare the entries for the years 19+2, 19+3, and 19+4 to record the pension expense under the maximum provision if the annual funding is $45,000.

Problem 19-17. George Ripple, president of Ripple Company, is interested in determining what effect a proposed employee pension plan will have on the company's earnings. The past-service cost has been computed to be $85,000 and the normal cost will be $20,000 annually. Interest will be earned at 6 percent.

Required:

(a) Compute for president Ripple, assuming that the past-service cost is not funded, the cost of the plan in the first and fifth year under (1) the maximum annual provision for pension expense; (2) the minimum annual provision for pension expense.

(b) Compute the same expenses as in (a) above assuming that the past-service costs are funded with a payment of $26,175 at the end of each year.

Problem 19-18. Saxon Manufacturing Company adopted an employee pension plan on January 1, 19+5. The data pertaining to the plan are listed below:

(1) The annual normal cost is estimated to be $75,000.
(2) The total actuarially determined past service cost is estimated to be $800,000.
(3) The rate of interest on the pension fund is estimated to be 5 percent.
(4) The company will fund the past-service cost at a rate of $100,000 a year.

Required:

(a) Prepare the entries for the years 19+5, 19+6, and 19+7 for the pension expense under (1) minimum provision, (2) maximum provision.
(b) Prepare the entries to record the entries for 19+5 and 19+6 under the minimum provision if the annual funding was $150,000.

Problem 19-19. Ultra Furniture Company has decided to start a pension plan for its employees after operating for several years without such a plan. If the plan is started on January 1, 19+3, the present value of the past service cost is actuarially determined to be $100,000.

Required (round to the nearest dollar):

(a) Prepare a table amortizing over twelve years and funding over ten years the past-service cost, assuming a 5 percent interest rate and payments at the end of each year.
(b) Ignoring maximum and minimum pension provisions per *Opinion No. 8,* and using the data developed in part (a), prepare journal entries to record pension expense and funding for: (1) First year of plan; (2) Second year of plan; (3) Tenth year of plan; (4) Twelfth year of plan.
(c) Prepare a table amortizing over twelve years and funding over fifteen years the past-service cost, assuming a 5 percent interest rate.
(d) Ignoring maximum and minimum pension provisions per *Opinion No. 8,* and using the data developed in part (c), prepare journal entries to record pension expense for: (1) First year of plan; (2) Second year of plan; (3) Twelfth year of plan; (4) Fifteenth year of plan.

CHAPTER 20

QUESTIONS

1. What are four basic rights of shareholders of a corporation?
2. Describe the concept of legal or stated capital.
3. In what ways may one class of stock have "preferences" over another class of stock?
4. Describe the participating feature contained in some preferred stock issues.
5. What are two reasons why the corporate form of business organization is so prevalent among large firms.
6. How should uncollected stock subscriptions receivable be reported on the balance sheet of a corporation?
7. What information pertaining to each class of stock outstanding should be reported in a firm's balance sheet?

8. When different types of securities are sold as a package by a corporation, how is the total selling price allocated to the different securities?

9. Discuss the procedures used for the valuation of stock issued for property.

10. Describe two alternative procedures that may be followed for the accounting records when an existing firm is incorporated.

11. What is the advantage to the preferred shareholder of the cumulative feature of preferred stock?

12. Can the legal or stated capital of a firm ever be reduced? If so, how is this accomplished?

PROBLEMS

Problem 20-1. Sunny Products Corporation was organized on January 20, 19+1, with capital stock authorized as follows: Cumulative 6 percent preferred, $15 par value; 200,000 shares. Common, no par value; stated value, $10; 1,000,000 shares.

The corporation issues stock certificates when subscriptions are fully paid. Journalize, in general journal form, the transactions listed below. You may omit explanations.

(1) 40,000 shares of common stock were issued for cash at $12 per share.
(2) 20,000 shares of preferred stock were issued at par for cash.
(3) 50,000 shares of preferred stock were subscribed at par value.
(4) $250,000 was received on the above subscription to preferred stock.
(5) 100 shares of preferred stock were issued in payment of attorneys' fees of $2,000 in connection with organizing the corporation.
(6) 200,000 shares of common stock were issued for plant and equipment which had a fair market value of $1,200,000.
(7) 30,000 shares of preferred stock were issued for cash at a 5 percent premium.
(8) 80,000 shares of common stock were subscribed for at $844,000.
(9) Fifty percent of the above common stock subscription was collected.
(10) The balance owing on the subscription described in (3) and (4) was collected and the preferred shares were issued.

Problem 20-2. Construct the Stockholders' Equity section of the June 30, 19+9 balance sheet to show correctly the information presented in each of the following unrelated situations:

(1) Alpha Corporation is authorized to issue 12,000 shares of $100 par value, 6 percent cumulative preferred stock and 25,000 shares of no-par common stock. The common stock has not been given a stated value.

On July 1, 19+1, 4,000 preferred shares were issued for cash at $103 per share. The remaining authorized preferred shares have not been issued.

12,000 common shares were issued for $30 per share, cash, on January 2, 19+1. An issuance of 6,000 shares, at $35 per share, was completed on August 1, 19+2. The remaining authorized common shares were issued at $50 per share on May 16, 19+4.

From the date of organization to June 30, 19+9, the company had total net income of $293,000, and had declared and paid dividends as follows:

Preferred	$192,000
Common	70,000

(2) Beta Corporation is authorized to issue 9,000 shares of 6 percent cumulative preferred stock, par value $50, and 18,000 shares of no-par common stock, which has been given a stated value of $10 per share by the board of directors.

The preferred stock is also preferred as to assets in the event of liquidation in an amount equal to par value plus dividends in arrears.

7,000 shares of preferred stock were issued on August 10, 19+2, at $54 per share. All of the authorized common shares were issued at $12 per share on March 1, 19+1.

As of June 30, 19+9, Beta Corporation had a deficit of $80,000.

Problem 20-3. On September 1, 19+1, Mr. R. Jensen subscribed to purchase 1,000 shares of Wallace Cement, Inc. preferred, 5 percent cumulative, $50 par value stock. The subscription price was $54 a share and equal payments were to be made over a four month period.

On October 1, 19+1 Mr. Jensen paid $13,500 on his subscription. Mr. Jensen notified Wallace on October 12 that he would not be able to pay any of the unpaid subscription contract. On October 15, the corporation sold these 1,000 shares at $52 a share with selling expenses of $30.

Prepare all journal entries to record the above transactions under the following independent assumptions:

(1) That Mr. Jensen forfeits any amount paid.
(2) That Mr. Jensen receives a refund on his subscription less the expenses incurred in reselling the stock.
(3) That Mr. Jensen receives the number of shares his partial payment will pay for in full.

Problem 20-4. On June 1, 19+1, Clinton Corporation received authorization to issue the following: 20,000 shares of nonvoting 6 percent cumulative, fully participating class A preferred stock, par value, $100; 10,000 shares of 6 percent cumulative, nonparticipating class B preferred stock, par value, $80; and 50,000 shares of no-par common stock.

The directors assigned a stated value of $40 per share to the common stock.

Class A preferred stock and common stock were to be offered to subscribers in units of one share of class A preferred and two shares of common.

On August 23, 19+1, 3,000 units were subscribed for; in addition, 7,000 units were issued for cash. Both transactions were completed at $200 per unit. Later the same day, class A preferred shares were traded on a stock exchange at $107 per share.

On November 18, 19+1, 6,000 shares of class B preferred stock were subscribed for at $85 per share.

First installments of $150,000 (one-fourth) on the units and $170,000 (one-third) on class B preferred shares were collected on January 31, 19+2.

The final three-quarters of the subscriptions for all but 100 units were received on April 1, 19+2, and the certificates for fully-paid shares were issued.

On April 15, 19+2, O. S. Hested notified the company that he would be unable to fulfill his subscription contract for 50 units. In accordance with state law, the company, on April 20, 19+2, sold the 50 units for $9,000 cash. The company paid selling expenses on this transaction in the amount of $60. The company then refunded the balance of Hested's installment payment after deducting therefrom the deficiency resulting from the default and the selling expenses.

Prepare journal entries for the preceding transactions.

Problem 20-5. On January 2, 19+1, the date of organization, The Bigelow Company issued 15,000 shares of $50 par, 5 percent cumulative preferred stock (authorized, 30,000 shares) at $54 per share and 10,000 shares of no-par common stock (authorized, 25,000 shares) at $23 per share. Stated value of the common stock is $20 per share.

On July 1, 19+2, 1,000 additional preferred shares were issued at $56 per share.

Net income and cash dividends, which are customarily declared yearly in December, were as follows:

	Net Income	Cash Dividends
19+1	$140,000	$60,000
19+2	145,000	90,000

Determine dividends for both 19+1 and 19+2 on each class of stock based on the following assumptions:

(1) Preferred stock is nonparticipating.
(2) Preferred stock is participating up to 7 percent.
(3) Preferred stock is fully participating.

Problem 20-6. Extra Corporation is authorized to issue two classes of capital stock: 5,000 shares of $10 par value, 6 percent cumulative preferred; 10,000 shares of no-par common.

The state in which the company is incorporated requires that a minimum of $5 per share shall be paid to a corporation for each share of no-par stock issued, and that at least this amount must be credited to the capital stock account. The directors of Extra Corporation have taken no action relative to a stated value per share.

On July 20, 19+3, 6,000 shares of common stock were issued for $39,000 in cash.

On August 11, 19+3, 3,000 shares of preferred stock were issued for $33,000 in cash.

On December 15, 19+3, subscriptions were received for 1,000 shares of common stock at $7 per share.

The corporation has selected the calendar year as its accounting year. For the fractional-year ending December 31, 19+3, the corporation operated at a loss of $14,300.

Required:

(a) Journal entries to record the transactions involving the capital stock of the corporation.
(b) The preferred stock account as it would appear in the general ledger as of December 31, 19+3.
(c) The Stockholders' Equity section of the December 31, 19+3 balance sheet.

Problem 20-7. Sussman Company has authorized capital stock as follows: $25 par value, 6 percent cumulative preferred stock, 10,000 shares authorized; No par value common stock, 50,000 shares authorized.

The applicable state laws specify that legal or stated capital includes the par value of shares issued. In the case of no par value stock, legal capital includes the total subscription or issue price of the shares.

The company issues stock certificates when subscriptions are received.

The following transactions took place during the first year of operations.

(1) Subscriptions are received from 5,000 shares of preferred stock at $28 per share and for 30,000 shares of common stock at $18 per share.

(2) Cash is collected from subscribers as follows:

Preferred stock	$100,000
Common stock	300,000

(3) Subscriptions are received for 2,000 shares of preferred stock at $31 per share.
(4) The remaining shares of authorized preferred stock are subscribed at $29 per share.
(5) Cash of $150,000 is received from subscribers to preferred stock.
(6) Land appraised for $18,000 is acquired in exchange for 1,000 shares of common stock.
(7) Subscriptions are received for 10,000 shares of common stock at $16 per share.
(8) Collections on common stock subscriptions are made in the amount of $300,000.

Required:

(a) Journal entries to record the foregoing transactions.
(b) Computation of the legal or stated capital of the firm.

Problem 20-8. Swan Corporation was organized on January 2, 19+1, with an authorized capital consisting of 15,000 shares of preferred stock of $100 par value and 60,000 shares of no-par common stock without stated value.

Transactions during 19+1 and 19+2, relative to capital stock, were:

19+1

(1) 20,000 shares of common stock were issued for cash at $10 per share.
(2) 4,000 shares of preferred were subscribed at par under the following conditions:
   (a) Subscriptions to preferred shares were accepted only for round lots in multiples of 100-share units.
   (b) Payment was to be made at the subscriber's convenience, but final settlement was to be made within six months of the subscription date. Shares were to be issued only when subscriptions had been collected in full.
   (c) Any amounts paid in on subscriptions not fully paid were to be returned, after deducting any expenses or deficiency incurred in the re-subscription of the shares.
(3) Collections on the subscriptions described in (2) are summarized below:
   (a) Subscriptions to 3,800 shares were collected in full within six months and the shares were issued.
   (b) Subscribers to 200 shares paid in only $12,700 within the six-month period. Expenses of $2,100 were incurred in securing subscribers for the shares of the defaulted subscribers. The new subscribers paid immediately a total of $18,000 for the shares covered in the defaulted subscription agreements.
(4) Late in 19+1, 10,000 shares of common stock were issued for cash at $15 per share.
(5) Shortly thereafter, 3,000 additional shares of preferred stock were subscribed at $105 on the same terms set forth under (2).
(6) When the year ended, collections in full had been received on 1,800 of the shares described in (5). $62,800 had been received on 900 of the remaining shares, and the corporation had reason to believe that subscribers to the other 300 shares, from whom no collections had been received, would default.

19+2

(7) Early in 19+2 the balance owing on the 900 shares was collected. No amounts were received from the subscribers to the 300 shares mentioned in (6).

Required:

(a) Journal entries to record all transactions related to capital stock during 19+1 and 19+2.

(b) The Stockholders' Equity section of the corporation's balance sheet as of December 31, 19+1. The company had a net loss of $21,600 in 19+1.

Problem 20-9. Prepare the necessary journal entries to record the change in authorized (and outstanding) common stock of Taylor Corporation from 1,000 shares with $25 par value to 2,000 shares of no par value, in each of the following unrelated cases:

(1) The corporation issued the 1,000 shares of $25 par value stock at par. A stated value of $10 per share has been assigned to the no par stock.

(2) The $25 par value stock was issued at a premium of $10 per share. The no par stock has been assigned a stated value of $15 per share.

(3) The $25 par value stock was issued at a premium of $15 per share. No stated value is assigned to the no par stock.

(4) The $25 par value stock was issued for $23 per share. No stated value is assigned to the no par stock.

Problem 20-10. Southwestern Transmission Corporation was organized on May 1, 19+1, to acquire facilities and contracts for the transmission of natural gas from producers to local utilities. Capital stock authorized consisted of $20,000,000 in $50 par value common, and $15,000,000 in 5 percent first preferred of $100 par value.

On May 5, forty percent of the common stock was subscribed at a 6 percent premium. Payment was to be made one-half at the date the subscriptions were received and the balance on May 25, 19+1. The balance was collected in full.

On May 6, 1,000 shares of common stock were issued to the law firm of Bell and Osmundson in payment of their bill for $50,000 for services in organizing the corporation.

On May 26, the corporation completed arrangements for the purchase of the assets and the assumption of the liabilities of Bridger Service Corporation, agreeing to pay $4,500,000 in preferred stock and the balance one-half in common stock (at par) and one-half in cash. The balance sheet of Bridger Service Corporation is presented below:

BRIDGER SERVICE CORPORATION
Balance Sheet
May 26, 19+1

Assets			Equities	
Cash		$ 675,000	Accounts payable	$ 3,330,000
Accounts receivable		2,205,000	Expenses payable	765,000
Sundry assets		2,880,000	5% debenture bonds payable	13,500,000
Plant and equipment	$23,238,000		Capital stock	7,200,000
Less accumulated depreciation	6,183,000	17,055,000	Retained earnings	1,620,000
Goodwill		3,600,000		
		$26,415,000		$26,415,000

By agreement:

An allowance for uncollectible accounts of $405,000 is to be set up.
Sundry assets are valued at $3,600,000.
Plant and equipment are valued at $21,600,000, net of accumulated depreciation.
Goodwill is to be removed from the accounts.

Required:

(a) Journal entries to adjust and close the books of Bridger Service Corporation.
(b) Journal entries to record all transactions of Southwestern Transmission Corporation through May 26, when the acquisition of Bridger Service Corporation was consummated.
(c) The balance sheet of Southwestern Transmission Corporation at the close of business, May 26, 19+1.

Problem 20-11. Johnson Company has the following stock authorization: 100,000 shares of 5 percent preferred stock; 300,000 shares of common stock.

The following account balances were taken from the records of the company at December 1, 19+2.

Preferred stock subscribed	$225,000
Preferred stock (par value, $75, non-cumulative)	2,250,000
Subscriptions receivable—Preferred	150,000
Subscriptions receivable—Common	165,000
Common stock subscribed	400,000
Common stock (stated value, $25)	250,000
Capital in excess of par value—From preferred stock issuances	50,000
Capital in excess of stated value—From common stock issuances	37,500
Retained earnings (as of December 31, 19+1)	500,000
Capital in excess of stated value—From forfeited subscriptions to common stock	500

The following transactions occurred during December 19+2.

6—Final installment on 10,000 common shares subscribed for at $26 per share was received; the certificates were issued. The subscriptions were collected in four equal installments.
13—Cash subscriptions of $156,000 were received for the issuance of 2,000 shares of preferred stock; the cash was received and the shares were issued.
14—Land was acquired in exchange for 2,500 shares of preferred stock.
16—3,000 shares of common stock were subscribed for $27 per share.
20—A machine was acquired for 2,000 shares of common stock.

Net income for 19+2 was $150,000. Dividends of $100,000 were declared and paid on the preferred stock during the first 11 months of 19+2. At year end it was determined that $15,000 of common stock subscriptions might prove to be uncollectible.

Required:

(a) Necessary journal entries for December 19+2 based on the information above.
(b) The Stockholders' Equity section of the December 31, 19+2 balance sheet.

Problem 20-12. Goss operated a small manufacturing concern as a single proprietor. The business needed additional cash in order to be in a position to accept larger orders. Goss interested Ellison and Newton in becoming stockholders and directors in a new corporation, called The Sun Corporation. The new corporation was authorized to issue 400,000 shares of $5 par value common stock.

On July 1, 19+9, The Sun Corporation received the following stock subscriptions:

Subscriber	Shares	Terms	
Ellison	50,000 shares	$260,000 cash.	
Newton	50,000 shares	$200,000 in cash and $60,000 in sixty days.	
Goss	100,000 shares	Transfer of the following assets used by Goss in his manufacturing business:	
		Accounts receivable, guaranteed by Goss to be collectible	$100,000
		Inventory, at cost or market, whichever is lower	200,000
		Machinery, original cost	300,000

Stock certificates were issued immediately to Ellison and Goss.

On September 15, 19+9, the corporation made an assessment on its stockholders in the amount of $.25 per share. The assessments were collected on that date.

As of December 31, 19+9, the corporation changed its stock from $5 par value to no par value with a stated value of $4 per share. The stockholders exchanged their shares as of this date.

Give the journal entries that would be made in the records of The Sun Corporation as a result of the facts stated above. You may assume that Newton honored his stock subscription agreement on August 30, 19+9.

CHAPTER 21

QUESTIONS

1. Why do corporations issue stock rights and warrants?
2. How is a valuation determined for stock warrants issued with other securities?
3. For what purposes are employee stock option plans adopted by corporations?
4. Distinguish between noncompensatory and compensatory stock option plans.
5. What are the characteristics of a noncompensatory stock option plan?
6. How is the compensation represented by compensatory stock option plans measured?
7. When should the compensation represented by compensatory stock option plans be charged against income of the firm?
8. What information concerning stock option plans should be disclosed in the corporation's financial statements?
9. Under what circumstances might a holder of convertible preferred stock wish to exercise the conversion privilege and exchange preferred shares for common shares?
10. State the general rules to be followed in accounting for the conversion of preferred stock into common stock.

11. How should the proceeds of debt securities issued with detachable stock warrants be accounted for?

12. What is the proper date for measuring the compensation cost associated with a stock option plan?

PROBLEMS

Problem 21-1. Heritage Corporation has the following transactions during 19+1:

January 1	Received subscriptions to 1,000 shares of $75 par value, 6 percent cumulative preferred stock at $77 a share. Each share has a warrant entitling the purchaser to buy one share of $50 par value common stock at $47 per share. The current market price of the common is $46 per share. The subscription requires a 30 percent down payment and the balance in two equal monthly installments.
January 30	Collected the first installment on the preferred stock subscriptions.
February 8	The market price of the common stock is now $48 per share and 250 warrants are exercised.
February 15	Sold 1,000 shares of preferred stock for $78 per share. The same warrant option is included in the sale of the preferred. The current market price of the common stock is $48.50.
February 28	Collected the final installment on all but 100 shares of the preferred stock subscribed on January 1. The warrants on these 100 shares have been exercised and the subscriber forfeits the amount paid on the subscription.
March 1	100 shares of preferred not issued under the forfeited subscription is sold for $76.
March 28	1,215 warrants are exercised. 750 warrants were from the first issue and the remainder from the February 15 issue.
July 1	All unexercised warrants lapse.

Prepare journal entries to record the above transactions.

Problem 21-2. Rich Corporation had the following stockholders' equity on December 31, 19+4:

Preferred stock—6%, cumulative, nonparticipating, convertible; par value, $50; 10,000 shares authorized and issued	$ 500,000
Common stock—$20 stated value; 50,000 shares authorized; 25,000 issued and outstanding	500,000
Capital in excess of par value—From preferred stock issuances	10,000
Capital in excess of stated value—From common stock issuances	50,000
Retained earnings	185,000
	$1,245,000

5,000 shares of common stock were issued on January 2, 19+3. All other shares indicated above were outstanding on December 31, 19+1, and there were no dividends in arrears as of that date.

The corporation has paid the following dividends:

19+2	$ 45,000
19+3	87,000
19+4	129,000

On January 2, 19+5, 1,000 shares of preferred stock were converted into common, the conversion basis being two shares of common for each share of preferred converted.

Required:

(a) The amount of dividends paid on each class of stock for each of the three years. Present working papers to support your answers.
(b) The entry for the conversion of shares on January 2, 19+5.

Problem 21-3. Dittrich Corporation's stockholders' equity as of December 31, 19+1, appears below:

DITTRICH CORPORATION
Partial Balance Sheet
December 31, 19+1

Stockholders' equity:	
Common stock, $25 par value; 500,000 shares authorized; 96,000 shares issued and outstanding	$2,400,000
Capital in excess of par value—From common stock issuances	120,000
Retained earnings	268,400

On January 1, 19+2, the corporation gave to the old shareholders 20,000 rights, each one permitting the purchase of one $25 par value share at $30. The rights were void after 60 days. The market price of the stock at this time was $32 per share.

All but 260 of the above rights were exercised by March 1, 19+2.

On July 1, 19+2, the corporation sold to the public a $100,000 6 percent bond issue at 106. One detachable stock purchase warrant was given for each $100 face value of bonds purchased. These warrants entitled the holder to acquire a share of the corporation's capital stock at $35 per share, any time within five years. The stock was selling at $33 on this date. Immediately after the sale of the bonds, the bonds were selling at a price of 105 without the warrants, and the warrants were selling at a price of $1 each.

By January 2, 19+3, the corporation's earnings had increased the retained earnings to $402,600 and the common stock was selling at $38. 230 warrants were exercised on this date.

On December 31, 19+3, with retained earnings up to $580,200, the corporation's stock rose to $42, and 720 warrants were exercised on this date.

In the ensuing year the market price of the corporation's stock fell below $35, and the price did not again go above this figure within the five-year period. The remaining warrants were never used by bondholders.

Required:

(a) Appropriate entries in general journal form to record the above transactions.
(b) The Stockholders' Equity section of the corporation's balance sheet on December 31, 19+3.

Problem 21-4. On January 1, 19+2, Milton Company granted stock options for 6,000 shares of $75 par value common stock to company executives. The market price of the stock on this date was $83 per share and the option price was $80. The options could be exercised no sooner than 18 months after they were granted and any unexercised options expired on December 31, 19+6.

Options for 4,000 shares were exercised on November 1, 19+3, when the market price was \$88 per share; and an additional 1,500 options were exercised on July 3, 19+5, when the market price was \$81 per share. No other options were exercised by the expiration date.

The company uses a calendar-year accounting period.

Required:

(a) A schedule showing the amount of compensation represented by the options and the way in which the compensation should be charged against income.

(b) All journal entries required during the period January 1, 19+2 to December 31, 19+6 to record the information above.

Problem 21-5. Robbins Corporation's board of directors approved the following stock option plan for certain key executives on July 1, 19+2:

(1) 13,000 shares of \$25 par value common are to be set aside for the executives as of July 1, 19+2.

(2) The option price per share is \$35.

(3) The options may be exercised at any time between July 1, 19+4 and June 30, 19+6. Options outstanding at July 1, 19+6 will expire.

(4) The options are non-transferable and lapse if the executive leaves the firm.

On July 1, 19+2 the market price of the common stock was \$30 per share.

The table below summarizes the transactions under the option plan.

		Options Exercised	
Officer	Options Issued	Date	Number
President	5,000	July 1, 19+4	2,500
		July 1, 19+5	2,000
Vice President—Marketing	2,000	July 1, 19+4	2,000
Vice President—Production	2,000	June 30, 19+6	2,000
Vice President—Finance	2,000	July 1, 19+4	1,000
		July 1, 19+5	500
		December 30, 19+5	500
Vice President—Personnel	2,000	July 1, 19+4	1,000

The vice president for personnel left the firm on July 1, 19+5.

Prepare journal entries to record the above transactions assuming that Robbins Corporation closes its books annually on December 31.

Problem 21-6. The Stockholders' Equity section of the December 31, 19+1 balance sheet of Nielsen Company contained the following:

Common stock—\$25 par value; 90,000 shares authorized; 30,000 shares issued and outstanding	\$750,000
Capital in excess of par value—From common stock issuances	30,000
Retained earnings	170,000
	\$950,000

On January 1, 19+2, the Company granted company executives stock options for 10,000 shares of common stock at $35 per share. On this date the stock was selling for $34 per share. The options must be exercised between January 1, 19+3 and December 31, 19+6.

On October 3, 19+3, 2,500 of the options were exercised.

Prepare the Stockholders' Equity section of the firm's balance sheet at December 31, 19+3. Assume that 19+2 and 19+3 income was $37,000 and $29,000, respectively, and that dividends of $1 per share were paid on July 1, 19+2 and November 30, 19+3. No other transactions affecting stockholders equity took place during this period.

Problem 21-7. The Neisbet Corporation entered into the following transactions during 19+1 in order to raise additional capital to expand its operations:

January 1—Issued pre-emptive stock rights to all common share holders entitling them to purchase no-par common stock with a stated value of $25 per share at $22 a share. There are currently 20,000 common shares outstanding and the firm has retained earnings of $800,000.

January 15—Sold 10,000 shares of 5 percent noncumulative, $50 par value preferred stock at $55 a share. Each share has a warrant entitling the purchaser to obtain one share of common stock at $25 a share within the next 6 months. The common stock has a market price of $27 on this date.

February 5—75 percent of the pre-emptive stock rights are exercised.

February 15—Sold 1,000, $1,000 face value 5½ percent 10-year bonds at 103 per bond. Each bond is convertible into 40 shares of common stock and has non-detachable warrants entitling the purchaser to acquire 10 additional shares of common stock upon conversion at $28 per share. The bonds can be converted only when the common stock reaches a market price of $30.

February 20—The remaining pre-emptive stock rights are exercised.

February 25—80 percent of the warrants issued with the preferred stock are exercised.

March 5—Sold 1,000, $1,000 face value 7 percent 10-year bonds at 101. Each bond has one detachable stock warrant entitling the holder to purchase one share of common stock at $26. After the sale the bonds are selling at 101 without the warrants and the warrants have a market price of $5 each.

March 21—630 of the warrants issued with the 7 percent bonds are exercised.

April 1—An additional 15 percent of the warrants issued with the preferred stock are exercised and the remainder lapse.

April 30—The market price of the common stock reaches $31 per share and 200 bonds are converted.

Prepare journal entries to record the above transactions.

Problem 21-8. Williams Company established on January 1, 19+1 a stock option plan for five executives that grants them options to purchase the company's stock. The options are to be granted over the next three years.

The total number of shares for which options will be granted each year will be determined by taking 5 percent of the firm's net income and dividing by the option price per share. The option price of the stock will be $2 less than the current market price of Williams' stock on December 31, the date the firm's books are closed. The number of shares available for purchase by each executive will be 20 percent of the total shares available in any given year. The options for any year are granted on the following January 1 and are exercisible one year after they are granted. They expire two years after they are first exercisible. If an executive resigns his position any unexercised options will terminate.

The information below summarizes the results of the option plan:

Year	Net Income	Market Value of Common Stock at December 31	Options Exercised
19+1	$400,000.....	$12	All options exercised on earliest date.
19+2	$504,000.....	$16	40% of options exercised on earliest date, remainder exercised one year later.
19+3	$760,000.....	$21	50% of options exercised on earliest date. One executive resigns two years after the options are granted without exercising one-half of his options. All others are exercised on the last date in the exercise period.

Prepare a schedule showing the way in which the total compensation represented by the plan should be allocated to the years 19+1–19+5.

Problem 21-9. Boulder Construction Company has outstanding 50,000 shares of 6 percent cumulative, convertible preferred stock, par value $100; 80,000 shares of $10 par common stock; and $2,000,000 of 5 percent bonds. The preferred stock was issued at $105 per share; the common stock was issued at $8 per share. The company is authorized to issue 1,000,000 shares of each class of stock. The company has a credit balance of $900,000 in its retained earnings account.

The following securities transactions took place during 19+4:

February 2—Collected an assessment of $3 per share from common stockholders.

March 11—Holders of 20,000 preferred shares elected to convert their holdings to common shares. Pursuant to the terms of the conversion agreement, nine shares of common were given in exchange for each share of preferred.

May 8—The directors voted to change the $10 par value stock to no par with a stated value of $10 per share and to issue 300,000 shares in exchange for the present number of outstanding shares.

July 26—Holders of $400,000 of bonds chose to exercise stock warrants which had been issued to all bondholders in 19+1. No entry was made for the issuance of the warrants. Each bondholder received one warrant for each $1,000 bond which he owned. One warrant could be used to purchase 25 common shares, at $12 per share, cash. In exchange for the warrants which were exercised, the aforementioned bondholders were issued 10,000 common shares.

September 14—Pre-emptive rights of preferred stockholders were mailed. The rights entitle each preferred stockholder to buy, at $96, one new share of preferred stock for each ten he now owns.

The controller reported 19+4 net income of $300,000; dividends of $250,000 were declared and paid during the year.

Required:

(a) All necessary journal entries for the transactions which occurred during 19+4, excluding entries for earnings and dividends.

(b) The Stockholders' Equity section of the December 31, 19+4 Boulder Construction Company balance sheet.

Problem 21-10. The Hudson Corporation adopted a stock option plan on March 30, 19+1, for its $15 par value common stock. The provisions of the plan are as follows:

(1) All non-executive employees as of March 30, 19+1 are eligible to participate.
(2) Each employee is entitled to purchase common shares at par value equal to 1 percent of his yearly salary. Any fractional amounts are to be rounded up to allow the purchase of whole shares. The current market price of the common stock is $16 a share.
(3) The employees are in the following salary scales: 600 earning $10,000 per year; 400 earning $11,000; and 250 earning $12,000.
(4) Payment for the stock will be accomplished by deducting from each electing employee's salary the cost of the common over 15 bi-weekly pay periods beginning the second pay period in April. The stock will be issued only after full payment has been made.
(5) Any employee who is terminated can continue to make payments on the stock or elect to receive a cash refund for the amount deducted previously less the cost of selling the stock to outsiders.
(6) Each employee must make an election to participate by April 6, 19+1.

By April 6, 19+1, 450 employees earning $10,000, 375 earning $11,000, and 240 earning $12,000 agreed to participate in the plan.

Between the start of the payroll deductions and the final payment the following terminations took place:

Salary	No. of Employees	No. of Payments Made	Election
$10,000	10	8	Continue plan
	7	10	Refund
	5	11	Refund
	4	13	Continue plan
11,000	9	7	Refund
	12	11	Continue plan
	7	13	Refund
12,000	3	4	Refund
	2	9	Continue plan
	5	14	Continue plan

All of the common stock not issued under the option agreement was sold to the public one week after the plan's expiration at $18 per share with selling expenses of $.15 per share.

Required:

(a) Calculate the total number of options in the plan as of April 6, 19+1
(b) Summary journal entries to record the following transactions:
 (1) Initial payment on the stock options.
 (2) Any entry or entries required due to employee termination.
 (3) Issuance of stock at end of payment period.
 (4) Sale of stock not issued under the plan and any refund to previous employees.

Problem 21-11. Southern Corporation had the following stockholders' equity as of December 31, 19+1:

Stockholders' equity:		
Capital stock:		
Preferred—6% cumulative, nonparticipating, convertible; par value, $50; authorized and issued, 10,000 shares .	$500,000	
Class A common—$20 stated value, with a cumulative dividend of $1; authorized, 60,000 shares; issued and outstanding, 25,000 shares	500,000	
Class B common—No par value; authorized, 100,000 shares; issued and outstanding, 30,000 shares	425,000	$1,425,000
Capital in excess of par or stated value:		
From preferred stock issuances..........	$ 10,000	
From class A common stock issuances...	87,000	97,000
Total................................		$1,522,000
Retained earnings		$2,400,000
Total stockholders' equity		$3,922,000

The preferred stock of the Southern Corporation is convertible into 3 shares of Class A common stock at the option of the preferred shareholder.

During 19+2 the following transactions affecting the stockholders' equity took place.

March 1—1,000 shares of preferred stock were converted into class A common.
July 1—One-half of the yearly preferred dividend was declared and paid.
July 15—A $2,000,000, 7 percent bond issue was sold at 102. Each $1,000 bond has a detachable warrant for the purchase of 1 share of class A common stock at $25 per share. Immediately after the sale the bonds have a market price of $1,015 without the warrant and the warrant has a market price of $10.
November 1—725 shares of preferred stock were converted into class A common.
November 25—475 warrants are exercised when the class A common has a market price of $28 per share.
December 31—The board of directors declares the following dividends to be paid on February 20, 19+3 to all stockholders of record as of February 1, 19+3:
(a) The remaining preferred dividend.
(b) The cumulative class A common dividend.
(c) A $1.50 dividend on the class B common stock.

Required:

(a) Journal entries to record the above transactions.
(b) The Stockholder's Equity section of the Southern Corporation's balance sheet as of December 31, 19+2. Assume net income for the year was $775,000.

Problem 21-12. A partial balance sheet of Block Company appears below.

BLOCK COMPANY
Partial Balance Sheet
June 30, 19+1

Stockholders' equity:		
Common stock—$20 stated value; authorized, 100,000 shares; issued and outstanding, 25,000 shares		$500,000
Capital in excess of stated value—From common stock issuances	$ 50,000	
Retained earnings	125,000	175,000
Total		$675,000

The common stock of Block Company is currently selling on the regional stock exchange for $27 per share.

On July 1, 19+1, the company receives authorization to issue 10,000 shares of $25 par value, 6 percent, cumulative preferred stock. The preferred shares are offered to the common stockholders at $28 per share, with each preferred share including a detachable warrant good until June 30, 19+2, entitling the holder to purchase one share of common stock for $25 per share.

Subscriptions receivable are due in thirty days and the shares are to be issued when the subscription has been collected.

Subscriptions, all dated July 15, 19+1, are received from the common stockholders for all of the authorized preferred stock. Cash therefor is collected on August 14, 19+1, and the shares are issued.

On September 1, 19+1, the board of directors grants nontransferable stock options for 1,000 common shares to the junior officers of the company under the following conditions: common shares may be purchased for $30 per share during the six months ended December 31, 19+2. Unexercised options lapse at that time.

The market price of the company's common shares on September 1, 19+1, is $27 per share.

On December 1, 19+1, when the market price of the common stock is $28 per share, the preferred stockholders present cash and warrants for 8,000 common shares, and the stock is issued to them.

During the six months ended June 30, 19+2, the company's common stock sells in the range of $21 to $23 per share, and the preferred stockholders allow the remaining detachable warrants to lapse.

On August 15, 19+2, when the market price of the common stock is $32 per share, junior officers present cash and options for 200 shares; the stock is issued to them.

On November 1, 19+2, when the market price of the common stock is $35 per share, other junior officers present cash and options for 500 shares; the stock is issued to them.

During November and December the market price of the common stock declines significantly and no options are exercised.

Prepare journal entries for the above, including any entries required as of June 30, 19+2, the close of the company's fiscal year.

CHAPTER 22

QUESTIONS

1. What are dividends? Do they always involve the outflow of assets of the firm?
2. List several different kinds of dividends.
3. What is the primary reason for stock dividends?
4. How are stock dividends accounted for?
5. How should stock dividends declared but not yet issued be reported in the balance sheet?
6. Distinguish between a stock dividend and a stock split.
7. List some of the reasons a corporation may find itself restricted as to the amount of dividends it can pay.
8. What is the purpose of retained earnings appropriations. List some specific reasons for which retained earnings may be restricted.
9. How should retained earnings appropriations be reported in the balance sheet?
10. When a company follows a policy of self-insurance, how should actual losses be accounted for?
11. What is the significance of the liquidating price of preferred stock?
12. What are fractional shares? How are they accounted for?

PROBLEMS

Problem 22-1. Cagle Company has the following stockholders' equity at December 31, 19+6.

6% cumulative, nonparticipating preferred stock, $100 par value		$ 600,000
Common stock—stated value, $100		900,000
Retained earnings:		
Appropriated for plant expansion	$600,000	
Unappropriated	200,000	800,000
Total		$2,300,000

During recent years, the corporation has reinvested most of its earnings in more modern plant facilities and additional sales branches. Consequently, dividends have not been paid on the preferred stock since December 31, 19+3, and on the common stock since December 31, 19+1. The company having completed its expansion program, the board of directors, on December 31, 19+6, declared dividends in the amount of $250,000 and voted to eliminate the reserve for plant expansion from the accounts.

Journalize the dividend declaration, with a computation showing the amount to be paid to each class of stockholders, and the entry required to eliminate the retained earnings appropriation.

Problem 22-2. Clifton Company was organized on July 1, 19+3 with the following authorized stock: 60,000 shares of $100 par value, 5 percent cumulative preferred; 50,000 shares of $25 par value common.

On the date of organization the firm sold 30,000 shares of preferred stock at $104 per share and 20,000 shares of common stock at $30 per share. The preferred stock has a liquidating price of $115 per share.

On November 1, 19+3, the company issued $5,000,000 of 7 percent bonds, requiring that $40,000 be set aside annually in a sinking fund and that retained earnings of this amount be appropriated each year, beginning in 19+4.

An appropriation of retained earnings for the retirement of preferred stock was established for $60,000 on May 1, 19+4; it is to be increased by $60,000 on each December 31, beginning on December 31, 19+4.

On July 1, 19+4, 10,000 additional preferred shares were issued at $106 per share.

Net income and cash dividends, which are customarily declared yearly in December, were as follows:

	Net Income	Cash Dividends
19+3	$280,000	$120,000
19+4	300,000	200,000

Present the Stockholders' Equity section of the December 31, 19+4 balance sheet.

Problem 22-3. The Stockholders' Equity section of the December 31, 19+6 balance sheet for Thomas Company was as follows:

Stockholders' equity:	
Capital stock—Par value, $100; authorized, 40,000 shares; issued and outstanding, 10,000 shares	$1,000,000
Capital in excess of par value	80,000
Retained earnings	300,000
	$1,380,000

On January 2, 19+7, the board of directors declared an 8 percent stock dividend. Market price on this date was $103 per share. The stock was to be issued on January 15, 19+7.

(a) Prepare entries for the declaration and issuance of the stock dividend.
(b) If the stock dividend was not to be issued until February 10, 19+7, state how it would be disclosed in the January 31, 19+7 balance sheet.

Problem 22-4. Jackson Company decided upon a program of self-insurance on October 1, 19+4, the beginning of its accounting period. It was estimated that losses for the next several years would average $12,000 per year. Based upon this, the firm followed the policy of charging this amount to insurance expense and crediting an account titled Reserve for Self-Insurance. Actual losses were debited to the reserve account.

Information concerning the program for the first five years is presented below.

Year Ended	Charge to Insurance Expense	Actual Losses	Net Income
9/30/+5	$12,000	$ 8,000	$183,000
9/30/+6	12,000	10,000	226,000
9/30/+7	12,000	15,000	95,000
9/30/+8	12,000	9,500	176,000
9/30/+9	12,000	16,400	293,000

Required:

(a) Calculate net income for each of the five years assuming the self-insurance program was accounted for by use of an appropriation of retained earnings account for $20,000, the maximum loss expected to be incurred at any one time.
(b) Journal entries for the year ended September 30, 19+5 under the assumption in part (a).

Problem 22-5. The following accounts appear in the December 31, 19+7 trial balance of Petty Company. On this date the market price of the common stock was $30 per share.

Common stock	$300,000
Fractional share certificates	6,500
Capital in excess of par value—From stock dividends	15,000
Capital in excess of par value—From common stock issuances	35,000
Retained earnings—Unappropriated	135,400
Retained earnings appropriated for retirement of preferred stock	50,000

Prepare whatever journal entries you believe necessary in view of the following information:

The common stock has a par value of $25 per share.
During 19+7, the retained earnings appropriated for retirement of preferred stock account was charged $50,000 for the write-off of obsolete parts being carried in the inventory.
The fractional share certificates, issued in connection with a stock dividend, have expired. The directors cannot rescind, in part, a stock dividend.
The preferred stock was retired as of July 1, 19+7.
As of December 31, 19+7, the board of directors declared a stock dividend of 2,000 shares, issuable as of January 10, 19+8.

Problem 22-6. Blackwelder Company had the following account balances on June 30, 19+4:

6% preferred stock—$50 par value; 20,000 shares authorized, issued, and outstanding	$1,000,000
Capital in excess of par value—From preferred stock issuances	20,000
Common stock—No par value; no stated value; 100,000 shares authorized; 80,000 shares issued and outstanding	845,500
Paid-in capital—Common—Stockholders' assessments	80,000
Common stock warrants outstanding (10,000 shares)	5,000
Retained earnings	378,900
Retained earnings appropriated for self-insurance	24,500

On July 10, 19+4, when the company's common stock was selling for $11 per share, the board of directors declared a common stock dividend of 4 percent, stock to be issued to holders of common stock on August 1, 19+4. The board also voted to increase the self-insurance appropriation to a balance of $30,000.
On August 1, 19+4, stock certificates representing the stock dividend were distributed.
On August 10, 19+4, the board of directors declared a 3 percent scrip dividend on the

preferred stock. The scrip, bearing 5 percent interest, is to be issued to stockholders of record on September 1.

On September 1, 19+4, the scrip was distributed to the preferred stockholders.

Prepare journal entries required by the information above.

Problem 22-7. Art, Incorporated was organized on January 1, 19+2 with an authorized capital of 50,000 shares of $50 par value, 6 percent non-cumulative preferred stock and 100,000 shares of no par value common stock with a stated value of $5 per share. The preferred stock has a liquidating price of $65 per share. The following transactions took place during the first two years of operations:

(1) Issued 10,000 shares of preferred stock at $55 per share.
(2) Issued 10,000 shares of common stock at $8 per share.
(3) Issued 500 shares of common stock in payment of attorneys fees. The stock was selling for $9 per share at this time.
(4) Declared and paid the annual dividend on the preferred stock, plus a dividend of $1 on the common stock.
(5) Split the common stock two-for-one.
(6) Issued 10,000 shares of common stock at $5 per share.
(7) Issued 5,000 shares of preferred stock at $60 per share.
(8) Distributed as a dividend one share of the stock of Public Company to each share of common stock outstanding. The Public Company stock is carried at $2 per share by Art, Incorporated.
(9) Declared a stock dividend of 10 percent on the common stock. The current market price of the stock is $9.
(10) Split the common stock two-for-one.

Required:

(a) Journal entries to record the transactions.
(b) The stockholders equity section of the firm's balance sheet at December 31, 19+2, assuming net income of $200,000 for the two-year period.

Problem 22-8. Prepare all journal entries required by the following information:

Martin Manufacturing Corporation had authorized capital of $500,000, representing 20,000 shares of $25 par value common stock, 16,000 shares of which were outstanding, having been issued for $28 per share on October 1, 19+4, when the corporation was organized.

On July 1, 19+9, when the common stock was selling for $30 per share and the corporation had retained earnings of $214,300, the board of directors declared a 10 percent stock dividend on the 16,000 shares outstanding on that date. The distribution of the outstanding shares indicated that certificates for 1,300 full shares would be issued and that fractional share certificates for the remaining shares would be necessary.

On August 1, 19+9, the dividend shares and fractional share certificates were issued.

As of August 10, 19+9, fractional share certificates equivalent to 260 shares were presented and certificates were issued. No additional fractional share certificates were presented.

The fractional share certificates expired on December 1, 19+9, and the board of directors voted to rescind this portion of the stock dividend.

Problem 22-9. As of October 31, 19+2, the stockholders' equity of Dudish Corporation was as follows:

Stockholders' equity:	
Capital stock:	
Preferred stock—6% cumulative; par value, $100; liquidating price, $110; authorized and issued, 20,000 shares	$2,000,000
Common stock—Par value, $80; authorized, 60,000 shares; issued and outstanding, 30,000 shares	2,400,000
Capital in excess of par value—From preferred stock issuances	20,000
Retained earnings	400,000
	$4,820,000

The following transactions, given in summary form, occurred between November 1, 19+2 and October 31, 19+3:

(1) The company acquired, at the liquidating price, all outstanding preferred shares; it thereupon cancelled the shares. No dividends were in arrears.

(2) A 5 percent stock dividend was declared on the common shares. On the date of declaration, the market price per share was $84. By October 31, 19+3, the dividend had not been issued.

(3) The company's counsel reported that unfavorable adjudication of pending litigation brought against the company could result in damages of $60,000. Accordingly, the board of directors authorized the appropriation of retained earnings for that amount.

(4) The reported net income for the fiscal year ended October 31, 19+3, was $200,000.

Required:

(a) A statement of retained earnings for the year ended October 31, 19+3.

(b) The Stockholders' Equity section of the October 31, 19+3 balance sheet, in proper form.

Problem 22-10. The board of directors of Campus Bike Company, which owns a manufacturing plant and leases sixty retail outlets, decided on January 1, 19+5, to cancel the existing fire insurance coverage on its buildings and equipment and establish a self-insurance policy. On this date an appropriation of retained earnings for self-insurance was made in the amount of $10,000, the maximum loss expected to occur at any one time.

On December 30, 19+7, a fire completely destroyed the equipment in one store. This equipment was purchased on January 2, 19+3, the date when the store was leased, and as of December 31, 19+6, when it was 40 percent depreciated, its book amount was $5,760. On February 1, 19+8, the company spent $10,500 to replace all of the equipment destroyed by the fire.

The accounting year for the company is the calendar year.

Prepare journal entries, with supporting computations where necessary, required as a result of the self-insurance program, the fire loss, and the equipment replacement.

Problem 22-11. River Corporation has outstanding on January 1, 19+5, 15,000 of its 20,000 authorized shares of common stock, par value $10 per share.

Retained earnings, unappropriated, on the above date amounted to $63,900, capital in excess of par value totaled $55,000, consisting of $30,000 from the original issuance of the stock, and $25,000 from stock dividends, and retained earnings appropriated for self-insurance was $10,000.

During the year 19+5 the corporation declared, December 1, and paid, December 8, a cash dividend of 80 cents per share and the net income was $34,800.

On January 2, 19+6, the corporation took title to a tract of unimproved real estate appraised for $20,000, received as a gift from the City of Y.

In order to conserve cash for building needs, a 10 percent stock dividend was declared as of December 1, 19+6, and issued on December 15, 19+6. It was necessary to issue fractional share certificates for 120 shares. During the latter part of November and the early part of December the corporation's stock had a market price of $16 per share.

The net income for 19+6 was $29,900. An appropriation of retained earnings for plant expansion was established for $30,000.

By December 31, 19+6, fractional share certificates had been presented and full share certificates issued for 90 shares. On June 15, 19+7, the remaining fractional share certificates expired and the board of directors took appropriate action (in conformity with state law) to give recognition to this fact in the accounts of the corporation. By law, the board of directors is not empowered to rescind any part of a stock dividend.

Required:

(a) Journal entries to record all activity affecting the stockholders' equity of the the firm from January 1, 19+5, through June 15, 19+7. (Debit Other Assets when recording net income.)

(b) The Stockholders' Equity section of the corporation's balance sheet at December 31, 19+6.

Problem 22-12. The condensed balance sheet of Dempsey Company on December 31, 19+1, was as follows:

DEMPSEY COMPANY
Balance Sheet
December 31, 19+1

Assets		
Cash		$261,400
Accounts receivable		88,600
Inventories		118,300
Unexpired insurance		12,000
Stock of *XY* Company		100,000
Property, plant, and equipment	$324,300	
Less accumulated depreciation	173,300	151,000
		$731,300
Equities		
Accounts payable		$ 78,400
Expenses payable		9,100
8% preferred stock—$100 par value	$200,000	
Common stock—No par value—Stated value, $10 per share	220,000	
Capital in excess of par value—From preferred stock issuances	13,600	
Capital in excess of stated value—From common stock issuances	44,000	
Retained earnings	166,200	643,800
		$731,300

Details of the capital stock of the corporation are shown below.

	Authorized	Issued
8% cumulative preferred with a liquidating price of $110 per share	2,000 shares	2,000 shares
Common..................................	25,000 shares	22,000 shares

The following transactions affecting the company's stockholders' equity accounts occurred during 19+2:

January 15—Necessary authorization was obtained to change the authorized common stock to 50,000 shares with a $5 stated value. The change was effective on this date and two new shares were issued for each share of outstanding common.

March 15—The regular quarterly dividend on the preferred stock was declared.

25—The quarterly preferred dividend was paid.

May 15—The board of directors took the necessary action to retire, as of this date, all of the preferred stock at its liquidating price plus cumulative dividend of 1 percent.

June 20—Subscriptions were received for 500 shares of common stock at $7 per share. Cash of $4 per share was received with the subscriptions. The shares are to be issued when the subscription price is received in full.

21—A 5 percent stock dividend was declared, to be issued June 30 on the basis of the number of shares outstanding as of June 26.

25—Subscribers to 200 shares of common paid the balance of their subscriptions and common shares were issued to them.

30—The common stock dividend was issued.

August 15—The directors authorized the appropriation of retained earnings for general contingencies of $20,000.

December 21—The directors voted to distribute, as of December 31, the stock of *XY* Company as a dividend to the common stockholders.

31—The stock of *XY* Company was distributed.

(1) Prepare journal entries to record all transactions indicated by the foregoing information.

(2) Prepare a statement of retained earnings for 19+2, assuming that the net income for the year amounted to $85,000.

(3) Show how the Stockholders' Equity section of the December 31, 19+2 balance sheet would appear.

CHAPTER 23

QUESTIONS

1. What requirements must stock meet in order to be classified as treasury stock?
2. Describe two methods of accounting for treasury stock.
3. When the amount paid for treasury stock is in excess of the par or stated value, what alternatives may be followed in accounting for the excess?

4. What is the major argument in favor of the par-value method of accounting for treasury stock?

5. What is the reason for restricting dividends payments in the amount of the cost of treasury stock?

6. How should treasury stock be reported in the balance sheet?

7. Describe the procedures to record the cancellation of preferred stock by a corporation.

8. How is the book value per share of stock calculated? Why are certain features of preferred stock important in calculating book value?

9. How are appraisal increments reported in the balance sheet?

10. List three different ways in which the restriction of retained earnings due to treasury stock acquisitions can be disclosed in the financial statements.

11. How is donated treasury stock accounted for?

PROBLEMS

Problem 23-1. On its organization date, January 2, 19+9, Kendrick Corporation sold 8,000 shares of $20 par capital stock at $22 per share. 20,000 shares were authorized. The following stock transactions occurred during 19+9:

February 21—Acquired 200 shares of capital stock at $23 per share.
March 15—Reissued 200 shares at $25 per share.
May 28—Acquired 200 shares of capital stock at $25 per share.
June 4—Reissued 200 shares at $24 per share.
September 12—Acquired 200 shares of capital stock at $27 per share.

The controller, on December 31, 19+9, reported earnings for the year of $50,000.

State law imposes a restriction on retained earnings equal in amount to the cost of treasury shares.

Required:

(a) Journal entries for the treasury stock transactions using the cost method.
(b) Stockholders' Equity section of the December 31, 19+9 balance sheet.

Problem 23-2. Powell Company uses the par-value method to account for treasury stock transactions. On December 31, 19+3, the company had 50,000 shares of $10 par value common stock outstanding, all of which had been sold for $15 per share. During 19+4, the following treasury stock transactions took place.

January 20—Acquired 500 shares at $18 per share.
June 10—Reissued 300 shares at $10 per share.
July 31—Reissued 150 shares at $12 per share.
October 3—Reissued 50 shares at $9 per share.

Prepare journal entries for the transactions.

Problem 23-3. For each of the following companies, present journal entries for the stock transactions and prepare the Stockholders' Equity section of each company's balance sheet, giving effect to the transactions. Assume that retained earnings restrictions are necessary in both cases.

(1) The Folsom Corporation, empowered to issue 10,000 shares of $30 par capital stock, issued 7,000 shares at $32 per share. 800 shares were acquired at $35 per share; 500 of these were reissued at $31 per share. Earnings of $50,000 were reported for the period. The company uses the par-value method in accounting for treasury stock.

(2) Pioneer, Inc., issued 2,000 of its 8,000 authorized $40 par shares for $65 per share. 300 shares were acquired by the company for $70 per share. 100 of such treasury shares were reissued at $68 per share. Earnings for the fiscal period were $15,000; the cost basis is used for treasury stock.

Problem 23-4. Super Dealers, Inc., issued 20,000 shares of $50 par capital stock at $51 per share on January 2, 19+7. 30,000 shares were authorized on that date. During the next three years, the company earned $100,000, and, on December 20 each year, paid a dividend of $1 per share.

On January 2, 19+8, the company purchased 1,000 shares of its capital stock at $50 per share. On December 31, 19+8, it sold 700 treasury shares at $48 per share. On January 2, 19+9, 500 shares were presented as a gift to the company.

State law requires that a restriction equal to the cost of treasury shares be placed on retained earnings.

Prepare the Stockholders' Equity section of the December 31, 19+9 balance sheet, using the cost method of accounting for treasury shares.

Problem 23-5. Fowler Company uses the cost method to account for treasury stock transactions. The following information is taken from the records of the company at December 31, 19+1.

Common stock, $25 par value	$50,000
Capital in excess of par value—From common stock issuances	5,000
Capital in excess of par value—From treasury stock transactions	300
Retained earnings	8,000

On February 3, 19+2, the company acquired 200 shares of treasury stock at $31 per share. All of the treasury stock was reissued for $26 per share on July 23, 19+2.

Prepare the entry to record the reissuance of the treasury shares under each of the following assumptions.

(a) Legal capital consists of the total par value of all shares issued.
(b) Legal capital consists of the total amount paid for stock when it is originally sold.
(c) Legal capital consists of all paid-in capital associated with the common stock.

Problem 23-6. Madison Machine Company was organized on January 2, 19+8. Considering the following summarized transactions, which occurred during 19+8, compute the book amount per share of the capital stock at December 31, 19+8.

January	2	—Sold 3,000 shares of $100 par value capital stock at $103 per share.
March	27	—Acquired 400 shares of the company's capital stock at $100 per share, cash.
April	20	—Reissued 100 treasury shares at $102 per share, cash.
June	30	—Reported earnings of $50,000 for the first six months.
August	31	—Declared and issued a 10 percent stock dividend.
October	3	—Reserved $40,000 of retained earnings for plant expansion.
December	10	—Declared a cash dividend of $3 per share, payable January 7, 19+9.
	31	—Reported earnings of $30,000 for preceding six months.

Problem 23-7. The following December 31, 19+8 balance sheet of Bryson Company was prepared by company officials.

BRYSON COMPANY
Balance Sheet
December 31, 19+8

Assets:		
Current assets:		
Cash	$ 920,000	
Accounts receivable	240,000	$1,160,000
Investments:		
Treasury stock, at cost		105,000
Long-lived assets:		
Equipment	$ 100,000	
Less accumulated depreciation	5,000	95,000
		$1,360,000
Liabilities:		
Current liabilities:		
Accounts payable	$ 20,000	
Reserve for plant expansion	80,000	$ 100,000
Stockholders' equity:		
Capital stock:		
Authorized, 30,000 shares; 2,000 issued shares are in the treasury	$1,040,000	
Retained earnings	220,000	1,260,000
		$1,360,000

The company was organized on January 2, 19+8. On examining the books and records of the company at December 31, 19+8, the auditor discovered:

(1) All acquisitions of treasury stock were completed at the same price. The only disposal of treasury shares, involving 500 shares reissued at $60 per share on June 1, was recorded by crediting Treasury Stock for the proceeds.
(2) The 20,000 issued shares of par value stock were sold on January 2 at a premium of $2 per share.
(3) Directors declared a dividend of $1 per share on December 29. Date of payment was set at January 18, 19+9. The credit was made to Accounts Payable.
(4) The equipment was presented to the company as a gift by a group of stockholders. The credit, for its fair value, was made to Retained Earnings.

State law requires that retained earnings be restricted to the extent of the cost of treasury stock.

Required:

(a) Journal entries as of December 31, 19+8, to correct the ledger accounts.
(b) The balance sheet as it should have appeared on December 31, 19+8.
(c) Compute the 19+8 net income.

Problem 23-8. Royal Plastics Corporation was incorporated on January 2, 19+9, and was authorized to issue 20,000 shares of $10 par value capital stock.

On February 26, 19+9, the company issued 8,000 shares of stock at $11 per share. 1,000 shares were acquired by the company on March 18, 19+9, at a cost per share of $9. On April 6, 19+9, stockholders donated 700 shares; the market price on this date was $10 per share. The company reissued 200 treasury shares, at $10 per share, on April 13, 19+9. 1,100 treasury shares were reissued on May 31, 19+9, at $5 per share.

On September 30, the board of directors declared a quarterly dividend of twenty cents per share, payable October 20. In the state of incorporation dividends can be declared from either retained earnings or paid-in capital, but retained earnings must be restricted to the extent of the cost of any treasury shares.

Nine months' earnings of $20,000 were reported on September 30, 19+9.

Required:

(a) Journal entries for the foregoing transactions (except recognition of earnings). Use the cost method for treasury stock transactions, and assume the first-in, first-out basis for sales of treasury shares.
(b) Stockholders' Equity section of the September 30, 19+9 balance sheet.
(c) Calculation of the book value per share at September 30, 19+9.

Problem 23-9. Kingman Company has the following common stock outstanding at January 1, 19+3: 10,000 shares sold at $25 per share; 15,000 shares sold at $28 per share; 9,000 shares sold at $30 per share.

On March 10, 19+4, the company acquired 500 of the shares at a price of $23 per share. The stock was reissued at a price of $31 per share one year later.

Required:

(a) Entries to record the acquisition and reissuance of the stock under the cost method, assuming the following about the stock:
   (1) The par value is $25 per share.
   (2) It is no par value stock and no stated value has been assigned.
   (3) It is no par value stock, with a stated value of $20.
(b) Entries to record the acquisition and reissuance of the stock under the par value method, assuming the three different situations presented in part (a). Assume a first-in, first-out flow in determining the cost of shares reissued.

Problem 23-10. Walton Mills, Inc., was organized on January 2, 19+3; authorized capital consisted of 20,000 5 percent cumulative preferred shares, par $50, and 30,000 common shares, par $20. The liquidation price of the preferred stock was set at $54 plus dividends in arrears. On that date, the company issued 8,000 preferred shares at $52 per share, and 10,000 common shares at par.

A 10 percent common stock dividend was declared on December 4, 19+6, and issued 30 days later. On the declaration date, the market price was $21 per share.

On January 2, 19+8, the company purchased 1,000 of its common shares at $24 per share. 400 of these shares were reissued at $25 per share on April 7, 19+8, and 500 shares were reissued at $20 per share on October 19, 19+8. The remaining treasury shares were retired on November 3, 19+8.

On January 2, 19+9, the company received as a gift 2,000 of its common shares. Of these shares, 500 were reissued at $25 per share on July 1, 19+9.

Accumulated earnings from the date of organization through December 31, 19+7, were $300,000. Dividends on preferred shares were not paid in 19+8 and 19+9; 5 percent was paid in all other years. Common dividends of $1 per share were paid on outstanding shares on December 31 in all years except those in which there was a preferred arrearage.

The retirement of shares does not reduce the shares authorized.

Required:

(a) Journal entries for transactions which occurred during 19+6, 19+7, 19+8, and 19+9 (except earnings and cash dividends). The firm uses the cost method to account for treasury stock transactions.
(b) Stockholders' Equity section of the December 31, 19+9 balance sheet.
(c) Book value per share of each class of stock on December 31, 19+9.

Problem 23-11. Using the following list of accounts from the records of Engel Company as of November 30, 19+8, prepare the Stockholders' Equity section of the company's balance sheet as it should appear on that date.

Retained earnings appropriated for bond retirement	$120,000
Treasury stock—Preferred (acquired January, 19+8)	28,800
Retained earnings	500,000
Common stock, par $40	800,000
Donated capital—19+8	16,400
Declared but unpaid 19+8 dividend on preferred stock (credit balance)	23,200
Treasury stock—Common (Held for distribution to officers)	30,000
Paid-in capital—From retirement of preferred stock	?
Capital in excess of par value—From preferred treasury stock transactions	1,500
Preferred stock, par $100	580,000
Common stock dividends payable	38,400

Additional information:

One preferred treasury stock purchase, 1,000 shares at $96, has been made; some of these shares were reissued at $3 per share above cost; some were retired; the latter shares can be reissued.

The cost method was used for all treasury stock transactions.

No debits have been made to paid-in capital accounts.

The stock dividend was to be issued on January 14, 19+9.

During 19+8, one stockholder presented to the company, as a gift, 900 common shares. Some of the shares were thereupon reissued at $41 per share.

40,000 preferred shares and 50,000 common shares have been authorized. The preferred stock is cumulative at an 8 percent rate.

State law requires that retained earnings be restricted to the extent of the cost of treasury shares.

Problem 23-12. The following transactions were completed by Baker Shops Company from the date of incorporation through December 31, 19+7.

January 2, 19+5	—Received subscriptions to 40,000 shares of the 100,000 authorized preferred shares, at $12 per share. The 6 percent preferred stock had a par value of $10 and was cumulative and convertible. The subscription contract provided for payment in two equal installments. Issued 10,000 shares of $20 par common stock at $23 per share, cash. 60,000 shares were authorized.
March 18, 19+5	—All preferred subscribers paid the first installment.
April 3, 19+5	—Subscriber reported that he could not fulfill his agreement for 300 shares. Accordingly, the company sold his shares at $11 per share, cash, and paid $20 selling expenses. No refund was required to be made to the original subscriber.
June 19, 19+5	—Remaining subscribers paid the second installment and certificates were issued.

August 1, 19+5—Under an employee stock option plan established by the directors on June 1, options for 5,000 common shares, to be purchased at $25 per share, were offered. Market price this date was $28 per share, and the options could not be exercised for 24 months from August 1. Expiration date was set as December 31, 19+8.

October 8, 19+5—Acquired 4,800 shares of common stock at a cash price of $29 per share.

November 17, 19+5—Issued stock warrants to holders of $100,000 of bonds. Two warrants were issued for every $1,000 bond. Each warrant entitled the holder to buy one share of common stock at $30 per share; warrants were to expire on December 30, 19+6.

December 31, 19+5—Controller reported 19+5 earnings of $50,000. The directors announced that when dividends are declared, present holders of preferred shares will be entitled to the full 19+5 dividend—as though the shares were issued on January 2, 19+5.

January 1, 19+6—Stockholders donated 1,000 common shares to the company. Market price this date was $29.50 per share.

January 2, 19+6—Issued 5,000 shares of common stock at $30 per share, cash. On the same date, issued 1,000 common shares for a tract of improved land, the market value of which could not be ascertained.

January 3, 19+6—Directors announced a 5 percent common stock dividend on shares outstanding as of January 15, 19+6. Issuance was effected on February 1, 19+6. Market price on January 3 was $30 per share. Preferred stockholders, who had not yet received dividends for 19+5, assented to the board action.

June 30, 19+6—Reissued 1,500 treasury shares at $35 per share, cash. (Assume first-in, first-out basis for sale of treasury shares.)

December 30, 19+6—Holders of $95,000 of bonds exercised their warrants. Cash was received. Remainder of warrants expired.

December 31, 19+6—Controller reported 19+6 earnings of $250,000.
Directors declared dividends of $64,000 to be paid to holders of outstanding shares on January 10, 19+7. Show how much goes to each class of stock.

January 12, 19+7—Holders of $120,000 (par) of preferred stock exchanged their holdings for common stock. One share of common was given for every three shares of preferred. The converted shares could not be reissued.

February 11, 19+7—Directors authorized, with stockholders' consent, a change in the common shares from $20 par to no par; stated value, $25. The same number of shares were to be issued.

March 20, 19+7—Directors instructed the controller to take proper accounting steps in order to withhold $100,000 from dividend use due to intended expansion of sales outlets.

August 1, 19+7—Holders of stock options to 4,800 common shares made purchases under the plan.

November 4, 19+7—Reissued 4,000 treasury shares at $26 per share, cash. (Assume first-in, first-out basis.)

December 31, 19+7—Controller reported 19+7 earnings of $100,000.

(a) Prepare all necessary journal entries for the foregoing transactions. (Omit entries for earnings.) Use the cost method for treasury stock transactions.

(b) Prepare the Stockholders' Equity section of the December 31, 19+7 balance sheet.

CHAPTER 24

QUESTIONS

1. With regard to income tax allocation, answer the following questions.

(**a**) What is income tax allocation?
(**b**) What is the objective of income tax allocation?

2. With regard to income tax allocation, what are the following distinctions?

(**a**) Intraperiod and interperiod income tax allocation
(**b**) Taxable and pretax accounting income
(**c**) Deferred income tax charge and credit

3. In general, why does taxable income differ from pretax accounting income?

4. Timing differences can be classified four different ways with regard to the effect of revenues and expenses on taxable and pretax accounting income. Can you construct such a classification with an example of each?

5. With regard to interperiod income tax allocation, what are the following distinctions?

(**a**) Timing and permanent differences
(**b**) Deferred method and liability method
(**c**) Comprehensive and partial allocation

6. What is the net-of-tax method of interperiod income tax allocation? Is it an acceptable method?

7. With respect to operating-loss carry-backs, answer the following questions.

(**a**) What is an operating-loss carry-back?
(**b**) Why is there an income tax allocation problem?
(**c**) Per *Opinion No. 11*, how are operating-loss carry-backs accounted for?

8. Per *Opinion No. 11*, what are the similarities and dissimilarities between the accounting for operating-loss carry-forwards and carry-backs? Why do the dissimilarities exist?

9. Since tax carry-forwards reflect operating losses of previous periods, why are they not deducted from, instead of added to, income before extraordinary items?

10. In current accounting practice is intraperiod income tax allocation followed with regard to operating and nonoperating items in a multistep income statement?

11. If a strict all-inclusive concept of income were used in current accounting practice, then there would be no need for intraperiod income tax allocation. Do you agree with this statement?

12. Since they are reported as such on the balance sheet, deferred income tax charges and credits are assets and liabilities, respectively. Do you agree with this statement?

13. Income taxes are not really expenses; hence, there is no need for interperiod income tax allocation. What does this statement mean?

14. When pretax accounting income is smaller than taxable income because of timing differences, a company has in effect prepaid income taxes. Similarly, when pretax accounting income is larger than taxable income because of timing difference, a company has in effect a future tax liability. What do these statements mean and do you agree with them?

15. Because timing differences are not really temporary, differences between pretax accounting income and taxable income can produce an indefinite postponement of income taxes. What does this statement mean?

16. A counter argument to the basic statement in question 15 above is that the deferred tax amounts revolve or turnover. What is this turnover argument? What are some problems with this argument?

17. Do permanent differences require intraperiod income tax allocation?

18. How does a change in income tax rates affect the accounting for interperiod income tax allocation?

PROBLEMS

Problem 24-1. You are given below six multiple choice statements. Select the correct answer to complete each statement and indicate the corresponding letter on a separate sheet of paper (e.g., 1-a, 2-a, etc.).

(1) Interperiod tax allocation results in a deferred credit (deferred income taxes) from (a) an income item partially recognized for financial purposes but fully recognized for tax purposes in any one year, (b) an income item partially recognized for tax purposes but fully recognized for financial purposes in any one year, (c) an income item fully recognized for tax and financial purposes in any one year, (d) an income item not recognized for tax or financial purposes in any one year, (e) none of the above.

(2) Income tax allocation procedures are *not* appropriate when (a) an extraordinary loss will cause the amount of income tax expense to be less than the tax on ordinary net income, (b) an extraordinary gain will cause the amount of income tax expense to be greater than the tax on ordinary net income, (c) differences between net income for tax purposes and financial reporting occur because tax laws and financial accounting principles do not concur on the items to be recognized as revenue and expense, (d) differences between net income for tax purposes and financial reporting occur because, even though financial accounting principles and tax laws concur on the items to be recognized as revenue and expenses, they do not concur on the timing of the recognition, (e) none of the above.

(3) Interperiod tax allocation would *not* be required when (a) research and development costs are written off in the year of the expenditure for tax purposes but capitalized for accounting purposes, (b) statutory (or percentage) depletion exceeds cost depletion for the period, (c) accelerated depreciation is used for tax purposes and the straight-line method is used for accounting purposes, (d) different methods of revenue recognition are used for tax purposes and accounting purposes, (e) none of the above.

(4) With respect to the allocation of income taxes, it is recommended that (a) because of the difficulty in making allocations and because of the uncertainty of tax rates, no allocation should be attempted, (b) because income taxes are an expense they should be allocated to income and retained earnings accounts of the same period, but they should not be allocated to other accounts which will affect the income of other periods, (c) allocation of income taxes should be made so long as the amount shown for income taxes in the income statement is not increased beyond the amount of the tax estimated to be actually payable, (d) because income taxes are an expense, they should be allocated to income and other accounts affecting the income of the current period or affecting the income of the current and future periods, (e) none of the above.

(5) With regard to income tax allocation, a timing difference (a) is the distribution of income taxes for a specific period, (b) reflects items reported on the financial statements but never reported on the tax return (or vice versa), (c) is the apportionment of income tax expense between accounting periods, (d) none of the above.

(6) With regard to income tax allocation, *one* of the following statements is true: (a) Income tax allocation has been criticized as a form of income smoothing; (b) it is generally recognized in accounting practice that income taxes are a distribution of profits; (c) it is generally recognized in accounting practice that deferred income tax charges and credits are assets and liabilities, respectively; (d) income tax allocation should reflect permanent differences; (e) none of the above.

Problem 24-2. A portion of the statement of income and retained earnings for Sturbottom Company is presented below:

STURBOTTOM COMPANY
Statement of Income and Retained Earnings
For the Year Ended December 31, 19+4

Net operating income		$100,000
Nonoperating item:		
Interest revenue		1,000
Income before taxes		$101,000
Income taxes		37,475
Net income		63,525
Retained earnings at beginning of year:		
As previously reported	$100,000	
Deduct: Prior-period adjustment for settlement of legal suit	15,500	
As restated		$ 84,500
Deduct: Plant destroyed by hurricane	$ 10,000	
Flood damage	11,100	21,100
Retained earnings at end of year		$ 63,400

	Income Tax Rate for Following Items
Net operating income	50%
Flood damage	25%
Hurricane damage	25%
Settlement of legal suit	50%
Interest revenue	50%

Restate the statement of income and retained earnings assuming intraperiod income tax allocation.

Problem 24-3. You are given below the net income figures for Premium Company:

	19+1	19+2	19+3	19+4	19+5	19+6	19+7
Income before taxes	$2,000	$3,000	$8,000	($25,000)	$3,000	$5,000	($12,000)

The income tax rates were 40 percent for the years 19+1 through 19+3 and 50 percent for the years 19+4 through 19+7.

Required:

(a) Prepare the carry-back and carry-forward entries that are required. Assume carry-forwards are recognized in the year of loss.

(b) Prepare the carry-forward entries that are required if one assumes carry-forwards are recognized in the year when realized.

Problem 24-4. Gray Whale Company purchases a long-lived asset for $1,500,000. The asset has an estimated life of five years and the company adopts the sum-of-the-years'-digits depreciation method for its books and the straight-line method for income tax purposes. Data regarding depreciation are presented below:

	Books		
Year	Amount	Over-Under Amount for Taxes	Tax Return Amount
19+1	$500,000	$200,000	$300,000
19+2	400,000	100,000	300,000
19+3	300,000	—	300,000
19+4	200,000	(100,000)	300,000
19+5	100,000	(200,000)	300,000

The income before federal income taxes for the five years are presented below (before deduction of depreciation):

19+1	19+2	19+3	19+4	19+5
$700,000	$600,000	$800,000	$700,000	$900,000

The income tax rate is 50 percent.

Required:

(a) Prepare the income tax entries for the five years assuming income tax allocation.

(b) Assuming that the company used straight-line depreciation for book purposes and sum-of-the-years' digits for income tax reporting, prepare the income tax entries for the five years assuming income tax allocation.

Problem 24-5. Circle Company has been depreciating its equipment over a five-year useful life by the straight-line method for both book and tax purposes. A partial lapsing schedule, relating to equipment owned on December 31, 19+4, is presented below.

Partial Lapsing Schedule—Equipment

		Depreciation					
Year Acquired	Cost	19+5	19+6	19+7	19+8	19+9	19+10
19+1	$100,000	$20,000					
19+2	120,000	24,000	$24,000				
19+3	120,000	24,000	24,000	$24,000			
19+4	125,000	25,000	25,000	25,000	$25,000		

As indicated by the above data, the equipment has no salvage, and a full year's depreciation is taken in the year of acquisition.

The equipment-acquisition plan of the company is as follows: 19+5, $150,000; 19+6, $180,000; 19+7, $180,000; 19+8, $210,000; 19+9, $210,000; and 19+10, $150,000.

Management has decided to adopt the sum-of-the-years' digits method for tax purposes only starting in 19+5 and applicable to assets acquired after December 31, 19+4.

Required:

(a) Prepare lapsing schedules for the 19+5–19+10 period for book depreciation and tax depreciation, assuming that assets are retired and acquired as planned. Also prepare a schedule showing the prospective cumulative deferred tax during this period. Assume a 40 percent income tax rate.

(b) Assuming that the company changed its method of depreciation for tax purposes as planned but failed to apply income tax-allocation procedures, compute the aggregate effect which the failure to adopt income tax-allocation procedures would have on the amount of net income shown in the income statements for the six-year period ending December 31, 19+10.

Problem 24-6. Dam Construction Company specializes in the building of dams. During the years 19+7, 19+8, and 19+9, three dams were completed. The first dam was started in 19+5 and completed in 19+7 at a profit before income taxes of $320,000. The second and third dams were started in 19+6. The second dam was completed in 19+8 at a profit before income taxes of $326,000, and the third dam was completed in 19+9 at a profit before income taxes of $350,000.

The company uses the percentage-of-completion method of accounting in its books and the completed-contract method for income tax purposes.

Data relating to the progress toward completion of work on each dam as reported by the company's engineers are set forth below.

Dam	19+5	19+6	19+7	19+8	19+9
1	20%	60%	20%		
2		30	60	10%	
3		10	30	50	10%

Prepare the income tax entries for the years 19+5, 19+6, 19+7, 19+8, and 19+9 assuming income tax allocation and a tax rate of 40 percent.

Problem 24-7. The only difference between the book and tax income figures for Widmark Whalers is caused by the depreciation of its ship. Sum-of-the-years'-digits depreciation is used for tax purposes and straight-line depreciation for book purposes. It is estimated that the ship will have an eight-year life and no salvage at the end of that period. The income before depreciation and income taxes for each year is presented below:

19+1	19+2	19+3	19+4	19+5	19+6	19+7	19+8
$300,000	$200,000	$270,000	$200,000	$180,000	$150,000	$ 80,000	$140,000

The income tax rates for the years 19+1 through 19+6 were 40 percent and were 60 percent in 19+7 through 19+8. The ship was acquired January 1, 19+1 for $1,080,000.

Required:

Prepare the income tax entries for the years 19+1 through 19+8 assuming income tax allocation. Prepare any income tax carry-forward and carry-back entries that are required assuming that carry-forwards are recorded when realized.

Problem 24-8. Weinstein Contractors, Inc. undertakes long-term large-scale construction projects and began operations on October 15, 19+0 with Contract No. 1, its only job during 19+0. A trial balance of the Company's general ledger at December 31, 19+1 follows:

WEINSTEIN CONTRACTORS, INC.
Trial Balance
December 31, 19+1

Cash	68,090	
Accounts receivable	136,480	
Costs of contracts in progress	421,320	
Plant and equipment	35,500	
Accumulated depreciation		8,000
Accounts payable		70,820
Deferred income tax credit		1,908
Progress billings		459,400
Capital stock		139,000
Retained earnings		2,862
Selling and administrative expenses	20,600	
	681,990	681,990

The following information is available:

(1) The Company has the approval of the Internal Revenue Service to determine income on the completed-contract basis for federal income tax reporting and on the percentage-of-completion basis for financial reporting purposes.

(2) At December 31, 19+1 there were three jobs in progress, the contract prices of which had been computed as follows:

	Contract 1	Contract 2	Contract 3
Labor and materials cost	$169,000	$34,500	$265,700
Indirect costs	30,000	5,500	48,000
Total costs	$199,000	$40,000	$313,700
Add: Gross margin in contract	40,000	3,000	30,300
Total contract price	$239,000	$43,000	$344,000

During the year, billings are credited to progress billings; at year-end this account is charged for the amount of revenue to be recognized.

(3) All job costs are charged to construction in progress. Cost estimates are carefully derived by engineers and architects and are considered reliable. Data on costs to December 31, 19+1 follow:

		Incurred to Date		
Contract	Estimate	Total	Labor & Materials	Indirect
1	$199,000	$115,420	$ 92,620	$22,800
2	40,000	32,000	26,950	5,050
3	313,700	313,700	265,700	48,000
	$552,700	$461,120	$385,270	$75,850

(4) At December 31, 19+0 accumulated costs on contract 1 were $39,800; no costs had accumulated on contracts 2 and 3.

(5) Assume that the federal income tax rate is 40 percent.

Required:

(a) Prepare a schedule computing the percentage of completion of contracts in progress at December 31, 19+1.

(b) Prepare a schedule computing the amounts of revenue related costs, and net income to be recognized in 19+1 from contracts in progress at December 31, 19+1.

(c) Prepare a schedule computing the income tax expense assuming income tax allocation for the year ended December 31, 19+1.

(d) Prepare the income tax entries for the year 19+1 assuming income tax allocation.

Problem 24-9. Equipment Hauling Company purchased five special trailers during the first five years of its business life. As shown by the schedule below, it adopted different depreciation methods for books and tax return purposes. This is the only instance where the company's tax return differs from its books.

	Trailer Number									
	1		2		3		4		5	
	Depreciation Per		Depreciation Per		Depreciation Per		Depreciation Per		Depreciation Per	
Year	Tax Return	Books	Tax Return	Books	Tax Return	Books	Tax Return	Books	Tax Return	Books
19+1	$25,000	$15,000	$20,000	$12,000						
19+2	20,000	15,000	16,000	12,000	$25,000	$15,000				
19+3	15,000	15,000	12,000	12,000	20,000	15,000	$20,000	$12,000		
19+4	10,000	15,000	8,000	12,000	15,000	15,000	16,000	12,000		
19+5	5,000	15,000	4,000	12,000	10,000	15,000	12,000	12,000	$30,000	$18,000

The income before income tax, as shown in the company's books, for each of five years, is set forth below:

Year	Amount	Tax Rate
19+1	$200,000	50%
19+2	220,000	50%
19+3	140,000	50%
19+4	300,000	50%
19+5	400,000	50%

Prepare the income tax entries for the years covered by the above data assuming income tax allocation.

Problem 24-10. The following data are taken from the adjusted trial balances of Spoiler Company.

	December 31,		
	19+5	19+6	19+7
Sales	2,100,000	2,250,000	2,300,000
Cost of goods sold	1,450,000	1,575,000	1,600,000
Operating expenses	430,000	455,000	480,000
Loss—Inventory obsolescence	100,000	50,000	—
Gain on sale of obsolete inventory	—	—	10,000
Income tax	88,000	58,000	62,000
Income taxes payable (40% rate)	88,000	58,000	62,000
Obsolete inventory (Asset)	100,000	25,000	—

In the latter part of 19+5 it became apparent that inventory costing $200,000 was obsolete. On the basis of the information then available to management, it seemed reasonable to expect that the obsolete inventory could be sold for $100,000. The following journal entry was authorized and recorded as of December 31, 19+5. Assume that the loss was *not* deductible for income tax purposes until a sale or other disposal occurred.

December 31, 19+5	Obsolete inventory	100,000	
	Loss—Inventory obsolescence .	100,000	
	Inventory....................		200,000

During 19+6, one-half of the obsolete inventory was sold for $25,000. In view of this experience, management directed that the obsolete inventory still on hand at the end of 19+6 be further written down to 25 percent of its original cost. The loss arising from the sale during 19+6 of one-half of the obsolete inventory was deductible for income tax purposes on the 19+6 tax return.

During 19+7, the remaining one-half of the obsolete inventory was sold for $35,000. The company did not use income tax-allocation procedures.

Required:

(a) A schedule comparing the net income as shown by the company's income statement for each of the three years with the net income that would have been shown if income tax-allocation procedures had been followed.

(b) The 19+5 income statement as it would have appeared if the company had followed income tax-allocation procedures.

(c) Prepare the income tax entries for the years 19+5, 19+6, and 19+7 assuming income tax allocation.

Problem 24-11. Gulf Shipbuilding Company has contracts for four super tankers. Data relating to these contracts are presented below:

Tanker Identification	Year Started	Year Completed	Profit
I	19+4	19+6	$40,000
II	19+5	19+7	42,000
III	19+5	19+8	50,000
IV...............................	19+6	19+8	30,000

	19+4	19+5	19+6	19+7	19+8
Percentage of completion during year:					
I	20%	60%	20%		
II		30	60	10%	
III		10	30	50	10%
IV			10	40	50

The company uses the percentage-of-completion method of accounting in its books and the completed-contract method for income tax purposes.

Assuming that the applicable income tax rate is 50 percent, prepare the income tax entries for the years 19+4 through 19+8 assuming income tax allocation.

Problem 24-12. Metro Construction Company commenced doing business in January, 19+1. Construction activities for the year 19+1 are summarized below:

Project	Total Contract Price	Contract Expenditures to December 31, 19+1	Estimated Additional Costs to Complete Contracts	Cash Collections to December 31, 19+1	Billings to December 31, 19+1
A	$ 310,000	$187,500	$ 12,500	$155,000	$155,000
B	415,000	195,000	255,000	210,000	249,000
C	350,000	320,000	—	300,000	350,000
D	300,000	16,500	183,500	—	4,000
	$1,375,000	$719,000	$451,000	$665,000	$758,000

The company has adopted the percentage-of-completion method for financial reporting purposes and the completed-contract method for income tax purposes. The income tax rate is 50 percent.

Required:

(a) Prepare a schedule computing the amount of income by project for the year ended December 31, 19+1 that would be reported under (1) the completed-contract method, (2) the percentage-of-completion method.

(b) Prepare the income tax entries for the year 19+1 assuming income tax allocation. Assume that income before provision for taxes for the year ended December 31, 19+1 under the percentage-of-completion method is $80,000 and the taxable income is $20,000.

Problem 24-13. Lewis Company, a manufacturer of whaleboats, grants a four-year warranty on its products. The Estimated Liability for Product Warranty account shows the following transactions for the year:

Opening balance	$45,000
Provision	20,000
	65,000
Cost of servicing claims	12,000
Ending balance	$53,000

A review of unsettled claims and the company's experience indicates that the required balance at the end of the year is $80,000 and that claims have averaged 1½ percent of net sales per year. For income tax purposes only, the cost of servicing claims may be deducted as an expense.

The following additional information is available from the company's records at the end of the current year:

Gross sales	$2,040,000
Sales returns and allowances	40,000
Cost of goods sold	1,350,000
Selling and administrative expense	600,000
Net Income per books before income taxes and warranty expense	50,000

The books have not been closed, the company has not allocated income taxes in the past, and the company has an income tax rate of 50 percent. Assume that the next year net sales are $3,000,000 and income per books before income taxes is $70,000. The cost for servicing claims the next year is $60,000.

Required:

(a) Prepare the adjusting journal entry to adjust the current year's provision for warranty costs.
(b) Prepare the income tax entry for the current year assuming income tax allocation.
(c) Prepare the journal entry to record the next year's provision for warranty costs.
(d) Prepare the income tax entry for the next year assuming income tax allocation.

Problem 24-14. Shuttle Service Company owns 10 motor coaches which it uses to haul airline passengers to and from the local airport. The company has been depreciating the vehicles on the straight-line method over a five-year useful life for both book purposes and income tax purposes.

The company is considering the adoption of the double-declining-balance method for the first three years with a change to the straight-line method for the remaining two years of useful life, for income tax purposes only and for new equipment purchased after January 1, 19+5.

The depreciation status of its present fleet is set forth below.

Number of Vehicles	Acquired	Aggregate Cost	Aggregate Salvage	Accumulated Depreciation December 31, 19+4
3	19+1	$ 60,000	$3,000	$45,600
3	19+2	60,000	3,000	34,200
4	19+4	84,000	4,000	16,000
10		$204,000		$95,800

The company takes a full year's depreciation in the year of acquisition and no depreciation in the year of disposal.

The company has prepared a projection of its motor-equipment needs for the next five years. The plan is submitted below:

Year	Number of Vehicles to be Purchased: Replacements	Additions	Per Unit: Cost	Salvage	Useful Life-Years
19+5		1	$22,000	$1,000	5
19+6	1		33,000	1,000	5
19+7	1		33,000	1,000	5
19+8		1	25,000	1,500	5
19+9	2		25,000	750	5

Prepare a schedule showing the potential cumulative income tax deferral from the adoption of the double-declining-balance method of depreciation for tax purposes only for the five-year period ending December 31, 19+9. You may assume that no gain or loss is realized upon disposal. Also assume an income tax rate of 40 percent.

Problem 24-15. In January 19+4 you began the examination of the financial statements for the year ended December 31, 19+3 of Hines Corporation, a new audit client. During your examination the following information was disclosed:

(1) Federal income tax reported on tax returns was:

Year	Amount Due per Tax Return
19+1	$33,850
19+2	77,020
19+3	51,966

(2) On January 2, 19+1 packaging equipment was purchased at a cost of $225,000. The equipment had an estimated useful life of five years and a salvage of $15,000. The sum-of-the-years'-digits method of depreciation was used for income tax reporting and the straight-line method was used on the financial statements.

(3) On January 8, 19+2 $60,000 was collected in advance rental of a building for a three-year period. The $60,000 was reported as taxable income in 19+2, but $40,000 was reported as deferred revenue in 19+2 in the financial statements. The building will continue to be rented for the foreseeable future.

(4) On January 5, 19+3 office equipment was purchased for $10,000. The office equipment has an estimated life of 10 years and no salvage. Straight-line depreciation was used for both financial and income tax reporting purposes. Management, however, elected to take the allowable additional first year depreciation of $2,000 for income tax reporting. As a result, the depreciation reported on the income tax return for this equipment was $2,800 in 19+3. (Ignore the investment credit for simplicity.)

(5) On February 12, 19+3 the Corporation sold land with a book and tax basis of $150,000 for $200,000. Assume the gain can be reported in full in 19+3 on the financial statements but was reported by the installment method on the income tax return equally over a period of 10 years and is taxable at the capital gains rate.

(6) On March 15, 19+3 a patent developed at a cost of $34,000 was granted. The Corporation is amortizing the patent over a period of 4 years on the financial statements and over 17 years on its income tax return. The Corporation elected to record a full year's amortization in 19+3 on both its financial statements and income tax return.

(7) The income tax rates for 19+1, 19+2 and 19+3 were:

	Rate
Ordinary income:	
First $25,000	22 percent
Excess over $25,000	48 percent
Long-term capital gains	25 percent

Required:

(a) Prepare a schedule computing the amount of the total net deferred tax charges or credits for each year ended December 31, 19+1, 19+2, and 19+3.

(b) Prepare a schedule computing the total amount of income tax expense for financial reporting purposes for each year ended December 31 for 19+1, 19+2, and 19+3 assuming income tax allocation.

Problem 24-16. Spindletop Oil Company was formed January 5, 19+1 with the purchase of an oil lease for $70,000. The 850,000 barrels of reserves were developed at a cost of $405,000. Direct costs of producing the oil are $.20 a barrel. No oil was produced in 19+1 and 100,000 barrels of oil were produced in 19+2 and 19+3. Spindletop estimates that once its production operations are completed the land can be sold for $50,000. For tax purposes the company will expense the intangible costs of developing the lease of $380,000 (incurred in 19+1). The company will use cost depletion for tax purposes in 19+2 and percentage (statutory) depletion in 19+3, which is 22 percent of sales revenue. Each barrel of oil is sold for $4.20 and the depletion claimed for tax purposes in 19+2 is $50,000. The income tax rate is 50 percent.

Required:

(a) Knowing that profitable operations are assured for 19+2 and 19+3, prepare the tax loss carry-forward entry for 19+1.

(b) Prepare the income tax entries for the years 19+2 and 19+3 assuming income tax allocation.

Problem 24-17. Your firm has been appointed to examine the financial statements of Clark Engineering, Inc. (CEI) for the two years ended December 31, 19+9 in conjunction with an application for a bank loan. CEI was formed on January 2, 19+0 by the nontaxable incorporation of the Clark family partnership.

Early in the engagement you learned that the controller was unfamiliar with income tax accounting and that no tax allocations have been recorded.

During the examination considerable information was gathered from the accounting records and client employees regarding interperiod tax allocation. This information has been audited and is as follows (with dollar amounts rounded to the nearest $100):

(1) In accounting for bad debts, CEI uses the direct write-off method for tax purposes and the percentage-of-sales method (full accrual) for book purposes. The balance of the Allowance for Uncollectibles account at December 31, 19+9 was $62,000. Following is a schedule of accounts written off and the corresponding year(s) in which the related sales were made.

Year(s) in Which Sales Were Made	Year in Which Accounts Written Off 19+9	19+8
19+7 and prior	$19,800	$29,000
19+8	7,200	
19+9		
	$27,000	$29,000

The following is a schedule of changes in the Allowance for Uncollectibles account for the two years ended December 31, 19+9:

	Year Ended December 31	
	19+9	19+8
Balance at beginning of year	$66,000	$62,000
Accounts written off during the year	(27,000)	(29,000)
Bad debt expense for the year	38,000	33,000
Balance at the end of year	$77,000	$66,000

(2) Following is a reconciliation between net income per books and taxable income:

	Year Ended December 31	
	19+9	19+8
1. Net income per books	$333,100	$262,800
2. Federal income tax payable during year	182,300	236,800
3. Taxable income not recorded on the books this year:		
Deferred sales commissions	10,000	
4. Expenses recorded on the books this year not deducted on the tax return:		
(a) Allowance for uncollectible receivables	11,000	4,000
(b) Amortization of goodwill	8,000	8,000
5. Total of lines 1 through 4	544,400	511,600
6. Income recorded on the books this year not included on the tax return:		
Tax exempt interest—Watertown 5% Municipal Bonds	5,000	
7. Deductions on the tax return not charged against book income this year:		
Depreciation	83,700	38,000
8. Total of lines 6 and 7	88,700	38,000
9. Taxable income (line 5 less line 8)	$455,700	$473,600

(3) Assume that the effective tax rates are as follows: 19+7 and prior years: 60%; 19+8: 50%; 19+9: 40%.

(4) In December 19+9 CEI entered into a contract to serve as distributor for Brown Manufacturer, Inc.'s engineering products. The contract became effective December 31, 19+9 and $10,000 of advance commissions on the contract were received and deposited on December 31, 19+9. Since the commissions had not been earned, they were accounted for as a deferred credit to income on the balance sheet at December 31, 19+9.

(5) Goodwill represents the excess of cost over fair value of the net tangible assets of a retiring competitor that were acquired for cash on January 2, 19+3. The original balance was $80,000.

(6) Depreciation on plant assets transferred at incorporation and acquisitions through December 31, 19+9 have been accounted for on a straight-line basis for both

Asset	Cost	Life	Annual Straight-line Amount*	Declining-Balance Depreciation 19+9	Declining-Balance Depreciation 19+8	Depreciation Taken Through December 31, 19+7
Buildings	$1,190,000	20 & 50 yrs.	$31,000			$380,000
Machinery and equipment:						
Transferred at incorporation or acquired through December 31, 19+7	834,000	Various	45,900			495,800
Acquisitions since December 31, 19+7						
19+8	267,000	6 yrs.	38,000	$ 63,700	$ 76,000	
19+9	395,000	6 yrs.	58,000	116,000		
Total Asset cost	$2,686,000					

	Total Depreciation Expense 19+9	Total Depreciation Expense 19+8	Total Depreciation Expense Through December 31, 19+7
For book purposes	$172,900	$114,900	$875,800
For tax purposes	$256,600	$152,900	$875,800

*After giving appropriate consideration to salvage value.

financial and tax reporting. Beginning in 19+8 all additions of machinery and equipment have been depreciated using the double-declining-balance method for tax reporting but the straight-line method for financial reporting. Company policy is to take a full year's depreciation in the year of acquisition and none in the year of retirement. There have been no sales, trade-ins, or retirements since incorporation. On page 918 is a schedule disclosing significant information about depreciable property and related depreciation.

Required:

(a) Prepare a schedule calculating (1) the balance of deferred income taxes at December 31, 19+8 and 19+9, and (2) the amount of the timing differences between actual income tax payable and financial income tax expense for 19+8 and 19+9.

(b) Independent of your solution to part (a) and assuming the data shown below, prepare the section of the income statement beginning with pretax accounting income to disclose properly income tax expense for the years ended December 31, 19+9 and 19+8.

	19+9	19+8
Pretax accounting income	$480,400	$465,600
Taxes payable currently	182,300	236,800
Year's net timing difference—Dr. (Cr.)	28,100	(24,500)
Balance of deferred tax at end of year—Dr. (Cr.)	(44,200)	(16,100)

CHAPTER 25

QUESTIONS

1. With regard to the statement of changes in financial position, answer the following questions.
   (**a**) What are the objectives of the statement?
   (**b**) Per GAAP, is the statement mandatory?

2. What information is provided by the statement of changes in financial position that is *not* found in the following statements?
   (**a**) Balance sheet
   (**b**) Comparative balance sheets
   (**c**) Income statement
   (**d**) Statement of retained earnings

3. Why is a financial-resource-flow (funds-flow) concept needed by the accountant to prepare a statement of changes in financial position?

4. Why is a financial-resource-flow concept based on cash or working capital too narrow of a concept to underlie the preparation of the statement of changes in financial position?

5. Per *Opinion No. 19,* what is the financial-resource-flow concept that underlies the statement of changes in financial position?

6. With regard to the statement of changes in financial position, what are the following distinctions?
   (a) Cash provided from operations and cash used in operations
   (b) Working capital provided from operations and working capital used in operations
   (c) Cash provided from operations and working capital provided from operations
7. What is the difference between net income and working capital provided from operations? What is the difference between net income and cash provided from operations?
8. What is the difference between a statement of changes in financial position based on a cash format and one based on a working-capital format?
9. What are noncash (nonworking-capital) investing and financing transactions? How are such transactions reported in the statement of changes in financial position?
10. With regard to cash (or working capital) provided from operations, answer the following questions.
    (a) Why are the following reported as additions to net income (or income before extraordinary items) in the statement of changes in financial position?
    (i) Depreciation (ii) Bond-discount amortization
    (iii) Loss on sale of equipment
    (b) Why are the following reported as deductions from net income (or income before extraordinary items) in the statement of changes in financial position?
    (i) Bond-premium amortization (ii) Gain on sale of equipment
    (c) Are the additions in part (a) above and the deductions in part (b) above sources and and uses, respectively, of cash or working capital?
11. Answer the following questions and show your computations.
    (a) If net sales were $100,000 for the period and the beginning and ending balances of net accounts receivable were $60,000 and $80,000, respectively, what would be the estimated cash collected from customers for the period?
    (b) If cost of goods sold were $80,000 for the period, if the beginning and ending balances of inventory were $85,000 and $100,000, respectively, and if the beginning and ending balances of accounts payable were $50,000 and $40,000, respectively, what would be the estimated cash paid for inventory purchases for the period?
    (c) If accrued expenses were $30,000 for the period and if the beginning and ending balances of accrued liabilities were $35,000 and $31,000, respectively, what would be the estimated cash paid for accrued expenses for the period?
12. Assuming that the following transactions took place during the current period, and assuming a working capital format, how would each transaction be reported in the statement of changes in financial position?

(a) Allowance for uncollectibles	1,000	
Accounts receivable		1,000
(b) Cash	9,000	
Loss on marketable securities	1,000	
Marketable securities		10,000
(c) Bonds payable	50,000	
Gain on bond retirement		2,000
Cash		48,000
(d) Inventory	45,000	
Cash		45,000
(e) Retained earnings	10,000	
Common stock		10,000

(**f**) Notes payable (long-term)	15,000	
Common stock		15,000
(**g**) Dividends payable	60,000	
Cash		60,000
(**h**) Land	40,000	
Notes payable (short-term)		10,000
Cash		30,000
(**i**) Insurance expense	3,000	
Prepaid insurance		3,000
(**j**) Deferred revenue	8,000	
Revenue		8,000

13. What would be your answers to question 12 above assuming a cash format, instead of a working-capital format?

14. Assuming that the following transactions took place during the current period and assuming a cash format, how would each transaction be reported in the statement of changes in financial position?

(**a**) Cash surrender value of life insurance	500	
Insurance expense		500
(**b**) Income tax expense	50,000	
Deferred income tax credit		10,000
Income taxes payable		40,000
(**c**) Pension expense	90,000	
Deferred pension cost—Payments in excess of pension expense	450,000	
Cash		540,000
(**d**) Land	15,000	
Donated capital		15,000
(**e**) Lease obligation	7,473	
Interest expense—Lease	2,527	
Amortization expense—Lease	8,425	
Cash		10,000
Lease rights—Equipment		8,425

15. What would be your answers to question 14 above assuming a working-capital format, instead of a cash format?

16. Some accountants argue that the statement of changes in financial position should not begin with net income (or income before extraordinary items). Instead the statement should begin with revenue that provided working capital or cash less operating costs and expenses that required working capital or cash during the period. What are the advantages and disadvantages of such a presentation? Is such presentation acceptable per GAAP?

17. What are the advantages and disadvantages of preparing a statement of changes in financial position based on the following financial-resource-flow concepts? (In your answers compare and contrast the different concepts with regard to the relevancy of the information provided and their measurement problems).

(**a**) Cash
(**b**) Net current monetary assets (current monetary assets minus current monetary liabilities)
(**c**) Working capital
(**d**) All significant financial resources arising from external transactions.

PROBLEMS

Problem 25-1. You are given below nine multiple choice questions. Select the correct answer to each question and indicate the corresponding letter on a separate sheet of paper (e.g., 1-a, 2-a, etc.).

(1) In a statement of changes in financial position, the "Sources of Financial Resources" section should report (a) the issuance of common stock in exchange for a factory building, (b) stock dividends received, (c) repairs to machinery charged to accumulated depreciation, (d) the assignment of accounts receivable, (e) none of the above.

(2) A transaction which would appear as an application of financial resources on a statement of changes in financial position, but not on a traditional statement of sources and uses of working capital, would be the (a) acquisition of property, plant and equipment for cash, (b) reacquisition of bonds issued by the reporting entity, (c) acquisition of property, plant and equipment with an issue of common stock, (d) declaration and payment of dividends, (e) none of the above.

(3) A major difference between a statement of changes in financial position with a working-capital format as opposed to a cash format would be in the treatment of (a) dividends declared and paid, (b) sales of noninventory assets for cash at a loss, (c) payment of long-term debt, (d) a change during the period in the accounts payable balance, (e) none of the above.

(4) A statement of changes in financial position typically would not disclose the effects of (a) capital stock issued to acquire productive facilities, (b) stock dividends declared, (c) cash dividends declared but not yet paid, (d) a purchase and immediate retirement of treasury stock, (e) none of the above.

(5) A basic objective of the statement of changes in financial position is to (a) supplant the income statement and balance sheet, (b) disclose changes during the period in all asset and all liability accounts, (c) disclose the change in working capital during the period, (d) provide essential information for financial statement users in making economic decisions, (e) none of the above.

(6) The financial-resource-flow concept embodied in the statement of changes in financial position is (a) cash, (b) working capital, (c) net quick assets, (d) net current monetary assets, (e) none of the above.

(7) A statement of changes in financial position would disclose the amortization of bond premium as (a) a use, (b) both a source and use, (c) a deduction in the computation of financial resources generated from operations, (d) a source, (e) none of the above.

(8) The major difference between a statement of changes in financial position with a working-capital format as opposed to a cash format would be in the treatment of (a) nonfund expenses, (b) important financing and investing activities that do not affect cash or working capital directly, (c) net changes in current accounts, (d) none of the above.

(9) On July 1, 1976, Wilkerson, Inc., issued at face amount \$100,000 in serial bonds with 5 percent interest payable January 1 and July 1 of each year and principal payable \$10,000 on July 1 of each year from 1980 through 1989. Transactions related to this issue decreased working capital during 1981 by (a) \$14,250, (b) \$14,500, (c) \$4,250, (d) \$4,500, (e) none of the above.

Problem 25-2. The following items relate to APB *Opinion No. 19.* Your answers pertain to data to be reported in the Statement of Changes in Financial Position of Retail Establishment, Inc. for the year ended December 31, 19+3. Balance sheets and income statements for 19+3 and 19+2 follow:

RETAIL ESTABLISHMENT, INC.
Comparative Balance Sheets
December 31, 19+3 and 19+2

Assets	19+3	19+2
Current assets:		
Cash	$ 150,000	$100,000
Marketable securities	40,000	
Accounts receivable—net	420,000	290,000
Merchandise inventory	330,000	210,000
Prepayments	50,000	25,000
	$ 990,000	$625,000
Land, buildings and fixtures	$ 565,000	$300,000
Less accumulated depreciation	55,000	25,000
	$ 510,000	$275,000
	$1,500,000	$900,000
Equities		
Current liabilities:		
Accounts payable	$ 265,000	$220,000
Accrued expenses	$ 70,000	$ 65,000
Dividends payable	$ 35,000	
	$ 370,000	$285,000
Note payable—due 19+5	$ 250,000	—
Stockholders' equity:		
Common stock	$ 600,000	$450,000
Retained earnings	280,000	165,000
	$ 880,000	$615,000
	$1,500,000	$900,000

RETAIL ESTABLISHMENT, INC.
Comparative Income Statements
For the Years Ended December 31, 19+3 and 19+2

	19+3	19+2
Net sales—including service charges	$3,200,000	$2,000,000
Cost of goods sold	2,500,000	1,600,000
Gross margin	$ 700,000	$ 400,000
Expenses (including income taxes)	500,000	260,000
Net income	$ 200,000	$ 140,000

Additional information available included the following:

Although Retail Establishment, Inc. will report all significant changes in financial position, management has adopted a cash format.

All accounts receivable and accounts payable relate to trade merchandise. Cash discounts are not allowed to customers but a service charge is added to an account for late payment. Accounts payable are recorded net and always are paid to take all of the discount allowed. The Allowance for Uncollectibles at the end of 19+3 was the same as at the end of 19+2; no receivables were charged against the Allowance during 19+3.

The proceeds from the note payable were used to finance a new store building. Capital stock was sold to provide additional working capital.

(1) Cash collected during 19+3 from accounts receivable amounted to (a) \$3,200,000, (b) \$3,070,000, (c) \$2,920,000, (d) \$2,780,000, (e) none of the above or not determinable from the above facts.

(2) Cash payments during 19+3 on accounts payable to suppliers amounted to (a) \$2,575,000, (b) \$2,500,000, (c) \$2,455,000, (d) \$2,335,000, (e) none of the above or not determinable from the above facts.

(3) Cash dividend payments during 19+3 amounted to (a) \$120,000, (b) \$115,000, (c) \$85,000, (d) \$35,000, (e) none of the above or not determinable from the above facts.

(4) Cash receipts during 19+3 that were not provided by operations totaled (a) \$400,000, (b) \$250,000, (c) \$150,000, (d) \$70,000, (e) none of the above or not determinable from the above facts.

(5) Cash payments for assets during 19+3 that were not reflected in operations totaled (a) \$305,000, (b) \$265,000, (c) \$185,000, (d) \$40,000, (e) none of the above or not determinable from the above facts.

Problem 25-3. The balance sheets of Karns Enterprises, Inc. for the years 19+3 and 19+4 are as follows:

	19+4	19+3
Cash	\$ 312,500	\$ 100,000
Land	75,000	25,000
Buildings	125,000	125,000
Plant equipment	1,475,000	1,250,000
Accumulated depreciation	(450,000)	(250,000)
	\$1,537,500	\$1,250,000
Bonds payable	\$ 625,000	\$ 500,000
Common Stock, \$100 par value	675,000	625,000
Retained earnings	237,500	125,000
	\$1,537,500	\$1,250,000

Additional information: Cash dividends of \$187,500 were charged to Retained Earnings in 19+4; net income accounted for the remaining change in Retained Earnings. Additional land was acquired during the year by the issuance of common stock. Prepare a statement of changes in financial position using a cash format for the year 19+4.

Problem 25-4. The comparative balance sheets and income statements for the years 19+1 and 19+2 for the Income Yes–Cash No Company are as follows. Assume that all purchases and all sales are made on account, and that the accounts payable represent suppliers of merchandise only.

INCOME YES–CASH NO COMPANY
Balance Sheet
December 31, 19+2 and 19+1

Assets	19+2	19+1	Change Dr.	Change Cr.
Cash	$ 5,000	$ 30,000		$25,000
Accounts receivable	45,000	24,000	$21,000	
Inventories	50,000	65,000		15,000
Plant & equipment	500,000	500,000	—	—
Accumulated depreciation	(150,000)	(100,000)		50,000
	$450,000	$519,000		
Equities				
Accounts payable	$ 15,000	$ 39,000	$24,000	
Salaries payable	5,000	30,000	25,000	
Common stock	300,000	300,000	—	—
Retained earnings	130,000	150,000	20,000	
	$450,000	$519,000	$90,000	$90,000

INCOME YES–CASH NO COMPANY
Income Statement
For the Year Ended December 31, 19+2

Net sales		$200,000
Cost of goods sold		110,000
Gross margin		$ 90,000
Operating expenses:		
Salaries expense	$10,000	
Depreciation expense	50,000	60,000
Net income		$ 30,000

You are asked to prepare a statement of changes in financial position, using a cash format, for the year 19+2.

Problem 25-5. The comparative financial condition of the Conrad Gilham Company on December 31, 19+3 and 19+4 is summarized below.

Assets	December 31, 19+4	December 31, 19+3	Increase (Decrease)
Working capital	$164,710	$125,300	$39,410
Plant and equipment	84,000	57,400	26,600
Accumulated depreciation	(11,480)	(8,610)	(2,870)
	$237,230	$174,090	$63,140
Equities			
Bonds payable	$ 80,000	$ 50,000	$30,000
Bond discount	(3,800)		(3,800)
Common Stock, $100 par value	100,000	70,000	30,000
Capital in excess of par	30,000	21,000	9,000
Retained earnings	31,030	33,090	(2,060)
	$237,230	$174,090	$63,140

Additional information: During the year equipment that cost $10,000 and that had a book amount (value) of $6,500 was sold for $5,000. On June 30 all of the outstanding bonds payable were purchased at 103. A new 10 year issue was sold at 95. Cash dividends of $7,000 were paid during the year. Plant and equipment costing $20,000 was acquired by the issuance of 200 shares of stock.

Required:

Prepare a statement of changes in financial position, using a working-capital format. Note that a schedule of working-capital changes is not required.

Problem 25-6. Dickson Company submitted the following comparative balance sheet.

DICKSON COMPANY
Comparative Balance Sheet
December 31, 19+9 and 19+8

	December 31,	
Assets	19+9	19+8
Cash	$ 2,600	$ 3,000
Accounts receivable	7,500	6,000
Allowance for uncollectibles	1,200*	950*
Inventory	23,600	22,000
Furniture and fixtures	20,000	15,000
Accumulated depreciation—Furniture & fixtures	4,500*	3,000*
Delivery equipment	15,000	10,000
Accumulated depreciation—Delivery equipment	7,500*	5,000*
Goodwill		5,000
	$55,500	$52,050
Liabilities and Stockholders' Equity		
Accounts payable	$ 5,750	$ 5,050
Notes payable	6,000	7,000
Capital stock	35,000	25,000
Capital in excess of par	1,000	
Retained earnings	7,750	15,000
	$55,500	$52,050

*Deduction

The decrease in retained earnings was caused by a net loss which was composed of an operating loss of $2,250 and the amortization of goodwill. The change in the balance of each of the other non-current accounts was caused by one entry only.

Required:

(a) A statement of changes in financial position, using a working-capital format.
(b) A schedule of working capital changes.
(c) A statement of changes in financial position, using a cash format.

Problem 25-7. The Osborne Company's balance sheets on December 31, 19+8 and 19+7 were:

	December 31, 19+8	December 31, 19+7
Cash	$ 6,000	$ 9,000
Accounts receivable	19,600	22,050
Allowance for uncollectibles	600*	700*
Merchandise	39,210	32,560
Investments in securities—Long term	13,000	8,000
Equipment	8,200	6,500
Accumulated depreciation	1,200*	850*
	$84,210	$76,560
Liabilities and Stockholders' Equity		
Accounts payable	$29,000	$31,000
Notes payable	7,500	10,000
Capital stock	35,000	30,000
Retained earnings	12,710	5,560
	$84,210	$76,560

*Deduction

The increase in equipment resulted from a purchase. A dividend of $5,000 was paid during the year. Capital stock of $5000 was issued in exchange for the securities acquired during the year.

Required:

(a) Prepare a statement of changes in financial position for the year 19+8 using a working-capital format and a schedule of working-capital changes.
(b) Prepare a statement of changes in financial position using a cash format.

Problem 25-8. During 19+6 Clear Air Company acquired control of Turbulence Company in order to assure itself of a supply of raw materials. Details of the transaction are shown below:

Securities acquired:	
Capital stock with a par value of $30,000 acquired at a valuation of	$32,500
Bonds at face amount	25,000
Total Turbulence Company securities acquired	$57,500
Payment:	
Clear Air Company capital stock:	
Preferred—Par	$50,000
Capital in excess of par	2,500
Total	$52,500
Common—Par	5,000
Total payment	$57,500

Corporation balance sheets for the last two years are presented below:

CLEAR AIR COMPANY
Condensed Comparative Balance Sheet
December 31, 19+6 and 19+5

	December 31, 19+6	December 31, 19+5
Assets		
Working capital	$ 93,200	$ 78,000
Land	10,000	8,000
Buildings	50,000	50,000
Accumulated depreciation—buildings	(8,000)	(6,000)
Equipment	40,000	35,000
Accumulated depreciation—equipment	(8,700)	(6,300)
Stock of Turbulence Company	32,500	
Bonds of Turbulence Company	25,000	
	$234,000	$158,700
Equities		
Mortgage payable	$ 30,000	$ 30,000
Capital stock—common	110,000	100,000
Capital stock—preferred	50,000	
Capital in excess of par value—preferred	2,500	
Retained earnings	41,500	28,700
	$234,000	$158,700

Clear Air Company had a net income of $21,900 during 19+6; it paid dividends of $6,600 on its common stock and $2,500 on its preferred stock. The company also issued $5,000 of its common stock for equipment.

Prepare a statement of changes in financial position, using a working-capital format. Note a schedule of working-capital changes is not required.

Problem 25-9. The net change in working capital and the net changes in the balance sheet accounts of United Company for the year ended December 30, 19+5, are shown below:

	Debit	Credit
Working capital	$23,400	
Investments		$30,000
Land	3,200	
Buildings	35,000	
Machinery	3,000	
Office equipment		1,500
Accumulated depreciation:		
Buildings		2,000
Machinery	2,100	
Office equipment	600	
Bond discount	1,000	
Bonds payable		20,000
Capital stock—Preferred	10,000	
Capital stock—Common		12,400
Capital in excess of par value—Common		5,600
Retained earnings		6,800
	$78,300	$78,300

Additional information:

(1) The net income for the year was $28,000.

(2) A cash dividend of $18,000 was declared December 15, 19+5, payable January 15, 19+6. A 2 percent stock dividend was issued March 31, 19+5, when the market price was $12.50 per share.

(3) The investments were sold for $32,500.

(4) A building and the land on which it stood were sold for $54,000. The land cost $4,000 and the buildings cost $45,000. There was accumulated depreciation on the building of $4,500.

(5) A new machine was purchased during the year on the following terms: $11,000 cash plus the trade-in of an old machine which cost $10,000 and on which there was accumulated depreciation of $8,000. No gain or loss was shown for the transaction.

(6) A fully depreciated office machine which cost $1,500 was written off.

(7) Preferred stock of $10,000 par value was retired for $10,200.

(8) The company issued 1,000 shares of its common stock (par value $10) on June 15, 19+5 for $15 per share. There were 13,240 shares outstanding on December 1, 19+5.

Required:

Prepare a statement of changes in financial position, using a working-capital format, for the year 19+5. Note that a schedule of working-capital changes is not required.

Problem 25-10. From the following information for Oread Company you are to prepare a statement of changes in financial position for the year 19+5, using a working-capital format, and a supporting schedule of working-capital changes.

	December 31,	
Debits	19+5	19+4
Cash	100,296	110,368
Temporary investments	148,000	175,500
Accounts receivable	123,902	125,450
Inventories	154,060	141,786
Prepayments	1,670	1,625
Cash surrender value of life insurance policies	11,000	10,250
Unamortized bond discount	3,255	4,200
Property, plant, and equipment	285,125	246,525
Treasury stock	5,750	
	833,058	815,704
Credits		
Accounts payable	92,056	95,324
Notes payable to banks	110,000	100,000
Accrued liabilities	24,163	15,427
First-mortgage 6 percent serial bonds	117,500	140,000
Allowance for uncollectibles	7,615	8,430
Accumulated depreciation	97,126	98,610
Allowance for inventory loss	6,162	4,253
Common stock—$100 par value	200,000	200,000
Additional paid-in capital	15,000	15,000
Retained earnings	122,236	106,260
Reserve for contingencies	41,200	32,400
	833,058	815,704

The information concerning the transactions during 19+5 is as follows:

(1) Net income for 19+5 was $60,476. There were no extraordinary items.

(2) Uncollectible accounts of $2,500 were written off against the allowance for uncollectibles.

(3) The allowance for inventory loss was created by a charge to expense in each year, and it was set up to reduce the inventory cost of obsolete items to estimated market value.

(4) The 19+5 premium on life insurance policies was $1,685, and expense was charged with $935 of this payment.

(5) Machinery was purchased for $23,875 and machinery costing $25,275 was retired. The retired machinery had accumulated depreciation of $21,484 at date of retirement and it was sold as scrap for $1,600. The remaining increase in property, plant, and equipment resulted from construction of a building.

(6) The serial bonds mature at the rate of $10,000 per year. In addition to the retirement of the $10,000 bonds due in 19+5, the company purchased and retired an additional $12,500 of the bonds due in 19+8 and 19+9 at 103. Both the premium on retirement and the applicable discount were charged to expense.

(7) The reserve for contingencies was provided by charges against retained earnings. A debit to the reserve of $16,200 was made during the year, which represented the final settlement of part of a 19+2 income tax liability.

Problem 25-11. The following comparative balance sheets are submitted to you. Prepare a statement of changes in financial position, using a cash format, for the year 19+9.

THORNDYKE COMPANY
Comparative Balance Sheets
December 31, 19+9 and 19+8

	December 31,	
Assets	19+9	19+8
Cash	$ 55,000	$ 21,080
Accounts receivable—net	25,000	22,700
Merchandise inventory	65,000	51,000
Prepayments	3,500	4,640
Funds impounded for completion of building	10,000	
Land	15,000	
Buildings	145,000	
Equipment	26,400	19,810
Accumulated depreciation—Buildings and equipment	17,600*	7,300*
	$327,300	$111,930
Liabilities and Stockholders' Equity		
Accounts payable	$ 26,000	$ 23,500
Accrued taxes and expenses	18,900	17,200
Bonds payable	100,000	
Unamortized premium on bonds payable	4,500	
Capital stock	85,000	35,000
Capital in excess of par	25,000	
Donated capital	15,000	
Retained earnings	42,900	28,230
Reserve for possible decline in inventory	10,000	8,000
	$327,300	$111,930

*Deduction.

Thorndyke Company had operated for several years in leased premises in Springfield. Late in 19+8 the city of York offered to donate land worth $15,000 to the company if it would build and operate a plant in that city. Title to the land was obtained early in 19+9.

To finance the construction of the plant, Thorndyke Company issued $100,000 par value of bonds at 105, and $50,000 par value of capital stock at 150. The proceeds of the bond issue were impounded for construction purposes. The building was occupied during 19+9, but a supplementary building remained to be constructed and $10,000 of cash continued to be impounded until the completion of this building.

A portion ($500) of the bond premium was amortized during 19+9.

Problem 25-12. The financial statements of Frank Manufacturing Corporation for 19+4 and 19+3 follow. The Corporation was formed on January 1, 19+1.

FRANK MANUFACTURING CORPORATION
Comparative Balance Sheets
December 31, 19+4 and 19+3

Assets	19+4	19+3	Increase (Decrease)
Current assets			
Cash	$ 33,500	$ 27,000	$ 6,500
Accounts receivable (net allowance for uncollectibles of $1,900 and $2,000)	89,900	79,700	10,200
Inventories (at lower of cost or market)	136,300	133,200	3,100
Prepayments	4,600	12,900	(8,300)
Total	$264,300	$252,800	$ 11,500
Investments			
Land held for future plant site	$ 35,000	—	$ 35,000
Property, plant, and equipment			
Land	$ 47,000	$ 47,000	—
Buildings and equipment (net of accumulated depreciation of $155,600 and $117,000)	551,900	425,000	126,900
Total	$598,900	$472,000	$126,900
Other assets			
Organization cost	1,500	3,000	(1,500)
Total	$899,700	$727,800	$171,900
Liabilities & Stockholders' Equity			
Current liabilities			
Accounts payable	$ 3,000	$ 7,800	$ (4,800)
Notes payable	8,000	5,000	3,000
Mortgage payable	3,600	3,600	—
Accrued liabilities	6,200	4,800	1,400
Income taxes payable	87,500	77,900	9,600
Total	$108,300	$ 99,100	$ 9,200
Long-term liabilities			
Notes payable	$ —	$ 18,000	$ (18,000)
Mortgage payable	70,200	73,800	(3,600)
Total	$ 70,200	$ 91,800	$ (21,600)
Deferred income—investment credit	$ 16,800	$ 18,900	$ (2,100)

Stockholders' equity			
Capital stock; $1 par value; shares authorized, 300,000 in 19+4 and 200,000 in 19+3; shares issued and outstanding, 162,000 in 19+4 and 120,000 in 19+3	$162,000	$120,000	$ 42,000
Capital in excess of par value	306,900	197,900	109,000
Reserve for contingencies	25,000	—	25,000
Retained earnings	210,500	200,100	10,400
Total	$704,400	$518,000	$186,400
Total	$899,700	$727,800	$171,900

FRANK MANUFACTURING COMPANY
Statement of Income and Retained Earnings
For the Years Ended December 31, 19+4 and 19+3

	19+4	19+3	Increase (Decrease)
Sales	$980,000	$900,000	$ 80,000
Cost of goods sold	540,000	490,000	50,000
Gross margin	$440,000	$410,000	30,000
Selling and administrative expenses	262,000	248,500	13,500
Net income from operations	$178,000	$161,500	$ 16,500
Other income and (deductions), (net)	(3,000)	(1,500)	1,500
Net income before income taxes	$175,000	$160,000	$ 15,000
Provision for income taxes	85,400	77,900	7,500
Net income after income taxes	$ 89,600	$ 82,100	$ 7,500
Retained earnings, January 1	200,100	118,000	82,100
Ten percent stock dividend distributed	(36,000)	—	(36,000)
Cash dividends paid	(18,200)	—	(18,200)
Appropriation for contingent loss	(25,000)	—	(25,000)
Retained earnings, December 31	$210,500	$200,100	$ 10,400

The following information was given effect in the preparation of the foregoing financial statements:

(1) The 10 percent stock dividend was distributed on August 1. The investment in land for a future plant site was obtained by the issuance of 10,000 shares of the Corporation's common stock on October 1. On December 1, 20,000 shares of common stock were sold to obtain additional working capital. There were no other 19+4 transactions affecting contributed capital.

(2) During 19+4 depreciable assets with a total cost of $17,500 were retired and sold as scrap for a nominal amount. These assets were fully depreciated at December 31, 19+3. The only depreciable asset acquired in 19+4 was a new building which was completed in December; no depreciation was taken on its cost.

(3) When new equipment, with an estimated life of 10 years, was purchased on January 2, 19+3, for $300,000, the decision was made to record the resulting investment

credit in a deferred income account with the benefit of the investment credit being allocated over the useful life of the machine by a reduction of the provision for income taxes. The income tax rate for 19+3 and 19+4 was 50 percent.

(4) In 19+4, $10,000 was paid in advance on a long-term notes payable. The balance of the long-term notes is due in 19+5.

(5) A reserve for a contingent loss of $25,000 arising from a law suit was established in 19+4.

Required:

Prepare a statement of changes in financial position, using a working-capital format, and a schedule of working-capital changes for the year 19+4.

Problem 25-13. From the following data prepare a statement of changes in financial position, using a working-capital format, and a schedule of working capital changes for the year 19+9.

HUDSON COMPANY
Comparative Balance Sheet
December 31, 19+9 and 19+8

	December 31,	
Assets	19+9	19+8
Cash	$ 5,150	$ 4,500
Accounts receivable	31,600	29,700
Allowance for uncollectibles	1,500*	1,200*
Finished goods	10,000	12,500
Goods in process	18,320	15,800
Materials	9,700	10,000
Advances to salesmen	1,000	750
Prepayments	250	300
Land	70,000	65,000
Buildings	155,000	110,000
Accumulated depreciation—Buildings	16,000*	10,000*
Machinery	110,000	100,000
Accumulated depreciation—Machinery	13,500*	11,000*
Tools—less depreciation	22,000	25,000
Patents—less amortization	37,000	30,000
Investment in stocks		25,000
	$439,020	$406,350
Liabilities and Stockholders' Equity		
Accounts payable	$ 12,000	$ 33,500
Notes payable	5,000	27,000
Bank loans		20,000
Bonds payable	300,000	200,000
Discount on bonds	1,800*	
Capital stock	109,000	100,000
Reserve for contingencies		16,000
Retained earnings	14,820	9,850
	$439,020	$406,350

*Deduction.

Analysis of Retained Earnings

Balance, December 31, 19+8	$ 9,850
Add: Net income—19+9	3,970
Return of Reserve for Contingencies	16,000
Total	$29,820
Deduct: Dividends paid	15,000
Balance, December 31, 19+9	$14,820

Bonds of $100,000 par value were issued at 98 at the beginning of 19+9.

Depreciation and amortization were charged to operations during the year as follows:

By credit to accumulated depreciation accounts:	
Buildings	$6,000
Machinery	6,500
By credit to long-lived asset accounts:	
Tools	$5,000
Patents	2,000
By credit to a contra account:	
Discount on bonds	$ 200

During the year, machinery which cost $10,000 was sold for $6,000. The accumulated depreciation account was debited $4,000 although depreciation of only $2,500 had been provided.

Land that cost $4,000 was sold for $4,300 and an additional parcel was acquired for $9,000 in capital stock.

The long-term investments were sold for $23,000.

Problem 25-14. Based on the information given below, prepare a statement of changes in financial position for Sunflower, Inc. using a cash format.

SUNFLOWER, INC.
Balance Sheet Accounts
December 31, 19+5 and 19+4

			Changes	
Debits	19+5	19+4	Debit	Credit
Cash	15,000	12,500	2,500	
Temporary investments	—	100,000		100,000
Accounts receivable	48,750	57,500		8,750
Other current assets	335,000	270,000	65,000	
Land	60,000	95,000		35,000
Building and equipment	250,000	350,000		100,000
Organization cost	45,000	60,000		15,000
Bond discount	3,200	2,000	1,200	
	756,950	947,000		
Credits				
Accounts payable	14,175	37,900	23,725	
Other current liabilities	103,000	93,000		10,000
Allowance for uncollectibles	900	1,100	200	
Accumulated depreciation	70,000	125,000	55,000	
Bonds payable	150,000	100,000		50,000
Common stock	400,000	550,000	150,000	
Retained earnings	18,875	40,000	21,125	
	756,950	947,000	318,750	318,750

SUNFLOWER, INC.
Statement of Income and Retained Earnings
For the Year Ended December 31, 19+5

Sales			$110,000
Cost of goods sold			70,000
Gross margin			$ 40,000
Operating expenses:			
Selling expenses		$ 2,100	
General and administrative expenses		1,700	
Depreciation expense		5,000	8,800
Net operating income			$ 31,200
Nonoperating items:			
Add: Gain on sale of equipment		$10,000	
Deduct: Loss on sale of temporary investments	$ 900		
Amortization of organization cost	15,000		
Bond interest expense (includes $800 bond discount amortization)	6,800	22,700	12,700
Net income before taxes			$ 18,500
Income taxes (25%)			4,625
Net income			$ 13,875
Beginning retained earnings, January 1			40,000
			$ 53,875
Deduct stock dividends on common			35,000
Ending retained earnings, December 31			$ 18,875

Problem 25-15. From the following data prepare a statement of changes in financial position, using a working-capital format, and a schedule of working-capital changes for the year 19+9.

TEMPLETON MANUFACTURING COMPANY
Comparative Balance Sheet
December 31, 19+9 and 19+8

	December 31,	
Assets	19+9	19+8
Cash	$ 50,300	$ 40,750
Accounts receivable	64,900	63,850
Allowance for uncollectibles	3,100*	3,400*
Notes receivable—Trade	10,000	12,000
Accrued interest receivable	200	150
Finished goods	31,000	29,950
Goods in process	5,100	4,975
Materials	20,720	19,850
Prepayments	700	680
Factory supplies	2,600	2,390
Property, plant, and equipment	845,000	915,000
Accumulated depreciation	160,000*	155,000*
Leasehold improvements	46,000	50,000
Sinking fund securities	19,755	9,875
Sinking fund cash	11,805	10,645
	$944,980	$1,001,715

Equities

Accounts payable	$ 39,540	$ 37,820
Bank loans	30,000	40,000
Federal income taxes payable	25,000	22,600
Revenue received in advance	2,360	2,195
Sinking fund bonds payable	100,000	100,000
Unamortized bond premium	2,100	2,400
Capital stock	400,000	400,000
Unearned increment per appraisal		75,000
Sinking fund reserve	30,000	20,000
Retained earnings	315,980	301,700
	$944,980	$1,001,715

*Deduction.

The bonds were issued at the beginning of 19+7 at 103, and were to mature in ten years.

The bond indenture required the creation of a sinking fund by annual deposits of $10,000. Interest on sinking fund investments and amortizations of discounts or premiums on the investments were to be recorded in the sinking fund accounts; when the sinking fund thus accumulated amounted to $100,000 additional contributions were to cease. Sinking fund transactions during 19+9 were:

Purchase of sinking fund securities from sinking fund cash	$ 9,820
Collection of interest	980
Amortization of discount	60
Sinking fund deposit	10,000

The bond indenture also required the creation of a sinking fund reserve by annual credits of $10,000.

Fully depreciated equipment acquired at a cost of $8,000 were written off during the year.

At the end of 19+7, an appraisal of property, plant, and equipment was recorded by the following entry:

Property, plant, and equipment	100,000	
Accumulated depreciation		25,000
Unearned increment per appraisal		75,000

Depreciation for 19+8 was computed on the basis of cost. New auditors, engaged at the end of 19+9, insisted on basing the depreciation expense on the appraised value, and the directors thereupon decided to reverse the appraisal.

The net income for the year was $44,280 (including interest on sinking fund securities), and a $20,000 cash dividend was paid.

Land was sold at cost, $15,000. Other property, plant, and equipment were purchased for $53,000.

Problem 25-16. The following financial data were furnished to you by the Relgne Corporation:

RELGNE CORPORATION
Comparative Trial Balances
At Beginning and End of Fiscal Year Ended October 31, 19+4

Debits	19+4	19+3
Cash	226,000	50,000
Accounts receivable	148,000	100,000
Inventories	291,000	300,000
Prepayments	2,500	2,000
Long-term investments at cost	10,000	40,000
Sinking Fund	90,000	80,000
Land and building	195,000	195,000
Equipment	215,000	90,000
Discount on bonds payable	8,500	9,000
Treasury stock	5,000	10,000
	1,191,000	876,000
Credits		
Allowance for uncollectibles	8,000	5,000
Accumulated depreciation—building	26,250	22,500
Accumulated depreciation—equipment	39,750	27,500
Accounts payable	55,000	60,000
Notes payable—current	70,000	20,000
Accrued expenses payable	18,000	15,000
Taxes payable	35,000	10,000
Unearned revenue	1,000	9,000
Notes payable—long term	40,000	60,000
Bonds payable—long term	250,000	250,000
Common stock	300,000	200,000
Appropriation for sinking fund	90,000	80,000
Unappropriated retained earnings	142,000	112,000
Paid-in capital in excess of par value	116,000	5,000
	1,191,000	876,000

The following information was also available:

(1) All purchases and sales were on account.
(2) Equipment with an original cost of $15,000 was sold for $7,000.
(3) A six-month note payable for $50,000 was issued towards the purchase of new equipment.
(4) Treasury stock was sold for $1000 more than its cost.
(5) Cash dividends were $8000.
(6) The following were included in miscellaneous expenses:

Loss on sale of equipment	$ 1,000
Expired prepayments	2,000
Building depreciation	3,750
Equipment depreciation	19,250
Bad debts expense	4,000
Interest expense	18,000
Gain on sale of investments	12,000

Required:

Prepare a statement of changes in financial position, using a cash-flow format, for the year 19+4.

CHAPTER 26

QUESTIONS

1. What are accountants assuming when they use money as the basic measuring unit?

2. In a modern economy money is a commodity. What is meant by this statement and of what significance is it?

3. What is meant by the "exchange value of money" and of what significance is it to accounting?

4. Is it possible to directly or indirectly measure the changes in the general purchasing power of the dollar?

5. What is the relationship between the general purchasing power of the dollar and the general price level?

6. Is there any difference between changes in specific prices and changes in general prices?

7. What are some of the implications of using accounting data for purposes of financial analysis when such data are affected by changes in the general price level?

8. Debtors lose and creditors gain during periods of inflation. Do you agree with this statement?

9. What are monetary assets and monetary liabilities? How are they affected by changes in the general price level?

10. What are some of the arguments used by accountants to support the conventional accounting use of the unadjusted dollar as the basic measuring unit?

11. What are general price-level financial statements?

12. It is often said that general price-level financial statements result in "current-dollar" reporting. Does this mean that such financial statements report current values?

13. Is the presentation of general price-level financial statements required in order to be in conformity with generally accepted accounting principles (GAAP)?

14. What are some general guidelines that should be followed in preparing general price-level financial statements?

15. Suppose that land was acquired for $25,000 when the general price-level index was 100. If the general price-level index is now 110, so that the land in terms of today's dollars is $27,500, has there been a gain of $2,500?

16. Suppose that 19+6 was the annual fiscal period just ended. Further suppose that land was acquired for $15,000 in 19+5. Given the following general price-level indexes, answer the questions below (show all calculations):

19+1	100
19+4	115
19+5	120
19+6	125

(**a**) What is the cost of the land in 19+5 dollars?
(**b**) What is the cost of the land in 19+6 dollars?
(**c**) What is the cost of the land in base-year dollars?
(**d**) What is the cost of the land in 19+6 dollars if the base period is switched from 19+1 to 19+4?

17. What is the general price-level gain or loss reported in general price-level income statements?

18. A friend of yours in analyzing a company's annual report, which includes supplementary comparative general price-level financial statements, cannot understand why monetary items for the current year are reported at the same dollar amounts on both the general price-level and historical-dollar balance sheets. Furthermore, he cannot understand why the reported dollar amounts for the monetary items in prior years are different in the comparative general price-level balance sheets from those of the comparative historical-dollar balance sheets. Can you explain to your friend why the monetary items are the same in the first case and different in the second case?

19. Such current monetary items as cash, receivables, and current payables are turning over so fast in many businesses that inflation does not affect them; hence, they should not be included in the computation of the general price-level gain or loss. Do you agree with this statement?

20. Some accountants do not believe that the effect of inflation or deflation on long-term liabilities should be included in the general price-level gain or loss reported in general price-level income statements. What must these accountants be arguing?

PROBLEMS

Problem 26-1. Equipment was purchased for $120,000 on January 1, Year 1 when the general price-level index was 100, and was sold on December 31, Year 3 at a price of $85,000. The equipment originally was expected to last six years with no estimated salvage and was depreciated on a straight-line basis. The general price-level index at the end of Year 1 was 125, at Year 2 was 150, and at Year 3 was 175.

Based on the above information, select the answer that you think will best complete each of the following four multiple choice statements and indicate the corresponding letter on a separate sheet of paper (e.g., 1-a, 2-c, etc.) along with summarized computations.

(1) The general price-level financial statements prepared at the end of Year 1 would include: (a) equipment of $150,000, accumulated depreciation of $25,000, and a gain of $30,000; (b) equipment of $150,000, accumulated depreciation of $25,000, and no gain or loss; (c) equipment of $150,000, accumulated depreciation of $20,000, and a gain of $30,000; (d) equipment of $120,000, accumulated depreciation of $20,000, and a gain of $30,000; (e) none of the above.

(2) In general price-level comparative financial statements prepared at the end of Year 2, the Year 1 financial statements should show equipment (net of accumulated depreciation) at: (a) $150,000, (b) $125,000, (c) $100,000, (d) $80,000, (e) none of the above.

(3) The general price-level financial statements prepared at the end of Year 2 should include depreciation expense of: (a) $35,000, (b) $30,000, (c) $25,000, (d) $20,000, (e) none of the above.

(4) The general price-level income statement prepared at the end of Year 3 should include: (a) a loss of $5,000, (b) a gain of $25,000, (c) no gain or loss, (d) a loss of $20,000, (e) none of the above.

Problem 26-2. Based on the seven multiple choice statements given below, select the answer that you think will best complete each statement and indicate the corresponding letter on a separate sheet of paper (e.g., 1-b, 2-a, etc.).

(1) An accountant who recommends the adjustment of financial statements for general price-level changes should *not* support his recommendation by stating that:

(a) purchasing power gains or losses should be recognized, (b) historical dollars are not comparable to present-day dollars, (c) the conversion of asset costs to a common-dollar basis is a useful extension of the original cost basis of asset valuation, (d) assets valuation should be based on selling prices, (e) none of the above.

(2) An unacceptable practice for presenting general price-level information is (a) the inclusion of general price-level gains and losses on monetary items in the general price-level statement of income, (b) the inclusion of extraordinary gains and losses in the general price-level statement of income, (c) the use of charts, ratios, and narrative information, (d) the use of specific-price indexes to restate inventories, plant, and equipment, (e) none of the above.

(3) When general price-level balance sheets are prepared, they should be presented in terms of (a) the general purchasing power of the dollar at the latest balance sheet date, (b) the general purchasing power of the dollar in the base period, (c) the average general purchasing power of the dollar for the latest fiscal period, (d) the general purchasing power of the dollar at the time the financial statements are issued, (e) none of the above.

(4) The restatement of historical-dollar financial statements to reflect general price-level changes results in presenting assets at (a) lower of cost or market, (b) current appraisal, (c) historical cost adjusted for general purchasing power changes, (d) current replacement cost, (e) none of the above.

(5) During a period of deflation an entity would have the greatest gain in general purchasing power by holding (a) cash, (b) plant and equipment, (c) accounts payable, (d) mortgages payable, (e) none of the above.

(6) In preparing general price-level financial statements a nonmonetary item would be (a) accounts payable, (b) long-term bonds payable, (c) accounts receivable, (d) allowance for uncollectibles, (e) none of the above.

(7) For purposes of adjusting financial statements for changes in the general level of prices, monetary items consist of (a) assets and liabilities whose amounts are fixed by contract or otherwise in terms of dollars regardless of general price-level changes, (b) assets and liabilities that are classified as current on the balance sheet, (c) cash items plus all receivables with a fixed maturity date, (d) cash, other assets expected to be converted into cash, and current liabilities, (e) none of the above.

Problem 26-3. Based on the seven multiple choice statements given below, select the answer that you think will best complete each statement and indicate the corresponding letter on a separate sheet of paper (e.g., 1-c, 2-a, etc.).

(1) When preparing general price-level financial statements, it would not be appropriate to use (a) cost or market, whichever is lower, in the valuation of inventories, (b) replacement cost in the valuation of plant assets, (c) the historical-cost basis in reporting income tax expense, (d) the actual amounts payable in reporting liabilities on the balance sheet, (e) none of the above.

(2) For comparison purposes general price-level financial statements of earlier periods should be restated to the general purchasing power dollars of (a) the beginning of the base period, (b) an average for the current period, (c) the beginning of the current period, (d) the end of the current period, (e) none of the above.

(3) Gains and losses on nonmonetary assets usually are reported in historical-dollar financial statements when the items are sold. Gains and losses on the sale of nonmonetary assets should be reported in general price-level financial statements

(a) in the same period, but the amount will probably differ, (b) in the same period and the same amount, (c) over the life of the nonmonetary asset, (d) partly over the life of the nonmonetary asset and the remainder when the asset is sold, (e) none of the above.

(4) If land was purchased in 19+1 for $100,000 when the general price-level index was 100 and sold at the end of 19+9 for $160,000 when the index was 170, the general price-level statement of income for 19+9 would show a (a) general price-level gain of $70,000 and a loss on sale of land of $10,000, (b) gain on sale of land of $60,000, (c) general price-level loss of $10,000, (d) loss on sale of land of $10,000, (e) none of the above.

(5) If the base year is 19+2 (when the general price-level index = 100) and land is purchased for $50,000 in 19+8 when the general price-level index is 108.5, the cost of the land restated to 19+2 general purchasing power (rounded to the nearest whole dollar) would be (a) $54,250, (b) $50,000, (c) $46,083, (d) $45,750, (e) none of the above.

(6) Assume the same facts as in the above problem. The cost of the land restated to December 31, 19+8 when the price index was 119.2 (rounded to the nearest whole dollar) would be (a) $59,600, (b) $54,931, (c) $46,083, (d) $45,512, (e) none of the above.

(7) If land was purchased at a cost of $20,000 in January, 19+4 when the general price-level index was 120 and sold in December, 19+8 when the index was 150, the selling price that would result in no gain or loss would be (a) $30,000, (b) $24,000, (c) $20,000, (d) $16,000, (e) none of the above.

Problem 26-4. On January 1, 19+1, Huffman Company purchased equipment for $50,000. The equipment had an estimated five-year life and no estimated salvage. General price-level changes are to be reflected in the supplementary financial statements. The general price index for each statement year during the equipment life was as follows:

January 1, 19+1	100	December 31, 19+3	125
December 31, 19+1	112	December 31, 19+4	120
December 31, 19+2	118	December 31, 19+5	132

Required:

Prepare a schedule for *each* year of the entire five-year life of the equipment adjusted for general price-level changes (i.e., show cost and accumulated depreciation that would appear in comparative balance sheets adjusted for general price-level changes).

Problem 26-5. The comparative income statement for Norse Village Laundry for 19+5 and 19+6 are as follows:

NORSE VILLAGE LAUNDRY
Comparative Income Statement
For the Year Ended December 31, 19+6 and 19+5

	19+6	19+5
Revenue from machines	$134,000	$126,000
Expenses:		
Depreciation—building	$ 6,400	$ 6,400
Depreciation—machines	3,240	3,240
All other expenses	103,830	98,360
Total expense	$113,470	$108,000
Net income	$ 20,530	$ 18,000

The building was acquired in 19+1. The machines are being depreciated at a rate of 10 percent per year. The asset account shows that $16,200 was invested in machines in 19+1 and another $16,200 was invested in 19+4. The general price-level indexes are as follows: (Assume that all changes in the price-level index took place at the beginning of each year.)

Year	General Price-Level
19+1	100
19+4	115
19+5	120
19+6	125

Required:

(a) Prepare a general price-level working statement of income for the years ended December 31, 19+5 and 19+6 in terms of 19+6 dollars.

(b) Prepare a comparative general price-level income statement for Norse Village Laundry in 19+6 dollars.

Problem 26-6. The income statement of Office Supply Company is presented below.

OFFICE SUPPLY COMPANY
Income Statement
For the Year Ended December 31, 19+4

Sales		$350,000
Less: Cost of goods sold		218,000
Gross margin		$132,000
Expenses:		
Depreciation—building	$ 34,000	
Depreciation—equipment	23,000	
All other expenses	48,000	105,000
Net income		$ 27,000

Selected accounts from the company's general ledger are set forth below in T-account form. The company uses the FIFO method.

Inventory

19+3 Inventory	28,750	19+4	218,000
19+4 Purchase	220,000		

Cost of Goods Sold

19+4	218,000		

Building

19+1	850,000		

Equipment

19+1	85,000		
19+3	30,000		

A general price index covering a recent number of years is set forth below. (Assume that all changes in the general price-level index took place at the beginning of each year.)

19+1	100	19+3	105
19+2	102	19+4	112

Required:

(a) Prepare a general price-level working income statement for the year ended December 31, 19+4.

(b) Prepare a general price-level income statement for the year ended December 31, 19+4.

Problem 26-7. You are asked to convert the financial statements of GPL Company into general-price-level statements. You ask for the balance sheet for 19+2 and the income statement for the year ended December 31, 19+3. You are provided with the following simplified statements.

GPL COMPANY
Balance Sheet
December 31, 19+2

Monetary assets	$ 50,000	Monetary liabilities	$ 20,000
Nonmonetary assets....	200,000	Common Stock.........	160,000
Less accumulated depreciation.........	(40,000)	Retained earnings	30,000
Total assets	$210,000	Total equities	$210,000

GPL COMPANY
Income Statement
For the Year Ended December 31, 19+3

Sales (cash)		$90,000
Operating expenses:		
Depreciation expense..............................	$20,000	
Miscellaneous expense (cash)....................	45,000	65,000
Net income		$25,000

You discover the company was started at the beginning of 19+1 when common stock ($160,000) was issued and nonmonetary assets ($200,000) acquired. The company depreciates its nonmonetary assets at the annual amount of $20,000. Revenue and expenses (other than depreciation) are on a cash basis and tend to occur fairly evenly throughout the year. The applicable GNP Deflators are as follows:

Year	Annual Average	Year-End Average
19+1	100	100
19+2...	108	110
19+3...	115	120

Required:

(a) Restate the 19+2 balance sheet into 19+3 dollars in order to derive the adjusted beginning retained earnings for 19+3.

(b) Determine the general-price-level gain or loss for the year ended December 31, 19+3.

(c) Prepare a general-price-level working statement of income and retained earnings for the year ended December 31, 19+3.

(d) Prepare a general-price-level working balance sheet for 19+3.

Problem 26-8. Data from the conventional, post-closing trial balances of Low Rise Apartment Company are presented below.

	December 31,	
Debits	19+6	19+5
Cash	17,000	9,000
Land	38,500	38,500
Apartment	252,000	252,000
	307,500	299,500
Credits		
Accumulated Depreciation	63,000	50,400
Accounts payable	3,000	1,500
Mortgage payable	150,000	160,000
Capital stock	75,000	75,000
Retained earnings	16,500	12,600
	307,500	299,500

A cash dividend of $5,000 was declared and paid during 19+6.

Additional Data

Year		Price Index
19–	Company organized and stock issued	100
19+1	Land purchased for cash	110
19+2	Apartment built and occupied; financed in part with a mortgage	120
19+5		140
19+6	Mortgage reduced as of December 31	147

Required:

(a) Restate the 19+5 balance sheet into 19+6 dollars in order to derive the adjusted beginning retained earnings for 19+5.

(b) Prepare a general price-level retained earnings statement for the year ended December 31, 19+6.

Problem 26-9. The financial statements for Fort's, Inc. appear below.

FORT'S, INC.
Balance Sheet
December 31, 19+5

Assets

Cash	$ 24,000
Accounts receivable	20,000
Inventories—fifo cost	28,000
Land	16,000
Building	40,000
Less accumulated depreciation	(4,000)
Equipment	40,000
Less accumulated depreciation	(15,000)
Total assets	$149,000

Equities

Current liabilities	$ 32,000
Bond payable—6 percent	40,000
Common stock	60,000
Retained earnings	17,000
Total equities	$149,000

FORT'S, INC.
Income Statement
For the Year Ended December 31, 19+5

Sales		$200,000
Less Cost of goods sold		140,000
Gross margin		$ 60,000
Expenses:		
Selling and general expenses	$32,000	
Interest	2,400	
Depreciation	4,800	
Income tax	5,200	44,400
Net income		$ 15,600
Dividends		6,000
Earnings retained in business		$ 9,600

OTHER DATA

(1) The land and building were acquired when the general price-level index was 70. The building is estimated to have a useful life of 50 years.

(2) One-half of the equipment was acquired when the general price-level index was 70, one-fourth when it was 90, and the final one fourth when it was 100. All of the equipment is assumed to have a 10-year life.

(3) The beginning inventory cost was $32,000 and was acquired when the general price-level index was 125. The ending inventory was acquired when the general price-level index was 160.

(4) Two-thirds of the accumulated depreciation relates to equipment acquired when the general-price-level-index was 70, one fifth to equipment acquired when the general-price-level index was 90 and two fifteenths to equipment acquired when the general-price-level-index was 100.

(5) All operating revenues and expenses, excluding depreciation, are assumed to have been incurred uniformly throughout the year.

(6) Dividends were declared on December 31 and payable the following January 15.

(7) The bonds and stock were issued at the same time the land and buildings were acquired. Bond interest is payable at midyear and year end. (Assume that the midyear average is the same as the average for the year.)

(8) The general-price-level index at the beginning of the year was 130, the average for the year was 150, and at the end of the year was 165.

(9) When the 19+4 balance sheet was adjusted to 19+5 dollars, the retained earnings was determined to be $19,503. The general-price-level gain on monetary items for 19+5 amounted to $14,607.

Required:

(a) Prepare a general-price-level working statement of income and retained earnings for the year ended December 31, 19+5.

(b) Prepare a general-price-level working balance sheet for 19+5.

Problem 26-10. To obtain a more realistic appraisal of his investment, Martin Arnett, your client, has asked you to adjust certain financial data of The Glo-Bright Company for general price-level changes. On January 1, 19+5 he invested $50,000 in The Glo-Bright Company in return for 10,000 shares of common stock. Immediately after his investment the trial balance appeared as follows:

	Dr.	Cr.
Cash and receivables	65,200	
Merchandise inventory	4,000	
Building	50,000	
Accumulated depreciation-building		8,000
Equipment	36,000	
Accumulated depreciation-equipment		7,200
Land	10,000	
Current liabilities		50,000
Common stock		100,000
	165,200	165,200

Balances in certain selected accounts as of December 31 of each of the next three years were as follows:

	19+7	19+6	19+5
Sales	$42,350	$39,000	$39,650
Inventory	5,347	5,600	4,500
Purchases	18,150	16,350	14,475
Operating expenses (excluding depreciation)	9,075	9,050	10,050

Assume that the 19+5 general price-level index is the base year and that all changes in the general price-level index took place at the beginning of each year. Further assume that the 19+6 general price-level index was 10 percent above the 19+5 general price-level index and that the 19+7 general price-level index was 10 percent above the 19+6 level.

The building was constructed in 19+1 at a cost of $50,000 with an estimated life of 25 years. The general price-level index at that time was 80 percent of the 19+5 general price-level index.

The equipment was purchased in 19+3 at a cost of $36,000 with an estimated life of ten years. The general price-level index at that time was 90 percent of the 19+5 general price-level index.

The LIFO inventory method is used. The original inventory was acquired in the same year the building was constructed and was maintained at a constant $4,000 until 19+5. In 19+5 a gradual buildup of the inventory was begun in anticipation of an increase in the volume of business.

Arnett considers the return on his investment as the dividend he actually receives. In 19+7 Glo-Bright paid cash dividends in the amount of $8,000.

There were 2,000 shares of common stock outstanding during the year.

Required:

(a) Compute the 19+7 earnings per share of common stock in terms of 19+5 dollars.

(b) Compute the percentage return on investment for 19+5 and 19+7 in terms of 19+5 dollars.

Problem 26-11. Skadden, Inc., a retailer, was organized during 19+1. Skadden's management has decided to supplement its December 31, 19+4 historical-dollar financial statements with general price-level financial statements. The following general ledger trial balance (historical dollar) and additional information have been furnished:

SKADDEN, INC.
Trial Balance
December 31, 19+4

	Debit	Credit
Cash and receivables (net)	540,000	
Marketable securities (common stock)	400,000	
Inventory	440,000	
Equipment	650,000	
Equipment—accumulated depreciation		164,000
Accounts payable		300,000
6% First mortgage bonds, due 19+9		500,000
Common stock, $10 par		1,000,000
Retained earnings, December 31, 19+3	46,000	
Sales		1,900,000
Cost of sales	1,508,000	
Depreciation	65,000	
Other operating expenses and interest	215,000	
	3,864,000	3,864,000

(1) Monetary assets (cash and receivables) exceeded monetary liabilities (accounts payable and bonds payable) by $445,000 at December 31, 19+3.

(2) Purchases ($1,840,000 in 19+4) and sales are made uniformly throughout the year.

(3) Depreciation is computed on a straight-line basis, with a full year's depreciation being taken in the year of acquisition and none in the year of retirement. The depreciation rate is 10 percent and no estimated salvage is anticipated. Acquisitions and retirements have been made fairly evenly over each year and the retirements in 19+4 consisted of assets purchased during 19+2 that were scrapped. An analysis of the equipment account reveals the following:

Year	Beginning Balance	Additions	Retirements	Ending Balance
19+2	—	$550,000	—	$550,000
19+3	$550,000	10,000	—	560,000
19+4	560,000	150,000	$60,000	650,000

(4) The bonds were issued in 19+2 and the marketable securities were purchased fairly evenly over 19+4. Other operating expenses and interest are assumed to be incurred evenly throughout the year.

(5) Assume that Gross National Product Implicit Price Deflators were as follows:

Annual Averages		Index	Conversion Factors (19+4 4th Qtr. = 1.000)
19+1		113.9	1.128
19+2		116.8	1.100
19+3		121.8	1.055
19+4		126.7	1.014
Quarterly Averages			
19+3	4th	123.5	1.040
19+4	1st	124.9	1.029
	2nd	126.1	1.019
	3rd	127.3	1.009
	4th	128.5	1.000

Required:

(a) Prepare a schedule to convert the Equipment account balance at December 31, 19+4 from historical dollars to general price-level adjusted dollars.

(b) Prepare a schedule to analyze in historical dollars the Equipment—accumulated depreciation account for the year 19+4.

(c) Prepare a schedule to analyze in general price-level dollars the Equipment—accumulated depreciation account for the year 19+4.

(d) Prepare a schedule to compute Skadden, Inc.'s general price-level gain or loss on its net holdings of monetary assets for 19+4 (ignore income tax implications). The schedule should give consideration to appropriate items on or related to the balance sheet and the income statement.

Problem 26-12. The Melgar Company purchased a tract of land as an investment in 19+4 for $100,000; late in that year the Company decided to construct a shopping center on the site. Construction began in 19+5 and was completed in 19+7; one third of the construction was completed each year. Melgar originally estimated the costs of the project would be $1,200,000 for materials, $750,000 for labor, $150,000 for variable overhead, and $600,000 for depreciation.

Actual costs (excluding depreciation) incurred for construction were:

	19+7	19+6	19+5
Materials	$462,000	$434,560	$418,950
Labor	282,000	274,400	236,250
Variable overhead	61,200	54,208	47,250

Shortly after construction began, Melgar sold the shopping center for $3,000,000 with payment to be made in full on completion in December 19+7. Of the sales price, $150,000 was allocated for the land.

The transaction was completed as scheduled and now a controversy has developed between the two major stockholders of the Company. One feels the Company should have invested in land because a high rate of return was earned on the land. The other feels the original decision was sound and that changes in the general price level which were not anticipated affected the original cost estimates.

You were engaged to furnish guidance to these stockholders in resolving their controversy. As an aid, you obtained the following information:

Using 19+4 as the base year, general-price-level indices for relevant years are: 19+1 = 90, 19+2 = 93, 19+3 = 96, 19+4 = 100, 19+5 = 105, 19+6 = 112, and 19+7 = 120. (Assume that all changes in the general-price-level index take place at the beginning of each year.)

The Company allocated $200,000 per year for depreciation of tangible, long-lived assets allocated to this construction project; of that amount $25,000 was for a building purchased in 19+1 and $175,000 was for equipment purchased in 19+3.

Required:

(a) Prepare a schedule to restate in base year (19+4) costs the actual costs, including depreciation, incurred each year. Disregard income taxes.

(b) Prepare a schedule comparing the originally estimated costs of the project with the total actual costs for each element of cost (materials, labor, variable overhead, and depreciation) adjusted to the 19+4 price-level.

(c) Prepare a schedule to restate the amount received on the sale in terms of base year (19+4) purchasing power. The gain or loss should be determined separately for the land and the building in terms of base-year purchasing power and should exclude depreciation.

Problem 26-13. The following data were taken from the conventional trial balances of Downtown Building Corporation. The corporation closes its books as of December 31.

	19+6	19+5
Cash	56,500	18,000
Rent receivable	3,000	2,400
Supplies on hand	900	1,200
Land	59,500	49,500
Building	550,000	550,000
Depreciation expense	22,000	22,000
Taxes expense	30,000	28,000
Repairs and maintenance	15,200	15,000
Supplies used	7,500	7,410
Salaries	18,900	18,000
	763,500	711,510
Accumulated depreciation	88,000	66,000
Accrued taxes	8,400	8,000
Mortgage payable	300,000	300,000
Capital stock	200,000	200,000
Retained earnings	47,100	17,510
Rent revenue	120,000	120,000
	763,500	711,510

The corporation was organized and the capital stock was issued when the general-price-level was indicated by an index number of 100. The land was acquired for cash; the first parcel was purchased when the general-price-level index was 105. The last parcel was purchased 12/20/+6. The building was completed and space rented when the general-price-level index was 110. The mortgage financing was secured when the index was at 107. The supplies on hand at the end of 19+4 cost $590. Assume all revenue and expense flows took place at the average-general-price-level index for the year.

The general-price-level index for recent years is set forth below:

19+4	118
19+5	120
19+6	126
19+6 average	123

Required:

(a) Prepare a 12/31/+5 working balance sheet restated in 12/31/+6 dollars.

(b) Prepare a statement of general price-level gain or loss for 19+6

(c) Prepare a general-price-level working statement of income and retained earnings for 19+6.

(d) Prepare a general-price-level working balance sheet as of December 31, 19+6.

Problem 26-14. The financial statements for Cusenbary Manufacturing Company are presented below:

CUSENBARY MANUFACTURING COMPANY

Balance Sheets

December 31, 19+6 and 19+5

Assets	19+6	19+5
Cash	$ 15,000	$ 30,000
Inventory	60,000	30,000
Land	72,000	72,000
Equipment	150,000	150,000
Less accumulated depreciation	(60,000)	(50,000)
Total assets	$237,000	$232,000
Equities		
Accounts payable	$ 12,000	$ 12,000
Bonds payable	60,000	60,000
Capital stock	150,000	150,000
Retained earnings	15,000	10,000
Total equities	$237,000	$232,000

CUSENBARY MANUFACTURING COMPANY

Income Statement

For the Year Ended December 31, 19+6

Sales		$300,000
Cost of goods sold:		
Inventory, December 31, 19+5	$ 30,000	
Purchases	240,000	
	$270,000	
Inventory, December 31, 19+6	60,000	210,000
Gross margin		$ 90,000
Depreciation	$ 10,000	
Other expenses and taxes	69,000	79,000
Net income		$ 11,000
Dividends		6,000
Increase in retained earnings		$ 5,000
Retained earnings, December 31, 19+5		10,000
Retained earnings, December 31, 19+6		$ 15,000

(1) At the time the land and equipment were acquired and the capital stock was issued, the general-price-level-index stood at 75.
(2) The general-price-level index stood at 125 on December 31, 19+5 and at 150 on December 31, 19+6.
(3) The inventories were accounted for on a FIFO basis and were acquired when the general price index for beginning inventory was 90 and the ending inventory at 144. Purchases were made evenly throughout the year.
(4) It is assumed that the dividends were declared and paid uniformly throughout the year. The average-general-price-level index for 19+6 was 137.5.

Required:

(a) Prepare a working balance sheet for Cusenbary Manufacturing Company for the year 19+5 stated in terms of December 31, 19+6 dollars. (This step is necessary to derive the beginning retained earnings for 19+6.)
(b) Prepare a general-price-level gain or loss statement for the year 19+6 stated in terms of December 31, 19+6 dollars.
(c) Prepare a working statement of income and retained earnings for 19+6.
(d) Prepare a working balance sheet as of 12/31/+6.

Problem 26-15. The comparative balance sheets of Research Company for the years 19+5 and 19+6 are presented below.

RESEARCH COMPANY
Comparative Balance Sheets
December 31, 19+6 and 19+5

	19+6	19+5
Cash	$ 42,800	$ 25,000
Accounts receivable	150,000	50,000
Merchandise	110,000	125,000
Land	40,000	40,000
Building (cost)	150,000	150,000
Accumulated depreciation	(45,000)	(37,500)
Total assets	$447,800	$352,500
Accounts payable	$ 67,500	$ 57,500
Mortgage payable	100,000	120,000
Common stock	137,500	137,500
Retained earnings	142,800	37,500
Total equities	$447,800	$352,500

The general-price-level index stood at 75 when the stockholders purchased their stock to start the company. When the land and buildings were acquired and the mortgage assumed, the general-price-level index was 80. The average general-price-level index for year 19+5 was 100 and for year 19+6 was 125. At December 31, 19+5 the general-price-level index was 110 and at December 31, 19+6 it was 143.

During the year 19+6 the following transactions took place in the Research Company.

(1) Sales, all on credit, $1,000,000.
(2) Wages paid, $125,000.
(3) Merchandise purchased on account, $690,000.
(4) Other expenses incurred for cash, $50,000.

(5) Payments on account, \$680,000.
(6) Interest paid on December 31, \$7,200.
(7) Principal paid on mortgage, December 31, \$20,000.
(8) Merchandise on hand at December 31, all from current purchases, \$110,000.
(9) The annual straight-line depreciation on the building is \$7,500.

During the year 19+5 the ending inventory was all from current purchases.

Required:

(a) Prepare a working balance sheet for 19+5 that restates the historical dollars into general purchasing power dollars as of 19+6. (This needs to be done to derive 19+5 retained earnings in 19+6 purchasing power; i.e., beginning retained earnings for 19+6.)
(b) Prepare a schedule showing the general-price-level gain or loss for 19+6.
(c) Prepare a general-price-level statement of income and retained earnings for 19+6.
(d) Prepare a general-price-level balance sheet as of 12/31/+6.

CHAPTER 27

QUESTIONS

1. Define an accounting error. List some examples of accounting errors.
2. Describe the two kinds of errors that affect the income statement for a period and the balance sheet at the end of the period.
3. Give an example of an error in computing the net income of one year that will be offset by a counterbalancing error in the following year, thus correcting the retained earnings but leaving the net income incorrectly stated by years.
4. Describe the use of the account titled Correction of Prior Period Errors.
5. What will be the effect upon the income statement of the present and future periods if: (a) prepayments of expenses are ignored; and (b) income collected in advance is ignored?
6. List three different alternative procedures that may be followed in correcting errors made in prior periods. What is the major consideration in determining the alternative to be followed?
7. Describe the closing procedure followed when the correction of errors is reported as a prior period adjustment.
8. What is the difference between the single-entry system and double-entry system of record keeping?
9. What are the minimum essentials of the single-entry record keeping system?
10. Describe the single-entry method of determining the net income for a period.
11. Under what circumstances might financial statements of prior years be revised to correct for accounting errors made in the prior years?

PROBLEMS

Problem 27-1. In each of the following cases, determine the net income or loss for the year 19+4.

(1)	Proprietorship equity—beginning of period	$23,000
	Additional investments during the period	1,000
	Withdrawals during the period	5,000
	Proprietorship equity—end of period	25,000
(2)	Proprietorship equity—beginning of period	$30,000
	Additional investments during the period	5,000
	Withdrawals during the period	3,000
	Proprietorship equity—end of period	31,000
(3)	Proprietorship equity—beginning of period	$20,000
	Additional investments during the period	1,000
	Withdrawals during the period	6,000
	Proprietorship equity—end of period	18,000
(4)	Proprietorship equity—beginning of period	$14,000
	Additional investments during the period	5,000
	Withdrawals during the period	2,000
	Proprietorship equity—end of period	11,000

Problem 27-2. The owner of Community Store has compiled the following comparative data.

	December 31,	
Assets	19+9	19+8
Cash in bank	$ 4,000	$ 6,000
Accounts receivable	30,000	20,000
Allowance for uncollectibles	1,500*	1,000*
Inventory	60,000	45,000
Investment securities	10,000	4,000
Store and delivery equipment	25,000	20,000
Accumulated depreciation	6,000*	5,000*
	$121,500	$89,000
Liabilities		
Accounts payable	$ 32,500	$15,000
Mortgage payable		10,000

*Deduction.

Upon inquiry you learn the following:

(1) The mortgage was on the owner's residence. It was paid by a store check, which included interest for 19+9 in the amount of $100.

(2) The investment securities were paid for by the owner's wife with her funds, and the securities are held by the owner and his wife jointly.

(3) Cash receipts from customers during 19+9 amounted to $185,000. Cash disbursements included drawings of $80 per week.

(4) The increase in equipment was accounted for by the acquisition of an additional delivery truck costing $5,000. Only $3,000 of the store's cash was spent for this

purpose, since a $2,000 trade-in allowance was granted on a convertible previously used by the owner's son while in college.

Compute the net income or loss for 19+9.

Problem 27-3. An audit of the records of Mixon Company disclosed the following:

(1) Inventory overstated (understated):	
December 31, 19+7	$11,600
December 31, 19+8	(22,200)
(2) Payable wages ignored at year end:	
December 31, 19+7	$ 1,230
December 31, 19+8	2,330
December 31, 19+9	850
(3) Depreciation overstated (understated):	
Year ended December 31, 19+8	$ 3,500
Year ended December 31, 19+9	(8,900)
(4) Interest expense overstated (understated):	
December 31, 19+7	$ (700)
December 31, 19+8	1,400

Prepare a work sheet to determine the effect of the above errors on the income statements for the years 19+7, 19+8, and 19+9 and the December 31, 19+9 balance sheet.

Problem 27-4. A. B. Coker, a single proprietor, does not maintain an adequate set of accounting records for his business. However, an analysis of his records establishes that the following increases and decreases occurred during the twelve months ended December 31, 19+9.

Increases:	
Cash	$4,200
Accounts receivable	2,430
Inventory	3,000
Decreases:	
Notes receivable	1,600
Accounts payable	150
Notes payable	2,000

Mr. Coker asks you to compute the net income (or loss) of his business during 19+9. In connection with this request, he gives you the following additional information:

(1) No long-lived assets were purchased during 19+9. Those owned were acquired at the beginning of 19+2 at a cost of $18,000 and, as of December 31, 19+9, are believed to have remaining useful lives of four years.

(2) At the end of 19+8, he had not paid the property taxes on his business assets. This tax bill, amounting to $185, and the current year's tax bill, amounting to $190, were both paid in 19+9.

(3) During 19+9 a $2,000 note payable matured and was paid, with interest of $120.

(4) During 19+9 he cashed some of his personal savings bonds and used the $3,500 thus obtained to enlarge the store's inventory.

(5) He regularly withdrew $100 each week for personal living expenses.

Problem 27-5. From the following data taken from the books of Claxton Corporation, prepare a work sheet showing the corrected net income before income taxes for the years 19+7, 19+8, and 19+9.

	Year Ended December 31,		
	19+7	19+8	19+9
Net income before income taxes, per books	$18,720	$24,190	$21,400
Payment of liabilities existing but not recorded at close of preceding year:			
Heat and light......................................	830	720	680
Merchandise (goods on hand and included in inventory)	1,200	1,050	810
Unrecorded liabilities as of December 31, 19+9:			
Heat and light			600
Merchandise (goods on hand but not included in inventory)...			760
Uncollectible accounts charged to expense, arising from sales of preceding year, for which no provision for bad debts was made		2,000	
Purchase of delivery equipment good for four years charged to Delivery Expense on July 1, 19+8		4,000	

Problem 27-6. As the result of an examination of the accounts of Duke Corporation by an internal revenue agent, it is discovered that, from time to time, certain items of new equipment have been debited to the repairs and maintenance expense account.

Information related to this matter is presented below:

Account Balances, December 31

	Equipment	Accumulated Depreciation	New Equipment Charged to Expense	Net Income Reported
19+5......................	$102,560	$31,810	$12,000	$80,500
19+6......................	116,980	48,360	8,800	72,111
19+7......................	120,100	54,200	-0-	65,432
19+8......................	124,320	59,600	10,000	78,900
19+9......................	126,400	62,240	6,440	75,115

It is the company's practice, which is approved by the internal revenue agent, to compute depreciation by applying the rate of 25 percent to the balance of the Equipment account at the end of each year.

The accounts have not been closed for the year 19+9.

Required:

(a) A schedule showing the necessary adjustments to net income, and the corrected net income for each of the above years.

(b) The adjusting entry necessary to record the corrections in the books as of December 31, 19+9, assuming that it is desired to disclose the corrections in the 19+9 statement of retained earnings. Ignore income tax considerations.

Problem 27-7. Assume that the following adjusted trial balance is that of Rowell Company on September 30, 19+9, the close of its fiscal year:

Adjusted Trial Balance
September 30, 19+9

Cash	4,618	
Accounts receivable	4,110	
Allowance for uncollectibles		420
Merchandise inventory—September 30, 19+8	12,130	
Unexpired insurance	320	
Prepaid rent	100	
Furniture and equipment	3,600	
Accumulated depreciation—Furniture and equipment		900
Accounts payable		3,030
Notes payable		1,000
Accrued interest payable		30
Accrued property taxes payable		80
Capital stock		10,000
Retained earnings (September 30, 19+8)		4,157
Dividends	1,000	
Sales		61,300
Purchases	42,469	
Wages	9,100	
Rent expense	1,200	
Repairs and maintenance	818	
Insurance expense	112	
Depreciation expense	290	
Taxes—Property	318	
Bad debts	150	
Utilities	508	
Interest expense	74	
	80,917	80,917

Inventory of merchandise, September 30, 19+9—$13,100.

An audit of the accounts of Rowell Company on September 30, 19+9, and for the year ended that date disclosed that adjustments for accruals and prepayments as of September 30, 19+9, had been properly computed and recorded and that the September 30, 19+9 inventory of merchandise was correct. However, the following errors had been made in preceding fiscal periods:

(1) The merchandise inventory on September 30, 19+8, was overstated $840 owing to an error in adding the inventory count sheets.

(2) Unexpired insurance and prepaid rent were not recorded at the close of preceding fiscal periods. An examination of insurance policies disclosed that the amount of unexpired insurance on September 30, 19+8, was $335, and that rent prepaid on that date amounted to $100.

(3) On June 30, 19+8, an item of equipment costing $400 had been debited to Repairs and Maintenance. This item was of a type which would be depreciated at a 10 percent rate.

(4) A sales invoice for $118 covering merchandise sold and shipped on September 20, 19+8, was not recorded until October 8, 19+8.

Required:

(a) Necessary adjusting journal entries as of September 30, 19+9, assuming that the results of any errors relating to prior periods will be absorbed in the current income statement without disclosure.
(b) The income statement for the year ended September 30, 19+9, prepared on the basis described in (a).
(c) A computation showing the net income that would be reported for the year ended September 30, 19+9, if the prior period errors were reported in the statement of retained earnings.

Problem 27-8. Ventura Corporation, by analyzing its incomplete records, has been able to supply the following information.

List of Increases—June 30, 19+9 Compared to June 30, 19+8

Accounts receivable	$ 240
Inventory	1,800
Accounts payable	80
Salesmen's commissions payable	160
Equipment	500

List of Decreases—June 30, 19+9 Compared to June 30, 19+8

Cash	$ 1,336
Notes receivable—Trade	700
Unexpired insurance	60

Summary of Cash Transactions—Year Ended June 30, 19+9

Receipts:	
Cash sales	$18,000
Collections from customers	52,000
Collections on notes receivable	1,400
Interest	90
Purchase returns	85
Disbursements:	
Cash purchases	915
Sales returns	202
Payments on accounts payable	31,104
Insurance premium	300
Salesmen's commissions	9,106
New equipment	3,000
Rent	2,400
Office expense	5,711
Other operating expenses	20,173

The bookkeeper reported that the principal amount of a $300 note proved to be uncollectible during the year just ended. No long-lived assets were sold or retired from use. Prepare the income statement for the year ended June 30, 19+9. Ignore income taxes.

Problem 27-9. The comparative balance sheets appearing below were prepared from the single-entry records and other data of Carter Company.

CARTER COMPANY
Comparative Balance Sheets
December 31, 19+8 and December 31, 19+9

Assets	December 31, 19+9		December 31, 19+8	
Current assets:				
Cash	$13,740		$12,825	
Accounts receivable	11,700		14,100	
Merchandise	15,000	$40,440	12,720	$39,645
Long-lived assets:				
Furniture and fixtures—less depreciation		24,360		22,980
		$64,800		$62,625
Equities				
Current liabilities:				
Accounts payable	$ 8,100		$ 3,300	
Notes payable:				
Bank	3,000		750	
Trade	—		4,500	
Total liabilities		$11,100		$ 8,550
Stockholders' equity:				
Capital stock	$49,500		$49,500	
Retained earnings	4,200	53,700	4,575	54,075
		$64,800		$62,625

A summary of cash receipts and payments for the year 19+9 is as follows:

Receipts:	
Cash sales	$ 5,850
From customers on account	62,700
From notes payable—bank	3,750
	$72,300
Payments:	
For furniture and fixtures	$ 3,000
To merchandise creditors on account	44,865
Retirement of notes payable (including interest of $350)	6,350
For operating expenses	14,200
For dividends	2,970
	$71,385

Bad debts were written off during 19+9 in the amount of $735.
There were no disposals or retirements of long-lived assets during 19+9.

Required:

(a) Compute the net income or loss for the year 19+9 by the single-entry method.
(b) Prepare an income statement using double-entry form.

Problem 27-10. The trial balance presented below was taken from the ledger of Lincoln Sales Company after regular adjusting journal entries had been recorded on June 30, 19+9.

LINCOLN SALES COMPANY
Adjusted Trial Balance
June 30, 19+9

Cash	16,615	
Inventory—end of year	15,200	
Office supplies on hand	300	
Automotive equipment	27,300	
Accumulated depreciation		11,305
Accounts payable		10,390
Wages payable		350
Common stock		30,000
Retained earnings		5,450
Dividends	3,000	
Sales		123,000
Cost of goods sold	88,935	
Wages	14,280	
Office supplies expense	1,475	
Depreciation	5,100	
Other expense	8,290	
	180,495	180,495

An examination of the accounts indicates that certain errors were made during prior periods and that these errors were never corrected. These errors are described below:

(1) The June 30, 19+8 inventory was understated by $1,200.

(2) A small car trailer acquired on September 30, 19+7, at a cost of $800, was charged to Other Expense. Such trailers have a use-life expectancy of five years. Since acquisition, the company has charged the depreciation account $280 for depreciation on the trailer.

(3) On July 10, 19+8, a delivery truck was wrecked in an accident. The truck was a total loss and its cost was removed from the accounts by the following entry:

Accumulated depreciation	3,600	
Automotive equipment		3,600
Cost of truck purchased on July 1, 19+3 removed from accounts.		

In each of the five years preceding the accident the company had recorded $900 depreciation on the truck.

(4) During the three-year period ending June 30, 19+8, the company had understated payable wages by an amount aggregating $1,000. The details are as follows:

	Amount	
	Booked	Ignored
Accrued wages, June 30, 19+6	$100	$ 350
Accrued wages, June 30, 19+7	150	500
Accrued wages, June 30, 19+8	50	150
		$1,000

Required:

(a) Working papers for the year ended June 30, 19+9, assuming that errors affecting prior years' earnings are to be disclosed in the statement of retained earnings.

(b) Income statement for the year ended June 30, 19+9 following the procedure in part (a).

Problem 27-11. The present bookkeeper of Nova Company started to work for the company at the beginning of 19+7. He has never recorded an adjusting entry. Except for this failing, his work has been satisfactory. By making use of the current trial balance and the additional information, prepare working papers for the year ended December 31, 19+9, assuming that any errors affecting prior years' earnings are to be disclosed in the statement of retained earnings. Also prepare the 19+9 statement of retained earnings.

NOVA COMPANY

Trial Balance—December 31, 19+9

Cash	7,650	
Bond investments, at par, 8%	10,000	
Inventory	13,170	
Equipment	36,000	
Accumulated depreciation		11,700
Accounts payable		6,120
Common stock		40,000
Retained earnings		5,560
Dividends	2,000	
Sales		94,300
Cost of goods sold	70,830	
Wages	16,140	
Insurance expense	180	
Other expense	2,110	
Interest revenue		400
	158,080	158,080

There has been no change in the bond investments since 19+5. The bonds pay interest semiannually on April 1 and October 1.

A record of the insurance premiums paid during the last six years is presented below.

Insurance Policies

Date	Coverage	Premium	Term
July 1, 19+4	Inventory	$156	2 years
July 1, 19+6	Inventory	156	2 years
October 1, 19+6	Equipment	180	3 years
July 1, 19+8	Inventory	156	2 years
October 1, 19+9	Equipment	180	3 years

The equipment was purchased on October 1, 19+3; its use life is ten years, and no scrap value is expected.

Wages payable at year end:

19+5	$300
19+6	-0-
19+7	200
19+8	275
19+9	225

Problem 27-12. Art Little, a merchant, kept only limited records. Purchases of merchandise were paid for by check, but most other disbursements were paid out of cash receipts. Any cash on hand at the end of the week was deposited in the bank. No record was kept of cash in bank nor was a record kept of sales. No record of accounts receivable was maintained other than by keeping a copy of the charge ticket, and this copy was given to the customer when he paid his account.

Little had started in business on January 1, 19+3, with $20,000 cash and a building which had cost $15,000, of which one-third was applicable to the building site. The building depreciated 4 percent a year. An analysis of the bank statements showed total deposits, including the original cash investment, of $120,500. The balance in the bank per bank statement on December 31, 19+3, was $5,300, but there were checks amounting to $2,150 dated in December but not paid by the bank until January. During the year, Little wrote checks amounting to $1,000 for personal expenses. All other checks were for merchandise. Cash on hand December 31 was $334.

An inventory of merchandise taken on December 31, 19+3, showed $21,710 of merchandise on a cost basis. Accounts receivable totaled $1,270, but $123 of that amount is probably not collectible. Customers may order special merchandise not carried in stock. A deposit equal to 50 percent of the selling price is required of the customer. Little has collected $150 of such deposits for merchandise still on order; the funds are included in the cash on hand. Unpaid suppliers' invoices for merchandise amounted to $3,780. Little has taken, from the collections, cash for personal expenses of $4,800. Expenses paid in cash were as follows:

Utilities	$554
Advertising	50
Sales help (part-time)	590
Office expense	100
Insurance (expires 12/31/+3)	234
Real estate taxes	350

Store fixtures with a list price of $7,200 were purchased on January 16 and Little signed a 6 percent, one-year note for the list price. The fixtures have an estimated useful life of ten years.

You are to prepare an income statement for 19+3, supported by all necessary computations. Any fractional-period depreciation should be computed to the nearest half-month.

Problem 27-13. The following financial statements have been prepared by Overby Company as a part of an application for a bank loan.

OVERBY COMPANY
Income Statement
For the Year Ended October 31, 19+9

Net sales		$81,315
Cost of goods sold:		
Inventory—beginning of year	$12,014	
Purchases	62,012	
Total	$74,026	
Inventory—end of year	13,100	
Cost of goods sold		60,926
Gross margin		$20,389
Expenses:		
Wages and salaries	$ 8,838	
Insurance	312	
Taxes	605	
Repairs	753	
Rent of building	1,200	
Depreciation	830	
Other expenses	610	
Total expenses		13,148
Net income		$ 7,241

OVERBY COMPANY
Statement of Retained Earnings
For the Year Ended October 31, 19+9

Balance at beginning of year	$ 9,233
Net income for the year	7,241
Total	$16,474
Dividends	2,000
Balance at end of year	$14,474

OVERBY COMPANY
Balance Sheet
October 31, 19+9

Assets

Cash		$ 4,230
Accounts receivable		11,930
Merchandise inventory		13,100
Unexpired insurance		710
Furniture and equipment	$ 8,040	
Accumulated depreciation	2,910	5,130
		$35,100

Equities

Accounts payable	$10,190
Taxes payable	436
Capital stock	10,000
Retained earnings	14,474
	$35,100

The bank has requested that the company have its financial statements audited, and you have been retained by Overby Company for this purpose. In the course of your audit you discover the following:

(1) The beginning inventory was understated $2,000.

(2) Unexpired insurance was overstated $200 on October 31, 19+8, and by the same amount on October 31, 19+9.

(3) Wages and salaries payable were overstated by $100 on October 31, 19+8. The wages and salaries payable account was closed by the following entry for the first payroll in the current fiscal year:

Wages and salaries	600	
Wages and salaries payable	150	
Cash		750

There were no wages or salaries payable as of October 31, 19+9.

(4) Repair supplies of $115 were included with the October 31, 19+9 merchandise inventory. No supplies were included in the merchandise inventory on October 31, 19+8.

Required:

(a) Working papers to revise the current financial statements, assuming that any errors affecting prior years' earnings are to be disclosed in the statement of retained earnings.

(b) Closing entries, as of October 31, 19+9.

Appendix
Tables of Amounts and Present Values

AMOUNT OF $1

$(1 + i)^n$

n \ i	½ %	1 %	1¼ %	1½ %	2 %	2½ %
1	1.0050 0000	1.0100 0000	1.0125 0000	1.0150 0000	1.0200 0000	1.0250 0000
2	1.0100 2500	1.0201 0000	1.0251 5625	1.0302 2500	1.0404 0000	1.0506 2500
3	1.0150 7513	1.0303 0100	1.0379 7070	1.0456 7838	1.0612 0800	1.0768 9063
4	1.0201 5050	1.0406 0401	1.0509 4534	1.0613 6355	1.0824 3216	1.1038 1289
5	1.0252 5125	1.0510 1005	1.0640 8215	1.0772 8400	1.1040 8080	1.1314 0821
6	1.0303 7751	1.0615 2015	1.0773 8318	1.0934 4326	1.1261 6242	1.1596 9342
7	1.0355 2940	1.0721 3535	1.0908 5047	1.1098 4491	1.1486 8567	1.1886 8575
8	1.0407 0704	1.0828 5671	1.1044 8610	1.1264 9259	1.1716 5938	1.2184 0290
9	1.0459 1058	1.0936 8527	1.1182 9218	1.1433 8998	1.1950 9257	1.2488 6297
10	1.0511 4013	1.1046 2213	1.1322 7083	1.1605 4083	1.2189 9442	1.2800 8454
11	1.0563 9583	1.1156 6835	1.1464 2422	1.1779 4894	1.2433 7431	1.3120 8666
12	1.0616 7781	1.1268 2503	1.1607 5452	1.1956 1817	1.2682 4179	1.3448 8882
13	1.0669 8620	1.1380 9328	1.1752 6395	1.2135 5244	1.2936 0663	1.3785 1104
14	1.0723 2113	1.1494 7421	1.1899 5475	1.2317 5573	1.3194 7876	1.4129 7382
15	1.0776 8274	1.1609 6896	1.2048 2918	1.2502 3207	1.3458 6834	1.4482 9817
16	1.0830 7115	1.1725 7864	1.2198 8955	1.2689 8555	1.3727 8571	1.4845 0562
17	1.0884 8651	1.1843 0443	1.2351 3817	1.2880 2033	1.4002 4142	1,5216 1826
18	1.0939 2894	1.1961 4748	1.2505 7739	1.3073 4064	1.4282 4625	1.5596 5872
19	1.0993 9858	1.2081 0895	1.2662 0961	1.3269 5075	1.4568 1117	1.5986 5019
20	1.1048 9558	1.2201 9004	1.2820 3723	1.3468 5501	1.4859 4740	1.6386 1644
21	1.1104 2006	1.2323 9194	1.2980 6270	1.3670 5783	1.5156 6634	1.6795 8185
22	1.1159 7216	1.2447 1586	1.3142 8848	1.3875 6370	1.5459 7967	1.7215 7140
23	1.1215 5202	1.2571 6302	1.3307 1709	1.4083 7715	1.5768 9926	1.7646 1068
24	1.1271 5978	1.2697 3465	1.3473 5105	1.4295 0281	1.6084 3725	1.8087 2595
25	1.1327 9558	1.2824 3200	1.3641 9294	1.4509 4535	1.6406 0599	1.8539 4410
26	1.1384 5955	1.2952 5631	1.3812 4535	1.4727 0953	1.6734 1811	1.9002 9270
27	1.1441 5185	1.3082 0888	1.3985 1092	1.4948 0018	1.7068 8648	1.9478 0002
28	1.1498 7261	1.3212 9097	1.4159 9230	1.5172 2218	1.7410 2421	1.9964 9502
29	1.1556 2197	1.3345 0388	1.4336 9221	1.5399 8051	1.7758 4469	2.0464 0739
30	1.1614 0008	1.3478 4892	1.4516 1336	1.5630 8022	1.8113 6158	2.0975 6758
31	1.1672 0708	1.3613 2740	1.4697 5853	1.5865 2642	1.8475 8882	2.1500 0677
32	1.1730 4312	1.3749 4068	1.4881 3051	1.6103 2432	1.8845 4059	2.2037 5694
33	1.1789 0833	1.3886 9009	1.5067 3214	1.6344 7918	1.9222 3140	2.2588 5086
34	1.1848 0288	1.4025 7699	1.5255 6629	1.6589 9637	1.9606 7603	2.3153 2213
35	1.1907 2689	1.4166 0276	1.5446 3587	1.6838 8132	1.9998 8955	2.3732 0519
36	1.1966 8052	1.4307 6878	1.5639 4382	1.7091 3954	2.0398 8734	2.4325 3532
37	1.2026 6393	1.4450 7647	1.5834 9312	1.7347 7663	2.0806 8509	2.4933 4870
38	1.2086 7725	1.4595 2724	1.6032 8678	1.7607 9828	2.1222 9879	2.5556 8242
39	1.2147 2063	1.4741 2251	1.6233 2787	1.7872 1025	2.1647 4477	2.6195 7448
40	1.2207 9424	1.4888 6373	1.6436 1946	1.8140 1841	2.2080 3966	2.6850 6384
41	1.2268 9821	1.5037 5237	1.6641 6471	1.8412 2868	2.2522 0046	2.7521 9043
42	1.2330 3270	1.5187 8989	1.6849 6677	1.8688 4712	2.2972 4447	2.8209 9520
43	1.2391 9786	1.5339 7779	1.7060 2885	1.8968 7982	2.3431 8936	2.8915 2008
44	1.2453 9385	1.5493 1757	1.7273 5421	1.9253 3302	2.3900 5314	2.9638 0808
45	1.2516 2082	1.5648 1075	1.7489 4614	1.9542 1301	2.4378 5421	3.0379 0328
46	1.2578 7892	1.5804 5885	1.7708 0797	1.9835 2621	2.4866 1129	3.1138 5086
47	1.2641 6832	1.5962 6344	1.7929 4306	2.0132 7910	2.5363 4351	3.1916 9713
48	1.2704 8916	1.6122 2608	1.8153 5485	2.0434 7829	2.5870 7039	3.2714 8956
49	1.2768 4161	1.6283 4834	1.8380 4679	2.0741 3046	2.6388 1179	3.3532 7680
50	1.2832 2581	1.6446 3182	1.8610 2237	2.1052 4242	2.6915 8803	3.4371 0872

AMOUNT OF $1 (CONTINUED)
$(1 + i)^n$

n \ i	3%	3½%	4%	5%	6%	7%
1	1.0300 0000	1.0350 0000	1.0400 0000	1.0500 0000	1.0600 0000	1.0700 0000
2	1.0609 0000	1.0712 2500	1.0816 0000	1.1025 0000	1.1236 0000	1.1449 0000
3	1.0927 2700	1.1087 1788	1.1248 6400	1.1576 2500	1.1910 1600	1.2250 4300
4	1.1255 0881	1.1475 2300	1.1698 5856	1.2155 0625	1.2624 7696	1.3107 9601
5	1.1592 7407	1.1876 8631	1.2166 5290	1.2762 8156	1.3382 2558	1.4025 5173
6	1.1940 5230	1.2292 5533	1.2653 1902	1.3400 9564	1.4185 1911	1.5007 3035
7	1.2298 7387	1.2722 7926	1.3159 3178	1.4071 0042	1.5036 3026	1.6057 8148
8	1.2667 7008	1.3168 0904	1.3685 6905	1.4774 5544	1.5938 4807	1.7181 8618
9	1.3047 7318	1.3628 9735	1.4233 1181	1.5513 2822	1.6894 7896	1.8384 5921
10	1.3439 1638	1.4105 9876	1.4802 4428	1.6288 9463	1.7908 4770	1.9671 5136
11	1.3842 3387	1.4599 6972	1.5394 5406	1.7103 3936	1.8982 9856	2.1048 5195
12	1.4257 6089	1.5110 6866	1.6010 3222	1.7958 5633	2.0121 9647	2.2521 9159
13	1.4685 3371	1.5639 5606	1.6650 7351	1.8856 4914	2.1329 2826	2.4098 4500
14	1.5125 8972	1.6186 9452	1.7316 7645	1.9799 3160	2.2609 0396	2.5785 3415
15	1.5579 6742	1.6753 4883	1.8009 4351	2.0789 2818	2.3965 5819	2.7590 3154
16	1.6047 0644	1.7339 8604	1.8729 8125	2.1828 7459	2.5403 5168	2.9521 6375
17	1.6528 4763	1.7946 7555	1.9479 0050	2.2920 1832	2.6927 7279	3.1588 1521
18	1.7024 3306	1.8574 8920	2.0258 1652	2.4066 1923	2.8543 3915	3.3799 3228
19	1.7535 0605	1.9225 0132	2.1068 4918	2.5269 5020	3.0255 9950	3.6165 2754
20	1.8061 1123	1.9897 8886	2.1911 2314	2.6532 9771	3.2071 3547	3.8696 8446
21	1.8602 9457	2.0594 3147	2.2787 6807	2.7859 6259	3.3995 6360	4.1405 6237
22	1.9161 0341	2.1315 1158	2.3699 1879	2.9252 6072	3.6035 3742	4.4304 0174
23	1.9735 8651	2.2061 1448	2.4647 1554	3.0715 2376	3.8197 4966	4.7405 2986
24	2.0327 9411	2.2833 2849	2.5633 0416	3.2250 9994	4.0489 3464	5.0723 6695
25	2.0937 7793	2.3632 4498	2.6658 3633	3.3863 5494	4.2918 7072	5.4274 3264
26	2.1565 9127	2.4459 5856	2.7724 6978	3.5556 7269	4.5493 8296	5.8073 5292
27	2.2212 8901	2.5315 6711	2.8833 6858	3.7334 5632	4.8223 4594	6.2138 6763
28	2.2879 2768	2.6201 7196	2.9987 0332	3.9201 2914	5.1116 8670	6.6488 3836
29	2.3565 6551	2.7118 7798	3.1186 5145	4.1161 3560	5.4183 8790	7.1142 5705
30	2.4272 6247	2.8067 9370	3.2433 9751	4.3219 4238	5.7434 9117	7.6122 5504
31	2.5000 8035	2.9050 3148	3.3731 3341	4.5380 3949	6.0881 0064	8.1451 1290
32	2.5750 8276	3.0067 0759	3.5080 5875	4.7649 4147	6.4533 8668	8.7152 7080
33	2.6523 3524	3.1119 4235	3.6483 8110	5.0031 8854	6.8405 8988	9.3253 3975
34	2.7319 0530	3.2208 6033	3.7943 1634	5.2533 4797	7.2510 2528	9.9781 1354
35	2.8138 6245	3.3335 9045	3.9460 8899	5.5160 1537	7.6860 8679	10.6765 8148
36	2.8982 7833	3.4502 6611	4.1039 3255	5.7918 1614	8.1472 5200	11.4239 4219
37	2.9852 2668	3.5710 2543	4.2680 8986	6.0814 0694	8.6360 8712	12.2236 1814
38	3.0747 8348	3.6960 1132	4.4388 1345	6.3854 7729	9.1542 5235	13.0792 7141
39	3.1670 2698	3.8253 7171	4.6163 6599	6.7047 5115	9.7035 0749	13.9948 2041
40	3.2620 3779	3.9592 5972	4.8010 2063	7.0399 8871	10.2857 1794	14.9744 5784
41	3.3598 9893	4.0978 3381	4.9930 6145	7.3919 8815	10.9028 6101	16.0226 6989
42	3.4606 9589	4.2412 5799	5.1927 8391	7.7615 8756	11.5570 3267	17.1442 5678
43	3.5645 1677	4.3897 0202	5.4004 9527	8.1496 6693	12.2504 5463	18.3443 5475
44	3.6714 5227	4.5433 4160	5.6165 1508	8.5571 5028	12.9854 8191	19.6284 5959
45	3.7815 9584	4.7023 5855	5.8411 7568	8.9850 0779	13.7646 1083	21.0024 5176
46	3.8950 4372	4.8669 4110	6.0748 2271	9.4342 5818	14.5904 8748	22.4726 2338
47	4.0118 9503	5.0372 8404	6.3178 1562	9.9059 7109	15.4659 1673	24.0457 0702
48	4.1322 5188	5.2135 8898	6.5705 2824	10.4012 6965	16.3938 7173	25.7289 0651
49	4.2562 1944	5.3960 6459	6.8333 4937	10.9213 3313	17.3775 0403	27.5299 2997
50	4.3839 0602	5.5849 2686	7.1066 8335	11.4673 9979	18.4201 5427	29.4570 2506

AMOUNT OF $1 (CONCLUDED)

$(1 + i)^n$

n \ i	8%	9%	10%	11%	12%	13%	14%	15%
1	1.080000	1.090000	1.100000	1.110000	1.120000	1.130000	1.140000	1.150000
2	1.166400	1.188100	1.210000	1.232100	1.254400	1.276900	1.299600	1.322500
3	1.259712	1.295029	1.331000	1.367631	1.404928	1.442897	1.481544	1.520875
4	1.360489	1.411582	1.464100	1.518070	1.573519	1.630474	1.688960	1.749006
5	1.469328	1.538624	1.610510	1.685058	1.762342	1.842435	1.925415	2.011357
6	1.586874	1.677100	1.771561	1.870415	1.973823	2.081952	2.194973	2.313061
7	1.713824	1.828039	1.948717	2.076160	2.210681	2.352605	2.502269	2.660020
8	1.850930	1.992563	2.143589	2.304538	2.475963	2.658444	2.852586	3.059023
9	1.999005	2.171893	2.357948	2.558037	2.773079	3.004042	3.251949	3.517876
10	2.158925	2.367364	2.593742	2.839421	3.105848	3.394567	3.707221	4.045558
11	2.331639	2.580426	2.853117	3.151757	3.478550	3.835861	4.226232	4.652391
12	2.518170	2.812665	3.138428	3.498451	3.895976	4.334523	4.817905	5.350250
13	2.719624	3.065805	3.452271	3.883280	4.363493	4.898011	5.492411	6.152788
14	2.937194	3.341727	3.797498	4.310441	4.887112	5.534753	6.261349	7.075706
15	3.172169	3.642482	4.177248	4.784589	5.473566	6.254270	7.137938	8.137062
16	3.425943	3.970306	4.594973	5.310894	6.130394	7.067326	8.137249	9.357621
17	3.700018	4.327633	5.054470	5.895093	6.866041	7.986078	9.276464	10.761264
18	3.996019	4.717120	5.559917	6.543553	7.689966	9.024268	10.575169	12.375454
19	4.315701	5.141661	6.115909	7.263344	8.612762	10.197423	12.055693	14.231772
20	4.660957	5.604411	6.727500	8.062312	9.646293	11.523088	13.743490	16.366537
21	5.033834	6.108808	7.400250	8.949166	10.803848	13.021089	15.667578	18.821518
22	5.436540	6.658600	8.140275	9.933574	12.100310	14.713831	17.861039	21.644746
23	5.871464	7.257874	8.954302	11.026267	13.552347	16.626629	20.361585	24.891458
24	6.341181	7.911083	9.849733	12.239157	15.178629	18.788091	23.212207	28.625176
25	6.848475	8.623081	10.834706	13.585464	17.000064	21.230542	26.461916	32.918953
26	7.396353	9.399158	11.918177	15.079865	19.040072	23.990513	30.166584	37.856796
27	7.988061	10.245082	13.109994	16.738650	21.324881	27.109279	34.389906	43.535315
28	8.627106	11.167140	14.420994	18.579901	23.883866	30.633486	39.204493	50.065612
29	9.317275	12.172182	15.863093	20.623691	26.749930	34.615839	44.693122	57.575454
30	10.062657	13.267678	17.449402	22.892297	29.959922	39.115898	50.950159	66.211772
31	10.867669	14.461770	19.194342	25.410449	33.555113	44.200965	58.083181	76.143538
32	11.737083	15.763329	21.113777	28.205599	37.581726	49.947090	66.214826	87.565068
33	12.676050	17.182028	23.225154	31.308214	42.091533	56.440212	75.484902	100.699829
34	13.690134	18.728411	25.547670	34.752118	47.142517	63.777439	86.052788	115.804803
35	14.785344	20.413968	28.102437	38.574851	52.799620	72.068506	98.100178	133.175523
36	15.968172	22.251225	30.912681	42.818085	59.135574	81.437412	111.834203	153.151852
37	17.245626	24.253835	34.003949	47.528074	66.231843	92.024276	127.490992	176.124630
38	18.625276	26.436680	37.404343	52.756162	74.179664	103.987432	145.339731	202.543324
39	20.115298	28.815982	41.144778	58.559340	83.081224	117.505798	165.687293	232.924823
40	21.724521	31.409420	45.259256	65.000867	93.050970	132.781552	188.883514	267.863546
41	23.462483	34.236268	49.785181	72.150963	104.217087	150.043153	215.327206	308.043078
42	25.339482	37.317532	54.763699	80.087569	116.723137	169.548763	245.473015	354.249540
43	27.366640	40.676110	60.240069	88.897201	130.729914	191.590103	279.839237	407.386971
44	29.555972	44.336960	66.264076	98.675893	146.417503	216.496816	319.016730	468.495017
45	31.920449	48.327286	72.890484	109.530242	163.987604	244.641402	363.679072	538.769269
46	34.474085	52.676742	80.179532	121.578568	183.666116	276.444784	414.594142	619.584659
47	37.232012	57.417649	88.197485	134.952211	205.706050	312.382606	472.637322	712.522358
48	40.210573	62.585237	97.017234	149.796954	230.390776	352.992345	538.806547	819.400712
49	43.427419	68.217908	106.718957	166.274619	258.037669	398.881350	614.239464	942.310819
50	46.901613	74.357520	117.390853	184.564827	289.002190	450.735925	700.232988	1083.657442

PRESENT VALUE OF $1

$(1 + i)^{-n}$

n \ i	½%	1%	1¼%	1½%	2%	2½%
1	0.9950 2488	0.9900 9901	0.9876 5432	0.9852 2167	0.9803 9216	0.9756 0976
2	0.9900 7450	0.9802 9605	0.9754 6106	0.9706 6175	0.9611 6878	0.9518 1440
3	0.9851 4876	0.9705 9015	0.9634 1833	0.9563 1699	0.9423 2233	0.9285 9941
4	0.9802 4752	0.9609 8034	0.9515 2428	0.9421 8423	0.9238 4543	0.9059 5064
5	0.9753 7067	0.9514 6569	0.9397 7706	0.9282 6033	0.9057 3081	0.8838 5429
6	0.9705 1808	0.9420 4524	0.9281 7488	0.9145 4219	0.8879 7138	0.8622 9687
7	0.9656 8963	0.9327 1805	0.9167 1593	0.9010 2679	0.8705 6018	0.8412 6524
8	0.9608 8520	0.9234 8322	0.9053 9845	0.8877 1112	0.8534 9037	0.8207 4657
9	0.9561 0468	0.9143 3982	0.8942 2069	0.8745 9224	0.8367 5527	0.8007 2836
10	0.9513 4794	0.9052 8695	0.8831 8093	0.8616 6723	0.8203 4830	0.7811 9840
11	0.9466 1489	0.8963 2372	0.8722 7746	0.8489 3323	0.8042 6304	0.7621 4478
12	0.9419 0534	0.8874 4923	0.8615 0860	0.8363 8742	0.7884 9318	0.7435 5589
13	0.9372 1924	0.8786 6260	0.8508 7269	0.8240 2702	0.7730 3253	0.7254 2038
14	0.9325 5646	0.8699 6297	0.8403 6809	0.8118 4928	0.7578 7502	0.7077 2720
15	0.9279 1688	0.8613 4947	0.8299 9318	0.7998 5150	0.7430 1473	0.6904 6556
16	0.9233 0037	0.8528 2126	0.8197 4635	0.7880 3104	0.7284 4581	0.6736 2493
17	0.9187 0684	0.8443 7749	0.8096 2602	0.7763 8526	0.7141 6256	0.6571 9506
18	0.9141 3616	0.8360 1731	0.7996 3064	0.7649 1159	0.7001 5937	0.6411 6591
19	0.9095 8822	0.8277 3992	0.7897 5866	0.7536 0747	0.6864 3076	0.6255 2772
20	0.9050 6290	0.8195 4447	0.7800 0855	0.7424 7042	0.6729 7133	0.6102 7094
21	0.9005 6010	0.8114 3017	0.7703 7881	0.7314 9795	0.6597 7582	0.5953 8629
22	0.8960 7971	0.8033 9621	0.7608 6796	0.7206 8763	0.6468 3904	0.5808 6467
23	0.8916 2160	0.7954 4179	0.7514 7453	0.7100 3708	0.6341 5592	0.5666 9724
24	0.8871 8567	0.7875 6613	0.7421 9707	0.6995 4392	0.6217 2149	0.5528 7535
25	0.8827 7181	0.7797 6844	0.7330 3414	0.6892 0583	0.6095 3087	0.5393 9059
26	0.8783 7991	0.7720 4796	0.7239 8434	0.6790 2052	0.5975 7928	0.5262 3472
27	0.8740 0986	0.7644 0392	0.7150 4626	0.6689 8574	0.5858 6204	0.5133 9973
28	0.8696 6155	0.7568 3557	0.7062 1853	0.6590 9925	0.5743 7455	0.5008 7778
29	0.8653 3488	0.7493 4215	0.6974 9978	0.6493 5887	0.5631 1231	0.4886 6125
30	0.8610 2973	0.7419 2292	0.6888 8867	0.6397 6243	0.5520 7089	0.4767 4269
31	0.8567 4600	0.7345 7715	0.6803 8387	0.6303 0781	0.5412 4597	0.4651 1481
32	0.8524 8358	0.7273 0411	0.6719 8407	0.6209 9292	0.5306 3330	0.4537 7055
33	0.8482 4237	0.7201 0307	0.6636 8797	0.6118 1568	0.5202 2873	0.4427 0298
34	0.8440 2226	0.7129 7334	0.6554 9429	0.6027 7407	0.5100 2817	0.4319 0534
35	0.8398 2314	0.7059 1420	0.6474 0177	0.5938 6608	0.5000 2761	0.4213 7107
36	0.8356 4492	0.6989 2495	0.6394 0916	0.5850 8974	0.4902 2315	0.4110 9372
37	0.8314 8748	0.6920 0490	0.6315 1522	0.5764 4309	0.4806 1093	0.4010 6705
38	0.8273 5073	0.6851 5337	0.6237 1873	0.5679 2423	0.4711 8719	0.3912 8492
39	0.8232 3455	0.6783 6967	0.6160 1850	0.5595 3126	0.4619 4822	0.3817 4139
40	0.8191 3886	0.6716 5314	0.6084 1334	0.5512 6232	0.4528 9042	0.3724 3062
41	0.8150 6354	0.6650 0311	0.6009 0206	0.5431 1559	0.4440 1021	0.3633 4695
42	0.8110 0850	0.6584 1892	0.5934 8352	0.5350 8925	0.4353 0413	0.3544 8483
43	0.8069 7363	0.6518 9992	0.5861 5656	0.5271 8153	0.4267 6875	0.3458 3886
44	0.8029 5884	0.6454 4546	0.5789 2006	0.5193 9067	0.4184 0074	0.3374 0376
45	0.7989 6402	0.6390 5492	0.5717 7290	0.5117 1494	0.4101 9680	0.3291 7440
46	0.7949 8907	0.6327 2764	0.5647 1397	0.5041 5265	0.4021 5373	0.3211 4576
47	0.7910 3390	0.6264 6301	0.5577 4219	0.4967 0212	0.3942 6836	0.3133 1294
48	0.7870 9841	0.6202 6041	0.5508 5649	0.4893 6170	0.3865 3761	0.3056 7116
49	0.7831 8250	0.6141 1921	0.5440 5579	0.4821 2975	0.3789 5844	0.2982 1576
50	0.7792 8607	0.6080 3882	0.5373 3905	0.4750 0468	0.3715 2788	0.2909 4221

PRESENT VALUE OF $1 (CONTINUED)

$(1 + i)^{-n}$

n \ i	3%	3½%	4%	5%	6%	7%
1	0.9708 7379	0.9661 8357	0.9615 3846	0.9523 8095	0.9433 9623	0.9345 7944
2	0.9425 9591	0.9335 1070	0.9245 5621	0.9070 2948	0.8899 9644	0.8734 3873
3	0.9151 4166	0.9019 4271	0.8889 9636	0.8638 3760	0.8396 1928	0.8162 9788
4	0.8884 8705	0.8714 4223	0.8548 0419	0.8227 0247	0.7920 9366	0.7628 9521
5	0.8626 0878	0.8419 7317	0.8219 2711	0.7835 2617	0.7472 5817	0.7129 8618
6	0.8374 8426	0.8135 0064	0.7903 1453	0.7462 1540	0.7049 6054	0.6663 4222
7	0.8130 9151	0.7859 9096	0.7599 1781	0.7106 8133	0.6650 5711	0.6227 4974
8	0.7894 0923	0.7594 1156	0.7306 9021	0.6768 3936	0.6274 1237	0.5820 0910
9	0.7664 1673	0.7337 3097	0.7025 8674	0.6446 0892	0.5918 9846	0.5439 3374
10	0.7440 9391	0.7089 1881	0.6755 6417	0.6139 1325	0.5583 9478	0.5083 4929
11	0.7224 2128	0.6849 4571	0.6495 8093	0.5846 7929	0.5267 8753	0.4750 9280
12	0.7013 7988	0.6617 8330	0.6245 9705	0.5568 3742	0.4969 6936	0.4440 1196
13	0.6809 5134	0.6394 0415	0.6005 7409	0.5303 2135	0.4688 3902	0.4149 6445
14	0.6611 1781	0.6177 8179	0.5774 7508	0.5050 6795	0.4423 0096	0.3878 1724
15	0.6418 6195	0.5968 9062	0.5552 6450	0.4810 1710	0.4172 6506	0.3624 4602
16	0.6231 6694	0.5767 0591	0.5339 0818	0.4581 1152	0.3936 4628	0.3387 3460
17	0.6050 1645	0.5572 0378	0.5133 7325	0.4362 9669	0.3713 6442	0.3165 7439
18	0.5873 9461	0.5383 6114	0.4936 2812	0.4155 2065	0.3503 4379	0.2958 6392
19	0.5702 8603	0.5201 5569	0.4746 4242	0.3957 3396	0.3305 1301	0.2765 0832
20	0.5536 7575	0.5025 6588	0.4563 8695	0.3768 8948	0.3118 0473	0.2584 1900
21	0.5375 4928	0.4855 7090	0.4388 3360	0.3589 4236	0.2941 5540	0.2415 1309
22	0.5218 9250	0.4691 5063	0.4219 5539	0.3418 4987	0.2775 0510	0.2257 1317
23	0.5066 9175	0.4532 8563	0.4057 2633	0.3255 7131	0.2617 9726	0.2109 4688
24	0.4919 3374	0.4379 5713	0.3901 2147	0.3100 6791	0.2469 7855	0.1971 4662
25	0.4776 0557	0.4231 4699	0.3751 1680	0.2953 0277	0.2329 9863	0.1842 4918
26	0.4636 9473	0.4088 3767	0.3606 8923	0.2812 4073	0.2198 1003	0.1721 9549
27	0.4501 8906	0.3950 1224	0.3468 1657	0.2678 4832	0.2073 6795	0.1609 3037
28	0.4370 7675	0.3816 5434	0.3334 7747	0.2550 9364	0.1956 3014	0.1504 0221
29	0.4243 4636	0.3687 4815	0.3206 5141	0.2429 4632	0.1845 5674	0.1405 6282
30	0.4119 8676	0.3562 7841	0.3083 1867	0.2313 7745	0.1741 1013	0.1313 6712
31	0.3999 8715	0.3442 3035	0.2964 6026	0.2203 5947	0.1642 5484	0.1227 7301
32	0.3883 3703	0.3325 8971	0.2850 5794	0.2098 6617	0.1549 5740	0.1147 4113
33	0.3770 2625	0.3213 4271	0.2740 9417	0.1998 7254	0.1461 8622	0.1072 3470
34	0.3660 4490	0.3104 7605	0.2635 5209	0.1903 5480	0.1379 1153	0.1002 1934
35	0.3553 8340	0.2999 7686	0.2534 1547	0.1812 9029	0.1301 0522	0.0936 6294
36	0.3450 3243	0.2898 3272	0.2436 6872	0.1726 5741	0.1227 4077	0.0875 3546
37	0.3349 8294	0.2800 3161	0.2342 9685	0.1644 3563	0.1157 9318	0.0818 0884
38	0.3252 2615	0.2705 6194	0.2252 8543	0.1566 0536	0.1092 3885	0.0764 5686
39	0.3157 5355	0.2614 1250	0.2166 2061	0.1491 4797	0.1030 5552	0.0714 5501
40	0.3065 5684	0.2525 7247	0.2082 8904	0.1420 4568	0.0972 2219	0.0667 8038
41	0.2976 2800	0.2440 3137	0.2002 7793	0.1352 8160	0.0917 1905	0.0624 1157
42	0.2889 5922	0.2357 7910	0.1925 7493	0.1288 3962	0.0865 2740	0.0583 2857
43	0.2805 4294	0.2278 0590	0.1851 6820	0.1227 0440	0.0816 2962	0.0545 1268
44	0.2723 7178	0.2201 0231	0.1780 4635	0.1168 6133	0.0770 0908	0.0509 4643
45	0.2644 3862	0.2126 5924	0.1711 9841	0.1112 9651	0.0726 5007	0.0476 1349
46	0.2567 3653	0.2054 6787	0.1646 1386	0.1059 9668	0.0685 3781	0.0444 9859
47	0.2492 5876	0.1985 1968	0.1582 8256	0.1009 4921	0.0646 5831	0.0415 8747
48	0.2419 9880	0.1918 0645	0.1521 9476	0.0961 4211	0.0609 9840	0.0388 6679
49	0.2349 5029	0.1853 2024	0.1463 4112	0.0915 6391	0.0575 4566	0.0363 2410
50	0.2281 0708	0.1790 5337	0.1407 1262	0.0872 0373	0.0542 8836	0.0339 4776

PRESENT VALUE OF $1 (CONCLUDED)

$(1 + i)^{-n}$

n \ i	8%	9%	10%	11%	12%	13%	14%	15%
1	0.925926	0.917431	0.909091	0.900901	0.892857	0.884956	0.877193	0.869565
2	0.857339	0.841680	0.826446	0.811622	0.797194	0.783147	0.769468	0.756144
3	0.793832	0.772183	0.751315	0.731191	0.711780	0.693050	0.674972	0.657516
4	0.735030	0.708425	0.683013	0.658731	0.635518	0.613319	0.592080	0.571753
5	0.680583	0.649931	0.620921	0.593451	0.567427	0.542760	0.519369	0.497177
6	0.630170	0.596267	0.564474	0.534641	0.506631	0.480319	0.455587	0.432328
7	0.583490	0.547034	0.513158	0.481658	0.452349	0.425061	0.399637	0.375937
8	0.540269	0.501866	0.466507	0.433926	0.403883	0.376160	0.350559	0.326902
9	0.500249	0.460428	0.424098	0.390925	0.360610	0.332885	0.307508	0.284262
10	0.463193	0.422411	0.385543	0.352184	0.321973	0.294588	0.269744	0.247185
11	0.428883	0.387533	0.350494	0.317283	0.287476	0.260698	0.236617	0.214943
12	0.397114	0.355535	0.318631	0.285841	0.256675	0.230706	0.207559	0.186907
13	0.367698	0.326179	0.289664	0.257514	0.229174	0.204165	0.182069	0.162528
14	0.340461	0.299246	0.263331	0.231995	0.204620	0.180677	0.159710	0.141329
15	0.315242	0.274538	0.239392	0.209004	0.182696	0.159891	0.140096	0.122894
16	0.291890	0.251870	0.217629	0.188292	0.163122	0.141496	0.122892	0.106865
17	0.270269	0.231073	0.197845	0.169633	0.145644	0.125218	0.107800	0.092926
18	0.250249	0.211994	0.179859	0.152822	0.130040	0.110812	0.094561	0.080805
19	0.231712	0.194490	0.163508	0.137678	0.116107	0.098064	0.082948	0.070265
20	0.214548	0.178431	0.148644	0.124034	0.103667	0.086782	0.072762	0.061100
21	0.198656	0.163698	0.135131	0.111742	0.092560	0.076798	0.063826	0.053131
22	0.183941	0.150182	0.122846	0.100669	0.082643	0.067963	0.055988	0.046201
23	0.170315	0.137781	0.111678	0.090693	0.073788	0.060144	0.049112	0.040174
24	0.157699	0.126405	0.101526	0.081705	0.065882	0.053225	0.043081	0.034934
25	0.146018	0.115968	0.092296	0.073608	0.058823	0.047102	0.037790	0.030378
26	0.135202	0.106393	0.083905	0.066314	0.052521	0.041683	0.033149	0.026415
27	0.125187	0.097608	0.076278	0.059742	0.046894	0.036888	0.029078	0.022970
28	0.115914	0.089548	0.069343	0.053822	0.041869	0.032644	0.025507	0.019974
29	0.107328	0.082155	0.063039	0.048488	0.037383	0.028889	0.022375	0.017369
30	0.099377	0.075371	0.057309	0.043683	0.033378	0.025565	0.019627	0.015103
31	0.092016	0.069148	0.052099	0.039354	0.029802	0.022624	0.017217	0.013133
32	0.085200	0.063438	0.047362	0.035454	0.026609	0.020021	0.015102	0.011420
33	0.078889	0.058200	0.043057	0.031940	0.023758	0.017718	0.013248	0.009931
34	0.073045	0.053395	0.039143	0.028775	0.021212	0.015680	0.011621	0.008635
35	0.067635	0.048986	0.035584	0.025924	0.018940	0.013876	0.010194	0.007509
36	0.062625	0.044941	0.032349	0.023355	0.016910	0.012279	0.008942	0.006529
37	0.057986	0.041231	0.029408	0.021040	0.015098	0.010867	0.007844	0.005678
38	0.053690	0.037826	0.026735	0.018955	0.013481	0.009617	0.006880	0.004937
39	0.049713	0.034703	0.024304	0.017077	0.012036	0.008510	0.006035	0.004293
40	0.046031	0.031838	0.022095	0.015384	0.010747	0.007531	0.005294	0.003733
41	0.042621	0.029209	0.020086	0.013860	0.009595	0.006665	0.004644	0.003246
42	0.039464	0.026797	0.018260	0.012486	0.008567	0.005898	0.004074	0.002823
43	0.036541	0.024584	0.016600	0.011249	0.007649	0.005219	0.003573	0.002455
44	0.033834	0.022555	0.015091	0.010134	0.006830	0.004619	0.003135	0.002134
45	0.031328	0.020692	0.013719	0.009130	0.006098	0.004088	0.002750	0.001856
46	0.029007	0.018984	0.012472	0.008225	0.005445	0.003617	0.002412	0.001614
47	0.026859	0.017416	0.011338	0.007410	0.004861	0.003201	0.002116	0.001403
48	0.024869	0.015978	0.010307	0.006676	0.004340	0.002833	0.001856	0.001220
49	0.023027	0.014659	0.009370	0.006014	0.003875	0.002507	0.001628	0.001061
50	0.021321	0.013449	0.008519	0.005418	0.003460	0.002219	0.001428	0.000923

AMOUNT OF ANNUITY OF $1

$$s_{\overline{n}|i} = \frac{(1 + i)^n - 1}{i}$$

n \ i	½%	1%	1¼%	1½%	2%	2½%
1	1.0000 0000	1.0000 0000	1.0000 0000	1.0000 0000	1.0000 0000	1.0000 0000
2	2.0050 0000	2.0100 0000	2.0125 0000	2.0150 0000	2.0200 0000	2.0250 0000
3	3.0150 2500	3.0301 0000	3.0376 5625	3.0452 2500	3.0604 0000	3.0756 2500
4	4.0301 0013	4.0604 0100	4.0756 2695	4.0909 0338	4.1216 0800	4.1525 1563
5	5.0502 5063	5.1010 0501	5.1265 7229	5.1522 6693	5.2040 4016	5.2563 2852
6	6.0755 0188	6.1520 1506	6.1906 5444	6.2295 5093	6.3081 2096	6.3877 3673
7	7.1058 7939	7.2135 3521	7.2680 3762	7.3229 9419	7.4342 8338	7.5474 3015
8	8.1414 0879	8.2856 7056	8.3588 8809	8.4328 3911	8.5829 6905	8.7361 1590
9	9.1821 1583	9.3685 2727	9.4633 7420	9.5593 3169	9.7546 2843	9.9545 1880
10	10.2280 2641	10.4622 1254	10.5816 6637	10.7027 2167	10.9497 2100	11.2033 8177
11	11.2791 6654	11.5668 3467	11.7139 3720	11.8632 6249	12.1687 1542	12.4834 6631
12	12.3355 6237	12.6825 0301	12.8603 6142	13.0412 1143	13.4120 8973	13.7955 5297
13	13.3972 4018	13.8093 2804	14.0211 1594	14.2368 2960	14.6803 3152	15.1404 4179
14	14.4642 2639	14.9474 2132	15.1963 7988	15.4503 8205	15.9739 3815	16.5189 5284
15	15.5365 4752	16.0968 9554	16.3863 3463	16.6821 3778	17.2934 1692	17.9319 2666
16	16.6142 3026	17.2578 6449	17.5911 6382	17.9323 6984	18.6392 8525	19.3802 2483
17	17.6973 0141	18.4304 4314	18.8110 5336	19.2013 5539	20.0120 7096	20.8647 3045
18	18.7857 8791	19.6147 4757	20.0461 9153	20.4893 7572	21.4123 1238	22.3863 4871
19	19.8797 1685	20.8108 9504	21.2967 6893	21.7967 1636	22.8405 5863	23.9460 0743
20	20.9791 1544	22.0190 0399	22.5629 7854	23.1236 6710	24.2973 6980	25.5446 5761
21	22.0840 1101	23.2391 9403	23.8450 1577	24.4705 2211	25.7833 1719	27.1832 7405
22	23.1944 3107	24.4715 8598	25.1430 7847	25.8375 7994	27.2989 8354	28.8628 5590
23	24.3104 0322	25.7163 0183	26.4573 6695	27.2251 4364	28.8449 6321	30.5844 2730
24	25.4319 5524	26.9734 6485	27.7880 8403	28.6335 2080	30.4218 6247	32.3490 3798
25	26.5591 1502	28.2431 9950	29.1354 3508	30.0630 2361	32.0302 9972	34.1577 6393
26	27.6919 1059	29.5256 3150	30.4996 2802	31.5139 6896	33.6709 0572	36.0117 0803
27	28.8303 7015	30.8208 8781	31.8808 7337	32.9866 7850	35.3443 2383	37.9120 0073
28	29.9745 2200	32.1290 9669	33.2793 8429	34.4814 7867	37.0512 1031	39.8598 0075
29	31.1243 9461	33.4503 8766	34.6953 7659	35.9987 0085	38.7922 3451	41.8562 9577
30	32.2800 1658	34.7848 9153	36.1290 6880	37.5386 8137	40.5680 7921	43.9027 0316
31	33.4414 1666	36.1327 4045	37.5806 8216	39.1017 6159	42.3794 4079	46.0002 7074
32	34.6086 2375	37.4940 6785	39.0504 4069	40.6882 8801	44.2270 2961	48.1502 7751
33	35.7816 6686	38.8690 0853	40.5385 7120	42.2986 1233	46.1115 7020	50.3540 3445
34	36.9605 7520	40.2576 9862	42.0453 0334	43.9330 9152	48.0338 0160	52.6128 8531
35	38.1453 7807	41.6602 7560	43.5708 6963	45.5920 8789	49.9944 7763	54.9282 0744
36	39.3361 0496	43.0768 7836	45.1155 0550	47.2759 6921	51.9943 6719	57.3014 1263
37	40.5327 8549	44.5076 4714	46.6794 4932	48.9851 0874	54.0342 5453	59.7339 4794
38	41.7354 4942	45.9527 2361	48.2926 4243	50.7198 8538	56.1149 3962	62.2272 9664
39	42.9441 2666	47.4122 5085	49.8862 2921	52.4806 8366	58.2372 3841	64.7829 7906
40	44.1588 4730	48.8863 7336	51.4895 5708	54.2678 9391	60.4019 8318	67.4025 5354
41	45.3796 4153	50.3752 3709	53.1331 7654	56.0819 1232	62.6100 2284	70.0876 1737
42	46.6065 3974	51.8789 8946	54.7973 4125	57.9231 4100	64.8622 2330	72.8398 0781
43	47.8395 7244	53.3977 7936	56.4823 0801	59.7919 8812	67.1594 6777	75.6608 0300
44	49.0787 7030	54.9317 5715	58.1883 3687	61.6888 6794	69.5026 5712	78.5523 2308
45	50.3241 6415	56.4810 7472	59.9156 9108	63.6142 0096	71.8927 1027	81.5161 3116
46	51.5757 8497	58.0458 8547	61.6646 3721	65.5684 1398	74.3305 6447	84.5540 3443
47	52.8336 6390	59.6263 4432	63.4354 4518	67.5519 4018	76.8171 7576	87.6678 8530
48	54.0978 3222	61.2226 0777	65.2283 8824	69.5652 1929	79.3535 1927	90.8595 8243
49	55.3683 2138	62.8348 3385	67.0437 4310	71.6086 9758	81.9405 8966	94.1310 7199
50	56.6451 6299	64.4631 8218	68.8817 8989	73.6828 2804	84.5794 0145	97.4843 4879

AMOUNT OF ANNUITY OF $1 (CONTINUED)

$$s_{\overline{n}|i} = \frac{(1+i)^n - 1}{i}$$

n \ i	3%	3½%	4%	5%	6%	7%
1	1.0000 0000	1.0000 0000	1.0000 0000	1.0000 0000	1.0000 0000	1.0000 0000
2	2.0300 0000	2.0350 0000	2.0400 0000	2.0500 0000	2.0600 0000	2.0700 0000
3	3.0909 0000	3.1062 2500	3.1216 0000	3.1525 0000	3.1836 0000	3.2149 0000
4	4.1836 2700	4.2149 4288	4.2464 6400	4.3101 2500	4.3746 1600	4.4399 4300
5	5.3091 3581	5.3624 6588	5.4163 2256	5.5256 3125	5.6370 9296	5.7507 3901
6	6.4684 0988	6.5501 5218	6.6329 7546	6.8019 1281	6.9753 1854	7.1532 9074
7	7.6624 6218	7.7794 0751	7.8982 9448	8.1420 0845	8.3938 3765	8.6540 2109
8	8.8923 3605	9.0516 8677	9.2142 2626	9.5491 0888	9.8974 6791	10.2598 0257
9	10.1591 0613	10.3684 9581	10.5827 9531	11.0265 6432	11.4913 1598	11.9779 8875
10	11.4638 7931	11.7313 9316	12.0061 0712	12.5778 9254	13.1807 9494	13.8164 4796
11	12.8077 9569	13.1419 9192	13.4863 5141	14.2067 8716	14.9716 4264	15.7835 9932
12	14.1920 2956	14.6019 6164	15.0258 0546	15.9171 2652	16.8699 4120	17.8884 5127
13	15.6177 9045	16.1130 3030	16.6268 3768	17.7129 8285	18.8821 3767	20.1406 4286
14	17.0863 2416	17.6769 8636	18.2919 1119	19.5986 3199	21.0150 6593	22.5504 8786
15	18.5989 1389	19.2956 8088	20.0235 8764	21.5785 6359	23.2759 6988	25.1290 2201
16	20.1568 8130	20.9710 2971	21.8245 3114	23.6574 9177	25.6725 2808	27.8880 5355
17	21.7615 8774	22.7050 1575	23.6975 1239	25.8403 6636	28.2128 7976	30.8402 1730
18	23.4144 3537	24.4996 9130	25.6454 1288	28.1323 8467	30.9056 5255	33.9990 3251
19	25.1168 6844	26.3571 8050	27.6712 2940	30.5390 0391	33.7599 9170	37.3789 6479
20	26.8703 7449	28.2796 8181	29.7780 7858	33.0659 5410	36.7855 9120	40.9954 9232
21	28.6764 8572	30.2694 7068	31.9692 0172	35.7192 5181	39.9927 2668	44.8651 7678
22	30.5367 8030	32.3289 0215	34.2479 6979	38.5052 1440	43.3922 9028	49.0057 3916
23	32.4528 8370	34.4604 1373	36.6178 8858	41.4304 7512	46.9958 2769	53.4361 4090
24	34.4264 7022	36.6665 2821	39.0826 0412	44.5019 9887	50.8155 7735	58.1766 7076
25	36.4592 6432	38.9498 5669	41.6459 0829	47.7270 9882	54.8645 1200	63.2490 3772
26	38.5530 4225	41.3131 0168	44.3117 4462	51.1134 5376	59.1563 8272	68.6764 7036
27	40.7096 3352	43.7590 6024	47.0842 1440	54.6691 2645	63.7057 6568	74.4838 2328
28	42.9309 2252	46.2906 2734	49.9675 8298	58.4025 8277	68.5281 1162	80.6976 9091
29	45.2188 5020	48.9107 9930	52.9662 8630	62.3227 1191	73.6397 9832	87.3465 2927
30	47.5754 1571	51.6226 7728	56.0849 3775	66.4388 4750	79.0581 8622	94.4607 8632
31	50.0026 7818	54.4294 7098	59.3283 3526	70.7607 8988	84.8016 7739	102.0730 4137
32	52.5027 5852	57.3345 0247	62.7014 6867	75.2988 2937	90.8897 7803	110.2181 5426
33	55.0778 4128	60.3412 1005	66.2095 2742	80.0637 7084	97.3431 6471	118.9334 2506
34	57.7301 7652	63.4531 5240	69.8579 0851	85.0669 5938	104.1837 5460	128.2587 6481
35	60.4620 8181	66.6740 1274	73.6522 2486	90.3203 0735	111.4347 7987	138.2368 7835
36	63.2759 4427	70.0076 0318	77.5983 1385	95.8363 2272	119.1208 6666	148.9134 5984
37	66.1742 2259	73.4578 6930	81.7022 4640	101.6281 3886	127.2681 1866	160.3374 0202
38	69.1594 4927	77.0288 9472	85.9703 3626	107.7095 4580	135.9042 0578	172.5610 2017
39	72.2342 3275	80.7249 0604	90.4091 4971	114.0950 2309	145.0584 5813	185.6402 9158
40	75.4012 5973	84.5502 7775	95.0255 1570	120.7997 7424	154.7619 6562	199.6351 1199
41	78.6632 9753	88.5095 3747	99.8265 3633	127.8397 6295	165.0476 8356	214.6095 6983
42	82.0231 9645	92.6073 7128	104.8195 9778	135.2317 5110	175.9505 4457	230.6322 3972
43	85.4838 9234	96.8486 2928	110.0123 8169	142.9933 3866	187.5075 7724	247.7764 9650
44	89.0484 0911	101.2383 3130	115.4128 7696	151.1430 0559	199.7580 3188	266.1208 5125
45	92.7198 6139	105.7816 7290	121.0293 9204	159.7001 5587	212.7435 1379	285.7493 1084
46	96.5014 5723	110.4840 3145	126.8705 6772	168.6851 6366	226.5081 2462	306.7517 6260
47	100.3965 0095	115.3509 7255	132.9453 9043	178.1194 2185	241.0986 1210	329.2243 8598
48	104.4083 9598	120.3882 5659	139.2632 0604	188.0253 9294	256.5645 2882	353.2700 9300
49	108.5406 4785	125.6018 4557	145.8337 3429	198.4266 6259	272.9584 0055	378.9989 9951
50	112.7968 6729	130.9979 1016	152.6670 8366	209.3479 9572	290.3359 0458	406.5289 2947

AMOUNT OF ANNUITY OF $1 (CONCLUDED)

$$s_{\overline{n}|i} = \frac{(1+i)^n - 1}{i}$$

n \ i	8%	9%	10%	11%	12%	13%	14%	15%
1	1.000000	1.000000	1.000000	1.000000	1.000000	1.000000	1.000000	1.000000
2	2.080000	2.090000	2.100000	2.110000	2.120000	2.130000	2.140000	2.150000
3	3.246400	3.278100	3.310000	3.342100	3.374400	3.406900	3.439600	3.472500
4	4.506112	4.573129	4.641000	4.709731	4.779328	4.849797	4.921144	4.993375
5	5.866601	5.984711	6.105100	6.227801	6.352847	6.480271	6.610104	6.742381
6	7.335929	7.523335	7.715610	7.912860	8.115189	8.322706	8.535519	8.753738
7	8.922803	9.200435	9.487171	9.783274	10.089012	10.404658	10.730491	11.066799
8	10.636628	11.028474	11.435888	11.859434	12.299693	12.757263	13.232760	13.726819
9	12.487558	13.021036	13.579477	14.163972	14.775656	15.415707	16.085347	16.785842
10	14.486562	15.192930	15.937425	16.722009	17.548735	18.419749	19.337295	20.303718
11	16.645487	17.560293	18.531167	19.561430	20.654583	21.814317	23.044516	24.349276
12	18.977126	20.140720	21.384284	22.713187	24.133133	25.650178	27.270749	29.001667
13	21.495297	22.953385	24.522712	26.211638	28.029109	29.984701	32.088654	34.351917
14	24.214920	26.019189	27.974983	30.094918	32.392602	34.882712	37.581065	40.504705
15	27.152114	29.360916	31.772482	34.405359	37.279715	40.417464	43.842414	47.580411
16	30.324283	33.003399	35.949730	39.189948	42.753280	46.671735	50.980352	55.717472
17	33.750226	36.973705	40.544703	44.500843	48.883674	53.739060	59.117601	65.075093
18	37.450244	41.301338	45.599173	50.395936	55.749715	61.725138	68.394066	75.836357
19	41.446263	46.018458	51.159090	56.939488	63.439681	70.749406	78.969235	88.211811
20	45.761964	51.160120	57.274999	64.202832	72.052442	80.946829	91.024928	102.443583
21	50.422921	56.764530	64.002499	72.265144	81.698736	92.469917	104.768418	118.810120
22	55.456755	62.873338	71.402749	81.214309	92.502584	105.491006	120.435996	137.631638
23	60.893296	69.531939	79.543024	91.147884	104.602894	120.204837	138.297035	159.276384
24	66.764759	76.789813	88.497327	102.174151	118.155241	136.831465	158.658620	184.167841
25	73.105940	84.700896	98.347059	114.413307	133.333870	155.619556	181.870827	212.793017
26	79.954415	93.323977	109.181765	127.998771	150.333934	176.850098	208.332743	245.711970
27	87.350768	102.723135	121.099942	143.078636	169.374007	200.840611	238.499327	283.568766
28	95.338830	112.968217	134.209936	159.817286	190.698887	227.949890	272.889233	327.104080
29	103.965936	124.135356	148.630930	178.397187	214.582754	258.583376	312.093725	377.169693
30	113.283211	136.307539	164.494023	199.020878	241.332684	293.199215	356.786847	434.745146
31	123.345868	149.575217	181.943425	221.913174	271.292606	332.315113	407.737006	500.956918
32	134.213537	164.036987	201.137767	247.323624	304.847719	376.516078	465.820186	577.100456
33	145.950620	179.800315	222.251544	275.529222	342.429446	426.463168	532.035012	644.665525
34	158.626670	196.982344	245.476699	306.837437	384.520979	482.903380	607.519914	765.365353
35	172.316804	215.710755	271.024368	341.589555	431.663496	546.680819	693.572702	881.170156
36	187.102148	236.124723	299.126805	380.164406	484.463116	618.749325	791.672881	1014.345680
37	203.070320	258.375948	330.039486	422.982490	543.598690	700.186738	903.507084	1167.497532
38	220.315945	282.629783	364.043434	470.510564	609.830533	792.211014	1030.998076	1343.622161
39	238.941221	309.066463	401.447778	523.266726	684.010197	896.198445	1176.337806	1546.165485
40	259.056519	337.882445	442.592556	581.826066	767.091420	1013.704243	1342.025099	1779.090308
41	280.781040	369.291865	487.851811	646.826934	860.142391	1146.485795	1530.908613	2046.953854
42	304.243523	403.528133	537.636992	718.977896	964.359478	1296.528948	1746.235819	2354.996933
43	329.583005	440.845665	592.400692	799.065465	1081.082615	1466.077712	1991.708833	2709.246473
44	356.949646	481.521775	652.640761	887.962666	1211.812529	1657.667814	2271.548070	3116.633443
45	386.505617	525.858734	718.904837	986.638559	1358.230032	1874.164630	2590.564800	3585.128460
46	418.426067	574.186021	791.795321	1096.168801	1522.217636	2118.806032	2954.243872	4123.897729
47	452.900152	626.862762	871.974853	1217.747369	1705.883752	2395.250816	3368.838014	4743.482388
48	490.132164	684.280411	960.172338	1352.699580	1911.589803	2707.633422	3841.475336	5466.004746
49	530.342737	746.865648	1057.189572	1502.496534	2141.980579	3060.625767	4380.281883	6275.405458
50	573.770156	815.083556	1163.908529	1668.771152	2400.018249	3459.507117	4994.521346	7217.716277

PRESENT VALUE OF ANNUITY OF $1

$$p_{\overline{n}|i} = \frac{1 - (1 + i)^{-n}}{i}$$

n \ i	½%	1%	1¼%	1½%	2%	2½%
1	0.9950 2488	0.9900 9901	0.9876 5432	0.9852 2167	0.9803 9216	0.9756 0976
2	1.9850 9938	1.9703 9506	1.9631 1538	1.9558 8342	1.9415 6094	1.9274 2415
3	2.9702 4814	2.9409 8521	2.9265 3371	2.9122 0042	2.8838 8327	2.8560 2356
4	3.9504 9566	3.9019 6555	3.8780 5798	3.8543 8465	3.8077 2870	3.7619 7421
5	4.9258 6633	4.8534 3124	4.8178 3504	4.7826 4497	4.7134 5951	4.6458 2850
6	5.8963 8441	5.7954 7647	5.7460 0992	5.6971 8717	5.6014 3089	5.5081 2536
7	6.8620 7404	6.7281 9453	6.6627 2585	6.5982 1396	6.4719 9107	6.3493 9060
8	7.8229 5924	7.6516 7775	7.5681 2429	7.4859 2508	7.3254 8144	7.1701 3717
9	8.7790 6392	8.5660 1758	8.4623 4498	8.3605 1732	8.1622 3671	7.9708 6553
10	9.7304 1186	9.4713 0453	9.3455 2591	9.2221 8455	8.9825 8501	8.7520 6393
11	10.6770 2673	10.3676 2825	10.2178 0337	10.0711 1779	9.7868 4805	9.5142 0871
12	11.6189 3207	11.2550 7747	11.0793 1197	10.9075 0521	10.5753 4122	10.2577 6460
13	12.5561 5131	12.1337 4007	11.9301 8466	11.7315 3222	11.3483 7375	10.9831 8497
14	13.4887 0777	13.0037 0304	12.7705 5275	12.5433 8150	12.1062 4877	11.6909 1217
15	14.4166 2465	13.8650 5252	13.6005 4592	13.3432 3301	12.8492 6350	12.3813 7773
16	15.3399 2502	14.7178 7378	14.4202 9227	14.1312 6405	13.5777 0931	13.0550 0266
17	16.2586 3186	15.5622 5127	15.2299 1829	14.9076 4931	14.2918 7188	13.7121 9772
18	17.1727 6802	16.3982 6858	16.0295 4893	15.6725 6089	14.9920 3125	14.3533 6363
19	18.0823 5624	17.2260 0850	16.8193 0759	16.4261 6837	15.6784 6201	14.9788 9134
20	18.9874 1915	18.0455 5297	17.5993 1613	17.1686 3879	16.3514 3334	15.5891 6229
21	19.8879 7925	18.8569 8313	18.3696 9495	17.9001 3673	17.0112 0916	16.1845 4857
22	20.7840 5896	19.6603 7934	19.1305 6291	18.6208 2437	17.6580 4820	16.7654 1324
23	21.6756 8055	20.4558 2113	19.8820 3744	19.3308 6145	18.2922 0412	17.3321 1048
24	22.5628 6622	21.2433 8726	20.6242 3451	20.0304 0537	18.9139 2560	17.8849 8583
25	23.4456 3803	22.0231 5570	21.3572 6865	20.7196 1120	19.5234 5647	18.4243 7642
26	24.3240 1794	22.7952 0366	22.0812 5299	21.3986 3172	20.1210 3576	18.9506 1114
27	25.1980 2780	23.5596 0759	22.7962 9925	22.0676 1746	20.7068 9780	19.4640 1087
28	26.0676 8936	24.3164 4316	23.5025 1778	22.7267 1671	21.2812 7236	19.9648 8866
29	26.9330 2423	25.0657 8530	24.2000 1756	23.3760 7558	21.8443 8466	20.4535 4991
30	27.7940 5397	25.8077 0822	24.8889 0623	24.0158 3801	22.3964 5555	20.9302 9259
31	28.6507 9997	26.5422 8537	25.5692 9010	24.6461 4582	22.9377 0152	21.3954 0741
32	29.5032 8355	27.2695 8947	26.2412 7418	25.2671 3874	23.4683 3482	21.8491 7796
33	30.3515 2592	27.9896 9255	26.9049 6215	25.8789 5442	23.9885 6355	22.2918 8094
34	31.1955 4818	28.7026 6589	27.5604 5644	26.4817 2849	24.4985 9172	22.7237 8628
35	32.0353 7132	29.4085 8009	28.2078 5822	27.0755 9458	24.9986 1933	23.1451 5734
36	32.8710 1624	30.1075 0504	28.8472 6737	27.6606 8431	25.4888 4248	23.5562 5107
37	33.7025 0372	30.7995 0994	29.4787 8259	28.2371 2740	25.9694 5341	23.9573 1812
38	34.5298 5445	31.4846 6330	30.1025 0133	28.8050 5163	26.4406 4060	24.3486 0304
39	35.3530 8900	32.1630 3298	30.7185 1983	29.3645 8288	26.9025 8883	24.7303 4443
40	36.1722 2786	32.8346 8611	31.3269 3316	29.9158 4520	27.3554 7924	25.1027 7505
41	36.9872 9141	33.4996 8922	31.9278 3522	30.4589 6079	27.7994 8945	25.4661 2200
42	37.7982 9991	34.1581 0814	32.5213 1874	30.9940 5004	28.2347 9358	25.8206 0683
43	38.6052 7354	34.8100 0806	33.1074 7530	31.5212 3157	28.6615 6233	26.1664 4569
44	39.4082 3238	35.4554 5352	33.6863 9536	32.0406 2223	29.0799 6307	26.5038 4945
45	40.2071 9640	36.0945 0844	34.2581 6825	32.5523 3718	29.4901 5987	26.8330 2386
46	41.0021 8547	36.7272 3608	34.8228 8222	33.0564 8983	29.8923 1360	27.1541 6962
47	41.7932 1937	37.3536 9909	35.3806 2442	33.5531 9195	30.2865 8196	27.4674 8255
48	42.5803 1778	37.9739 5949	35.9314 8091	34.0425 5365	30.6731 1957	27.7731 5371
49	43.3635 0028	38.5880 7871	36.4755 3670	34.5246 8339	31.0520 7801	28.0713 6947
50	44.1427 8635	39.1961 1753	37.0128 7574	34.9996 8807	31.4236 0589	28.3623 1168

PRESENT VALUE OF ANNUITY OF $1 (CONTINUED)

$$p_{\overline{n}|i} = \frac{1 - (1 + i)^{-n}}{i}$$

n \ i	3%	3½%	4%	5%	6%	7%
1	0.9708 7379	0.9661 8357	0.9615 3846	0.9523 8095	0.9433 9623	0.9345 7944
2	1.9134 6970	1.8996 9428	1.8860 9467	1.8594 1043	1.8333 9267	1.8080 1817
3	2.8286 1135	2.8016 3698	2.7750 9103	2.7232 4803	2.6730 1195	2.6243 1604
4	3.7170 9840	3.6730 7921	3.6298 9522	3.5459 5050	3.4651 0561	3.3872 1126
5	4.5797 0719	4.5150 5238	4.4518 2233	4.3294 7667	4.2123 6379	4.1001 9744
6	5.4171 9144	5.3285 5302	5.2421 3686	5.0756 9206	4.9173 2433	4.7665 3966
7	6.2302 8296	6.1145 4398	6.0020 5467	5.7863 7340	5.5823 8144	5.3892 8940
8	7.0196 9219	6.8739 5554	6.7327 4487	6.4632 1276	6.2097 9381	5.9712 9851
9	7.7861 0892	7.6076 8651	7.4353 3161	7.1078 2168	6.8016 9227	6.5152 3225
10	8.5302 0284	8.3166 0532	8.1108 9578	7.7217 3493	7.3600 8705	7.0235 8154
11	9.2526 2411	9.0015 5104	8.7604 7671	8.3064 1422	7.8868 7458	7.4986 7434
12	9.9540 0399	9.6633 3433	9.3850 7376	8.8632 5164	8.3838 4394	7.9426 8630
13	10.6349 5533	10.3027 3849	9.9856 4785	9.3935 7299	8.8526 8296	8.3576 5074
14	11.2960 7314	10.9205 2028	10.5631 2293	9.8986 4094	9.2949 8393	8.7454 6799
15	11.9379 3509	11.5174 1090	11.1183 8743	10.3796 5804	9.7122 4899	9.1079 1401
16	12.5611 0203	12.0941 1681	11.6522 9561	10.8377 6956	10.1058 9527	9.4466 4860
17	13.1661 1847	12.6513 2059	12.1656 6885	11.2740 6625	10.4772 5969	9.7632 2299
18	13.7535 1308	13.1896 8173	12.6592 9697	11.6895 8690	10.8276 0348	10.0590 8691
19	14.3237 9911	13.7098 3742	13.1339 3940	12.0853 2086	11.1581 1649	10.3355 9524
20	14.8774 7486	14.2124 0330	13.5903 2634	12.4622 1034	11.4699 2122	10.5940 1425
21	15.4150 2414	14.6979 7420	14.0291 5995	12.8211 5271	11.7640 7662	10.8355 2733
22	15.9369 1664	15.1671 2484	14.4511 1533	13.1630 0258	12.0415 8172	11.0612 4050
23	16.4436 0839	15.6204 1047	14.8568 4167	13.4885 7388	12.3033 7898	11.2721 8738
24	16.9355 4212	16.0583 6760	15.2469 6314	13.7986 4179	12.5503 5753	11.4693 3400
25	17.4131 4769	16.4815 1459	15.6220 7994	14.0939 4457	12.7833 5616	11.6535 8318
26	17.8768 4242	16.8903 5226	15.9827 6918	14.3751 8530	13.0031 6619	11.8257 7867
27	18.3270 3147	17.2853 6451	16.3295 8575	14.6430 3362	13.2105 3414	11.9867 0904
28	18.7641 0823	17.6670 1885	16.6630 6322	14.8981 2726	13.4061 6428	12.1371 1125
29	19.1884 5459	18.0357 6700	16.9837 1463	15.1410 7358	13.5907 2102	12.2776 7407
30	19.6004 4135	18.3920 4541	17.2920 3330	15.3724 5103	13.7648 3115	12.4090 4118
31	20.0004 2849	18.7362 7576	17.5884 9356	15.5928 1050	13.9290 8599	12.5318 1419
32	20.3887 6553	19.0688 6547	17.8735 5150	15.8026 7667	14.0840 4339	12.6465 5532
33	20.7657 9178	19.3902 0818	18.1476 4567	16.0025 4921	14.2302 2961	12.7537 9002
34	21.1318 3668	19.7006 8423	18.4111 9776	16.1929 0401	14.3681 4114	12.8540 0936
35	21.4872 2007	20.0006 6110	18.6646 1323	16.3741 9429	14.4982 4636	12.9476 7230
36	21.8322 5250	20.2904 9381	18.9082 8195	16.5468 5171	14.6209 8713	13.0352 0776
37	22.1672 3544	20.5705 2542	19.1425 7880	16.7112 8734	14.7367 8031	13.1170 1660
38	22.4924 6159	20.8410 8736	19.3678 6423	16.8678 9271	14.8460 1916	13.1934 7345
39	22.8082 1513	21.1024 9987	19.5844 8484	17.0170 4067	14.9490 7468	13.2649 2846
40	23.1147 7197	21.3550 7234	19.7927 7388	17.1590 8635	15.0462 9687	13.3317 0884
41	23.4123 9997	21.5991 0371	19.9930 5181	17.2943 6796	15.1380 1592	13.3941 2041
42	23.7013 5920	21.8348 8281	20.1856 2674	17.4232 0758	15.2245 4332	13.4524 4898
43	23.9819 0213	22.0626 8870	20.3707 9494	17.5459 1198	15.3061 7294	13.5069 6167
44	24.2542 7392	22.2827 9102	20.5488 4129	17.6627 7331	15.3831 8202	13.5579 0810
45	24.5187 1254	22.4954 5026	20.7200 3970	17.7740 6982	15.4558 3209	13.6055 2159
46	24.7754 4907	22.7009 1813	20.8846 5356	17.8800 6650	15.5243 6990	13.6500 2018
47	25.0247 0783	22.8994 3780	21.0429 3612	17.9810 1571	15.5890 2821	13.6916 0764
48	25.2667 0664	23.0912 4425	21.1951 3088	18.0771 5782	15.6500 2661	13.7304 7443
49	25.5016 5693	23.2765 6450	21.3414 7200	18.1687 2173	15.7075 7227	13.7667 9853
50	25.7297 6401	23.4556 1787	21.4821 8462	18.2559 2546	15.7618 6064	13.8007 4629

PRESENT VALUE OF ANNUITY OF $1 (CONCLUDED)

$$p_{\overline{n}|i} = \frac{1 - (1 + i)^{-n}}{i}$$

n \ i	8%	9%	10%	11%	12%	13%	14%	15%
1	0.925926	0.917431	0.909091	0.900901	0.892857	0.884956	0.877193	0.869565
2	1.783265	1.759111	1.735537	1.712523	1.690051	1.668102	1.646661	1.625709
3	2.577097	2.531295	2.486852	2.443715	2.401831	2.361153	2.321632	2.283225
4	3.312127	3.239720	3.169865	3.102446	3.037349	2.974471	2.913712	2.854978
5	3.992710	3.889651	3.790787	3.695897	3.604776	3.517231	3.433081	3.352155
6	4.622880	4.485919	4.355261	4.230538	4.111407	3.997550	3.888668	3.784483
7	5.206370	5.032953	4.868419	4.712196	4.563757	4.422610	4.288305	4.160420
8	5.746639	5.534819	5.334926	5.146123	4.967640	4.798770	4.638864	4.487322
9	6.246888	5.995247	5.759024	5.537048	5.328250	5.131655	4.946372	4.771584
10	6.710081	6.417658	6.144567	5.889232	5.650223	5.426243	5.216116	5.018769
11	7.138964	6.805191	6.495061	6.206515	5.937699	5.686941	5.452733	5.233712
12	7.536078	7.160725	6.813692	6.492356	6.194374	5.917647	5.660292	5.420619
13	7.903776	7.486904	7.103356	6.749870	6.423548	6.121812	5.842362	5.583147
14	8.244237	7.786150	7.366687	6.981865	6.628168	6.302488	6.002072	5.724476
15	8.559479	8.060688	7.606080	7.190870	6.810864	6.462379	6.142168	5.847370
16	8.851369	8.312558	7.823709	7.379162	6.973986	6.603875	6.265060	5.954235
17	9.121638	8.543631	8.021553	7.548794	7.119630	6.729093	6.372859	6.047161
18	9.371887	8.755625	8.201412	7.701617	7.249670	6.839905	6.467420	6.127966
19	9.603599	8.950115	8.364920	7.839294	7.365777	6.937969	6.550369	6.198231
20	9.818147	9.128546	8.513564	7.963328	7.469444	7.024752	6.623131	6.259331
21	10.016803	9.292244	8.648694	8.075070	7.562003	7.101550	6.686957	6.312462
22	10.200744	9.442425	8.771540	8.175739	7.644646	7.169513	6.742944	6.358663
23	10.371059	9.580207	8.883218	8.266432	7.718434	7.229658	6.792056	6.398837
24	10.528758	9.706612	8.984744	8.348137	7.784316	7.282883	6.835137	6.433771
25	10.674776	9.822580	9.077040	8.421745	7.843139	7.329985	6.872927	6.464149
26	10.809978	9.928972	9.160945	8.488058	7.895660	7.371668	6.906077	6.490564
27	10.935165	10.026580	9.237223	8.547800	7.942554	7.408556	6.935155	6.513534
28	11.051078	10.116128	9.306567	8.601622	7.984423	7.441200	6.960662	6.533508
29	11.158406	10.198283	9.369606	8.650110	8.021806	7.470088	6.983037	6.550877
30	11.257783	10.273654	9.426914	8.693793	8.055184	7.495653	7.002664	6.565980
31	11.349799	10.342802	9.479013	8.733146	8.084986	7.518277	7.019881	6.579113
32	11.434999	10.406240	9.526376	8.768600	8.111594	7.538299	7.034983	6.590533
33	11.513888	10.464441	9.569432	8.800541	8.135352	7.556016	7.048231	6.600463
34	11.586934	10.517835	9.608575	8.829316	8.156564	7.571696	7.059852	6.609099
35	11.654568	10.566821	9.644159	8.855240	8.175504	7.585572	7.070045	6.616607
36	11.717193	10.611763	9.676508	8.878594	8.192414	7.597851	7.078987	6.623137
37	11.775179	10.652993	9.705917	8.899635	8.207513	7.608718	7.086831	6.628815
38	11.828869	10.690820	9.732651	8.918590	8.220993	7.618334	7.093711	6.633752
39	11.878582	10.725523	9.756956	8.935666	8.233030	7.626844	7.099747	6.638045
40	11.924613	10.757360	9.779051	8.951051	8.243777	7.634376	7.105041	6.641778
41	11.967235	10.786569	9.799137	8.964911	8.253372	7.641040	7.109685	6.645025
42	12.006699	10.813366	9.817397	8.977397	8.261939	7.646938	7.113759	6.647848
43	12.043240	10.837950	9.833998	8.988646	8.269589	7.652158	7.117332	6.650302
44	12.077074	10.860505	9.849089	8.998780	8.276418	7.656777	7.120467	6.652437
45	12.108402	10.881197	9.862808	9.007910	8.282516	7.660864	7.123217	6.654293
46	12.137409	10.900181	9.875280	9.016135	8.287961	7.664482	7.125629	6.655907
47	12.164267	10.917597	9.886618	9.023545	8.292822	7.667683	7.127744	6.657310
48	12.189136	10.933575	9.896926	9.030221	8.297163	7.670516	7.129600	6.658531
49	12.212163	10.948234	9.906296	9.036235	8.301038	7.673023	7.131228	6.659592
50	12.233485	10.961683	9.914814	9.041653	8.304498	7.675242	7.132656	6.660515

INDEX

M

R

S

T